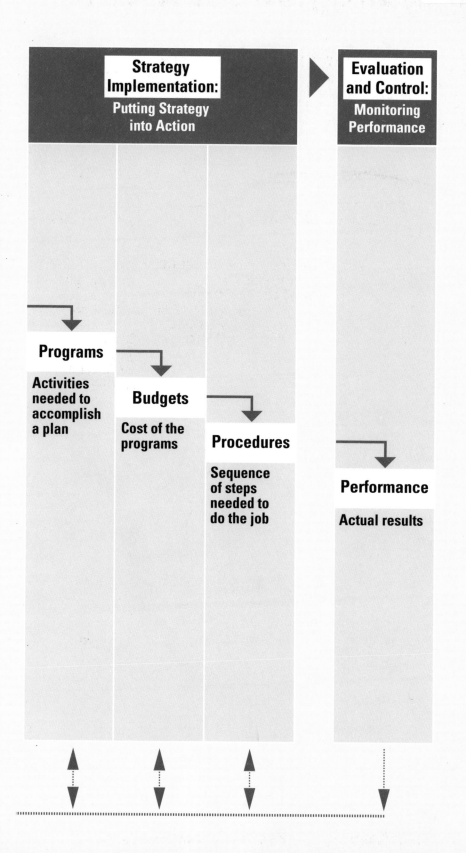

TWELFTH EDITION

Strategic Management and **Business Policy**

ACHIEVING SUSTAINABILITY

INTERNATIONAL EDITION

TWELFTH EDITION

Strategic Management and Business Policy

ACHIEVING SUSTAINABILITY
INTERNATIONAL EDITION

Thomas L. Wheelen
Formerly with University of Virginia
Trinity College, Dublin Ireland

J. David Hunger
Iowa State University
St. John's University

Prentice Hall
Boston   Columbus   Indianapolis   New York   San Francisco   Upper Saddle River
Amsterdam   Cape Town   Dubai   London   Madrid   Milan   Munich   Paris   Montreal   Toronto
Delhi Mexico City   Sao Paulo   Sydney   Hong Kong   Seoul   Singapore   Taipei   Tokyo

Editorial Director: Sally Yagan
Editor in Chief: Eric Svendsen
Acquisitions Editor, International Edition:
  Steven Jackson
Editorial Project Manager: Claudia Fernandes
Director of Marketing: Patrice Lumumba Jones
Marketing Manager: Nikki Jones
Marketing Assistant: Ian Gold
Senior Managing Editor: Judy Leale
Project Manager: Becca Richter
Senior Operations Supervisor: Arnold Vila
Operations Specialist: Ilene Kahn
Senior Art Director: Janet Slowik
Art Director: Steve Frim

Interior Designer: Maureen Eide
Cover Designer: Jodi Notowitz
Manager, Visual Research: Beth Brenzel
Manager, Rights and Permissions: Zina Arabia
Image Permission Coordinator: Silvana Attanasio
Permissions Project Manager: Charles Morris
Media Project Manager, Editorial: Denise Vaughn
Media Project Manager, Production: Lisa Rinaldi
Full-Service Project Management: Emily Bush,
  S4Carlisle
Printer/Binder: Courier/Kendalville
Cover Printer: Lehigh-Phoenix Color/Hagerstown
Text Font: 10/12 Times

Credits and acknowledgments borrowed from other sources and reproduced, with permission, in this textbook appear on appropriate page within text.

If you purchased this book within the United States or Canada you should be aware that it has been imported without the approval of the Publisher or the Author.

Prentice Hall
is an imprint of

PEARSON

10 9 8 7 6 5 4 3 2 1
ISBN 10:   0-13-702915-2
ISBN 13: 978-0-13-702915-0

Dedicated to

Kathy, Richard and Tom

Betty, Kari and Jeff, Maddie and Megan, Suzi and Nick, Summer and Kacey, Lori and Dave, Merry and Dylan, and Woofie

This book is also dedicated to the following Prentice Hall sales representatives who work so hard to promote this book:

NOLA AKALA
YEZAN ALAYAN
DAVID ALEVY
GEORGE ALEXANDRIS
TARA ALGEO
HECTOR AMAYA
LAUREN ANDERSON
LAURA ARBLASTER
DAVID ARMSTRONG
LAURA BAILEY
NICK BAKER
ASHLEY BARNES
ALICE BARR
SHERRY BARTEL
KATHRYN BASS
JAY BECKENSTEIN
CATHY BENNETT
BILL BEVILLE
SCOTT BORDEN
JENNIFER BOYLE
CRISTIN BRAUN
JAKE BROWN
KYLE BURDETTE
AMANDA CAGLE
FRANCESCA CALOGERO
ERICA CAPOGRECO
RUTH CARDIFF
CHRIS CARDONA
ANDREA CATULLO-LINN
MEREDITH CHANDLER
BEVERLY CHANNING
DAVE CHWALIK
KARA CLARK
ROCHELLE CLARKE
DAN COHEN
VANESSA COLEY
TARYLL CONNOLLY
DONNA CONROY
GEORGE COOK

CYNDI CRIMMINS
KASEY CROCKETT
DAN CURRIER
KELLY DAN
MICHLENE DAOUD
STACY DAVIS
CHRIS DELANEY
MATT DENHAM
GEORGE DEVENNEY
NORRIN DIAS
WENDY DiLEONARDO
DANA DODGE
KATE DOLDER
RYAN DOMBROWSKI
BARBARA DONLON
MICHELLE DOWNEY
DEBI DOYLE
MATTHEW EARLY
TRISH EICHHOLD
SARA EILERT
CYNDI ELLER
MELANIE EVELAND
SUSAN FACKERT
LEEANNE FISHER
RACHEL FLANNERY
CANDAS FLETCHER
MARCIA FLYNN
JULIE FORD
BRAD FORRESTER
EVELYN FORTE
DIANNE FORTIER
KRISTEN FRANK
JOHN FREDERICK
STEPHANIE FRITSON
MARK GAFFNEY
MICHELLE GARCIA-JUCHTER
SARAH BETH GARY
KRISTINE GEBHARDT
ALLI GENTILE

BURKE GEORGE
SYBIL GERAUD
SUE GERRISH
GINA GIMELLI
AMBER GOECKE
CAROLYN GOGOLIN
ADAM GOLDSTEIN
BRIAN GRAVEL
MARGARET GREENE
MATT GRIER
DAVID GROSSMAN
GREG HAITH
ERIC HAKANSON
SANDI HAKANSON
DEMETRIUS HALL
TARA HARTLEY
PHOENIX HARVEY
ALISON HASKINS
CAROL HAWKS
JESSICA HECTOR
JENNIFER HEILBRUNN
CHRISTINE HENRY
LYNN HICKS
JULIE HILDEBRAND
DAUNNE HINGLE
WENDI HOLLAND
LEXI HULL
CHRISTINE HUMENIUK
ANDREA IORIO
ADAM JAY
PAM JEFFRIES
BILL JENNINGS
TOM JOHNSON
STACY JONES
CHERYL KABB
KIMBERLY KANDEL
SUSAN KAPFF
GIA KAUL
ALICIA KELLY

FRANNY KELLY
JULIE KESTENBAUM
KIMBERLY KIEHLER
AMANDA KILLEEN
KELLY KIMBALL
WALT KIRBY
CARRIE KITCHER
TANYA KNAUSS
MARY-JO KOVACH
GREG KRAMP
DANIEL KRAUSS
MICHAEL KRISANDA
GINA LaMANTIA
JOE LEE
TRACEY LEEBROOK
APRIL LEMONS
GENEVIEVE LIENKE
TRICIA LISCIO
TODD LOVVORN
BETH LUDWIG
CARY LUNA
KATE LYNCH
KATIE MAHAN
LAURA MANN
PATRICIA MARTINEZ
STACEY MARTINEZ
BROOK MATTHEWS
GEORGIA MAY
MASON McCARTNEY
KAREN McFADYEN
BRIAN McGARRY
CAROLINE McGILLEN
IRENE McGUINNESS
RYAN McHENRY
KRISTI McHUGH
JEFF McILROY
KATE McKAIN
RAY MEDINA
MOLLY MEINERS
BRENDA MENDOZA
MATT MESAROS
ANDREA MESSINEO
BRIAN MICKELSON

SHALON MILLER
WILLIAM MINERICH
JULIE MOREL
TRACY MORSE
LINDA NELSON
LYNNE NICLAIR
NIKKI NIMS
BOB NISBET
BETSY NIXON
TOM NIXON
LAURA NOAH
LAUREN O'CONNOR
COLLEEN O'DELL
DEBBIE OGILIVE
DAVE OSTROW
TONI PAYNE
ANNE PESCETTO
JULIANNE PETERSON
MELISSA PFISTNER
CARRIE PIZZUTI
MICHAEL POKRYWKA
BELEN POLTORAK
ELIZABETH POPIELARZ
JENNIFER POTTER
JILL PROMESSO
LENNY ANN RAPER
MARY RHODES
TORIAN RICHARDSON
LACEY ROBERTS
DAN ROBERTSON
GARY RODGERS
TESSA ROHDE
JENNIFER ROSEN
DOROTHY ROSENE
RICH ROWE
KATIE ROWLAND
JOANNA SABELLA
STEVE SARTORI
BOB SCANLON
JAYSEN SCHAFFER
BRAD SCHICK
CHRIS SCHMIDT
DEB SCHMIDT

MOLLY SCHMIDT
BILL SCHOOF
CORRINA SCHULTZ
ERIC SEVERSON
SCOTT SHAFER
MARY SHAPIRO
KEN SHIPBAUGH
PAMELA SHIPLEY
KRISTINA SHUBEL
LEA SILVERMAN
AUTUMN SLAUGHTER
ELIZABETH SMITH
LEIGH SMITH
SCOTT SMITH
LEE SOLOMONIDES
VERONICA SPARKS
ASHLEY SPICER
WHITTNEY STAUFFER
BEN STEPHEN
MELANIE STEPHENS
MOLLIE STEPHENSON
TORI STEPOWOY
KATHLEEN STERN
JOE STURINO
ALISON SULLENBERGER
DAN SULLIVAN
LORI SULLIVAN
STEPHANIE SURFUS
CHRISTINA TATE
RICK TAYLOR
ERICA TEICHMAN
KEVIN TEMPLE
SARAH THOMAS
AMANDA TILLEY
FRANK TIMONEY
LAURANNE TOMASZEWSKI
KATY TOWNLEY
ELIZABETH TREPKOWSKI
TARA TRIPP
EMILY TRUMBOLD
JULIE TYLMAN
JOE VIRZI
BALLARD WARD

JENNY WEBER
SHANNON WEIR
ERIC WEISS
DANIEL WELLS
LIZ WILDES

BRIAN WILLIAMS
ERIN WILLIAMS
WILLIAM WILSON
THEISEN WOJAK
KARA WRIGHT

GEORGE YOUNG
SHARON YOUNG
MARY ZIMMERMANN

Brief Contents

Contents

PART SEVEN Cases in Strategic Management   441

SECTION A   Corporate Governance and Social Responsibility

(Contributors: Dan R. Dalton, Richard A. Cosier, and Cathy A. Enz)

A plant location decision forces a confrontation between the board of directors and the CEO regarding an issue in social responsibility and ethics.

(Contributor: Laurence J. Stybel)

Managers question the strategic direction of the company and how it is being managed by its founder and CEO. Company growth has resulted not only in disorganization and confusion among employees, but in poor overall performance. How should the board deal with the founder of the company?

(Contributor: Cynthia Clark Williams)

The CEO of the not-for-profit Hershey Trust Company (HTC), which owned 77% voting control of the for-profit Hershey Foods Company, was facing one of the most challenging decisions of his 25-year career as a trust officer: whether or not to recommend to his board that the American chocolate-making icon be sold. Hershey Foods' profit margins had been steadily declining against strong competition from competitors Nestlé and Mars, but the firm's new CEO had introduced a turnaround strategy.

SECTION B   Business Ethics

(Contributors: Gamewell D. Gantt, George A. Johnson and John A. Kilpatrick)

A questionable accounting practice by the company being audited puts a new CPA in a difficult position. Although the practice is clearly wrong, she is being pressured by her manager to ignore it because it is common in the industry.

SECTION F   Web Mini-Cases

Additional Mini-Cases Available on the Companion Web Site at
www.pearsonglobaleditions.com/wheelen

Preface

Welcome to the 12th edition of *Strategic Management and Business Policy: Achieving Sustainability*! We have examined the latest books, academic journals, and business publications to find the most relevant research, concepts, and techniques in the growing field of strategic management for inclusion in this edition. We have also found some of the latest strategy cases—comprehensive as well as special issue cases—presenting well-known companies facing strategic decisions. We reduced the size of the book to make it more usable by moving some cases and special issue chapters (dealing with technology, entrepreneurship, and not-for-profit) to the Web site (www.pearsonglobaleditions.com/wheelen). We continue to be the most comprehensive strategy book on the market, with chapters ranging from corporate governance and social responsibility to competitive strategy, functional strategy, and strategic alliances.

This edition introduces a new theme that runs throughout all 12 chapters: *environmental sustainability*. This new theme complements the existing global issues theme carried forward from past editions. Environmental sustainability has become a strategic issue and one that will become even more important in the years ahead, as all of us struggle to deal with the consequences of climate change, global warming, and energy availability.

FEATURES NEW TO THIS 12TH EDITION

New to the Concepts Portion

- Each chapter contains a boxed insert dealing with an issue in environmental sustainability.
- Each chapter ends with *Eco Bits*, interesting tidbits of ecological information, such as the number of plastic bags added to landfills each year.
- Each part ends with a short case dealing with topics and issues from that part's chapters on companies ranging from Chiquita Bananas to Boeing and Airbus, Kmart and Sears, to Hewlett-Packard and EDS.
- Special sections on sustainability have been added to Chapters 1 and 3.
- A section on the natural environment has been added to the societal and task environments in Chapter 4.
- A section on managing strategic alliances has been added to Chapter 7.
- Offshoring has been added to the outsourcing section in Chapter 8.

New to the Cases Portion: Ten New Cases

Ten comprehensive cases have been added to support twenty popular full-length cases and four mini-cases carried forward from past editions. Nine of them are brand new cases. One (Harley-Davidson) is a newly-revised favorite from the 11th edition. Of the thirty full-length cases appearing in this book, ten are exclusive and do not appear in other books.

- Two of the new cases deal with international issues (**Li & Fung** and **Starbucks**).
- One of the new cases deals with the Internet (**Yahoo!**).
- Two new cases are in entertainment (**TiVo** and **Marvel Entertainment**).

- Two new cases are of well-known transportation firms (**Harley-Davidson** and **JetBlue Airways**).

- Two new specialty retailing cases offer clothes (**Gap**) and candy (**Rocky Mountain Chocolate Factory**).

- A new case comes from the food industry (**Wal-Mart and Vlasic Pickles**).

HOW THIS BOOK IS DIFFERENT FROM OTHER STRATEGY TEXTBOOKS

This book contains a **Strategic Management Model** that runs through the first eleven chapters and is made operational through the **Strategic Audit**, a complete case analysis methodology. The Strategic Audit provides a professional framework for case analysis in terms of external and internal factors and takes the student through the generation of strategic alternatives and implementation programs.

To help the student synthesize the many factors in a complex strategy case, we developed three useful techniques:

- **External Factor Analysis (EFAS) Table in Chapter 4**
  This reduces the external Opportunities and Threats to the 8–10 most important external factors facing management.

- **Internal Factor Analysis (IFAS) Table in Chapter 5**
  This reduces the internal Strengths and Weaknesses to the 8–10 most important internal factors facing management.

- **Strategic Factor Analysis Summary (SFAS) Matrix in Chapter 6**
  This condenses the 16–20 factors generated in the EFAS and IFAS Tables into the 8–10 most important (strategic) factors facing the company. These strategic factors become the basis for generating alternatives and a recommendation for the company's future direction.

Suggestions for Case Analysis are provided in **Appendix 12.B (end of Chapter 12)** and contain step-by-step procedures for how to use the Strategic Audit in analyzing a case. This appendix includes an example of a student-written Strategic Audit. Thousands of students around the world have applied this methodology to case analysis with great success. *The Case Instructor's Manual* contains examples of student-written Strategic Audits for most of the comprehensive strategy cases.

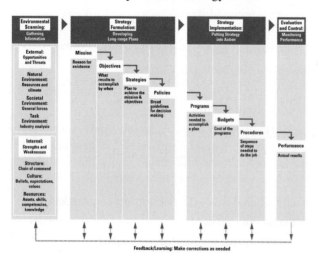

TIME-TESTED FEATURES

This edition contains many of the same features and content that helped make previous editions successful. Some of the features are the following:

- A **strategic management model** runs throughout the first eleven chapters as a unifying concept. (Explained in *Chapter 1*)

APPENDIX 1.A
Strategic Audit
of a Corporation

I. Current Situation

A. Current Performance

How did the corporation perform the past year overall in terms of return on investment, market share, and profitability?

B. Strategic Posture

What are the corporation's current mission, objectives, strategies, and policies?

1. Are they clearly stated, or are they merely implied from performance?
2. **Mission:** What business(es) is the corporation in? Why?
3. **Objectives:** What are the corporate, business, and functional objectives? Are they consistent with each other, with the mission, and with the internal and external environments?
4. **Strategies:** What strategy or mix of strategies is the corporation following? Are they consistent with each other, with the mission and objectives, and with the internal and external environments?
5. **Policies:** What are the corporation's policies? Are they consistent with each other, with the mission, objectives, and strategies, and with the internal and external environments?
6. Do the current mission, objectives, strategies, and policies reflect the corporation's international operations, whether global or multidomestic?

II. Corporate Governance

A. Board of Directors

1. Who is on the board? Are they internal (employees) or external members?
2. Do they own significant shares of stock?
3. Is the stock privately held or publicly traded? Are there different classes of stock with different voting rights?
4. What do the board members contribute to the corporation in terms of knowledge, skills, background, and connections? If the corporation has international operations, do board members have international experience? Are board members concerned with environmental sustainability?

SOURCE: T. L. Wheelen and J. D. Hunger, *Strategic Audit of a Corporation*, Copyright © 1982 by Wheelen and Hunger Associates. Originally in T. L. Wheelen and J. D. Hunger, "The Strategic Audit," 1979, 1977, 1979, and 2005. Presented by J. D. Hunger and T. L. Wheelen in "The Strategic Audit: An Integrative Approach to Teaching Business Policy," to *Academy of Management*, August 1983. Published as "Using the Strategic Audit," by T. L. Wheelen and J. D. Hunger in *SAM Advanced Management Journal* (Winter 1987), pp. 4–12. Reprinted by permission. Revised 1988, 1991, 1994, 1997, 2000, 2002, 2005, and 2008.

- The **strategic audit**, a way to operationalize the strategic decision-making process, serves as a checklist in case analysis. (*Chapter 1*)

- **Corporate governance** is examined in terms of the roles, responsibilities, and interactions of top management and the board of directors and includes the impact of the Sarbanes-Oxley Act. (*Chapter 2*)

FIGURE 2–1   Board of Directors Continuum

DEGREE OF INVOLVEMENT IN STRATEGIC MANAGEMENT						
Low (Passive) →						High (Active)
Phantom	**Rubber Stamp**	**Minimal Review**	**Nominal Participation**	**Active Participation**		**Catalyst**
Never knows what to do, if anything; no degree of involvement.	Permits officers to make all decisions. It votes as the officers recommend on action issues.	Formally reviews selected issues that officers bring to its attention.	Involved to a limited degree in the performance or review of selected key decisions, indicators, or programs of managment.	Approves, questions, and makes final decisions on mission, strategy, policies, and objectives. Has active board committees. Performs fiscal and management audits.		Takes the leading role in establishing and modifying the mission, objectives, strategy, and policies. It has a very active strategy committee.

SOURCE: T. L. Wheelen and J. D. Hunger, "Board of Directors Continuum," Copyright © 1994 by Wheelen and Hunger Associates. Reprinted by permission.

FIGURE 3–1
Responsibilities
of Business

		Social Responsibilities	
Economic	**Legal**	**Ethical**	**Discretionary**
(Must Do)	(Have to Do)	(Should Do)	(Might Do)

SOURCE: Adapted from A. B. Carroll, "A Three Dimensional Conceptual Model of Corporate Performance," *Academy of Management Review* (October 1979), p. 499. Reprinted with permission.

- **Social responsibility and managerial ethics** are examined in detail in terms of how they affect strategic decision making. They include the process of stakeholder analysis and the concept of social capital. (*Chapter 3*)

4.1 Environmental Scanning

Before an organization can begin strategy formulation, it must scan the external environment to identify possible opportunities and threats and its internal environment for strengths and weaknesses. **Environmental scanning** is the monitoring, evaluation, and dissemination of information from the external and internal environments to key people within the corporation. A corporation uses this tool to avoid strategic surprise and to ensure its long-term health. Research has found a positive relationship between environmental scanning and profits.[2] Approximately 70% of executives around the world state that global social, environmental, and business trends are increasingly important to corporate strategy, according to a 2008 survey by McKinsey & Company.[3]

IDENTIFYING EXTERNAL ENVIRONMENTAL VARIABLES

In undertaking environmental scanning, strategic managers must first be aware of the many variables within a corporation's natural, societal, and task environments (see **Figure 1–3**). The

- Equal emphasis is placed on **environmental scanning** of the natural and societal environments as well as on the task environment. Topics include forecasting and Miles and Snow's typology in addition to competitive intelligence techniques and Porter's industry analysis. (*Chapter 4*)

- **Core and distinctive competencies** are examined within the framework of the resource-based view of the firm. (*Chapter 5*)

- **Organizational analysis** includes material on business models, supply chain management, and corporate reputation. (*Chapter 5*)

- Internal and external strategic factors are emphasized through the use of specially-designed **EFAS, IFAS,** and **SFAS tables.** (*Chapters 4, 5, and 6*)

- **Functional strategies** are examined in light of **outsourcing.** (*Chapter 8*)

CHAPTER 9

strategy implementation: organizing for Action

For nearly five decades, Wal-Mart's "everyday low prices" and low cost position had enabled it to rapidly grow to dominate North America's retailing landscape. By 2006, however, its U.S. division generated only 1.9% growth in its same-store sales. By 2007, Target, Costco, Kroger, Safeway, Walgreens, CVS, and Best Buy were all growing faster than Wal-Mart. At about the same time, Microsoft, whose software had grown to dominate personal computers worldwide, saw its revenue growth slow to just 8% in 2005. The company's stock price had been flat since 2002, an indication that investors no longer perceived Microsoft as a growth company. What had happened to these two successful companies? Was this an isolated phenomenon? What could be done, if anything, to reinvigorate these giants?¹

A research study by Matthew Olson, Derek van Bever, and Seth Verry attempts to provide an answer. After analyzing the experiences of 500 successful companies over a 50-year period, they found that 87% of the firms had suffered one or more serious declines in sales and profits. This included a diverse set of corporations, such as Levi Strauss, 3M, Apple, Bank One, Caterpillar, Daimler-Benz, Toys"R"Us, and Volvo. After years of prolonged growth in sales and profits, revenue growth at each of these firms suddenly stopped and even turned negative! Olson, van Bever, and Verry called these long-term reversals in company growth *stall points*. On average, corporations lost 74% of their market capitalization in the decade surrounding a growth stall. Even though the CEO and other members of top management were typically replaced, only 46% of the firms were able to return to moderate or high growth within the decade. When slow growth was allowed to persist for more than 10 years, the delay was usually fatal. Only 7% of this group was able to return to moderate or high growth.²

At Levi Strauss & Company, for example, sales topped $7 billion in 1996—extending growth that had more than doubled over the previous decade. From that high-water mark, sales plummeted until they reached $4.6 in 2000—a 35% decline. Market share in its U.S. jeans market dropped from 31% in 1990 to 14% by 2000. Its market value fell from $14 billion to $8 billion during these four years. After replacing management, the company underwent a companywide transformation, but by 2008 it had yet to return to growth.

■ Two chapters deal with issues in **strategy implementation**, such as organizational and job design plus strategy-manager fit, action planning, corporate culture, and international strategic alliances. (*Chapters 9 and 10*)

CHAPTER 10

strategy implementation: staffing and Directing

Have you heard of Enterprise Rent-A-Car? Hertz, Avis, and National Car Rental operations are much more visible at airports. Yet Enterprise owns more cars and operates in more locations than Hertz or Avis. Enterprise began operations in St. Louis in 1957, but didn't locate at an airport until 1995. It is the largest rental car company in North America, but only 230 out of its 7,000 worldwide offices are at airports. In virtually ignoring the highly competitive airport market, Enterprise has chosen a cost-leadership competitive strategy by marketing to people in need of a spare car at neighborhood locations. Its offices are within 15 miles of 90% of the U.S. population. Instead of locating many cars at a few high-priced locations at airports, Enterprise sets up inexpensive offices throughout metropolitan areas. As a result, cars are rented for 30% less than they cost at airports. As soon as one branch office grows to about 150 cars, the company opens another rental office a few miles away. People are increasingly renting from Enterprise even when their current car works fine. According to CEO Andy Taylor, "We call it a 'virtual car.' Small-business people who have to pick up clients call us when they want something better than their own car." Why is this competitive strategy so successful for Enterprise even though its locations are now being imitated by Hertz and Avis?

The secret to Enterprise's success is its well-executed strategy implementation. Clearly laid out programs, budgets, and procedures support the company's competitive strategy by making Enterprise stand out in the mind of the consumer. It was ranked on *Business Week*'s list of "Customer Service Champs" in both 2007 and 2008. When a new rental office opens, employees spend time developing relationships with the service managers of every auto dealership and body shop in the area. Enterprise employees bring pizza and doughnuts to workers at the auto garages across the country. Enterprise forms agreements with dealers to provide replacements for cars brought in for service. At major accounts, the company actually staffs an office at the dealership and has cars parked outside so customers don't have to go to an Enterprise office to complete paperwork.

One key to implementation at Enterprise is staffing—hiring and promoting a certain kind of person. Virtually every Enterprise employee is a college graduate, usually from the bottom

■ A separate chapter on **evaluation and control** explains the importance of measurement and incentives to organizational performance. (*Chapter 11*)

■ **Suggestions for in-depth case analysis** provide a complete listing of financial ratios, recommendations for oral and written analysis, and ideas for further research. (*Chapter 12*)

TABLE 12–1   Financial Ratio Analysis

	Formula	How Expressed	Meaning
1. Liquidity Ratios Current ratio	$\dfrac{\text{Current assets}}{\text{Current liabilities}}$	Decimal	A short-term indicator of the company's ability to pay its short-term liabilities from short-term assets; how much of current assets are available to cover each dollar of current liabilities.
Quick (acid test) ratio	$\dfrac{\text{Current assets} - \text{Inventory}}{\text{Current liabilities}}$	Decimal	Measures the company's ability to pay off its short-term obligations from current assets, excluding inventories.
Inventory to net working capital	$\dfrac{\text{Inventory}}{\text{Current assets} - \text{Current liabilities}}$	Decimal	A measure of inventory balance; measures the extent to which the cushion of excess current assets over current liabilities may be threatened by unfavorable changes in inventory.
Cash ratio	$\dfrac{\text{Cash} + \text{Cash equivalents}}{\text{Current liabilities}}$	Decimal	Measures the extent to which the company's capital is in cash or cash equivalents; shows how much of the current obligations can be paid from cash or near-cash assets.
2. Profitability Ratios Net profit margin	$\dfrac{\text{Net profit after taxes}}{\text{Net sales}}$	Percentage	Shows how much after-tax profits are generated by each dollar of sales.
Gross profit margin	$\dfrac{\text{Sales} - \text{Cost of goods sold}}{\text{Net sales}}$	Percentage	Indicates the total margin available to cover other expenses beyond cost of goods sold and still yield a profit.
Return on investment (ROI)	$\dfrac{\text{Net profit after taxes}}{\text{Total assets}}$	Percentage	Measures the rate of return on the total assets utilized in the company; a measure of management's efficiency, it shows the return on all the assets under its control, regardless of source of financing.
Return on equity (ROE)	$\dfrac{\text{Net profit after taxes}}{\text{Shareholders' equity}}$	Percentage	Measures the rate of return on the book value of shareholders' total investment in the company.
Earnings per share (EPS)	$\dfrac{\text{Net profit after taxes} - \text{Preferred stock dividends}}{\text{Average number of common shares}}$	Dollars per share	Shows the after-tax earnings generated for each share of common stock.
3. Activity Ratios Inventory turnover	$\dfrac{\text{Net sales}}{\text{Inventory}}$	Decimal	Measures the number of times that average inventory of finished goods was turned over or sold during a period of time, usually a year.
Days of inventory	$\dfrac{\text{Inventory}}{\text{Cost of goods sold} \div 365}$	Days	Measures the number of one day's worth of inventory that a company has on hand at any given time.

FIGURE 12–1
Strategic Audit
Worksheet

Strategic Audit Heading	Analysis		Comments
	(+) Factors	(–) Factors	
I. Current Situation			
A. Past Corporate Performance Indexes			
B. Strategic Posture:			
Current Mission			
Current Objectives			
Current Strategies			
Current Policies			
SWOT Analysis Begins:			
II. Corporate Governance			
A. Board of Directors			
B. Top Management			
III. External Environment (EFAS): Opportunities and Threats (SWOT)			
A. Societal Environment			
B. Task Environment (Industry Analysis)			
IV. Internal Environment (IFAS): Strengths and Weaknesses (SWOT)			
A. Corporate Structure			
B. Corporate Culture			
C. Corporate Resources			
1. Marketing			
2. Finance			
3. Research and Development			
4. Operations and Logistics			
5. Human Resources			
6. Information Systems			
V. Analysis of Strategic Factors (SFAS)			
A. Key Internal and External Strategic Factors (SWOT)			
B. Review of Mission and Objectives			
SWOT Analysis Ends. Recommendation Begins:			
VI. Alternatives and Recommendations			
A. Strategic Alternatives—pros and cons			
B. Recommended Strategy			
VII. Implementation			
VIII. Evaluation and Control			

NOTE: See the complete Strategic Audit on pages 26–33. It lists the pages in the book that discuss each of the eight headings.

SOURCE: T. L. Wheelen and J. D. Hunger, "Strategic Audit Worksheet." Copyright © 1985, 1986, 1987, 1988, 1989, 2005, and 2009 by T. L. Wheelen. Copyright © 1989, 2005, and 2009 by Wheelen and Hunger Associates. Revised 1991, 1994, and 1997. Reprinted by permission. Additional copies available for classroom use in Part D of Case Instructors Manual and on the Prentice Hall Web site (www.prenhall.com/wheelen).

■ An **experiential exercise** focusing on the material covered in each chapter helps the reader to apply strategic concepts to an actual situation.

■ The **Strategic Audit Worksheet** is based on the time-tested strategic audit and is designed to help students organize and structure daily case preparation in a brief period of time. The worksheet works exceedingly well for checking the level of daily student case preparation—especially for open class discussions of cases. (*Chapter 12*)

■ Special chapters deal with strategic issues in **managing technology and innovation**, **entrepreneurial ventures and small businesses**, and **not-for-profit organizations**. (*Web Chapters A, B, and C*, respectively) These issues are often ignored by other strategy textbooks, but are available on this book's Web site at www.pearsonglobaleditions.com/wheelen.

STRATEGIC PRACTICE EXERCISE

Each year, *Fortune* magazine publishes an article entitled, "America's Most Admired Companies." It lists the 10 most admired companies in the United States and in the world. *Fortune*'s rankings are based on scoring publicly held companies on what it calls "eight key attributes of reputation": innovation, people management, use of corporate assets, social responsibility, quality of management, financial soundness, long-term investment value, and quality of products/services. In 2008, *Fortune* asked Hay Group to survey more than 3,700 people from multiple industries. Respondents were asked to choose the companies they admired most, regardless of industry. *Fortune* has been publishing this list since 1982. The 2008 *Fortune* list of the top 10 most admired U.S. companies were (starting with #1): Apple, Berkshire Hathaway, General Electric, Google, Toyota Motor, Starbucks, FedEx, Procter & Gamble, Johnson & Johnson, and Goldman Sachs Group. The next 10 most admired were (from 11 to 20): Target, Southwest Airlines, American Express, BMW, Costco Wholesale, Microsoft, United Parcel Service, Cisco Systems, 3M, and Nordstrom.[114]

Four years earlier in 2004, the list of 10 most admired U.S. companies was: Wal-Mart, Berkshire Hathaway, Southwest Airlines, General Electric, Dell Computer, Microsoft, Johnson & Johnson, Starbucks, FedEx, and IBM.[115]

■ Why did the most admired U.S. firm in 2004 (Wal-Mart) drop off the 10 ten listing in 2008?

■ Why did Apple go from not even being on the 10 ten U.S. listing in 2004 to No. 1 in 2008?

■ Which firms appeared on both top 10 lists? Why?

■ Why did some firms drop off the list from 2004 to 2008 and why did others get included?

■ What companies should be on the most admired list this year? Why?

Try One of These Exercises

1. Go to the library and find a "Most Admired Companies" *Fortune* article from the 1980s or early 1990s and compare that list to the latest one. (See www.fortune.com for the latest list.) Which companies have fallen out of the top 10? Pick one of the companies and investigate why it is no longer on the list.

■ A list of **key terms** and the pages in which they are discussed enable the reader to keep track of important concepts as they are introduced in each chapter.

■ **Learning objectives** begin each chapter.

■ **Timely, well-researched, and class-tested cases** deal with interesting companies and industries. Many of the cases are about well-known, publicly held corporations—ideal subjects for further research by students wishing to update the cases.

Both the text and the cases have been class-tested in strategy courses and revised based on feedback from students and instructors. The first eleven chapters are organized around a strategic management model that begins each chapter and provides a structure for both content and case analysis. We emphasize those concepts that have proven to be most useful in understanding strategic decision making and in conducting case analysis. Our goal was to make the text as comprehensive as possible without getting bogged down in any one area. Endnote references are provided for those who wish to learn more about any particular topic. All cases are about actual organizations. The firms range in size from large, established multinationals to small, entrepreneurial ventures, and cover a broad variety of issues. As an aid to case analysis, we propose the strategic audit as an analytical technique.

MyManagementLab

MyManagementLab (www.mymanagementlab.com) is an easy-to-use online tool that personalizes course content and provides robust assessment and reporting to measure student and class performance. All the resources you need for course success are in one place—flexible and easily adapted for your course experience. Some of the resources include: an eBook version of all chapters, special issue chapters (dealing with technology, entrepreneurship, and not-for-profit), additional cases, quizzes, video clips, and PowerPoint presentations that engage students while helping them to study independently.

Acknowledgments

We thank the many people at Prentice Hall who helped to make this edition possible. We thank our new editor, Kim Norbuta. We are especially grateful to Kim's project manager, Claudia Fernandes, who managed to keep everything on an even keel. We also thank Becca Richter and Emily Bush, who took the book through the production process.

We are very thankful to Lindle Hatton, California State University – Sacramento; J. Kay Keels, Coastal Carolina University; Carol K. Jacobson, Purdue University; Xia Zhao, California State University – Dominguez Hills; Steven A. Frankforter, Winthrop University; Charles M. Byles, Virginia Commonwealth University; and Doreen J. Gooden, Florida International University for their constructive criticism of the 11th edition concepts and cases. We have incorporated many of their ideas in this edition by reducing the size of the book, moving special issue cases to the Web site, and deciding which of our favorite cases to keep and which to delete or update.

We are very grateful to Kathy Wheelen for her first-rate administrative support of the cases and *Case Instructor's Manual* and to Betty Hunger for her preparation of the indexes and the glossary. We are especially thankful to the many students who tried out the cases we chose to include in this book. Their comments helped us find any flaws in the cases before the book went to the printer.

In addition, we express our appreciation to John Hasselberg and Wendy Klepetar, Management Department Chairs of St. John's University, for their support and provision of the resources so helpful to revise a textbook. Both of us acknowledge our debt to Dr. William Shenkir and Dr. Frank S. Kaulback, former Deans of the McIntire School of Commerce of the University of Virginia for the provision of a work climate most supportive to the original development of this book.

We offer a special thanks to the hundreds of case authors who have provided us with excellent cases for the twelve editions of this book. We consider many of these case authors to be our friends. A special thanks to you!! The adage is true: The path to greatness is through others.

Lastly, to the many strategy instructors and students who have moaned to us about their problems with the strategy course: We have tried to respond to your problems and concerns as best we could by providing a comprehensive yet usable text coupled with recent and complex cases. To you, the people who work hard in the strategy trenches, we acknowledge our debt. This book is yours.

T. L. Wheelen
Saint Petersburg, Florida

J. D. Hunger
St. Joseph, Minnesota

About the Contributors

MOUSTAFA H. ABDELSAMAD, DBA (George Washington University), is Dean of the College of Business at Texas A&M University–Corpus Christi. He previously served as Dean of the College of Business and Industry at the University of Massachsetts–Dartmouth and as Professor of Finance and Associate Dean of Graduate Studies in Business at Virginia Commonthwealth University. He is Editor-in-Chief of the *SAM Advanced Managament Journal* and International President of the Society of Advancement of Management. He is author of *A Guide to Capital Expenditure Analysis* and of two chapters in the *Dow Jones –Irwin Capital Budgeting Handbook.* He is the author and coauthor of numerous articles in various publications.

HITESH (JOHN) P. ADHIA, CPA, MS and BA, (University of South Florida), is the President and Chief Investment Officer of Adhia Investment Advisors, Inc. (the "Firm"). Mr. Adhia is a CPA and has been in the finance industry since 1982. Mr. Adhia is the founder and Investment Manager for the Adhia Twenty Fund, the Adhia Health Care Fund, the Adhia Short Term Advantage Fund, the Adhia Arbitrage Fund, and the Adhia Derivative Fund. Prior to forming Adhia Investment Advisors, Mr. Adhia owned a Tampa-based public accounting practice and also served as Acting CFO and Independent Advisor to the Well Care Group of Companies. Mr. Adhia has over twenty years experience in managing fixed income strategies.

KAREN A. BERGER, M.Phil and PhD (New York University), MBA (University of Connecticut), MA (Columbia University), and BA (SUNY at Buffalo), is Chairperson of the Marketing Department and Associate Professor of Marketing at Pace University; she also held previous academic positions with New York University, Stern School of Business, and Mercy College. Dr. Berger has published in Marketing and has several teaching awards.

JAMES W. CAMERIUS, MS (University of North Dakota), is Professor of Marketing at Northern Michigan University. He has served as President of the Society for Case Research, Marketing Track Chair of the North American Case Research Association, and Workshop and Colloquium Director of the World Association for Case Method Research. He is a research grant recipient of the Walker L. Cisler College of Business at Northern Michigan University and also a 1995 recipient of the Distinguished Faculty Award of the Michigan Association of Governing Boards of State Universities. His cases appear in more than 90 management, marketing, and retailing textbooks in addition to *Annual Advances in Business Cases,* a publication of the Society for Case Research. His studies of corporate situations include Kmart Corporation; Tanner Companies, Inc.; Mary Kay Cosmetics, Inc.; Sasco Products,Inc.; The Fuller Brush Company; Wal-Mart Stores, Inc.; Longaberger Marketing, Inc.; Encyclopaedia Britannica International; RWC, Inc.; and several others. His writings include several studies of the case method of instruction. He is an award and grant recipient of the Direct Selling Educational Foundation, Washington, DC, and is listed in *Who's Who in the World, America, Midwest, American Education, and Finance and Industry.*

RICHARD A. COISER, PhD (University of Iowa), is Dean and Leeds Professor of Management at Purdue University. He formerly was Dean and Fred B. Brown Chair at the University of Oklahoma and was Associate Dean for Academics and Professor of Business Administration at Indiana University. He served as Chairperson of the Department of Management at Indiana University. He was formerly a Planning Engineer with Western Electric Company and Instructor of Management and Quantitative Methods at the University of Notre Dame.

Dr. Coiser is interested in researching the managerial decision-making process, organization responses to external forces, and participative management. He has published in *Behavior Science, Academy of Management Journal, Academy of Management Review, Organizational Behavior and Human Performance, Management Science, Strategic Management Journal, Business Horizons, Decision Sciences, Personnel Pyschology, Journal of Creative Behavior, International Journal of Management, The Business Quarterly, Public Administration Quarterly, Human Relations,* and other journals. In addition, Dr. Coiser has presented numerous papers at professional meetings and has coauthored a management text. He has been active in many executive development programs and has acted as management-education consultant for several organizations. Dr. Coiser is the recipient of teaching Excellence Awards in the MBA Program at Indiana and a Richard D. Irwin Fellowship. He belongs to the Institute of Management, Sigma Iota Epsilon, and the Decision Sciences Institute.

ROY A. COOK, DBA (Mississippi State University), is Associate Dean of the School of Business Administration, and formerly was a Professor at Fort Lewis College, Durango, Colorado. He has written a best-selling textbook, *Tourism: The Business of Travel,* now in its second edition, and has two forthcoming textbooks: *Cases and Experiential Exercises in Human Resource Management* and *Guide to Business Etiquette.* He has authored numerous articles, cases, and papers based on his extensive experience in the hospitality industry and research interests in the areas of strategy, small business management, human resource management, and communication. Dr. Cook is the Director of Colorado's Center for Tourism Research®, Editor of *The Annual Advances in Business Cases,* and also serves on the editorial boards of the *Business Case Journal,* the *Journal of Business Strategies,* and the *Journal of Teaching and Tourism.* He is member of the Academy of Management, Society for Case Research (past President), and the International Society of Travel and Tourism Educators. Dr. Cook teaches courses in Strategic Management, Small Business Management, Tourism and Resort Management, and Human Resource Management.

STEVEN M. COX, PhD (University of Nebraska) is an Associate Professor of Marketing, McColl School of Business, Queens University of Charlotte. He had a twenty-five-year career in executive level marketing and sales positions with AT&T, GE, and several satellite imaging companies. He owns and manages LSI, a geographic information system company. He currently serves as a case reviewer for the *Business Case Journal* and the *Southeast Case Research Journal.*

DAVID B. CROLL, PhD (Pennsylvania State University), is Professor Emeritus of Accounting at the McIntire School of Commerce, the University of Virginia. He was Visiting Associate Professor at the Graduate Business School, the University of Michigan. He is on the editorial board of *SAM Advanced Management Journal.* He has published in the *Accounting Review* and the *Case Research Journal.* His cases appear in twelve accounting and management textbooks.

DAN R. DALTON, PhD (University of California, Irvine), is the Dean the Graduate School of Business, Indiana University, and Harold A. Polipl Chair of Strategic Management. He was formerly with General Telephone & Electronics for thirteen years. Widely published in business and psychology periodicals, his articles have appeared in the *Academy of Management Journal, Journal of Applied Psychology, Personnel Psychology, Academy of Management Review,* and *Strategic Management Journal.*

CATHY A. ENZ, PhD (Ohio State University), is the Lewis G. Schaeneman Jr. Professor of Innovation and Dynamic Management at Cornell University's School of Hotel Administration, where she is also the Executive Director of the Center for Hospitality Research. Her doctoral degree is in organization theory and behavior. Professor Enz has written numerous articles, cases, and books on corporate culture, value sharing, change management, and strategic human resource management effects on performance. Professor Enz consults extensively in the service sector and serves on the Board of Directors for two hospitality-related organizations.

ELLIE A. FOGARTY, EdD (University of Pennsylvania), MBA (Temple University), MLS (University of Pittsburgh), and BA (Immaculata University), is the Director of Compliance and Ethics at The College of New Jersey (TCNJ). Previously, she served as the Associate Provost for Planning and Resource Allocation, Executive Assistant to the Provost, and Business and Economics Librarian, all at TCNJ. She has written five cases used in earlier editions of Strategic Management and Business Policy. She has taught management courses at TCNJ and Rutgers University.

GAMEWELL D. GANTT, JD, CPA, is Professor of Accounting and Management in the College of Business at Idaho State University in Pocatello, Idaho, where he teaches a variety of legal studies courses. He is past President of the Rocky Mountain Academy of Legal Studies in Business and a past Chair of the Idaho Endowment Investment Fund Board. His published articles and papers have appeared in journals including *Midwest Law Review, Business Law Review, Copyright World,* and *Intellectual Property World.* His published cases have appeared in several textbooks and in *Annual Advances in Business Cases.*

MARC GARTENFELD, BS, MBA (St. John's University), is the Associate Director of The Strategic Management Research Group and the Center for Case Development and Use. He has coauthored more than seventy-five books, monographs, instructor's guides, case studies, journal articles, conference presentations, and table topic papers in the areas of Multinational Strategic Management, E-Business, Expert Knowledge-Based Systems, Entrepreneurship, and Application Service Providers. One of his coauthored papers won a Distinguished Paper Award, and various case studies won national and international awards. He is also the recipient of the 2001 Teaching Excellence Award and Professor of the Year Award both from the Tobin College of Business, St. John's University.

S.S. GEORGE, Dean, ICMR *Case Studies and Management Resources.* S.S. George is a Faculty Member at the ICFAI Center for Management Research (ICMR).

NORMAN J. GIERLASINSKI, DBA, CPA, CFE, CIA, is Professor of Accounting at Central Washington University. He served as Chairman of the Small Business Division of the Midwest Business Administration Association. He has authored and coauthored cases for professional associations and the Harvard Case Study Series. He has authored various articles in professional journals as well as serving as a contributing author for textbooks and as a consultant to many organizations. He also served as a reviewer for various publications.

WALTER E. GREENE, Ph.D., PHR, Owner & President, Greene and Associates, Professional Human Resource Manager (SHRM Lifetime Award), Ph.D. University of Arkansas, College Management Certificate, 1967 University of Nebraska, Omaha, M.S. University of North Dakota, 1967 (Industrial Management), B.S. University of Maryland, 1959 (Military Science–Logistics). Dr. Greene was on the graduate faculty at The University of Texas Pan American from 1985, teaching Doctoral, MBA and Undergraduate classes until his retirement on September 1, 2005, from the College of Business Administration, as Full Professor of Strategic Management & International Business. Dr. Greene has over three dozen refereed articles in such journals as *The Review of Business, Journal of World Business, Journal of Management Systems, The Journal of Big Bend Studies, International Journal of Manpower, The Journal of Services in Marketing, Southwest Journal of Business & Economics, The Journal of Business & Entrepreneurship, International Journal of Commerce and Management,* and *The International Journal of Case Studies and Research.* Prior to entering the teaching profession, Dr. Greene was a retired USAF Commissioned Officer, seeing service in the U.S. Army of Occupation of Germany,

WWII. Capt. Greene was on active duty during both the Korean War and the SE Asian conflicts, and held the highest possible security clearances through top secret, cryptographic, and EWO clearances. Captain Greene was awarded several decorations, including the USAF Commendation Medal, Presidential Citation, National Defense Medal, AF Outstanding Unit Award, Armed Forces Medal, Cold War Victory and the AF 50th Anniversary Medals. Dr. Greene was also an Expert Marksman with both the carbine rifle and pistol.

SUE GREENFELD, DBA (University of Southern California), is a Professor of Management and Associate Dean for Student Affairs in the College of Business Administration, California State University, San Bernardino. She is twice a recipient of a Fulbright Senior Fellowship where she has taught at the National Chengchi University in Taipei, Taiwan, and at the Marmara University in Istanbul, Turkey. She has written numerous cases on business policy and strategic issues, and has served on the editorial board of the *Case Research Journal.*

VIVEK GUPTA is a faculty member at the ICFAI Center for Management Research. (ICMR).

RENDY HALIM, MBA and BS(Bentley College), is currently focusing on equity and commodity trading, as well as venturing a new start-up company. Actively involved in his church ministry, he is also contributing his time and thought on how to properly manage the church's management and financial report effectively.

PATRICIA HARASTA, MBA (Bentley McCallum Graduate School of Business), is Director of Quality Assurance at CA (formerly Computer Associates). She manages a distributed team responsible for new development and maintenance of QA activities for products that provide management of applications such as SAP, Microsoft Exchange, Lotus Domino, WebSphere, WebLogic, MQ, and Web Servers.

ALAN N. HOFFMAN, DBA (Indiana University), is Professor Emeritus of Strategic Management and Director of the MBA program at the McCallum Graduate School, Bentley University. Major areas of interest include strategic management, global competition, investment strategy and technology. Professor Hoffman is coauthor of *The Strategic Management Casebook* and *Skill Builder* textbook. Recent publications have appeared in the *Academy of Management Journal*, *Human Relations*, the *Journal of Business Ethics*, the *Journal of Business Research*, and *Business Horizons*. He has authored more than twenty strategic management cases, including: The Boston YWCA, Ryka, Inc., Liz Claiborne, Ben & Jerry's, Cisco Systems, Sun Microsystems, Palm Inc., Handspring, Ebay, AOL/Time Warner, McAfee, Apple Computer, Tivo, Inc. and Wynn Resorts. He is the recipient of the 2004 Bentley University Teaching Innovation award for his course "The Organizational Life Cycle–The Boston Beer Company Brewers of Samuel Adams Lager Beer."

J. DAVID HUNGER, PhD (Ohio State University), is Professor Emeritus of Strategic Management at Iowa State University. He is also Strategic Management Scholar in Residence at Saint John's University (MN). He previously taught at George Mason University, the University of Virginia, and Baldwin-Wallace College. His research interests lie in strategic management, corporate governance, and entrepreneurship. He served as Academic Director of the Pappajohn Center for Entrepreneurship at Iowa State University. He worked in brand management at Procter & Gamble Company, as a selling supervisor at Lazarus Department Store, and served as a Captain in U.S. Army Military Intelligence. He has been active as consultant and trainer to business corporations, as well as to state and federal government agencies. He has written numerous articles and cases that have appeared in the *Academy of Management Journal*, *International Journal of Management*, *Human Resource Management*, *Journal of Business Strategies*, *Case Research Journal*, *Business Case Journal*, *Handbook of Business Strategy*, *Journal of Management Case Studies*, *Annual Advances in Business Cases*, *Journal of Retail Banking*, *SAM Advanced Management Journal*, and *Journal of Management*, among others. Dr. Hunger is a member of the Academy of Management, North American Case Research Association, Society for Case Research, North American Management Society, Textbook and Academic Authors Association, and the Strategic Management Society. He is past President of the North American Case Research Association, Society for Case Research and the Iowa State University Board of Directors. He was elected as a Fellow in the North American Case Research Association. He also served as Vice President of the U.S. Association for Small Business and Entrepreneurship (USASBE). He has served on the editorial review boards of *SAM Advanced Management Journal*, *Journal of Business Strategies*, and *Case Research Journal*. He is also a member of the Board of Directors of the North American Management Society. He is coauthor with Thomas L. Wheelen of *Strategic Management and Business Policy* and *Essentials of Strategic Management* plus *Concepts in Strategic Management and Business Policy* and *Cases in Strategic =Management and Business Policy*, as well as *Strategic Management Cases* (*PIC: Preferred Individualized Cases*), and a monograph assessing undergraduate business education in the United States. The 8th edition of *Strategic Management and Business Policy* received the McGuffey Award for Excellence and Longevity in 1999 from the Text and Academic Authors Association. Dr. Hunger received the Best Case Award given by the McGraw-Hill Publishing Company and the Society for Case Research in 1991 for outstanding case development. He is listed in various versions of Who's Who, including *Who's Who in the United States* and *Who's Who in the World*. He was also recognized in 1999 by the Iowa State University College of Business with its Innovation in Teaching Award and was elected a Fellow of the Teaching and Academic Authors Association in 2001.

P. INDU wrote this case under the direction Vivek Gupta at the ICFAI Center of Management Research (ICMR).

GEORGE A. JOHNSON, PhD, is Professor of Management and Director of the Idaho State University MBA program. He has published in the fields of management education, ethics, project management, and simulation. He is also active in developing and publishing case material for educational purposes. His industry experience includes several years as a Project Manager in the development and procurement of aircraft systems.

SHAWANA P. JOHNSON, Doctorate (Case Western Reserve University), is President of Global Marketing Insights, Inc.

MICHAEL J. KEEFFE, PhD (University of Arkansas), is Associate Professor of Management at Southwest Texas State University. He has served as Chair of the Department of Management and Marketing, Co-Director of AACSB–International Accreditation at SWTU, authored numerous cases in the field of strategic management, published in several journals, and served as an independent consultant since 1982. He currently teaches and conducts research in the fields of strategic management and human resource management.

JOHN A. KILPATRICK, PhD (University of Iowa), is Professor of Management and International Business, Idaho State University. He has taught in the areas of business and business ethics for more than twenty-five years. He served as Co-Chair of the management track of the Institute for Behavioral and Applied Management from its inception and continues as a board member for that organization. He is author of *The Labor Content of American Foreign Trade,* and coauthor of *Issues in International Business.* His cases have appeared in a number of organizational behavior and strategy texts and casebooks, and in *Annual Advances in Business Cases.*

DONALD F. KURATKO is the Jack M. Gill Chair of Entrepreneurship, Professor of Entrepreneurship, and Executive Director of the Johnson Center for Entrepreneurship & Innovation at The Kelley School of Business, Indiana University–Bloomington. Dr. Kuratko is a preeminent scholar and national leader in the field of entrepreneurship. He has published over 150 articles on aspects of entrepreneurship, new venture development, and corporate entrepreneurship. His work has been published in journals such as *Strategic Management Journal, Academy of Management Executive, Journal of Business Venturing, Entrepreneurship Theory & Practice, Journal of Small Business Management, Journal of Small Business Strategy, Family Business Review, and Advanced Management Journal*. Dr. Kuratko has authored twenty books, including the leading entrepreneurship book in American universities today, *Entrepreneurship: Theory, Process, Practice*, 7th ed., as well as *Strategic Entrepreneurial Growth*, 2nd ed*., Corporate Entrepreneurship*, and *Effective Small Business Management*, 7th ed.. In addition, Dr. Kuratko has been consultant on Corporate Entrepreneurship and Entrepreneurial Strategies to a number of major corporations such as Anthem Blue Cross/Blue Shield, AT&T, United Technologies, Ameritech, The Associated Group (Acordia), Union Carbide Corporation, ServiceMaster, and TruServ.

Dr. Kuratko's honors include earning the Ball State University College of Business *Teaching Award 15* consecutive years as well as being the only professor in the history of Ball State University to achieve all four of the university's major lifetime awards which included: *Outstanding Young Faculty* (1987); *Outstanding Teaching Award* (1990); *Outstanding Faculty Award* (1996); and *Outstanding Researcher Award* (1999). He was also honored as the *Entrepreneur of the Year* for the state of Indiana and was inducted into the *Institute of American Entrepreneurs Hall of Fame* (1990). He has been honored with *The George Washington Medal of Honor*; the *Leavey Foundation Award for Excellence in Private Enterprise*; the *NFIB Entrepreneurship Excellence Award*; and the *National Model Innovative Pedagogy Award for Entrepreneurship*. In addition, Dr. Kuratko was named the *National Outstanding Entrepreneurship Educator* (by the U.S. Association for Small Business and Entrepreneurship) and he was selected one of the *Top Three Entrepreneurship Professors in the U.S.* by the Kauffman Foundation, Ernst & Young, *Inc.* magazine, and Merrill Lynch. He received the *Thomas W. Binford Memorial Award for Outstanding Contribution to Entrepreneurial Development* from the Indiana Health Industry Forum. Dr. Kuratko has been named a *21st Century Entrepreneurship Research Fellow* by the National Consortium of Entrepreneurship Centers as well as the U.S. Association for Small Business & Entrepreneurship *Scholar for Corporate Entrepreneurship* in 2003. Finally, he has been honored by his peers in *Entrepreneur* magazine as one of the Top Two Entrepreneurship Program Directors in the nation for three consecutive years, including the *#1 Entrepreneurship Program Director* in 2003.

YONGJUN LU is a Graduate Research Assistant at the Tobin School of Business at St. John's.

RUCHI MANKAD is a Faculty Member at the ICFAI Center for Management Research (ICMR).

BILL J. MIDDLEBROOK, PhD (University of North Texas), is Professor of Management at Southwest Texas State University. He has served as Acting Chair of the Department of Management and Marketing, published in numerous journals, served as a consultant in industry, and is currently teaching and researching in the fields of Strategic Management and Human Resources.

ROBERT J. MOCKLER, Ph.D. (Columbia), BA and MBA (Harvard), is the Joseph F. Adams Professor of Management at St. John's University's Graduate School of Business. He is the director of the Strategic Management Research Group and its Centers of Knowledge-Based Systems for Business (one of the largest databases of prototype expert systems for management decision making in the United States), Case Study Development and Use Program (the third largest case study development program in the United States), and Cross-Cultural Management. He has authored, coauthored, or edited more than 50 books and monographs, some 230 case studies, more than 70 articles, more than 50 book chapters, and more than 200 presentations covering such areas as strategic management, case study development and use, competitive market analysis, new venture management, multinational planning, business ethics, management decision making, modeling of cognitive and behavioral management processes, contingency theory, business process reengineering, computer information systems, group decision support systems for management, expert knowledge-base systems, and innovative teaching. His first articles on strategic management and situational decision theory were published in *Harvard Business Review* in 1970 and 1971. His first book on strategic management was published in 1969. His books include three on expert systems and computer information systems development in 1992, five on strategic management, information systems, and case study development and use in 1993 and 1994; and four on multinational strategic management in 1997, 1998, 1999, and 2003, with various major publishers. Three of his books have been translated into Chinese and published in China, two into Romanian and published in Romania, one into Greek and published in Greece, and one into Russian and published in Russia. He has lectured, consulted and taught worldwide (in China, Russia, Finland, Japan, England, Poland, Germany, Brazil, Argentina, Costa Rica, Ireland, Italy, Taiwan, Philippines, India, Egypt, Mexico, Canada, and Romania), received national awards for innovative teaching (Decision Sciences Institute), been a Fulbright Scholar, and taught MBA courses in Rome, Milan, Latin America, and Beijing, and won numerous other awards for his work. He has also successfully started, run and eventually sold his own multimillion dollar business ventures. He has developed and published more than 120 presentations, case studies, and articles with other faculty at St. John's University. In addition, more than 80 joint publications have been done with professors of other domestic and overseas universities.

NATHAN NEBBE, MBA and MA (Iowa State University), has significant interests in the indigenous peoples of the Americas. With an undergraduate degree in Animal Ecology, he served as a Peace Corps Volunteer in Honduras, where he worked at the Hondouran national forestry school ESNAACIFORE (Escuela National de Ciencias Forestales). After the Peace Corps, Mr. Nebbe worked for a year on a recycling project for the Town of Ignacio and the Southern Ute Indian Tribe in southwestern Colorado. Following his experience in Colorado, Nathan returned to Iowa State University where he obtained his MBA followed by an MA in Anthropology. He is currently studying how globalization of the Chilian forestry industry is affecting the culture of the indigenous Mapuche people of south central Chile.

ANNE PHAN, BS (The College of New Jersey), is currently an analyst at Goldman Sachs & Co. She has also assisted with research for a book on global corporate branding.

A. NEELA RADHIKA is a former Faculty Associate at the ICFAI Center for Management Research.

SHIRISHA REGANI is a Faculty Associate at the ICFAI Center for Management Research.

TED REPETTI, BS (The College of New Jersey), is currently a valuation analyst at Management Planning, Inc., in Princeton. Management Planning renders financial advice to corporations, and specializes in the valuation of closely held corporations.

JOHN K. ROSS, III, PhD (University of North Texas), is Associate Professor of Management at Southwest Texas State University. He has served as SBI Director, Associate Dean, Chair of the Department of Management and Marketing, published in numerous journals, and is currently teaching and researching in the fields of strategic management and human resource.

MARYANNE M. ROUSE, CPA, MBA (University of South Florida), BA in English, Romance Languages, and Political Science (Syracuse University), joined the faculty of the College of Business Administration at the University of South Florida in 1971. She served as the College's Assistant Dean from 1974 to 1976 and as Director of Executive Education and Management Development from 1981 to 1994. Ms. Rouse's current teaching assignments include Strategic Management, the undergraduate capstone course, Measuring Organization Performance in the Graduate Leadership Program, Integrative Business Applications II in the MBA, and Managerial Accounting in the Executive MBA and the MBA Program for Physicians. She has also taught in the USF/EDC French executive MBA Program in Paris. The recipient of a number of MBA teaching awards, including MVP by the Physicians MBA class and Outstanding Professor for the executive MBA, she is a frequent program speaker and continuing education faculty member. A consultant in strategic planning and accounting in several industries, including the not-for-profit sector and health care, she served as one of four international accreditation fellows for the Accreditation Commission for Education in Health Services Administration (ACEHSA.) Ms. Rouse is a member of the Board of Directors and Vice Chair of the Tampa Economic Development Corporation, and CDC, and serves on the board of the University's Small Business Development Center, and chairs the college's Undergraduate Programs Committee.

PATRICIA A. RYAN, PhD. (University of South Florida), is an Associate Professor of Finance, Colorado State University. She currently serves on the Board of the Midwest Finance Association and was the Associate Editor of the *Business Case Journal*. Her research interests lie in corporate finance, specifically initial public offerings, capital budgeting, and case writing. She has published in the *Journal of Business and Management*, the *Business Case Journal*, *Educational and Psychological Measurement*, the *Journal of Research in Finance*, the *Journal of Financial and Strategic Decisions*, and the *Journal of Accounting and Finance Research*. Her research has been cited in the *Wall Street Journal*, *CFO Magazine*, and *Investment Dealers Digest*.

RANGKI SON, MBA Finance (McCallum Graduate School of Business, Bentley University), is currently working for KPMG Korea as a business performance service consultant.

LAURENCE J. STYBEL, EdD (Harvard University), is Cofounder of Stybel Peabody Lincolnshire, a Boston-based management consulting firm devoted to enhancing career effectiveness of executives who report to boards of directors. Services include search, outplacement, outplacement avoidance, and valued executive career consulting. Stybel Peabody Lincolnshire was voted Best Outplacement Firm by the readers of *Massachusetts Lawyers Weekly*. Its programs are the only ones officially endorsed by the Massachusetts Hospital Association and the Financial Executives Institute. He serves on the Board of Directors of the New England Chapter of the National Association of Corporate Directors and the Boston Human Resources Association. His home page can be found at www.stybelpeabody.com. The "Your Career" department of the home page contains downloadable back issues of his monthly *Boston Business Journal* column, "Your Career."

BETHANY SWEESY, MBA (McCallum School of Business, Bentley College), has received several awards, including *The National Dean's List 2002/2003*, *The 2004 Wall Street Journal Student Achievement Award,* and a research assistantship position at Bentley College. She has worked as a writer and editor in both financial services and medical devices. She is studying cardiac rhythm management at Arrhythmia Technologies Institute.

JOEL SAROSH THADAMALLA is a Faculty Member at the ICFAI Center for Management Research (ICMR).

JOSEPH TEYE-KOFI is a Graduate Research Assistant at the Tobin School of Business at Saint Johns.

JEFFREY W. TOTTEN, DBA (Louisiana Tech University), PCM, MBA, and BS (Northwestern State University), is an Assistant Professor of Marketing at McNeese State University in Lake Charles, Louisiana. Mr. Totten especially enjoys teaching marketing research, and has taught several other marketing courses, including principles, retailing, personal selling, and promotion strategy. His research interests include fast food nutrition, students' use and perceptions of mobile phones and body art, case research and writing, and students' perceptions of personal selling as a career choice. He has published in *Services Marketing Quarterly, International Journal of Consumer Studies, Journal of Healthcare Marketing,* and *Marketing Intelligence & Planning,* among others.

MRS. MIRDA VERMA serves as a consulting Editor at ICFAI Business School (ICMR).

JOYCE P. VINCELETTE, DBA (Indiana University), is a Professor of Management and the Coordinator of Management and Interdisciplinary Business Programs at The College of New Jersey. She was previously a faculty member at the University of South Florida. She has authored and coauthored various articles, chapters and cases that have appeared in management journals and strategic management texts and casebooks. She is also active as a consultant and trainer for a number of local and national business organizations as well as for a variety of not-for-profit and government agencies. She teaches and conducts research in the fields of strategic management and leadership.

KATHRYN E. WHEELEN, BA, LMT (University of Tampa), has worked as an Administrative Assistant for case and textbook development with the Thomas L. Wheelen Company (circa 1879). She is working on her Master's in Educational Leadership at Nova Southern University and works as a Reading Teacher at Dorothy Thomas, Tampa, Florida.

RICHARD D. WHEELEN, BS (University of South Florida), has worked as a case research assistant. He is currently practicing in the field of Health Care. He lives in Everett, Washington.

THOMAS L. WHEELEN II, BA (Boston College), has worked as a case research assistant. He is working and living in Boulder, Colorado.

THOMAS L. WHEELEN, DBA (George Washington University), MBA (Babson College), BS cum laude (Boston College). **Teaching experience:** Visiting Professorat Trinity College–University of Dublin; Professor of Strategic Management at University of South Florida, University of Virginia–McIntire School of Commerce, and Ralph A. Beeton Professor of Free Enterprise; Professor, Associate Professor, Assistant Professor, and Visiting Professor at University of Arizona and Northeastern University. **Academic, Industry and Military Experience:** Coordinator for Business Education at the University of Virginia College of Continuing Education; approve all undergraduate courses offered at seven Regional Centers and approved faculty, Liaison Faculty and Consultant to the National Academy of the FBI Academy, and developed, sold, and conducted over 200 seminars for local, state, and national governments, and companies for McIntire School of Commerce and Continuing Education. Held various management positions at General Electric Company; Assistant Supply Officer aboard nuclear support tender *U.S. Navy Supply Corps* (SC)–Lt. (SC) USNR. **Publications:** (1) *Monograph,* <u>An Assessment of Undergraduate Business Education in the United States</u> (with J. D. Hunger), 1980; (2) 60 books published; 14 books translated into 10 languages (Arabic, Bahasa, Indonesia, Chinese, Chinese Simplified, Greek, Italian, Japanese, Portuguese, and Thai); (3) coauthor with J. D. Hunger—5 active books: *Strategic Management and Business Policy*, 12th ed. (2010); *Cases in Strategic Management and Business Policy*, 12th Edition (2010); *Concepts in Strategic Management and Business Policy*, 12th ed. (2010); *Strategic Management and Business Policy*, 12th ed.; *International Edition* (2010); and *Essentials of Strategic Management*, 4th ed. (2007); (3) Co-editor *Developments in Information Systems* (1974) and *Collective Bargaining in the Public Sector* (1977); (4) Co-developer of software: STrategic Financial ANalyzer (ST. FAN) (1993, 1990, 1989); (5) Articles: authored more than forty articles that have appeared in such journals as the *Journal of Management, Business Quarterly, Personnel Journal, SAM Advanced Management Journal, Journal of Retailing, International Journal of Management,* and the *Handbook of Business Strategy.* (6) Cases: Have about 280 cases appearing in over 83 text and case books, as well as the *Business Case Journal, Journal of Management Case Studies, International Journal of Case Studies and Research and Case Research Journal.* **Awards:** (1) Fellow elected by the Society for Advancement of Management in 2002 (2) Fellow elected by North American Case Research Association in 2000; (3) Fellow elected by Text and Academic Authors Association in 2000; (4) 1999 Phil Carroll Advancement of Management Award in Strategic Management from the Society for Advancement of Management; (5) 1999 McGuffey Award for Excellence and Longevity for *Strategic Management and Business Policy*, 6th ed. from the Text and Academic Authors Association; (6) 1996/97 Teaching Incentive Program Award for teaching undergraduate strategic management; (7) Fulbright, 1996–1997, to Ireland but had to turn it down; (8) Endowed Chair, Ralph A. Beeton Professor, at University of Virginia (1981–1985); (9) Sesquicentennial Associateship research grant from the Center for Advanced Studies at the University of Virginia, 1979–1980; (10) *Small Business Administration* (Small Business Institute) supervised undergraduate team that won District, Regional III, and Honorable Mention Awards; and (11) awards for two articles. **Associations:** Dr. Wheelen serves on the Board of Directors of Adhia Mutual Fund, Society for Advancement of Management, and on the Editorial Board and the Associate Editor of *SAM Advanced Management Journal*. He served on the Board of Directors of Lazer Surgical Software, Inc., and Southern Management Association and on the Editorial Boards of the *Journal of Management* and *Journal of Management Case Studies, Journal of Retail Banking, Case Research Journal,* and *Business Case Journal.* He was Vice President of Strategic Management for the Society for the Advancement of Management, and President of the North American Case Research Association. Dr. Wheelen *is* a member of the Academy of Management, Beta Gamma Sigma, Southern Management Association, North American Case Research Association, Society for Advancement of Management, Society for Case Research, Strategic Management Association, and World Association for Case Method Research and Application. He has been listed in *Who's Who in Finance and Industry, Who's Who in the South and Southwest,* and *Who's Who in American Education.*

CYNTHIA CLARK WILLIAMS, MA (Northwestern University), PhD (Boston University), is an assistant professor of management and serves as the assistant director of the doctoral programs at Bentley College. Her research interests focus on various topics including corporate disclosures, governance, management strategy and organizational ethics. Prior to joining Bentley, she was a member of the faculty at Merrimack College and Boston University following a career in the securities industry. She is a member of the Academy of Management, the International Association of Business & Society, the Society for Business Ethics and the North American Case

Research Association. She is a reviewer for several journals and has presented numerous papers at conferences both in the United States and Europe. Recent published work has appeared in *Business & Society*, the *Case Research Journal, Investor Relations Quarterly,* and *Public Relations Review.*

SUZANNE WONG, BSBA Finance and Marketing (Northeastern University), MBA Finance (Bentley University), was born and raised in Jakarta, Indonesia. Upon graduation, Suzanne joined Fidelity Investments' parent company FMRCo in Boston as an Analyst in Technology Risk Management–Information Security. She plans to continue the operational success of her parents' pharmaceutical company in Indonesia.

TWELFTH EDITION

Strategic Management and Business Policy

ACHIEVING SUSTAINABILITY

INTERNATIONAL EDITION

PART 1

Introduction to Strategic Management and Business Policy

basic concepts of
Strategic Management

How does a company become successful and stay successful? Certainly not by playing it safe and following the traditional ways of doing business! Taking a strategic risk is what General Electric (GE) did when it launched its *Ecomagination* strategic initiative in 2005. According to Jeffrey Immelt, Chairman and CEO:

Ecomagination is GE's commitment to address challenges, such as the need for cleaner, more efficient sources of energy, reduced emissions, and abundant sources of clean water. And we plan to make money doing it. Increasingly for business, "green" is green.[1]

Immelt announced in a May 9, 2005, conference call that the company planned to more than double its spending on research and development from $700 million in 2004 to $1.5 billion by 2010 for cleaner products ranging from power generation to locomotives to water processing. The company intended to introduce 30 to 40 new products, including more efficient lighting and appliances, over the next two years. It also expected to double revenues from businesses that made wind turbines, treat water, and reduce greenhouse-emitting gases to at least $20 billion by 2010. In addition to working with customers to develop more efficient power generators, the company planned to reduce its own emission of greenhouse gases by 1% by 2012 and reduce the intensity of those gases 30% by 2008.[2] In 2006, GE's top management informed the many managers of its global business units that in the future they would be judged not only by the usual measures, such as return on capital, but that they would also be accountable for achieving corporate environmental objectives.

Ecomagination was a strategic change for GE, a company that had previously been condemned by environmentalists for its emphasis on coal and nuclear power and for polluting the Hudson and Housatonic rivers with polychlorinated biphenyls (PCBs) in the 1980s. Over the years, GE had been criticized for its lack of social responsibility and for its emphasis on profitability and financial performance over social and environmental objectives. What caused GE's management to make this strategic change?

In the 18 months before launching its new environmental strategy, GE invited managers from companies in various industries to participate in two-day "dreaming sessions" during which they were asked to imagine life in 2015—and the products they, as customers, would need from GE. The consensus was a future of rising fuel costs, restrictive environmental regulations, and growing consumer expectations for cleaner technologies, especially in the energy industry. Based on this conclusion, GE's management made the strategic decision to move in a new

Learning Objectives

After reading this chapter, you should be able to:

- Understand the benefits of strategic management
- Explain how globalization and environmental sustainability influence strategic management
- Understand the basic model of strategic management and its components
- Identify some common triggering events that act as stimuli for strategic change
- Understand strategic decision-making modes
- Use the strategic audit as a method of analyzing corporate functions and activities

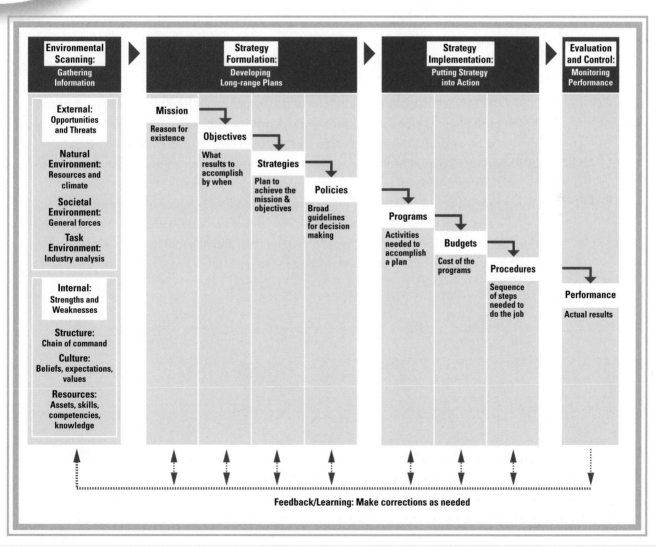

Environmental Scanning: Gathering Information	Strategy Formulation: Developing Long-range Plans	Strategy Implementation: Putting Strategy into Action	Evaluation and Control: Monitoring Performance

External: Opportunities and Threats

Natural Environment: Resources and climate

Societal Environment: General forces

Task Environment: Industry analysis

Internal: Strengths and Weaknesses

Structure: Chain of command

Culture: Beliefs, expectations, values

Resources: Assets, skills, competencies, knowledge

Mission — Reason for existence

Objectives — What results to accomplish by when

Strategies — Plan to achieve the mission & objectives

Policies — Broad guidelines for decision making

Programs — Activities needed to accomplish a plan

Budgets — Cost of the programs

Procedures — Sequence of steps needed to do the job

Performance — Actual results

Feedback/Learning: Make corrections as needed

direction. According to Vice Chairman David Calhoun, "We decided that if this is what our customers want, let's stop putting our heads in the sand, dodging environmental interests, and go from defense to offense."[3]

Following GE's announcement of its new strategic initiative, analysts raised questions regarding the company's ability to make Ecomagination successful. They not only questioned CEO Immelt's claim that green could be profitable as well as socially responsible, but they also wondered if Immelt could transform GE's incremental approach to innovation to one of pursuing riskier technologies, such as fuel cells, solar energy, hydrogen storage, and nanotechnology.[4] Other companies had made announcements of green initiatives, only to leave them withering on the vine when they interfered with profits. For example, FedEx had announced in 2003 that it would soon be deploying clean-burning hybrid trucks at a rate of 3,000 per year, eventually cutting emissions by 250,000 tons of greenhouse gases. Four years later, FedEx had purchased fewer than 100 hybrid vehicles, less than 1% of its fleet! With hybrid trucks costing 75% more than conventional trucks, it would take 10 years for the fuel savings to pay for the costly vehicles. FedEx management concluded that breaking even over a 10-year period was not the best use of company capital. As a result of this and other experiences, skeptics felt that most large companies were only indulging in *greenwash* when they talked loudly about their sustainability efforts, but followed through with very little actual results.[5]

CEO Immelt had put his reputation at risk by personally leading GE's Ecomagination initiative. Skeptics wondered if the environmental markets would materialize and if they would be as profitable as demanded by GE's shareholders. Would a corporate culture known for its pursuit of the Six Sigma statistics-based approach to quality control be able to create technological breakthroughs and new green businesses? If Immelt was correct, not only would GE benefit, but other companies would soon follow GE's lead. If, however, he was wrong, Immelt would have led his company down a dead end where it would be difficult to recover from the damage to its reputation and financial standing. According to a 25-year veteran of GE, "Jeff is asking us to take a really big swing . . . . This is hard for us."[6]

1.1 The Study of Strategic Management

Strategic management is a set of managerial decisions and actions that determines the long-run performance of a corporation. It includes environmental scanning (both external and internal), strategy formulation (strategic or long-range planning), strategy implementation, and evaluation and control. The study of strategic management, therefore, emphasizes the monitoring and evaluating of external opportunities and threats in light of a corporation's strengths and weaknesses. Originally called *business policy*, strategic management incorporates such topics as strategic planning, environmental scanning, and industry analysis.

PHASES OF STRATEGIC MANAGEMENT

Many of the concepts and techniques that deal with strategic management have been developed and used successfully by business corporations such as General Electric and the Boston Consulting Group. Over time, business practitioners and academic researchers have expanded and refined these concepts. Initially, strategic management was of most use to large corporations operating in multiple industries. Increasing risks of error, costly mistakes, and even economic ruin are causing today's professional managers in all organizations to take strategic management seriously in order to keep their companies competitive in an increasingly volatile environment.

As managers attempt to better deal with their changing world, a firm generally evolves through the following four **phases of strategic management**:[7]

Phase 1—Basic financial planning: Managers initiate serious planning when they are requested to propose the following year's budget. Projects are proposed on the basis of very little analysis, with most information coming from within the firm. The sales force usually provides the small amount of environmental information. Such simplistic operational planning only pretends to be strategic management, yet it is quite time consuming. Normal company activities are often suspended for weeks while managers try to cram ideas into the proposed budget. The time horizon is usually one year.

Phase 2—Forecast-based planning: As annual budgets become less useful at stimulating long-term planning, managers attempt to propose five-year plans. At this point they consider projects that may take more than one year. In addition to internal information, managers gather any available environmental data—usually on an ad hoc basis—and extrapolate current trends five years into the future. This phase is also time consuming, often involving a full month of managerial activity to make sure all the proposed budgets fit together. The process gets very political as managers compete for larger shares of funds. Endless meetings take place to evaluate proposals and justify assumptions. The time horizon is usually three to five years.

Phase 3—Externally oriented (strategic) planning: Frustrated with highly political yet ineffectual five-year plans, top management takes control of the planning process by initiating strategic planning. The company seeks to increase its responsiveness to changing markets and competition by thinking strategically. Planning is taken out of the hands of lower-level managers and concentrated in a planning staff whose task is to develop strategic plans for the corporation. Consultants often provide the sophisticated and innovative techniques that the planning staff uses to gather information and forecast future trends. Ex-military experts develop competitive intelligence units. Upper-level managers meet once a year at a resort "retreat" led by key members of the planning staff to evaluate and update the current strategic plan. Such top-down planning emphasizes formal strategy formulation and leaves the implementation issues to lower management levels. Top management typically develops five-year plans with help from consultants but minimal input from lower levels.

Phase 4—Strategic management: Realizing that even the best strategic plans are worthless without the input and commitment of lower-level managers, top management forms planning groups of managers and key employees at many levels, from various departments and workgroups. They develop and integrate a series of strategic plans aimed at achieving the company's primary objectives. Strategic plans at this point detail the implementation, evaluation, and control issues. Rather than attempting to perfectly forecast the future, the plans emphasize probable scenarios and contingency strategies. The sophisticated annual five-year strategic plan is replaced with strategic thinking at all levels of the organization throughout the year. Strategic information, previously available only centrally to top management, is available via local area networks and intranets to people throughout the organization. Instead of a large centralized planning staff, internal and external planning consultants are available to help guide group strategy discussions. Although top management may still initiate the strategic planning process, the resulting strategies may come from anywhere in the organization. Planning is typically interactive across levels and is no longer top down. People at all levels are now involved.

General Electric, one of the pioneers of strategic planning, led the transition from strategic planning to strategic management during the 1980s.[8] By the 1990s, most other corporations around the world had also begun the conversion to strategic management.

BENEFITS OF STRATEGIC MANAGEMENT

Strategic management emphasizes long-term performance. Many companies can manage short-term bursts of high performance, but only a few can sustain it over a longer period of time. For example, of the original *Forbes 100* companies listed in 1917, only 13 have survived to the present day. To be successful in the long-run, companies must not only be able to *execute* current activities to satisfy an existing market, but they must also *adapt* those activities to satisfy new and changing markets.[9]

Research reveals that organizations that engage in strategic management generally outperform those that do not.[10] The attainment of an appropriate match, or "fit," between an organization's environment and its strategy, structure, and processes has positive effects on the organization's performance.[11] Strategic planning becomes increasingly important as the environment becomes more unstable.[12] For example, studies of the impact of deregulation on the U.S. railroad and trucking industries found that companies that changed their strategies and structures as their environment changed outperformed companies that did not change.[13]

A survey of nearly 50 corporations in a variety of countries and industries found the three most highly rated benefits of strategic management to be:

- Clearer sense of strategic vision for the firm.
- Sharper focus on what is strategically important.
- Improved understanding of a rapidly changing environment.[14]

A recent survey by McKinsey & Company of 800 executives found that formal strategic planning processes improve overall satisfaction with strategy development.[15] To be effective, however, strategic management need not always be a formal process. It can begin with a few simple questions:

1. Where is the organization now? (Not where do we hope it is!)
2. If no changes are made, where will the organization be in one year? two years? five years? 10 years? Are the answers acceptable?
3. If the answers are not acceptable, what specific actions should management undertake? What are the risks and payoffs involved?

Bain & Company's *2007 Management Tools and Trends* survey of 1,221 global executives revealed strategic planning to be the most used management tool—used by 88% of respondents. Strategic planning is particularly effective at identifying new opportunities for growth and in ensuring that all managers have the same goals.[16] Other highly-ranked strategic management tools were mission and vision statements (used by 79% of respondents), core competencies (79%), scenario and contingency planning (69%), knowledge management (69%), strategic alliances (68%), and growth strategy tools (65%).[17] A study by Joyce, Nohria, and Roberson of 200 firms in 50 subindustries found that devising and maintaining an engaged, focused strategy was the first of four essential management practices that best differentiated between successful and unsuccessful companies.[18] Based on these and other studies, it can be concluded that strategic management is crucial for long-term organizational success.

Research into the planning practices of companies in the oil industry concludes that the real value of modern strategic planning is more in the *strategic thinking* and *organizational learning* that is part of a future-oriented planning process than in any resulting written strategic plan.[19] Small companies, in particular, may plan informally and irregularly. Nevertheless, studies of small- and medium-sized businesses reveal that the greater the level of planning intensity, as measured by the presence of a formal strategic plan, the greater the level of financial performance, especially when measured in terms of sales increases.[20]

Planning the strategy of large, multidivisional corporations can be complex and time consuming. It often takes slightly more than a year for a large company to move from situation assessment to a final decision agreement. For example, strategic plans in the global oil industry tend to cover four to five years. The planning horizon for oil exploration is even longer—up to 15 years.[21] Because of the relatively large number of people affected by a strategic decision in a large firm, a formalized, more sophisticated system is needed to ensure that strategic planning leads to successful performance. Otherwise, top management becomes isolated from developments in the business units, and lower-level managers lose sight of the corporate mission and objectives.

1.2 Globalization and Environmental Sustainability: Challenges to Strategic Management

Not too long ago, a business corporation could be successful by focusing only on making and selling goods and services within its national boundaries. International considerations were minimal. Profits earned from exporting products to foreign lands were considered frosting on the cake, but not really essential to corporate success. During the 1960s, for example, most U.S. companies organized themselves around a number of product divisions that made and sold goods only in the United States. All manufacturing and sales outside the United States were typically managed through one international division. An international assignment was usually considered a message that the person was no longer promotable and should be looking for another job.

Similarly, until the later part of the 20th century, a business firm could be very successful without being environmentally sensitive. Companies dumped their waste products in nearby streams or lakes and freely polluted the air with smoke containing noxious gases. Responding to complaints, governments eventually passed laws restricting the freedom to pollute the environment. Lawsuits forced companies to stop old practices. Nevertheless, until the dawn of the 21st century, most executives considered pollution abatement measures to be a cost of business that should be either minimized or avoided. Rather than clean up a polluting manufacturing site, they often closed the plant and moved manufacturing offshore to a developing nation with fewer environmental restrictions. Sustainability, as a term, was used to describe competitive advantage, not the environment.

IMPACT OF GLOBALIZATION

Today, everything has changed. **Globalization**, the integrated internationalization of markets and corporations, has changed the way modern corporations do business. As Thomas Friedman points out in *The World Is Flat*, jobs, knowledge, and capital are now able to move across borders with far greater speed and far less friction than was possible only a few years ago.[22] For example, the inter-connected nature of the global financial community meant that the mortgage lending problems of U.S. banks led to a global financial crisis in 2008. The worldwide availability of the Internet and supply-chain logistical improvements, such as containerized shipping, mean that companies can now locate anywhere and work with multiple partners to serve any market. To reach the economies of scale necessary to achieve the low costs, and thus the low prices, needed to be competitive, companies are now thinking of a global market instead of national markets. Nike and Reebok, for example, manufacture their athletic shoes in various countries throughout Asia for sale on every continent. Many other companies in North America and Western Europe are outsourcing their manufacturing, software development, or customer service to companies in China, Eastern Europe, or India. Large pools of talented software programmers, English language proficiency, and lower wages in India enables IBM to employ 75,000 people in its global delivery centers in Bangalore, Delhi, or Kolkata to serve the needs of clients in Atlanta, Munich, or Melbourne.[23] Instead of using one international division to manage everything outside the home country, large corporations are now using matrix structures in which product units are interwoven with country or regional units. International assignments are now considered key for anyone interested in reaching top management.

As more industries become global, strategic management is becoming an increasingly important way to keep track of international developments and position a company for long-term competitive advantage. For example, General Electric moved a major research and development lab for its medical systems division from Japan to China in order to learn more about developing new products for developing economies. Microsoft's largest research center outside Redmond, Washington, is in Beijing. According to Wilbur Chung, a Wharton professor, "Whatever China develops is rolled out to the rest of the world. China may have a lower GDP per-capita than developed countries, but the Chinese have a strong sense of how products should be designed for their market."[24]

The formation of regional trade associations and agreements, such as the European Union, NAFTA, Mercosur, Andean Community, CAFTA, and ASEAN, is changing how international business is being conducted. See the **Global Issue** feature to learn how regional trade associations are forcing corporations to establish a manufacturing presence wherever they wish to market goods or else face significant tariffs. These associations have led to the increasing harmonization of standards so that products can more easily be sold and moved across national boundaries. International considerations have led to the strategic alliance between British Airways and American Airlines and to the acquisition of the Miller Brewing Company by South African Breweries (SAB), among others.

IMPACT OF ENVIRONMENTAL SUSTAINABILITY

Environmental sustainability refers to the use of business practices to reduce a company's impact upon the natural, physical environment. Climate change is playing a growing role in business decisions. More than half of the global executives surveyed by McKinsey & Company in 2007 selected "environmental issues, including climate change," as the most important issue facing them over the next five years.[25] A 2005 survey of 27 large, publicly-held, multinational corporations based in North America revealed that 90% believed that government regulation was

GLOBAL issue

REGIONAL TRADE ASSOCIATIONS REPLACE NATIONAL TRADE BARRIERS

Formed as the European Economic Community in 1957, the **European Union (EU)** is the most significant trade association in the world. The goal of the EU is the complete economic integration of its 27 member countries so that goods made in one part of Europe can move freely without ever stopping for a customs inspection. The EU includes Austria, Belgium, Bulgaria, Cyprus, Czech Republic, Denmark, Estonia, Finland, France, Germany, Greece, Hungary, Ireland, Italy, Latvia, Lithuania, Luxembourg, Malta, Netherlands, Poland, Portugal, Romania, Slovakia, Slovenia, Spain, Sweden, and the United Kingdom. Others, including Croatia, Macedonia, and Turkey, have either recently applied or are in the process of applying. The EU is less than half the size of the United States of America, but has 50% more population. One currency, the euro, is being used throughout the region as members integrate their monetary systems. The steady elimination of barriers to free trade is providing the impetus for a series of mergers, acquisitions, and joint ventures among business corporations. The requirement of at least 60% local content to avoid tariffs has forced many U.S. and Asian companies to abandon exporting in favor of having a strong local presence in Europe.

Canada, the United States, and Mexico are affiliated economically under the **North American Free Trade Agreement (NAFTA)**. The goal of NAFTA is improved trade among the three member countries rather than complete economic integration. Launched in 1994, the agreement required all three members to remove all tariffs among themselves over 15 years, but they were allowed to have their own tariff arrangements with nonmember countries. Cars and trucks must have 62.5% North American content to qualify for duty-free status. Transportation restrictions and other regulations have been being significantly reduced. A number of Asian and European corporations, such as Sweden's Electrolux, have built manufacturing facilities in Mexico to take advantage of the country's lower wages and easy access to the entire North American region.

South American countries are also working to harmonize their trading relationships with each other and to form trade associations. The establishment of the **Mercosur** (**Mercosul** in Portuguese) free-trade area among Argentina, Brazil, Uruguay, and Paraguay means that a manufacturing presence within these countries is becoming essential to avoid tariffs for nonmember countries. Venezuela has applied for admission to Mercosur. The **Andean Community** (Comunidad Andina de Naciones) is a free-trade alliance composed of Columbia, Ecuador, Peru, Bolivia, and Chile. On May 23, 2008, the **Union of South American Nations** was formed to unite the two existing free-trade areas with a secretariat in Ecuador and a parliament in Bolivia.

In 2004, the five Central American countries of El Salvador, Guatemala, Honduras, Nicaragua, and Costa Rica plus the United States signed the **Central American Free Trade Agreement (CAFTA)**. The Dominican Republic joined soon thereafter. Previously, Central American textile manufacturers had to pay import duties of 18%–28% to sell their clothes in the United States unless they bought their raw material from U.S. companies. Under CAFTA, members can buy raw material from anywhere and their exports are duty free. In addition, CAFTA eliminated import duties on 80% of U.S. goods exported to the region, with the remaining tariffs being phased out over 10 years.

The **Association of Southeast Asian Nations (ASEAN)**—composed of Brunei Darussalam, Cambodia, Indonesia, Laos, Malaysia, Myanmar, Philippines, Singapore, Thailand, and Vietnam—is in the process of linking its members into a borderless economic zone by 2020. Tariffs had been significantly reduced among member countries by 2008. Increasingly referred to as ASEAN+3, ASEAN now includes China, Japan, and South Korea in its annual summit meetings. The ASEAN nations negotiated linkage of the ASEAN Free Trade Area (AFTA) with the existing free-trade area of Australia and New Zealand. With the EU extending eastward and NAFTA extending southward to someday connect with CAFTA and the Union of South American Nations, pressure is building on the independent Asian nations to join ASEAN.

imminent and 67% believed that such regulation would come between 2010 and 2015.[26] According to Eileen Claussen, President of the Pew Center on Global Climate Change:

> *There is a growing consensus among corporate leaders that taking action on climate change is a responsible business decision. From market shifts to regulatory constraints, climate change poses real risks and opportunities that companies must begin planning for today, or risk losing ground*

to their more forward-thinking competitors. Prudent steps taken now to address climate change can improve a company's competitive position relative to its peers and earn it a seat at the table to influence climate policy. With more and more action at the state level and increasing scientific clarity, it is time for businesses to craft corporate strategies that address climate change.[27]

Porter and Reinhardt warn that "in addition to understanding its emissions costs, every firm needs to evaluate its vulnerability to climate-related effects such as regional shifts in the availability of energy and water, the reliability of infrastructures and supply chains, and the prevalence of infectious diseases."[28] Swiss Re, the world's second-largest reinsurer, estimated that the overall economic costs of climate catastrophes related to climate change threatens to double to $150 billion per year by 2014. The insurance industry's share of this loss would be $30–$40 billion annually.[29]

The effects of climate change on industries and companies throughout the world can be grouped into six categories of risks: regulatory, supply chain, product and technology, litigation, reputational, and physical.[30]

1. **Regulatory Risk:** Companies in much of the world are already subject to the *Kyoto Protocol*, which requires the developed countries (and thus the companies operating within them) to reduce carbon dioxide and other greenhouse gases by an average of 6% from 1990 levels by 2012. The European Union has an emissions trading program that allows companies that emit greenhouse gases beyond a certain point to buy additional allowances from other companies whose emissions are lower than that allowed. Companies can also earn credits toward their emissions by investing in emissions abatement projects outside their own firms. Although the United States withdrew from the Kyoto Protocol, various regional, state, and local government policies affect company activities in the U.S. For example, seven Northeastern states, six Western states, and four Canadian provinces have adopted proposals to cap carbon emissions and establish carbon-trading programs.

2. **Supply Chain Risk:** Suppliers will be increasingly vulnerable to government regulations—leading to higher component and energy costs as they pass along increasing carbon-related costs to their customers. Global supply chains will be at risk from an increasing intensity of major storms and flooding. Higher sea levels resulting from the melting of polar ice will create problems for seaports. China, where much of the world's manufacturing is currently being outsourced, is becoming concerned with environmental degradation. In 2006, 12 Chinese ministries produced a report on global warming foreseeing a 5%–10% reduction in agricultural output by 2030; more droughts, floods, typhoons, and sandstorms; and a 40% increase in population threatened by plague.[31]

    The increasing scarcity of fossil-based fuel is already boosting transportation costs significantly. For example, Tesla Motors, the maker of an electric-powered sports car, transferred assembly of battery packs from Thailand to California because Thailand's low wages were more than offset by the costs of shipping thousand-pound battery packs across the Pacific Ocean.[32] Although the world production of oil had leveled off at 85 million barrels a day by 2008, the International Energy Agency predicted global demand to increase to 116 million barrels by 2030. Given that output from existing fields was falling 8% annually, oil companies must develop up to seven million barrels a day in additional capacity to meet projected demand. Nevertheless, James Mulva, CEO of ConocoPhilips, estimated in late 2007 that the output of oil will realistically stall at around 100 million barrels a day.[33]

3. **Product and Technology Risk:** Environmental sustainability can be a prerequisite to profitable growth. For example, worldwide investments in sustainable energy (including wind, solar, and water power) more than doubled to $70.9 billion from 2004 to 2006.[34] Sixty percent of U.S. respondents to an Environics study stated that knowing a company is mindful of its impact on the environment and society makes them more likely to buy their products

and services.[35] Carbon-friendly products using new technologies are becoming increasingly popular with consumers. Those automobile companies, for example, that were quick to introduce hybrid or alternative energy cars gained a competitive advantage.

4. **Litigation Risk:** Companies that generate significant carbon emissions face the threat of lawsuits similar to those in the tobacco, pharmaceutical, and building supplies (e.g., asbestos) industries. For example, oil and gas companies were sued for greenhouse gas emissions in the federal district court of Mississippi, based on the assertion that these companies contributed to the severity of Hurricane Katrina. As of October 2006, at least 16 cases were pending in federal or state courts in the U.S. "This boomlet in global warming litigation represents frustration with the White House's and Congress' failure to come to grips with the issue," explained John Echeverria, executive director of Georgetown University's Environmental Law & Policy Institute.[36]

5. **Reputational Risk:** A company's impact on the environment can heavily affect its overall reputation. The Carbon Trust, a consulting group, found that in some sectors the value of a company's brand could be at risk because of negative perceptions related to climate change. In contrast, a company with a good record of environmental sustainability may create a competitive advantage in terms of attracting and keeping loyal consumers, employees, and investors. For example, Wal-Mart's pursuit of environmental sustainability as a core business strategy has helped soften its negative reputation as a low-wage, low-benefit employer. By setting objectives for its retail stores of reducing greenhouse gases by 20%, reducing solid waste by 25%, increasing truck fleet efficiency by 25%, and using 100% renewable energy, it is also forcing its suppliers to become more environmentally sustainable.[37] Tools have recently been developed to measure sustainability on a variety of factors. For example, the SAM (Sustainable Asset Management) Group of Zurich, Switzerland, has been assessing and documenting the sustainability performance of over 1,000 corporations annually since 1999. SAM lists the top 15% of firms in its *Sustainability Yearbook* and classifies them into gold, silver, and bronze categories.[38] *Business Week* published its first list of the world's 100 most sustainable corporations January 29, 2007. The *Dow Jones Sustainability Indexes* and the *KLD Broad Market Social Index*, which evaluate companies on a range of environmental, social, and governance criteria are used for investment decisions.[39] Financial services firms, such as Goldman Sachs, Bank of America, JPMorgan Chase, and Citigroup have adopted guidelines for lending and asset management aimed at promoting clean-energy alternatives.[40]

6. **Physical Risk:** The direct risk posed by climate change includes the physical effects of droughts, floods, storms, and rising sea levels. Average Arctic temperatures have risen four to five degrees Fahrenheit (two to three degrees Celsius) in the past 50 years, leading to melting glaciers and sea levels rising one inch per decade.[41] Industries most likely to be affected are insurance, agriculture, fishing, forestry, real estate, and tourism. Physical risk can also affect other industries, such as oil and gas, through higher insurance premiums paid on facilities in vulnerable areas. Coca-Cola, for example, studies the linkages between climate change and water availability in terms of how this will affect the location of its new bottling plants. The warming of the Tibetan plateau has led to a thawing of the permafrost—thereby threatening the newly-completed railway line between China and Tibet.[42] (See the **Environmental Sustainability Issue** feature for a more complete list of projected effects of climate change.)

Although global warming remains a controversial topic, the best argument in favor of working toward environmental sustainability is a variation of Pascal's Wager on the existence of God:

> *The same goes for global warming. If you accept it as reality, adapting your strategy and practices, your plants will use less energy and emit fewer effluents. Your packaging will be more*

ENVIRONMENTAL sustainability issue

PROJECTED EFFECTS OF CLIMATE CHANGE

According to the Intergovernmental Panel on Climate Change (IPCC), the global climate system is projected to include a number of changes during the 21st century:

TEMPERATURE INCREASE

- Global average warming of approximately 0.2 degrees Celsius each decade.
- Long-term warming associated with doubled carbon dioxide concentrations in the range of 2 to 4.5 degrees Celsius.
- Fewer cold days and nights; warmer and more frequent hot days and nights.
- Increased frequency, intensity, and duration of heat waves in central Europe, western U.S., East Asia, and Korea.

SEA LEVEL RISE

- Sea level will continue to rise due to thermal expansion of seawater and loss of land ice at greater rates.
- Sea level rise of 18 to 59 centimeters by the end of the 21st century.
- Warming will continue contributing to sea level rise for many centuries even if greenhouse gas concentrations are stabilized.

PRECIPITATION AND HUMIDITY

- Increasing numbers of wet days in high latitudes; increasing numbers of dry spells in subtropical areas.

- Annual precipitation increases in most of northern Europe, Canada, northeastern U.S., and the Arctic.
- Winter precipitation increases in northern Asia and the Tibetan Plateau.
- Dry spells increase in length and frequency in the Mediterranean, Australia, and New Zealand; seasonal droughts increase in many mid-latitude continent interiors.

EXTREME WEATHER-RELATED EVENTS

- Increasing intense tropical cyclone activity.
- Increasing frequency of flash floods and large-area floods in many regions.
- Increasing risk of drought in Australia, eastern New Zealand, and the Mediterranean, with seasonal droughts in central Europe and Central America.
- Increasing wildfires in arid and semi-arid areas such as Australia and the western U.S.

OTHER RELATED EFFECTS

- Decreasing snow season length and depth in Europe and North America.
- Fewer cold days and nights leading to decreasing frosts.
- Accelerated glacier loss.
- Reduction in and warming of permafrost.

....

SOURCE: F. G. Sussman and J. R. Freed, "Adapting to Climate Change: A Business Approach," Paper prepared for the Pew Center on Global Climate Change (April 2008), pp. 5–6.

biodegradable, and your new products will be able to capture any markets created by severe weather effects. Yes, global warming might not be as damaging as some predict, and you might have invested more than you needed, but it's just as Pascal said: Given all the possible outcomes, the upside of being ready and prepared for a "fearsome event" surely beats the alternative.[43]

1.3 Theories of Organizational Adaptation

Globalization and environmental sustainability present real challenges to the strategic management of business corporations. How can any one company keep track of all the changing technological, economic, political–legal, and sociocultural trends around the world and make the necessary adjustments? This is not an easy task. Various theories have been proposed to account for how organizations obtain fit with their environment. The theory of **population ecology,** for example, proposes that once an organization is successfully established in a particular environmental niche, it is unable to adapt to changing conditions. Inertia prevents the organization from changing. The company is thus replaced (is bought out or goes bankrupt) by other organizations more suited to the new environment. Although it is a popular theory in sociology, research fails to support the arguments of population ecology.[44] **Institution theory,** in contrast, proposes that organizations can and do adapt to changing conditions by imitating other successful organizations. To its credit, many examples can be found of companies that have adapted to changing circumstances by imitating an admired firm's strategies and management techniques.[45] The theory does not, however, explain how or by whom successful new strategies are developed in the first place. The **strategic choice perspective** goes one step further by proposing that not only do organizations adapt to a changing environment, but they also have the opportunity and power to reshape their environment. This perspective is supported by research indicating that the decisions of a firm's management have at least as great an impact on firm performance as overall industry factors.[46] Because of its emphasis on managers making rational strategic decisions, the strategic choice perspective is the dominant one taken in strategic management. Its argument that adaptation is a dynamic process fits with the view of **organizational learning theory,** which says that an organization adjusts defensively to a changing environment and uses knowledge offensively to improve the fit between itself and its environment. This perspective expands the strategic choice perspective to include people at all levels becoming involved in providing input into strategic decisions.[47]

In agreement with the concepts of organizational learning theory, an increasing number of companies are realizing that they must shift from a vertically organized, top-down type of organization to a more horizontally managed, interactive organization. They are attempting to adapt more quickly to changing conditions by becoming "learning organizations."

1.4 Creating a Learning Organization

Strategic management has now evolved to the point that its primary value is in helping an organization operate successfully in a dynamic, complex environment. To be competitive in dynamic environments, corporations are becoming less bureaucratic and more flexible. In stable environments such as those that existed in years past, a competitive strategy simply involved defining a competitive position and then defending it. As it takes less and less time for one product or technology to replace another, companies are finding that there is no such thing as a permanent competitive advantage. Many agree with Richard D'Aveni, who says in his book *Hypercompetition* that any sustainable competitive advantage lies not in doggedly following a centrally managed five-year plan but in stringing together a series of strategic short-term thrusts (as Intel does by cutting into the sales of its own offerings with periodic introductions of new products).[48] This means that corporations must develop *strategic flexibility*—the ability to shift from one dominant strategy to another.[49]

Strategic flexibility demands a long-term commitment to the development and nurturing of critical resources. It also demands that the company become a **learning organization**—an organization skilled at creating, acquiring, and transferring knowledge and at modifying its behavior to reflect new knowledge and insights. Organizational learning is a critical component of competitiveness in a dynamic environment. It is particularly important to innovation and new product development.[50] For example, both Hewlett-Packard and British Petroleum (BP) use an extensive network of informal committees to transfer knowledge among their cross-functional teams and to help spread new sources of knowledge quickly.[51] Siemens, a major electronics company, created a global knowledge-sharing network, called ShareNet, in order to quickly spread information technology throughout the firm. Based on its experience with ShareNet, Siemens established PeopleShareNet, a system that serves as a virtual expert marketplace for facilitating the creation of cross-cultural teams composed of members with specific knowledge and competencies.[52]

Learning organizations are skilled at four main activities:

- Solving problems systematically
- Experimenting with new approaches
- Learning from their own experiences and past history as well as from the experiences of others
- Transferring knowledge quickly and efficiently throughout the organization[53]

Business historian Alfred Chandler proposes that high-technology industries are defined by "paths of learning" in which organizational strengths derive from learned capabilities.[54] According to Chandler, companies spring from an individual entrepreneur's knowledge, which then evolves into organizational knowledge. This organizational knowledge is composed of three basic strengths: technical skills, mainly in research; functional knowledge, such as production and marketing; and managerial expertise. This knowledge leads to new businesses where the company can succeed and creates an entry barrier to new competitors. Chandler points out that once a corporation has built its learning base to the point where it has become a core company in its industry, entrepreneurial startups are rarely able to successfully enter. Thus, organizational knowledge becomes a competitive advantage.

Strategic management is essential for learning organizations to avoid stagnation through continuous self-examination and experimentation. People at all levels, not just top management, participate in strategic management—helping to scan the environment for critical information, suggesting changes to strategies and programs to take advantage of environmental shifts, and working with others to continuously improve work methods, procedures, and evaluation techniques. For example, Motorola developed an action learning format in which people from marketing, product development, and manufacturing meet to argue and reach agreement about the needs of the market, the best new product, and the schedules of each group producing it. This action learning approach overcame the problems that arose previously when the three departments met and formally agreed on plans but continued with their work as if nothing had happened.[55] Research indicates that involving more people in the strategy process results in people not only viewing the process more positively, but also acting in ways that make the process more effective.[56]

Organizations that are willing to experiment and are able to learn from their experiences are more successful than those that are not.[57] For example, in a study of U.S. manufacturers of diagnostic imaging equipment, the most successful firms were those that improved products sold in the United States by incorporating some of what they had learned from their manufacturing and sales experiences in other nations. The less successful firms used the foreign operations primarily as sales outlets, not as important sources of technical knowledge.[58] Research also reveals that multidivisional corporations that establish ways to transfer knowledge across divisions are more innovative than other diversified corporations that do not.[59]

1.5 Basic Model of Strategic Management

Strategic management consists of four basic elements:

- **Environmental scanning**
- **Strategy formulation**
- **Strategy implementation**
- **Evaluation and control**

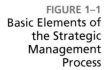

FIGURE 1–1
Basic Elements of
the Strategic
Management
Process

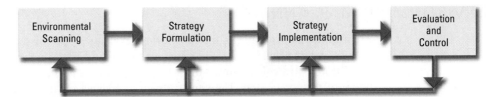

Figure 1–1 illustrates how these four elements interact; **Figure 1–2** expands each of these elements and serves as the model for this book. This model is both rational and prescriptive. It is a planning model that presents what a corporation *should* do in terms of the strategic management process, not what any particular firm may actually do. The rational planning model predicts that as environmental uncertainty increases, corporations that work more diligently to analyze and predict more accurately the changing situation in which they operate will outperform those that do not. Empirical research studies support this model.[60] The terms used in Figure 1–2 are explained in the following pages.

FIGURE 1–2   Strategic Management Model

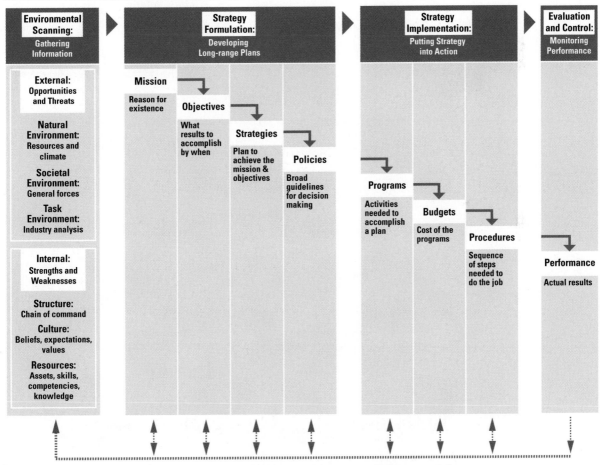

SOURCE: T. L. Wheelen, "Strategic Management Model," adapted from "Concepts of Management," presented to Society for Advancement of Management (SAM), International Meeting, Richmond, VA, 1981. Kathryn E. Wheelen solely owns all of (Dr) Thomas L. Wheelen's copyright materials. Kathryn E. Wheelen requires written reprint permission for each book that this material is to be printed in. Copyright © 1981 by T. L. Wheelen and SAM. Copyright © 1982, 1985, 1988, and 2005 by T. L. Wheelen and J. D. Hunger. Revised 1989, 1995, 1998, 2000, 2005, and 2009. Reprinted by permission of the copyright holders.

ENVIRONMENTAL SCANNING

Environmental scanning is the monitoring, evaluating, and disseminating of information from the external and internal environments to key people within the corporation. Its purpose is to identify **strategic factors**—those external and internal elements that will determine the future of the corporation. The simplest way to conduct environmental scanning is through **SWOT analysis**. SWOT is an acronym used to describe the particular **S**trengths, **W**eaknesses, **O**pportunities, and **T**hreats that are strategic factors for a specific company. The **external environment** consists of variables (**O**pportunities and **T**hreats) that are outside the organization and not typically within the short-run control of top management. These variables form the context within which the corporation exists. **Figure 1–3** depicts key environmental variables. They may be general forces and trends within the natural or societal environments or specific factors that operate within an organization's specific task environment—often called its *industry*. (These external variables are defined and discussed in more detail in **Chapter 4**.)

The **internal environment** of a corporation consists of variables (**S**trengths and **W**eaknesses) that are within the organization itself and are not usually within the short-run

FIGURE 1–3   Environmental Variables

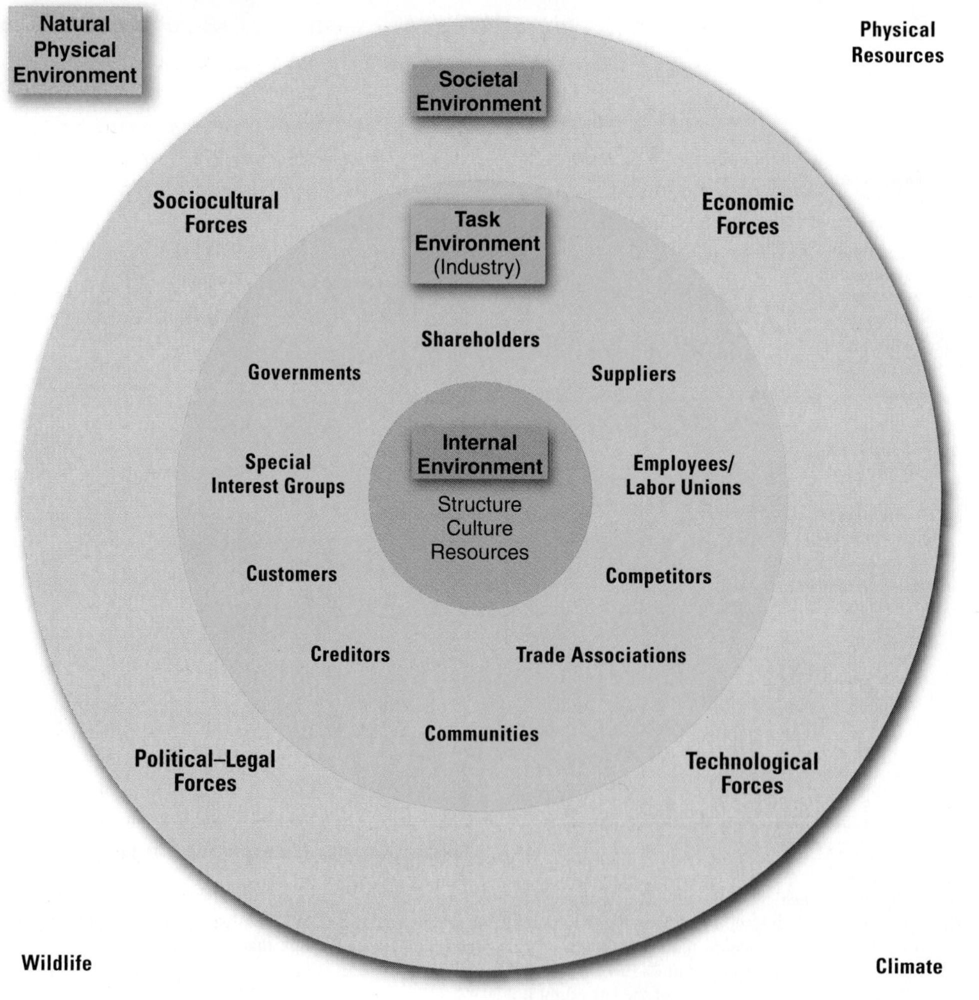

control of top management. These variables form the context in which work is done. They include the corporation's structure, culture, and resources. Key strengths form a set of core competencies that the corporation can use to gain competitive advantage. (These internal variables and core competencies are defined and discussed in more detail in **Chapter 5**.)

STRATEGY FORMULATION

Strategy formulation is the development of long-range plans for the effective management of environmental opportunities and threats, in light of corporate strengths and weaknesses (SWOT). It includes defining the corporate mission, specifying achievable objectives, developing strategies, and setting policy guidelines.

Mission

An organization's **mission** is the purpose or reason for the organization's existence. It tells what the company is providing to society—either a service such as housecleaning or a product such as automobiles. A well-conceived mission statement defines the fundamental, unique purpose that sets a company apart from other firms of its type and identifies the scope or domain of the company's operations in terms of products (including services) offered and markets served. Research reveals that firms with mission statements containing explicit descriptions of customers served and technologies used have significantly higher growth than firms without such statements.[61] A mission statement may also include the firm's values and philosophy about how it does business and treats its employees. It puts into words not only what the company is now but what it wants to become—management's strategic vision of the firm's future. The mission statement promotes a sense of shared expectations in employees and communicates a public image to important stakeholder groups in the company's task environment. Some people like to consider vision and mission as two different concepts: Mission describes what the organization is now; **vision** describes what the organization would like to become. We prefer to combine these ideas into a single mission statement.[62] Some companies prefer to list their values and philosophy of doing business in a separate publication called a *values statement*. For a listing of the many things that could go into a mission statement, see **Strategy Highlight 1.1**.

One example of a mission statement is that of Google:

> *To organize the world's information and make it universally accessible and useful.*[63]

Another classic example is that etched in bronze at Newport News Shipbuilding, unchanged since its founding in 1886:

> *We shall build good ships here—at a profit if we can—at a loss if we must—but always good ships.*[64]

A mission may be defined narrowly or broadly in scope. An example of a *broad* mission statement is that used by many corporations: "Serve the best interests of shareowners, customers, and employees." A broadly defined mission statement such as this keeps the company from restricting itself to one field or product line, but it fails to clearly identify either what it makes or which products/markets it plans to emphasize. Because this broad statement is so general, a *narrow* mission statement, such as the preceding examples by Google and Newport News Shipbuilding, is generally more useful. A narrow mission very clearly states the organization's primary business, but it may limit the scope of the firm's activities in terms of the product or service offered, the technology used, and the market served. Research indicates that a narrow mission statement may be best in a turbulent industry because it keeps the firm focused on what it does best; whereas, a broad mission statement may be best in a stable environment that lacks growth opportunities.[65]

STRATEGY highlight 1.1

DO YOU HAVE A GOOD MISSION STATEMENT?

Andrew Campbell, a director of Ashridge Strategic Management Centre and a long-time contributor to *Long Range Planning*, proposes a means for evaluating a mission statement. Arguing that mission statements can be more than just an expression of a company's purpose and ambition, he suggests that they can also be a company flag to rally around, a signpost for all stakeholders, a guide to behavior, and a celebration of a company's culture. For a company trying to achieve all of the above, evaluate its mission statement using the following 10-question test. Score each question 0 for no, 1 for somewhat, or 2 for yes. According to Campbell, a score of over 15 is exceptional, and a score of less than 10 suggests that more work needs to be done.

1. Does the statement describe an inspiring purpose that avoids playing to the selfish interests of the stakeholders?

2. Does the statement describe the company's responsibility to its stakeholders?

3. Does the statement define a business domain and explain why it is attractive?

4. Does the statement describe the strategic positioning that the company prefers in a way that helps to identify the sort of competitive advantage it will look for?

5. Does the statement identify values that link with the organization's purpose and act as beliefs with which employees can feel proud?

6. Do the values resonate with and reinforce the organization's strategy?

7. Does the statement describe important behavior standards that serve as beacons of the strategy and the values?

8. Are the behavior standards described in a way that enables individual employees to judge whether they are behaving correctly?

9. Does the statement give a portrait of the company, capturing the culture of the organization?

10. Is the statement easy to read?

SOURCE: Reprinted from Long Range Planning, Vol. 30, No. 6, 1997, Campbell "Mission Statements", pp. 931–932, Copyright © 1997 with permission of Elsevier.

Objectives

Objectives are the end results of planned activity. They should be stated as *action verbs* and tell what is to be accomplished by when and quantified if possible. The achievement of corporate objectives should result in the fulfillment of a corporation's mission. In effect, this is what society gives back to the corporation when the corporation does a good job of fulfilling its mission. For example, by providing society with gums, candy, iced tea, and carbonated drinks, Cadbury Schweppes, has become the world's largest confectioner by sales. One of its prime objectives is to increase sales 4%–6% each year. Even though its profit margins were lower than those of Nestlé, Kraft, and Wrigley, its rivals in confectionary, or those of Coca-Cola or Pepsi, its rivals in soft drinks, Cadbury Schweppes' management established the objective of increasing profit margins from around 10% in 2007 to the mid-teens by 2011.[66]

The term *goal* is often used interchangeably with the term objective. In this book, we prefer to differentiate the two terms. In contrast to an objective, we consider a *goal* as an open-ended statement of what one wants to accomplish, with no quantification of what is to be achieved and no time criteria for completion. For example, a simple statement of "increased profitability" is thus a goal, not an objective, because it does not state how much profit the firm wants to make the next year. A good objective should be action-oriented and begin with the word *to*. An example of an objective is "to increase the firm's profitability in 2010 by 10% over 2009."

Some of the areas in which a corporation might establish its goals and objectives are:

- Profitability (net profits)
- Efficiency (low costs, etc.)
- Growth (increase in total assets, sales, etc.)
- Shareholder wealth (dividends plus stock price appreciation)
- Utilization of resources (ROE or ROI)
- Reputation (being considered a "top" firm)
- Contributions to employees (employment security, wages, diversity)
- Contributions to society (taxes paid, participation in charities, providing a needed product or service)
- Market leadership (market share)
- Technological leadership (innovations, creativity)
- Survival (avoiding bankruptcy)
- Personal needs of top management (using the firm for personal purposes, such as providing jobs for relatives)

Strategies

A **strategy** of a corporation forms a comprehensive master plan that states how the corporation will achieve its mission and objectives. It maximizes competitive advantage and minimizes competitive disadvantage. For example, even though Cadbury Schweppes was a major competitor in confectionary and soft drinks, it was not likely to achieve its challenging objective of significantly increasing its profit margin within four years without making a major change in strategy. Management therefore decided to cut costs by closing 33 factories and reducing staff by 10%. It also made the strategic decision to concentrate on the confectionary business by divesting its less-profitable Dr. Pepper/Snapple soft drinks unit. Management was also considering acquisitions as a means of building on its existing strengths in confectionary by purchasing either Kraft's confectionary unit or the Hershey Company.

The typical business firm usually considers three types of strategy: corporate, business, and functional.

1. **Corporate strategy** describes a company's overall direction in terms of its general attitude toward growth and the management of its various businesses and product lines. Corporate strategies typically fit within the three main categories of stability, growth, and retrenchment. Cadbury Schweppes, for example, was following a corporate strategy of retrenchment by selling its marginally profitable soft drink business and concentrating on its very successful confectionary business.

2. **Business strategy** usually occurs at the business unit or product level, and it emphasizes improvement of the competitive position of a corporation's products or services in the specific industry or market segment served by that business unit. Business strategies may fit within the two overall categories, *competitive* and *cooperative* strategies. For example, Staples, the U.S. office supply store chain, has used a competitive strategy to differentiate its retail stores from its competitors by adding services to its stores, such as copying, UPS shipping, and hiring mobile technicians who can fix computers and install networks. British Airways has followed a cooperative strategy by forming an alliance with American Airlines in order to provide global service. Cooperative strategy may thus be used to

provide a competitive advantage. Intel, a manufacturer of computer microprocessors, uses its alliance (cooperative strategy) with Microsoft to differentiate itself (competitive strategy) from AMD, its primary competitor.

3. **Functional strategy** is the approach taken by a functional area to achieve corporate and business unit objectives and strategies by maximizing resource productivity. It is concerned with developing and nurturing a distinctive competence to provide a company or business unit with a competitive advantage. Examples of research and development (R&D) functional strategies are technological followership (imitation of the products of other companies) and technological leadership (pioneering an innovation). For years, Magic Chef had been a successful appliance maker by spending little on R&D but by quickly imitating the innovations of other competitors. This helped the company to keep its costs lower than those of its competitors and consequently to compete with lower prices. In terms of marketing functional strategies, Procter & Gamble (P&G) is a master of marketing "pull"—the process of spending huge amounts on advertising in order to create customer demand. This supports P&G's competitive strategy of differentiating its products from those of its competitors.

Business firms use all three types of strategy simultaneously. A **hierarchy of strategy** is a grouping of strategy types by level in the organization. Hierarchy of strategy is a nesting of one strategy within another so that they complement and support one another. (See **Figure 1–4**.) Functional strategies support business strategies, which, in turn, support the corporate strategy(ies).

Just as many firms often have no formally stated objectives, many firms have unstated, incremental, or intuitive strategies that have never been articulated or analyzed. Often the only way to spot a corporation's implicit strategies is to look not at what management says but at what it does. Implicit strategies can be derived from corporate policies, programs approved (and disapproved), and authorized budgets. Programs and divisions favored by budget increases and staffed by managers who are considered to be on the fast promotion track reveal where the corporation is putting its money and its energy.

FIGURE 1–4
Hierarchy
of Strategy

Corporate Strategy:
Overall Direction of
Company and Management
of Its Businesses

Business
Strategy:
Competitive and
Cooperative Strategies

Functional
Strategy:
Maximize Resource
Productivity

Policies

A **policy** is a broad guideline for decision making that links the formulation of a strategy with its implementation. Companies use policies to make sure that employees throughout the firm make decisions and take actions that support the corporation's mission, objectives, and strategies. For example, when Cisco decided on a strategy of growth through acquisitions, it established a policy to consider only companies with no more than 75 employees, 75% of whom were engineers.[67] Consider the following company policies:

- **3M:** 3M says researchers should spend 15% of their time working on something other than their primary project. (This supports 3M's strong product development strategy.)
- **Intel:** Intel cannibalizes its own product line (undercuts the sales of its current products) with better products before a competitor does so. (This supports Intel's objective of market leadership.)
- **General Electric:** GE must be number one or two wherever it competes. (This supports GE's objective to be number one in market capitalization.)
- **Southwest Airlines:** Southwest offers no meals or reserved seating on airplanes. (This supports Southwest's competitive strategy of having the lowest costs in the industry.)
- **Exxon:** Exxon pursues only projects that will be profitable even when the price of oil drops to a low level. (This supports Exxon's profitability objective.)

Policies such as these provide clear guidance to managers throughout the organization. (Strategy formulation is discussed in greater detail in **Chapters 6, 7,** and **8**.)

STRATEGY IMPLEMENTATION

Strategy implementation is a process by which strategies and policies are put into action through the development of programs, budgets, and procedures. This process might involve changes within the overall culture, structure, and/or management system of the entire organization. Except when such drastic corporatewide changes are needed, however, the implementation of strategy is typically conducted by middle- and lower-level managers, with review by top management. Sometimes referred to as *operational planning*, strategy implementation often involves day-to-day decisions in resource allocation.

Programs

A **program** is a statement of the activities or steps needed to accomplish a single-use plan. It makes a strategy action oriented. It may involve restructuring the corporation, changing the company's internal culture, or beginning a new research effort. For example, Boeing's strategy to regain industry leadership with its proposed 787 Dreamliner meant that the company had to increase its manufacturing efficiency in order to keep the price low. To significantly cut costs, management decided to implement a series of programs:

- Outsource approximately 70% of manufacturing.
- Reduce final assembly time to three days (compared to 20 for its 737 plane) by having suppliers build completed plane sections.
- Use new, lightweight composite materials in place of aluminum to reduce inspection time.
- Resolve poor relations with labor unions caused by downsizing and outsourcing.

Another example is a set of programs used by automaker BMW to achieve its objective of increasing production efficiency by 5% each year: (a) shorten new model development time from 60 to 30 months, (b) reduce preproduction time from a year to no more than five months, and (c) build at least two vehicles in each plant so that production can shift among models depending upon demand.

Budgets

A **budget** is a statement of a corporation's programs in terms of dollars. Used in planning and control, a budget lists the detailed cost of each program. Many corporations demand a certain percentage return on investment, often called a "hurdle rate," before management will approve a new program. This ensures that the new program will significantly add to the corporation's profit performance and thus build shareholder value. The budget thus not only serves as a detailed plan of the new strategy in action, it also specifies through pro forma financial statements the expected impact on the firm's financial future.

For example, General Motors budgeted $4.3 billion to update and expand its Cadillac line of automobiles. With this money, the company was able to increase the number of models from five to nine and to offer more powerful engines, sportier handling, and edgier styling. The company reversed its declining market share by appealing to a younger market. (The average Cadillac buyer in 2000 was 67 years old.)[68] Another example is the $8 billion budget that General Electric established to invest in new jet engine technology for regional-jet airplanes. Management decided that an anticipated growth in regional jets should be the company's target market. The program paid off when GE won a $3 billion contract to provide jet engines for China's new fleet of 500 regional jets in time for the 2008 Beijing Olympics.[69]

Procedures

Procedures, sometimes termed Standard Operating Procedures (SOP), are a system of sequential steps or techniques that describe in detail how a particular task or job is to be done. They typically detail the various activities that must be carried out in order to complete the corporation's program. For example, when the home improvement retailer Home Depot noted that sales were lagging because its stores were full of clogged aisles, long checkout times, and too few salespeople, management changed its procedures for restocking shelves and pricing the products. Instead of requiring its employees to do these activities at the same time they were working with customers, management moved these activities to when the stores were closed at night. Employees were then able to focus on increasing customer sales during the day. Both UPS and FedEx put such an emphasis on consistent, quality service that both companies have strict rules for employee behavior, ranging from how a driver dresses to how keys are held when approaching a customer's door. (Strategy implementation is discussed in more detail in **Chapters 9** and **10**.)

EVALUATION AND CONTROL

Evaluation and control is a process in which corporate activities and performance results are monitored so that actual performance can be compared with desired performance. Managers at all levels use the resulting information to take corrective action and resolve problems. Although evaluation and control is the final major element of strategic management, it can also pinpoint weaknesses in previously implemented strategic plans and thus stimulate the entire process to begin again.

Performance is the end result of activities.[70] It includes the actual outcomes of the strategic management process. The practice of strategic management is justified in terms of its ability to improve an organization's performance, typically measured in terms of profits and return on investment. For evaluation and control to be effective, managers must obtain clear, prompt, and unbiased information from the people below them in the corporation's hierarchy. Using this information, managers compare what is actually happening with what was originally planned in the formulation stage.

For example, when market share (followed by profits) declined at Dell in 2007, Michael Dell, founder, returned to the CEO position and reevaluated his company's strategy and operations. Planning for continued growth, the company's expansion of its computer product line into new types of hardware, such as storage, printers, and televisions, had not worked as planned. In some areas, like televisions and printers, Dell's customization ability did not add much value. In other areas, like services, lower-cost competitors were already established. Michael Dell concluded, "I think you're going to see a more streamlined organization, with a much clearer strategy."[71]

The evaluation and control of performance completes the strategic management model. Based on performance results, management may need to make adjustments in its strategy formulation, in implementation, or in both. (Evaluation and control is discussed in more detail in **Chapter 11**.)

FEEDBACK/LEARNING PROCESS

Note that the strategic management model depicted in **Figure 1–2** includes a feedback/learning process. Arrows are drawn coming out of each part of the model and taking information to each of the previous parts of the model. As a firm or business unit develops strategies, programs, and the like, it often must go back to revise or correct decisions made earlier in the process. For example, poor performance (as measured in evaluation and control) usually indicates that something has gone wrong with either strategy formulation or implementation. It could also mean that a key variable, such as a new competitor, was ignored during environmental scanning and assessment. In the case of Dell, the personal computer market had matured and by 2007 there were fewer growth opportunities available within the industry. Even Jim Cramer, host of the popular television program, *Mad Money*, was referring to computers in 2008 as "old technology" having few growth prospects. Dell's management needed to reassess the company's environment and find better opportunities to profitably apply its core competencies.

1.6 Initiation of Strategy: Triggering Events

After much research, Henry Mintzberg discovered that strategy formulation is typically not a regular, continuous process: "It is most often an irregular, discontinuous process, proceeding in fits and starts. There are periods of stability in strategy development, but also there are periods of flux, of groping, of piecemeal change, and of global change."[72] This view of strategy formulation as an irregular process can be explained by the very human tendency to continue on a particular course of action until something goes wrong or a person is forced to question his or her actions. This period of strategic drift may result from inertia on the part of the organization, or it may reflect management's belief that the current strategy is still appropriate and needs only some fine-tuning.

Most large organizations tend to follow a particular strategic orientation for about 15 to 20 years before making a significant change in direction.[73] This phenomenon, called *punctuated equilibrium*, describes corporations as evolving through relatively long periods of stability (equilibrium periods) punctuated by relatively short bursts of fundamental change (revolutionary periods).[74] After this rather long period of fine-tuning an existing strategy, some sort of shock to the system is needed to motivate management to seriously reassess the corporation's situation.

A **triggering event** is something that acts as a stimulus for a change in strategy. Some possible triggering events are:[75]

- **New CEO:** By asking a series of embarrassing questions, a new CEO cuts through the veil of complacency and forces people to question the very reason for the corporation's existence.

- **External intervention:** A firm's bank suddenly refuses to approve a new loan or suddenly demands payment in full on an old one. A key customer complains about a serious product defect.

- **Threat of a change in ownership:** Another firm may initiate a takeover by buying a company's common stock.

- **Performance gap:** A *performance gap* exists when performance does not meet expectations. Sales and profits either are no longer increasing or may even be falling.

- **Strategic inflection point:** Coined by Andy Grove, past-CEO of Intel Corporation, a *strategic inflection point* is what happens to a business when a major change takes place due to the introduction of new technologies, a different regulatory environment, a change in customers' values, or a change in what customers prefer.[76]

Unilever is an example of one company in which a triggering event forced management to radically rethink what it was doing. See **Strategy Highlight 1.2** to learn how a slumping stock price stimulated a change in strategy at Unilever.

STRATEGY highlight 1.2

TRIGGERING EVENT AT UNILEVER

Unilever, the world's second-largest consumer goods company, received a jolt in 2004 when its stock price fell sharply after management had warned investors that profits would be lower than anticipated. Even though the company had been the first consumer goods company to enter the world's emerging economies in Africa, China, India, and Latin America with a formidable range of products and local knowledge, its sales faltered when rivals began to attack its entrenched position in these markets. Procter & Gamble's (P&G) acquisition of Gillette had greatly bolstered P&G's growing portfolio of global brands and allowed it to undermine Unilever's global market share. For example, when P&G targeted India for a sales initiative in 2003–04, profit margins fell at Unilever's Indian subsidiary from 20% to 13%.

An in-depth review of Unilever's brands revealed that its brands were doing as well as were those of its rivals. Something else was wrong. According to Richard Rivers, Unilever's head of corporate strategy, "We were just not executing as well as we should have."

Unilever's management realized that it had no choice but to make-over the company from top to bottom. Over decades of operating in almost every country in the world, the company had become fat with unnecessary bureaucracy and complexity. Unilever's traditional emphasis on the autonomy of its country managers had led to a lack of synergy and a duplication of corporate structures. Country managers had been making strategic decisions without regard for their effect on other regions or on the corporation as a whole. Starting at the top, two joint chairmen were replaced by one sole chief executive. In China, three companies with three chief executives were replaced by one company with one person in charge. Overall staff was cut from 223,000 in 2004 to 179,000 in 2008. By 2010, management planned close to 50 of its 300 factories and to eliminate 75 of 100 regional centers. Twenty thousand more jobs were selected to be eliminated over a four-year period. Ralph Kugler, manager of Unilever's home and personal care division, exhibited confidence that after these changes, the company was better prepared to face competition. "We are much better organized now to defend ourselves," he stated.

SOURCE: Summarized from "The Legacy that Got Left on the Shelf," *The Economist* (February 2, 2008), pp. 77–79.

1.7 Strategic Decision Making

The distinguishing characteristic of strategic management is its emphasis on strategic decision making. As organizations grow larger and more complex, with more uncertain environments, decisions become increasingly complicated and difficult to make. In agreement with the strategic choice perspective mentioned earlier, this book proposes a strategic decision-making framework that can help people make these decisions regardless of their level and function in the corporation.

WHAT MAKES A DECISION STRATEGIC

Unlike many other decisions, **strategic decisions** deal with the long-run future of an entire organization and have three characteristics:

1. **Rare:** Strategic decisions are unusual and typically have no precedent to follow.
2. **Consequential:** Strategic decisions commit substantial resources and demand a great deal of commitment from people at all levels.
3. **Directive:** Strategic decisions set precedents for lesser decisions and future actions throughout an organization.[77]

One example of a strategic decision with all of these characteristics was that made by Genentech, a biotechnology company that had been founded in 1976 to produce protein-based drugs from cloned genes. After building sales to $9 billion and profits to $2 billion in 2006, the company's sales growth slowed and its stock price dropped in 2007. The company's products were reaching maturity with few new ones in the pipeline. To regain revenue growth, management decided to target autoimmune diseases, such as multiple sclerosis, rheumatoid arthritis, lupus, and 80 other ailments for which there was no known lasting treatment. This was an enormous opportunity, but also a very large risk for the company. Existing drugs in this area either weren't effective for many patients or caused side effects that were worse than the disease. Competition from companies like Amgen and Novartis were already vying for leadership in this area. A number of Genentech's first attempts in the area had failed to do well against the competition.

The strategic decision to commit resources to this new area was based on a report from a British physician that the Genentech's cancer drug Rituxan eased the agony of rheumatoid arthritis in five of his patients. CEO Arthur Levinson was so impressed with this report that he immediately informed Genentech's board of directors. He urged them to support a full research program for Rituxan in autoimmune disease. With the board's blessing, Levinson launched a program to study the drug as a treatment for rheumatoid arthritis, MS, and lupus. The company deployed a third of its 1,000 researchers to pursue new drugs to fight autoimmune diseases. In 2006, Rituxan was approved to treat rheumatoid arthritis and captured 10% of the market. The company was working on some completely new approaches to autoimmune disease. The research mandate was to consider ideas others might overlook. "There's this tremendous herd instinct out there," said Levinson. "That's a great opportunity, because often the crowd is wrong."[78]

MINTZBERG'S MODES OF STRATEGIC DECISION MAKING

Some strategic decisions are made in a flash by one person (often an entrepreneur or a powerful chief executive officer) who has a brilliant insight and is quickly able to convince others to adopt his or her idea. Other strategic decisions seem to develop out of a series of small incremental choices that over time push an organization more in one direction than another.

According to Henry Mintzberg, the three most typical approaches, or modes, of strategic decision making are entrepreneurial, adaptive, and planning (a fourth mode, logical incrementalism, was added later by Quinn):[79]

- **Entrepreneurial mode:** Strategy is made by one powerful individual. The focus is on opportunities; problems are secondary. Strategy is guided by the founder's own vision of direction and is exemplified by large, bold decisions. The dominant goal is growth of the corporation. Amazon.com, founded by Jeff Bezos, is an example of this mode of strategic decision making. The company reflected Bezos' vision of using the Internet to market books and more. Although Amazon's clear growth strategy was certainly an advantage of the entrepreneurial mode, Bezos' eccentric management style made it difficult to retain senior executives.[80]

- **Adaptive mode:** Sometimes referred to as "muddling through," this decision-making mode is characterized by reactive solutions to existing problems, rather than a proactive search for new opportunities. Much bargaining goes on concerning priorities of objectives. Strategy is fragmented and is developed to move a corporation forward incrementally. This mode is typical of most universities, many large hospitals, a large number of governmental agencies, and a surprising number of large corporations. Encyclopaedia Britannica Inc., operated successfully for many years in this mode, but it continued to rely on the door-to-door selling of its prestigious books long after dual-career couples made that marketing approach obsolete. Only after it was acquired in 1996 did the company change its door-to-door sales to television advertising and Internet marketing. The company now charges libraries and individual subscribers for complete access to Brittanica.com and offers CD-ROMs in addition to a small number of its 32-volume print set.[81]

- **Planning mode:** This decision-making mode involves the systematic gathering of appropriate information for situation analysis, the generation of feasible alternative strategies, and the rational selection of the most appropriate strategy. It includes both the proactive search for new opportunities and the reactive solution of existing problems. IBM under CEO Louis Gerstner is an example of the planning mode. When Gerstner accepted the position of CEO in 1993, he realized that IBM was in serious difficulty. Mainframe computers, the company's primary product line, were suffering a rapid decline both in sales and market share. One of Gerstner's first actions was to convene a two-day meeting on corporate strategy with senior executives. An in-depth analysis of IBM's product lines revealed that the only part of the company that was growing was services, but it was a relatively small segment and not very profitable. Rather than focusing on making and selling its own computer hardware, IBM made the strategic decision to invest in services that integrated information technology. IBM thus decided to provide a complete set of services from building systems to defining architecture to actually running and managing the computers for the customer—regardless of who made the products. Because it was no longer important that the company be completely vertically integrated, it sold off its DRAM, disk-drive, and laptop computer businesses and exited software application development. Since making this strategic decision in 1993, 80% of IBM's revenue growth has come from services.[82]

- **Logical incrementalism:** A fourth decision-making mode can be viewed as a synthesis of the planning, adaptive, and, to a lesser extent, the entrepreneurial modes. In this mode, top management has a reasonably clear idea of the corporation's mission and objectives, but, in its development of strategies, it chooses to use "an interactive process in which the organization probes the future, experiments and learns from a series of partial (incremental) commitments rather than through global formulations of total strategies."[83] Thus, although the mission and objectives are set, the strategy is allowed to emerge out of debate, discussion, and experimentation. This approach appears to be useful when the environment is changing rapidly and when it is important to build consensus and develop needed resources before committing an entire corporation to a specific strategy. In his analysis of the petroleum industry, Grant described strategic planning in this industry as "planned emergence." Corporate headquarters established the mission and objectives but allowed the business units to propose strategies to achieve them.[84]

STRATEGIC DECISION-MAKING PROCESS: AID TO BETTER DECISIONS

Good arguments can be made for using either the entrepreneurial or adaptive modes (or logical incrementalism) in certain situations.[85] This book proposes, however, that in most situations the planning mode, which includes the basic elements of the strategic management process, is a more rational and thus better way of making strategic decisions. Research indicates that the planning mode is not only more analytical and less political than are the other modes, but it is also more appropriate for dealing with complex, changing environments.[86] We therefore propose the following eight-step **strategic decision-making process** to improve the making of strategic decisions (see **Figure 1–5**):

1. **Evaluate current performance results** in terms of (a) return on investment, profitability, and so forth, and (b) the current mission, objectives, strategies, and policies.

2. **Review corporate governance**—that is, the performance of the firm's board of directors and top management.

3. **Scan and assess the external environment** to determine the strategic factors that pose **O**pportunities and **T**hreats.

4. **Scan and assess the internal corporate environment** to determine the strategic factors that are **S**trengths (especially core competencies) and **W**eaknesses.

5. **Analyze strategic (SWOT) factors** to (a) pinpoint problem areas and (b) review and revise the corporate mission and objectives, as necessary.

6. **Generate, evaluate, and select the best alternative strategy** in light of the analysis conducted in step 5.

7. **Implement selected strategies** via programs, budgets, and procedures.

8. **Evaluate implemented strategies** via feedback systems, and the control of activities to ensure their minimum deviation from plans.

This rational approach to strategic decision making has been used successfully by corporations such as Warner-Lambert, Target, General Electric, IBM, Avon Products, Bechtel Group Inc., and Taisei Corporation.

FIGURE 1–5
Strategic Decision-Making Process

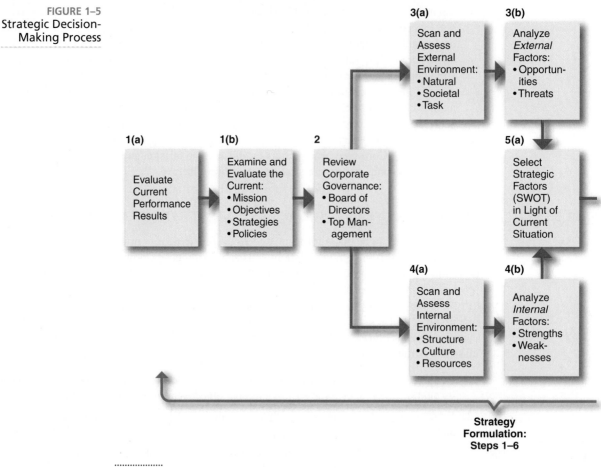

SOURCE: T. L. Wheelen and J. D. Hunger, "Strategic Decision-Making Process." Copyright © 1994 and 1977 by Wheelen and Hunger Associates. Reprinted by permission.

1.8 The Strategic Audit: Aid to Strategic Decision-Making

The strategic decision-making process is put into action through a technique known as the strategic audit. A **strategic audit** provides a checklist of questions, by area or issue, that enables a systematic analysis to be made of various corporate functions and activities. (See **Appendix 1.A** at the end of this chapter.) Note that the numbered primary headings in the audit are the same as the numbered blocks in the strategic decision-making process in **Figure 1–5**. Beginning with an evaluation of current performance, the audit continues with environmental scanning, strategy formulation, and strategy implementation, and it concludes with evaluation and control. A strategic audit is a type of management audit and is extremely useful as a diagnostic tool to pinpoint corporatewide problem areas and to highlight organizational strengths and weaknesses.[87] A strategic audit can help determine why a certain area is creating problems for a corporation and help generate solutions to the problem.

A strategic audit is not an all-inclusive list, but it presents many of the critical questions needed for a detailed strategic analysis of any business corporation. Some questions or even some areas might be inappropriate for a particular company; in other cases, the questions may

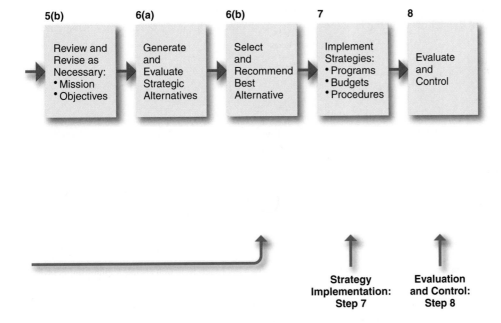

be insufficient for a complete analysis. However, each question in a particular area of a strategic audit can be broken down into an additional series of sub-questions. An analyst can develop these sub-questions when they are needed for a complete strategic analysis of a company.

End of Chapter SUMMARY

Strategy scholars Donald Hambrick and James Fredrickson propose that a good strategy has five elements, providing answers to five questions:

1. Arenas: Where will we be active?
2. Vehicles: How will we get there?
3. Differentiators: How will we win in the marketplace?
4. Staging: What will be our speed and sequence of moves?
5. Economic logic: How will we obtain our returns?[88]

This chapter introduces you to a well-accepted model of strategic management (**Figure 1–2**) in which environmental scanning leads to strategy formulation, strategy implementation, and evaluation and control. It further shows how that model can be put into action through the strategic decision-making process (**Figure 1–5**) and a strategic audit (**Appendix 1.A**). As pointed out by Hambrick and Fredrickson, "strategy consists of an integrated set of choices."[89] The questions "Where will we be active?" and "How will we get there?" are dealt with by a company's mission, objectives, and corporate strategy. The question "How will we win in the marketplace?" is the concern of business strategy. The question "What will be our speed and sequence of moves?" is answered not only by business strategy and tactics but also by functional strategy and by implemented programs, budgets, and procedures. The question "How will we obtain our returns?" is the primary emphasis of the evaluation and control element of the strategic management model. Each of these questions and topics will be dealt with in greater detail in the chapters to come. Welcome to the study of strategic management!

ECO-BITS

- The world's primary energy consumption by fuel in 2004 was 35% oil, 25% coal, 21% natural gas, 10% biomass and waste, 6% nuclear, 2% hydroelectric, and 1% other renewable.[90]

- The price per watt of photovoltaic modules used in solar power dropped from $18 in 1980 to $4 in 2007.[91]

- Since 1869 world crude oil prices, adjusted for inflation, have averaged $21.66 per barrel in 2006 dollars. By 2008, the price per barrel reached $140 for the first time in history.[92]

DISCUSSION QUESTIONS

1. Why has strategic management become so important to today's corporations?

2. How does strategic management typically evolve in a corporation?

3. What is a learning organization? Is this approach to strategic management better than the more traditional top-down approach in which strategic planning is primarily done by top management?

4. Why are strategic decisions different from other kinds of decisions?

5. When is the planning mode of strategic decision making superior to the entrepreneurial and adaptive modes?

STRATEGIC PRACTICE EXERCISES

Mission statements vary widely from one company to another. Why is one mission statement better than another? Using Campbell's questions in **Strategy Highlight 1.2** as a starting point, develop criteria for evaluating any mission statement. Then do one or both of the following exercises:

1. Evaluate the following mission statement of Celestial Seasonings. How many points would Campbell give it?

   Our mission is to grow and dominate the U.S. specialty tea market by exceeding consumer expectations with the best tasting, 100% natural hot and iced teas, packaged with Celestial art and philosophy, creating the most valued tea experience. Through leadership, innovation, focus, and teamwork, we are dedicated to continuously improving value to our consumers, customers, employees, and stakeholders with a quality-first organization.[93]

2. Using the Internet, find the mission statements of three different organizations, which can be business or not-for-profit. (Hint: Check annual reports and 10K forms. They can often be found via a link on a company's Web page or through Hoovers.com.) Which mission statement is best? Why?

KEY TERMS

budget (p. 70)
business strategy (p. 67)
corporate strategy (p. 67)

environmental scanning (p. 64)
environmental sustainability (p. 56)
evaluation and control (p. 70)

external environment (p. 64)
functional strategy (p. 68)
globalization (p. 56)

NOTES

1. "GE Launches Ecomagination to Develop Environmental Technologies," www.nema.org (May 13, 2005), in S. Regani, "'Ecomagination' at Work: GE's Sustainability Initiative," ICFAI Center for Management Research (2006).

2. R. Layne, "GE Plans to Double Spending on 'Environmental' Products," *Des Moines Register* (May 10, 2005), p. 6D.

3. "A Lean, Clean Electric Machine," *The Economist* (December 10, 2005), p. 78.

4. "A Lean, Clean Electric Machine," *The Economist* (December 10, 2005), pp. 77–79.

5. B. Elgin, "Little Green Lies," *Business Week* (October 29, 2007), pp. 45–52.

6. "A Lean, Clean Electric Machine," *The Economist* (December 10, 2005), p. 79.

7. F. W. Gluck, S. P. Kaufman, and A. S. Walleck, "The Four Phases of Strategic Management," *Journal of Business Strategy* (Winter 1982), pp. 9–21.

8. M. R. Vaghefi and A. B Huellmantel, "Strategic Leadership at General Electric," *Long Range Planning* (April 1998), pp. 280–294. For a detailed description of the evolution of strategic management at GE, see W. Ocasio and J. Joseph, "Rise and Fall—or Transformation?" *Long Range Planning* (June 2008), pp. 248–272.

9. E. D. Beinhocker, "The Adaptable Corporation," *McKinsey Quarterly* (2006, Number 2), pp. 77–87.

10. B. W. Wirtz, A. Mathieu, and O. Schilke, "Strategy in High-Velocity Environments," *Long Range Planning* (June 2007), pp. 295–313; L. F. Teagarden, Y. Sarason, J. S. Childers, and D. E. Hatfield, "The Engagement of Employees in the Strategy Process and Firm Performance: The Role of Strategic Goals and Environment," *Journal of Business Strategies* (Spring 2005), pp. 75–99; T. J. Andersen, "Strategic Planning, Autonomous Actions and Corporate Performance," *Long Range Planning* (April 2000), pp. 184–200; C. C. Miller and L. B. Cardinal, "Strategic Planning and Firm Performance: A Synthesis of More Than Two Decades of Research," *Academy of Management Journal* (December 1994), pp. 1649–1665; P. Pekar Jr., and S. Abraham, "Is Strategic Management Living Up to Its Promise?" *Long Range Planning* (October 1995), pp. 32–44; W. E. Hopkins and S. A. Hopkins, "Strategic Planning—Financial Performance Relationship in Banks: A Causal Examination," *Strategic Management Journal* (September 1997), pp. 635–652.

11. E. J. Zajac, M. S. Kraatz, and R. F. Bresser, "Modeling the Dynamics of Strategic Fit: A Normative Approach to Strategic Change," *Strategic Management Journal* (April 2000), pp. 429–453; M. Peteraf and R. Reed, "Managerial Discretion and Internal Alignment Under Regulatory Constraints and Change," *Strategic Management Journal* (November 2007), pp. 1089–1112; C. S. Katsikeas, S. Samiee, and M. Theodosiou, "Strategy Fit and Performance Consequences of International Marketing Standardization," *Strategic Management Journal* (September 2006), pp. 867–890.

12. P. Brews and D. Purohit, "Strategic Planning in Unstable Environments," *Long Range Planning* (February 2007), pp. 64–83.

13. K. G. Smith and C. M. Grimm, "Environmental Variation, Strategic Change and Firm Performance: A Study of Railroad Deregulation," *Strategic Management Journal* (July–August 1987), pp. 363–376; J. A. Nickerson and B. S. Silverman, "Why Firms Want to Organize Efficiently and What Keeps Them from Doing So: Inappropriate Governance, Performance, and Adaptation in a Deregulated Industry," *Administrative Science Quarterly* (September 2003), pp. 433–465.

14. I. Wilson, "Strategic Planning Isn't Dead—It Changed," *Long Range Planning* (August 1994), p. 20.

15. R. Dye and O. Sibony, "How to Improve Strategic Planning," *McKinsey Quarterly* (2007, Number 3), pp. 40–48.

16. W. M. Becker and V. M. Freeman, "Going from Global Trends to Corporate Strategy," *McKinsey Quarterly* (2006, Number 2), pp. 17–27.

17. D. Rigby and B. Bilodeau, *Management Tools and Trends 2007*, Bain & Company (2007).

18. W. Joyce, "What Really Works: Building the 4+2 Organization," *Organizational Dynamics* (Vol. 34, Issue 2, 2005), pp. 118–129. See also W. Joyce, N. Nohria, and B. Roberson, *What Really Works: The 4+2 Formula for Sustained Business Success* (HarperBusiness), 2003.

19. R. M. Grant, "Strategic Planning in a Turbulent Environment: Evidence from the Oil Majors," *Strategic Management Journal* (June 2003), pp. 491–517.

20. M. J. Peel and J. Bridge, "How Planning and Capital Budgeting Improve SME Performance," *Long Range Planning* (December 1998), pp. 848–856; L. W. Rue and N. A. Ibrahim, "The Relationship Between Planning Sophistication and Performance in Small Businesses," *Journal of Small Business Management* (October 1998), pp. 24–32; J. C. Carland and J. W. Carland, "A Model of Entrepreneurial Planning and Its Effect on Performance," paper presented to Association for Small Business and Entrepreneurship (Houston, TX, 2003).

21. R. M. Grant, "Strategic Planning in a Turbulent Environment: Evidence from the Oil Majors," *Strategic Management Journal* (June 2003), pp. 491–517.

22. T. L. Friedman, *The World Is Flat* (NY: Farrar, Strauss & Giroux), 2005.

23. A. K. Gupta, V. Govindarajan, and H. Wang, *The Quest for Global Dominance*, 2nd ed. (San Francisco: Jossey-Bass, 2008).

24. Quoted in "Companies that Expand Abroad: 'Knowledge Seekers' vs. Conquerors," *Knowledge @ Wharton.com* (March 24, 2004), p. 1.

25. S. M. J. Bonini, G. Hintz, and L. T. Mendonca, "Addressing Consumer Concerns about Climate Change," *McKinsey Quarterly* (March 2008), pp. 1–9.

26. A. J. Hoffman, *Getting Ahead of the Curve: Corporate Strategies that Address Climate Change* (Ann Arbor: University of Michigan, 2006), p. 1.

27. A. J. Hoffman, *Getting Ahead of the Curve: Corporate Strategies that Address Climate Change* (Ann Arbor: University of Michigan, 2006), p. iii.

28. M. E. Porter and F. L. Reinhardt, "A Strategic Approach to Climate," *Harvard Business Review* (October 2007), p. 22.

29. "The Rising Costs of Global Warming," *Futurist* (November–December 2005), p. 13.

30. J. Lash and F. Wellington, "Competitive Advantage on a Warming Planet," *Harvard Business Review* (March 2007), pp. 95–102.

31. "Melting Asia," *The Economist* (June 7, 2008), pp. 29–32.

32. P. Engardio, "Can the U.S. Bring Jobs Back from China?" *Business Week* (June 30, 2008), pp. 39–43.

33. P. Roberts, "Tapped Out," *National Geographic* (June 2008), pp. 87–91.

34. T. Rooselt IV and J. Llewelyn, "Investors Hunger for Clean Energy," *Harvard Business Review* (October 2007), p. 38.

35. D. Rigby, "Growth through Sustainability," Presentation to the 2008 Annual Meeting of the Consumer Industries Governors, World Economic Forum (January 24, 2008).

36. J. Carey and L. Woellert, "Global Warming: Here Comes the Lawyers," *Business Week* (October 30, 2006), pp. 34–36.

37. C. Laszlo, *Sustainable Value: How the World's Leading Companies Are Doing Well by Doing Good* (Stanford: Stanford University Press, 2008), pp. 89–99.

38. R. Ringger and S. A. DiPiazza, *Sustainability Yearbook 2008* (PricewaterhouseCoopers, 2008).

39. L. T. Mendonca and J. Oppenheim, "Investing in Sustainability: An Interview with Al Gore and David Blood," *McKinsey Quarterly* (May 2007).

40. A. J. Hoffman, *Getting Ahead of the Curve: Corporate Strategies that Address Climate Change* (Ann Arbor: University of Michigan, 2006), p. 2.

41. J. K. Bourne, Jr., "Signs of Change," *National Geographic* (Special Report on Changing Climate, 2008), pp. 7–21.

42. "Melting Asia," *The Economist* (June 7, 2008), pp. 29–32.

43. J. Welch and S. Welch, "The Global Warming Wager," *Business Week* (February 26, 2007), p. 130.

44. J. A. C. Baum, "Organizational Ecology," in *Handbook of Organization Studies*, edited by S. R. Clegg, C. Handy, and W. Nord (London: Sage, 1996), pp. 77–114.

45. B. M. Staw and L. D. Epstein, "What Bandwagons Bring: Effects of Popular Management Techniques on Corporate Performance, Reputation, and CEO Pay," *Administrative Science Quarterly* (September 2000), pp. 523–556; M. B. Lieberman and S. Asaba, "Why Do Firms Imitate Each Other?" *Academy of Management Review* (April 2006), pp. 366–385.

46. T. W. Ruefli and R. R. Wiggins, "Industry, Corporate, and Segment Effects and Business Performance: A Non-Parametric Approach," *Strategic Management Journal* (September 2003), pp. 861–879; Y. E. Spanos, G. Zaralis, and S. Lioukas, "Strategy and Industry Effects on Profitability: Evidence from Greece," *Strategic Management Journal* (February 2004), pp. 139–165; E. H. Bowman and C. E. Helfat, "Does Corporate Strategy Matter?" *Strategic Management Journal* (January 2001), pp. 1–23; T. H. Brush, P. Bromiley, and M. Hendrickx, "The Relative Influence of Industry and Corporation on Business Segment Performance: An Alternative Estimate," *Strategic Management Journal* (June 1999), pp. 519–547; K. M. Gilley, B. A. Walters, and B. J. Olson, "Top Management Team Risk Taking Propensities and Firm Performance: Direct and Moderating Effects," *Journal of Business Strategies* (Fall 2002), pp. 95–114.

47. For more information on these theories, see A. Y. Lewin and H. W. Voloberda, "Prolegomena on Coevolution: A Framework for Research on Strategy and New Organizational Forms," *Organization Science* (October 1999), pp. 519–534, and H. Aldrich, *Organizations Evolving* (London: Sage, 1999), pp. 43–74.

48. R. A. D'Aveni, *Hypercompetition* (New York: The Free Press, 1994). Hypercompetition is discussed in more detail in Chapter 4.

49. R. S. M. Lau, "Strategic Flexibility: A New Reality for World-Class Manufacturing," *SAM Advanced Management Journal* (Spring 1996), pp. 11–15.

50. M. A. Hitt, B. W. Keats, and S. M. DeMarie, "Navigating in the New Competitive Landscape: Building Strategic Flexibility and Competitive Advantage in the 21st Century," *Academy of Management Executive* (November 1998), pp. 22–42.

51. D. Lei, J. W. Slocum, and R. A. Pitts, "Designing Organizations for Competitive Advantage: The Power of Unlearning and Learning," *Organizational Dynamics* (Winter 1999), pp. 24–38; M. Goold, "Making Peer Groups Effective: Lessons from BP's Experience," *Long Range Planning* (October 2005), pp. 429–443.

52. S. C. Voelpel, M. Dous, and T. H. Davenport, "Five Steps to Creating a Global Knowledge-Sharing System: Siemens' ShareNet," *Academy of Management Executive* (May 2005), pp. 9–23.

53. D. A. Garvin, "Building a Learning Organization," *Harvard Business Review* (July/August 1993), p. 80. See also P. M. Senge, *The Fifth Discipline: The Art and Practice of the Learning Organization* (New York: Doubleday, 1990).

54. A. D. Chandler, *Inventing the Electronic Century* (New York: The Free Press, 2001).

55. T. T. Baldwin, C. Danielson, and W. Wiggenhorn, "The Evolution of Learning Strategies in Organizations: From Employee Development to Business Redefinition," *Academy of Management Executive* (November 1997), pp. 47–58.

56. N. Collier, F. Fishwick, and S. W. Floyd, "Managerial Involvement and Perceptions of Strategy Process," *Long Range Planning* (February 2004), pp. 67–83; J. A. Parnell, S. Carraher, and K. Holt, "Participative Management's Influence on Effective Strategic Planning," *Journal of Business Strategies* (Fall 2002), pp. 161–179; M. Ketokivi and X. Castaner, "Strategic Planning as an Integrative Device," *Administrative Science Quarterly* (September 2004), pp. 337–365.

57. E. W. K. Tsang, "Internationalization as a Learning Process: Singapore MNCs in China," *Academy of Management Executive* (February 1999), pp. 91–101; J. M. Shaver, W. Mitchell, and

B. Yeung, "The Effect of Own-Firm and Other Firm Experience on Foreign Direct Investment Survival in the U.S., 1987–92," *Strategic Management Journal* (November 1997), pp. 811–824; P. Kale and H. Singh, "Building Firm Capabilities through Learning: The Role of the Alliance Learning Process in Alliance Capability and Firm-Level Alliance Success," *Strategic Management Journal* (October 2007), pp. 981–1000; H. Barkema and M. Schijven, "How Do Firms Learn to Make Acquisitions? A Review of Past Research and an Agenda for the Future," *Journal of Management* (June 2008), pp. 594–634; D. D. Bergh and E. N-K Lim, "Learning How to Restructure: Absorptive Capacity and Improvisational Views of Restructuring Actions and Performance," *Strategic Management Journal* (June 2008), pp. 593–616.

58. W. Mitchell, J. M. Shaver, and B. Yeung, "Getting There in a Global Industry: Impacts on Performance of Changing International Presence," *Strategic Management Journal* (September 1992), pp. 419–432.

59. D. J. Miller, M. J. Fern, and L. B. Cardinal, "The Use of Knowledge for Technological Innovation Within Diversified Firms," *Academy of Management Journal* (April 2007), pp. 308–326.

60. R. Wiltbank, N. Dew, S. Read, and S. D. Sarasvathy, "What To Do Next? The Case for Non-Predictive Strategy," *Strategic Management Journal* (October 2006), pp. 981–998; J. A. Smith, "Strategies for Start-Ups," *Long Range Planning* (December 1998), pp. 857–872.

61. J. S. Sidhu, "Business-Domain Definition and Performance: An Empirical Study," *SAM Advanced Management Journal* (Autumn 2004), pp. 40–45.

62. See A. Campbell and S. Yeung, "Brief Case: Mission, Vision, and Strategic Intent," *Long Range Planning* (August 1991), pp. 145–147; S. Cummings and J. Davies, "Mission, Vision, Fusion," *Long Range Planning* (December 1994), pp. 147–150.

63. S. Baker, "Google and the Wisdom of Clouds," *Business Week* (December 24, 2007), pp. 49–55.

64. J. Cosco, "Down to the Sea in Ships," *Journal of Business Strategy* (November/December 1995), p. 48.

65. J. S. Sidhu, E. J. Nijssen, and H. R. Commandeur, "Business Domain Definition Practice: Does It Affect Organizational Performance?" *Long Range Planning* (June 2000), pp. 376–401.

66. "Time to Break Off a Chunk," *The Economist* (December 15, 2007), pp. 75–76.

67. K. M. Eisenhardt and D. N. Sull, "Strategy as Simple Rules," *Harvard Business Review* (January 2001), p. 110.

68. D. Welch, "Cadillac Hits the Gas," *Business Week* (September 4, 2000), p. 50.

69. S. Holmes, "GE: Little Engines That Could," *Business Week* (January 20, 2003), pp. 62–63.

70. H. A. Simon, *Administrative Behavior*, 2nd edition (New York: The Free Press, 1957), p. 231.

71. L. Lee and P. Burrows, "Is Dell Too Big for Michael Dell?" *Business Week* (February 12, 2007), p. 33.

72. H. Mintzberg, "Planning on the Left Side and Managing on the Right," *Harvard Business Review* (July–August 1976), p. 56.

73. R. A. Burgelman and A. S. Grove, "Let Chaos Reign, Then Reign In Chaos—Repeatedly: Managing Strategic Dynamics for Corporate Longevity," *Strategic Management Journal* (October 2007), pp. 965–979.

74. See E. Romanelli and M. L. Tushman, "Organizational Transformation as Punctuated Equilibrium: An Empirical Test," *Academy of Management Journal* (October 1994), pp. 1141–1166.

75. S. S. Gordon, W. H. Stewart, Jr., R. Sweo, and W. A. Luker, "Convergence versus Strategic Reorientation: The Antecedents of Fast-Paced Organizational Change," *Journal of Management*, Vol. 26, No. 5 (2000), pp. 911–945.

76. Speech to the 1998 Academy of Management, reported by S. M. Puffer, "Global Executive: Intel's Andrew Grove on Competitiveness," *Academy of Management Executive* (February 1999), pp. 15–24.

77. D. J. Hickson, R. J. Butler, D. Cray, G. R. Mallory, and D. C. Wilson, *Top Decisions: Strategic Decision Making in Organizations* (San Francisco: Jossey-Bass, 1986), pp. 26–42.

78. A. Weintraub, "Genentech's Gamble," *Business Week* (December 17, 2007), pp. 44–48.

79. H. Mintzberg, "Strategy-Making in Three Modes," *California Management Review* (Winter 1973), pp. 44–53.

80. F. Vogelstein, "Mighty Amazon," *Fortune* (May 26, 2003), pp. 60–74.

81. M. Wong, "Once-Prized Encyclopedias Fall into Disuse," *Des Moines Register* (March 9, 2004), p. 3D.

82. L. V. Gerstner, *Who Says Elephants Can't Dance?* (New York: HarperCollins, 2002).

83. J. B. Quinn, *Strategies for Change: Logical Incrementalism* (Homewood, IL.: Irwin, 1980), p. 58.

84. R. M. Grant, "Strategic Planning in a Turbulent Environment: Evidence from the Oil Majors," *Strategic Management Journal* (June 2003), pp. 491–517.

85. G. Gavetti and J. W. Rivkin, "Seek Strategy the Right Way at the Right Time," *Harvard Business Review* (January 2008), pp. 22–23.

86. P. J. Brews and M. R. Hunt, "Learning to Plan and Planning to Learn: Resolving the Planning School/Learning School Debate," *Strategic Management Journal* (October 1999), pp. 889–913; I. Gold and A. M. A. Rasheed, "Rational Decision-Making and Firm Performance: The Moderating Role of the Environment," *Strategic Management Journal* (August 1997), pp. 583–591; R. L. Priem, A. M. A. Rasheed, and A. G. Kotulic, "Rationality in Strategic Decision Processes, Environmental Dynamism and Firm Performance," *Journal of Management*, Vol. 21, No. 5 (1995), pp. 913–929; J. W. Dean, Jr., and M. P. Sharfman, "Does Decision Process Matter? A Study of Strategic Decision-Making Effectiveness," *Academy of Management Journal* (April 1996), pp. 368–396.

87. T. L. Wheelen and J. D. Hunger, "Using the Strategic Audit," *SAM Advanced Management Journal* (Winter 1987), pp. 4–12; G. Donaldson, "A New Tool for Boards: The Strategic Audit," *Harvard Business Review* (July–August 1995), pp. 99–107.

88. D. C. Hambrick and J. W. Fredrickson, "Are You Sure You Have a Strategy?" *Academy of Management Executive* (November, 2001), pp. 48–59.

89. Hambrick and Fredrickson, p. 49.

90. "The Power and the Glory," *The Economist*, Special Report on Energy (June 21, 2008), pp. 3–6.

91. "Another Silicon Valley?" *The Economist*, Special Report on Energy (June 21, 2008), pp. 14–15.

92. J. L. Williams, "Oil Price History and Analysis," *WTRG Economics* (http://www.wtrg.com/prices.htm, accessed June 27, 2008).

93. P. Jones and L. Kahaner, *Say It & Live It: 50 Corporate Mission Statements That Hit the Mark* (New York: Currency Doubleday, 1995), p. 53.

Strategic Audit of a Corporation

I. Current Situation

A. Current Performance

How did the corporation perform the past year overall in terms of return on investment, market share, and profitability?

B. Strategic Posture

What are the corporation's current mission, objectives, strategies, and policies?

1. Are they clearly stated, or are they merely implied from performance?

2. **Mission:** What business(es) is the corporation in? Why?

3. **Objectives:** What are the corporate, business, and functional objectives? Are they consistent with each other, with the mission, and with the internal and external environments?

4. **Strategies:** What strategy or mix of strategies is the corporation following? Are they consistent with each other, with the mission and objectives, and with the internal and external environments?

5. **Policies:** What are the corporation's policies? Are they consistent with each other, with the mission, objectives, and strategies, and with the internal and external environments?

6. Do the current mission, objectives, strategies, and policies reflect the corporation's international operations, whether global or multidomestic?

II. Corporate Governance

A. Board of Directors

1. Who is on the board? Are they internal (employees) or external members?

2. Do they own significant shares of stock?

3. Is the stock privately held or publicly traded? Are there different classes of stock with different voting rights?

4. What do the board members contribute to the corporation in terms of knowledge, skills, background, and connections? If the corporation has international operations, do board members have international experience? Are board members concerned with environmental sustainability?

SOURCE: T. L. Wheelen and J. D. Hunger, *Strategic Audit of a Corporation*, Copyright © 1982 and 2005 by Wheelen and Hunger Associates. Thomas L. Wheelen, "A Strategic Audit," paper presented to Society for Advancement of Management (SAM). Presented by J. D. Hunger and T. L. Wheelen in "The Strategic Audit: An Integrative Approach to Teaching Business Policy," to *Academy of Management*, August 1983. Published in "Using the Strategic Audit," by T. L. Wheelen and J. D. Hunger in *SAM Advanced Management Journal* (Winter 1987), pp. 4–12. Reprinted by permission of the copyright holders. Revised 1988, 1994, 1997, 2000, 2002, 2004, 2005, and 2009.

5. How long have the board members served on the board?

6. What is their level of involvement in strategic management? Do they merely rubber-stamp top management's proposals or do they actively participate and suggest future directions? Do they evaluate management's proposals in terms of environmental sustainability?

B. Top Management

1. What person or group constitutes top management?

2. What are top management's chief characteristics in terms of knowledge, skills, background, and style? If the corporation has international operations, does top management have international experience? Are executives from acquired companies considered part of the top management team?

3. Has top management been responsible for the corporation's performance over the past few years? How many managers have been in their current position for less than three years? Were they promoted internally or externally hired?

4. Has top management established a systematic approach to strategic management?

5. What is top management's level of involvement in the strategic management process?

6. How well does top management interact with lower-level managers and with the board of directors?

7. Are strategic decisions made ethically in a socially responsible manner?

8. Are strategic decisions made in an environmentally sustainable manner?

9. Do top executives own significant amounts of stock in the corporation?

10. Is top management sufficiently skilled to cope with likely future challenges?

III. External Environment: Opportunities and Threats (SW**OT**)

A. Natural Physical Environment: Sustainability Issues

1. What forces from the natural physical environmental are currently affecting the corporation and the industries in which it competes? Which present current or future threats? Opportunities?
   a. Climate, including global temperature, sea level, and fresh water availability
   b. Weather-related events, such as severe storms, floods, and droughts
   c. Solar phenomena, such as sun spots and solar wind

2. Do these forces have different effects in other regions of the world?

B. Societal Environment

1. What general environmental forces are currently affecting both the corporation and the industries in which it competes? Which present current or future threats? Opportunities?
   a. Economic
   b. Technological
   c. Political–legal
   d. Sociocultural

2. Are these forces different in other regions of the world?

C. Task Environment

1. What forces drive industry competition? Are these forces the same globally or do they vary from country to country? Rate each force as **high, medium,** or **low.**
   a. Threat of new entrants
   b. Bargaining power of buyers
   c. Threat of substitute products or services
   d. Bargaining power of suppliers
   e. Rivalry among competing firms
   f. Relative power of unions, governments, special interest groups, etc.

2. What key factors in the immediate environment (that is, customers, competitors, suppliers, creditors, labor unions, governments, trade associations, interest groups, local communities, and shareholders) are currently affecting the corporation? Which are current or future Threats? Opportunities?

D. Summary of External Factors
(List in the EFAS Table 4–5, p. 174)

Which of these forces and factors are the most important to the corporation and to the industries in which it competes at the present time? Which will be important in the future?

IV. Internal Environment: Strengths and Weaknesses (**SW**OT)

A. Corporate Structure

1. How is the corporation structured at present?
   a. Is the decision-making authority centralized around one group or decentralized to many units?
   b. Is the corporation organized on the basis of functions, projects, geography, or some combination of these?

2. Is the structure clearly understood by everyone in the corporation?

3. Is the present structure consistent with current corporate objectives, strategies, policies, and programs, as well as with the firm's international operations?

4. In what ways does this structure compare with those of similar corporations?

B. Corporate Culture

1. Is there a well-defined or emerging culture composed of shared beliefs, expectations, and values?

2. Is the culture consistent with the current objectives, strategies, policies, and programs?

3. What is the culture's position on environmental sustainability?

4. What is the culture's position on other important issues facing the corporation (that is, on productivity, quality of performance, adaptability to changing conditions, and internationalization)?

5. Is the culture compatible with the employees' diversity of backgrounds?

6. Does the company take into consideration the values of the culture of each nation in which the firm operates?

C. Corporate Resources

1. **Marketing**
   a. What are the corporation's current marketing objectives, strategies, policies, and programs?
      i. Are they clearly stated or merely implied from performance and/or budgets?
      ii. Are they consistent with the corporation's mission, objectives, strategies, and policies and with internal and external environments?
   b. How well is the corporation performing in terms of analysis of market position and marketing mix (that is, product, price, place, and promotion) in both domestic and international markets? How dependent is the corporation on a few customers? How big is its market? Where is it gaining or losing market share? What percentage of sales comes from developed versus developing regions? Where are current products in the product life cycle?
      i. What trends emerge from this analysis?
      ii. What impact have these trends had on past performance and how might these trends affect future performance?
      iii. Does this analysis support the corporation's past and pending strategic decisions?
      iv. Does marketing provide the company with a competitive advantage?
   c. How well does the corporation's marketing performance compare with that of similar corporations?
   d. Are marketing managers using accepted marketing concepts and techniques to evaluate and improve product performance? (Consider product life cycle, market segmentation, market research, and product portfolios.)
   e. Does marketing adjust to the conditions in each country in which it operates?
   f. Does marketing consider environmental sustainability when making decisions?
   g. What is the role of the marketing manager in the strategic management process?

2. **Finance**
   a. What are the corporation's current financial objectives, strategies, and policies and programs?
      i. Are they clearly stated or merely implied from performance and/or budgets?
      ii. Are they consistent with the corporation's mission, objectives, strategies, and policies and with internal and external environments?
   b. How well is the corporation performing in terms of financial analysis? (Consider ratio analysis, common size statements, and capitalization structure.) How balanced, in terms of cash flow, is the company's portfolio of products and businesses? What are investor expectations in terms of share price?
      i. What trends emerge from this analysis?
      ii. Are there any significant differences when statements are calculated in constant versus reported dollars?
      iii. What impact have these trends had on past performance and how might these trends affect future performance?
      iv. Does this analysis support the corporation's past and pending strategic decisions?
      v. Does finance provide the company with a competitive advantage?
   c. How well does the corporation's financial performance compare with that of similar corporations?
   d. Are financial managers using accepted financial concepts and techniques to evaluate and improve current corporate and divisional performance? (Consider financial leverage, capital budgeting, ratio analysis, and managing foreign currencies.)
   e. Does finance adjust to the conditions in each country in which the company operates?
   f. Does finance cope with global financial issues?
   g. What is the role of the financial manager in the strategic management process?

3. **Research and Development (R&D)**
   a. What are the corporation's current R&D objectives, strategies, policies, and programs?
      i. Are they clearly stated or merely implied from performance or budgets?
      ii. Are they consistent with the corporation's mission, objectives, strategies and policies and with internal and external environments?
      iii. What is the role of technology in corporate performance?
      iv. Is the mix of basic, applied, and engineering research appropriate given the corporate mission and strategies?
      v. Does R&D provide the company with a competitive advantage?
   b. What return is the corporation receiving from its investment in R&D?
   c. Is the corporation competent in technology transfer? Does it use concurrent engineering and cross-functional work teams in product and process design?
   d. What role does technological discontinuity play in the company's products?
   e. How well does the corporation's investment in R&D compare with the investments of similar corporations? How much R&D is being outsourced? Is the corporation using value-chain alliances appropriately for innovation and competitive advantage?
   f. Does R&D adjust to the conditions in each country in which the company operates?
   g. Does R&D consider environmental sustainability in product development and packaging?
   h. What is the role of the R&D manager in the strategic management process?

4. **Operations and Logistics**
   a. What are the corporation's current manufacturing/service objectives, strategies, policies, and programs?
      i. Are they clearly stated or merely implied from performance or budgets?
      ii. Are they consistent with the corporation's mission, objectives, strategies, and policies and with internal and external environments?
   b. What are the type and extent of operations capabilities of the corporation? How much is done domestically versus internationally? Is the amount of outsourcing appropriate to be competitive? Is purchasing being handled appropriately? Are suppliers and distributors operating in an environmentally sustainable manner? Which products have the highest and lowest profit margins?
      i. If the corporation is product oriented, consider plant facilities, type of manufacturing system (continuous mass production, intermittent job shop, or flexible manufacturing), age and type of equipment, degree and role of automation and/or robots, plant capacities and utilization, productivity ratings, and availability and type of transportation.
      ii. If the corporation is service oriented, consider service facilities (hospital, theater, or school buildings), type of operations systems (continuous service over time to same clientele or intermittent service over time to varied clientele), age and type of supporting equipment, degree and role of automation and use of mass communication devices (diagnostic machinery, video machines), facility capacities and utilization rates, efficiency ratings of professional and service personnel, and availability and type of transportation to bring service staff and clientele together.
   c. Are manufacturing or service facilities vulnerable to natural disasters, local or national strikes, reduction or limitation of resources from suppliers, substantial cost increases of materials, or nationalization by governments?
   d. Is there an appropriate mix of people and machines (in manufacturing firms) or of support staff to professionals (in service firms)?
   e. How well does the corporation perform relative to the competition? Is it balancing inventory costs (warehousing) with logistical costs (just-in-time)? Consider costs per unit of labor, material, and overhead; downtime; inventory control management and scheduling of service staff; production ratings; facility utilization percentages; and number of clients successfully treated by category (if service firm) or percentage of orders shipped on time (if product firm).

      i. What trends emerge from this analysis?

      ii. What impact have these trends had on past performance and how might these trends affect future performance?

      iii. Does this analysis support the corporation's past and pending strategic decisions?

      iv. Does operations provide the company with a competitive advantage?

  f. Are operations managers using appropriate concepts and techniques to evaluate and improve current performance? Consider cost systems, quality control and reliability systems, inventory control management, personnel scheduling, TQM, learning curves, safety programs, and engineering programs that can improve efficiency of manufacturing or of service.

  g. Do operations adjust to the conditions in each country in which it has facilities?

  h. Do operations consider environmental sustainability when making decisions?

  i. What is the role of the operations manager in the strategic management process?

5. **Human Resources Management (HRM)**

  a. What are the corporation's current HRM objectives, strategies, policies, and programs?

      i. Are they clearly stated or merely implied from performance and/or budgets?

      ii. Are they consistent with the corporation's mission, objectives, strategies, and policies and with internal and external environments?

  b. How well is the corporation's HRM performing in terms of improving the fit between the individual employee and the job? Consider turnover, grievances, strikes, layoffs, employee training, and quality of work life.

      i. What trends emerge from this analysis?

      ii. What impact have these trends had on past performance and how might these trends affect future performance?

      iii. Does this analysis support the corporation's past and pending strategic decisions?

      iv. Does HRM provide the company with a competitive advantage?

  c. How does this corporation's HRM performance compare with that of similar corporations?

  d. Are HRM managers using appropriate concepts and techniques to evaluate and improve corporate performance? Consider the job analysis program, performance appraisal system, up-to-date job descriptions, training and development programs, attitude surveys, job design programs, quality of relationships with unions, and use of autonomous work teams.

  e. How well is the company managing the diversity of its workforce? What is the company's record on human rights? Does the company monitor the human rights record of key suppliers and distributors?

  f. Does HRM adjust to the conditions in each country in which the company operates? Does the company have a code of conduct for HRM for itself and key suppliers in developing nations? Are employees receiving international assignments to prepare them for managerial positions?

  g. What is the role of outsourcing in HRM planning?

  h. What is the role of the HRM manager in the strategic management process?

6. **Information Technology (IT)**

  a. What are the corporation's current IT objectives, strategies, policies, and programs?

      i. Are they clearly stated or merely implied from performance and/or budgets?

      ii. Are they consistent with the corporation's mission, objectives, strategies, and policies and with internal and external environments?

  b. How well is the corporation's IT performing in terms of providing a useful database, automating routine clerical operations, assisting managers in making routine decisions, and providing information necessary for strategic decisions?

      i. What trends emerge from this analysis?

      ii. What impact have these trends had on past performance and how might these trends affect future performance?

    iii. Does this analysis support the corporation's past and pending strategic decisions?

    iv. Does IT provide the company with a competitive advantage?

c. How does this corporation's IT performance and stage of development compare with that of similar corporations? Is it appropriately using the Internet, intranet, and extranets?

d. Are IT managers using appropriate concepts and techniques to evaluate and improve corporate performance? Do they know how to build and manage a complex database, establish Web sites with firewalls and virus protection, conduct system analyses, and implement interactive decision-support systems?

e. Does the company have a global IT and Internet presence? Does it have difficulty with getting data across national boundaries?

f. What is the role of the IT manager in the strategic management process?

D. Summary of Internal Factors (List in the IFAS Table 5–2, p. 212)

Which of these factors are core competencies? Which, if any, are distinctive competencies? Which of these factors are the most important to the corporation and to the industries in which it competes at the present time? Which might be important in the future? Which functions or activities are candidates for outsourcing?

V. Analysis of Strategic Factors (SWOT)

A. Situational Analysis (List in SFAS Matrix, Figure 6–1, pp. 226–227)

Of the external (EFAS) and internal (IFAS) factors listed in III.D and IV.D, which are the strategic (most important) factors that strongly affect the corporation's present and future performance?

B. Review of Mission and Objectives

1. Are the current mission and objectives appropriate in light of the key strategic factors and problems?

2. Should the mission and objectives be changed? If so, how?

3. If they are changed, what will be the effects on the firm?

VI. Strategic Alternatives and Recommended Strategy

A. Strategic Alternatives (See the TOWS Matrix, Figure 6–3, p. 230)

1. Can the current or revised objectives be met through more careful implementation of those strategies presently in use (for example, fine-tuning the strategies)?

2. What are the major feasible alternative strategies available to the corporation? What are the pros and cons of each? Can corporate scenarios be developed and agreed on? (Alternatives must fit the natural physical environment, societal environment, industry, and corporation for the next three to five years.)

    a. Consider *stability*, *growth*, and *retrenchment* as corporate strategies.

    b. Consider *cost leadership* and *differentiation* as business strategies.

c. Consider any functional strategic alternatives that might be needed for reinforcement of an important corporate or business strategic alternative.

B. Recommended Strategy

1. Specify which of the strategic alternatives you are recommending for the corporate, business, and functional levels of the corporation. Do you recommend different business or functional strategies for different units of the corporation?

2. Justify your recommendation in terms of its ability to resolve both long- and short-term problems and effectively deal with the strategic factors.

3. What policies should be developed or revised to guide effective implementation?

4. What is the impact of your recommended strategy on the company's core and distinctive competencies?

VII. Implementation

A. What Kinds of Programs (for Example, Restructuring the Corporation or Instituting TQM) Should Be Developed to Implement the Recommended Strategy?

1. Who should develop these programs?

2. Who should be in charge of these programs?

B. Are the Programs Financially Feasible? Can Pro Forma Budgets Be Developed and Agreed On? Are Priorities and Timetables Appropriate to Individual Programs?

C. Will New Standard Operating Procedures Need to Be Developed?

VIII. Evaluation and Control

A. Is the Current Information System Capable of Providing Sufficient Feedback on Implementation Activities and Performance? Can It Measure Strategic Factors?

1. Can performance results be pinpointed by area, unit, project, or function?

2. Is the information timely?

3. Is the corporation using benchmarking to evaluate its functions and activities?

B. Are Adequate Control Measures in Place to Ensure Conformance with the Recommended Strategic Plan?

1. Are appropriate standards and measures being used?

2. Are reward systems capable of recognizing and rewarding good performance?

corporate Governance

On paper, Robert Nardelli, seemed to be doing everything right. Selected personally by the founders, Arthur Blank, Kenneth Langone, and Bernard Marcus, the board of directors felt that the company was lucky to have hired Nardelli from General Electric to be CEO of Home Depot in December 2000. Between 2000 and 2005, the company opened more than 900 stores, doubled sales to $81.5 billion, and achieved earnings per share growth of at least 20% every year. According to Nardelli, the company had the strongest balance sheet in the industry and tremendous potential for future growth. The board loved Nardelli and had been happy to support his decisions.

The stockholders, however, were not as satisfied with Nardelli's performance. They wondered why Home Depot's common stock had fallen 30% since Nardelli had taken charge of the company. In addition, Nardelli was increasingly being attacked for having "excessive compensation," given the firm's poor stock performance. People questioned why he was receiving $38.1 million annually in salary, cash bonuses, and stock options. Nardelli was one of the six executives highlighted in a July 24, 2006 *Fortune* article entitled "The Real CEO Pay Problem."[1]

Stockholders were unhappy with Nardelli's tendency to manipulate negative performance data. For example, when same-store sales failed to increase in 2005, he announced that management would no longer report that figure. When a *Business Week* reporter questioned his persuading the board not to use stock price to decide his compensation, Nardelli responded that he and the board had felt that the leadership team should be measured on things over which the team had direct control, such as earnings per share instead of stock price compared to the retail index.[2]

Since Nardelli saw little growth opportunity in the company's retail stores, he pushed to make the stores run more efficiently. Importing ideas, people, and management concepts from the military was one way to reshape an increasingly unwieldy Home Depot into a more centralized and efficient organization. Under Nardelli, the emphasis was on building a disciplined manager corps, one predisposed to following orders, operating in high-pressure environments, and executing with high standards.[3] He hired ex-military to be store managers. The previous constant flow of ideas and suggestions flowing up the organization from Home Depot's many employees was replaced by major decisions and goals flowing down from top management.

Former Home Depot executives reported that a "culture of fear" had caused customer service to decline. The once-heavy ranks of full-time store employees had been replaced with part-timers to reduce labor costs. Since 2001, 98% of Home Depot's 170 top executives had left the

Learning Objectives

After reading this chapter, you should be able to:

- Describe the role and responsibilities of the board of directors in corporate governance
- Understand how the composition of a board can affect its operation
- Describe the impact of the Sarbanes-Oxley Act on corporate governance in the United States

- Discuss trends in corporate governance
- Explain how executive leadership is an important part of strategic management

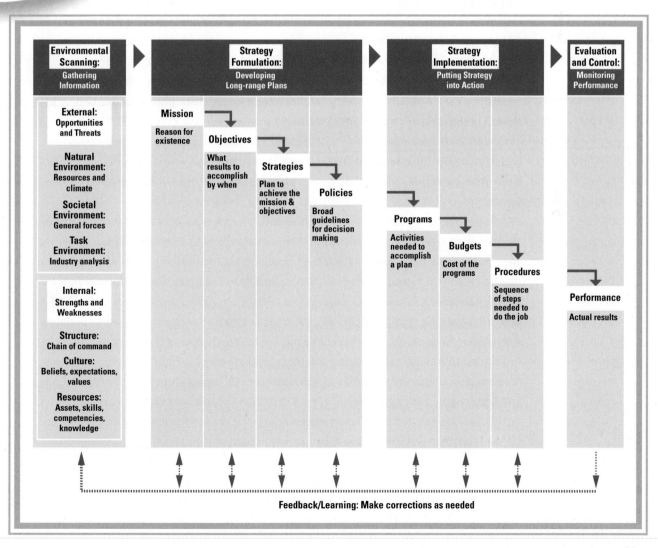

company. The University of Michigan's *American Customer Satisfaction Index*, compiled in 2005, revealed that Home Depot, with a score of 67, had slipped to last place among major U.S. retailers.

Nardelli did not react well to criticism. For example, the agenda for the May 2006 shareholders meeting contained a number of shareholder proposals dealing with "excessive" senior management compensation, separating the position of Chairman of the Board from another management position, requiring a majority (instead of plurality) vote for board member elections, shareholder approval for future "extraordinary" retirement benefits for senior executives, and disclosure of the monetary value of executive benefits. The votes on these proposals indicated an unusually high level of shareholder dissent, with at least one-third of shareholders voting for every proposal—votes cast before the meeting. Upon arriving at the annual shareholders meeting, people were surprised to note a number of changes from previous annual meetings. For one thing, except for CEO Nardelli, none of the members of the board of directors were present. For another, shareholders were allowed to speak about their shareholder proposals, but each had a time limit that was carefully tracked by a giant clock. Nardelli did not present a performance review, refused to acknowledge comments or answer questions, and adjourned the meeting after 30 minutes. Many of the shareholders were enraged by Nardelli's arrogance.

Pushed by the shareholders to reduce the CEO's large compensation package, the board of directors finally asked Nardelli to accept future stock awards being tied to increases in the company's stock price. Nardelli flatly refused and instead quit the company in January 2007—taking with him a $210 million retirement package. Observers could not understand why the board had been so generous with a CEO who during his tenure had been more concerned with building his own compensation than in building shareholder wealth.[4]

Home Depot's shareholders are not the only ones who are concerned with questionable top managers and weak boards of directors. A record 1,169 shareholder resolutions were proposed in the U.S. during 2007. Proposals on CEO pay and other governance issues received record high support votes of 30% to 60% from investors.[5] Successful shareholder activist campaigns increased in Europe from less than 10 in 2001 to over 50 in 2007.[6] Research revealing that managers at 29% of all U.S. public corporations had back-dated stock options in order to boost executive pay led to civil charges and shareholder lawsuits in addition to criminal indictments.[7] Board members are increasingly being held accountable for poor corporate governance. For example, 10 former directors from WorldCom and Enron agreed to pay $18 million and $13 million, respectively, of their own money to settle lawsuits launched by enraged stockholders over the unethical and even criminal actions of top management overseen by a passive board of directors.[8]

2.1 Role of the Board of Directors

A *corporation* is a mechanism established to allow different parties to contribute capital, expertise, and labor for their mutual benefit. The investor/shareholder participates in the profits of the enterprise without taking responsibility for the operations. Management runs the company without being responsible for personally providing the funds. To make this possible, laws have been passed that give shareholders limited liability and, correspondingly, limited involvement in a corporation's activities. That involvement does include, however, the right to elect directors who have a legal duty to represent the shareholders and protect their interests. As representatives of the shareholders, directors have both the authority and the responsibility to establish basic corporate policies and to ensure that they are followed.[9]

The board of directors, therefore, has an obligation to approve all decisions that might affect the long-run performance of the corporation. This means that the corporation is fundamentally governed by the *board of directors* overseeing *top management*, with the concurrence of the *shareholder*. The term **corporate governance** refers to the relationship among these three groups in determining the direction and performance of the corporation.[10]

Over the past decade, shareholders and various interest groups have seriously questioned the role of the board of directors in corporations. They are concerned that inside board members may use their position to feather their own nests and that outside board members often lack sufficient knowledge, involvement, and enthusiasm to do an adequate job of monitoring and providing guidance to top management. Instances of widespread corruption and questionable accounting practices at Enron, Global Crossing, WorldCom, Tyco, and Qwest, among others, seem to justify their concerns. Home Depot's board, for example, seemed more interested in keeping CEO Nardelli happy than in promoting shareholder interests.

The general public has not only become more aware and more critical of many boards' apparent lack of responsibility for corporate activities, it has begun to push government to demand accountability. As a result, the board as a rubber stamp of the CEO or as a bastion of the "old-boy" selection system is being replaced by more active, more professional boards.

RESPONSIBILITIES OF THE BOARD

Laws and standards defining the responsibilities of boards of directors vary from country to country. For example, board members in Ontario, Canada, face more than 100 provincial and federal laws governing director liability. The United States, however, has no clear national standards or federal laws. Specific requirements of directors vary, depending on the state in which the corporate charter is issued. There is, nevertheless, a developing worldwide consensus concerning the major responsibilities of a board. Interviews with 200 directors from eight countries (Canada, France, Germany, Finland, Switzerland, the Netherlands, the United Kingdom, and Venezuela) revealed strong agreement on the following five **board of director responsibilities**, listed in order of importance:

1. Setting corporate strategy, overall direction, mission, or vision
2. Hiring and firing the CEO and top management
3. Controlling, monitoring, or supervising top management
4. Reviewing and approving the use of resources
5. Caring for shareholder interests[11]

These results are in agreement with a survey by the National Association of Corporate Directors, in which U.S. CEOs reported that the four most important issues boards should address are corporate performance, CEO succession, strategic planning, and corporate governance.[12] Directors in the United States must make certain, in addition to the duties just listed, that the corporation is managed in accordance with the laws of the state in which it is incorporated. Because more than half of all publicly traded companies in the United States are incorporated in the state of Delaware, this state's laws and rulings have more impact than do those of any other state.[13] Directors must also ensure management's adherence to laws and regulations, such as those dealing with the issuance of securities, insider trading, and other conflict-of-interest situations. They must also be aware of the needs and demands of constituent groups so that they can achieve a judicious balance among the interests of these diverse groups while ensuring the continued functioning of the corporation.

In a legal sense, the board is required to direct the affairs of the corporation but not to manage them. It is charged by law to act with **due care**. If a director or the board as a whole fails to act with due care and, as a result, the corporation is in some way harmed, the careless director or directors can be held personally liable for the harm done. This is no small concern given that one survey of outside directors revealed that more than 40% had been named as part of lawsuits against corporations.[14] For example, board members of Equitable Life in Britain were sued for up to $5.4 billion for failure to question the CEO's reckless policies.[15] For this reason, corporations have found that they need directors and officers' liability insurance in order to attract people to become members of boards of directors.

A 2008 global survey of directors by McKinsey & Company revealed the average amount of time boards spend on a given issue during their meetings:[16]

- Strategy (development and analysis of strategies)—24%
- Execution (prioritizing programs and approving mergers and acquisitions)—24%
- Performance management (development of incentives and measuring performance)—20%
- Governance and compliance (nominations, compensation, audits)—17%
- Talent management—11%

Role of the Board in Strategic Management

How does a board of directors fulfill these many responsibilities? The *role of the board of directors in strategic management* is to carry out three basic tasks:

- **Monitor:** By acting through its committees, a board can keep abreast of developments inside and outside the corporation, bringing to management's attention developments it might have overlooked. A board should at the minimum carry out this task.

- **Evaluate and influence:** A board can examine management's proposals, decisions, and actions; agree or disagree with them; give advice and offer suggestions; and outline alternatives. More active boards perform this task in addition to monitoring.

- **Initiate and determine:** A board can delineate a corporation's mission and specify strategic options to its management. Only the most active boards take on this task in addition to the two previous ones.

Board of Directors' Continuum

A board of directors is involved in strategic management to the extent that it carries out the three tasks of monitoring, evaluating and influencing, and initiating and determining. The **board of directors' continuum** shown in **Figure 2–1** shows the possible degree of involvement (from low to high) in the strategic management process. Boards can range from phantom boards with no real involvement to catalyst boards with a very high degree of involvement.[17] Research suggests that active board involvement in strategic management is positively related to a corporation's financial performance and its credit rating.[18]

FIGURE 2–1 Board of Directors' Continuum

DEGREE OF INVOLVEMENT IN STRATEGIC MANAGEMENT

Low
(Passive)

High
(Active)

Phantom	Rubber Stamp	Minimal Review	Nominal Participation	Active Participation	Catalyst
Never knows what to do, if anything; no degree of involvement.	Permits officers to make all decisions. It votes as the officers recommend on action issues.	Formally reviews selected issues that officers bring to its attention.	Involved to a limited degree in the performance or review of selected key decisions, indicators, or programs of managment.	Approves, questions, and makes final decisions on mission, strategy, policies, and objectives. Has active board committees. Performs fiscal and management audits.	Takes the leading role in establishing and modifying the mission, objectives, strategy, and policies. It has a very active strategy committee.

SOURCE: T. L. Wheelen and J. D. Hunger, "Board of Directors' Continuum," Copyright © 1994 by Wheelen and Hunger Associates. Reprinted by permission.

Highly involved boards tend to be very active. They take their tasks of monitoring, evaluating and influencing, and initiating and determining very seriously; they provide advice when necessary and keep management alert. As depicted in **Figure 2–1**, their heavy involvement in the strategic management process places them in the active participation or even catalyst positions. Although 74% of public corporations have periodic board meetings devoted primarily to the review of overall company strategy, the boards may not have had much influence in generating the plan itself.[19] A 2008 global survey of directors by McKinsey & Company found that 43% of respondents had high to very high influence in creating corporate value. Thirty-eight percent stated that they had moderate influence and 18% reported that they had little to very little influence. Those boards reporting high influence typically shared a common plan for creating value and had healthy debate about what actions the company should take to create value. Together with top management, these high-influence boards considered global trends and future scenarios and developed plans. In contrast, those boards with low influence tended not to do any of these things.[20] These results are supported by a 2006 survey by Korn/Ferry International revealing that 30% of directors felt that their CEO was not utilizing them to their full capacity. In the same study, 73% of the directors indicated that were not content with an oversight role mandated by regulation and wanted to be more involved in setting strategic plans.[21] Nevertheless, studies indicate that boards are becoming increasingly active. For example, in a global survey of directors conducted by McKinsey & Company in 2005, 64% of the respondents indicated that they were more actively involved in the core areas of company performance and value creation than they had been five years earlier. This percentage was higher in large companies (77%) and in publicly held companies (75%).[22]

These and other studies suggest that most large publicly owned corporations have boards that operate at some point between nominal and active participation. Some corporations with actively participating boards are Target, Medtronic, Best Western, Service Corporation International, Bank of Montreal, Mead Corporation, Rolm and Haas, Whirlpool, 3M, Apria Healthcare, General Electric, Pfizer, and Texas Instruments.[23] Target, a corporate governance leader, has a board that each year sets three top priorities, such as strategic direction, capital allocation, and succession planning. Each of these priority topics is placed at the top of the agenda for at least one meeting. Target's board also devotes one meeting a year to setting the strategic direction for each major operating division.[24]

As a board becomes less involved in the affairs of the corporation, it moves farther to the left on the continuum (see **Figure 2–1**). On the far left are passive phantom or rubber-stamp boards that typically never initiate or determine strategy unless a crisis occurs. In these situations, the CEO also serves as Chairman of the Board, personally nominates all directors, and works to keep board members under his or her control by giving them the "mushroom treatment"—throw manure on them and keep them in the dark!

Generally, the smaller the corporation, the less active is its board of directors in strategic management.[25] In an entrepreneurial venture, for example, the privately held corporation may be 100% owned by the founders—who also manage the company. In this case, there is no need for an active board to protect the interests of the owner-manager shareholders—the interests of the owners and the managers are identical. In this instance, a board is really unnecessary and only meets to satisfy legal requirements. If stock is sold to outsiders to finance growth, however, the board becomes more active. Key investors want seats on the board so they can oversee their investment. To the extent that they still control most of the stock, however, the founders dominate the board. Friends, family members, and key shareholders usually become members, but the board acts primarily as a rubber stamp for any proposals put forward by the owner-managers. In this type of company, the founder tends to be both CEO and Chairman of the Board and the board includes few people who are not affiliated with the firm or family.[26] This cozy relationship between the board and management should change, however, when the corporation goes public and stock is more widely dispersed. The founders, who are still acting as management, may sometimes make decisions that conflict with the needs of the other shareholders (especially if the founders own less than 50% of the common stock). In this instance, problems could occur if the board fails to become more active in terms of its roles and responsibilities.

MEMBERS OF A BOARD OF DIRECTORS

The boards of most publicly owned corporations are composed of both inside and outside directors. **Inside directors** (sometimes called management directors) are typically officers or executives employed by the corporation. **Outside directors** (sometimes called non-management directors) may be executives of other firms but are not employees of the board's corporation. Although there is yet no clear evidence indicating that a high proportion of outsiders on a board results in improved financial performance,[27] there is a trend in the United States to increase the number of outsiders on boards and to reduce the total size of the board.[28] The board of directors of a typical large U.S. corporation has an average of 10 directors, 2 of whom are insiders.[29] Outsiders thus account for 80% of the board members in large U.S. corporations (approximately the same as in Canada). Boards in the UK typically have 5 inside and 5 outside directors, whereas in France boards usually consist of 3 insiders and 8 outsiders. Japanese boards, in contrast, contain 2 outsiders and 12 insiders.[30] The board of directors in a typical small U.S. corporation has four to five members, of whom only one or two are outsiders.[31] Research from large and small corporations reveals a negative relationship between board size and firm profitability.[32]

People who favor a high proportion of outsiders state that outside directors are less biased and more likely to evaluate management's performance objectively than are inside directors. This is the main reason why the U.S. Securities and Exchange Commission (SEC) in 2003 required that a majority of directors on the board be independent outsiders. The SEC also required that all listed companies staff their audit, compensation, and nominating/corporate governance committees entirely with independent, outside members. This view is in agreement with **agency theory**, which states that problems arise in corporations because the agents (top management) are not willing to bear responsibility for their decisions unless they own a substantial amount of stock in the corporation. The theory suggests that a majority of a board needs to be from outside the firm so that top management is prevented from acting selfishly to the detriment of the shareholders. For example, proponents of agency theory argue that managers in management-controlled firms (contrasted with owner-controlled firms in which the founder or family still own a significant amount of stock) select less risky strategies with quick payoffs in order to keep their jobs.[33] This view is supported by research revealing that manager-controlled firms (with weak boards) are more likely to go into debt to diversify into unrelated markets (thus quickly boosting sales and assets to justify higher salaries for themselves), thus resulting in poorer long-term performance than owner-controlled firms.[34] Boards with a larger proportion of outside directors tend to favor growth through international expansion and innovative venturing activities than do boards with a smaller proportion of outsiders.[35] Outsiders tend to be more objective and critical of corporate activities. For example, research reveals that the likelihood of a firm engaging in illegal behavior or being sued declines with the addition of outsiders on the board.[36] Research on family businesses has found that boards with a larger number of outsiders on the board tended to have better corporate governance and better performance than did boards with fewer outsiders.[37]

In contrast, those who prefer inside over outside directors contend that outside directors are less effective than are insiders because the outsiders are less likely to have the necessary interest, availability, or competency. **Stewardship theory** proposes that, because of their long tenure with the corporation, insiders (senior executives) tend to identify with the corporation and its success. Rather than use the firm for their own ends, these executives are thus most interested in guaranteeing the continued life and success of the corporation. (See Strategy Highlight 2.1 for a discussion of Agency Theory contrasted with Stewardship Theory.) Excluding all insiders but the CEO reduces the opportunity for outside directors to see potential successors in action or to obtain alternate points of view of management decisions. Outside directors may sometimes serve on so many boards that they spread their time and interest too thin to actively fulfill their responsibilities. The average board member of a U.S. Fortune 500 firm serves on three boards. Research indicates that firm performance decreases as the number of directorships held by the average board member increases.[38] Although only 40% of surveyed U.S. boards currently limit the number of directorships a board member may hold in other corporations, 60% limit the number of boards on which their CEO may be a member.[39]

Those who question the value of having more outside board members point out that the term *outsider* is too simplistic because some outsiders are not truly objective and should be considered more as insiders than as outsiders. For example, there can be:

1. **Affiliated directors**, who, though not really employed by the corporation, handle the legal or insurance work for the company or are important suppliers (thus dependent on the current management for a key part of their business). These outsiders face a conflict of interest and are not likely to be objective. As a result of recent actions by the U.S. Congress, Securities and Exchange Commission, New York Stock Exchange, and NASDAQ, affiliated directors are being banned from U.S. corporate boardrooms. U.S. boards can no longer include representatives of major suppliers or customers or even professional organizations that might do business with the firm, even though these people could provide valuable knowledge and expertise.[40] The New York Stock Exchange decided in 2004 that anyone paid by the company during the previous three years could not be classified as an independent outside director.[41]

2. **Retired executive directors**, who used to work for the company, such as the past CEO who is partly responsible for much of the corporation's current strategy and who probably groomed the current CEO as his or her replacement. In the recent past, many boards of large firms kept the firm's recently retired CEO on the board for a year or two after retirement as

STRATEGY highlight 2.1

AGENCY THEORY VERSUS STEWARDSHIP THEORY IN CORPORATE GOVERNANCE

Managers of large, modern publicly held corporations are typically not the owners. In fact, most of today's top managers own only nominal amounts of stock in the corporation they manage. The real owners (shareholders) elect boards of directors who hire managers as their agents to run the firm's day-to-day activities. Once hired, how trustworthy are these executives? Do they put themselves or the firm first?

Agency Theory. As suggested in the classic study by Berle and Means, top managers are, in effect, "hired hands" who may very likely be more interested in their personal welfare than that of the shareholders. For example, management might emphasize strategies, such as acquisitions, that increase the size of the firm (to become more powerful and to demand increased pay and benefits) or that diversify the firm into unrelated businesses (to reduce short-term risk and to allow them to put less effort into a core product line that may be facing difficulty) but that result in a reduction of dividends and/or stock price.

Agency theory is concerned with analyzing and resolving two problems that occur in relationships between principals (owners/shareholders) and their agents (top management):

1. The agency problem that arises when (a) the desires or objectives of the owners and the agents conflict or (b) it is difficult or expensive for the owners to verify what the agent is actually doing. One example is when top management is more interested in raising its own salary than in increasing stock dividends.

2. The risk-sharing problem that arises when the owners and agents have different attitudes toward risk. Executives may not select risky strategies because they fear losing their jobs if the strategy fails.

According to agency theory, the likelihood that these problems will occur increases when stock is widely held (that is, when no one shareholder owns more than a small percentage of the total common stock), when the board of directors is composed of people who know little of the company or who are personal friends of top management, and when a high percentage of board members are inside (management) directors.

To better align the interests of the agents with those of the owners and to increase the corporation's overall perfor-

mance, agency theory suggests that top management have a significant degree of ownership in the firm and/or have a strong financial stake in its long-term performance. In support of this argument, research indicates a positive relationship between corporate performance and the amount of stock owned by directors.

Stewardship Theory. In contrast, stewardship theory suggests that executives tend to be more motivated to act in the best interests of the corporation than in their own self-interests. Whereas agency theory focuses on extrinsic rewards that serve the lower-level needs, such as pay and security, stewardship theory focuses on the higher-order needs, such as achievement and self-actualization. Stewardship theory argues that senior executives over time tend to view the corporation as an extension of themselves. Rather than use the firm for their own ends, these executives are most interested in guaranteeing the continued life and success of the corporation. The relationship between the board and top management is thus one of principal and steward, not principal and agent ("hired hand"). Stewardship theory notes that in a widely held corporation, the shareholder is free to sell his or her stock at any time. In fact, the average share of stock is held less than 10 months. A diversified investor or speculator may care little about risk at the company level—preferring management to assume extraordinary risk so long as the return is adequate. Because executives in a firm cannot easily leave their jobs when in difficulty, they are more interested in a merely satisfactory return and put heavy emphasis on the firm's continued survival. Thus, stewardship theory argues that in many instances top management may care more about a company's long-term success than do more short-term oriented shareholders.

....

For more information about agency and stewardship theory, see A. A. Berle and G. C. Means, *The Modern Corporation and Private Property* (NY: Macmillan, 1936). Also see J. H. Davis, F. D. Schoorman, and L. Donaldson, "Toward a Stewardship Theory of Management," *Academy of Management Review* (January 1997), pp. 20–47; P. J. Lane, A. A. Cannella, Jr. & M. H. Lubatkin, "Agency Problems as Antecedents to Unrelated Mergers and Diversification: Amihud and Lev Reconsidered," *Strategic Management Journal* (June 1998), pp. 555–578; M. L. Hayward and D. C. Hambrick, "Explaining the Premiums Paid for Large Acquisitions: Evidence of CEO Hubris," *Administrative Science Quarterly* (March 1997), pp. 103–127; and C. M. Christensen and S. D. Anthony, "Put Investors in their Place," *Business Week* (May 28, 2007), p. 108.

a courtesy, especially if he/she had performed well as the CEO. It is almost certain, however, that this person will not be able to objectively evaluate the corporation's performance. Because of the likelihood of a conflict of interest, only 31% of boards in the Americas, 25% in Europe, and 20% in Australasia now include the former CEO on their boards.[42]

3. **Family directors**, who are descendants of the founder and own significant blocks of stock (with personal agendas based on a family relationship with the current CEO). The Schlitz Brewing Company, for example, was unable to complete its turnaround strategy with a non-family CEO because family members serving on the board wanted their money out of the company, forcing it to be sold.[43]

The majority of outside directors are active or retired CEOs and COOs of other corporations. Others are major investors/shareholders, academicians, attorneys, consultants, former government officials, and bankers. Given that 66% of the outstanding stock in the largest U.S. and UK corporations is now owned by institutional investors, such as mutual funds and pension plans, these investors are taking an increasingly active role in board membership and activities.[44] For example, TIAA-CREF's Corporate Governance team monitors governance practices of the 4,000 companies in which it invests its pension funds through its Corporate Assessment Program. If its analysis of a company reveals problems, TIAA-CREF first sends letters stating its concerns, followed up by visits, and it finally sponsors a shareholder resolution in opposition to management's actions.[45] Institutional investors are also powerful in many other countries. In Germany, bankers are represented on almost every board—primarily because they own large blocks of stock in German corporations. In Denmark, Sweden, Belgium, and Italy, however, investment companies assume this role. For example, the investment company Investor casts 42.5% of the Electrolux shareholder votes, thus guaranteeing itself positions on the Electrolux board.

Boards of directors have been working to increase the number of women and minorities serving on boards. Korn/Ferry International reports that of the Fortune 1000 largest U.S. firms, 85% had at least one woman director in 2006 (compared to 69% in 1995), comprising 15% of total directors. Approximately one-half of the boards in Europe included a female director, comprising 9% of total directors. (The percentage of female directors in Europe in 2006 ranged from less than 1% in Portugal to almost 40% in Norway.)[46] Korn/Ferry's survey also revealed that 76% of the U.S. boards had at least one ethnic minority in 2006 (African-American, 47%; Latino, 19%; Asian, 10%) as director compared to only 47% in 1995, comprising around 14% of total directors.[47] Among the top 200 S&P companies in the U.S., however, 84% have at least one African-American director.[48] The globalization of business is having an impact on board membership. According to the Spencer Stuart executive recruiting firm, 33% of U.S. boards had an international director.[49] Europe was the most "globalized" region of the world, with most companies reporting one or more non-national directors.[50] Although Asian and Latin American boards are still predominantly staffed by nationals, they are working to add more international directors.[51]

Outside directors serving on the boards of large Fortune 1000 U.S. corporations annually earned on average $58,217 in cash plus an average of $75,499 in stock options. Most of the companies (63%) paid their outside directors an annual retainer plus a fee for every meeting attended.[52] Directors serving on the boards of small companies usually received much less compensation (around $10,000). One study found directors of a sample of large U.S. firms to hold on average 3% of their corporations' outstanding stock.[53]

The vast majority of inside directors are the chief executive officer and either the chief operating officer (if not also the CEO) or the chief financial officer. Presidents or vice presidents of key operating divisions or functional units sometimes serve on the board. Few, if any, inside directors receive any extra compensation for assuming this extra duty. Very rarely does a U.S. board include any lower-level operating employees.

Codetermination: Should Employees Serve on Boards?

Codetermination, the inclusion of a corporation's workers on its board, began only recently in the United States. Corporations such as Chrysler, Northwest Airlines, United Airlines (UAL), and Wheeling-Pittsburgh Steel added representatives from employee associations to their boards as part of union agreements or Employee Stock Ownership Plans (ESOPs). For example, United Airlines workers traded 15% in pay cuts for 55% of the company (through an ESOP) and 3 of the firm's 12 board seats. In this instance, workers represent themselves on the board not so much as employees but primarily as owners. At Chrysler, however, the United Auto Workers union obtained a temporary seat on the board as part of a union contract agreement in exchange for changes in work rules and reductions in benefits. This was at a time when Chrysler was facing bankruptcy in the late 1970s. In situations like this when a director represents an internal stakeholder, critics raise the issue of conflict of interest. Can a member of the board, who is privy to confidential managerial information, function, for example, as a union leader whose primary duty is to fight for the best benefits for his or her members? Although the movement to place employees on the boards of directors of U.S. companies shows little likelihood of increasing (except through employee stock ownership), the European experience reveals an increasing acceptance of worker participation (without ownership) on corporate boards.

Germany pioneered codetermination during the 1950s with a two-tiered system: (1) a supervisory board elected by shareholders and employees to approve or decide corporate strategy and policy and (2) a management board (composed primarily of top management) appointed by the supervisory board to manage the company's activities. Most other Western European countries have either passed similar codetermination legislation (as in Sweden, Denmark, Norway, and Austria) or use worker councils to work closely with management (as in Belgium, Luxembourg, France, Italy, Ireland, and the Netherlands).

Interlocking Directorates

CEOs often nominate chief executives (as well as board members) from other firms to membership on their own boards in order to create an interlocking directorate. A *direct* **interlocking directorate** occurs when two firms share a director or when an executive of one firm sits on the board of a second firm. An *indirect* interlock occurs when two corporations have directors who also serve on the board of a third firm, such as a bank.

Although the Clayton Act and the Banking Act of 1933 prohibit interlocking directorates by U.S. companies competing in the same industry, interlocking continues to occur in almost all corporations, especially large ones. Interlocking occurs because large firms have a large impact on other corporations and these other corporations, in turn, have some control over the firm's inputs and marketplace. For example, most large corporations in the United States, Japan, and Germany are interlocked either directly or indirectly with financial institutions.[54] Eleven of the 15 largest U.S. corporations have at least two board members who sit together on another board. Twenty percent of the 1,000 largest U.S. firms share at least one board member.[55]

Interlocking directorates are useful for gaining both inside information about an uncertain environment and objective expertise about potential strategies and tactics.[56] For example, Kleiner Perkins, a high-tech venture capital firm, not only has seats on the boards of the companies in which it invests, but it also has executives (which Kleiner Perkins hired) from one entrepreneurial venture who serve as directors on others. Kleiner Perkins refers to its network of interlocked firms as its *keiretsu*, a Japanese term for a set of companies with interlocking business relationships and share-holdings.[57] Family-owned corporations, however, are less likely to have interlocking directorates than are corporations with highly dispersed stock ownership, probably because family-owned corporations do not like to dilute their corporate control by adding outsiders to boardroom discussions.

There is some concern, however, when the chairs of separate corporations serve on each other's boards. Twenty-two such pairs of corporate chairs (who typically also served as their firm's CEO) existed in 2003. In one instance, the three chairmen of Anheuser-Busch, SBC Communications, and Emerson Electric served on all three of the boards. Typically a CEO sits on only one board in addition to his or her own—down from two additional boards in previous years. Although such interlocks may provide valuable information, they are increasingly frowned upon because of the possibility of collusion.[58] Nevertheless, evidence indicates that well-interlocked corporations are better able to survive in a highly competitive environment.[59]

NOMINATION AND ELECTION OF BOARD MEMBERS

Traditionally the CEO of a corporation decided whom to invite to board membership and merely asked the shareholders for approval in the annual proxy statement. All nominees were usually elected. There are some dangers, however, in allowing the CEO free rein in nominating directors. The CEO might select only board members who, in the CEO's opinion, will not disturb the company's policies and functioning. Given that the average length of service of a U.S. board member is for three three-year terms (but can range up to 20 years for some boards), CEO-friendly, passive boards are likely to result. This is especially likely given that only 7% of surveyed directors indicated that their company had term limits for board members. Nevertheless, 60% of U.S. boards and 58% of European boards have a mandatory retirement age—typically around 70.[60] Research reveals that boards rated as least effective by the Corporate Library, a corporate governance research firm, tend to have members serving longer (an average of 9.7 years) than boards rated as most effective (7.5 years).[61] Directors selected by the CEO often feel that they should go along with any proposal the CEO makes. Thus board members find themselves accountable to the very management they are charged to oversee. Because this is likely to happen, more boards are using a nominating committee to nominate new outside board members for the shareholders to elect. Ninety-seven percent of large U.S. corporations now use nominating committees to identify potential directors. This practice is less common in Europe where 60% of boards use nominating committees.[62]

Many corporations whose directors serve terms of more than one year divides the board into classes and staggers elections so that only a portion of the board stands for election each year. This is called a *staggered board*. Sixty-three percent of U.S. boards currently have staggered boards.[63] Arguments in favor of this practice are that it provides continuity by reducing the chance of an abrupt turnover in its membership and that it reduces the likelihood of electing people unfriendly to management (who might be interested in a hostile takeover) through cumulative voting. An argument against staggered boards is that they make it more difficult for concerned shareholders to curb a CEO's power—especially when that CEO is also Chairman of the Board. An increasing number of shareholder resolutions to replace staggered boards with annual elections of all board members are currently being passed at annual meetings.

When nominating people for election to a board of directors, it is important that nominees have previous experience dealing with corporate issues. For example, research reveals that a firm makes better acquisition decisions when the firm's outside directors have had experience with such decisions.[64]

A survey of directors of U.S. corporations revealed the following criteria in a good director:

- Willing to challenge management when necessary—95%
- Special expertise important to the company—67%
- Available outside meetings to advise management—57%
- Expertise on global business issues—41%

- Understands the firm's key technologies and processes—39%
- Brings external contacts that are potentially valuable to the firm—33%
- Has detailed knowledge of the firm's industry—31%
- Has high visibility in his or her field—31%
- Is accomplished at representing the firm to stakeholders—18%[65]

ORGANIZATION OF THE BOARD

The size of a board in the United States is determined by the corporation's charter and its by-laws, in compliance with state laws. Although some states require a minimum number of board members, most corporations have quite a bit of discretion in determining board size. The average large, publicly held U.S. firm has 10 directors on its board. The average small, privately-held company has four to five members. The average size of boards elsewhere is Japan, 14; Non-Japan Asia, 9; Germany, 16; UK, 10; and France, 11.[66]

Approximately 70% of the top executives of U.S. publicly held corporations hold the dual designation of Chairman and CEO. (Only 5% of the firms in the UK have a combined Chair/CEO.)[67] The combined Chair/CEO position is being increasingly criticized because of the potential for conflict of interest. The CEO is supposed to concentrate on strategy, planning, external relations, and responsibility to the board. The Chairman's responsibility is to ensure that the board and its committees perform their functions as stated in the board's charter. Further, the Chairman schedules board meetings and presides over the annual shareholders' meeting. Critics of having one person in the two offices ask how the board can properly oversee top management if the Chairman is also a part of top management. For this reason, the Chairman and CEO roles are separated by law in Germany, the Netherlands, South Africa, and Finland. A similar law has been considered in the United Kingdom and Australia. Although research is mixed regarding the impact of the combined Chair/CEO position on overall corporate financial performance, firm stock price and credit ratings both respond negatively to announcements of CEOs also assuming the Chairman position.[68] Research also shows that corporations with a combined Chair/CEO have a greater likelihood of fraudulent financial reporting when CEO stock options are not present.[69]

Many of those who prefer that the Chairman and CEO positions be combined agree that the outside directors should elect a **lead director**. This person is consulted by the Chair/CEO regarding board affairs and coordinates the annual evaluation of the CEO.[70] The lead director position is very popular in the United Kingdom, where it originated. Of those U.S. companies combining the Chairman and CEO positions, 96% had a lead director.[71] This is one way to give the board more power without undermining the power of the Chair/CEO. The lead director becomes increasingly important because 94% of U.S. boards in 2006 (compared to only 41% in 2002) held regular executive sessions without the CEO being present.[72] Nevertheless, there are many ways in which an unscrupulous Chair/CEO can guarantee a director's loyalty. Research indicates that an increase in board independence often results in higher levels of CEO ingratiation behavior aimed at persuading directors to support CEO proposals. Long-tenured directors who support the CEO may use social pressure to persuade a new board member to conform to the group. Directors are more likely to be recommended for membership on other boards if they "don't rock the boat" and engage in low levels of monitoring and control behavior.[73] Even in those situations when the board has a nominating committee composed only of outsiders, the committee often obtains the CEO's approval for each new board candidate.[74]

The most effective boards accomplish much of their work through committees. Although they do not usually have legal duties, most committees are granted full power to act with the authority of the board between board meetings. Typical standing committees (in order of prevalence) are the audit (100%), compensation (99%), nominating (97%), corporate governance (94%), stock options (84%), director compensation (52%), and executive (43%) committees.[75] The executive committee is usually composed of two inside and two outside directors located nearby who can meet between board meetings to attend to matters that must be settled quickly. This committee acts as an extension of the board and, consequently, may have almost unrestricted authority in certain areas.[76] Except for the executive, finance, and investment committees, board committees are now typically staffed only by outside directors. Although each board committee typically meets four to five times annually, the average audit committee met nine times during 2006.[77]

IMPACT OF THE SARBANES-OXLEY ACT ON U.S. CORPORATE GOVERNANCE

In response to the many corporate scandals uncovered since 2000, the U.S. Congress passed the **Sarbanes-Oxley Act** in June 2002. This act was designed to protect shareholders from the excesses and failed oversight that characterized failures at Enron, Tyco, WorldCom, Adelphia Communications, Qwest, and Global Crossing, among other prominent firms. Several key elements of Sarbanes-Oxley were designed to formalize greater board independence and oversight. For example, the act requires that all directors serving on the audit committee be independent of the firm and receive no fees other than for services of the director. In addition, boards may no longer grant loans to corporate officers. The act has also established formal procedures for individuals (known as "whistleblowers") to report incidents of questionable accounting or auditing. Firms are prohibited from retaliating against anyone reporting wrongdoing. Both the CEO and CFO must certify the corporation's financial information. The act bans auditors from providing both external and internal audit services to the same company. It also requires that a firm identify whether it has a "financial expert" serving on the audit committee who is independent from management.

Although the cost to a large corporation of implementing the provisions of the law was $8.5 million in 2004, the first year of compliance, the costs to a large firm fell to $1–$5 million annually during the following years as accounting and information processes were refined and made more efficient.[78] Pitney Bowes, for example, saved more than $500,000 in 2005 simply by consolidating four accounts receivable offices into one. Similar savings were realized at Cisco and Genentech.[79] An additional benefit of the increased disclosure requirements is more reliable corporate financial statements. Companies are now reporting numbers with fewer adjustments for unusual charges and write-offs, which in the past have been used to boost reported earnings.[80] The new rules have also made it more difficult for firms to post-date executive stock options. "This is an unintended consequence of disclosure," remarked Gregory Taxin, CEO of Glass, Lewis & Company, a stock research firm.[81] See the **Global Issue** feature to learn how corporate governance is being improved in other parts of the world.

Improving Governance

In implementing the Sarbanes-Oxley Act, the U.S. Securities and Exchange Commission (SEC) required in 2003 that a company disclose whether it has adopted a code of ethics that applies to the CEO and to the company's principal financial officer. Among other things, the SEC requires that the audit, nominating, and compensation committees be staffed entirely by outside directors. The New York Stock Exchange reinforced the mandates of Sarbanes-Oxley by requiring that companies have a nominating/governance committee composed entirely of independent outside directors. Similarly, NASDAQ rules require that nominations for new directors be made by either a nominating committee of independent outsiders or by a majority of independent outside directors.[82]

GLOBAL issue

CORPORATE GOVERNANCE IMPROVEMENTS THROUGHOUT THE WORLD

Countries throughout the world are working to improve corporate governance. Provisions that are roughly equivalent to Sarbanes-Oxley are in place in France and Japan, while both China and Canada are implementing similar rules. In the UK, the Cadbury Report has led to revisions to the Combined Code of Conduct that have placed additional responsibilities on non-management directors, altered board and committee composition, and modified the roles of the CEO and Chairman. The adoption of recommendations from the government-sponsored Cromme Commission has reduced the power of management directors and increased the transparency of Germany's two-tier system of governance. Italy has implemented the Draghi Law of 1998 and the Preda Code of Conduct. Since many corporations in non-Japan Asia are family-controlled or have stock that is at least partially owned by the state, the Anglo-American system of corporate governance does not quite fit. Nevertheless, many of the changes in other parts of the world, such as CEO performance reviews and executive succession planning, are taking place in Asian corporations.

In an attempt to make Korean businesses more attractive to foreign investors, for example, the South Korean government recommended that companies listed on the stock exchange introduce a two-tiered structure. One structure was to consist entirely of non-executive (outside) directors. One of the few companies to immediately adopt this new system of governance was Pohang Iron & Steel Company Ltd. (POSCO), the world's largest steelmaker. POSCO was listed on the New York Stock Exchange and had significant operations in the United States, plus a joint venture with U.S. Steel. According to Youn-Gil Ro, Corporate Information Team Manager, "We needed professional advice on international business practices as well as American practices."

SOURCES: A. L. Nazareth, "Keeping SarbOx Is Crucial," *Business Week* (November 13, 2006), p. 134; *33rd Annual Board of Directors Study* (New York: Korn/Ferry International, 2007); C. A. Mallin, editor, *Handbook on International Corporate Governance* (Northampton, Massachusetts: Edward Elgar Publishing, 2006). *Globalizing the Board of Directors: Trends and Strategies* (New York: Conference Board, 1999), p. 16.

Partially in response to Sarbanes-Oxley, a survey of directors of Fortune 1000 U.S. companies by Mercer Delta Consulting and the University of Southern California revealed that 60% of directors were spending more time on board matters than before Sarbanes-Oxley, with 85% spending more time on their company's accounts, 83% more on governance practices, and 52% on monitoring financial performance.[83] Newly elected outside directors with financial management experience increased to 10% of all outside directors in 2003 from only 1% of outsiders in 1998.[84] Seventy-eight percent of Fortune 1000 U.S. boards in 2006 required that directors own stock in the corporation, compared to just 36% in Europe, and 26% in Asia.[85]

Evaluating Governance

To help investors evaluate a firm's corporate governance, a number of independent rating services, such as Standard & Poor's (S&P), Moody's, Morningstar, The Corporate Library, Institutional Shareholder Services (ISS), and Governance Metrics International (GMI), have established criteria for good governance. *Business Week* annually publishes a list of the best and worst boards of U.S. corporations. Whereas rating service firms like S&P, Moody's, and The Corporate Library use a wide mix of research data and criteria to evaluate companies, ISS and GMI have been criticized because they primarily use public records to score firms, using simple checklists.[86] In contrast, the S&P Corporate Governance Scoring System researches four major issues:

- Ownership Structure and Influence
- Financial Stakeholder Rights and Relations

- Financial Transparency and Information Disclosure
- Board Structure and Processes

Although the S&P scoring system is proprietary and confidential, independent research using generally accepted measures of S&P's four issues revealed that moving from the poorest- to the best-governed categories nearly doubled a firm's likelihood of receiving an investment-grade credit rating.[87]

Avoiding Governance Improvements

A number of corporations are concerned that various requirements to improve corporate governance will constrain top management's ability to effectively manage the company. For example, more U.S. public corporations have gone private in the years since the passage of Sarbanes-Oxley than before its passage. Other companies use multiple classes of stock to keep outsiders from having sufficient voting power to change the company. Insiders, usually the company's founders, get stock with extra votes, while others get second-class stock with fewer votes. For example, Brian Roberts, CEO of Comcast, owns "superstock" that represents only 0.4% of outstanding common stock but guarantees him one-third of the voting stock. The Investor Responsibility Research Center reports that 11.3% of the companies it monitored in 2004 had multiple classes, up from 7.5% in 1990.[88]

Another approach to sidestepping new governance requirements is being used by corporations such as Google, Infrasource Services, Orbitz, and W&T Offshore. If a corporation in which an individual group or another company controls more than 50% of the voting shares decides to become a "controlled company," the firm is then exempt from requirements by the New York Stock Exchange and NASDAQ that a majority of the board and all members of key board committees be independent outsiders. According to governance authority Jay Lorsch, this will result in a situation in which "the majority shareholders can walk all over the minority."[89]

TRENDS IN CORPORATE GOVERNANCE

The role of the board of directors in the strategic management of a corporation is likely to be more active in the future. Although neither the composition of boards nor the board leadership structure has been consistently linked to firm financial performance, better governance does lead to higher credit ratings and stock prices. A McKinsey survey reveals that investors are willing to pay 16% more for a corporation's stock if it is known to have good corporate governance. The investors explained that they would pay more because, in their opinion (1) good governance leads to better performance over time, (2) good governance reduces the risk of the company getting into trouble, and (3) governance is a major strategic issue.[90]

Some of today's trends in governance (particularly prevalent in the United States and the United Kingdom) that are likely to continue include the following:

- Boards are getting more involved not only in reviewing and evaluating company strategy but also in shaping it.
- Institutional investors, such as pension funds, mutual funds, and insurance companies, are becoming active on boards and are putting increasing pressure on top management to improve corporate performance. This trend is supported by a U.S. SEC requirement that a mutual fund must publicly disclose the proxy votes cast at company board meetings in its portfolio. This reduces the tendency for mutual funds to rubber-stamp management proposals.[91]
- Shareholders are demanding that directors and top managers own more than token amounts of stock in the corporation. Research indicates that boards with equity ownership use quantifiable, verifiable criteria (instead of vague, qualitative criteria) to evaluate the CEO.[92] When compensation committee members are significant shareholders, they tend

to offer the CEO less salary but with a higher incentive component than do compensation committee members who own little to no stock.[93]

■ Non-affiliated outside (non-management) directors are increasing their numbers and power in publicly held corporations as CEOs loosen their grip on boards. Outside members are taking charge of annual CEO evaluations.

■ Women and minorities are being increasingly represented on boards.

■ Boards are establishing mandatory retirement ages for board members—typically around age 70.

■ Boards are evaluating not only their own overall performance, but also that of individual directors.

■ Boards are getting smaller—partially because of the reduction in the number of insiders but also because boards desire new directors to have specialized knowledge and expertise instead of general experience.

■ Boards continue to take more control of board functions by either splitting the combined Chair/CEO into two separate positions or establishing a lead outside director position.

■ Boards are eliminating 1970s anti-takeover defenses that served to entrench current management. In just one year, for example, 66 boards repealed their staggered boards and 25 eliminated poison pills.[94]

■ As corporations become more global, they are increasingly looking for board members with international experience.

■ Instead of merely being able to vote for or against directors nominated by the board's nominating committee, shareholders may eventually be allowed to nominate board members. This was originally proposed by the U.S. Securities and Exchange Commission in 2004, but was not implemented. Supported by the AFL-CIO, a more open nominating process would enable shareholders to vote out directors who ignore shareholder interests.[95]

■ Society, in the form of special interest groups, increasingly expects boards of directors to balance the economic goal of profitability with the social needs of society. Issues dealing with workforce diversity and environmental sustainability are now reaching the board level. (See the **Environmental Sustainability Issue** feature for an example of a conflict between a CEO and the board of directors over environmental issues.)

2.2 The Role of Top Management

The top management function is usually conducted by the CEO of the corporation in coordination with the COO (Chief Operating Officer) or president, executive vice president, and vice presidents of divisions and functional areas.[96] Even though strategic management involves everyone in the organization, the board of directors holds top management primarily responsible for the strategic management of a firm.[97]

RESPONSIBILITIES OF TOP MANAGEMENT

Top management responsibilities, especially those of the CEO, involve getting things accomplished through and with others in order to meet the corporate objectives. Top management's job is thus multidimensional and is oriented toward the welfare of the total

ENVIRONMENTAL sustainability issue

CONFLICT AT THE BODY SHOP

When Anita Roddick opened the first Body Shop in 1976, she probably had no idea that she would become one of the first "green" business executives. She simply liked the idea of selling cosmetics in small sizes that were made from natural ingredients. By 1998, her entrepreneurial venture grew through franchising into a global business with 1,594 shops in 47 countries. Roddick's personal philosophy in favor of human rights, endangered wildlife, and the environment, while being strongly against the use of animals in testing cosmetics, became an inherent part of the company's philosophy of business. Reflecting an environmental awareness far in advance of other firms, the company's publication, *This Is the Body Shop,* stated: "We aim to avoid excessive packaging, to refill our bottles, and to recycle our packaging and use raw materials from renewable sources when technologically and economically feasible." The company drafted the European Union's *Eco-Management and Audit Regulation* in 1991 and the company's first environmental statement, *The Green Book*, in 1992.

The Body Shop became a publicly traded corporation in 1984 when it was listed on London's Unlisted Securities Market for just 95 pence per stock. By 1986, the stock price had increased ten-fold in value and was listed on the London Stock Exchange. The company grew quickly to be worth 700 million British pounds in 1991. Although the influx of money from the sale of stock enabled the company to expand throughout the world, there were disadvantages to having shareholders and a board of directors. Some shareholders began to complain that the company was diverting money into social projects instead of maximizing profits. Roddick had used her position as CEO to join the Body Shop with Greenpeace's "Save the Whales" campaign and to form alliances with Amnesty International and Friends of the Earth. Although the company continued to grow in size, its market value was declining by 1998. Tiring

of Roddick's social and environmental "radicalism," the board forced her to resign as CEO. Roddick and her husband (with just 18% of the stock) remained on the board as co-chairmen until 2002, when they were replaced. Roddick continued to carry out public relations functions for the company and traveled the world in search of new product ideas, but no longer had any control over the strategic direction of the firm she had founded.

On March 17, 2006, the Body Shop's board agreed to the company's sale to L'Oreal for a premium of 34.2% over the company's stock price. The sale was perceived by observers as quite ironic, given that for years Anita Roddick had criticized L'Oreal for its animal testing practices and for its exploitation of women in the workplace. On its Web site, Naturewatch said: "We feel that the Body Shop has 'sold out' and is not standing on its principles." Animal rights activists and some consumers vowed to boycott Body Shop stores. Within three weeks of the announcement, the Body Shop's "satisfaction" rating compiled by BrandIndex fell 11 points, to 14, its "buzz" rating fell by 10 points, to −4, and its "general impression" fell by 3 points, to 19. One Body Shop customer reflected the widespread dissatisfaction: "The Body Shop used to be my high street "safe house," a place where I could walk into and know that what I bought was okay, that people were actually benefiting from my purchase. . . . By buying from the Body Shop, you are now no longer supporting ethical consumerism. If I want legitimate fair-trade, non-animal tested products, I can find them easily, at the same price, elsewhere."

....
SOURCES: E. A. Fogarty, J. P. Vincelette, and T. L. Wheelen, "The Body Shop International PLC: Anita Roddick, OBE," in T. L. Wheelen and J. D. Hunger, *Strategic Management and Business Policy*, 8th ed. (Upper Saddle River, NJ: Prentice Hall, 2002), pp. 7.1–7.26; D. Purkayastha and R. Fernando, *The Body Shop: Social Responsibility or Sustained Greenwashing?* (Hyderabad, India: ICFAI Center for Management Research, 2006).

organization. Specific top management tasks vary from firm to firm and are developed from an analysis of the mission, objectives, strategies, and key activities of the corporation. Tasks are typically divided among the members of the top management team. A diversity of skills can thus be very important. Research indicates that top management teams with a diversity of functional backgrounds, experiences, and length of time with the company tend to be significantly related to improvements in corporate market share and profitability.[98] In addition, highly diverse teams with some international experience tend to emphasize international growth strategies and strategic innovation, especially in uncertain environments, to boost financial performance.[99] The CEO, with the support of the rest of the top management team, must successfully handle two primary responsibilities that are crucial to the effective strategic management of the corporation: (1) provide executive leadership and a strategic vision and (2) manage the strategic planning process.

Executive Leadership and Strategic Vision

Executive leadership is the directing of activities toward the accomplishment of corporate objectives. Executive leadership is important because it sets the tone for the entire corporation. A **strategic vision** is a description of what the company is capable of becoming. It is often communicated in the company's mission and vision statements (as described in **Chapter 1**). People in an organization want to have a sense of mission, but only top management is in the position to specify and communicate this strategic vision to the general workforce. Top management's enthusiasm (or lack of it) about the corporation tends to be contagious. The importance of executive leadership is illustrated by Steve Reinemund, past-CEO of PepsiCo: "A leader's job is to define overall direction and motivate others to get there."[100]

Successful CEOs are noted for having a clear strategic vision, a strong passion for their company, and an ability to communicate with others. They are often perceived to be dynamic and charismatic leaders—which is especially important for high firm performance and investor confidence in uncertain environments.[101] They have many of the characteristics of **transformational leaders**—that is, leaders who provide change and movement in an organization by providing a vision for that change.[102] For instance, the positive attitude characterizing many well-known industrial leaders—such as Bill Gates at Microsoft, Anita Roddick at the Body Shop, Richard Branson at Virgin, Steve Jobs at Apple Computer, Phil Knight at Nike, Bob Lutz at General Motors, and Louis Gerstner at IBM—has energized their respective corporations. These transformational leaders have been able to command respect and to influence strategy formulation and implementation because they tend to have three key characteristics:[103]

1. **The CEO articulates a strategic vision for the corporation:** The CEO envisions the company not as it currently is but as it can become. The new perspective that the CEO's vision brings to activities and conflicts gives renewed meaning to everyone's work and enables employees to see beyond the details of their own jobs to the functioning of the total corporation.[104] Louis Gerstner proposed a new vision for IBM when he proposed that the company change its business model from computer hardware to services: "If customers were going to look to an integrator to help them envision, design, and build end-to-end solutions, then the companies playing that role would exert tremendous influence over the full range of technology decisions—from architecture and applications to hardware and software choices."[105] In a survey of 1,500 senior executives from 20 different countries, when asked the most important behavioral trait a CEO must have, 98% responded that the CEO must convey "a strong sense of vision."[106]

2. **The CEO presents a role for others to identify with and to follow:** The leader empathizes with followers and sets an example in terms of behavior, dress, and actions. The CEO's attitudes and values concerning the corporation's purpose and activities are clear-cut and constantly communicated in words and deeds. For example, when design engineers at General Motors had problems with monitor resolution using the Windows operating system, Steve Ballmer, CEO of Microsoft, personally crawled under conference room tables to plug in PC monitors and diagnose the problem.[107] People know what to expect and have trust in their CEO. Research indicates that businesses in which the general manager has the trust of the employees have higher sales and profits with lower turnover than do businesses in which there is a lesser amount of trust.[108]

3. **The CEO communicates high performance standards and also shows confidence in the followers' abilities to meet these standards:** The leader empowers followers by raising their beliefs in their own capabilities. No leader ever improved performance by setting easily attainable goals that provided no challenge. Communicating high expectations to others can often lead to high performance.[109] The CEO must be willing to follow through by coaching people. As a result, employees view their work as very important and thus motivating.[110] Ivan Seidenberg, chief executive of Verizon Communications, was closely involved in deciding Verizon's strategic direction, and he showed his faith in his people by letting his key managers handle important projects and represent the company in public forums. "All of these people could be CEOs in their own right. They are warriors and they are on a mission," explained Seidenberg. Grateful for his faith in them, his managers were fiercely loyal both to him and the company.[111]

The negative side of confident executive leaders is that their very confidence may lead to *hubris*, in which their confidence blinds them to information that is contrary to a decided course of action. For example, overconfident CEOs tend to charge ahead with mergers and acquisitions even though they are aware that most acquisitions destroy shareholder value. Research by Tate and Malmendier found that "overconfident CEOs are more likely to conduct mergers than rational CEOs at any point in time. Overconfident CEOs view their company as undervalued by outside investors who are less optimistic about the prospects of the firm." Overconfident CEOs were most likely to make acquisitions when they could avoid selling new stock to finance them, and they were more likely to do deals that diversified their firm's lines of businesses.[112]

Managing the Strategic Planning Process

As business corporations adopt more of the characteristics of the learning organization, strategic planning initiatives can come from any part of an organization. A survey of 156 large corporations throughout the world revealed that, in two-thirds of the firms, strategies were first proposed in the business units and sent to headquarters for approval.[113] However, unless top management encourages and supports the planning process, strategic management is not likely to result. In most corporations, top management must initiate and manage the strategic planning process. It may do so by first asking business units and functional areas to propose strategic plans for themselves, or it may begin by drafting an overall corporate plan within which the units can then build their own plans. Research suggests that bottom-up strategic planing may be most appropriate in multidivisional corporations operating in relatively stable environments but that top-down strategic planning may be most appropriate for firms operating in turbulent environments.[114] Other organizations engage in concurrent strategic planning in which all the organization's units draft plans for themselves after they have been provided with the organization's overall mission and objectives.

Regardless of the approach taken, the typical board of directors expects top management to manage the overall strategic planning process so that the plans of all the units and functional areas fit together into an overall corporate plan. Top management's job therefore includes the tasks of evaluating unit plans and providing feedback. To do this, it may require each unit to justify its proposed objectives, strategies, and programs in terms of how well they satisfy the organization's overall objectives in light of available resources. If a company is not organized into business units, top managers may work together as a team to do strategic planning. CEO Jeff Bezos tells how this is done at Amazon.com:

> We have a group called the S Team—S meaning "senior" [management]—that stays abreast of what the company is working on and delves into strategy issues. It meets for about four hours every Tuesday. Once or twice a year the S Team also gets together in a two-day meeting where

different ideas are explored. Homework is assigned ahead of time. . . . Eventually we have to choose just a couple of things, if they're big, and make bets.[115]

In contrast to the seemingly continuous strategic planning being done at Amazon.com, most large corporations conduct the strategic planning process just once a year—often at off-site strategy workshops attended by senior executives.[116]

Many large organizations have a *strategic planning staff* charged with supporting both top management and the business units in the strategic planning process. This staff may prepare the background materials used in senior management's off-site strategy workshop. This planning staff typically consists of fewer than ten people, headed by a senior executive with the title of Director of Corporate Development or Chief Strategy Officer. The staff's major responsibilities are to:

1. Identify and analyze companywide strategic issues, and suggest corporate strategic alternatives to top management.

2. Work as facilitators with business units to guide them through the strategic planning process.[117]

End of Chapter SUMMARY

Who determines a corporation's performance? According to the popular press, it is the chief executive officer who seems to be personally responsible for a company's success or failure. When a company is in trouble, one of the first alternatives usually presented is to fire the CEO. That was certainly the case at the Walt Disney Company under Michael Eisner and Hewlett-Packard under Carly Fiorina. Both CEOs were first viewed as transformational leaders who made needed strategic changes to their companies. After a few years, both were perceived to be the primary reason for their company's poor performance and were fired by their boards. The truth is rarely this simple.

According to research by Margarethe Wiersema, firing the CEO rarely solves a corporation's problems. In a study of CEO turnover caused by dismissals and retirements in the 500 largest public U.S. companies, 71% of the departures were involuntary. In those firms in which the CEO was fired or asked to resign and replaced by another, Wiersema found *no* significant improvement in the company's operating earnings or stock price. She couldn't find a single measure suggesting that CEO dismissal had a positive effect on corporate performance! Wiersema placed the blame for the poor results squarely on the shoulders of the boards of directors. Boards typically lack an in-depth understanding of the business and consequently rely too heavily on executive search firms that know even less about the business. According to Wiersema, boards that successfully managed the executive succession process had three things in common:

- The board set the criteria for candidate selection based on the strategic needs of the company.

- The board set realistic performance expectations rather than demanding a quick fix to please the investment community.

- The board developed a deep understanding of the business and provided strong strategic oversight of top management, including thoughtful annual reviews of CEO performance.[118]

As noted at the beginning of this chapter, corporate governance involves not just the CEO or the board of directors. It involves the combined active participation of the board, top management, and shareholders. One positive result of the many corporate scandals occurring over the past decade is the increased interest in governance. Institutional investors are no longer content to be passive shareholders. Thanks to new regulations, boards of directors are taking their responsibilities more seriously and including more independent outsiders on key oversight committees. Top managers are beginning to understand the value of working with boards as partners, not just as adversaries or as people to be manipulated. Although there will always be passive shareholders, rubber-stamp boards, and dominating CEOs, the simple truth is that good corporate governance means better strategic management.

ECO-BITS

- DuPont, originally founded in 1802 to make gunpowder and explosives, was a major producer in 1990 of nitrous oxides and fluorocarbons—gases with a global warming potential 310 and 11,700 times that of carbon dioxide, respectively.

- DuPont was the first company to phase-out CFCs and the first to develop and commercialize CFC alternatives for refrigeration and air conditioning.

- DuPont's reputation changed from "Top U.S. Polluter of 1995" to *Business Week*'s list of "Top Green Companies" in 2005; meanwhile, its earnings per share increased from $1 in 2003 to $3.25 in 2007.[119]

DISCUSSION QUESTIONS

1. When does a corporation need a board of directors?

2. Who should and should not serve on a board of directors? What about environmentalists or union leaders?

3. Should a CEO be allowed to serve on another company's board of directors?

4. What would be the result if the only insider on a corporation's board were the CEO?

5. Should all CEOs be transformational leaders? Would you like to work for a transformational leader?

STRATEGIC PRACTICE EXERCISE

A. Think of the **best manager** for whom you have ever worked. What was it about this person that made him or her such a good manager? Consider the following statements as they pertain to that person. Fill in the blank *in front of each statement* with one of the following values:

**STRONGLY AGREE = 5; AGREE = 4; NEUTRAL = 3;
DISAGREE = 2; STRONGLY DISAGREE = 1.**

1. ___ I respect him/her personally, and want to act in a way that merits his/her respect and admiration. ___

2. ___ I respect her/his competence about things she/he is more experienced about than I. ___

3. ___ He/she can give special help to those who cooperate with him/her. ___

4. ___ He/she can apply pressure on those who cooperate with him/her. ___

5. ___ He/she has a legitimate right, considering his/her position, to expect that his/her suggestions will be carried out. ___

6. ___ I defer to his/her judgment in areas with which he/she is more familiar than I. ___

7. ___ He/she can make things difficult for me if I fail to follow his/her advice. ___

8. ___ Because of his/her job title and rank, I am obligated to follow his/her suggestions. ___

9. ___ I can personally benefit by cooperating with him/her. ___

10. ___ Following his/her advice results in better decisions. ___

11. ___ I cooperate with him/her because I have high regard for him/her as an individual. ___

12. ___ He/she can penalize those who do not follow his/her suggestions. ___

13. ___ I feel I have to cooperate with him/her. ___

14. ___ I cooperate with him/her because I wish to be identified with him/her. ___

15. ___ Cooperating with him/her can positively affect my performance. ___

....

SOURCE: Questionnaire developed by J. D. Hunger from the article "Influence and Information: An Exploratory Investigation of the Boundary Role Person's Bases of Power" by Robert Spekman, *Academy of Management Journal*, March 1979. Copyright © 2004 by J. David Hunger.

B. Now think of the **worst manager** for whom you have ever worked. What was it about this person that made him or her such a poor manager? Please consider the statements above as they pertain to that person. Please place a number *after each statement* with one of the values from 5 = strongly agree to 1 = strongly disagree.

C. Add the values you marked for the best manager within each of the five categories of power below. Then do the same for the values you marked for the worst manager.

BEST MANAGER

Reward	Coercive	Legitimate	Referent	Expert
3.	4.	5.	1.	2.
9.	7.	8.	11.	6.
15.	12.	13.	14.	10.
Total	Total	Total	Total	Total

WORST MANAGER

Reward	Coercive	Legitimate	Referent	Expert
3.	4.	5.	1.	2.
9.	7.	8.	11.	6.
15.	12.	13.	14.	10.
Total	Total	Total	Total	Total

D. Consider the differences between how you rated your best and your worst manager. How different are the two profiles? In many cases, the best manager's profile tends to be similar to that of transformational leaders in that the best manager tends to score highest on referent, followed by expert and reward, power—especially when compared to the worst manager's profile. The worst manager often scores highest on coercive and legitimate power, followed by reward power. The results of this survey may help you to answer the fifth discussion question for this chapter.

KEY TERMS

affiliated director (p. 97)

agency theory (p. 96)

board of directors' continuum (p. 94)

board of director responsibilities (p. 93)

codetermination (p. 100)

corporate governance (p. 93)

due care (p. 94)

executive leadership (p. 108)

inside director (p. 96)

interlocking directorate (p. 100)

lead director (p. 102)

outside director (p. 96)

Sarbanes-Oxley Act (p. 103)

stewardship theory (p. 97)

strategic vision (p. 108)

top management responsibilities (p. 106)

transformational leader (p. 108)

NOTES

1. R. Kirkland, "The Real CEO Pay Problem," *Fortune* (July 10, 2006), pp. 78–81.
2. M. Bartiromo, "Bob Nardelli Explains Himself," *Business Week* (July 24, 2006), pp. 98–100.
3. B. Grow, "Renovating Home Depot," *Business Week* (March 6, 2006), pp. 50–58.
4. B. Grow, "Out at Home Depot," *Business Week* (January 15, 2007), pp. 56–62.
5. M. Fetterman, "Boardrooms Open Up to Investors' Input," *USA Today* (September 7, 2007), pp. 1B–2B.
6. "Raising Their Voices," *The Economist* (March 22, 2008), p. 72.
7. P. Burrows, "He's Making Hay as CEOs Squirm," *Business Week* (January 15, 2007), pp. 64–65.
8. "The Price of Prominence," *The Economist* (January 15, 2005), p. 69.
9. A. G. Monks and N. Minow, *Corporate Governance* (Cambridge, MA: Blackwell Business, 1995), pp. 8–32.
10. Ibid., p. 1.
11. A. Demb, and F. F. Neubauer, "The Corporate Board: Confronting the Paradoxes," *Long Range Planning* (June 1992), p. 13. These results are supported by a 1995 Korn/Ferry International survey in which chairs and directors agreed that strategy and management succession, in that order, are the most important issues the board expects to face.
12. Reported by E. L. Biggs in "CEO Succession Planning: An Emerging Challenge for Boards of Directors," *Academy of Management Executive* (February 2004), pp. 105–107.
13. A. Borrus, "Less Laissez-Faire in Delaware?" *Business Week* (March 22, 2004), pp. 80–82.
14. L. Light, "Why Outside Directors Have Nightmares," *Business Week* (October 23, 1996), p. 6.
15. "Where's All the Fun Gone?" *Economist* (March 20, 2004), p. 76.
16. A. Chen, J. Osofsky, and E. Stephenson, "Making the Board More Strategic: A McKinsey Global Survey," *McKinsey Quarterly* (March 2008), pp. 1–10.
17. Nadler proposes a similar five-step continuum for board involvement ranging from the least involved "passive board" to the most involved "operating board," plus a form for measuring board involvement in D. A. Nadler, "Building Better Boards," *Harvard Business Review* (May 2004), pp. 102–111.
18. H. Ashbaugh, D. W. Collins, and R. LaFond, "The Effects of Corporate Governance on Firms' Credit Ratings," unpublished paper (March, 2004); W. Q. Judge Jr., and C. P. Zeithaml, "Institutional and Strategic Choice Perspectives on Board Involvement in the Strategic Choice Process," *Academy of Management Journal* (October 1992), pp. 766–794; J. A. Pearce II, and S. A. Zahra, "Effective Power-Sharing Between the Board of Directors and the CEO," *Handbook of Business Strategy*, 1992/93 Yearbook (Boston: Warren, Gorham, and Lamont, 1992), pp. 1.1–1.16.
19. *Current Board Practices,* American Society of Corporate Secretaries, 2002 as reported by B. Atkins in "Directors Don't Deserve such a Punitive Policy,"*Directors & Boards* (Summer 2002), p. 23.
20. A. Chen, J. Osofsky, and E. Stephenson, "Making the Board More Strategic: A McKinsey Global Survey," *McKinsey Quarterly* (March 2008), pp. 1–10.
21. *33rd Annual Board of Directors Study* (New York: Korn/Ferry International, 2007).
22. "What Directors Know About their Companies: A McKinsey Survey," *McKinsey Quarterly Web Exclusive* (March 2006).
23. D. A. Nadler, "Building Better Boards," *Harvard Business Review* (May 2004), pp. 102–111; L. Lavelle, "The Best and Worst Boards," *Business Week* (October 7, 2002), pp. 104–114.
24. Nadler, p. 109.
25. M. K. Fiegener, "Determinants of Board Participation in the Strategic Decisions of Small Corporations,"*Entrepreneurship Theory and Practice* (September 2005), pp. 627–650.
26. Fiegener; A. L. Ranft and H. M. O'Neill, "Board Composition and High-Flying Founders: Hints of Trouble to Come?" *Academy of Management Executive* (February 2001), pp. 126–138.
27. D. R. Dalton, M. A. Hitt, S. Trevis Certo, and C. M. Dalton, "The Fundamental Agency Problem and Its Mitigation," Chapter One in *Academy of Management Annals*, edited by J. F. Westfall and A. F. Brief (London: Rutledge, 2007); Y. Deutsch, "The Impact of Board Composition on Firms' Critical Decisions: A Meta-Analytic Review," *Journal of Management* (June 2005), pp. 424–444; D. F. Larcher, S. A. Richardson, and I. Tuna, "Does Corporate Governance Really Matter?" *Knowledge @ Wharton* (September 8–21, 2004); J. Merritt and L. Lavelle, "A Different Kind of Governance Guru," *Business Week* (August 9, 2004), pp. 46–47; A. Dehaene, V. DeVuyst, and H. Ooghe, "Corporate Performance and Board Structure in Belgian Companies," *Long Range Planning* (June 2001), pp. 383–398; M. W. Peng, "Outside Directors and Firm Performance During Institutional Transitions," *Strategic Management Journal* (May 2004), pp. 453–471.
28. D. R. Dalton, M. A. Hitt, S. Trevis Certo, and C. M. Dalton, "The Fundamental Agency Problem and Its Mitigation," Chapter One in *Academy of Management Annals*, edited by J. F. Westfall and A. F. Brief (London: Rutledge, 2007).
29. *33rd Annual Board of Directors Study* (New York: Korn/Ferry International, 2007), p. 11.
30. *30th Annual Board of Directors Study* (New York: Korn/Ferry International, 2003).
31. M. K. Fiegerer, "Determinants of Board Participation in the Strategic Decisions of Small Corporations," *Entrepreneurship Theory and Practice* (September 2005), pp. 627–650; S. K. Lee and G. Filbeck, "Board Size and Firm Performance: Case of Small Firms," *Proceedings of the Academy of Accounting and Financial Studies* (2006), pp. 43–46; W. S. Schulze, M. H. Lubatkin, R. N. Dino, and A. K. Buchholtz, "Agency Relationships in Family Firms: Theory and Evidence," *Organization Science* (March–April, 2001), pp. 99–116.

32. S. K. Lee and G. Filbeck, "Board Size and Firm Performance: The Case of Small Firms," *Proceedings of the Academy of Accounting and Financial Studies* (2006), pp. 43–46.

33. J. J. Reur and R. Ragozzino, "Agency Hazards and Alliance Portfolios," *Strategic Management Journal* (January 2006), pp. 27–43.

34. M. Goranova, T. M. Alessandri, P. Brades, and R. Dharwadkar, "Managerial Ownership and Corporate Diversification: A Longitudinal View," *Strategic Management Journal* (March 2007), pp. 211–225; B. K. Boyd, S. Gove, and M. A. Hitt, "Consequences of Measurement Problems in Strategic Management Research: The Case of Amihud and Lev," *Strategic Management Journal* (April 2005), pp. 367–375; J. P. Katz and B. P. Niehoff, "How Owners Influence Strategy—A Comparison of Owner-Controlled and Manager-Controlled Firms," *Long Range Planning* (October 1998), pp. 755–761; M. Kroll, P. Wright, L. Toombs, and H. Leavell, "Form of Control: A Critical Determinant of Acquisition Performance and CEO Rewards," *Strategic Management Journal* (February 1997), pp. 85–96.

35. L. Tihanyi, R. A. Johnson, R. E. Hoskisson, and M. A. Hitt, "Institutional Ownership Differences and International Diversification: The Effects of Boards of Directors and Technological Opportunity," *Academy of Management Journal* (April 2003), pp. 195–211; A. E. Ellstrand, L. Tihanyi, and J. L. Johnson, "Board Structure and International Political Risk," *Academy of Management Journal* (August 2002), pp. 769–777); S. A. Zahra, D. O. Neubaum, and M. Huse, "Entrepreneurship in Medium-Size Companies: Exploring the Effects of Ownership and Governance Systems," *Journal of Management*, Vol. 26, No. 5 (2000), pp. 947–976.

36. G. Kassinis and N. Vafeas, "Corporate Boards and Outside Stakeholders as Determinants of Environmental Litigation," *Strategic Management Journal* (May 2002), pp. 399–415; P. Dunn, "The Impact of Insider Power on Fraudulent Financial Reporting," *Journal of Management*, Vol. 30, No. 3 (2004), pp. 397–412.

37. R. C. Anderson and D. M. Reeb, "Board Composition: Balancing Family Influence in S&P 500 Firms," *Administrative Science Quarterly* (June 2004), pp. 209–237; W. S. Schulze, M. H. Lubatkin, R. N. Dino, and A. K. Buckholtz, "Agency Relationships in Family Firms: Theory and Evidence," *Organization Science* (March–April, 2001), pp. 99–116.

38. M. N. Young, A. K. Bushholtz, and D. Ahlstrom, "How Can Board Members Be Empowered If They Are Spread Too Thin?" *SAM Advanced Management Journal* (Autumn 2003), pp. 4–11.

39. *33rd Annual Board of Directors Study* (New York: Korn/Ferry International, 2007), p. 21.

40. C. M. Daily and D. R. Dalton, "The Endangered Director," *Journal of Business Strategy*, Vol. 25, No. 3 (2004), pp. 8–9.

41. I. Sager, "The Boardroom: New Rules, New Loopholes," *Business Week* (November 29, 2004), p. 13.

42. *33rd Annual Board of Directors Study* (New York: Korn/Ferry International, 2007), p. 43.

43. See S. Finkelstein, and D. C. Hambrick, *Strategic Leadership: Top Executives and Their Impact on Organizations* (St. Paul, MN: West, 1996), p. 213.

44. D. R. Dalton, M. A. Hitt, S. Trevis Certo, and C. M. Dalton, "The Fundamental Agency Problem and Its Mitigation," Chapter One in *Academy of Management Annals*, edited by J. F. Westfall and A. F. Brief (London: Rutledge, 2007).

45. "TIAA-CREF's Role in Corporate Governance," *Investment Forum* (June 2003), p. 13.

46. "Jobs for the Girls," *The Economist* (May 3, 2008), p. 73; "Girl Power," *The Economist* (January 5, 2008), p. 54.

47. *33rd Annual Board of Directors Study* (New York: Korn/Ferry International, 2007), p. 11; T. Neff and J. H. Daum, "The Empty Boardroom," *Strategy + Business* (Summer 2007), pp. 57–61.

48. R. O. Crockett, "The Rising Stock of Black Directors," *Business Week* (February 27, 2006), p. 34.

49. J. Daum, "Portrait of Boards on the Cusp of Historic Change," *Directors & Boards* (Winter 2003), p. 56; J. Daum, "SSBI: Audit Committees Are Leading the Change," *Directors & Boards* (Winter 2004), p. 59.

50. *30th Annual Board of Directors Study* (New York: Korn/Ferry International, 2003) p. 38.

51. *Globalizing the Board of Directors: Trends and Strategies* (New York: The Conference Board, 1999).

52. *33rd Annual Board of Directors Study* (New York: Korn/Ferry International, 2007), p. 15.

53. R. W. Pouder and R. S. Cantrell, "Corporate Governance Reform: Influence on Shareholder Wealth," *Journal of Business Strategies* (Spring 1999), pp. 48–66.

54. M. L. Gerlach, "The Japanese Corporate Network: A Blockmodel Analysis," *Administrative Science Quarterly* (March 1992), pp. 105–139.

55. W. E. Stead and J. G. Stead, *Sustainable Strategic Management* (Armonk, NY: M. E. Sharp, 2004), p. 47.

56. J. D. Westphal, M. L. Seidel, and K. J. Stewart, "Second-Order Imitation: Uncovering Latent Effects of Board Network Ties," *Administrative Science Quarterly* (December 2001), pp. 717–747; M. A. Geletkanycz, B. K. Boyd, and S. Finkelstein, "The Strategic Value of CEO External Directorate Networks: Implications for CEO Compensation," *Strategic Management Journal* (September 2001), pp. 889–898; M. A. Carpenter and J. D. Westphal, "The Strategic Context of External Network Ties: Examining the Impact of Director Appointments on Board Involvement in Strategic Decision Making," *Academy of Management Journal* (August 2001), pp. 639–660.

57. M. Warner, "Inside the Silicon Valley Money Machine," *Fortune* (October 26, 1998), pp. 128–140.

58. D. Jones and B. Hansen, "Chairmen Still Doing Do-Si-Do," *USA Today* (November 5, 2003), p. 3B; J. H. Daum and T. J. Neff, "SSBI: Audit Committees Are Leading the Charge," *Directors & Boards* (Winter 2003), p. 59.

59. J. A. C. Baum and C. Oliver, "Institutional Linkages and Organizational Mortality," *Administrative Science Quarterly* (June 1991) pp. 187–218; J. P. Sheppard, "Strategy and Bankruptcy: An Exploration into Organizational Death," *Journal of Management* (Winter 1994), pp. 795–833.

60. *33rd Annual Board of Directors Study* (New York: Korn/Ferry International, 2007), p. 44 and *Directors' Compensation and*

Board Practices in 2003, Research Report R-1339-03-RR (New York: Conference Board, 2003) Table 49, p. 38.

61. J. Canavan, B. Jones, and M. J. Potter, "Board Tenure: How Long Is Too Long?" *Boards & Directors* (Winter 2004), pp. 39–42.

62. *33rd Annual Board of Directors Study* (New York: Korn/Ferry International, 2007), p. 17 and *30th Annual Board of Directors Study Supplement: Governance Trends of the Fortune 1000* (New York: Korn/Ferry International, 2004), p. 5.

63. D. F. Larcker and S. A. Richardson, "Does Governance Really Matter?" *Knowledge @ Wharton* (September 8–21, 2004).

64. M. L. McDonald, J. D. Westphal, and M. E. Graebner, "What Do they Know? The Effects of Outside Director Acquisition Experience on Firm Acquisition Experience," *Strategic Management Journal* (November 2008), pp. 1155–1177.

65. *26th Annual Board of Directors Study* (New York: Korn/Ferry International, 1999), p. 30.

66. *30th Annual Board of Directors Study* (New York: Korn/Ferry International, 2003), pp. 8, 31, 44.

67. D. R. Dalton, M. A. Hitt, S. Trevis Certo, and C. M. Dalton, "The Fundamental Agency Problem and Its Mitigation," Chapter One in *Academy of Management Annals*, edited by J. F. Westfall and A. F. Brief (London: Rutledge, 2007); P. Coombes and S. C-Y Wong, "Chairman and CEO—One Job or Two?" *McKinsey Quarterly* (2004, No. 2), pp. 43–47.

68. A. Desai, M. Kroll, and P. Wright, "CEO Duality, Board Monitoring, and Acquisition Performance," *Journal of Business Strategies* (Fall 2003), pp. 147–156; D. Harris and C. E. Helfat, "CEO Duality, Succession, Capabilities and Agency Theory: Commentary and Research Agenda," *Strategic Management Journal* (September 1998), pp. 901–904; C. M. Daily and D. R. Dalton, "CEO and Board Chair Roles Held Jointly or Separately: Much Ado About Nothing," *Academy of Management Executive* (August 1997), pp. 11–20; D. L. Worrell, C. Nemec, and W. N. Davidson III, "One Hat Too Many: Key Executive Plurality and Shareholder Wealth," *Strategic Management Journal* (June 1997), pp. 499–507; J. W. Coles and W. S. Hesterly, "Independence of the Chairman and Board Composition: Firm Choices and Shareholder Value," *Journal of Management*, Vol. 26, No. 2 (2000), pp. 195–214; H. Ashbaugh, D. W. Collins, and R. LaFond, "The Effects of Corporate Governance on Firms' Credit Ratings," unpublished paper, March 2004.

69. J. P. O'Connor, R. I. Priem, J. E. Coombs, and K. M. Gilley, "Do CEO Stock Options Prevent or Promote Fraudulent Financial Reporting?" *Academy of Management Journal* (June 2006), pp. 483–500.

70. N. R. Augustine, "How Leading a Role for the Lead Director?" *Directors & Boards* (Winter 2004), pp. 20–23.

71. D. R. Dalton, M. A. Hitt, S. Trevis Certo, and C. M. Dalton, "The Fundamental Agency Problem and Its Mitigation," Chapter One in *Academy of Management Annals*, edited by J. F. Westfall and A. F. Brief (London: Rutledge, 2007).

72. *33rd Annual Board of Directors Study* (New York: Korn/Ferry International, 2007), p. 21.

73. J. D. Westphal and I. Stern, "Flattery Will Get You Everywhere (Especially If You Are a Male Caucasian): How Ingratiation, Boardroom Behavior, and Demographic Minority Status Affect Additional Board Appointments at U.S. Companies," *Academy of Management Journal* (April 2007), pp. 267–288; J. D. Westphal, "Board Games: How CEOs Adapt to Increases in Structural Board Independence from Management," *Administrative Science Quarterly* (September 1998), pp. 511–537; J. D. Westphal and P. Khanna, "Keeping Directors in Line: Social Distancing as a Control Mechanism in the Corporate Elite," *Administrative Science Quarterly* (September 2003), pp. 361–398.

74. H. L. Tosi, W. Shen, and R. J. Gentry, "Why Outsiders on Boards Can't Solve the Corporate Governance Problem," *Organizational Dynamics*, Vol. 32, No. 2 (2003), pp. 180–192.

75. *33rd Annual Board of Directors Study* (New York: Korn/Ferry International, 2007), p. 12. Other committees are succession planning (39%), finance (30%), corporate responsibility (17%), and investment (15%).

76. Perhaps because of their potential to usurp the power of the board, executive committees are being used less often.

77. *33rd Annual Board of Directors Study* (New York: Korn/Ferry International, 2007), p. 14.

78. "The Trial of Sarbanes-Oxley," *The Economist* (April 22, 2006), pp. 59–60; *33rd Annual Board of Directors Study* (New York: Korn/Ferry International, 2007), p. 14; S. Wagner and L. Dittmar, "The Unexpected Benefits of Sarbanes-Oxley," *Harvard Business Review* (April 2006), pp. 133–140.

79. A. Borrus, "Learning to Love Sarbanes-Oxley," *Business Week* (November 21, 2005), pp. 126–128.

80. D. Henry, "Not Everyone Hates SarbOx," *Business Week* (January 29, 2007), p. 37.

81. D. Henry, "A SarbOx Surprise," *Business Week* (January 12, 2006), p. 38.

82. *30th Annual Board of Directors Study Supplement: Governance Trends of the Fortune 1000* (New York: Korn/Ferry International, 2004), p. 5.

83. "Where's All the Fun Gone?" *Economist* (March 20, 2004), pp. 75–77.

84. Daum and Neff (2004), p. 58.

85. *33rd Annual Board of Directors Study* (New York: Korn/Ferry International, 2007), p. 7.

86. J. Sonnenfeld, "Good Governance and the Misleading Myths of Bad Metrics." *Academy of Management Executive* (February 2004), pp. 108–113.

87. H. Ashbaugh, D. W. Collins, and R. LaFond, "The Effects of Corporate Governance on Firms' Credit Ratings," unpublished paper (March 2002).

88. I. Sager, "Access Denied: A Private Matter," *Business Week* (January 26, 2004), p. 13; J. Weber, "One Share, Many Votes," *Business Week* (March 29, 2004), pp. 94–95.

89. E. Thorton, "Corporate Control Freaks," *Business Week* (May 31, 2004), p. 86.

90. D. R. Dalton, C. M. Daily, A. E. Ellstrand, and J. L. Johnson, "Meta-Analytic Reviews of Board Composition, Leadership Structure, and Financial Performance," *Strategic Management Journal* (March 1998), pp. 269–290; G. Beaver, "Competitive Advantage and Corporate Governance—Shop Soiled and Needing Attention!" *Strategic Change* (September–October 1999), p. 330.

91. A. Borrus and L. Young, "Nothing Like a Little Exposure," *Business Week* (September 13, 2004), p. 92.

92. P. Silva, "Do Motivation and Equity Ownership Matter in Board of Directors' Evaluation of CEO Performance?" *Journal of Management Issues* (Fall 2005), pp. 346–362.

93. L. He and M. J. Conyon, "The Role of Compensation Committees in CEO and Committee Compensation Decisions," paper presented to *Academy of Management* (Seattle, WA, 2003).

94. P. Coy, E. Thornton, M. Arndt, B. Grow, and A. Park, "Shake, Rattle, and Merge," *Business Week* (January 10, 2005), pp. 32–35.

95. L. Lavelle, "A Fighting Chance for Boardroom Democracy," *Business Week* (June 9, 2003), p. 50; L. Lavelle, "So That's Why Boards Are Waking Up," *Business Week* (January 19, 2004), pp. 72–73.

96. For a detailed description of the COO's role, see N. Bennett and S. A. Miles, "Second in Command," *Harvard Business Review* (May 2006), pp. 71–78.

97. S. Finkelstein and D. C. Hambrick, *Strategic Leadership: Top Executives and Their Impact on Organizations* (St. Louis: West, 1996).

98. H. G. Barkema and O. Shvyrkov, "Does Top Management Team Diversity Promote or Hamper Foreign Expansion?" *Strategic Management Journal* (July 2007), pp. 663–680; D. C. Hambrick, T. S. Cho, and M-J Chen, "The Influence of Top Management Team Heterogeneity on Firms' Competitive Moves," *Administrative Science Quarterly* (December 1996), pp. 659–684.

99. P. Pitcher and A. D. Smith, "Top Management Heterogeneity: Personality, Power, and Proxies," *Organization Science* (January–February 2001), pp. 1–18; M. A. Carpenter and J. W. Fredrickson, "Top Management Teams, Global Strategic Posture, and the Moderating Role of Uncertainty," *Academy of Management Journal* (June 2001), pp. 533–545; M. A. Carpenter, "The Implications of Strategy and Social Context for the Relationship Between Top Management Team Heterogeneity and Firm Performance," *Strategic Management Journal* (March 2002), pp. 275–284; L. Tihanyi, A. E. Ellstrand, C. M. Daily, and D. R. Dalton, "Composition of the Top Management Team and Firm International Expansion," *Journal of Management*, Vol. 26, No. 6 (2000), pp. 1157–1177.

100. "One on One with Steve Reinemund," *Business Week* (December 17, 2001), Special advertising insert on leadership by Heidrick & Struggles, executive search firm.

101. D. A. Waldman, G. G. Ramirez, R. J. House, and P. Puranam, "Does Leadership Matter? CEO Leadership Attributes and Profitability Under Conditions of Perceived Environmental Uncertainty," *Academy of Management Journal* (February 2001), pp. 134–143; F. J. Flynn and B. M. Staw, "Lend Me Your Wallets: The Effect of Charismatic Leadership on External Support for an Organization," *Strategic Management Journal* (April 2004), pp. 309–330.

102. J. Burns, *Leadership* (New York: HarperCollins, 1978); B. Bass, "From Transactional to Transformational Leadership: Learning to Share the Vision," *Organizational Dynamics*, Vol. 18 (1990), pp. 19–31; W. Bennis and B. Nanus, *Leaders: Strategies for Taking Charge* (New York: HarperCollins, 1997).

103. Based on R. J. House, "A 1976 Theory of Charismatic Leadership," in J. G. Hunt and L. L. Larson (Eds.), *Leadership: The Cutting Edge* (Carbondale, IL: Southern Illinois University Press, 1976), pp. 189–207. Also see J. Choi, "A Motivational Theory of Charismatic Leadership: Envisioning, Empathy, and Empowerment," *Journal of Leadership and Organizational Studies* (2006), Vol. 13, No. 1, pp. 24–43.

104. I. D. Colville and A. J. Murphy, "Leadership as the Enabler of Strategizing and Organizing," *Long Range Planning* (December 2006), pp. 663–677.

105. L. V. Gerstner Jr., *Who Says Elephants Can't Dance?* (New York: HarperCollins, 2002), p. 124.

106. M. Lipton, "Demystifying the Development of an Organizational Vision," *Sloan Management Review* (Summer 1996), p. 84.

107. S. Hahn, "Why High Tech Has to Stay Humble," *Business Week* (January 19, 2004), pp. 76–77.

108. J. H. David, F. D. Schoorman, R. Mayer, and H. H. Tan, "The Trusted General Manager and Business Unit Performance: Empirical Evidence of a Competitive Advantage," *Strategic Management Journal* (May 2000), pp. 563–576.

109. D. B. McNatt and T. A. Judge, "Boundary Conditions of the Galatea Effect: A Field Experiment and Constructive Replication," *Academy of Management Journal* (August 2004), pp. 550–565.

110. R. F. Piccolo and J. A. Colquitt, "Transformational Leadership and Job Behaviors: The Mediating Role of Core Job Characteristics," *Academy of Management Journal* (April 2006), pp. 327–340; J. E. Bono and T. A. Judge, "Self-Concordance at Work: Toward Understanding the Motivational Effects of Transformational Leaders," *Academy of Management Journal* (October 2003), pp. 554–571.

111. T. Lowry, R. O. Crockett, and I. M. Kunii, "Verizon's Gutsy Bet," *Business Week* (August 4, 2003), pp. 52–62.

112. G. Tate and U. Malmendier, "Who Makes Acquisitions? CEO Overconfidence and the Market's Reaction," summarized by *Knowledge @ Wharton* (February 25, 2004).

113. M. C. Mankins and R. Steele, "Stop Making Plans, Start Making Decisions," *Harvard Business Review* (January 2006), pp. 76–84.

114. T. R. Eisenmann and J. L. Bower, "The Entrepreneurial M Form: Strategic Integration in Global Media Firms," *Organization Science* (May–June 2000), pp. 348–355.

115. J. Kirby and T. A. Stewart, "The Institutional Yes," *Harvard Business Review* (October 2007), p. 76.

116. M. C. Mankins and R. Steele, "Stop Making Plans, Start Making Decisions," *Harvard Business Review* (January 2006), pp. 76–84; G. P. Hodgkinson, R. Whittington, G. Johnson, and M. Schwarz, "The Role of Strategy Workshops in Strategy Development Processes: Formality, Communication, Co-ordination and Inclusion," *Long Range Planning* (October 2006), pp. 479–496; B. Frisch and L. Chandler, "Off-Sites That Work," *Harvard Business Review* (June 2006), pp. 117–126.

117. For a description of the Chief Strategy Officer, see R. T. S. Breene, P. F. Nunes, and W. E. Shill, "The Chief Strategy Officer," *Harvard Business Review* (October 2007), pp. 84–93; R. Dye, "How Chief Strategy Officers Think about their Role: A Roundtable," *McKinsey Quarterly* (May 2008), pp. 1–8.

118. M. Wiersema, "Holes at the Top: Why CEO Firings Backfire," *Harvard Business Review* (December 2002), pp. 70–77.

119. C. Laszlo, *Sustainable Value: How the World's Leading Companies Are Doing Well by Doing Good* (Stanford, CA: Stanford University Press, 2008), pp. 81–88.

social responsibility and ethics in Strategic Management

Only a few miles from the gleaming skyscrapers of prosperous Minneapolis was a neighborhood littered with shattered glass from stolen cars and derelict houses used by drug lords. During the 1990s, the Hawthorne neighborhood became a no-man's-land where gun battles terrified local residents and raised the per capita murder rate 70% higher than that of New York.

Executives at General Mills became concerned when the murder rate reached a record high in 1996. The company's headquarters was located just five miles away from Hawthorne, then the city's most violent neighborhood. Working with law enforcement, politicians, community leaders, and residents, General Mills spent $2.5 million and donated thousands of employee hours to help clean up Hawthorne. Crack houses were demolished to make way for a new elementary school. Dilapidated houses in the neighborhood's core were rebuilt. General Mills provided grants to help people buy Hawthorne's houses. By 2003, homicides were down 32% and robberies had declined 56% in Hawthorne.

This story was nothing new for General Mills, a company often listed in *Fortune* magazine's "Most Admired Companies," ranked third most socially responsible company in a survey conducted by *The Wall Street Journal* and Harris Interactive, and fourth in *Business Week*'s 2007 survey of "most generous corporate donors." Since 2000, the company has annually contributed 5% of pretax profits to a wide variety of social causes. In 2007, for example, the company donated $82 million to causes ranging from education and the arts to social services. Every day, the company ships three truckloads of Cheerios, Wheaties, and other packaged goods to food banks throughout the nation. Community performance is even reflected in the performance reviews of top management. According to Christina Shea, president of General Mills Foundation, "We take as innovative approach to giving back to our communities as we do in our business." For joining with a nonprofit organization and a minority-owned food company to create 150 inner-city jobs, General Mills received *Business Ethics*' annual corporate citizenship award.[1]

Was this the best use of General Mills' time and money? At a time when companies were being pressured to cut costs and outsource jobs to countries with cheaper labor, what do business corporations owe their local communities? Should business firms give away shareholders' money, support social causes, and ask employees to donate their time to the community? Critics argue that this sort of thing is done best by government and not-for-profit charities. Isn't the primary goal of business to maximize profits, not to be a social worker?

Learning Objectives

After reading this chapter, you should be able to:

- Compare and contrast Friedman's traditional view with Carroll's contemporary view of social responsibility
- Understand the relationship between social responsibility and corporate performance
- Explain the concept of sustainability
- Conduct a stakeholder analysis
- Explain why people may act unethically
- Describe different views of ethics according to the utilitarian, individual rights, and justice approaches

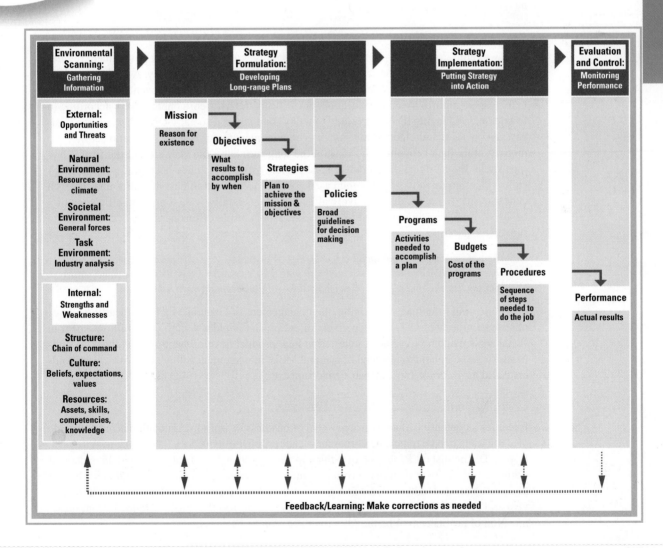

3.1 Social Responsibilities of Strategic Decision Makers

Should strategic decision makers be responsible only to shareholders, or do they have broader responsibilities? The concept of **social responsibility** proposes that a private corporation has responsibilities to society that extend beyond making a profit. Strategic decisions often affect more than just the corporation. A decision to retrench by closing some plants and discontinuing product lines, for example, affects not only the firm's workforce but also the communities where the plants are located and the customers with no other source for the discontinued product. Such situations raise questions of the appropriateness of certain missions, objectives, and strategies of business corporations. Managers must be able to deal with these conflicting interests in an ethical manner to formulate a viable strategic plan.

RESPONSIBILITIES OF A BUSINESS FIRM

What are the responsibilities of a business firm and how many of them must be fulfilled? Milton Friedman and Archie Carroll offer two contrasting views of the responsibilities of business firms to society.

Friedman's Traditional View of Business Responsibility

Urging a return to a laissez-faire worldwide economy with a minimum of government regulation, Milton Friedman argues against the concept of social responsibility. A business person who acts "responsibly" by cutting the price of the firm's product to prevent inflation, or by making expenditures to reduce pollution, or by hiring the hard-core unemployed, according to Friedman, is spending the shareholder's money for a general social interest. Even if the businessperson has shareholder permission or encouragement to do so, he or she is still acting from motives other than economic and may, in the long run, harm the very society the firm is trying to help. By taking on the burden of these social costs, the business becomes less efficient—either prices go up to pay for the increased costs or investment in new activities and research is postponed. These results negatively affect—perhaps fatally—the long-term efficiency of a business. Friedman thus referred to the social responsibility of business as a "fundamentally subversive doctrine" and stated that:

> There is one and only one social responsibility of business—to use its resources and engage in activities designed to increase its profits so long as it stays within the rules of the game, which is to say, engages in open and free competition without deception or fraud.[2]

Following Friedman's reasoning, the management of General Mills was clearly guilty of misusing corporate assets and negatively affecting shareholder wealth. The millions spent in social services could have been invested in new product development or given back as dividends to the shareholders. Instead of General Mills' management acting on its own, shareholders could have decided which charities to support.

Carroll's Four Responsibilities of Business

Friedman's contention that the primary goal of business is profit maximization is only one side of an ongoing debate regarding corporate social responsibility (CSR). According to William J. Byron, Distinguished Professor of Ethics at Georgetown University and past-President of Catholic University of America, profits are merely a means to an end, not an end in itself. Just as a person needs food to survive and grow, so does a business corporation need profits to survive and grow. "Maximizing profits is like maximizing food." Thus, contends Byron, maximization of profits cannot be the primary obligation of business.[3]

FIGURE 3–1
Responsibilities
of Business

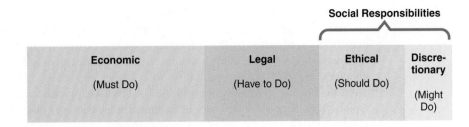

SOURCE: *Adapted from A. B. Carroll, "A Three Dimensional Conceptual Model of Corporate Performance,"* Academy of Management Review *(October 1979), p. 499. Reprinted with permission.*

As shown in **Figure 3–1,** Archie Carroll proposes that the managers of business organizations have four responsibilities: economic, legal, ethical, and discretionary.[4]

1. **Economic** responsibilities of a business organization's management are to produce goods and services of value to society so that the firm may repay its creditors and shareholders.

2. **Legal** responsibilities are defined by governments in laws that management is expected to obey. For example, U.S. business firms are required to hire and promote people based on their credentials rather than to discriminate on non-job-related characteristics such as race, gender, or religion.

3. **Ethical** responsibilities of an organization's management are to follow the generally held beliefs about behavior in a society. For example, society generally expects firms to work with the employees and the community in planning for layoffs, even though no law may require this. The affected people can get very upset if an organization's management fails to act according to generally prevailing ethical values.

4. **Discretionary** responsibilities are the purely voluntary obligations a corporation assumes. Examples are philanthropic contributions, training the hard-core unemployed, and providing day-care centers. The difference between ethical and discretionary responsibilities is that few people expect an organization to fulfill discretionary responsibilities, whereas many expect an organization to fulfill ethical ones.[5]

Carroll lists these four responsibilities *in order of priority.* A business firm must first make a profit to satisfy its economic responsibilities. To continue in existence, the firm must follow the laws, thus fulfilling its legal responsibilities. There is evidence that companies found guilty of violating laws have lower profits and sales growth after conviction.[6] To this point Carroll and Friedman are in agreement. Carroll, however, goes further by arguing that business managers have responsibilities beyond economic and legal ones.

Having satisfied the two basic responsibilities, according to Carroll, a firm should look to fulfilling its social responsibilities. Social responsibility, therefore, includes both ethical and discretionary, but not economic and legal, responsibilities. A firm can fulfill its ethical responsibilities by taking actions that society tends to value but has not yet put into law. When ethical responsibilities are satisfied, a firm can focus on discretionary responsibilities—purely voluntary actions that society has not yet decided are important. For example, when Cisco Systems decided to dismiss 6,000 full-time employees, it provided a novel severance package. Those employees who agreed to work for a local nonprofit organization for a year would receive one-third of their salaries plus benefits and stock options and be the first to be rehired. Nonprofits were delighted to hire such highly qualified people and Cisco was able to maintain its talent pool for when it could hire once again.[7]

As societal values evolve, the discretionary responsibilities of today may become the ethical responsibilities of tomorrow. For example, in 1990, 86% of people in the U.S. believed that obesity was caused by the individuals themselves, with only 14% blaming either corporate marketing or government guidelines. By 2003, however, only 54% blamed obesity on individuals and 46% put responsibility on corporate marketing and government guidelines. Thus, the offering of healthy, low-calorie food by food processors and restaurants is moving rapidly from being a discretionary to an ethical responsibility.[8] One example of this change in values is the film documentary *Super Size Me*, which criticizes the health benefits of eating McDonald's deep-fried fast food. (McDonald's responded by offering more healthy food items.)

Carroll suggests that to the extent that business corporations fail to acknowledge discretionary or ethical responsibilities, society, through government, will act, making them legal responsibilities. Government may do this, moreover, without regard to an organization's economic responsibilities. As a result, the organization may have greater difficulty in earning a profit than it would have if it had voluntarily assumed some ethical and discretionary responsibilities.

Both Friedman and Carroll argue their positions based on the impact of socially responsible actions on a firm's profits. Friedman says that socially responsible actions hurt a firm's efficiency. Carroll proposes that a lack of social responsibility results in increased government regulations, which reduce a firm's efficiency.

Friedman's position on social responsibility appears to be losing traction with business executives. For example, a 2006 survey of business executives across the world by McKinsey & Company revealed that only 16% felt that business should focus solely on providing the highest possible returns to investors while obeying all laws and regulations, contrasted with 84% who stated that business should generate high returns to investors but balance it with contributions to the broader public good.[9] A 2007 survey of global executives by the Economist Intelligence Unit found that the percentage of companies giving either high or very high priority to corporate social responsibility had risen from less than 40% in 2004 to over 50% in 2007 and was expected to increase to almost 70% by 2010.[10]

Empirical research now indicates that socially responsible actions may have a positive effect on a firm's financial performance. Although a number of studies in the past have found no significant relationship,[11] an increasing number are finding a small, but positive relationship.[12] A recent in-depth analysis by Margolis and Walsh of 127 studies found that "there is a positive association and very little evidence of a negative association between a company's social performance and its financial performance."[13] Another meta-analysis of 52 studies on social responsibility and performance reached this same conclusion.[14]

According to Porter and Kramer, "social and economic goals are not inherently conflicting, but integrally connected."[15] Being known as a socially responsible firm may provide a company with *social capital*, the goodwill of key stakeholders, that can be used for competitive advantage.[16] Target, for example, tries to attract socially concerned younger consumers by offering brands from companies that can boost ethical track records and community involvement.[17] In a 2004 study conducted by the strategic marketing firm Cone, Inc., eight in ten Americans said that corporate support of social causes helps earn their loyalty. This was a 21% increase since 1997.[18]

Being socially responsible does provide a firm a more positive overall reputation.[19] A survey of more than 700 global companies by the Conference Board reported that 60% of the managers state that citizenship activities had led to (1) goodwill that opened doors in local communities and (2) an enhanced reputation with consumers.[20] Another survey of 140 U.S. firms revealed that being more socially responsible regarding environmental sustainability resulted not only in competitive advantages but also in cost savings.[21] For example, companies that take the lead in being environmentally friendly, such as by using recycled materials, preempt attacks from environmental groups and enhance their corporate image. Programs to reduce pollution, for example, can actually reduce waste and maximize resource productivity. One study that examined 70 ecological initiatives taken by 43 companies found the average payback period to be 18 months.[22] Other examples of benefits received from being socially responsible are:[23]

- Their environmental concerns may enable them to charge premium prices and gain brand loyalty (for example, Ben & Jerry's Ice Cream).

- Their trustworthiness may help them generate enduring relationships with suppliers and distributors without requiring them to spend a lot of time and money policing contracts.

- They can attract outstanding employees who prefer working for a responsible firm (for example, Procter & Gamble and Starbucks).

- They are more likely to be welcomed into a foreign country (for example, Levi Strauss).

- They can utilize the goodwill of public officials for support in difficult times.

- They are more likely to attract capital infusions from investors who view reputable companies as desirable long-term investments. For example, mutual funds investing only in socially responsible companies more than doubled in size from 1995 to 2007 and outperformed the S&P 500 list of stocks.[24]

SUSTAINABILITY: MORE THAN ENVIRONMENTAL?

As a term, sustainability may include more than just ecological concerns and the natural environment. Crane and Matten point out that the concept of sustainability can be broadened to include economic and social as well as environmental concerns. They argue that it is sometimes impossible to address the sustainability of the natural environment without considering the social and economic aspects of relevant communities and their activities. For example, even though environmentalists may oppose road-building programs because of their effect on wildlife and conservation efforts, others point to the benefits to local communities of less traffic congestion and more jobs.[25] Dow Jones & Company, a leading provider of global business news and information, developed a sustainability index that considers not only environmental, but also economic and social factors. See the **Environmental Sustainability Issue** feature to learn the criteria Dow Jones uses in its index.

The broader concept of sustainability has much in common with Carroll's list of business responsibilities presented earlier. In order for a business corporation to be sustainable, that is, to be successful over a long period of time, it must satisfy all of its economic, legal, ethical, and discretionary responsibilities. Sustainability thus involves many issues, concerns, and tradeoffs—leading us to an examination of corporate stakeholders.

CORPORATE STAKEHOLDERS

The concept that business must be socially responsible sounds appealing until we ask, "Responsible to whom?" A corporation's task environment includes a large number of groups with interest in a business organization's activities. These groups are referred to as **stakeholders** because they affect or are affected by the achievement of the firm's objectives.[26] Should a corporation be responsible only to some of these groups, or does business have an equal responsibility to all of them?

A survey of the U.S. general public by Harris Poll revealed that 95% of the respondents felt that U.S. corporations owe something to their workers and the communities in which they operate and that they should sometimes sacrifice some profit for the sake of making things better for their workers and communities. People were concerned that business executives seemed to

ENVIRONMENTAL sustainability issue

THE DOW JONES SUSTAINABILITY INDEX

Dow Jones & Company, a leading provider of global business news and information, pioneered in 1999 the first index of common stocks that rates corporations according to their performance on sustainability. This index has grown to include multiple sustainability indexes, such as a World Index, North America Index, and United States Index, among others. The Dow Jones Sustainability Index (DJSI) follows a "best in class" approach that identifies sustainability leaders in each industry. Companies are evaluated against general and industry-specific criteria and ranked with their peers. Data come from questionnaires, submitted documentation, corporate policies, reports, and available public information. Since its inception, the Dow Jones Sustainability Index has slightly outperformed its well-known Dow Jones Industrial Index. Based on SAM (Sustainable Asset Management AG) Research's corporate sustainability assessment, Dow Jones includes not only environmental, but also economic and social criteria in its sustainability index.

■ **Environmental sustainability.** This includes environmental reporting, eco-design and efficiency, environmental management systems, and executive commitment to environmental issues.

■ **Economic sustainability.** This includes codes of conduct and compliance, anti-corruption policies, corporate governance, risk and crisis management, strategic planning, quality and knowledge management, and supply chain management.

■ **Social sustainability.** This includes corporate citizenship, philanthropy, labor practices, human capital development, social reporting, talent attraction and retention, and stakeholder dialogue.

....

NOTE: For more information on SAM Sustainable Asset Management, see *Sustainability Yearbook 2008*, available from PriceWaterHouseCoopers (www.pwc.com).

SOURCES: Dow Jones Indexes Web site (www.djindexes.com/) as of July 15, 2008 and A. Crane and D. Matten, *Business Ethics: A European Perspective* (Oxford: Oxford University Press, 2004), pp. 214–215.

---

be more interested in making profits and boosting their own pay than they were in the safety and quality of the products made by their companies.[27] The percentage of the U.S. general public that agreed that business leaders could be trusted to do what is right "most of the time or almost always" fell from 36% in 2002 to 28% in 2006.[28] These negative feelings receive some support from a study that revealed that the CEOs at the 50 U.S. companies that outsourced the greatest number of jobs received a greater increase in pay than did the CEOs of 365 U.S. firms overall.[29]

In any one strategic decision, the interests of one stakeholder group can conflict with those of another. For example, a business firm's decision to use only recycled materials in its manufacturing process may have a positive effect on environmental groups but a negative effect on shareholder dividends. In another example, Maytag Corporation's top management decided to move refrigerator production from Galesburg, Illinois, to a lower-wage location in Mexico. On the one hand, shareholders were generally pleased with the decision because it would lower costs. On the other hand, officials and local union people were very unhappy at the loss of jobs when the Galesburg plant closed. Which group's interests should have priority?

In order to answer this question, the corporation may need to craft an *enterprise strategy*—an overarching strategy that explicitly articulates the firm's ethical relationship with its stakeholders. This requires not only that management clearly state the firm's key ethical values, but also that it understands the firm's societal context, and undertakes stakeholder analysis to identify the concerns and abilities of each stakeholder.[30]

Stakeholder Analysis

Stakeholder analysis is the identification and evaluation of corporate stakeholders. This can be done in a three-step process.

The *first step* in stakeholder analysis is to identify primary stakeholders, those who have a *direct connection* with the corporation and who have sufficient bargaining power to *directly* affect corporate activities. Primary stakeholders are directly affected by the corporation and usually include customers, employees, suppliers, shareholders, and creditors.

But who exactly are a firm's customers or employees and what do they want? This is not always a simple exercise. For example, Intel's customers were clearly computer manufacturers because that's to whom Intel sold its electronic chips. When a math professor found a small flaw in Intel's Pentium microprocessor in 1994, computer users demanded that Intel replace the defective chips. At first Intel refused to do so because it hadn't sold to these individuals. According to then-CEO Andy Grove, "I got irritated and angry because of user demands that we take back a device we didn't sell." Intel wanted the PC users to follow the supply chain and complain to the firms from whom they had bought the computers. Gradually Grove was persuaded that Intel had a direct duty to these consumers. "Although we didn't sell to these individuals directly, we marketed to them. . . . It took me a while to understand this," explained Grove. In the end, Intel paid $450 million to replace the defective parts.[31]

Aside from the Intel example, business corporations usually know their primary stakeholders and what they want. The corporation systematically monitors these stakeholders because they are important to a firm's meeting its economic and legal responsibilities. Employees want a fair day's pay and fringe benefits. Customers want safe products and value for price paid. Shareholders want dividends and stock price appreciation. Suppliers want predictable orders and bills paid. Creditors want commitments to be met on time. In the normal course of affairs, the relationship between a firm and each of its primary stakeholders is regulated by written or verbal agreements and laws. Once a problem is identified, negotiation takes place based on costs and benefits to each party. (Government is not usually considered a primary stakeholder because laws apply to all in a category and usually cannot be negotiated.)

The *second step* in stakeholder analysis is to identify the *secondary stakeholders*—those who have only an *indirect* stake in the corporation but who are also affected by corporate activities. These usually include nongovernmental organizations (NGOs, such as Greenpeace), activists, local communities, trade associations, competitors, and governments. Because the corporation's relationship with each of these stakeholders is usually not covered by any written or verbal agreement, there is room for misunderstanding. As in the case of NGOs and activists, there actually may be no relationship until a problem develops—usually brought up by the stakeholder. In the normal course of events, these stakeholders do not affect the corporation's ability to meet its economic or legal responsibilities. Aside from competitors, these secondary stakeholders are not usually monitored by the corporation in any systematic fashion. As a result, relationships are usually based on a set of questionable assumptions about each other's needs and wants. Although these stakeholders may not directly affect a firm's short-term profitability, their actions could determine a corporation's reputation and thus its long-term performance.

The *third step* in stakeholder analysis is to estimate the effect on each stakeholder group from any particular strategic decision. Because the primary decision criteria are typically economic, this is the point where secondary stakeholders may be ignored or discounted as unimportant. For a firm to fulfill its ethical or discretionary responsibilities, it must seriously consider the needs and wants of its secondary stakeholders in any strategic decision. For example, how much will specific stakeholder groups lose or gain? What other alternatives do they have to replace what may be lost?

Stakeholder Input

Once stakeholder impacts have been identified, managers should decide whether stakeholder input should be invited into the discussion of the strategic alternatives. A group is more likely to accept or even help implement a decision if it has some input into which alternative is chosen and how it is to be implemented. In the case of Maytag's decision to close its Galesburg, Illinois, refrigeration plant, the community was not a part of the decision. Nevertheless, management decided to inform the local community of its decision three years in advance of the closing instead of the 60 days required by law. Although the announcement created negative attention, it gave the Galesburg employees and townspeople more time to adjust to the eventual closing.

Given the wide range of interests and concerns present in any organization's task environment, one or more groups, at any one time, probably will be dissatisfied with an organization's activities—even if management is trying to be socially responsible. A company may have some stakeholders of which it is only marginally aware. For example, when Ford Motor Company extended its advertising to magazines read by gay and lesbian readers in 2005, management had no idea that the American Family Association (AFA) would argue that this was tantamount to promoting a homosexual agenda and call for a boycott of all Ford products. In response, Ford pulled its ads. Gay and lesbian groups then protested Ford's backpedaling. Ford then placed corporate ads in many of the same publications, which gays saw as clumsy and the AFA saw as backsliding.[32]

Therefore, before making a strategic decision, strategic managers should consider how each alternative will affect various stakeholder groups. What seems at first to be the best decision because it appears to be the most profitable may actually result in the worst set of consequences to the corporation. One example of a company that does its best to consider its responsibilities to its primary and secondary stakeholders when making strategic decisions is Johnson & Johnson. See **Strategic Highlight 3.1** for the J & J Credo.

STRATEGY highlight 3.1

JOHNSON & JOHNSON CREDO

We believe our first responsibility is to the doctors, nurses, and patients, to mothers and fathers and all others who use our products and services. In meeting their needs everything we do must be of high quality. We must constantly strive to reduce our costs in order to maintain reasonable prices. Customers' orders must be serviced promptly and accurately. Our suppliers and distributors must have an opportunity to make a fair profit.

We are responsible to our employees, the men and women who work with us throughout the world. Everyone must be considered as an individual. We must respect their dignity and recognize their merit. They must have a sense of security in their jobs. Compensation must be fair and adequate, and working conditions clean, orderly, and safe. We must be mindful of ways to help our employees fulfill their family responsibilities. Employees must feel free to make suggestions and complaints. There must be equal opportunity for employment, development, and advance-

ment for those qualified. We must provide competent management, and their actions must be just and ethical.

We are responsible to the communities where we live and work and to the world community as well. We must be good citizens—support good works and charities and bear our fair share of taxes. We must encourage civic improvements and better health and education. We must maintain in good order the property we are privileged to use, and protecting the environment and natural resources.

Our final responsibility is to our stockholders. Business must make a sound profit. We must experiment with new ideas. Research must be carried on, innovative programs developed, and mistakes paid for. New equipment must be purchased, new facilities provided, and new products launched. Reserves must be created for adverse times. When we operate according to these principles, the stockholders should realize a fair return.

....

3.2 Ethical Decision Making

Some people joke that there is no such thing as "business ethics." They call it an oxymoron—a concept that combines opposite or contradictory ideas. Unfortunately, there is some truth to this sarcastic comment. For example, a survey by the Ethics Resource Center of 1,324 employees of 747 U.S. companies found that 48% of employees surveyed said that they had engaged in one or more unethical and/or illegal actions during the past year. The most common questionable behaviors involved cutting corners on quality (16%), covering up incidents (14%), abusing or lying about sick days (11%), and lying to or deceiving customers (9%).[33] Some 52% of workers reported observing at least one type of misconduct in the workplace, but only 55% reported it.[34] From 1996 to 2005, top managers at 2,270 firms (29.2% of the firms analyzed) had backdated or otherwise manipulated stock option grants to take advantage of favorable share-price movements.[35] In a survey, 53% of employees in corporations of all sizes admitted that they would be willing to misrepresent corporate financial statements if asked to do so by a superior.[36] A survey of 141 chief financial executives (CFOs) revealed that 17% had been pressured by their CEOs over a five-year period to misrepresent the company's financial results. Five percent admitted that they had succumbed to the request.[37]

Around 53,000 cases of suspected mortgage fraud were reported by banks in 2007. The most common type of mortgage fraud was misstatement of income or assets, followed by forged documents, inflated appraisals, and misrepresentation of a buyer's intent to occupy a property as a primary residence.[38] In one instance, Allison Bice, office manager at Leonard Fazio's RE/MAX A-1 Best Realtors in Urbandale, Iowa, admitted that she submitted fake invoices and copies of checks drawn on a closed account as part of a scheme to obtain more money from Homecoming Financial, a mortgage company that had hired Fazio's agency to resell foreclosed homes. "I was directed by Mr. Fazio to have the bills be larger to Homecomings because we didn't make much money on commissions," Bice told a federal jury in Des Moines. "He told me that everybody in the business does it."[39]

A study of more than 5,000 graduate students at 32 colleges and universities in the United States and Canada revealed that 56% of business students and 47% of non-business students admitted to cheating at least once during the past year. Cheating was more likely when a student's peers also cheated.[40] In another example, 6,000 people paid $30 to enter a VIP section on ScoreTop.com's Web site to obtain access to actual test questions posted by those who had recently taken the Graduate Management Admission Test (GMAT). In response, the Graduate Management Admission Council promised to cancel the scores of anyone who posted "live" questions to the site or knowingly read them.[41] Given this lack of ethical behavior among students, it is easy to understand why some could run into trouble if they obtained a job at a corporation having an unethical culture, such as Enron, WorldCom, or Tyco. (See Strategy Highlight 3.2 for examples of unethical practices at Enron and Worldcom.)

SOME REASONS FOR UNETHICAL BEHAVIOR

Why are many business people perceived to be acting unethically? It may be that the involved people are not even aware that they are doing something questionable. There is no worldwide standard of conduct for business people. This is especially important given the global nature of business activities. Cultural norms and values vary between countries and even between different geographic regions and ethnic groups within a country. For example, what is considered in one country to be a bribe to expedite service is sometimes considered in another country to be normal business practice. Some of these differences may derive from whether a country's

STRATEGY highlight 3.2

UNETHICAL PRACTICES AT ENRON AND WORLDCOM EXPOSED BY "WHISTLE-BLOWERS"

Corporate scandals at Enron, WorldCom, and Tyco, among other international companies, have caused people around the world to seriously question the ethics of business executives. Enron, in particular, has become infamous for the questionable actions of its top executives in the form of (1) off-balance sheet partnerships used to hide the company's deteriorating finances, (2) revenue from long-term contracts being recorded in the first year instead of being spread over multiple years, (3) financial reports being falsified to inflate executive bonuses, and (4) manipulation of the electricity market—leading to a California energy crisis. Only Sherron Watkins, an Enron accountant, was willing to speak out regarding the questionable nature of these practices. In a now-famous memo to then-CEO Kenneth Lay, Watkins warned:

*I realize that we have had a lot of smart people looking at this and a lot of accountants including AA & Co. [Arthur Andersen] have blessed the accounting treat-*ment. None of that will protect Enron if these transactions are ever disclosed in the bright light of day.*

At WorldCom, Cynthia Cooper, an internal auditor, noted that some of the company's capital expenditures should have been listed on the second-quarter financial statements as expenses. When she mentioned this to both WorldCom's controller and its chief financial officer, she was told to stop what she was doing and to delay the audit until the third quarter (when expensing the transactions would not be noticed). Instead, Cooper informed the board of directors' audit committee. Two weeks later, WorldCom announced that it was reducing earnings by $3.9 billion, the largest restatement in history.

SOURCES: G. Colvin, "Wonder Women of Whistleblowers," *Fortune* (August 12, 2002), p. 56; W. Zellner, "The Deadly Sins of Enron," *Business Week* (October 14, 2002), pp. 26–28; M. J. Mandel, "And the Enron Award Goes to . . . Enron," *Business Week* (May 20, 2002), p. 46.

governance system is *rule-based* or *relationship-based*. Relationship-based countries tend to be less transparent and have a higher degree of corruption than do rule-based countries.[42] See the **Global Issue** feature for an explanation of country governance systems and how they may affect business practices.

Another possible reason for what is often perceived to be unethical behavior lies in differences in values between business people and key stakeholders. Some businesspeople may believe profit maximization is the key goal of their firm, whereas concerned interest groups may have other priorities, such as the hiring of minorities and women or the safety of their neighborhoods. Of the six values measured by the Allport-Vernon-Lindzey Study of Values test (aesthetic, economic, political, religious, social, and theoretical), both U.S. and UK executives consistently score highest on economic and political values and lowest on social and religious ones. This is similar to the value profile of managers from Japan, Korea, India, and Australia, as well as those of U.S. business school students. U.S. Protestant ministers, in contrast, score highest on religious and social values and very low on economic values.[43]

This difference in values can make it difficult for one group of people to understand another's actions. For example, even though some people feel that the advertising of cigarettes and alcoholic drinks (especially to youth) is unethical, the people managing these companies can respond that they are simply offering a product; *"Let the buyer beware"* is a traditional saying in free-market capitalism. They argue that customers in a free market democracy have the right to choose how they spend their money and live their lives. Social progressives may contend that business people working in tobacco, alcoholic beverages, and gambling industries are acting unethically by making and advertising products with potentially dangerous and expensive side effects, such as cancer, alcoholism, and addiction. People working in these industries could respond by asking whether it is ethical for people who don't smoke, drink, or

GLOBAL issue

HOW RULE-BASED AND RELATIONSHIP-BASED GOVERNANCE SYSTEMS AFFECT ETHICAL BEHAVIOR

The developed nations of the world operate under governance systems quite different from those used by developing nations. The developed nations and the business firms within them follow well-recognized rules in their dealings and financial reporting. To the extent that a country's rules force business corporations to publicly disclose in-depth information about the company to potential shareholders and others, that country's financial and legal system is said to be *transparent*. Transparency is said to simplify transactions and reduce the temptation to behave illegally or unethically. Finland, the United Kingdom, Hong Kong, the United States, and Australia have very transparent business climates. The Kurtzman Group, a consulting firm, developed an *opacity index* that measures the risks associated with unclear legal systems, regulations, economic policies, corporate governance standards, and corruption in 48 countries. The countries with the most opaque/least transparent ratings are Indonesia, Venezuela, China, Nigeria, India, Egypt, and Russia.

Developing nations tend to have *relationship-based governance*. Transactions are based on personal and implicit agreements, not on formal contracts enforceable by a court. Information about a business is largely local and private—thus cannot be easily verified by a third party. In contrast, *rule-based governance* relies on publicly verifiable information—the type of information that is typically not available in a developing country. The rule-based system has an infrastructure, based on accounting, auditing, ratings systems, legal cases, and codes, to provide and monitor this information. If present in a developing nation, the infrastructure is not very sophisticated. This is why investing in a developing country is very risky. The relationship-based system in a developing nation is inherently nontransparent due to the local and non-verifiable nature of its information. A business person needs to develop and nurture a wide network of personal relationships. *What* you know is less important than *who* you know.

The investment in time and money needed to build the necessary relationships to conduct business in a developing nation creates a high entry barrier for any newcomers to an industry. Thus, key industries in developing nations tend to be controlled by a small number of companies, usually privately owned, family-controlled conglomerates. Because public information is unreliable and insufficient for decisions, strategic decisions may depend more on a CEO playing golf with the prime minister than with questionable market share data. In a relationship-based system, the culture of the country (and the founder's family) strongly affects corporate culture and business ethics. What is "fair" depends on whether one is a family member, a close friend, a neighbor, or a stranger. Because behavior tends to be less controlled by laws and agreed-upon standards than by tradition, businesspeople from a rule-based developed nation perceive the relationship-based system in a developing nation to be less ethical and more corrupt. According to Larry Smeltzer, ethics professor at Arizona State University: "The lack of openness and predictable business standards drives companies away. Why would you want to do business in, say Libya, where you don't know the rules?"

....

SOURCES: S. Li, S. H. Park, and S. Li, "The Great Leap Forward: The Transition from Relation-Based Governance to Rule-Based Governance," *Organizational Dynamics*, Vol. 33, No. 1 (2003), pp. 63–78; M. Davids, "Global Standards, Local Problems," *Journal of Business Strategy* (January/February 1999), pp. 38–43; "The Opacity Index," *Economist* (September 18, 2004), p. 106.

gamble to reject another person's right to do so. One example is the recent controversy over the marketing of "alcopops," caffeinated malt beverages containing twice as much alcohol as many beers in the U.S. Critics of Sparks and Tilt call them alcoholic beverages disguised as energy drinks aimed at luring underage drinkers.[44]

Seventy percent of executives representing 111 diverse national and multinational corporations reported that they bend the rules to attain their objectives.[45] The three most common reasons given were:

- Organizational performance required it—74%
- Rules were ambiguous or out of date—70%
- Pressure from others and everyone does it—47%

The financial community's emphasis on short-term earnings performance is a significant pressure for executives to "manage" quarterly earnings. For example, a company achieving its forecasted quarterly earnings figure signals the investment community that its strategy and operations are proceeding as planned. Failing to meet its targeted objective signals that the company is in trouble—thus causing the stock price to fall and shareholders to become worried. Research by Degeorge and Patel involving more than 100,000 quarterly earnings reports revealed that a preponderance (82%) of reported earnings *exactly* matched analysts' expectations or exceeded them by 1%. The disparity between the number of earnings reports that missed estimates by a penny and the number that exceeded them by a penny suggests that executives who risked falling short of forecasts "borrowed" earnings from future quarters.[46]

In explaining why executives and accountants at Enron engaged in unethical and illegal actions, former Enron vice president Sherron Watkins used the *"frogs in boiling water"* analogy. If, for example, one were to toss a frog into a pan of boiling water, according to the folk tale, the frog would quickly jump out. It might be burned, but the frog would survive. However, if one put a frog in a pan of cold water and turned up the heat very slowly, the frog would not sense the increasing heat until it was too lethargic to jump out and would be boiled. According to Watkins:

> *Enron's accounting moved from creative to aggressive, to fraudulent, like the pot of water moving from cool to lukewarm to boiling; those involved with the creative transactions soon found themselves working on the aggressive transactions and were finally in the uncomfortable situation of working on fraudulent deals.[47]*

Moral Relativism

Some people justify their seemingly unethical positions by arguing that there is no one absolute code of ethics and that morality is relative. Simply put, **moral relativism** claims that morality is relative to some personal, social, or cultural standard and that there is no method for deciding whether one decision is better than another.

At one time or another, most managers have probably used one of the four types of moral relativism—naïve, role, social group, or cultural—to justify questionable behavior.[48]

Naïve relativism: Based on the belief that all moral decisions are deeply personal and that individuals have the right to run their own lives, adherents of moral relativism argue that each person should be allowed to interpret situations and act on his or her own moral values. This is not so much a belief as it is an excuse for not having a belief or is a common excuse for not taking action when observing others lying or cheating.

Role relativism: Based on the belief that social roles carry with them certain obligations to that role, adherents of role relativism argue that a manager in charge of a work unit must put aside his or her personal beliefs and do instead what the role requires, that is, act in the best interests of the unit. Blindly following orders was a common excuse provided by Nazi war criminals after World War II.

Social group relativism: Based on a belief that morality is simply a matter of following the norms of an individual's peer group, social group relativism argues that a decision is considered legitimate if it is common practice, regardless of other considerations ("everyone's doing it"). A real danger in embracing this view is that the person may incorrectly believe that a certain action is commonly accepted practice in an industry when it is not.

Cultural relativism: Based on the belief that morality is relative to a particular culture, society, or community, adherents of cultural relativism argue that people should understand the practices of other societies, but not judge them. This view not only suggests that one should not criticize another culture's norms and customs, but also that it is acceptable to personally follow these norms and customs ("When in Rome, do as the Romans do.").

Although these arguments make some sense, moral relativism could enable a person to justify almost any sort of decision or action, so long as it is not declared illegal.

Kohlberg's Levels of Moral Development

Another reason why some business people might be seen as unethical is that they may have no well-developed personal sense of ethics. A person's ethical behavior is affected by his or her level of moral development, certain personality variables, and such situational factors as the job itself, the supervisor, and the organizational culture.[49] Kohlberg proposes that a person progresses through three **levels of moral development.**[50] Similar in some ways to Maslow's hierarchy of needs, in Kohlberg's system, the individual moves from total self-centeredness to a concern for universal values. Kohlberg's three levels are as follows:

1. **The preconventional level:** This level is characterized by a concern for self. Small children and others who have not progressed beyond this stage evaluate behaviors on the basis of personal interest—avoiding punishment or quid pro quo.

2. **The conventional level:** This level is characterized by considerations of society's laws and norms. Actions are justified by an external code of conduct.

3. **The principled level:** This level is characterized by a person's adherence to an internal moral code. An individual at this level looks beyond norms or laws to find universal values or principles.

Kohlberg places most people in the conventional level, with fewer than 20% of U.S. adults in the principled level of development.[51] Research appears to support Kohlberg's concept. For example, one study found that individuals higher in cognitive moral development, lower in Machiavellianism, with a more internal locus of control, a less-relativistic moral philosophy, and higher job satisfaction are less likely to plan and enact unethical choices.[52]

ENCOURAGING ETHICAL BEHAVIOR

Following Carroll's work, if business people do not act ethically, government will be forced to pass laws regulating their actions—and usually increasing their costs. For self-interest, if for no other reason, managers should be more ethical in their decision making. One way to do that is by developing codes of ethics. Another is by providing guidelines for ethical behavior.

Codes of Ethics

A **code of ethics** specifies how an organization expects its employees to behave while on the job. Developing codes of ethics can be a useful way to promote ethical behavior, especially for people who are operating at Kohlberg's conventional level of moral development. Such codes are currently being used by more than half of U.S. business corporations. A code of ethics (1) clarifies company expectations of employee conduct in various situations and (2) makes clear that the company expects its people to recognize the ethical dimensions in decisions and actions.[53]

Various studies indicate that an increasing number of companies are developing codes of ethics and implementing ethics training workshops and seminars. However, research also indicates that when faced with a question of ethics, managers tend to ignore codes of ethics and try to solve dilemmas on their own.[54] To combat this tendency, the management of a company that wants to improve its employees' ethical behavior should not only develop a comprehensive code of ethics but also communicate the code in its training programs, in its performance appraisal system, policies and procedures, and through its own actions.[55] It may even include key values in its values and mission statements. According to a 2004 survey of CEOs by the Business Roundtable Institute for Corporate Ethics, 74% of CEOs confirmed that their companies had made changes within the previous two years in how they handled or reported ethics issues. Specific changes reported were:

- Enhanced internal reporting and communications—33%
- Ethics hotlines—17%
- Improved compliance procedures—12%
- Greater oversight by the board of directors—10%[56]

In addition, U.S. corporations have attempted to support **whistle-blowers,** those employees who report illegal or unethical behavior on the part of others. The U.S. False Claims Act gives whistle-blowers 15% to 30% of any damages recovered in cases where the government is defrauded. Even though the Sarbanes-Oxley Act forbids firms from retaliating against anyone reporting wrongdoing, 82% of those who uncovered fraud from 1996 to 2004 reported being ostracized, demoted, or pressured to quit.[57]

Corporations appear to benefit from well-conceived and implemented ethics programs. For example, companies with strong ethical cultures and enforced codes of conduct have fewer unethical choices available to employees—thus fewer temptations.[58] A study by the Open Compliance and Ethics Group found that no company with an ethics program in place for 10 years or more experienced "reputational damage" in the last five years.[59] Some of the companies identified in surveys as having strong moral cultures are Canon, Hewlett-Packard, Johnson & Johnson, Levi Strauss, Medtronic, Motorola, Newman's Own, Patagonia, S. C. Johnson, Shorebank, Smucker, and Sony.[60]

A corporation's management should consider establishing and enforcing a code of ethical behavior for those companies with which it does business—especially if it outsources its manufacturing to a company in another country. For example, Gap International, one of American's largest fashion retailers, developed one of the most rigorous codes of conduct for its suppliers. Its suppliers must comply with all child-labor laws on hiring, working hours, overtime, and working conditions. Workers must be at least 14 years of age. Rather than simply canceling business with suppliers using child labor, Gap requires suppliers to stop using child workers and to provide them with schooling instead, while continuing to pay them regularly and guaranteeing them a job once they reach legal age. In one year, Gap canceled contracts with 23 factories that did not meet its standards.[61]

Gap's experience, however, may be unusual. Recent surveys of over one hundred companies in the Global 2000 uncovered that 64% have some code of conduct that regulates supplier conduct, but only 40% require suppliers to actually take any action with respect to the code, such as disseminating it to employees, offering training, certifying compliance, or even reading or acknowledging receipt of the code.[62]

It is important to note that having a code of ethics for suppliers does not prevent harm to a corporation's reputation if one of its offshore suppliers is able to conceal abuses. Numerous Chinese factories, for example, keep double sets of books to fool auditors and distribute scripts for employees to recite if they are questioned. Consultants have found new business helping Chinese companies evade audits.[63]

Guidelines for Ethical Behavior

Ethics is defined as the consensually accepted standards of behavior for an occupation, a trade, or a profession. *Morality,* in contrast, is the precepts of personal behavior based on religious or philosophical grounds. *Law* refers to formal codes that permit or forbid certain behaviors and may or may not enforce ethics or morality.[64] Given these definitions, how do we arrive at a comprehensive statement of ethics to use in making decisions in a specific occupation, trade, or profession? A starting point for such a code of ethics is to consider the three basic approaches to ethical behavior:[65]

1. **Utilitarian approach:** The **utilitarian approach** proposes that actions and plans should be judged by their consequences. People should therefore behave in a way that will produce the greatest benefit to society and produce the least harm or the lowest cost. A problem with this approach is the difficulty in recognizing all the benefits and the costs of any particular decision. Research reveals that only the stakeholders who have the most *power* (ability to affect the company), *legitimacy* (legal or moral claim on company resources), and *urgency* (demand for immediate attention) are given priority by CEOs.[66] It is therefore likely that only the most obvious stakeholders will be considered, while others are ignored.

2. **Individual rights approach:** The **individual rights approach** proposes that human beings have certain fundamental rights that should be respected in all decisions. A particular decision or behavior should be avoided if it interferes with the rights of others. A problem with this approach is in defining "fundamental rights." The U.S. Constitution includes a Bill of Rights that may or may not be accepted throughout the world. The approach can also encourage selfish behavior when a person defines a personal need or want as a "right."

3. **Justice approach:** The **justice approach** proposes that decision makers be equitable, fair, and impartial in the distribution of costs and benefits to individuals and groups. It follows the principles of *distributive justice* (people who are similar on relevant dimensions such as job seniority should be treated in the same way) and *fairness* (liberty should be equal for all persons). The justice approach can also include the concepts of *retributive justice* (punishment should be proportional to the offense) and *compensatory justice* (wrongs should be compensated in proportion to the offense). Affirmative action issues such as reverse discrimination are examples of conflicts between distributive and compensatory justice.

Cavanagh proposes that we solve ethical problems by asking the following three questions regarding an act or a decision:

1. **Utility:** Does it optimize the satisfactions of all stakeholders?
2. **Rights:** Does it respect the rights of the individuals involved?
3. **Justice:** Is it consistent with the canons of justice?

For example, is padding an expense account ethical? Using the utility criterion, this action increases the company's costs and thus does not optimize benefits for shareholders or customers. Using the rights approach, a person has no right to the money (otherwise, we wouldn't call it "padding"). Using the justice criterion, salary and commissions constitute ordinary compensation, but expense accounts compensate a person only for expenses incurred in doing his or her job—expenses that the person would not normally incur except in doing the job.[67]

Another approach to resolving ethical dilemmas is by applying the logic of the philosopher Immanuel Kant. Kant presents two principles (called **categorical imperatives**) to guide our actions:

1. A person's action is ethical only if that person is willing for that same action to be taken by everyone who is in a similar situation. This is the same as the Golden Rule: Treat others as you would like them to treat you. For example, padding an expense account would be considered ethical if the person were also willing for everyone else to do the same if they were the boss. Because it is very doubtful that any manager would be pleased with expense account padding, the action must be considered unethical.

2. A person should never treat another human being simply as a means but always as an end. This means that an action is morally wrong for a person if that person uses others merely as means for advancing his or her own interests. To be moral, the act should not restrict other people's actions so that they are disadvantaged in some way.[68]

End of Chapter SUMMARY

In his book *Defining Moments*, Joseph Badaracco states that most ethics problems deal with "right versus right" problems in which neither choice is wrong. These are what he calls "dirty hands problems" in which a person has to deal with very specific situations that are covered only vaguely in corporate credos or mission statements. For example, many mission statements endorse fairness but fail to define the term. At the personal level, *fairness* could mean playing by the rules of the game, following basic morality, treating everyone alike and not playing favorites, treating others as you would want to be treated, being sensitive to individual needs, providing equal opportunity for everyone, or creating a level playing field for the disadvantaged. According to Badaracco, codes of ethics are not always helpful because they tend to emphasize problems of misconduct and wrongdoing, not a choice between two acceptable alternatives, such as keeping an inefficient plant operating for the good of the community or closing the plant and relocating to a more efficient location to lower costs.[69]

This chapter provides a framework for understanding the social responsibilities of a business corporation. Following Carroll, it proposes that a manager should consider not only the economic and legal responsibilities of a firm but also its ethical and discretionary responsibilities. It also provides a method for making ethical choices, whether they are right versus right or some combination of right and wrong. It is important to consider Cavanaugh's questions using the three approaches of utilitarian, rights, and justice plus Kant's categorical imperatives when making a strategic decision. A corporation should try to move from Kohlberg's conventional to a principled level of ethical development. If nothing else, the frameworks should contribute to well-reasoned strategic decisions that a person can defend when interviewed by hostile media or questioned in a court room.

ECO-BITS

- An Australian nut orchard converts the shells of old Macintosh computers into houses for pest-eating birds.
- Nike gathers old athletic shoes and turns them into raw material for "sports surfaces" like tennis courts and running tracks.

- The British company Ecopods sells stylish coffins made from hardened recycled paper.
- It takes three months for a recycled aluminum can to return to the supermarket shelf in reincarnated form.[70]

DISCUSSION QUESTIONS

1. What is the relationship between corporate governance and social responsibility?

2. What is your opinion of Gap International's having a code of conduct for its suppliers? What would Milton Friedman say? Contrast his view with Archie Carroll's view.

3. Does a company have to act selflessly to be considered socially responsible? For example, when building a new plant, a corporation voluntarily invested in additional equipment that enabled it to reduce its pollution emissions beyond any current laws. Knowing that it would be very expensive for its competitors to do the same, the firm lobbied the government to make pollution regulations more restrictive on the entire industry. Is this company socially responsible? Were its managers acting ethically?

4. Are people living in a relationship-based governance system likely to be unethical in business dealings?

5. Given that people rarely use a company's code of ethics to guide their decision making, what good are the codes?

STRATEGIC PRACTICE EXERCISE

It is 1982. Zombie Savings and Loan is in trouble. This is a time when many savings and loans (S&Ls) are in financial difficulty. Zombie holds many 30-year mortgages at low fixed-interest rates in its loan portfolio. Interest rates have risen significantly, and the Deregulation Act of 1980 has given Zombie and other S&Ls the right to make business loans and hold up to 20% of its assets as such. Because interest rates in general have risen, but the rate that Zombie receives on its old mortgages has not, Zombie must now pay out higher interest rates to its deposit customers or see them leave, and it has negative cash flow until rates fall below the rates in its mortgage portfolio or Zombie itself fails.

In present value terms, Zombie is insolvent, but the accounting rules of the time do not require marking assets to market, so Zombie is allowed to continue to operate and is faced with two choices: It can wait and hope interest rates fall before it is declared insolvent and is closed down, or it can raise fresh (insured) deposits and make risky loans that have high interest rates. Risky loans promise high payoffs (if they are repaid), but the probability of loss to Zombie and being closed later with greater loss to the Federal Savings & Loan Insurance Corpora-

tion (FSLIC) is high. Zombie stays in business if its gamble pays off, and it loses no more than it has already lost if the gamble does not pay off. Indeed, if not closed, Zombie will raise increasingly greater new deposits and make more risky loans until it either wins or is shut down by the regulators.

Waiting for lower interest rates and accepting early closure if lower rates do not arrive is certainly in the best interest of the FSLIC and of the taxpayers, but the manager of Zombie has more immediate responsibilities, such as employees' jobs, mortgage customers, depositors, the local neighborhood, and his or her job. As a typical S&L, Zombie's depositors are its shareholders and vote according to how much money they have in savings accounts with Zombie. If Zombie closes, depositors may lose some, but not all of their money, because their deposits are insured by the FSLIC. There is no other provider of home mortgages in the immediate area. What should the manager do?

....

SOURCE: Adapted from D. W. Swanton, "Teaching Students the Nature of Moral Hazard: An Ethical Component for Finance Classes," paper presented to the annual meeting of the *Academy of Finance*, Chicago (March 13, 2003). Reprinted with permission.

KEY TERMS

categorical imperatives (p. 133)
code of ethics (p. 131)
ethics (p. 132)
individual rights approach (p. 133)
justice approach (p. 133)

law (p. 132)
levels of moral development (p. 131)
morality (p. 132)
moral relativism (p. 130)
social responsibility (p. 120)

stakeholder analysis (p. 124)
stakeholders (p. 123)
utilitarian approach (p. 133)
whistle-blowers (p. 132)

NOTES

1. *2008 Corporate Social Responsibility Report*, General Mills Inc., Minneapolis, MN; M. Conlin, J. Hempel, J. Tanzer, and D. Poole, "The Corporate Donors," *Business Week* (December 1, 2003), pp. 92–96; I. Sager, "The List: Angels in the Boardroom," *Business Week* (July 7, 2003), p. 12.

2. M. Friedman, "The Social Responsibility of Business Is to Increase Its Profits," *New York Times Magazine* (September 13, 1970), pp. 30, 126–127; M. Friedman *Capitalism and Freedom* (Chicago: University of Chicago Press, 1963), p. 133.

3. W. J. Byron, *Old Ethical Principles for the New Corporate Culture*, presentation to the College of Business, Iowa State University, Ames, Iowa (March 31, 2003).

4. A. B. Carroll, "A Three-Dimensional Conceptual Model of Corporate Performance," *Academy of Management Review* (October 1979), pp. 497–505. This model of business responsibilities was reaffirmed in A. B. Carroll, "Managing Ethically with Global Stakeholders: A Present and Future Challenge," *Academy of Management Executive* (May 2004), pp. 114–120.

5. Carroll refers to discretionary responsibilities as philanthropic responsibilities in A. B. Carroll, "The Pyramid of Corporate Social Responsibility: Toward the Moral Management of Organizational Stakeholders," *Business Horizons* (July–August 1991), pp. 39–48.

6. M. S. Baucus and D. A. Baucus, "Paying the Piper: An Empirical Examination of Longer-Term Financial Consequences of Illegal Corporate Behavior," *Academy of Management Journal* (February 1997), pp. 129–151.

7. J. Oleck, "Pink Slips with a Silver Lining," *Business Week* (June 4, 2001), p. 14.

8. S. M. J. Bonini, L. T. Mendonca, and J. M. Oppenheim, "When Social Issues Become Strategic," *McKinsey Quarterly* (2006, Number 2), pp. 20–31.

9. "The McKinsey Global Survey of Business Executives: Business and Society," *McKinsey Quarterly*, Web edition (March 31, 2006).

10. "Just Good Business," *The Economist*, Special Report on Social Responsibility (January 19, 2008), p. 4.

11. A. McWilliams and D. Siegel, "Corporate Social Responsibility and Financial Performance: Correlation or Misspecification?" *Strategic Management Journal* (May 2000), pp. 603–609; P. Rechner and K. Roth, "Social Responsibility and Financial Performance: A Structural Equation Methodology," *International Journal of Management* (December 1990), pp. 382–391; K. E. Aupperle, A. B. Carroll, and J. D. Hatfield, "An Empirical Examination of the Relationship Between Corporate Social Responsibility and Profitability," *Academy of Management Journal* (June 1985), p. 459.

12. M. M. Arthur, "Share Price Reactions to Work-Family Initiatives: An Institutional Perspective," *Academy of Management Journal* (April 2003), pp. 497–505; S. A. Waddock and S. B. Graves, "The Corporate Social Performance—Financial Performance Link," *Strategic Management Journal* (April 1997), pp. 303–319; M. V. Russo and P. A. Fouts, "Resource Based Perspective on Corporate Environmental Performance and Profitability" *Academy of Management Journal* (July 1997), pp. 534–559; H. Meyer, "The Greening of Corporate America," *Journal of Business Strategy* (January/February 2000), pp. 38–43.

13. J. D. Margolis and J. P. Walsh, "Misery Loves Companies: Rethinking Social Initiatives by Business," *Administrative Science Quarterly* (June 2003), pp. 268–305.

14. M. F. L. Orlitzky, F. L. Schmidt, and S. L. Rynes, "Corporate Social and Financial Performance: A Meta Analysis," *Organization Studies*, Vol. 24 (2003), pp. 403–441.

15. M. Porter and M. R. Kramer, "The Competitive Advantage of Corporate Philanthropy," *Harvard Business Review* (December 2002), p. 59.

16. P. S. Adler and S. W. Kwon, "Social Capital: Prospects for a New Concept," *Academy of Management Journal* (January 2002), pp. 17–40. Also called "moral capital" in P. C. Godfrey, "The Relationship Between Corporate Philanthropy and Shareholder Wealth: A Risk Management Perspective," *Academy of Management Review* (October 2005), pp. 777–799.

17. L. Gard, "We're Good Guys, Buy from Us," *Business Week* (November 22, 2004), pp. 72–74.

18. C. J. Prince, "Give and Receive," *Entrepreneur* (November 2005), pp. 76–78.

19. C. J. Fombrun, "Corporate Reputation as an Economic Asset," in M. A. Hitt, E. R. Freeman, and J. S. Harrison (Eds.), *The Blackwell Handbook of Strategic Management* (Oxford: Blackwell Publishers, 2001), pp. 289–310.

20. S. A. Muirhead, C. J. Bennett, R. E. Berenbeim, A. Kao, and D. J. Vidal, *Corporate Citizenship in the New Century* (New York: The Conference Board, 2002), p. 6.

21. *2002 Sustainability Survey Report*, PriceWaterhouseCoopers, reported in "Corporate America's Social Conscience," Special Advertising Section, *Fortune* (May 26, 2003), pp. 149–157.

22. C. L. Harman and E. R. Stafford, "Green Alliances: Building New Business with Environmental Groups" *Long Range Planning* (April 1997), pp. 184–196.

23. D. B. Turner and D. W. Greening, "Corporate Social Performance and Organizational Attractiveness to Prospective Employees," *Academy of Management Journal* (July 1997), pp. 658–672; S. Preece, C. Fleisher, and J. Toccacelli, "Building a Reputation Along the Value Chain at Levi Strauss," *Long Range Planning* (December 1995), pp. 88–98; J. B. Barney and M. H. Hansen, "Trustworthiness as a Source of Competitive Advantage," *Strategic Management Journal* (Special Winter Issue, 1994), pp. 175–190: R. V. Aguilera, D. E. Rupp, C. A. Williams, and J. Ganapathi, "Putting the S Back in Corporate Social Responsibility: A Multilevel Theory of Social Change in Organizations," *Academy of Management Review* (July 2007), pp. 836–863; S. Bonini and S. Chenevert, "The State of Corporate Philanthropy: A McKinsey Global Survey," *McKinsey Quarterly*, Web edition (March 1, 2008); P. Kotler and N. Lee, eds., *Corporate Social Responsibility: Doing the Most Good for Your Company and Your Cause* (Hoboken, NJ: Wiley, 2005).

24. "Numbers: Do-Good Investments Are Holding Up Better," *Business Week* (July 14 & 21, 2008), p. 15.

25. A. Crane and D. Matten, *Business Ethics: A European Perspective* (Oxford: Oxford University Press, 2004), p. 22.

26. R. E. Freeman and D. R. Gilbert, *Corporate Strategy and the Search for Ethics* (Upper Saddle River, NJ: Prentice Hall, 1988), p. 6.

27. M. Arndt, W. Zellner, and P. Coy, "Too Much Corporate Power?" *Business Week* (September 11, 2000), pp. 144–158.

28. L. T. Mendonca and M. Miller, "Exploring Business's Social Contract: An Interview with Daniel Yankellvich," *McKinsey Quarterly* (2007, Number 2).

29. "Report: CEOs of Companies with Greatest Outsourcing Got Biggest Pay," *Des Moines Register* (August 31, 2004), p. B5.

30. W. E. Stead and J. G. Stead, *Sustainable Strategic Management* (Armonk, NY: M. E. Sharpe, 2004), p. 41.

31. "Andy Grove to Corporate Boards: It's Time to Take Charge," *Knowledge @ Wharton* (September 9–October 5, 2004).

32. "Ford Flip-Flop Annoys both Gays and Fundamentalists," *Roundel* (February 2006), p. 23.

33. "Nearly Half of Workers Take Unethical Actions—Survey," *Des Moines Register* (April 7, 1997), p. 18B.

34. M. Hendricks, "Well, Honestly!" *Entrepreneur* (December 2006), pp. 103–104.

35. "Dates from Hell," *The Economist* (July 22, 2006), pp. 59–60.

36. J. Kurlantzick, "Liar, Liar," *Entrepreneur* (October 2003), p. 70.

37. M. Roman, "True Confessions from CFOs," *Business Week* (August 12, 2002), p. 40.

38. "Fraud Arrests Net 406," *Saint Cloud Times* (June 20, 2008), pp. 3A–4A.

39. J. Eckhoff, "Realtor Faked Invoices, Ex-Employee Says," *Des Moines Register* (October 5, 2005), p. 5B.

40. D. L. McCabe, K. D. Butterfield, and L. K. Trevino, "Academic Dishonesty in Graduate Business Programs: Prevalence, Causes, and Proposed Action," *Academy of Management Learning & Education* (September 2006), pp. 294–305.

41. L. Lavelle, "The GMAT Cheat Sheet," *Business Week* (July 14 & 21, 2008), p. 34.

42. S. Li, S. H. Park, and S. Li, "The Great Leap Forward: The Transition from Relation-Based Governance to Rule-Based Governance," *Organizational Dynamics*, Vol. 33, No. 1 (2004), pp. 63–78; M. Davids, "Global Standards, Local Problems," *Journal of Business Strategy* (January/February 1999), pp. 38–43; "The Opacity Index," *Economist* (September 18, 2004), p. 106.

43. K. Kumar, "Ethical Orientation of Future American Executives: What the Value Profiles of Business School Students Portend," *SAM Advanced Management Journal* (Autumn 1995), pp. 32–36, 47; M. Gable and P. Arlow, "A Comparative Examination of the Value Orientations of British and American Executives," *International Journal of Management* (September 1986), pp. 97–106; W. D. Guth and R. Tagiuri, "Personal Values and Corporate Strategy," *Harvard Business Review* (September–October 1965), pp. 126–127; G. W. England, "Managers and

Their Value Systems: A Five Country Comparative Study," *Columbia Journal of World Business* (Summer 1978), p. 35.

44. I. Penn, "Bad Buzz," *St. Petersburg Times* (June 21, 2008), pp. 1A, 0A.

45. J. F. Veiga, T. D. Golden, and K. Dechant, "Why Managers Bend Company Rules," *Academy of Management Executive* (May 2004), pp. 84–91.

46. H. Collingwood, "The Earnings Game," *Harvard Business Review* (June 2001), pp. 65–74; J. Fox, "Can We Trust Them Now?" *Fortune* (March 3, 2003), pp. 97–99.

47. S. Watkins, "Former Enron Vice President Sherron Watkins on the Enron Collapse," *Academy of Management Executive* (November 2003), p. 122.

48. R. E. Freeman and D. R. Gilbert, Jr., *Corporate Strategy and the Search for Ethics* (Englewood Cliffs, NJ: Prentice Hall, 1988), pp. 24–41.

49. L. K. Trevino, "Ethical Decision Making in Organizations: A Person-Situation Interactionist Model," *Academy of Management Review* (July 1986), pp. 601–617.

50. L. Kohlberg, "Moral Stage and Moralization: The Cognitive-Development Approach," in *Moral Development and Behavior*, edited by T. Lickona (New York: Holt, Rinehart & Winston, 1976).

51. L. K. Trevino, "Ethical Decision Making in Organizations: A Person-Situation Interactionist Model," *Academy of Management Review* (July 1986), p. 606; L. K. Trevino, G. R. Weaver, and S. J. Reynolds, "Behavioral Ethics in Organizations: A Review," *Journal of Management* (December 2006), pp. 951–990.

52. J. K. Gephart, D. A. Harrison, and L. K. Trevino, "The Who, When, and Where of Unethical Choices: Meta-Analytic Answers to Fundamental Ethics Questions." Paper presented to the *Academy of Management* annual meeting, Philadelphia, PA (2007).

53. J. Keogh, ed., *Corporate Ethics: A Prime Business Asset* (New York: The Business Roundtable, 1988), p. 5.

54. G. F. Kohut, and S. E. Corriher, "The Relationship of Age, Gender, Experience and Awareness of Written Ethics Policies to Business Decision Making," *SAM Advanced Management Journal* (Winter 1994), pp. 32–39; J. C. Lere and B. R. Gaumitz, "The Impact of Codes of Ethics on Decision Making: Some Insights from Information Economics," *Journal of Business Ethics*, Vol. 48 (2003), pp. 365–379.

55. W. I. Sauser, "Business Ethics: Back to Basics," *Management in Practice* (2005, No. 2), pp. 2–3; J. M. Stevens, H. K. Steensma, D. A. Harrison, and P. L. Cochran, "Symbolic or Substantive Document? The Influence of Ethics Codes on Financial Executives' Decisions," *Strategic Management Journal* (February 2005), pp. 181–195.

56. *Business Roundtable Institute for Corporate Ethics Announces Key Findings from "Mapping the Terrain" Survey of CEOs*, press release (Charlottesville, VA: Business Roundtable Institute for Corporate Ethics, June 10, 2004).

57. B. Levinson, "Getting More Workers to Whistle," *Business Week* (January 28, 2008), p. 18.

58. J. K. Gephart, D. A. Harrison, and L. K. Trevino, "The Who, When, and Where of Unethical Choices: Meta-Analytic Answers to Fundamental Ethics Questions." Paper presented to the *Academy of Management* annual meeting, Philadelphia, PA (2007).

59. "A 'How Am I Doing?' Guide for Ethics Czars," *Business Ethics* (Fall 2005), p. 11.

60. S. P. Feldman, "Moral Business Cultures: The Keys to Creating and Maintaining Them," *Organizational Dynamics* (2007, Vol. 36, No. 2), pp. 156–170. Also see the "World's Most Ethical Companies," published annually by Ethisphere at http://ethisphere.com.

61. "Clean, Wholesome and American?" *The Economist* (November 3, 2007), pp. 78–79.

62. M. Levin, "Building an Ethical Supply Chain," *Sarbanes-Oxley Compliance Journal* (April 3, 2008).

63. A. Bernstein, S. Holmes, and X. Ji, "Secrets, Lies, and Sweatshops," *Business Week* (November 27, 2006), pp. 50–58.

64. T. J. Von der Embse, and R. A. Wagley, "Managerial Ethics: Hard Decisions on Soft Criteria," *SAM Advanced Management Journal* (Winter 1988), p. 6.

65. G. F. Cavanagh, *American Business Values*, 3rd ed. (Upper Saddle River, NJ: Prentice Hall, 1990), pp. 186–199.

66. B. R. Agle, R. K. Mitchell, and J. A. Sonnenfeld, "Who Matters Most to CEOs? An Investigation of Stakeholder Attributes and Salience, Corporate Performance, and CEO Values," *Academy of Management Journal* (October 1999), pp. 507–525.

67. G. F. Cavanagh, *American Business Values*, 3rd ed. (Upper Saddle River, NJ: Prentice Hall, 1990, pp. 195–196.

68. I. Kant, "The Foundations of the Metaphysic of Morals," in *Ethical Theory: Classical and Contemporary Readings*, 2nd ed., by L. P. Pojman (Belmont, CA: Wadsworth Publishing, 1995), pp. 255–279.

69. J. L. Badaracco, Jr., *Defining Moments* (Boston: Harvard Business School Press, 1997).

70. J. Rice and A. Fields, "20 Things You Didn't Know About Recycling." *Discover* (May 2008), p. 80.

Ending Case for Part One

BLOOD BANANAS

Every company hates to be blackmailed, but that was exactly what was happening to one of America's largest fruit growing and processing companies, Chiquita Brands. Carlos Castaño, leader of the United Self Defense Forces of Columbia (AUC), a Colombian paramilitary organization, had just proposed that it would be in the best interests of Chiquita Brands and its subsidiary in Colombia, Banadex, to pay the AUC a few thousand dollars per month for "security" services. The security services were little more than protection from the AUC itself. Unfortunately, the local law enforcement agencies as well as the U.S. government were in no position to offer legitimate protection from paramilitary groups like the AUC. Chiquita was forced to decide whether to pay the AUC for protection or risk the lives of Chiquita employees in Colombia.

Chiquita Brands International Inc., headquartered in Cincinnati, Ohio, was a leading international marketer and distributor of high-quality fresh produce that was sold under the Chiquita® premium brand and related trademarks. The company was one of the largest banana producers in the world and a major supplier of bananas in Europe and North America. The company had revenues of approximately $4.5 billion and employed about 25,000 people in 70 countries in 2006.

Chiquita Brands, formerly United Brands and United Fruit, had been operating fruit plantations in Colombia for nearly 100 years. Chiquita's Banadex was responsible for 4,400 direct and an additional 8,000 indirect jobs in Colombia, jobs that were almost entirely performed by local (Colombian) workers. The company "contributed almost $70 million annually to the Colombian economy in the form of capital expenditures, payroll, taxes, social security, pensions, and local purchases of goods and services." Banadex was responsible for managing Chiquita's extensive plantation holding and was Chiquita's most profitable international operation.

....
This case was written by Steven M. Cox, Bradley W. Brooks, and S. Catherine Anderson of the Queens University of Charlotte and appeared in the *Journal of Critical Incidents*, Volume 1 (2008). Copyright © 2008 by Steven M. Cox, Bradley W. Brooks, and S. Catherine Anderson. Edited for publication in *Strategic Management and Business Policy*, 12th edition and *Concepts in Strategic Management and Business Policy*, 12th edition. Reprinted by permission of the authors and the Society for Case Research.

By the 1990s, Colombia had become a very violent country. Kidnappings and murders of wealthy Colombians and foreigners had become commonplace. The U.S. State Department had issued several advisories warning U.S. citizens about the dangers of travel to the country. In 1997, Carlos Castaño, leader of the AUC, met with senior officials of Banadex and offered to provide security services to the Banadex workers and property in Colombia. The AUC, often described as a "death squad," was one of the most violent, paramilitary organizations that existed in Colombia. Estimated by the U.S. State Department to number between 8,000 and 11,000 members, their activities included assassinations, guerrilla warfare, and drug trafficking. So far the AUC had not been designated a Foreign Terrorist Organization by the U.S. State Department, so it was not illegal to do business with the AUC. The implication of the offer for Banadex employees was obvious. Extortion or not, the implication of non-participation by Banadex would put employees at serious risk.

The options for Chiquita were straightforward: agree to pay, refuse to pay, or exit the country. The ramifications of any of the actions, however, were not pleasant.

Agree to Pay: If Chiquita agreed to pay for "protection" they might forestall killings and kidnappings; however, they would be financing a group of terrorists. The money it paid would be used to further the activities of AUC.

Refuse to Pay: If Chiquita chose to reject the offer of "protection" from Castaño, then there was the real likelihood that Banadex employees would be kidnapped and/or executed. There was ample evidence of the brutality of the AUC and similar organizations currently operating in Colombia. While a legitimate security company might be found to protect the plantations and employees, the cost to hire sufficient men to withstand a force of 8,000–11,000 paramilitary fighters would be inordinately expensive. Only governments had the strength to mount such a protective service and neither the U.S. nor Colombian governments were willing to support such an effort. Furthermore, it was unlikely that the Colombian government would welcome a mercenary force hired by Chiquita into the country.

Exit the Country: If the decision was made to abandon the plantations in Colombia what would happen to the 12,000 individuals whose livelihoods depended upon the work or workers on the plantation? Contributing $70 million annually to the economy, a rapid exit would represent a significant loss to the Colombian people. Further, Banadex exports represented a significant portion of the bananas sold by Chiquita brands. The loss of this supply would not only affect Chiquita Brands' profitability and shareholder value but also the profitability of numerous Chiquita distributors around the world.

Study Question

1. What should Chiquita do?

PART 2

Scanning the Environment

environmental scanning and Industry Analysis

The Arctic is undergoing an extraordinary transformation—a transformation that will have global impact not only on wildlife, but upon many countries and a number of industries. Some of the most significant environmental changes are retreating sea ice, melting glaciers, thawing permafrost, increasing coastal erosion, and shifting vegetation zones. The average temperature of the Arctic has risen at twice the rate of the rest of the planet. According to *Impacts of a Warming Arctic: Arctic Climate Impact Assessment*, a 2004 report by the eight-nation Arctic Council, the melting of the area's highly reflective snow and sea ice is uncovering darker land and ocean surfaces, further increasing the absorption of the sun's heat. Reductions in Arctic sea ice will drastically shrink marine habitats for polar bears, ice seals, and some seabirds. The warming of the tundra will likely boost greenhouse gases by releasing long-stored quantities of methane and carbon dioxide.

In addition to containing a large percentage of the world's water as ice, the Arctic is a large storehouse of natural resources. Given that the Arctic Ocean could be ice-free in the summer by 2040, countries bordering the Arctic are already positioning themselves for exploitation of these resources. Lawson Brigham, Alaska Office Director of the U.S. Arctic Research Commission and a former chief of strategic planning for the U.S. Coast Guard, examined how regional warming will affect transportation systems, resource development, indigenous Arctic peoples, regional environmental degradation and protection schemes, and overall geopolitical issues. From this, he proposes four possible scenarios for the Arctic in 2040:

1. **Globalized frontier:** In this scenario, the Arctic by 2040 has become an integral component of the global economic system, but is itself a semi-lawless frontier with participants jockeying for control. The summer sea ice has completely disappeared for a two-week period, allowing greater marine access and commercial shipping throughout the area. The famous "Northwest Passage" dreamed by 16th century navigators is now a reality. Rising prices for oil, natural gas, nickel, copper, zinc, and freshwater in conjunction with an easily accessible and less-harsh climate have made Arctic natural resource exploitation economically viable. Even though overfishing has reduced fish stocks, Arctic tourism is flourishing. By now, well-worn oil and gas pipelines in western Siberia and Alaska are experiencing recurring serious

Learning Objectives

After reading this chapter, you should be able to:

- Recognize aspects of an organization's environment that can influence its long-term decisions

- Identify the aspects of an organization's environment that are most strategically important

- Conduct an industry analysis to understand the competitive forces that influence the intensity of rivalry within an industry

- Understand how industry maturity affects industry competitive forces

- Categorize international industries based on their pressures for coordination and local responsiveness

- Construct strategic group maps to assess the competitive positions of firms in an industry

- Identify key success factors and develop an industry matrix

- Use publicly available information to conduct competitive intelligence

- Know how to develop an industry scenario

- Be able to construct an EFAS table that summarizes external environmental factors

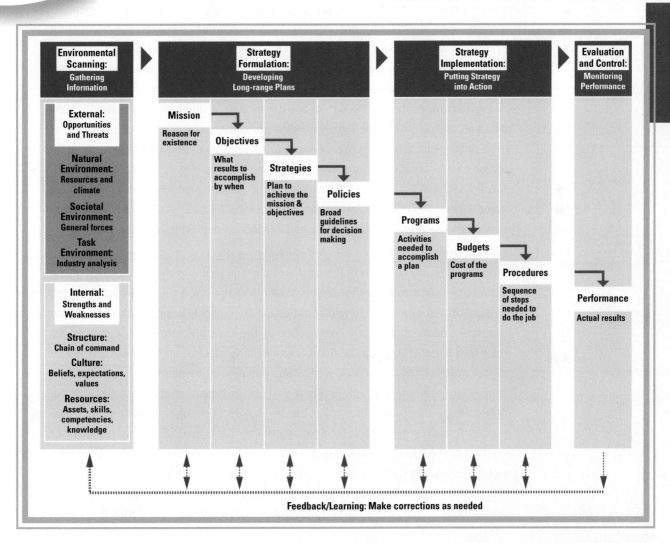

spills. By 2020, Canada, Denmark (Greenland), Norway, Russia, and the United States had asserted their sovereignty over sea bed resources beyond 200 nautical miles—leaving only two small regions in the central Arctic Ocean under international jurisdiction. Environmental concerns that once fostered polar cooperation have been replaced by economic and political interests. The protection, development, and governance of the Svalbard Islands became a problem when Russia refused to recognize Norway's 200-nautical mile exclusive economic zone around the islands. Issues regarding freedom of navigation and commercial access rights are highly contentious. The eight permanent members of the Arctic Council have increasingly excluded outside participation in the Council's deliberations.

2. **Adaptive frontier:** In this scenario, the Arctic in 2040 is being drawn much more slowly into the global economy. The area is viewed as an international resource. Competition among the Arctic countries for control of the region's resources never grew beyond a low level and the region is the scene of international cooperation among many international stakeholders. The indigenous peoples throughout the area have organized and now have significant influence over decisions relating to regional environmental protection and economic development. The exploitation of Arctic oil and gas is restricted to the few key areas that are most cost-competitive. Air and water transportation systems flourish throughout the area. Commercially viable fishing has continued, thanks to stringent harvesting quotas and other bilateral agreements. The Arctic Council is a proactive forum resolving several disputes and engaging the indigenous peoples in all deliberations. Nevertheless, the impact of global warming on the Arctic is widespread and serious. Contingency planning for manmade and natural emergencies is advanced and well coordinated. Sustainable development is widely supported by most stakeholders. The Arctic region has become a model for habitat protection. Arctic national parks have expanded modestly and adapted to deal with increased tourism.

3. **Fortress frontier:** In this scenario, widespread resource exploitation and increased international tension exist throughout the Arctic. The region is viewed by much of the global community as a storehouse of natural resources that is being jealously guarded by a handful of wealthy circumpolar nations. Although the Arctic is part of the global economic system, any linkage is controlled by the most powerful Arctic countries for their own benefit. By 2040, the Arctic is undergoing extreme environmental stress, as global warming continues unabated. Many indigenous peoples have been displaced from their traditional homelands due to extreme environmental events. Illegal immigration becomes an issue in many subarctic regions. Although air and marine transportation routes are open, foreign access has been periodically suspended for political or security reasons. Russia and Canada, in particular, continue to tightly control marine access through the Northern Sea Route and Northwest Passage. Fishing rights have been suspended to all but the Arctic countries. Oil and gas exploration and production has intensified throughout the Arctic. The Svalbard Islands, claimed

by Norway, have been a source of potential conflict over access to living and nonliving resources. Norway, Russia, and the United States have increased military forces in the region. Rather than dealing with sustainable development, the Arctic Council focuses on economic and security concerns, such as illegal immigrants and controlling the flow of exports from the Arctic consortium. Early in the 21st century, the five countries bordering the Arctic declared their sovereignty over resources beyond 200 nautical miles to the edge of the continental shelf extensions. By 2030, the Arctic Council unilaterally took jurisdiction over the two small regions that remained within international jurisdiction. Arctic tourism thrives, since many other traditional destinations are experiencing turmoil and a shortage of necessities.

4. **Equitable frontier:** In this scenario, the Arctic is integrated with the global economic system by 2040, but international concern for sustainable development has slowed the region's economic development. Mutual respect and cooperation among the circumpolar nations allows for the development of a respected Arctic governance system. Even though the world is working hard to reduce greenhouse gas emissions, the Arctic continues to warm. Transport user fees and other eco-taxes are used to support endangered wildlife and impacted indigenous communities. The growth of the Northern Sea Route and Northwest Passage has enabled significant efficiencies in commercial shipping. Canada and Russia have maintained stringent marine regulations that emphasize environmental protection. Despite differences over freedom of navigation, the United States, Canada, and Russia have negotiated an agreement that allows a seamless voyage around Alaska and through the routes under a uniform set of operational procedures. The Arctic Council has created regional disaster teams to respond to maritime and other emergencies. Boundary disputes have been resolved and fishing rights have been allocated to various nations. The University of the Arctic has brought quality online education to easy reach of all northern citizens. The Arctic Council has brokered an agreement to allow 30,000 environmental refugees to settle in subarctic territories. Oil exploration and production in the Arctic has slowed considerably. Arctic tourism continues its steady growth, prompting national and regional parliaments to establish additional wilderness lands funded by tourist fees. There is low military presence in the region, thanks to the diplomatic efforts of the Arctic Council.

The Arctic is a complex, but relatively small region. These four scenarios suggest how climate change combined with a growing need for natural resources might impact this region and the world.[1]

- Which of the four preceding scenarios is most likely?
- Which industries are likely to be affected (either positively or negatively) by the warming of the Arctic?
- If in an affected industry, how could a business corporation prepare for each of these scenarios?

A changing environment can help as well as hurt a company. Many pioneering companies have gone out of business because of their failure to adapt to environmental change or, even worse, because of their failure to create change. For example, Baldwin Locomotive, the major manufacturer of steam locomotives, was very slow in making the switch to diesel locomotives. General Electric and General Motors soon dominated the diesel locomotive business and Baldwin went out of business. The dominant manufacturers of vacuum tubes failed to make the change to transistors and consequently lost this market. Eastman Kodak, the pioneer and market leader of chemical-based film photography, continues to struggle with its transition to the newer digital technology. Failure to adapt is, however, only one side of the coin. The aforementioned Arctic warming example shows how a changing environment can create new opportunities at the same time it destroys old ones. The lesson is simple: To be successful over time, an organization needs to be in tune with its external environment. There must be a strategic fit between what the environment wants and what the corporation has to offer, as well as between what the corporation needs and what the environment can provide.

Current predictions are that the environment for all organizations will become even more uncertain with every passing year. What is **environmental uncertainty**? It is the *degree of complexity* plus the *degree of change* that exists in an organization's external environment. As more and more markets become global, the number of factors a company must consider in any decision becomes huge and much more complex. With new technologies being discovered every year, markets change and products must change with them.

On the one hand, environmental uncertainty is a threat to strategic managers because it hampers their ability to develop long-range plans and to make strategic decisions to keep the corporation in equilibrium with its external environment. On the other hand, environmental uncertainty is an opportunity because it creates a new playing field in which creativity and innovation can play a major part in strategic decisions.

4.1 Environmental Scanning

Before an organization can begin strategy formulation, it must scan the external environment to identify possible opportunities and threats and its internal environment for strengths and weaknesses. **Environmental scanning** is the monitoring, evaluation, and dissemination of information from the external and internal environments to key people within the corporation. A corporation uses this tool to avoid strategic surprise and to ensure its long-term health. Research has found a positive relationship between environmental scanning and profits.[2] Approximately 70% of executives around the world state that global social, environmental, and business trends are increasingly important to corporate strategy, according to a 2008 survey by McKinsey & Company.[3]

IDENTIFYING EXTERNAL ENVIRONMENTAL VARIABLES

In undertaking environmental scanning, strategic managers must first be aware of the many variables within a corporation's natural, societal, and task environments (see **Figure 1–3**). The

natural environment includes physical resources, wildlife, and climate that are an inherent part of existence on Earth. These factors form an ecological system of interrelated life. The **societal environment** is mankind's social system that includes general forces that do not directly touch on the short-run activities of the organization that can, and often do, influence its long-run decisions. These factors affect multiple industries and are as follows:

- **Economic forces** that regulate the exchange of materials, money, energy, and information.
- **Technological forces** that generate problem-solving inventions.
- **Political–legal forces** that allocate power and provide constraining and protecting laws and regulations.
- **Sociocultural forces** that regulate the values, mores, and customs of society.

The **task environment** includes those elements or groups that directly affect a corporation and, in turn, are affected by it. These are governments, local communities, suppliers, competitors, customers, creditors, employees/labor unions, special-interest groups, and trade associations. A corporation's task environment is typically the industry within which the firm operates. **Industry analysis** (popularized by Michael Porter) refers to an in-depth examination of key factors within a corporation's task environment. The natural, societal, and task environments must be monitored to detect the strategic factors that are likely in the future to have a strong impact on corporate success or failure. Changes in the natural environment usually affect a business corporation first through its impact on the societal environment in terms of resource availability and costs and then upon the task environment in terms of the growth or decline of particular industries.

Scanning the Natural Environment

The natural environment includes physical resources, wildlife, and climate that are an inherent part of existence on Earth. Until the 20th century, the natural environment was generally perceived by business people to be a given—something to exploit, not conserve. It was viewed as a free resource, something to be taken or fought over, like arable land, diamond mines, deep water harbors, or fresh water. Once they were controlled by a person or entity, these resources were considered assets and thus valued as part of the general economic system—a resource to be bought, sold, or sometimes shared. Side effects, such as pollution, were considered to be *externalities*, costs not included in a business firm's accounting system, but felt by others. Eventually these externalities were identified by governments, which passed regulations to force business corporations to deal with the side effects of their activities.

The concept of sustainability argues that a firm's ability to continuously renew itself for long-term success and survival is dependent not only upon the greater economic and social system of which it is a part, but also upon the natural ecosystem in which the firm is embedded.[4] A business corporation must thus scan the natural environment for factors that might previously have been taken for granted, such as the availability of fresh water and clean air. Global warming means that aspects of the natural environment, such as sea level, weather, and climate, are becoming increasingly uncertain and difficult to predict. Management must therefore scan not only the natural environment for possible strategic factors, but also include in its strategic decision-making processes the impact of its activities upon the natural environment. In a world concerned with global warming, a company should measure and reduce its *carbon footprint*— the amount of greenhouse gases it is emitting into the air. Research reveals that scanning the market for environmental issues is positively related to firm performance because it helps management identify opportunities to fulfill future market demand based upon environmentally friendly products or processes.[5] See the **Environmental Sustainability Issue** feature to learn how individuals can also measure and shrink their personal carbon footprints.

ENVIRONMENTAL sustainability issue

MEASURING AND SHRINKING
YOUR PERSONAL CARBON FOOTPRINT

As people become more "green," that is more conscious of environmental sustainability, they wonder what they can do as individuals to reduce the emission of greenhouse gases. This is an important issue given that a typical American produces more than 20 tons of carbon dioxide annually—a very large carbon footprint. Even a homeless American has a carbon footprint of 8.5 tons, more than twice the global average! The first problem for concerned individuals is finding a way to measure the size of their own carbon footprint. The second problem is developing feasible programs to reduce that footprint in some meaningful way.

The Web site *carbonrally.com* solves these problems by presenting competitive environmental challenges and keeping score by translating green actions into pounds of carbon dioxide averted. For instance, cutting the time of a daily shower by two minutes for a month reduces CO_2 emissions by 15.3 pounds. According to Kelsey Schroeder, who has logged savings of more than 1,000 pounds of emissions, "This has been a great motivational technique. We just want to keep going and see if we can do better."

How does Carbonrally calculate someone's carbon shoe size? Since everything a person does that is powered by fossil fuels has a carbon dioxide cost, many activities have the potential of being counted. Commuting in a gasoline powered car has obvious carbon costs, but so does eating a hamburger. Since livestock are responsible for an esti-

mated 18% of global carbon emissions, eating a hamburger results in carbon emissions by the consumer. Something as small as an iPod adds to a person's carbon footprint due not only to the energy used to produce and transport the product, but also to the energy used to charge it over its lifetime—approximately 68 pounds of CO_2. Both the Nature Conservancy and the U.S. Environmental Protection Agency provide ways to measure an individual carbon footprint. The EPA even offers a carbon calculator on its Web site, epa.gov.

Carbonrally offers concrete ways to start cutting carbon emissions. One 2008 contest challenged people to avoid bottled soda, tea, and sports drinks for a month for an average individual savings of 25.7 pounds of CO_2.

Other challenges were using a clothesline to dry one laundry load a week, unplugging computers every night for one month, and using a personal cup for coffee instead of using a disposable cup. By the end of 2008, nearly 15,000 individuals had completed a challenge, effectively reducing over 1,622.57 tons of CO_2.

Given that global carbon dioxide emissions total more than 28 billion tons annually, one person's reductions can seem very small. Why bother? Carbonrally might respond that the best way to change the world is one person at a time.

....
SOURCES: B. Walsh and T. Sharples, "Sizing Up Carbon Footprints," *Time* (May 26, 2008), pp. 53–55 and www.carbonrally.com.

Scanning the Societal Environment: STEEP Analysis

The number of possible strategic factors in the societal environment is very high. The number becomes enormous when we realize that, generally speaking, each country in the world can be represented by its own unique set of societal forces—some of which are very similar to those of neighboring countries and some of which are very different.

For example, even though Korea and China share Asia's Pacific Rim area with Thailand, Taiwan, and Hong Kong (sharing many similar cultural values), they have very different views about the role of business in society. It is generally believed in Korea and China (and to a lesser extent in Japan) that the role of business is primarily to contribute to national development; however in Hong Kong, Taiwan, and Thailand (and to a lesser extent in the Philippines, Indonesia, Singapore, and Malaysia), the role of business is primarily to make profits for the shareholders.[6] Such differences may translate into different trade regulations and varying difficulty in the *repatriation of profits* (the transfer of profits from a foreign subsidiary to a corporation's headquarters) from one group of Pacific Rim countries to another.

STEEP Analysis: Monitoring Trends in the Societal and Natural Environments. As shown in **Table 4–1**, large corporations categorize the societal environment in any one geographic region into four areas and focus their scanning in each area on trends that have corporatewide relevance. By including trends from the natural environment, this scanning can be called **STEEP Analysis**, the scanning of Sociocultural, Technological, Economic, Ecological, and Political-legal environmental forces.[7] (It may also be called *PESTEL Analysis* for Political, Economic, Sociocultural, Technological, Ecological, and Legal forces.) Obviously, trends in any one area may be very important to firms in one industry but of lesser importance to firms in other industries.

Trends in the *economic* part of the societal environment can have an obvious impact on business activity. For example, an increase in interest rates means fewer sales of major home appliances. Why? A rising interest rate tends to be reflected in higher mortgage rates. Because higher mortgage rates increase the cost of buying a house, the demand for new and used houses tends to fall. Because most major home appliances are sold when people change houses, a reduction in house sales soon translates into a decline in sales of refrigerators, stoves, and dishwashers and reduced profits for everyone in the appliance industry. Changes in the price of oil have a similar impact upon multiple industries, from packaging and automobiles to hospitality and shipping.

The rapid economic development of Brazil, Russia, India, and China (often called the *BRIC* countries) is having a major impact on the rest of the world. By 2007, China had become the world's second-largest economy according to the World Bank. With India graduating more English-speaking scientists, engineers, and technicians than all other nations combined, it has become the primary location for the outsourcing of services, computer software, and telecommunications.[8] Eastern Europe has become a major manufacturing supplier to the European Union countries. According to the International Monetary Fund, emerging markets make up less than one-third of total world gross domestic product (GDP), but account for more than half of GDP growth.[9]

TABLE 4–1	Some Important Variables in the Societal Environment		
Economic	**Technological**	**Political–Legal**	**Sociocultural**
GDP trends	Total government spending for R&D	Antitrust regulations	Lifestyle changes
Interest rates	Total industry spending for R&D	Environmental protection laws	Career expectations
Money supply	Focus of technological efforts	Global warming legislation	Consumer activism
Inflation rates	Patent protection	Immigration laws	Rate of family formation
Unemployment levels	New products	Tax laws	Growth rate of population
Wage/price controls	New developments in technology transfer from lab to marketplace	Special incentives	Age distribution of population
Devaluation/revaluation	Productivity improvements through automation	Foreign trade regulations	Regional shifts in population
Energy alternatives	Internet availability	Attitudes toward foreign companies	Life expectancies
Energy availability and cost	Telecommunication infrastructure	Laws on hiring and promotion	Birthrates
Disposable and discretionary income	Computer hacking activity	Stability of government	Pension plans
Currency markets		Outsourcing regulation	Health care
Global financial system		Foreign "sweat shops"	Level of education
			Living wage
			Unionization

Changes in the *technological* part of the societal environment can also have a great impact on multiple industries. Improvements in computer microprocessors have not only led to the widespread use of personal computers but also to better automobile engine performance in terms of power and fuel economy through the use of microprocessors to monitor fuel injection. Digital technology allows movies and music to be available instantly over the Internet or through cable service, but it also means falling fortunes for video rental shops such as the Movie Gallery and CD stores such as Tower Records. Advances in nanotechnology are enabling companies to manufacture extremely small devices that are very energy efficient. Developing biotechnology, including gene manipulation techniques, is already providing new approaches to dealing with disease and agriculture. Researchers at George Washington University have identified a number of technological breakthroughs that are already having a significant impact on many industries:

- **Portable information devices and electronic networking:** Combining the computing power of the personal computer, the networking of the Internet, the images of the television, and the convenience of the telephone, these appliances will soon be used by a majority of the population of industrialized nations to make phone calls, send e-mail, and transmit documents and other data. Even now, homes, autos, and offices are being connected (via wires and wirelessly) into intelligent networks that interact with one another. This trend is being supported by the development of *cloud computing*, in which a person can tap into computing power elsewhere through a Web connection.[10] The traditional stand-alone desktop computer may soon join the manual typewriter as a historical curiosity.

- **Alternative energy sources:** The use of wind, geothermal, hydroelectric, solar, biomass, and other alternative energy sources should increase considerably. Over the past two decades, the cost of manufacturing and installing a photovoltaic solar-power system has decreased by 20% with every doubling of installed capacity. The cost of generating electricity from conventional sources, in contrast, has been rising along with the price of petroleum and natural gas.[11]

- **Precision farming:** The computerized management of crops to suit variations in land characteristics will make farming more efficient and sustainable. Farm equipment dealers such as Case and John Deere add this equipment to tractors for an additional $6,000 or so. It enables farmers to reduce costs, increase yields, and decrease environmental impact. The old system of small, low-tech farming is becoming less viable as large corporate farms increase crop yields on limited farmland for a growing population.

- **Virtual personal assistants:** Very smart computer programs that monitor e-mail, faxes, and phone calls will be able to take over routine tasks, such as writing a letter, retrieving a file, making a phone call, or screening requests. Acting like a secretary, a person's virtual assistant could substitute for a person at meetings or in dealing with routine actions.

- **Genetically altered organisms:** A convergence of biotechnology and agriculture is creating a new field of life sciences. Plant seeds can be genetically modified to produce more needed vitamins or to be less attractive to pests and more able to survive. Animals (including people) could be similarly modified for desirable characteristics and to eliminate genetic disabilities and diseases.

- **Smart, mobile robots:** Robot development has been limited by a lack of sensory devices and sophisticated artificial intelligence systems. Improvements in these areas mean that robots will be created to perform more sophisticated factory work, run errands, do household chores, and assist the disabled.[12]

Trends in the *political–legal* part of the societal environment have a significant impact not only on the level of competition within an industry but also on which strategies might be successful.[13] For example, periods of strict enforcement of U.S. antitrust laws directly affect corporate growth strategy. As large companies find it more difficult to acquire another firm in the same or a related industry, they are typically driven to diversify into unrelated industries.[14] High levels of taxation and constraining labor laws in Western European countries stimulate companies to alter their competitive strategies or find better locations elsewhere. It is because Germany has some of the highest labor and tax costs in Europe that German companies have been forced to compete at the top end of the market with high-quality products or else move their manufacturing to lower-cost countries.[15] Government bureaucracy can create multiple regulations and make it almost impossible for a business firm to operate profitably in some countries. For example, the number of days needed to obtain the government approvals necessary to start a new business vary from only one day in Singapore to 14 in Mexico, 59 in Saudi Arabia, 87 in Indonesia, to 481 in the Congo.[16]

The $66 trillion global economy operates through a set of rules established by the World Trade Organization (WTO). Composed of 153 member nations and 30 observer nations, the WTO is a forum for governments to negotiate trade agreements and settle trade disputes. Originally founded in 1947 as the General Agreement on Tariffs and Trade (GATT), the WTO was created in 1995 to extend the ground rules for international commerce. The system's purpose is to encourage free trade among nations with the least undesirable side effects. Among its principles is trade without discrimination. This is exemplified by its *most-favored nation* clause, which states that a country cannot grant a trading partner lower customs duties without granting them to all other WTO member nations. Another principle is that of lowering trade barriers gradually though negotiation. It implements this principle through a series of rounds of trade negotiations. As a result of these negotiations, industrial countries' tariff rates on industrial goods had fallen steadily to less than 4% by the mid-1990s. The WTO is currently negotiating its ninth round of negotiations, called the Doha Round. The WTO is also in favor of fair competition, predictability of member markets, and the encouragement of economic development and reform. As a result of many negotiations, developed nations have started to allow duty-free and quota-free imports from almost all products from the least-developed countries.[17]

Demographic trends are part of the *sociocultural* aspect of the societal environment. Even though the world's population is growing from 3.71 billion people in 1970 to 6.82 billion in 2010 to 8.72 billion by 2040, not all regions will grow equally. Most of the growth will be in the developing nations. The population of the developed nations will fall from 14% of the total world population in 2000 to only 10% in 2050.[18] Around 75% of the world will live in a city by 2050 compared to little more than half in 2008.[19] Developing nations will continue to have more young than old people, but it will be the reverse in the industrialized nations. For example, the demographic bulge in the U.S. population caused by the baby boom in the 1950s continues to affect market demand in many industries. This group of 77 million people now in their 50s and 60s is the largest age group in all developed countries, especially in Europe. **(See Table 4–2.)** Although the median age in the United States will rise from 35 in 2000 to 40 by 2050, it will increase from 40 to 47 during the same time period in Germany, and it will increase up to 50 in Italy as soon as 2025.[20] By 2050, one in three Italians will be over 65, nearly

TABLE 4–2	Generation	Born	Age in 2005	Number
Current U.S. Generations	WWII/Silent Generation	1932–1945	60–73	32 million
	Baby Boomers	1946–1964	41–59	77 million
	Generation X	1965–1977	28–40	45 million
	Generation Y	1978–1994	11–27	70 million

SOURCE: Developed from data listed in D. Parkinson, *Voices of Experience: Mature Workers in the Future Workforce* (New York: The Conference Board, 2002), p. 19.

double the number in 2005.[21] With its low birthrate, Japan's population is expected to fall from 127.6 million in 2004 to around 100 million by 2050.[22] China's stringent birth control policy is causing the ratio of workers to retirees to fall from 20 to 1 during the early 1980s to 2.5 to one by 2020.[23] Companies with an eye on the future can find many opportunities to offer products and services to the growing number of "woofies" (well-off old folks—defined as people over 50 with money to spend.[24] These people are very likely to purchase recreational vehicles (RVs), take ocean cruises, and enjoy leisure sports, such as boating, fishing, and bowling, in addition to needing financial services and health care. Anticipating the needs of seniors for prescription drugs is one reason the Walgreen Company has been opening a new corner pharmacy every 19 hours![25]

To attract older customers, retailers will need to place seats in their larger stores so aging shoppers can rest. Washrooms need to be more accessible. Signs need to be larger. Restaurants need to raise the level of lighting so people can read their menus. Home appliances need simpler and larger controls. Automobiles need larger door openings and more comfortable seats. Zimmer Holdings, an innovative manufacturer of artificial joints, is looking forward to its market growing rapidly over the next 20 years. According to J. Raymond Elliot, chair and CEO of Zimmer, "It's simple math. Our best years are still in front of us."[26]

Eight current sociocultural trends are transforming North America and the rest of the world:

1. **Increasing environmental awareness:** Recycling and conservation are becoming more than slogans. Busch Gardens, for example, has eliminated the use of disposable styrofoam trays in favor of washing and reusing plastic trays.

2. **Growing health consciousness:** Concerns about personal health fuel the trend toward physical fitness and healthier living. As a result, sales growth is slowing at fast-food "burgers and fries" retailers such as McDonald's. Changing public tastes away from sugar-laden processed foods forced Interstate Bakeries, the maker of Twinkies and Wonder Bread, to declare bankruptcy in 2004. In 2008, the French government was considering increasing sales taxes on extra-fatty, salty, or sugary products.[27] The European Union forbade the importation of genetically altered grain ("Frankenfood") because of possible side effects. The spread of AIDS to more than 40 million people worldwide adds even further impetus to the health movement.

3. **Expanding seniors market:** As their numbers increase, people over age 55 will become an even more important market. Already some companies are segmenting the senior population into Young Matures, Older Matures, and the Elderly—each having a different set of attitudes and interests. Both mature segments, for example, are good markets for the health care and tourism industries; whereas, the elderly are the key market for long-term care facilities. The desire for companionship by people whose children are grown is causing the pet care industry to grow 4.5% annually in the United States. In 2007, for example, 71.1 million households in the U.S. spent $41 billion on their pets—more than the gross domestic product of all but 16 countries in the world.[28]

4. **Impact of Generation Y Boomlet:** Born between 1978 and 1994 to the baby boom and X generations, this cohort is almost as large as the baby boom generation. In 1957, the peak year of the postwar boom, 4.3 million babies were born. In 1990, there were 4.2 million births in Generation Y's peak year. By 2000, they were overcrowding elementary and high schools and entering college in numbers not seen since the baby boomers. Now in its teens and 20s, this cohort is expected to have a strong impact on future products and services.

5. **Declining mass market:** Niche markets are defining the marketers' environment. People want products and services that are adapted more to their personal needs. For example, Estée Lauder's "All Skin" and Maybelline's "Shades of You" lines of cosmetic products are specifically made for African-American women. "Mass customization"—the making

and marketing of products tailored to a person's requirements (Dell for example, and Gateway computers)—is replacing the mass production and marketing of the same product in some markets. Only 10% of the 6,200 magazines sold in the United States in 2004 were aimed at the mass market, down from 30% in the 1970s.[29]

6. **Changing pace and location of life:** Instant communication via e-mail, cell phones, and overnight mail enhances efficiency, but it also puts more pressure on people. Merging the personal computer with the communication and entertainment industries through telephone lines, satellite dishes, and cable television increases consumers' choices and allows workers to leave overcrowded urban areas for small towns and telecommute via personal computers and modems.

7. **Changing household composition:** Single-person households, especially those of single women with children, could soon become the most common household type in the United States. Married-couple households slipped from nearly 80% in the 1950s to 50.7% of all households in 2002.[30] By 2007, for the first time in U.S. history, more than half of women were single.[31] Thirty-eight percent of U.S. children are currently being born out of wedlock.[32] A typical family household is no longer the same as it was once portrayed in *The Brady Bunch* in the 1970s or *The Cosby Show* in the 1980s.

8. **Increasing diversity of workforce and markets:** Between now and 2050, minorities will account for nearly 90% of population growth in the United States. Over time, group percentages of the total United States population are expected to change as follows: Non-Hispanic Whites—from 90% in 1950 to 74% in 1995 to 53% by 2050; Hispanic Whites—from 9% in 1995 to 22% in 2050; Blacks—from 13% in 1995 to 15% in 2050; Asians—from 4% in 1995 to 9% in 2050; American Indians—1%, with slight increase.[33]

   Heavy immigration from the developing to the developed nations is increasing the number of minorities in all developed countries and forcing an acceptance of the value of diversity in races, religions, and life style. For example, 24% of the Swiss population was born elsewhere.[34] Traditional minority groups are increasing their numbers in the workforce and are being identified as desirable target markets. For example, Sears, Roebuck transformed 97 of its stores in October 2004 into "multicultural stores" containing fashions for Hispanic, African-American, and Asian shoppers.[35]

International Societal Considerations. Each country or group of countries in which a company operates presents a unique societal environment with a different set of economic, technological, political–legal, and sociocultural variables for the company to face. International societal environments vary so widely that a corporation's internal environment and strategic management process must be very flexible. Cultural trends in Germany, for example, have resulted in the inclusion of worker representatives in corporate strategic planning. Because Islamic law (*sharia*) forbids interest (*riba*), loans of capital in Islamic countries must be arranged on the basis of profit-sharing instead of interest rates.[36]

Differences in societal environments strongly affect the ways in which a **multinational corporation (MNC)**, a company with significant assets and activities in multiple countries, conducts its marketing, financial, manufacturing, and other functional activities. For example, Europe's lower labor productivity, due to a shorter work week and restrictions on the ability to lay off unproductive workers, forces European-based MNCs to expand operations in countries where labor is cheaper and productivity is higher.[37] Moving manufacturing to a lower-cost location, such as China, was a successful strategy during the 1990s, but a country's labor costs rise as it develops economically. For example, China required all firms in January 2008 to consult employees on material work-related issues, enabling the country to achieve its stated objective of having trade unions in all of China's non-state-owned enterprises. By September 2008, the All-China Federation of Trade Unions had signed with 80% of the largest foreign companies.[38]

To account for the many differences among societal environments from one country to another, consider **Table 4–3**. It includes a list of economic, technological, political–legal, and sociocultural variables for any particular country or region. For example, an important economic variable for any firm investing in a foreign country is currency convertibility. Without convertibility, a company operating in Russia cannot convert its profits from rubles to dollars or euros. In terms of sociocultural variables, many Asian cultures (especially China) are less concerned with the values of human rights than are European and North American cultures. Some Asians actually contend that U.S. companies are trying to impose Western human rights requirements on them in an attempt to make Asian products less competitive by raising their costs.[39]

Before planning its strategy for a particular international location, a company must scan the particular country environment(s) in question for opportunities and threats, and it must compare those with its own organizational strengths and weaknesses. Focusing only on the developed nations may cause a corporation to miss important market opportunities in the developing nations of the world. Although those nations may not have developed to the point that they have significant demand for a broad spectrum of products, they may very likely be on the threshold of rapid growth in the demand for specific products like cell phones. This would be the ideal time for a company to enter this market—before competition is established. The key is to be able to identify the *trigger point* when demand for a particular product or service is ready to boom. See the **Global Issue** boxed highlight for an in-depth explanation of a technique to identify the optimum time to enter a particular market in a developing nation.

Creating a Scanning System. How can anyone monitor and keep track of all the trends and factors in the worldwide societal environment? With the existence of the Internet, it is now possible to scan the entire world. Nevertheless, the vast amount of raw data makes scanning

TABLE 4–3	Some Important Variables in *International* Societal Environments		
Economic	**Technological**	**Political–Legal**	**Sociocultural**
Economic development	Regulations on technology transfer	Form of government	Customs, norms, values
Per capita income	Energy availability/cost	Political ideology	Language
Climate	Natural resource availability	Tax laws	Demographics
GDP trends	Transportation network	Stability of government	Life expectancies
Monetary and fiscal policies	Skill level of workforce	Government attitude toward foreign companies	Social institutions
Unemployment levels	Patent-trademark protection	Regulations on foreign ownership of assets	Status symbols
Currency convertibility	Internet availability	Strength of opposition groups	Lifestyle
Wage levels	Telecommunication infrastructure	Trade regulations	Religious beliefs
Nature of competition	Computer hacking technology	Protectionist sentiment	Attitudes toward foreigners
Membership in regional economic associations, e.g., EU, NAFTA, ASEAN	New energy sources	Foreign policies	Literacy level
Membership in World Trade Organization (WTO)		Terrorist activity	Human rights
Outsourcing capability		Legal system	Environmentalism
Global financial system		Global warming laws	"Sweat shops"
		Immigration laws	Pension plans
			Health care
			Slavery

GLOBAL issue

IDENTIFYING POTENTIAL MARKETS IN DEVELOPING NATIONS

Research by the Deloitte & Touche Consulting Group reveals that the demand for a specific product increases exponentially at certain points in a country's development. Identifying this trigger point of demand is thus critical to entering emerging markets at the best time. A *trigger point* is the time when enough people have enough money to buy what a company has to sell but before competition is established. This can be determined by using the concept of *purchasing power parity (PPP)*, which measures the cost in dollars of the U.S.–produced equivalent volume of goods that an economy produces.

PPP offers an estimate of the material wealth a nation can purchase, rather than the financial wealth it creates as typically measured by Gross Domestic Product (GDP). As a result, restating a nation's GDP in PPP terms reveals much greater spending power than market exchange rates would suggest. For example, a shoe shine costing $5 to $10 in New York City can be purchased for 50¢ in Mexico City. Consequently the people of Mexico City can enjoy the same standard of living (with respect to shoe shines) as people in New York City with only 5% to 10% of the money. Correcting for PPP restates all Mexican shoe shines at their U.S. purchase value of $5. If one million shoe shines were purchased in Mexico last year, using the PPP model would effectively increase the Mexican GDP by $5 million to $10 million. Using PPP, China becomes the world's second-largest economy after the United States, followed by Japan, India, and Germany.

A trigger point identifies when demand for a particular product is about to rapidly increase in a country. Identifying a trigger point can be a very useful technique for determining when to enter a new market in a developing nation. Trigger points vary for different products. For example, an apparent trigger point for long-distance telephone services is at $7,500 in GDP per capita—a point when demand for telecommunications services increases rapidly. Once national wealth surpasses $15,000 per capita, demand increases at a much slower rate with further increases in wealth. The trigger point for life insurance is around $8,000 in GDP per capita. At this point, the demand for life insurance increases between 200% and 300% above those countries with GDP per capita below the trigger point.

....
SOURCE: D. Fraser and M. Raynor, "The Power of Parity," *Forecast* (May/June, 1996), pp. 8–12; "A Survey of the World Economy: The Dragon and the Eagle," Special Insert, *Economist* (October 2, 2004), p. 8; "The Big Mac Index: Food for Thought," *Economist* (May 29, 2004), pp. 71–72.

---

for information similar to drinking from a fire hose. It is a daunting task for even a large corporation with many resources. To deal with this problem, in 2002 IBM created a tool called *WebFountain* to help the company analyze the vast amounts of environmental data available on the Internet. WebFountain is an advanced information discovery system designed to help extract trends, detect patterns, and find relationships within vast amounts of raw data. For example, IBM sought to learn whether there was a trend toward more positive discussions about e-business. Within a week, the company had data that experts within the company used to replace their hunches with valid conclusions. The company uses WebFountain to:

- Locate negative publicity or investor discontent
- Track general trends
- Learn competitive information
- Identify emerging competitive threats
- Unravel consumer attitudes[40]

Scanning the Task Environment

As shown in **Figure 4–1**, a corporation's scanning of the environment includes analyses of all the relevant elements in the task environment. These analyses take the form of individual reports written by various people in different parts of the firm. At Procter & Gamble (P&G), for

FIGURE 4–1
Scanning External
Environment

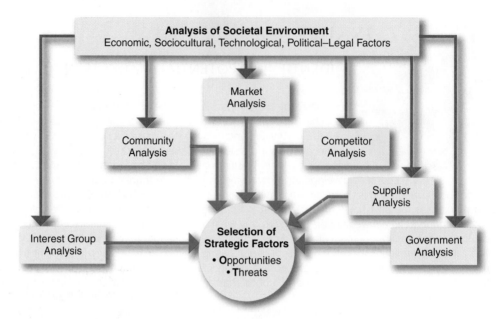

example, people from each of the brand management teams work with key people from the sales and market research departments to research and write a "competitive activity report" each quarter on each of the product categories in which P&G competes. People in purchasing also write similar reports concerning new developments in the industries that supply P&G. These and other reports are then summarized and transmitted up the corporate hierarchy for top management to use in strategic decision making. If a new development is reported regarding a particular product category, top management may then send memos asking people throughout the organization to watch for and report on developments in related product areas. The many reports resulting from these scanning efforts, when boiled down to their essentials, act as a detailed list of external strategic factors.

IDENTIFYING EXTERNAL STRATEGIC FACTORS

The origin of competitive advantage lies in the ability to identify and respond to environmental change well in advance of competition.[41] Although this seems obvious, why are some companies better able to adapt than others? One reason is because of differences in the ability of managers to recognize and understand external strategic issues and factors. For example, in a global survey conducted by the Fuld-Gilad-Herring Academy of Competitive Intelligence, two-thirds of 140 corporate strategists admitted that their firms had been surprised by as many as three high-impact events in the past five years. Moreover, as recently as 2003, 97% stated that their companies had no early warning system in place.[42]

No firm can successfully monitor all external factors. Choices must be made regarding which factors are important and which are not. Even though managers agree that strategic importance determines what variables are consistently tracked, they sometimes miss or choose to ignore crucial new developments.[43] Personal values and functional experiences of a corporation's managers as well as the success of current strategies are likely to bias both their perception of what is important to monitor in the external environment and their interpretations of what they perceive.[44]

This willingness to reject unfamiliar as well as negative information is called *strategic myopia*.[45] If a firm needs to change its strategy, it might not be gathering the appropriate external

FIGURE 4–2
Issues Priority
Matrix

Probable Impact on Corporation

	High	Medium	Low
High	High Priority	High Priority	Medium Priority
Medium	High Priority	Medium Priority	Low Priority
Low	Medium Priority	Low Priority	Low Priority

Probability of Occurrence

SOURCE: *Reprinted from* Long-Range Planning, *Vol. 17, No. 3, 1984, Campbell, "Foresight Activities in the U.S.A.: Time for a Re-Assessment?" pp. 46. Copyright © 1984 with permission from Elsevier.*

information to change strategies successfully. For example, when Daniel Hesse became CEO of Sprint Nextel in December 2007, he assumed that improving customer service would be one of his biggest challenges. He quickly discovered that none of the current Sprint Nextel executives were even thinking about the topic. "We weren't talking about the customer when I first joined," said Hesse. "Now this is the No. 1 priority of the company."[46]

One way to identify and analyze developments in the external environment is to use the **issues priority matrix** (see **Figure 4–2**) as follows:

1. Identify a number of likely trends emerging in the natural, societal, and task environments. These are strategic environmental issues—those important trends that, if they occur, determine what the industry or the world will look like in the near future.

2. Assess the probability of these trends actually occurring, from low to medium to high.

3. Attempt to ascertain the likely impact (from low to high) of each of these trends on the corporation being examined.

A corporation's *external strategic factors* are the key environmental trends that are judged to have both a medium to high probability of occurrence and a medium to high probability of impact on the corporation. The issues priority matrix can then be used to help managers decide which environmental trends should be merely scanned (low priority) and which should be monitored as strategic factors (high priority). Those environmental trends judged to be a corporation's strategic factors are then categorized as opportunities and threats and are included in strategy formulation.

4.2 Industry Analysis: Analyzing the Task Environment

An **industry** is a group of firms that produces a similar product or service, such as soft drinks or financial services. An examination of the important stakeholder groups, such as suppliers and customers, in a particular corporation's task environment is a part of industry analysis.

PORTER'S APPROACH TO INDUSTRY ANALYSIS

Michael Porter, an authority on competitive strategy, contends that a corporation is most concerned with the intensity of competition within its industry. The level of this intensity is determined by basic competitive forces, as depicted in **Figure 4–3.** "The collective strength of these forces," he contends, "determines the ultimate profit potential in the industry, where profit potential is measured in terms of long-run return on invested capital."[47] In carefully scanning its industry, a corporation must assess the importance to its success of each of six forces: threat of new entrants, rivalry among existing firms, threat of substitute products or services, bargaining power of buyers, bargaining power of suppliers, and relative power of other stakeholders.[48] The stronger each of these forces, the more limited companies are in their ability to raise prices and earn greater profits. Although Porter mentions only five forces, a sixth—other stakeholders—is added here to reflect the power that governments, local communities, and other groups from the task environment wield over industry activities.

Using the model in **Figure 4–3,** a high force can be regarded as a threat because it is likely to reduce profits. A low force, in contrast, can be viewed as an opportunity because it may allow the company to earn greater profits. In the short run, these forces act as constraints on a company's activities. In the long run, however, it may be possible for a company, through its choice of strategy, to change the strength of one or more of the forces to the company's advantage. For example, Dell's early use of the Internet to market its computers was an effective way to negate the bargaining power of distributors in the PC industry.

A strategist can analyze any industry by rating each competitive force as high, medium, or low in strength. For example, the global athletic shoe industry could be rated as follows:

FIGURE 4–3
Forces Driving Industry Competition

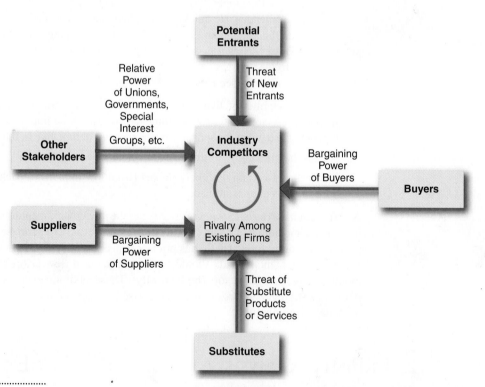

rivalry is high (Nike, Reebok, New Balance, Converse, and Adidas are strong competitors worldwide), threat of potential entrants is low (the industry has reached maturity/sales growth rate has slowed), threat of substitutes is low (other shoes don't provide support for sports activities), bargaining power of suppliers is medium but rising (suppliers in Asian countries are increasing in size and ability), bargaining power of buyers is medium but increasing (prices are falling as the low-priced shoe market has grown to be half of the U.S. branded athletic shoe market), and threat of other stakeholders is medium to high (government regulations and human rights concerns are growing). Based on current trends in each of these competitive forces, the industry's level of competitive intensity will continue to be high—meaning that sales increases and profit margins should continue to be modest for the industry as a whole.[49]

Threat of New Entrants

New entrants to an industry typically bring to it new capacity, a desire to gain market share, and substantial resources. They are, therefore, threats to an established corporation. The threat of entry depends on the presence of entry barriers and the reaction that can be expected from existing competitors. An **entry barrier** is an obstruction that makes it difficult for a company to enter an industry. For example, no new domestic automobile companies have been successfully established in the United States since the 1930s because of the high capital requirements to build production facilities and to develop a dealer distribution network. Some of the possible barriers to entry are:

- **Economies of scale:** Scale economies in the production and sale of microprocessors, for example, gave Intel a significant cost advantage over any new rival.
- **Product differentiation:** Corporations such as Procter & Gamble and General Mills, which manufacture products such as Tide and Cheerios, create high entry barriers through their high levels of advertising and promotion.
- **Capital requirements:** The need to invest huge financial resources in manufacturing facilities in order to produce large commercial airplanes creates a significant barrier to entry to any competitor for Boeing and Airbus.
- **Switching costs:** Once a software program such as Excel or Word becomes established in an office, office managers are very reluctant to switch to a new program because of the high training costs.
- **Access to distribution channels:** Small entrepreneurs often have difficulty obtaining supermarket shelf space for their goods because large retailers charge for space on their shelves and give priority to the established firms who can pay for the advertising needed to generate high customer demand.
- **Cost disadvantages independent of size:** Once a new product earns sufficient market share to be accepted as the *standard* for that type of product, the maker has a key advantage. Microsoft's development of the first widely adopted operating system (MS-DOS) for the IBM-type personal computer gave it a significant competitive advantage over potential competitors. Its introduction of Windows helped to cement that advantage so that the Microsoft operating system is now on more than 90% of personal computers worldwide.
- **Government policy:** Governments can limit entry into an industry through licensing requirements by restricting access to raw materials, such as oil-drilling sites in protected areas.

Rivalry Among Existing Firms

In most industries, corporations are mutually dependent. A competitive move by one firm can be expected to have a noticeable effect on its competitors and thus may cause retaliation. For example, the entry by mail order companies such as Dell and Gateway into a PC industry previously dominated by IBM, Apple, and Compaq increased the level of competitive activity to such an extent that any price reduction or new product introduction was quickly followed by similar moves from other PC makers. The same is true of prices in the United States airline industry. According to Porter, intense rivalry is related to the presence of several factors, including:

- **Number of competitors:** When competitors are few and roughly equal in size, such as in the auto and major home appliance industries, they watch each other carefully to make sure that they match any move by another firm with an equal countermove.

- **Rate of industry growth:** Any slowing in passenger traffic tends to set off price wars in the airline industry because the only path to growth is to take sales away from a competitor.

- **Product or service characteristics:** A product can be very unique, with many qualities differentiating it from others of its kind or it may be a *commodity*, a product whose characteristics are the same, regardless of who sells it. For example, most people choose a gas station based on location and pricing because they view gasoline as a commodity.

- **Amount of fixed costs:** Because airlines must fly their planes on a schedule, regardless of the number of paying passengers for any one flight, they offer cheap standby fares whenever a plane has empty seats.

- **Capacity:** If the only way a manufacturer can increase capacity is in a large increment by building a new plant (as in the paper industry), it will run that new plant at full capacity to keep its unit costs as low as possible—thus producing so much that the selling price falls throughout the industry.

- **Height of exit barriers: Exit barriers** keep a company from leaving an industry. The brewing industry, for example, has a low percentage of companies that voluntarily leave the industry because breweries are specialized assets with few uses except for making beer.

- **Diversity of rivals:** Rivals that have very different ideas of how to compete are likely to cross paths often and unknowingly challenge each other's position. This happens often in the retail clothing industry when a number of retailers open outlets in the same location—thus taking sales away from each other. This is also likely to happen in some countries or regions when multinational corporations compete in an increasingly global economy.

Threat of Substitute Products or Services

A **substitute product** is a product that appears to be different but can satisfy the same need as another product. For example, e-mail is a substitute for the fax, Nutrasweet is a substitute for sugar, the Internet is a substitute for video stores, and bottled water is a substitute for a cola. According to Porter, "Substitutes limit the potential returns of an industry by placing a ceiling on the prices firms in the industry can profitably charge."[50] To the extent that switching costs are low, substitutes may have a strong effect on an industry. Tea can be considered a substitute for coffee. If the price of coffee goes up high enough, coffee drinkers will slowly begin switching to tea. The price of tea thus puts a price ceiling on the price of coffee. Sometimes a difficult task, the identification of possible substitute products or services means searching for products or services that can perform the same function, even though they have a different appearance and may not appear to be easily substitutable.

Bargaining Power of Buyers

Buyers affect an industry through their ability to force down prices, bargain for higher quality or more services, and play competitors against each other. A buyer or a group of buyers is powerful if some of the following factors hold true:

- A buyer purchases a large proportion of the seller's product or service (for example, oil filters purchased by a major auto maker).

- A buyer has the potential to integrate backward by producing the product itself (for example, a newspaper chain could make its own paper).

- Alternative suppliers are plentiful because the product is standard or undifferentiated (for example, motorists can choose among many gas stations).

- Changing suppliers costs very little (for example, office supplies are easy to find).

- The purchased product represents a high percentage of a buyer's costs, thus providing an incentive to shop around for a lower price (for example, gasoline purchased for resale by convenience stores makes up half their total costs).

- A buyer earns low profits and is thus very sensitive to costs and service differences (for example, grocery stores have very small margins).

- The purchased product is unimportant to the final quality or price of a buyer's products or services and thus can be easily substituted without affecting the final product adversely (for example, electric wire bought for use in lamps).

Bargaining Power of Suppliers

Suppliers can affect an industry through their ability to raise prices or reduce the quality of purchased goods and services. A supplier or supplier group is powerful if some of the following factors apply:

- The supplier industry is dominated by a few companies, but it sells to many (for example, the petroleum industry).

- Its product or service is unique and/or it has built up switching costs (for example, word processing software).

- Substitutes are not readily available (for example, electricity).

- Suppliers are able to integrate forward and compete directly with their present customers (for example, a microprocessor producer such as Intel can make PCs).

- A purchasing industry buys only a small portion of the supplier group's goods and services and is thus unimportant to the supplier (for example, sales of lawn mower tires are less important to the tire industry than are sales of auto tires).

Relative Power of Other Stakeholders

A sixth force should be added to Porter's list to include a variety of stakeholder groups from the task environment. Some of these groups are governments (if not explicitly included elsewhere), local communities, creditors (if not included with suppliers), trade associations, special-interest groups, unions (if not included with suppliers), shareholders, and complementors. According to Andy Grove, Chairman and past CEO of Intel, a **complementor** is a company (e.g., Microsoft) or an industry whose product works well with a firm's (e.g., Intel's) product and without which the product would lose much of its value.[51] An example of complementary industries is the tire and automobile industries. Key international stakeholders who determine many of the international trade regulations and standards are the World Trade Organization, the European Union, NAFTA, ASEAN, and Mercosur.

The importance of these stakeholders varies by industry. For example, environmental groups in Maine, Michigan, Oregon, and Iowa successfully fought to pass bills outlawing disposable bottles and cans, and thus deposits for most drink containers are now required. This effectively raised costs across the board, with the most impact on the marginal producers who could not internally absorb all these costs. The traditionally strong power of national unions in the United States' auto and railroad industries has effectively raised costs throughout these industries but is of little importance in computer software.

INDUSTRY EVOLUTION

Over time, most industries evolve through a series of stages from growth through maturity to eventual decline. The strength of each of the six forces mentioned earlier varies according to the stage of industry evolution. The industry life cycle is useful for explaining and predicting trends among the six forces that drive industry competition. For example, when an industry is new, people often buy the product, regardless of price, because it fulfills a unique need. This usually occurs in a **fragmented industry**—where no firm has large market share, and each firm serves only a small piece of the total market in competition with others (for example, cleaning services).[52] As new competitors enter the industry, prices drop as a result of competition. Companies use the experience curve (discussed in **Chapter 5**) and economies of scale to reduce costs faster than the competition. Companies integrate to reduce costs even further by acquiring their suppliers and distributors. Competitors try to differentiate their products from one another's in order to avoid the fierce price competition common to a maturing industry.

By the time an industry enters maturity, products tend to become more like commodities. This is now a **consolidated industry**—dominated by a few large firms, each of which struggles to differentiate its products from those of the competition. As buyers become more sophisticated over time, purchasing decisions are based on better information. Price becomes a dominant concern, given a minimum level of quality and features, and profit margins decline. The automobile, petroleum, and major home appliance industries are examples of mature, consolidated industries each controlled by a few large competitors. In the case of the United States major home appliance industry, the industry changed from being a fragmented industry (pure competition) composed of hundreds of appliance manufacturers in the industry's early years to a consolidated industry (mature oligopoly) composed of three companies controlling over 90% of United States appliance sales. A similar consolidation is occurring now in European major home appliances.

As an industry moves through maturity toward possible decline, its products' growth rate of sales slows and may even begin to decrease. To the extent that exit barriers are low, firms begin converting their facilities to alternate uses or sell them to other firms. The industry tends to consolidate around fewer but larger competitors. The tobacco industry is an example of an industry currently in decline.

CATEGORIZING INTERNATIONAL INDUSTRIES

According to Porter, world industries vary on a continuum from multidomestic to global (see **Figure 4–4**).[53] **Multidomestic industries** are specific to each country or group of countries. This type of international industry is a collection of essentially domestic industries, such as

FIGURE 4–4
Continuum
of International
Industries

Multidomestic ⟷ **Global**

Industry in which companies tailor
their products to the specific needs
of consumers in a particular country.
• Retailing
• Insurance
• Banking

Industry in which companies manufacture
and sell the same products, with only minor
adjustments made for individual countries
around the world.
• Automobiles
• Tires
• Television sets

retailing and insurance. The activities in a subsidiary of a multinational corporation (MNC) in this type of industry are essentially independent of the activities of the MNC's subsidiaries in other countries. Within each country, it has a manufacturing facility to produce goods for sale within that country. The MNC is thus able to tailor its products or services to the very specific needs of consumers in a particular country or group of countries having similar societal environments.

Global industries, in contrast, operate worldwide, with MNCs making only small adjustments for country-specific circumstances. In a global industry an MNC's activities in one country are significantly affected by its activities in other countries. MNCs in global industries produce products or services in various locations throughout the world and sell them, making only minor adjustments for specific country requirements. Examples of global industries are commercial aircraft, television sets, semiconductors, copiers, automobiles, watches, and tires. The largest industrial corporations in the world in terms of sales revenue are, for the most part, MNCs operating in global industries.

The factors that tend to determine whether an industry will be primarily multidomestic or primarily global are:

1. *Pressure for coordination* within the MNCs operating in that industry
2. *Pressure for local responsiveness* on the part of individual country markets

To the extent that the pressure for coordination is strong and the pressure for local responsiveness is weak for MNCs within a particular industry, that industry will tend to become global. In contrast, when the pressure for local responsiveness is strong and the pressure for coordination is weak for multinational corporations in an industry, that industry will tend to be multidomestic. Between these two extremes lie a number of industries with varying characteristics of both multidomestic and global industries. These are **regional industries**, in which MNCs primarily coordinate their activities within regions, such as the Americas or Asia.[54] The major home appliance industry is a current example of a regional industry becoming a global industry. Japanese appliance makers, for example, are major competitors in Asia, but only minor players in Europe or America. The dynamic tension between the pressure for coordination and the pressure for local responsiveness is contained in the phrase, "*Think globally but act locally.*"

INTERNATIONAL RISK ASSESSMENT

Some firms develop elaborate information networks and computerized systems to evaluate and rank investment risks. Small companies may hire outside consultants, such as Boston's Arthur D. Little Inc., to provide political-risk assessments. Among the many systems that exist to assess political and economic risks are the Business Environment Risk Index, the Economist Intelligence Unit, and Frost and Sullivan's World Political Risk Forecasts. The Economist Intelligence Unit, for example, provides a constant flow of analysis and forecasts on more than 200 countries and eight key industries. Regardless of the source of data, a firm must develop its own method of assessing risk. It must decide on its most important risk factors and then assign weights to each.

STRATEGIC GROUPS

A **strategic group** is a set of business units or firms that "pursue similar strategies with similar resources."[55] Categorizing firms in any one industry into a set of strategic groups is very useful as a way of better understanding the competitive environment.[56] Research shows that some strategic groups in the same industry are more profitable than others.[57] Because a corporation's structure and culture tend to reflect the kinds of strategies it follows, companies or business units belonging to a particular strategic group within the same industry tend to be strong rivals and tend to be more similar to each other than to competitors in other strategic groups within the same industry.[58]

For example, although McDonald's and Olive Garden are a part of the same industry, the restaurant industry, they have different missions, objectives, and strategies, and thus they belong to different strategic groups. They generally have very little in common and pay little attention to each other when planning competitive actions. Burger King and Hardee's, however, have a great deal in common with McDonald's in terms of their similar strategy of producing a high volume of low-priced meals targeted for sale to the average family. Consequently, they are strong rivals and are organized to operate similarly.

Strategic groups in a particular industry can be mapped by plotting the market positions of industry competitors on a two-dimensional graph, using two strategic variables as the vertical and horizontal axes (See **Figure 4–5**):

1. Select two broad characteristics, such as price and menu, that differentiate the companies in an industry from one another.

2. Plot the firms, using these two characteristics as the dimensions.

3. Draw a circle around those companies that are closest to one another as one strategic group, varying the size of the circle in proportion to the group's share of total industry sales. (You could also name each strategic group in the restaurant industry with an identifying title, such as quick fast food or buffet-style service.)

FIGURE 4–5
Mapping Strategic Groups in the U.S. Restaurant Chain Industry

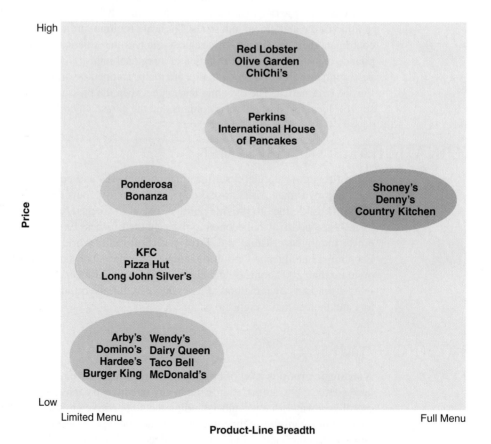

Other dimensions, such as quality, service, location, or degree of vertical integration, could also be used in additional graphs of the restaurant industry to gain a better understanding of how the various firms in the industry compete. Keep in mind, however, that the two dimensions should not be highly correlated; otherwise, the circles on the map will simply lie along the diagonal, providing very little new information other than the obvious.

STRATEGIC TYPES

In analyzing the level of competitive intensity within a particular industry or strategic group, it is useful to characterize the various competitors for predictive purposes. A **strategic type** is a category of firms based on a common strategic orientation and a combination of structure, culture, and processes consistent with that strategy. According to Miles and Snow, competing firms within a single industry can be categorized into one of four basic types on the basis of their general strategic orientation.[59] This distinction helps explain why companies facing similar situations behave differently and why they continue to do so over long periods of time.[60] These general types have the following characteristics:

- **Defenders** are companies with a limited product line that *focus on improving the efficiency of their existing operations*. This cost orientation makes them unlikely to innovate in new areas. With its emphasis on efficiency, Lincoln Electric is an example of a defender.

- **Prospectors** are companies with fairly broad product lines that *focus on product innovation and market opportunities*. This sales orientation makes them somewhat inefficient. They tend to emphasize creativity over efficiency. Rubbermaid's emphasis on new product development makes it an example of a prospector.

- **Analyzers** are corporations that *operate in at least two different product-market areas*, one stable and one variable. In the stable areas, efficiency is emphasized. In the variable areas, innovation is emphasized. Multidivisional firms, such as IBM and Procter & Gamble, which operate in multiple industries, tend to be analyzers.

- **Reactors** are corporations that *lack a consistent strategy-structure-culture relationship*. Their (often ineffective) responses to environmental pressures tend to be piecemeal strategic changes. Most major U.S. airlines have recently tended to be reactors—given the way they have been forced to respond to new entrants such as Southwest and JetBlue.

Dividing the competition into these four categories enables the strategic manager not only to monitor the effectiveness of certain strategic orientations, but also to develop scenarios of future industry developments (discussed later in this chapter).

HYPERCOMPETITION

Most industries today are facing an ever-increasing level of environmental uncertainty. They are becoming more complex and more dynamic. Industries that used to be multidomestic are becoming global. New flexible, aggressive, innovative competitors are moving into established markets to rapidly erode the advantages of large previously dominant firms. Distribution channels vary from country to country and are being altered daily through the use of sophisticated information systems. Closer relationships with suppliers are being forged to reduce costs, increase quality, and gain access to new technology. Companies learn to quickly imitate the successful strategies of market leaders, and it becomes harder to sustain any competitive advantage for very long. Consequently, the level of competitive intensity is increasing in most industries.

Richard D'Aveni contends that as this type of environmental turbulence reaches more industries, competition becomes **hypercompetition**. According to D'Aveni:

> *In hypercompetition the frequency, boldness, and aggressiveness of dynamic movement by the players accelerates to create a condition of constant disequilibrium and change. Market stability is threatened by short product life cycles, short product design cycles, new technologies, frequent entry by unexpected outsiders, repositioning by incumbents, and tactical redefinitions of market boundaries as diverse industries merge. In other words, environments escalate toward higher and higher levels of uncertainty, dynamism, heterogeneity of the players and hostility.*[61]

In hypercompetitive industries such as computers, competitive advantage comes from an up-to-date knowledge of environmental trends and competitive activity coupled with a willingness to risk a current advantage for a possible new advantage. Companies must be willing to *cannibalize* their own products (that is, replace popular products before competitors do so) in order to sustain their competitive advantage. See Strategy Highlight 4.1 to learn how Microsoft is operating in the hypercompetitive industry of computer software. (Hypercompetition is discussed in more detail in **Chapter 6**.)

USING KEY SUCCESS FACTORS TO CREATE AN INDUSTRY MATRIX

Within any industry there are usually certain variables—key success factors—that a company's management must understand in order to be successful. **Key success factors** are variables that can significantly affect the overall competitive positions of companies within any particular industry. They typically vary from industry to industry and are crucial to determining a company's ability to succeed within that industry. They are usually determined by the

STRATEGY highlight 4.1

MICROSOFT IN A HYPERCOMPETITIVE INDUSTRY

Microsoft is a hypercompetitive firm operating in a hypercompetitive industry. It has used its dominance in operating systems (DOS and Windows) to move into a very strong position in application programs such as word processing and spreadsheets (Word and Excel). Even though Microsoft held 90% of the market for personal computer operating systems in 1992, it still invested millions in developing the next generation—Windows 95 and Windows NT. These were soon followed by Windows Me, XP, and Vista. Instead of trying to protect its advantage in the profitable DOS operating system, Microsoft actively sought to replace DOS with various versions of Windows. Before hypercompetition, most experts argued against *cannibalization* of a company's own product line because it destroys a very profitable product instead of harvesting it like a "cash cow." According to this line of thought, a company would be better off defending its older products. New products would be introduced only if it could be proven that they would not take sales away

from current products. Microsoft was one of the first companies to disprove this argument against cannibalization.

Bill Gates, Microsoft's co-founder, chair, and CEO, realized that if his company didn't replace its own DOS product line with a better product, someone else would (such as Linux or IBM's OS/2 Warp). He knew that success in the software industry depends not so much on company size as on moving aggressively to the next competitive advantage before a competitor does. "This is a hypercompetitive market," explained Gates. "Scale is not all positive in this business. Cleverness is the position in this business." By 2008, Microsoft still controlled over 90% of operating systems software and had achieved a dominant position in applications software as well.

....

TABLE 4–4   Industry Matrix

Key Success Factors	Weight	Company A Rating	Company A Weighted Score	Company B Rating	Company B Weighted Score
	1	2	3	4	5	6
Total	1.00		===		===

SOURCE: T. L. Wheelen and J. D. Hunger, *Industry Matrix*. Copyright © 1997, 2001, and 2005 by Wheelen & Hunger Associates. Reprinted with permission.

economic and technological characteristics of the industry and by the competitive weapons on which the firms in the industry have built their strategies.[62] For example, in the major home appliance industry, a firm must achieve low costs, typically by building large manufacturing facilities dedicated to making multiple versions of one type of appliance, such as washing machines. Because 60% of major home appliances in the United States are sold through "power retailers" such as Sears and Best Buy, a firm must have a strong presence in the mass merchandiser distribution channel. It must offer a full line of appliances and provide a just-in-time delivery system to keep store inventory and ordering costs to a minimum. Because the consumer expects reliability and durability in an appliance, a firm must have excellent process R&D. Any appliance manufacturer that is unable to deal successfully with these key success factors will not survive long in the U.S. market.

An **industry matrix** summarizes the key success factors within a particular industry. As shown in **Table 4–4**, the matrix gives a weight for each factor based on how important that factor is for success within the industry. The matrix also specifies how well various competitors in the industry are responding to each factor. To generate an industry matrix using two industry competitors (called A and B), complete the following steps for the industry being analyzed:

1. In **Column 1** (*Key Success Factors*), list the 8 to 10 factors that appear to determine success in the industry.

2. In **Column 2** (*Weight*), assign a weight to each factor, from **1.0** (*Most Important*) to **0.0** (*Not Important*) based on that factor's probable impact on the overall industry's current and future success. **(All weights must sum to 1.0 regardless of the number of strategic factors.)**

3. In **Column 3** (*Company A Rating*), examine a particular company within the industry—for example, Company A. Assign a rating to each factor from **5** (*Outstanding*) to **1** (*Poor*) based on Company A's current response to that particular factor. Each rating is a judgment regarding how well that company is specifically dealing with each key success factor.

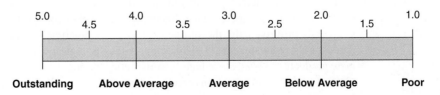

4. In **Column 4** (*Company A Weighted Score*) multiply the weight in **Column 2** for each factor by its rating in **Column 3** to obtain that factor's weighted score for Company A.

5. In **Column 5** (*Company B Rating*) examine a second company within the industry - in this case, Company B. Assign a rating to each key success factor from **5.0** (Outstanding) to **1.0** (Poor), based on Company B's current response to each particular factor.

6. In **Column 6** (*Company B Weighted Score*) multiply the weight in **Column 2** for each factor times its rating in **Column 5** to obtain that factor's weighted score for Company B.

7. Finally, add the weighted scores for all the factors in **Columns 4** and **6** to determine the total weighted scores for companies A and B. **The total weighted score indicates how well each company is responding to current and expected key success factors in the industry's environment.** Check to ensure that the total weighted score truly reflects the company's current performance in terms of profitability and market share. (An average company should have a total weighted score of 3.)

The industry matrix can be expanded to include all the major competitors within an industry through the addition of two additional columns for each additional competitor.

4.3 Competitive Intelligence

Much external environmental scanning is done on an informal and individual basis. Information is obtained from a variety of sources—suppliers, customers, industry publications, employees, industry experts, industry conferences, and the Internet.[63] For example, scientists and engineers working in a firm's R&D lab can learn about new products and competitors' ideas at professional meetings; someone from the purchasing department, speaking with supplier-representatives' personnel, may also uncover valuable bits of information about a competitor. A study of product innovation found that 77% of all product innovations in scientific instruments and 67% in semiconductors and printed circuit boards were initiated by the customer in the form of inquiries and complaints.[64] In these industries, the sales force and service departments must be especially vigilant.

A recent survey of global executives by McKinsey & Company found that the single factor contributing most to the increasing competitive intensity in their industries was the improved capabilities of competitors.[65] Yet, without competitive intelligence, companies run the risk of flying blind in the marketplace. In a 2008 survey of global executives, the majority revealed that their companies typically learned about a competitor's price change or significant innovation too late to respond before it was introduced into the market.[66] According to work by Ryall, firms can have competitive advantages simply because their rivals have erroneous beliefs about them.[67] This is why competitive intelligence has become an important part of environmental scanning in most companies.

Competitive intelligence is a formal program of gathering information on a company's competitors. Often called *business intelligence*, it is one of the fastest growing fields within strategic management. Research indicates that there is a strong association between corporate performance and competitive intelligence activities.[68] According to a survey of competitive intelligence professionals, the primary reasons for practicing competitive intelligence are to build industry awareness (90.6%), support the strategic planning process (79.2%), develop new products (73.6%), and create new marketing strategies and tactics.[69] As early as the 1990s, 78% of large U.S. corporations conducted competitive intelligence activities.[70] In about a third of the firms, the competitive/business intelligence function is housed in its own unit, with the remainder being housed within marketing, strategic planning, information services, business development (merger & acquisitions), product development, or other units.[71] According to a

2007 survey of 141 large American corporations, spending on competitive intelligence activities was rising from $1 billion in 2007 to $10 billion by 2012.[72] At General Mills, for example, all employees have been trained to recognize and tap sources of competitive information. Janitors no longer simply place orders with suppliers of cleaning materials; they also ask about relevant practices at competing firms!

SOURCES OF COMPETITIVE INTELLIGENCE

Most corporations use outside organizations to provide them with environmental data. Firms such as A. C. Nielsen Co. provide subscribers with bimonthly data on brand share, retail prices, percentages of stores stocking an item, and percentages of stock-out stores. Strategists can use this data to spot regional and national trends as well as to assess market share. Information on market conditions, government regulations, industry competitors, and new products can be bought from "information brokers" such as Market Research.com (Findex), LexisNexis (company and country analyses), and Finsbury Data Services. Company and industry profiles are generally available from the Hoover's Web site, at www.hoovers.com. Many business corporations have established their own in-house libraries and computerized information systems to deal with the growing mass of available information.

The Internet has changed the way strategists engage in environmental scanning. It provides the quickest means to obtain data on almost any subject. Although the scope and quality of Internet information is increasing geometrically, it is also littered with "noise," misinformation, and utter nonsense. For example, a number of corporate Web sites are sending unwanted guests to specially constructed bogus Web sites.[73] Unlike the library, the Internet lacks the tight bibliographic control standards that exist in the print world. There is no ISBN or Dewey Decimal System to identify, search, and retrieve a document. Many Web documents lack the name of the author and the date of publication. A Web page providing useful information may be accessible on the Web one day and gone the next. Unhappy ex-employees, far-out environmentalists, and prank-prone hackers create "blog" Web sites to attack and discredit an otherwise reputable corporation. Rumors with no basis in fact are spread via chat rooms and personal Web sites. This creates a serious problem for researchers. How can one evaluate the information found on the Internet? For a way to evaluate intelligence information, see Strategy Highlight 4.2.

Some companies choose to use industrial espionage or other intelligence-gathering techniques to get their information straight from their competitors. According to a survey by the American Society for Industrial Security, PricewaterhouseCoopers, and the United States Chamber of Commerce, Fortune 1000 companies lost an estimated $59 billion in one year alone due to the theft of trade secrets.[74] By using current or former competitors' employees and private contractors, some firms attempt to steal trade secrets, technology, business plans, and pricing strategies. For example, Avon Products hired private investigators to retrieve from a public dumpster documents (some of them shredded) that Mary Kay Corporation had thrown away. Oracle Corporation also hired detectives to obtain the trash of a think tank that had defended the pricing practices of its rival Microsoft. Studies reveal that 32% of the trash typically found next to copy machines contains confidential company data, in addition to personal data (29%) and gossip (39%).[75] Even P&G, which defends itself like a fortress from information leaks, is vulnerable. A competitor was able to learn the precise launch date of a concentrated laundry detergent in Europe when one of its people visited the factory where machinery was being made. Simply asking a few questions about what a certain machine did, whom it was for, and when it would be delivered was all that was necessary.

Some of the firms providing investigatory services are Kroll Inc. with 4,000 employees in 25 countries, Fairfax, Security Outsourcing Solutions, Trident Group, and Diligence Inc.[76] Trident, for example, specializes in helping American companies enter the Russian market and

STRATEGY highlight 4.2

EVALUATING COMPETITIVE INTELLIGENCE

A basic rule in intelligence gathering is that before a piece of information can be used in any report or briefing, it must first be evaluated in two ways. *First*, the source of the information should be judged in terms of its truthfulness and reliability. How trustworthy is the source? How well can a researcher rely upon it for truthful and correct information? One approach is to rank the reliability of the source on a scale from A (extremely reliable), B (reliable), C (unknown reliability), D (probably unreliable), to E (very questionable reliability). The reliability of a source can be judged on the basis of the author's credentials, the organization sponsoring the information, and past performance, among other factors. *Second*, the information or data should be judged in terms of its likelihood of being correct. The correctness of the data may be ranked on a scale from 1 (correct), 2 (probably correct), 3 (unknown), 4 (doubtful), to 5 (extremely doubtful). The correctness of a piece of data or information can be judged on the basis of its agreement with other bits of separately-obtained information or with a general trend supported by previous data. For every piece of information found on the Internet, for example, list not only the URL of the Web page, but also the evaluation of the information from A1 (good stuff) to E5 (bad doodoo). Information found through library research in sources such as Moody's Industrials, Standard & Poor's, or Value Line can generally be evaluated as having a reliability of A. The correctness of the data can still range anywhere from 1 to 5, but in most instances is likely to be either 1 or 2, but probably no worse than 3 or 4. Web sites are quite different.

Web sites, such as those sponsored by the U.S. Securities and Exchange Commission (www.sec.gov), the Economist (www.economist.com), or Hoovers Online (www.hoovers.com) are extremely reliable. Company-sponsored Web sites are generally reliable, but are not the place to go for trade secrets, strategic plans, or proprietary information. For one thing, many firms think of their Web sites primarily in terms of marketing and provide little data aside from product descriptions and distributors. Other companies provide their latest financial statements and links to other useful Web sites. Nevertheless, some companies in very competitive industries may install software on their Web site to ascertain a visitor's web address. Visitors from a competitor's domain name are thus screened before they are allowed to access certain Web sites. They may not be allowed beyond the product information page or they may be sent to a bogus Web site containing misinformation. Cisco Systems, for example, uses its Web site to send visitors from other high-tech firms to a special Web page asking if they would like to apply for a job at Cisco!

is a U.S.-based corporate intelligence firm founded and managed by former veterans of Russian intelligence services, like the KGB.[77]

To combat the increasing theft of company secrets, the United States government passed the Economic Espionage Act in 1996. The law makes it illegal (with fines up to $5 million and 10 years in jail) to steal any material that a business has taken "reasonable efforts" to keep secret and that derives its value from not being known.[78] The Society of Competitive Intelligence Professionals (www.scip.org) urges strategists to stay within the law and to act ethically when searching for information. The society states that illegal activities are foolish because the vast majority of worthwhile competitive intelligence is available publicly via annual reports, Web sites, and libraries. Unfortunately, a number of firms hire "kites," consultants with questionable reputations, who do what is necessary to get information when the selected methods do not meet SPIC ethical standards or are illegal. This allows the company that initiated the action to deny that it did anything wrong.[79]

MONITORING COMPETITORS FOR STRATEGIC PLANNING

The primary activity of a competitive intelligence unit is to monitor **competitors**—organizations that offer same, similar, or substitutable products or services in the business area in which a particular company operates. To understand a competitor, it is important to answer the following 10 questions:

1. Why do your competitors exist? Do they exist to make profits or just to support another unit?

2. Where do they add customer value—higher quality, lower price, excellent credit terms, or better service?

3. Which of your customers are the competitors most interested in? Are they cherry-picking your best customers, picking the ones you don't want, or going after all of them?

4. What is their cost base and liquidity? How much cash do they have? How do they get their supplies?

5. Are they less exposed with their suppliers than your firm? Are their suppliers better than yours?

6. What do they intend to do in the future? Do they have a strategic plan to target your market segments? How committed are they to growth? Are there any succession issues?

7. How will their activity affect your strategies? Should you adjust your plans and operations?

8. How much better than your competitor do you need to be in order to win customers? Do either of you have a competitive advantage in the marketplace?

9. Will new competitors or new ways of doing things appear over the next few years? Who is a potential new entrant?

10. If you were a customer, would you choose your product over those offered by your competitors? What irritates your current customers? What competitors solve these particular customer complaints?[80]

To answer these and other questions, competitive intelligence professionals utilize a number of analytical techniques. In addition to the previously discussed SWOT analysis, Michael Porter's industry forces analysis, and strategic group analysis, some of these techniques are Porter's four-corner exercise, Treacy and Wiersema's value disciplines, Gilad's blind spot analysis, and war gaming.[81] See **Appendix 4.A** for more information about these competitive analysis techniques.

Done right, competitive intelligence is a key input to strategic planning. Avnet Inc., one of the world's largest distributors of electronic components, uses competitive intelligence in its growth by acquisition strategy. According to John Hovis, Avnet's senior vice president of corporate planning and investor relations:

> *Our competitive intelligence team has a significant responsibility in tracking all of the varied competitors, not just our direct competitors, but all the peripheral competitors that have a potential to impact our ability to create value. . . . One of the things we are about is finding new acquisition candidates, and our competitive intelligence unit is very much involved with our acquisition team, in helping to profile potential acquisition candidates.*[82]

4.4 Forecasting

Environmental scanning provides reasonably hard data on the present situation and current trends, but intuition and luck are needed to accurately predict whether these trends will continue. The resulting forecasts are, however, usually based on a set of assumptions that may or may not be valid.

DANGER OF ASSUMPTIONS

Faulty underlying assumptions are the most frequent cause of forecasting errors. Nevertheless, many managers who formulate and implement strategic plans rarely consider that their success is based on a series of basic assumptions. Many strategic plans are simply based on projections of the current situation. For example, few people in 2007 expected the price of oil (light, sweet crude, also called West Texas intermediate) to rise above $80 per barrel and were extremely surprised to see the price approach $150 by July 2008, especially since the price had been around $20 per barrel in 2002. U.S. auto companies, in particular, had continued to design and manufacture large cars, pick-up trucks, and SUVs under the assumption of gasoline being available for around $2.00 a gallon. Market demand for these types of cars collapsed when the price of gasoline passed $3.00 to reach $4.00 a gallon in July 2008. In another example, many banks made a number of questionable mortgages based on the assumption that housing prices would continue to rise as they had in the past. When housing prices fell in 2007, these "sub-prime" mortgages were almost worthless—causing a number of banks to sell out or fail in 2008. Assumptions like these can be dangerous to your health!

USEFUL FORECASTING TECHNIQUES

Various techniques are used to forecast future situations. They do not tell the future; they merely state what can be, not what will be. As such, they can be used to form a set of reasonable assumptions about the future. Each technique has its proponents and its critics. A study of nearly 500 of the world's largest corporations revealed trend extrapolation to be the most widely practiced form of forecasting—over 70% use this technique either occasionally or frequently.[83] Simply stated, *extrapolation* is the extension of present trends into the future. It rests on the assumption that the world is reasonably consistent and changes slowly in the short run. Time-series methods are approaches of this type; they attempt to carry a series of historical events forward into the future. The basic problem with extrapolation is that a historical trend is based on a series of patterns or relationships among so many different variables that a change in any one can drastically alter the future direction of the trend. As a rule of thumb, the further back into the past you can find relevant data supporting the trend, the more confidence you can have in the prediction.

Brainstorming, expert opinion, and statistical modeling are also very popular forecasting techniques. *Brainstorming* is a non-quantitative approach that requires simply the presence of people with some knowledge of the situation to be predicted. The basic ground rule is to propose ideas without first mentally screening them. No criticism is allowed. "Wild" ideas are encouraged. Ideas should build on previous ideas until a consensus is reached.[84] This is a good technique to use with operating managers who have more faith in "gut feel" than in more quantitative number-crunching techniques. *Expert opinion* is a nonquantitative technique in which experts in a particular area attempt to forecast likely developments. This type of forecast is based on the ability of a knowledgeable person(s) to construct probable future developments based on the interaction of key variables. One application, developed by the RAND Corporation, is the *Delphi technique,* in which separated experts independently assess the likelihoods of specified events. These assessments are combined and sent back to each expert for fine-tuning until agreement is reached. These assessments are most useful if they are shaped into several possible scenarios that allow decision makers to more fully understand their implication.[85] *Statistical modeling* is a quantitative technique that attempts to discover causal or at least explanatory factors that link two or more time series together. Examples of statistical modeling are regression analysis and other econometric methods. Although very useful in the grasping of historic trends, statistical modeling, such as trend extrapolation, is based on historical data. As the patterns of relationships change, the accuracy of the forecast deteriorates.

Prediction markets is a recent forecasting technique enabled by easy access to the Internet. As emphasized by James Surowiecki in *The Wisdom of Crowds*, the conclusions of large groups can often be better than those of experts because such groups can aggregate a large amount of dispersed wisdom.[86] Prediction markets are small-scale electronic markets, frequently open to any employee, that tie payoffs to measurable future events, such as sales data for a computer workstation, the number of bugs in an application, or a product usage patterns. These markets yield prices on prediction contracts—prices that can be interpreted as market-aggregated forecasts.[87] Companies including Microsoft, Google, and Eli Lilly have asked their employees to participate in prediction markets by betting on whether products will sell, when new offices will open, and whether profits will be high in the next quarter. Early predictions have been exceedingly accurate.[88] Intrade.com offers a free Web site in which people can buy or sell various predictions in a manner similar to buying or selling common stock. On May 26, 2008, for example, Intrade.com listed the buying price for democratic presidential candidate Barack Obama as $91.50 compared to $8.00 for Hillary Clinton, and $37.70 for John McCain. Thus far, prediction markets have not been documented for long-term forecasting, so its value in strategic planning has not yet been established. Other forecasting techniques, such as *cross-impact analysis (CIA)* and *trend-impact analysis (TIA)*, have not established themselves successfully as regularly employed tools.[89]

Scenario writing is the most widely used forecasting technique after trend extrapolation. Originated by Royal Dutch Shell, *scenarios* are focused descriptions of different likely futures presented in a narrative fashion. A scenario thus may be merely a written description of some future state, in terms of key variables and issues, or it may be generated in combination with other forecasting techniques. Often called scenario planning, this technique has been successfully used by 3M, Levi-Strauss, General Electric, United Distillers, Electrolux, British Airways, and Pacific Gas and Electricity, among others.[90] According to Mike Eskew, Chairman and CEO of United Parcel Service, UPS uses scenario writing to envision what its customers might need five to ten years in the future.[91] The four Arctic scenarios that began this chapter are an example of scenario writing that should be an input to a transportation company's strategic planning.

An **industry scenario** is a forecasted description of a particular industry's likely future. Such a scenario is developed by analyzing the probable impact of future societal forces on key groups in a particular industry. The process may operate as follows:[92]

1. Examine possible shifts in the natural environment and in societal variables globally.
2. Identify uncertainties in each of the six forces of the task environment (that is, potential entrants, competitors, likely substitutes, buyers, suppliers, and other key stakeholders).
3. Make a range of plausible assumptions about future trends.
4. Combine assumptions about individual trends into internally consistent scenarios.
5. Analyze the industry situation that would prevail under each scenario.
6. Determine the sources of competitive advantage under each scenario.
7. Predict competitors' behavior under each scenario.
8. Select the scenarios that are either most likely to occur or most likely to have a strong impact on the future of the company. Use these scenarios as assumptions in strategy formulation.

4.5 The Strategic Audit: A Checklist for Environmental Scanning

One way of scanning the environment to identify opportunities and threats is by using the Strategic Audit found in **Appendix 1.A** at the end of Chapter 1. The audit provides a checklist of questions by area of concern. For example, Part III of the audit examines the natural, societal, and task environments. It looks at the societal environment in terms of economic, technological, political-legal, and sociocultural forces. It also considers the task environment (industry) in terms of threat of new entrants, bargaining power of buyers and suppliers, threat of substitute products, rivalry among existing firms, and the relative power of other stakeholders.

4.6 Synthesis of External Factors—EFAS

After strategic managers have scanned the societal and task environments and identified a number of likely external factors for their particular corporation, they may want to refine their analysis of these factors by using a form such as that given in **Table 4–5**. Using an **EFAS (External Factors Analysis Summary) Table** is one way to organize the external factors into the generally accepted categories of opportunities and threats as well as to analyze how well a particular company's management (rating) is responding to these specific factors in light of the perceived importance (weight) of these factors to the company. To generate an EFAS Table for the company being analyzed, complete the following steps:

1. In **Column 1 (*External Factors*)**, list the eight to ten most important opportunities and threats facing the company.

TABLE 4–5 External Factor Analysis Summary (EFAS Table): Maytag as Example

External Factors	Weight	Rating	Weighted Score	Comments
1	2	3	4	5
Opportunities				
■ Economic integration of European Community	.20	4.1	.82	Acquisition of Hoover
■ Demographics favor quality appliances	.10	5.0	.50	Maytag quality
■ Economic development of Asia	.05	1.0	.05	Low Maytag presence
■ Opening of Eastern Europe	.05	2.0	.10	Will take time
■ Trend to "Super Stores"	.10	1.8	.18	Maytag weak in this channel
Threats				
■ Increasing government regulations	.10	4.3	.43	Well positioned
■ Strong U.S. competition	.10	4.0	.40	Well positioned
■ Whirlpool and Electrolux strong globally	.15	3.0	.45	Hoover weak globally
■ New product advances	.05	1.2	.06	Questionable
■ Japanese appliance companies	.10	1.6	.16	Only Asian presence in Australia
Total Scores	1.00		3.15	

NOTES:

1. List opportunities and threats (8–10) in Column 1.
2. Weight each factor from 1.0 (Most Important) to 0.0 (Not Important) in Column 2 based on that factor's probable impact on the company's strategic position. **The total weights must sum to 1.00.**
3. Rate each factor from 5.0 (Outstanding) to 1.0 (Poor) in Column 3 based on the company's response to that factor.
4. Multiply each factor's weight times its rating to obtain each factor's weighted score in Column 4.
5. Use Column 5 (comments) for rationale used for each factor.
6. Add the individual weighted scores to obtain the total weighted score for the company in Column 4. This tells how well the company is responding to the factors in its external environment.

SOURCE: Thomas L. Wheelen. Copyright © 1982, 1985, 1987, 1988, 1989, 1990, 1991, 1998, and every year after that. Kathryn E. Wheelen solely owns all of (Dr.) Thomas L. Wheelan's copyright materials. Kathryn E. Wheelen requires written reprint permission for each book that this material is to be printed in. Thomas L. Wheelen and J. David Hunger, copyright © 1991–first year "External Factor Analysis Summary" (EFAS) appeared in this text (4th ed.). Reprinted by permission of the copyright holders.

2. In **Column 2 (*Weight*)**, assign a weight to each factor from **1.0** (*Most Important*) to **0.0** (*Not Important*) based on that factor's probable impact on a particular company's current strategic position. The higher the weight, the more important is this factor to the current and future success of the company. **(All weights must sum to 1.0 regardless of the number of factors.)**

3. In **Column 3 (*Rating*)**, assign a rating to each factor from **5.0** (*Outstanding*) to **1.0** (*Poor*) based on that particular company's specific response to that particular factor. Each rating is a judgment regarding how well the company is currently dealing with each specific external factor.

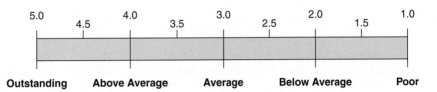

| 5.0 | | 4.0 | | 3.0 | | 2.0 | | 1.0 |
| | 4.5 | | 3.5 | | 2.5 | | 1.5 | |

Outstanding   Above Average   Average   Below Average   Poor

4. In **Column 4 (*Weighted Score*)**, multiply the weight in **Column 2** for each factor times its rating in **Column 3** to obtain that factor's weighted score.

5. In **Column 5 (*Comments*)**, note why a particular factor was selected and how its weight and rating were estimated.

6. Finally, add the weighted scores for all the external factors in **Column 4** to determine the total weighted score for that particular company. The **total weighted** score indicates how well a particular company is responding to current and expected factors in its external environment. The score can be used to compare that firm to other firms in the industry. Check to ensure that the total weighted score truly reflects the company's current performance in terms of profitability and market share. **The total weighted score for an average firm in an industry is always 3.0.**

As an example of this procedure, **Table 4–5** includes a number of external factors for Maytag Corporation with corresponding weights, ratings, and weighted scores provided. This table is appropriate for 1995, long before Maytag was acquired by Whirlpool. Note that Maytag's total weight was 3.15, meaning that the corporation was slightly above average in the major home appliance industry at that time.

End of Chapter SUMMARY

Wayne Gretzky was one of the most famous people ever to play professional ice hockey. He wasn't very fast. His shot was fairly weak. He was usually last in his team in strength training. He tended to operate in the back of his opponent's goal, anticipating where his team members would be long before they got there and fed them passes so unsuspected that he would often surprise his own team members. In an interview with *Time* magazine, Gretzky stated that the key to winning is skating not to where the puck is but to where it is going to be. "People talk about skating, puck handling and shooting, but the whole sport is angles and caroms, forgetting the straight direction the puck is going, calculating where it will be diverted, factoring in all the interruptions," explained Gretzky.[93]

Environmental scanning involves monitoring, collecting, and evaluating information in order to understand the current trends in the natural, societal, and task environments. The information is then used to forecast whether these trends will continue or whether others will take their place. How will developments in the natural environment affect the world? What kind of developments can we expect in the societal environment to affect our industry? What will an industry look like in 10 to 20 years? Who will be the key competitors? Who is likely to fall by the wayside? We use this information to make certain assumptions about the future—assumptions that are then used in strategic planning. In many ways, success in the business world is like ice hockey: The key to winning is not to assume that your industry will continue as it is now but to assume that the industry will change and to make sure that your company will be in position to take advantage of those changes.

ECO-BITS

- The International Panel on Climate Change reports that carbon dioxide emissions are rising faster than its worst-case scenario and that without new government action greenhouse gases will rise 25% to 90% over 2000 levels by 2030.

- China surpassed the United States in carbon emissions in 2006 by producing 6.6 billion tons of carbon dioxide, 24% of the world's annual production of CO_2.

- The total number of people affected by natural disasters has tripled over the past decade to two billion people.

- By 2025, 1.8 billion people could be living in water-scarce areas with the likely result being mass migrations out of these areas.[94]

DISCUSSION QUESTIONS

1. Discuss how a development in a corporation's natural and societal environments can affect the corporation through its task environment.

2. According to Porter, what determines the level of competitive intensity in an industry?

3. According to Porter's discussion of industry analysis, is Pepsi Cola a substitute for Coca-Cola?

4. How can a decision maker identify strategic factors in a corporation's external international environment?

5. Compare and contrast trend extrapolation with the writing of scenarios as forecasting techniques.

STRATEGIC PRACTICE EXERCISE

How far should people in a business firm go in gathering competitive intelligence? Where do you draw the line?

Evaluate each of the following approaches that a person could use to gather information about competitors. For each approach, mark your feeling about its appropriateness:

1 (DEFINITELY NOT APPROPRIATE), 2 (PROBABLY NOT APPROPRIATE), 3 (UNDECIDED), 4 (PROBABLY APPROPRIATE), OR 5 (DEFINITELY APPROPRIATE).

The business firm should try to get useful information about competitors by:

_____ Carefully studying trade journals

_____ Wiretapping the telephones of competitors

_____ Posing as a potential customer to competitors

_____ Getting loyal customers to put out a phony "request for proposal" soliciting competitors' bids

_____ Buying competitors' products and taking them apart

_____ Hiring management consultants who have worked for competitors

_____ Rewarding competitors' employees for useful "tips"

_____ Questioning competitors' customers and/or suppliers

_____ Buying and analyzing competitors' garbage

_____ Advertising and interviewing for nonexistent jobs

_____   Taking public tours of competitors' facilities

_____   Releasing false information about the company in order to confuse competitors

_____   Questioning competitors' technical people at trade shows and conferences

_____   Hiring key people away from competitors

....

SOURCE: Developed from W. A. Jones, Jr., and N. B. Bryan, Jr., "Business Ethics and Business Intelligence: An Empirical Study of Information-Gathering Alternatives," *International Journal of Management* (June 1995), pp. 204–208. For actual examples of some of these activities, see J. Kerstetter, P. Burrows, J. Greene, G. Smith, and M. Conlin, "The Dark Side of the Valley," *Business Week* (July 17, 2000), pp. 42–43.

_____   Analyzing competitors' labor union contracts

_____   Having employees date persons who work for competitors

_____   Studying aerial photographs of competitors' facilities

After marking each of the preceding approaches, compare your responses to those of other people in your class. For each approach, the people marking 4 or 5 should say why they thought this particular act would be appropriate. Those who marked 1 or 2 should then state why they thought this act would be inappropriate.

Go to the Web site of the Society for Competitive Intelligence Professionals (www.scip.org). What does SCIP say about these approaches?

KEY TERMS

competitive intelligence (p. 168)

competitors (p. 170)

complementor (p. 161)

consolidated industry (p. 162)

EFAS Table (p. 174)

entry barrier (p. 159)

environmental scanning (p. 146)

environmental uncertainty (p. 146)

exit barrier (p. 160)

fragmented industry (p. 162)

global industry (p. 163)

hypercompetition (p. 166)

industry (p. 157)

industry analysis (p. 147)

industry matrix (p. 167)

industry scenario (p. 173)

issues priority matrix (p. 157)

key success factor (p. 166)

multidomestic industry (p. 162)

multinational corporation (MNC) (p. 153)

natural environment (p. 147)

new entrant (p. 159)

regional industries (p. 163)

societal environment (p. 147)

STEEP analysis (p. 149)

strategic group (p. 163)

strategic type (p. 165)

substitute product (p. 160)

task environment (p. 147)

NOTES

1. L. W. Brigham, "Thinking about the Arctic's Future: Scenarios for 2040," *The Futurist* (September–October 2007), pp. 27–34.

2. J. B. Thomas, S. M. Clark, and D. A. Gioia, "Strategic Sensemaking and Organizational Performance: Linkages Among Scanning, Interpretation, Action, Outcomes," *Academy of Management Journal* (April 1993), pp. 239–270; J. A. Smith, "Strategies for Start-Ups," *Long Range Planning* (December 1998), pp. 857–872.

3. E. Stephenson and A. Pandit, "How Companies Act on Global Trends: A McKinsey Global Survey," *McKinsey Quarterly* (April 2008).

4. W. E. Stead and J. G. Stead, *Sustainable Strategic Management* (Armonk, NY: M. E. Sharpe, 2004), p. 6.

5. F. Montabon, R. Sroufe, and R. Narasimhan, "An Examination of Corporate Reporting, Environmental Management Practices and Firm Performance," *Journal of Operations Management* (August 2007), pp. 998–1014.

6. P. Lasserre and J. Probert, "Competing on the Pacific Rim: High Risks and High Returns," *Long Range Planning* (April 1994), pp. 12–35.

7. J. J. McGonagle, "Mapping and Anticipating the Competitive Landscape," *Competitive Intelligence Magazine* (March–April 2007), p. 49.

8. M. J. Cetron, "Economics: Prospects for the 'Dragon' and the 'Tiger,'" *Futurist* (July–August 2004), pp. 10–11; "A Less Fiery Dragon," *The Economist* (December 1, 2007), p. 92.

9. "Investing Without Borders: A Different Approach to Global Investing," *T. Rowe Price Report* (Fall 2007), p. 1.

10. S. Hamm, "Cloud Computing Made Clear," *Business Week* (May 5, 2008), p. 59.

11. P. Lorenz, D. Pinner, and T. Seitz, "The Economics of Solar Power," *McKinsey Quarterly* (June 2008), p. 2.

12. W. E. Halal, "The Top 10 Emerging Technologies," *Special Report* (World Future Society, 2000).

13. F. Dobbin and T. J. Dowd, "How Policy Shapes Competition: Early Railroad Foundings in Massachusetts," *Administrative Science Quarterly* (September 1997), pp. 501–529.

14. A. Shleifer and R. W. Viskny, "Takeovers in the 1960s and the 1980s: Evidence and Implications," in *Fundamental Issues in Strategy: A Research Agenda*, edited by R. P. Rumelt, D. E.

Schendel, and D. J. Teece (Boston: Harvard Business School Press, 1994), pp. 403–418.

15. "The Problem with Solid Engineering," *The Economist* (May 20, 2006), pp. 71–73.

16. "Doing Business," *The Economist* (September 9, 2006), p. 98.

17. Web site, *World Trade Organization*, www.wto.org (accessed July 31, 2008).

18. M. J. Cetron and O. Davies, "Trends Now Shaping the Future," *The Futurist* (March–April 2005), pp. 28–29; M. Cetron and O. Davies, "Trends Shaping Tomorrow's World," *The Futurist* (March–April 2008), pp. 35–52.

19. "Trend: Urbane Urban Portraits," *Business Week* (April 28, 2008), p. 57.

20. "Old Europe," *Economist* (October 2, 2004), pp. 49–50.

21. M. J. Cetron and O. Davies, "Trends Now Shaping the Future," *The Futurist* (March–April 2005), p. 30.

22. "The Incredible Shrinking Country," *Economist* (November 13, 2004), pp. 45–46.

23. D. Levin, "Tradition Under Stress," *AARP Bulletin* (July–August 2008), pp. 16–18.

24. J. Wyatt, "Playing the Woofie Card," *Fortune* (February 6, 1995), pp. 130–132.

25. D. Carpenter, "Walgreen Pursues 12,000 Corners of Market," *Des Moines Register* (May 9, 2004), pp. 1D, 5D.

26. M. Arndt, "Zimmer: Growing Older Gracefully," *Business Week* (June 9, 2003), pp. 82–84.

27. "France Considering Raising Tax on Fatty, Sugary Foods," *(Minneapolis) Star Tribune* (August 7, 2008), p. A7.

28. H. Yen, "Empty Nesters Push Growth of Pet Health Care Businesses," *The (Ames, IA) Tribune* (September 27, 2003), p. C8; D. Brady and C. Palmeri, "The Pet Economy," *Business Week* (August 6, 2007), pp. 45–54; "Pampering Your Pet," *St. Cloud (MN) Times* (September 8, 2007), p. 3A.

29. A. Bianco, "The Vanishing Mass Market," *Business Week* (July 12, 2004), pp. 61–68.

30. M. Conlin, "UnMarried America," *Business Week* (October 20, 2003), pp. 106–116.

31. "The Power of One," *Entrepreneur* (June 2007), p. 28.

32. "BGSU Is Leader in Marriage Research," *BGSU Magazine* (Spring 2008), p. 18.

33. N. Irvin, II, "The Arrival of the Thrivals," *Futurist* (March–April 2004), pp. 16–23.

34. "The Trouble with Migrants," *The Economist* (November 24, 2007), pp. 56–57.

35. "Multicultural Retailing," *Arizona Republic* (October 10, 2004), p. D4.

36. "Islamic Finance: West Meets East," *Economist* (October 25, 2003), p. 69.

37. "Giants Forced to Dance," *The Economist* (May 26, 2007), pp. 67–68.

38. "Membership Required," *The Economist* (August 2, 2008), p. 66.

39. J. Naisbitt, *Megatrends Asia* (New York: Simon & Schuster, 1996), p. 79.

40. A. Menon and A. Tomkins, "Learning About the Market's Periphery: IBM's WebFountain," *Long Range Planning* (April 2004), pp. 153–162.

41. I. M. Cockburn, R. M. Henderson, and S. Stern, "Untangling the Origins of Competitive Advantage," *Strategic Management Journal* (October–November, 2000), Special Issue, pp. 1123–1145.

42. L. Fuld, "Be Prepared," *Harvard Business Review* (November 2003), pp. 20–21.

43. H. Wissema, "Driving through Red Lights," *Long Range Planning* (October 2002), pp. 521–539; B. K. Boyd and J. Fulk, "Executive Scanning and Perceived Uncertainty: A Multidimensional Model," *Journal of Management*, Vol. 22, No. 1 (1996), pp. 1–21.

44. P. G. Audia, E. A. Locke, and K. G. Smith, "The Paradox of Success: An Archival and a Laboratory Study of Strategic Persistence Following Radical Environmental Change," *Academy of Management Journal* (October 2000), pp. 837–853; M. L. McDonald and J. D. Westphal, "Getting By with the Advice of Their Friends" CEOs Advice Networks and Firms' Strategic Responses to Poor Performance," *Administrative Science Quarterly* (March 2003), pp. 1–32; R. A. Bettis and C. K. Prahalad, "The Dominant Logic: Retrospective and Extension," *Strategic Management Journal* (January 1995), pp. 5–14; J. M. Stofford and C. W. F. Baden-Fuller, "Creating Corporate Entrepreneurship," *Strategic Management Journal* (September 1994), pp. 521–536; J. M. Beyer, P. Chattopadhyay, E. George, W. H. Glick, and D. Pugliese, "The Selective Perception of Managers Revisited," *Academy of Management Journal* (June 1997), pp. 716–737.

45. H. I. Ansoff, "Strategic Management in a Historical Perspective," in *International Review of Strategic Management*, Vol. 2, No. 1 (1991), edited by D. E. Hussey (Chichester, England: Wiley, 1991), p. 61.

46. S. E. Ante, "Sprint's Wake-Up Call," *Business Week* (March 3, 2008), p. 54.

47. M. E. Porter, *Competitive Strategy* (New York: The Free Press, 1980), p. 3.

48. This summary of the forces driving competitive strategy is taken from Porter, *Competitive Strategy*, pp. 7–29.

49. M. McCarthy, "Rivals Scramble to Topple Nike's Sneaker Supremacy," *USA Today* (April 3, 2003), pp. B1–B2; S. Holmes, "Changing the Game on Nike," *Business Week* (January 22, 2007), p. 80.

50. Porter, *Competitive Strategy*, (New York: The Free Press, 1980), p. 23.

51. A. S. Grove, "Surviving a 10x Force," *Strategy & Leadership* (January/February 1997), pp. 35–37.

52. A fragmented industry is defined as one whose market share for the leading four firms is equal to or less than 40% of total industry sales. See M. J. Dollinger, "The Evolution of Collective Strategies in Fragmented Industries," *Academy of Management Review* (April 1990), pp. 266–285.

53. M. E. Porter, "Changing Patterns of International Competition," *California Management Review* (Winter 1986), pp. 9–40.

54. A. M. Rugman, *The Regional Multinationals: MNEs and Global Strategic Management* (Cambridge: Cambridge University Press, 2005).

55. K. J. Hatten and M. L. Hatten, "Strategic Groups, Asymmetrical Mobility Barriers, and Contestability," *Strategic Management Journal* (July–August 1987), p. 329.

56. J. C. Short, D. J. Ketchen Jr., T. B. Palmer, and G. T. M. Hult, "Firm, Strategic Group, and Industry Influences on Performance," *Strategic Management Journal* (February 2007), pp. 147–167; J. D. Osborne, C. I. Stubbart, and A. Ramaprasad, "Strategic Groups and Competitive Enactment: A Study of Dynamic Relationships Between Mental Models and

Performance," *Strategic Management Journal* (May 2001), pp. 435–454; A. Fiegenbaum and H. Thomas, "Strategic Groups as Reference Groups: Theory, Modeling and Empirical Examination of Industry and Competitive Strategy," *Strategic Management Journal* (September 1995), pp. 461–476; H. R. Greve, "Managerial Cognition and the Mimities Adoption of Market Positions: What You See Is What You Do," *Strategic Management Journal* (October 1998), pp. 967–988.

57. G. Leask and D. Parker, "Strategic Groups, Competitive Groups and Performance Within the U.K. Pharmaceutical Industry: Improving Our Understanding of the Competitive Process," *Strategic Management Journal* (July 2007), pp. 723–745.

58. C. C. Pegels, Y. I. Song, and B. Yang, "Management Heterogeneity, Competitive Interaction Groups, and Firm Performance," *Strategic Management Journal* (September 2000), pp. 911–923; W. S. Desarbo and R. Grewal, "Hybrid Strategic Groups," *Strategic Management Journal* (March 2008), pp. 293–317.

59. R. E. Miles and C. C. Snow, *Organizational Strategy, Structure, and Process* (New York: McGraw-Hill, 1978). See also D. J. Ketchen, Jr., "An Interview with Raymond E. Miles and Charles C. Snow," *Academy of Management Executive* (November 2003), pp. 97–104.

60. B. Kabanoff and S. Brown, "Knowledge Structures of Prospectors, Analyzers, and Defenders: Content, Structure, Stability, and Performance," *Strategic Management Journal* (February 2008), pp. 149–171.

61. R. A. D'Aveni, *Hypercompetition* (New York: The Free Press, 1994), pp. xiii–xiv.

62. C. W. Hofer and D. Schendel, *Strategy Formulation: Analytical Concepts* (St. Paul: West Publishing Co., 1978), p. 77.

63. "Information Overload," *Journal of Business Strategy* (January–February 1998), p. 4.

64. E. Von Hipple, *Sources of Innovation* (New York: Oxford University Press, 1988), p. 4.

65. "An Executive Takes on the Top Business Trends: A McKinsey Global Survey," *McKinsey Quarterly* (April 2006).

66. K. Coyne and J. Horn, "How Companies Respond to Competitors: A McKinsey Global Survey," *McKinsey Quarterly* (August 2008).

67. M. D. Ryall, "Subjective Rationality, Self-Confirming Equilibrium, and Corporate Strategy", *Management Science* (Vol. 49, 2003), pp. 936–949.

68. C. H. Wee and M. L. Leow, "Competitive Business Intelligence in Singapore," *Journal of Strategic Marketing* (Vol. 2, 1994), pp. 112–139.

69. A. Badr, E. Madden, and S. Wright, "The Contributions of CI to the Strategic Decision Making Process: Empirical Study of the European Pharmaceutical Industry," *Journal of Competitive Intelligence and Management* (Vol. 3, No. 4, 2006), pp. 15–35.

70. R. G. Vedder, "CEO and CIO Attitudes about Competitive Intelligence," *Competitive Intelligence Magazine* (October–December 1999), pp. 39–41.

71. D. Fehringer, B. Hohhof, and T. Johnson, "State of the Art: Competitive Intelligence," Research Report of the *Competitive Intelligence Foundation* (2006), p. 6.

72. "Competitive Intelligence Spending 'to Rise Tenfold' in 5 Years," *Daily Research News* (June 19, 2007).

73. S. H. Miller, "Beware Rival's Web Site Subterfuge," *Competitive Intelligence Magazine* (January–March 2000), p. 8.

74. E. Iwata, "More U.S. Trade Secrets Walk Out Door with Foreign Spies," *USA Today* (February 13, 2003), pp. B1, B2.

75. Twenty-nine Percent Spy on Co-Workers," *USA Today* (August 19, 2003), p. B1.

76. M. Orey, "Corporate Snoops," *Business Week* (October 9, 2006), pp. 46–49; E. Javers, "Spies, Lies, & KPMG," *Business Week* (February 26, 2007), pp. 86–88.

77. E. Javers, "I Spy—For Capitalism," *Business Week* (August 13, 2007), pp. 54–56.

78. B. Flora, "Ethical Business Intelligence in NOT Mission Impossible," *Strategy & Leadership* (January/February 1998), pp. 40–41.

79. A. L. Penenberg and M. Berry, *Spooked: Espionage in Corporate America* (Cambridge, MA: Perseus Publishing, 2000).

80. T. Kendrick and J. Blackmore, "Ten Things You Really Need to Know About Competitors," *Competitive Intelligence Magazine* (September–October 2001), pp. 12–15.

81. For the percentage of CI professionals using each analytical technique, see A. Badr, E. Madden, and S. Wright, "The Contributions of CI to the Strategic Decision Making Process: Empirical Study of the European Pharmaceutical Industry," *Journal of Competitive Intelligence and Management* (Vol. 3, No. 4, 2006), pp. 15–35; and D. Fehringer, B. Hohhof, and T. Johnson, "State of the Art: Competitive Intelligence," Research Report of the *Competitive Intelligence Foundation* (2006).

82. "CI at Avnet: A Bottom-Line Impact," *Competitive Intelligence Magazine* (July–September 2000), p. 5. For further information on competitive intelligence, see C. S. Fleisher and D. L. Blenkhorn, *Controversies in Competitive Intelligence: The Enduring Issues* (Westport, CT: Praeger Publishers, 2003); C. Vibert, *Competitive Intelligence: A Framework for Web-Based Analysis and Decision Making* (Mason, OH: Thomson/Southwestern, 2004); and C. S. Fleisher and B. E. Bensoussan, *Strategic and Competitive Analysis* (Upper Saddle River, NJ: Prentice Hall, 2003).

83. H. E. Klein and R. E. Linneman, "Environmental Assessment: An International Study of Corporate Practices," *Journal of Business Strategy* (Summer 1984), p. 72.

84. A. F. Osborn, *Applied Imagination* (NY: Scribner, 1957); R. C. Litchfield, "Brainstorming Reconsidered: A Goal-Based View," *Academy of Management Review* (July 2008), pp. 649–668; R. I. Sutton, "The Truth About Brainstorming," *Inside Innovation*, insert to *Business Week* (September 26, 2006), pp. 17–21.

85. R. S. Duboff, "The Wisdom of Expert Crowds," *Harvard Business Review* (September 2007), p. 28.

86. J. Surowiecki, *The Wisdom of Crowds* (NY: Doubleday, 2004).

87. R. Dye, "The Promise of Prediction Markets: A Roundtable," *McKinsey Quarterly* (April 2008), pp. 83–93.

88. C. R. Sunstein, "When Crowds Aren't Wise," *Harvard Business Review* (September 2006), pp. 20–21.

89. See L. E. Schlange and U. Juttner, "Helping Managers to Identify the Key Strategic Issues," *Long Range Planning* (October 1997), pp. 777–786, for an explanation and application of the cross-impact matrix.

90. G. Ringland, *Scenario Planning: Managing for the Future* (Chichester, England: Wiley, 1998); N. C. Georgantzas and W. Acar, *Scenario-Driven Planning: Learning to Manage Strategic Uncertainty* (Westport, CN: Quorum Books, 1995); L. Fahey and R. M. Randall (eds), *Learning from the Future: Competitive Foresight Scenarios* (New York: John Wiley & Sons, 1998).

91. M. Eskew, "Stick with Your Vision," *Harvard Business Review* (July–August 2007), pp. 56–57.

92. This process of scenario development is adapted from M. E. Porter, *Competitive Advantage* (New York: The Free Press, 1985), pp. 448–470.

93. H. C. Sashittal and A. R. Jassawalla, "Learning from Wayne Gretzky," *Organizational Dynamics* (Spring 2002), pp. 341–355.

94. J. C. Glenn, "Scanning the Global Situation and Prospects for the Future," *The Futurist* (January–February 2008), pp. 41–46.

95. M. E. Porter, *Competitive Strategy: Techniques for Analyzing Industries and Competitors* (New York: The Free Press, 1980), pp. 47–75.

96. M. Treacy and F. Wiersema, *The Discipline of Market Leaders* (Reading, MA: Addison-Wesley, 1995).

97. Presentation by W. A. Rosenkrans, Jr., to the Iowa Chapter of the Society of Competitive Intelligence Professionals, Des Moines, IA (August 5, 2004).

98. B. Gilad, *Early Warning* (New York: AMACOM, 2004), pp. 97–103. Also see C. S. Fleisher and B. E. Bensoussan, *Strategic and Competitive Analysis* (Upper Saddle River, NJ: Prentice Hall, 2003), pp. 122–143.

99. Presentation by W. A. Rosenkrans, Jr., to the Iowa Chapter of the Society of Competitive Intelligence Professionals, Des Moines, IA (August 5, 2004). See also S. M. Shaker and M. P. Gembicki, *War Room Guide to Competitive Intelligence* (New York: McGraw-Hill, 1999).

100. L. Fahey, "Invented Competitors: A New Competitor Analysis Methodology," *Strategy & Leadership*, Vol. 30, No. 6 (2002), pp. 5–12.

101. A. Beurschgens, "Using Business War Gaming to Generate Actionable Intelligence," *Competitive Intelligence Magazine* (January–February 2008), pp. 43–45.

APPENDIX 4.A
Competitive Analysis Techniques

Analytical techniques commonly used in competitive intelligence are *SWOT analysis, Porter's industry forces, ratio analysis*, and *strategic group analysis* (also called *competitive cluster analysis*). In addition to these are Porter's *four-corner exercise*, Treacy and Wiersema's *value disciplines*, and Gilad's *blind spot analysis*. These can be used in a *war game simulation* in which people role-play different competitors and their possible future strategies.

Porter's four-corner exercise involves analyzing a specific competitor's future goals, assumptions, current strategies, and capabilities in order to compile a competitor's response profile. See **Figure 4–6.** Having knowledge of a competitor's goals allows predictions about how likely the competitor is to change strategy and respond to changing conditions. Identifying a competitor's assumptions about itself and the industry can reveal blind spots about how management perceives its environment. Considering a competitor's current strategy and how long it has been in place may indicate whether the company is likely to continue in its current direction. If a strategy is not stated explicitly, one should consider its actions and policies in order to note its implicit strategy. The last step is to objectively evaluate a competitor's capabilities in terms of strengths and weaknesses. The competitor's goals, assumptions, and current strategy influence the likelihood, timing, nature, and intensity of a competitor's reactions. Its strengths and weaknesses determine its ability to initiate or react to strategic moves and to deal with environmental changes.[95]

Treacy and Wiersema's value disciplines involves the evaluation of a competitor in terms of three dimensions: product leadership, operational excellence, and customer intimacy. (See **Figure 4–7**.) After analyzing 80 market-leading companies, Treacy and Wiersema noted that each of these firms developed a compelling and unmatched value proposition on one dimension but was able to maintain acceptable standards on the other two dimensions. *Operationally excellent* companies deliver a combination of quality, price, and ease of purchase that no other can match in their market. An example is Dell Computer, a master of operational excellence. A *product leader* consistently strives to provide its market with leading-edge products or new applications of existing products or services. Johnson & Johnson is an example of a product leader that finds new ideas, develops them quickly, and then looks for ways to improve them. A company that delivers value through *customer intimacy* bonds with its customers and develops high customer loyalty. IBM is an example of a company that pursues excellence in customer intimacy. IBM's current strategy is to provide a total information technology service to its customers so that customers can totally rely on IBM to take care of any Information Technology (IT) problems.[96] According to Wayne Rosenkrans, past president of SCIP, it is possible to mark a spot on each of the three value dimensions shown in **Figure 4–7** for each competitor being analyzed. Then one can draw lines connecting each of the marks, resulting in a triangle that reveals that competitor's overall value proposition.[97]

Gilad's blind spot analysis is based on the premise that the assumptions held by decision makers regarding their own company and their industry may act as perceptual biases or blind spots. As a result, (1) the firm may not be aware of strategically important developments, (2) the firm may inaccurately perceive strategically important developments, or (3) even if the firm is aware of important developments, it may learn too slowly to allow for a timely response. It is important to gather sufficient information about a competitor and its executives to be able to list top management's assumptions about buyers' preferences, the nature of the supply chain, the industry's key success factors, barriers to entry, and the threat appeal of substitutes to customers. One should analyze the industry objectively without regard to these assumptions. Any gap between an objective industry analysis and a competitor's top management assumptions is a potential blind spot. One should include these blind spots when considering how this competitor might respond to environmental change.[98]

FIGURE 4–6
Four-Corner
Exercise: Porter's
Components
of Competitor
Analysis

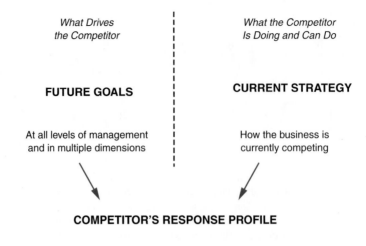

FUTURE GOALS

*What Drives
the Competitor*

At all levels of management
and in multiple dimensions

CURRENT STRATEGY

*What the Competitor
Is Doing and Can Do*

How the business is
currently competing

COMPETITOR'S RESPONSE PROFILE

Is the competitor satisfied with current position?

What likely moves or strategy shifts will the competitor make?

Where is the competitor vulnerable?

What will provoke the greatest and most effective retaliation by the competitor?

ASSUMPTIONS

Held about itself
and the industry

CAPABILITIES

Both strengths
and weaknesses

Rosenkrans suggests that an analyst should first use Porter's industry forces technique to develop the four-corner analysis. Then the analyst should use the four-corner analysis to generate a strategic group (cluster) analysis. Finally, the analyst should include the three value dimensions to develop a blind spot analysis.

These techniques can be used to conduct a war game simulating the various competitors in the industry. Gather people from various functional areas in your own corporation and put them into teams identified as industry competitors. Each company team should perform a complete analysis of the competitor it is role-playing. Each company team first creates starting strategies for its company and presents it to the entire group. Each company team then creates counter-strategies and presents them to the entire group. After all the presentations are complete, the full group creates new strategic considerations to be included as items to monitor in future environmental scanning.[99] Some of the companies that have used war gaming successfully are Kimberly Clark, Baxter Healthcare, Lockheed Martin, Hewlett-Packard, and Dow Corning. If a corporation does not have the expertise needed to run a war game, it can utilize management consultants, like KappaWest, who prepare and facilitate a complete war game simulation.

Some competitive intelligence analysts take the war game approach one step further by creating an "invented" company that could appear in the future but does not exist today. A team brainstorms what type of strategy the invented competitor might employ. The strategy is often based on a new breakthrough product that is radically different from current offerings. Its goals, strategies, and competitive

FIGURE 4–7   Value
Discipline Triad

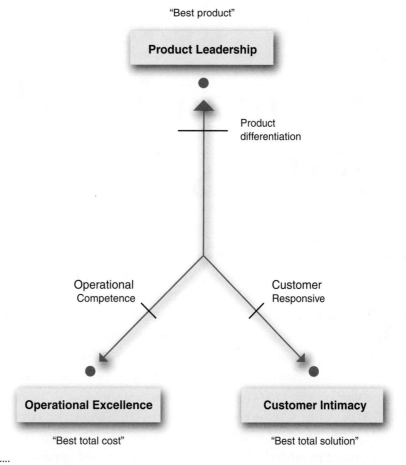

"Best product"

Product Leadership

Product
differentiation

Operational
Competence

Customer
Responsive

Operational Excellence

Customer Intimacy

"Best total cost"

"Best total solution"

SOURCE: From DISCIPLINE OF MARKET LEADERS by Michael Treacy. Copyright © 1997 Michael Treacy.
Reprinted by permission of Perseus Books Group.

posture should be different from any currently being used in the industry. According to Liam Fahey, an authority on competitive intelligence, "the invented competitor is proving to be a spur to bold and innovative thinking."[100] War games are especially useful when (externally) the market is shifting, competitive rules are changing, new competitors are entering the industry, a significant competitor is changing its strategy, a firm's competitive position is weakening, the "uncontrollables" are getting stronger, and/or when (internally) the company is "flying blind," its current strategy is stale or confused, managers are over-confident or arrogant, and/or the firm suffers from a "silo" mentality.[101]

internal scanning: Organizational Analysis

On January 10, 2008, a new automobile from Tata Motors was introduced to the world at the Indian Auto Show in New Delhi. Called the *People's Car*, the new auto was planned to sell for $2,500 in India. Even though many manufacturers were hoping to introduce cheap small cars into India and other developing nations, Tata Motors seemed to have significant advantages that other companies lacked. India's low labor costs meant that Tata could engineer a new model for 20% of the $350 million it would cost in developed nations. A factory worker in Mumbai earned just $1.20 per hour, less than auto workers earned in China. The car was kept very simple. The company would save about $900 per car by skipping equipment that the U.S., Europe, and Japan required for emissions control. The People's Car did not have features like antilock brakes, air bags, or support beams to protect passengers in case of a crash. The dashboard contained just a speedometer, fuel gauge, and oil light. It lacked a radio, reclining seats, or power steering. It came with a small 650 cc engine that generated only 70 horsepower, but obtained 50 to 60 miles per gallon. The car's suspension system used old technology that was cheap, but resulted in a rougher ride than in more expensive cars. More importantly, Tata Motors would save money by using an innovative distribution strategy. Instead of selling completed cars to dealers, Tata planned to supply kits that would then be assembled by the dealers. By eliminating large, centralized assembly plants, Tata could cut the car's retail price by 20%.

Although Tata Motors intended to initially sell the people's car in India and then offer it in other developing markets, management felt that they could build a car that would meet U.S. or European specifications for around $6,000—still a low price for an automobile. Given that Tata Motors was able to acquire Jaguar and Land Rover from Ford later in the year, other auto companies had to admit that Tata was on its way to becoming a major competitor in the industry.[1]

Learning Objectives

After reading this chapter, you should be able to:

- Apply the resource view of the firm to determine core and distinctive competencies
- Use the VRIO framework and the value chain to assess an organization's competitive advantage and how it can be sustained
- Understand a company's business model and how it could be imitated

- Assess a company's corporate culture and how it might affect a proposed strategy
- Scan functional resources to determine their fit with a firm's strategy
- Construct an IFAS Table that summarizes internal factors

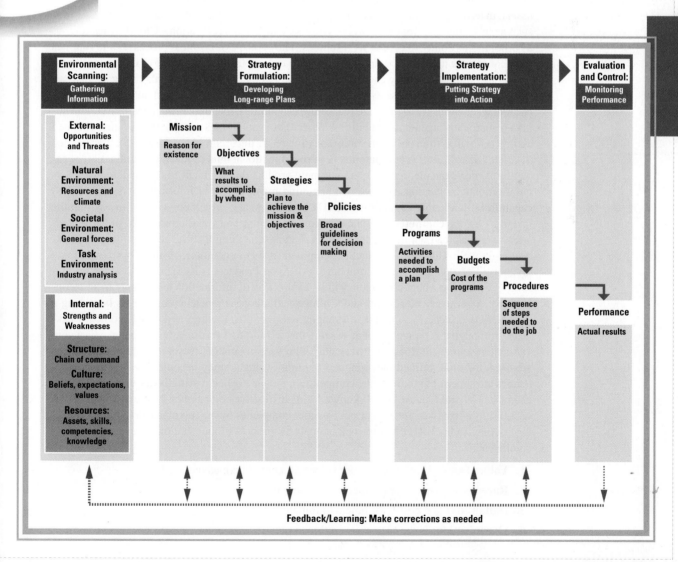

5.1 A Resource-Based Approach to Organizational Analysis

Scanning and analyzing the external environment for opportunities and threats is not enough to provide an organization a competitive advantage. Analysts must also look within the corporation itself to identify *internal strategic factors*—critical *strengths and weaknesses* that are likely to determine whether a firm will be able to take advantage of opportunities while avoiding threats. This internal scanning, often referred to as **organizational analysis**, is concerned with identifying and developing an organization's resources and competencies.

CORE AND DISTINCTIVE COMPETENCIES

Resources are an organization's assets and are thus the basic building blocks of the organization. They include *tangible assets*, such as its plant, equipment, finances, and location, *human assets*, in terms of the number of employees, their skills, and motivation, and *intangible assets*, such as its technology (patents and copyrights), culture, and reputation.[2] **Capabilities** refer to a corporation's ability to exploit its resources. They consist of business processes and routines that manage the interaction among resources to turn inputs into outputs. For example, a company's marketing capability can be based on the interaction among its marketing specialists, distribution channels, and sales people. A capability is functionally based and is resident in a particular function. Thus, there are marketing capabilities, manufacturing capabilities, and human resource management capabilities. When these capabilities are constantly being changed and reconfigured to make them more adaptive to an uncertain environment, they are called *dynamic capabilities*.[3] A **competency** is a cross-functional integration and coordination of capabilities. For example, a competency in new product development in one division of a corporation may be the consequence of integrating management of information systems (MIS) capabilities, marketing capabilities, R&D capabilities, and production capabilities within the division. A **core competency** is a collection of competencies that crosses divisional boundaries, is widespread within the corporation, and is something that the corporation can do exceedingly well. Thus, new product development is a core competency if it goes beyond one division.[4] For example, a core competency of Avon Products is its expertise in door-to-door selling. FedEx has a core competency in its application of information technology to all its operations. A company must continually reinvest in a core competency or risk its becoming a *core rigidity* or *deficiency,* that is, a strength that over time matures and may become a weakness.[5] Although it is typically not an asset in the accounting sense, a core competency is a very valuable resource—it does not "wear out" with use. In general, the more core competencies are used, the more refined they get, and the more valuable they become. When core competencies are superior to those of the competition, they are called **distinctive competencies**. For example, General Electric is well known for its distinctive competency in management development. Its executives are sought out by other companies hiring top managers.[6]

Barney, in his **VRIO framework** of analysis, proposes four questions to evaluate a firm's competencies:

1. **Value:** Does it provide customer value and competitive advantage?

2. **Rareness:** Do no other competitors possess it?

3. **Imitability:** Is it costly for others to imitate?

4. **Organization:** Is the firm organized to exploit the resource?

If the answer to each of these questions is *yes* for a particular competency, it is considered to be a strength and thus a distinctive competence.[7] This should give the company a competitive advantage and lead to higher performance.[8]

It is important to evaluate the importance of a company's resources, capabilities, and competencies to ascertain whether they are internal strategic factors—that is, particular strengths and weaknesses that will help determine the future of the company. This can be done by comparing measures of these factors with measures of (1) the company's past performance, (2) the company's key competitors, and (3) the industry as a whole. To the extent that a resource (such as a firm's cash situation), capability, or competency is significantly different from the firm's own past, its key competitors, or the industry average, that resource is likely to be a strategic factor and should be considered in strategic decisions.

Even though a distinctive competency is certainly considered to be a corporation's key strength, a key strength may not always be a distinctive competency. As competitors attempt to imitate another company's competency (especially during hypercompetition), what was once a distinctive competency becomes a minimum requirement to compete in the industry.[9] Even though the competency may still be a core competency and thus a strength, it is no longer unique. For example, when Maytag Company alone made high-quality home appliances, this ability was a distinctive competency. As other appliance makers imitated Maytag's quality control and design processes, this continued to be a key strength (that is, a core competency) of Maytag, but it was less and less a distinctive competency.

USING RESOURCES TO GAIN COMPETITIVE ADVANTAGE

Proposing that a company's sustained competitive advantage is primarily determined by its resource endowments, Grant proposes a five-step, resource-based approach to strategy analysis.

1. Identify and classify the firm's resources in terms of strengths and weaknesses.

2. Combine the firm's strengths into specific capabilities and core competencies.

3. Appraise the profit potential of these capabilities and competencies in terms of their potential for sustainable competitive advantage and the ability to harvest the profits resulting from their use. Are there any distinctive competencies?

4. Select the strategy that best exploits the firm's capabilities and competencies relative to external opportunities.

5. Identify resource gaps and invest in upgrading weaknesses.[10]

Where do these competencies come from? A corporation can gain access to a distinctive competency in four ways:

- It may be an asset endowment, such as a key patent, coming from the founding of the company. For example, Xerox grew on the basis of its original copying patent.

- It may be acquired from someone else. For example, Whirlpool bought a worldwide distribution system when it purchased Philips's appliance division.

- It may be shared with another business unit or alliance partner. For example, Apple Computer worked with a design firm to create the special appeal of its personal computers and iPods.

- It may be carefully built and accumulated over time within the company. For example, Honda carefully extended its expertise in small motor manufacturing from motorcycles to autos and lawnmowers.[11]

There is some evidence that the best corporations prefer organic internal growth over acquisitions. One study of large global companies identified firms that outperformed their peers on both revenue growth and profitability over a decade. These excellent performers generated value from knowledge-intensive intangibles, such as copyrights, trade secrets, or strong brands, not from acquisitions.[12]

The desire to build or upgrade a core competency is one reason entrepreneurial and other fast-growing firms often tend to locate close to their competitors. They form *clusters*—geographic concentrations of interconnected companies and industries. Examples in the United States are computer technology in Silicon Valley in northern California; light aircraft in Wichita, Kansas; financial services in New York City; agricultural equipment in Iowa and Illinois; and home furniture in North Carolina. According to Michael Porter, clusters provide access to employees, suppliers, specialized information, and complementary products.[13] Being close to one's competitors makes it easier to measure and compare performance against rivals. Capabilities may thus be formed externally through a firm's network resources. An example is the presence of many venture capitalists located in Silicon Valley who provide financial support and assistance to high-tech startup firms in the region. Employees from competitive firms in these clusters often socialize. As a result, companies learn from each other while competing with each other. Interestingly, research reveals that companies with core competencies have little to gain from locating in a cluster with other firms and therefore do not do so. In contrast, firms with the weakest technologies, human resources, training programs, suppliers, and distributors are strongly motivated to cluster. They have little to lose and a lot to gain from locating close to their competitors.[14]

DETERMINING THE SUSTAINABILITY OF AN ADVANTAGE

Just because a firm is able to use its resources, capabilities, and competencies to develop a competitive advantage does not mean it will be able to sustain it. Two characteristics determine the sustainability of a firm's distinctive competency(ies): durability and imitability.

Durability is the rate at which a firm's underlying resources, capabilities, or core competencies depreciate or become obsolete. New technology can make a company's core competency obsolete or irrelevant. For example, Intel's skills in using basic technology developed by others to manufacture and market quality microprocessors was a crucial capability until management realized that the firm had taken current technology as far as possible with the Pentium chip. Without basic R&D of its own, it would slowly lose its competitive advantage to others. It thus formed a strategic alliance with HP to gain access to a needed technology.

Imitability is the rate at which a firm's underlying resources, capabilities, or core competencies can be duplicated by others. To the extent that a firm's distinctive competency gives it competitive advantage in the marketplace, competitors will do what they can to learn and imitate that set of skills and capabilities. Competitors' efforts may range from *reverse engineering* (which involves taking apart a competitor's product in order to find out how it works), to hiring employees from the competitor, to outright patent infringement. A core competency can be easily imitated to the extent that it is transparent, transferable, and replicable.

- **Transparency** is the speed with which other firms can understand the relationship of resources and capabilities supporting a successful firm's strategy. For example, Gillette has always supported its dominance in the marketing of razors with excellent R&D. A competitor could never understand how the Sensor or Mach 3 razor was produced simply by taking one apart. Gillette's razor design was very difficult to copy, partially because the manufacturing equipment needed to produce it was so expensive and complicated.

- **Transferability** is the ability of competitors to gather the resources and capabilities necessary to support a competitive challenge. For example, it may be very difficult for a wine maker to duplicate a French winery's key resources of land and climate, especially if the imitator is located in Iowa.

■ **Replicability** is the ability of competitors to use duplicated resources and capabilities to imitate the other firm's success. For example, even though many companies have tried to imitate Procter & Gamble's success with brand management by hiring brand managers away from P&G, they have often failed to duplicate P&G's success. The competitors failed to identify less visible P&G coordination mechanisms or to realize that P&G's brand management style conflicted with the competitor's own corporate culture.

It is relatively easy to learn and imitate another company's core competency or capability if it comes from **explicit knowledge**, that is, knowledge that can be easily articulated and communicated. This is the type of knowledge that competitive intelligence activities can quickly identify and communicate. **Tacit knowledge**, in contrast, is knowledge that is *not* easily communicated because it is deeply rooted in employee experience or in a corporation's culture.[15] Tacit knowledge is more valuable and more likely to lead to a sustainable competitive advantage than is explicit knowledge because it is much harder for competitors to imitate.[16] As explained by Michael Dell, founder of the Dell computer company, "others can understand what they do, but they can't do it."[17] The knowledge may be complex and combined with other types of knowledge in an unclear fashion in such a way that even management cannot clearly explain the competency.[18] Tacit knowledge is thus subject to a paradox. For a corporation to be successful and grow, its tacit knowledge must be clearly identified and codified if the knowledge is to be spread throughout the firm. Once tacit knowledge is identified and written down, however, it is easily imitable by competitors.[19] This forces companies to establish complex security systems to safeguard their key knowledge.

An organization's resources and capabilities can be placed on a continuum to the extent they are durable and can't be imitated (that is, aren't transparent, transferable, or replicable) by another firm. This **continuum of sustainability** is depicted in **Figure 5–1**. At one extreme are slow-cycle resources, which are sustainable because they are shielded by patents, geography, strong brand names, or tacit knowledge. These resources and capabilities are distinctive competencies because they provide a sustainable competitive advantage. Gillette's razor technology is a good example of a product built around slow-cycle resources. The other extreme includes fast-cycle resources, which face the highest imitation pressures because they are

FIGURE 5–1
Continuum of Resource Sustainability

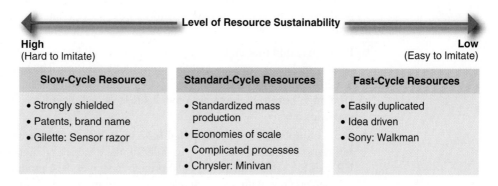

SOURCE: Copyright © 1992 by the Regents of the University of California. Reprinted from the California Management Review, Vol. 34, No. 3. By permission of The Regents.

based on a concept or technology that can be easily duplicated, such as Sony's walkman. To the extent that a company has fast-cycle resources, the primary way it can compete successfully is through increased speed from lab to marketplace. Otherwise, it has no real sustainable competitive advantage.

With its low-cost position and innovative marketing strategy, Tata Motors appeared to have a competitive advantage in making and selling its new People's Car at the lowest price in the industry. Would this low-cost competitive advantage be sustainable? In terms of durability, the car's lack of safety or emissions equipment could be a disadvantage when India and other developing nations begin to require such technology. Given that most developing nations also have low labor costs, Tata's low wages could be easily imitated—probably fairly quickly. For example, the Renault—Nissan auto firm had already formed an alliance in 2008 with Indian motorcycle maker Bajal Auto to launch a $3,000 car in India in 2009.[20] Tata Motor's strategy of selling its new car in kit form was highly imitable, assuming that a competitor's car could be kept simple enough for dealers to assemble easily. Overall, the sustainability of Tata Motors' competitive advantage seemed fairly low, given the fast-cycle nature of its resources.

5.2 Business Models

When analyzing a company, it is helpful to learn what sort of business model it is following. This is especially important when analyzing Internet-based companies. A **business model** is a company's method for making money in the current business environment. It includes the key structural and operational characteristics of a firm—how it earns revenue and makes a profit. A business model is usually composed of five elements:

- Who it serves
- What it provides
- How it makes money
- How it differentiates and sustains competitive advantage
- How it provides its product/service[21]

The simplest business model is to provide a good or service that can be sold so that revenues exceed costs and expenses. Other models can be much more complicated. Some of the many possible business models are:

- **Customer solutions model:** IBM uses this model to make money not by selling IBM products, but by selling its expertise to improve its customers' operations. This is a consulting model.

- **Profit pyramid model:** General Motors offers a full line of automobiles in order to close out any niches where a competitor might find a position. The key is to get customers to buy in at the low-priced, low-margin entry point (Saturn's basic sedans) and move them up to high-priced, high-margin products (SUVs and pickup trucks) where the company makes its money.

- **Multi-component system/installed base model:** Gillette invented this classic model to sell razors at break-even pricing in order to make money on higher-margin razor blades. HP does the same with printers and printer cartridges. The product is thus a system, not just one product, with one component providing most of the profits.

- **Advertising model:** Similar to the multi-component system/installed base model, this model offers its basic product free in order to make money on advertising. Originating in the newspaper industry, this model is used heavily in commercial radio and television. Internet-based firms, such as Google, offer free services to users in order to expose them to the advertising that pays the bills. This model is analogous to Mary Poppins' "spoonful of sugar (content) helps the medicine (advertising) go down."

- **Switchboard model:** In this model a firm acts as an intermediary to connect multiple sellers to multiple buyers. Financial planners juggle a wide range of products for sale to multiple customers with different needs. This model has been successfully used by eBay and Amazon.com.

- **Time model:** Product R&D and speed are the keys to success in the time model. Being the first to market with a new innovation allows a pioneer like Sony to earn high margins. Once others enter the market with process R&D and lower margins, it's time to move on.

- **Efficiency model:** In this model a company waits until a product becomes standardized and then enters the market with a low-priced, low-margin product that appeals to the mass market. This model is used by Wal-Mart, Dell, and Southwest Airlines.

- **Blockbuster model:** In some industries, such as pharmaceuticals and motion picture studios, profitability is driven by a few key products. The focus is on high investment in a few products with high potential payoffs—especially if they can be protected by patents.

- **Profit multiplier model:** The idea of this model is to develop a concept that may or may not make money on its own but, through synergy, can spin off many profitable products. Walt Disney invented this concept by using cartoon characters to develop high-margin theme parks, merchandise, and licensing opportunities.

- **Entrepreneurial model:** In this model, a company offers specialized products/services to market niches that are too small to be worthwhile to large competitors but have the potential to grow quickly. Small, local brew pubs have been very successful in a mature industry dominated by Anheuser-Busch. This model has often been used by small high-tech firms that develop innovative prototypes in order to sell off the companies (without ever selling a product) to Microsoft or DuPont.

- **De Facto industry standard model:** In this model, a company offers products free or at a very low price in order to saturate the market and become the industry standard. Once users are locked in, the company offers higher-margin products using this standard. For example, Microsoft packaged Internet Explorer free with its Windows software in order to take market share from Netscape's Web browser.[22]

In order to understand how some of these business models work, it is important to learn where on the value chain the company makes its money. Although a company might offer a large number of products and services, one product line might contribute most of the profits. For example, ink and toner supplies for Hewlett-Packard's printers make up more than half of the company's profits while accounting for less than 25% of its sales.[23] For an example of a new business model at SmartyPig, see Strategy Highlight 5.1.

5.3 Value-Chain Analysis

A **value chain** is a linked set of value-creating activities that begin with basic raw materials coming from suppliers, moving on to a series of value-added activities involved in producing and marketing a product or service, and ending with distributors getting the final goods into the hands of the ultimate consumer. See **Figure 5–2** for an example of a typical value chain for a manufactured product. The focus of value-chain analysis is to examine the corporation in the context of the overall chain of value-creating activities, of which the firm may be only a small part.

STRATEGY highlight 5.1

A NEW BUSINESS MODEL AT SMARTYPIG

Are you having difficulty saving up for an important purchase like a trip or a car or a big-screen television? Would savings go faster if your friends and family could contribute to your savings account? What if they lived far away from your current bank?

Mike Ferari and Jon Gaskell of Des Moines, Iowa, are co-founders of SmartyPig, an online company that promotes savings through social networking. According to Gaskell, it's the 21st century version of a piggy bank—a new business model for motivating people to save money (instead of going into debt) for specific purchases. It's not a bank, but it works in partnership with West Bank of Des Moines, Iowa to provide an innovative service at its www.smartypig.com Web site.

- It creates an online way for a person to save money (and earn interest) for a specific goal, like a vacation, a big-screen TV, or even a house.

- It merges a savings account with digital social networking so that friends and family can contribute money to

a saver's goal, such as a birthday or Christmas present. They can even view how close the saver is to reaching a goal.

- It creates rewards for reaching a savings goal by offering 5% discounts from merchants, like Best Buy or Circuit City, who offer the product being saved for.

- It offers the option for a saver to collect the money saved on an ATM debit card.

SmartyPig also offers gift cards for a friend or family member to purchase using e-mail or regular mail; cards that are not redeemable until an account has been opened and a goal has been selected.

The company's co-founders spent over a year dealing with regulatory and security issues. "The hurdles to make it work were huge, but it's the neatest savings device I've ever seen," reported Tom Stanberry, Chairman and CEO of SmartyPig's bank partner, West Bank.

....

SOURCE: "Online Company Promotes Savings," Saint Cloud Times (April 27, 2008), p. 11A; A. Kamenetz, "Making Banking Fun," Fast Company (September 2008); Corporate Web sites at www.smartpig.com and www.westbankiowa.com.

Very few corporations include a product's entire value chain. Ford Motor Company did when it was managed by its founder, Henry Ford I. During the 1920s and 1930s, the company owned its own iron mines, ore-carrying ships, and a small rail line to bring ore to its mile-long River Rouge plant in Detroit. Visitors to the plant would walk along an elevated walkway, where they could watch iron ore being dumped from the rail cars into huge furnaces. The resulting steel was poured and rolled out onto a moving belt to be fabricated into auto frames and parts while the visitors watched in awe. As visitors walked along the walkway, they observed an automobile being built piece by piece. Reaching the end of the moving line, the finished automobile was driven out of the plant into a vast adjoining parking lot. Ford trucks would then load the cars for delivery to dealers. Although the Ford dealers were not employees of the company, they had almost no power in the arrangement. Dealerships were awarded by the company and taken away if a dealer was at all disloyal. Ford Motor Company at that time was completely vertically integrated, that is, it controlled (usually by ownership) every stage of the value chain, from the iron mines to the retailers.

FIGURE 5–2
Typical Value Chain for a Manufactured Product

| Raw Materials | Primary Manufacturing | Fabrication | Distributor | Retailer |

INDUSTRY VALUE-CHAIN ANALYSIS

The value chains of most industries can be split into two segments, *upstream* and *downstream* segments. In the petroleum industry, for example, *upstream* refers to oil exploration, drilling, and moving of the crude oil to the refinery, and *downstream* refers to refining the oil plus transporting and marketing gasoline and refined oil to distributors and gas station retailers. Even though most large oil companies are completely integrated, they often vary in the amount of expertise they have at each part of the value chain. Amoco, for example, had strong expertise downstream in marketing and retailing. British Petroleum, in contrast, was more dominant in upstream activities like exploration. That's one reason the two companies merged to form BP Amoco.

An industry can be analyzed in terms of the profit margin available at any point along the value chain. For example, the U.S. auto industry's revenues and profits are divided among many value-chain activities, including manufacturing, new and used car sales, gasoline retailing, insurance, after-sales service and parts, and lease financing. From a revenue standpoint, auto manufacturers dominate the industry, accounting for almost 60% of total industry revenues. Profits, however, are a different matter. Auto leasing has been the most profitable activity in the value chain, followed by insurance and auto loans. The core activities of manufacturing and distribution, however, earn significantly smaller shares of the total industry profits than they do of total revenues. For example, because auto sales have become marginally profitable, dealerships are now emphasizing service and repair. As a result of various differences along the industry value chain, manufacturers have moved aggressively into auto financing.[24] Ford, for example, generated $1.2 billion in profits from financial services in 2007 compared to a loss of $5 billion from automobiles, even though financing accounted for only 10.5% of the company's revenues!

In analyzing the complete value chain of a product, note that even if a firm operates up and down the entire industry chain, it usually has an area of expertise where its primary activities lie. A company's *center of gravity* is the part of the chain that is most important to the company and the point where its greatest expertise and capabilities lie—its core competencies. According to Galbraith, a company's center of gravity is usually the point at which the company started. After a firm successfully establishes itself at this point by obtaining a competitive advantage, one of its first strategic moves is to move forward or backward along the value chain in order to reduce costs, guarantee access to key raw materials, or to guarantee distribution.[25] This process, called *vertical integration,* is discussed in more detail in **Chapter 7**.

In the paper industry, for example, Weyerhauser's center of gravity is in the raw materials and primary manufacturing parts of the value chain as shown in **Figure 5–2**. Weyerhauser's expertise is in lumbering and pulp mills, which is where the company started. It integrated forward by using its wood pulp to make paper and boxes, but its greatest capability still lay in getting the greatest return from its lumbering activities. In contrast, P&G is primarily a consumer products company that also owned timberland and operated pulp mills. Its expertise is in the fabrication and distribution parts of the **Figure 5–2** value chain. P&G purchased these assets to guarantee access to the large quantities of wood pulp it needed to expand its disposable diaper, toilet tissue, and napkin products. P&G's strongest capabilities have always been in the downstream activities of product development, marketing, and brand management. It has never been as efficient in upstream paper activities as Weyerhauser. It had no real distinctive competency on that part of the value chain. When paper supplies became more plentiful (and competition got rougher), P&G gladly sold its land and mills to focus more on the part of the value chain where it could provide the greatest value at the lowest cost—creating and marketing innovative consumer products. As was the case with P&G's experience in the paper industry, it makes sense for a company to outsource any weak areas it may control internally on the industry value chain.

CORPORATE VALUE-CHAIN ANALYSIS

Each corporation has its own internal value chain of activities. See **Figure 5–3** for an example of a corporate value chain. Porter proposes that a manufacturing firm's *primary activities* usually begin with inbound logistics (raw materials handling and warehousing), go through an operations process in which a product is manufactured, and continue on to outbound logistics (warehousing and distribution), to marketing and sales, and finally to service (installation, repair, and sale of parts). Several *support activities,* such as procurement (purchasing), technology development (R&D), human resource management, and firm infrastructure (accounting, finance, strategic planning), ensure that the primary value chain activities operate effectively and efficiently. Each of a company's product lines has its own distinctive value chain. Because most corporations make several different products or services, an internal analysis of the firm involves analyzing a series of different value chains.

The systematic examination of individual value activities can lead to a better understanding of a corporation's strengths and weaknesses. According to Porter, "Differences among competitor value chains are a key source of competitive advantage."[26] Corporate value chain analysis involves the following three steps:

1. **Examine each product line's value chain in terms of the various activities involved in producing that product or service:** Which activities can be considered strengths (core competencies) or weaknesses (core deficiencies)? Do any of the strengths provide competitive advantage and can they thus be labeled distinctive competencies?

2. **Examine the "linkages" within each product line's value chain:** *Linkages* are the connections between the way one value activity (for example, marketing) is performed and the cost of performance of another activity (for example, quality control). In seeking ways for a corporation to gain competitive advantage in the marketplace, the same function can be performed in different ways with different results. For example, quality inspection of 100% of output by the workers themselves instead of the usual 10% by quality control

FIGURE 5–3
A Corporation's
Value Chain

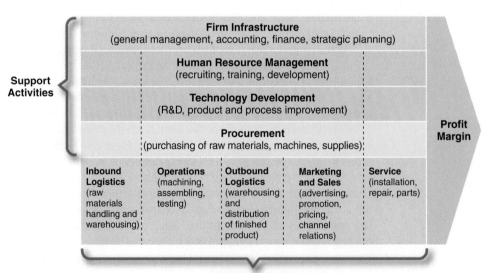

inspectors might increase production costs, but that increase could be more than offset by the savings obtained from reducing the number of repair people needed to fix defective products and increasing the amount of salespeople's time devoted to selling instead of exchanging already-sold but defective products.

3. **Examine the potential synergies among the value chains of different product lines or business units:** Each value element, such as advertising or manufacturing, has an inherent economy of scale in which activities are conducted at their lowest possible cost per unit of output. If a particular product is not being produced at a high enough level to reach economies of scale in distribution, another product could be used to share the same distribution channel. This is an example of **economies of scope**, which result when the value chains of two separate products or services share activities, such as the same marketing channels or manufacturing facilities. The cost of joint production of multiple products can be lower than the cost of separate production.

5.4 Scanning Functional Resources and Capabilities

The simplest way to begin an analysis of a corporation's value chain is by carefully examining its traditional functional areas for potential strengths and weaknesses. Functional resources and capabilities include not only the financial, physical, and human assets in each area but also the ability of the people in each area to formulate and implement the necessary functional objectives, strategies, and policies. These resources and capabilities include the knowledge of analytical concepts and procedural techniques common to each area as well as the ability of the people in each area to use them effectively. If used properly, these resources and capabilities serve as strengths to carry out value-added activities and support strategic decisions. In addition to the usual business functions of marketing, finance, R&D, operations, human resources, and information systems/technology, we also discuss structure and culture as key parts of a business corporation's value chain.

BASIC ORGANIZATIONAL STRUCTURES

Although there is an almost infinite variety of structural forms, certain basic types predominate in modern complex organizations. **Figure 5–4** illustrates three basic **organizational structures**. The conglomerate structure is a variant of divisional structure and is thus not depicted as a fourth structure. Generally speaking, each structure tends to support some corporate strategies over others:

- **Simple structure** has no functional or product categories and is appropriate for a small, entrepreneur-dominated company with one or two product lines that operates in a reasonably small, easily identifiable market niche. Employees tend to be generalists and jacks-of-all-trades. In terms of stages of development (to be discussed in **Chapter 9**), this is a Stage I company.

- **Functional structure** is appropriate for a medium-sized firm with several product lines in one industry. Employees tend to be specialists in the business functions that are important to that industry, such as manufacturing, marketing, finance, and human resources. In terms of stages of development (discussed in **Chapter 9**), this is a Stage II company.

- **Divisional structure** is appropriate for a large corporation with many product lines in several related industries. Employees tend to be functional specialists organized according to product/market distinctions. General Motors, for example, groups its various auto lines into the separate divisions of Saturn, Chevrolet, Pontiac, Buick, and Cadillac. Management

FIGURE 5–4
Basic
Organizational
Structures

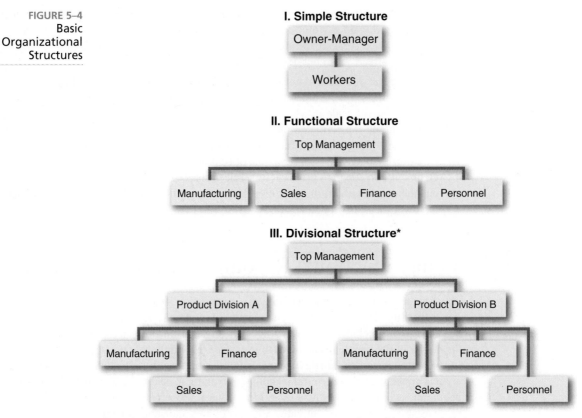

I. Simple Structure

Owner-Manager

Workers

II. Functional Structure

Top Management

Manufacturing   Sales   Finance   Personnel

III. Divisional Structure*

Top Management

Product Division A   Product Division B

Manufacturing   Finance   Manufacturing   Finance

Sales   Personnel   Sales   Personnel

*Strategic Business Units and the conglomerate structure are variants of the divisional structure.

attempts to find some synergy among divisional activities through the use of committees and horizontal linkages. In terms of stages of development (to be discussed in **Chapter 9**), this is a Stage III company.

■ **Strategic business units (SBUs)** are a modification of the divisional structure. Strategic business units are divisions or groups of divisions composed of independent product-market segments that are given primary responsibility and authority for the management of their own functional areas. *An SBU may be of any size or level, but it must have (1) a unique mission, (2) identifiable competitors, (3) an external market focus, and (4) control of its business functions.*[27] The idea is to decentralize on the basis of strategic elements rather than on the basis of size, product characteristics, or span of control and to create horizontal linkages among units previously kept separate. For example, rather than organize products on the basis of packaging technology like frozen foods, canned foods, and bagged foods, General Foods organized its products into SBUs on the basis of consumer-oriented menu segments: breakfast food, beverage, main meal, dessert, and pet foods. In terms of stages of development (to be discussed in **Chapter 9**), this is also a Stage III company.

■ **Conglomerate structure** is appropriate for a large corporation with many product lines in several unrelated industries. A variant of the divisional structure, the conglomerate structure (sometimes called a holding company) is typically an assemblage of legally independent firms (subsidiaries) operating under one corporate umbrella but controlled through the subsidiaries' boards of directors. The unrelated nature of the subsidiaries prevents any attempt at gaining synergy among them. In terms of stages of development (discussed in **Chapter 9**), this is also a Stage III company.

If the current basic structure of a corporation does not easily support a strategy under consideration, top management must decide whether the proposed strategy is feasible or whether the structure should be changed to a more advanced structure such as a matrix or network. (Advanced structural designs such as the matrix and network are discussed in **Chapter 9**.)

CORPORATE CULTURE: THE COMPANY WAY

There is an oft-told story of a person new to a company asking an experienced co-worker what an employee should do when a customer calls. The old-timer responded: "There are three ways to do any job—the right way, the wrong way, and the company way. Around here, we always do things the company way." In most organizations, the "company way" is derived from the corporation's culture. **Corporate culture** is the collection of beliefs, expectations, and values learned and shared by a corporation's members and transmitted from one generation of employees to another. The corporate culture generally reflects the values of the founder(s) and the mission of the firm.[28] It gives a company a sense of identity: "This is who we are. This is what we do. This is what we stand for." The culture includes the dominant orientation of the company, such as R&D at HP, high productivity at Nucor, customer service at Nordstrom, innovation at Google, or product quality at BMW. It often includes a number of informal work rules (forming the "company way") that employees follow without question. These work practices over time become part of a company's unquestioned tradition. The culture, therefore, reflects the company's values.

Corporate culture has two distinct attributes, intensity and integration.[29] *Cultural intensity* is the degree to which members of a unit accept the norms, values, or other culture content associated with the unit. This shows the culture's depth. Organizations with strong norms promoting a particular value, such as quality at BMW, have intensive cultures, whereas new firms (or those in transition) have weaker, less intensive cultures. Employees in an intensive culture tend to exhibit consistent behavior, that is, they tend to act similarly over time. *Cultural integration* is the extent to which units throughout an organization share a common culture. This is the culture's breadth. Organizations with a pervasive dominant culture may be hierarchically controlled and power-oriented, such as a military unit, and have highly integrated cultures. All employees tend to hold the same cultural values and norms. In contrast, a company that is structured into diverse units by functions or divisions usually exhibits some strong subcultures (for example, R&D versus manufacturing) and a less integrated corporate culture.

Corporate culture fulfills several important functions in an organization:

1. Conveys a sense of identity for employees.
2. Helps generate employee commitment to something greater than themselves.
3. Adds to the stability of the organization as a social system.
4. Serves as a frame of reference for employees to use to make sense of organizational activities and to use as a guide for appropriate behavior.[30]

Corporate culture shapes the behavior of people in a corporation, thus affecting corporate performance. For example, corporate cultures that emphasize the socialization of new employees have less employee turnover, leading to lower costs.[31] Because corporate cultures have a powerful influence on the behavior of people at all levels, they can strongly affect a corporation's ability to shift its strategic direction. A strong culture should not only promote survival, but it should also create the basis for a superior competitive position by increasing motivation

GLOBAL issue

MANAGING CORPORATE CULTURE FOR GLOBAL COMPETITIVE ADVANTAGE: ABB VERSUS MATSUSHITA

Zurich-based ABB Asea Brown Boveri AG is a worldwide builder of power plants, electrical equipment, and industrial factories in 140 countries. By establishing one set of multicultural values throughout its global operations, ABB's management believes that the company will gain an advantage over its rivals Siemens AG of Germany, France's Alcatel-Alsthom NV, and the U.S.'s General Electric Company. ABB is a company with no geographic base. Instead, it has many "home" markets that can draw on expertise from around the globe. ABB created a set of 500 global managers who could adapt to local cultures while executing ABB's global strategies. These people are multilingual and move around each of ABB's 5,000 profit centers in 140 countries. Their assignment is to cut costs, improve efficiency, and integrate local businesses with the ABB worldview.

Few multinational corporations are as successful as ABB in getting global strategies to work with local operations. In agreement with the resource-based view of the firm, the past Chairman of ABB, Percy Barnevik stated, "Our strength comes from pulling together. . . . If you can make this work real well, then you get a competitive edge out of the organization which is very, very difficult to copy."

Contrast ABB's globally-oriented corporate culture with the more Japanese-oriented parochial culture of Matsushita Electric Industrial Corporation (MEI) of Japan. Operating under the brand names of Panasonic and Technic,

MEI is the third-largest electrical company in the world. Konosuke Matsushita founded the company in 1918. His management philosophy led to the company's success but became institutionalized in the corporate culture—a culture that was more focused on Japanese values than on cross-cultural globalization. As a result, MEI's corporate culture does not adapt well to local conditions. Not only is MEI's top management *exclusively* Japanese, its subsidiary managers are *overwhelmingly* Japanese. The company's distrust of non-Japanese managers in the United States and some European countries results in a "rice-paper ceiling" that prevents non-Japanese people from being promoted into MEI subsidiaries' top management. Foreign employees are often confused by the corporate philosophy that has not been adapted to suit local realities. MEI's corporate culture perpetuates a cross-cultural divide that separates the Japanese from the non-Japanese managers, leaving the non-Japanese managers feeling frustrated and undervalued. This divide prevents the flow of knowledge and experience from regional operations to the headquarters and may hinder MEI's ability to compete globally.

....

SOURCES: Summarized from J. Guyon, "ABB Fuses Units with One Set of Values," *Wall Street Journal* (October 2, 1996), p. A15 and N. Holden, "Why Globalizing with a Conservative Corporate Culture Inhibits Localization of Management: The Telling Case of Matsushita Electric," *International Journal of Cross Cultural Management*, Vol. 1, No. 1 (2001), pp. 53–72.

and facilitating coordination and control.[32] For example, a culture emphasizing constant renewal may help a company adapt to a changing, hypercompetitive environment.[33] To the extent that a corporation's distinctive competence is embedded in an organization's culture, it will be a form of tacit knowledge and very difficult for a competitor to imitate. The **Global Issue** feature shows the differences between ABB Asea Brown Boveri AG and Matsushita Electric in terms of how they manage their corporate cultures in a global industry.

A change in mission, objectives, strategies, or policies is not likely to be successful if it is in opposition to the accepted culture of a firm. Foot-dragging and even sabotage may result, as employees fight to resist a radical change in corporate philosophy. As with structure, if an organization's culture is compatible with a new strategy, it is an internal strength. But if the corporate culture is not compatible with the proposed strategy, it is a serious weakness. For example, when General Motors created a collaborative effort in 1996 among the three internal units of Saturn, International Operations, and Small Car Group for its proposed Delta Small Car Program, it caused a conflict with the company's long-standing cultural tradition of unit autonomy. GM employees found that they were expected to cooperate with other GM employees who did not share their views regarding vehicle requirements and architecture or of work practices and processes. Significant cultural differences among the three units led to the program being abandoned in 2000.[34]

Corporate culture is also important when considering an acquisition. The merging of two dissimilar cultures, if not handled wisely, can create some serious internal conflicts. Procter & Gamble's management knew, for example, that their 2005 acquisition of Gillette might create some cultural problems. Even though both companies were strong consumer goods marketers, they each had a fundamental difference that led to many, subtle differences between the cultures: Gillette sold its razors, toothbrushes, and batteries to men; whereas, P&G sold its health and beauty aids to women. Art Lafley, P&G's CEO, admitted a year after the merger that it would take an additional year to 15 months to align the two companies.[35]

STRATEGIC MARKETING ISSUES

The marketing manager is a company's primary link to the customer and the competition. The manager, therefore, must be especially concerned with the market position and marketing mix of the firm as well as with the overall reputation of the company and its brands.

Market Position and Segmentation

Market position deals with the question, "Who are our customers?" It refers to the selection of specific areas for marketing concentration and can be expressed in terms of market, product, and geographic locations. Through market research, corporations are able to practice *market segmentation* with various products or services so that managers can discover what niches to seek, which new types of products to develop, and how to ensure that a company's many products do not directly compete with one another.

Marketing Mix

Marketing mix refers to the particular combination of key variables under a corporation's control that can be used to affect demand and to gain competitive advantage. These variables are product, place, promotion, and price. Within each of these four variables are several subvariables, listed in **Table 5–1**, that should be analyzed in terms of their effects on divisional and corporate performance.

TABLE 5–1	Product	Place	Promotion	Price
Marketing Mix Variables	Quality	Channels	Advertising	List price
	Features	Coverage	Personal selling	Discounts
	Options	Locations	Sales promotion	Allowances
	Style	Inventory	Publicity	Payment periods
	Brand name	Transport		Credit items
	Packaging			
	Sizes			
	Services			
	Warranties			
	Returns			

SOURCE: KOTLER, PHILIP, MARKETING MANAGEMENT, 11th edition © 2003, p. 16. Reprinted by Pearson Education, Inc., Upper Saddle River, NJ.

Product Life Cycle

One of the most useful concepts in marketing, insofar as strategic management is concerned, is the **product life cycle**. As depicted in **Figure 5–5**, the product life cycle is a graph showing time plotted against the monetary sales of a product as it moves from introduction through growth and maturity to decline. This concept enables a marketing manager to examine the marketing mix of a particular product or group of products in terms of its position in its life cycle.

Brand and Corporate Reputation

A **brand** is a name given to a company's product which identifies that item in the mind of the consumer. Over time and with proper advertising, a brand connotes various characteristics in the consumers' minds. For example, Disney stands for family entertainment. Ivory suggests "pure" soap. BMW means high-performance autos. A brand can thus be an important corporate resource. If done well, a brand name is connected to the product to such an extent that a brand may stand for an entire product category, such as Kleenex for facial tissue. The objective is for the customer to ask for the brand name (Coke or Pepsi) instead of the product category (cola). The world's 10 most valuable brands in 2007 were Coca-Cola, Microsoft, IBM, GE, Nokia, Toyota, Intel, McDonald's, Disney, and Mercedes-Benz, in that order. According to *Business Week*, the value of the Coca-Cola brand is worth $65.3 billion.[36]

A *corporate brand* is a type of brand in which the company's name serves as the brand. Of the world's top 10 world brands listed previously, all are company names. The value of a corporate brand is that it typically stands for consumers' impressions of a company and can thus be extended onto products not currently offered—regardless of the company's actual expertise. For example, Caterpillar, a manufacturer of heavy earth-moving equipment, used consumer associations with the Caterpillar brand (*rugged, masculine, construction-related*) to market work boots. Thus, consumer impressions of a brand can suggest new product categories to enter even though a company may have no competencies in making or marketing that type of product or service.[37]

A **corporate reputation** is a widely held perception of a company by the general public. It consists of two attributes: (1) stakeholders' perceptions of a corporation's ability to produce quality goods and (2) a corporation's prominence in the minds of stakeholders.[38] A

FIGURE 5–5
Product Life Cycle

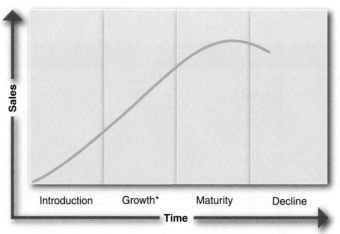

* The right end of the Growth stage is often called Competitive Turbulence because of price and distribution competition that shakes out the weaker competitors. For further information, see C. R. Wasson, *Dynamic Competitive Strategy and Product Life Cycles.* 3rd ed. (Austin, TX: Austin Press, 1978).

good corporate reputation can be a strategic resource. It can serve in marketing as both a signal and an entry barrier. It contributes to its goods having a price premium.[39] Reputation is especially important when the quality of a company's product or service is not directly observable and can be learned only through experience. For example, retail stores are willing to stock a new product from P&G or Anheuser-Busch because they know that both companies market only good-quality products that are highly advertised. Like tacit knowledge, reputation tends to be long-lasting and hard for others to duplicate—thus providing sustainable competitive advantage.[40] It can have a significant impact on a firm's stock price.[41] Research reveals a positive relationship between corporate reputation and financial performance.[42]

STRATEGIC FINANCIAL ISSUES

A financial manager must ascertain the best sources of funds, uses of funds, and control of funds. All strategic issues have financial implications. Cash must be raised from internal or external (local and global) sources and allocated for different uses. The flow of funds in the operations of an organization must be monitored. To the extent that a corporation is involved in international activities, currency fluctuations must be dealt with to ensure that profits aren't wiped out by the rise or fall of the dollar versus the yen, euro, or other currencies. Benefits in the form of returns, repayments, or products and services must be given to the sources of outside financing. All these tasks must be handled in a way that complements and supports overall corporate strategy. A firm's capital structure (amounts of debt and equity) can influence its strategic choices. For example, increased debt tends to increase risk aversion and decrease the willingness of management to invest in R&D.[43]

Financial Leverage

The mix of externally generated short-term and long-term funds in relation to the amount and timing of internally generated funds should be appropriate to the corporate objectives, strategies, and policies. The concept of **financial leverage** (the ratio of total debt to total assets) is helpful in describing how debt is used to increase the earnings available to common shareholders. When the company finances its activities by sales of bonds or notes instead of through stock, the earnings per share are boosted: the interest paid on the debt reduces taxable income, but fewer shareholders share the profits than if the company had sold more stock to finance its activities. The debt, however, does raise the firm's break-even point above what it would have been if the firm had financed from internally generated funds only. High leverage may therefore be perceived as a corporate strength in times of prosperity and ever-increasing sales, or as a weakness in times of a recession and falling sales. This is because leverage acts to magnify the effect on earnings per share of an increase or decrease in dollar sales. Research indicates that greater leverage has a positive impact on performance for firms in stable environments, but a negative impact for firms in dynamic environments.[44]

Capital Budgeting

Capital budgeting is the analyzing and ranking of possible investments in fixed assets such as land, buildings, and equipment in terms of the additional outlays and additional receipts that will result from each investment. A good finance department will be able to prepare such capital budgets and to rank them on the basis of some accepted criteria or *hurdle rate* (for example, years to pay back investment, rate of return, or time to break-even point) for the purpose of strategic decision making. Most firms have more than one hurdle rate and vary it as a function of the type of project being considered. Projects with high strategic significance, such as entering new markets or defending market share, will often have low hurdle rates.[45]

STRATEGIC RESEARCH AND DEVELOPMENT (R&D) ISSUES

The R&D manager is responsible for suggesting and implementing a company's technological strategy in light of its corporate objectives and policies. The manager's job, therefore, involves (1) choosing among alternative new technologies to use within the corporation, (2) developing methods of embodying the new technology in new products and processes, and (3) deploying resources so that the new technology can be successfully implemented.

R&D Intensity, Technological Competence, and Technology Transfer

The company must make available the resources necessary for effective research and development. A company's **R&D intensity** (its spending on R&D as a percentage of sales revenue) is a principal means of gaining market share in global competition. The amount spent on R&D often varies by industry. For example, the U.S. computer software industry traditionally spends 13.5% of its sales dollar for R&D, whereas the paper and forest products industry spends only 1.0%.[46] A good rule of thumb for R&D spending is that a corporation should spend at a "normal" rate for that particular industry unless its strategic plan calls for unusual expenditures.

Simply spending money on R&D or new projects does not mean, however, that the money will produce useful results. For example, Pharmacia Upjohn spent more of its revenues on research than any other company in any industry (18%), but it was ranked low in innovation.[47] A company's R&D unit should be evaluated for **technological competence** in both the development and the use of innovative technology. Not only should the corporation make a consistent research effort (as measured by reasonably constant corporate expenditures that result in usable innovations), it should also be proficient in managing research personnel and integrating their innovations into its day-to-day operations. A company should also be proficient in **technology transfer**, the process of taking a new technology from the laboratory to the marketplace. Aerospace parts maker Rockwell Collins, for example, is a master of developing new technology, such as the "heads-up display" (transparent screens in an airplane cockpit that tell pilots speed, altitude, and direction), for the military and then using it in products built for the civilian market.[48]

R&D Mix

Basic R&D is conducted by scientists in well-equipped laboratories where the focus is on theoretical problem areas. The best indicators of a company's capability in this area are its patents and research publications. *Product R&D* concentrates on marketing and is concerned with product or product-packaging improvements. The best measurements of ability in this area are the number of successful new products introduced and the percentage of total sales and profits coming from products introduced within the past five years. *Engineering (or process) R&D* is concerned with engineering, concentrating on quality control, and the development of design specifications and improved production equipment. A company's capability in this area can be measured by consistent reductions in unit manufacturing costs and by the number of product defects.

Most corporations will have a mix of basic, product, and process R&D, which varies by industry, company, and product line. The balance of these types of research is known as the **R&D mix** and should be appropriate to the strategy being considered and to each product's life cycle. For example, it is generally accepted that product R&D normally dominates the early stages of a product's life cycle (when the product's optimal form and features are still being debated), whereas process R&D becomes especially important in the later stages (when the product's design is solidified and the emphasis is on reducing costs and improving quality).

Impact of Technological Discontinuity on Strategy

The R&D manager must determine when to abandon present technology and when to develop or adopt new technology. Richard Foster of McKinsey and Company states that the displacement of one technology by another (**technological discontinuity**) is a frequent and strategically important phenomenon. Such a discontinuity occurs when a new technology cannot simply be used to enhance the current technology, but actually substitutes for that technology to yield better performance. For each technology within a given field or industry, according to Foster, the plotting of product performance against research effort/expenditures on a graph results in an S-shaped curve. He describes the process depicted in **Figure 5–6**:

> *Early in the development of the technology a knowledge base is being built and progress requires a relatively large amount of effort. Later, progress comes more easily. And then, as the limits of that technology are approached, progress becomes slow and expensive. That is when R&D dollars should be allocated to technology with more potential. That is also—not so incidentally—when a competitor who has bet on a new technology can sweep away your business or topple an entire industry.[49]*

Computerized information technology is currently on the steep upward slope of its S-curve in which relatively small increments in R&D effort result in significant improvement in performance. This is an example of *Moore's Law*, which states that silicon chips (microprocessors) double in complexity every 18 months.[50] The presence of a technological discontinuity in the world's steel industry during the 1960s explains why the large capital expenditures by U.S. steel companies failed to keep them competitive with the Japanese firms that adopted the new technologies. As Foster points out, "History has shown that as one technology nears the end of its S-curve, competitive leadership in a market generally changes hands."[51]

FIGURE 5–6
Technological Discontinuity

What the S-Curves Reveal

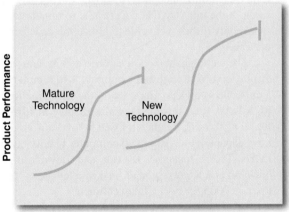

Product Performance

Mature Technology

New Technology

Research Effort/Expenditure

In the corporate planning process, it is generally assumed that incremental progress in technology will occur. But past developments in a given technology cannot be extrapolated into the future because every technology has its limits. The key to competitiveness is to determine when to shift resources to a technology that has more potential.

SOURCE: *From "Are You Investing in the Wrong Technology?" P. Pascarella,* Industry Week, *July 25, 1983. Reprinted by permission of Penton Media, Inc.*

Christensen explains in *The Innovator's Dilemma* why this transition occurs when a "disruptive technology" enters an industry. In a study of computer disk drive manufacturers, he explains that established market leaders are typically reluctant to move in a timely manner to a new technology. This reluctance to switch technologies (even when the firm is aware of the new technology and may have even invented it!) is because the resource allocation process in most companies gives priority to those projects (typically based on the old technology) with the greatest likelihood of generating a good return on investment—those projects appealing to the firm's current customers (whose products are also based on the characteristics of the old technology). For example, in the 1980s a disk drive manufacturer's customers (PC manufacturers) wanted a better (faster) 5 1/4″ drive with greater capacity. These PC makers were not interested in the new 3 1/2″ drives based on the new technology because (at that time) the smaller drives were slower and had less capacity. Smaller size was irrelevant since these companies primarily made desk top personal computers which were designed to hold large drives.

The new technology is generally riskier and of little appeal to the current customers of established firms. Products derived from the new technology are more expensive and do not meet the customers' requirements—requirements based on the old technology. New entrepreneurial firms are typically more interested in the new technology because it is one way to appeal to a developing market niche in a market currently dominated by established companies. Even though the new technology may be more expensive to develop, it offers performance improvements in areas that are attractive to this small niche, but of no consequence to the customers of the established competitors.

This was the case with the entrepreneurial manufacturers of 3 1/2″ disk drives. These smaller drives appealed to the PC makers who were trying to increase their small PC market share by offering laptop computers. Size and weight were more important to these customers than were capacity and speed. By the time the new technology was developed to the point that the 3 1/2″ drive matched and even surpassed the 5 1/4″ drive in terms of speed and capacity (in addition to size and weight), it was too late for the established 5 1/4″ disk drive firms to switch to the new technology. Once their customers begin demanding smaller products using the new technology, the established firms were unable to respond quickly and lost their leadership position in the industry. They were able to remain in the industry (with a much reduced market share) only if they were able to utilize the new technology to be competitive in the new product line.[52]

The same phenomenon can be seen in many product categories ranging from flat-panel display screens to railroad locomotives to digital photography to musical recordings. For example, George Heilmeier created the first practical liquid-crystal display (LCD) in 1964 at RCA Labs. RCA unveiled the new display in 1968 with much fanfare about LCDs being the future of TV sets, but then refused to fund further development of the new technology. In contrast, Japanese television and computer manufacturers invested in long-term development of LCDs. Today, Japanese, Korean, and Taiwanese companies dominate the $39 billion LCD business and RCA no longer makes televisions. Interestingly, Heilmeier received the Kyoto Prize in 2005 for his LCD invention.[53]

STRATEGIC OPERATIONS ISSUES

The primary task of the operations (manufacturing or service) manager is to develop and operate a system that will produce the required number of products or services, with a certain quality, at a given cost, within an allotted time. Many of the key concepts and techniques popularly used in manufacturing can be applied to service businesses.

In very general terms, manufacturing can be intermittent or continuous. In *intermittent systems* (job shops), the item is normally processed sequentially, but the work and sequence of the process vary. An example is an auto body repair shop. At each location, the tasks determine the details of processing and the time required for them. These job shops can be very labor intensive. For example, a job shop usually has little automated machinery and thus a small amount of fixed costs. It has a fairly low break-even point, but its variable cost line (composed of wages and costs of special parts) has a relatively steep slope. Because most of the costs associated with the product are variable (many employees earn piece-rate wages), a job shop's variable costs are higher than those of automated firms. Its advantage over other firms is that it can operate at low levels and still be profitable. After a job shop's sales reach break-even, however, the huge variable costs as a percentage of total costs keep the profit per unit at a relatively low level. In terms of strategy, this firm should look for a niche in the marketplace for which it can produce and sell a reasonably small quantity of custom-made goods.

In contrast, *continuous systems* are those laid out as lines on which products can be continuously assembled or processed. An example is an automobile assembly line. A firm using continuous systems invests heavily in fixed investments such as automated processes and highly sophisticated machinery. Its labor force, relatively small but highly skilled, earns salaries rather than piece-rate wages. Consequently, this firm has a high amount of fixed costs. It also has a relatively high break-even point, but its variable cost line rises slowly. This is an example of **operating leverage**, the impact of a specific change in sales volume on net operating income. The advantage of high operating leverage is that once the firm reaches break-even, its profits rise faster than do those of less automated firms having lower operating leverage. Continuous systems reap benefits from economies of scale. In terms of strategy, this firm needs to find a high-demand niche in the marketplace for which it can produce and sell a large quantity of goods. However, a firm with high operating leverage is likely to suffer huge losses during a recession. During an economic downturn, the firm with less automation and thus less leverage is more likely to survive comfortably because a drop in sales primarily affects variable costs. It is often easier to lay off labor than to sell off specialized plants and machines.

Experience Curve

A conceptual framework that many large corporations have used successfully is the experience curve (originally called the learning curve). The **experience curve** suggests that unit production costs decline by some fixed percentage (commonly 20%–30%) each time the total accumulated volume of production in units doubles. The actual percentage varies by industry and is based on many variables: the amount of time it takes a person to learn a new task, scale economies, product and process improvements, and lower raw materials cost, among others. For example, in an industry with an 85% experience curve, a corporation might expect a 15% reduction in unit costs for every doubling of volume. The total costs per unit can be expected to drop from $100 when the total production is 10 units, to $85 ($100 x 85%) when production increases to 20 units, and to $72.25 ($85 x 85%) when it reaches 40 units. Achieving these results often means investing in R&D and fixed assets; higher fixed costs and less flexibility thus result. Nevertheless the manufacturing strategy is one of building capacity ahead of demand in order to achieve the lower unit costs that develop from the experience curve. On the basis of some future point on the experience curve, the corporation should price the product or service very low to preempt competition and increase market demand. The resulting high number of units sold and high market share should result in high profits, based on the low unit costs.

Management commonly uses the experience curve in estimating the production costs of (1) a product never before made with the present techniques and processes or (2) current products produced by newly introduced techniques or processes. The concept was first applied in the airframe industry and can be applied in the service industry as well. For example, a cleaning company can reduce its costs per employee by having its workers use the same equipment and techniques to clean many adjacent offices in one office building rather than just cleaning a few offices in multiple buildings. Although many firms have used experience curves extensively, an unquestioning acceptance of the industry norm (such as 80% for the airframe industry or 70% for integrated circuits) is very risky. The experience curve of the industry as a whole might not hold true for a particular company for a variety of reasons.[54]

Flexible Manufacturing for Mass Customization

The use of large, continuous, mass-production facilities to take advantage of experience-curve economies has recently been criticized. The use of **C**omputer-**A**ssisted **D**esign and **C**omputer-**A**ssisted **M**anufacturing (CAD/CAM) and robot technology means that learning times are shorter and products can be economically manufactured in small, customized batches in a process called *mass customization*—the low-cost production of individually customized goods and services.[55] Economies of scope (in which common parts of the manufacturing activities of various products are combined to gain economies even though small numbers of each product are made) replace **Economies of scale** (in which unit costs are reduced by making large numbers of the same product) in flexible manufacturing. *Flexible manufacturing* permits the low-volume output of custom-tailored products at relatively low unit costs through economies of scope. It is thus possible to have the cost advantages of continuous systems with the customer-oriented advantages of intermittent systems. The auto maker, BMW, for example, uses flexible manufacturing to customize cars to suit each buyer's preference. It replaced its two assembly lines in its Spartanburg, South Carolina, plant with one flexible assembly line in 2006. According to spokesperson Bunny Richardson, "Until now, if we wanted to introduce an additional model, we'd have to construct a new line."[56]

STRATEGIC HUMAN RESOURCE (HRM) ISSUES

The primary task of the manager of human resources is to improve the match between individuals and jobs. Research indicates that companies with good HRM practices have higher profits and a better survival rate than do firms without these practices.[57] A good HRM department should know how to use attitude surveys and other feedback devices to assess employees' satisfaction with their jobs and with the corporation as a whole. HRM managers should also use job analysis to obtain job description information about what each job needs to accomplish in terms of quality and quantity. Up-to-date job descriptions are essential not only for proper employee selection, appraisal, training, and development for wage and salary administration, and for labor negotiations, but also for summarizing the corporate-wide human resources in terms of employee-skill categories. Just as a company must know the number, type, and quality of its manufacturing facilities, it must also know the kinds of people it employs and the skills they possess. The best strategies are meaningless if employees do not have the skills to carry them out or if jobs cannot be designed to accommodate the available workers. IBM, Procter & Gamble, and Hewlett-Packard, for example, use employee profiles to ensure that they have the best mix of talents to implement their planned strategies. Because project managers at IBM are now able to scan the company's databases to identify employee capabilities and availability, the average time needed to assemble a team has declined 20% for a savings of $500 million overall.[58]

Increasing Use of Teams

Management is beginning to realize that it must be more flexible in its utilization of employees in order for human resources to be classified as a strength. Human resource managers, therefore, need to be knowledgeable about work options such as part-time work, job sharing, flex-time, extended leaves, and contract work, and especially about the proper use of teams. Over two-thirds of large U.S. companies are successfully using *autonomous (self-managing) work teams* in which a group of people work together without a supervisor to plan, coordinate, and evaluate their own work.[59] Northern Telecom found productivity and quality to increase with work teams to such an extent that it was able to reduce the number of quality inspectors by 40%.[60]

As a way to move a product more quickly through its development stage, companies like Motorola, Chrysler, NCR, Boeing, and General Electric are using *cross-functional work teams*. Instead of developing products in a series of steps—beginning with a request from sales, which leads to design, then to engineering and on to purchasing, and finally to manufacturing (and often resulting in a costly product rejected by the customer)—companies are tearing down the traditional walls separating the departments so that people from each discipline can get involved in projects early on. In a process called *concurrent engineering*, the once-isolated specialists now work side by side and compare notes constantly in an effort to design cost-effective products with features customers want. Taking this approach enabled Chrysler Corporation to reduce its product development cycle from 60 to 36 months.[61] For such cross-functional work teams to be successful, the groups must receive training and coaching. Otherwise, poorly implemented teams may worsen morale, create divisiveness, and raise the level of cynicism among workers.[62]

Virtual teams are groups of geographically and/or organizationally dispersed coworkers that are assembled using a combination of telecommunications and information technologies to accomplish an organizational task.[63] In the U.S. alone, more than half of companies having over 5,000 employees use virtual teams involving around 8.4 million people.[64] According to the Gartner Group, more than 60% of professional employees now work in virtual teams.[65] Internet, intranet, and extranet systems are combining with other new technologies, such as desktop video conferencing and collaborative software, to create a new workplace in which teams of workers are no longer restrained by geography, time, or organizational boundaries. This technology allows about 12% of the U.S. workforce, who have no permanent office at their companies, to do team projects over the Internet and report to a manager thousands of miles away. More than 20 million people in the U.S. are engaged in telecommuting.[66] Charles Grantham of Work Design Collaborative predicts that 40% of the workforce will be working remotely by 2012.[67]

As more companies outsource some of the activities previously conducted internally, the traditional organizational structure is being replaced by a series of virtual teams, which rarely, if ever, meet face-to-face. Such teams may be established as temporary groups to accomplish a specific task or may be more permanent to address continuing issues such as strategic planning. Membership on these teams is often fluid, depending upon the task to be accomplished. They may include not only employees from different functions within a company, but also members of various stakeholder groups, such as suppliers, customers, and law or consulting firms. The use of virtual teams to replace traditional face-to-face work groups is being driven by five trends:

1. Flatter organizational structures with increasing cross-functional coordination need
2. Turbulent environments requiring more inter-organizational cooperation
3. Increasing employee autonomy and participation in decision making
4. Higher knowledge requirements derived from a greater emphasis on service
5. Increasing globalization of trade and corporate activity[68]

Union Relations and Temporary/Part-Time Workers

If the corporation is unionized, a good human resource manager should be able to work closely with the union. Even though union membership had dropped to only 12.1% of the U.S. workforce by 2007 compared to 20.1% in 1983, it still included 15.7 million people. Nevertheless, only 7.5% of the 108,714 million private sector employees belonged to a union (compared to 35.9% of public sector employees).[69] To save jobs, U.S. unions are increasingly willing to support new strategic initiatives and employee involvement programs. For example, United Steel Workers hired Ron Bloom, an investment banker, to propose a strategic plan to make Goodyear Tire & Rubber globally competitive in a way that would preserve as many jobs as possible. In a recent contract, the union gave up $1.15 billion in wage and benefit concessions over three years in return for a promise by Goodyear's top management to invest in 12 of its 14 U.S. factories, to limit imports from its factories in Brazil and Asia, and to maintain 85% of its 19,000-person workforce. The company also agreed to aggressively restructure the firm's $5 billion debt. According to Bloom, "We told Goodyear, 'We'll make you profitable, but you're going to adopt this strategy.'. . . We think the company should be a patient, long-term builder of value for the employees and shareholders."[70]

Outside the United States, the average proportion of unionized workers among major industrialized nations is around 50%. European unions tend to be militant, politically oriented, and much less interested in working with management to increase efficiency. Nationwide strikes can occur quickly. In contrast, Japanese unions are typically tied to individual companies and are usually supportive of management. These differences among countries have significant implications for the management of multinational corporations.

To increase flexibility, avoid layoffs, and reduce labor costs, corporations are using more temporary (also known as contingent) workers. Over 90% of U.S. and European firms use temporary workers in some capacity; 43% use them in professional and technical functions.[71] Approximately 13% of the U.S. workforce are part-time workers. The percentage is even higher in Japan, where 26% of workers are part-time, and in the Netherlands, where 36% of all employees work part-time.[72] Labor unions are concerned that companies use temps to avoid hiring costlier unionized workers. At United Parcel Service, for example, 80% of the jobs created from 1993 to 1997 were staffed by part-timers, whose pay rates hadn't changed since 1982. Fully 10% of the company's 128,000 part-timers worked 30 hours or more per week, but were still paid at a lower rate than were full-time employees.[73]

Quality of Work Life and Human Diversity

Human resource departments have found that to reduce employee dissatisfaction and unionization efforts (or, conversely, to improve employee satisfaction and existing union relations), they must consider the *quality of work life* in the design of jobs. Partially a reaction to the traditionally heavy emphasis on technical and economic factors in job design, quality of work life emphasizes improving the human dimension of work. The knowledgeable human resource manager, therefore, should be able to improve the corporation's quality of work life by (1) introducing participative problem solving, (2) restructuring work, (3) introducing innovative reward systems, and (4) improving the work environment. It is hoped that these improvements will lead to a more participative corporate culture and thus higher productivity and quality products. Ford Motor Company, for example, rebuilt and modernized its famous River Rouge plant using flexible equipment and new processes. Employees work in teams and use Internet-connected PCs on the shop floor to share their concerns instantly with suppliers or product engineers. Workstations were redesigned to make them more ergonomic and reduce repetitive-strain injuries. "If you feel good while you're working, I think quality and productivity will increase, and Ford thinks that too, otherwise, they wouldn't do this," observed Jerry Sullivan, president of United Auto Workers Local 600.[74]

Companies are also discovering that by redesigning their plants and offices for improved energy efficiency, they can receive a side effect of improving their employees' quality of work life—thus raising labor productivity. See the **Environmental Sustainability Issue** feature to learn how improved energy efficiency can not only cut costs, but also boost employee morale.

ENVIRONMENTAL sustainability issue

USING ENERGY EFFICIENCY FOR COMPETITIVE ADVANTAGE AND QUALITY OF WORK LIFE

Amory Lovins, Co-founder and Chairman of the Rocky Mountain Institute, works to educate business executives on how the efficient use of energy can lead not only to lower costs, but also to competitive advantage and increased labor productivity. His Rocky Mountain Institute is a nonprofit organization that develops and implements programs for energy and resource efficiency. According to Lovins:

In my team's latest redesigns for $30 billion worth of facilities in 29 sectors, we consistently found about 30 to 60 percent energy savings that could be captured through retrofits, which paid for themselves in two to three years. In new facilities, 40 to 90 percent savings could be gleaned—and with nearly always lower capital cost.

Lovins' Rocky Mountain Institute promotes the use of *micropower*, on-site or decentralized energy production, such as waste-heat, or gas-fired cogeneration, wind and solar power, geothermal, small hydro, and waste- or biomass-fueled plants. Lovins points out that a sixth of the world's electricity and a third of new electricity now comes from micropower because it's cheaper with lower financial risk.

Lovins points out that energy redesigns often have side effects that may be far more valuable than the direct savings. For example, a typical office pays around 160 times more in payroll than for energy. According to Lovins, his programs routinely get a 6% to 16% increase gain in labor productivity in more efficient buildings having improved thermal, visual, and acoustic comfort. "When people can see what they are doing, hear themselves think, breathe cleaner air, and feel more comfortable, they do more and better work," says Lovins.

....

SOURCE: Material based on M. Hirschland, J. M. Oppenheim, and A. P. Webb, "Using Energy More Efficiently: An Interview with the Rocky Mountain Institute's Amory Lovins," *McKinsey Quarterly* (July 2008), pp. 1–7.

Human diversity refers to the mix in the workplace of people from different races, cultures, and backgrounds. Realizing that the demographics are changing toward an increasing percentage of minorities and women in the U.S. workforce, companies are now concerned with hiring and promoting people without regard to ethnic background. Research does indicate that an increase in racial diversity leads to an increase in firm performance.[75] In a survey of 131 leading European companies, 67.2% stated that a diverse work force can provide competitive advantage.[76] A manager from Nestlé stated: "To deliver products that meet the needs of individual consumers, we need people who respect other cultures, embrace diversity, and never discriminate on any basis."[77] Good human resource managers should be working to ensure that people are treated fairly on the job and not harassed by prejudiced co-workers or managers. Otherwise, they may find themselves subject to lawsuits. Coca-Cola Company, for example, agreed to pay $192.5 million because of discrimination against African-American salaried employees in pay, promotions, and evaluations from 1995 and 2000. According to Chairman and CEO Douglas Daft, "Sometimes things happen in an unintentional manner. And I've made it clear that can't happen anymore."[78]

An organization's human resources may be a key to achieving a sustainable competitive advantage. Advances in technology are copied almost immediately by competitors around the world. People, however, are not as willing to move to other companies in other countries. This means that the only long-term resource advantage remaining to corporations operating in the industrialized nations may lie in the area of skilled human resources.[79] Research does reveal that competitive strategies are more successfully executed in those companies with a high level of commitment to their employees than in those firms with less commitment.[80]

STRATEGIC INFORMATION SYSTEMS/TECHNOLOGY ISSUES

The primary task of the manager of information systems/technology is to design and manage the flow of information in an organization in ways that improve productivity and decision making. Information must be collected, stored, and synthesized in such a manner that it will answer important operating and strategic questions. A corporation's information system can be a strength or a weakness in multiple areas of strategic management. It can not only aid in environmental scanning and in controlling a company's many activities, it can also be used as a strategic weapon in gaining competitive advantage.

Impact on Performance

Information systems/technology offers four main contributions to corporate performance. *First,* (beginning in the 1970s with mainframe computers) it is used to automate existing back-office processes, such as payroll, human resource records, accounts payable and receivable, and to establish huge databases. *Second,* (beginning in the 1980s) it is used to automate individual tasks, such as keeping track of clients and expenses, through the use of personal computers with word processing and spreadsheet software. Corporate databases are accessed to provide sufficient data to analyze the data and create what-if scenarios. These first two contributions tend to focus on reducing costs. *Third,* (beginning in the 1990s) it is used to enhance key business functions, such as marketing and operations. This third contribution focuses on productivity improvements. The system provides customer support and help in distribution and logistics. For example, Federal Express found that by allowing customers to directly access its package-tracking database via its Internet Web site instead of their having to ask a human operator, the company saved up to $2 million annually.[81] Business processes are analyzed to increase efficiency and productivity via reengineering. Enterprise resource planning (ERP) application software, such as SAP, PeopleSoft, Oracle, Baan, and J.D. Edwards, (discussed further in **Chapter 10**) is used to integrate worldwide business activities so that employees need to enter information only once and that information is available to all corporate systems (including accounting) around the world. *Fourth,* (beginning in 2000) it is used to develop competitive advantage. For example, American Hospital Supply (AHS), a leading manufacturer and distributor of a broad line of products for doctors, laboratories, and hospitals, developed an order entry distribution system that directly linked the majority of its customers to AHS computers. The system was successful because it simplified ordering processes for customers, reduced costs for both AHS and the customer, and allowed AHS to provide pricing incentives to the customer. As a result, customer loyalty was high and AHS's share of the market became large.

A current trend in corporate information systems/technology is the increasing use of the Internet for marketing, intranets for internal communication, and extranets for logistics and distribution. An *intranet* is an information network within an organization that also has access to the external worldwide Internet. Intranets typically begin as ways to provide employees with company information such as lists of product prices, fringe benefits, and company policies. They are then converted into extranets for supply chain management. An *extranet* is an information network within an organization that is available to key suppliers and customers. The key issue in building an extranet is the creation of "fire walls" to block extranet users from accessing the firm's or other users' confidential data. Once this is accomplished, companies can allow employees, customers, and suppliers to access information and conduct business on the Internet in a completely automated manner. By connecting these groups, companies hope to obtain a competitive advantage by reducing the time needed to design and bring new products to market, slashing inventories, customizing manufacturing, and entering new markets.[82]

A recent development in information systems/technology is Web 2.0. *Web 2.0* refers to the use of wikis, blogs, RSS (Really Simple Syndication), social networks (e.g., MySpace and Facebook), podcasts, and mash-ups through company Web sites to forge tighter links with customers and suppliers and to engage employees more successfully. A 2008 survey by McKinsey revealed the percentage of companies using individual Web 2.0 technologies to be Web services (58%), blogs (34%), RSS (33%), wikis (32%), podcasts (29%), social networking (28%), peer-to-peer (18%), and mash-ups (10%). The most heavily used tool is Web services, software that makes it easier to exchange information and conduct transactions. Wikis and blogs are being increasingly used in companies throughout the world. Satisfied users of these information technologies report that they are using these tools to interact with their customers, suppliers, and outside experts in product development efforts known as *co-creation*. For example, LEGO invited customers to suggest new models interactively and then financially rewarded the people whose ideas proved marketable.[83]

Supply Chain Management

The expansion of the marketing-oriented Internet into intranets and extranets is making significant contributions to organizational performance through supply chain management. **Supply chain management** is the forming of networks for sourcing raw materials, manufacturing products or creating services, storing and distributing the goods, and delivering them to customers and consumers.[84] Research indicates that supplier network resources have a significant impact on firm performance.[85] A survey of global executives revealed that their interest in supply chains was first to reduce costs, and then to improve customer service and get new products to market faster.[86] More than 85% of senior executives stated that improving their firm's supply-chain performance was a top priority. Companies, like Wal-Mart, Dell, and Toyota, who are known to be exemplars in supply-chain management, spend only 4% of their revenues on supply chain costs compared to 10% by the average firm.[87]

Industry leaders are integrating modern information systems into their corporate value chains to harmonize companywide efforts and to achieve competitive advantage. For example, Heineken beer distributors input actual depletion figures and replenishment orders to the Netherlands brewer through their linked Web pages. This interactive planning system generates time-phased orders based on actual usage rather than on projected demand. Distributors are then able to modify plans based on local conditions or changes in marketing. Heineken uses these modifications to adjust brewing and supply schedules. As a result of this system, lead times have been reduced from the traditional 10–12 weeks to 4–6 weeks. This time savings is especially useful in an industry competing on product freshness. In another example, Procter & Gamble participates in an information network to move the company's line of consumer products through Wal-Mart's many stores. *Radio-frequency identification (RFID)* tags containing product information is used to track goods through inventory and distribution channels. As part of the network with Wal-Mart, P&G knows by cash register and by store what products have passed through the system every hour of each day. The network is linked by satellite communications on a real-time basis. With actual point-of-sale information, products are replenished to meet current demand and minimize stockouts while maintaining exceptionally low inventories.[88]

5.5 The Strategic Audit: A Checklist for Organizational Analysis

One way of conducting an organizational analysis to ascertain a company's strengths and weakness is by using the Strategic Audit found in **Appendix 1.A** at the end of Chapter 1. The audit provides a checklist of questions by area of concern. For example, Part IV of the audit examines corporate structure, culture, and resources. It looks at organizational resources and capabilities in terms of the functional areas of marketing, finance, R&D, operations, human resources, and information systems, among others.

5.6 Synthesis of Internal Factors

After strategists have scanned the internal organizational environment and identified factors for their particular corporation, they may want to summarize their analysis of these factors using a form such as that given in **Table 5–2**. This **IFAS (Internal Factor Analysis Summary) Table** is one way to organize the internal factors into the generally accepted categories of strengths and weaknesses as well as to analyze how well a particular company's management is responding to these specific factors in light of the perceived importance of these factors to the company. Use the VRIO framework (**V**alue, **R**areness, **I**mitability, & **O**rganization) to assess the importance of each of the factors that might be considered strengths. Except for its internal orientation, this IFAS Table is built the same way as the EFAS Table described in **Chapter 4** (in **Table 4–5**). To use the IFAS Table, complete the following steps:

1. In **Column 1** (*Internal Factors*), list the eight to ten most important strengths and weaknesses facing the company.

TABLE 5–2 Internal Factor Analysis Summary (IFAS Table): Maytag as Example

Internal Factors	Weight	Rating	Weighted Score	Comments
	1	2	3	4	5
Strengths				
▪ Quality Maytag culture	.15	5.0	.75	Quality key to success
▪ Experienced top management	.05	4.2	.21	Know appliances
▪ Vertical integration	.10	3.9	.39	Dedicated factories
▪ Employer relations	.05	3.0	.15	Good, but deteriorating
▪ Hoover's international orientation	.15	2.8	.42	Hoover name in cleaners
Weaknesses				
▪ Process-oriented R&D	.05	2.2	.11	Slow on new products
▪ Distribution channels	.05	2.0	.10	Superstores replacing small dealers
▪ Financial position	.15	2.0	.30	High debt load
▪ Global positioning	.20	2.1	.42	Hoover weak outside the United Kingdom and Australia
▪ Manufacturing facilities	.05	4.0	.20	Investing now
Total Scores	**1.00**		**3.05**	

NOTES:
1. List strengths and weaknesses (8–10) in Column 1.
2. Weight each factor from **1.0** (Most Important) to **0.0** (Not Important) in Column 2 based on that factor's probable impact on the company's strategic position. **The total weights must sum to 1.00**.
3. Rate each factor from **5.0** (Outstanding) to **1.0** (Poor) in Column 3 based on the company's response to that factor.
4. Multiply each factor's weight times its rating to obtain each factor's weighted score in Column 4.
5. Use Column 5 (comments) for rationale used for each factor.
6. Add the individual weighted scores to obtain the total weighted score for the company in Column 4. This tells how well the company is responding to the factors in its internal environment.

SOURCE: Thomas L. Wheelen, Copyright © 1982, 1985, 1987, 1988, 1989, 1990, 1991, 1995, and every year after that. Kathryn E. Wheelen solely owns all of (Dr.) Thomas L. Wheelen's copyright materials. Kathryn E. Wheelen requires written reprint permission for each book that this material is to be printed in. Thomas L. Wheelen and J. David Hunger, copyright © 1991–first year "Internal Factor Analysis Summary (IFAS) appeared in this text (4th ed.) Rerprinted by permission of the copyright holders.

2. In **Column 2** (*Weight*), assign a weight to each factor from **1.0** (*Most Important*) to **0.0** (*Not Important*) based on that factor's probable impact on a particular company's current strategic position. The higher the weight, the more important is this factor to the current and future success of the company. **All weights must sum to 1.0 regardless of the number of factors.**

3. In **Column 3** (*Rating*), assign a rating to each factor from **5.0** (*Outstanding*) to **1.0** (*Poor*) based on management's specific response to that particular factor. Each rating is a judgment regarding how well the company's management is currently dealing with each specific internal factor.

4. In **Column 4** (*Weighted Score*), multiply the weight in **Column 2** for each factor times its rating in **Column 3** to obtain that factor's weighted score.

5. In **Column 5** (*Comments*), note why a particular factor was selected and/or how its weight and rating were estimated.

6. Finally, add the weighted scores for all the internal factors in **Column 4** to determine the total weighted score for that particular company. The **total weighted score** indicates how well a particular company is responding to current and expected factors in its internal environment. The score can be used to compare that firm to other firms in its industry. Check to ensure that the total weighted score truly reflects the company's current performance in terms of profitability and market share. **The total weighted score for an average firm in an industry is always 3.0.**

As an example of this procedure, **Table 5–2** includes a number of internal factors for Maytag Corporation in 1995 (before Maytag was acquired by Whirlpool) with corresponding weights, ratings, and weighted scores provided. Note that Maytag's total weighted score is 3.05, meaning that the corporation is about average compared to the strengths and weaknesses of others in the major home appliance industry.

End of Chapter SUMMARY

Every day, about 17 truckloads of used diesel engines and other parts are dumped at a receiving facility at Caterpillar's remanufacturing plant in Corinth, Mississippi. The filthy iron engines are then broken down by two workers, who manually hammer and drill for half a day until they have taken every bolt off the engine and put each component into its own bin. The engines are then cleaned and re-made at a half the cost of a new engine and sold for a tidy profit. This system works at Caterpillar because as a general rule, 70% of the cost to build something new is in the materials and 30% is in the labor. Remanufacturing simply starts the manufacturing process over again with materials that are essentially free and which already contain most of the energy costs needed to make them. The would-be discards become fodder for the next product, eliminating waste, and cutting costs. Caterpillar's management was so impressed by the remanufacturing operation that they made the business a separate division in 2005. The unit earned more than $1 billion in sales in 2005 and expects 15% growth for many more years—given the steadily increasing cost of oil and raw materials.

Caterpillar's remanufacturing unit was successful not only because of its capability of wringing productivity out of materials and labor, but also because it designed its products for re-use. Before they are built new, remanufactured products must be designed for disassembly. In order to achieve this, Caterpillar asks its designers to check a "Reman" box on Caterpillar's product development checklist. The company also needs to know where its products are being used in order to take them back—known as the art of *reverse logistics*. This is achieved by Caterpillar's excellent relationship with its dealers throughout the world as well as through financial incentives. For example, when a customer orders a crankshaft, that customer is offered a remanufactured one for half the cost of a new one—assuming the customer turns in the old crankshaft to Caterpillar. The products also should be built for performance with little regard for changing fashion. Since diesel engines change little from year to year, a remanufactured engine is very similar to a new engine and might perform even better.

Monitoring the external environment is only one part of environmental scanning. Strategists also need to scan a corporation's internal environment to identify its resources, capabilities, and competencies. What are its strengths and weaknesses? At Caterpillar, management clearly noted that the environment was changing in a way to make its remanufactured product more desirable. It took advantage of its strengths in manufacturing and distribution to offer a recycling service for its current customers and a low-cost alternative product for those who could not afford a new Caterpillar engine. It also happened to be an environmentally friendly, sustainable business model. Caterpillar's management felt that remanufacturing thus provided them with a strategic advantage over competitors who don't remanufacture. This is an example of a company using its capabilities in key functional areas to expand its business by moving into a new profitable position on its value chain.[89]

ECO-BITS

- The average number of plastic bottles used each year in the U.S. per person: 200
- The average number of plastic bottles recycled each year in the U.S. per person: 40

- Revenue produced in 2007 by recycling and ancillary industries: $236 billion
- Share of electronic waste that is hauled overseas, stripped unsafely, and dumped: 80%[90]

DISCUSSION QUESTIONS

1. What is the relevance of the resource-based view of the firm to strategic management in a global environment?

2. How can value-chain analysis help identify a company's strengths and weaknesses?

3. In what ways can a corporation's structure and culture be internal strengths or weaknesses?

4. What are the pros and cons of management's using the experience curve to determine strategy?

5. How might a firm's management decide whether it should continue to invest in current known technology or in new, but untested technology? What factors might encourage or discourage such a shift?

STRATEGIC PRACTICE EXERCISES

Can you analyze a corporation using the Internet? Try the following exercise.

1. Form into teams of around three to five people. Select a well-known publicly owned company to research. Inform the instructor of your choice.

2. Assign each person a separate task. One task might be to find the latest financial statements. Another would be to learn as much as possible about its top management and board of directors. Another might be to identify its business model. Another might be to identify its key competitors.

3. Conduct research on the company *using the Internet only*.

4. Meet with your team members to discuss what you have found. What are the company's opportunities, threats, strengths, and weaknesses? Go back to the Internet for more information, if needed.

5. Prepare a 3- to 5-page typed report of the company. The report should include the following:
   a. Does the firm have any core competencies? Are any of these distinctive (better than the competition) competencies? Does the firm have any competitive

advantage? Provide a SWOT analysis using EFAS and IFAS Tables.

   b. What is the likely future of this firm if it continues on its current path?

   c. Would you buy stock in this company? Assume that your team has $25,000 to invest. Allocate the money

among the four to five primary competitors in this industry. List the companies, the number of shares purchased of each, the cost of each share as of a given date, and the total cost for each purchase assuming a typical commission used by an Internet broker, such as E-Trade or Scottrade.

KEY TERMS

brand (p. 200)
business model (p. 190)
capabilities (p. 186)
capital budgeting (p. 201)
competency (p. 186)
conglomerate structure (p. 196)
continuum of sustainability (p. 189)
core competencies (p. 186)
corporate culture (p. 197)
corporate reputation (p. 200)
distinctive competencies (p. 186)
divisional structure (p. 195)
durability (p. 188)
economies of scale (p. 206)
economies of scope (p. 195)

experience curve (p. 205)
explicit knowledge (p. 189)
financial leverage (p. 201)
functional structure (p. 195)
IFAS Table (p. 212)
imitability (p. 188)
marketing mix (p. 199)
operating leverage (p. 205)
organizational analysis (p. 186)
organizational structures (p. 195)
product life cycle (p. 200)
R&D intensity (p. 202)
R&D mix (p. 202)
replicability (p. 189)

resource (p. 186)
simple structure (p. 195)
strategic business units (SBUs) (p. 196)
supply chain management (p. 211)
tacit knowledge (p. 189)
technological competence (p. 202)
technological discontinuity (p. 203)
technology transfer (p. 202)
transferability (p. 188)
transparency (p. 188)
value chain (p. 191)
virtual teams (p. 207)
VRIO framework (p. 186)

NOTES

1. D. Welch and N. Lakshman, "My Other Car Is a Tata," *Business Week* (January 14, 2008), pp. 33–34.

2. R. M. Grant, *Contemporary Strategy Analysis*, 6th edition (Malden, MA: Blackwell Publishing, 2008), pp. 130–131.

3. G. Schreyogg and M. Kliesch-Eberl, "How Dynamic Can Organizational Capabilities Be? Towards a Dual-Process Model of Capability Dynamization," *Strategic Management Journal* (September 2007), pp. 913–933.

4. M. Javidan, "Core Competence: What Does It Mean in Practice?" *Long Range Planning* (February 1998), pp. 60–71.

5. M. A. Hitt, B. W. Keats, and S. M. DeMarie, "Navigating in the New Competitive Landscape: Building Strategic Flexibility and Competitive Advantage in the 21st Century," *Academy of Management Executive* (November 1998), pp. 22–42; C. E. Helfat and M. A. Peteraf, "The Dynamic Resources-Based View: Capability Life Cycles," *Strategic Management Journal* (October 2003), pp. 997–1010.

6. D. Brady and K. Capell, "GE Breaks the Mold to Spur Innovation," *Business Week* (April 26, 2004), pp. 88–89.

7. J. B. Barney, *Gaining and Sustaining Competitive Advantage*. 2nd ed. (Upper Saddle River, NJ: Prentice Hall, 2002), pp. 159–172. Barney's VRIO questions are very similar to those proposed by G. Hamel and S. K. Prahalad in their book, *Competing for the Future* (Boston: Harvard Business School Press, 1994) on pages 202–207 in which they state that to be distinctive, a competency must (a) provide customer value, (b) be competitor unique, and (c) be extendable to develop new products and/or markets.

8. S. L. Newbert, "Value, Rareness, Competitive Advantage, and Performance: A Conceptual-Level Empirical Investigation of the Resource-Based View of the Firm," *Strategic Management Journal* (July 2008), pp. 745–768.

9. Barney, p. 161.

10. R. M. Grant, "The Resource-Based Theory of Competitive Advantage: Implications for Strategy Formulation," *California Management Review* (Spring 1991), pp. 114–135.

11. P. J. Verdin and P. J. Williamson, "Core Competencies, Competitive Advantage and Market Analysis: Forging the Links," in *Competence-Based Competition*, edited by G. Hamel and A. Heene (New York: John Wiley and Sons, 1994), pp. 83–84; S. K. Ethiraj, P. Kale, M. S. Krishnan, and J. V. Singh, "Where Do Capabilities Come From and How Do They Matter? A Study in the Software Services Industry," *Strategic Management Journal* (January 2005), pp. 701–719.

12. J. Devan, M. B. Klusas, and T. W. Ruefli, "The Elusive Goal of Corporate Outperformance," *McKinsey Quarterly Online* (April 2007).

13. M. E. Porter, "Clusters and the New Economics of Competition," *Harvard Business Review* (November–December 1998), pp. 77–90.

14. J. M. Shaver and F. Flyer, "Agglomeration Economies, Firm Heterogeneity, and Foreign Direct Investment in the United States," *Strategic Management Journal* (December 2000), pp. 1175–1193; W. Chung and A. Kalnins, "Agglomeration Effects and Performance: A Test of the Texas Lodging Industry," *Strategic Management Journal* (October 2001), pp. 969–988.

15. M. Polanyi, *The Tacit Dimension* (London: Routledge & Kegan Paul, 1966).

16. S. K. McEvily and B. Chakravarthy, "The Persistence of Knowledge-Based Advantage: An Empirical Test for Product

Performance and Technological Knowledge," *Strategic Management Journal* (April 2002), pp. 285–305.

17. K. Maney, "Dell Business Model Turns to Muscle as Rivals Struggle," *USA Today* (January 20, 2003), p. 2B.

18. P. E. Bierly III, "Development of a Generic Knowledge Strategy Typology," *Journal of Business Strategies* (Spring 1999), p. 3.

19. R. W. Coff, D. C. Coff, and R. Eastvold, "The Knowledge-Leveraging Paradox: How to Achieve Scale Without Making Knowledge Imitable," *Academy of Management Review* (April 2006), pp. 452–465.

20. D. Welch and N. Lakshman, p. 33.

21. S. Abraham, "Experiencing Strategic Conversations about the Central Forces of our Time," *Strategy & Leadership*, Vol. 31, No. 2 (2003), pp. 61–62.

22. C. A. de Kluyver and J. A. Pearce II, *Strategy: A View from the Top* (Upper Saddle River, NJ: Prentice Hall, 2003), pp. 63–66.

23. P. Burrows, "Ever Wonder Why Ink Costs So Much?" *Business Week* (November 14, 2005), pp. 42–44.

24. O. Gadiesh and J. L. Gilbert, "Profit Pools: A Fresh Look at Strategy," *Harvard Business Review* (May–June, 1998). pp. 139–147.

25. J. R. Galbraith, "Strategy and Organization Planning," in *The Strategy Process: Concepts, Contexts, and Cases*, 2nd ed., edited by H. Mintzberg and J. B. Quinn (Englewood Cliffs, N.J.: Prentice Hall, 1991), pp. 315–324.

26. M. Porter, *Competitive Advantage: Creating and Sustaining Superior Performance* (New York: The Free Press, 1985), p. 36.

27. M. Leontiades, "A Diagnostic Framework for Planning," *Strategic Management Journal* (January–March 1983), p. 14.

28. E. H. Schein, *The Corporate Culture Survival Guide* (San Francisco: Jossey-Bass, 1999), p. 12; L. C. Harris and E. Ogbonna, "The Strategic Legacy of Company Founders," *Long Range Planning* (June 1999), pp. 333–343.

29. D. M. Rousseau, "Assessing Organizational Culture: The Case for Multiple Methods," in *Organizational Climate and Culture*, edited by B. Schneider (San Francisco: Jossey-Bass, 1990), pp. 153–192.

30. L. Smircich, "Concepts of Culture and Organizational Analysis," *Administrative Science Quarterly* (September 1983), pp. 345–346; D. Ravasi and M. Schultz, "Responding to Organizational Identity Threats: Exploring the Role of Organizational Culture," *Academy of Management Journal* (June 2006), pp. 433–458.

31. D. G. Allen, "Do Organizational Socialization Tactics Influence Newcomer Embeddedness and Turnover?" *Journal of Management* (April 2006), pp. 237–256.

32. J. B. Sorensen, "The Strength of Corporate Culture and the Reliability of Firm Performance," *Administrative Science Quarterly* (March 2002), pp. 70–91; R. E. Smerek and D. R. Denison, "Social Capital in Organizations: Understanding the Link to Firm Performance," presentation to the *Academy of Management* (Philadelphia, 2007).

33. K. E. Aupperle, "Spontaneous Organizational Reconfiguration: A Historical Example Based on Xenophon's Anabasis," *Organization Science* (July–August 1996), pp. 445–460.

34. E. K. Briody, S. T. Cavusgil, and S. R. Miller, "Turning Three Sides into a Delta at General Motors: Enhancing Partnership Integration on Corporate Ventures," *Long Range Planning* (October 2004), pp. 421–434.

35. "Face Value: A Post-Modern Proctoid," *The Economist* (April 15, 2006), p. 68.

36. D. Kiley, B. Helm, L. Lee, G. Edmundson, C. Edwards, and M. Scott, "Best Global Brands," *Business Week* (August 6, 2007), pp. 56–64.

37. R. T. Wilcox, "The Hidden Potential of Powerful Brands," *Batten Briefings* (Summer 2003), pp. 1, 4–5.

38. V. P. Rindova, I. O. Williamson, A. P. Petkova, and J. M. Sever, "Being Good or Being Known: An Empirical Examination of the Dimensions, Antecedents, and Consequences of Organizational Reputation," *Academy of Management Journal* (December 2005), pp. 1033–1049.

39. V. P. Rindova, I. O. Williamson, A. P. Petkova, and J. M. Sever, "Being Good or Being Known: An Empirical Examination of the Dimensions, Antecedents, and Consequences of Organizational Reputation," *Academy of Management Journal* (December 2005), pp. 1033–1049.

40. C. Fombrun and C. Van Riel, "The Reputational Landscape," Corporate Reputation Review, Vol. 1, Nos. 1&2 (1997), pp. 5–13.

41. P. Engardio and M. Arndt, "What Price Reputation?" *Business Week* (July 9 & 16, 2007), pp. 70–79.

42. P. W. Roberts and G. R. Dowling, "Corporate Reputation and Sustained Financial Performance," *Strategic Management Journal* (December 2002), pp. 1077–1093; J. Shamsie, "The Context of Dominance: An Industry-Driven Framework for Exploiting Reputation," *Strategic Management Journal* (March 2003), pp. 199–215; M. D. Michalisin, D. M. Kline, and R. D. Smith, "Intangible Strategic Assets and Firm Performance: A Multi-Industry Study of the Resource-Based View," *Journal of Business Strategies* (Fall 2000), pp. 91–117; S. S. Standifird, "Reputation and E-Commerce: eBay Auctions and the Asymmetrical Impact of Positive and Negative Ratings," *Journal of Management*, Vol. 27, No. 3 (2001), pp. 279–295.

43. R. L. Simerly and M. Li, "Environmental Dynamism, Capital Structure and Performance: A Theoretical Integration and an Empirical Test," *Strategic Management Journal* (January 2000), pp. 31–49.

44. R. L. Simerly and M. Li, "Environmental Dynamism, Capital Structure and Performance: A Theoretical Integration and an Empirical Test," *Strategic Management Journal* (January 2000), pp. 31–49; A. Heisz and S. LaRochelle-Cote, "Corporate Financial Leverage in Canadian Manufacturing: Consequences for Employment and Inventories," *Canadian Journal of Administrative Science* (June 2004), pp. 111–128.

45. J. M. Poterba and L. H. Summers, "A CEO Survey of U.S. Companies' Time Horizons and Hurdle Rates," *Sloan Management Review* (Fall 1995), pp. 43–53.

46. "R&D Scoreboard," *Business Week* (June 27, 1994), pp. 81–103.

47. B. O'Reilly, "The Secrets of America's Most Admired Corporations: New Ideas and New Products," *Fortune* (March 3, 1997), p. 62.

48. C. Palmeri, "Swords to Plowshares—And Back Again," *Business Week* (February 11, 2008), p. 66.

49. P. Pascarella, "Are You Investing in the Wrong Technology?" *Industry Week* (July 25, 1983), p. 37.

50. D. J. Yang, "Leaving Moore's Law in the Dust," *U.S. News & World Report* (July 10, 2000), pp. 37–38; R. Fishburne and M. Malone, "Laying Down the Laws: Gordon Moore and Bob Metcalfe in Conversation," *Forbes ASAP* (February 21, 2000), pp. 97–100.

51. Pascarella, p. 38.

52. C. M. Christensen, *The Innovator's Dilemma* (Boston: Harvard Business School Press, 1997).

53. O. Port, "Flat-Panel Pioneer," *Business Week* (December 12, 2005), p. 22. This phenomenon has also been discussed in terms of paradigm shifts in which a new development makes the old

game obsolete—See Joel A. Barker, *Future Edge* (New York: William Morrow and Company, 1992).

54. For examples of experience curves for various products, see M. Gottfredson, S. Schaubert, and H. Saenz, "The New Leader's Guide to Diagnosing the Business," *Harvard Business Review* (February 2008), pp. 63–73.

55. B. J. Pine, *Mass Customization: The New Frontier in Business Competition* (Boston: Harvard Business School Press, 1993).

56. D. Coates, "The Art of Assembly," *Sports Car International* (September 2007), p. 14; "One Line for Two: Spartanburg Revamps Assembly Process," *Roundel* (January 2006), p. 31.

57. S. L Rynes, K. G. Brown, and A. E. Colbert, "Seven Common Misconceptions about Human Resource Practices: Research Findings Versus Practitioner Belief," *Academy of Management Executive* (August 2002), pp. 92–103; R. S. Schuler and S. E. Jackson, "A Quarter-Century Review of Human Resource Management in the U.S.: The Growth in Importance of the International Perspective," in *Strategic Human Resource Management*, 2nd ed., edited by R. S. Schuler and S. E. Jackson (Malden, MA: Blackwell Publishing, 2007), pp. 214–240; M. Guthridge and A. B. Komm, "Why Multinationals Struggle to Manage Talent," *McKinsey Quarterly* (May 2008), pp. 1–5.

58. J. McGregor and S. Hamm, "Managing the Global Workforce," *Business Week* (January 28, 2008), pp. 34–48; D. A. Ready and J. A. Conger, "Make Your Company a Talent Factory," *Harvard Business Review* (June 2007), pp. 68–77.

59. E. E. Lawler, S. A. Mohrman, and G. E. Ledford, Jr., *Creating High Performance Organizations* (San Francisco: Jossey-Bass, 1995), p. 29.

60. A. Versteeg, "Self-Directed Work Teams Yield Long-Term Benefits," *Journal of Business Strategy* (November/December 1990), pp. 9–12.

61. R. Sanchez, "Strategic Flexibility in Product Competition," *Strategic Management Journal* (Summer 1995), p. 147.

62. A. R. Jassawalla and H. C. Sashittal, "Building Collaborative Cross-Functional New Product Teams," *Academy of Management Executive* (August 1999), pp. 50–63.

63. A. M. Townsend, S. M. DeMarie, and A. R. Hendrickson, "Virtual Teams' Technology and the Workplace of the Future," *Academy of Management Executive* (August 1998), pp. 17–29.

64. S. A. Furst, M. Reeves, B. Rosen, and R. S. Blackburn, "Managing the Life Cycle of Virtual Teams," *Academy of Management Executive* (May 2004), pp. 6–20; L. L. Martins, L. L. Gilson, and M. T. Maynard, "Virtual Teams: What Do We Know and Where Do We Go From Here?" *Journal of Management*, Vol. 30, No. 6 (2004), pp. 805–835.

65. C. B. Gibson and J. L. Gibbs, "Unpacking the Concept of Virtuality: The Effects of Geographic Dispersion, Electronic Dependence, Dynamic Structure, and National Diversity on Team Innovation," *Administrative Science Quarterly* (September 2006), pp. 451–495.

66. T. D. Golden and J. F. Veiga, "The Impact of Extent of Telecommuting on Job Satisfaction: Resolving Inconsistent Findings," *Journal of Management* (April 2005), pp. 301–318.

67. M. Conlin, "The Easiest Commute of All," *Business Week* (December 12, 2005), pp. 78–80.

68. Townsend, DeMarie, and Hendrickson, p. 18.

69. "News," *Bureau of Labor Statistics*, U.S. Department of Labor (January 25, 2008).

70. D. Welsh, "What Goodyear Got from Its Union," *Business Week* (October 20, 2003), pp. 148–149.

71. S. F. Matusik and C. W. L. Hill, "The Utilization of Contingent Work, Knowledge Creation, and Competitive Advantage," *Academy of Management Executive* (October 1998), pp. 680–697; W. Mayrhofer and C. Brewster, "European Human Resource Management: Researching Developments Over Time," in *Strategic Human Resource Management*, 2nd ed. (Malden, MA: Blackwell Publishing, 2007), pp. 241–269.

72. "Part-time Work," *The Economist* (June 24, 2006), p. 112.

73. A. Bernstein, "At UPS, Part-Time Work Is a Full-Time Issue," *Business Week* (June 16, 1997), pp. 88–90.

74. J. Muller, "A Ford Redesign," *Business Week* (November 13, 2000), Special Report.

75. O. C. Richard, B. P. S. Murthi, and K. Ismail, "The Impact of Racial Diversity on Intermediate and Long-Term Performance: The Moderating Role of Environmental Context," *Strategic Management Journal* (December 2007), pp. 1213–1233; G. Colvin, "The 50 Best Companies for Asians, Blacks, and Hispanics," *Fortune* (July 19, 1999), pp. 53–58.

76. V. Singh and S. Point, "Strategic Responses by European Companies to the Diversity Challenge: An Online Comparison," *Long Range Planning* (August 2004), pp. 295–318.

77. Singh and Point, p. 310.

78. J. Bachman, "Coke to Pay $192.5 Million to Settle Lawsuit," *The (Ames) Tribune* (November 20, 2000), p. D4.

79. O. Gottschalg and M. Zollo, "Interest Alignment and Competitive Advantage," *Academy of Management Review* (April 2007), pp. 418–437.

80. J. Lee and D. Miller, "People Matter: Commitment to Employees, Strategy, and Performance in Korean Firms," *Strategic Management Journal* (June 1999), pp. 579–593.

81. A. Cortese, "Here Comes the Intranet," *Business Week* (February 26, 1996), p. 76.

82. D. Bartholomew, "Blue-Collar Computing," *Information Week* (June 19, 1995), pp. 34–43.

83. J. Bughin, J. Manyika, A. Miller, and M. Cjhui, "Building the Web 2.0 Enterprise," *McKinsey Quarterly Online* (July 2008); J. Bughin, M. Chui, and B. Johnson, "The Next Step in Open Innovation," *McKinsey Quarterly Online* (June 2008), pp. 1–8.

84. C. C. Poirier, *Advanced Supply Chain Management* (San Francisco: Berrett-Koehler Publishers, 1999), p. 2.

85. J. H. Dyer and N. W. Hatch, "Relation-Specific Capabilities and Barriers to Knowledge Transfers: Creating Advantage through Network Relationships," *Strategic Management Journal* (August 2006), pp. 701–719.

86. D. Paulonis and S. Norton, "Managing Global Supply Chains," *McKinsey Quarterly Online* (August 2008).

87. M. Cook and R. Hagey, "Why Companies Flunk Supply-Chain 101: Only 33 Percent Correctly Measure Supply-Chain Performance; Few Use the Right Incentives," *Journal of Business Strategy*, Vol. 24, No. 4 (2003), pp. 35–42.

88. C. C. Poirer, pp. 3–5. For further information on RFID technology, see F. Taghaboni-Dutta and B. Velthouse, "RFID Technology is Revolutionary: Who Should Be Involved in This Game of Tag?" *Academy of Management Perspectives* (November 2006), pp. 65–78.

89. M. Arndt, "Everything Old Is New Again," *Business Week* (September 25, 2006), pp. 64–70.

90. R. Farzad, "Cash for Trash," *Business Week* (August 4, 2008), pp. 36–46.

Ending Case for Part Two

BOEING BETS THE COMPANY

The Boeing Company, a well-known U.S.-based manufacturer of commercial and military aircraft, faced a dilemma in 2004. Long the leader of the global airframe manufacturing industry, Boeing had been slowly losing market share since the 1990s to the European-based Airbus Industrie—now incorporated as the European Aeronautic & Space Company (EADS). In December 2001, the EADS board of directors had committed the corporation to an objective it had never before achieved—taking from Boeing the leadership of the commercial aviation industry by building the largest commercial jet plane in the world, the Airbus 380. The A380 would carry 481 passengers in a normal multiple-class seating configuration compared to the 416 passengers carried by Boeing's 747—400 in a similar seating configuration. The A380 would not only fly 621 miles farther than the 747, but it would cost airlines 15%–20% less per passenger to operate. With orders for 50 A380 aircraft in hand, the EADS board announced that the new plane would be ready for delivery during 2006. The proposed A380 program decimated the sales of Boeing's jumbo jet. Since 2000, airlines had ordered only 10 Boeing 747s configured for passengers.

Boeing was clearly a company in difficulty in 2004. Distracted by the 1996 acquisitions of McDonnell Douglas and Rockwell Aerospace, Boeing's top management had spent the next few years strengthening the corporation's historically weak position in aerospace and defense and had allowed its traditional competency in commercial aviation to deteriorate. Boeing, once the manufacturing marvel of the world, was now spending 10%–20% more than EADS (Airbus) to build a plane. The prices it asked for its planes were thus also higher. As a result, Boeing's estimated market share of the commercial market slid from nearly 70% in 1996 to less than half that by the end of 2003. EADS claimed to have delivered 300 aircraft to Boeing's 285 and to have won 56% of the 396 orders placed by airlines in 2003—quite an improvement from 1994, when EADS controlled only one-fifth of the market! This was quite an

accomplishment, given that the A380 was so large that the modifications needed to accommodate it at airports would cost $80 to $100 million.

Even though defense sales now accounted for more than half of the company's revenues, Boeing's CEO realized that he needed to quickly act to regain Boeing's leadership of the commercial part of the industry. In December 2003, the board approved the strategic decision to promote a new commercial airplane, the Boeing 787, for sale to airlines. The 787 was a midrange aircraft, not a jumbo jet such as the A380. The 787 would carry between 220 and 250 passengers but consume 20% less fuel and be 10% cheaper to operate than its competitor, EADS' current midrange plane, the smaller wide-body A330-200. It was to be made from a graphite/epoxy resin instead of aluminum. It was designed to fly faster, higher, farther, cleaner, more quietly, and more efficiently than any other medium-sized jet. This was the first time since approving the 777 jet in 1990 that the company had launched an all-new plane program. Development costs were estimated at $8 billion over five years. Depending on the results of these sales efforts, the board would decide sometime during 2004 to either begin or cancel the 787 construction program. If approved, the planes could be delivered in 2008—two years after the delivery of the A380.

The Boeing 787 decision was based on a completely different set of assumptions from those used by the EADS board to approve the A380. EADS top management believed that the commercial market wanted even larger jumbo jets to travel long international routes. Airports in Asia, the Middle East, and Europe were becoming heavily congested. In these locations, the "hub-and-spoke" method of creating major airline hubs was flourishing. Using larger planes was a way of dealing with that congestion by flying more passengers per plane out of these hubs. EADS management believed that over the next 20 years, airlines and freight carriers would need a minimum of 1,500 more aircraft at least as big as the B747. EADS management had concluded that the key to controlling the future commercial market was by using larger, more expensive planes. The A380 was a very large bet on that future scenario. The A380 program would cost EADS almost $13 million before the first plane was delivered.

In contrast, Boeing's management believed in a very different future scenario. Noting the success of Southwest and JetBlue, among other airlines in North America, it concluded that no more than 320 extra-large planes would be

This case was written by J. David Hunger for *Strategic Management and Business Policy*, 12th edition and for *Concepts in Strategic Management and Business Policy*, 12th edition. Copyright © 2008 by J. David Hunger. Reprinted by permission. References available upon request.

sold in the future as the airline industry moved away from hub-and-spoke networks toward more direct flights between smaller airports. The fragmentation of the airline industry, with its emphasis on competing through lower costs was the primary rationale for Boeing's fuel-efficient 787. A secondary reason was to deal with increasing passenger complaints about shrinking legroom and seat room on current planes flown by cost-conscious airlines. The 787 was designed with larger windows, seats, lavatories, and overhead bins. The plane was being designed in both short- and long-range versions. Boeing's management predicted a market for 2,000 to 3,000 such planes. Additional support for the midrange plane came from some industry analysts who predicted that the huge A380 would give new meaning to the term "cattle class." To reach necessary economies of scale, the A380 would likely devote a large portion of both of its decks to economy class, with passengers sitting three or four across, the same configuration as most of Boeing's 747s.

Boeing's strategy to regain industry leadership with its proposed 787 airplane meant that the company would have to increase its manufacturing efficiency in order to keep the price low. To significantly cut costs, management would be forced to implement a series of new programs:

- Outsource approximately 70% of manufacturing. Could it find suppliers who could consistently make the high-quality parts needed by Boeing?

- Reduce final assembly time to three days (compared to 20 for its 737 plane) by having suppliers build completed plane sections. Could this many suppliers meet Boeing's exacting deadlines?

- Use new, lightweight composite materials in place of aluminum to reduce inspection time. Would the plane be as dependable and as easy to maintain as Boeing's aluminum airplanes?

- Resolve poor relations with labor unions caused by downsizing and outsourcing. The machinists' union would have to be given a greater voice in specifying manufacturing procedures. Would Boeing's middle managers be willing to share power with an antagonistic union?

Which vision of the future was correct? The long-term fortunes of both Boeing and EADS depended on two contrasting strategic decisions, based on two very different assessments of the market. If EADS was correct, the market would continue to demand ever-larger airplanes. If Boeing was correct, the current wave of jumbo jets had crested, and a new wave of fuel-saving midrange jets would soon replace them. Which company's strategy had the best chance of succeeding?

PART 3

Strategy
Formulation

strategy formulation: situation analysis and Business Strategy

Midamar Corporation is a family-owned company in Cedar Rapids, Iowa, that has carved out a growing niche for itself in the world food industry: supplying food prepared according to strict religious standards. The company specializes in *halal foods*, which are produced and processed according to Islamic law for sale to Muslims. Why did it focus on this one type of food? According to owner-founder Bill Aossey, "It's a big world, and you can only specialize in so many places." Although halal foods are not as widely known as kosher foods (processed according to Judaic law), their market is growing along with Islam, the world's fastest-growing religion. Midamar purchases halal-certified meat from Midwestern companies certified to conduct halal processing. Certification requires practicing Muslims schooled in halal processing to slaughter the livestock and to oversee meat and poultry processing.

Aossey is a practicing Muslim who did not imagine such a vast market when he founded his business in 1974. "People thought it would be a passing fad," remarked Aossey. The company has grown to the point where it now exports halal-certified beef, lamb, and poultry to hotels, restaurants, and distributors in 30 countries throughout Asia, Africa, Europe, and North America. Its customers include McDonald's, Pizza Hut, and KFC. McDonald's, for example, uses Midamar's turkey strips as a bacon-alternative in a breakfast product in Singapore.[1]

Midamar is successful because its chief executive formulated a strategy designed to give it an advantage in a very competitive industry. It is an example of a differentiation focus competitive strategy in which a company focuses on a particular target market to provide a differentiated product or service. This strategy is one of the business competitive strategies discussed in this chapter.

Learning Objectives

After reading this chapter, you should be able to:

- Organize environmental and organizational information using SWOT analysis and a SFAS matrix
- Generate strategic options by using the TOWS matrix
- Understand the competitive and cooperative strategies available to corporations

- List the competitive tactics that would accompany competitive strategies
- Identify the basic types of strategic alliances

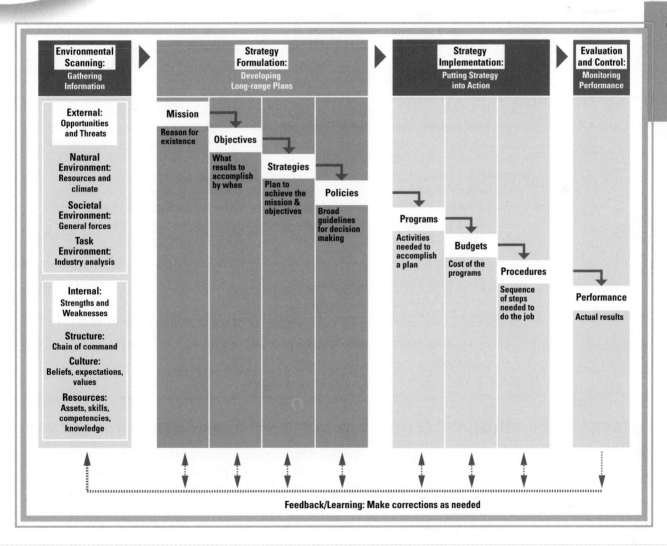

6.1 Situational Analysis: SWOT Analysis

Strategy formulation, often referred to as strategic planning or long-range planning, is concerned with developing a corporation's mission, objectives, strategies, and policies. It begins with situation analysis: the process of finding a strategic fit between external opportunities and internal strengths while working around external threats and internal weaknesses. As shown in the Strategic Decision-Making Process in Figure 1–5, step 5(a) is analyzing strategic factors in light of the current situation using SWOT analysis. **SWOT** is an acronym used to describe the particular **S**trengths, **W**eaknesses, **O**pportunities, and **T**hreats that are strategic factors for a specific company. SWOT analysis should not only result in the identification of a corporation's distinctive competencies—the particular capabilities and resources that a firm possesses and the superior way in which they are used—but also in the identification of opportunities that the firm is not currently able to take advantage of due to a lack of appropriate resources. Over the years, SWOT analysis has proven to be the most enduring analytical technique used in strategic management. For example, in a 2007 McKinsey & Company global survey of 2,700 executives, 82% of the executives stated that the most relevant activities for strategy formulation were evaluating the strengths and weaknesses of the organization and identifying top environmental trends affecting business unit performance over the next three to five years.[2] A 2005 survey of competitive intelligence professionals found that SWOT analysis was used by 82.7% of the respondents, the second most frequently used technique, trailing only competitor analysis.[3]

It can be said that the essence of strategy is opportunity divided by capacity.[4] An opportunity by itself has no real value unless a company has the capacity (i.e., resources) to take advantage of that opportunity. This approach, however, considers only opportunities and strengths when considering alternative strategies. By itself, a distinctive competency in a key resource or capability is no guarantee of competitive advantage. Weaknesses in other resource areas can prevent a strategy from being successful. SWOT can thus be used to take a broader view of strategy through the formula $SA = O/(S – W)$ that is, (Strategic Alternative equals Opportunity divided by Strengths minus Weaknesses). This reflects an important issue strategic managers face: Should we invest more in our strengths to make them even stronger (a distinctive competence) or should we invest in our weaknesses to at least make them competitive?

SWOT analysis, by itself, is not a panacea. Some of the primary criticisms of SWOT analysis are:

- It generates lengthy lists.
- It uses no weights to reflect priorities.
- It uses ambiguous words and phrases.
- The same factor can be placed in two categories (e.g., a strength may also be a weakness).
- There is no obligation to verify opinions with data or analysis.
- It requires only a single level of analysis.
- There is no logical link to strategy implementation.[5]

GENERATING A STRATEGIC FACTORS ANALYSIS SUMMARY (SFAS) MATRIX

The EFAS and IFAS Tables plus the SFAS Matrix have been developed to deal with the criticisms of SWOT analysis. When used together, they are a powerful analytical set of tools for strategic analysis. The **SFAS (Strategic Factors Analysis Summary) Matrix** summarizes an organization's strategic factors by combining the external factors from the EFAS Table with the internal factors from the IFAS Table. The EFAS and IFAS examples given of Maytag Corporation (as it was in 1995) in **Tables 4–5** and **5–2** list a total of 20 internal and external factors. These are too many factors for most people to use in strategy formulation. The SFAS Matrix requires a strategic decision maker to condense these strengths, weaknesses, opportunities, and threats into fewer than 10 strategic factors. This is done by reviewing and revising the weight given each factor. The revised weights reflect the priority of each factor as a determinant of the company's future success. The highest-weighted EFAS and IFAS factors should appear in the SFAS Matrix.

As shown in **Figure 6–1** , you can create an SFAS Matrix by following these steps:

1. In **Column 1** *(Strategic Factors)*, list the most important EFAS and IFAS items. After each factor, indicate whether it is a Strength **(S)**, Weakness **(W)**, an Opportunity **(O)**, or a Threat **(T)**.

2. In **Column 2** *(Weight)*, assign weights for all of the internal and external strategic factors. As with the EFAS and IFAS Tables presented earlier, the **weight column must total 1.00**. This means that the weights calculated earlier for EFAS and IFAS will probably have to be adjusted.

3. In **Column 3** *(Rating)* assign a rating of how the company's management is responding to each of the strategic factors. These ratings will probably (but not always) be the same as those listed in the EFAS and IFAS Tables.

4. In **Column 4** *(Weighted Score)* multiply the weight in **Column 2** for each factor by its rating in **Column 3** to obtain the factor's rated score.

5. In **Column 5** *(Duration)*, depicted in **Figure 6–1**, indicate **short-term** (less than one year), **intermediate-term** (one to three years), or **long-term** (three years and beyond).

6. In **Column 6** *(Comments)*, repeat or revise your comments for each strategic factor from the previous EFAS and IFAS Tables. **The total weighted score for the average firm in an industry is always 3.0.**

The resulting SFAS Matrix is a listing of the firm's external and internal strategic factors in one table. The example given in **Figure 6–1** is for Maytag Corporation in 1995, before the firm sold its European and Australian operations and it was acquired by Whirlpool. The SFAS Matrix includes only the most important factors gathered from environmental scanning and thus provides information that is essential for strategy formulation. The use of EFAS and IFAS Tables together with the SFAS Matrix deals with some of the criticisms of SWOT analysis. For example, the use of the SFAS Matrix reduces the list of factors to a manageable number, puts weights on each factor, and allows one factor to be listed as both a strength and a weakness (or as an opportunity and a threat).

FINDING A PROPITIOUS NICHE

One desired outcome of analyzing strategic factors is identifying a niche where an organization can use its core competencies to take advantage of a particular market opportunity. A niche is a need in the marketplace that is currently unsatisfied. The goal is to find a *propitious niche*—an extremely favorable niche—that is so well suited to the firm's internal and external environment that other corporations are not likely to challenge or dislodge it.[6] A niche is propitious to the extent that it currently is just large enough for one firm to satisfy its demand. After a firm has found and filled that niche, it is not worth a potential competitor's time or money to also go after the same niche. Such a niche may also be called a *strategic sweet spot*

FIGURE 6–1   Strategic Factor Analysis Summary (SFAS) Matrix

Internal Strategic Factors	Weight	Rating	Weighted Score	Comments
	1	2	3	4		5
Strengths				
S1 Quality Maytag culture	.15	5.0	.75	Quality key to success
S2 Experienced top management	.05	4.2	.21	Know appliances
S3 Vertical integration	.10	3.9	.39	Dedicated factories
S4 Employee relations	.05	3.0	.15	Good, but deteriorating
S5 Hoover's international orientation	.15	2.8	.42	Hoover name in cleaners
Weaknesses				
W1 Process-oriented R&D	.05	2.2	.11	Slow on new products
W2 Distribution channels	.05	2.0	.10	Superstores replacing small dealers
W3 Financial position	.15	2.0	.30	High debt load
W4 Global positioning	.20	2.1	.42	Hoover weak outside the United Kingdom and Australia
W5 Manufacturing facilities	.05	4.0	.20	Investing now
Total Scores	1.00		3.05	

External Strategic Factors	Weight	Rating	Weighted Score	Comments
	1	2	3	4		5
Opportunities				
O1 Economic integration of European Community	.20	4.1	.82	Acquisition of Hoover
O2 Demographics favor quality appliances	.10	5.0	.50	Maytag quality
O3 Economic development of Asia	.05	1.0	.05	Low Maytag presence
O4 Opening of Eastern Europe	.05	2.0	.10	Will take time
O5 Trend to "Super Stores"	.10	1.8	.18	Maytag weak in this channel
Threats				
T1 Increasing government regulations	.10	4.3	.43	Well positioned
T2 Strong U.S. competition	.10	4.0	.40	Well positioned
T3 Whirlpool and Electrolux strong globally	.15	3.0	.45	Hoover weak globally
T4 New product advances	.05	1.2	.06	Questionable
T5 Japanese appliance companies	.10	1.6	.16	Only Asian presence is Australia
Total Scores	1.00		3.15	

*The most important external and internal factors are identified in the EFAS and IFAS tables as shown here by shading these factors.

	1	2	3	4 Weighted	Duration 5			6
Strategic Factors (Select the most important opportunities/threats from EFAS, Table 4–5 and the most important strengths and weaknesses from IFAS, Table 5–2)		**Weight**	**Rating**	**Weighted Score**	**SHORT**	**INTERMEDIATE**	**LONG**	**Comments**
S1	Quality Maytag culture (S)	.10	5.0	.50			X	Quality key to success
S5	Hoover's international orientation (S)	.10	2.8	.28	X	X		Name recognition
W3	Financial position (W)	.10	2.0	.20	X	X		High debt
W4	Global positioning (W)	.15	2.2	.33		X	X	Only in N.A., U.K., and Australia
O1	Economic integration of European Community (O)	.10	4.1	.41			X	Acquisition of Hoover
O2	Demographics favor quality (O)	.10	5.0	.50		X		Maytag quality
O5	Trend to super stores (O + T)	.10	1.8	.18	X			Weak in this channel
T3	Whirlpool and Electrolux (T)	.15	3.0	.45	X			Dominate industry
T5	Japanese appliance companies (T)	.10	1.6	.16			X	Asian presence
Total Scores		**1.00**		**3.01**				

Notes:
1. List each of the most important factors developed in your IFAS and EFAS Tables in Column 1.
2. Weight each factor from 1.0 (Most Important) to 0.0 (Not Important) in Column 2 based on that factor's probable impact on the company's strategic position. **The total weights must sum to 1.00.**
3. Rate each factor from 5.0 (Outstanding) to 1.0 (Poor) in Column 3 based on the company's response to that factor.
4. Multiply each factor's weight times its rating to obtain each factor's weighted score in Column 4.
5. For duration in Column 5, check appropriate column (short term—less than 1 year; intermediate—1 to 3 years; long term—over 3 years).
6. Use Column 6 (comments) for rationale used for each factor.

(see **Figure 6–2**)—where a company is able to satisfy customers' needs in a way that rivals cannot, given the context in which it operates.[7]

Finding such a niche or sweet spot is not always easy. A firm's management must be always looking for a *strategic window*—that is, a unique market opportunity that is available only for a particular time. The first firm through a strategic window can occupy a propitious niche and discourage competition (if the firm has the required internal strengths). One company that successfully found a propitious niche was Frank J. Zamboni & Company, the manufacturer of the machines that smooth the ice at ice skating rinks. Frank Zamboni invented the

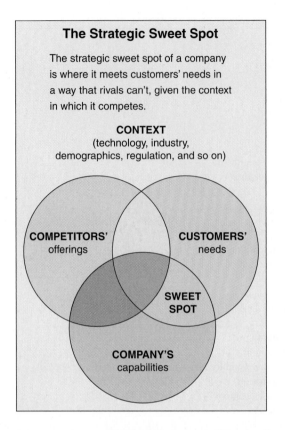

The Strategic Sweet Spot

The strategic sweet spot of a company is where it meets customers' needs in a way that rivals can't, given the context in which it competes.

CONTEXT
(technology, industry, demographics, regulation, and so on)

COMPETITORS' offerings

CUSTOMERS' needs

SWEET SPOT

COMPANY'S capabilities

SOURCE: D. J. Collis and M. G. Rukstad, "Can You Say What Your Strategy Is?" Reprinted by permission of Harvard Business Review. 'The Strategic Sweet Spot' from "Can You Say What Strategy is?" by D. J. Collis & M. G. Rukstad April 2008. Copyright © 2008 by the Harvard Business School Publishing Corporation. All rights reserved.

unique tractor-like machine in 1949 and no one has found a substitute for what it does. Before the machine was invented, people had to clean and scrape the ice by hand to prepare the surface for skating. Now hockey fans look forward to intermissions just to watch "the Zamboni" slowly drive up and down the ice rink, turning rough, scraped ice into a smooth mirror surface—almost like magic. So long as Zamboni's company was able to produce the machines in the quantity and quality desired, at a reasonable price, it was not worth another company's while to go after Frank Zamboni & Company's propitious niche.

As a niche grows, so can a company within that niche—by increasing its operations' capacity or through alliances with larger firms. The key is to identify a market opportunity in which the first firm to reach that market segment can obtain and keep dominant market share. For example, Church & Dwight was the first company in the United States to successfully market sodium bicarbonate for use in cooking. Its Arm & Hammer brand baking soda is still found in 95% of all U.S. households. The propitious niche concept is crucial to the software industry. Small initial demand in emerging markets allows new entrepreneurial ventures to go after niches too small to be noticed by established companies. When Microsoft developed its first disk operating system (DOS) in 1980 for IBM's personal computers, for example, the demand for such open systems software was very small—a small niche for a then very small Microsoft. The company was able to fill that niche and to successfully grow with it.

Niches can also change—sometimes faster than a firm can adapt to that change. A company's management may discover in their situation analysis that they need to invest heavily in the firm's capabilities to keep them competitively strong in a changing niche. South African

GLOBAL issue

SAB DEFENDS ITS PROPITIOUS NICHE

Out of 50 beers drunk by South Africans, 49 are brewed by South African Breweries (SAB). Founded more than a century ago, SAB controlled most of the local beer market by 1950 with brands such as Castle and Lion. When the government repealed the ban on the sale of alcohol to blacks in the 1960s, SAB and other brewers competed for the rapidly growing market. SAB fought successfully to retain its dominance of the market. With the end of apartheid, foreign brewers have been tempted to break SAB's near-monopoly but have been deterred by the entry barriers SAB has erected:

Entry Barrier #1: Every year for the past two decades SAB has reduced its prices. The "real" (adjusted for inflation) price of its beer is now half what it was during the 1970s. SAB has been able to achieve this through a continuous emphasis on productivity improvements— boosting production while cutting the workforce almost in half. Keeping prices low has been key to SAB's avoiding charges of abusing its monopoly.

Entry Barrier #2: In South Africa's poor and rural areas, roads are rough, and electricity is undependable. SAB has long experience in transporting crates to remote villages along bad roads and making sure that distributors have refrigerators (and electricity generators if needed). Many of its distributors are former employees who have been helped by the company to start their own trucking businesses.

Entry Barrier #3: Most of the beer sold in South Africa is sold through unlicensed pubs called *shebeens*—most of which date back to apartheid, when blacks were not allowed licenses. Although the current government of South Africa would be pleased to grant pub licenses to blacks, the shebeen owners don't want them. They enjoy not paying any taxes. SAB cannot sell directly to the shebeens, but it does so indirectly through wholesalers. The government, in turn, ignores the situation, preferring that people drink SAB beer than potentially deadly moonshine.

To break into South Africa, a new entrant would have to build large breweries and a substantial distribution network. SAB would, in turn, probably reduce its prices still further to defend its market. The difficulties of operating in South Africa are too great, the market is growing too slowly, and (given SAB's low cost position) the likely profit margin is too low to justify entering the market. Some foreign brewers, such as Heineken, would rather use SAB to distribute their products throughout South Africa. With its home market secure, SAB purchased Miller Brewing to secure a strong presence in North America.

SOURCE: Summarized from "Big Lion, Small Cage," *The Economist* (August 12, 2000), p. 56, and other sources.

Breweries (SAB), for example, took this approach when management realized that the only way to keep competitors out of its market was to continuously invest in increased productivity and infrastructure in order to keep its prices very low. See the **Global Issue** feature to see how SAB was able to successfully defend its market niche during significant changes in its environment.

6.2 Review of Mission and Objectives

A reexamination of an organization's current mission and objectives must be made before alternative strategies can be generated and evaluated. Even when formulating strategy, decision makers tend to concentrate on the alternatives—the action possibilities—rather than on a mission to be fulfilled and objectives to be achieved. This tendency is so attractive because it is much easier to deal with alternative courses of action that exist right here and now than to really think about what you want to accomplish in the future. The end result is that we often choose strategies that set our objectives for us rather than having our choices incorporate clear objectives and a mission statement.

Problems in performance can derive from an inappropriate statement of mission, which may be too narrow or too broad. If the mission does not provide a *common thread* (a unifying theme) for a corporation's businesses, managers may be unclear about where the company is heading. Objectives and strategies might be in conflict with each other. Divisions might be competing against one another rather than against outside competition—to the detriment of the corporation as a whole.

A company's objectives can also be inappropriately stated. They can either focus too much on short-term operational goals or be so general that they provide little real guidance. There may be a gap between planned and achieved objectives. When such a gap occurs, either the strategies have to be changed to improve performance or the objectives need to be adjusted downward to be more realistic. Consequently, objectives should be constantly reviewed to ensure their usefulness. This is what happened at Boeing when management decided to change its primary objective from being the largest in the industry to being the most profitable. This had a significant effect on its strategies and policies. Following its new objective, the company cancelled its policy of competing with Airbus on price and abandoned its commitment to maintaining a manufacturing capacity that could produce more than half a peak year's demand for airplanes.[8]

6.3 Generating Alternative Strategies by Using a TOWS Matrix

Thus far we have discussed how a firm uses SWOT analysis to assess its situation. SWOT can also be used to generate a number of possible alternative strategies. The **TOWS Matrix** (TOWS is just another way of saying SWOT) illustrates how the external opportunities and threats facing a particular corporation can be matched with that company's internal strengths and weaknesses to result in four sets of possible strategic alternatives. (See **Figure 6–3**.) This is a good way to use brainstorming to create alternative strategies that might not otherwise be considered. It forces strategic managers to create various kinds of growth as well as retrenchment strategies. It can be used to generate corporate as well as business strategies.

FIGURE 6–3
TOWS Matrix

INTERNAL FACTORS (IFAS) / EXTERNAL FACTORS (EFAS)	Strengths (S) List 5 – 10 *internal* strengths here	Weaknesses (W) List 5 – 10 *internal* weaknesses here
Opportunities (O) List 5 – 10 *external* opportunities here	SO Strategies Generate strategies here that use **strengths** to take **advantage of opportunities**	WO Strategies Generate strategies here that take **advantage** of **opportunities** by **overcoming weaknesses**
Threats (T) List 5 – 10 *external* threats here	ST Strategies Generate strategies here that use **strengths** to **avoid threats**	WT Strategies Generate strategies here that **minimize weaknesses** and **avoid threats**

SOURCE: *Reprinted from* Long-Range Planning, *Vol. 15, No. 2, 1982, Weihrich "The TOWS Matrix—A Tool For Situational Analysis," p. 60. Copyright © 1982 with permission of Elsevier and H. Weihrich.*

To generate a TOWS Matrix for Maytag Corporation in 1995, for example, use the External Factor Analysis Summary (EFAS) Table listed in **Table 4–5** from **Chapter 4** and the Internal Factor Analysis Summary (IFAS) Table listed in **Table 5–2** from **Chapter 5**. To build **Figure 6–4**, take the following steps:

1. In the **Opportunities (O)** block, list the external opportunities available in the company's or business unit's current and future environment from the EFAS Table (**Table 4–5**).

2. In the **Threats (T)** block, list the external threats facing the company or unit now and in the future from the EFAS Table (**Table 4–5**).

3. In the **Strengths (S)** block, list the specific areas of current and future strength for the company or unit from the IFAS Table (**Table 5–2**).

4. In the **Weaknesses (W)** block, list the specific areas of current and future weakness for the company or unit from the IFAS Table (**Table 5–2**).

5. Generate a series of possible strategies for the company or business unit under consideration based on particular combinations of the four sets of factors:
   - **SO Strategies** are generated by thinking of ways in which a company or business unit could use its strengths to take advantage of opportunities.
   - **ST Strategies** consider a company's or unit's strengths as a way to avoid threats.
   - **WO Strategies** attempt to take advantage of opportunities by overcoming weaknesses.
   - **WT Strategies** are basically defensive and primarily act to minimize weaknesses and avoid threats.

The TOWS Matrix is very useful for generating a series of alternatives that the decision makers of a company or business unit might not otherwise have considered. It can be used for the corporation as a whole (as is done in **Figure 6–4** with Maytag Corporation before it sold Hoover Europe), or it can be used for a specific business unit within a corporation (such as Hoover's floor care products). Nevertheless using a TOWS Matrix is only one of many ways to generate alternative strategies. Another approach is to evaluate each business unit within a corporation in terms of possible competitive and cooperative strategies.

6.4 Business Strategies

Business strategy focuses on improving the competitive position of a company's or business unit's products or services within the specific industry or market segment that the company or business unit serves. Business strategy is extremely important because research shows that business unit effects have double the impact on overall company performance than do either corporate or industry effects.[9] Business strategy can be competitive (battling against all competitors for advantage) and/or cooperative (working with one or more companies to gain advantage against other competitors). Just as corporate strategy asks what industry(ies) the company should be in, business strategy asks how the company or its units should compete or cooperate in each industry.

PORTER'S COMPETITIVE STRATEGIES

Competitive strategy raises the following questions:

- Should we compete on the basis of lower cost (and thus price), or should we differentiate our products or services on some basis other than cost, such as quality or service?

FIGURE 6–4   Generating a TOWS Matrix for Maytag Corporation

Internal Strategic Factors	Weight	Rating	Weighted Score	Comments
	1	2	3	4 5
Strengths				
S1 Quality Maytag culture	.15	5.0	.75	Quality key to success
S2 Experienced top management	.05	4.2	.21	Know appliances
S3 Vertical integration	.10	3.9	.39	Dedicated factories
S4 Employee relations	.05	3.0	.15	Good, but deteriorating
S5 Hoover's international orientation	.15	2.8	.42	Hoover name in cleaners
Weaknesses				
W1 Process-oriented R&D	.05	2.2	.11	Slow on new products
W2 Distribution channels	.05	2.0	.10	Superstores replacing small dealers
W3 Financial position	.15	2.0	.30	High debt load
W4 Global positioning	.20	2.1	.42	Hoover weak outside the United Kingdom and Australia
W5 Manufacturing facilities	.05	4.0	.20	Investing now
Total Scores	**1.00**		**3.05**	

External Strategic Factors	Weight	Rating	Weighted Score	Comments
	1	2	3	4 5
Opportunities				
O1 Economic integration of European Community	.20	4.1	.82	Acquisition of Hoover
O2 Demographics favor quality appliances	.10	5.0	.50	Maytag quality
O3 Economic development of Asia	.05	1.0	.05	Low Maytag presence
O4 Opening of Eastern Europe	.05	2.0	.10	Will take time
O5 Trend to "Super Stores"	.10	1.8	.18	Maytag weak in this channel
Threats				
T1 Increasing government regulations	.10	4.3	.43	Well positioned
T2 Strong U.S. competition	.10	4.0	.40	Well positioned
T3 Whirlpool and Electrolux strong globally	.15	3.0	.45	Hoover weak globally
T4 New product advances	.05	1.2	.06	Questionable
T5 Japanese appliance companies	.10	1.6	.16	Only Asian presence is Australia
Total Scores	**1.00**		**3.15**	

*The most important external and internal factors are identified in the EFAS and IFAS Tables as shown here by shading these factors.

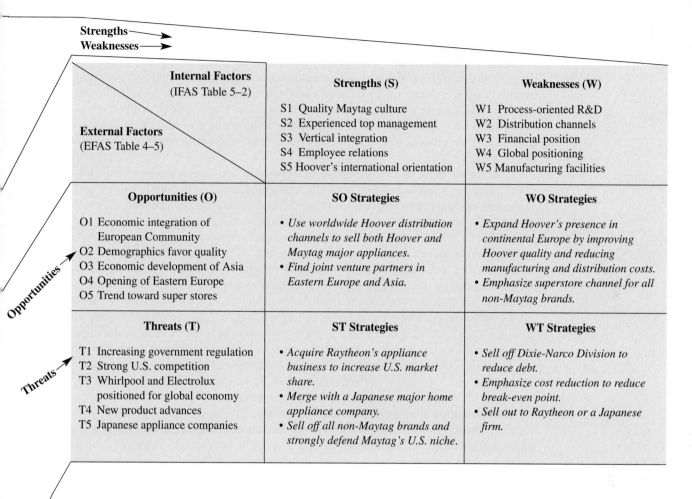

Strengths——→
Weaknesses——→

Internal Factors (IFAS Table 5–2) External Factors (EFAS Table 4–5)	Strengths (S) S1 Quality Maytag culture S2 Experienced top management S3 Vertical integration S4 Employee relations S5 Hoover's international orientation	Weaknesses (W) W1 Process-oriented R&D W2 Distribution channels W3 Financial position W4 Global positioning W5 Manufacturing facilities
Opportunities (O) O1 Economic integration of European Community O2 Demographics favor quality O3 Economic development of Asia O4 Opening of Eastern Europe O5 Trend toward super stores	**SO Strategies** • *Use worldwide Hoover distribution channels to sell both Hoover and Maytag major appliances.* • *Find joint venture partners in Eastern Europe and Asia.*	**WO Strategies** • *Expand Hoover's presence in continental Europe by improving Hoover quality and reducing manufacturing and distribution costs.* • *Emphasize superstore channel for all non-Maytag brands.*
Threats (T) T1 Increasing government regulation T2 Strong U.S. competition T3 Whirlpool and Electrolux positioned for global economy T4 New product advances T5 Japanese appliance companies	**ST Strategies** • *Acquire Raytheon's appliance business to increase U.S. market share.* • *Merge with a Japanese major home appliance company.* • *Sell off all non-Maytag brands and strongly defend Maytag's U.S. niche.*	**WT Strategies** • *Sell off Dixie-Narco Division to reduce debt.* • *Emphasize cost reduction to reduce break-even point.* • *Sell out to Raytheon or a Japanese firm.*

Opportunities

Threats

- ■ Should we compete head to head with our major competitors for the biggest but most sought-after share of the market, or should we focus on a niche in which we can satisfy a less sought-after but also profitable segment of the market?

Michael Porter proposes two "generic" competitive strategies for outperforming other corporations in a particular industry: lower cost and differentiation.[10] These strategies are called generic because they can be pursued by any type or size of business firm, even by not-for-profit organizations:

- ■ **Lower cost strategy** is the ability of a company or a business unit to design, produce, and market a comparable product more efficiently than its competitors.
- ■ **Differentiation strategy** is the ability of a company to provide unique and superior value to the buyer in terms of product quality, special features, or after-sale service.

Porter further proposes that a firm's competitive advantage in an industry is determined by its **competitive scope**, that is, the breadth of the company's or business unit's target market. Before using one of the two generic competitive strategies (lower cost or differentiation), the firm or unit must choose the range of product varieties it will produce, the distribution channels it will employ, the types of buyers it will serve, the geographic areas in which it will sell, and the array of related industries in which it will also compete. This should reflect an understanding of the firm's unique resources. Simply put, a company or business unit can choose a broad target (that is, aim at the middle of the mass market) or a narrow target (that is, aim at a market niche). Combining these two types of target markets with the two competitive strategies results in the four variations of generic strategies depicted in **Figure 6–5**. When the lower-cost and differentiation strategies have a broad mass-market target, they are simply called *cost leadership* and *differentiation*. When they are focused on a market niche (narrow target), however, they are called *cost focus* and *differentiation focus*. Although research does indicate that established firms pursuing broad-scope strategies outperform firms following narrow-scope strategies in terms of ROA (Return on Assets), new entrepreneurial firms have a better chance of surviving if they follow a narrow-scope rather than a broad-scope strategy.[11]

Cost leadership is a lower-cost competitive strategy that aims at the broad mass market and requires "aggressive construction of efficient-scale facilities, vigorous pursuit of cost reductions from experience, tight cost and overhead control, avoidance of marginal customer accounts, and cost minimization in areas like R&D, service, sales force, advertising, and so on."[12] Because of its lower costs, the cost leader is able to charge a lower price for its products than its competitors and still make a satisfactory profit. Although it may not necessarily have the lowest costs in the industry, it has lower costs than its competitors. Some companies successfully following this strategy are Wal-Mart (discount retailing), McDonald's (fast-food restaurants), Dell (computers), Alamo (rental cars), Aldi (grocery stores), Southwest Airlines, and Timex (watches). Having a lower-cost position also gives a company or business unit a defense against rivals. Its lower costs allow it to continue to earn profits during times of heavy competition. Its high market share means that it will have high bargaining power relative to its suppliers (because it buys in large quantities). Its low price will also serve as a barrier to entry because few new entrants will be able to match the leader's cost advantage. As a result, cost leaders are likely to earn above-average returns on investment.

Differentiation is aimed at the broad mass market and involves the creation of a product or service that is perceived throughout its industry as unique. The company or business unit may then charge a premium for its product. This specialty can be associated with design or brand image, technology, features, a dealer network, or customer service. Differentiation is a viable strat-

FIGURE 6–5
Porter's Generic Competitive Strategies

Competitive Advantage

	Lower Cost	Differentiation
Broad Target	**Cost Leadership**	**Differentiation**
Narrow Target	**Cost Focus**	**Differentiation Focus**

Competitive Scope

egy for earning above-average returns in a specific business because the resulting brand loyalty lowers customers' sensitivity to price. Increased costs can usually be passed on to the buyers. Buyer loyalty also serves as an entry barrier; new firms must develop their own distinctive competence to differentiate their products in some way in order to compete successfully. Examples of companies that successfully use a differentiation strategy are Walt Disney Productions (entertainment), BMW (automobiles), Nike (athletic shoes), Apple Computer (computers and cell phones), and Pacar (trucks). Pacar Inc., for example, charges 10% more for its Kenworth and Peterbilt 10-wheel diesel trucks than does market-leader Chrysler's Freightliner because of its focus on product quality and a superior dealer experience.[13] Research does suggest that a differentiation strategy is more likely to generate higher profits than does a low-cost strategy because differentiation creates a better entry barrier. A low-cost strategy is more likely, however, to generate increases in market share.[14] For an example of a differentiation strategy based upon environmental sustainability, see the **Environmental Sustainability Issue** feature on Patagonia.

Cost focus is a low-cost competitive strategy that focuses on a particular buyer group or geographic market and attempts to serve only this niche, to the exclusion of others. In using cost focus, the company or business unit seeks a cost advantage in its target segment. A good example of this strategy is Potlach Corporation, a manufacturer of toilet tissue. Rather than

ENVIRONMENTAL sustainability issue

PATAGONIA USES SUSTAINABILITY AS DIFFERENTIATION COMPETITIVE STRATEGY

Patagonia is a highly respected designer and manufacturer of outdoor clothing, outdoor gear, footwear, and luggage. Founded by Yvon Chouinard, an avid surfer and outdoorsman, the company reflects his commitment to both quality clothing and sustainable business practices. Since its founding in 1973, Patagonia has grown at a healthy rate and retained an excellent reputation in a highly competitive industry. It uses a differentiation competitive strategy emphasizing quality, but defines quality in a way differently from most other companies.

Our definition of quality includes a mandate for building products and working with processes that cause the least harm to the environment. We evaluate raw materials, invest in innovative technologies, rigorously police our waste and use a portion (1%) of our sales to support groups working to make a real difference. We acknowledge that the wild world we love best is disappearing. That is why those of us who work here share a strong commitment to protecting undomesticated lands and waters. We believe in using business to inspire solutions to the environmental crisis.

Patagonia's Web site includes not only the usual information about its products lines, but also an environmental section that examines the company's business practices. Its

Footprint Chronicles is an interactive mini-site that allows the viewer to track the impact of 10 specific Patagonia products from design through delivery. For example, the down sweater page tells how the company uses high-quality goose down from humanely raised geese. The down is minimally processed and the shell is made of recycled polyester. One problem is that the company had to increase the weight of the shell fabric when it switched to recycled polyester. Another problem is that the zipper is treated with a water repellent that contains perfluorooctanoic acid (PFOA), which has been found to persist in the environment and is not recyclable. The Web page tells that the company is investigating alternatives to the use of PFOA in water repellents and looking for ways to recycle down garments. The page then asks for feedback and gives the viewer the opportunity to see what others are saying.

Chairman Chouinard is proud of his company's reputation as a "green" company, but also wants the firm to be economically sustainable as well. According to Chouinard, "I look at this company as an experiment to see if we can run it so it's here 100 years from now and always makes the best-quality stuff."

SOURCE: S. Hamm, "A Passion for the Plan," *Business Week* (August 21/28, 2006), pp. 92–93 and corporate Web site accessed September 17, 2008, www.patagonia.com.

compete directly against Procter & Gamble's Charmin, Potlach makes the house brands for Al-bertson's, Safeway, Jewel, and many other grocery store chains. It matches the quality of the well-known brands, but keeps costs low by eliminating advertising and promotion expenses. As a result, Spokane-based Potlach makes 92% of the private-label bathroom tissue and one-third of all bathroom tissue sold in Western U.S. grocery stores.[15]

Differentiation focus, like cost focus, concentrates on a particular buyer group, product line segment, or geographic market. This is the strategy successfully followed by Midamar Corporation (distributor of halal foods), Morgan Motor Car Company (a manufacturer of clas-sic British sports cars), Nickelodeon (a cable channel for children), Orphagenix (pharmaceu-ticals), and local ethnic grocery stores. In using differentiation focus, a company or business unit seeks differentiation in a targeted market segment. This strategy is valued by those who believe that a company or a unit that focuses its efforts is better able to serve the special needs of a narrow strategic target more effectively than can its competition. For example, Orpha-genix is a small biotech pharmaceutical company that avoids head-to-head competition with big companies like AstraZenica and Merck by developing "orphan" drugs to target diseases that affect fewer than 200,000 people—diseases such as sickle cell anemia and spinal muscu-lar atrophy that big drug makers are overlooking.[16]

Risks in Competitive Strategies

No one competitive strategy is guaranteed to achieve success, and some companies that have successfully implemented one of Porter's competitive strategies have found that they could not sustain the strategy. As shown in **Table 6–1**, each of the generic strategies has risks. For ex-ample, a company following a differentiation strategy must ensure that the higher price it charges for its higher quality is not too far above the price of the competition; otherwise cus-tomers will not see the extra quality as worth the extra cost. This is what is meant in **Table 6.1** by the term *cost proximity*. For years, Deere & Company was the leader in farm machinery until low-cost competitors from India and other developing countries began making low-priced products. Deere responded by building high-tech flexible manufacturing plants using mass-customization to cut its manufacturing costs and using innovation to create differenti-ated products which, although higher-priced, reduced customers' labor and fuel expenses.[17]

TABLE 6–1   Risks of Generic Competitive Strategies

Risks of Cost Leadership	Risks of Differentiation	Risks of Focus
Cost leadership is not sustained: ■ Competitors imitate. ■ Technology changes. ■ Other bases for cost leadership erode.	Differentiation is not sustained: ■ Competitors imitate. ■ Bases for differentiation become less important to buyers.	The focus strategy is imitated. The target segment becomes structurally unattractive: ■ Structure erodes. ■ Demand disappears.
Proximity in differentiation is lost.	Cost proximity is lost.	Broadly targeted competitors overwhelm the segment: ■ The segment's differences from other segments narrow. ■ The advantages of a broad line increase.
Cost focusers achieve even lower cost in segments.	Differentiation focusers achieve even greater differentiation in segments.	New focusers subsegment the industry.

SOURCE: Reprinted with permission of The Free Press, a Division of Simon & Schuster, Inc. from COMPETITIVE ADVANTAGE: Creating and Sustaining Superior Performance by Michael E. Porter. Copyright © 1985, 1998 by The Free Press. All rights reserved.

Issues in Competitive Strategies

Porter argues that to be successful, a company or business unit must achieve one of the previously mentioned generic competitive strategies. Otherwise, the company or business unit is *stuck in the middle* of the competitive marketplace with no competitive advantage and is doomed to below-average performance. A classic example of a company that found itself stuck in the middle was K-Mart. The company spent a lot of money trying to imitate both Wal-Mart's low-cost strategy and Target's quality differentiation strategy—only to end up in bankruptcy with no clear competitive advantage. Although some studies do support Porter's argument that companies tend to sort themselves into either lower cost or differentiation strategies and that successful companies emphasize only one strategy,[18] other research suggests that some combination of the two competitive strategies may also be successful.[19]

The Toyota and Honda auto companies are often presented as examples of successful firms able to achieve both of these generic competitive strategies. Thanks to advances in technology, a company may be able to design quality into a product or service in such a way that it can achieve both high quality and high market share—thus lowering costs.[20] Although Porter agrees that it is possible for a company or a business unit to achieve low cost and differentiation simultaneously, he continues to argue that this state is often temporary.[21] Porter does admit, however, that many different kinds of potentially profitable competitive strategies exist. Although there is generally room for only one company to successfully pursue the mass-market cost leadership strategy (because it is so dependent on achieving dominant market share), there is room for an almost unlimited number of differentiation and focus strategies (depending on the range of possible desirable features and the number of identifiable market niches). Quality, alone, has eight different dimensions—each with the potential of providing a product with a competitive advantage (see **Table 6–2**).

Most entrepreneurial ventures follow focus strategies. The successful ones differentiate their product from those of other competitors in the areas of quality and service, and they focus the product on customer needs in a segment of the market, thereby achieving a dominant

TABLE 6–2 The Eight Dimensions of Quality		
	1. **Performance**	Primary operating characteristics, such as a washing machine's cleaning ability.
	2. **Features**	"Bells and whistles," such as cruise control in a car, that supplement the basic functions.
	3. **Reliability**	Probability that the product will continue functioning without any significant maintenance.
	4. **Conformance**	Degree to which a product meets standards. When a customer buys a product out of the warehouse, it should perform identically to that viewed on the showroom floor.
	5. **Durability**	Number of years of service a consumer can expect from a product before it significantly deteriorates. Differs from reliability in that a product can be durable but still need a lot of maintenance.
	6. **Serviceability**	Product's ease of repair.
	7. **Aesthetics**	How a product looks, feels, sounds, tastes, or smells.
	8. **Perceived Quality**	Product's overall reputation. Especially important if there are no objective, easily used measures of quality.

SOURCE: Adapted with the permission of The Free Press, A Division of Simon & Schuster Adult Publishing Group, from *MANAGING QUALITY: The Strategic and Competitive Edge* by David A. Garvin. Copyright © 1988 by David A. Garvin. All rights reserved.

share of that part of the market. Adopting guerrilla warfare tactics, these companies go after opportunities in market niches too small to justify retaliation from the market leaders.

Industry Structure and Competitive Strategy

Although each of Porter's generic competitive strategies may be used in any industry, certain strategies are more likely to succeed than others in some instances. In a **fragmented industry**, for example, where many small- and medium-sized local companies compete for relatively small shares of the total market, focus strategies will likely predominate. Fragmented industries are typical for products in the early stages of their life cycles. If few economies are to be gained through size, no large firms will emerge and entry barriers will be low—allowing a stream of new entrants into the industry. Chinese restaurants, veterinary care, used-car sales, ethnic grocery stores, and funeral homes are examples. Even though P.F. Chang's and the Panda Restaurant Group have firmly established themselves as chains in the United States, lo-cal, family-owned restaurants still comprise 87% of Asian casual dining restaurants.[22]

If a company is able to overcome the limitations of a fragmented market, however, it can reap the benefits of a broadly targeted cost-leadership or differentiation strategy. Until Pizza Hut was able to use advertising to differentiate itself from local competitors, the pizza fast-food business was a fragmented industry composed primarily of locally owned pizza parlors, each with its own distinctive product and service offering. Subsequently Domino's used the cost-leader strategy to achieve U.S. national market share.

As an industry matures, fragmentation is overcome, and the industry tends to become a **consolidated industry** dominated by a few large companies. Although many industries start out being fragmented, battles for market share and creative attempts to overcome local or niche market boundaries often increase the market share of a few companies. After product standards become established for minimum quality and features, competition shifts to a greater empha-sis on cost and service. Slower growth, overcapacity, and knowledgeable buyers combine to put a premium on a firm's ability to achieve cost leadership or differentiation along the dimen-sions most desired by the market. R&D shifts from product to process improvements. Overall product quality improves, and costs are reduced significantly.

The *strategic rollup* was developed in the mid-1990s as an efficient way to quickly consoli-date a fragmented industry. With the aid of money from venture capitalists, an entrepreneur ac-quires hundreds of owner-operated small businesses. The resulting large firm creates economies of scale by building regional or national brands, applies best practices across all aspects of mar-keting and operations, and hires more sophisticated managers than the small businesses could pre-viously afford. Rollups differ from conventional mergers and acquisitions in three ways: (1) they involve large numbers of firms, (2) the acquired firms are typically owner operated, and (3) the objective is not to gain incremental advantage, but to reinvent an entire industry.[23] Rollups are cur-rently under way in the funeral industry led by Service Corporation International, Stewart Enter-prises, and the Loewen Group; and in the veterinary care industries by VCA (Veterinary Centers of America) Antech Inc. Of the 22,000 pet hospitals in the U.S., VCA Antech had acquired 465 by July 2008 with plans to continue acquisitions for the foreseeable future.[24]

Once consolidated, an industry has become one in which cost leadership and differentia-tion tend to be combined to various degrees, even though one competitive strategy may be pri-marily emphasized. A firm can no longer gain and keep high market share simply through low price. The buyers are more sophisticated and demand a certain minimum level of quality for price paid. For example, low-cost office supplies retailer Staples introduced in 2007 a line of premium office supplies called "My Style, My Way" in order to halt sliding sales.[25] Even Mc-Donald's, long the leader in low-cost fast-food restaurants, has been forced to add healthier and more upscale food items, such as Asian chicken salad, comfortable chairs, and Wi-Fi In-ternet access in order to keep its increasingly sophisticated customer base.[26] The same is true for firms emphasizing high quality. Either the quality must be high enough and valued by the customer enough to justify the higher price or the price must be dropped (through lowering costs) to compete effectively with the lower priced products. Hewlett-Packard, for example, spent years restructuring its computer business in order to cut Dell's cost advantage from 20% to just 10%.[27] Consolidation is taking place worldwide in the automobile, airline, computer, and home appliance industries.

Hypercompetition and Competitive Advantage Sustainability

Some firms are able to sustain their competitive advantage for many years,[28] but most find that competitive advantage erodes over time. In his book *Hypercompetition*, D'Aveni proposes that it is becoming increasingly difficult to sustain a competitive advantage for very long. "Market stability is threatened by short product life cycles, short product design cycles, new technologies, frequent entry by unexpected outsiders, repositioning by incumbents, and tactical redefinitions of market boundaries as diverse industries merge."[29] Consequently, a company or business unit must constantly work to improve its competitive advantage. It is not enough to be just the lowest-cost competitor. Through continuous improvement programs, competitors are usually working to lower their costs as well. Firms must find new ways not only to reduce costs further but also to add value to the product or service being provided.

The same is true of a firm or unit that is following a differentiation strategy. Maytag Corporation, for example, was successful for many years by offering the most reliable brand in North American major home appliances. It was able to charge the highest prices for Maytag brand washing machines. When other competitors improved the quality of their products, however, it became increasingly difficult for customers to justify Maytag's significantly higher price. Consequently Maytag Corporation was forced not only to add new features to its products but also to reduce costs through improved manufacturing processes so that its prices were no longer out of line with those of the competition. D'Aveni's theory of hypercompetition is supported by developing research on the importance of building *dynamic capabilities* to better cope with uncertain environments (discussed previously in Chapter 5 in the resource-based view of the firm).

D'Aveni contends that when industries become hypercompetitive, they tend to go through escalating stages of competition. Firms initially compete on cost and quality, until an abundance of high-quality, low-priced goods result. This occurred in the U.S. major home appliance industry by 1980. In a second stage of competition, the competitors move into untapped markets. Others usually imitate these moves until the moves become too risky or expensive. This epitomized the major home appliance industry during the 1980s and 1990s, as strong U.S. and European firms like Whirlpool, Electrolux, and Bosch-Siemens established presences in both Europe and the Americas and then moved into Asia. Strong Asian firms like LG and Haier likewise entered Europe and the Americas in the late 1990s.

According to D'Aveni, firms then raise entry barriers to limit competitors. Economies of scale, distribution agreements, and strategic alliances made it all but impossible for a new firm to enter the major home appliance industry by the end of the 20th century. After the established players have entered and consolidated all new markets, the next stage is for the remaining firms to attack and destroy the strongholds of other firms. Maytag's inability to hold onto its North American stronghold led to its acquisition by Whirlpool in 2006. Eventually, according to D'Aveni, the remaining large global competitors work their way to a situation of perfect competition in which no one has any advantage and profits are minimal.

Before hypercompetition, strategic initiatives provided competitive advantage for many years, perhaps for decades. Except for a few stable industries, this is no longer the case. According to D'Aveni, as industries become hypercompetitive, there is no such thing as a sustainable competitive advantage. Successful strategic initiatives in this type of industry typically last only months to a few years. According to D'Aveni, the only way a firm in this kind of dynamic industry can sustain any competitive advantage is through a continuous series of multiple short-term initiatives aimed at replacing a firm's current successful products with the next generation of products before the competitors can do so. Intel and Microsoft are taking this approach in the hypercompetitive computer industry.

Hypercompetition views competition, in effect, as a distinct series of ocean waves on what used to be a fairly calm stretch of water. As industry competition becomes more intense, the waves grow higher and require more dexterity to handle. Although a strategy is still needed to sail from point A to point B, more turbulent water means that a craft must continually adjust course to suit each new large wave. One danger of D'Aveni's concept of hypercompetition, however, is that it may lead to an overemphasis on short-term tactics (discussed in the next section) over long-term strategy. Too much of an orientation on the individual waves of hyper-competition could cause a company to focus too much on short-term temporary advantage and not enough on achieving its long-term objectives through building sustainable competitive advantage. Nevertheless, research supports D'Aveni's argument that sustained competitive advantage is increasingly a matter not of a single advantage maintained over time, but more a matter of sequencing advantages over time.[30]

Which Competitive Strategy Is Best?

Before selecting one of Porter's generic competitive strategies for a company or business unit, management should assess its feasibility in terms of company or business unit resources and capabilities. Porter lists some of the commonly required skills and resources, as well as organizational requirements, in **Table 6–3**.

Competitive Tactics

Studies of decision making report that half the decisions made in organizations fail because of poor tactics.[31] A **tactic** is a specific operating plan that details how a strategy is to be implemented in terms of when and where it is to be put into action. By their nature, tactics are narrower in scope and shorter in time horizon than are strategies. Tactics, therefore, may be viewed

TABLE 6–3	Requirements for Generic Competitive Strategies	
Generic Strategy	**Commonly Required Skills and Resources**	**Common Organizational Requirements**
Overall Cost Leadership	■ Sustained capital investment and access to capital ■ Process engineering skills ■ Intense supervision of labor ■ Products designed for ease of manufacture ■ Low-cost distribution system	■ Tight cost control ■ Frequent, detailed control reports ■ Structured organization and responsibilities ■ Incentives based on meeting strict quantitative targets
Differentiation	■ Strong marketing abilities ■ Product engineering ■ Creative flair ■ Strong capability in basic research ■ Corporate reputation for quality or technological leadership ■ Long tradition in the industry or unique combination of skills drawn from other businesses ■ Strong cooperation from channels	■ Strong coordination among functions in R&D, product development, and marketing ■ Subjective measurement and incentives instead of quantitative measures ■ Amenities to attract highly skilled labor, scientists, or creative people
Focus	■ Combination of the above policies directed at the particular strategic target	■ Combination of the above policies directed at the particular strategic target

SOURCE: Reprinted with the permission of The Free Press, A Division of Simon & Schuster, from *COMPETITIVE STRATEGY: Techniques for Analyzing Industries and Competitors* by Michael E. Porter. Copyright © 1980, 1998 by The Free Press. All rights reserved.

(like policies) as a link between the formulation and implementation of strategy. Some of the tactics available to implement competitive strategies are timing tactics and market location tactics.

Timing Tactics: When to Compete

A **timing tactic** deals with *when* a company implements a strategy. The first company to manufacture and sell a new product or service is called the **first mover** (or pioneer). Some of the advantages of being a first mover are that the company is able to establish a reputation as an industry leader, move down the learning curve to assume the cost-leader position, and earn temporarily high profits from buyers who value the product or service very highly. A successful first mover can also set the standard for all subsequent products in the industry. A company that sets the standard "locks in" customers and is then able to offer further products based on that standard.[32] Microsoft was able to do this in software with its Windows operating system, and Netscape garnered over an 80% share of the Internet browser market by being first to commercialize the product successfully. Research does indicate that moving first or second into a new industry or foreign country results in greater market share and shareholder wealth than does moving later.[33] Being first provides a company profit advantages for about 10 years in consumer goods and about 12 years in industrial goods.[34] This is true, however, only if the first mover has sufficient resources to both exploit the new market and to defend its position against later arrivals with greater resources.[35] Gillette, for example, has been able to keep its leadership of the razor category (70% market share) by continuously introducing new products.[36]

Being a first mover does, however, have its disadvantages. These disadvantages can be, conversely, advantages enjoyed by late-mover firms. **Late movers** may be able to imitate the technological advances of others (and thus keep R&D costs low), keep risks down by waiting until a new technological standard or market is established, and take advantage of the first mover's natural inclination to ignore market segments.[37] Research indicates that successful late movers tend to be large firms with considerable resources and related experience.[38] Microsoft is one example. Once Netscape had established itself as the standard for Internet browsers in the 1990s, Microsoft used its huge resources to directly attack Netscape's position with its Internet Explorer. It did not want Netscape to also set the standard in the developing and highly lucrative intranet market inside corporations. By 2004, Microsoft's Internet Explorer dominated Web browsers, and Netscape was only a minor presence. Nevertheless, research suggests that the advantages and disadvantages of first and late movers may not always generalize across industries because of differences in entry barriers and the resources of the specific competitors.[39]

Market Location Tactics: Where to Compete

A **market location tactic** deals with *where* a company implements a strategy. A company or business unit can implement a competitive strategy either offensively or defensively. An *offensive tactic* usually takes place in an established competitor's market location. A *defensive tactic* usually takes place in the firm's own current market position as a defense against possible attack by a rival.[40]

Offensive Tactics. Some of the methods used to attack a competitor's position are:

- **Frontal assault:** The attacking firm goes head to head with its competitor. It matches the competitor in every category from price to promotion to distribution channel. To be successful, the attacker must have not only superior resources, but also the willingness to persevere. This is generally a very expensive tactic and may serve to awaken a sleeping giant, depressing profits for the whole industry. This is what Kimberly-Clark did when it introduced Huggies disposable diapers against P&G's market-leading Pampers. The resulting competitive battle between the two firms depressed Kimberly-Clark's profits.[41]

- **Flanking maneuver:** Rather than going straight for a competitor's position of strength with a frontal assault, a firm may attack a part of the market where the competitor is weak. Texas Instruments, for example, avoided competing directly with Intel by developing microprocessors for consumer electronics, cell phones, and medical devices instead of computers. Taken together, these other applications are worth more in terms of dollars and influence than are computers, where Intel dominates.[42]

- **Bypass attack:** Rather than directly attacking the established competitor frontally or on its flanks, a company or business unit may choose to change the rules of the game. This tactic attempts to cut the market out from under the established defender by offering a new type of product that makes the competitor's product unnecessary. For example, instead of competing directly against Microsoft's Pocket PC and Palm Pilot for the handheld computer market, Apple introduced the iPod as a personal digital music player. It was the most radical change to the way people listen to music since the Sony Walkman. By redefining the market, Apple successfully sidestepped both Intel and Microsoft, leaving them to play "catch-up."[43]

- **Encirclement:** Usually evolving out of a frontal assault or flanking maneuver, encirclement occurs as an attacking company or unit encircles the competitor's position in terms of products or markets or both. The encircler has greater product variety (e.g., a complete product line, ranging from low to high price) and/or serves more markets (e.g., it dominates every secondary market). For example, Steinway was a major manufacturer of pianos in the United States until Yamaha entered the market with a broader range of pianos, keyboards, and other musical instruments. Although Steinway still dominates concert halls, it has only a 2% share of the U.S. market.[44] Oracle is using this strategy in its battle against market leader SAP for enterprise resource planning (ERP) software by "surrounding" SAP with acquisitions.[45]

- **Guerrilla warfare:** Instead of a continual and extensive resource-expensive attack on a competitor, a firm or business unit may choose to "hit and run." Guerrilla warfare is characterized by the use of small, intermittent assaults on different market segments held by the competitor. In this way, a new entrant or small firm can make some gains without seriously threatening a large, established competitor and evoking some form of retaliation. To be successful, the firm or unit conducting guerrilla warfare must be patient enough to accept small gains and to avoid pushing the established competitor to the point that it must respond or else lose face. Microbreweries, which make beer for sale to local customers, use this tactic against major brewers such as Anheuser-Busch.

Defensive Tactics. According to Porter, defensive tactics aim to lower the probability of attack, divert attacks to less threatening avenues, or lessen the intensity of an attack. Instead of increasing competitive advantage per se, they make a company's or business unit's competitive advantage more sustainable by causing a challenger to conclude that an attack is unattractive. These tactics deliberately reduce short-term profitability to ensure long-term profitability:[46]

- **Raise structural barriers.** Entry barriers act to block a challenger's logical avenues of attack. Some of the most important, according to Porter, are to:
    1. Offer a full line of products in every profitable market segment to close off any entry points (for example, Coca Cola offers unprofitable noncarbonated beverages to keep competitors off store shelves);
    2. Block channel access by signing exclusive agreements with distributors;
    3. Raise buyer switching costs by offering low-cost training to users;
    4. Raise the cost of gaining trial users by keeping prices low on items new users are most likely to purchase;

5. Increase scale economies to reduce unit costs;
6. Foreclose alternative technologies through patenting or licensing;
7. Limit outside access to facilities and personnel;
8. Tie up suppliers by obtaining exclusive contracts or purchasing key locations;
9. Avoid suppliers that also serve competitors; and
10. Encourage the government to raise barriers, such as safety and pollution standards or favorable trade policies.

■ **Increase expected retaliation:** This tactic is any action that increases the perceived threat of retaliation for an attack. For example, management may strongly defend any erosion of market share by drastically cutting prices or matching a challenger's promotion through a policy of accepting any price-reduction coupons for a competitor's product. This counterattack is especially important in markets that are very important to the defending company or business unit. For example, when Clorox Company challenged P&G in the detergent market with Clorox Super Detergent, P&G retaliated by test marketing its liquid bleach, Lemon Fresh Comet, in an attempt to scare Clorox into retreating from the detergent market. Research suggests that retaliating quickly is not as successful in slowing market share loss as a slower, but more concentrated and aggressive response.[47]

■ **Lower the inducement for attack:** A third type of defensive tactic is to reduce a challenger's expectations of future profits in the industry. Like Southwest Airlines, a company can deliberately keep prices low and constantly invest in cost-reducing measures. With prices kept very low, there is little profit incentive for a new entrant.[48]

COOPERATIVE STRATEGIES

A company uses competitive strategies and tactics are used to gain competitive advantage within an industry by battling against other firms. These are not, however, the only business strategy options available to a company or business unit for competing successfully within an industry. A company can also use **cooperative strategies** to gain competitive advantage within an industry by working with other firms. The two general types of cooperative strategies are collusion and strategic alliances.

Collusion

Collusion is the active cooperation of firms within an industry to reduce output and raise prices in order to get around the normal economic law of supply and demand. Collusion may be explicit, in which case firms cooperate through direct communication and negotiation, or tacit, in which case firms cooperate indirectly through an informal system of signals. Explicit collusion is illegal in most countries and in a number of regional trade associations, such as the European Union. For example, Archer Daniels Midland (ADM), the large U.S. agricultural products firm, conspired with its competitors to limit the sales volume and raise the price of the food additive lysine. Executives from three Japanese and South Korean lysine manufacturers admitted meeting in hotels in major cities throughout the world to form a "lysine trade association." The three companies were fined more than $20 million by the U.S. federal government.[49] In another example, Denver-based Qwest signed agreements favoring competitors that agreed not to oppose Qwest's merger with U.S. West or its entry into the long-distance business in its 14-state region. In one agreement, Qwest agreed to pay McLeodUSA almost $30 million to settle a billing dispute in return for McLeod's withdrawing its objections to Qwest's purchase of U.S. West.[50]

Collusion can also be tacit, in which case there is no direct communication among competing firms. According to Barney, tacit collusion in an industry is most likely to be successful if (1) there are a small number of identifiable competitors, (2) costs are similar among firms, (3) one firm tends to act as the price leader, (4) there is a common industry culture that accepts cooperation, (5) sales are characterized by a high frequency of small orders, (6) large inventories and order backlogs are normal ways of dealing with fluctuations in demand, and (7) there are high entry barriers to keep out new competitors.[51]

Even tacit collusion can, however, be illegal. For example, when General Electric wanted to ease price competition in the steam turbine industry, it widely advertised its prices and publicly committed not to sell below those prices. Customers were even told that if GE reduced turbine prices in the future, it would give customers a refund equal to the price reduction. GE's message was not lost on Westinghouse, the major competitor in steam turbines. Both prices and profit margins remained stable for the next 10 years in this industry. The U.S. Department of Justice then sued both firms for engaging in "conscious parallelism" (following each other's lead to reduce the level of competition) in order to reduce competition.

Strategic Alliances

A **strategic alliance** is a long-term cooperative arrangement between two or more independent firms or business units that engage in business activities for mutual economic gain.[52] Alliances between companies or business units have become a fact of life in modern business. In the U.S. software industry, for example, the percentage of publicly traded firms that engaged in alliances increased from 32% in 1990 to 95% in 2001. During the same time period, the average number of alliances grew from four to more than 30 per firm.[53] Each of the top 500 global business firms now averages 60 major alliances.[54] Some alliances are very short term, only lasting long enough for one partner to establish a beachhead in a new market. Over time, conflicts over objectives and control often develop among the partners. For these and other reasons, around half of all alliances (including international alliances) perform unsatisfactorily.[55] Others are more long lasting and may even be preludes to full mergers between companies.

Many alliances do increase profitability of the members and have a positive effect on firm value.[56] A study by Cooper & Lybrand found that firms involved in strategic alliances had 11% higher revenue and 20% higher growth rate than did companies not involved in alliances.[57] Forming and managing strategic alliances is a capability that is learned over time. Research reveals that the more experience a firm has with strategic alliances, the more likely that its alliances will be successful.[58] (There is some evidence, however, that too much partnering experience with the same partners generates diminishing returns over time and leads to reduced performance.)[59] Consequently, leading firms are making investments in building and developing their partnering capabilities.[60]

Companies or business units may form a strategic alliance for a number of reasons, including:

1. **To obtain or learn new capabilities:** For example, General Motors and Chrysler formed an alliance in 2004 to develop new fuel-saving hybrid engines for their automobiles.[61] Alliances are especially useful if the desired knowledge or capability is based on tacit knowledge or on new poorly-understood technology.[62] A study found that firms with strategic alliances had more modern manufacturing technologies than did firms without alliances.[63]

2. **To obtain access to specific markets:** Rather than buy a foreign company or build breweries of its own in other countries, Anheuser-Busch chose to license the right to brew and market Budweiser to other brewers, such as Labatt in Canada, Modelo in Mexico, and Kirin in Japan. As another example, U.S. defense contractors and aircraft manufacturers selling to foreign governments are typically required by these governments to spend a percentage of the contract/purchase value, either by purchasing parts or obtaining sub-contractors, in that

country. This is often achieved by forming value-chain alliances with foreign companies either as parts suppliers or as sub-contractors.[64] In a survey by the *Economist Intelligence Unit*, 59% of executives stated that their primary reason for engaging in alliances was the need for fast and low-cost expansion into new markets.[65]

3. **To reduce financial risk:** Alliances take less financial resources than do acquisitions or going it alone and are easier to exit if necessary.[66] For example, because the costs of developing new large jet airplanes were becoming too high for any one manufacturer, Aerospatiale of France, British Aerospace, Construcciones Aeronáuticas of Spain, and Daimler-Benz Aerospace of Germany formed a joint consortium called Airbus Industrie to design and build such planes. Using alliances with suppliers is a popular means of outsourcing an expensive activity.

4. **To reduce political risk:** Forming alliances with local partners is a good way to overcome deficiencies in resources and capabilities when expanding into international markets.[67] To gain access to China while ensuring a positive relationship with the often restrictive Chinese government, Maytag Corporation formed a joint venture with the Chinese appliance maker, RSD.

Cooperative arrangements between companies and business units fall along a continuum from weak and distant to strong and close. (See **Figure 6–6**.) The types of alliances range from mutual service consortia to joint ventures and licensing arrangements to value-chain partnerships.[68]

Mutual Service Consortia. A **mutual service consortium** is a partnership of similar companies in similar industries that pool their resources to gain a benefit that is too expensive to develop alone, such as access to advanced technology. For example, IBM established a research alliance with Sony Electronics and Toshiba to build its next generation of computer chips. The result was the "cell" chip, a microprocessor running at 256 gigaflops—around ten times the performance of the fastest chips currently used in desktop computers. Referred to as a "supercomputer on a chip," cell chips were to be used by Sony in its PlayStation 3, by Toshiba in its high-definition televisions, and by IBM in its super computers.[69] The mutual service consortia is a fairly weak and distant alliance—appropriate for partners that wish to work together but not share their core competencies. There is very little interaction or communication among the partners.

Joint Venture. A **joint venture** is a "cooperative business activity, formed by two or more separate organizations for strategic purposes, that creates an independent business entity and allocates ownership, operational responsibilities, and financial risks and rewards to each member, while preserving their separate identity/autonomy."[70] Along with licensing arrangements, joint ventures lie at the midpoint of the continuum and are formed to pursue an

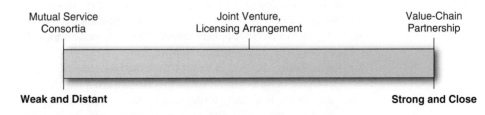

FIGURE 6–6
Continuum of Strategic Alliances

Mutual Service Consortia	Joint Venture, Licensing Arrangement	Value-Chain Partnership

Weak and Distant   **Strong and Close**

opportunity that needs a capability from two or more companies or business units, such as the technology of one and the distribution channels of another.

Joint ventures are the most popular form of strategic alliance. They often occur because the companies involved do not want to or cannot legally merge permanently. Joint ventures provide a way to temporarily combine the different strengths of partners to achieve an outcome of value to all. For example, Proctor & Gamble formed a joint venture with Clorox to produce food-storage wraps. P&G brought its cling-film technology and 20 full-time employees to the venture, while Clorox contributed its bags, containers, and wraps business.[71]

Extremely popular in international undertakings because of financial and political–legal constraints, forming joint ventures is a convenient way for corporations to work together without losing their independence. Around 30% to 55% of international joint ventures include three or more partners.[72] Disadvantages of joint ventures include loss of control, lower profits, probability of conflicts with partners, and the likely transfer of technological advantage to the partner. Joint ventures are often meant to be temporary, especially by some companies that may view them as a way to rectify a competitive weakness until they can achieve long-term dominance in the partnership. Partially for this reason, joint ventures have a high failure rate. Research indicates, however, that joint ventures tend to be more successful when both partners have equal ownership in the venture and are mutually dependent on each other for results.[73]

Licensing Arrangements. A **licensing arrangement** is an agreement in which the licensing firm grants rights to another firm in another country or market to produce and/or sell a product. The licensee pays compensation to the licensing firm in return for technical expertise. Licensing is an especially useful strategy if the trademark or brand name is well known but the MNC does not have sufficient funds to finance its entering the country directly. For example, Yum! Brands successfully used franchising and licensing to establish its KFC, Pizza Hut, Taco Bell, Long John Silvers, and A&W restaurants throughout the world. In 2007 alone, it opened 471 restaurants in China alone plus 852 more across six continents.[74] This strategy also becomes important if the country makes entry via investment either difficult or impossible. The danger always exists, however, that the licensee might develop its competence to the point that it becomes a competitor to the licensing firm. Therefore, a company should never license its distinctive competence, even for some short-run advantage.

Value-Chain Partnerships. A **value-chain partnership** is a strong and close alliance in which one company or unit forms a long-term arrangement with a key supplier or distributor for mutual advantage. For example, P&G, the maker of Folgers and Millstone coffee, worked with coffee appliance makers Mr. Coffee, Krups, and Hamilton Beach to use technology licensed from Black & Decker to market a pressurized, single-serve coffee-making system called Home Cafe. This was an attempt to reverse declining at-home coffee consumption at a time when coffeehouse sales were rising.[75]

To improve the quality of parts it purchases, companies in the U.S. auto industry, for example, have decided to work more closely with fewer suppliers and to involve them more in product design decisions. Activities that had previously been done internally by an automaker are being outsourced to suppliers specializing in those activities. The benefits of such relationships do not just accrue to the purchasing firm. Research suggests that suppliers that engage in long-term relationships are more profitable than suppliers with multiple short-term contracts.[76]

All forms of strategic alliances involve uncertainty. Many issues need to be dealt with when an alliance is initially formed, and others, which emerge later. Many problems revolve around the fact that a firm's alliance partners may also be its competitors, either immediately or in the future. According to Peter Lorange, an authority in strategy, one thorny issue in any strategic alliance is how to cooperate without giving away the company or business unit's core

TABLE 6–4	
Strategic Alliance Success Factors	■ Have a clear strategic purpose. Integrate the alliance with each partner's strategy. Ensure that mutual value is created for all partners.
	■ Find a fitting partner with compatible goals and complementary capabilities.
	■ Identify likely partnering risks and deal with them when the alliance is formed.
	■ Allocate tasks and responsibilities so that each partner can specialize in what it does best.
	■ Create incentives for cooperation to minimize differences in corporate culture or organization fit.
	■ Minimize conflicts among the partners by clarifying objectives and avoiding direct competition in the marketplace.
	■ In an international alliance, ensure that those managing it have comprehensive cross-cultural knowledge.
	■ Exchange human resources to maintain communication and trust. Don't allow individual egos to dominate.
	■ Operate with long-term time horizons. The expectation of future gains can minimize short-term conflicts.
	■ Develop multiple joint projects so that any failures are counterbalanced by successes.
	■ Agree on a monitoring process. Share information to build trust and keep projects on target. Monitor customer responses and service complaints.
	■ Be flexible in terms of willingness to renegotiate the relationship in terms of environmental changes and new opportunities.
	■ Agree on an exit strategy for when the partners' objectives are achieved or the alliance is judged a failure.

SOURCE: Compiled from B. Gomes-Casseres, "Do You Really Have an Alliance Strategy?" *Strategy & Leadership* (September/October 1998), pp. 6–11; L. Segil, "Strategic Alliances for the 21st Century," *Strategy & Leadership* (September/October 1998), pp. 12–16; and A. C. Inkpen and K-Q Li, "Joint Venture Formation: Planning and Knowledge Gathering for Success," *Organizational Dynamics* (Spring 1999), pp. 33–47. Inkpen and Li provide a checklist of 17 questions on p. 46.

competence: "Particularly when advanced technology is involved, it can be difficult for partners in an alliance to cooperate and openly share strategic know-how, but it is mandatory if the joint venture is to succeed."[77] It is therefore important that a company or business unit that is interested in joining or forming a strategic alliance consider the strategic alliance success factors listed in **Table 6–4**.

End of Chapter SUMMARY

Once environmental scanning is completed, situational analysis calls for the integration of this information. SWOT analysis is the most popular method for examining external and internal information. We recommend using the SFAS Matrix as one way to identify a corporation's strategic factors. Using the TOWS Matrix to identify a propitious niche is one way to develop a sustainable competitive advantage using those strategic factors.

Business strategy is composed of both competitive and cooperative strategy. As the external environment becomes more uncertain, an increasing number of corporations are choosing to simultaneously compete *and* cooperate with their competitors. These firms may cooperate to obtain efficiency in some areas, while each firm simultaneously tries to differentiate itself for competitive purposes. Raymond Noorda, Novell's founder and former CEO, coined the term *co-opetition* to describe such simultaneous competition and cooperation among firms.[78] One example is the collaboration between competitors DHL and UPS in the express delivery market. DHL's American delivery business was losing money and UPS' costly airfreight network had excess capacity. Under the terms of a 10-year agreement signed in 2008, UPS carried DHL packages in its American airfreight network for a fee. The agreement covered only air freight, leaving both firms free to compete in the rest of the express-parcel business.[79] A careful balancing act, co-opetition involves the careful management of alliance partners so that each partner obtains sufficient benefits to keep the alliance together. A long-term view is crucial. An unintended transfer of knowledge could be enough to provide one partner a significant competitive advantage over the others.[80] Unless that company forebears from using that knowledge against its partners, the alliance will be doomed.

ECO-BITS

- Target became a certified organic produce retailer in 2006 and now offers more than 500 choices of organic certified food. The company reduces waste by giving away 7 million pounds of food annually.
- Home Depot offers more than 2,500 environmentally friendly products, ranging from all-natural insect repellants to front-loading washing machines, specially tagged as Eco Options.
- Vowing to become "carbon neutral" by 2010, Timberland introduced Green Index tags, which rate its products on the use of greenhouse gas emissions, solvents, and organic materials.[81]

DISCUSSION QUESTIONS

1. What industry forces might cause a propitious niche to disappear?

2. Is it possible for a company or business unit to follow a cost leadership strategy and a differentiation strategy simultaneously? Why or why not?

3. Is it possible for a company to have a sustainable competitive advantage when its industry becomes hyper-competitive?

4. What are the advantages and disadvantages of being a first mover in an industry? Give some examples of first mover and late mover firms. Were they successful?

5. Why are many strategic alliances temporary?

STRATEGIC PRACTICE EXERCISE

Select an industry to analyze. Identify companies for each of Porter's four competitive strategies. How many different kinds of differentiation strategies can you find?

INDUSTRY: _____

Cost Leadership: _____

Differentiation: _____

Cost Focus: _____

Differentiation Focus: _____

KEY TERMS

business strategy (p. 231)

collusion (p. 243)

common thread (p. 230)

competitive scope (p. 233)

competitive strategy (p. 231)

consolidated industry (p. 238)

cooperative strategy (p. 243)

cost focus (p. 235)

cost leadership (p. 234)

differentiation (p. 234)

differentiation focus (p. 236)

differentiation strategy (p. 233)

first mover (p. 241)

fragmented industry (p. 238)

joint venture (p. 245)

late mover (p. 241)

licensing arrangement (p. 246)

lower cost strategy (p. 233)

market location tactics (p. 241)

mutual service consortium (p. 245)

propitious niche (p. 225)

SFAS (Strategic Factors Analysis Summary) Matrix (p. 224)

strategic alliance (p. 244)

strategy formulation (p. 224)

SWOT (p. 224)

tactic (p. 240)

timing tactic (p. 241)

TOWS Matrix (p. 230)

value-chain partnership (p. 246)

NOTES

1. A. Fitzgerald, "Cedar Rapids Export Company Serves Muslims Worldwide," *Des Moines Register* (October 26, 2003), pp. 1M–2M. See also corporate Web site at www.midamar.com.

2. J. Choi, D. Lovallo, and A. Tarasova, "Better Strategy for Business Units: A McKinsey Global Survey," *McKinsey Quarterly Online* (July 2007).

3. D. Fehringer, "Six Steps to Better SWOTs," *Competitive Intelligence Magazine* (January–February, 2007), p. 54.

4. T. Brown, "The Essence of Strategy," *Management Review* (April 1997), pp. 8–13.

5. T. Hill and R. Westbrook, "SWOT Analysis: It's Time for a Product Recall," *Long Range Planning* (February 1997), pp. 46–52.

6. W. H. Newman, "Shaping the Master Strategy of Your Firm," *California Management Review*, Vol. 9, No. 3 (1967), pp. 77–88.

7. D. J. Collis and M. G. Rukstad, "Can You Say What Your Strategy Is?" *Harvard Business Review* (April 2008), pp. 82–90.

8. D. J. Collis and M. G. Rukstad, "Can You Say What Your Strategy Is?" *Harvard Business Review* (April 2008), p. 86.

9. V. F. Misangyi, H. Elms, T. Greckhamer, and J. A Lepine, "A New Perspective on a Fundamental Debate: A Multilevel Approach to Industry, Corporate, and Business Unit Effects," *Strategic Management Journal* (June 2006), pp. 571–590.

10. M. E. Porter, *Competitive Strategy* (New York: The Free Press, 1980), pp. 34–41 as revised in M. E. Porter, *The Competitive Advantage of Nations* (New York: The Free Press, 1990), pp. 37–40.

11. J. O. DeCastro and J. J. Chrisman, "Narrow-Scope Strategies and Firm Performance: An Empirical Investigation," *Journal of Business Strategies* (Spring 1998), pp. 1–16; T. M. Stearns, N. M. Carter, P. D. Reynolds, and M. L. Williams, "New Firm Survival: Industry, Strategy, and Location," *Journal of Business Venturing* (January 1995), pp. 23–42.

12. Porter, *Competitive Strategy* (New York: The Free Press, 1980), p. 35.

13. M. Arndt, "Built for the Long Haul," *Business Week* (January 30, 2006), p. 66.

14. R. E. Caves, and P. Ghemawat, "Identifying Mobility Barriers," *Strategic Management Journal* (January 1992), pp. 1–12.

15. N. K. Geranios, "Potlach Aims to Squeeze Toilet Tissue Leaders," *Des Moines Register* (October 22, 2003), p. 3D.

16. "Company Targets 'Orphan Drugs,'" *St. Cloud (MN) Times* (May 9, 2007), p. 2A.

17. M. Arndt, "Deere's Revolution on Wheels," *Business Week* (July 2, 2007), pp. 78–79.

18. S. Thornhill and R. E. White, "Strategic Purity: A Multi-Industry Evaluation of Pure Vs. Hybrid Business Strategies," *Strategic Management Journal* (May 2007), pp. 553–561; M. Delmas, M. V. Russo, and M. J. Montes-Sancho, "Deregulation and Environmental Differentiation in the Electric Utility Industry," *Strategic Management Journal* (February 2007), pp. 189–209.

19. C. Campbell-Hunt, "What Have We Learned About Generic Competitive Strategy? A Meta Analysis," *Strategic Management Journal* (February 2000), pp. 127–154.

20. M. Kroll, P. Wright, and R. A. Heiens, "The Contribution of Product Quality to Competitive Advantage: Impacts on Systematic Variance and Unexplained Variance in Returns," *Strategic Management Journal* (April 1999), pp. 375–384.

21. R. M. Hodgetts, "A Conversation with Michael E. Porter: A 'Significant Extension' Toward Operational Improvement and Positioning," *Organizational Dynamics* (Summer 1999), pp. 24–33.

22. M. Rushlo, "P. F. Chang's Plans Succeed Where Others Have Failed," *Des Moines Register* (May 18, 2004), p. 1D, 6D.

23. P. F. Kocourek, S. Y. Chung, and M. G. McKenna, "Strategic Rollups: Overhauling the Multi-Merger Machine," *Strategy + Business* (2nd Quarter 2000), pp. 45–53.

24. J. A. Tannenbaum, "Acquisitive Companies Set Out to 'Roll Up' Fragmented Industries," *Wall Street Journal* (March 3, 1997), pp. A1, A6; 2007 Form 10-K and Quarterly Report (July 2008), VCA Antech, Inc.

25. A. Pressman, "Upwardly Mobile Stationary," *Business Week* (March 17, 2008), pp. 60–61.

26. P. Gogoi, "Mickey D's McMakeover," *Business Week* (May 15, 2006), pp. 42–43.

27. N. Kumar, "Strategies to Fight Low-Cost Rivals," *Harvard Business Review* (December 2006), pp. 104–112.

28. J. C. Bou and A. Satorra, "The Presistence of Abnormal Returns at Industry and Firm Levels: Evidence from Spain," *Strategic Management Journal* (July 2007), pp. 707–722.

29. R. A. D'Aveni, *Hypercompetition* (New York: The Free Press, 1994), pp. xiii–xiv.

30. R. R. Wiggins and T. W. Ruefli, "Schumpeter's Ghost: Is Hypercompetition Making the Best of Times Shorter?" *Strategic Management Journal* (October 2005), pp. 887–911.

31. P. C. Nutt, "Surprising But True: Half the Decisions in Organizations Fail," *Academy of Management Executive* (November 1999), pp. 75–90.

32. Some refer to this as the economic concept of "increasing returns." Instead of the curve leveling off when the company reaches a point of diminishing returns when a product saturates a market, the curve continues to go up as the company takes advantage of setting the standard to spin off new products that use the new standard to achieve higher performance than competitors. See J. Alley, "The Theory That Made Microsoft," *Fortune* (April 29, 1996), pp. 65–66.

33. H. Lee, K. G. Smith, C. M. Grimm and A. Schomburg, "Timing, Order and Durability of New Product Advantages with Imitation," *Strategic Management Journal* (January 2000), pp. 23–30; Y. Pan and P. C. K. Chi, "Financial Performance and Survival of Multinational Corporations in China," *Strategic Management Journal* (April 1999), pp. 359–374; R. Makadok, "Can First-Mover and Early-Mover Advantages Be Sustained in an Industry with Low Barriers to Entry/Imitation?" *Strategic Management Journal* (July 1998), pp. 683–696; B. Mascarenhas, "The Order and Size of Entry into International Markets," *Journal of Business Venturing* (July 1997), pp. 287–299.

34. At these respective points, cost disadvantages vis-à-vis later entrants fully eroded the earlier returns to first movers. See W. Boulding and M. Christen, "Idea—First Mover Disadvantage," *Harvard Business Review*, Vol. 79, No. 9 (2001), pp. 20–21 as reported by D. J. Ketchen, Jr., C. C. Snow, and V. L. Hoover, "Research on Competitive Dynamics: Recent Accomplishments and Future Challenges," *Journal of Management*, Vol. 30, No. 6 (2004), pp. 779–804.

35. M. B. Lieberman and D. B. Montgomery, "First-Mover (Dis) Advantages: Retrospective and Link with the Resource-Based View," *Strategic Management Journal* (December, 1998), pp. 1111–1125; G. J. Tellis and P. N. Golder, "First to Market, First to Fail? Real Causes of Enduring Market Leadership," *Sloan Management Review* (Winter 1996), pp. 65–75.

36. J. Pope, "Schick Entry May Work Industry into a Lather," *Des Moines Register* (May 15, 2003), p. 6D.

37. S. K. Ethiraj and D. H. Zhu, "Performance Effects of Imitative Entry," *Strategic Management Journal* (August 2008), pp. 797–817; G. Dowell and A. Swaminathan, "Entry Timing, Exploration, and Firm Survival in the Early U.S. Bicycle Industry," *Strategic Management Journal* (December 2006), pp. 1159–1182. For an in-depth discussion of first and late mover advantages and disadvantages, see D. S. Cho, D. J. Kim, and D. K. Rhee, "Latecomer Strategies: Evidence from the Semiconductor Industry in Japan and Korea," *Organization Science* (July–August 1998), pp. 489–505.

38. J. Shamsie, C. Phelps, and J. Kuperman, "Better Late Than Never: A Study of Late Entrants in Household Electrical Equipment," *Strategic Management Journal* (January 2004), pp. 69–84.

39. T. S. Schoenecker and A. C. Cooper, "The Role of Firm Resources and Organizational Attributes in Determining Entry Timing: A Cross-Industry Study," *Strategic Management Journal* (December 1998), pp. 1127–1143.

40. Summarized from various articles by L. Fahey in *The Strategic Management Reader*, edited by L. Fahey (Englewood Cliffs, NJ: Prentice Hall, 1989), pp. 178–205.

41. M. Boyle, "Dueling Diapers," *Fortune* (February 17, 2003), pp. 115–116.

42. C. Edwards, "To See Where Tech Is Headed, Watch TI," *Business Week* (November 6, 2006), p. 74.

43. P. Burrows, "Show Time," *Business Week* (February 2, 2004), pp. 56–64.

44. A. Serwer, "Happy Birthday, Steinway," *Fortune* (March 17, 2003), pp. 94–97.

45. "Programmed for a Fight," *The Economist* (October 20, 2007), p. 85.

46. This information on defensive tactics is summarized from M. E. Porter, *Competitive Advantage* (New York: The Free Press, 1985), pp. 482–512.

47. H. D. Hopkins, "The Response Strategies of Dominant U.S. Firms to Japanese Challengers," *Journal of Management*, Vol. 29, No. 1 (2003), pp. 5–25.

48. For additional information on defensive competitive tactics, see G. Stalk, "Curveball Strategies to Fool the Competition," *Harvard Business Review* (September 2006), pp. 115–122.

49. T. M. Burton, "Archer-Daniels Faces a Potential Blow As Three Firms Admit Price-Fixing Plot," *Wall Street Journal* (August 28, 1996), pp. A3, A6; R. Henkoff, "The ADM Tale Gets Even Stranger," *Fortune* (May 13, 1996), pp. 113–120.

50. B. Gordon, "Qwest Defends Pacts with Competitors," *Des Moines Register* (April 30, 2002), p. 1D.

51. Much of the content on cooperative strategies was summarized from J. B. Barney, *Gaining and Sustaining Competitive Advantage* (Reading, MA: Addison-Wesley, 1997), pp. 255–278.

52. A. C. Inkpen and E. W. K. Tsang, "Learning and Strategic Alliances," *Academy of Management Annals*, Vol. 1, edited by J. F. Walsh and A. F. Brief (December 2007), pp. 479–511.

53. D. Lavie, "Alliance Portfolios and Firm Performance: A Study of Value Creation and Appropriation in the U.S. Software Industry." *Strategic Management Journal* (December 2007), pp. 1187–1212.

54. R. D. Ireland, M. A. Hitt, and D. Vaidyanath, "Alliance Management as a Source of Competitive Advantage," *Journal of Management*, Vol. 28, No. 3 (2002), pp. 413–446.

55. S. H. Park and G. R. Ungson, "Interfirm Rivalry and Managerial Complexity: A Conceptual Framework of Alliance Failure," *Organization Science* (January–February 2001), pp. 37–53.; D. C. Hambrick, J. Li, K. Xin, and A. S. Tsui, "Compositional Gaps and Downward Spirals in International Joint Venture Management Groups," *Strategic Management Journal* (November 2001), pp. 1033–1053; T. K. Das and B. S. Teng, "Instabilities of Strategic Alliances: An Internal Tensions Perspective," *Organization Science* (January–February 2000), pp. 77–101; J. F. Hennart, D. J. Kim, and M. Zeng, "The Impact of Joint Venture Status on the Longevity of Japanese Stakes in U.S. Manufacturing Affiliates," *Organization Science* (May–June 1998), pp. 382–395.

56. N. K. Park, J. M. Mezias, and J. Song, "A Resource-based View of Strategic Alliances and Firm Value in the Electronic Marketplace," *Journal of Management*, Vol. 30, No. 1 (2004), pp. 7–27; T. Khanna and J. W. Rivkin, "Estimating the Performance Effects of Business Groups in Emerging Markets," *Strategic Management Journal* (January 2001), pp. 45–74; G. Garai, "Leveraging the Rewards of Strategic Alliances," *Journal of Business Strategy* (March–April 1999), pp. 40–43.

57. L. Segil, "Strategic Alliances for the 21st Century," *Strategy & Leadership* (September/October 1998), pp. 12–16.

58. R. C. Sampson, "Experience Effects and Collaborative Returns in R&D Alliances," *Strategic Management Journal* (November 2005), pp. 1009–1031; J. Draulans, A-P deMan, and H. W. Volberda, "Building Alliance Capability: Management Techniques for Superior Alliance Performance," *Long Range Planning* (April 2003), pp. 151–166; P. Kale, J. H. Dyer, and H. Singh, "Alliance Capability, Stock Market Response, and Long-Term Alliance Success: The Role of the Alliance Function," *Strategic Management Journal* (August 2002), pp. 747–767.

59. H. Hoang and F. T. Rothaermel, "The Effect of General and Partner-Specific Alliance Experience on Joint R&D Project Performance," *Academy of Management Journal* (April 2005), pp. 332–345; A. Goerzen, "Alliance Networks and Firm Performance: The Impact of Repeated Partnerships," *Strategic Management Journal* (May 2007), pp. 487–509.

60. A. MacCormack and T. Forbath, "Learning the Fine Art of Global Collaboration," *Harvard Business Review* (January 2008), pp. 24–26.

61. J. Porretto, "Rival Automakers Team Up to Catch Up," *Des Moines Register* (December 14, 2004), pp. 1D–2D.

62. H. Bapuji and M. Crossan, "Knowledge Types and Knowledge Management Strategies," in *Strategic Networks: Learning to Compete*, M. Gibbert and T. Durand, eds. (Malden, MA: Blackwell Publishing, 2007), pp. 8–25; F. T. Rothaermel and W. Boeker, "Old Technology Meets New Technology: Complementarities, Similarities, and Alliance Formation," *Strategic Management Journal* (January 2008), pp. 47–77.

63. M. M. Bear, "How Japanese Partners Help U.S. Manufacturers to Raise Productivity," *Long Range Planning* (December 1998), pp. 919–926.

64. According to M. J. Thome of Rockwell Collins in a June 26, 2008, e-mail, these are called "international offsets."

65. P. Anslinger and J. Jenk, "Creating Successful Alliances," *Journal of Business Strategy*, Vol. 25, No. 2 (2004), p. 18.

66. X. Yin and M. Shanley, "Industry Determinants of the 'Merger Versus Alliance' Decision," *Academy of Management Review* (April 2008), pp. 473–491.

67. J. W. Lu and P. W. Beamish, "The Internationalization and Performance of SMEs," *Strategic Management Journal* (June–July 2001), pp. 565–586.

68. R. M. Kanter, "Collaborative Advantage: The Art of Alliances," *Harvard Business Review* (July–August 1994), pp. 96–108.

69. "The Cell of the New Machine," *The Economist* (February 12, 2005), pp. 77–78.

70. R. P. Lynch, *The Practical Guide to Joint Ventures and Corporate Alliances* (New York: John Wiley and Sons, 1989), p. 7.

71. "Will She, Won't She? *The Economist* (August 11, 2007), pp. 61–63.

72. Y Gong, O Shenkar, Y. Luo, and M-K Nyaw, "Do Multiple Parents Help or Hinder International Joint Venture Performance? The Mediating Roles of Contract Completeness and Partner Cooperation," *Strategic Management Journal* (October 2007), pp. 1021–1034.

73. L. L. Blodgett, "Factors in the Instability of International Joint Ventures: An Event History Analysis," *Strategic Management Journal* (September 1992), pp. 475–481; J. Bleeke and D. Ernst, "The Way to Win in Cross-Border Alliances," *Harvard Business Review* (November–December 1991), pp. 127–135; J. M. Geringer, "Partner Selection Criteria for Developed Country Joint Ventures," in *International Management Behavior*, 2nd ed., edited by H. W. Lane and J. J. DiStephano (Boston: PWS-Kent, 1992), pp. 206–216.

74. 2007 Annual Report, *Yum! Brands*.

75. B. Horovitz, "New Coffee Maker May Jolt Industry," *USA Today* (February 18, 2004), pp. 1E–2E.

76. K. Z. Andrews, "Manufacturer/Supplier Relationships: The Supplier Payoff," *Harvard Business Review* (September–October 1995), pp. 14–15.

77. P. Lorange, "Black-Box Protection of Your Core Competencies in Strategic Alliances," in *Cooperative Strategies: European Perspectives*, edited by P. W. Beamish and J. P. Killing (San Francisco: The New Lexington Press, 1997), pp. 59–99.

78. E. P. Gee, "Co-opetition: The New Market Milieu," *Journal of Healthcare Management*, Vol. 45 (2000), pp. 359–363.

79. "Make Love—and War," *The Economist* (August 9, 2008), pp. 57–58.

80. D. J. Ketchen, Jr., C. C. Snow, and V. L. Hoover, "Research on Competitive Dynamics: Recent Accomplishments and Future Challenges," *Journal of Management*, Vol. 30, No. 6 (2004), pp. 779–804.

81. J. O'Donnell and C. Dugas, "More Retailers Go for Green—the Eco Kind," *USA Today* (April 18, 2007), p. 3B.

strategy formulation: corporate Strategy

What is the best way for a company to grow if its primary business is maturing? A study of 1,850 companies by Zook and Allen revealed two conclusions: First, the most sustained profitable growth occurs when a corporation pushes out of the boundary around its core business into adjacent businesses. Second, corporations that consistently outgrow their rivals do so by developing a formula for expanding those boundaries in a predicable, repeatable manner.[1]

Nike is a classic example of this process. Despite its success in athletic shoes, no one expected Nike to be successful when it diversified in 1995 from shoes into golf apparel, balls, and equipment. Only a few years later, it was acknowledged to be a major player in the new business. According to researchers Zook and Allen, the key to Nike's success was a formula for growth that the company had applied and adapted successfully in a series of entries into sports markets, from jogging to volleyball to tennis to basketball to soccer and, most recently, to golf. First, Nike established a leading position in athletic shoes in the target market, in this case, golf shoes. Second, Nike launched a clothing line endorsed by the sports' top athletes—in this case, Tiger Woods. Third, the company formed new distribution channels and contracts with key suppliers in the new business. Nike's reputation as a strong marketer of new products gave it credibility. Fourth, the company introduced higher-margin equipment into the new market. In the case of golf clubs, it started with irons and then moved to drivers. Once it had captured a significant share in the U.S. market, Nike's next step was global distribution.

Zook and Allen propose that this formula was the reason Nike moved past Reebok in the sporting goods industry. In 1987, Nike's operating profits were only $164 million compared to Reebok's much larger $309 million. Fifteen years later, Nike's operating profits had grown to $1.1 billion while Reebok's had declined to $247 million.[2] Reebok was subsequently acquired by Adidas in 2005 while Nike went on to generate operating profits of $2.4 billion in 2008.

Learning Objectives

After reading this chapter, you should be able to:

- Understand the three aspects of corporate strategy
- Apply the directional strategies of growth, stability, and retrenchment
- Understand the differences between vertical and horizontal growth as well as concentric and conglomerate diversification

- Identify strategic options to enter a foreign country
- Apply portfolio analysis to guide decisions in companies with multiple products and businesses
- Develop a parenting strategy for a multiple-business corporation

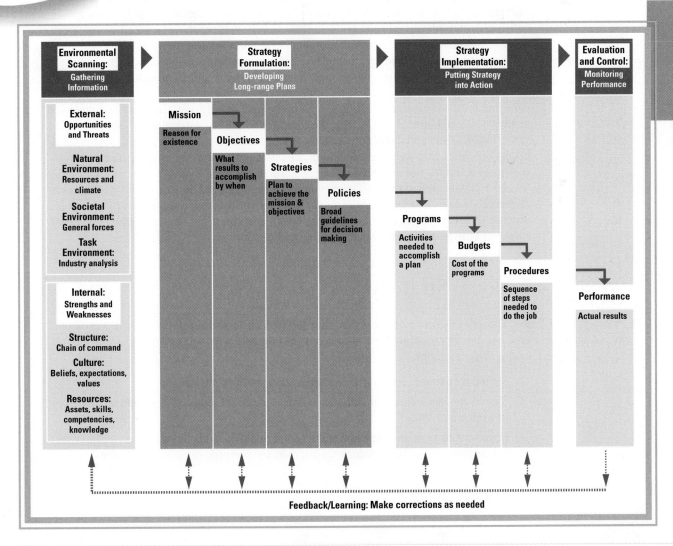

7.1 Corporate Strategy

The vignette about Nike illustrates the importance of corporate strategy to a firm's survival and success. Corporate strategy deals with three key issues facing the corporation as a whole:

1. The firm's overall orientation toward growth, stability, or retrenchment (**directional strategy**)
2. The industries or markets in which the firm competes through its products and business units (**portfolio analysis**)
3. The manner in which management coordinates activities and transfers resources and cultivates capabilities among product lines and business units (**parenting strategy**)

Corporate strategy is primarily about the choice of direction for a firm as a whole and the management of its business or product portfolio.[3] This is true whether the firm is a small company or a large multinational corporation (MNC). In a large multiple-business company, in particular, corporate strategy is concerned with managing various product lines and business units for maximum value. In this instance, corporate headquarters must play the role of the organizational "parent," in that it must deal with various product and business unit "children." Even though each product line or business unit has its own competitive or cooperative strategy that it uses to obtain its own competitive advantage in the marketplace, the corporation must coordinate these different business strategies so that the corporation as a whole succeeds as a "family."[4]

Corporate strategy, therefore, includes decisions regarding the flow of financial and other resources to and from a company's product lines and business units. Through a series of coordinating devices, a company transfers skills and capabilities developed in one unit to other units that need such resources. In this way, it attempts to obtain synergy among numerous product lines and business units so that the corporate whole is greater than the sum of its individual business unit parts.[5] All corporations, from the smallest company offering one product in only one industry to the largest conglomerate operating in many industries with many products, must at one time or another consider one or more of these issues.

To deal with each of the key issues, this chapter is organized into three parts that examine corporate strategy in terms of *directional strategy* (orientation toward growth), *portfolio analysis* (coordination of cash flow among units), and *corporate parenting* (the building of corporate synergies through resource sharing and development).[6]

7.2 Directional Strategy

Just as every product or business unit must follow a business strategy to improve its competitive position, every corporation must decide its orientation toward growth by asking the following three questions:

1. Should we expand, cut back, or continue our operations unchanged?
2. Should we concentrate our activities within our current industry, or should we diversify into other industries?
3. If we want to grow and expand nationally and/or globally, should we do so through internal development or through external acquisitions, mergers, or strategic alliances?

FIGURE 7–1
Corporate
Directional
Strategies

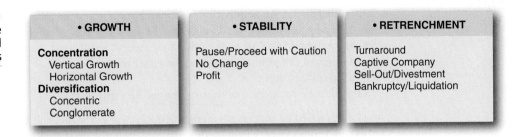

• GROWTH	• STABILITY	• RETRENCHMENT

Concentration
    Vertical Growth
    Horizontal Growth
Diversification
    Concentric
    Conglomerate
	Pause/Proceed with Caution
	No Change
	Profit
		Turnaround
		Captive Company
		Sell-Out/Divestment
		Bankruptcy/Liquidation

A corporation's **directional strategy** is composed of three general orientations (sometimes called *grand strategies*):

- **Growth strategies** expand the company's activities.
- **Stability strategies** make no change to the company's current activities.
- **Retrenchment strategies** reduce the company's level of activities.

Having chosen the general orientation (such as growth), a company's managers can select from several more specific corporate strategies such as concentration within one product line/industry or diversification into other products/industries. (See **Figure 7–1**.) These strategies are useful both to corporations operating in only one industry with one product line and to those operating in many industries with many product lines.

GROWTH STRATEGIES

By far the most widely pursued corporate directional strategies are those designed to achieve growth in sales, assets, profits, or some combination. Companies that do business in expanding industries must grow to survive. Continuing growth means increasing sales and a chance to take advantage of the experience curve to reduce the per-unit cost of products sold, thereby increasing profits. This cost reduction becomes extremely important if a corporation's industry is growing quickly or consolidating and if competitors are engaging in price wars in attempts to increase their shares of the market. Firms that have not reached "critical mass" (that is, gained the necessary economy of large-scale production) face large losses unless they can find and fill a small, but profitable, niche where higher prices can be offset by special product or service features. That is why Oracle acquired PeopleSoft, a rival software firm, in 2005. Although still growing, the software industry was maturing around a handful of large firms. According to CEO Larry Ellison, Oracle needed to double or even triple in size by buying smaller and weaker rivals if it was to compete with SAP and Microsoft.[7] Growth is a popular strategy because larger businesses tend to survive longer than smaller companies due to the greater availability of financial resources, organizational routines, and external ties.[8]

A corporation can grow internally by expanding its operations both globally and domestically, or it can grow externally through mergers, acquisitions, and strategic alliances. A **merger** is a transaction involving two or more corporations in which stock is exchanged but in which only one corporation survives. Mergers usually occur between firms of somewhat similar size and are usually "friendly." The resulting firm is likely to have a name derived from its composite firms. One example is the merging of Allied Corporation and Signal Companies to form Allied Signal. An **acquisition** is the purchase of a company that is completely absorbed as an operating subsidiary or division of the acquiring corporation. Procter & Gamble's (P&G's) purchase of Gillette is an example of a recent acquisition. Acquisitions usually occur between firms of different sizes and can be either friendly or hostile. Hostile acquisitions are often called *takeovers*.

Growth is a very attractive strategy for two key reasons:

- Growth based on increasing market demand may mask flaws in a company—flaws that would be immediately evident in a stable or declining market. A growing flow of revenue into a highly leveraged corporation can create a large amount of *organization slack* (unused resources) that can be used to quickly resolve problems and conflicts between departments and divisions. Growth also provides a big cushion for turnaround in case a strategic error is made. Larger firms also have more bargaining power than do small firms and are more likely to obtain support from key stakeholders in case of difficulty.

- A growing firm offers more opportunities for advancement, promotion, and interesting jobs. Growth itself is exciting and ego-enhancing for CEOs. The marketplace and potential investors tend to view a growing corporation as a "winner" or "on the move." Executive compensation tends to get bigger as an organization increases in size. Large firms are also more difficult to acquire than are smaller ones; thus an executive's job in a large firm is more secure.

The two basic growth strategies are **concentration** on the current product line(s) in one industry and **diversification** into other product lines in other industries.

Concentration

If a company's current product lines have real growth potential, concentration of resources on those product lines makes sense as a strategy for growth. The two basic concentration strategies are vertical growth and horizontal growth. Growing firms in a growing industry tend to choose these strategies before they try diversification.

Vertical Growth. **Vertical growth** can be achieved by taking over a function previously provided by a supplier or by a distributor. The company, in effect, grows by making its own supplies and/or by distributing its own products. This may be done in order to reduce costs, gain control over a scarce resource, guarantee quality of a key input, or obtain access to potential customers. This growth can be achieved either internally by expanding current operations or externally through acquisitions. Henry Ford, for example, used internal company resources to build his River Rouge plant outside Detroit. The manufacturing process was integrated to the point that iron ore entered one end of the long plant, and finished automobiles rolled out the other end, into a huge parking lot. In contrast, Cisco Systems, a maker of Internet hardware, chose the external route to vertical growth by purchasing Scientific-Atlanta Inc., a maker of set-top boxes for television programs and movies-on-demand. This acquisition gave Cisco access to technology for distributing television to living rooms through the Internet.[9]

Vertical growth results in **vertical integration**—the degree to which a firm operates vertically in multiple locations on an industry's value chain from extracting raw materials to manufacturing to retailing. More specifically, assuming a function previously provided by a supplier is called **backward integration** (going backward on an industry's value chain). The purchase of Carroll's Foods for its hog-growing facilities by Smithfield Foods, the world's largest pork processor, is an example of backward integration.[10] Assuming a function previously provided by a distributor is labeled **forward integration** (going forward on an industry's value chain). FedEx, for example, used forward integration when it purchased Kinko's in order to provide store-front package drop-off and delivery services for the small-business market.[11]

Vertical growth is a logical strategy for a corporation or business unit with a strong competitive position in a highly attractive industry—especially when technology is predictable and markets are growing.[12] To keep and even improve its competitive position, a company may use backward integration to minimize resource acquisition costs and inefficient operations as well as forward integration to gain more control over product distribution. The firm, in effect, builds on its distinctive competence by expanding along the industry's value chain to gain greater competitive advantage.

Although backward integration is often more profitable than forward integration (because of typical low margins in retailing), it can reduce a corporation's strategic flexibility. The resulting encumbrance of expensive assets that might be hard to sell could create an exit barrier, preventing the corporation from leaving that particular industry. Examples of single-use assets are blast furnaces and breweries. When demand drops in either of these industries (steel or beer), these assets have no alternative use, but continue to cost money in terms of debt payments, property taxes, and security expenses.

Transaction cost economics proposes that vertical integration is more efficient than contracting for goods and services in the marketplace when the transaction costs of buying goods on the open market become too great. When highly vertically integrated firms become excessively large and bureaucratic, however, the costs of managing the internal transactions may become greater than simply purchasing the needed goods externally—thus justifying outsourcing over vertical integration. This is why vertical integration and outsourcing are situation specific. Neither approach is best for all companies in all situations.[13] See the Strategy Highlight 7.1 feature on how transaction cost economics helps explain why firms vertically integrate or outsource important activities. Research thus far provides mixed support for the predictions of transaction cost economics.[14]

Harrigan proposes that a company's degree of vertical integration can range from total ownership of the value chain needed to make and sell a product to no ownership at all.[15] (See **Figure 7–2**.) Under **full integration**, a firm internally makes 100% of its key supplies and completely controls its distributors. Large oil companies, such as British Petroleum and Royal Dutch Shell, are fully integrated. They own the oil rigs that pump the oil out of the ground, the ships and pipelines that transport the oil, the refineries that convert the oil to gasoline, and the trucks that deliver the gasoline to company-owned and franchised gas stations. Sherwin-Williams Company, which not only manufacturers paint, but also sells it in its own chain of 3,000 retail stores, is another example of a fully-integrated firm.[16] If a corporation does not want the disadvantages of full vertical integration, it may choose either taper or quasi-integration strategies.

With **taper integration** (also called concurrent sourcing), a firm internally produces less than half of its own requirements and buys the rest from outside suppliers (backward taper integration).[17] In the case of Smithfield Foods, its purchase of Carroll's allowed it to produce 27% of the hogs it needed to process into pork. In terms of forward taper integration, a firm sells part of its goods through company-owned stores and the rest through general wholesalers. Although Apple had 216 of its own retain stores in 2008, much of the company's sales continued to be through national chains such as Best Buy and through independent local and regional dealers.

With **quasi-integration**, a company does not make any of its key supplies but purchases most of its requirements from outside suppliers that are under its partial control (backward

FIGURE 7–2
Vertical
Integration
Continuum

Full Integration	Taper Integration	Quasi-Integration	Long-Term Contract

SOURCE: *Suggested by K. R. Harrigan,* Strategies for Vertical Integration *(Lexington, Mass.: Lexington Books, D.C. Heath, 1983), pp. 16–21.*

STRATEGY highlight 7.1

TRANSACTION COST ECONOMICS
ANALYZES VERTICAL GROWTH STRATEGY

Why do corporations use vertical growth to permanently own suppliers or distributors when they could simply purchase individual items when needed on the open market? Transaction cost economics is a branch of institutional economics that attempts to answer this question. Transaction cost economics proposes that owning resources through vertical growth is more efficient than contracting for goods and services in the marketplace when the transaction costs of buying goods on the open market become too great. Transaction costs include the basic costs of drafting, negotiating, and safeguarding a market agreement (a contract) as well as the later managerial costs when the agreement is creating problems (goods aren't being delivered on time or quality is lower than needed), renegotiation costs (e.g., costs of meetings and phone calls), and the costs of settling disputes (e.g., lawyers' fees and court costs).

According to Williamson, three conditions must be met before a corporation will prefer internalizing a vertical transaction through ownership over contracting for the transaction in the marketplace: (1) a high level of uncertainty must surround the transaction, (2) assets involved in the transaction must be highly specialized to the transaction, and (3) the transaction must occur frequently. If there is a high level of uncertainty, it will be impossible to write a contract covering all contingencies, and it is likely that the contractor will act opportunistically to exploit any gaps in the written agreement—thus creating problems and increasing costs. If the assets being contracted for are highly

specialized (e.g., goods or services with few alternate uses), there are likely to be few alternative suppliers—thus allowing the contractor to take advantage of the situation and increase costs. The more frequent the transactions, the more opportunity for the contractor to demand special treatment and thus increase costs further.

Vertical integration is not always more efficient than the marketplace, however. When highly vertically integrated firms become excessively large and bureaucratic, the costs of managing the internal transactions may become greater than simply purchasing the needed goods externally—thus justifying outsourcing over ownership. The usually hidden management costs (e.g., excessive layers of management, endless committee meetings needed for interdepartmental coordination, and delayed decision making due to excessively detailed rules and policies) add to the internal transaction costs—thus reducing the effectiveness and efficiency of vertical integration. The decision to own or to outsource is, therefore, based on the particular situation surrounding the transaction and the ability of the corporation to manage the transaction internally both effectively and efficiently.

....
SOURCES: O. E. Williamson and S. G. Winter, eds., *The Nature of the Firm: Origins, Evolution, and Development* (New York: Oxford University Press, 1991); E. Mosakowski, "Organizational Boundaries and Economic Performance: An Empirical Study of Entrepreneurial Computer Firms," *Strategic Management Journal* (February 1991), pp. 115–133; P. S. Ring and A. H. Van de Ven, "Structuring Cooperative Relationships Between Organizations," *Strategic Management Journal* (October 1992), pp. 483–498.

quasi-integration). A company may not want to purchase outright a supplier or distributor, but it still may want to guarantee access to needed supplies, new products, technologies, or distribution channels. For example, the pharmaceutical company Bristol-Myers Squibb purchased 17% of the common stock of ImClone in order to gain access to new drug products being developed through biotechnology. An example of forward quasi-integration would be a paper company acquiring part interest in an office products chain in order to guarantee that its products had access to the distribution channel. Purchasing part interest in another company usually provides a company with a seat on the other firm's board of directors, thus guaranteeing the acquiring firm both information and control. As in the case of Bristol-Myers Squibb and ImClone, a quasi-integrated firm may later decide to buy the rest of a key supplier that it did not already own.[18]

Long-term contracts are agreements between two firms to provide agreed-upon goods and services to each other for a specified period of time. This cannot really be considered to be vertical integration unless it is an *exclusive* contract that specifies that the supplier or distributor cannot have a similar relationship with a competitive firm. In that case, the supplier or distributor is really a *captive company* that, although officially independent, does most of its business with the contracted firm and is formally tied to the other company through a long-term contract.

Recently there has been a movement away from vertical growth strategies (and thus vertical integration) toward cooperative contractual relationships with suppliers and even with competitors.[19] These relationships range from *outsourcing*, in which resources are purchased from outsiders through long-term contracts instead of being made in-house (for example, Hewlett-Packard bought its laser engines from Canon for HP's laser jet printers), to strategic alliances, in which partnerships, technology licensing agreements, and joint ventures supplement a firm's capabilities (for example, Toshiba has used strategic alliances with GE, Siemens, Motorola, and Ericsson to become one of the world's leading electronic companies).[20]

Horizontal Growth. A firm can achieve **horizontal growth** by expanding its operations into other geographic locations and/or by increasing the range of products and services offered to current markets. Research indicates that firms that grow horizontally by broadening their product lines have high survival rates.[21] Horizontal growth results in **horizontal integration**—the degree to which a firm operates in multiple geographic locations at the same point on an industry's value chain. For example, Procter & Gamble (P&G) continually adds additional sizes and multiple variations to its existing product lines to reduce possible niches competitors may enter. In addition, it introduces successful products from one part of the world to other regions. P&G has been introducing into China a steady stream of popular American brands, such as Head & Shoulders, Crest, Olay, Tide, Pampers, and Whisper. By 2007, it had 6,300 employees in China and the extensive distribution network it needed to prosper in the world's fastest growing market.[22]

Horizontal growth can be achieved through internal development or externally through acquisitions and strategic alliances with other firms in the same industry. For example, Delta Airlines acquired Northwest Airlines in 2008 to obtain access to Northwest's Asian markets and those American markets that Delta was not then serving. In contrast, many small commuter airlines engage in long-term contracts with major airlines in order to offer a complete arrangement for travelers. For example, the regional carrier Mesa Airlines arranged contractual agreements with United Airlines, U.S. Airways, and America West to be listed on their computer reservations, respectively, as United Express, U.S. Airways Express, and America West Express.

Horizontal growth is increasingly being achieved in today's world through international expansion. American's Wal-Mart, France's Carrefour, and Britain's Tesco are examples of national supermarket discount chains expanding horizontally throughout the world. This type of growth can be achieved internationally through many different strategies.

International Entry Options for Horizontal Growth

Research indicates that growing internationally is positively associated with firm profitability.[23] A corporation can select from several strategic options the most appropriate method for entering a foreign market or establishing manufacturing facilities in another country. The options vary from simple exporting to acquisitions to management contracts. See the **Global Issue** feature to see how U.S.-based firms are using international entry options in a horizontal growth strategy to expand throughout the world.

Some of the most popular options for international entry are as follows:

■ **Exporting:** A good way to minimize risk and experiment with a specific product is **exporting**, shipping goods produced in the company's home country to other countries for marketing. The company could choose to handle all critical functions itself, or it could contract these functions to an export management company. Exporting is becoming increasingly

GLOBAL issue

COMPANIES LOOK TO INTERNATIONAL MARKETS FOR HORIZONTAL GROWTH

What do Wal-Mart, Starbucks, and International Paper have in common? For one thing, they are successful U.S. companies that grew to the point that eventually their products saturated the domestic market—resulting in slower growth in domestic sales and profits. For another, all are companies that have chosen the corporate growth strategy of concentrating in one industry. A third thing in common is that all of them are using international markets as a key growth opportunity.

From its humble beginnings in Bentonville, Arkansas, Wal-Mart has successfully grown such that its discount stores can now be found in most every corner of the nation. Knowing that Wal-Mart had fewer locations left in the United States on which to build stores, the company's management knew that the company's domestic growth could not be sustained past 2007. Consequently, the company began acquiring retail chains in other countries to eventually become the largest company in the world in terms of sales.

Growing from its base in Seattle, Washington, Starbucks expanded its coffee shops to every city in the coun-try in only a few years. Soon imitators began opening their own versions until the U.S. market was completely saturated with coffee shops. Facing slow growth in its domestic market, Starbucks' management made the strategic decision to add fewer U.S. stores and to make international expansion its top priority.

Until recently, International Paper (IP) was international in name only. Founded in 1898, the company had once supplied 60% of the newsprint for American newspapers. After years of slow growth and weak financial performance, IP's management decided to divest unrelated businesses and to branch out from its North American roots to developing international markets. Acquisitions in Russia and green-field development in Brazil now positioned the company within low-cost, high-growth markets. IP's management hoped to soon control about half the office paper market in Latin America.

....

SOURCES: B. Helm and J. McGregor, "Howard Schultz's Grande Challenge," *Business Week* (January 21, 2008), p. 28; J. Bush, "Now It's Really International Paper," *Business Week* (December 17, 2007).

popular for small businesses because of the Internet, fax machines, toll-free numbers, and overnight express services, which reduce the once-formidable costs of going international.

- **Licensing:** Under a **licensing** agreement, the licensing firm grants rights to another firm in the host country to produce and/or sell a product. The licensee pays compensation to the licensing firm in return for technical expertise. This is an especially useful strategy if the trademark or brand name is well known, but the company does not have sufficient funds to finance its entering the country directly. Anheuser-Busch used this strategy to produce and market Budweiser beer in the United Kingdom, Japan, Israel, Australia, Korea, and the Philippines. This strategy is also important if the country makes entry via investment either difficult or impossible.

- **Franchising:** Under a **franchising** agreement, the franchiser grants rights to another company to open a retail store using the franchiser's name and operating system. In exchange, the franchisee pays the franchiser a percentage of its sales as a royalty. Franchising provides an opportunity for a firm to establish a presence in countries where the population or per capita spending is not sufficient for a major expansion effort.[24] Franchising accounts for 40% of total U.S. retail sales. Close to half of U.S. franchisers, such as Yum! Brands, franchise internationally.[25]

- **Joint Ventures:** Forming a **joint venture** between a foreign corporation and a domestic company is the most popular strategy used to enter a new country.[26] Companies often form joint ventures to combine the resources and expertise needed to develop new products or technologies. A joint venture may be an association between a company and a firm in the host country or a government agency in that country. A quick method of obtaining local management, it also reduces the risks of expropriation and harassment by host country officials. A joint venture may also enable a firm to enter a country that restricts foreign ownership. The corporation can enter another country with fewer assets at stake and thus lower risk. Under Indian law, for example, foreign retailers are permitted to own no more than 51% of shops selling single-brand products, or to sell to others on a wholesale basis. These and other restrictions deterred supermarket giants Tesco and Carrefour from entering India. As a result, 97% of Indian retailing is composed of small, family-run stores. Eager to enter India, Wal-Mart's management formed an equal partnership joint venture in 2007 with Bharti Enterprises to start wholesale operations. Under the name Bharti-Mart, the new company planned to open a dozen small retail stores by 2015.[27]

- **Acquisitions:** A relatively quick way to move into an international area is through acquisitions—purchasing another company already operating in that area. Synergistic benefits can result if the company acquires a firm with strong complementary product lines and a good distribution network. For example, Belgium's InBev purchased Anheuser-Busch in 2008 for $52 billion to obtain a solid position in the profitable North American beer market. Before the acquisition, InBev had only a small presence in the U.S., but a strong one in Europe and Latin American, where Anheuser-Busch was weak.[28] Research suggests that wholly owned subsidiaries are more successful in international undertakings than are strategic alliances, such as joint ventures.[29] This is one reason why firms more experienced in international markets take a higher ownership position when making a foreign investment.[30] Cross-border acquisitions now account for 19% of all acquisitions in the United States—up from only 6% in 1985.[31] In some countries, however, acquisitions can be difficult to arrange because of a lack of available information about potential candidates. Government restrictions on ownership, such as the U.S. requirement that limits foreign ownership of U.S. airlines to 49% of nonvoting and 25% of voting stock, can also discourage acquisitions.

- **Green-Field Development:** If a company doesn't want to purchase another company's problems along with its assets, it may choose **green-field development** and build its own manufacturing plant and distribution system. Research indicates that firms possessing high levels of technology, multinational experience, and diverse product lines prefer green-field development to acquisitions.[32] This is usually a far more complicated and expensive operation than acquisition, but it allows a company more freedom in designing the plant, choosing suppliers, and hiring a workforce. For example, Nissan, Honda, and Toyota built auto factories in rural areas of Great Britain and then hired a young workforce with no experience in the industry. BMW did the same thing when it built its auto plant in Spartanburg, South Carolina, to make its Z3 and Z4 sports cars.

- **Production Sharing:** Coined by Peter Drucker, the term **production sharing** means the process of combining the higher labor skills and technology available in developed countries with the lower-cost labor available in developing countries. Often called *outsourcing*, one example is Maytag's moving some of its refrigeration production to a new plant in Reynosa, Mexico, in order to reduce labor costs. Many companies have moved data processing, programming, and customer service activities "offshore" to Ireland, India, Barbados, Jamaica, the Philippines, and Singapore, where wages are lower, English is spoken, and telecommunications are in place. As the number of technology services employees in India grew to be 15% of IBM's total tech services employees by 2007, the company has been able to eliminate 20,000 jobs in high-cost locations in the U.S., Europe, and Japan.[33]

- **Turnkey Operations: Turnkey operations** are typically contracts for the construction of operating facilities in exchange for a fee. The facilities are transferred to the host country or firm when they are complete. The customer is usually a government agency of, for example, a Middle Eastern country that has decreed that a particular product must be produced locally and under its control. For example, Fiat built an auto plant in Tagliatti,

Russia, for the Soviet Union in the late 1960s to produce an older model of Fiat under the brand name of Lada. MNCs that perform turnkey operations are frequently industrial equipment manufacturers that supply some of their own equipment for the project and that commonly sell replacement parts and maintenance services to the host country. They thereby create customers as well as future competitors. Interestingly, Renault purchased in 2008 a 25% stake in the same Tagliatti factory built by Fiat to help the Russian carmaker modernize, using Renault's low cost Logan as the base for the plant's new Lada model.[34]

- **BOT Concept:** The **BOT (Build, Operate, Transfer) concept** is a variation of the turnkey operation. Instead of turning the facility (usually a power plant or toll road) over to the host country when completed, the company operates the facility for a fixed period of time during which it earns back its investment plus a profit. It then turns the facility over to the government at little or no cost to the host country.[35]

- **Management Contracts:** A large corporation operating throughout the world is likely to have a large amount of management talent at its disposal. **Management contracts** offer a means through which a corporation can use some of its personnel to assist a firm in a host country for a specified fee and period of time. Management contracts are common when a host government expropriates part or all of a foreign-owned company's holdings in its country. The contracts allow the firm to continue to earn some income from its investment and keep the operations going until local management is trained.[36]

Diversification Strategies

According to strategist Richard Rumelt, companies begin thinking about diversification when their growth has plateaued and opportunities for growth in the original business have been depleted.[37] This often occurs when an industry consolidates, becomes mature, and most of the surviving firms have reached the limits of growth using vertical and horizontal growth strategies. Unless the competitors are able to expand internationally into less mature markets, they may have no choice but to diversify into different industries if they want to continue growing. The two basic diversification strategies are concentric and conglomerate.

Concentric (Related) Diversification. Growth through **concentric diversification** into a related industry may be a very appropriate corporate strategy when a firm has a strong competitive position but industry attractiveness is low.

Research indicates that the probability of succeeding by moving into a related business is a function of a company's position in its core business. For companies in leadership positions, the chances for success are nearly three times higher than those for followers.[38] By focusing on the characteristics that have given the company its distinctive competence, the company uses those very strengths as its means of diversification. The firm attempts to secure strategic fit in a new industry where the firm's product knowledge, its manufacturing capabilities, and the marketing skills it used so effectively in the original industry can be put to good use.[39] The corporation's products or processes are related in some way: they possess some common thread.

The search is for **synergy**, the concept that two businesses will generate more profits together than they could separately. The point of commonality may be similar technology, customer usage, distribution, managerial skills, or product similarity. This is the rationale taken by Quebec-based Bombardier, the world's third-largest aircraft manufacturer. In the 1980s, the company expanded beyond snowmobiles into making light rail equipment. Defining itself as a transportation company, it entered the aircraft business in 1986, with its purchase of Canadair, then best known for its fire-fighting airplanes. It later bought Learjet, a well-known maker of business jets. Over a 14-year period, Bombardier launched 14 new aircraft. In July 2008, the company announced its C Series Aircraft Program to manufacture a 110–130-seat "green" single-aisle family of airplanes to directly compete with Airbus and Boeing.[40]

A firm may choose to diversify concentrically through either internal or external means. Bombardier, for example, diversified externally through acquisitions. Toro, in contrast, grew internally in North America by using its current manufacturing processes and distributors to make and market snow blowers in addition to lawn mowers. When considering concentric diversification alternatives, see the criteria presented in **Strategy Highlight 7.2.**

Conglomerate (Unrelated) Diversification. When management realizes that the current industry is unattractive and that the firm lacks outstanding abilities or skills that it could easily transfer to related products or services in other industries, the most likely strategy is **conglomerate diversification**—diversifying into an industry unrelated to its current one. Rather than maintaining a common thread throughout their organization, strategic managers who adopt this strategy are primarily concerned with financial considerations of cash flow or risk reduction. This is also a good strategy for a firm that is able to transfer its own excellent management system into less-well-managed acquired firms. General Electric and Berkshire Hathaway are examples of companies that have used conglomerate diversification to grow successfully. Managed by Warren Buffet, Berkshire Hathaway has interests in furniture retailing, razor blades, airlines, paper, broadcasting, soft drinks, and publishing.[41]

The emphasis in conglomerate diversification is on sound investment and value-oriented management rather than on the product-market synergy common to concentric diversification. A cash-rich company with few opportunities for growth in its industry might, for example, move into another industry where opportunities are great but cash is hard to find. Another instance of conglomerate diversification might be when a company with a seasonal and,

STRATEGY highlight 7.2

SCREENING CRITERIA FOR CONCENTRIC DIVERSIFICATION

Market Attractiveness

1. Is the market large enough to be attractive?
2. Is the market growing faster than the economy?
3. Does it offer the potential to increase revenue from current customers?
4. Does it provide the ability to sell existing services to new customers?
5. Does it create a recurring revenue stream?
6. Are average earnings in the industry/market higher than in current businesses?
7. Is the market already taken by strong competitors?
8. Does it strengthen relationships with existing value-chain players?

Market Feasibility

1. Can the company enter the market within a year?
2. Are there any synergies in the geographic region where the market is located?
3. Can existing capabilities be leveraged for market entry?
4. Can existing assets be leveraged for market entry?
5. Can existing employees be used to support this opportunity?
6. Will current and future laws and regulations affect entry?
7. Is there a need for a strong brand in the new market?
8. If there is a need for partners, can the company secure and manage partner relationships?

SOURCE: Summarized from N. J. Kaplan, "Surviving and Thriving When Your Customers Contract," *Journal of Business Strategy* (January/February, 2003), p. 20.

therefore, uneven cash flow purchases a firm in an unrelated industry with complementing seasonal sales that will level out the cash flow. CSX management considered the purchase of a natural gas transmission business (Texas Gas Resources) by CSX Corporation (a railroad-dominated transportation company) to be a good fit because most of the gas transmission revenue was realized in the winter months—the lean period in the railroad business.

CONTROVERSIES IN DIRECTIONAL GROWTH STRATEGIES

Is vertical growth better than horizontal growth? Is concentration better than diversification? Is concentric diversification better than conglomerate diversification? Research reveals that companies following a related diversification strategy appear to be higher performers and survive longer than do companies with narrower scope following a pure concentration strategy.[42] Although the research is not in complete agreement, growth into areas related to a company's current product lines is generally more successful than is growth into completely unrelated areas.[43] For example, one study of various growth projects examined how many were considered successful, that is, still in existence after 22 years. The results were vertical growth, 80%; horizontal growth, 50%; concentric diversification, 35%; and conglomerate diversification, 28%.[44] This supports the conclusion from a study of 40 successful European companies that companies should first exploit their existing assets and capabilities before exploring for new ones, but that they should also diversify their portfolio of products.[45]

In terms of diversification strategies, research suggests that the relationship between relatedness and performance is curvilinear in the shape of an inverted U-shaped curve. If a new business is very similar to that of the acquiring firm, it adds little new to the corporation and only marginally improves performance. If the new business is completely different from the acquiring company's businesses, there may be very little potential for any synergy. If, however, the new business provides new resources and capabilities in a different, but similar, business, the likelihood of a significant performance improvement is high.[46]

Is internal growth better than external growth? Corporations can follow the growth strategies of either concentration or diversification through the internal development of new products and services, or through external acquisitions, mergers, and strategic alliances. The value of global acquisitions and mergers has steadily increased from less than $1 trillion in 1990 to $3.5 trillion in 2000.[47] According to a McKinsey & Company survey, managers are primarily motivated to purchase other companies in order to add capabilities, expand geographically, and buy growth.[48] Research generally concludes, however, that firms growing through acquisitions do not perform financially as well as firms that grow through internal means.[49] For example, on September 3, 2001, the day *before* HP announced that it was purchasing Compaq, HP's stock was selling at $23.11. After the announcement, the stock price fell to $18.87. Three years later, on September 21, 2004, the shares sold at $18.70.[50] One reason for this poor performance may be that acquiring firms tend to spend less on R&D than do other firms.[51] Another reason may be the typically high price of the acquisition itself. Studies reveal that over half to two-thirds of acquisitions are failures primarily because the premiums paid were too high for them to earn their cost of capital.[52] Another reason for the poor stock performance is that 50% of the customers of a merged firm are less satisfied with the combined company's service two years after the merger.[53] It is likely that neither strategy is best by itself and that some combination of internal and external growth strategies is better than using one or the other.[54]

What can improve acquisition performance? For one thing, the acquisition should be linked to strategic objectives and support corporate strategy. In addition, a corporation must be prepared to identify roughly 100 candidates and conduct due diligence investigation on around 40 companies in order to ultimately purchase 10 companies. This kind of effort requires the capacity to sift through many candidates while simultaneously integrating previous acquisitions.[55] A study by Bain & Company of more than 11,000 acquisitions by companies throughout the world concluded that successful acquirers make small, low-risk acquisitions before moving on to larger ones.[56] Previous experience between an acquirer and a target firm in terms of R&D, manufacturing, or marketing alliances improves the likelihood of a successful acquisition.[57] Realizing that an acquired company must be carefully assimilated into the acquiring firm's operations, Cisco uses three criteria to judge whether a company is a suitable candidate for takeover:

- It must be relatively small.
- It must be comparable in organizational culture.
- It must be physically close to one of the existing affiliates.[58]

STABILITY STRATEGIES

A corporation may choose stability over growth by continuing its current activities without any significant change in direction. Although sometimes viewed as a lack of strategy, the stability family of corporate strategies can be appropriate for a successful corporation operating in a reasonably predictable environment.[59] They are very popular with small business owners who have found a niche and are happy with their success and the manageable size of their firms. Stability strategies can be very useful in the short run, but they can be dangerous if followed for too long. Some of the more popular of these strategies are the pause/proceed-with-caution, no-change, and profit strategies.

Pause/Proceed with Caution Strategy

A **pause/proceed-with-caution strategy** is, in effect, a timeout—an opportunity to rest before continuing a growth or retrenchment strategy. It is a very deliberate attempt to make only incremental improvements until a particular environmental situation changes. It is typically conceived as a temporary strategy to be used until the environment becomes more hospitable or to enable a company to consolidate its resources after prolonged rapid growth. This was the strategy Dell followed after its growth strategy had resulted in more growth than it could handle. Explained CEO Michael Dell, "We grew 285% in two years, and we're having some growing pains." Selling personal computers by mail enabled Dell to underprice competitors, but it could not keep up with the needs of a $2 billion, 5,600-employee company selling PCs in 95 countries. Dell did not give up on its growth strategy; it merely put it temporarily in limbo until the company was able to hire new managers, improve the structure, and build new facilities.[60] This was a popular strategy in late-2008 during a U.S. financial crisis when banks were freezing their lending and awaiting a rescue package from the federal government.

No-Change Strategy

A **no-change strategy** is a decision to do nothing new—a choice to continue current operations and policies for the foreseeable future. Rarely articulated as a definite strategy, a no-change strategy's success depends on a lack of significant change in a corporation's situation. The relative stability created by the firm's modest competitive position in an industry facing little or no growth encourages the company to continue on its current course, making only small adjustments for inflation in its sales and profit objectives. There are no obvious opportunities or threats, nor is there much in the way of significant strengths or weaknesses. Few aggressive new competitors are likely to enter such an industry. The corporation has probably found a reasonably profitable and stable niche for its products. Unless the industry is undergoing consolidation, the relative comfort a company in this situation experiences is likely to encourage the company to follow a no-change strategy in which the future is expected to continue as an extension of the present. Many small-town businesses followed this strategy before Wal-Mart moved into their areas and forced them to rethink their strategy.

Profit Strategy

A **profit strategy** is a decision to do nothing new in a worsening situation but instead to act as though the company's problems are only temporary. The profit strategy is an attempt to artificially support profits when a company's sales are declining by reducing investment and short-term discretionary expenditures. Rather than announce the company's poor position to shareholders and the investment community at large, top management may be tempted to follow this very seductive strategy. Blaming the company's problems on a hostile environment (such as anti-business government policies, unethical competitors, finicky customers, and/or greedy lenders), management defers investments and/or cuts expenses (such as R&D, maintenance, and advertising) to stabilize profits during this period. It may even sell one of its product lines for the cash-flow benefits.

The profit strategy is useful only to help a company get through a temporary difficulty. It may also be a way to boost the value of a company in preparation for going public via an initial public offering (IPO). Unfortunately, the strategy is seductive and if continued long enough it will lead to a serious deterioration in a corporation's competitive position. The profit strategy is typically top management's passive, short-term, and often self-serving response to a difficult situation. In such situations, it is often better to face the problem directly by choosing a retrenchment strategy.

RETRENCHMENT STRATEGIES

A company may pursue retrenchment strategies when it has a weak competitive position in some or all of its product lines resulting in poor performance—sales are down and profits are becoming losses. These strategies impose a great deal of pressure to improve performance. In an attempt to eliminate the weaknesses that are dragging the company down, management may follow one of several retrenchment strategies, ranging from turnaround or becoming a captive company to selling out, bankruptcy, or liquidation.

Turnaround Strategy

Turnaround strategy emphasizes the improvement of operational efficiency and is probably most appropriate when a corporation's problems are pervasive but not yet critical. Research shows that poorly performing firms in mature industries have been able to improve their performance by cutting costs and expenses and by selling off assets.[61] Analogous to a weight-reduction diet, the two basic phases of a turnaround strategy are contraction and consolidation.[62]

Contraction is the initial effort to quickly "stop the bleeding" with a general, across-the-board cutback in size and costs. For example, when Howard Stringer was selected to be CEO of Sony Corporation in 2005, he immediately implemented the first stage of a turnaround plan by eliminating 10,000 jobs, closing 11 of 65 plants, and divesting many unprofitable electronics businesses. [63] The second phase, *consolidation*, implements a program to stabilize the now-leaner corporation. To streamline the company, plans are developed to reduce unnecessary overhead and to make functional activities cost-justified. This is a crucial time for the organization. If the consolidation phase is not conducted in a positive manner, many of the best people leave the organization. An overemphasis on downsizing and cutting costs coupled with a heavy hand by top management is usually counterproductive and can actually hurt performance.[64] If, however, all employees are encouraged to get involved in productivity improvements, the firm is likely to emerge from this retrenchment period a much stronger and better-organized company. It has improved its competitive position and is able once again to expand the business.[65]

Captive Company Strategy

A **captive company strategy** involves giving up independence in exchange for security. A company with a weak competitive position may not be able to engage in a full-blown turnaround strategy. The industry may not be sufficiently attractive to justify such an effort from either the current management or investors. Nevertheless, a company in this situation faces poor sales and increasing losses unless it takes some action. Management desperately searches for an "angel" by offering to be a captive company to one of its larger customers in order to guarantee the company's continued existence with a long-term contract. In this way, the corporation may be able to reduce the scope of some of its functional activities, such as marketing, thus significantly reducing costs. The weaker company gains certainty of sales and production in return for becoming heavily dependent on another firm for at least 75% of its sales. For example, to become the sole supplier of an auto part to General Motors, Simpson Industries of Birmingham, Michigan, agreed to let a special team from GM inspect its engine parts facilities and books and interview its employees. In return, nearly 80% of the company's production was sold to GM through long-term contracts.[66]

Sell-Out/Divestment Strategy

If a corporation with a weak competitive position in an industry is unable either to pull itself up by its bootstraps or to find a customer to which it can become a captive company, it may have no choice but to sell out. The **sell-out strategy** makes sense if management can still obtain a good price for its shareholders and the employees can keep their jobs by selling the entire company to another firm. The hope is that another company will have the necessary resources and determination to return the company to profitability. Marginal performance in a troubled industry was one reason Northwest Airlines was willing to be acquired by Delta Airlines in 2008.

If the corporation has multiple business lines and it chooses to sell off a division with low growth potential, this is called **divestment**. This was the strategy Ford used when it sold its struggling Jaguar and Land Rover units to Tata Motors in 2008 for $2 billion. Ford had spent $10 billion trying to turn around Jaguar after spending $2.5 billion to buy it in 1990. In addition, Ford had paid $2.8 billion for Land Rover in 2000. Ford's management hoped to use the proceeds of the sale to help the company reach profitability in 2009.[67] General Electric's management used the same reasoning when it decided to sell or spin off its slow-growth appliance business in 2008.

Divestment is often used after a corporation acquires a multi-unit corporation in order to shed the units that do not fit with the corporation's new strategy. This is why Whirlpool sold Maytag's Hoover vacuum cleaner unit after Whirlpool purchased Maytag. Divestment was also a key part of Lego's turnaround strategy when management decided to divest its theme parks to concentrate more on its core business of making toys.[68]

Bankruptcy/Liquidation Strategy

When a company finds itself in the worst possible situation with a poor competitive position in an industry with few prospects, management has only a few alternatives—all of them distasteful. Because no one is interested in buying a weak company in an unattractive industry, the firm must pursue a bankruptcy or liquidation strategy. **Bankruptcy** involves giving up management of the firm to the courts in return for some settlement of the corporation's obligations. Top management hopes that once the court decides the claims on the company, the company will be stronger and better able to compete in a more attractive industry. Faced with a recessionary economy and falling market demand for casual dining, restaurants like Bennigan's Grill & Tavern and Steak & Ale, that once thrived by offering mid-priced menus with potato skins and thick hamburgers, filed for bankruptcy in July 2008. Within the troubled airline industry, at least 30 airlines went bankrupt during just the first half of 2008 with 30 more bankruptcies expected by the end of the year.[69] A controversial approach was used by Delphi Corporation when it filed for Chapter 11 bankruptcy only for its U.S. operations, which employed 32,000 high-wage union workers, but not for its foreign factories in low-wage countries.[70]

In contrast to bankruptcy, which seeks to perpetuate a corporation, **liquidation** is the termination of the firm. When the industry is unattractive and the company too weak to be sold as a going concern, management may choose to convert as many saleable assets as possible to cash, which is then distributed to the shareholders after all obligations are paid. Liquidation is a prudent strategy for distressed firms with a small number of choices, all of which are problematic.[71] This was Circuit City's situation in 2008, when it liquidated its retail stores. The benefit of liquidation over bankruptcy is that the board of directors, as representatives of the shareholders, together with top management make the decisions instead of turning them over to the bankruptcy court, which may choose to ignore shareholders completely.

At times, top management must be willing to select one of these less desirable retrenchment strategies. Unfortunately, many top managers are unwilling to admit that their company has serious weaknesses for fear that they may be personally blamed. Even worse, top management may not even perceive that crises are developing. When these top managers eventually notice trouble, they are prone to attribute the problems to temporary environmental disturbances and tend to follow profit strategies. Even when things are going terribly wrong, top management is greatly tempted to avoid liquidation in the hope of a miracle. Top management enters a *cycle of decline,* in which it goes through a process of secrecy and denial, followed by blame and scorn, avoidance and turf protection, ending with passivity and helplessness.[72] Thus, a corporation needs a strong board of directors who, to safeguard shareholders' interests, can tell top management when to quit.

7.3 Portfolio Analysis

Chapter 6 dealt with how individual product lines and business units can gain competitive advantage in the marketplace by using competitive and cooperative strategies. Companies with multiple product lines or business units must also ask themselves how these various products and business units should be managed to boost overall corporate performance:

- How much of our time and money should we spend on our best products and business units to ensure that they continue to be successful?

- How much of our time and money should we spend developing new costly products, most of which will never be successful?

One of the most popular aids to developing corporate strategy in a multiple-business corporation is portfolio analysis. Although its popularity has dropped since the 1970s and 1980s, when more than half of the largest business corporations used portfolio analysis, it is still used by around 27% of Fortune 500 firms in corporate strategy formulation.[73] Portfolio analysis puts corporate headquarters into the role of an internal banker. In **portfolio analysis**, top management views its product lines and business units as a series of investments from which it expects a profitable return. The product lines/business units form a portfolio of investments that top management must constantly juggle to ensure the best return on the corporation's invested money. A McKinsey & Company study of the performance of the 200 largest U.S. corporations found that companies that actively managed their business portfolios through acquisitions and divestitures created substantially more shareholder value than those companies that passively held their businesses.[74] Given the increasing number of strategic alliances in today's corporations, portfolio analysis is also being used to evaluate the contribution of alliances to corporate and business unit objectives.

Two of the most popular portfolio techniques are the BCG Growth-Share Matrix and GE Business Screen.

BCG GROWTH-SHARE MATRIX

Using the **BCG (Boston Consulting Group) Growth-Share Matrix** depicted in **Figure 7–3** is the simplest way to portray a corporation's portfolio of investments. Each of the corporation's product lines or business units is plotted on the matrix according to both the growth rate of the industry in which it competes and its relative market share. A unit's relative competitive position is defined as its market share in the industry divided by that of the largest other competitor. By this calculation, a relative market share above 1.0 belongs to the market leader. The business growth rate is the percentage of market growth, that is, the percentage by which sales of a particular business unit classification of products have increased. The matrix assumes that, other things being equal, a growing market is attractive.

The line separating areas of high and low relative competitive position is set at 1.5 times. A product line or business unit must have relative strengths of this magnitude to ensure that it will have the dominant position needed to be a "star" or "cash cow." On the other hand, a product line or unit having a relative competitive position less than 1.0 has "dog" status.[75] Each product or unit is represented in Figure 7–3 by a circle. The area of the circle represents the relative significance of each business unit or product line to the corporation in terms of assets used or sales generated.

FIGURE 7–3
BCG Growth-Share Matrix

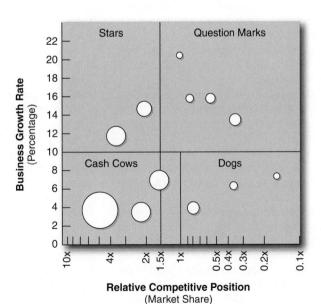

SOURCE: *Reprinted from* Long Range Planning, *Vol. 10, No. 2, 1977, Hedley, "Strategy and the Business Portfolio," p. 12. Copyright © 1977 with permission from Elsevier.*

The BCG Growth-Share Matrix has a lot in common with the product life cycle. As a product moves through its life cycle, it is categorized into one of four types for the purpose of funding decisions:

- **Question marks** (sometimes called "problem children" or "wildcats") are new products with the potential for success, but they need a lot of cash for development. If such a product is to gain enough market share to become a market leader and thus a star, money must be taken from more mature products and spent on the question mark. This is a "fish or cut bait" decision in which management must decide if the business is worth the investment needed. For example, after years of fruitlessly experimenting with an electric car, General Motors finally decided in 2006 to take a chance on developing the Chevrolet Volt.[76] To learn more of GM's decision to build the electric car, see the **Environmental Sustainability Issue** feature.

- **Stars** are market leaders that are typically at the peak of their product life cycle and are able to generate enough cash to maintain their high share of the market and usually contribute to the company's profits. HP's printer business has been called HP's "crown jewel" because of its 41% market share in printers and its control of the replacement cartridge

ENVIRONMENTAL sustainability issue

GENERAL MOTORS AND THE ELECTRIC CAR

In 2003, top management at General Motors (GM) decided to discontinue further work on its EV1 electric automobile. Working versions of the car had been leased to a limited number of people, but never sold. Environmentalists protested that GM stopped making the car just to send a message to government policy makers that an electric car was bad business. Management responded by stating that the car would never have made a profit.

In an April 2005 meeting of GM's top management team, Vice Chairman Robert Lutz suggested that it might be time to build another electric car. He noted that Toyota's Prius hybrid had made Toyota look environmentally sensitive; whereas, GM was viewed as making gas "hogs." The response was negative. Lutz recalled one executive saying, "We lost $1 billion on the last one. Do you want to lose $1 billion on the next one?"

Even though worldwide car ownership was growing 5% annually, rising fuel prices in 2005 reduced sales of GM's profitable SUVs—resulting in a loss of $11 billion. Board members began signaling that it was time for management to take some riskier bets to get the company out of financial trouble. In February 2006, management reluctantly approved developmental work on another electric car. At the time, no one in GM knew if batteries could be made small enough to power a car, but they knew that

choices were limited. According to Larry Burns, Vice President of R&D and Strategic Planning, "This industry is 98% dependent on petroleum. GM has concluded that that's not sustainable."

Chairman and CEO Richard Wagoner, Jr. surprised the world at the January 2007 Detroit Auto Show with a vow to start developing an electric car called the Chevrolet Volt. It would plug into a regular electric outlet, leapfrog the competition, and be on sale in 2010. The company not only needed to build a radical new car, but had to convert as much as 75% of its current fleet to hybrid engines to meet fuel economy rules taking effect in 2017.

Management created a new team dedicated to getting hybrid and electric cars to market. The R&D budget was increased from $6.6 billion in 2006 to $8.1 billion in 2007. Several new models were canceled to free resources. The battery lab was under pressure to design batteries that could propel the Volt 40 miles before a small gasoline engine would re-charge the battery and extend the range to 600 miles. Douglas Drauch, battery lab manager, promised that the batteries would be ready on schedule. "We're making history," he said. "Fifty years from now, people will remember the Volt—like they remember a '53 Corvette."

SOURCES: D. Welch, "GM: Live Green or Die," *Business Week* (May 26, 2008), pp. 36–41; "The Drive for Low Emissions," *The Economist's Special Report on Business and Climate Change* (June 2, 2007), pp. 26–28.

market. On its own, it accounted for more than half of HP's operating profit.[77] When a star's market growth rate slows, it becomes a cash cow.

■ **Cash cows** typically bring in far more money than is needed to maintain their market share. In this declining stage of their life cycle, these products are "milked" for cash that will be invested in new question marks. Expenses such as advertising and R&D are reduced. Panasonic's video cassette recorders (VCRs) moved to this category when sales declined and DVD player/recorders replaced them. Question marks unable to obtain dominant market share (and thus become stars) by the time the industry growth rate inevitably slows become dogs.

■ **Dogs** have low market share and do not have the potential (because they are in an unattractive industry) to bring in much cash. According to the BCG Growth-Share Matrix, dogs should be either sold off or managed carefully for the small amount of cash they can generate. For example, DuPont, the inventor of nylon, sold its textiles unit in 2003 because the company wanted to eliminate its low-margin products and focus more on its growing biotech business.[78] The same was true of IBM when it sold its PC business to China's Lenovo Group in order to emphasize its growing services business.

Underlying the BCG Growth-Share Matrix is the concept of the experience curve (discussed in **Chapter 5**). The key to success is assumed to be market share. Firms with the highest market share tend to have a cost leadership position based on economies of scale, among other things. If a company is able to use the experience curve to its advantage, it should be able to manufacture and sell new products at a price low enough to garner early market share leadership (assuming no successful imitation by competitors). Once the product becomes a star, it is destined to be very profitable, considering its inevitable future as a cash cow.

Having plotted the current positions of its product lines or business units on a matrix, a company can project its future positions, assuming no change in strategy. Present and projected matrixes can thus be used to help identify major strategic issues facing the organization. The goal of any company is to maintain a balanced portfolio so it can be self-sufficient in cash and always working to harvest mature products in declining industries to support new ones in growing industries.

The BCG Growth-Share Matrix is a very well-known portfolio concept with some clear advantages. It is quantifiable and easy to use. *Cash cow, dog, question mark,* and *star* are easy-to-remember terms for referring to a corporation's business units or products. Unfortunately, the BCG Growth-Share Matrix also has some serious limitations:

■ The use of highs and lows to form four categories is too simplistic.

■ The link between market share and profitability is questionable.[79] Low-share businesses can also be profitable.[80] For example, Olivetti is still profitably selling manual typewriters through mail-order catalogs.

■ Growth rate is only one aspect of industry attractiveness.

■ Product lines or business units are considered only in relation to one competitor: the market leader. Small competitors with fast-growing market shares are ignored.

■ Market share is only one aspect of overall competitive position.

GE BUSINESS SCREEN

General Electric, with the assistance of the McKinsey & Company consulting firm, developed a more complicated matrix. As depicted in **Figure 7–4**, the **GE Business Screen** includes nine cells based on long-term industry attractiveness and business strength competitive position. The GE Business Screen, in contrast to the BCG Growth-Share Matrix, includes much more

FIGURE 7–4
General Electric's
Business Screen

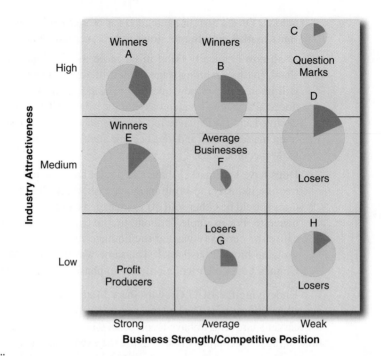

SOURCE: *Adapted from* Strategic Management in GE, *Corporate Planning and Development, General Electric Corporation, Reprinted by permission of General Electric Company.*

data in its two key factors than just business growth rate and comparable market share. For example, at GE, industry attractiveness includes market growth rate, industry profitability, size, and pricing practices, among other possible opportunities and threats. Business strength or competitive position includes market share as well as technological position, profitability, and size, among other possible strengths and weaknesses.[81]

The individual product lines or business units are identified by a letter and plotted as circles on the GE Business Screen. The area of each circle is in proportion to the size of the industry in terms of sales. The pie slices within the circles depict the market shares of the product lines or business units.

To plot product lines or business units on the GE Business Screen, follow these four steps:

1. Select criteria to rate the industry for each product line or business unit. Assess overall industry attractiveness for each product line or business unit on a scale from 1 (very unattractive) to 5 (very attractive).

2. Select the key factors needed for success in each product line or business unit. Assess business strength/competitive position for each product line or business unit on a scale of 1 (very weak) to 5 (very strong).

3. Plot each product line's or business unit's current position on a matrix as that depicted in Figure 7–4.

4. Plot the firm's future portfolio, assuming that present corporate and business strategies remain unchanged. Is there a performance gap between projected and desired portfolios? If so, this gap should serve as a stimulus to seriously review the corporation's current mission, objectives, strategies, and policies.

Overall, the nine-cell GE Business Screen is an improvement over the BCG Growth-Share Matrix. The GE Business Screen considers many more variables and does not lead to such simplistic conclusions. It recognizes, for example, that the attractiveness of an industry can be assessed in many different ways (other than simply using growth rate), and it thus allows users to select whatever criteria they feel are most appropriate to their situation. This portfolio matrix, however, does have some shortcomings:

- It can get quite complicated and cumbersome.
- The numerical estimates of industry attractiveness and business strength/competitive position give the appearance of objectivity, but they are in reality subjective judgments that may vary from one person to another.
- It cannot effectively depict the positions of new products or business units in developing industries.

ADVANTAGES AND LIMITATIONS OF PORTFOLIO ANALYSIS

Portfolio analysis is commonly used in strategy formulation because it offers certain *advantages:*

- It encourages top management to evaluate each of the corporation's businesses individually and to set objectives and allocate resources for each.
- It stimulates the use of externally oriented data to supplement management's judgment.
- It raises the issue of cash-flow availability for use in expansion and growth.
- Its graphic depiction facilitates communication.

Portfolio analysis does, however, have some very real *limitations* that have caused some companies to reduce their use of this approach:

- Defining product/market segments is difficult.
- It suggests the use of standard strategies that can miss opportunities or be impractical.
- It provides an illusion of scientific rigor when in reality positions are based on subjective judgments.
- Its value-laden terms such as cash cow and dog can lead to self-fulfilling prophecies.
- It is not always clear what makes an industry attractive or where a product is in its life cycle.
- Naively following the prescriptions of a portfolio model may actually reduce corporate profits if they are used inappropriately. For example, General Mills' Chief Executive H. Brewster Atwater cited his company's Bisquick brand of baking mix as a product that would have been written off years ago based on portfolio analysis. "This product is 57 years old. By all rights it should have been overtaken by newer products. But with the proper research to improve the product and promotion to keep customers excited, it's doing very well."[82]

MANAGING A STRATEGIC ALLIANCE PORTFOLIO

Just as product lines/business units form a portfolio of investments that top management must constantly juggle to ensure the best return on the corporation's invested money, strategic alliances can also be viewed as a portfolio of investments—investments of money, time, and energy. The way a company manages these intertwined relationships can significantly influence corporate competitiveness. Alliances are thus recognized as an important source of competitive advantage and superior performance.[83]

Managing groups of strategic alliances is primarily the job of the business unit. Its decisions may escalate, however, to the corporate level. Toman Corporation, for example, has

195 international joint ventures containing 422 alliance partners. According to a Toman executive, "If headquarters is trying to bring us and some other company closer together, they should understand not only our business unit, but also other business units. Sometimes the whole of our company may benefit (from an alliance) but it may not be good for one of our business units. And if it proceeds, headquarters must give some credit to our business unit so that we can agree. But it is not acceptable if they say to us that we are to lose something as a result of the alliance and now we have to make up the difference in one of our other businesses." In this instance the stage is set for negotiations across business units at the corporate level to achieve a broadly supported alliance network management system.[84]

A study of 25 leading European corporations found four tasks of multi-alliance management that are necessary for successful alliance portfolio management:

1. **Developing and implementing a portfolio strategy for each business unit and a corporate policy for managing all the alliances of the entire company:** Alliances are primarily determined by business units. The corporate level develops general rules concerning when, how, and with whom to cooperate. The task of alliance policy is to strategically align all of the corporation's alliance activities with corporate strategy and corporate values. Every new alliance is thus checked against corporate policy before it is approved.

2. **Monitoring the alliance portfolio in terms of implementing business unit strategies and corporate strategy and policies:** Each alliance is measured in terms of achievement of objectives (e.g., market share), financial measures (e.g., profits and cash flow), contributed resource quality and quantity, and the overall relationship. The more a firm is diversified, the less the need for monitoring at the corporate level.

3. **Coordinating the portfolio to obtain synergies and avoid conflicts among alliances:** Because the interdependencies among alliances within a business unit are usually greater than among different businesses, the need for coordination is greater at the business level than at the corporate level. The need for coordination increases as the number of alliances in one business unit and the company as a whole increases, the average number of partners per alliance increases, and/or the overlap of the alliances increases.

4. **Establishing an alliance management system to support other tasks of multi-alliance management:** This infrastructure consists of formalized processes, standardized tools and specialized organizational units. All but two of the 25 companies established centers of competence for alliance management. The centers were often part of a department for corporate development or a department of alliance management at the corporate level. In other corporations, specialized positions for alliance management were created at both the corporate and business unit levels or only at the business unit level. Most corporations prefer a system in which the corporate level provides the methods and tools to support alliances centrally, but decentralizes day-to-day alliance management to the business units.[85]

7.4 Corporate Parenting

Campbell, Goold, and Alexander, authors of *Corporate-Level Strategy: Creating Value in the Multibusiness Company*, contend that corporate strategists must address two crucial questions:

- What businesses should this company own and why?
- What organizational structure, management processes, and philosophy will foster superior performance from the company's business units?[86]

Portfolio analysis typically attempts to answer these questions by examining the attractiveness of various industries and by managing business units for cash flow, that is, by using cash generated from mature units to build new product lines. Unfortunately, portfolio analysis fails to deal with the question of what industries a corporation should enter or with how a corporation can attain synergy among its product lines and business units. As suggested by its name, portfolio analysis tends to primarily view matters financially, regarding business units and product lines as separate and independent investments.

Corporate parenting, in contrast, views a corporation in terms of resources and capabilities that can be used to build business unit value as well as generate synergies across business units. According to Campbell, Goold, and Alexander:

> *Multibusiness companies create value by influencing—or parenting—the businesses they own. The best parent companies create more value than any of their rivals would if they owned the same businesses. Those companies have what we call parenting advantage.*[87]

Corporate parenting generates corporate strategy by focusing on the core competencies of the parent corporation and on the value created from the relationship between the parent and its businesses. In the form of corporate headquarters, the parent has a great deal of power in this relationship. According to Campbell, Goold, and Alexander, if there is a good fit between the parent's skills and resources and the needs and opportunities of the business units, the corporation is likely to create value. If, however, there is not a good fit, the corporation is likely to destroy value.[88] Research indicates that companies that have a good fit between their strategy and their parenting roles are better performers than those companies that do not have a good fit.[89] This approach to corporate strategy is useful not only in deciding what new businesses to acquire but also in choosing how each existing business unit should be best managed. This appears to have been the secret to the success of General Electric under CEO Jack Welch. According to one analyst in 2000, "He and his managers really add value by imposing tough standards of profitability and by disseminating knowledge and best practice quickly around the GE empire. If some manufacturing trick cuts costs in GE's aero-engine repair shops in Wales, he insists it be applied across the group."[90]

The primary job of corporate headquarters is, therefore, to obtain synergy among the business units by providing needed resources to units, transferring skills and capabilities among the units, and coordinating the activities of shared unit functions to attain economies of scope (as in centralized purchasing).[91] This is in agreement with the concept of the learning organization discussed in **Chapter 1** in which the role of a large firm is to facilitate and transfer the knowledge assets and services throughout the corporation.[92] This is especially important given that 75% or more of a modern company's market value stems from its intangible assets—the organization's knowledge and capabilities.[93] At Proctor & Gamble, for example, the various business units are expected to work together to develop innovative products. Crest Whitestrips, which controls 68% of the at-home tooth-whitening market, was based on the P&G laundry division's knowledge of whitening agents.[94]

DEVELOPING A CORPORATE PARENTING STRATEGY

Campbell, Goold, and Alexander recommend that the search for appropriate corporate strategy involves three analytical steps:

1. **Examine each business unit (or target firm in the case of acquisition) in terms of its strategic factors:** People in the business units probably identified the strategic factors when they were generating business strategies for their units. One popular approach is to

establish centers of excellence throughout the corporation. According to Frost, Birkinshaw, and Ensign, a *center of excellence* is "an organizational unit that embodies a set of capabilities that has been explicitly recognized by the firm as an important source of value creation, with the intention that these capabilities be leveraged by and/or disseminated to other parts of the firm."[95]

2. **Examine each business unit (or target firm) in terms of areas in which performance can be improved:** These are considered to be parenting opportunities. For example, two business units might be able to gain economies of scope by combining their sales forces. In another instance, a unit may have good, but not great, manufacturing and logistics skills. A parent company having world-class expertise in these areas could improve that unit's performance. The corporate parent could also transfer some people from one business unit who have the desired skills to another unit that is in need of those skills. People at corporate headquarters may, because of their experience in many industries, spot areas where improvements are possible that even people in the business unit may not have noticed. Unless specific areas are significantly weaker than the competition, people in the business units may not even be aware that these areas could be improved, especially if each business unit monitors only its own particular industry.

3. **Analyze how well the parent corporation fits with the business unit (or target firm):** Corporate headquarters must be aware of its own strengths and weaknesses in terms of resources, skills, and capabilities. To do this, the corporate parent must ask whether it has the characteristics that fit the parenting opportunities in each business unit. It must also ask whether there is a misfit between the parent's characteristics and the critical success factors of each business unit.

HORIZONTAL STRATEGY AND MULTIPOINT COMPETITION

A **horizontal strategy** is a corporate strategy that cuts across business unit boundaries to build synergy across business units and to improve the competitive position of one or more business units.[96] When used to build synergy, it acts like a parenting strategy. When used to improve the competitive position of one or more business units, it can be thought of as a corporate competitive strategy. In **multipoint competition,** large multi-business corporations compete against other large multi-business firms in a number of markets. These multipoint competitors are firms that compete with each other not only in one business unit, but also in a number of business units. At one time or another, a cash-rich competitor may choose to build its own market share in a particular market to the disadvantage of another corporation's business unit. Although each business unit has primary responsibility for its own business strategy, it may sometimes need some help from its corporate parent, especially if the competitor business unit is getting heavy financial support from its corporate parent. In this instance, corporate headquarters develops a horizontal strategy to coordinate the various goals and strategies of related business units.

For example, P&G, Kimberly-Clark, Scott Paper, and Johnson & Johnson (J&J) compete with one another in varying combinations of consumer paper products, from disposable diapers to facial tissue. If (purely hypothetically) J&J had just developed a toilet tissue with which it chose to challenge Procter & Gamble's high-share Charmin brand in a particular district, it might charge a low price for its new brand to build sales quickly. P&G might not choose to respond to this attack on its share by cutting prices on Charmin. Because of Charmin's high market share, P&G would lose significantly more sales dollars in a price war than J&J would with its initially low-share brand. To retaliate, P&G might thus challenge J&J's high-share baby shampoo with P&G's own low-share brand of baby shampoo in a different district. Once J&J had perceived P&G's response, it might choose to stop challenging Charmin so that P&G would stop challenging J&J's baby shampoo.

Multipoint competition and the resulting use of horizontal strategy may actually slow the development of hypercompetition in an industry. The realization that an attack on a market leader's position could result in a response in another market leads to mutual forbearance in which managers behave more conservatively toward multimarket rivals and competitive rivalry is reduced.[97] In one industry, for example, multipoint competition resulted in firms being less likely to exit a market. "Live and let live" replaced strong competitive rivalry.[98] Multipoint competition is likely to become even more prevalent in the future, as corporations become global competitors and expand into more markets through strategic alliances.[99]

End of Chapter SUMMARY

Corporate strategy is primarily about the choice of direction for the firm as a whole. It deals with three key issues that a corporation faces: (1) the firm's overall orientation toward growth, stability, or retrenchment; (2) the industries or markets in which the firm competes through its products and business units; and (3) the manner in which management coordinates activities and transfers resources and cultivates capabilities among product lines and business units. These issues are dealt with through directional strategy, portfolio analysis, and corporate parenting.

Managers must constantly examine their corporation's entire portfolio of products, businesses, and opportunities as if they were planning to reinvest all of its capital.[100] One example is Cummins, Inc. in 2003 when management decided to invest heavily in the firm's power generation business. Management realized at the time that the global appetite for power was growing far faster than local power grids could provide, especially in the fast-growing developing countries. Unfortunately, power generation was the only one of Cummins' four business units to lose money. Tom Linebarger, Cummins' CFO, took over the power generation unit, cut costs, and reorganized the division around product lines rather than territories. Over the next four years, sales of the company's power generators, ranging from portables for RVs to house-sized machines for factories, more than tripled to $3 billion—20% of the company's total sales. Cummins achieved second place, behind Caterpillar, in the global power generator market. Management decided to grow horizontally by building plants in China and India and making small home generators to sell through mass merchandisers.[101]

ECO-BITS

- Bosch Appliances, the German multinational corporation, was the only U.S. appliance manufacturer whose entire line of major appliances in 2008 was Energy Star qualified in the categories that the program rates. According to Bosch, if the more than 8 million U.S. consumers who purchased a new dishwasher in 2007 had bought a Bosch 800 model instead of a conventional unit, the lifetime energy savings would be equal to preventing 21 billion pounds of CO_2 emissions.[102]

- The green building industry is projected to grow from $2.2 billion in 2006 to $4.7 billion by 2011.[103]

DISCUSSION QUESTIONS

1. How does horizontal growth differ from vertical growth as a corporate strategy? From concentric diversification?

2. What are the tradeoffs between an internal and an external growth strategy? Which approach is best as an international entry strategy?

3. Is stability really a strategy or just a term for no strategy?

4. Compare and contrast SWOT analysis with portfolio analysis.

5. How is corporate parenting different from portfolio analysis? How is it alike? Is it a useful concept in a global industry?

STRATEGIC PRACTICE EXERCISE

On March 14, 2000, Stephen King, the horror writer, published his new book, *Riding the Bullet*, on the Internet before it appeared in print. Within 24 hours, around 400,000 people had downloaded the book—even though most of them needed to download software in order to read the book. The unexpected demand crashed servers. According to Jack Romanos, president of Simon & Schuster, "I don't think anybody could have anticipated how many people were out there who are willing to accept the written word in a paperless format." To many, this announced the coming of the electronic novel. Environmentalists applauded that e-books would soon replace paper books and newspapers, thus reducing pollution coming from paper mills and landfills. The King book was easy to download and took less time than a trip to the bookstore. Critics argued that the King book used the Internet because at 66 pages, it was too short to be a standard printed novel. It was also free, so there was nothing to discourage natural curiosity. Some people in the industry estimated that 75% of those who downloaded the book did not read it.[104]

By 2008, HarperCollins and Random House were offering free online book content. Amazon was selling a $399 Kindle e-book reader for downloadable books costing $10 each, but Apple CEO Steve Jobs described the Kindle as something that filled no void and would "go nowhere." Sales in electronic trade books increased from $5.8 million in 2002 to $20 million in 2006 compared to total 2006 book sales of $25–$30 billion. Borders was market testing the downloading of digital purchases. Tim O'Reilly, coiner of the term *Web 2.0*, had been urging publishers to go digital since the early 1980s, but pub-

lishers and authors were still concerned with how they would be paid for the intellectual property they created. Om Malik, senior writer for *Business 2.0* magazine reported that the money earned from advertising clicks related to their blog content was barely enough to cover the costs of blogging. Flat World Knowledge, a new entrepreneurial digital textbook publisher, announced that in 2009 it planned to offer free online textbooks with the hope that the firm would make money selling supplementary materials like study guides. Publishers wondered how an industry built on a 15th century paper technology could make a profitable transition to a 21st century paperless electronic technology.[105]

1. Form into small groups in the class to discuss the future of Internet publishing.

2. Consider the following questions as discussion guides:
   - What are the pros and cons of electronic publishing?
   - What is the impact of electronic publishing on the environment?
   - Should newspaper and book publishers completely convert to electronic publishing over paper? (The *Wall Street Journal* and others publish in both paper and electronic formats. Is this a success?)
   - Would you prefer this textbook and others in an electronic format? How would you prefer to read the book?
   - What business model should publishers use to make money publishing on the Internet?

3. Present your group's conclusions to the class.

KEY TERMS

acquisition (p. 256)

backward integration (p. 256)

bankruptcy (p. 267)

BCG (Boston Consulting Group) Growth-Share Matrix (p. 269)

BOT (Build, Operate, Transfer) concept (p. 262)

captive company strategy (p. 267)

cash cows (p. 271)

concentration (p. 256)

concentric diversification (p. 262)

conglomerate diversification (p. 263)

corporate parenting (p. 275)

corporate strategy (p. 254)

directional strategy (p. 255)

diversification (p. 256)

divestment (p. 267)

dogs (p. 271)

exporting (p. 259)

forward integration (p. 256)

franchising (p. 260)

full integration (p. 257)

GE business screen (p. 271)

green-field development (p. 261)

growth strategy (p. 255)

horizontal growth (p. 259)

horizontal integration (p. 259)

horizontal strategy (p. 276)

joint venture (p. 260)

licensing (p. 260)

liquidation (p. 268)

long-term contracts (p. 258)

management contracts (p. 262)

merger (p. 255)

multipoint competition (p. 276)

no-change strategy (p. 265)

parenting strategy (p. 254)

pause/proceed with caution strategy (p. 265)

portfolio analysis (p. 268)

production sharing (p. 261)

profit strategy (p. 266)

quasi-integration (p. 257)

question marks (p. 270)

retrenchment strategies (p. 255)

sell-out strategy (p. 267)

stability strategy (p. 255)

stars (p. 270)

synergy (p. 262)

taper integration (p. 257)

transaction cost economics (p. 257)

turnaround strategy (p. 266)

turnkey operations (p. 261)

vertical growth (p. 256)

vertical integration (p. 256)

NOTES

1. C. Zook and J. Allen, "Growth Outside the Core," *Harvard Business Review* (December 2003), pp. 66–73.

2. Ibid., p. 67.

3. R. P. Rumelt, D. E. Schendel, and D. J. Teece, "Fundamental Issues in Strategy," in *Fundamental Issues in Strategy: A Research Agenda*, edited by R. P. Rumelt, D. E. Schendel, and D. J. Teece (Boston: HBS Press, 1994), p. 42.

4. This analogy of corporate parent and business unit children was initially proposed by A. Campbell, M. Goold, and M. Alexander. See "Corporate Strategy: The Quest for Parenting Advantage," *Harvard Business Review* (March–April, 1995), pp. 120–132.

5. M. E. Porter, "From Competitive Strategy to Corporate Strategy," in *International Review of Strategic Management*, Vol. 1, edited by D. E. Husey (Chicester, UK: John Wiley & Sons, 1990), p. 29.

6. This is in agreement with Toyohiro Kono when he proposes that corporate headquarters has three main functions: formulate corporate strategy, identify and develop the company's core competencies, and provide central resources. See T. Kono, "A

Strong Head Office Makes a Strong Company," *Long Range Planning* (April 1999), pp. 225–236.

7. "Larry Ups the Ante," *Economist* (February 7, 2004), pp. 59–60.

8. J. Bercovitz and W. Mitchell, "When Is More Better? The Impact of Business Scale and Scope on Long-Term Business Survival, While Controlling for Profitability," *Strategic Management Journal* (January 2007), pp. 61–79.

9. "Cisco Inc. Buys Top Technology Innovator," *St. Cloud (MN) Times* (November 19, 2005), p. 6A.

10. J. Perkins, "It's a Hog Predicament," *Des Moines Register* (April 11, 1999), pp. J1–J2.

11. C. Woodyard, "FedEx Ponies Up $2.4B for Kinko's," *USA Today* (December 31, 2003), p. B1.

12. J. W. Slocum, Jr., M. McGill, and D. T. Lei, "The New Learning Strategy: Anytime, Anything, Anywhere," *Organizational Dynamics* (Autumn 1994), p. 36.

13. M. J. Leiblein, J. J. Reuer, and F. Dalsace, "Do Make or Buy Decisions Matter? The Influence of Organizational Governance

on Technological Performance," *Strategic Management Journal* (September 2002), pp. 817–833.

14. I. Geyskens, J-B. E. M. Steenkamp, and N. Kumar, "Make, Buy, or Ally: A Transaction Cost Theory Meta-Analysis," *Academy of Management Journal* (June 2006), pp. 519–543; R. Carter and G. M. Hodgson, "The Impact of Empirical Tests of Transaction Cost Economics on the Debate on the Nature of the Firm," *Strategic Management Journal* (May 2006), pp. 461–476; T. A. Shervani, G. Frazier, and G. Challagalla, "The Moderating Influence of Firm Market Power on the Transaction Cost Economics Model: An Empirical Test in a Forward Channel Integration Context," *Strategic Management Journal* (June 2007), pp. 635–652; K. J. Mayer and R. M. Solomon, "Capabilities, Contractual Hazards, and Governance: Integrating Resource-Based and Transaction Cost Perspectives," *Academy of Management Journal* (October 2006), pp. 942–959.

15. K. R. Harrigan, *Strategies for Vertical Integration* (Lexington, MA.: Lexington Books, 1983), pp. 16–21.

16. M. Arndt, "Who's Afraid of a Housing Slump?" *Business Week* (April 30, 2007), p. 76.

17. A. Parmigiani, "Why Do Firms Both Make and Buy? An Investigation of Concurrent Sourcing," *Strategic Management Journal* (March 2007), pp. 285–311; F. T. Rothaermel, M. A. Hitt, and L. A. Jobe, "Balancing Vertical Integration and Strategic Outsourcing: Effects on Product Portfolio, Product Success, and Firm Performance," *Strategic Management Journal* (November 2006), pp. 1033–1056.

18. "Converge or Conflict?" *The Economist* (August 30, 2008), pp. 61–62.

19. M. G. Jacobides, "Industry Change Through Vertical Disintegration: How and Why Markets Emerged in Mortgage Banking," *Academy of Management Journal* (June 2005), pp. 465–498.

20. For a discussion of the pros and cons of contracting versus vertical integration, see J. T. Mahoney, "The Choice of Organizational Form: Vertical Financial Ownership Versus Other Methods of Vertical Integration," *Strategic Management Journal* (November 1992), pp. 559–584.

21. G. Dowell, "Product Line Strategies of New Entrants in an Established Industry: Evidence from the U.S. Bicycle Industry," *Strategic Management Journal* (October 2006), pp. 959–979; C. Sorenson, S. McEvily, C. R. Ren, and R. Roy, "Niche Width Revisited: Organizational Scope, Behavior and Performance," *Strategic Management Journal* (October 2006), pp. 915–936.

22. D. Roberts, "Scrambling to Bring Crest to the Masses," *Business Week* (June 25, 2007), pp. 72–73.

23. A. Delios and P. W. Beamish, "Geographic Scope, Product Diversification, and the Corporate Performance of Japanese Firms," *Strategic Management Journal* (August 1999), pp. 711–727.

24. E. Elango and V. H. Fried, "Franchising Research: A Literature Review and Synthesis," *Journal of Small Business Management* (July 1997), pp. 68–81.

25. T. Thilgen, "Corporate Clout Replaces 'Small Is Beautiful,'" *Wall Street Journal* (March 27, 1997), p. B14.

26. J. E. McCann III, "The Growth of Acquisitions in Services," *Long Range Planning* (December 1996), pp. 835–841.

27. "Gently Does It," *The Economist* (August 11, 2007), p. 59.

28. "A Bid for Bud," *The Economist* (June 21, 2008), p. 77.

29. B. Voss, "Strategic Federations Frequently Falter in Far East," *Journal of Business Strategy* (July/August 1993), p. 6; S. Douma, "Success and Failure in New Ventures," *Long Range Planning* (April 1991), pp. 54–60.

30. A. Delios and P. W. Beamish, "Ownership Strategy of Japanese Firms: Transactional, Institutional, and Experience Approaches," *Strategic Management Journal* (October 1999), pp. 915–933.

31. A. Seth, K. P. Song, and R. R. Pettit, "Value Creation and Destruction in Cross-Border Acquisitions: An Empirical Analysis of Foreign Acquisitions of U.S. Firms," *Strategic Management Journal* (October 2002), pp. 921–940.

32. K. D. Brouthers and L. E. Brouthers, "Acquisition or Greenfield Start-up? Institutional, Cultural, and Transaction Cost Influences," *Strategic Management Journal* (January 2000), pp. 89–97.

33. M. Kripalani, "A Red-Hot Big Blue in India," *Business Week* (September 3, 2007), p. 52.

34. C. Matlack, "Carlos Ghosn's Russian Gambit," *Business Week* (March 17, 2008), pp. 57–58.

35. J. Naisbitt, *Megatrends Asia* (New York: Simon & Schuster, 1996), p. 143.

36. For additional information on international entry modes, see D. F. Spulber, *Global Competitive Strategy* (Cambridge, UK: Cambridge University Press, 2007) and K. D. Brouthers and J-F Hennart, "Boundaries of the Firm: Insights from International Entry Mode Research," *Journal of Management* (June 2007), pp. 395–425.

37. D. P. Lovallo and L. T. Mendonca, "Strategy's Strategist: An Interview with Richard Rumelt," *McKinsey Quarterly Online* (2007, No. 4).

38. C. Zook, "Increasing the Odds of Successful Growth: The Critical Prelude to Moving 'Beyond the Core.'" *Strategy & Leadership*, Vol. 32, No. 4 (2004), pp. 17–23.

39. A. Y. Ilinich and C. P. Zeithaml, "Operationalizing and Testing Galbraith's Center of Gravity Theory," *Strategic Management Journal* (June 1995), pp. 401–410; H. Tanriverdi and N. Venkatraman, "Knowledge Relatedness and the Performance of Multibusiness Firms," *Strategic Management Journal* (February 2005), pp. 97–119.

40. "Flying into Battle," *Economist* (May 8, 2004), p. 60 and Corporate Web site (www.bombardier.com) accessed September 27, 2008.

41. R. F. Bruner, "Corporation Diversification May Be Okay After All," *Batten Briefings* (Spring 2003), pp. 2–3, 12.

42. J. Bercovitz and W. Mitchell, "When Is More Better? The Impact of Business Scale and Scope on Long-Term Business Survival, While Controlling for Profitability," *Strategic Management Journal* (January 2007), pp. 61–79; D. J. Miller, "Technological Diversity, Related Diversification, and Firm Performance," *Strategic Management Journal* (July 2006), pp. 601–619; C. Stadler, "The Four Principles of Enduring Success," *Harvard Business Review* (July–August 2007), pp. 62–72.

43. K. Carow, R. Heron, and T. Saxton, "Do Early Birds Get the Returns? An Empirical Investigation of Early-Mover Advantages in Acquisitions," *Strategic Management Journal* (June 2004), pp. 563–585; K. Ramaswamy, "The Performance Impact of Strategic Similarity in Horizontal Mergers: Evidence from the

U.S. Banking Industry," *Academy of Management Journal* (July 1997), pp. 697–715; D. J. Flanagan, "Announcements of Purely Related and Purely Unrelated Mergers and Shareholder Returns: Reconciling the Relatedness Paradox," *Journal of Management*, Vol. 22, No. 6 (1996), pp. 823–835; D. D. Bergh, "Predicting Diversification of Unrelated Acquisitions: An Integrated Model of Ex Ante Conditions," *Strategic Management Journal* (October 1997), pp. 715–731.

44. J. M. Pennings, H. Barkema, and S. Douma, "Organizational Learning and Diversification," *Academy of Management Journal* (June 1994), pp. 608–640.

45. C. Stadler, "The Four Principles of Enduring Success," *Harvard Business Review* (July–August 2007), pp. 62–72.

46. L. E. Palich, L. B. Cardinal, and C. C. Miller, "Curvilinearity in the Diversification-Performance Linkage: An Examination of over Three Decades of Research," *Strategic Management Journal* (February 2000), pp. 155–174; M. S. Gary, "Implementation Strategy and Performance Outcomes in Related Diversification," *Strategic Management Journal* (July 2005), pp. 643–664; G. Yip and G. Johnson, "Transforming Strategy," *Business Strategy Review* (Spring 2007), pp. 11–15.

47. "The Great Merger Wave Breaks," *The Economist* (January 27, 2001), pp. 59–60.

48. R. N. Palter and D. Srinivasan, "Habits of Busiest Acquirers," *McKinsey on Finance* (Summer 2006), pp. 8–13.

49. D. R. King, D. R. Dalton, C. M. Daily, and J. G. Covin, "Meta-Analyses of Post-Acquisition Performance: Indications of Unidentified Moderators," *Strategic Management Journal* (February 2004), pp. 187–200; W. B. Carper, "Corporate Acquisitions and Shareholder Wealth: A Review and Exploratory Analysis" *Journal of Management* (December 1990), pp. 807–823; P. G. Simmonds, "Using Diversification as a Tool for Effective Performance," *Handbook of Business Strategy, 1992/93 Yearbook*, edited by H. E. Glass and M. A. Hovde (Boston: Warren, Gorham & Lamont, 1992), pp. 3.1–3.7; B. T. Lamont and C. A. Anderson, "Mode of Corporate Diversification and Economic Performance," *Academy of Management Journal* (December 1985), pp. 926–936.

50. "The HP–Compaq Merger Two Years Out: Still Waiting for the Upside," *Knowledge @Wharton* (October 6–19, 2004).

51. D. J. Miller, "Firms' Technological Resources and the Performance Effects of Diversification: A Longitudinal Study," *Strategic Management Journal* (November 2004), pp. 1097–1119.

52. A. Hinterhuber, "When Two Companies Become One," in *Financial Times Handbook of Management*, 3rd ed., S. Crainer and D. Dearlove, Eds. (Harlow, UK: Pearson Education, 2004), pp. 824–833; D. L. Laurie, Y. L. Doz, and C. P. Sheer, "Creating New Growth Platforms," *Harvard Business Review* (May 2006), pp. 80–90; R. Langford and C. Brown III, "Making M&A Pay: Lessons from the World's Most Successful Acquirers," *Strategy & Leadership*, Vol. 32, No. 1 (2004), pp. 5–14; J. G. Lynch and B. Lind, "Escaping Merger and Acquisition Madness," *Strategy & Leadership*, Vol. 30, No. 2 (2002), pp. 5–12; M. L. Sirower, *The Synergy Trap* (New York: Free Press, 1997); B. Jensen, "Make It Simple! How Simplicity Could Become Your Ultimate Strategy," *Strategy & Leadership* (March/April 1997), p. 35.

53. E. Thornton, "Why Consumers Hate Mergers," *Business Week* (December 6, 2004), pp. 58–64.

54. S. Karim and W. Mitchell, "Innovating through Acquisition and Internal Development: A Quarter-century of Boundary Evolution at Johnson & Johnson," *Long Range Planning* (December 2004), pp. 525–547; L. Selden and G. Colvin, "M&A Needn't Be a Loser's Game," *Harvard Business Review* (June 2003), pp. 70–79; E. C. Busija, H. M. O'Neill, and C. P. Zeithaml, "Diversification Strategy, Entry Mode, and Performance: Evidence of Choice and Constraints," *Strategic Management Journal* (April 1997), pp. 321–327; A. Sharma, "Mode of Entry and Ex-Post Performance," *Strategic Management Journal* (September 1998), pp. 879–900.

55. R. T. Uhlaner and A. S. West, "Running a Winning M&A Shop," *McKinsey Quarterly* (March 2008), pp.1–7.

56. S. Rovitt, D. Harding, and C. Lemire, "A Simple M&A Model for All Seasons," *Strategy & Leadership*, Vol. 32, No. 5 (2004), pp. 18–24.

57. P. Porrini, "Can a Previous Alliance Between an Acquirer and a Target Affect Acquisition Performance?" *Journal of Management*, Vol. 30, No. 4 (2004), pp. 545–562; L. Wang and E. J. Zajac, "Alliance or Acquisition? A Dyadic Perspective on Interfirm Resource Combinations," *Strategic Management Journal* (December 2007), pp. 1291–1317.

58. F. Vermeulen, "Controlling International Expansion," *Business Strategy Review* (September 2001), pp. 29–36.

59. A. Inkpen and N. Choudhury, "The Seeking of Strategy Where It Is Not: Towards a Theory of Strategy Absence," *Strategic Management Journal* (May 1995), pp. 313–323.

60. P. Burrows and S. Anderson, "Dell Computer Goes Into the Shop," *Business Week* (July 12, 1993), pp. 138–140.

61. M. Brauer, "What Have We Acquired and What Should We Acquire in Divestiture Research? A Review and Research Agenda," Journal of Management (December 2006), pp. 751–785; J. L. Morrow, Jr., R. A. Johnson, and L. W. Busenitz, "The Effects of Cost and Asset Retrenchment on Firm Performance: The Overlooked Role of a Firm's Competitive Environment," *Journal of Management*, Vol. 30, No. 2 (2004), pp. 189–208.

62. J. A. Pearce II and D. K. Robbins, "Retrenchment Remains the Foundation of Business Turnaround," *Strategic Management Journal* (June 1994), pp. 407–417.

63. Y. Kageyama, "Sony Turnaround Plan Draws Yawns," *Des Moines Register* (September 23, 2005), p. 3D.

64. F. Gandolfi, "Reflecting on Downsizing: What Have We Learned?" *SAM Advanced Management Journal* (Spring 2008), pp. 46–55; C. Chadwick, L. W. Hunter, and S. L. Walston, "Effects of Downsizing Practices on the Performance of Hospitals," *Strategic Management Journal* (May 2004), pp. 405–427; J. R. Morris, W. F. Cascio, and C. E. Young, "Downsizing After All These Years," *Organizational Dynamics* (Winter 1999), pp. 78–87; P. H. Mirvis, "Human Resource Management: Leaders, Laggards, and Followers," *Academy of Management Executive* (May 1997), pp. 43–56; J. K. DeDee and D. W. Vorhies, "Retrenchment Activities of Small Firms During Economic Downturn: An Empirical Investigation," *Journal of Small Business Management* (July 1998), pp. 46–61.

65. C. Chadwick, L. W. Hunter, and S. L Walston, "Effects of Downsizing Practices on the Performance of Hospitals," *Strategic Management Journal* (May 2004), pp. 405–427.

66. J. B. Treece, "U.S. Parts Makers Just Won't Say 'Uncle,'" *Business Week* (August 10, 1987), pp. 76–77.

67. S. S. Carty, "Ford Plans to Park Jaguar, Land Rover with Tata Motors," *USA Today* (March 26, 2008), p. 1B–2B.

68. For more on divestment, see C. Dexter and T. Mellewight, "Thirty Years After Michael E. Porter: What Do We Know about Business Exit?" *Academy of Management Perspectives* (May 2007), pp. 41–55.

69. "Shredding Money," *The Economist* (September 20, 2008), pp. 77–78.

70. D. Welch, "Go Bankrupt, Then Go Overseas," *Business Week* (April 24, 2006), pp. 52–55.

71. D. D. Dawley, J. J. Hoffman, and B. T. Lamont, "Choice Situation, Refocusing, and Post-Bankruptcy Performance," *Journal of Management*, Vol. 28, No. 5 (2002), pp. 695–717.

72. R. M. Kanter, "Leadership and the Psychology of Turnarounds," *Harvard Business Review* (June 2003), pp. 58–67.

73. B. C. Reimann and A. Reichert, "Portfolio Planning Methods for Strategic Capital Allocation: A Survey of Fortune 500 Firms," *International Journal of Management* (March 1996), pp. 84–93; D. K. Sinha, "Strategic Planning in the Fortune 500," *Handbook of Business Strategy, 1991/92 Yearbook*, edited by H. E. Glass and M. A. Hovde (Boston: Warren, Gorham & Lamont, 1991), p. 9.6.

74. L. Dranikoff, T. Koller, and A. Schneider, "Divestiture: Strategy's Missing Link," *Harvard Business Review* (May 2002), pp. 74–83.

75. B. Hedley, "Strategy and the Business Portfolio," *Long Range Planning* (February 1977), p. 9.

76. D. Welch, "GM: Live Green or Die," *Business Week* (May 26, 2008), pp. 36–41.

77. P. Burrows and S. Hamm, "Tech Has a New Top Dog," *Business Week* (June 19, 2006), p. 60.

78. A. Fitzgerald, "Going Global," *Des Moines Register* (March 14, 2004), pp. 1M, 3M.

79. C. Anterasian, J. L. Graham, and R. B. Money, "Are U.S. Managers Superstitious About Market Share?" *Sloan Management Review* (Summer 1996), pp. 67–77.

80. D. Rosenblum, D. Tomlinson, and L. Scott, "Bottom-Feeding for Blockbuster Businesses," *Harvard Business Review* (March 2003), pp. 52–59.

81. R. G. Hamermesh, *Making Strategy Work* (New York: John Wiley & Sons, 1986), p. 14.

82. J. J. Curran, "Companies That Rob the Future," *Fortune* (July 4, 1988), p. 84.

83. W. H. Hoffmann, "Strategies for Managing a Portfolio of Alliances," *Strategic Management Journal* (August 2007), pp. 827–856; D. Lavie, "Alliance Portfolios and Firm Performance: A Study of Value Creation and Appropriation in the U.S. Software Industry," *Strategic Management Journal* (December 2007), pp. 1187–1212.

84. A. Goerzen, "Managing Alliance Networks: Emerging Practices of Multinational Corporations," *Academy of Management Executive* (May 2005), pp. 94–107; S. Lazzarini, "The Impact of Membership in Competing Alliance Constellations: Evidence on the Operational Performance of Global Airlines," *Strategic Management Journal* (April 2007), pp. 345–367.

85. W. H. Hoffmann, "How to Manage a Portfolio of Alliances," *Long Range Planning* (April 2005), pp. 121–143.

86. A. Campbell, M. Goold, and M. Alexander, *Corporate-Level Strategy: Creating Value in the Multibusiness Company* (New York: John Wiley & Sons, 1994). See also M. Goold, A. Campbell, and M. Alexander, "Corporate Strategy and Parenting Theory," *Long Range Planning* (April 1998), pp. 308–318, and M. Goold and A. Campbell, "Parenting in Complex Structures," *Long Range Planning* (June 2002), pp. 219–243.

87. A. Campbell, M. Goold, and M. Alexander, "Corporate Strategy: The Quest for Parenting Advantage," *Harvard Business Review* (March–April 1995), p. 121.

88. Ibid., p. 122.

89. A. van Oijen and S. Douma, "Diversification Strategy and the Roles of the Centre," *Long Range Planning* (August 2000), pp. 560–578.

90. "Jack's Gamble," *The Economist* (October 28, 2000), pp. 13–14.

91. D. J. Collis, "Corporate Strategy in Multibusiness Firms," *Long Range Planning* (June 1996), pp. 416–418; D. Lei, M. A. Hitt, and R. Bettis, "Dynamic Core Competencies Through Meta-Learning and Strategic Context," *Journal of Management*, Vol. 22, No. 4 (1996), pp. 549–569.

92. D. J. Teece, "Strategies for Managing Knowledge Assets: The Role of Firm Structure and Industrial Context," *Long Range Planning* (February 2000), pp. 35–54.

93. R. S. Kaplan and D. P. Norton, "The Strategy Map: Guide to Aligning Intangible Assets," *Strategy & Leadership*, Vol. 32, No. 5 (2004), pp. 10–17; L. Edvinsson, "The New Knowledge Economics," *Business Strategy Review* (September 2002), pp. 72–76; C. Havens and E. Knapp, "Easing into Knowledge Management," *Strategy & Leadership* (March/April 1999), pp. 4–9.

94. J. Scanlon, "Cross-Pollinators," *Business Week's Inside Innovation* (September 2007), pp. 8–11.

95. T. S. Frost, J. M. Birkinshaw, and P. C. Ensign, "Centers of Excellence in Multinational Corporations," *Strategic Management Journal* (November 2002), pp. 997–1018.

96. M. E. Porter, *Competitive Advantage* (New York: The Free Press, 1985), pp. 317–382.

97. H. R. Greve, "Multimarket Contact and Sales Growth: Evidence from Insurance," *Strategic Management Journal* (March 2008), pp. 229–249; L. Fuentelsaz and J. Gomez, "Multipoint Competition, Strategic Similarity and Entry Into Geographic Markets," *Strategic Management Journal* (May 2006), pp. 477–499; J. Gimeno, "Reciprocal Threats in Multimarket Rivalry: Staking Out 'Spheres of Influence' in the U.S. Airline Industry," *Strategic Management Journal* (February 1999), pp. 101–128; J. Baum and H. J. Korn, "Dynamics of Dyadic Competitive Interaction," *Strategic Management Journal* (March 1999), pp. 251–278; J. Gimeno and C. Y. Woo, "Hypercompetition in a Multimarket Environment: The Role of Strategic Similarity and Multimarket Contact in Competitive De-escalation," *Organization Science* (May/June 1996), pp. 322–341.

98. W. Boeker, J. Goodstein, J. Stephan, and J. P. Murmann, "Competition in a Multimarket Environment: The Case of Market Exit," *Organization Science* (March/April 1997), pp. 126–142.

99. J. Gimeno and C. Y. Woo, "Multimarket Contact, Economies of Scope, and Firm Performance," *Academy of Management Journal* (June 1999), pp. 239–259.

100. L. Carlesi, B. Verster, and F. Wenger, "The New Dynamics of Managing the Corporate Portfolio," *McKinsey Quarterly Online* (April 2007).

101. B. Hindo, "Generating Power for Cummins," *Business Week* (September 24, 2007), p. 90.

102. "Energy Efficiency Update," *Appliance Magazine Online* (April 2008).

103. "Sustainability Living Grows Up," *St. Cloud (MN) Times* (July 11, 2008), p. 5C.

104. "Learning to E-Read," *The Economist Survey E-Entertainment* (October 7, 2000), p. 22.

105. P. Tucker, "The 21st-Century Writer," *The Futurist* (July–August 2008), pp. 25–31; M. J. Perenson, "Amazon Kindles Interest in E-Books," *PC World* (February 2008), p. 64; M. R. Nelson, "E-Books in Higher Education: Nearing the End of the Era of Hype?" *EDUCAUSE Review* (March/April 2008), pp. 40–56.

CHAPTER 8

strategy formulation: functional strategy and Strategic Choice

For almost 150 years, the Church & Dwight Company has been building market share on a brand name whose products are in 95% of all U.S. households. Yet if you asked the average person what products this company makes, few would know. Although Church & Dwight may not be a household name, the company's ubiquitous orange box of Arm & Hammer[1] brand baking soda is common throughout North America. Church & Dwight provides a classic example of a marketing functional strategy called *market development*—finding new uses/markets for an existing product. Shortly after its introduction in 1878, Arm & Hammer Baking Soda became a fundamental item on the pantry shelf as people found many uses for sodium bicarbonate other than baking, such as cleaning, deodorizing, and tooth brushing. Hearing of the many uses people were finding for its product, the company advertised that its baking soda was good not only for baking but also for deodorizing refrigerators—simply by leaving an open box in the refrigerator. In a brilliant marketing move, the firm then suggested that consumers buy the product and throw it away—deodorize a kitchen sink by dumping Arm & Hammer baking soda down the drain!

The company did not stop there. It initiated a *product development* strategy by looking for other uses of its sodium bicarbonate in new products. Church & Dwight has achieved consistent growth in sales and earnings through the use of *line extensions,* putting the Arm & Hammer brand first on baking soda and then on laundry detergents, toothpaste, and deodorants. By the beginning of the 21st century, Church & Dwight had become a significant competitor in markets previously dominated only by giants such as Procter & Gamble, Unilever, and Colgate-Palmolive—using only one brand name. Was there a limit to this growth? Was there a point at which these continuous line extensions would begin to eat away at the integrity of the Arm & Hammer name?

Learning Objectives

After reading this chapter, you should be able to:

- Identify a variety of functional strategies that can be used to achieve organizational goals and objectives
- Understand what activities and functions are appropriate to outsource in order to gain or strengthen competitive advantage
- Recognize strategies to avoid and understand why they are dangerous
- Construct corporate scenarios to evaluate strategic options
- Use a stakeholder priority matrix to aid in strategic decision making
- Develop policies to implement corporate, business, and functional strategies

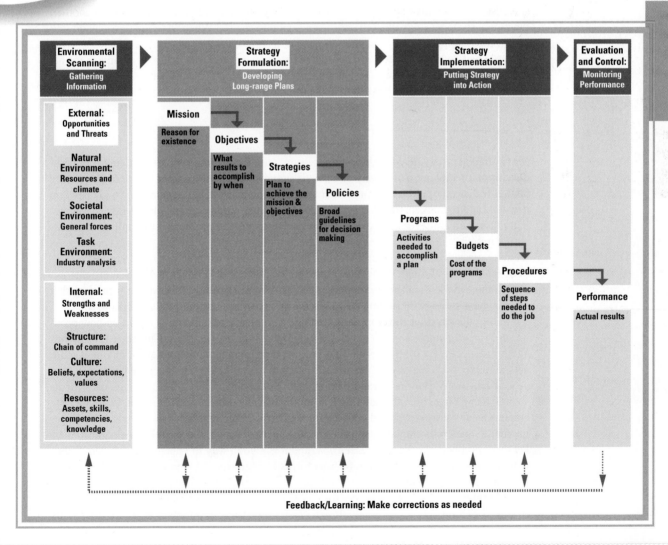

8.1 Functional Strategy

Functional strategy is the approach a functional area takes to achieve corporate and business unit objectives and strategies by maximizing resource productivity. It is concerned with developing and nurturing a distinctive competence to provide a company or business unit with a competitive advantage. Just as a multidivisional corporation has several business units, each with its own business strategy, each business unit has its own set of departments, each with its own functional strategy.

The orientation of a functional strategy is dictated by its parent business unit's strategy.[2] For example, a business unit following a competitive strategy of differentiation through high quality needs a manufacturing functional strategy that emphasizes expensive quality assurance processes over cheaper, high-volume production; a human resource functional strategy that emphasizes the hiring and training of a highly skilled, but costly, workforce; and a marketing functional strategy that emphasizes distribution channel "pull," using advertising to increase consumer demand, over "push," using promotional allowances to retailers. If a business unit were to follow a low-cost competitive strategy, however, a different set of functional strategies would be needed to support the business strategy.

Just as competitive strategies may need to vary from one region of the world to another, functional strategies may need to vary from region to region. When Mr. Donut expanded into Japan, for example, it had to market donuts not as breakfast, but as snack food. Because the Japanese had no breakfast coffee-and-donut custom, they preferred to eat the donuts in the afternoon or evening. Mr. Donut restaurants were thus located near railroad stations and supermarkets. All signs were in English to appeal to the Western interests of the Japanese.

MARKETING STRATEGY

Marketing strategy deals with pricing, selling, and distributing a product. Using a **market development** strategy, a company or business unit can (1) capture a larger share of an existing market for current products through market saturation and market penetration or (2) develop new uses and/or markets for current products. Consumer product giants such as P&G, Colgate-Palmolive, and Unilever are experts at using advertising and promotion to implement a market saturation/penetration strategy to gain the dominant market share in a product category. As seeming masters of the product life cycle, these companies are able to extend product life almost indefinitely through "new and improved" variations of product and packaging that appeal to most market niches. A company, such as Arm & Hammer, follows the second market development strategy by finding new uses for its successful current product, baking soda.

Using the **product development** strategy, a company or unit can (1) develop new products for *existing markets* or (2) develop new products for *new markets*. Church & Dwight has had great success by following the first product development strategy developing new products to sell to its current customers in its existing markets. Acknowledging the widespread appeal of its Arm & Hammer brand baking soda, the company has generated new uses for its sodium bicarbonate by reformulating it as toothpaste, deodorant, and detergent. In another example, Ocean Spray developed craisans, mock berries, light cranberry juices, and juice boxes in order to market its cranberries to current customers.[3] Using a successful brand name to market other products is called *line extension*, and it is a good way to appeal to a company's current customers. Smith & Wesson, famous for its handguns, has taken this approach by using licensing to put its name on men's cologne and other products like the Smith & Wesson 357 Magnum Wood Pellet Smoker (for smoking meats).[4] Arm & Hammer has successfully followed the second product development strategy (new products for new markets) by developing new pollution-reduction products (using sodium bicarbonate compounds) for sale to coal-fired electric utility plants—a very different market from grocery stores.

There are numerous other marketing strategies. For advertising and promotion, for example, a company or business unit can choose between "push" and "pull" marketing strategies. Many large food and consumer products companies in the United States and Canada follow a *push strategy* by spending a large amount of money on trade promotion in order to gain or hold shelf space in retail outlets. Trade promotion includes discounts, in-store special offers, and advertising allowances designed to "push" products through the distribution system. The Kellogg Company decided a few years ago to change its emphasis from a push to a *pull strategy*, in which advertising "pulls" the products through the distribution channels. The company now spends more money on consumer advertising designed to build brand awareness so that shoppers will ask for the products. Research has found that a high level of advertising (a key part of a pull strategy) is beneficial to leading brands in a market.[5] Strong brands provide a competitive advantage to a firm because they act as entry barriers and usually generate high market share.[6]

Other marketing strategies deal with distribution and pricing. Should a company use distributors and dealers to sell its products, or should it sell directly to mass merchandisers or use the direct marketing model by selling straight to the consumers via the Internet? Using multiple channels simultaneously can lead to problems. In order to increase the sales of its lawn tractors and mowers, for example, John Deere decided to sell the products not only through its current dealer network but also through mass merchandisers such as Home Depot. Deere's dealers, however, were furious. They considered Home Depot to be a key competitor. The dealers were concerned that Home Depot's ability to underprice them would eventually lead to their becoming little more than repair facilities for their competition and left with insufficient sales to stay in business.[7]

When pricing a new product, a company or business unit can follow one of two strategies. For new-product pioneers, *skim pricing* offers the opportunity to "skim the cream" from the top of the demand curve with a high price while the product is novel and competitors are few. *Penetration pricing*, in contrast, attempts to hasten market development and offers the pioneer the opportunity to use the experience curve to gain market share with a low price and then dominate the industry. Depending on corporate and business unit objectives and strategies, either of these choices may be desirable to a particular company or unit. Penetration pricing is, however, more likely than skim pricing to raise a unit's operating profit in the long term.[8] The use of the Internet to market goods directly to consumers allows a company to use *dynamic pricing*, a practice in which prices vary frequently based upon demand, market segment, and product availability.[9]

FINANCIAL STRATEGY

Financial strategy examines the financial implications of corporate and business-level strategic options and identifies the best financial course of action. It can also provide competitive advantage through a lower cost of funds and a flexible ability to raise capital to support a business strategy. Financial strategy usually attempts to maximize the financial value of a firm.

The trade-off between achieving the desired debt-to-equity ratio and relying on internal long-term financing via cash flow is a key issue in financial strategy. Many small- and medium-sized family-owned companies such as Urschel Laboratories try to avoid all external sources of funds in order to avoid outside entanglements and to keep control of the company within the family. Few large publicly-held firms have no long-term debt and instead keep a large amount of money in cash and short-term investments. One of these is Apple, Inc. According to Apple's Chief Financial Officer, Peter Oppenheimer, "Our preference is to maintain a strong balance sheet in order to preserve our flexibility."[10] Many financial analysts believe, however, that only by financing through long-term debt can a corporation use financial leverage to boost earnings per share—thus raising stock price and the overall value of the company. Research indicates that higher debt levels not only deter takeover by other firms (by making the company less attractive) but also lead to improved productivity and improved cash flows by forcing management to focus on core businesses.[11] High debt can be a problem, however, when the economy falters and a company's cash flow drops.

Research reveals that a firm's financial strategy is influenced by its corporate diversification strategy. Equity financing, for example, is preferred for related diversification, whereas debt financing is preferred for unrelated diversification.[12] The trend away from unrelated to related acquisitions explains why the number of acquisitions being paid for entirely with stock increased from only 2% in 1988 to 50% in 1998.[13]

A very popular financial strategy is the leveraged buyout (LBO). During 2006 and 2007, for example, the total value of LBOs was $1.4 trillion, about one-third of all the buyouts ever done.[14] In a **leveraged buyout**, a company is acquired in a transaction financed largely by debt, usually obtained from a third party, such as an insurance company or an investment banker. Ultimately the debt is paid with money generated from the acquired company's operations or by sales of its assets. The acquired company, in effect, pays for its own acquisition. Management of the LBO is then under tremendous pressure to keep the highly leveraged company profitable. Unfortunately, the huge amount of debt on the acquired company's books may actually cause its eventual decline by focusing management's attention on short-term matters. For example, one year after the buyout, the cash flow of eight of the largest LBOs made during 2006–2007 was barely enough to cover interest payments.[15] One study of LBOs (also called MBOs—Management BuyOuts) revealed that the financial performance of the typical LBO usually falls below the industry average in the fourth year after the buyout. The firm declines because of inflated expectations, utilization of all slack, management burnout, and a lack of strategic management.[16] Often the only solutions are to sell the company or to again go public by selling stock to finance growth.[17]

The management of dividends and stock price is an important part of a corporation's financial strategy. Corporations in fast-growing industries such as computers and computer software often do not declare dividends. They use the money they might have spent on dividends to finance rapid growth. If the company is successful, its growth in sales and profits is reflected in a higher stock price, eventually resulting in a hefty capital gain when shareholders sell their common stock. Other corporations, such as Whirlpool Corporation, that do not face rapid growth, must support the value of their stock by offering consistent dividends. Instead of raising dividends when profits are high, a popular financial strategy is to use excess cash (or even use debt) to buy back a company's own shares of stock. During 2005, for example, 1,012 U.S.-based publicly traded companies declared $446 billion worth of stock repurchase plans. Because stock buybacks increase earnings per share, they typically increase a firm's stock price and make unwanted takeover attempts more difficult. Such buybacks do signal, however, that either management may not have been able to find any profitable investment opportunities for the company or that it is anticipating reduced future earnings.[18]

A number of firms have been supporting the price of their stock by using *reverse stock splits*. Contrasted with a typical forward 2-for-1 stock split in which an investor receives an additional share for every share owned (with each share being worth only half as much), in a reverse 1-for-2 stock split, an investor's shares are split in half for the same total amount of money (with each share now being worth twice as much). Thus, 100 shares of stock worth $10 each are exchanged for 50 shares worth $20 each. A reverse stock split may successfully raise a company's stock price, but it does not solve underlying problems. A study by Credit Suisse First Boston revealed that almost all 800 companies that had reverse stock splits in a five-year period underperformed their peers over the long term.[19]

A rather novel financial strategy is the selling of a company's patents. Companies such as AT&T, Bellsouth, American Express, Kimberly Clark, and 3Com have been selling patents for products that they no longer wish to commercialize or are not a part of their core business.

They use an intermediary, like Chicago-based Ocean Tomo, to group the patents into lots related to a common area and sell them to the highest bidder.[20]

RESEARCH AND DEVELOPMENT (R&D) STRATEGY

R&D strategy deals with product and process innovation and improvement. It also deals with the appropriate mix of different types of R&D (basic, product, or process) and with the question of how new technology should be accessed—through internal development, external acquisition, or strategic alliances.

One of the R&D choices is to be either a **technological leader,** pioneering an innovation, or a **technological follower,** imitating the products of competitors. Porter suggests that deciding to become a technological leader or follower can be a way of achieving either overall low cost or differentiation. (See **Table 8–1.**)

One example of an effective use of the *leader* R&D functional strategy to achieve a differentiation competitive advantage is Nike, Inc. Nike spends more than most in the industry on R&D to differentiate the performance of its athletic shoes from that of its competitors. As a result, its products have become the favorite of serious athletes. An example of the use of the *follower* R&D functional strategy to achieve a low-cost competitive advantage is Dean Foods Company. "We're able to have the customer come to us and say, 'If you can produce X, Y, and Z product for the same quality and service, but at a lower price and without that expensive label on it, you can have the business,'" says Howard Dean, president of the company.[21]

An increasing number of companies are working with their suppliers to help them keep up with changing technology. They are beginning to realize that a firm cannot be competitive technologically only through internal development. For example, Chrysler Corporation's skillful use of parts suppliers to design everything from car seats to drive shafts has enabled it to spend consistently less money than its competitors to develop new car models. Using strategic technology alliances is one way to combine the R&D capabilities of two companies. Maytag Company worked with one of its suppliers to apply fuzzy logic technology to its IntelliSense™ dishwasher. The partnership enabled Maytag to complete the project in a shorter amount of time than if it had tried to do it alone.[22] One UK study found that 93% of UK auto assemblers and component manufacturers use their suppliers as technology suppliers.[23]

A new approach to R&D is *open innovation*, in which a firm uses alliances and connections with corporate, government, academic labs, and even consumers to develop new products and processes. For example, Intel opened four small-scale research facilities adjacent to universities to promote the cross-pollination of ideas. Thirteen U.S. university labs engaging

TABLE 8–1		Technological Leadership	Technological Followership
Research and Development Strategy and Competitive Advantage	**Cost Advantage**	Pioneer the lowest-cost production design. Be the first down the learning curve. Create low cost ways of performing value activities.	Lower the cost of the product or value activities by learning from the leader's experience. Avoid R & D costs through imitation.
	Differentiation	Pioneer a unique product that increases buyer value. Innovate in other activities to increase buyer value.	Adapt the product or delivery system more closely to buyer needs by learning from the leader's experience.

SOURCE: Adapted with the permission of The Free Press, A Division of Simon & Schuster, from *COMPETITIVE ADVANTAGE. Creating and Sustaining Superior Performance* by Michael E. Porter. Copyright © 1985, 1988 by The Free Press. All rights reserved.

in nanotechnology research have formed the National Nanotechnology Infrastructure Network in order to offer their resources to businesses for a fee.[24] Mattel, Wal-Mart, and other toy manufacturers and retailers use idea brokers such as Big Idea Group to scout for new toy ideas. Big Idea Group invites inventors to submit ideas to its Web site (www.bigideagroup.net). It then refines and promotes to its clients the most promising ideas.[25] IBM adopted the open operating system Linux for some of its computer products and systems, drawing on a core code base that is continually improved and enhanced by a massive global community of software developers, of whom only a fraction work for IBM.[26] To open its own labs to ideas being generated elsewhere, P&G's CEO Art Lafley decreed that half of the company's ideas must come from outside, up from 10% in 2000. P&G instituted the use of *technology scouts* to search beyond the company for promising innovations. By 2007, the objective was achieved: 50% of the company's innovations originated outside P&G.[27]

A slightly different approach to technology development is for a large firm such as IBM or Microsoft to purchase minority stakes in relatively new high-tech entrepreneurial ventures that need capital to continue operation. Investing corporate venture capital is one way to gain access to promising innovations at a lower cost than by developing them internally.[28]

OPERATIONS STRATEGY

Operations strategy determines how and where a product or service is to be manufactured, the level of vertical integration in the production process, the deployment of physical resources, and relationships with suppliers. It should also deal with the optimum level of technology the firm should use in its operations processes. See the **Global Issue** feature to see how differences in national conditions can lead to differences in product design and manufacturing facilities from one country to another.

Advanced Manufacturing Technology (AMT) is revolutionizing operations worldwide and should continue to have a major impact as corporations strive to integrate diverse business activities by using computer assisted design and manufacturing (CAD/CAM) principles. The use of CAD/CAM, flexible manufacturing systems, computer numerically controlled systems, automatically guided vehicles, robotics, manufacturing resource planning (MRP II), optimized production technology, and just-in-time techniques contribute to increased flexibility, quick response time, and higher productivity. Such investments also act to increase the company's fixed costs and could cause significant problems if the company is unable to achieve economies of scale or scope. Baldor Electric Company, the largest maker of industrial electric motors in the United States, built a new factory by using the new technology to eliminate undesirable jobs with high employee turnover. With one-tenth the employees of its foreign plants, the plant was cost-competitive with motors produced in Mexico or China.[29]

A firm's manufacturing strategy is often affected by a product's life cycle. As the sales of a product increase, there will be an increase in production volume ranging from lot sizes as low as one in a *job shop* (one-of-a-kind production using skilled labor) through *connected line batch flow* (components are standardized; each machine functions such as a job shop but is positioned in the same order as the parts are processed) to lot sizes as high as 100,000 or more per year for *flexible manufacturing systems* (parts are grouped into manufacturing families to produce a wide variety of mass-produced items) and *dedicated transfer lines* (highly automated assembly lines making one mass-produced product using little human labor). According to this concept, the product becomes standardized into a commodity over time in conjunction with increasing demand. Flexibility thus gives way to efficiency.[30]

Increasing competitive intensity in many industries has forced companies to switch from traditional mass production using dedicated transfer lines to a continuous improvement production strategy. A *mass-production* system was an excellent method to produce a large number of low-cost, standard goods and services. Employees worked on narrowly defined,

GLOBAL issue

INTERNATIONAL DIFFERENCES ALTER WHIRLPOOL'S OPERATIONS STRATEGY

To better penetrate the growing markets in developing nations, Whirlpool decided to build a "world washer." This new type of washing machine was to be produced in Brazil, Mexico, and India. Lightweight, with substantially fewer parts than its U.S. counterpart, its performance was to be equal to or better than anything on the world market while being competitive in price with the most popular models in these markets. The goal was to develop a complete product, process, and facility design package that could be used in different countries with low initial investment. Originally the plan had been to make the same low-cost washer in identical plants in each of the three countries.

Significant differences in each of the three countries forced Whirlpool to change its product design to adapt to each nation's situation. According to Lawrence Kremer, Senior Vice President of Global Technology and Operations, "Our Mexican affiliate, Vitromatic, has porcelain and glassmaking capabilities. Porcelain baskets made sense for them. Stainless steel became the preferred material for the others." Costs also affected decisions. "In India, for exam-

ple, material costs may run as much as 200% to 800% higher than elsewhere, while labor and overhead costs are comparatively minimal," added Kremer. Another consideration was the garments to be washed in each country. For example, saris—the 18-foot lengths of cotton or silk with which Indian women drape themselves—needed special treatment in an Indian washing machine, forcing additional modifications.

Manufacturing facilities also varied from country to country. Brastemp, Whirlpool's Brazilian partner, built its plant of precast concrete to address the problems of high humidity. In India, however, the construction crew cast the concrete, allowed it to cure, and then using chain, block, and tackle, five or six men raised each three-ton slab into place. Instead of using one building, Mexican operations used two, one housing the flexible assembly lines and stamping operations, and an adjacent facility housing the injection molding and extrusion processes.

....

SOURCE: WHEELEN, TOM; HUNGER, J. DAVID, STRATEGIC MANAGEMENT AND BUSINESS POLICY, 9th Edition, © 2004, p. 172. Reprinted by permission of Pearson Education, Inc. Upper Saddle River, NJ.

repetitive tasks under close supervision in a bureaucratic and hierarchical structure. Quality, however, often tended to be fairly low. Learning how to do something better was the prerogative of management; workers were expected only to learn what was assigned to them. This system tended to dominate manufacturing until the 1970s. Under the *continuous improvement* system developed by Japanese firms, empowered cross-functional teams strive constantly to improve production processes. Managers are more like coaches than like bosses. The result is a large quantity of low-cost, standard goods and services, but with high quality. The key to continuous improvement is the acknowledgment that workers' experience and knowledge can help managers solve production problems and contribute to tightening variances and reducing errors. Because continuous improvement enables firms to use the same low-cost competitive strategy as do mass-production firms but at a significantly higher level of quality, it is rapidly replacing mass production as an operations strategy.

The automobile industry is currently experimenting with the strategy of *modular manufacturing* in which preassembled subassemblies are delivered as they are needed (i.e., Just-in-Time) to a company's assembly-line workers, who quickly piece the modules together into a finished product. For example, General Motors built a new automotive complex in Brazil to make its new subcompact, the Celta. Sixteen of the 17 buildings were occupied by suppliers, including Delphi, Lear, and Goodyear. These suppliers delivered preassembled modules (which comprised 85% of the final value of each car) to GM's building for assembly. In a process new to the industry, the suppliers acted as a team to build a single module comprising the motor, transmission, fuel lines, rear axle, brake-fluid lines, and exhaust system, which was then installed as one piece. GM hoped that this manufacturing strategy would enable it to produce 100 vehicles annually per worker compared to the standard rate of 30 to 50 autos per worker.[31] Ford and Chrysler have also opened similar modular facilities in Brazil.

The concept of a product's life cycle eventually leading to one-size-fits-all mass production is being increasingly challenged by the new concept of mass customization. Appropriate for an ever-changing environment, *mass customization* requires that people, processes, units, and technology reconfigure themselves to give customers exactly what they want, when they want it. In the case of Dell Computer, customers use the Internet to design their own computers. In contrast to continuous improvement, mass customization requires flexibility and quick responsiveness. Managers coordinate independent, capable individuals. An efficient linkage system is crucial. The result is low-cost, high-quality, customized goods and services appropriate for a large number of market niches.

A contentious issue for manufacturing companies throughout the world is the availability of resources needed to operate a modern factory. The increasing cost of oil during 2007 and 2008 drastically boosted costs, only some of which could be passed on to the customers in a competitive environment. The likelihood that fresh water could become an equally scarce resource is causing many companies to rethink water-intensive manufacturing processes. To learn how companies are beginning to deal with increasing fresh water scarcity, see the **Environmental Sustainability Issue** feature.

PURCHASING STRATEGY

Purchasing strategy deals with obtaining the raw materials, parts, and supplies needed to perform the operations function. Purchasing strategy is important because materials and components purchased from suppliers comprise 50% of total manufacturing costs of manufacturing companies in the United Kingdom, United States, Australia, Belgium, and Finland.[32] The basic purchasing choices are multiple, sole, and parallel sourcing. Under *multiple sourcing,* the purchasing company orders a particular part from several vendors. Multiple sourcing has traditionally been considered superior to other purchasing approaches because (1) it forces suppliers to compete for the business of an important buyer, thus reducing purchasing costs, and (2) if one supplier cannot deliver, another usually can, thus guaranteeing that parts and supplies are always on hand when needed. Multiple sourcing has been one way for a purchasing firm to control the relationship with its suppliers. So long as suppliers can provide evidence that they can meet the product specifications, they are kept on the purchaser's list of acceptable vendors for specific parts and supplies. Unfortunately, the common practice of accepting the lowest bid often compromises quality.

W. Edward Deming, a well-known management consultant, strongly recommended *sole sourcing* as the only manageable way to obtain high supplier quality. Sole sourcing relies on only one supplier for a particular part. Given his concern with designing quality into a product in its early stages of development, Deming argued that the buyer should work closely with the supplier at all stages. This reduces both cost and time spent on product design and it also improves quality. It can also simplify the purchasing company's production process by using the *Just-In-Time* (JIT) concept of having the purchased parts arrive at the plant just when they are needed rather than keeping inventories. The concept of sole sourcing is taken one step further in JIT II, in which vendor sales representatives actually have desks next to the purchasing company's factory floor, attend production status meetings, visit the R&D lab, and analyze the purchasing company's sales forecasts. These in-house suppliers then write sales orders for which the purchasing company is billed. Developed by Lance Dixon at Bose Corporation, JIT II is also being used at IBM, Honeywell, and Ingersoll-Rand. Karen Dale, purchasing manager for Honeywell's office supplies, said she was very concerned about confidentiality when JIT II was first suggested to her. Soon she had five suppliers working with her 20 buyers and reported few problems.[33]

ENVIRONMENTAL sustainability issue

OPERATIONS NEED FRESH WATER AND LOTS OF IT!

The U.S. Department of Energy (DOE) plans to build a rail line more than 300 miles long through the Nevada wilderness to move spent nuclear fuel from 121 sites in 39 states to a geologic repository at Yucca Mountain. One of the biggest issues to overcome will be water supply. The DOE estimates that the construction phase would require 5,500 acre feet of water for earthwork compaction, 370 acre-feet for construction personnel, 200 acre-feet for dust control along access roads, and 30 acre-feet for quarry operations, totaling 6,100 acre-feet, or two billion gallons, of water to support a four-year construction period. To meet this need, DOE wants to drill 150 to 176 new wells. The state of Nevada, however, has rejected a permit request to use water for drilling on the Yucca Mountain site, stating that water has to be used for the benefit of the public. Negotiations continue.

This is just one of the ways that organizations need fresh water for their operations. Nestlé, Unilever, Coca-Cola, Anheuser-Busch, and Danone consume almost 575 billion liters of water a year, enough to satisfy the daily water needs of every person on the planet. It takes about 13 cubic meters of freshwater to produce a single 200 mm semiconductor wafer. As a result, chip making is believed to account for 25% of the water consumption in Silicon Valley. According to Jose Lopez, Nestlé's COO, it takes four liters of water to make one liter of product in Nestlé's factories, but 3,000 liters of water are needed to grow the agricultural produce that supplies them. Each year, around 40% of the freshwater withdrawn from lakes and aquifers in America is used to cool power plants. Separating one liter of oil from Canada's tar sands requires up to five liters of water!

"Water is the oil of the 21st century," contends Andrew Liveris, CEO of the chemical company Dow. Like oil, supplies of clean, easily accessible fresh water are under a growing strain because of the growing population and widespread improvements in living standards. Industrialization in developing nations is contaminating rivers and aquifers. Climate change is altering the patterns of fresh water availability so that droughts are more likely in many parts of the world. According to a survey by the Marsh Center for Risk Insights, 40% of Fortune 1000 companies stated that the impact of a water shortage on their business would be "severe" or "catastrophic," but only 17% said that they were prepared for such a crisis. Of Nestlé's 481 factories worldwide, 49 are located in water-scarce regions. Environmental activists have attacked PepsiCo and Coca-Cola for allegedly depleting groundwater in India to make bottled drinks.

There are a number of companies that are taking action to protect their future supply of freshwater. Dow has reduced the amount of water it uses by over a third since 1995. During 1997–2006, when Nestle almost doubled the volume of food it produced, it reduced the amount of water used by 29%. By 2008, Coca-Cola had achieved 85% of its objective to clean all of the wastewater generated at its bottling plants by 2010. China's Elion Chemical is working with General Electric to recycle 90% of its wastewater to comply with the government's new "zero-liquid" discharge rules.

SOURCE: K. Kube, "Into the Wild Brown Yonder," *Trains* (November 2008), pp. 68–73; "Running Dry," *The Economist* (August 23, 2008), pp. 53–54.

Sole sourcing reduces transaction costs and builds quality by having the purchaser and supplier work together as partners rather than as adversaries. With sole sourcing, more companies will have longer relationships with fewer suppliers. Research has found that buyer-supplier collaboration and joint problem solving with both parties dependent upon the other results in the development of competitive capabilities, higher quality, lower costs, and better scheduling.[34] Sole sourcing does, however, have limitations. If a supplier is unable to deliver a part, the purchaser has no alternative but to delay production. Multiple suppliers can provide the purchaser with better information about new technology and performance capabilities. The limitations of sole sourcing have led to the development of parallel sourcing. In *parallel sourcing*, two suppliers are the sole suppliers of two different parts, but they are also backup suppliers for each other's parts. If one vendor cannot supply all of its parts on time, the other vendor is asked to make up the difference.[35]

The Internet is being increasingly used both to find new sources of supply and to keep inventories replenished. For example, Hewlett-Packard introduced a Web-based procurement system to enable its 84,000 employees to buy office supplies from a standard set of suppliers. The new system enabled the company to save $60 to $100 million annually in purchasing costs.[36] Research indicates that companies using Internet-based technologies are able to lower administrative costs and purchase prices.[37]

LOGISTICS STRATEGY

Logistics strategy deals with the flow of products into and out of the manufacturing process. Three trends related to this strategy are evident: centralization, outsourcing, and the use of the Internet. To gain logistical synergies across business units, corporations began centralizing logistics in the headquarters group. This centralized logistics group usually contains specialists with expertise in different transportation modes such as rail or trucking. They work to aggregate shipping volumes across the entire corporation to gain better contracts with shippers. Companies such as Georgia-Pacific, Marriott, and Union Carbide view the logistics function as an important way to differentiate themselves from the competition, to add value, and to reduce costs.

Many companies have found that outsourcing logistics reduces costs and improves delivery time. For example, HP contracted with Roadway Logistics to manage its inbound raw materials warehousing in Vancouver, Canada. Nearly 140 Roadway employees replaced 250 HP workers, who were transferred to other HP activities.[38]

Many companies are using the Internet to simplify their logistical system. For example, Ace Hardware created an online system for its retailers and suppliers. An individual hardware store can now see on the Web site that ordering 210 cases of wrenches is cheaper than ordering 200 cases. Because a full pallet is composed of 210 cases of wrenches, an order for a full pallet means that the supplier doesn't have to pull 10 cases off a pallet and repackage them for storage. There is less chance that loose cases will be lost in delivery, and the paperwork doesn't have to be redone. As a result, Ace's transportation costs are down 18%, and warehouse costs have been cut 28%.[39]

HUMAN RESOURCE MANAGEMENT (HRM) STRATEGY

HRM strategy, among other things, addresses the issue of whether a company or business unit should hire a large number of low-skilled employees who receive low pay, perform repetitive jobs, and are most likely quit after a short time (the McDonald's restaurant strategy) or hire skilled employees who receive relatively high pay and are cross-trained to participate in *self-managing work teams*. As work increases in complexity, the more suited it is for teams, especially in the case of innovative product development efforts. Multinational corporations are increasingly using self-managing work teams in their foreign affiliates as well as in home-country operations.[40] Research indicates that the use of work teams leads to increased quality and productivity as well as to higher employee satisfaction and commitment.[41]

Companies following a competitive strategy of differentiation through high quality use input from subordinates and peers in performance appraisals to a greater extent than do firms following other business strategies.[42] A complete *360-degree appraisal*, in which input is gathered from multiple sources, is now being used by more than 10% of U.S. corporations and has become one of the most popular and effective tools in developing employees and new managers.[43] One Indian company, HCL Technologies, publishes the appraisal ratings for the top 20 managers on the company's intranet for all to see.[44]

Companies are finding that having a *diverse workforce* can be a competitive advantage. Research reveals that firms with a high degree of racial diversity following a growth strategy have higher productivity than do firms with less racial diversity.[45] Avon Company, for example, was able to turn around its unprofitable inner-city markets by putting African-American and Hispanic managers in charge of marketing to these markets.[46] Diversity in terms of age and national origin also offers benefits. DuPont's use of multinational teams has helped the company develop and market products internationally. McDonald's has discovered that older workers perform as well as, if not better than, younger employees. According to Edward Rensi, CEO of McDonald's USA, "We find these people to be particularly well motivated, with a sort of discipline and work habits hard to find in younger employees."[47]

INFORMATION TECHNOLOGY STRATEGY

Corporations are increasingly using **information technology strategy** to provide business units with competitive advantage. When FedEx first provided its customers with PowerShip computer software to store addresses, print shipping labels, and track package location, its sales jumped significantly. UPS soon followed with its own MaxiShips software. Viewing its information system as a distinctive competency, FedEx continued to push for further advantage over UPS by using its Web site to enable customers to track their packages. FedEx uses this competency in its advertisements by showing how customers can track the progress of their shipments. Soon thereafter, UPS provided the same service. Although it can be argued that information technology has now become so pervasive that it no longer offers companies a competitive advantage, corporations worldwide continue to spend over $2 trillion annually on information technology.[48]

Multinational corporations are finding that having a sophisticated intranet allows employees to practice *follow-the-sun management*, in which project team members living in one country can pass their work to team members in another country in which the work day is just beginning. Thus, night shifts are no longer needed.[49] The development of instant translation software is also enabling workers to have online communication with co-workers in other countries who use a different language.[50] For example, Mattel has cut the time it takes to develop new products by 10% by enabling designers and licensees in other countries to collaborate on toy design. IBM uses its intranet to allow its employees to collaborate and improve their skills, thus reducing its training and travel expenses.[51]

Many companies, such as Lockheed Martin, General Electric, and Whirlpool, use information technology to form closer relationships with both their customers and suppliers through sophisticated extranets. For example, General Electric's Trading Process Network allows suppliers to electronically download GE's requests for proposals, view diagrams of parts specifications, and communicate with GE purchasing managers. According to Robert Livingston, GE's head of worldwide sourcing for the Lighting Division, going on the Web reduces processing time by one-third.[52] Thus, the use of information technology through extranets makes it easier for a company to buy from others (outsource) rather than make it themselves (vertically integrate).[53]

8.2   The Sourcing Decision: Location of Functions

For a functional strategy to have the best chance of success, it should be built on a distinctive competency residing within that functional area. If a corporation does not have a distinctive competency in a particular functional area, that functional area could be a candidate for outsourcing.

Outsourcing is purchasing from someone else a product or service that had been previously provided internally. Thus, it is the reverse of vertical integration. Outsourcing is becoming an increasingly important part of strategic decision making and an important way to increase efficiency and often quality. In a study of 30 firms, outsourcing resulted on average in a 9% reduction in costs and a 15% increase in capacity and quality.[54] For example, Boeing used outsourcing as a way to reduce the cost of designing and manufacturing its new 787 Dreamliner. Up to 70% of the plane was outsourced. In a break from past practice, suppliers make large parts of the fuselage, including plumbing, electrical, and computer systems, and ship them to Seattle for assembly by Boeing. Outsourcing enabled Boeing to build a 787 in 4 months instead of the usual 12.[55]

According to an American Management Association survey of member companies, 94% of the responding firms outsource at least one activity. The outsourced activities are general and administrative (78%), human resources (77%), transportation and distribution (66%), information systems (63%), manufacturing (56%), marketing (51%), and finance and accounting (18%). The survey also reveals that 25% of the respondents have been disappointed in their outsourcing results. Fifty-one percent of the firms reported bringing an outsourced activity back in-house. Nevertheless, authorities not only expect the number of companies engaging in outsourcing to increase, they also expect companies to outsource an increasing number of functions, especially those in customer service, bookkeeping, financial/clerical, sales/telemarketing, and the mailroom.[56] It is estimated that 50% of U.S. manufacturing will be outsourced to firms in 28 developing countries by 2015.[57]

Offshoring is the outsourcing of an activity or a function to a wholly owned company or an independent provider in another country. Offshoring is a global phenomenon that has been supported by advances in information and communication technologies, the development of stable, secure, and high-speed data transmission systems, and logistical advances like containerized shipping. According to Bain & Company, 51% of large firms in North America, Europe, and Asia outsource offshore.[58] Although India currently has 70% of the offshoring market, countries such as Brazil, China, Russia, the Phillipines, Malaysia, Hungary, the Czech Republic, and Israel are growing in importance. These countries have low-cost qualified labor and an educated workforce. These are important considerations because more than 93% of offshoring companies do so to reduce costs.[59] For example, Mexican assembly line workers average $3.50 an hour plus benefits compared to $27 an hour plus benefits at a GM or Ford plant in the U.S. Less skilled Mexican workers at auto parts makers earn as little as $1.50 per hour with fewer benefits.[60]

Software programming and customer service, in particular, are being outsourced to India. For example, General Electric's back-office services unit, GE Capital International Services, is one of the oldest and biggest of India's outsourcing companies. From only $26 million in 1999, its annual revenues grew to over $420 million by 2004.[61] As part of this trend, IBM acquired Daksh eServices Ltd., one of India's biggest suppliers of remote business services.[62]

Outsourcing, including offshoring, has significant disadvantages. For example, mounting complaints forced Dell Computer to stop routing corporate customers to a technical support call center in Bangalore, India.[63] GE's introduction of a new washing machine was delayed three weeks because of production problems at a supplier's company to which it had contracted out key work. Some companies have found themselves locked into long-term contracts with outside suppliers that were no longer competitive.[64] Some authorities propose that the cumulative effects of continued outsourcing steadily reduces a firm's ability to learn new skills and to develop new core competencies.[65] One survey of 129 outsourcing firms revealed that half the outsourcing projects undertaken in one year failed to deliver anticipated savings. This is in agreement with a survey by Bain & Company in which 51% of large North American, European, and Asian firms stated that outsourcing (including offshoring) did not meet their expectations.[66] Another survey of software projects, by MIT, found that the median Indian project had 10% more software bugs than did comparable U.S. projects.[67] During 2007–2008, tainted goods made by Chinese manufacturers, ranging from lead paint on toys, contaminated heparin, and melamine-laced milk caused their customers to reevaluate the manner in which they engaged in offshore outsourcing.[68] The increasing cost of oil was making offshoring less economical. Since 2003, crude oil increased in price from $28 to over $100 a barrel in 2008, causing the cost to ship a standard 40-foot container to triple. By 2008 it cost about $100 to ship a ton of iron from Brazil to China, more than the cost of the mineral itself.[69]

A study of 91 outsourcing efforts conducted by European and North American firms found seven major errors that should be avoided:

1. **Outsourcing activities that should not be outsourced:** Companies failed to keep core activities in-house.

2. **Selecting the wrong vendor:** Vendors were not trustworthy or lacked state-of-the-art processes.

3. **Writing a poor contract:** Companies failed to establish a balance of power in the relationship.

4. **Overlooking personnel issues:** Employees lost commitment to the firm.

5. **Losing control over the outsourced activity:** Qualified managers failed to manage the outsourced activity.[70]

6. **Overlooking the hidden costs of outsourcing:** Transaction costs overwhelmed other savings.

7. **Failing to plan an exit strategy:** Companies failed to build reversibility clauses into the contract.[71]

The key to outsourcing is to purchase from outside only those activities that are not key to the company's distinctive competencies. Otherwise, the company may give up the very capabilities that made it successful in the first place—thus putting itself on the road to eventual decline. This is supported by research reporting that companies that have more experience with a particular manufacturing technology tend to keep manufacturing in-house.[72] J. P. Morgan Chase & Company terminated a seven-year technology outsourcing agreement with IBM because the bank's management realized that information technology (IT) was too important strategically to be outsourced.[73]

In determining functional strategy, the strategist must:

- Identify the company's or business unit's core competencies
- Ensure that the competencies are continually being strengthened
- Manage the competencies in such a way that best preserves the competitive advantage they create

An outsourcing decision depends on the fraction of total value added that the activity under consideration represents and on the amount of potential competitive advantage in that activity for the company or business unit. See the outsourcing matrix in **Figure 8–1**. A firm should consider outsourcing any activity or function that has low potential for competitive advantage. If that activity constitutes only a small part of the total value of the firm's products or services, it should be purchased on the open market (assuming that quality providers of the activity are plentiful). If, however, the activity contributes highly to the company's products or services, the firm should purchase it through long-term contracts with trusted suppliers or distributors. A firm should always produce at least some of the activity or function (i.e., taper vertical integration) if that activity has the potential for providing the company some competitive advantage. However, full vertical integration should be considered only when that activity or function adds significant value to the company's products or services in addition to providing competitive advantage.[74]

FIGURE 8–1
Proposed
Outsourcing
Matrix

Activity's Total Value-Added to Firm's Products and Services

	Low	High
High	**Taper Vertical Integration:** Produce Some Internally	**Full Vertical Integration:** Produce All Internally
Low	**Outsource Completely:** Buy on Open Market	**Outsource Completely:** Purchase with Long-Term Contracts

Activity's Potential for Competitive Advantage

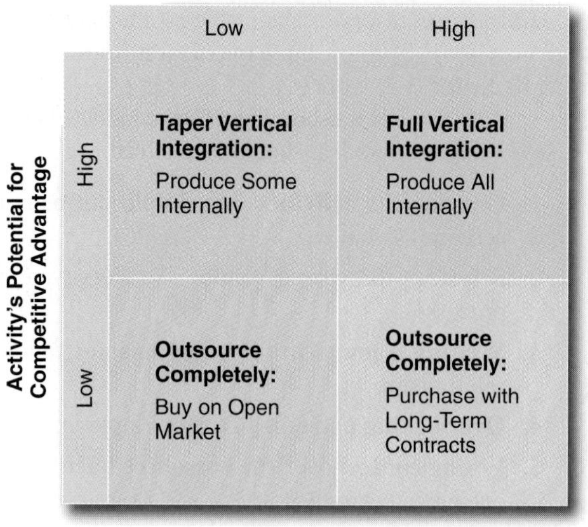

SOURCE: *J. D. Hunger and T. L. Wheelen, "Proposed Outsourcing Matrix." Copyright © 1996 and 2005 by Wheelen and Hunger Associates. Reprinted by permission.*

8.3 Strategies to Avoid

Several strategies, that could be considered corporate, business, or functional are very dangerous. Managers who have made poor analyses or lack creativity may be trapped into considering some of the following strategies to avoid:

■ **Follow the leader:** Imitating a leading competitor's strategy might seem to be a good idea, but it ignores a firm's particular strengths and weaknesses and the possibility that the leader may be wrong. Fujitsu Ltd., the world's second-largest computer maker, had been driven since the 1960s by the sole ambition of catching up to IBM. Like IBM, Fujitsu competed primarily as a mainframe computer maker. So devoted was it to catching IBM, however, that it failed to notice that the mainframe business had reached maturity by 1990 and was no longer growing.

■ **Hit another home run:** If a company is successful because it pioneered an extremely successful product, it tends to search for another super product that will ensure growth and prosperity. As in betting on long shots in horse races, the probability of finding a second winner is slight. Polaroid spent a lot of money developing an "instant" movie camera, but the public ignored it in favor of the camcorder.

■ **Arms race:** Entering into a spirited battle with another firm for increased market share might increase sales revenue, but that increase will probably be more than offset by increases in advertising, promotion, R&D, and manufacturing costs. Since the deregulation of airlines, price wars and rate specials have contributed to the low profit margins and bankruptcies of many major airlines, such as Eastern, Pan American, TWA, and United.

■ **Do everything:** When faced with several interesting opportunities, management might tend to leap at all of them. At first, a corporation might have enough resources to develop each idea into a project, but money, time, and energy are soon exhausted as the many projects demand large infusions of resources. The Walt Disney Company's expertise in the entertainment industry led it to acquire the ABC network. As the company churned out new motion pictures and television programs such as *Who Wants to Be a Millionaire?* it spent $750 million to build new theme parks and buy a cruise line and a hockey team. By 2000, even though corporate sales had continued to increase, net income was falling.[75]

- **Losing hand:** A corporation might have invested so much in a particular strategy that top management is unwilling to accept its failure. Believing that it has too much invested to quit, management may continue to throw "good money after bad." Pan American Airlines, for example, chose to sell its Pan Am Building and Intercontinental Hotels, the most profitable parts of the corporation, to keep its money-losing airline flying. Continuing to suffer losses, the company followed this profit strategy of shedding assets for cash until it had sold off everything and went bankrupt.

8.4 Strategic Choice: Selecting the Best Strategy

After the pros and cons of the potential strategic alternatives have been identified and evaluated, one must be selected for implementation. By now, it is likely that many feasible alternatives will have emerged. How is the best strategy determined?

Perhaps the most important criterion is the capability of the proposed strategy to deal with the specific strategic factors developed earlier, in the SWOT analysis. If the alternative doesn't take advantage of environmental opportunities and corporate strengths/competencies, and lead away from environmental threats and corporate weaknesses, it will probably fail.

Another important consideration in the selection of a strategy is the ability of each alternative to satisfy agreed-on objectives with the least resources and the fewest negative side effects. It is, therefore, important to develop a tentative implementation plan in order to address the difficulties that management is likely to face. This should be done in light of societal trends, the industry, and the company's situation based on the construction of scenarios.

CONSTRUCTING CORPORATE SCENARIOS

Corporate scenarios are *pro forma* (estimated future) balance sheets and income statements that forecast the effect each alternative strategy and its various programs will likely have on division and corporate return on investment. (Pro forma financial statements are discussed in **Chapter 12**.) In a survey of Fortune 500 firms, 84% reported using computer simulation models in strategic planning. Most of these were simply spreadsheet-based simulation models dealing with what-if questions.[76]

The recommended scenarios are simply extensions of the industry scenarios discussed in **Chapter 4**. If, for example, industry scenarios suggest the probable emergence of a strong market demand in a specific country for certain products, a series of alternative strategy scenarios can be developed. The alternative of acquiring another firm having these products in that country can be compared with the alternative of a green-field development (e.g., building new operations in that country). Using three sets of estimated sales figures (Optimistic, Pessimistic, and Most Likely) for the new products over the next five years, the two alternatives can be evaluated in terms of their effect on future company performance as reflected in the company's probable future financial statements. Pro forma balance sheets and income statements can be generated with spreadsheet software, such as Excel, on a personal computer. Pro forma statements are based on financial and economic scenarios.

To construct a corporate scenario, follow these steps:

1. Use industry scenarios (as discussed in **Chapter 4**) to develop a set of assumptions about the task environment (in the specific country under consideration). For example, 3M requires the general manager of each business unit to describe annually what his or her industry will look like in 15 years. List *optimistic, pessimistic*, and *most likely* assumptions for key economic factors such as the GDP (Gross Domestic Product), CPI (Consumer Price Index), and prime interest rate and for other key external strategic factors such as governmental regulation and industry trends. This should be done for every country/region in which the corporation has significant operations that will be affected by each strategic alternative. These same underlying assumptions should be listed for each of the alternative scenarios to be developed.

2. Develop common-size financial statements (as discussed in **Chapter 12**) for the company's or business unit's previous years, to serve as the basis for the trend analysis projections of pro forma financial statements. Use the *Scenario Box* form shown in **Table 8–2**:
   a. Use the historical common-size percentages to estimate the level of revenues, expenses, and other categories in estimated pro forma statements for future years.
   b. Develop for each strategic alternative a set of *Optimistic(O), Pessimistic(P)*, and *Most Likely(ML)* assumptions about the impact of key variables on the company's future financial statements.
   c. Forecast three sets of sales and cost of goods sold figures for at least five years into the future.
   d. Analyze historical data and make adjustments based on the environmental assumptions listed earlier. Do the same for other figures that can vary significantly.

TABLE 8–2   Scenario Box for Use in Generating Financial Pro Forma Statements

Factor	Last Year	Historical Average	Trend Analysis	Projections[1] 200– O	P	ML	200– O	P	ML	200– O	P	ML	Comments
GDP													
CPI													
Other													
Sales units													
Dollars													
COGS													
Advertising and marketing													
Interest expense													
Plant expansion													
Dividends													
Net profits													
EPS													
ROI													
ROE													
Other													

NOTE 1:   **O** = Optimistic; **P** = Pessimistic; **ML** = Most Likely.

SOURCE: T. L. Wheelen and J. D. Hunger. Copyright © 1987, 1988, 1989, 1990, 1992, 2005, and 2009 by T. L. Wheelen. Copyright © 1993 and 2005 by Wheelen and Hunger Associates. Reprinted with permission.

    e. Assume for other figures that they will continue in their historical relationship to sales or some other key determining factor. Plug in expected inventory levels, accounts receivable, accounts payable, R&D expenses, advertising and promotion expenses, capital expenditures, and debt payments (assuming that debt is used to finance the strategy), among others.

    f. Consider not only historical trends but also programs that might be needed to implement each alternative strategy (such as building a new manufacturing facility or expanding the sales force).

3. Construct detailed pro forma financial statements for each strategic alternative:

    a. List the actual figures from this year's financial statements in the left column of the spreadsheet.

    b. List to the right of this column the optimistic figures for years 1 through 5.

    c. Go through this same process with the same strategic alternative, but now list the pessimistic figures for the next five years.

    d. Do the same with the most likely figures.

    e. Develop a similar set of *optimistic* (O), *pessimistic* (P), and *most likely* (ML) pro forma statements for the second strategic alternative. This process generates six different pro forma scenarios reflecting three different situations (O, P, and ML) for two strategic alternatives.

    f. Calculate financial ratios and common-size income statements, and create balance sheets to accompany the pro forma statements.

    g. Compare the assumptions underlying the scenarios with the financial statements and ratios to determine the feasibility of the scenarios. For example, if cost of goods sold drops from 70% to 50% of total sales revenue in the pro forma income statements, this drop should result from a change in the production process or a shift to cheaper raw materials or labor costs rather than from a failure to keep the cost of goods sold in its usual percentage relationship to sales revenue when the predicted statement was developed.

The result of this detailed scenario construction should be anticipated net profits, cash flow, and net working capital for each of three versions of the two alternatives for five years into the future. A strategist might want to go further into the future if the strategy is expected to have a major impact on the company's financial statements beyond five years. The result of this work should provide sufficient information on which forecasts of the likely feasibility and probable profitability of each of the strategic alternatives could be based.

Obviously, these scenarios can quickly become very complicated, especially if three sets of acquisition prices and development costs are calculated. Nevertheless, this sort of detailed what-if analysis is needed to realistically compare the projected outcome of each reasonable alternative strategy and its attendant programs, budgets, and procedures. Regardless of the quantifiable pros and cons of each alternative, the actual decision will probably be influenced by several subjective factors such as those described in the following sections.

Management's Attitude Toward Risk

The attractiveness of a particular strategic alternative is partially a function of the amount of risk it entails. **Risk** is composed not only of the *probability* that the strategy will be effective but also of the *amount of assets* the corporation must allocate to that strategy and the *length of time* the assets will be unavailable for other uses. Because of variation among countries in terms of customs, regulations, and resources, companies operating in global industries must deal with a greater amount of risk than firms operating only in one country.[77] The greater the assets involved and the longer they are committed, the more likely top management is to demand a high probability of success. Managers with no ownership position in a company are unlikely to have much interest in putting their jobs in danger with risky decisions. Research indicates that managers who own a significant amount of stock in their firms are more likely to engage in risk-taking actions than are managers with no stock.[78]

A high level of risk was why Intel's board of directors found it difficult to vote for a proposal in the early 1990s to commit $5 billion to making the Pentium microprocessor chip—five times the amount of money needed for its previous chip. In looking back on that board meeting, then-CEO Andy Grove remarked, "I remember people's eyes looking at that chart and getting big. I wasn't even sure I believed those numbers at the time." The proposal committed the company to building new factories—something Intel had been reluctant to do. A wrong decision would mean that the company would end up with a killing amount of overcapacity. Based on Grove's presentation, the board decided to take the gamble. Intel's resulting manufacturing expansion eventually cost $10 billion but resulted in Intel's obtaining 75% of the microprocessor business and huge cash profits.[79]

Risk might be one reason that significant innovations occur more often in small firms than in large, established corporations. A small firm managed by an entrepreneur is often willing to accept greater risk than is a large firm of diversified ownership run by professional managers.[80] It is one thing to take a chance if you are the primary shareholder and are not concerned with periodic changes in the value of the company's common stock. It is something else if the corporation's stock is widely held and acquisition-hungry competitors or takeover artists surround the company like sharks every time the company's stock price falls below some external assessment of the firm's value.

A new approach to evaluating alternatives under conditions of high environmental uncertainty is to use real-options theory. According to the **real-options** approach, when the future is highly uncertain, it pays to have a broad range of options open. This is in contrast to using *net present value (NPV)* to calculate the value of a project by predicting its payouts, adjusting them for risk, and subtracting the amount invested. By boiling everything down to one scenario, NPV doesn't provide any flexibility in case circumstances change. NPV is also difficult to apply to projects in which the potential payoffs are currently unknown. The real-options approach, however, deals with these issues by breaking the investment into stages. Management allocates a small amount of funding to initiate multiple projects, monitors their development, and then cancels the projects that aren't successful and funds those that are doing well.[81] This approach is very similar to the way venture capitalists fund an entrepreneurial venture in stages of funding based on the venture's performance.

A survey of 4,000 CFOs found that 27% of them always or almost always used some sort of options approach to evaluating and deciding upon growth opportunities.[82] Research indicates that the use of the real-options approach does improve organizational performance.[83] Some of the corporations using the real-options approach are Chevron for bidding on petroleum reserves, Airbus for calculating the costs of airlines changing their orders at the last minute, and the Tennessee Valley Authority for outsourcing electricity generation instead of building its own plant. Because of its complexity, the real-options approach is not worthwhile for minor decisions or for projects requiring a full commitment at the beginning.[84]

Pressures from Stakeholders

The attractiveness of a strategic alternative is affected by its perceived compatibility with the key stakeholders in a corporation's task environment. Creditors want to be paid on time. Unions exert pressure for comparable wage and employment security. Governments and interest groups demand social responsibility. Shareholders want dividends. All these pressures must be given some consideration in the selection of the best alternative.

Stakeholders can be categorized in terms of their (1) interest in the corporation's activities and (2) relative power to influence the corporation's activities.[85] With the **Stakeholder Priority Matrix** depicted in **Figure 8–2**, each stakeholder group can be placed in one of the nine cells.

FIGURE 8–2
Stakeholder
Priority Matrix

	Low Power	Medium Power	High Power
High Interest	Medium Priority	High Priority	High Priority
Medium Interest	Low Priority	Medium Priority	High Priority
Low Interest	Low Priority	Low Priority	Medium Priority

SOURCE: ACADEMY OF MANAGEMENT EXECUTIVE: THE THINKING MANAGER'S SOURCE *by C. ANDERSON. Copyright 1997 by ACAD OF MGMT. Reproduced with permission of ACAD OF MGMT in the format Textbook via Copyright Clearance Center.*

Strategic managers should ask four questions to assess the importance of stakeholder concerns in a particular decision:

1. How will this decision affect each stakeholder, especially those given high and medium priority?
2. How much of what each stakeholder wants is he or she likely to get under this alternative?
3. What are the stakeholders likely to do if they don't get what they want?
4. What is the probability that they will do it?

Strategy makers should choose strategic alternatives that minimize external pressures and maximize the probability of gaining stakeholder support. Managers may, however, ignore or take some stakeholders for granted—leading to serious problems later. The Tata Group, for example, failed to consider the unwillingness of farmers in Singur, India, to accept the West Bengal government's compensation for expropriating their land so that Tata could build its Nano auto plant. Farmers formed rallies against the plant, blocked roads, and even assaulted an employee of a Tata supplier.[86]

Top management can also propose a political strategy to influence its key stakeholders. A **political strategy** is a plan to bring stakeholders into agreement with a corporation's actions. Some of the most commonly used political strategies are constituency building, political action committee contributions, advocacy advertising, lobbying, and coalition building. Research reveals that large firms, those operating in concentrated industries, and firms that are highly dependent upon government regulation are more politically active.[87] Political support can be critical in entering a new international market, especially in transition economies where free market competition did not previously exist.[88]

Pressures from the Corporate Culture

If a strategy is incompatible with a company's corporate culture, the likelihood of its success is very low. Foot-dragging and even sabotage will result as employees fight to resist a radical change in corporate philosophy. Precedents from the past tend to restrict the kinds of objectives and strategies that are seriously considered.[89] The "aura" of the founders of a corporation can linger long past their lifetimes because their values are imprinted on a corporation's members.

In evaluating a strategic alternative, strategy makers must consider pressures from the corporate culture and assess a strategy's compatibility with that culture. If there is little fit, management must decide if it should:

- Take a chance on ignoring the culture
- Manage around the culture and change the implementation plan
- Try to change the culture to fit the strategy
- Change the strategy to fit the culture

Further, a decision to proceed with a particular strategy without a commitment to change the culture or manage around the culture (both very tricky and time consuming) is dangerous. Nevertheless, restricting a corporation to only those strategies that are completely compatible with its culture might eliminate from consideration the most profitable alternatives. (See **Chapter 10** for more information on managing corporate culture.)

Needs and Desires of Key Managers

Even the most attractive alternative might not be selected if it is contrary to the needs and desires of important top managers. Personal characteristics and experience affect a person's assessment of an alternative's attractiveness.[90] For example, one study found that narcissistic (self-absorbed and arrogant) CEOs favor bold actions that attract attention, like many large acquisitions—resulting in either big wins or big losses.[91] A person's ego may be tied to a particular proposal to the extent that all other alternatives are strongly lobbied against. As a result, the person may have unfavorable forecasts altered so that they are more in agreement with the desired alternative.[92] In a study by McKinsey & Company of 2,507 executives from around the world, 36% responded that managers hide, restrict, or misrepresent information at least "somewhat" frequently when submitting capital-investment proposals. In addition, an executive might influence other people in top management to favor a particular alternative so that objections to it are overruled. In the same McKinsey study of global executives, more than 60% of the managers reported that business unit and divisional heads form alliances with peers or lobby someone more senior in the organization at least "somewhat" frequently when resource allocation decisions are being made.[93]

Industry and cultural backgrounds affect strategic choice. For example, executives with strong ties within an industry tend to choose strategies commonly used in that industry. Other executives who have come to the firm from another industry and have strong ties outside the industry tend to choose different strategies from what is being currently used in their industry.[94] Country of origin often affects preferences. For example, Japanese managers prefer a cost-leadership strategy more than do United States managers.[95] Research reveals that executives from Korea, the U.S., Japan, and Germany tend to make different strategic choices in similar situations because they use different decision criteria and weights. For example, Korean executives emphasize industry attractiveness, sales, and market share in their decisions; whereas, U.S. executives emphasize projected demand, discounted cash flow, and ROI.[96]

There is a tendency to maintain the status quo, which means that decision makers continue with existing goals and plans beyond the point when an objective observer would recommend a change in course.[97] Some executives show a self-serving tendency to attribute the firm's problems not to their own poor decisions but to environmental events out of their control, such as government policies or a poor economic climate.[98] For example, a CEO is more likely to divest a poorly performing unit when its poor performance does not incriminate that same CEO who had acquired it.[99] Negative information about a particular course of action to which a person is committed may be ignored because of a desire to appear competent or because of strongly held values regarding consistency. It may take a crisis or an unlikely event to cause strategic decision makers to seriously consider an alternative they had previously ignored or discounted.[100] For example, it wasn't until the CEO of ConAgra, a multinational food products company, had a heart attack that ConAgra started producing the Healthy Choice line of low-fat, low-cholesterol, low-sodium frozen-food entrees.

PROCESS OF STRATEGIC CHOICE

There is an old story told at General Motors:

> At a meeting with his key executives, CEO Alfred Sloan proposed a controversial strategic decision. When asked for comments, each executive responded with supportive comments and praise. After announcing that they were all in apparent agreement, Sloan stated that they were not going to proceed with the decision. Either his executives didn't know enough to point out potential downsides of the decision, or they were agreeing to avoid upsetting the boss and disrupting the cohesion of the group. The decision was delayed until a debate could occur over the pros and cons.[101]

Strategic choice is the evaluation of alternative strategies and selection of the best alternative. According to Paul Nutt, an authority in decision making, half of the decisions made by managers are failures.[102] After analyzing 400 decisions, Nutt found that failure almost always stems from the actions of the decision maker, not from bad luck or situational limitations. In these instances, managers commit one or more key blunders: (1) their desire for speedy actions leads to a rush to judgment, (2) they apply failure-prone decision-making practices such as adopting the claim of an influential stakeholder, and (3) they make poor use of resources by investigating only one or two options. These three blunders cause executives to limit their search for feasible alternatives and look for quick consensus. Only 4% of the 400 managers set an objective and considered several alternatives. The search for innovative options was attempted in only 24% of the decisions studied.[103] Another study of 68 divestiture decisions found a strong tendency for managers to rely heavily on past experience when developing strategic alternatives.[104]

There is mounting evidence that when an organization is facing a dynamic environment, the best strategic decisions are not arrived at through **consensus** when everyone agrees on one alternative. They actually involve a certain amount of heated disagreement, and even conflict.[105] Many diverse opinions are presented, participants trust in one another's abilities and competences, and conflict is task-oriented, not personal.[106] This is certainly the case for firms operating in global industries. Because unmanaged conflict often carries a high emotional cost, authorities in decision making propose that strategic managers use "programmed conflict" to raise different opinions, regardless of the personal feelings of the people involved.[107] Two techniques help strategic managers avoid the consensus trap that Alfred Sloan found:

1. **Devil's advocate:** The idea of the **devil's advocate** originated in the medieval Roman Catholic Church as a way of ensuring that impostors were not canonized as saints. One trusted person was selected to find and present all the reasons why a person should not be canonized. When this process is applied to strategic decision making, a devil's advocate (who may be an individual or a group) is assigned to identify potential pitfalls and problems with a proposed alternative strategy in a formal presentation.

2. **Dialectical inquiry:** The dialectical philosophy, which can be traced back to Plato and Aristotle and more recently to Hegel, involves combining two conflicting views—the thesis and the antithesis—into a synthesis. When applied to strategic decision making, **dialectical inquiry** requires that two proposals using different assumptions be generated for each alternative strategy under consideration. After advocates of each position present and debate the merits of their arguments before key decision makers, either one of the alternatives or a new compromise alternative is selected as the strategy to be implemented.

Research generally supports the conclusion that the devil's advocate and dialectical inquiry methods are equally superior to consensus in decision making, especially when the firm's environment is dynamic. The debate itself, rather than its particular format, appears to improve the quality of decisions by formalizing and legitimizing constructive conflict and by encouraging critical evaluation. Both lead to better assumptions and recommendations and to a higher level of critical thinking among the people involved.[108]

Regardless of the process used to generate strategic alternatives, each resulting alternative must be rigorously evaluated in terms of its ability to meet four criteria:

1. **Mutual Exclusivity:** Doing any one alternative would preclude doing any other.
2. **Success:** It must be feasible and have a good probability of success.
3. **Completeness:** It must take into account all the key strategic issues.
4. **Internal Consistency:** It must make sense on its own as a strategic decision for the entire firm and not contradict key goals, policies, and strategies currently being pursued by the firm or its units.[109]

8.5 Developing Policies

The selection of the best strategic alternative is not the end of strategy formulation. The organization must then engage in developing policies. Policies define the broad guidelines for implementation. Flowing from the selected strategy, policies provide guidance for decision making and actions throughout the organization. They are the principles under which the corporation operates on a day-to-day basis. At General Electric, for example, Chairman Jack Welch initiated the policy that any GE business unit must be Number One or Number Two in whatever market it competes. This policy gave clear guidance to managers throughout the organization. Another example of such a policy is Casey's General Stores' policy that a new service or product line may be added to its stores only when the product or service can be justified in terms of increasing store traffic.

When crafted correctly, an effective policy accomplishes three things:

- It forces trade-offs between competing resource demands.
- It tests the strategic soundness of a particular action.
- It sets clear boundaries within which employees must operate while granting them freedom to experiment within those constraints.[110]

Policies tend to be rather long lived and can even outlast the particular strategy that created them. These general policies—such as "The customer is always right" (Nordstrom) or "Low prices, every day" (Wal-Mart)—can become, in time, part of a corporation's culture. Such policies can make the implementation of specific strategies easier. They can also restrict top management's strategic options in the future. Thus a change in strategy should be followed quickly by a change in policies. Managing policy is one way to manage the corporate culture.

End of Chapter SUMMARY

This chapter completes the part of this book on strategy formulation and sets the stage for strategy implementation. Functional strategies must be formulated to support business and corporate strategies; otherwise, the company will move in multiple directions and eventually pull itself apart. For a functional strategy to have the best chance of success, it should be built on a distinctive competency residing within that functional area. If a corporation does not have a distinctive competency in a particular functional area, that functional area could be a candidate for outsourcing.

When evaluating a strategic alternative, the most important criterion is the ability of the proposed strategy to deal with the specific strategic factors developed earlier, in the SWOT analysis. If the alternative doesn't take advantage of environmental opportunities and corporate strengths/competencies, and lead away from environmental threats and corporate weaknesses, it will probably fail. Developing corporate scenarios and pro forma projections for each alternative are rational aids for strategic decision making. This logical approach fits Mintzberg's planning mode of strategic decision making, as discussed earlier in **Chapter 1**. Nevertheless, some strategic decisions are inherently risky and may be resolved on the basis of one person's "gut feel." This is an aspect of the entrepreneurial mode and may be used in large established corporations as well as in new venture startups. Various management studies have found that executives routinely rely on their intuition to solve complex problems. The effective use of intuition has been found to differentiate successful top executives and board members from lower-level managers and dysfunctional boards.[111] According to Ralph Larsen, Chair and CEO of Johnson & Johnson, "Often there is absolutely no way that you could have the time to thoroughly analyze every one of the options or alternatives available to you. So you have to rely on your business judgment."[112] For managerial intuition to be effective, however, it requires years of experience in problem solving and is founded upon a complete understanding of the details of the business.[113]

For example, when Bob Lutz, President of Chrysler Corporation, was enjoying a fast drive in his Cobra roadster one weekend in 1988, he wondered why Chrysler's cars were so dull. "I felt guilty: there I was, the president of Chrysler, driving this great car that had such a strong Ford association," said Lutz, referring to the original Cobra's Ford V-8 engine. That Monday, Lutz enlisted allies at Chrysler to develop a muscular, outrageous sports car that would turn heads and stop traffic. Others in management argued that the $80 million investment would be better spent elsewhere. The sales force warned that no U.S. auto maker had ever succeeded in selling a $50,000 car. With only his gut instincts to support him, he pushed the project forward with unwavering commitment. The result was the Dodge Viper—a car that single-handedly changed the public's perception of Chrysler. Years later, Lutz had trouble describing exactly how he had made this critical decision. "It was this subconscious, visceral feeling. And it just felt right," explained Lutz.[114]

ECO-BITS

- In the two-day period after joining the U.S. Environmental Protection Agency's voluntary Climate Leader's initiative, which requires members to reduce or offset emissions over the next 5 to 10 years, the average company's stock price dropped 0.9% more than it would have from normal market factors.[115]

- General Motors states that its facilities recycle 89% of the waste they generate and that GM is one of the world's largest industrial users of solar power.[116]

DISCUSSION QUESTIONS

1. Are functional strategies interdependent, or can they be formulated independently of other functions?

2. Why is penetration pricing more likely than skim pricing to raise a company's or a business unit's operating profit in the long run?

3. How does mass customization support a business unit's competitive strategy?

4. When should a corporation or business unit outsource a function or an activity?

5. What is the relationship of policies to strategies?

STRATEGIC PRACTICE EXERCISE

Pierre Omidyar founded a sole proprietorship in September 1995 called Auction Web to allow people to buy and sell goods over the Internet. The new venture was based on the idea of developing a community-driven process, where an organic, evolving, self-organizing web of individual relationships, formed around shared interests, would handle tasks that other companies handle with customer service operations. By May 1996, Omidyar had added Jeff Skoll as a partner and the venture was incorporated as eBay. Two years later, Omidyar asked Meg Whitman to direct corporate strategy to continue the accelerated growth rate of the company. Whitman brought to the company global management and marketing experience and soon became President and CEO. In almost no time, the company became one of the Web's most successful sites, with 233 million registered users. By 2007, the average eBay user spent nearly two hours a month on the site—more than five times the time spent on Amazon.com.[117]

Whitman expanded the company's operations and spent more than $6 billion to acquire companies, such as Internet-phone operation Skype, online payments service PayPal, ticket reseller StubHub, property rental and roommate search firm Rent.com, comparison shopping site Shopping.com, Web site recommender Stumbleupon, and 25% interest in Craigslist. Expansion and diversification provided revenue and profit growth plus stock price appreciation. Although financial analysts wondered how all these businesses would fit together, Whitman argued that she wanted eBay to be everywhere users wanted to be. At developer conferences, company representatives unveiled new services that let buyers shop for and purchase eBay items outside of the core eBay.com site.

By 2008, eBay was in trouble. Its stock price had lost half its value over the past three years. The core auction and retail businesses, which accounted for the majority of revenue, were showing signs of weakness. The number of active users had been flat for three quarters, at 83 million. The number of new products listed on the site had increased only 4% from the previous year. The number of stores selling goods at fixed prices on eBay declined from a year earlier to 532,000. The company had not done a good job of integrating Skype with its main business. Since its acquisition, Skype's service had actually deteriorated.[118] Competition had increased as rival Web sites, particularly Amazon, now provided similar Web services and eroded eBay's competitive advantage.

On January 23, 2008, CEO Whitman announced that John Donahoe would take over as the company's CEO. Donahoe stated that his first priority would be to revitalize eBay's core business, even at the expense of investors. "We need to aggressively change our product, our customer approach, and our business model," announced the new CEO.[119]

1. What is eBay's problem?

2. Which marketing strategy was eBay following: market development or product development? Do you agree with it?

3. What decision-making process should CEO Donahoe utilize to make the decisions necessary to change the company's product, customer approach, and business model?

KEY TERMS

consensus (p. 305)

corporate scenarios (p. 299)

devil's advocate (p. 305)

dialectical inquiry (p. 305)

financial strategy (p. 287)

functional strategy (p. 286)

HRM strategy (p. 294)

information technology strategy (p. 295)

leveraged buyout (p. 288)

logistics strategy (p. 294)

market development (p. 286)

marketing strategy (p. 286)

offshoring (p. 296)

operations strategy (p. 290)

outsourcing (p. 295)

political strategy (p. 303)

product development (p. 286)

purchasing strategy (p. 292)

R&D strategy (p. 289)

real options (p. 302)

risk (p. 301)

Stakeholder Priority Matrix (p. 302)

strategic choice (p. 305)

technological follower (p. 289)

technological leader (p. 289)

NOTES

1. Arm & Hammer is a registered trademark of Church & Dwight Company, Inc.

2. S. F. Slater and E. M. Olson, "Market's Contribution to the Implementation of Business Strategy: An Empirical Analysis," *Strategic Management Journal* (November 2001), pp. 1055–1067; B. C. Skaggs and T. R. Huffman, "A Customer Interaction Approach to Strategy and Production Complexity Alignment in Service Firms," *Academy of Management Journal* (December 2003), pp. 775–786.

3. A. Pressman, "Ocean Spray's Creative Juices," *Business Week* (May 15, 2006), pp. 88–89.

4. A. Pressman, "Smith & Wesson: A Gunmaker Loaded with Offshoots," *Business Week* (June 4, 2007), p. 66.

5. S. M. Oster, *Modern Competitive Analysis*, 2nd ed. (New York: Oxford University Press, 1994), p. 93.

6. J. M. de Figueiredo and M. K. Kyle, "Surviving the Gales of Creative Destruction: The Determinants of Product Turnover," *Strategic Management Journal* (March 2006), pp. 241–264.

7. M. Springer, "Plowed Under," *Forbes* (February 21, 2000), p. 56.

8. W. Redmond, "The Strategic Pricing of Innovative Products," *Handbook of Business Strategy, 1992/1993 Yearbook*, edited by H. E. Glass and M. A. Hovde (Boston: Warren, Gorham & Lamont, 1992), pp. 16.1–16.13; A. Hinterhuber, "Towards Value-Based Pricing—An Integrative Framework for Decision Making," *Industrial Marketing Management*, Vol. 33 (2004), pp. 765–778.

9. A. Kambil, H. J. Wilson III, and V. Agrawal, "Are You Leaving Money on the Table?" *Journal of Business Strategy* (January/February 2002), pp. 40–43.

10. P. Burrows, "Apple's Cash Conundrum," *Business Week* (August 11, 2008), p. 32.

11. A. Safieddine and S. Titman in April 1999 *Journal of Finance,* as summarized by D. Champion, "The Joy of Leverage," *Harvard Business Review* (July–August 1999), pp. 19–22.

12. R. Kochhar and M. A. Hitt, "Linking Corporate Strategy to Capital Structure: Diversification Strategy, Type and Source of Financing," *Strategic Management Journal* (June 1998), pp. 601–610.

13. A. Rappaport and M. L. Sirower, "Stock or Cash?" *Harvard Business Review* (November–December 1999), pp. 147–158.

14. "Private Investigations," *The Economist* (July 5, 2008), pp. 84–85.

15. "Private Investigations," *The Economist* (July 5, 2008), pp. 84–85.

16. D. Angwin and I. Contardo, "Unleashing Cerberus: Don't Let Your MBOs Turn on Themselves," *Long Range Planning* (October 1999), pp. 494–504.

17. For information on different types of LBOs, see M. Wright, R. E. Hoskisson, and L. W. Busenitz, "Firm Rebirth: Buyouts as Facilitators of Strategic Growth and Entrepreneurship," *Academy of Management Executive* (February 2001), pp. 111–125.

18. D. N. Hurtt, J. G. Kreuze, and S. A. Langsam, "Stock Buybacks and Their Association with Stock Options Exercised in the IT Industry," *American Journal of Business* (Spring 2008), pp. 13–21.

19. B. Deener, "Back Up and Look at Reasons for Reverse Stock Split," *The (St. Petersburg, FL) Times* (December 29, 2002), p. 3H.

20. M. Orey, "A Sotheby's for Investors," *Business Week* (February 13, 2006), p. 39.

21. T. Due, "Dean Foods Thrives on Regional Off-Brand Products," *Wall Street Journal* (September 17, 1987), p. A6.

22. S. Stevens, "Speeding the Signals of Change," *Appliance* (February 1995), p. 7.

23. L-E. Gadde and H. Hakansson, "Teaching in Supplier Networks," in *Strategic Networks: Learning to Compete*, by M. Gibbert and T. Durand, eds. (Malden, MA: Blackwell Publishing, 2007), pp. 40–57.

24. "Schools Rent Out Labs to Businesses," *St. Cloud (MN) Times* (December 11, 2007), p. 3A.

25. H. W. Chesbrough, "A Better Way to Innovate," *Harvard Business Review* (July 2003), pp. 12–13.

26. J. Bughin, M. Chui, and B. Johnson, "The Next Step in Open Innovation," *McKinsey Quarterly* (June 2008), pp. 1–8.

27. J. Greene, J. Carey, M. Arndt, and O. Port, "Reinventing Corporate R&D," *Business Week* (September 22, 2003), pp. 74–76; J. Birkinshaw, S. Crainer, and M. Mol, "From

R&D to Connect + Develop at P&G," *Business Strategy Review* (Spring 2007), pp. 66–69; L. Huston and N. Sakkab, "Connect and Develop: Inside Proctor & Gamble's New Model for Innovation," *Harvard Business Review* (March 2006), pp. 58–66.

28. G. Dushnitsky and M. J. Lenox, "When Do Firms Undertake R&D by Investing in New Ventures?" Paper presented to annual meeting of the *Academy of Management*, Seattle, WA (August 2003).

29. A. Aston and M. Arndt, "The Flexible Factory," *Business Week* (May 5, 2003), pp. 90–91.

30. J. R. Williams and R. S. Novak, "Aligning CIM Strategies to Different Markets," *Long Range Planning* (February 1990), pp. 126–135.

31. J. Wheatley, "Super Factory—or Super Headache," *Business Week* (July 31, 2000), p. 66.

32. M. Tayles and C. Drury, "Moving from Make/Buy to Strategic Sourcing: The Outsource Decision Process," *Long Range Planning* (October 2001), pp. 605–622.

33. F. R. Bleakley, "Some Companies Let Supplies Work on Site and Even Place Orders," *Wall Street Journal* (January 13, 1995), pp. A1, A6.

34. M. Hoegl and S. M. Wagner, "Buyer-Supplier Collaboration in Product Development Projects," *Journal of Management* (August 2005), pp. 530–548; B. McEvily and A. Marcus, "Embedded Ties and the Acquisition of Competitive Capabilities," *Strategic Management Journal* (November 2005), pp. 1033–1055; R. Gulati and M. Sytch, "Dependence Asymmetry and Joint Dependence in Interorganizational Relationships: Effects of Embeddedness on a Manufacturer's Performance in Procurement Relationships," *Administrative Science Quarterly* (March 2007), pp. 32–69.

35. J. Richardson, "Parallel Sourcing and Supplier Performance in the Japanese Automobile Industry," *Strategic Management Journal* (July 1993), pp. 339–350.

36. S. Roberts-Witt, "Procurement: The HP Way," *PC Magazine* (November 21, 2000), pp. 21–22.

37. D. H. Pearcy, D. B. Parker, and L. C. Giunipero, "Using Electronic Procurement to Facilitate Supply Chain Integration: An Exploratory Study of U.S.-based Firms," *American Journal of Business* (Spring 2008), pp. 23–35.

38. J. Bigness, "In Today's Economy, There Is Big Money to Be Made in Logistics," *Wall Street Journal* (September 6, 1995), pp. A1, A9.

39. F. Keenan, "Logistics Gets a Little Respect," *Business Week* (November 20, 2000), pp. 112–116.

40. B. L. Kirkman and Debra L. Shapiro, "The Impact of Cultural Values on Employee Resistance to Teams: Toward a Model of Globalized Self-Managing Work Team Effectiveness," *Academy of Management Review* (July 1997), pp. 730–757.

41. R. D. Banker, J. M. Field, R. G. Schroeder, and K. K. Sinha, "Impact of Work Teams on Manufacturing Performance: A Longitudinal Field Study," *Academy of Management Journal*

(August 1996), pp. 867–890; B. L. Kirkman and B. Rosen, "Beyond Self-Management: Antecedents and Consequences of Team Empowerment," *Academy of Management Journal* (February 1999), pp. 58–74.

42. V. Y. Haines III, S. St. Onge, and A. Marcoux, "Performance Management Design and Effectiveness in Quality-Driven Organizations," *Canadian Journal of Administrative Sciences* (June 2004), pp. 146–160.

43. A. S. DeNisi and A. N. Kluger, "Feedback Effectiveness: Can 360-Degree Appraisals Be Improved?" *Academy of Management Executive* (February 2000), pp. 129–139; G. Toegel and J. A. Conger, "360-Degree Assessment: Time for Reinvention," *Academy of Management Learning and Education* (September 2003), pp. 297–311; F. Shipper, R. C. Hoffman, and D. M. Rotondo, "Does the 360 Feedback Process Create Actionable Knowledge Equally Across Cultures?" *Academy of Management Learning & Education* (March 2007), pp. 33–50.

44. J. McGregor, "The Employee Is Always Right," *Business Week* (November 19, 2007), pp. 80–82.

45. O. C. Richard, "Racial Diversity, Business Strategy, and Firm Performance: A Resource-Based View," *Academy of Management Journal* (April 2000), pp. 164–177.

46. G. Robinson and K. Dechant, "Building a Business Case for Diversity," *Academy of Management Executive* (August 1997), pp. 21–31.

47. K. Labich, "Making Diversity Pay," *Fortune* (September 9, 1996), pp. 177–180.

48. N. G. Carr, "IT Doesn't Matter," *Harvard Business Review* (May 2003), pp. 41–50.

49. J. Greco, "Good Day Sunshine," *Journal of Business Strategy* (July/August 1998), pp. 4–5.

50. W. Howard, "Translate Now," *PC Magazine* (September 19, 2000), p. 81.

51. H. Green, "The Web Smart 50," *Business Week* (November 24, 2003), p. 84.

52. T. Smart, "Jack Welch's Cyber-Czar," *Business Week* (August 5, 1996), p. 83.

53. S. M. Kim and J. T. Mahoney, "Mutual Commitment to Support Exchange: Relation-Specific IT System as a Substitute for Managerial Hierarchy," *Strategic Management Journal* (May 2006), pp. 401–423.

54. B. Kelley, "Outsourcing Marches On," *Journal of Business Strategy* (July/August 1995), p. 40.

55. S. Holmes and M. Arndt, "A Plane that Could Change the Game," *Business Week* (August 9, 2004), p. 33.

56. J. Greco, "Outsourcing: The New Partnership," *Journal of Business Strategy* (July/August 1997), pp. 48–54.

57. W. M. Fitzpatrick and S. A. DiLullo, "Outsourcing and the Personnel Paradox," *SAM Advanced Management Journal* (Summer 2007), pp. 4–12.

58. Outsourcing: Time to Bring It Back Home?" *The Economist* (March 5, 2005), p. 63.

59. A. Y. Lewin and C. Peeters, "Offshoring Work: Business Hype or the Onset of Fundamental Transformation?" *Long Range Planning* (June 2006), pp. 221–239; A. Y. Lewing and C. Peeters, "The Top-Line Allure of Offshoring," *Harvard Business Review* (March 2006), pp. 22–24.

60. G. Smith, "Factories Go South; So Does Pay," *Business Week* (April 9, 2007), p. 76.

61. "Out of Captivity," *Economist* (November 13, 2004), p. 68.

62. "IBM's Plan to Buy India Firm Points to Demand for Outsourcing," *Des Moines Register* (April 11, 2004), p. 2D.

63. A. Castro, "Complaints Push Dell to Use U.S. Call Centers," *Des Moines Register* (November 25, 2003), p. 1D.

64. J. A. Byrne, "Has Outsourcing Gone Too Far?" *Business Week* (April 1, 1996), pp. 26–28.

65. R. C. Insinga and M. J. Werle, "Linking Outsourcing to Business Strategy," *Academy of Management Executive* (November 2000), pp. 58–70; D. Lei and M. A. Hitt, "Strategic Restructuring and Outsourcing: The Effect of Mergers and Acquisitions and LBOs on Building Firm Skills and Capabilities," *Journal of Management*, Vol. 21, No. 5 (1995), pp. 835–859.

66. "Outsourcing: Time to Bring It Back Home*?" The Economist* (May 5, 2005), p. 63.

67. S. E. Ante, "Shifting Work Offshore? Outsourcer Beware," *Business Week* (January 12, 2004), pp. 36–37.

68. J. Carey, "Not Made in China," *Business Week* (July 30, 2007), pp. 41–43; "The Poison Spreads," *The Economist* (September 27, 2008), pp. 77–78; "Plenty of Blame to Go Around," *The Economist* (September 29, 2007), pp. 68–70; J. Schmit, "Heparin Plant in China Passed 'In-Depth' Review," *USA Today* (April 30, 2008), p. B1.

69. A. Goel, N. Moussavi, and V. N. Srivatsan, "Time to Rethink Offshoring?" *McKinsey Quarterly* (September 2008), pp. 1–5.

70. A. Takeishi, "Bridging Inter- and Intra-Firm Boundaries: Management of Supplier Involvement in Automobile Product Development," *Strategic Management Journal* (May 2001), pp. 403–433.

71. J. Barthelemy, "The Seven Deadly Sins of Outsourcing," *Academy of Management Executive* (May 2003), pp. 87–98.

72. M. J. Leiblein and D. J. Miller, "An Empirical Examination of Transaction and Firm-Level Influences on the Vertical Boundaries of the Firm," *Strategic Management Journal* (September 2003), pp. 839–859.

73. S. Hamm, "Is Outsourcing on the Outs?" *Business Week* (October 4, 2004), p. 42.

74. For further information on effective offshoring, see R. Aron and J. V. Singh, "Getting Offshoring Right," *Harvard Business Review* (December 2005), pp. 135–143.

75. R. Grover and D. Polek, "Millionaire Buys Disney Time," *Business Week* (June 26, 2000), pp. 141–144.

76. D. K. Sinha, "Strategic Planning in the Fortune 500," *Handbook of Business Strategy, 1991/1992 Yearbook*, edited by H. E. Glass and M. A. Hovde (Boston: Warren, Gorham & Lamont, 1991), pp. 9.6–9.8.

77. N. Checa, J. Maguire, and J. Berry, "The New World Disorder," *Harvard Business Review* (August 2003), pp. 70–79.

78. T. B. Palmer and R. M. Wiseman, "Decoupling Risk Taking from Income Stream Uncertainty: A Holistic Model of Risk," *Strategic Management Journal* (November 1999), pp. 1037–1062; W. G. Sanders and D. C. Hambrick, "Swinging for the Fences: The Effects of CEO Stock Options on Company Risk Taking and Performance," *Academy of Management Journal* (October 2007), pp. 1055–1078.

79. D. Clark, "All the Chips: A Big Bet Made Intel What It Is Today; Now It Wagers Again," *Wall Street Journal* (June 6, 1995), pp. A1, A5.

80. L. W. Busenitz and J. B. Barney, "Differences Between Entrepreneurs and Managers in Large Organizations: Biases and Heuristics in Strategic Decision-Making," *Journal of Business Venturing* (January 1997), pp. 9–30.

81. J. J. Janney and G. G. Dess, "Can Real-Options Analysis Improve Decision-Making? Promises and Pitfalls," *Academy of Management Executive* (November 2004), pp. 60–75; S. Maklan, S. Knox, and L. Ryals, "Using Real Options to Help Build the Business Case for CRM Investment," *Long Range Planning* (August 2005), pp. 393–410.

82. T. Copeland and P. Tufano, "A Real-World Way to Manage Real Options," *Harvard Business Review* (March 2004), pp. 90–99.

83. J. Rosenberger and K. Eisenhardt, "What Are Real Options: A Review of Empirical Research," Paper presented to annual meeting of the *Academy of Management*, Seattle, WA (August 2003).

84. P. Coy, "Exploiting Uncertainty," *Business Week* (June 7, 1999), pp. 118–124. For further information on real options, see M. Amram and N. Kulatilaka, *Real Options* (Boston, Harvard University Press, 1999). For a simpler summary, see R. M. Grant, *Contemporary Strategy Analysis*, 5th edition (Malden, MA: Blackwell Publishing, 2005), pp. 48–50.

85. C. Anderson, "Values-Based Management," *Academy of Management Executive* (November 1997), pp. 25–46.

86. "Nano Wars," *The Economist* (August 30, 2008), p. 63.

87. J-P. Bonardi, A. J. Hillman, and G. D. Keim, "The Attractiveness of Political Markets: Implications for Firm Strategy," *Academy of Management Review* (April 2005), pp. 397–413.

88. J. G. Frynas, K. Mellahi, and G. A. Pigman, "First Mover Advantages in International Business and Firm-Specific Political Resources," *Strategic Management Journal* (April 2006), pp. 321–345. For additional information about political strategies, see C. Oliver and I. Holzinger, "The Effectiveness of Strategic Political Management: A Dynamic Capabilities Framework," *Academy of Management Review* (April 2008), pp. 496–520.

89. H. M. O'Neill, R. W. Pouder, and A. K. Buchholtz, "Patterns in the Diffusion of Strategies Across Organizations: Insights from the Innovation Diffusion Literature," *Academy of Management Executive* (January 1998), pp. 98–114; C. G. Gilbert, "Unbundling the Structure of Inertia: Resource Versus Routine Rigidity," *Academy of Management Journal* (October 2005), pp. 741–763.

90. B. B. Tyler and H. K. Steensma. "Evaluating Technological Collaborative Opportunities: A Cognitive Modeling Perspective," *Strategic Management Journal* (Summer 1995), pp. 43–70; D. Duchan, D. P. Ashman, and M. Nathan, "Mavericks, Visionaries, Protestors, and Sages: Toward a Typology of Cognitive Structures for Decision Making in Organizations," *Journal of Business Strategies* (Fall 1997), pp. 106–125; P. Chattopadhyay, W. H. Glick, C. C. Miller, and G. P. Huber, "Determinants of Executive Beliefs: Comparing Functional Conditioning and Social Influence," *Strategic Management Journal* (August 1999), pp. 763–789; B. Katey and G. G. Meredith, "Relationship Among Owner/Manager Personal Values, Business Strategies, and Enterprise Performance," *Journal of Small Business Management* (April 1997), pp. 37–64.

91. A. Chatterjee and D. C. Hambrick, "It's All About Me: Narcissistic Executive Officers and Their Effects on Company Strategy and Performance," *Administrative Science Quarterly* (September 2007), pp. 351–386.

92. C. S. Galbraith and G. B. Merrill, "The Politics of Forecasting: Managing the Truth," *California Management Review* (Winter 1996), pp. 29–43.

93. M. Garbuio, D. Lovallo, and P. Viguerie, "How Companies Spend Their Money: A McKinsey Global Survey," *McKinsey Quarterly Online* (June 2007).

94. M. A. Geletkanycz and D. C. Hambrick, "The External Ties of Top Executives: Implications for Strategic Choice and Performance," *Administrative Science Quarterly* (December 1997), pp. 654–681.

95. M. Song, R. J. Calantone, and C. A. Di Benedetto, "Competitive Forces and Strategic Choice Decisions: An Experimental Investigation in the United States and Japan," *Strategic Management Journal* (October 2002), pp. 969–978.

96. M. A. Hitt, M. T. Dacin, B. B. Tyler, and D. Park, "Understanding the Differences in Korean and U.S. Executives' Strategic Orientation," *Strategic Management Journal* (February 1997), pp. 159–167; L. G. Thomas III and G. Waring, "Competing Capitalisms: Capital Investment in American, German, and Japanese Firms," *Strategic Management Journal* (August 1999), pp. 729–748.

97. M. H. Bazerman and D. Chugh, "Decisions Without Blinders," *Harvard Business Review* (January 2006), pp. 88–97.

98. J. A. Wagner III and R. Z. Gooding, "Equivocal Information and Attribution: An Investigation of Patterns of Managerial Sensemaking," *Strategic Management Journal* (April 1997), pp. 275–286; K. Shimizu and M. A. Hitt, "Strategic Flexibility: Organizational Preparedness to Reverse Ineffective Strategic Decisions," *Academy of Management Executive* (November 2004), pp. 44–59.

99. M. L. A. Hayward and K. Shimizu, "De-Commitment to Losing Strategic Action: Evidence from the Divestiture of Poorly Performing Acquisitions," *Strategic Management Journal* (June 2006), pp. 541–557.

100. J. Ross and B. M. Staw, "Organizational Escalation and Exit: Lessons from the Shoreham Nuclear Power Plant," *Academy of Management Journal* (August 1993), pp. 701–732; P. W. Mulvey, J. F. Veiga, and P. M. Elsass, "When Teammates Raise a White Flag," *Academy of Management Executive* (February 1996), pp. 40–49.

101. R. A. Cosier and C. R. Schwenk, "Agreement and Thinking Alike: Ingredients for Poor Decisions," *Academy of Management Executive* (February 1990), p. 69.

102. P. C. Nutt, *Why Decisions Fail* (San Francisco: Berrett-Koehler, 2002).

103. P. C. Nutt, "Expanding the Search for Alternatives During Strategic Decision-Making," *Academy of Management Executive* (November 2004), pp. 13–28.

104. K. Shimizu, "Prospect Theory, Behavioral Theory, and the Threat-Rigidity Thesis: Combinative Effects on Organizational Decisions to Divest Formerly Acquired Units," *Academy of Management Journal* (December 2007), pp. 1495–1514.

105. G. P. West III and G. D. Meyer, "To Agree or Not to Agree? Consensus and Performance in New Ventures," *Journal of Business Venturing* (September 1998), pp. 395–422; L. Markoczy, "Consensus Formation During Strategic Change," *Strategic Management Journal* (November 2001), pp. 1013–1031.

106. B. J. Olson, S. Parayitam, and Y. Bao, "Strategic Decision Making: The Effects of Cognitive Diversity, Conflict, and Trust on Decision Outcomes," *Journal of Management* (April 2007), pp. 196–222.

107. A. C. Amason, "Distinguishing the Effects of Functional and Dysfunctional Conflict on Strategic Decision Making: Resolving a Paradox for Top Management Teams," *Academy of Management Journal* (February 1996), pp. 123–148; A. C. Amason and H. J. Sapienza, "The Effects of Top Management Team Size and Interaction Norms on Cognitive and Affective Conflict," *Journal of Management*, Vol. 23, No. 4 (1997), pp. 495–516.

108. D. M. Schweiger, W. R. Sandberg, and P. L. Rechner, "Experiential Effects of Dialectical Inquiry, Devil's Advocacy, and Consensus Approaches to Strategic Decision Making," *Academy of Management Journal* (December 1989), pp. 745–772; G. Whyte, "Decision Failures: Why They Occur and How to Prevent Them," *Academy of Management Executive* (August 1991), pp. 23–31; R. L. Priem, D. A. Harrison, and N. K. Muir, "Structured Conflict and Consensus Outcomes in Group Decision Making," *Journal of Management*, Vol. 21, No. 4 (1995), pp. 691–710.

109. S. C. Abraham, "Using Bundles to Find the Best Strategy," *Strategy & Leadership* (July/August/September 1999), pp. 53–55.

110. O. Gadiesh and J. L Gilbert, "Transforming Corner-Office Strategy into Frontline Action," *Harvard Business Review* (May 2001), pp. 73–79.

111. E. Dane and M. G. Pratt, "Exploring Intuition and Its Role in Managerial Decision Making," *Academy of Management Review* (January 2007), pp. 33–54.

112. A. M. Hayashi, "When to Trust Your Gut," *Harvard Business Review* (February 2001), pp. 59–65.

113. E. Dane and M. G. Pratt, "Exploring Intuition and Its Role in Managerial Decision Making," *Academy of Management Review* (January 2007), pp. 33–54.

114. A. M. Hayashi, pp. 59–60.

115. "Losing Green By Going Green," *Business Week* (June 30, 2008), p. 61.

116. Advertisement by General Motors appearing in *National Geographic Magazine* (June 2008).

117. C. Holahan, "Going, Going...Everywhere," *Business Week* (June 18, 2007), pp. 62–64.

118. "The Skype Hyper," *The Economist* (October 6, 2007), p. 80.

119. C. Holahan, "EBay's New Tough Love CEO," Business Week (February 4, 2008), pp. 58–59.

Ending Case for Part Three

KMART AND SEARS: STILL STUCK IN THE MIDDLE?

On January 22, 2002, Kmart Corporation became the largest retailer in U.S. history to seek bankruptcy protection. In Kmart's petition for reorganization under Chapter 11 of the U.S. Bankruptcy Code, Kmart management announced that they would outline a plan for repaying Kmart's creditors, reducing its size, and restructuring its business so that it could leave court protection as a viable competitor in discount mass-market retailing. Emerging from bankruptcy in May 2003, Kmart still lacked a business strategy to succeed in an extremely competitive marketplace.

The U.S. discount department store industry had reached maturity by 2004 and Kmart no longer possessed a clearly-defined position within that industry. Its primary competitors were Wal-Mart, Sears, Target, Kohl's, and J.C. Penney, with secondary competitors in certain categories. Wal-Mart, an extremely efficient retailer, was known for consistently having the lowest costs (reflected in low prices) and the highest sales in the industry. Having started in rural America, Wal-Mart was now actively growing internationally. Sears, with the second-highest annual sales, had a strong position in hard goods, such as home appliances and tools. Around 40% of all major home appliance sales continued to be controlled by Sears. Nevertheless, Sears was struggling with slumping sales as customers turned from Sears mall stores to stand-alone, big-box retailers, such as Lowe's and Home Depot, to buy their hard goods. Target, third in sales but second in profits, behind Wal-Mart, had distinguished itself as a merchandiser of stylish upscale products. Along with Wal-Mart, Target had flourished to such an extent that Dayton-Hudson, its parent company, had changed its corporate name to Target. Kohl's, a relatively new entrant to the industry, operated 420 family-oriented stores in 32 states. J.C. Penney operated more than 1,000 stores in all 50 states. Both Kohl's and J.C. Penney emphasized soft goods, such as clothing and related items.

....
This case was written by J. David Hunger for *Strategic Management and Business Policy*, 12th edition and for *Concepts in Strategic Management and Business Policy*, 12th edition. Copyright © 2008 by J. David Hunger. Reprinted by permission. References available upon request.

Kmart was also challenged by "category killers" that competed in only one or a few industry categories, but in greater depth within any category than could any department store. Some of these were Toys "R" Us, Home Depot, Lowe's, and drug stores such as Rite Aid, CVS, Eckerd, and Walgreens.

Kmart had been established in 1962 by its parent company S.S. Kresge as a discount department store offering the most variety of goods at the lowest prices. Unlike Sears, the company chose not to locate in large shopping malls but to establish its discount stores in highly visible corner locations. During the 1960s, '70s, and '80s, Kmart prospered. By 1990, however, when Wal-Mart first surpassed Kmart in annual sales, Kmart's stores had become dated and lost their appeal. Other well-known discount stores, such as Korvette's, Grant's, Woolco, Ames, Bradlees, and Montgomery Ward, had gone out of business as the industry had consolidated and reached maturity. Attempting to avoid this fate, Kmart management updated and enlarged the stores, added name brands, and hired Martha Stewart as its lifestyle consultant. None of these changes improved Kmart's financial situation. By the time it declared bankruptcy, it had lost money in five of the past 10 years.

Out of bankruptcy, Kmart became profitable—primarily by closing or selling (to Sears and Home Depot) around 600 of its retail stores. Management had been unable to invigorate sales in its stores. Declared guilty of insider trading, Martha Stewart went to prison just before the 2004 Christmas season. In a surprise move, Edward Lampert, Kmart's Chairman of the Board and a controlling shareholder of Kmart, initiated the acquisition of Sears by Kmart for $11 billion in November 2004. The new company was to be called Sears Holdings Corporation. Even though management predicted that the combined company's costs could be reduced by $500 million annually within three years through supplier and administrative economies, analysts wondered how these two struggling firms could ever be successful.

By the end of 2007, the stock of Sears Holdings had fallen to 111 from its peak of 195 earlier in the year. Like many retailers, both Sears and Kmart struggled to attract shoppers in an overcrowded industry and a slumping economy. Sears Holdings did, however, have $1.5 billion in cash, a significant advantage during lean times, and more than its rivals J.C. Penney, Kohl's, and Macy's combined. The company's debt load was only 25% of the total capital on its balance sheet, compared to 46% for Penney's and 53% for Macy's. It also had significant real estate assets on its balance sheet. For example, Sears owned outright 518 of its 816 locations and many of the Kmart stores were located in strip malls close to large cities. Since fewer shopping malls were now being built, it was becoming harder to find space for "big-box" retailers in metropolitan areas.

The most recent quarterly results for 2007 of Sears Holdings reported the third straight quarter of deteriorating profit margins and same-store sales. After months of cutting the number of employees and reducing other expenses, industry analysts felt that there was little left to cut. They were also concerned that management had failed to invest in store improvements. Sears Holdings had just launched a bid in November 2007 to purchase Restoration Hardware, a home-goods retailer. Even though Restoration Hardware was also facing sluggish sales, it was thought that Sears' management could use the acquisition to create an upscale boutique within its stores.

PART 4

Strategy
Implementation
and
Control

CHAPTER 9

strategy implementation: organizing for Action

For nearly five decades, Wal-Mart's "everyday low prices" and low cost position had enabled it to rapidly grow to dominate North America's retailing landscape. By 2006, however, its U.S. division generated only 1.9% growth in its same-store sales. By 2007, Target, Costco, Kroger, Safeway, Walgreens, CVS, and Best Buy were all growing faster than Wal-Mart. At about the same time, Microsoft, whose software had grown to dominate personal computers worldwide, saw its revenue growth slow to just 8% in 2005. The company's stock price had been flat since 2002, an indication that investors no longer perceived Microsoft as a growth company. What had happened to these two successful companies? Was this an isolated phenomenon? What could be done, if anything, to reinvigorate these giants?[1]

A research study by Matthew Olson, Derek van Bever, and Seth Verry attempts to provide an answer. After analyzing the experiences of 500 successful companies over a 50-year period, they found that 87% of the firms had suffered one or more serious declines in sales and profits. This included a diverse set of corporations, such as Levi Strauss, 3M, Apple, Bank One, Caterpillar, Daimler-Benz, Toys"R"Us, and Volvo. After years of prolonged growth in sales and profits, revenue growth at each of these firms suddenly stopped and even turned negative! Olson, van Bever, and Verry called these long-term reversals in company growth *stall points*. On average, corporations lost 74% of their market capitalization in the decade surrounding a growth stall. Even though the CEO and other members of top management were typically replaced, only 46% of the firms were able to return to moderate or high growth within the decade. When slow growth was allowed to persist for more than 10 years, the delay was usually fatal. Only 7% of this group was able to return to moderate or high growth.[2]

At Levi Strauss & Company, for example, sales topped $7 billion in 1996—extending growth that had more than doubled over the previous decade. From that high-water mark, sales plummeted until they reached $4.6 in 2000—a 35% decline. Market share in its U.S. jeans market dropped from 31% in 1990 to 14% by 2000. Its market value fell from $14 billion to $8 billion during these four years. After replacing management, the company underwent a companywide transformation, but by 2008 it had yet to return to growth.

Learning Objectives

After reading this chapter, you should be able to:

- Develop programs, budgets, and procedures to implement strategic change
- Understand the importance of achieving synergy during strategy implementation
- List the stages of corporate development and the structure that characterizes each stage
- Identify the blocks to changing from one stage to another

- Construct matrix and network structures to support flexible and nimble organizational strategies
- Decide when and if programs such as reengineering, Six Sigma, and job redesign are appropriate methods of strategy implementation
- Understand the centralization versus decentralization issue in multinational corporations

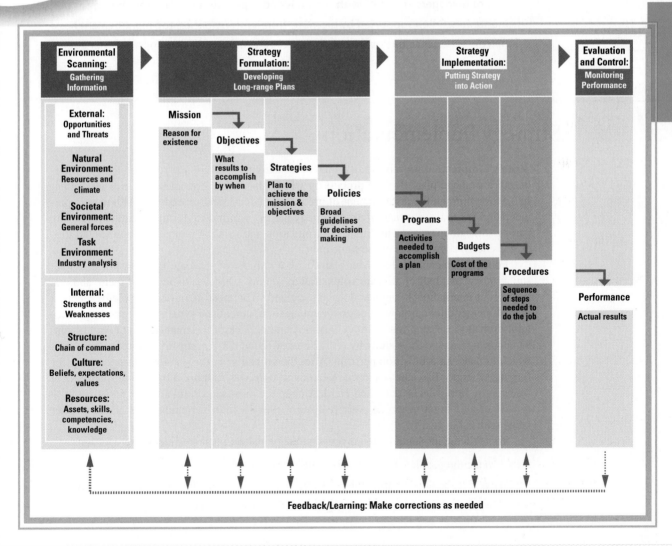

| Environmental Scanning: Gathering Information | Strategy Formulation: Developing Long-range Plans | Strategy Implementation: Putting Strategy into Action | Evaluation and Control: Monitoring Performance |

External: Opportunities and Threats

Natural Environment: Resources and climate

Societal Environment: General forces

Task Environment: Industry analysis

Internal: Strengths and Weaknesses

Structure: Chain of command

Culture: Beliefs, expectations, values

Resources: Assets, skills, competencies, knowledge

Mission — Reason for existence

Objectives — What results to accomplish by when

Strategies — Plan to achieve the mission & objectives

Policies — Broad guidelines for decision making

Programs — Activities needed to accomplish a plan

Budgets — Cost of the programs

Procedures — Sequence of steps needed to do the job

Performance — Actual results

Feedback/Learning: Make corrections as needed

According to Olson, van Bever, and Verry, these stall points occurred primarily because of a poor choice in strategy or organizational design. The root causes fell into four categories:

1. **Premium position backfires:** This happens to a firm that has developed a premium position in the market, but is unable to respond effectively to new, low-cost competitors or a shift in customer valuation of product features. Management teams go through a process of disdain, denial, and rationalization that precedes the fall.

2. **Innovation management breaks down:** Management processes for updating existing products and creating new ones falter and become systemic inefficiencies.

3. **Core business abandoned:** Management fails to exploit growth opportunities in existing core businesses and instead engages in growth initiatives in areas remote from existing customers, products, and distribution channels.

4. **Talent and capabilities run short:** Strategies are not executed properly because of a lack of managers and staff with the skills and capabilities needed for strategy implementation. Often supported by promote-from-within policies, top management has a narrow experience base, which too often replicates the skill set of past top managers.[3]

9.1 Strategy Implementation

Strategy implementation is the sum total of the activities and choices required for the execution of a strategic plan. It is the process by which objectives, strategies, and policies are put into action through the development of programs, budgets, and procedures. Although implementation is usually considered after strategy has been formulated, implementation is a key part of strategic management. Strategy formulation and strategy implementation should thus be considered as two sides of the same coin.

Poor implementation has been blamed for a number of strategic failures. For example, studies show that half of all acquisitions fail to achieve what was expected of them, and one out of four international ventures does not succeed.[4] The most-mentioned problems reported in post-merger integration were poor communication, unrealistic synergy expectations, structural problems, missing master plan, lost momentum, lack of top management commitment, and unclear strategic fit. A study by A. T. Kearney found that a company has just two years in which to make an acquisition perform. After the second year, the window of opportunity for forging synergies has mostly closed. Kearney's study was supported by further independent research by Bert, MacDonald, and Herd. Among the most successful acquirers studied, 70% to 85% of all merger synergies were realized within the first 12 months, with the remainder being realized in year two.[5]

To begin the implementation process, strategy makers must consider these questions:

- *Who* are the people who will carry out the strategic plan?
- *What* must be done to align the company's operations in the new intended direction?
- *How* is everyone going to work together to do what is needed?

These questions and similar ones should have been addressed initially when the pros and cons of strategic alternatives were analyzed. They must also be addressed again before appropriate implementation plans can be made. Unless top management can answer these basic questions satisfactorily, even the best planned strategy is unlikely to provide the desired outcome.

A survey of 93 Fortune 500 firms revealed that more than half of the corporations experienced the following 10 problems when they attempted to implement a strategic change. These problems are listed in order of frequency:

1. Implementation took more time than originally planned.
2. Unanticipated major problems arose.
3. Activities were ineffectively coordinated.
4. Competing activities and crises took attention away from implementation.
5. The involved employees had insufficient capabilities to perform their jobs.
6. Lower-level employees were inadequately trained.
7. Uncontrollable external environmental factors created problems.
8. Departmental managers provided inadequate leadership and direction.
9. Key implementation tasks and activities were poorly defined.
10. The information system inadequately monitored activities.[6]

9.2 Who Implements Strategy?

Depending on how a corporation is organized, those who implement strategy will probably be a much more diverse set of people than those who formulate it. In most large, multi-industry corporations, the implementers are everyone in the organization. Vice presidents of functional areas and directors of divisions or strategic business units (SBUs) work with their subordinates to put together large-scale implementation plans. Plant managers, project managers, and unit heads put together plans for their specific plants, departments, and units. Therefore, every operational manager down to the first-line supervisor and every employee is involved in some way in the implementation of corporate, business, and functional strategies.

Many of the people in the organization who are crucial to successful strategy implementation probably had little to do with the development of the corporate and even business strategy. Therefore, they might be entirely ignorant of the vast amount of data and work that went into the formulation process. Unless changes in mission, objectives, strategies, and policies and their importance to the company are communicated clearly to all operational managers, there can be a lot of resistance and foot-dragging. Managers might hope to influence top management into abandoning its new plans and returning to its old ways. This is one reason why involving people from all organizational levels in the formulation and implementation of strategy tends to result in better organizational performance.[7]

9.3 What Must Be Done?

The managers of divisions and functional areas work with their fellow managers to develop programs, budgets, and procedures for the implementation of strategy. They also work to achieve synergy among the divisions and functional areas in order to establish and maintain a company's distinctive competence.

DEVELOPING PROGRAMS, BUDGETS, AND PROCEDURES

Strategy implementation involves establishing programs to create a series of new organizational activities, budgets to allocate funds to the new activities, and procedures to handle the day-to-day details.

Programs

The purpose of a **program** is to make a strategy action oriented. For example, when Xerox Corporation undertook a turnaround strategy, it needed to significantly reduce its costs and expenses. Management introduced a program called *Lean Six Sigma*. This program was developed to identify and improve a poorly performing process. Xerox first trained its top executives in the program and then launched around 250 individual Six Sigma projects throughout the corporation. The result was $6 million in savings in one year, with even more expected the next.[8] (Six Sigma is explained later in this chapter.)

Most corporate headquarters have around 10 to 30 programs in effect at any one time.[9] One of the programs initiated by Ford Motor Company was to find an organic substitute for petroleum-based foam being used in vehicle seats. For more information on Ford's innovative soybean seat program, see the **Environment Sustainability Issue** feature.

One way to examine the likely impact new programs will have on an existing organization is to compare proposed programs and activities with current programs and activities. Brynjolfsson, Renshaw, and Van Alstyne proposed a **matrix of change** to help managers decide how quickly change should proceed, in what order changes should take place, whether to start at a new site, and whether the proposed systems are stable and coherent. As shown in **Figure 9–1**, target practices (new programs) for a manufacturing plant are drawn on the

ENVIRONMENTAL sustainability issue

FORD'S SOYBEAN SEAT FOAM PROGRAM

The Model T Ford once contained 60 pounds of soybeans in its paint and molded plastic parts. Since that time, petroleum has become the primary ingredient in most plastic parts, including the foam currently used in car and truck seats. Nevertheless, today's manufacturers are looking for ways to replace petroleum-based products with ones made from agricultural crops, as the political, environmental, and economic costs of oil increase. According to Larry Johnson, Director of the Center for Crops Utilization Research at Iowa State University, soy is usually cheaper and more environmentally friendly than petroleum and comes from a renewable agricultural source. With this in mind, Ford's management initiated a program in 2001 with seat supplier Lear Corporation to research soy-based foam as a possible substitute for petroleum-based foam. The program was a huge success. A complete seating system, including suspension systems, contains about 20% soy oil. The new seats were used in the Mustang and other Ford vehicles delivered to auto showrooms beginning August 2007.

Sears Manufacturing Company, a seat supplier to Deere and other companies, licensed the Ford technology to work with Deere in developing soy-based foam for seats on Deere's farm and construction equipment. Deere was already using soy-based materials for parts such as hoods, side panels, and doors on some models of tractors, combines, cotton pickers, and backhoes. According to John Koutsky, Vice President of Product Development, Sears started commercial production of the new seats in 2009 and planned to use soy foam throughout its product line being sold to heavy truck manufacturers like Freightliner and International. "It's good to be green," commented Koutsky.

SOURCE: "Manufacturers Turn to Soy for Cushy Seats," *St. Cloud (MN) Times* (January 26, 2008), p. 3A, and Ford Motor Company Web site (www.Ford.com).

FIGURE 9–1
The Matrix of Change

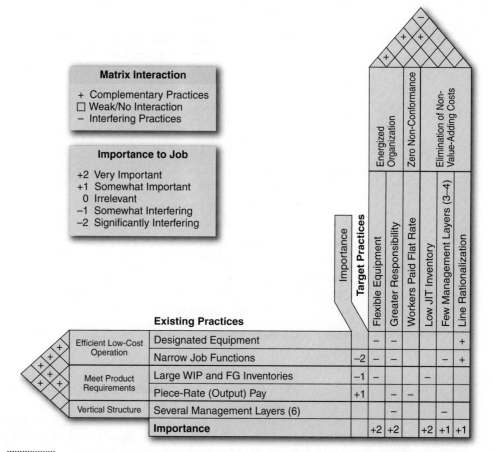

vertical axis and existing practices (current activities) are drawn on the horizontal axis. As shown, any new strategy will likely involve a sequence of new programs and activities. Any one of these may conflict with existing practices/activities—and that creates implementation problems. Use the following steps to create the matrix:

1. Compare the new programs/target practices with each other to see if they are complementary (+), interfering (−), or have no effect on each other (leave blank).

2. Examine existing practices/activities for their interactions with each other using the same symbols as in step 1.

3. Compare each new program/target practice with each existing practice/activity for any interaction effects. Place the appropriate symbols in the cells in the lower-right part of the matrix.

4. Evaluate each program/activity in terms of its relative importance to achieving the strategy or getting the job accomplished.

5. Examine the overall matrix to identify problem areas where proposed programs are likely to either interfere with each other or with existing practices/activities. Note in **Figure 9–1** that the proposed program of installing flexible equipment interferes with the proposed

program of assembly line rationalization. The two new programs need to be changed so that they no longer conflict with each other. Note also that the amount of change necessary to carry out the proposed implementation programs (target practices) is a function of the number of times each program interferes with existing practices/activities. That is, the more minus signs and the fewer plus signs in the matrix, the more implementation problems can be expected.

The matrix of change can be used to address the following types of questions:

- **Feasibility:** Do the proposed programs and activities constitute a coherent, stable system? Are the current activities coherent and stable? Is the transition likely to be difficult?
- **Sequence of execution:** Where should the change begin? How does the sequence affect success? Are there reasonable stopping points?
- **Location:** Are we better off instituting the new programs at a new site, or can we reorganize the existing facilities at a reasonable cost?
- **Pace and nature of change:** Should the change be slow or fast, incremental or radical? Which blocks of current activities must be changed at the same time?
- **Stakeholder evaluations:** Have we overlooked any important activities or interactions? Should we get further input from interested stakeholders? Which new programs and current activities offer the greatest sources of value?

The matrix offers useful guidelines on where, when, and how fast to implement change.[10]

Budgets

After programs have been developed, the **budget** process begins. Planning a budget is the last real check a corporation has on the feasibility of its selected strategy. An ideal strategy might be found to be completely impractical only after specific implementation programs are costed in detail. As an example, once Cadbury Schweppes' management realized how dependent the company was on cocoa from Ghana to continue the company's growth strategy, it developed a program to show cocoa farmers how to increase yields using fertilizers and by working with each other. Ghana produced 70% of Cadbury's worldwide supply of the high-quality cocoa necessary to provide the distinctive taste of Dairy Milk, Crème Egg, and other treats. Management introduced the "Cadbury Cocoa Partnership" on January 28, 2008, and budgeted $87 million for this program over a 10-year period.[11]

Procedures

After the program, divisional, and corporate budgets are approved, **procedures** must be developed. Often called *Standard Operating Procedures (SOPs)*, they typically detail the various activities that must be carried out to complete a corporation's programs. Also known as *organizational routines*, procedures are the primary means by which organizations accomplish much of what they do.[12] Once in place, procedures must be updated to reflect any changes in technology as well as in strategy. For example, a company following a differentiation competitive strategy manages its sales force more closely than does a firm following a low-cost strategy. Differentiation requires long-term customer relationships created out of close interaction with the sales force. An in-depth understanding of the customer's needs provides the foundation for product development and improvement.[13]

In a retail store, procedures ensure that the day-to-day store operations will be consistent over time (that is, next week's work activities will be the same as this week's) and consistent among stores (that is, each store will operate in the same manner as the others). Properly planned procedures can help eliminate poor service by making sure that employees do use not excuses to justify poor behavior toward customers. Even though McDonald's, the fast-food restaurant, has developed very detailed procedures to ensure that customers have high quality service, not every business is so well managed. See **Strategy Highlight 9.1** for the top 10 excuses for bad service.

Before a new strategy can be successfully implemented, current procedures may need to be changed. For example, in order to implement Home Depot's strategic move into services, such as kitchen and bathroom installation, the company had to first improve its productivity. Store managers were drowning in paperwork designed for a smaller and simpler company. "We'd get a fax, an e-mail, a call, and a memo, all on the same project," reported store manager Michael Jones. One executive used just three weeks of memos to wallpaper an entire conference room, floor to ceiling, windows included. CEO Robert Nardelli told his top managers

STRATEGY highlight 9.1

THE TOP TEN EXCUSES FOR BAD SERVICE

Corporations may have official policies stating that the "customer is always right" or "customer is number one," but these quickly become meaningless platitudes unless procedures are developed and communicated to all employees for them to follow when confronted with a problem or a question from a customer. Beware of the top ten excuses for bad service. They can sabotage a company's strategy and send valued customers to the competition. How many times have you heard the following excuses when you received poor service? Or even worse, how many times have you personally given one or all of these excuses?

#10. Customer complaint: Why do I have to wait so long for service? **Excuse:** To get service as good as ours, sometimes you have to wait; our guests expect that.

#9. Customer complaint: Why didn't your service meet what I expected? **Excuse:** Nobody's perfect; we simply can't make every customer happy.

#8. Customer complaint: Why didn't you let us have it "our way"? **Excuse:** We're sorry, but if we did it "your way" for all our customers, we would crash our systems and overextend our already overworked employees.

#7. Customer complaint: Service wasn't as good this time as it was the last time we were here. **Excuse:** Everybody has good days and bad days; we're doing our best to please you, but we can't always be perfect.

#6. Customer complaint: Your place is dirty, dated, and worn. **Excuse:** We do our best to keep it clean and up to date, but we can't afford to follow every customer around to make sure we pick up everything, nor can we refurbish our place all the time.

#5. Customer complaint: I placed my order a while ago, why is it taking so long? **Excuse:** Sorry, but we are very busy right now. You came at our "busy" time and you must be patient.

#4. Customer complaint: Your server did not seem to know what he/she was doing and made a mess of my experience. **Excuse:** Unfortunately, with all the turnover we are having right now, we just didn't have the time to train everyone up to our standards.

#3. Customer complaint: Your employee was rude to me and has a bad attitude. **Excuse:** We do apologize for the unfortunate attitude of a few employees.

#2. Customer complaint: The server didn't seem to be interested in doing what he/she was supposed to do. Why can't she/he do it the right way? **Excuse:** We are sorry. While we trained them to do it the right way, sometimes they just seem to ignore what we taught them.

#1. Customer complaint: We expected something different from your company and we are really disappointed. **Excuse:** You must be misinformed, as we have been successful for a long time and obviously know exactly what our customers want and need.

SOURCE: D. Dickson, R. C. Ford, and B. Laval, "The Top Ten Excuses for Bad Service (and How to Avoid Needing Them)" *Organizational Dynamics*, Vol. 34, Issue 2 (2005), pp. 168–181.

to eliminate duplicate communications and streamline work projects. Directives not related to work orders had to be sent separately and only once a month. The company also spent $2 million on workload-management software.[14]

ACHIEVING SYNERGY

One of the goals to be achieved in strategy implementation is synergy between and among functions and business units. This is the reason corporations commonly reorganize after an acquisition. **Synergy** is said to exist for a divisional corporation if the return on investment (ROI) of each division is greater than what the return would be if each division were an independent business. According to Goold and Campbell, synergy can take place in one of six forms:

- **Shared know-how:** Combined units often benefit from sharing knowledge or skills. This is a leveraging of core competencies. One reason that Procter & Gamble purchased Gillette was to combine P&G's knowledge of the female consumer with Gillette's knowledge of the male consumer.

- **Coordinated strategies:** Aligning the business strategies of two or more business units may provide a corporation significant advantage by reducing inter-unit competition and developing a coordinated response to common competitors (horizontal strategy). The merger between Arcelor and Mittal Steel, for example, gave the combined company enhanced R&D capabilities and wider global coverage while presenting a common face to the market.

- **Shared tangible resources:** Combined units can sometimes save money by sharing resources, such as a common manufacturing facility or R&D lab. The alliance between Renault and Nissan allowed it to build new factories that would build both Nissan and Renault vehicles.

- **Economies of scale or scope:** Coordinating the flow of products or services of one unit with that of another unit can reduce inventory, increase capacity utilization, and improve market access. This was a reason Delta Airlines bought Northwest Airlines.

- **Pooled negotiating power:** Combined units can combine their purchasing to gain bargaining power over common suppliers to reduce costs and improve quality. The same can be done with common distributors. The acquisitions of Macy's and the May Company enabled Federated Department Stores (which changed its name to Macy's in 2007) to gain purchasing economies for all of its stores.

- **New business creation:** Exchanging knowledge and skills can facilitate new products or services by extracting discrete activities from various units and combining them in a new unit or by establishing joint ventures among internal business units. Oracle, for example, purchased a number of software companies in order to create a suite of software code-named "Project Fusion" to help corporations run everything from accounting and sales to customer relations and supply-chain management.[15]

9.4 How Is Strategy to Be Implemented? Organizing for Action

Before plans can lead to actual performance, a corporation should be appropriately organized, programs should be adequately staffed, and activities should be directed toward achieving desired objectives. (Organizing activities are reviewed briefly in this chapter; staffing, directing, and control activities are discussed in **Chapters 10** and **11**.)

Any change in corporate strategy is very likely to require some sort of change in the way an organization is structured and in the kind of skills needed in particular positions. Managers must, therefore, closely examine the way their company is structured in order to decide what, if any, changes should be made in the way work is accomplished. Should activities be grouped differently? Should the authority to make key decisions be centralized at headquarters or decentralized to managers in distant locations? Should the company be managed like a "tight ship" with many rules and controls, or "loosely" with few rules and controls? Should the corporation be organized into a "tall" structure with many layers of managers, each having a narrow span of control (that is, few employees per supervisor) to better control his or her subordinates; or should it be organized into a "flat" structure with fewer layers of managers, each having a wide span of control (that is, more employees per supervisor) to give more freedom to his or her subordinates?

STRUCTURE FOLLOWS STRATEGY

In a classic study of large U.S. corporations such as DuPont, General Motors, Sears, and Standard Oil, Alfred Chandler concluded that **structure follows strategy**—that is, changes in corporate strategy lead to changes in organizational structure.[16] He also concluded that organizations follow a pattern of development from one kind of structural arrangement to another as they expand. According to Chandler, these structural changes occur because the old structure, having been pushed too far, has caused inefficiencies that have become too obviously detrimental to bear. Chandler, therefore, proposed the following as the sequence of what occurs:

1. New strategy is created.
2. New administrative problems emerge.
3. Economic performance declines.
4. New appropriate structure is invented.
5. Profit returns to its previous level.

Chandler found that in their early years, corporations such as DuPont tend to have a centralized functional organizational structure that is well suited to producing and selling a limited range of products. As they add new product lines, purchase their own sources of supply, and create their own distribution networks, they become too complex for highly centralized structures. To remain successful, this type of organization needs to shift to a decentralized structure with several semiautonomous divisions (referred to in **Chapter 5** as *divisional structure*).

Alfred P. Sloan, past CEO of General Motors, detailed how GM conducted such structural changes in the 1920s.[17] He saw decentralization of structure as "centralized policy determination coupled with decentralized operating management." After top management had developed a strategy for the total corporation, the individual divisions (Chevrolet, Buick, and so on) were free to choose how to implement that strategy. Patterned after DuPont, GM found the decentralized multidivisional structure to be extremely effective in allowing the maximum amount of freedom for product development. Return on investment was used as a financial control. (ROI is discussed in more detail in **Chapter 11**.)

Research generally supports Chandler's proposition that structure follows strategy (as well as the reverse proposition that structure influences strategy).[18] As mentioned earlier, changes in the environment tend to be reflected in changes in a corporation's strategy, thus leading to changes in a corporation's structure. In 2008, Arctic Cat, the recreational vehicles firm, reorganized its ATV (all terrain vehicles), snowmobile and parts, and garments and accessories product lines into three separate business units, each led by a general manager focused on expanding the business. True to Chandler's findings, the restructuring of Arctic Cat came after seven consecutive years of record growth followed by its first loss in 25 years.

Strategy, structure, and the environment need to be closely aligned; otherwise, organizational performance will likely suffer.[19] For example, a business unit following a differentiation strategy needs more freedom from headquarters to be successful than does another unit following a low-cost strategy.[20]

Although it is agreed that organizational structure must vary with different environmental conditions, which, in turn, affect an organization's strategy, there is no agreement about an optimal organizational design. What was appropriate for DuPont and General Motors in the 1920s might not be appropriate today. Firms in the same industry do, however, tend to organize themselves similarly to one another. For example, automobile manufacturers tend to emulate General Motors' divisional concept, whereas consumer-goods producers tend to emulate the brand-management concept (a type of matrix structure) pioneered by Procter & Gamble Company. The general conclusion seems to be that firms following similar strategies in similar industries tend to adopt similar structures.

STAGES OF CORPORATE DEVELOPMENT

Successful corporations tend to follow a pattern of structural development as they grow and expand. Beginning with the simple structure of the entrepreneurial firm (in which everybody does everything), successful corporations usually get larger and organize along functional lines, with marketing, production, and finance departments. With continuing success, the company adds new product lines in different industries and organizes itself into interconnected divisions. The differences among these three structural **stages of corporate development** in terms of typical problems, objectives, strategies, reward systems, and other characteristics are specified in detail in **Table 9–1**.

Stage I: Simple Structure

Stage I is typified by the entrepreneur, who founds a company to promote an idea (a product or a service). The entrepreneur tends to make all the important decisions personally and is involved in every detail and phase of the organization. The Stage I company has little formal structure, which allows the entrepreneur to directly supervise the activities of every employee (see **Figure 5–4** for an illustration of the simple, functional, and divisional structures). Planning is usually short range or reactive. The typical managerial functions of planning, organizing, directing, staffing, and controlling are usually performed to a very limited degree, if at all. The greatest strengths of a Stage I corporation are its flexibility and dynamism. The drive of the entrepreneur energizes the organization in its struggle for growth. Its greatest weakness is its extreme reliance on the entrepreneur to decide general strategies as well as detailed procedures. If the entrepreneur falters, the company usually flounders. This is labeled by Greiner as a *crisis of leadership*.[21]

Stage I describes Oracle Corporation, the computer software firm, under the management of its co-founder and CEO Lawrence Ellison. The company adopted a pioneering approach to retrieving data, called Structured Query Language (SQL). When IBM made SQL its standard, Oracle's success was assured. Unfortunately, Ellison's technical wizardry was not sufficient to manage the company. Often working at home, he lost sight of details outside his technical interests. Although the company's sales were rapidly increasing, its financial controls were so weak that management had to restate an entire year's results to rectify irregularities. After the company recorded its first loss, Ellison hired a set of functional managers to run the company while he retreated to focus on new product development.

TABLE 9–1	Factors Differentiating Stage I, II, and III Companies		
Function	**Stage I**	**Stage II**	**Stage III**
1. Sizing up: Major problems	Survival and growth dealing with short-term operating problems.	Growth, rationalization, and expansion of resources, providing for adequate attention to product problems.	Trusteeship in management and investment and control of large, increasing, and diversified resources. Also, important to diagnose and take action on problems at division level.
2. Objectives	Personal and subjective.	Profits and meeting functionally oriented budgets and performance targets.	ROI, profits, earnings per share.
3. Strategy	Implicit and personal; exploitation of immediate opportunities seen by owner-manager.	Functionally oriented moves restricted to "one product" scope; exploitation of one basic product or service field.	Growth and product diversification; exploitation of general business opportunities.
4. Organization: Major characteristic of structure	One unit, "one-man show."	One unit, functionally specialized group.	Multiunit general staff office and decentralized operating divisions.
5. (a) Measurement and control	Personal, subjective control based on simple accounting system and daily communication and observation.	Control grows beyond one person; assessment of functional operations necessary; structured control systems evolve.	Complex formal system geared to comparative assessment of performance measures, indicating problems and opportunities and assessing management ability of division managers.
5. (b) Key performance indicators	Personal criteria, relationships with owner, operating efficiency, ability to solve operating problems.	Functional and internal criteria such as sales, performance compared to budget, size of empire, status in group, personal, relationships, etc.	More impersonal application of comparisons such as profits, ROI, P/E ratio, sales, market share, productivity, product leadership, personnel development, employee attitudes, public responsibility.
6. Reward-punishment system	Informal, personal, subjective; used to maintain control and divide small pool of resources for key performers to provide personal incentives.	More structured; usually based to a greater extent on agreed policies as opposed to personal opinion and relationships.	Allotment by "due process" of a wide variety of different rewards and punishments on a formal and systematic basis. Companywide policies usually apply to many different classes of managers and workers with few major exceptions for individual cases.

SOURCE: Donald H. Thain, "Stages of Corporate Development," *Ivey Business Journal* (formerly *Ivey Business Quarterly*), Winter 1969, p. 37. Copyright © 1969, Ivey Management Services. One time permission to reproduce granted by Ivey Management Services.

Stage II: Functional Structure

Stage II is the point when the entrepreneur is replaced by a team of managers who have functional specializations. The transition to this stage requires a substantial managerial style change for the chief officer of the company, especially if he or she was the Stage I entrepreneur. He or she must learn to delegate; otherwise, having additional staff members yields no benefits to the organization. The previous example of Ellison's retreat from top management at Oracle Corporation to new product development manager is one way that technically brilliant founders are able to get out of the way of the newly empowered functional managers. In Stage II, the corporate strategy favors protectionism through dominance of the industry, often through vertical and horizontal growth. The great strength of a Stage II corporation lies in its concentration and specialization in one industry. Its great weakness is that all its eggs are in one basket.

By concentrating on one industry while that industry remains attractive, a Stage II company, such as Oracle Corporation in computer software, can be very successful. Once a functionally structured firm diversifies into other products in different industries, however, the advantages of the functional structure break down. A *crisis of autonomy* can now develop, in which people managing diversified product lines need more decision-making freedom than top management is willing to delegate to them. The company needs to move to a different structure.

Stage III: Divisional Structure

Stage III is typified by the corporation's managing diverse product lines in numerous industries; it decentralizes the decision-making authority. Stage III organizations grow by diversifying their product lines and expanding to cover wider geographical areas. They move to a divisional structure with a central headquarters and decentralized operating divisions—with each division or business unit a functionally organized Stage II company. They may also use a conglomerate structure if top management chooses to keep its collection of Stage II subsidiaries operating autonomously. A *crisis of control* can now develop, in which the various units act to optimize their own sales and profits without regard to the overall corporation, whose headquarters seems far away and almost irrelevant.

Recently, divisions have been evolving into SBUs to better reflect product-market considerations. Headquarters attempts to coordinate the activities of its operating divisions or SBUs through performance- and results-oriented control and reporting systems and by stressing corporate planning techniques. The units are not tightly controlled but are held responsible for their own performance results. Therefore, to be effective, the company has to have a decentralized decision process. The greatest strength of a Stage III corporation is its almost unlimited resources. Its most significant weakness is that it is usually so large and complex that it tends to become relatively inflexible. General Electric, DuPont, and General Motors are examples of Stage III corporations.

Stage IV: Beyond SBUs

Even with its evolution into SBUs during the 1970s and 1980s, the divisional structure is not the last word in organization structure. The use of SBUs may result in a *red tape crisis* in which the corporation has grown too large and complex to be managed through formal programs and rigid systems, and procedures take precedence over problem solving.[22] For example, Pfizer's acquisitions of Warner-Lambert and Pharmacia resulted in 14 layers of management between scientists and top executives and forced researchers to spend most of their time in meetings.[23] Under conditions of (1) increasing environmental uncertainty, (2) greater use of sophisticated technological production methods and information systems, (3) the increasing size and scope of worldwide business corporations, (4) a greater emphasis on multi-industry competitive strategy, and (5) a more educated cadre of managers and employees, new advanced forms of organizational structure are emerging. These structures emphasize collaboration over competition in the managing of an organization's multiple overlapping projects and developing businesses.

The matrix and the network are two possible candidates for a fourth stage in corporate development—a stage that not only emphasizes horizontal over vertical connections between people and groups but also organizes work around temporary projects in which sophisticated information systems support collaborative activities. According to Greiner, it is likely that this stage of development will have its own crisis as well—a sort of *pressure-cooker crisis*. He predicts that employees in these collaborative organizations will eventually grow emotionally and physically exhausted from the intensity of teamwork and the heavy pressure for innovative solutions.[24]

Blocks to Changing Stages

Corporations often find themselves in difficulty because they are blocked from moving into the next logical stage of development. Blocks to development may be internal (such as lack of resources, lack of ability, or refusal of top management to delegate decision making to others) or external (such as economic conditions, labor shortages, and lack of market growth). For example, Chandler noted in his study that the successful founder/CEO in one stage was rarely the person who created the new structure to fit the new strategy, and as a result, the transition from one stage to another was often painful. This was true of General Motors Corporation under the management of William Durant, Ford Motor Company under Henry Ford I, Polaroid Corporation under Edwin Land, Apple Computer under Steven Jobs, and Sun Microsystems under Scott McNealy.

Entrepreneurs who start businesses generally have four tendencies that work very well for small new ventures but become Achilles' heels for these same individuals when they try to manage a larger firm with diverse needs, departments, priorities, and constituencies:

- **Loyalty to comrades:** This is good at the beginning but soon becomes a liability as "favoritism."
- **Task oriented:** Focusing on the job is critical at first but then becomes excessive attention to detail.
- **Single-mindedness:** A grand vision is needed to introduce a new product but can become tunnel vision as the company grows into more markets and products.
- **Working in isolation:** This is good for a brilliant scientist but disastrous for a CEO with multiple constituencies.[25]

This difficulty in moving to a new stage is compounded by the founder's tendency to maneuver around the need to delegate by carefully hiring, training, and grooming his or her own team of managers. The team tends to maintain the founder's influence throughout the organization long after the founder is gone. This is what happened at Walt Disney Productions when the family continued to emphasize Walt's policies and plans long after he was dead. Although this may often be an organization's strength, it may also be a weakness—to the extent that the culture supports the status quo and blocks needed change.

ORGANIZATIONAL LIFE CYCLE

Instead of considering stages of development in terms of structure, the organizational life cycle approach places the primary emphasis on the dominant issue facing the corporation. Organizational structure is only a secondary concern. The **organizational life cycle** describes how organizations grow, develop, and eventually decline. It is the organizational equivalent of the product life cycle in marketing. These stages are Birth (Stage I), Growth (Stage II), Maturity (Stage III), Decline (Stage IV), and Death (Stage V). The impact of these stages on corporate strategy and structure is summarized in **Table 9–2.** Note that the first three stages of the organizational life cycle are similar to the three commonly accepted stages of corporate development mentioned previously. The only significant difference is the addition of the Decline and Death stages to complete the cycle. Even though a company's strategy may still be sound, its

TABLE 9–2 Organizational Life Cycle

	Stage I	Stage II	Stage III*	Stage IV	Stage V
Dominant Issue	Birth	Growth	Maturity	Decline	Death
Popular Strategies	Concentration in a niche	Horizontal and vertical growth	Concentric and conglomerate diversification	Profit strategy followed by retrenchment	Liquidation or bankruptcy
Likely Structure	Entrepreneur dominated	Functional management emphasized	Decentralization into profit or investment centers	Structural surgery	Dismemberment of structure

NOTE: *An organization may enter a Revival phase either during the Maturity or Decline stages and thus extend the organization's life.

aging structure, culture, and processes may be such that they prevent the strategy from being executed properly. Its core competencies become *core rigidities* that are no longer able to adapt to changing conditions—thus the company moves into Decline.[26]

Movement from Growth to Maturity to Decline and finally to Death is not, however, inevitable. A Revival phase may occur sometime during the Maturity or Decline stages. The corporation's life cycle can be extended by managerial and product innovations.[27] Developing new combinations of existing resources to introduce new products or acquiring new resources through acquisitions can enable firms with declining performance to regain growth—so long as the action is valuable and difficult to imitate.[28] This can occur during the implementation of a turnaround strategy.[29] Nevertheless, the fact that firms in decline are less likely to search for new technologies suggests that it is difficult to revive a company in decline.[30]

Eastman Kodak is an example of a firm in decline that has been attempting to develop new combinations of its existing resources to introduce new products, and thus, revive the corporation. When Antonio Perez left Hewlett-Packard to become Kodak's President in 2003, Kodak was in the midst of its struggle to make the transition from chemical film technology to digital technology and digital cameras. Instead of focusing the company's efforts on acquisitions to find growth, Perez looked at technologies that Kodak already owned, but was not utilizing. He noticed that Kodak scientists had developed new ink to yield photo prints with vivid colors that would last a lifetime. He suddenly realized that Kodak's distinctive competence was not in digital photography, where other competitors led the market, but in color printing. Perez initiated project *Goza* to go head to head with HP in the consumer inkjet printer business. In 2007, Kodak unveiled its new line of multipurpose machines that not only handled photographs and documents, but also made copies and sent faxes. The printers were designed to print high-quality photos with ink that would stay vibrant for 100 rather than the usual 15 years. Most importantly, replacement ink cartridges would cost half the price of competitors' cartridges. According to Perez, "We think it will give us the opportunity to disrupt the industry's business model and address consumers' key dissatisfaction: the high cost of ink." Perez then predicted that Kodak's inkjet printers would become a multibillion-dollar product line.[31]

Unless a company is able to resolve the critical issues facing it in the Decline stage, it is likely to move into Stage V, Death—also known as bankruptcy. This is what happened to Montgomery Ward, Pan American Airlines, Macy's Department Stores, Baldwin-United, Eastern Airlines, Colt's Manufacturing, Orion Pictures, and Wheeling-Pittsburgh Steel, as well as many other firms. As in the cases of Johns-Manville, International Harvester, Macy's, and Kmart—all of which went bankrupt—a corporation can rise like a phoenix from its own ashes and live again under the same or a different name. The company may be reorganized or liquidated, depending on individual circumstances. For example, Kmart emerged from Chapter 11 bankruptcy in 2003 with a new CEO and a plan to sell a number of its stores to

Home Depot and Sears. These sales earned the company close to $1 billion. Although store sales continued to erode, Kmart had sufficient cash reserves to continue with its turnaround.[32] It used that money to acquire Sears in 2005. Unfortunately, however, fewer than 20% of firms entering Chapter 11 bankruptcy in the United States emerge as going concerns; the rest are forced into liquidation.[33]

Few corporations will move through these five stages in order. Some corporations, for example, might never move past Stage II. Others, such as General Motors, might go directly from Stage I to Stage III. A large number of entrepreneurial ventures jump from Stage I or II directly into Stage IV or V. Hayes Microcomputer Products, for example, went from the Growth to Decline stage under its founder Dennis Hayes. The key is to be able to identify indications that a firm is in the process of changing stages and to make the appropriate strategic and structural adjustments to ensure that corporate performance is maintained or even improved.

ADVANCED TYPES OF ORGANIZATIONAL STRUCTURES

The basic structures (simple, functional, divisional, and conglomerate) are discussed in **Chapter 5** and summarized under the first three stages of corporate development in this chapter. A new strategy may require more flexible characteristics than the traditional functional or divisional structure can offer. Today's business organizations are becoming less centralized with a greater use of cross-functional work teams. **Table 9–3** depicts some of the changing structural characteristics of modern corporations. Although many variations and hybrid structures contain these characteristics, two forms stand out: the matrix structure and the network structure.

Matrix Structure

Most organizations find that organizing around either functions (in the functional structure) or products and geography (in the divisional structure) provides an appropriate organizational structure. The matrix structure, in contrast, may be very appropriate when organizations conclude that neither functional nor divisional forms, even when combined with horizontal linking mechanisms such as SBUs, are right for their situations. In **matrix structures,** functional and product forms are combined simultaneously at the same level of the organization. (See **Figure 9–2.**) Employees have two superiors, a product or project manager, and a functional manager. The "home" department—that is, engineering, manufacturing, or sales—is usually functional and is reasonably permanent. People from these functional units are often assigned temporarily to one or more product units or projects. The product units or projects are usually temporary and act like divisions in that they are differentiated on a product-market basis.

TABLE 9–3	Old Organization Design	New Organization Design
Changing Structural Characteristics of Modern Corporations	One large corporation	Minibusiness units and cooperative relationships
	Vertical communication	Horizontal communication
	Centralized, top-down decision making	Decentralized participative decision making
	Vertical integration	Outsourcing and virtual organizations
	Work/quality teams	Autonomous work teams
	Functional work teams	Cross-functional work teams
	Minimal training	Extensive training
	Specialized job design focused on individuals	Value-chain team-focused job design

SOURCE: Reprinted from *RESEARCH IN ORGANIZATIONAL CHANGE AND DEVELOPMENT*, Vol. 7, No. 1, 1993, Macy and Izumi, "Organizational Change, Design, and Work Innovation: A Meta-Analysis of 131 North American Field Studies—1961–1991," p. 298. Copyright © 1993 with permission from Elsevier.

FIGURE 9–2
**Matrix
and Network
Structures**

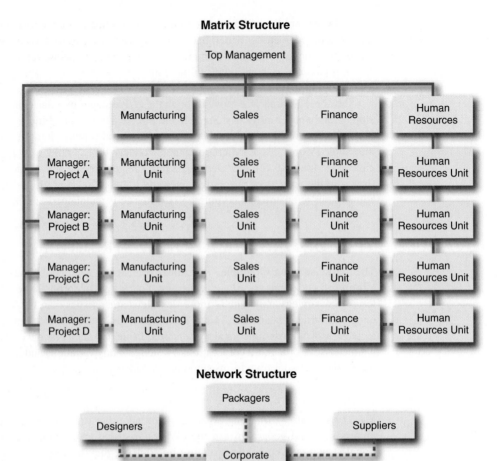

Pioneered in the aerospace industry, the matrix structure was developed to combine the stability of the functional structure with the flexibility of the product form. The matrix structure is very useful when the external environment (especially its technological and market aspects) is very complex and changeable. It does, however, produce conflicts revolving around duties, authority, and resource allocation. To the extent that the goals to be achieved are vague and the technology used is poorly understood, a continuous battle for power between product and functional managers is likely. The matrix structure is often found in an organization or SBU when the following three conditions exist:

- Ideas need to be cross-fertilized across projects or products.

- Resources are scarce.

- Abilities to process information and to make decisions need to be improved.[34]

Davis and Lawrence, authorities on the matrix form of organization, propose that *three distinct phases* exist in the development of the matrix structure:[35]

1. **Temporary cross-functional task forces:** These are initially used when a new product line is being introduced. A project manager is in charge as the key horizontal link. J&J's experience with cross-functional teams in its drug group led it to emphasize teams crossing multiple units.

2. **Product/brand management:** If the cross-functional task forces become more permanent, the project manager becomes a product or brand manager and a second phase begins. In this arrangement, function is still the primary organizational structure, but product or brand managers act as the integrators of semi-permanent products or brands. Considered by many a key to the success of P&G, brand management has been widely imitated by other consumer products firms around the world.

3. **Mature matrix:** The third and final phase of matrix development involves a true dual-authority structure. Both the functional and product structures are permanent. All employees are connected to both a vertical functional superior and a horizontal product manager. Functional and product managers have equal authority and must work well together to resolve disagreements over resources and priorities. Boeing, Philips, and TRW Systems are example of companies that use a mature matrix.

Network Structure–The Virtual Organization

A newer and somewhat more radical organizational design, the **network structure** (see **Figure 9–2**) is an example of what could be termed a "non-structure" because of its virtual elimination of in-house business functions. Many activities are outsourced. A corporation organized in this manner is often called a **virtual organization** because it is composed of a series of project groups or collaborations linked by constantly changing nonhierarchical, cobweb-like electronic networks.[36]

The network structure becomes most useful when the environment of a firm is unstable and is expected to remain so.[37] Under such conditions, there is usually a strong need for innovation and quick response. Instead of having salaried employees, the company may contract with people for a specific project or length of time. Long-term contracts with suppliers and distributors replace services that the company could provide for itself through vertical integration. Electronic markets and sophisticated information systems reduce the transaction costs of the marketplace, thus justifying a "buy" over a "make" decision. Rather than being located in a single building or area, the organization's business functions are scattered worldwide. The organization is, in effect, only a shell, with a small headquarters acting as a "broker," electronically connected to some completely owned divisions, partially owned subsidiaries, and other independent companies. In its ultimate form, a network organization is a series of independent firms or business units linked together by computers in an information system that designs, produces, and markets a product or service.[38]

Entrepreneurial ventures often start out as network organizations. For example, Randy and Nicole Wilburn of Dorchester, Massachusetts, run real estate, consulting, design, and baby food companies out of their home. Nicole, a stay-at-home mom and graphic designer, farms out design work to freelancers and cooks her own line of organic baby food. For $300, an Indian artist designed the logo for Nicole's "Baby Fresh Organic Baby Foods." A London freelancer wrote promotional materials. Instead of hiring a secretary, Randy hired "virtual assistants" in Jerusalem to transcribe voice mail, update his Web site, and design PowerPoint graphics. Retired brokers in Virginia and Michigan deal with his real estate paperwork.[39]

Large companies such as Nike, Reebok, and Benetton use the network structure in their operations function by subcontracting (outsourcing) manufacturing to other companies in low-cost locations around the world. For control purposes, the Italian-based Benetton maintains what it calls an "umbilical cord" by assuring production planning for all its subcontractors, planning materials requirements for them, and providing them with bills of labor and standard prices and costs, as well as technical assistance to make sure their quality is up to Benetton's standards.

The network organizational structure provides an organization with increased flexibility and adaptability to cope with rapid technological change and shifting patterns of international trade and competition. It allows a company to concentrate on its distinctive competencies, while gathering efficiencies from other firms that are concentrating their efforts in their areas of expertise. The network does, however, have disadvantages. Some believe that the network is really only a transitional structure because it is inherently unstable and subject to tensions.[40] The availability of numerous potential partners can be a source of trouble. Contracting out individual activities to separate suppliers/distributors may keep the firm from discovering any internal synergies by combining these activities. If a particular firm overspecializes on only a few functions, it runs the risk of choosing the wrong functions and thus becoming noncompetitive.

Cellular/Modular Organization: A New Type of Structure?

Some authorities in the field propose that the evolution of organizational forms is leading from the matrix and the network to the cellular (also called modular) organizational form. According to Miles and Snow et al., "a **cellular organization** is composed of cells (self-managing teams, autonomous business units, etc.) which can operate alone but which can interact with other cells to produce a more potent and competent business mechanism." This combination of independence and interdependence allows the cellular/modular organizational form to generate and share the knowledge and expertise needed to produce continuous innovation. The cellular/modular form includes the dispersed entrepreneurship of the divisional structure, customer responsiveness of the matrix, and self-organizing knowledge and asset sharing of the network.[41] Bombardier, for example, broke up the design of its Continental business jet into 12 parts provided by internal divisions and external contractors. The cockpit, center, and forward fuselage were produced in-house, but other major parts were supplied by manufacturers spread around the globe. The cellular/modular structure is used when it is possible to break up a company's products into self-contained modules or cells and where interfaces can be specified such that the cells/modules work when they are joined together.[42] The cellular/modular structure is similar to a current trend in industry of using internal joint ventures to temporarily combine specialized expertise and skills within a corporation to accomplish a task which individual units alone could not accomplish.[43]

The impetus for such a new structure is the pressure for a continuous process of innovation in all industries. Each cell/module has an entrepreneurial responsibility to the larger organization. Beyond knowledge creation and sharing, the cellular/modular form adds value by keeping the firm's total knowledge assets more fully in use than any other type of structure.[44] It is beginning to appear in firms that are focused on rapid product and service innovation—providing unique or state-of-the-art offerings in industries such as automobile manufacture, bicycle production, consumer electronics, household appliances, power tools, computing products, and software.[45]

REENGINEERING AND STRATEGY IMPLEMENTATION

Reengineering is the radical redesign of business processes to achieve major gains in cost, service, or time. It is not in itself a type of structure, but it is an effective program to implement a turnaround strategy.

Business process reengineering strives to break away from the old rules and procedures that develop and become ingrained in every organization over the years. They may be a combination of policies, rules, and procedures that have never been seriously questioned because they were established years earlier. These may range from "Credit decisions are made by the credit department" to "Local inventory is needed for good customer service." These rules of organization and work design may have been based on assumptions about technology, people, and organizational goals that may no longer be relevant. Rather than attempting to fix existing problems through minor adjustments and fine-tuning of existing processes, the key to reengineering is asking "If this were a new company, how would we run this place?"

Michael Hammer, who popularized the concept of reengineering, suggests the following principles for reengineering:

- **Organize around outcomes, not tasks:** Design a person's or a department's job around an objective or outcome instead of a single task or series of tasks.

- **Have those who use the output of the process perform the process:** With computer-based information systems, processes can now be reengineered so that the people who need the result of the process can do it themselves.

- **Subsume information-processing work into the real work that produces the information:** People or departments that produce information can also process it for use instead of just sending raw data to others in the organization to interpret.

- **Treat geographically dispersed resources as though they were centralized:** With modern information systems, companies can provide flexible service locally while keeping the actual resources in a centralized location for coordination purposes.

- **Link parallel activities instead of integrating their results:** Instead of having separate units perform different activities that must eventually come together, have them communicate while they work so that they can do the integrating.

- **Put the decision point where the work is performed and build control into the process:** The people who do the work should make the decisions and be self-controlling.

- **Capture information once and at the source:** Instead of having each unit develop its own database and information processing activities, the information can be put on a network so that all can access it.[46]

Studies of the performance of reengineering programs show mixed results. Several companies have had success with business process reengineering. For example, the Mossville Engine Center, a business unit of Caterpillar Inc., used reengineering to decrease process cycle times by 50%, reduce the number of process steps by 45%, reduce human effort by 8%, and improve cross-divisional interactions and overall employee decision making.[47]

One study of North American financial firms found that "the average reengineering project took 15 months, consumed 66 person-months of effort, and delivered cost savings of 24%."[48] In a survey of 782 corporations using reengineering, 75% of the executives said their companies had succeeded in reducing operating expenses and increasing productivity.[49] A study of 134 large and small Canadian companies found that reengineering programs resulted in (1) an increase in productivity and product quality, (2) cost reductions, and (3) an increase in overall organization quality, for both large and small firms.[50] Other studies report, however, that anywhere from 50% to 70% of reengineering programs fail to achieve their objectives.[51] Reengineering thus appears to be more useful for redesigning specific processes like order entry, than for changing an entire organization.[52]

SIX SIGMA

Originally conceived by Motorola as a quality improvement program in the mid-1980s, Six Sigma has become a cost-saving program for all types of manufacturers. Briefly, **Six Sigma** is an analytical method for achieving near-perfect results on a production line. Although the emphasis is on reducing product variance in order to boost quality and efficiency, it is increasingly being applied to accounts receivable, sales, and R&D. In statistics, the Greek letter *sigma* denotes variation in the standard bell-shaped curve. One sigma equals 690,000 defects per 1 million. Most companies are able to achieve only three sigma, or 66,000 errors per million. Six Sigma reduces the defects to only 3.4 per million—thus saving money by preventing waste. The process of Six Sigma encompasses five steps.

1. *Define* a process where results are poorer than average.
2. *Measure* the process to determine exact current performance.
3. *Analyze* the information to pinpoint where things are going wrong.
4. *Improve* the process and eliminate the error.
5. *Establish* controls to prevent future defects from occurring.[53]

Savings attributed to Six Sigma programs have ranged from 1.2% to 4.5% of annual revenue for a number of Fortune 500 firms. Firms that have successfully employed Six Sigma are General Electric, Allied Signal, ABB, and Ford Motor Company.[54] About 35% of U.S. companies now have a Six Sigma program in place.[55] At Dow Chemical, each Six Sigma project has resulted in cost savings of $500,000 in the first year. According to Jack Welch, GE's past CEO, Six Sigma is an appropriate change program for the entire organization.[56] Six Sigma experts at 3M have been able to speed up R&D and analyze why its top sales people sold more than others. A disadvantage of the program is that training costs in the beginning may outweigh any savings. The expense of compiling and analyzing data, especially in areas where a process cannot be easily standardized, may exceed what is saved.[57] Another disadvantage is that Six Sigma can lead to less-risky incremental innovation based on previous work than on riskier "blue-sky" projects.[58]

A new program called *Lean Six Sigma* is becoming increasingly popular in companies. This program incorporates the statistical approach of Six Sigma with the lean manufacturing program originally developed by Toyota. Like reengineering, it includes the removal of unnecessary steps in any process and fixing those that remain. This is the "lean" addition to Six Sigma. Xerox used Lean Six Sigma to resolve a problem with a $500,000 printing press it had just introduced. Teams from supply, manufacturing, and R&D used Lean Six Sigma to find the cause of the problem and to resolve it by working with a supplier to change the chemistry of the oil on a roller.[59]

DESIGNING JOBS TO IMPLEMENT STRATEGY

Organizing a company's activities and people to implement strategy involves more than simply redesigning a corporation's overall structure; it also involves redesigning the way jobs are done. With the increasing emphasis on reengineering, many companies are beginning to rethink their work processes with an eye toward phasing unnecessary people and activities out of the process. Process steps that have traditionally been performed sequentially can be improved by performing them concurrently using cross-functional work teams. Harley-Davidson, for example, has managed to reduce total plant employment by 25% while reducing by 50% the time needed to build a motorcycle. Restructuring through needing fewer people requires broadening the scope of jobs and encouraging teamwork. The design of jobs and subsequent job performance are, therefore, increasingly being considered as sources of competitive advantage.

Job design refers to the study of individual tasks in an attempt to make them more relevant to the company and to the employee(s). To minimize some of the adverse consequences of task specialization, corporations have turned to new job design techniques: *job enlargement* (combining tasks to give a worker more of the same type of duties to perform), *job rotation* (moving workers through several jobs to increase variety), and *job enrichment* (altering the jobs by giving the worker more autonomy and control over activities). The *job characteristics*

STRATEGY highlight 9.2

DESIGNING JOBS WITH THE JOB CHARACTERISTICS MODEL

The job characteristics model is an advanced approach to job design based on the belief that tasks can be described in terms of certain objective characteristics and that these characteristics affect employee motivation. In order for a job to be motivating, (1) the worker needs to feel a sense of responsibility, feel the task to be meaningful, and receive useful feedback on his or her performance, and (2) the job has to satisfy needs that are important to the worker. The model proposes that managers follow five principles for redesigning work:

1. Combine tasks to increase task variety and to enable workers to identify with what they are doing.

2. Form natural work units to make a worker more responsible and accountable for the performance of the job.

3. Establish client relationships so the worker will know what performance is required and why.

4. Vertically load the job by giving workers increased authority and responsibility over their activities.

5. Open feedback channels by providing workers with information on how they are performing.

Research supports the job characteristics model as a way to improve job performance through job enrichment. Although there are several other approaches to job design, practicing managers seem increasingly to follow the prescriptions of this model as a way of improving productivity and product quality.

....

SOURCE: J. R. Hackman and G. R. Oldham, *Work Redesign* (Reading, MA: Addison-Wesley, 1980), pp. 135–141; G. Johns, J. L. Xie, and Y. Fang, "Mediating and Moderating Effects in Job Design," *Journal of Management* (December 1992), pp. 657–676; R. W. Griffin, "Effects of Work Redesign on Employee Perceptions, Attitudes, and Behaviors: A Long-Term Investigation," *Academy of Management Journal* (June 1991), pp. 425–435.

model is a good example of job enrichment. (See **Strategy Highlight 9.2**.) Although each of these methods has its adherents, no one method seems to work in all situations.

A good example of modern job design is the introduction of team-based production by the glass manufacturer Corning Inc., in its Blacksburg, Virginia, plant. With union approval, Corning reduced job classifications from 47 to 4 to enable production workers to rotate jobs after learning new skills. The workers were divided into 14-member teams that, in effect, managed themselves. The plant had only two levels of management: Plant Manager Robert Hoover and two line leaders who only advised the teams. Employees worked demanding 12 ½-hour shifts, alternating three-day and four-day weeks. The teams made managerial decisions, imposed discipline on fellow workers, and were required to learn three "skill modules" within two years or else lose their jobs. As a result of this new job design, a Blacksburg team, made up of workers with interchangeable skills, can retool a line to produce a different type of filter in only 10 minutes—six times faster than workers in a traditionally designed filter plant. The Blacksburg plant earned a $2 million profit in its first eight months of production instead of losing the $2.3 million projected for the startup period. The plant performed so well that Corning's top management acted to convert the company's 27 other factories to team-based production.[60]

9.5 International Issues in Strategy Implementation

An international company is one that engages in any combination of activities, from exporting/importing to full-scale manufacturing, in foreign countries. A **multinational corporation (MNC)**, in contrast, is a highly developed international company with a deep involvement throughout the world, plus a worldwide perspective in its management and decision making.

For an MNC to be considered global, it must manage its worldwide operations as if they were totally interconnected. This approach works best when the industry has moved from being *multidomestic* (each country's industry is essentially separate from the same industry in other countries) to *global* (each country is a part of one worldwide industry).

The global MNC faces the dual challenge of achieving scale economies through standardization while at the same time responding to local customer differences. According to Spulber in his book, *Global Competitive Strategy*, the forces pushing for *standardization* are:

- Convergence in customer preferences and income across target countries.
- Competition from successful global products.
- Growing customer awareness of international brands.
- Economies of scale.
- Falling trading costs across countries.
- Cultural exchange and business interactions among countries.

The forces pushing for *customization* to local markets are:

- Persistent differences in customer preferences.
- Persistent differences in customer incomes.
- The need to build local brand reputation.
- Competition from successful, innovative domestic companies.
- Variations in trading costs across countries.
- Local regulatory requirements.[61]

The design of an organization's structure is strongly affected by the company's stage of development in international activities and the types of industries in which the company is involved. Strategic alliances may complement or even substitute for an internal functional activity. The issue of centralization versus decentralization becomes especially important for an MNC operating in both multidomestic and global industries.

INTERNATIONAL STRATEGIC ALLIANCES

Strategic alliances, such as joint ventures and licensing agreements, between an MNC and a local partner in a host country are becoming increasingly popular as a means by which a corporation can gain entry into other countries, especially less developed countries. The key to the successful implementation of these strategies is the selection of the local partner. Each party needs to assess not only the strategic fit of each company's project strategy but also the fit of each company's respective resources. A successful joint venture may require as much as two years of prior contacts between the parties. A prior relationship helps to develop a level of trust, which facilitates openness in sharing knowledge and a reduced fear of opportunistic behavior by the alliance partners. This is especially important when the environmental uncertainty is high.[62] Research reveals that firms favor past partners when forming new alliances.[63] Key drivers for strategic fit between alliance partners are the following:

- Partners must agree on fundamental values and have a shared vision about the potential for joint value creation.
- Alliance strategy must be derived from business, corporate, and functional strategy.
- The alliance must be important to both partners, especially to top management.
- Partners must be mutually dependent for achieving clear and realistic objectives.

■ Joint activities must have added value for customers and the partners.

■ The alliance must be accepted by key stakeholders.

■ Partners contribute key strengths but protect core competencies.[64]

STAGES OF INTERNATIONAL DEVELOPMENT

Corporations operating internationally tend to evolve through five common stages, both in their relationships with widely dispersed geographic markets and in the manner in which they structure their operations and programs. These **stages of international development** are:

■ **Stage 1 (Domestic company):** The primarily domestic company exports some of its products through local dealers and distributors in the foreign countries. The impact on the organization's structure is minimal because an export department at corporate headquarters handles everything.

■ **Stage 2 (Domestic company with export division):** Success in Stage 1 leads the company to establish its own sales company with offices in other countries to eliminate the middlemen and to better control marketing. Because exports have now become more important, the company establishes an export division to oversee foreign sales offices.

■ **Stage 3 (Primarily domestic company with international division):** Success in earlier stages leads the company to establish manufacturing facilities in addition to sales and service offices in key countries. The company now adds an international division with responsibilities for most of the business functions conducted in other countries.

■ **Stage 4 (Multinational corporation with multidomestic emphasis):** Now a full-fledged MNC, the company increases its investments in other countries. The company establishes a local operating division or company in the host country, such as Ford of Britain, to better serve the market. The product line is expanded, and local manufacturing capacity is established. Managerial functions (product development, finance, marketing, and so on) are organized locally. Over time, the parent company acquires other related businesses, broadening the base of the local operating division. As the subsidiary in the host country successfully develops a strong regional presence, it achieves greater autonomy and self-sufficiency. The operations in each country are, nevertheless, managed separately as if each is a domestic company.

■ **Stage 5 (MNC with global emphasis):** The most successful MNCs move into a fifth stage in which they have worldwide human resources, R&D, and financing strategies. Typically operating in a global industry, the MNC denationalizes its operations and plans product design, manufacturing, and marketing around worldwide considerations. Global considerations now dominate organizational design. The global MNC structures itself in a matrix form around some combination of geographic areas, product lines, and functions. All managers are responsible for dealing with international as well as domestic issues.

Research provides some support for stages of international development, but it does not necessarily support the preceding sequence of stages. For example, a company may initiate production and sales in multiple countries without having gone through the steps of exporting or having local sales subsidiaries. In addition, any one corporation can be at different stages simultaneously, with different products in different markets at different levels. Firms may also leapfrog across stages to a global emphasis. In addition, most firms that are considered to be stage 5 global MNCs are actually regional. Around 88% of the world's biggest MNCs derive at least half of their sales from their home regions. Just 2% (a total of nine firms) derive 20% or more of their sales from each of the North American, European, and Asian regions.[65]

Developments in information technology are changing the way business is being done internationally. See the **Global Issue** feature for a possible sixth stage of international development, in

GLOBAL issue

MULTIPLE HEADQUARTERS: A SIXTH STAGE OF INTERNATIONAL DEVELOPMENT?

In what could be a sixth stage of international development, an increasing number of MNCs are relocating their headquarters and headquarters functions at multiple locations around the world. Of the 800 corporate headquarters established in 2002, 200 of them were in developing nations. The antivirus software company Trend Micro, for example, spreads its top executives, engineers, and support staff throughout the world to improve its ability to respond to new virus threats. "With the Internet, viruses became global. To fight them, we had to become a global company," explained Chairman Steve Chang. Trend Micro's financial headquarters is in Tokyo, where it went public. Its product development is in Taiwan, and its sales headquarters is in America's Silicon Valley.

C. K. Prahalad, strategy professor at the University of Michigan, proposes that this is a new stage of international development. "There is a fundamental rethinking about what is a multinational company. Does it have a home country? What does headquarters mean? Can you fragment your corporate functions globally?" Corporate headquarters are now becoming virtual with executives and core corporate functions dispersed throughout various world regions. These primarily technology companies are using geography to obtain competitive advantage through the availability of talent or capital, low costs, or proximity to most important customers. Logitech, for example, has its manufacturing headquarters in Taiwan to capitalize on low-cost Asian manufacturing, its business-development headquarters in Switzerland where it has a series of strategic technology partnerships, and a third headquarters in Fremont, California.

....

SOURCES: S. Hamm, "Borders Are So 20th Century," *Business Week* (January 22, 2003), pp. 68–70; "Globalization from the Top Down," *Futurist* (November–December 2003), p. 13.

which an MNC locates its headquarters and key functions at multiple locations around the world.[66] Nevertheless, the stages concept provides a useful way to illustrate some of the structural changes corporations undergo when they increase their involvement in international activities.

CENTRALIZATION VERSUS DECENTRALIZATION

A basic dilemma an MNC faces is how to organize authority centrally so that it operates as a vast interlocking system that achieves synergy and at the same time decentralize authority so that local managers can make the decisions necessary to meet the demands of the local market or host government.[67] To deal with this problem, MNCs tend to structure themselves either along product groups or geographic areas. They may even combine both in a matrix structure—the design chosen by 3M Corporation, Philips, and Asea Brown Boveri (ABB), among others.[68] One side of 3M's matrix represents the company's product divisions; the other side includes the company's international country and regional subsidiaries.

Two examples of the usual international structure are Nestlé and American Cyanamid. Nestlé's structure is one in which significant power and authority have been decentralized to geographic entities. This structure is similar to that depicted in **Figure 9–3,** in which each geographic set of operating companies has a different group of products. In contrast, American Cyanamid has a series of centralized product groups with worldwide responsibilities. To depict Cyanamid's structure, the geographical entities in **Figure 9–3** would have to be replaced by product groups or SBUs.

FIGURE 9–3
Geographic Area
Structure
for an MNC

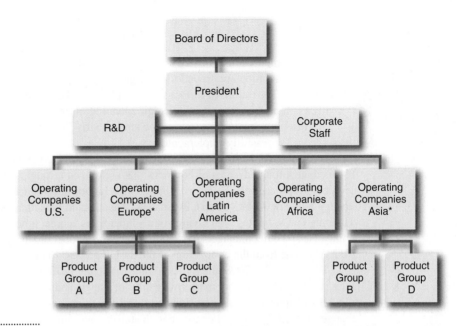

*NOTE: Because of space limitations, product groups for only Europe and Asia are shown here.

The **product-group structure** of American Cyanamid enables the company to introduce and manage a similar line of products around the world. This enables the corporation to centralize decision making along product lines and to reduce costs. The **geographic-area structure** of Nestlé, in contrast, allows the company to tailor products to regional differences and to achieve regional coordination. For instance, Nestlé markets 200 different varieties of its instant coffee, Nescafé. The geographic-area structure decentralizes decision making to the local subsidiaries.

As industries move from being multidomestic to more globally integrated, MNCs are increasingly switching from the geographic-area to the product-group structure. Nestlé, for example, has found that its decentralized area structure had become increasingly inefficient. As a result, operating margins at Nestlé have trailed those at rivals Unilever, Group Danone, and Kraft Foods by as much as 50%. CEO Peter Brabeck-Letmathe acted to eliminate country-by-country responsibilities for many functions. In one instance, he established five centers worldwide to handle most coffee and cocoa purchasing. Nevertheless, Nestlé is still using three different versions of accounting, planning, and inventory software for each of its main regions—Europe, the Americas, and Asia, Oceania, and Africa.[69]

Simultaneous pressures for decentralization to be locally responsive and centralization to be maximally efficient are causing interesting structural adjustments in most large corporations. This is what is meant by the phrase "think globally, act locally." Companies are attempting to decentralize those operations that are culturally oriented and closest to the customers—manufacturing, marketing, and human resources. At the same time, the companies are consolidating less visible internal functions, such as research and development, finance, and information systems, where there can be significant economies of scale.

End of Chapter SUMMARY

Strategy implementation is where "the rubber hits the road." Environmental scanning and strategy formulation are crucial to strategic management but are only the beginning of the process. The failure to carry a strategic plan into the day-to-day operations of the workplace is a major reason why strategic planning often fails to achieve its objectives. It is discouraging to note that in one study nearly 70% of the strategic plans were never successfully implemented.[70]

For a strategy to be successfully implemented, it must be made action oriented. This is done through a series of programs that are funded through specific budgets and contain new detailed procedures. This is what Sergio Marchionne did when he implemented a turnaround strategy as the new Fiat Group CEO in 2004. He attacked the lethargic, bureaucratic system by flattening Fiat's structure and giving younger managers a larger amount of authority and responsibility. He and other managers worked to reduce the number of auto platforms from 19 to six by 2012. The time from the completion of the design process to new car production was cut from 26 to 18 months. By 2008, the Fiat auto unit was again profitable. Marchionne's next step was to revive the other two underperforming units of Lancia and Alfa Romeo.[71]

This chapter explains how jobs and organizational units can be designed to support a change in strategy. We will continue with staffing and directing issues in strategy implementation in the next chapter.

ECO-BITS

- Only 5% of the 30 million tons of annual plastic waste in the U.S. is currently being recycled.[72]
- Cargill is building the first large-scale manufacturing plant to make soybean-based "polyols," the building

blocks of polyurethane. The company says that the use of polyols is a more sustainable option for manufacturers of plastic and ultimately for consumers interested in reducing their environmental footprint.[73]

DISCUSSION QUESTIONS

1. How should a corporation attempt to achieve synergy among functions and business units?

2. How should an owner-manager prepare a company for its movement from Stage I to Stage II?

3. How can a corporation keep from sliding into the Decline stage of the organizational life cycle?

4. Is reengineering just another management fad, or does it offer something of lasting value?

5. How is the cellular/modular structure different from the network structure?

STRATEGIC PRACTICE EXERCISE

The Synergy Game
Yolanda Sarason and Catherine Banbury

Setup

Put three to five chairs on either side of a room, facing each other, in the front of the class. Put a table in the middle, with a bell in the middle of the table.

Procedure

The instructor/moderator divides the class into teams of three to five people. Each team selects a name for itself. The instructor/moderator lists the team names on the board. The first two teams come to the front and sit in the chairs facing each other. The instructor/moderator reads a list of products or services being provided by an actual company. The winning team must identify (1) possible sources of synergy and (2) the actual company being described. For example, if the products/services listed are family restaurants, airline catering, hotels, and retirement centers, the synergy is **standardized food service and hospitality settings** and the company is **The Marriott Corporation**. The first team to successfully name the company *and* the synergy wins the round.

After one practice session, the game begins. Each of the teams is free to discuss the question with other team members. When one of the two teams thinks that it has the answer to both parts of the question, it must be the first to ring the bell in order to announce its answer. If it gives the correct answer, it is deemed the winner of round one. Both parts of the answer must be given for a team to have the correct answer. If a team correctly provides only one part, that answer is still wrong—no partial credit. The instructor/moderator does not say which part of the answer, if either, was correct. The second team then has the opportunity to state the answer. If the second team is wrong, both teams may try once more. If neither chooses to try again, the instructor/moderator may (1) declare

....

SOURCE: This exercise was developed by Professors Yolanda Sarason of Colorado State University and Catherine Banbury of St. Mary's College and Purdue University and presented at the Organizational Behavior Teaching Conference, June 1999. Copyright © 1999 by Yolanda Sarason and Catherine Banbury. Adapted with permission.

no round winner and both teams sit down, (2) allow the next two teams to provide the answer to round one, or (3) go on to the next round with the same two teams. Two new teams then come to the front for the next round. Once all groups have played once, the winning teams play each other. Rounds continue until there is a grand champion. The instructor should provide a suitable prize, such as candy bars, for the winning team.

Note from Wheelen and Hunger

The *Instructors' Manual* for this book contains a list of products and services with their synergy and the name of the company. In case your instructor does not use this exercise, try the following examples:

Example 1: Motorcycles, autos, lawn mowers, generators

Example 2: Athletic footwear, Rockport shoes, Greg Norman clothing, sportswear

For each example, did you guess the company providing these products/services and the synergy obtained? The answers are printed here, upside-down:

Example 2: Marketing and distribution for the athletically-oriented by Reebok

Example 1: Engine technology by Honda

KEY TERMS

budget (p. 324)

cellular/modular organization (p. 336)

geographic-area structure (p. 343)

job design (p. 338)

matrix of change (p. 322)

matrix structure (p. 333)

multinational corporation (MNC) (p. 339)

network structure (p. 335)

organizational life cycle (p. 331)

procedures (p. 324)

product-group structure (p. 343)

program (p. 322)

reengineering (p. 336)

Six Sigma (p. 337)

stages of corporate development (p. 328)

stages of international development (p. 341)

strategy implementation (p. 320)

structure follows strategy (p. 327)

synergy (p. 326)

virtual organization (p. 335)

NOTES

1. A. Bianco, M. Der Hovanesian, L. Young, and P. Gogoi, "Wal-Mart's Midlife Crisis," *Business Week* (April 30, 2007), pp. 46–56; "The Bulldozer of Bentonville Slows," *The Economist* (February 17, 2007), p. 64; D. Kirkpatrick, "Microsoft's New Brain," *Fortune* (May 1, 2006), pp. 56–68; "Spot the Dinosaur," *The Economist* (April 1, 2006), pp. 53–54; J. Greene, "Microsoft's Midlife Crisis," *Business Week* (April 19, 2004), pp. 88–98.

2. M. S. Olson, D. van Bever, and S. Verry, "When Growth Stalls," *Harvard Business Review* (March 2008), pp. 50–61. This phenomenon was called the "burnout syndrome" by G. Probst and S. Raisch in "Organizational Crisis: The Logic of Failure," *Academy of Management Executive* (February 2005), pp. 90–105.

3. Ibid.

4. J. W. Gadella, "Avoiding Expensive Mistakes in Capital Investment," *Long Range Planning* (April 1994), pp. 103–110; B. Voss, "World Market Is Not for Everyone," *Journal of Business Strategy* (July/August 1993), p. 4.

5. A. Bert, T. MacDonald, and T. Herd, "Two Merger Integration Imperatives: Urgency and Execution," *Strategy & Leadership*, Vol. 31, No. 3 (2003), pp. 42–49.

6. L. D. Alexander, "Strategy Implementation: Nature of the Problem," *International Review of Strategic Management*, Vol. 2, No. 1, edited by D. E. Hussey (New York: John Wiley & Sons, 1991), pp. 73–113. See also L. G. Hrebiniak, "Obstacles to Effective Strategy Implementation," *Organizational Dynamics*, Vol. 35, Issue 1 (2006), pp. 12–31 for six obstacles to implementation.

7. L. G. Hrebiniak (2006).

8. F. Arner and A. Aston, "How Xerox Got Up to Speed," *Business Week* (May 3, 2004), pp. 103–104.

9. J. Darragh and A. Campbell, "Why Corporate Initiatives Get Stuck?" *Long Range Planning* (February 2001), pp. 33–52.

10. E. Brynjolfsson, A. A. Renshaw, and M. Van Alstyne, "The Matrix of Change," *Sloan Management Review* (Winter 1997), pp. 37–54.

11. "Cocoa Farming: Fair Enough?" *The Economist* (February 2, 2008), p. 74.

12. M. S. Feldman and B. T. Pentland, "Reconceptualizing Organizational Routines as a Source of Flexibility and Change," *Administrative Science Quarterly* (March 2003), pp. 94–118.

13. S. F. Slater and E. M. Olson, "Strategy Type and Performance: The Influence of Sales Force Management," *Strategic Management Journal* (August 2000), pp. 813–829.

14. B. Grow, "Thinking Outside the Box," *Business Week* (October 25, 2004), pp. 70–72.

15. M. Goold and A. Campbell, "Desperately Seeking Synergy," *Harvard Business Review* (September–October 1998), pp. 131–143.

16. A. D. Chandler, *Strategy and Structure* (Cambridge, MA: MIT Press, 1962).

17. A. P. Sloan, Jr., *My Years with General Motors* (Garden City, NY: Doubleday, 1964).

18. T. L. Amburgey and T. Dacin, "As the Left Foot Follows the Right? The Dynamics of Strategic and Structural Change," *Academy of Management Journal* (December 1994), pp. 1427–1452; M. Ollinger, "The Limits of Growth of the Multidivisional Firm: A Case Study of the U.S. Oil Industry from 1930–90," *Strategic Management Journal* (September 1994), pp. 503–520.

19. D. F. Jennings and S. L. Seaman, "High and Low Levels of Organizational Adaptation: An Empirical Analysis of Strategy, Structure, and Performance," *Strategic Management Journal* (July 1994), pp. 459–475; L. Donaldson, "The Normal Science of Structured Contingency Theory," in *Handbook of Organization Studies*, edited by S. R. Clegg, C. Hardy, and W. R. Nord (London: Sage Publications, 1996), pp. 57–76.

20. A. K. Gupta, "SBU Strategies, Corporate-SBU Relations, and SBU Effectiveness in Strategy Implementation," *Academy of Management Journal* (September 1987), pp. 477–500.

21. L. E. Greiner, "Evolution and Revolution As Organizations Grow," *Harvard Business Review* (May–June 1998), pp. 55–67. This is an updated version of Greiner's classic 1972 article.

22. K. Shimizu and M. A. Hitt, "What Constrains or Facilitates Divestitures of Formerly Acquired Firms? The Effects of Organizational Inertia," *Journal of Management* (February 2005), pp. 50–72.

23. A. Weintraub, "Can Pfizer Prime the Pipeline?" *Business Week* (December 31, 2007), pp. 90–91.

24. Ibid, p. 64. Although Greiner simply labeled this as the "*?" crisis*, the term *pressure-cooker* seems apt.

25. J. Hamm, "Why Entrepreneurs Don't Scale," *Harvard Business Review* (December 2002), pp. 110–115. See also C. B. Gibson and R. M. Rottner, "The Social Foundations for Building a Company Around an Inventor," *Organizational Dynamics*, Vol. 37, Issue 1 (January–March 2008), pp. 21–34.

26. W. P. Barnett, "The Dynamics of Competitive Intensity," *Administrative Science Quarterly* (March 1997), pp. 128–160; D. Miller, *The Icarus Paradox: How Exceptional Companies Bring About Their Own Downfall* (New York: Harper Business, 1990).

27. D. Miller and P. H. Friesen, "A Longitudinal Study of the Corporate Life Cycle," *Management Science* (October 1984), pp. 1161–1183.

28. J. L. Morrow, Jr., D. G. Sirmon, M. A. Hitt, and T. R. Holcomb, "Creating Value in the Face of Declining Performance: Firm Strategies and Organizational Recovery," *Strategic Management Journal* (March 2007), pp. 271–283; C. Zook, "Finding Your Next Core Business," *Harvard Business Review* (April 2007), pp. 66–75.

29. J. P. Sheppard and S. D. Chowdhury, "Riding the Wrong Wave: Organizational Failure as a Failed Turnaround," *Long Range Planning* (June 2005), pp. 239–260.

30. W-R. Chen and K. D. Miller, "Situational and Institutional Determinants of Firms' R&D Search Intensity," *Strategic Management Journal* (April 2007), pp. 369–381.

31. S. Hamm, "Kodak's Moment of Truth," *Business Week* (February 19, 2007), pp. 42–49.

32. R. Berner, "Turning Kmart into a Cash Cow," *Business Week* (July 12, 2004), p. 81.

33. H. Tavakolian, "Bankruptcy: An Emerging Corporate Strategy," *SAM Advanced Management Journal* (Spring 1995), p. 19.

34. L. G. Hrebiniak and W. F. Joyce, *Implementing Strategy* (New York: Macmillan, 1984), pp. 85–86.

35. S. M. Davis and P. R. Lawrence, *Matrix* (Reading, MA: Addison-Wesley, 1977), pp. 11–24.

36. J. G. March, "The Future Disposable Organizations and the Rigidities of Imagination," *Organization* (August/November 1995), p. 434.

37. M. A. Schilling and H. K. Steensma, "The Use of Modular Organizational Forms: An Industry-Level Analysis," *Academy of Management Journal* (December 2001), pp. 1149–1168.

38. M. P. Koza and A. Y. Lewin, "The Coevolution of Network Alliances: A Longitudinal Analysis of an International Professional Service Network," *Organization Science* (September/October 1999), pp. 638–653.

39. P. Engardio, "Mom-and-Pop Multinationals," *Business Week* (July 14 & 21, 2008), pp. 77–78.

40. For more information on managing a network organization, see G. Lorenzoni and C Baden-Fuller, "Creating a Strategic Center to Manage a Web of Partners," *California Management Review* (Spring 1995), pp. 146–163.

41. R. E. Miles, C. C. Snow, J. A. Mathews, G. Miles, and H. J. Coleman, Jr., "Organizing in the Knowledge Age: Anticipating the Cellular Form," *Academy of Management Executive* (November 1997), pp. 7–24.

42. N. Anand and R. L. Daft, "What Is the Right Organization Design?" *Organizational Dynamics*, Vol. 36, No. 4 (2007), pp. 329–344.

43. J. Naylor and M. Lewis, "Internal Alliances: Using Joint Ventures in a Diversified Company," *Long Range Planning* (October 1997), pp. 678–688.

44. G. Hoetker, "Do Modular Products Lead to Modular Organizations?" *Strategic Management Journal* (June 2006), pp. 501–518.

45. Anand and Daft, pp. 336–338.

46. Summarized from M. Hammer, "Reengineering Work: Don't Automate, Obliterate," *Harvard Business Review* (July–August 1990), pp. 104–112.

47. D. Paper, "BPR: Creating the Conditions for Success," *Long Range Planning* (June 1998), pp. 426–435.

48. S. Drew, "BPR in Financial Services: Factors for Success," *Long Range Planning* (October 1994), pp. 25–41.

49. "Do As I Say, Not As I Do," *Journal of Business Strategy* (May/June 1997), pp. 3–4.

50. L. Raymond and S. Rivard, "Determinants of Business Process Reengineering Success in Small and Large Enterprises: An Empirical Study in the Canadian Context," *Journal of Small Business Management* (January 1998), pp. 72–85.

51. K. Grint, "Reengineering History: Social Resonances and Business Process Reengineering," *Organization* (July 1994), pp. 179–201; A. Kleiner, "Revisiting Reengineering," *Strategy + Business* (3rd Quarter 2000), pp. 27–31.

52. E. A. Hall, J. Rosenthal, and J. Wade, "How to Make Reengineering *Really* Work," McKinsey Quarterly (1994, No.2), pp. 107–128.

53. M. Arndt, "Quality Isn't Just for Widgets," *Business Week* (July 22, 2002), pp. 72–73.

54. T. M. Box, "Six Sigma Quality: Experiential Learning," *SAM Advanced Management Journal* (Winter 2006), pp. 20–23.

55. R. O. Crockett, "Six Sigma Still Pays Off at Motorola," *Business Week* (December 4, 2006), p. 50.

56. J. Welch and S. Welch, "The Six Sigma Shotgun," *Business Week* (May 21, 2007), p. 110.

57. Arndt, p. 73.

58. B. Hindo, "At 3M, A Struggle Between Efficiency and Creativity," *Business Week IN* (June 11, 2007), pp. 8–16.

59. F. Arner and A. Aston, "How Xerox Got Up to Speed," *Business Week* (May 3, 2004), pp. 103–104.

60. J. Hoerr, "Sharpening Minds for a Competitive Edge," *Business Week* (December 17, 1990), pp. 72–78.

61. D. Spulberg, *Global Competitive Strategy* (Cambridge, UK: Cambridge University Press, 2007), p. 257; See also A. K. Gupta, V. Govindarajan, and H. Wang, *The Quest for Global Dominance*, 2nd ed. (San Francisco: Jossey-Bass, 2007) for a similar set of forces.

62. R. Krishnan, X. Martin, and N. G. Noorderhaven, "When Does Trust Matter to Alliance Performance," *Academy of Management Journal* (October 2006), pp. 894–917.

63. S. X. Li and T. J. Rowley, "Inertia and Evaluation Mechanisms in Interorganizational Partner Selection: Syndicate Formation Among U.S. Investment Banks," *Academy of Management Journal* (December 2002), pp. 1104–1119.

64. M. U. Douma, J. Bilderbeek, P. J. Idenburg, and J. K. Loise, "Strategic Alliances: Managing the Dynamics of Fit," *Long Range Planning* (August 2000), pp. 579–598; W. Hoffmann and R. Schlosser, "Success Factors of Strategic Alliances in Small and Medium-Sized Enterprises—An Empirical Survey," *Long Range Planning* (June 2001), pp. 357–381; Y. Luo, "How Important Are Shared Perceptions of Procedural Justice in Cooperative Alliances?" *Academy of Management Journal* (August 2005), pp. 695–709.

65. Alan M. Rugman, *The Regional Multinationals* (Cambridge, UK: Cambridge University Press, 2005); P. Ghemawat, "Regional Strategies for Global Leadership," *Harvard Business Review* (December 2005), pp. 98–108.

66. J. Birkinshaw, P. Braunerhjelm, U. Holm, and S. Terjesen, "Why Do Some Multinational Corporations Relocate Their Headquarters Overseas?" *Strategic Management Journal* (July 2006), pp. 681–700.

67. J. H. Taggart, "Strategy Shifts in MNC Subsidiaries," *Strategic Management Journal* (July 1998), pp. 663–681.

68. C. A. Bartlett and S. Ghoshal, "Beyond the M-Form: Toward a Managerial Theory of the Firm," *Strategic Management Journal* (Winter 1993), pp. 23–46.

69. C. Matlack, "Nestle Is Starting to Slim Down at Last," *Business Week* (October 27, 2003), pp. 56–57; "Daring, Defying to Grow," *Economist* (August 7, 2004), pp. 55–58.

70. J. Sterling, "Translating Strategy into Effective Implementation: Dispelling the Myths and Highlighting What Works," *Strategy & Leadership*, Vol. 31, No. 3 (2003), pp. 27–34.

71. "Rebirth of a Carmaker," *The Economist* (April 26, 2008), pp. 87–89.

72. M. Der Hovanesian, "I Have One Word for You: Bioplastics," *Business Week* (June 30, 2008), pp. 44–47.

73. "Cargill Begins to Build Chicago Plant," *St. Cloud* (MN) *Times* (July 9, 2008), p. 3A.

strategy implementation: staffing and Directing

Have you heard of Enterprise Rent-A-Car? Hertz, Avis, and National Car Rental operations are much more visible at airports. Yet Enterprise owns more cars and operates in more locations than Hertz or Avis. Enterprise began operations in St. Louis in 1957, but didn't locate at an airport until 1995. It is the largest rental car company in North America, but only 230 out of its 7,000 worldwide offices are at airports. In virtually ignoring the highly competitive airport market, Enterprise has chosen a cost-leadership competitive strategy by marketing to people in need of a spare car at neighborhood locations. Its offices are within 15 miles of 90% of the U.S. population. Instead of locating many cars at a few high-priced locations at airports, Enterprise sets up inexpensive offices throughout metropolitan areas. As a result, cars are rented for 30% less than they cost at airports. As soon as one branch office grows to about 150 cars, the company opens another rental office a few miles away. People are increasingly renting from Enterprise even when their current car works fine. According to CEO Andy Taylor, "We call it a 'virtual car.' Small-business people who have to pick up clients call us when they want something better than their own car." Why is this competitive strategy so successful for Enterprise even though its locations are now being imitated by Hertz and Avis?

The secret to Enterprise's success is its well-executed strategy implementation. Clearly laid out programs, budgets, and procedures support the company's competitive strategy by making Enterprise stand out in the mind of the consumer. It was ranked on *Business Week*'s list of "Customer Service Champs" in both 2007 and 2008. When a new rental office opens, employees spend time developing relationships with the service managers of every auto dealership and body shop in the area. Enterprise employees bring pizza and doughnuts to workers at the auto garages across the country. Enterprise forms agreements with dealers to provide replacements for cars brought in for service. At major accounts, the company actually staffs an office at the dealership and has cars parked outside so customers don't have to go to an Enterprise office to complete paperwork.

One key to implementation at Enterprise is *staffing*—hiring and promoting a certain kind of person. Virtually every Enterprise employee is a college graduate, usually from the bottom

Learning Objectives

After reading this chapter, you should be able to:

- Understand the link between strategy and staffing decisions
- Match the appropriate manager to the strategy
- Understand how to implement an effective downsizing program
- Discuss important issues in effectively staffing and directing international expansion

- Assess and manage the corporate culture's fit with a new strategy
- Decide when and if programs such as MBO and TQM are appropriate methods of strategy implementation
- Formulate action plans

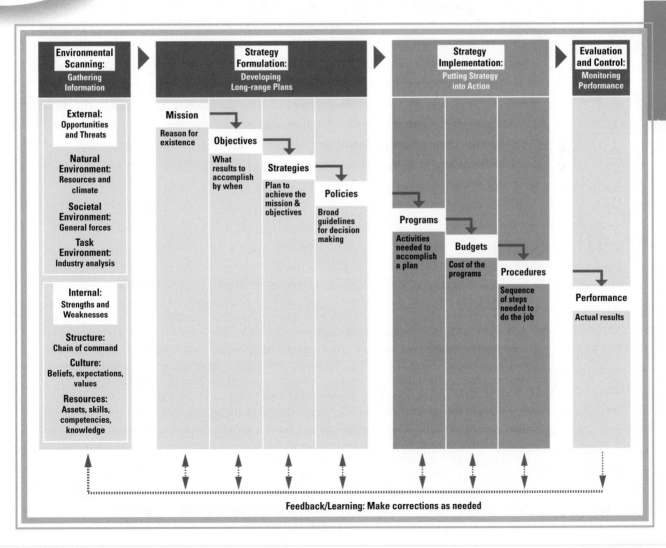

| Environmental Scanning: Gathering Information | Strategy Formulation: Developing Long-range Plans | Strategy Implementation: Putting Strategy into Action | Evaluation and Control: Monitoring Performance |

External: Opportunities and Threats

Natural Environment: Resources and climate

Societal Environment: General forces

Task Environment: Industry analysis

Internal: Strengths and Weaknesses

Structure: Chain of command

Culture: Beliefs, expectations, values

Resources: Assets, skills, competencies, knowledge

Mission — Reason for existence

Objectives — What results to accomplish by when

Strategies — Plan to achieve the mission & objectives

Policies — Broad guidelines for decision making

Programs — Activities needed to accomplish a plan

Budgets — Cost of the programs

Procedures — Sequence of steps needed to do the job

Performance — Actual results

Feedback/Learning: Make corrections as needed

half of the class. According to COO Donald Ross, "We hire from the half of the college class that makes the upper half possible. We want athletes, fraternity types—especially fraternity presidents and social directors. People people." These new employees begin as management trainees. Instead of regular raises, their pay is tied to branch office profits.

Another key to implementation at Enterprise is *leading*—specifying clear performance objectives and promoting a team-oriented corporate culture. The company stresses promotion from within and advancement based on performance. Every Enterprise employee, including top executives, starts at the bottom. As a result, a bond of shared experience connects all employees and managers. Enterprise was included in *Business Week's* "50 Best Places to Launch a Career" three years in a row. To reinforce a cohesive culture of camaraderie, senior executives routinely do "grunt work" at branch offices. Even Andy Taylor, the CEO, joins the work. "We were visiting an office in Berkeley and it was mobbed, so I started cleaning cars," says Taylor. "As it was happening, I wondered if it was a good use of my time, but the effect on morale was tremendous." Because the financial results of every branch office and every region are available to all, the collegial culture stimulates good-natured competition. "We're this close to beating out Middlesex," grins Woody Erhardt, an area manager in New Jersey. "I want to pound them into the ground. If they lose, they have to throw a party for us, and we get to decide what they wear."[1]

This example from Enterprise Rent-A-Car illustrates how a strategy must be implemented with carefully considered programs in order to succeed. This chapter discusses strategy implementation in terms of staffing and leading. **Staffing** focuses on the selection and use of employees. **Leading** emphasizes the use of programs to better align employee interests and attitudes with a new strategy.

10.1 Staffing

The implementation of new strategies and policies often calls for new human resource management priorities and a different use of personnel. Such staffing issues can involve hiring new people with new skills, firing people with inappropriate or substandard skills, and/or training existing employees to learn new skills. Research demonstrates that companies with enlightened talent-management policies and programs have higher returns on sales, investments, assets, and equity.[2] This is especially important given that it takes an average of 48 days for an American company to fill a job vacancy at an average cost per hire of $3,270.[3]

If growth strategies are to be implemented, new people may need to be hired and trained. Experienced people with the necessary skills need to be found for promotion to newly created managerial positions. When a corporation follows a growth through acquisition strategy, it may find that it needs to replace several managers in the acquired company. The percentage of an acquired company's top management team that either quit or was asked to leave is around 25% after the first year, 35% after the second year, 48% after the third year, 55% after the fourth year, and 61% after five years.[4] In addition, executives who join an acquired company after the acquisition quit at significantly higher-than-normal rates beginning in their second year. Executives continue to depart at higher-than-normal rates for nine years after the acquisition.[5] Turnover rates of executives in firms acquired by foreign firms are significantly higher than for firms acquired by domestic firms, primarily in the fourth and fifth years after the acquisition.[6]

It is one thing to lose excess employees after a merger, but it is something else to lose highly skilled people who are difficult to replace. In a study of 40 mergers, 90% of the acquiring companies in the 15 successful mergers identified key employees and targeted them for retention within 30 days after the announcement. In contrast, this task was carried out only in one-third of the unsuccessful acquisitions.[7] To deal with integration issues such as these, some companies are appointing special **integration managers to** shepherd companies through the implementation process. The job of the integrator is to prepare a competitive profile of the combined company in terms of its strengths and weaknesses, draft an ideal profile of what the combined company should look like, develop action plans to close the gap between the actuality and the ideal, and establish training programs to unite the combined company and to make it more competitive.[8] To be a successful integration manager, a person should have (1) a deep knowledge of the acquiring company, (2) a flexible management style, (3) an ability to work in cross-functional project teams, (4) a willingness to work independently, and (5) sufficient emotional and cultural intelligence to work well with people from all backgrounds.[9]

If a corporation adopts a retrenchment strategy, however, a large number of people may need to be laid off or fired (in many instances, being laid off is the same as being fired); and top management, as well as the divisional managers, needs to specify the criteria to be used in making these personnel decisions. Should employees be fired on the basis of low seniority or on the basis of poor performance? Sometimes corporations find it easier to close or sell off an entire division than to choose which individuals to fire.

STAFFING FOLLOWS STRATEGY

As in the case of structure, staffing requirements are likely to follow a change in strategy. For example, promotions should be based not only on current job performance but also on whether a person has the skills and abilities to do what is needed to implement the new strategy.

Changing Hiring and Training Requirements

Having formulated a new strategy, a corporation may find that it needs to either hire different people or retrain current employees to implement the new strategy. Consider the introduction of team-based production at Corning's filter plant mentioned in **Chapter 9**. Employee selection and training were crucial to the success of the new manufacturing strategy. Plant Manager Robert Hoover sorted through 8,000 job applications before hiring 150 people with the best problem-solving ability and a willingness to work in a team setting. Those selected received extensive training in technical and interpersonal skills. During the first year of production, 25% of all hours worked were devoted to training, at a cost of $750,000.[10]

One way to implement a company's business strategy, such as overall low cost, is through training and development. According to the American Society of Training and Development, the average annual expenditure per employee on corporate training and development is $1,000 per employee.[11] A study of 51 corporations in the UK found that 71% of "leading" companies rated staff learning and training as important or very important compared to 62% of the other companies.[12] Another study of 155 U. S. manufacturing firms revealed that those with training programs had 19% higher productivity than did those without such programs. Another study found that a doubling of formal training per employee resulted in a 7% reduction in scrap.[13] Training is especially important for a differentiation strategy emphasizing quality or customer service. For example, Motorola, with annual sales of $17 billion, spends 4% of its payroll on training by providing at least 40 hours of training a year to each employee. There is a very strong connection between strategy and training at Motorola. For example, after setting a goal to reduce product development cycle time, Motorola created a two-week course to teach its employees how to accomplish that goal. It brought together marketing, product development, and manufacturing managers to create an action learning format in which the managers worked together instead of separately. The company is especially concerned with attaining the highest quality possible in all its operations. Realizing that it couldn't hit quality targets with poor parts, Motorola developed a class for its suppliers on statistical process control. The company estimates that every $1 it spends on training delivers $30 in productivity gains within three years.[14]

Training is also important when implementing a retrenchment strategy. As suggested earlier, successful downsizing means that a company has to invest in its remaining employees. General Electric's Aircraft Engine Group used training to maintain its share of the market even though it had cut its workforce from 42,000 to 33,000 in the 1990s.[15]

Matching the Manager to the Strategy

Executive characteristics influence strategic outcomes for a corporation.[16] It is possible that a current CEO may not be appropriate to implement a new strategy. Research indicates that there may be a career life cycle for top executives. During the early years of executives' tenure, for example, they tend to experiment intensively with product lines to learn about their business. This is their learning stage. Later, their accumulated knowledge allows them to reduce experimentation and increase performance. This is their harvest stage. They enter a decline stage in their later years, when they reduce experimentation still further, and performance declines. Thus, there is an inverted U-shaped relationship between top executive tenure and the firm's financial performance. Some executives retire before any decline occurs. Others stave off decline longer than their counterparts. Because the length of time spent in each stage varies among CEOs, it is up to the board to decide when a top executive should be replaced.[17]

The most appropriate type of general manager needed to effectively implement a new corporate or business strategy depends on the desired strategic direction of that firm or business unit. Executives with a particular mix of skills and experiences may be classified as an **executive type** and paired with a specific corporate strategy. For example, a corporation following a concentration strategy emphasizing vertical or horizontal growth would probably want an aggressive new chief executive with a great deal of experience in that particular industry—a *dynamic industry expert*. A diversification strategy, in contrast, might call for someone with an analytical mind who is highly knowledgeable in other industries and can manage diverse product lines—an *analytical portfolio manager*. A corporation choosing to follow a stability strategy would probably want as its CEO a *cautious profit planner*, a person with a conservative style, a production or engineering background, and experience with controlling budgets, capital expenditures, inventories, and standardization procedures.

Weak companies in a relatively attractive industry tend to turn to a type of challenge-oriented executive known as a *turnaround specialist* to save the company. For example, when former IHOP (International House of Pancakes) waitress Julia Stewart left Applebee's restaurant chain to become CEO of IHOP, she worked to rebuild the company with better food, better ads, and better atmosphere. Six years later, a much improved IHOP acquired the struggling Applebee's restaurant chain. CEO Stewart vowed to turnaround Applebee's within a year by improving service, food quality and focusing the menu on what the restaurant does best: riblets, burgers, and salads. She wanted Applebee's to again be the friendly, neighborhood bar and grill that it once was.[18]

If a company cannot be saved, a *professional liquidator* might be called on by a bankruptcy court to close the firm and liquidate its assets. This is what happened to Montgomery Ward, Inc., the nation's first catalog retailer, which closed its stores for good in 2001, after declaring bankruptcy for the second time.[19] Research tends to support the conclusion that as a firm's environment changes, it tends to change the type of top executive to implement a new strategy.[20] For example, during the 1990s when the emphasis was on growth in a company's core products/services, the most desired background for a U.S. CEO was either in marketing or international experience. With the current decade's emphasis on mergers, acquisitions, and divestitures, the most desired background is finance. Currently, one out of five American and UK CEOs are former Chief Financial Officers, twice the percentage during the previous decade.[21]

This approach is in agreement with Chandler, who proposes (see **Chapter 9**) that the most appropriate CEO of a company changes as a firm moves from one stage of development to another. Because priorities certainly change over an organization's life, successful corporations need to select managers who have skills and characteristics appropriate to the organization's particular stage of development and position in its life cycle. For example, founders of firms tend to have functional backgrounds in technological specialties, whereas successors tend to have backgrounds in marketing and administration.[22] A change in the environment leading to a change in a company's strategy also leads to a change in the top management team. For example, a change in the U.S. utility industry's environment in 1992 supporting internally focused, efficiency-oriented strategies, led to top management teams being dominated by older managers with longer company and industry tenure, with efficiency-oriented backgrounds in operations, engineering, and accounting.[23] Research reveals that executives having a specific personality characteristic (external locus of control) are more effective in regulated industries than are executives with a different characteristic (internal locus of control).[24]

Other studies have found a link between the type of CEO and a firm's overall strategic type. (Strategic types were presented in **Chapter 4**). For example, successful prospector firms tended to be headed by CEOs from research/engineering and general management backgrounds. High performance defenders tended to have CEOs with accounting/finance, manufacturing/production, and general management experience. Analyzers tended to have CEOs with a marketing/sales background.[25]

A study of 173 firms over a 25-year period revealed that CEOs in these companies tended to have the same functional specialization as the former CEO, especially when the past CEO's strategy continued to be successful. This may be a pattern for successful corporations.[26] In particular, it explains why so many prosperous companies tend to recruit their top executives from one particular area. At Procter & Gamble (P&G)—a good example of an analyzer firm—for example, the route to the CEO's position has traditionally been through brand management, with a strong emphasis on marketing—and more recently international experience. In other firms, the route may be through manufacturing, marketing, accounting, or finance—depending on what the corporation has always considered its core capability (and its overall strategic orientation).

SELECTION AND MANAGEMENT DEVELOPMENT

Selection and development are important not only to ensure that people with the right mix of skills and experiences are initially hired but also to help them grow on the job so that they might be prepared for future promotions.

Executive Succession: Insiders versus Outsiders

Executive succession is the process of replacing a key top manager. The average tenure of a chief executive of a large U.S. company declined from nearly nine years in 1980 to six years in 2006.[27] Given that two-thirds of all major corporations worldwide replace their CEO at least once in a five-year period, it is important that the firm plan for this eventuality.[28] It is especially important for a company that usually promotes from within to prepare its current managers for promotion. For example, companies using relay executive succession, in which a candidate is groomed to take over the CEO position, have significantly higher performance than those that hire someone from the outside or hold a competition between internal candidates.[29] These "heirs apparent" are provided special assignments including membership on other firms' boards of directors.[30] Nevertheless, only half of large U.S. companies have CEO succession plans in place.[31]

Companies known for being excellent training grounds for executive talent are AlliedSignal, Bain & Company, Bankers Trust, Bristol Myers Squibb, Cititcorp, General Electric, Hewlett-Packard, McDonald's, McKinsey & Company, Microsoft, Nike, PepsiCo, Pfizer, and P&G. For example, one study showed that hiring 19 GE executives into CEO positions added $24.5 billion to the share prices of the companies that hired them. One year after people from GE started their new jobs, 11 of the 19 companies they joined were outperforming their competitors and the overall market.[32]

Some of the best practices for top management succession are encouraging boards to help the CEO create a succession plan, identifying succession candidates below the top layer, measuring internal candidates against outside candidates to ensure the development of a comprehensive set of skills, and providing appropriate financial incentives.[33] Succession planning has become the most important topic discussed by boards of directors.[34] See **Strategy Highlight 10.1** to see how Hewlett-Packard identifies those with potential for executive leadership positions.

Prosperous firms tend to look outside for CEO candidates only if they have no obvious internal candidates.[35] For example, 85% of the CEOs selected to run S&P 500 companies in 2006 were insiders, according to executive search firm Spencer Stuart.[36] Hiring an outsider to be a CEO is a risky gamble. CEOs from the outside tend to introduce significant change and high turnover among the current top management.[37] For example, in one study, the percentage of senior executives that left a firm after a new CEO took office was 20% when the new CEO

STRATEGY highlight 10.1

HOW HEWLETT-PACKARD IDENTIFIES POTENTIAL EXECUTIVES

Hewlett-Packard identifies those with high potential for executive leadership by looking for six broad competencies that the company believes are necessary:

1. *Practice the HP Way* by building trust and respect, focusing on achievement, demonstrating integrity, being innovative with customers, contributing to the community, and developing organizational decision making.

2. *Lead change and learning* by recognizing and acting on signals for change, leading organizational change, learning from organizational experience, removing barriers to change, developing self, and challenging and developing others.

3. *Know the internal and external environments* by anticipating global trends, acting on trends, and learning from others.

4. *Lead strategy setting* by inspiring breakthrough business strategy, leading the strategy-making process, committing to business vision, creating long-range strategies, building financial strategies, and defining a business-planning system.

5. *Align the organization* by working across boundaries, implementing competitive cost structures, developing alliances and partnerships, planning and managing core business, and designing the organization.

6. *Achieve results* by building a track record, establishing accountability, supporting calculated risks, making tough individual decisions, and resolving performance problems.

....

SOURCE: Summarized from R. M. Fulmer, P. A. Gibbs, and M. Goldsmith, "The New HP Way: Leveraging Strategy with Diversity, Leadership Development and Decentralization," *Strategy & Leadership* (October/November/December, 1999), pp. 21–29.

was an insider, but increased to 34% when the new CEO was an outsider.[38] CEOs hired from outside the firm tend to have a low survival rate. According to RHR International, 40% to 60% of high-level executives brought in from outside a company failed within two years.[39] A study of 392 large U.S. firms revealed that only 16.6% of them had hired outsiders to be their CEOs. The outsiders tended to perform slightly worse than insiders but had a very high variance in performance. Compared to that of insiders, the performance of outsiders tended to be either very good or very poor. Although outsiders performed much better (in terms of shareholder returns) than insiders in the first half of their tenures, they did much worse in their second half. As a result, the average tenure of an outsider was significantly less than for insiders.[40]

Firms in trouble, however, overwhelmingly choose outsiders to lead them.[41] For example, one study of 22 firms undertaking turnaround strategies over a 13-year period found that the CEO was replaced in all but two companies. Of 27 changes of CEO (several firms had more than one CEO during this period), only seven were insiders—20 were outsiders.[42] The probability of an outsider being chosen to lead a firm in difficulty increases if there is no internal heir apparent, if the last CEO was fired, and if the board of directors is composed of a large percentage of outsiders.[43] Boards realize that the best way to force a change in strategy is to hire a new CEO who has no connections to the current strategy.[44] For example, outsiders have been found to be very effective in leading strategic change for firms in Chapter 11 bankruptcy.[45]

Identifying Abilities and Potential

A company can identify and prepare its people for important positions in several ways. One approach is to establish a sound *performance appraisal system* to identify good performers with promotion potential. A survey of 34 corporate planners and human resource executives from 24 large U.S. corporations revealed that approximately 80% made some attempt to identify managers' talents and behavioral tendencies so that they could place a manager with a likely fit to a given competitive strategy.[46] Companies select those people with promotion potential to be in their executive development training program. Approximately 10,000 of GE's 276,000 employees take at least one class at the company's famous Leadership Development Center in Crotonville, New York.[47] Doug Pelino, chief talent officer at Xerox, keeps a list of about 100 managers in middle management and at the vice presidential levels who have been selected to receive special training, leadership experience, and mentorship to become the next generation of top management.[48]

A company should examine its human resource system to ensure not only that people are being hired without regard to their racial, ethnic, or religious background, but also that they are being identified for training and promotion in the same manner. Management diversity could be a competitive advantage in a multi-ethnic world. With more women in the workplace, an increasing number are moving into top management, but are demanding more flexible career ladders to allow for family responsibilities.

Many large organizations are using *assessment centers* to evaluate a person's suitability for an advanced position. Corporations such as AT&T, Standard Oil, IBM, Sears, and GE have successfully used assessment centers. Because each is specifically tailored to its corporation, these assessment centers are unique. They use special interviews, management games, in-basket exercises, leaderless group discussions, case analyses, decision-making exercises, and oral presentations to assess the potential of employees for specific positions. Promotions into these positions are based on performance levels in the assessment center. Assessment centers have generally been able to accurately predict subsequent job performance and career success.[49]

Job rotation—moving people from one job to another—is also used in many large corporations to ensure that employees are gaining the appropriate mix of experiences to prepare them for future responsibilities. Rotating people among divisions is one way that a corporation can improve the level of organizational learning. General Electric, for example, routinely rotates its executives from one sector to a completely different one to learn the skills of managing in different industries. Jeffrey Immelt, who took over as CEO from Jack Welch, had managed businesses in plastics, appliances, and medical systems.[50] Companies that pursue related diversification strategies through internal development make greater use of interdivisional transfers of people than do companies that grow through unrelated acquisitions. Apparently, the companies that grow internally attempt to transfer important knowledge and skills throughout the corporation in order to achieve some sort of synergy.[51]

PROBLEMS IN RETRENCHMENT

On January 28, 2009, Starbucks announced that it was closing 300 stores in addition to the 600 closures it had announced earlier and thus reduce its workforce by 7,000 people. Meanwhile, Hershey Foods closed six plants in the U.S. and Canada and eliminated 3,000 U.S. jobs. Like other companies at the time, both firms were experiencing declining sales and profits and attempting to cut costs. Due to a poor economy, more than 2.1 million U.S. workers were laid off in 2008. **Downsizing** (sometimes called "rightsizing" or "resizing") refers to the planned elimination of positions or jobs. This program is often used to implement retrenchment strategies. Because the financial community is likely to react favorably to announcements of downsizing from a company in difficulty, such a program may provide some short-term benefits such as raising the company's stock price. If not done properly, however, downsizing may result in less, rather than more, productivity. One study found that a 10% reduction in people resulted in only a 1.5% reduction in costs, profits increased in only half the firms downsizing, and the stock prices of downsized firms increased over three years, but not as much as did those of firms that did not downsize.[52] Why were the results so marginal?

A study of downsizing at automobile-related U.S. industrial companies revealed that at 20 out of 30 companies, either the wrong jobs were eliminated or blanket offers of early retirement prompted managers, even those considered invaluable, to leave. After the layoffs, the remaining employees had to do not only their work but also the work of the people who had gone. Because the survivors often didn't know how to do the departeds' work, morale and productivity plummeted.[53] Downsizing can seriously damage the learning capacity of organizations.[54] Creativity drops significantly (affecting new product development), and it becomes very difficult to keep high performers from leaving the company.[55] In addition, cost-conscious executives tend to defer maintenance, skimp on training, delay new product introductions, and avoid risky new businesses—all of which leads to lower sales and eventually to lower profits.[56] These are some of the reasons why layoffs worry customers and have a negative effect on a firm's reputation.[57]

A good retrenchment strategy can thus be implemented well in terms of organizing but poorly in terms of staffing. A situation can develop in which retrenchment feeds on itself and acts to further weaken instead of strengthen the company. Research indicates that companies undertaking cost-cutting programs are four times more likely than others to cut costs again, typically by reducing staff.[58] This happened at Eastman Kodak, Xerox, Ford, and General Motors during the 1990s, but 10 years later the companies were still downsizing and working to regain their profitable past performance. In contrast, successful downsizing firms undertake a strategic reorientation, not just a bloodletting of employees. Research shows that when companies use downsizing as part of a larger restructuring program to narrow company focus, they enjoy better performance.[59]

Consider the following guidelines that have been proposed for successful downsizing:

■ **Eliminate unnecessary work instead of making across-the-board cuts:** Spend the time to research where money is going and eliminate the task, not the workers, if it doesn't add value to what the firm is producing. Reduce the number of administrative levels rather than the number of individual positions. Look for interdependent relationships before eliminating activities. Identify and protect core competencies.

■ **Contract out work that others can do cheaper:** For example, Bankers Trust of New York contracted out its mailroom and printing services and some of its payroll and accounts payable activities to a division of Xerox. Outsourcing may be cheaper than vertical integration.

■ **Plan for long-run efficiencies:** Don't simply eliminate all postponable expenses, such as maintenance, R&D, and advertising, in the unjustifiable hope that the environment will become more supportive. Continue to hire, grow, and develop—particularly in critical areas.

■ **Communicate the reasons for actions:** Tell employees not only why the company is downsizing but also what the company is trying to achieve. Promote educational programs.

■ **Invest in the remaining employees:** Because most "survivors" in a corporate downsizing will probably be doing different tasks from what they were doing before the change, firms need to draft new job specifications, performance standards, appraisal techniques, and compensation packages. Additional training is needed to ensure that everyone has the proper skills to deal with expanded jobs and responsibilities. Empower key individuals/groups and emphasize team building. Identify, protect, and mentor people who have leadership talent.

■ **Develop value-added jobs to balance out job elimination:** When no other jobs are currently available within the organization to transfer employees to, management must consider other staffing alternatives. For example, Harley-Davidson worked with the company's unions to find other work for surplus employees by moving into Harley plants work that had previously been done by suppliers.[60]

INTERNATIONAL ISSUES IN STAFFING

Implementing a strategy of international expansion takes a lot of planning and can be very expensive. Nearly 80% of midsize and larger companies send their employees abroad, and 45% plan to increase the number they have on foreign assignment. A complete package for one executive working in another country costs from $300,000 to $1 million annually. Nevertheless, between 10% and 20% of all U.S. managers sent abroad returned early because of job dissatisfaction or difficulties in adjusting to a foreign country. Of those who stayed for the duration of their assignment, nearly one-third did not perform as well as expected. One-fourth of those completing an assignment left their company within one year of returning home—often leaving to join a competitor.[61] One common mistake is failing to educate the person about the customs and values in other countries.

Because of cultural differences, managerial style and human resource practices must be tailored to fit the particular situations in other countries. Because only 11% of human resource managers have ever worked abroad, most have little understanding of a global assignment's unique personal and professional challenges and thus fail to develop the training necessary for such an assignment.[62] Ninety percent of companies select employees for an international assignment based on their technical expertise while ignoring other areas.[63] A lack of knowledge of national and ethnic differences can make managing an international operation extremely difficult. For example, the three ethnic groups living in Malaysia (Malay, Chinese, and Indian) share different religions, attend different schools, and do not like to work in the same factories with each other. Because of the importance of cultural distinctions such as these, multinational corporations (MNCs) are now putting more emphasis on intercultural training for managers being sent on an assignment to a foreign country. This type of training is one of the commonly cited reasons for the lower expatriate failure rates—6% or less—for European and Japanese MNCs, which have emphasized cross-cultural experiences, compared with a 35% failure rate for U.S.-based MNCs.[64]

To improve organizational learning, many MNCs are providing their managers with international assignments lasting as long as five years. Upon their return to headquarters, these expatriates have an in-depth understanding of the company's operations in another part of the world. This has value to the extent that these employees communicate this understanding to others in decision-making positions. Research indicates that an MNC performs at a higher level when its CEO has international experience.[65] Global MNCs, in particular, emphasize international experience, have a greater number of senior managers who have been expatriates, and have a strong focus on leadership development through the expatriate experience.[66] Unfortunately, not all corporations appropriately manage international assignments. While out of the country, a person may be overlooked for an important promotion (out of sight, out of mind). Upon his or her return to the home country, co-workers may deprecate the out-of country experience as a waste of time. The perceived lack of organizational support for international assignments increases the likelihood that an expatriate will return home early.[67]

From their study of 750 U.S., Japanese, and European companies, Black and Gregersen found that the companies that do a good job of managing foreign assignments follow three general practices:

- When making international assignments, they focus on transferring knowledge and developing global leadership.

- They make foreign assignments to people whose technical skills are matched or exceeded by their cross-cultural abilities.

- They end foreign assignments with a deliberate repatriation process, with career guidance and jobs where the employees can apply what they learned in their assignments.[68]

Once a corporation has established itself in another country, it hires and promotes people from the host country into higher-level positions. For example, most large MNCs attempt to fill managerial positions in their subsidiaries with well-qualified citizens of the host countries. Unilever and IBM have traditionally taken this approach to international staffing. This policy serves to placate nationalistic governments and to better attune management practices to the host country's culture. The danger in using primarily foreign nationals to staff managerial positions in subsidiaries is the increased likelihood of suboptimization (the local subsidiary ignores the needs of the larger parent corporation). This makes it difficult for an MNC to meet its long-term, worldwide objectives. To a local national in an MNC subsidiary, the corporation as a whole is an abstraction. Communication and coordination across subsidiaries become more difficult. As it becomes harder to coordinate the activities of several international subsidiaries, an MNC will have serious problems operating in a global industry.

Another approach to staffing the managerial positions of MNCs is to use people with an "international" orientation, regardless of their country of origin or host country assignment. This is a widespread practice among European firms. For example, Electrolux, a Swedish firm, had a French director in its Singapore factory. Using third-country "nationals" can allow for more opportunities for promotion than does Unilever's policy of hiring local people, but it can also result in more misunderstandings and conflicts with the local employees and with the host country's government.

Some corporations take advantage of immigrants and their children to staff key positions when negotiating entry into another country and when selecting an executive to manage the company's new foreign operations. For example, when General Motors wanted to learn more about business opportunities in China, it turned to Shirley Young, a Vice President of Marketing at GM. Born in Shanghai and fluent in Chinese language and customs, Young was instrumental in helping GM negotiate a $1 billion joint venture with Shanghai Automotive to build a Buick plant in China. With other Chinese-Americans, Young formed a committee to advise GM on relations with China. Although just a part of a larger team of GM employees working on the joint venture, Young coached GM employees on Chinese customs and traditions.[69]

MNCs with a high level of international interdependence among activities need to provide their managers with significant international assignments and experiences as part of their training and development. Such assignments provide future corporate leaders with a series of valuable international contacts in additional to a better personal understanding of international issues and global linkages among corporate activities.[70] Research reveals that corporations using cross-national teams, whose members have international experience and communicate frequently with overseas managers, have greater product development capabilities than others.[71] Executive recruiters report that more major corporations are now requiring candidates to have international experience.[72] To increase its own top management's global expertise, Cisco Systems introduced a staffing program in 2007 with the objective of locating 20% of its senior managers at its new Bangalore, India, Globalization Center by 2010.[73]

Since an increasing number of multinational corporations are primarily organized around business units and product lines instead of geographic areas, product and SBU managers who are based at corporate headquarters are often traveling around the world to work personally with country managers. These managers and other mobile workers are being called *stealth expatriates* because they are either cross-border commuters (especially in the EU) or the accidental expatriate who goes on many business trips or temporary assignments due to offshoring and/or international joint ventures.[74]

10.2 Leading

Implementation also involves leading through coaching people to use their abilities and skills most effectively and efficiently to achieve organizational objectives. Without direction, people tend to do their work according to their personal view of what tasks should be done, how, and in what order. They may approach their work as they have in the past or emphasize those tasks that they most enjoy—regardless of the corporation's priorities. This can create real problems, particularly if the company is operating internationally and must adjust to customs and traditions in other countries. This direction may take the form of management leadership, communicated norms of behavior from the corporate culture, or agreements among workers in autonomous work groups. It may be accomplished more formally through action planning or through programs, such as Management By Objectives and Total Quality Management. Procedures can be changed to provide incentives to motivate employees to align their behavior with corporate objectives. For an example of Abbott Laboratories' new procedures to motivate employees to drive carbon neutral autos, see the **Environmental Sustainability Issue** feature.

MANAGING CORPORATE CULTURE

Because an organization's culture can exert a powerful influence on the behavior of all employees, it can strongly affect a company's ability to shift its strategic direction. A problem for a strong culture is that a change in mission, objectives, strategies, or policies is not likely to be successful if it is in opposition to the accepted culture of the company. Corporate culture has a strong tendency to resist change because its very reason for existence often rests on preserving stable relationships and patterns of behavior. For example, when Robert Nardelli became

ENVIRONMENTAL sustainability issue

ABBOTT LABORATORIES' NEW PROCEDURES FOR GREENER COMPANY CARS

Abbott Laboratories, which provides its sales staff with 6,000 vehicles, has changed its procedures for mileage reimbursement in order to make its car fleet more carbon neutral. Under previous rules, Abbott's employees reimbursed the company for *personal* use of company cars at 17.3¢ per mile. Starting January 2009, those choosing SUVs were re-quired to pay **72.3¢** per mile. As a result, 48% of the sales reps selected sedans compared to only 25% in 2008. Requests for SUVs dropped from 44% of the sales reps the previous year to 29% in 2009. Requests for hybrid autos increased from 6% in 2008 to 18% in 2009.

....

SOURCE: Summarized from D. Kiley, "Steering Workers into the Green Lane," *Business Week* (October 27, 2008), p. 18.

CEO at Home Depot in 2000, he changed the corporate strategy to growing the company's small professional supply business (sales to building contractors) through acquisitions and making the mature retail business cost-effective. He attempted to replace the old informal en-trepreneurial collaborative culture with one of military efficiency. Before Nardelli's arrival, most store managers had based their decisions upon their personal knowledge of their cus-tomers' preferences. Under Nardelli, they were instead given weekly sales and profit targets. Underperforming managers were asked to leave the company. The once-heavy ranks of full-time employees were replaced with cheaper part-timers. In this "culture of fear," morale fell and Home Depot's customer satisfaction score dropped to last place among major U.S. retail-ers. By 2007, Nardelli was asked to leave the company.

There is no one best corporate culture. An optimal culture is one that best supports the mission and strategy of the company of which it is a part. This means that *corporate culture should support the strategy*. Unless strategy is in complete agreement with the culture, any sig-nificant change in strategy should be followed by a modification of the organization's culture. Although corporate culture can be changed, it may often take a long time, and it requires much effort. At Home Depot, for example, CEO Nardelli attempted to change the corporate culture by hiring GE veterans like himself into top management positions, hiring ex-military officers as store managers, and instituting a top-down command structure.

A key job of management involves managing corporate culture. In doing so, management must evaluate what a particular change in strategy means to the corporate culture, assess whether a change in culture is needed, and decide whether an attempt to change the culture is worth the likely costs.

Assessing Strategy-Culture Compatibility

When implementing a new strategy, a company should take the time to assess *strategy-culture compatibility*. (See **Figure 10–1**.) Consider the following questions regarding a corporation's culture:

1. **Is the proposed strategy compatible with the company's current culture?** *If yes*, full steam ahead. Tie organizational changes into the company's culture by identifying how the new strategy will achieve the mission better than the current strategy does. *If not . . .*

2. **Can the culture be easily modified to make it more compatible with the new strat-egy?** *If yes,* move forward carefully by introducing a set of culture-changing activities such as minor structural modifications, training and development activities, and/or hiring new managers who are more compatible with the new strategy. When Procter & Gamble's

FIGURE 10–1   Assessing Strategy–Culture Compatibility

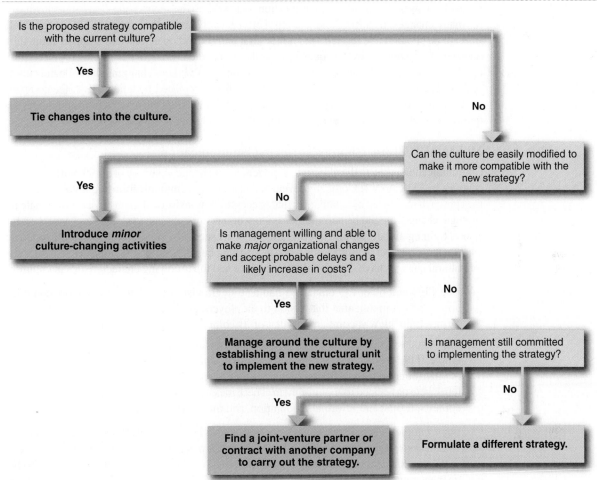

top management decided to implement a strategy aimed at reducing costs, for example, it made some changes in how things were done, but it did not eliminate its brand-management system. The culture adapted to these modifications over a couple years and productivity increased. *If not . . .*

3. **Is management willing and able to make major organizational changes and accept probable delays and a likely increase in costs?** *If yes,* manage around the culture by establishing a new structural unit to implement the new strategy. At General Motors, for example, top management realized the company had to make some radical changes to be more competitive. Because the current structure, culture, and procedures were very inflexible, management decided to establish a completely new Saturn division (GM's first new division since 1918) to build its new auto. In cooperation with the United Auto Workers, an entirely new labor agreement was developed, based on decisions reached by consensus. Carefully selected employees received from 100 to 750 hours of training, and a whole new culture was built, piece by piece. *If not . . .*

4. **Is management still committed to implementing the strategy?** *If yes,* find a joint-venture partner or contract with another company to carry out the strategy. *If not,* formulate a different strategy.

Based on Robert Nardelli's decisions when he initially started as Home Depot's CEO, he probably answered "no" to the first question and "yes" to the second question—thus justifying his many changes in staffing and leading. Unfortunately, these changes didn't work very well. Instead, he should have replied "no" to the first and second questions and stopped at the third question. As suggested by this question, he should have considered a different corporate strategy, such as growing the professional side of the business without changing the collegial culture of the retail stores. Not surprisingly, once Nardelli was replaced by a new CEO, the company divested the professional supply companies that Nardelli had spent so much time and money acquiring and returned to its previous strategy of concentrating on Home Depot retail stores.

Managing Cultural Change Through Communication

Communication is key to the effective management of change. A survey of 3,199 world-wide executives by McKinsey & Company revealed that ongoing communication and involvement was the approach most used by companies that successfully transformed themselves.[75] Rationale for strategic changes should be communicated to workers not only in newsletters and speeches, but also in training and development programs. This is especially important in decentralized firms where a large number of employees work in far-flung business units.[76] Companies in which major cultural changes have successfully taken place had the following characteristics in common:

- The CEO and other top managers had a strategic vision of what the company could become and communicated that vision to employees at all levels. The current performance of the company was compared to that of its competition and constantly updated.

- The vision was translated into the key elements necessary to accomplish that vision. For example, if the vision called for the company to become a leader in quality or service, aspects of quality and service were pinpointed for improvement, and appropriate measurement systems were developed to monitor them. These measures were communicated widely through contests, formal and informal recognition, and monetary rewards, among other devices.[77]

For example, when Pizza Hut, Taco Bell, and KFC were purchased by Tricon Global Restaurants (now Yum! Brands) from PepsiCo, the new management knew that it had to create a radically different culture than the one at PepsiCo if the company was to succeed. To begin, management formulated a statement of shared values—"How We Work Together" principles. They declared their differences with the "mother country" (PepsiCo) and wrote a "Declaration of Independence" stating what the new company would stand for. Restaurant managers participated in team-building activities at the corporate headquarters and finished by signing the company's "Declaration of Independence" as "founders" of the company. Since then, "Founder's Day" has become an annual event celebrating the culture of the company. Headquarters was renamed the "Restaurant Support Center," signifying the cultural value that the restaurants were the central focus of the company. People measures were added to financial measures and customer measures, reinforcing the "putting people first" value. In an unprecedented move in the industry, restaurant managers were given stock options and added to the list of performance incentives. The company created values-focused 360-degree performance reviews, which were eventually pushed to the restaurant manager level.[78]

Managing Diverse Cultures Following an Acquisition

When merging with or acquiring another company, top management must give some consideration to a potential clash of corporate cultures. According to a Hewitt Associates survey of 218 major U.S. corporations, integrating culture was a top challenge for 69% of the reporting companies.[79] Cultural differences are even more problematic when a company acquires a firm in another country. DaimlerChrysler's purchase of a controlling interest in Mitsubishi Motors in 2001 was insufficient to overcome Mitsubishi's resistance to change. After investing

FIGURE 10–2
Methods
of Managing
the Culture
of an
Acquired Firm

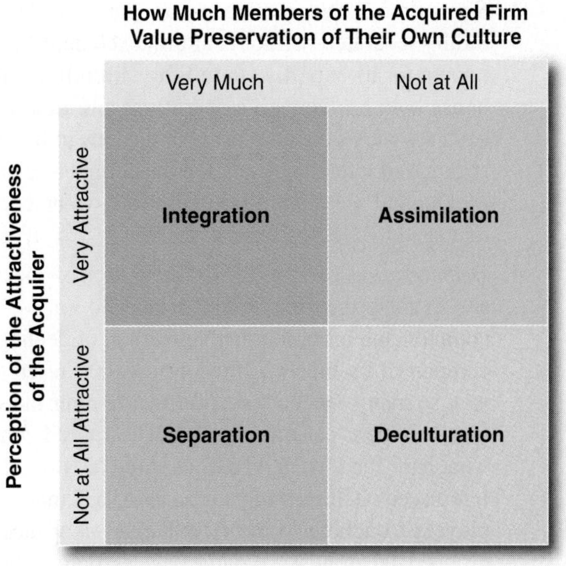

**How Much Members of the Acquired Firm
Value Preservation of Their Own Culture**

	Very Much	Not at All
Very Attractive	Integration	Assimilation
Not at All Attractive	Separation	Deculturation

Perception of the Attractiveness
of the Acquirer

$2 billion to cut Mitsubishi's costs and improve its product development, DaimlerChrysler gave up.[80] It's dangerous to assume that the firms can simply be integrated into the same reporting structure. The greater the gap between the cultures of the acquired firm and the acquiring firm, the faster executives in the acquired firm quit their jobs and valuable talent is lost. Conversely, when corporate cultures are similar, performance problems are minimized.[81]

There are four general methods of managing two different cultures. (See **Figure 10–2**.) The choice of which method to use should be based on (1) how much members of the acquired firm value preserving their own culture and (2) how attractive they perceive the culture of the acquirer to be.[82]

1. *Integration* involves a relatively balanced give-and-take of cultural and managerial practices between the merger partners, and no strong imposition of cultural change on either company. It merges the two cultures in such a way that the separate cultures of both firms are preserved in the resulting culture. This is what occurred when France's Renault purchased a controlling interest in Japan's Nissan Motor Company and installed Carlos Ghosn as Nissan's new CEO to turn around the company. Ghosn was very sensitive to Nissan's culture and allowed the company room to develop a new corporate culture based on the best elements of Japan's national culture. His goal was to form one successful auto group from two very distinct companies.[83]

2. *Assimilation* involves the domination of one organization over the other. The domination is not forced, but it is welcomed by members of the acquired firm, who may feel for many reasons that their culture and managerial practices have not produced success. The acquired firm surrenders its culture and adopts the culture of the acquiring company. This was the case when Maytag Company (now part of Whirlpool) acquired Admiral. Because Admiral's previous owners had not kept the manufacturing facilities up to date, quality had drastically fallen over the years. Admiral's employees were willing to accept the dominance of Maytag's strong quality-oriented culture because they respected it and knew that without significant changes at Admiral, they would soon be out of work. In turn, they expected to be treated with some respect for their skills in refrigeration technology.

3. *Separation* is characterized by a separation of the two companies' cultures. They are structurally separated, without cultural exchange. When Boeing acquired McDonnell-Douglas, known for its expertise in military aircraft and missiles, Boeing created a separate unit to house both McDonnell's operations and Boeing's own military business. McDonnell executives were given top posts in the new unit and other measures were taken to protect the strong McDonnell culture. On the commercial side, where Boeing had the most expertise, McDonnell's commercial operations were combined with Boeing's in a separate unit managed by Boeing executives.[84]

4. *Deculturation* involves the disintegration of one company's culture resulting from unwanted and extreme pressure from the other to impose its culture and practices. This is the most common and most destructive method of dealing with two different cultures. It is often accompanied by much confusion, conflict, resentment, and stress. This is a primary reason why so many executives tend to leave after their firm is acquired. Such a merger typically results in poor performance by the acquired company and its eventual divestment. This is what happened when AT&T acquired NCR Corporation in 1990 for its computer business. It replaced NCR managers with an AT&T management team, reorganized sales, forced employees to adhere to the AT&T code of values (called the "Common Bond"), and even dropped the proud NCR name (successor to National Cash Register) in favor of a sterile GIS (Global Information Solutions) nonidentity. By 1995, AT&T was forced to take a $1.2 billion loss and lay off 10,000 people.[85] The NCR unit was consequently sold.

ACTION PLANNING

Activities can be directed toward accomplishing strategic goals through action planning. At a minimum, an **action plan** states what actions are going to be taken, by whom, during what time frame, and with what expected results. After a program has been selected to implement a particular strategy, an action plan should be developed to put the program in place. **Table 10–1** shows an example of an action plan for a new advertising and promotion program.

Take the example of a company choosing forward vertical integration through the acquisition of a retailing chain as its growth strategy. Once it owns its own retail outlets, it must integrate the stores into the company. One of the many programs it would have to develop is a new advertising program for the stores. The resulting action plan to develop a new advertising program should include much of the following information:

1. **Specific actions to be taken to make the program operational:** One action might be to contact three reputable advertising agencies and ask them to prepare a proposal for a new radio and newspaper ad campaign based on the theme "Jones Surplus is now a part of Ajax Continental. Prices are lower. Selection is better."

2. **Dates to begin and end each action:** Time would have to be allotted not only to select and contact three agencies, but to allow them sufficient time to prepare a detailed proposal. For example, allow one week to select and contact the agencies plus three months for them to prepare detailed proposals to present to the company's marketing director. Also allow some time to decide which proposal to accept.

3. **Person (identified by name and title) responsible for carrying out each action:** List someone—such as Jan Lewis, advertising manager—who can be put in charge of the program.

4. **Person responsible for monitoring the timeliness and effectiveness of each action:** Indicate that Jan Lewis is responsible for ensuring that the proposals are of good quality and are priced within the planned program budget. She will be the primary company contact for the ad agencies and will report on the progress of the program once a week to the company's marketing director.

TABLE 10–1   Example of an Action Plan

Action Plan for Jan Lewis, Advertising Manager, and Rick Carter, Advertising Assistant, Ajax Continental

Program Objective: To Run a New Advertising and Promotion Campaign for the Combined Jones Surplus/Ajax Continental Retail Stores for the Coming Christmas Season within a Budget of $XX.

Program Activities:
1. Identify Three Best Ad Agencies for New Campaign.
2. Ask Three Ad Agencies to Submit a Proposal for a New Advertising and Promotion Campaign for Combined Stores.
3. Agencies Present Proposals to Marketing Manager.
4. Select Best Proposal and Inform Agencies of Decision.
5. Agency Presents Winning Proposal to Top Management.
6. Ads Air on TV and Promotions Appear in Stores.
7. Measure Results of Campaign in Terms of Viewer Recall and Increase in Store Sales.

Action Steps	Responsibility	Start–End
1. A. Review previous programs	Lewis & Carter	1/1–2/1
B. Discuss with boss	Lewis & Smith	2/1–2/3
C. Decide on three agencies	Lewis	2/4
2. A. Write specifications for ad	Lewis	1/15–1/20
B. Assistant writes ad request	Carter	1/20–1/30
C. Contact ad agencies	Lewis	2/5–2/8
D. Send request to three agencies	Carter	2/10
E. Meet with agency acct. execs	Lewis & Carter	2/16–2/20
3. A. Agencies work on proposals	Acct. Execs	2/23–5/1
B. Agencies present proposals	Carter	5/1–5/15
4. A. Select best proposal	Lewis	5/15–5/20
B. Meet with winning agency	Lewis	5/22–5/30
C. Inform losers	Carter	6/1
5. A. Fine-tune proposal	Acct. Exec	6/1–7/1
B. Presentation to management	Lewis	7/1–7/3
6. A. Ads air on TV	Lewis	9/1–12/24
B. Floor displays in stores	Carter	8/20–8/30
7. A. Gather recall measures of ads	Carter	9/1–12/24
B. Evaluate sales data	Carter	1/1–1/10
C. Prepare analysis of campaign	Carter	1/10–2/15

5. **Expected financial and physical consequences of each action:** Estimate when a completed ad campaign will be ready to show top management and how long it will take after approval to begin to air the ads. Estimate also the expected increase in store sales over the six-month period after the ads are first aired. Indicate whether "recall" measures will be used to help assess the ad campaign's effectiveness plus how, when, and by whom the recall data will be collected and analyzed.

6. **Contingency plans:** Indicate how long it will take to get an acceptable ad campaign to show top management if none of the initial proposals is acceptable.

Action plans are important for several reasons. First, action plans serve as a link between strategy formulation and evaluation and control. Second, the action plan specifies what needs to be done differently from the way operations are currently carried out. Third, during the evaluation and control process that comes later, an action plan helps in both the appraisal of performance and in the identification of any remedial actions, as needed. In addition, the explicit assignment of responsibilities for implementing and monitoring the programs may contribute to better motivation.

MANAGEMENT BY OBJECTIVES

Management By Objectives (MBO) is a technique that encourages participative decision making through shared goal setting at all organizational levels and performance assessment based on the achievement of stated objectives.[86] MBO links organizational objectives and the behavior of individuals. Because it is a system that links plans with performance, it is a powerful implementation technique.

The MBO process involves:

1. Establishing and communicating organizational objectives.
2. Setting individual objectives (through superior-subordinate interaction) that help implement organizational ones.
3. Developing an action plan of activities needed to achieve the objectives.
4. Periodically (at least quarterly) reviewing performance as it relates to the objectives and including the results in the annual performance appraisal.[87]

MBO provides an opportunity for the corporation to connect the objectives of people at each level to those at the next higher level. MBO, therefore, acts to tie together corporate, business, and functional objectives, as well as the strategies developed to achieve them. Although MBO originated the 1950s, 90% of surveyed practicing managers feel that MBO is applicable today.[88] The principles of MBO are a part of self-managing work teams and quality circles.[89]

One of the real benefits of MBO is that it can reduce the amount of internal politics operating within a large corporation. Political actions within a firm can cause conflict and create divisions between the very people and groups who should be working together to implement strategy. People are less likely to jockey for position if the company's mission and objectives are clear and they know that the reward system is based not on game playing, but on achieving clearly communicated, measurable objectives.

TOTAL QUALITY MANAGEMENT

Total Quality Management (TQM) is an operational philosophy committed to *customer satisfaction* and *continuous improvement*. TQM is committed to quality/excellence and to being the best in all functions. Because TQM aims to reduce costs and improve quality, it can be used as a program to implement an overall low-cost or a differentiation business strategy. About 92% of manufacturing companies and 69% of service firms have implemented some form of quality management practices.[90] Not all TQM programs have been successes. Nevertheless, a recent survey of 325 manufacturing firms in Canada, Hungary, Italy, Lebanon, Taiwan, and the United States revealed that total quality management and just-in-time were the two highest-ranked improvement programs to improve company performance. This study agreed with a 2004 Census of Manufacturing survey that identified total quality management and lean manufacturing as the top improvement methodologies in both the U.S. and China.[91] An analysis of the successes and failures of TQM concluded that the key ingredient is top management. Successful TQM programs occur in those companies in which "top managers move beyond defensive and tactical orientations to embrace a developmental orientation."[92]

TQM has four objectives:

1. Better, less variable quality of the product and service
2. Quicker, less variable response in processes to customer needs

3. Greater flexibility in adjusting to customers' shifting requirements

4. Lower cost through quality improvement and elimination of non-value-adding work[93]

According to TQM, faulty processes, not poorly motivated employees, are the cause of defects in quality. The program involves a significant change in corporate culture, requiring strong leadership from top management, employee training, empowerment of lower-level employees (giving people more control over their work), and teamwork in order to succeed in a company. TQM emphasizes prevention, not correction. Inspection for quality still takes place, but the emphasis is on improving the process to prevent errors and deficiencies. Thus, quality circles or quality improvement teams are formed to identify problems and to suggest how to improve the processes that may be causing the problems.

TQM's essential ingredients are:

- **An intense focus on customer satisfaction:** Everyone (not just people in the sales and marketing departments) understands that their jobs exist only because of customer needs. Thus all jobs must be approached in terms of how they will affect customer satisfaction.

- **Internal as well as external customers:** An employee in the shipping department may be the internal customer of another employee who completes the assembly of a product, just as a person who buys the product is a customer of the entire company. An employee must be just as concerned with pleasing the internal customer as in satisfying the external customer.

- **Accurate measurement of every critical variable in a company's operations:** This means that employees have to be trained in what to measure, how to measure, and how to interpret the data. A rule of TQM is that *you only improve what you measure.*

- **Continuous improvement of products and services:** Everyone realizes that operations need to be continuously monitored to find ways to improve products and services.

- **New work relationships based on trust and teamwork:** Important is the idea of empowerment—giving employees wide latitude in how they go about achieving the company's goals. Research indicates that the keys to TQM success lie in executive commitment, an open organizational culture, and employee empowerment.[94]

INTERNATIONAL CONSIDERATIONS IN LEADING

In a study of 53 different national cultures, Hofstede found that each nation's unique culture could be identified using five dimensions. He found that national culture is so influential that it tends to overwhelm even a strong corporate culture. (See the numerous sociocultural societal variables that compose another country's culture that are listed in **Table 4–3**.) In measuring the differences among these **dimensions of national culture** from country to country, he was able to explain why a certain management practice might be successful in one nation but fail in another:[95]

1. **Power distance (PD)** is the extent to which a society accepts an unequal distribution of power in organizations. Malaysia and Mexico scored highest, whereas Germany and Austria scored lowest. People in those countries scoring high on this dimension tend to prefer autocratic to more participative managers.

2. **Uncertainty avoidance (UA)** is the extent to which a society feels threatened by uncertain and ambiguous situations. Greece and Japan scored highest on disliking ambiguity, whereas the United States and Singapore scored lowest. People in those nations scoring high on this dimension tend to want career stability, formal rules, and clear-cut measures of performance.

3. **Individualism-collectivism (I-C)** is the extent to which a society values individual freedom and independence of action compared with a tight social framework and loyalty to the group. The United States and Canada scored highest on individualism, whereas Mexico

and Guatemala scored lowest. People in nations scoring high on individualism tend to value individual success through competition, whereas people scoring low on individualism (thus high on collectivism) tend to value group success through collective cooperation.

4. **Masculinity-femininity (M-F)** is the extent to which society is oriented toward money and things (which Hofstede labels masculine) or toward people (which Hofstede labels feminine). Japan and Mexico scored highest on masculinity, whereas France and Sweden scored lowest (thus highest on femininity). People in nations scoring high on masculinity tend to value clearly defined sex roles where men dominate, and to emphasize performance and independence, whereas people scoring low on masculinity (and thus high on femininity) tend to value equality of the sexes where power is shared, and to emphasize the quality of life and interdependence.

5. **Long-term orientation (LT)** is the extent to which society is oriented toward the long-versus the short-term. Hong Kong and Japan scored highest on long-term orientation, whereas Pakistan scored the lowest. A long-term time orientation emphasizes the importance of hard work, education, and persistence as well as the importance of thrift. Nations with a long-term time orientation tend to value strategic planning and other management techniques with a long-term payback.

Hofstede's work was extended by Project GLOBE, a team of 150 researchers who collected data on cultural values and practices and leadership attributes from 18,000 managers in 62 countries. The project studied the nine cultural dimensions of assertiveness, future orientation, gender differentiation, uncertainty avoidance, power distance, institutional emphasis on collectivism versus individualism, in-group collectivism, performance orientation, and humane orientation.[96]

The dimensions of national culture help explain why some management practices work well in some countries but not in others. For example, MBO, which originated in the United States, succeeded in Germany, according to Hofstede, because the idea of replacing the arbitrary authority of the boss with the impersonal authority of mutually agreed-upon objectives fits the low power distance that is a dimension of the German culture. It failed in France, however, because the French are used to high power distances; they are used to accepting orders from a highly personalized authority. In countries with high levels of uncertainty avoidance, such as Switzerland and Austria, communication should be clear and explicit, based on facts. Meetings should be planned in advance and have clear agendas. In contrast, in low-uncertainty-avoidance countries such as Greece or Russia, people are not used to structured communication and prefer more open-ended meetings. Because Thailand has a high level of power distance, Thai managers feel that communication should go from the top to the bottom of a corporation. As a result, 360-degree performance appraisals are seen as dysfunctional.[97] Some of the difficulties experienced by U.S. companies in using Japanese-style quality circles in TQM may stem from the extremely high value U.S. culture places on individualism. The differences between the United States and Mexico in terms of the power distance (Mexico 104 vs. U.S. 46) and individualism-collectivism (U.S. 91 vs. Mexico 30) dimensions may help explain why some companies operating in both countries have difficulty adapting to the differences in customs.[98] In addition, research has found that technology alliance formation is strongest in countries that value cooperation and avoid uncertainty.[99]

When one successful company in one country merges with another successful company in another country, the clash of corporate cultures is compounded by the clash of national cultures. For example, when two companies, one from a high-uncertainty-avoidance society and one from a low-uncertainty-avoidance country, are considering a merger, they should investigate each other's management practices to determine potential areas of conflict. Given the growing number of cross-border mergers and acquisitions, the management of cultures is becoming a key issue in strategy implementation. See the **Global Issue** feature to learn how differences in national and corporate cultures created conflict when Upjohn Company of the United States and Pharmacia AB of Sweden merged.

MNCs must pay attention to the many differences in cultural dimensions around the world and adjust their management practices accordingly. Cultural differences can easily go unrecognized by a headquarters staff that may interpret these differences as personality defects, whether the people in the subsidiaries are locals or expatriates. When conducting strategic planning in an MNC, top management must be aware that the process will vary based upon the national culture where a subsidiary is located. For example, in one MNC, the French expect concepts and key questions and answers. North American managers provide heavy financial analysis. Germans give precise dates and financial analysis. Information is usually late from Spanish and Moroccan operations and quotas are typically inflated. It is up to management to adapt to the differences.[100] The values embedded in his or her national culture have a profound and enduring effect on an executive's orientation, regardless of the impact of industry experience or corporate culture.[101] Hofstede and Bond conclude: "Whether they like it or not, the headquarters of multinationals are in the business of multicultural management."[102]

GLOBAL issue

CULTURAL DIFFERENCES CREATE IMPLEMENTATION PROBLEMS IN MERGER

When Upjohn Pharmaceuticals of Kalamazoo, Michigan, and Pharmacia AB of Stockholm, Sweden, merged in 1995, employees of both sides were optimistic for the newly formed Pharmacia & Upjohn, Inc. Both companies were second-tier competitors fighting for survival in a global industry. Together, the firms would create a global company that could compete scientifically with its bigger rivals.

Because Pharmacia had acquired an Italian firm in 1993, it also had a large operation in Milan. U.S. executives scheduled meetings throughout the summer of 1996—only to cancel them when their European counterparts could not attend. Although it was common knowledge in Europe that most Swedes take the entire month of July for vacation and that Italians take off all of August, this was not common knowledge in Michigan. Differences in management styles became a special irritant. Swedes were used to an open system, with autonomous work teams. Executives sought the whole group's approval before making an important decision. Upjohn executives followed the more traditional American top-down approach. Upon taking command of the newly merged firm, Dr. Zabriskie (who had been Upjohn's CEO), divided the company into departments reporting to the new London headquarters. He required frequent reports, budgets, and staffing updates. The Swedes reacted negatively to this top-down management hierarchical style. "It was degrading," said Stener Kvinnsland, head of Pharmacia's cancer research in Italy before he quit the new company.

The Italian operations baffled the Americans, even though the Italians felt comfortable with a hierarchical management style. Italy's laws and unions made layoffs difficult. Italian data and accounting were often inaccurate. Because the Americans didn't trust the data, they were constantly asking for verification. In turn, the Italians were concerned that the Americans were trying to take over Italian operations. At Upjohn, all workers were subject to testing for drug and alcohol abuse. Upjohn also banned smoking. At Pharmacia's Italian business center, however, waiters poured wine freely every afternoon in the company dining room. Pharmacia's boardrooms were stocked with humidors for executives who smoked cigars during long meetings. After a brief attempt to enforce Upjohn's policies, the company dropped both the no-drinking and no-smoking policies for European workers.

Although the combined company had cut annual costs by $200 million, overall costs of the merger reached $800 million, some $200 million more than projected. Nevertheless, Jan Eckberg, CEO of Pharmacia before the merger, remained confident of the new company's ability to succeed. He admitted, however, that "we have to make some smaller changes to release the full power of the two companies."

SOURCE: Summarized from R. Frank and T. M. Burton, "Cross-Border Merger Results in Headaches for a Drug Company," *Wall Street Journal* (February 4, 1997), pp. A1, A12.

End of Chapter SUMMARY

Strategy is implemented by modifying structure (organizing), selecting the appropriate people to carry out the strategy (staffing), and communicating clearly how the strategy can be put into action (leading). A number of programs, such as organizational and job design, reengineering, Six Sigma, MBO, TQM, and action planning, can be used to implement a new strategy. Executives must manage the corporate culture and find the right mix of qualified people to put a strategy in place.

Research on executive succession reveals that it is very risky to hire new top managers from outside the corporation. Although this is often done when a company is in trouble, it can be dangerous for a successful firm. This is also true when hiring people for non-executive positions. An in-depth study of 1,052 stock analysts at 78 investment banks revealed that hiring a star (an outstanding performer) from another company did not improve the hiring company's performance. When a company hires a star, the star's performance plunges, there is a sharp decline in the functioning of the team the person works with, and the company's market value declines. Their performance dropped about 20% and did not return to the level before the job change—even after five years. Interestingly, around 36% of the stars left the investment banks that hired them within 36 months. Another 29% quit in the next 24 months.

This phenomenon occurs not because a star doesn't suddenly become less intelligent when switching firms, but because the star cannot take to the new firm the firm-specific resources that contributed to her or his achievements at the previous company. As a result, the star is unable to repeat the high performance in another company until he/she learns the new system. This may take years, but only if the new company has a good support system in place. Otherwise, the performance may never improve. For these reasons, companies cannot obtain competitive advantage by hiring stars from the outside. Instead, they should emphasize growing their own talent and developing the infrastructure necessary for high performance.[103]

It is important to not ignore the 75% of the workforce who, while not being stars, are the solid performers that keep a company going over the years. An undue emphasis on attracting stars wastes money and destroys morale. The CEO of McKesson, a pharmaceutical wholesaler, calls these B players "performers in place. . . .They are happy living in Dubuque. I have more time and admiration for them than the A player who is at my desk every six months asking for the next promotion." Coaches who try to forge a sports team composed of stars court disaster. According to Karen Freeman, former head coach of women's basketball at Wake Forest University, "During my coaching days, the most dysfunctional teams were the ones who had no respect for the B players." In basketball or business, when the team goes into a slump, the stars are the first to whine, Freeman reports.[104]

ECO-BITS

- The U.S. Climate Action Partnership (USCAP), composed of General Electric, Caterpillar, Alcoa, General Motors, Chrysler, and Duke Energy plus 21 other major corporations, endorses reducing greenhouse gas emissions by 10% to 30% within 15 years and 60% to 80% by 2050 to avert the severest consequences of global warming. 😊

- General Electric, Caterpillar, and Alcoa also sit on the board of the Center for Energy & Economic Development (CEED), an organization that opposes a federal cli-

mate bill requiring a 65% reduction in emissions by 2050. 😖

- USCAP members General Motors and Chrysler are also members of the Heartland Institute, an organization that disputes humanity's role in global warming. 😖

- Duke Energy, a USCAP member, is currently building two coal-burning power plants and also belongs to Americans for Balanced Energy Choices, a group that advocates expanded coal use.[105] 😖

DISCUSSION QUESTIONS

1. What skills should a person have for managing a business unit following a differentiation strategy? Why? What should a company do if no one is available internally and the company has a policy of promotion from within?

2. When should someone from outside a company be hired to manage the company or one of its business units?

3. What are some ways to implement a retrenchment strategy without creating a lot of resentment and conflict with labor unions?

4. How can corporate culture be changed?

5. Why is an understanding of national cultures important in strategic management?

STRATEGIC PRACTICE EXERCISE

Staffing involves finding the person with the right blend of characteristics, such as personality, training, and experience, to implement a particular strategy. The Keirsey Temperament Sorter is designed to identify different kinds of personality temperament. It is similar to other instruments derived from Carl Jung's theory of psychological types, such as the Myers-Briggs, the Singer-Loomis, and the Grey-Wheelright. The questionnaire identifies four temperament types: **Guardian (SJ), Artisan (SP), Idealist (NF),** and **Rational (NT).** *Guardians* have natural talent in managing goods and services. They are dependable and trustworthy. *Artisans* have keen senses and are at home with tools, instruments, and vehicles. They are risk-takers and like action. *Idealists* are concerned with growth and development and like to work with people. They prefer friendly cooperation over confrontation and conflict. *Rationalists* are problem solvers who like to know how things work. They work tirelessly to accomplish their goals. Each of these four types has four variants.[106]

Keirsey challenges the assumption that people are basically the same in the ways that they think, feel, and approach problems. Keirsey argues that it is far less desirable to attempt to change others (because it has little likelihood of success) than to attempt to understand, work with, and take advantage of normal differences. Companies can use this type of questionnaire to help team members understand how each person can contribute to team performance. For example, Lucent Technology used the Myers-Briggs Type Indicator to help build trust and understanding among 500 engineers in 13 time zones and three continents in a distributed development project.

1. Access the Keirsey Temperament Sorter using your Internet browser. Type in the following URL: **www.advisorteam.com**

2. Complete and score the questionnaire. Print the description of your personality type.

3. Read the information on the Web site about each personality type. Become familiar with each.

4. Bring to class a sheet of paper containing your name and your personality type: *Guardian, Artisan, Idealist,* or *Rational.* Your instructor will either put you into a group containing people with the same predominant style or into a group with representatives from each type. He or she may then give each group a number. The instructor will then give the teams a task to accomplish. Each group will have approximately 30 minutes to do the task. It may be to solve a problem, analyze a short case, or propose a new entrepreneurial venture. The instructor will provide you with very little guidance other than to form and number the groups, give them a task, and keep track of time. He or she may move from group to group to sit in on each team's progress. When the time is up, the instructor will ask a spokesperson from each group to (1) describe the process the group went through and (2) present orally each group's ideas. After each group makes its presentation, the instructor may choose one or more of the following:

   ▪ On a sheet of paper, each person in the class identifies his/her personality type and votes which team did the best on the assignment.

   ▪ The class as a whole tries to identify each group's dominant decision-making style in terms of how they did their assignment. See how many people vote for one of the four types for each team.

   ▪ Each member of a group guesses if she/he was put into a team composed of the same personality types or in one composed of all four personality types.

KEY TERMS

action plan (p. 364)

dimensions of national culture (p. 367)

downsizing (p. 356)

executive succession (p. 353)

executive type (p. 352)

individualism-collectivism (I-C) (p. 367)

integration manager (p. 351)

leading (p. 350)

long-term orientation (LT) (p. 368)

Management By Objectives (MBO) (p. 366)

masculinity-femininity (M-F) (p. 368)

power distance (PD) (p. 367)

staffing (p. 350)

Total Quality Management (TQM) (p. 366)

uncertainty avoidance (UA) (p. 367)

NOTES

1. B. O'Reilly, "The Rent-A-Car Jocks Who Made Enterprise #1," *Fortune* (October 28, 1996), pp. 125–128; J. Schlereth, "Putting People First," an interview with Andrew Taylor, *BizEd* (July/August 2003), pp. 16–20; P. Lehman, "A Clear Road to the Top," *Business Week* (September 18, 2006), p. 72; Company Web site at www.enterprise.com.

2. S. Caudron, "How HR Drives Profits," *Workforce Management* (December 2001), pp. 26–31 as reported by L. L. Bryan, C. I. Joyce, and L. M. Weiss in "Making a Market in Talent," *McKinsey Quarterly* (2006, No. 2), pp. 1–7.

3. "The Stat," *Business Week* (October 24, 2005), p. 16.

4. The numbers are approximate averages from three separate studies of top management turnover after mergers. See M. Lubatkin, D. Schweiger, and Y. Weber, "Top Management Turnover in Related M&Ss: An Additional Test of the Theory of Relative Standing," *Journal of Management*, Vol. 25, No. 1 (1999), pp. 55–73.

5. J. A. Krug, "Executive Turnover in Acquired Firms: A Longitudinal Analysis of Long-Term Interaction Effects," paper presented to annual meeting of *Academy of Management*, Seattle, WA (2003).

6. J. A. Krug and W. H. Hegarty, "Post-Acquisition Turnover Among U.S. Top Management Teams: An Analysis of the Effects of Foreign vs. Domestic Acquisitions of U.S. Targets," *Strategic Management Journal* (September 1997), pp. 667–675; J. A. Jrug and W. H. Hegarty, "Predicting Who Stays and Leaves After an Acquisition: A Study of Top Managers in Multinational Firms," *Strategic Management Journal* (February 2001), pp. 185–196.

7. D. Harding and T. Rouse, "Human Due Diligence," *Harvard Business Review* (April 2007), pp. 124–131.

8. A. Hinterhuber, "Making M&A Work," *Business Strategy Review* (September 2002), pp. 7–9.

9. R. N. Ashkenas and S. C. Francis, "Integration Managers: Special Leaders for Special Times," *Harvard Business Review* (November–December 2000), pp. 108–116.

10. J. Hoerr, "Sharpening Minds for a Competitive Edge," *Business Week* (December 17, 1990), pp. 72–78.

11. K. Hess and N. J. Nentl, "Strategic Training for Managers," *SAM Management in Practice* (2006, No. 4).

12. "Training and Human Resources," *Business Strategy News Review* (July 2000), p. 6.

13. *High Performance Work Practices and Firm Performance* (Washington, DC: U.S. Department of Labor, Office of the American Workplace, 1993), pp. i, 4.

14. T. T. Baldwin, C. Danielson, and W. Wiggenhorn, "The Evolution of Learning Strategies in Organizations: From Employee Development to Business Redefinition," *Academy of Management Executive* (November 1997), pp. 47–58; K. Kelly, "Motorola: Training for the Millennium," *Business Week* (March 28, 1996), pp. 158–161.

15. R. Henkoff, "Companies That Train Best," *Fortune* (March 22, 1993), pp. 62–75.

16. D. C. Hambrick, "Upper Echelons Theory: An Update," *Academy of Management Review* (April 2007), pp. 334–343.

17. D. Miller and J. Shamsie, "Learning Across the Life Cycle: Experimentation and Performance Among the Hollywood Studio Heads," *Strategic Management Journal* (August 2001), pp. 725–745). An exception to these findings may be the computer software industry in which CEOs are at their best when they start their jobs and steadily decline during their tenures. See A. D. Henderson, D. Miller, and D. C. Hambrick, "How Quickly Do CEOs Become Obsolete? Industry Dynamism, CEO Tenure, and Company Performance," *Strategic Management Journal* (May 2006), pp. 447–460.

18. B. Hrowvitz, "New CEO Puts Comeback on the Menu at Applebee's," *USA Today* (April 28, 2008), pp. 1B, 2B.

19. A study of former General Electric executives who became CEOs categorized them as cost controllers, growers, or cycle managers on the basis of their line experience at GE. See B. Groysberg, A. N. McLean, and N. Nohria, "Are Leaders Portable?" *Harvard Business Review* (May 2006), pp. 92–100.

20. D. K. Datta and N. Rajagopalan, "Industry Structure and CEO Characteristics: An Empirical Study of Succession Events," *Strategic Management Journal* (September 1998), pp. 833–852; A. S. Thomas and K. Ramaswamy, "Environmental Change and Management Staffing: A Comment," *Journal of Management* (Winter 1993), pp. 877–887; J. P. Guthrie, C. M. Grimm, and K. G. Smith, "Environmental Change and Management Staffing: An Empirical Study," *Journal of Management* (December 1991), pp. 735–748.

21. J. Greco, "The Search Goes On," *Journal of Business Strategy* (September/October 1997), pp. 22–25; W. Ocasio and H. Kim, "The Circulation of Corporate Control: Selection of Functional Backgrounds on New CEOs in Large U.S. Manufacturing Firms, 1981–1992," *Administrative Science Quarterly* (September 1999), pp. 532–562; R. Dobbs, D. Harris, and A. Rasmussen, "When Should CFOs Take the Helm?" *McKinsey Quarterly Online* (November 2006); "How to Get to the Top," *The Economist* (May 31, 2008), p. 70.

22. R. Drazin and R. K. Kazanjian, "Applying the Del Technique to the Analysis of Cross-Classification Data: A Test of CEO Succession and Top Management Team Development," *Academy of Management Journal* (December 1993), pp. 1374–1399; W. E. Rothschild, "A Portfolio of Strategic Leaders," *Planning Review* (January/February 1996), pp. 16–19.

23. R. Subramanian and C. M. Sanchez, "Environmental Change and Management Staffing: An Empirical Examination of the Electric Utilities Industry," *Journal of Business Strategies* (Spring 1998), pp. 17–34.

24. M. A. Carpenter and B. R. Golden, "Perceived Managerial Discretion: A Study of Cause and Effect," *Strategic Management Journal* (March 1997), pp. 187–206.

25. J. A. Parnell, "Functional Background and Business Strategy: The Impact of Executive-Strategy Fit on Performance," *Journal of Business Strategies* (Spring 1994), pp. 49–62.

26. M. Smith and M. C. White, "Strategy, CEO Specialization, and Succession," *Administrative Science Quarterly* (June 1987), pp. 263–280.

27. "Making Companies Work," *Economist* (October 25, 2003), p. 14; C. H. Mooney, C. M. Dalton, D. R. Dalton, and S. T. Certo, "CEO Succession as a Funnel: The Critical, and Changing Role of Inside Directors," *Organizational Dynamics*, Vol. 36, No. 4 (2007), pp. 418–428. Note, however, that the tenures of CEOs of family firms typically exceed 15 years. See I. Le Breton-Miller and D. Miller, "Why Do Some Family Businesses Out-Compete? Governance, Long-Term Orientations, and Sustainable Capability," *Entrepreneurship Theory and Practice* (November 2006), pp. 731–746.

28. A. Bianco, L. Lavelle, J. Merrit, and A. Barrett, "The CEO Trap," *Business Week* (December 11, 2000), pp. 86–92.

29. Y. Zhang and N. Rajagopalan, "When the Known Devil Is Better Than an Unknown God: An Empirical Study of the Antecedents and Consequences of Relay CEO Succession," *Academy of Management Journal* (August 2004), pp. 483–500; W. Shen and A. A. Cannella, Jr., "Will Succession Planning Increase Shareholder Wealth? Evidence from Investor Reactions to Relay CEO Successions," *Strategic Management Journal* (February 2003), pp. 191–198.

30. G. A. Bigley and M. F. Wiersema, "New CEOs and Corporate Strategic Refocusing: How Experience as Heir Apparent Influences the Use of Power," *Administrative Science Quarterly* (December 2002), pp. 707–727.

31. J. L. Bower, "Solve the Succession Crisis by Growing Inside-Outside Leaders," *Harvard Business Review* (November 2007), pp. 91–96; Y. Zhang and N. Rajagopalan, "Grooming for the Top Post and Ending the CEO Succession Crisis," *Organizational Dynamics*, Vol. 35, Issue 1 (2006), pp. 96–105.

32. "Coming and Going," Survey of Corporate Leadership, *Economist* (October 25, 2003), pp. 12–14.

33. D. C. Carey and D. Ogden, *CEO Succession: A Window on How Boards Do It Right When Choosing a New Chief Executive* (New York: Oxford University Press, 2000).

34. "The King Lear Syndrome," *Economist* (December 13, 2003), p. 65.

35. Y. Zang and N. Rajagopalan, "Grooming for the Top Post and Ending the CEO Succession Crisis," *Organizational Dynamics*, Vol. 35, Issue 1 (2006), pp. 96–105.

36. J. Weber, "The Accidental CEO," *Business Week* (April 23, 2007), pp. 64–72.

37. M. S. Kraatz and J. H. Moore, "Executive Migration and Institutional Change," *Academy of Management Journal* (February 2002), pp. 120–143; Y. Zhang and N. Rajagopalan, "When the Known Devil Is Better Than an Unknown God: An Empirical Study of the Antecedents and Consequences of Relay CEO Succession," *Academy of Management Journal* (August 2004), pp. 483–500; W. Shen and A. A. Cannella, Jr., "Revisiting the Performance Consequences of CEO Succession: The Impacts of Successor Type, Post-Succession Senior Executive Turnover, and Departing CEO Tenure," *Academy of Management Journal* (August 2002), pp. 717–733.

38. K. P. Coyne and E. J. Coyne, Sr., "Surviving Your New CEO," *Harvard Business Review* (May 2007), pp. 62–69.

39. N. Byrnes and D. Kiley, "Hello, You Must Be Going," *Business Week* (February 12, 2007), pp. 30–32.

40. C. Lucier and J. Dyer, "Hiring an Outside CEO: A Board's Best Moves," *Directors & Boards* (Winter 2004), pp. 36–38. These findings are supported by a later study by Booz Allen Hamilton in which 1,595 worldwide companies during 1995 to 2005 showed the same results. See J. Webber, "The Accidental CEO," *Business Week* (April 23, 2007), pp. 64–72.

41. Q. Yue, "Antecedents of Top Management Successor Origin in China," paper presented to the annual meeting of the *Academy of Management*, Seattle, WA (2003); A. A. Buchko and D. DiVerde, "Antecedents, Moderators, and Consequences of CEO Turnover: A Review and Reconceptualization," Paper presented to *Midwest Academy of Management* (Lincoln, NE: 1997), p. 10; W. Ocasio, "Institutionalized Action and Corporate Governance: The Reliance on Rules of CEO Succession," *Administrative Science Quarterly* (June 1999), pp. 384–416.

42. C. Gopinath, "Turnaround: Recognizing Decline and Initiating Intervention," *Long Range Planning* (December 1991), pp. 96–101.

43. K. B. Schwartz and K. Menon, "Executive Succession in Failing Firms," *Academy of Management Journal* (September 1985), pp. 680–686; A. A. Cannella Jr., and M. Lubatkin, "Succession as a Sociopolitical Process: Internal Impediments to Outsider Selection," *Academy of Management Journal* (August 1993), pp. 763–793; W. Boeker and J. Goodstein, "Performance and Succession Choice: The Moderating Effects of Governance and Ownership," *Academy of Management Journal* (February 1993), pp. 172–186.

44. W. Boeker, "Executive Migration and Strategic Change: The Effect of Top Manager Movement on Product-Market Entry," *Administrative Science Quarterly* (June 1997), pp. 213–236.

45. E. Brockmann, J. J. Hoffman, and D. Dawley, "A Contingency Theory of CEO Successor Choice and Post-Bankruptcy Strategic Change," Paper presented to annual meeting of *Academy of Management*, Seattle, WA (2003).

46. P. Lorange, and D. Murphy, "Bringing Human Resources Into Strategic Planning: System Design Characteristics," in *Strategic Human Resource Management*, edited by C. J. Fombrun, N. M. Tichy, and M. A. Devanna (New York: John Wiley & Sons, 1984), pp. 281–283.

47. M. Leuchter, "Management Farm Teams," *Journal of Business Strategy* (May/June 1998), pp. 29–32.

48. S. Armour, "Playing the Succession Game," *USA Today* (November 24, 2003), p. 3B.

49. D. A. Waldman and T. Korbar, "Student Assessment Center Performance in the Prediction of Early Career Success," *Academy of Management Learning and Education* (June 2004), pp. 151–167.

50. "Coming and Going," Survey of Corporate Leadership, *Economist* (October 25, 2003), pp. 12–14.

51. R. A. Pitts, "Strategies and Structures for Diversification," *Academy of Management Journal* (June 1997), pp. 197–208.

52. K. E. Mishra, G. M. Spreitzer, and A. K. Mishra, "Preserving Employee Morale During Downsizing," *Sloan Management Review* (Winter 1998), pp. 83–95.

53. B. O'Reilly, "Is Your Company Asking Too Much?" *Fortune* (March 12, 1990), p. 41. For more information on the emotional reactions of survivors of downsizing, see C. R. Stoner and R. I. Hartman, "Organizational Therapy: Building Survivor Health & Competitiveness," *SAM Advanced Management Journal* (Summer 1997), pp. 15–31, 41.

54. S. R. Fisher and M. A. White, "Downsizing in a Learning Organization: Are There Hidden Costs?" *Academy of Management Review* (January 2000), pp. 244–251.

55. T. M. Amabile and R. Conti, "Changes in the Work Environment for Creativity During Downsizing," *Academy of Management Journal* (December 1999), pp. 630–640; A. G. Bedeian and A. A. Armenakis, "The Cesspool Syndrome: How Dreck Floats to the Top of Declining Organizations," *Academy of Management Executive* (February 1998), pp. 58–67.

56. For a more complete listing of the psychological and behavioral reactions to downsizing, see M. L. Marks and K. P. De Meuse, "Resizing the Organization: Maximizing the Gain While Minimizing the Pain of Layoffs, Divestitures, and Closings," *Organizational Dynamics*, Vol. 34, No. 1 (2005), pp. 19–35.

57. D. J. Flanagan and K. C. O'Shaughnessy, "The Effect of Layoffs on Firm Reputation," *Journal of Management* (June 2005), pp. 445–463.

58. *Wall Street Journal* (December 22, 1992), p. B1.

59. R. D. Nixon, M. A. Hitt, H. Lee, and E. Jeong, "Market Reactions to Announcements of Corporate Downsizing Actions and Implementation Strategies," *Strategic Management Journal* (November 2004), pp. 1121–1129; G. D. Bruton, J. K. Keels, and C. L. Shook, "Downsizing the Firm: Answering the Strategic Questions," *Academy of Management Executive* (May 1996), pp. 38–45; E. G. Love and N. Nohria, "Reducing Slack: The Performance Consequences of Downsizing by Large Industrial Firms, 1977–93," *Strategic Management Journal* (December 2005), pp. 1087–1108; C. D. Zatzick and R. D. Iverson, "High-Involvement Management and Workforce Reduction: Competitive Advantage or Disadvantage?" *Academy of Management Journal* (October 2006), pp. 999–1015.

60. M. A. Hitt, B. W. Keats, H. F. Harback, and R. D. Nixon, "Rightsizing: Building and Maintaining Strategic Leadership and Long-Term Competitiveness," *Organizational Dynamics* (Autumn 1994), pp. 18–32. For additional suggestions, see W. F. Cascio, "Strategies for Responsible Restructuring," *Academy of Management Executive* (August 2002), pp. 80–91, and T. Mroczkowski and M. Hanaoka, "Effective Rightsizing Strategies in Japan and America: Is There a Convergence of Employment Practices?" *Academy of Management Executive* (May 1997), pp. 57–67. For an excellent list of cost-reduction programs for use in short, medium, and long-term time horizons, see F. Gandolfi, "Cost Reductions, Downsizing-related Layoffs, and HR Practices," *SAM Advanced Management Journal* (Spring 2008), pp. 52–58.

61. J. S. Black and H. B. Gregersen, "The Right Way to Manage Expats," *Harvard Business Review* (March–April 1999), pp. 52–61.

62. Ibid, p. 54.

63. J. I. Sanchez, P. E. Spector, and C. L. Cooper, "Adapting to a Boundaryless World: A Developmental Expatriate Model," *Academy of Management Executive* (May 2000), pp. 96–106.

64. R. L. Tung, *The New Expatriates* (Cambridge, MA.: Ballinger, 1988); J. S. Black, M. Mendenhall, and G. Oddou, "Toward a Comprehensive Model of International Adjustment: An Integration of Multiple Theoretical Perspectives," *Academy of Management Review* (April 1991), pp. 291–317.

65. M. A. Carpenter, W. G. Sanders, and H. B. Gregersen, "Bundling Human Capital with Organizational Context: The Impact of International Assignment Experience on Multinational Firm Performance and CEO Pay," *Academy of Management Journal* (June 2001), pp. 493–511.

66. P. M. Caligiuri and S. Colakoglu, "A Strategic Contingency Approach to Expatriate Assignment Management," *Human Resource Management Journal*, Vol. 17, No. 4 (2007), pp. 393–410.

67. M. A. Shaffer, D. A. Harrison, K. M. Gilley, and D. M. Luk, "Struggling for Balance Amid Turbulence on International Assignments: Work-Family Conflict, Support, and Commitment," *Journal of Management*, Vol. 27, No. 1 (2001), pp. 99–121.

68. J. S. Black and H. B. Gregersen, "The Right Way to Manage Expats," *Harvard Business Review* (March–April 1999), p. 54.

69. G. Stern, "GM Executive's Ties to Native Country Help Auto Maker Clinch Deal in China," *Wall Street Journal* (November 2, 1995), p. B7.

70. K. Roth, "Managing International Interdependence: CEO Characteristics in a Resource-Based Framework," *Academy of Management Journal* (February 1995), pp. 200–231.

71. M. Subramaniam and N. Venkatraman, "Determinants of Transnational New Product Development Capability: Testing the Influence of Transferring and Deploying Tacit Overseas Knowledge," *Strategic Management Journal* (April 2001), pp. 359–378.

72. J. S. Lublin, "An Overseas Stint Can Be a Ticket to the Top," *Wall Street Journal* (January 29, 1996), pp. B1, B2.

73. "Cisco Shifts Senior Executives to India," *St. Cloud* (MN) *Times* (January 13, 2007), p. 6A.

74. "Expatriate Employees: In Search of Stealth," *The Economist* (April 23, 2005), pp. 62–64.

75. M. Meaney, C. Pung, and S. Kamath, "Creating Organizational Transformations," *McKinsey Quarterly Online* (September 10, 2008).

76. L. G. Love, R. L. Priem, and G. T. Lumpkin, "Explicitly Articulated Strategy and Firm Performance Under Alternative Levels of Centralization," *Journal of Management*, Vol. 28, No. 5 (2002), pp. 611–627.

77. G. G. Gordon, "The Relationship of Corporate Culture to Industry Sector and Corporate Performance," in *Gaining Control of the Corporate Culture,* edited by R. H. Kilmann, M. J. Saxton, R. Serpa, and Associates (San Francisco: Jossey-Bass, 1985), p. 123; T. Kono, "Corporate Culture and Long-Range Planning," *Long Range Planning* (August 1990), pp. 9–19.

78. B. Mike and J. W. Slocum, Jr., "Changing Culture at Pizza Hut and Yum! Brands," *Organizational Dynamics*, Vol. 32, No. 4 (2003), pp. 319–330.

79. T. J. Tetenbaum, "Seven Key Practices That Improve the Chance for Expected Integration and Synergies," *Organizational Dynamics* (Autumn 1999), pp. 22–35.

80. B. Bremner and G. Edmondson, "Japan: A Tale of Two Mergers," *Business Week* (May 10, 2004), p. 42.

81. P. Very, M. Lubatkin, R. Calori, and J. Veiga, "Relative Standing and the Performance of Recently Acquired European Firms," *Strategic Management Journal* (September 1997), pp. 593–614.

82. A. R. Malekzadeh and A. Nahavandi, "Making Mergers Work by Managing Cultures," *Journal of Business Strategy* (May/June 1990), pp. 53–57; A. Nahavandi, and A. R. Malekzadeh, "Acculturation in Mergers and Acquisitions," *Academy of Management Review* (January 1988), pp. 79–90.

83. C. Ghosn, "Saving the Business Without Losing the Company," *Harvard Business Review* (January 2002), pp. 37–45; B. Bremner, G. Edmondson, C. Dawson, D. Welch, and K. Kerwin, "Nissan's Boss," *Business Week* (October 4, 2004), pp. 50–60.

84. D. Harding and T. Rouse, "Human Due Diligence," *Harvard Business Review* (April 2007), pp. 124–131.

85. J. J. Keller, "Why AT&T Takeover of NCR Hasn't Been a Real Bell Ringer," *Wall Street Journal* (September 19, 1995), pp. A1, A5.

86. J. W. Gibson and D. V. Tesone, "Management Fads: Emergence, Evolution, and Implications for Managers," *Academy of Management Executive* (November 2001), pp. 122–133.

87. For additional information, see S. J. Carroll, Jr., and M. L. Tosi, Jr., *Management by Objectives: Applications and Research* (New York: Macmillan, 1973), and A. P. Raia, *Managing by Objectives* (Glenview, IL: Scott, Foresman, and Company, 1974).

88. J. W. Gibson, D. V. Tesone, and C. W. Blackwell, "Management Fads: Here Yesterday, Gone Today?" *SAM Advanced Management Journal* (Autumn 2003), pp. 12–17.

89. J. W. Gibson and D. V. Tesone, "Management Fads: Emergence, Evolution, and Implications fdor Managers," *Academy of Management Executive* (November 2001), p. 125.

90. S. S. Masterson, and M. S. Taylor, "Total Quality Management and Performance Appraisal: An Integrative Perspective," *Journal of Quality Management*, Vol. 1, No. 1 (1996), pp. 67–89.

91. R. J. Vokurka, R. R. Lummus, and D. Krumwiede, "Improving Manufacturing Flexibility: The Enduring Value of JIT and TQM," *SAM Advanced Management Journal* (Winter 2007), pp. 14–21.

92. T. Y. Choi and O. C. Behling, "Top Managers and TQM Success: One More Look After All These Years," *Academy of Management Executive* (February 1997), pp. 37–47.

93. R. J. Schonberger, "Total Quality Management Cuts a Broad Swath—Through Manufacturing and Beyond," *Organizational Dynamics* (Spring 1992), pp. 16–28.

94. T. C. Powell, "Total Quality Management as Competitive Advantage: A Review and Empirical Study," *Strategic Management Journal* (January 1995), pp. 15–37.

95. G. Hofstede, "Culture's Recent Consequences: Using Dimensional Scores in Theory and Research," *International Journal of Cross Cultural Management*, Vol. 1, No. 1 (2001), pp. 11–17; G. Hofstede, *Cultures and Organizations: Software of the Mind* (London: McGraw-Hill, 1991); G. Hofstede and M. H. Bond, "The Confucius Connection: From Cultural Roots to Economic Growth," *Organizational Dynamics* (Spring 1988), pp. 5–21; R. Hodgetts, "A Conversation with Geert Hofstede," *Organizational Dynamics* (Spring 1993), pp. 53–61.

96. M. Javidan and R. J. House, "Cultural Acumen for the Global Manager: Lessons from Project GLOBE," *Organizational Dynamics*, Vol. 29, No. 4 (2001), pp. 289–305; R. J. House, P. J. Hanges, M. Javidan, P. W. Dorfman, and V. Gupta, eds., *Culture, Leadership and Organizations: The GLOBE Study of 62 Societies* (Thousand Oaks, CA: Sage, 2004).

97. M. Javidan and R. J. House, "Cultural Acumen for the Global Manager: Lessons from Project GLOBE," *Organizational Dynamics*, Vol. 29, No. 4 (2001), p. 303.

98. See G. Hofstede and M. H. Bond, "The Confucius Connection, From Cultural Roots to Economic Growth," *Organizational Dynamics*, (Spring 1988), pp. 12–13.

99. H. K. Steensma, L. Marino, K. M. Weaver, and P. H. Dickson, "The Influence of National Culture on the Formation of Technology Alliances by Entrepreneurial Firms," *Academy of Management Journal* (October 2000), pp. 951–973.

100. T. T. Herbert, "Multinational Strategic Planning: Matching Central Expectations to Local Realities," *Long Range Planning* (February 1999), pp. 81–87.

101. M. A. Geletkancz, "The Salience of 'Culture's Consequences': The Effects of Cultural Values on Top Executive Commitment to the Status Quo," *Strategic Management Journal* (September 1997), pp. 615–634.

102. G. Hofstede and M. H. Bond, "The Confucius Connection, From Cultural Roots to Economic Growth," *Organizational Dynamics*, (Spring 1988), p. 20.

103. B. Groysberg, A. Nanda, and N. Nohria, "The Risky Business of Hiring Stars," *Harvard Business Review* (May 2004), pp. 92–100.

104. D. Jones, "Employers Learning That 'B Players' Hold the Cards," *USA Today* (September 9, 2003), pp. 1B–2B.

105. B. Elgin, "Green—Up to a Point," *Business Week* (March 3, 2008), pp. 25–26.

106. D. Keirsey, *Please Understand Me II* (Del Mar, CA: Prometheus Nemesis Book Co., 1998).

evaluation and Control

Nucor Corporation, one of the most successful steel firms operating in the United States, keeps its evaluation and control process simple and easy to manage. According to Kenneth Iverson, Chairman of the Board:

We try to keep our focus on what really matters—bottom-line performance and long-term survival. That's what we want our people to be thinking about. Management takes care not to distract the company with a lot of talk about other issues. We don't clutter the picture with lofty vision statements or ask employees to pursue vague, intermediate objectives such as "excellence" or burden them with complex business strategies. Our competitive strategy is to build manufacturing facilities economically and to operate them efficiently. Period. Basically, we ask our employees to produce more product for less money. Then we reward them for doing that well.[1]

The **evaluation and control process** ensures that a company is achieving what it set out to accomplish. It compares performance with desired results and provides the feedback necessary for management to evaluate results and take corrective action, as needed. This process can be viewed as a five-step feedback model, as depicted in **Figure 11–1.**

1. **Determine what to measure:** Top managers and operational managers need to specify what implementation processes and results will be monitored and evaluated. The processes and results must be capable of being measured in a reasonably objective and consistent manner. The focus should be on the most significant elements in a process—the ones that account for the highest proportion of expense or the greatest number of problems. Measurements must be found for all important areas, regardless of difficulty.

2. **Establish standards of performance:** Standards used to measure performance are detailed expressions of strategic objectives. They are measures of acceptable performance results. Each standard usually includes a tolerance range, which defines acceptable deviations. Standards can be set not only for final output but also for intermediate stages of production output.

3. **Measure actual performance:** Measurements must be made at predetermined times.

4. **Compare actual performance with the standard:** If actual performance results are within the desired tolerance range, the measurement process stops here.

Learning Objectives

After reading this chapter, you should be able to:

- Understand the basic control process
- Choose among traditional measures, such as ROI, and shareholder value measures, such as economic value added, to properly assess performance
- Use the balanced scorecard approach to develop key performance measures
- Apply the benchmarking process to a function or an activity
- Understand the impact of problems with measuring performance
- Develop appropriate control systems to support specific strategies

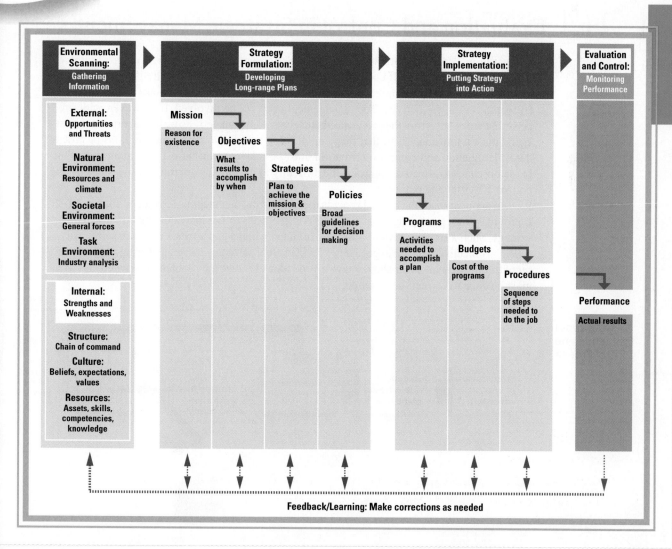

5. **Take corrective action:** If actual results fall outside the desired tolerance range, action must be taken to correct the deviation. The following questions must be answered:

   a. Is the deviation only a chance fluctuation?

   b. Are the processes being carried out incorrectly?

   c. Are the processes appropriate to the achievement of the desired standard? Action must be taken that will not only correct the deviation but also prevent its happening again.

   d. Who is the best person to take corrective action?

Top management is often better at the first two steps of the control model than it is at the last two follow-through steps. It tends to establish a control system and then delegate the implementation to others. This can have unfortunate results. Nucor is unusual in its ability to deal with the entire evaluation and control process.

11.1 Evaluation and Control in Strategic Management

Evaluation and control information consists of performance data and activity reports (gathered in Step 3 in **Figure 11–1**). If undesired performance results because the strategic management processes were inappropriately used, operational managers must know about it so that they can correct the employee activity. Top management need not be involved. If, however, undesired performance results from the processes themselves, top managers, as well as operational managers, must know about it so that they can develop new implementation programs or procedures. Evaluation and control information must be relevant to what is being monitored. One of the obstacles to effective control is the difficulty in developing appropriate measures of important activities and outputs.

An application of the control process to strategic management is depicted in **Figure 11–2.** It provides strategic managers with a series of questions to use in evaluating an implemented strategy. Such a strategy review is usually initiated when a gap appears between a company's financial objectives and the expected results of current activities. After answering the proposed set of questions, a manager should have a good idea of where the problem originated and what must be done to correct the situation.

FIGURE 11–1
Evaluation and Control Process

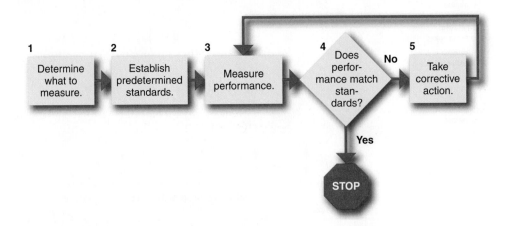

FIGURE 11–2
Evaluating an
Implemented
Strategy

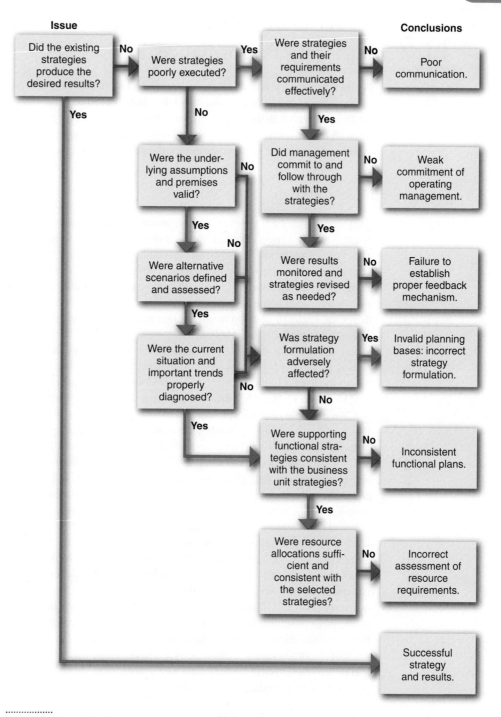

SOURCE: *From "The Strategic Review,"* Planning Review, *Jeffrey A. Schmidt, 1998 © MCB University Press Limited.
Republished with permission of Emerald Group Publishing Ltd.*

11.2 Measuring Performance

Performance is the end result of activity. Select measures to assess performance based on the organizational unit to be appraised and the objectives to be achieved. The objectives that were established earlier in the strategy formulation part of the strategic management process (dealing with profitability, market share, and cost reduction, among others) should certainly be used to measure corporate performance once the strategies have been implemented.

APPROPRIATE MEASURES

Some measures, such as return on investment (ROI) and earnings per share (EPS), are appropriate for evaluating a corporation's or a division's ability to achieve a profitability objective. This type of measure, however, is inadequate for evaluating additional corporate objectives such as social responsibility or employee development. Even though profitability is a corporation's major objective, ROI and EPS can be computed only after profits are totaled for a period. It tells what happened after the fact—not what is happening or what will happen. A firm, therefore, needs to develop measures that predict likely profitability. These are referred to as **steering controls** because they measure variables that influence future profitability. Every industry has its own set of key metrics which tend to predict profits. Airlines, for example, closely monitor cost per passenger mile. In the 1990s, Southwest's cost per passenger mile was 6.43¢, the lowest in the industry, contrasted with American's 12.95¢, the highest in the industry.[2] Its low costs gave Southwest a significant competitive advantage.

An example of a steering control used by retail stores is the *inventory turnover ratio*, in which a retailer's cost of goods sold is divided by the average value of its inventories. This measure shows how hard an investment in inventory is working; the higher the ratio, the better. Not only does quicker moving inventory tie up less cash in inventories, it also reduces the risk that the goods will grow obsolete before they're sold—a crucial measure for computers and other technology items. For example, Office Depot increased its inventory turnover ratio from 6.9 in one year to 7.5 the next year, leading to improved annual profits.[3]

Another steering control is customer satisfaction. Research reveals that companies that score high on the *American Customer Satisfaction Index (ACSI)*, a measure developed by the University of Michigan's National Research Center, have higher stock returns and better cash flows than do those companies that score low on the ACSI. A change in a firm's customer satisfaction typically works its way through a firm's value chain and is eventually reflected in quarterly profits.[4] Other approaches to measuring customer satisfaction include Oracle's use of the ratio of quarterly sales divided by customer service requests and the total number of hours that technicians spend on the phone solving customer problems. To help executives keep track of important steering controls, Netsuite developed *dashboard* software that displays critical information in easy-to-read computer graphics assembled from data pulled from other corporate software programs.[5]

TYPES OF CONTROLS

Controls can be established to focus on actual performance results (output), the activities that generate the performance (behavior), or on resources that are used in performance (input). **Output controls** specify what is to be accomplished by focusing on the end result of the behaviors through the use of objectives and performance targets or milestones. **Behavior controls** specify how something is to be done through policies, rules, standard operating procedures, and orders from a superior. **Input controls** emphasize resources, such as knowledge, skills, abilities, values, and motives of employees.[6]

Output, behavior, and input controls are not interchangeable. Output controls (such as sales quotas, specific cost-reduction or profit objectives, and surveys of customer satisfaction) are most appropriate when specific output measures have been agreed on but the cause–effect connection between activities and results is not clear. Behavior controls (such as following company procedures, making sales calls to potential customers, and getting to work on time) are most appropriate when performance results are hard to measure, but the cause–effect connection between activities and results is clear. Input controls (such as number of years of education and experience) are most appropriate when output is difficult to measure and there is no clear cause–effect relationship between behavior and performance (such as in college teaching). Corporations following the strategy of conglomerate diversification tend to emphasize output controls with their divisions and subsidiaries (presumably because they are managed independently of each other), whereas, corporations following concentric diversification use all three types of controls (presumably because synergy is desired).[7] Even if all three types of control are used, one or two of them may be emphasized more than another depending on the circumstances. For example, Muralidharan and Hamilton propose that as a multinational corporation moves through its stages of development, its emphasis on control should shift from being primarily output at first, to behavioral, and finally to input control.[8]

Examples of increasingly popular behavior controls are the ISO 9000 and 14000 Standards Series on quality and environmental assurance, developed by the International Standards Association of Geneva, Switzerland. Using the **ISO 9000 Standards Series** (composed of five sections from 9000 to 9004) is a way of objectively documenting a company's high level of quality operations. Using the **ISO 14000 Standards Series** is a way to document the company's impact on the environment. A company wanting ISO 9000 certification would document its process for product introductions, among other things. ISO 9001 would require this firm to separately document design input, design process, design output, and design verification—a large amount of work. ISO 14001 would specify how companies should establish, maintain and continually improve an environmental management system. Although the average total cost for a company to be ISO 9000 certified is close to $250,000, the annual savings are around $175,000 per company.[9] Overall, ISO 14001-related savings are about equal to the costs, reports Tim Delawder, Vice President of SWD, Inc., a metal finishing company in Addison, Illinois.[10]

Many corporations view ISO 9000 certification as assurance that a supplier sells quality products. Firms such as DuPont, Hewlett-Packard, and 3M have facilities registered to ISO standards. Companies in more than 60 countries, including Canada, Mexico, Japan, the United States (including the entire U.S. auto industry), and the European Union, require ISO 9000 certification of their suppliers.[11] The same is happening for ISO 14000. Both Ford and General Motors require their suppliers to follow ISO 14001. In a survey of manufacturing executives, 51% of the executives found that ISO 9000 certification increased their international competitiveness. Other executives noted that it signaled their commitment to quality and gave them a strategic advantage over noncertified competitors.[12]

Since its ISO 14000 certification, SWD Inc. has become a showplace for environmental awareness. According to SWD's Delawder, ISO 14000 certification improves environmental awareness among employees, reduces risks of violating regulations, and improves the firm's image among customers and the local community.[13]

Another example of a behavior control is a company's monitoring of employee phone calls and PCs to ensure that employees are behaving according to company guidelines. In a study by the American Management Association, nearly 75% of U.S. companies actively monitored their workers' communications and on-the-job activities. Around 54% tracked individual employees' Internet connections and 38% admitted storing and reviewing their employees' e-mail. About 45% of the companies surveyed had disciplined workers (16% had fired them). For example, Xerox fired 40 employees for visiting pornographic Web sites.[14]

ACTIVITY-BASED COSTING

Activity-based costing (ABC) is a recently developed accounting method for allocating indirect and fixed costs to individual products or product lines based on the value-added activities going into that product.[15] This accounting method is thus very useful in doing a value-chain analysis of a firm's activities for making outsourcing decisions. Traditional cost accounting, in contrast, focuses on valuing a company's inventory for financial reporting purposes. To obtain a unit's cost, cost accountants typically add direct labor to the cost of materials. Then they compute overhead from rent to R&D expenses, based on the number of direct labor hours it takes to make a product. To obtain unit cost, they divide the total by the number of items made during the period under consideration.

Traditional cost accounting is useful when direct labor accounts for most of total costs and a company produces just a few products requiring the same processes. This may have been true of companies during the early part of the twentieth century, but it is no longer relevant today, when overhead may account for as much as 70% of manufacturing costs. According to Bob Van Der Linde, CEO of a contract manufacturing services firm in San Diego, California: "Overhead is 80% to 90% in our industry, so allocation errors lead to pricing errors, which could easily bankrupt the company."[16] The appropriate allocation of indirect costs and overhead has thus become crucial for decision making. The traditional volume-based cost-driven system systematically understates the cost per unit of products with low sales volumes and products with a high degree of complexity. Similarly, it overstates the cost per unit of products with high sales volumes and a low degree of complexity.[17] When Chrysler used ABC, it discovered that the true cost of some of the parts used in making cars was 30 times what the company had previously estimated.[18]

ABC accounting allows accountants to charge costs more accurately than the traditional method because it allocates overhead far more precisely. For example, imagine a production line in a pen factory where black pens are made in high volume and blue pens in low volume. Assume that it takes eight hours to retool (reprogram the machinery) to shift production from one kind of pen to the other. The total costs include supplies (the same for both pens), the direct labor of the line workers, and factory overhead. In this instance, a very significant part of the overhead cost is the cost of reprogramming the machinery to switch from one pen to another. If the company produces 10 times as many black pens as blue pens, 10 times the cost of the reprogramming expenses will be allocated to the black pens as to the blue pens under traditional cost accounting methods. This approach underestimates, however, the true cost of making the blue pens.

ABC accounting, in contrast, first breaks down pen manufacturing into its activities. It is then very easy to see that it is the activity of changing pens that triggers the cost of retooling. The ABC accountant calculates an average cost of setting up the machinery and charges it against each batch of pens that requires retooling, regardless of the size of the run. Thus a product carries only those costs for the overhead it actually consumes. Management is now able to discover that its blue pens cost almost twice as much as do the black pens. Unless the company is able to charge a higher price for its blue pens, it cannot make a profit on these pens. Unless there is a strategic reason why it must offer blue pens (such as a key customer who must have a small number of blue pens with every large order of black pens or a marketing trend away from black to blue pens), the company will earn significantly greater profits if it completely stops making blue pens.[19]

ENTERPRISE RISK MANAGEMENT

Enterprise Risk Management (ERM) is a corporatewide, integrated process for managing the uncertainties that could negatively or positively influence the achievement of the corporation's objectives. In the past, managing risk was done in a fragmented manner within functions or business units. Individuals would manage process risk, safety risk, and insurance, financial, and other assorted risks. As a result of this fragmented approach, companies would take huge risks in some areas of the business while over-managing substantially smaller risks in other areas. ERM is being adopted because of the increasing amount of environmental uncertainty that can affect an entire corporation. As a result, the position Chief Risk Officer is one of the fastest growing executive positions in U.S. corporations.[20] Microsoft uses scenario analysis to identify key business risks. According to Microsoft's treasurer, Brent Callinicos, "The scenarios are really what we're trying to protect against."[21] The scenarios were the possibility of an earthquake in the Seattle region and a major downturn in the stock market.

The process of rating risks involves three steps:

1. Identify the risks using scenario analysis or brainstorming or by performing risk self-assessments.

2. Rank the risks, using some scale of impact and likelihood.

3. Measure the risks, using some agreed-upon standard.

Some companies are using value at risk, or VAR (effect of unlikely events in normal markets), and stress testing (effect of plausible events in abnormal markets) methodologies to measure the potential impact of the financial risks they face. DuPont uses earnings at risk (EAR) measuring tools to measure the effect of risk on reported earnings. It can then manage risk to a specified earnings level based on the company's "risk appetite." With this integrated view, DuPont can view how risks affect the likelihood of achieving certain earnings targets.[22] Research has shown that companies with integrative risk management capabilities achieve superior economic performance.[23]

PRIMARY MEASURES OF CORPORATE PERFORMANCE

The days when simple financial measures such as ROI or EPS were used alone to assess overall corporate performance are coming to an end. Analysts now recommend a broad range of methods to evaluate the success or failure of a strategy. Some of these methods are stakeholder measures, shareholder value, and the balanced scorecard approach. Even though each of these methods has supporters as well as detractors, the current trend is clearly toward more complicated financial measures and an increasing use of non-financial measures of corporate performance. For example, research indicates that companies pursuing strategies founded on innovation and new product development now tend to favor non-financial over financial measures.[24]

Traditional Financial Measures

The most commonly used measure of corporate performance (in terms of profits) is **Return On Investment (ROI).** It is simply the result of dividing net income before taxes by the total amount invested in the company (typically measured by total assets). Although using ROI has several advantages, it also has several distinct limitations. (See **Table 11–1.**) Although ROI gives the impression of objectivity and precision, it can be easily manipulated.

Earnings Per Share (EPS), which involves dividing net earnings by the amount of common stock, also has several deficiencies as an evaluation of past and future performance. First, because alternative accounting principles are available, EPS can have several different but

TABLE 11–1	Before using Return on Investment (ROI) as a measure of corporate performance, consider its advantages and limitations.
Advantages and Limitations of Using ROI as a Measure of Corporate Performance	**Advantages** ■ ROI is a single, comprehensive number that includes all revenues, costs, and expenses. ■ It can be used to evaluate the performance of a general manager of a division or SBU. ■ It can be compared across companies to see which firms are performing better. ■ It provides an incentive to use current assets efficiently and to acquire new assets only when they would increase profits significantly. **Limitations** ■ ROI is very sensitive to depreciation policy. ROI can be increased by writing down the value of assets through accelerated depreciation. ■ It can discourage investment in new facilities or the upgrading of old ones. Older plants with depreciated assets have an advantage over newer plants in earning a higher ROI. ■ It provides an incentive for division managers to set transfer prices for goods sold to other divisions as high as possible and to lobby for corporate policy favoring in-house transfers over purchases from other firms. ■ Managers tend to focus more on ROI in the short-run over its use in the long-run. This provides an incentive for goal displacement and other dysfunctional consequences. ■ ROI is not comparable across industries which operate under different conditions of favorability. ■ It is influenced by the overall economy and will tend to be higher in prosperity and lower in a recession.

SOURCE: Adapted from "Advantages and Limitations of ROI as a measure of Corporate Performance" from *Organizational Policy and Strategic Management: Text and Cases*, and ed. by James M. Higgins, copyright © 1983. By permission of South-Western College Publishing, a division of Thomson Learning.

equally acceptable values, depending on the principle selected for its computation. Second, because EPS is based on accrual income, the conversion of income to cash can be near term or delayed. Therefore, EPS does not consider the time value of money. **Return On Equity (ROE)**, which involves dividing net income by total equity, also has limitations because it is also derived from accounting-based data. In addition, EPS and ROE are often unrelated to a company's stock price.

Operating cash flow, the amount of money generated by a company before the cost of financing and taxes, is a broad measure of a company's funds. This is the company's net income plus depreciation, depletion, amortization, interest expense, and income tax expense.[25] Some takeover specialists look at a much narrower **free cash flow**: the amount of money a new owner can take out of the firm without harming the business. This is net income plus depreciation, depletion, and amortization less capital expenditures and dividends. The free cash flow ratio is very useful in evaluating the stability of an entrepreneurial venture.[26] Although cash flow may be harder to manipulate than earnings, the number can be increased by selling accounts receivable, classifying outstanding checks as accounts payable, trading securities, and capitalizing certain expenses, such as direct-response advertising.[27]

Because of these and other limitations, ROI, EPS, ROE, and operating cash flow are not by themselves adequate measures of corporate performance. At the same time, these traditional financial measures are very appropriate when used with complementary financial and non-financial measures. For example, some non–financial performance measures often used by Internet business ventures are *stickiness* (length of Web site visit), *eyeballs* (number of people who visit a Web site), and *mindshare* (brand awareness). Mergers and acquisitions may be priced on multiples of *MUUs* (monthly unique users) or even on registered users.

TABLE 11–2   A Sample Scorecard for "Keeping Score" with Stakeholders

Stakeholder Category	Possible Near-Term Measures	Possible Long-Term Measures
Customers	Sales ($ and volume) New customers Number of new customer needs met ("tries")	Growth in sales Turnover of customer base Ability to control price

Suppliers	Cost of raw material
	Delivery time
	Inventory
	Availability of raw material
		Growth rates of:
		   Raw material costs
		   Delivery time
		   Inventory
		New ideas from suppliers

Financial community	EPS Stock price Number of "buy" lists ROE	Ability to convince Wall Street of strategy Growth in ROE
Employees	Number of suggestions Productivity Number of grievances	Number of internal promotions Turnover
Congress	Number of new pieces of legislation that affect the firm Access to key members and staff	Number of new regulations that affect industry Ratio of "cooperative" vs. "competitive" encounters
Consumer advocate (CA)	Number of meetings Number of "hostile" encounters Number of times coalitions formed Number of legal actions	Number of changes in policy due to CA Number of CA-initiated "calls for help"
Environmentalists	Number of meetings Number of hostile encounters Number of times coalitions formed Number of EPA complaints Number of legal actions	Number of changes in policy due to environmentalists Number of environmentalist "calls for help"

SOURCE: R. E. Freeman, *Strategic Management: A Stakeholder Approach* (Boston: Ballinger Publishing Company, 1984), p. 179. Copyright © 1984 by R. E. Freeman. Reprinted by permission of R. Edward Freeman.

Stakeholder Measures

Each stakeholder has its own set of criteria to determine how well the corporation is performing. These criteria typically deal with the direct and indirect impacts of corporate activities on stakeholder interests. Top management should establish one or more stakeholder measures for each stakeholder category so that it can keep track of stakeholder concerns. (See **Table 11–2**.)

Shareholder Value

Because of the belief that accounting-based numbers such as ROI, ROE, and EPS are not reliable indicators of a corporation's economic value, many corporations are using shareholder value as a better measure of corporate performance and strategic management effectiveness.

Shareholder value can be defined as the present value of the anticipated future stream of cash flows from the business plus the value of the company if liquidated. Arguing that the purpose of a company is to increase shareholder wealth, shareholder value analysis concentrates on cash flow as the key measure of performance. The value of a corporation is thus the value of its cash flows discounted back to their present value, using the business's cost of capital as the discount rate. As long as the returns from a business exceed its cost of capital, the business will create value and be worth more than the capital invested in it. For example, Deere and Company charges each business unit a cost of capital of 1% of assets a month. Each business unit is required to earn a shareholder value-added profit margin of 20% on average over the business cycle. Financial rewards are linked to this measure.[28]

The New York consulting firm Stern Stewart & Company devised and popularized two shareholder value measures: economic value added (EVA) and market value added (MVA). A basic tenet of EVA and MVA is that businesses should not invest in projects unless they can generate a profit above the cost of capital. Stern Stewart argues that a deficiency of traditional accounting-based measures is that they assume the cost of capital to be zero.[29] Well-known companies, such as Coca-Cola, General Electric, AT&T, Whirlpool, Quaker Oats, Eli Lilly, Georgia-Pacific, Polaroid, Sprint, Teledyne, and Tenneco have adopted MVA and/or EVA as the best yardstick for corporate performance.

Economic Value Added (EVA) has become an extremely popular shareholder value method of measuring corporate and divisional performance and may be on its way to replacing ROI as the standard performance measure. EVA measures the difference between the pre-strategy and post-strategy values for the business. Simply put, EVA is after-tax operating income minus the total annual cost of capital. The formula to measure EVA is:

$$\text{EVA} = \text{after tax operating income} - (\text{investment in assets} \times \text{weighted average cost of capital})\text{[30]}$$

The cost of capital combines the cost of debt and equity. The annual cost of borrowed capital is the interest charged by the firm's banks and bondholders. To calculate the cost of equity, assume that shareholders generally earn about 6% more on stocks than on government bonds. If long-term treasury bills are selling at 7.5%, the firm's cost of equity should be 13.5%—more if the firm is in a risky industry. A corporation's overall cost of capital is the weighted-average cost of the firm's debt and equity capital. The investment in assets is the total amount of capital invested in the business, including buildings, machines, computers, and investments in R&D and training (allocating costs annually over their useful life). Because the typical balance sheet understates the investment made in a company, Stern Stewart has identified 150 possible adjustments, before EVA is calculated.[31] Multiply the firm's total investment in assets by the weighted-average cost of capital. Subtract that figure from after-tax operating income. If the difference is positive, the strategy (and the management employing it) is generating value for the shareholders. If it is negative, the strategy is destroying shareholder value.[32]

Roberto Goizueta, past-CEO of Coca-Cola, explained, "We raise capital to make concentrate, and sell it at an operating profit. Then we pay the cost of that capital. Shareholders pocket the difference."[33] Managers can improve their company's or business unit's EVA by: (1) earning more profit without using more capital, (2) using less capital, and (3) investing capital in high-return projects. Studies have found that companies using EVA outperform their median competitor by an average of 8.43% of total return annually.[34] EVA does, however, have some limitations. For one thing, it does not control for size differences across plants or divisions. As with ROI, managers can manipulate the numbers. As with ROI, EVA is an after-the-fact measure and cannot be used like a steering control.[35] Although proponents of EVA argue that EVA (unlike Return on Investment, Equity, or Sales) has a strong relationship to stock price, other studies do not support this contention.[36]

Market Value Added (MVA) is the difference between the market value of a corporation and the capital contributed by shareholders and lenders. Like net present value, it measures the stock market's estimate of the net present value of a firm's past and expected capital investment projects. As such, MVA is the present value of future EVA.[37] To calculate MVA,

1. Add all the capital that has been put into a company—from shareholders, bondholders, and retained earnings.

2. Reclassify certain accounting expenses, such as R&D, to reflect that they are actually investments in future earnings. This provides the firm's total capital. So far, this is the same approach taken in calculating EVA.

3. Using the current stock price, total the value of all outstanding stock, adding it to the company's debt. This is the company's market value. If the company's market value is greater than all the capital invested in it, the firm has a positive MVA—meaning that management (and the strategy it is following) has created wealth. In some cases, however, the market value of the company is actually less than the capital put into it, which means shareholder wealth is being destroyed.

Microsoft, General Electric, Intel, and Coca-Cola have tended to have high MVAs in the United States, whereas, General Motors and RJR Nabisco have had low ones.[38] Studies have shown that EVA is a predictor of MVA. Consecutive years of positive EVA generally lead to a soaring MVA.[39] Research also reveals that CEO turnover is significantly correlated with MVA and EVA, whereas ROA and ROE are not. This suggests that EVA and MVA may be more appropriate measures of the market's evaluation of a firm's strategy and its management than are the traditional measures of corporate performance.[40] Nevertheless, these measures consider only the financial interests of the shareholder and ignore other stakeholders, such as environmentalists and employees.

Climate change is likely to lead to new regulations, technological remedies, and shifts in consumer behavior. It will thus have a significant impact on the financial performance of many corporations. To learn how global warming is likely to affect different industrial sectors and corporations, see the **Environmental Sustainability Issue** feature.

Balanced Scorecard Approach: Using Key Performance Measures

Rather than evaluate a corporation using a few financial measures, Kaplan and Norton argue for a "balanced scorecard," that includes non-financial as well as financial measures.[41] This approach is especially useful given that research indicates that non-financial assets explain 50% to 80% of a firm's value.[42] The **balanced scorecard** combines financial measures that tell the results of actions already taken with operational measures on customer satisfaction, internal processes, and the corporation's innovation and improvement activities—the drivers of future financial performance. Thus steering controls are combined with output controls. In the balanced scorecard, management develops goals or objectives in each of four areas:

1. **Financial:** How do we appear to shareholders?
2. **Customer:** How do customers view us?
3. **Internal business perspective:** What must we excel at?
4. **Innovation and learning:** Can we continue to improve and create value?[43]

Each goal in each area (for example, avoiding bankruptcy in the financial area) is then assigned one or more measures, as well as a target and an initiative. These measures can be thought of as **key performance measures**—measures that are essential for achieving a desired strategic option.[44] For example, a company could include cash flow, quarterly sales growth, and ROE as measures for success in the financial area. It could include market share (competitive position goal), customer satisfaction, and percentage of new sales coming from new products (customer acceptance goal) as measures under the customer perspective. It could include cycle time and unit cost (manufacturing excellence goal) as measures under the internal business perspective. It could include time to develop next generation products (technology leadership objective) under the innovation and learning perspective.

ENVIRONMENTAL sustainability issue

HOW GLOBAL WARMING COULD AFFECT CORPORATE VALUATION

How will global warming affect the value of a corporation's stock? To answer this question, the U.S.-based consulting firm McKinsey & Company undertook a joint project with the Carbon Trust, a UK research organization. The resulting research found that the large reductions in greenhouse gas emissions needed to stop climate change will create significant opportunities and risks for most companies. Well-positioned, forward-thinking corporations could, for example, increase company value (stock price × number of shares outstanding) by up to 80%. The research found that as much as 65% of company value was at risk in some industrial sectors.

Industrial Sector	Maximum Company Value Creation Opportunity for Prepared Company	Maximum Company Value at Risk for a Company Failing to Adapt
Aluminum	30%	65%
Automotive	60%	65%
Oil & Gas (Exploration & Production)	0%	35%
Oil & Gas (Refining)	7%	30%
Consumer Electronics	35%	7%
Building Materials	80%	20%
Beer	0%	15%

The joint study investigated the industrial sectors of aluminum, automotive, oil and gas, consumer electronics, building materials, and beer. It quantified the impacts on each industrial sector and found that the impact of climate change will vary by sector. The resulting report lists both the maximum value creation opportunity for a prepared company and the maximum company value at risk for a company that fails to adapt.

Note that the oil and gas sectors will have very few opportunities (especially in exploration and production), but many risks. This overall negative impact will mean falling cash flows and stock prices for the companies in those sectors. In contrast, the building materials sector will benefit from rising demand for improved energy efficiency and insulation products, leading to increasing cash flows and stock prices. The consumer electronics sector is also in a good position. Using current technology, consumer electronics companies can make their products significantly more energy efficient (by reducing active and standby power consumption) at low and diminishing costs. Automobile companies, in contrast, face both a high level of opportunities and threats. The better prepared companies should do well, but the laggards will likely face serious cash flow problems and falling stock prices.

Tom Delay, Carbon Trust's CEO warns: "We have a short window of opportunity to act but at present business and investor actions are way out of step with the need to tackle climate change. They must be urgently re-aligned by developing new business and investment strategies and by working with governments to develop policy frameworks that reward early and effective action to rapidly reduce carbon emissions."

SOURCES: M. W. Brinkman, N. Hoffman, J. M. Oppenheim, "How Climate Change Could Affect Corporate Valuations," *McKinsey Quarterly* (Autumn 2008), pp. 1–7; "Climate Change: The Trillion Dollar Wake-Up Call," *Carbon Trust* Web site (September 22, 2008), www.carbontrust.com.

A survey by Bain & Company reported that 50% of *Fortune 1,000* companies in North America and about 40% in Europe use a version of the balanced scorecard.[45] Another survey reported that the balanced scorecard is used by over half of *Fortune's Global 1000* companies.[46] A study of the *Fortune 500* firms in the U.S. and the *Post 300* firms in Canada revealed the most popular non-financial measures to be customer satisfaction, customer service, product quality, market share, productivity, service quality, and core competencies. New product development, corporate culture, and market growth were not far behind.[47] DuPont's Engineering Polymers Division uses the balanced scorecard to align employees, business units, and shared services around a common strategy involving productivity improvements and revenue growth.[48] Corporate experience with the balanced scorecard reveals that a firm should tailor the system to suit its situation, not just adopt it as a cookbook approach. When the balanced scorecard complements corporate strategy, it improves performance. Using the method in a mechanistic fashion without any link to strategy hinders performance and may even decrease it.[49]

Evaluating Top Management and the Board of Directors

Through its strategy, audit, and compensation committees, a board of directors closely evaluates the job performance of the CEO and the top management team. The vast majority of American (91%), European (75%), and Asian (75%) boards review the CEO's performance using a formalized process.[50] Objective evaluations of the CEO by the board are very important given that CEOs tend to evaluate senior management's performance significantly more positively than do other executives.[51] The board is concerned primarily with overall corporate profitability as measured quantitatively by ROI, ROE, EPS, and shareholder value. The absence of short-run profitability certainly contributes to the firing of any CEO. The board, however, is also concerned with other factors.

Members of the compensation committees of today's boards of directors generally agree that a CEO's ability to establish strategic direction, build a management team, and provide leadership are more critical in the long run than are a few quantitative measures. The board should evaluate top management not only on the typical output-oriented quantitative measures, but also on behavioral measures—factors relating to its strategic management practices. According to a survey by Korn/Ferry International, the criteria used by American boards are financial (81%), ethical behavior (63%), thought leadership (58%), corporate reputation (32%), stock price performance (22%), and meeting participation (10%).[52] The specific items that a board uses to evaluate its top management should be derived from the objectives that both the board and top management agreed on earlier. If better relations with the local community and improved safety practices in work areas were selected as objectives for the year (or for five years), these items should be included in the evaluation. In addition, other factors that tend to lead to profitability might be included, such as market share, product quality, or investment intensity.

Performance evaluations of the overall board's performance are standard practice for 87% of directors in the Americas, 72% in Europe, and 62% in Asia.[53] Evaluations of individual directors are less common. According to a PriceWaterhouseCoopers survey of 1,100 directors, 77% of the directors agreed that individual directors should be appraised regularly on their performance, but only 37% responded that they actually do so.[54] Corporations that have successfully used board performance appraisal systems are Target, Radio Shack, Eastman Chemical Company, Bell South, Raytheon, and Gillette.[55]

Chairman-CEO Feedback Instrument. An increasing number of companies are evaluating their CEO by using a 17-item questionnaire developed by Ram Charan, an authority on corporate governance. The questionnaire focuses on four key areas: (1) company performance, (2) leadership of the organization, (3) team-building and management succession, and (4) leadership of external constituencies.[56] After taking an hour to complete the questionnaire, the board of KeraVision, Inc., used it as a basis for a lengthy discussion with the CEO, Thomas Loarie. The board criticized Loarie for "not tempering enthusiasm with reality" and urged Loarie to develop a clear management succession plan. The evaluation caused Loarie to more closely involve the board in setting the company's primary objectives and discussing "where we are, where we want to go, and the operating environment."[57]

Management Audit. **Management audits** are very useful to boards of directors in evaluating management's handling of various corporate activities. Management audits have been developed to evaluate activities such as corporate social responsibility, functional areas such as the marketing department, and divisions such as the international division. These can be helpful if the board has selected particular functional areas or activities for improvement.

Strategic Audit. The strategic audit, presented in the **Chapter 1 Appendix 1.A**, is a type of management audit. The strategic audit provides a checklist of questions, by area or issue, that enables a systematic analysis of various corporate functions and activities to be made. It is a type of management audit and is extremely useful as a diagnostic tool to pinpoint corporate-wide problem areas and to highlight organizational strengths and weaknesses.[58] A strategic audit can help determine why a certain area is creating problems for a corporation and help generate solutions to the problem. As such, it can be very useful in evaluating the performance of top management.

PRIMARY MEASURES OF DIVISIONAL AND FUNCTIONAL PERFORMANCE

Companies use a variety of techniques to evaluate and control performance in divisions, strategic business units (SBUs), and functional areas. If a corporation is composed of SBUs or divisions, it will use many of the same performance measures (ROI or EVA, for instance) that it uses to assess overall corporate performance. To the extent that it can isolate specific functional units such as R&D, the corporation may develop responsibility centers. It will also use typical functional measures, such as market share and sales per employee (marketing), unit costs and percentage of defects (operations), percentage of sales from new products and number of patents (R&D), and turnover and job satisfaction (HRM). For example, FedEx uses Enhanced Tracker software with its COSMOS database to track the progress of its 2.5 to 3.5 million shipments daily. As a courier is completing her or his day's activities, the Enhanced Tracker asks whether the person's package count equals the Enhanced Tracker's count. If the count is off, the software helps reconcile the differences.[59]

During strategy formulation and implementation, top management approves a series of programs and supporting *operating budgets* from its business units. During evaluation and control, actual expenses are contrasted with planned expenditures, and the degree of variance is assessed. This is typically done on a monthly basis. In addition, top management will probably require *periodic statistical reports* summarizing data on such key factors as the number of new customer contracts, the volume of received orders, and productivity figures.

Responsibility Centers

Control systems can be established to monitor specific functions, projects, or divisions. Budgets are one type of control system that is typically used to control the financial indicators of performance. **Responsibility centers** are used to isolate a unit so that it can be evaluated separately from the rest of the corporation. Each responsibility center, therefore, has its own budget and is evaluated on its use of budgeted resources. It is headed by the manager responsible for the center's performance. The center uses resources (measured in terms of costs or expenses) to produce a service or a product (measured in terms of volume or revenues). There are five major types of responsibility centers. The type is determined by the way the corporation's control system measures these resources and services or products.

1. **Standard cost centers: Standard cost centers** are primarily used in manufacturing facilities. Standard (or expected) costs are computed for each operation on the basis of historical data. In evaluating the center's performance, its total standard costs are multiplied by the units produced. The result is the *expected* cost of production, which is then compared to the *actual* cost of production.

2. **Revenue centers:** With **revenue centers**, production, usually in terms of unit or dollar sales, is measured without consideration of resource costs (for example, salaries). The center is thus judged in terms of effectiveness rather than efficiency. The effectiveness of a sales region, for example, is determined by comparing its actual sales to its projected or previous year's sales. Profits are not considered because sales departments have very limited influence over the cost of the products they sell.

3. **Expense centers:** Resources are measured in dollars, without consideration for service or product costs. Thus budgets will have been prepared for engineered expenses (costs that can be calculated) and for discretionary expenses (costs that can be only estimated). Typical **expense centers** are administrative, service, and research departments. They cost a company money, but they only indirectly contribute to revenues.

4. **Profit centers:** Performance is measured in terms of the difference between revenues (which measure production) and expenditures (which measure resources). A **profit center** is typically established whenever an organizational unit has control over both its resources and its products or services. By having such centers, a company can be organized into divisions of separate product lines. The manager of each division is given autonomy to the extent that he or she is able to keep profits at a satisfactory (or better) level.

    Some organizational units that are not usually considered potentially autonomous can, for the purpose of profit center evaluations, be made so. A manufacturing department, for example, can be converted from a standard cost center (or expense center) into a profit center; it is allowed to charge a transfer price for each product it "sells" to the sales department. The difference between the manufacturing cost per unit and the agreed-upon transfer price is the unit's "profit."

    Transfer pricing is commonly used in vertically integrated corporations and can work well when a price can be easily determined for a designated amount of product. Even though most experts agree that market-based transfer prices are the best choice, only 30%–40% of companies use market price to set the transfer price. (Of the rest, 50% use cost; 10%–20% use negotiation.)[60] When a price cannot be set easily, however, the relative bargaining power of the centers, rather than strategic considerations, tends to influence the agreed-upon price. Top management has an obligation to make sure that these political considerations do not overwhelm the strategic ones. Otherwise, profit figures for each center will be biased and provide poor information for strategic decisions at both the corporate and divisional levels.

5. **Investment centers:** Because many divisions in large manufacturing corporations use significant assets to make their products, their asset base should be factored into their performance evaluation. Thus it is insufficient to focus only on profits, as in the case of profit centers. An **investment center's** performance is measured in terms of the difference between its resources and its services or products. For example, two divisions in a corporation made identical profits, but one division owns a $3 million plant, whereas the other owns a $1 million plant. Both make the same profits, but one is obviously more efficient; the smaller plant provides the shareholders with a better return on their investment. The most widely used measure of investment center performance is ROI.

Most single-business corporations, such as Apple, tend to use a combination of cost, expense, and revenue centers. In these corporations, most managers are functional specialists and manage against a budget. Total profitability is integrated at the corporate level. Multidivisional corporations with one dominating product line (such as Anheuser-Busch), that have diversified into a few businesses but that still depend on a single product line (such as beer) for most of their revenue and income, generally use a combination of cost, expense, revenue, and profit centers. Multidivisional corporations, such as General Electric, tend to emphasize investment centers—although in various units throughout the corporation other types of responsibility centers are also used. One problem with using responsibility centers, however, is that the separation needed to measure and evaluate a division's performance can diminish the level of cooperation among divisions that is needed to attain synergy for the corporation as a whole. (This problem is discussed later in this chapter, under "Suboptimization.")

Using Benchmarking to Evaluate Performance

According to Xerox Corporation, the company that pioneered this concept in the United States, **benchmarking** is "the continual process of measuring products, services, and practices against the toughest competitors or those companies recognized as industry leaders."[61] Benchmarking, an increasingly popular program, is based on the concept that it makes no sense to reinvent something that someone else is already using. It involves openly learning how others do something better than one's own company so that the company not only can imitate, but perhaps even improve on its techniques. The benchmarking process usually involves the following steps:

1. Identify the area or process to be examined. It should be an activity that has the potential to determine a business unit's competitive advantage.

2. Find behavioral and output measures of the area or process and obtain measurements.

3. Select an accessible set of competitors and best-in-class companies against which to benchmark. These may very often be companies that are in completely different industries, but perform similar activities. For example, when Xerox wanted to improve its order fulfillment, it went to L. L. Bean, the successful mail order firm, to learn how it achieved excellence in this area.

4. Calculate the differences among the company's performance measurements and those of the best-in-class and determine why the differences exist.

5. Develop tactical programs for closing performance gaps.

6. Implement the programs and then compare the resulting new measurements with those of the best-in-class companies.

Benchmarking has been found to produce best results in companies that are already well managed. Apparently poorer performing firms tend to be overwhelmed by the discrepancy between their performance and the benchmark—and tend to view the benchmark as too difficult to reach.[62] Nevertheless, a survey by Bain & Company of 460 companies of various sizes across all U.S. industries indicated that more than 70% were using benchmarking in either a major or limited manner.[63] Cost reductions range from 15% to 45%.[64] Benchmarking can also increase sales, improve goal setting, and boost employee motivation.[65] The average cost of a benchmarking study is around $100,000 and involves 30 weeks of effort.[66] Manco, Inc., a small Cleveland-area producer of duct tape regularly benchmarks itself against Wal-Mart, Rubbermaid, and Pepsico to enable it to better compete with giant 3M. APQC (American Productivity & Quality Center), a Houston research group, established the Open Standards Benchmarking Collaborative database, composed of more than 1,200 commonly used measures and individual benchmarks, to track the performance of core operational functions. Firms can submit their performance data to this online database to learn how they compare to top performers and industry peers (see www.apqc.org).

INTERNATIONAL MEASUREMENT ISSUES

The three most widely used techniques for international performance evaluation are ROI, budget analysis, and historical comparisons. In one study, 95% of the corporate officers interviewed stated that they use the same evaluation techniques for foreign and domestic operations.

Rate of return was mentioned as the single most important measure.[67] However, ROI can cause problems when it is applied to international operations: Because of foreign currencies, different accounting systems, different rates of inflation, different tax laws, and the use of transfer pricing, both the net income figure and the investment base may be seriously distorted.[68] To deal with different accounting systems throughout the world, the London-based International Accounting Standards Board developed International Financial Reporting Standards (IFRS) to harmonize accounting practices. Over 100 countries have thus far adopted the rules. Foreign-based companies operating in the U.S. have a choice starting 2009 of using IFRS accounting standards or continuing the costly process translating their accounts using America's Generally Accepted Accounting Principles (GAAP). Nevertheless, enforcement and cultural interpretations of the international rules can still vary by country and may undercut what is hoped to be a uniform accounting system.[69]

A study of 79 MNCs revealed that *international transfer pricing* from one country unit to another is primarily used not to evaluate performance but to minimize taxes.[70] Taxes are an important issue for MNCs, given that corporate tax rates vary from 55% in Kuwait, 41%% in Japan, 40% in the United States, and 34% in Canada and India, to 28% in the UK, South Korea, and Mexico, 25% in China, 18% in Singapore, 10% in Albania, and 0% in Bahrain and the Cayman Islands.[71] For example, the U.S. Internal Revenue Service contended in the early 1990s that many Japanese firms doing business in the United States artificially inflated the value of U.S. deliveries in order to reduce the profits and thus the taxes of their American subsidiaries.[72] Parts made in a subsidiary of a Japanese MNC in a low-tax country such as Singapore could be shipped to its subsidiary in a high-tax country such as the United States at such a high price that the U.S. subsidiary reports very little profit (and thus pays few taxes), while the Singapore subsidiary reports a very high profit (but also pays few taxes because of the lower tax rate). A Japanese MNC could, therefore, earn more profit worldwide by reporting less profit in high-tax countries and more profit in low-tax countries. Transfer pricing can thus be one way the parent company can reduce taxes and "capture profits" from a subsidiary. Other common ways of transferring profits to the parent company (often referred to as the *repatriation of profits*) are through dividends, royalties, and management fees.[73]

Among the most important barriers to international trade are the different standards for products and services. There are at least three categories of standards: safety/environmental, energy efficiency, and testing procedures. Existing standards have been drafted by such bodies as the British Standards Institute (BSI-UK) in the United Kingdom, Japanese Industrial Standards Committee (JISC), AFNOR in France, DIN in Germany, CSA in Canada, and American Standards Institute in the United States. These standards traditionally created entry barriers that served to fragment various industries, such as major home appliances, by country. The International Electrotechnical Commission (IEC) standards were created to harmonize standards in the European Union and eventually to serve as worldwide standards, with some national deviations to satisfy specific needs. Because the European Union (EU) was the first to harmonize the many different standards of its member countries, the EU is shaping standards for the rest of the world. In addition, the International Organization for Standardization (ISO) is preparing and publishing international standards. These standards provide a foundation for regional associations to build upon. CANENA, the Council for Harmonization of Electrotechnical Standards of the Nations of the Americas, was created in 1992 to further coordinate the harmonization of standards in North and South America. Efforts are also under way in Asia to harmonize standards.[74]

An important issue in international trade is counterfeiting/piracy. Firms in developing nations around the world make money by making counterfeit/pirated copies of well-known name-brand products and selling them globally as well as locally. See the **Global Issue** feature to learn how this is being done.

Authorities in international business recommend that the control and reward systems used by a global MNC be different from those used by a multidomestic MNC.[75] A *multidomestic*

GLOBAL issue

COUNTERFEIT GOODS & PIRATED SOFTWARE: A GLOBAL PROBLEM

"We know that 15 to 20 percent of all goods in China are counterfeit," states Dan Chow, a law professor at Ohio State University. This includes products from Tide detergent and Budweiser beer to Marlboro cigarettes. There is a saying in Shanghai, China: "We can copy everything except your mother." Yamaha estimates that five out of every six bikes bearing its brand name are fake. Fake Cisco network routers (known as "Chiscos") and counterfeit Nokia mobile phones can be easily found throughout China. Procter & Gamble estimates that 15% of the soaps and detergents under its Head & Shoulders, Vidal Sassoon, Safeguard, and Tide brands in China are counterfeit, costing the company $150 million in lost sales.

In Yiwu, a few hours from Shanghai, one person admitted to a *60 Minutes* reporter that she could make 1,000 pairs of counterfeit Nike shoes in 10 days for $4.00 a pair. According to the market research firm Automotive Resources, the profit margins on counterfeit shock absorbers can reach 80% versus only 15% for the real ones. The World Custom Organization estimates that 7% of the world's merchandise is bogus.

Tens of thousands of counterfeiters are active in China. They range from factories mixing shampoo and soap in back rooms to large state-owned enterprises making copies of soft drinks and beer. Other factories make everything from car batteries to automobiles. Mobile CD factories with optical disc-mastering machines counterfeit music and software. *60 Minutes* found a small factory in Donguan making fake Callaway golf clubs and bags at a rate of 500 bags per week. Factories in southern Guangdong or Fujian provinces truck their products to a central distribution center, such as the one in Yiwu. They may also be shipped across the border into Russia, Pakistan, Vietnam, or Burma. Chinese counterfeiters have developed a global reach through their connections with organized crime.

As much as 35% of software on personal computers worldwide is pirated, according to the Business Software Alliance and ISDC, a market research firm. The worldwide cost of software piracy was around $34 billion in 2005. For example, 21% of the software sold in the United States is pirated. That figure increases to 26%–30% in the European Union, 83% in Russia, Algeria, and Bolivia, to 86% in China, 87% in Indonesia, and 90% in Vietnam.

SOURCES: "The Sincerest Form of Flattery," *The Economist* (April 7, 2007), pp. 64–65; F. Balfour, "Fakes!" Business Week (February 7, 2005), pp. 54–64; "PC Software Piracy," *The Economist* (June 10, 2006), p. 102; "The World's Greatest Fakes," *60 Minutes*, CBS News (August 8, 2004); "Business Software Piracy," *Pocket World in Figures 2004* (London: Economist & Profile Book, 2003), p. 60; D. Roberts, F. Balfour, P. Magnusson, P. Engardio, and J. Lee, "China's Piracy Plague," *Business Week* (June 5, 2000), pp. 44–48.

MNC should use loose controls on its foreign units. The management of each geographic unit should be given considerable operational latitude, but it should be expected to meet some performance targets. Because profit and ROI measures are often unreliable in international operations, it is recommended that the MNC's top management, in this instance, emphasize budgets and non-financial measures of performance such as market share, productivity, public image, employee morale, and relations with the host country government.[76] Multiple measures should be used to differentiate between the worth of the subsidiary and the performance of its management.

A *global MNC*, however, needs tight controls over its many units. To reduce costs and gain competitive advantage, it is trying to spread the manufacturing and marketing operations of a few fairly uniform products around the world. Therefore, its key operational decisions must be centralized. Its environmental scanning must include research not only into each of the national markets in which the MNC competes but also into the "global arena" of the interaction between markets. Foreign units are thus evaluated more as cost centers, revenue centers, or expense centers than as investment or profit centers because MNCs operating in a global industry do not often make the entire product in the country in which it is sold.

11.3 Strategic Information Systems

Before performance measures can have any impact on strategic management, they must first be communicated to the people responsible for formulating and implementing strategic plans. Strategic information systems can perform this function. They can be computer based or manual, formal or informal. One of the key reasons given for the bankruptcy of International Harvester was the inability of the corporation's top management to precisely determine income by major class of similar products. Because of this inability, management kept trying to fix ailing businesses and was unable to respond flexibly to major changes and unexpected events. In contrast, one of the key reasons for the success of Wal-Mart has been management's use of the company's sophisticated information system to control purchasing decisions. Cash registers in Wal-Mart retail stores transmit information hourly to computers at company headquarters. Consequently, managers know every morning exactly how many of each item were sold the day before, how many have been sold so far in the year, and how this year's sales compare to last year's. The information system allows all reordering to be done automatically by computers, without any managerial input. It also allows the company to experiment with new products without committing to big orders in advance. In effect, the system allows the customers to decide through their purchases what gets reordered.

ENTERPRISE RESOURCE PLANNING (ERP)

Many corporations around the world have adopted **enterprise resource planning (ERP)** software. ERP unites all of a company's major business activities, from order processing to production, within a single family of software modules. The system provides instant access to critical information to everyone in the organization, from the CEO to the factory floor worker. Because of the ability of ERP software to use a common information system throughout a company's many operations around the world, it is becoming the business information systems' global standard. The major providers of this software are SAP AG, Oracle (including People-Soft), J. D. Edwards, Baan, and SSA.

The German company SAP AG originated the concept with its R/3 software system. Microsoft, for example, used R/3 to replace a tangle of 33 financial tracking systems in 26 subsidiaries. Even though it cost the company $25 million and took 10 months to install, R/3 annually saves Microsoft $18 million. Coca-Cola uses the R/3 system to enable a manager in Atlanta to use her personal computer to check the latest sales of 20-ounce bottles of Coke Classic in India. Owens-Corning envisioned that its R/3 system allowed salespeople to learn what was available at any plant or warehouse and to quickly assemble orders for customers.

ERP may not fit every company, however. The system is extremely complicated and demands a high level of standardization throughout a corporation. Its demanding nature often forces companies to change the way they do business. There are three reasons ERP could fail: (1) insufficient tailoring of the software to fit the company, (2) inadequate training, and (3) insufficient implementation support.[77] Over the two-year period of installing R/3, Owens-Corning had to completely overhaul its operations. Because R/3 was incompatible with Apple's very organic corporate culture, the company was able to apply it only to its order management and financial operations, but not to manufacturing. Other companies that had difficulty installing and using ERP are Whirlpool, Hershey Foods, Volkswagen, and Stanley Works. At Whirlpool, SAP's software led to missed and delayed shipments, causing Home Depot to cancel its agreement for selling Whirlpool products.[78] One survey found that 65% of executives believed that ERP had a moderate chance of hurting their business because of implementation problems. Nevertheless, the payoff from ERP software is likely to be worth the effort. ERP is a key ingredient for gaining competitive advantage, streamlining operations, and managing a lean manufacturing system.[79]

RADIO FREQUENCY IDENTIFICATION (RFID)

Radio frequency identification (RFID) is an electronic tagging technology used in a number of companies to improve supply-chain efficiency. By tagging containers and items with tiny chips, companies use the tags as wireless bar-codes to track inventory more efficiently. Both Wal-Mart and the U.S. Department of Defense began requiring their largest suppliers to incorporate RFID tags in their goods in 2003. Although Tesco has experimented with RFID in Europe, full-scale use of the technology proved unfeasible because of incompatible standards. Nevertheless, some suppliers and retailers of expensive consumer products view the cost of the tag as worthwhile because it reduces losses from counterfeiting and theft. RFID technology is currently in wide use as wireless commuter passes for toll roads, tunnels, and bridges. Even though RFID standards may vary among companies, individual firms like Audi, Sony, and Dole Food use the tags to track goods within their own factories and warehouses.[80] According to Dan Mullen of AIM Global, "RFID will go through a process similar to what happened in bar code technology 20 years ago. . . . As companies implement the technology deeper within their operations, the return on investment will grow and applications will expand."[81]

DIVISIONAL AND FUNCTIONAL IS SUPPORT

At the divisional or SBU level of a corporation, the information system should be used to support, reinforce, or enlarge its business-level strategy through its decision support system. An SBU pursuing a strategy of overall cost leadership could use its information system to reduce costs either by improving labor productivity or improving the use of other resources such as inventory or machinery. Merrill Lynch took this approach when it developed PRISM software to provide its 500 U.S. retail offices with quick access to financial information in order to boost brokers' efficiency. Another SBU, in contrast, might want to pursue a differentiation strategy. It could use its information system to add uniqueness to the product or service and contribute to quality, service, or image through the functional areas. FedEx wanted to use superior service to gain a competitive advantage. It invested significantly in several types of information systems to measure and track the performance of its delivery service. Together, these information systems gave FedEx the fastest error-response time in the overnight delivery business.

11.4 Problems in Measuring Performance

The measurement of performance is a crucial part of evaluation and control. The lack of quantifiable objectives or performance standards and the inability of the information system to provide timely and valid information are two obvious control problems. According to Meg Whitman, past-CEO of eBay, "If you can't measure it, you can't control it." That's why eBay has a multitude of measures, from total revenues and profits to *take rate*, the ratio of revenues to the value of goods traded on the site.[82] Without objective and timely measurements, it would be extremely difficult to make operational, let alone strategic, decisions. Nevertheless, the use of timely, quantifiable standards does not guarantee good performance. The very act of monitoring and measuring performance can cause side effects that interfere with overall corporate performance. Among the most frequent negative side effects are a short-term orientation and goal displacement.

SHORT-TERM ORIENTATION

Top executives report that in many situations, they analyze neither the long-term implications of present operations on the strategy they have adopted nor the operational impact of a strategy on the corporate mission. Long-run evaluations may not be conducted because executives (1) don't realize their importance, (2) believe that short-run considerations are more important than long-run considerations, (3) aren't personally evaluated on a long-term basis, or (4) don't have the time to make a long-run analysis.[83] There is no real justification for the first and last reasons. If executives realize the importance of long-run evaluations, they make the time needed to conduct them. Even though many chief executives point to immediate pressures from the investment community and to short-term incentive and promotion plans to support the second and third reasons, evidence does not always support their claims.[84]

At one international heavy-equipment manufacturer, managers were so strongly motivated to achieve their quarterly revenue target that they shipped unfinished products from their plant in England to a warehouse in the Netherlands for final assembly. By shipping the incomplete products, they were able to realize the sales before the end of the quarter—thus fulfilling their budgeted objective and making their bonuses. Unfortunately, the high cost of assembling the goods at a distant location (requiring not only the renting the warehouse but also paying additional labor) ended up reducing the company's overall profit.[85]

Many accounting-based measures, such as EPS and ROI, encourage a **short-term orientation** in which managers consider only current tactical or operational issues and ignore long-term strategic ones. Because growth in EPS (earnings per share) is an important driver of near-term stock price, top managers are biased against investments that might reduce short-term EPS.[86] This is compounded by pressure from financial analysts and investors for quarterly *earnings guidance*, that is, estimates of future corporate earnings.[87] For example, in a $303 million law suit settled in 2008, General Motors admitted that its top managers and auditor had misstated its revenue, earnings, and cash flow in order to artificially inflate the company's stock price and debt securities.[88]

Table 11.1 indicates that one of the limitations of ROI as a performance measure is its short-term nature. In theory, ROI is not limited to the short run, but in practice it is often difficult to use this measure to realize long-term benefits for a company. Because managers can often manipulate both the numerator (earnings) and the denominator (investment), the resulting ROI figure can be meaningless. Advertising, maintenance, and research efforts can be reduced. Estimates of pension-fund profits, unpaid receivables, and old inventory, are easy to adjust. Optimistic estimates of returned products, bad debts, and obsolete inventory inflate the present year's sales and earnings.[89] Expensive retooling and plant modernization can be delayed as long as a manager can manipulate figures on production defects and absenteeism. In a recent survey of financial executives, 80% of the managers stated that they would decrease spending on research and development, advertising, maintenance, and hiring in order to meet earnings targets. More than half said that they would delay a new project even if it meant sacrificing value.[90]

Mergers can be undertaken that will do more for the present year's earnings (and the next year's paycheck) than for the division's or corporation's future profits. For example, research on 55 firms that engaged in major acquisitions revealed that even though the firms performed poorly after the acquisition, the acquiring firms' top management still received significant increases in compensation.[91] Determining CEO compensation on the basis of firm size rather than performance is typical and is particularly likely for firms that are not monitored closely by independent analysts.[92]

Research supports the conclusion that many CEOs and their friends on the board of directors' compensation committee manipulate information to provide themselves a pay raise.[93] For example, CEOs tend to announce bad news—thus reducing the company's stock price—just before the issuance of stock options. Once the options are issued, the CEOs tend to announce good news—thus raising the stock price and making their options more valuable.[94] Board compensation committees tend to expand the peer group comparison outside their industry to include lower-performing firms to justify a high raise to the CEO. They tend to do this when the company performs poorly, the industry performs well, the CEO is already highly paid, and shareholders are powerful and active.[95]

GOAL DISPLACEMENT

If not carefully done, monitoring and measuring of performance can actually result in a decline in overall corporate performance. **Goal displacement** is the confusion of means with ends and occurs when activities originally intended to help managers attain corporate objectives become ends in themselves—or are adapted to meet ends other than those for which they were intended. Two types of goal displacement are behavior substitution and suboptimization.

Behavior Substitution

Behavior substitution refers to a phenomenon when people substitute activities that do not lead to goal accomplishment for activities that do lead to goal accomplishment because the wrong activities are being rewarded. Managers, like most other people, tend to focus more of their attention on behaviors that are clearly measurable than on those that are not. Employees often receive little or no reward for engaging in hard-to-measure activities such as cooperation and initiative. However, easy-to-measure activities might have little or no relationship to the desired good performance. Rational people, nevertheless, tend to work for the rewards that the system has to offer. Therefore, people tend to substitute behaviors that are recognized and rewarded for behaviors that are ignored, without regard to their contribution to goal accomplishment. A research study of 157 corporations revealed that most of the companies made little attempt to identify areas of non-financial performance that might advance their chosen strategy. Only 23% consistently built and verified cause-and-effect relationships between intermediate controls (such as number of patents filed or product flaws) and company performance.[96]

A U.S. Navy quip sums up this situation: "What you inspect (or reward) is what you get." If the reward system emphasizes quantity while merely asking for quality and cooperation, the system is likely to produce a large number of low-quality products and unsatisfied customers.[97] A proposed law governing the effect of measurement on behavior is that *quantifiable measures drive out non-quantifiable measures*.

A classic example of behavior substitution happened a few years ago at Sears. Sears' management thought that it could improve employee productivity by tying performance to rewards. It, therefore, paid commissions to its auto shop employees as a percentage of each repair bill. Behavior substitution resulted as employees altered their behavior to fit the reward system. The results were over-billed customers, charges for work never done, and a scandal that tarnished Sears' reputation for many years.[98]

Suboptimization

Suboptimization refers to the phenomenon of a unit optimizing its goal accomplishment to the detriment of the organization as a whole. The emphasis in large corporations on developing separate responsibility centers can create some problems for the corporation as a whole. To the extent that a division or functional unit views itself as a separate entity, it might refuse to cooperate with other units or divisions in the same corporation if cooperation could in some way negatively affect its performance evaluation. The competition between divisions to achieve a high ROI can result in one division's refusal to share its new technology or work process improvements. One division's attempt to optimize the accomplishment of its goals can cause other divisions to fall behind and thus negatively affect overall corporate performance. One common example of suboptimization occurs when a marketing department approves an early shipment date to a customer as a means of getting an order and forces the manufacturing department into overtime production for that one order. Production costs are raised, which reduces the manu-facturing department's overall efficiency. The end result might be that, although marketing achieves its sales goal, the corporation as a whole fails to achieve its expected profitability.[99]

11.5 Guidelines for Proper Control

In designing a control system, top management should remember that controls should follow strategy. Unless controls ensure the use of the proper strategy to achieve objectives, there is a strong likelihood that dysfunctional side effects will completely undermine the implementation of the objectives. The following guidelines are recommended:

1. **Control should involve only the minimum amount of information needed to give a reliable picture of events:** Too many controls create confusion. Focus on the strategic factors by following the **80/20 rule**: *Monitor those 20% of the factors that determine 80% of the results.* See Strategy Highlight 11.1 for some additional rules of thumb used by strategists.

2. **Controls should monitor only meaningful activities and results, regardless of measurement difficulty:** If cooperation between divisions is important to corporate performance, some form of qualitative or quantitative measure should be established to monitor cooperation.

3. **Controls should be timely so that corrective action can be taken before it is too late:** Steering controls, controls that monitor or measure the factors influencing performance, should be stressed so that advance notice of problems is given.

STRATEGY highlight 11.1

SOME RULES OF THUMB IN STRATEGY

Managers use many *rules of thumb,* such as the 80/20 rule, in making strategic decisions. These "rules" are primarily approximations based on years of practical experience by many managers. Although most of these rules have no objective data to support them, they are often accepted by practicing managers as a way of estimating the cost or time necessary to conduct certain activities. They may be useful because they can help narrow the number of alternatives into a shorter list for more detailed analysis. Some of the rules of thumb used by experienced strategists are described here.

INDIRECT COSTS OF STRATEGIC INITIATIVES

■ The R&D *Rule of Sevens* is that for every $1 spent in developing a new prototype, $7 will be needed to get a product ready for market, and $7 additional dollars will be required to get to the first sale. These estimates don't cover working capital requirements for stocking distributor inventories.

■ First-year costs for promoting a new consumer goods product are 33% of anticipated first-year sales. Second-year costs should be 20%, and third-year costs 15%.

■ A reasonably successful patent-based innovation will require $2 million in legal defense costs.

SAFETY MARGINS FOR NEW BUSINESS INITIATIVES

■ A new manufacturing business should have sufficient startup capital to cover one year of costs.

■ A new consumer goods business should have sufficient capital to cover two years of business.

■ A new professional services business should have sufficient capital to cover three years of costs.

SOURCE: R. West and F. Wolek, "Rules of Thumb in Strategic Thinking," *Strategy & Leadership* (March/April 1999), p. 34. Copyright © 1999 by Emerald Group Publishing Ltd. Reprinted by permission.

4. **Long-term *and* short-term controls should be used:** If only short-term measures are emphasized, a short-term managerial orientation is likely.

5. **Controls should aim at pinpointing exceptions:** Only activities or results that fall outside a predetermined tolerance range should call for action.

6. **Emphasize the reward of meeting or exceeding standards rather than punishment for failing to meet standards:** Heavy punishment of failure typically results in goal displacement. Managers will "fudge" reports and lobby for lower standards.

If corporate culture complements and reinforces the strategic orientation of a firm, there is less need for an extensive formal control system. In their book *In Search of Excellence*, Peters and Waterman state that "the stronger the culture and the more it was directed toward the marketplace, the less need was there for policy manuals, organization charts, or detailed procedures and rules. In these companies, people way down the line know what they are supposed to do in most situations because the handful of guiding values is crystal clear."[100] For example, at Eaton Corporation, the employees are expected to enforce the rules themselves. If someone misses too much work or picks fights with co-workers, other members of the production team point out the problem. According to Randy Savage, a long-time Eaton employee, "They say there are no bosses here, but if you screw up, you find one pretty fast."[101]

11.6 Strategic Incentive Management

To ensure congruence between the needs of a corporation as a whole and the needs of the employees as individuals, management and the board of directors should develop an incentive program that rewards desired performance. This reduces the likelihood of the agency problems (when employees act to feather their own nests instead of building shareholder value) mentioned earlier in **Chapter 2**. Incentive plans should be linked in some way to corporate and divisional strategy. Research reveals that firm performance is affected by its compensation policies.[102] Companies using different strategies tend to adopt different pay policies. For example, a survey of 600 business units indicates that the pay mix associated with a growth strategy emphasizes bonuses and other incentives over salary and benefits, whereas the pay mix associated with a stability strategy has the reverse emphasis.[103] Research indicates that SBU managers having long-term performance elements in their compensation program favor a long-term perspective and thus greater investments in R&D, capital equipment, and employee training.[104] Although the typical CEO pay package is composed of 21% salary, 27% short-term annual incentives, 16% long-term incentives, and 36% stock options,[105] there is some evidence that stock options are being replaced by greater emphasis on performance-related pay.[106]

The following three approaches are tailored to help match measurements and rewards with explicit strategic objectives and time frames:[107]

1. **Weighted-factor method:** The **weighted-factor method** is particularly appropriate for measuring and rewarding the performance of top SBU managers and group-level executives when performance factors and their importance vary from one SBU to another. One corporation's measurements might contain the following variations: the performance of high-growth SBUs is measured in terms of market share, sales growth, designated future payoff, and progress on several future-oriented strategic projects; the performance of low-growth SBUs, in contrast, is measured in terms of ROI and cash generation; and the performance of medium-growth SBUs is measured for a combination of these factors. (Refer to **Table 11–3.**)

2. **Long-term evaluation method:** The **long-term evaluation method** compensates managers for achieving objectives set over a multiyear period. An executive is promised some company stock or "performance units" (convertible into money or stock) in amounts to be

TABLE 11–3	Strategic Business Unit Category	Factor	Weight
Weighted-Factor Approach to Strategic Incentive Management	**High Growth**	Return on assets	10%
		Cash flow	0%
		Strategic-funds programs (developmental expenses)	45%
		Market-share increase	45%
		Total	<u>100</u>%
	Medium Growth	Return on assets	25%
		Cash flow	25%
		Strategic-funds programs (developmental expenses)	25%
		Market-share increase	25%
		Total	<u>100</u>%
	Low Growth	Return on assets	50%
		Cash flow	50%
		Strategic-funds programs (developmental expenses)	0%
		Market-share increase	0%
		Total	<u>100</u>%

SOURCE: Reprinted from *ORGANIZATIONAL DYNAMICS,* Vol. 13, No. 4, 1984, Paul J. Stonich, "The Performance Measurement and Reward System: Critical to Strategic Management," p. 51. Copyright © 1984 with permission of Elsevier.

based on long-term performance. A board of directors, for example, might set a particular objective in terms of growth in earnings per share during a five-year period. The giving of awards would be contingent on the corporation's meeting that objective within the designated time. Any executive who leaves the corporation before the objective is met receives nothing. The typical emphasis on stock prices makes this approach more applicable to top management than to business unit managers. Because rising stock markets tend to raise the stock price of mediocre companies, there is a developing trend to index stock options to competitors or to the *Standard & Poor's 500*.[108] General Electric, for example, offered its CEO 250,000 performance share units (PSUs) tied to performance targets achieved over five years. Half of the PSUs convert into GE stock only if GE achieves 10% average annual growth in operations. The other half converts to stock only if total shareholder return meets or beats the *S&P 500*.[109]

3. **Strategic-funds method:** The **strategic-funds method** encourages executives to look at developmental expenses as being different from expenses required for current operations. The accounting statement for a corporate unit enters strategic funds as a separate entry below the current ROI. It is, therefore, possible to distinguish between expense dollars consumed in the generation of current revenues and those invested in the future of a business. Therefore, a manager can be evaluated on both a short- and a long-term basis and has an incentive to invest strategic funds in the future. (See **Table 11–4**.)

An effective way to achieve the desired strategic results through a reward system is to combine the three approaches:

1. Segregate strategic funds from short-term funds, as is done in the strategic-funds method.

2. Develop a weighted-factor chart for each SBU.

3. Measure performance on three bases: The pretax profit indicated by the strategic-funds approach, the weighted factors, and the long-term evaluation of the SBUs' and the corporation's performance.

TABLE 11–4		
Strategic-Funds Approach to an SBU's Profit-and-Loss Statement	**Sales**	$12,300,000
	Cost of sales	−6,900,000
	Gross margin	$ 5,400,000
	General and administrative expenses	−3,700,000
	Operating profit (return on sales)	$ 1,700,000
	Strategic funds (development expenses)	−1,000,000
	Pretax profit	$ 700,000

SOURCE: Reprinted from *ORGANIZATIONAL DYNAMICS,* Vol. 13, No. 4, 1984, Paul J. Stonich, "The Performance Measurement and Reward System: Critical to Strategic Management," p. 52. Copyright © 1984 with permission of Elsevier.

Genentech, General Electric, Adobe, IBM, and Textron are some firms in which top management compensation is contingent upon the company's achieving strategic objectives.[110]

The board of directors and top management must be careful to develop a compensation plan that achieves the appropriate objectives. One reason why top executives are often criticized for being overpaid (the ratio of CEO to average worker pay is currently 400 to 1)[111] is that in a large number of corporations the incentives for sales growth exceed those for shareholder wealth, resulting in too many executives pursuing growth to the detriment of shareholder value.[112]

End of Chapter SUMMARY

Having strategic management without evaluation and control is like playing football without any goalposts. Unless strategic management improves performance, it is only an exercise. In business, the bottom-line measure of performance is making a profit. If people aren't willing to pay more than what it costs to make a product or provide a service, that business will not continue to exist. **Chapter 1** explains that organizations engaging in strategic management outperform those that do not. The sticky issue is: How should we measure performance? Is measuring profits sufficient? Does an income statement tell us what we need to know? The accrual method of accounting enables us to count a sale even when the cash has not yet been received. Therefore, a firm might be profitable, but still go bankrupt because it can't pay its bills. Is profit the amount of cash on hand at the end of the year after paying costs and expenses? But what if you made a big sale in December and must wait until January to get paid? Like retail stores, perhaps we need to use a fiscal year ending January 31 (to include returned Christmas items that were bought in December) instead of a calendar year ending December 31. Should two managers receive the same bonus when their divisions earn the same profit, even though one division is much smaller than the other? What of the manager who is managing a new product introduction that won't make a profit for another two years?

Evaluation and control is one of the most difficult parts of strategic management. No one measure can tell us what we need to know. That's why we need to use not only the traditional measures of financial performance, such as net earnings, ROI, and EPS, but we need to consider using EVA or MVA and a balanced scorecard, among other possibilities. On top of that, science informs us that just attempting to measure something changes what is being measured. The measurement of performance can and does result in short-term oriented actions and goal displacement. That's why experts suggest that we use multiple measures of only those things that provide a meaningful and reliable picture of events: Measure those 20% of the factors that determine 80% of the results. Once the appropriate performance measurements are taken, it is possible to learn whether the strategy was successful. As shown in the model of strategic management depicted at the beginning this chapter, the measured results of corporate performance allow us to decide whether we need to reformulate the strategy, improve its implementation, or gather more information about our competition.

ECO-BITS

- In 2007, 64% of the Fortune Global 100 published a Corporate Social Responsibility report explaining their economic, environmental, and social performance.
- More than 4,000 organizations from over 100 countries are members of the United Nations Global Compact. Three of the 10 principles are:
  - Support a precautionary approach to environmental challenges.

- Undertake initiatives to promote greater environmental responsibility.
- Encourage the development and diffusion of environmentally friendly technologies.[113]

DISCUSSION QUESTIONS

1. Is Figure 11–1 a realistic model of the evaluation and control process?

2. What are some examples of behavior controls? Output controls? Input controls?

3. Is EVA an improvement over ROI, ROE, or EPS?

4. How much faith can a manager place in a transfer price as a substitute for a market price in measuring a profit center's performance?

5. Is the evaluation and control process appropriate for a corporation that emphasizes creativity? Are control and creativity compatible?

STRATEGIC PRACTICE EXERCISE

Each year, *Fortune* magazine publishes an article entitled, "America's Most Admired Companies." It lists the 10 most admired companies in the United States and in the world. *Fortune*'s rankings are based on scoring publicly held companies on what it calls "eight key attributes of reputation": innovation, people management, use of corporate assets, social responsibility, quality of management, financial soundness, long-term investment value, and quality of products/services. In 2008, *Fortune* asked Hay Group to survey more than 3,700 people from multiple industries. Respondents were asked to choose the companies they admired most, regardless of industry. *Fortune* has been publishing this list since 1982. The *2008 Fortune* list of the top 10 most admired U.S. companies were (starting with #1): Apple, Berkshire Hathaway, General Electric, Google, Toyota Motor, Starbucks, FedEx, Procter & Gamble, Johnson & Johnson, and Goldman Sachs Group. The next 10 most admired were (from 11 to 20): Target, Southwest Airlines, American Express, BMW, Costco Wholesale, Microsoft, United Parcel Service, Cisco Systems, 3M, and Nordstrom.[114]

Four years earlier in 2004, the list of 10 most admired U.S. companies was: Wal-Mart, Berkshire Hathaway, South-

west Airlines, General Electric, Dell Computer, Microsoft, Johnson & Johnson, Starbucks, FedEx, and IBM.[115]

- Why did the most admired U.S. firm in 2004 (Wal-Mart) drop off the 10 listing in 2008?
- Why did Apple go from not even being on the 10 U.S. listing in 2004 to No. 1 in 2008?
- Which firms appeared on both top 10 lists? Why?
- Why did some firms drop off the list from 2004 to 2008 and why did others get included?
- What companies should be on the most admired list this year? Why?

Try One of These Exercises

1. Go to the library and find a "Most Admired Companies" *Fortune* article from the 1980s or early 1990s and compare that list to the latest one. (See www.fortune.com for the latest list.) Which companies have fallen out of the top 10? Pick one of the companies and investigate why it is no longer on the list.

2. Given the likely impact of global warming on various industrial sectors, which companies are likely to be on *Fortune's* "Most Admired Companies" in 10 years?

3. Compare *Fortune's* list to that compiled by the Reputation Institute (www.reputationinstitute.com). Why is there a difference between the ratings?

KEY TERMS

80/20 rule (p. 399)

activity-based costing (ABC) (p. 382)

balanced scorecard (p. 387)

behavior control (p. 380)

behavior substitution (p. 398)

benchmarking (p. 392)

earnings per share (EPS) (p. 383)

economic value added (EVA) (p. 386)

enterprise resource planning (ERP) (p. 395)

enterprise risk management (ERM) (p. 383)

evaluation and control process (p. 376)

expense center (p. 391)

free cash flow (p. 384)

goal displacement (p. 398)

input controls (p. 381)

investment center (p. 391)

ISO 9000 Standards Service (p. 381)

ISO 14000 Standards Service (p. 381)

key performance measures (p. 387)

long-term evaluation method (p. 400)

management audit (p. 389)

market value added (p. 386)

operating cash flow (p. 384)

output controls (p. 380)

performance (p. 380)

profit center (p. 391)

responsibility center (p. 390)

return on equity (ROE) (p. 384)

return on investment (ROI) (p. 383)

revenue center (p. 391)

shareholder value (p. 385)

short-term orientation (p. 397)

standard cost center (p. 390)

steering control (p. 380)

strategic-funds method (p. 401)

suboptimization (p. 398)

transfer pricing (p. 391)

weighted-factor method (p. 400)

NOTES

1. K. F. Iverson with T. Varian, "Plain Talk," *Inc.* (October 1997), p. 81. Excerpted from Iverson's book, *Plain Talk: Lessons from a Business Maverick*, (New York: John Wiley & Sons, 1997).

2. R. Roach & Associates, cited in *Air Transport World* (June 1996), p. 1.

3. R. Barker, "A Surprise in Office Depot's In-Box," *Business Week* (October 25, 2004), p. 122.

4. C. W. Hart, "Customer Service: Beating the Market with Customer Satisfaction," *Harvard Business Review* (March 2007), pp. 30–32.

5. S. E. Ante, "Giving the Boss the Big Picture," *Business Week* (February 13, 2006), pp. 48–51.

6. R. Muralidharan and R. D. Hamilton III, "Aligning Multinational Control Systems," *Long Range Planning* (June 1999), pp. 352–361. These types are based on W. G. Ouchi, "The Relationship Between Organizational Structure and Organizational Control," *Administrative Science Quarterly*, Vol. 20 (1977), pp. 95–113 and W. G. Ouchi, "A Conceptual Framework for the Design of Organizational Control Mechanisms," *Management Science*, Vol. 25 (1979), pp. 833–848. Muralidhara and Hamilton refer to Ouchi's clan control as input control.

7. W. G. Rowe and P. M. Wright, "Related and Unrelated Diversification and Their Effect on Human Resource Management Controls," *Strategic Management Journal* (April 1997), pp. 329–338.

8. R. Muralidharan and R. D. Hamilton III, "Aligning Multinational Control Systems," *Long Range* Planning (June 1999) pp. 356–359.

9. F. C. Barnes, "ISO 9000 Myth and Reality: A Reasonable Approach to ISO 9000," *SAM Advanced Management Journal* (Spring 1998), pp. 23–30.

10. M. Henricks, "A New Standard," *Entrepreneur* (October 2002), pp. 83–84.

11. M. V. Uzumeri, "ISO 9000 and Other Metastandards: Principles for Management Practice*?*" *Academy of Management Executive* (February 1997), pp. 21–36.

12. A. M. Hormozi, "Understanding and Implementing ISO 9000: A Manager's Guide," *SAM Advanced Management Journal* (Autumn 1995), pp. 4–11.

13. M. Henricks, "A New Standard," *Entrepreneur* (October 2002) p. 84.

14. L. Armstrong, "Someone to Watch Over You," *Business Week* (July 10, 2000), pp. 189–190.

15. J. K. Shank and V. Govindarajan, *Strategic Cost Management* (New York: The Free Press, 1993).

16. S. S. Rao, "ABCs of Cost Control," *Inc. Technology*, No. 2 (1997), pp. 79–81.

17. R. Gruber, "Why You Should Consider Activity-Based Costing," *Small Business Forum* (Spring 1994), pp. 20–36.

18. "Easier Than ABC," *Economist* (October 25, 2003), p. 56.

19. T. P. Pare, "A New Tool for Managing Costs," *Fortune* (June 14, 1993), pp. 124–129. For further information on the use of ABC with EVA, see T. L. Pohlen and B. J. Coleman, "Evaluating Internal Operations and Supply Chain Performance Using EVA and ABC," *SAM Advanced Management Journal* (Spring 2005), pp. 45–58.

20. K. Hopkins, "The Risk Agenda," *Business Week*, Special Advertising Section (November 22, 2004), pp. 166–170.

21. T. L. Barton, W. G. Shenkir, and P. L. Walker, "Managing Risk: An Enterprise-wide Approach," *Financial Executive* (March/April 2001), p. 51.

22. T. L. Barton, W. G. Shenkir, and P. L. Walker, "Managing Risk: An Enterprise-Wide Approach," *Financial Executive*

(March/April 2001), pp. 48–51; P. L. Walker, W. G. Shenkir, and T. L. Barton, "Enterprise Risk Management: Putting It All Together," *Internal Auditor* (August 2003), pp. 50–55.

23. T. J. Andersen, "The Performance Relationship of Effective Risk Management: Exploring the Firm-Specific Investment Rationale," *Long Range Planning* (April 2008), pp. 155–176.

24. C. K. Brancato, *New Corporate Performance* Measures (New York: Conference Board, 1995); C. D. Ittner, D. F. Larcker, and M. V. Rajan, "The Choice of Performance Measures in Annual Bonus Contracts," working paper reported by K. Z. Andrews in "Executive Bonuses," *Harvard Business Review* (January–February 1996), pp. 8–9; J. Low and T. Siesfeld, "Measures That Matter: Wall Street Considers Non-Financial Performance More Than You Think," *Startegy & Leadership* (March/April 1998), pp. 24–30.

25. A similar measure, EBITDA (Earnings Before Interest, Taxes, Depreciation, and Amortization), is sometimes used, but is *not* determined in accordance with generally accepted accounting principles and is thus subject to varying calculations.

26. J. M. Laderman, "Earnings, Schmernings: Look at the Cash," *Business Week* (July 24, 1989), pp. 56–57.

27. H. Greenberg, "Don't Count on Cash Flow," *Fortune* (May 13, 2002), p. 176; A. Tergesen, "Cash-Flow Hocus-Pocus," *Business Week* (July 15, 2002), pp. 130–132.

28. "Green Revolutionary," *The Economist* (April 7, 2007), p. 66.

29. E. H. Hall, Jr., and J. Lee, "Diversification Strategies: Creating Value of Generating Profits?" paper presented to the annual meeting of the *Decision Sciences Institute*, Orlando, FL (November 18–21, 2000).

30. P. C. Brewer, G. Chandra, and C. A. Hock, "Economic Value Added (EVA): Its Uses and Limitations," SAM *Advanced Management Journal* (Spring 1999), pp. 4–11.

31. D. J. Skyrme and D. M. Amidon, "New Measures of Success," *Journal of Business Strategy* (January/February 1998), p. 23.

32. G. B. Stewart III, "EVA Works—But Not if You Make These Common Mistakes," *Fortune* (May 1, 1995), pp. 117–118.

33. S. Tully, "The Real Key to Creating Wealth," *Fortune* (September 20, 1993), p. 38.

34. A. Ehrbar, "Using EVA to Measure Performance and Assess Strategy," *Strategy & Leadership* (May/June 1999), pp. 20–24.

35. P. C. Brewer, G. Chandra, and C. A. Hock, "Economic Value Added (EVA): Its Uses and Limitations," *SAM Advanced Management Journal* (Spring 1999), pp. 7–9.

36. Pro: K. Lehn, and A. K. Makhija, "EVA & MVA As Performance Measures and Signals for Strategic Change," *Strategy & Leadership* (May/June 1996), pp. 34–38. Con: D. I. Goldberg, "Shareholder Value Debunked," *Strategy & Leadership* (January/February 2000), pp. 30–36.

37. A. Ehrbar, "Using EVA to Measure Performance and Assess Strategy," *Strategy &* Leadership (May/June 1999), p. 21.

38. S. Tully, "America's Wealth Creators," *Fortune* (November 22, 1999), pp. 275–284; A. B. Fisher, "Creating Stockholder Wealth: Market Value Added," *Fortune* (December 11, 1995), pp. 105–116.

39. A. B. Fisher, "Creating Stockholder Wealth: Market Value Added," *Fortune* (December 11, 1995), pp. 105–116.

40. K. Lehn and A. K. Makhija, "EVA & MVA As Performance Measures and Signals for Strategic Change," *Strategy &* Leadership (May/June, 1996), p. 37.

41. R. S. Kaplan and D. P. Norton, "Using the Balanced Scorecard as a Strategic Management System," *Harvard Business Review* (January–February 1996), pp. 75–85; R. S. Kaplan and D. P. Norton, "The Balanced Scorecard—Measures That Drive Performance," *Harvard Business Review* (January–February, 1992), pp. 71–79.

42. D. I. Goldenberg, "Shareholder Value Debunked," *Strategy & Leadership* (January/February 2000), p. 34.

43. In later work, Kaplan and Norton used the term "perspectives" and replaced "internal business perspective" with "process perspective" and "innovation and learning" to "learning and growth perspective." See R. S. Norton and D. P. Norton, "How to Implement a New Strategy Without Disrupting Your Organization," *Harvard Business Review* (March 2006), pp. 100–109.

44. C. K. Brancato, *New Performance Measures* (New York: Conference Board, 1995).

45. A. Gumpus and B. Lyons, "The Balanced Scorecard at Philips Electronics," *Strategic Finance*, Vol. 84 (2002), pp. 92–101.

46. P. D. Heaney, "Can Performance Be Measured*?" Progressive Grocer*, Vol. 82 (2003), pp. 11–13.

47. B. P. Stivers and T. Joyce, "Building a Balanced Performance Management System," *SAM Advanced Management Journal* (Spring 2000), pp. 22–29.

48. Kaplan and Norton (March, 2006), p. 107.

49. G. J. M. Braam and E. Nijssen, "Performance Effects of Using the Balanced Scorecard: A Note on the Dutch Experience," *Long Range Planning* (August 2004), pp. 335–349; H. Ahn, "Applying the Balanced Scorecard Concept: An Experience Report," *Long Range Planning* (August 2001), pp. 441–461.

50. S. P. Mader, D. Vuchot, and S. Fukushima of Korn/Ferry International, *33rd Annual Board of Directors Study* (2006), p. 9.

51. R. M. Rosen and F. Adair, "CEOs Misperceive Top Teams' Performance," *Harvard Business Review* (September 2007), p. 30.

52. S. P. Mader, D. Vuchot, and S. Fukushima of Korn/Ferry International, *33rd Annual Board of Directors Study* (2006), p. 33.

53. Ibid., p. 9.

54. J. L. Kerr and W. B. Werther, Jr., "The Next Frontier in Corporate Governance: Engaging the Board in Strategy," *Organizational Dynamics*, Vol. 37, No. 2 (2008), pp. 112–124. This agrees with figures (73% and 38%, respectively) reported by Korn/Ferry International in its *33rd Annual Board of Directors Study* from data gathered in 2006, p. 8.

55. J. M. Ivancevich, T. N. Duening, J. A. Gilbert, and R. Konopaske, "Deterring White-Collar Crime," *Academy of Management Executive* (May 2003), pp. 114–127. Also Kerr and Werther (2008).

56. R. Charan, *Boards at Work* (San Francisco: Jossey-Bass, 1998), pp. 176–177.

57. T. D. Schellhardt, "Directors Get Tough: Inside a CEO Performance Review," *Wall Street Journal Interactive Edition* (April 27, 1998).

58. T. L. Wheelen and J. D. Hunger, "Using the Strategic Audit," *SAM Advanced Management Journal* (Winter 1987), pp. 4–12; G. Donaldson, "A New Tool for Boards: The Strategic Audit," *Harvard Business Review* (July–August 1995), pp. 99–107.

59. H. Threat, "Measurement Is Free," *Strategy & Leadership* (May/June 1999), pp. 16–19.

60. Z. U. Khan, S. K. Chawla, M. F. Smith, and M. F. Sharif, "Transfer Pricing Policy Issues in Europe 1992," *International Journal of Management* (September 1992), pp. 230–241.

61. H. Rothman, "You Need Not Be Big to Benchmark," *Nation's Business* (December 1992), p. 64.

62. C. W. Von Bergen and B. Soper, "A Problem with Benchmarking: Using Shaping as a Solution," *SAM Advanced Management Journal* (Autumn 1995), pp. 16–19.

63. "Tool Usage Rates," *Journal of Business Strategy* (March/April 1995), p. 12.

64. R. J. Kennedy, "Benchmarking and Its Myths," *Competitive Intelligence Magazine* (April–June 2000), pp. 28–33.

65. "Just the Facts: Numbers Runners," *Journal of Business Strategy* (July/August 2002), p. 3; L. Mann, D. Samson, and D. Dow, "A Field Experiment on the Effects of Benchmarking & Goal Setting on Company Sales Performance," *Journal of Management*, Vol. 24, No. 1 (1998), pp. 73–96.

66. S. A. W. Drew, "From Knowledge to Action: The Impact of Benchmarking on Organizational Performance," *Long Range Planning* (June 1997), pp. 427–441.

67. S. M. Robbins and R. B. Stobaugh, "The Bent Measuring Stick for Foreign Subsidiaries," *Harvard Business Review* (September–October 1973), p. 82.

68. J. D. Daniels and L. H. Radebaugh, *International Business*, 5th ed. (Reading, MA: Addison-Wesley, 1989), pp. 673–674.

69. D. Henry, "A Better Way to Keep the Books," *Business Week* (September 15, 2008), p. 35; "International Accounting: Speaking in Tongues," *The Economist* (May 19, 2007), pp. 77–78.

70. W. A. Johnson and R. J. Kirsch, "International Transfer Pricing and Decision Making in United States Multinationals," *International Journal of Management* (June 1991), pp. 554–561.

71. L. Hickey, *KPMG's Corporate and Indirect Tax Rate Survey 2008*, pp. 11 & 13.

72. "Fixing the Bottom Line," *Time* (November 23, 1992), p. 20.

73. J. M. L. Poon, R. Ainuddin, and H. Affrim, "Management Policies and Practices of American, British, European, and Japanese Subsidiaries in Malaysia: A Comparative Study*," International Journal of Management* (December 1990), pp. 467–474.

74. M. Egan, "Setting Standards: Strategic Advantages in International Trade," *Business Strategy Review*, Vol. 13, No. 1 (2002), pp. 51–64; L. Swatkowski, "Building Towards International Standards," *Appliance* (December 1999), p. 30.

75. C. W. L. Hill, P. Hwang, and W. C. Kim, "An Eclectic Theory of the Choice of International Entry Mode," *Strategic Management Journal* (February 1990), pp. 117–128; D. Lei, J. W. Slocum, Jr., and R. W. Slater, "Global Strategy and Reward Systems: The Key Roles of Management Development and Corporate Culture," *Organizational Dynamics* (Autumn 1990), pp. 27–41; W. R. Fannin, and A. F. Rodriques, "National or Global?—Control vs. Flexibility," *Long Range Planning* (October 1986), pp. 84–188.

76. A. V. Phatak, *International Dimensions of Management*, 2nd ed. (Boston: Kent, 1989), pp. 155–157.

77. S. McAlary, "Three Pitfalls in ERP Implementation," *Strategy & Leadership* (October/November/December 1999), pp. 49–50.

78. J. B. White, D. Clark, and S. Ascarelli, "This German Software Is Complex, Expensive—And Wildly Popular," *Wall Street Journal* (March 14, 1997), pp. A1, A8; D. Ward, "Whirlpool Takes a Dive with Software Snarl," *Des Moines Register* (April 29, 2000), p. 8D.

79. J. Verville, R. Palanisamy, C. Bernadas, and A. Halingten, "ERP Acquisition Planning: A Critical Dimension for Making the Right Choice," *Long Range Planning* (February 2007), pp. 45–63.

80. "Radio Silence," *The Economist* (June 9, 2007), pp. 20–21.

81. C. Krivda, "RFID After Compliance: Integration and Payback," Special Advertising Section, *Business Week* (December 20, 2004), pp. 91–98.

82. A. Lashinsky, "Meg and the Machine," *Fortune* (September 1, 2003), pp. 68–78.

83. R. M. Hodgetts and M. S. Wortman, *Administrative Policy*, 2nd ed. (New York: John Wiley & Sons, 1980), p. 128.

84. J. R. Wooldridge and C. C. Snow, "Stock Market Reaction to Strategic Investment Decisions," *Strategic Management Journal* (September 1990), pp. 353–363.

85. M. C. Jensen, "Corporate Budgeting Is Broken—Let's Fix It," *Harvard Business Review* (November 2001), pp. 94–101.

86. C. M. Christensen, S. P. Kaufman, and W. C. Smith, "Innovation Killers: How Financial Tools Destroy Your Capacity to Do New Things," *Harvard Business Review* (January 2008), pp. 98–105.

87. P. Hsieh, T. Koller, and S. R. Rajan, "The Misguided Practice of Earnings Guidance," *McKinsey Quarterly* (Spring 2006), pp. 1–5.

88. "GM, Auditor Will Pay $303 Million in Suit," *Saint Cloud* (MN) *Times* (August 9, 2008), p. 3A.

89. D. Henry "Fuzzy Numbers," *Business Week* (October 4, 2004), pp. 79–88.

90. A. Rappaport, "10 Ways to Create Shareholder Value," *Harvard Business Review* (September 2006), pp. 66–77.

91. D. R. Schmidt and K. L. Fowler, "Post-Acquisition Financial Performance and Executive Compensation," *Strategic Management Journal* (November–December 1990), pp. 559–569.

92. H. L. Tosi, S. Werner, J. P. Katz, and L. R. Gomez-Mejia, "How Much Does Performance Matter? A Meta-Analysis of CEO Pay Studies," *Journal of Management*, Vol. 26, No. 2 (2000), pp. 301–339.; P. Wright, M. Kroll, and D. Elenkov, "Acquisition Returns, Increase in Firm Size, and Chief Executive Officer Compensation: The Moderating Role of Monitoring," *Academy of Management Journal* (June 2002), pp. 599–608; S. Werner, H. L. Tosi, and L. Gomez-Mejia, "Organizational Governance and Employee Pay: How Ownership Structure Affects the Firm's Compensation Strategy," *Strategic Management Journal* (April 2005), pp. 377–384.

93. X. Zhang, K. M. Bartol, K. G. Smith, M. D. Pfarrer, and D. M. Khanin, "CEOs on the Edge: Earnings Manipulation and Stock-based Incentive Misalignment," *Academy of Management Journal* (April 2008), pp. 241–258; L. Bebchuk and J. Fried, *Pay Without Performance: The Unfulfilled Promise of Executive Compensation* (Boston: Harvard University Press, 2004); L. A. Benchuk and J. M. Fried, "Pay Without Performance: Overview of the Issues," *Academy of Management Perspectives* (February 2006), pp. 5–24.

94. D. Jones, "Bad News Can Enrich Executives," *Des Moines Register* (November 26, 1999), p. 8S.

95. J. F. Porac, J. B. Wade, and T. G. Pollock, "Industry Categories and the Politics of the Comparable Firm in CEO Compensation," *Administrative Science Quarterly* (March 1999), pp. 112–144. For summaries of current research on executive compensation and performance, see C. E. Devers, A. A. Cannella Jr., G. P. Reilly, and M. E. Yoder, "Executive Compensation: A Multidisciplinary Review of Recent Developments," *Journal of Management* (December 2007), pp. 1016–1072; M. Chan, "Executive Compensation," *Business and Society Review* (March 2008), pp. 129–161; and S. N. Kaplan, "Are CEOs Overpaid?" *Academy of Management Perspective* (May 2008), pp. 5–20.

96. C. D. Ittner and D. F. Larcker, "Coming Up Short," *Harvard Business Review* (November 2003), pp. 88–95.

97. See the classic article by S. Kerr, "On the Folly of Rewarding A, While Hoping for B," *Academy of Management Journal*, Vol. 18 (December 1975), 769–783.

98. W. Zellner, E. Schine, and G. Smith, "Trickle-Down Is Trickling Down at Work," *Business Week* (March 18, 1996), p. 34.

99. For more information on how goals can have dysfunctional side effects, see D. C. Kayes, "The Destructive Pursuit of Idealized Goals," *Organizational Dynamics*, Vol. 34, Issue 4 (2005), pp. 391–401.

100. T. J. Peters and R. H. Waterman, *In Search of Excellence* (New York: HarperCollins, 1982), pp. 75–76.

101. T. Aeppel, "Not All Workers Find Idea of Empowerment as Neat as It Sounds," *Wall Street Journal* (September 8, 1997), pp. A1, A13.

102. R. S. Allen and M. M. Helms, "Employee Perceptions of the Relationship Between Strategy, Rewards, and Organizational Performance," *Journal of Business Strategies* (Fall 2002), pp. 115–140; M. A. Carpenter, "The Price of Change: The Role of CEO Compensation in Strategic Variation and Deviation from Industry Strategy Norms," *Journal of Management*, Vol. 26, No. 6 (2000), pp. 1179–1198; M. A. Carpenter and W. G. Sanders, "The Effects of Top Management Team Pay and Firm Internationalization on MNC Performance," *Journal of Management*, Vol. 30, No. 4 (2004), pp. 509–528; J. D. Shaw, N. Gupta, and J. E. Delery, "Congruence Between Technology and Compensation Systems: Implications for Strategy Implementation," *Strategic Management Journal* (April 2001), pp. 379–386; E. F. Montemazon, "Congruence Between Pay Policy and Competitive Strategy in High-Performing Organizations," *Journal of Management*, Vol. 22, No. 6 (1996), pp. 889–908.

103. D. B. Balkin and L. R. Gomez-Mejia, "Matching Compensation and Organizational Strategies," *Strategic Management Journal* (February 1990), pp. 153–169.

104. C. S. Galbraith, "The Effect of Compensation Programs and Structure on SBU Competitive Strategy: A Study of Technology-Intensive Firms," *Strategic Management Journal* (July 1991), pp. 353–370.

105. T. A. Stewart, "CEO Pay: Mom Wouldn't Approve," *Fortune* (March 31, 1997), pp. 119–120.

106. "The Politics of Pay," *The Economist* (March 24, 2007), pp. 71–72.

107. P. J. Stonich, "The Performance Measurement and Reward System: Critical to Strategic Management," *Organizational Dynamics* (Winter 1984), pp. 45–57.

108. A. Rappaport, "New Thinking on How to Link Executive Pay with Performance," *Harvard Business Review* (March–April 1999), pp. 91–101.

109. Motley Fool, "Fool's School: Hooray for GE," *The (Ames, IA) Tribune* (October 27, 2003), p. 1D.

110. E. Iwata and B. Hansen, "Pay, Performance Don't Always Add Up," *USA Today* (April 30, 2004), pp. 1B–2B; W. Grossman and R. E. Hoskisson, "CEO Pay at the Crossroads of Wall Street and Main: Toward the Strategic Design of Executive Compensation," *Academy of Management Executive* (February 1998), pp. 43–57.

111. M. Chan, "Executive Compensation," *Business and Society Review* (March 2008), pp. 129–161.

112. S. E. O'Byrne and S. D. Young, "Why Executive Pay Is Failing," *Harvard Business Review* (June 2006), p. 28.

113. P. A. Heslin and J. D. Ochoa, "Understanding and Developing Strategic Corporate Social Responsibility," *Organizational Dynamics* (April–June 2008), pp. 125–144.

114. *Fortune* magazine Web site accessed on November 7, 2008 at http://money.cnn.com/magazines/fortune/mostadmired/2008/top20/index.html.

115. A. Harrington, "America's Most Admired Companies," *Fortune* (March 8, 2004), pp. 80–81.

Ending Case for Part Four

HEWLETT-PACKARD BUYS EDS

On May 13, 2008, Hewlett-Packard (HP) announced its $13.9 billion acquisition of Electronic Data Systems (EDS), a technology services company. Together, HP and EDS formed a formidable tech services provider with $38 billion in revenues. It enabled HP to better compete with IBM, which controlled more than 7% market share of the $748 billion market for services. Tech services included managing the data centers of large companies and governments, or handling entire functions such as personnel or claims processing. At the time of the acquisition, IBM was the leading firm in the area, with EDS in second place with much lower profit margins, and HP following in fifth place.

Founded by Ross Perot in 1962, EDS pioneered the business of outsourced data management. Perot sold EDS to General Motors (GM) in 1984, but GM was unable to obtain any synergy with the purchase and spun off the company in 1996. EDS profits turned to losses during the technology downturn in 2000. The company eventually became profitable once again, but with smaller margins. EDS had been slow to respond to the threat of Indian rivals offering services at sharply lower prices. The company did increase its overseas hiring and bought control of MphasiS, an Indian services company. Since MphasiS was allowed to operate independently, with its own sales force and customer base, EDS did not gain much synergy from the acquisition. By 2008, EDS had 45,000 people working offshore and planned to hire more. Nevertheless, the best services companies had a large, low-cost workforce with tightly integrated operations so that employees with diverse skills could collaborate smoothly. This was the case with IBM, Accenture, and Indian companies like Tata Consultancy Services, but not with EDS or HP. Commenting on HP's purchase of EDS, N. Venkat Venktraman, chair of the Information Systems Department at Boston University's School of Management said, "The services sector is going through a shift, and this merger doesn't address the global service-delivery challenges that HP faces."

....
This case was written by J. David Hunger for *Strategic Management and Business Policy*, 12th edition and for *Concepts in Strategic Management and Business Policy*, 12th edition. Copyright © 2008 by J. David Hunger. Reprinted by permission.

Founded in 1940 by Dave Packard and Bill Hewlett in a garage in Palo Alto, California, Hewlett-Packard soon developed a reputation for making high-quality testing and measurement devices. Emphasizing their engineering roots, the two founders worked hard to develop the company's strong corporate culture. Their philosophy of managing became known as the "HP Way," composed of five basic values:

☐ We have trust and respect for individuals.

☐ We focus on a high level of achievement and contribution.

☐ We focus on a high level of business with uncompromising integrity.

☐ We achieve our common objectives through teamwork.

☐ We encourage flexibility and innovation.

These values continued to be emphasized by the CEOs following in the founder's footsteps. Until Carleton (Carly) Fiorina was hired as CEO in 1999, HP had been primarily known for its engineering excellence, but not for its marketing. For example, it developed the first handheld calculator, a quality product long cherished by engineers, but never developed or priced for the mass market. Fiorina lamented that Dell offered information technology products that were "low-tech and low cost; and IBM offered "high-tech and high cost," but HP was stuck somewhere in between them. She wanted to offer customers "high-tech and low cost" by improving the marketing of the company's outstanding products. During her tenure, HP acquired Compaq, the personal computer company. She also tried to buy the computer services unit of PriceWaterhouseCoopers in 2000, but lost out to IBM. Problems with integrating Compaq's middle-market orientation with HP's top-end orientation led to her firing by the board in 2005.

Fiorina was replaced by Mark Hurd, known to be a disciplined operations manager, who vowed to focus on implementation. Hurd had come to the company from Dayton, Ohio's NCR, where he had been President and CEO. Hurd dumped the matrix management structure initiated by Fiorina and gave responsibility back to the business unit managers. According to Hurd, "the more accountable I can make you, the easier it is for you to show you're a great performer. The more I use a matrix, the easier I make it to blame someone else." He also broke up the centralized sales force and assigned sales people to each business unit. The SBUs now controlled over 70% of their own budget expenses, up from just 30% under Fiorina. Among other changes, Hurd hired executives from outside the company and cut costs by laying off 14,500 workers from a workforce of 150,000. Prith Banerjee, HP's new director of R&D, worked to make HP's famed research lab more efficient by cutting the number of projects from 150 to 20 or 30. Researchers would now be competing for money and manpower by proposing projects, complete with business plans to a central review board. Hurd knew that he had to make further changes to improve HP's competitive position. HP's corporate computing business seemed incapable of competing against IBM and Dell. Margins were slipping in the printer business, the source of 85% of HP's profits.

Hewlett-Packard was organized into three main groups: Imaging & Printing (27% of revenues), Personal Systems (35%), and Technology Solutions, which was composed of the Enterprise Storage & Servers segment (18%), HP Services segment (16%), and HP Software segment (2%). An additional business segment was Financial Services & Other (2% of revenues).

Even though Hurd was working hard to change the company by tightening up HP's operations, many of HP's middle managers still subscribed to the gentle, collegiate "HP Way." This culture fit the relaxed and casual style common to California's Silicon Valley and was part of the company's soul. People ate ahi tuna in the cafeteria. In contrast, EDS was founded in Plano, Texas, by the hard-charging entrepreneur, Ross Perot, who ran for U.S. president as an independent in 1992 and 1996. Reflecting Perot's no-nonsense style, the EDS corporate culture was military, buttoned-down, and staid. People wore ties and ate steak and fries in the EDS cafeteria.

One advantage of EDS was that it was the largest services firm that was independent of any hardware or software vendor. According to CEO Hurd, even though EDS would continue to advise clients to buy systems from all vendors, those clients would now be more likely to pay more attention when the boxes came from HP. Nevertheless, one disadvantage of the acquisition was the likely culture clash that would result from integrating EDS into HP's operations. Even though one analyst commented that Hurd's operations style made him "an EDS guy sitting on top of the HP Way," others wondered if the EDS acquisition would be as problematic as was the Compaq merger.

PART 5

Introduction to
Case Analysis

suggestions for Case Analysis

Howard Schilit, founder of the Center for Financial Research & Analysis (CFRA), works with a staff of 15 analysts to screen financial databases and analyze public financial filings of 3,600 companies, looking for inconsistencies and aggressive accounting methods. Schilit calls this search for hidden weaknesses in a company's performance *forensic accounting*. "I'm like an investigative reporter," explains Schilit. "I'm interested in finding companies where the conventional wisdom is that they're very healthy, but if you dig a bit deeper, you find the emperor is not wearing the clothes you thought."[1] He advises anyone interested in analyzing a company to look deeply into its financial statements. For example, when the CFRA noticed that Kraft Foods made $122 million in acquisitions in 2002, but claimed $539 million as "goodwill" assets related to the purchases, it concluded that Kraft was padding its earnings with one-time gains. According to Schilit, unusually high goodwill gains related to recent acquisitions is a *red flag* that suggests an underlying problem.

Schilit proposes a short checklist of items to examine for red flags:

- **Cash flow from operations should exceed net income:** If cash flow from operations drops below net income, it could mean that the company is propping up its earnings by selling assets, borrowing cash, or shuffling numbers. Says Schilit, "You could have spotted the problems at Enron by just doing this."[2]

- **Accounts receivable should not grow faster than sales:** A firm facing slowing sales can make itself look better by inflating accounts receivable with expected future sales and by making sales to customers who are not credit worthy. "It's like mailing a contract to a dead person and then counting it as a sale," says Schilit.[3]

- **Gross margins should not fluctuate over time:** A change of more than 2% in either direction from year to year is worth a closer look. It could mean that the company is using other revenue, such as sales of assets or write-offs to boost profits. Sunbeam reported an increase of 10% in gross margins just before it was investigated by the SEC.

- **Examine carefully information about top management and the board:** When Schilit learned that the chairman of Checkers Restaurants had put his two young sons on the board, he warned investors of nepotism. Two years later, Checkers' huge debt caused its stock to fall 85% and all three family members were forced out of the company.

Learning Objectives

After reading this chapter, you should be able to:

- Research the case situation as needed
- Analyze financial statements by using ratios and common-size statements
- Use the strategic audit as a method of organizing and analyzing case information

- **Footnotes are important:** When companies change their accounting assumptions to make the statements more attractive, they often bury their rationale in the footnotes. Schilit dislikes companies that extend the depreciable life of their assets. "There's only one reason to do that—to add a penny or two to earnings—and it makes me very mistrustful of management."[4]

Schilit makes his living analyzing companies and selling his reports to investors. Annual reports and financial statements provide a lot of information about a company's health, but it's hard to find problem areas when management is massaging the numbers to make the company appear more attractive than it is. That's why Michelle Leder created her Web site, www.footnoted.org. She likes to highlight "the things that companies bury in their routine SEC filings."[5] This type of in-depth, investigative analysis is a key part of analyzing strategy cases. This chapter provides various analytical techniques and suggestions for conducting this kind of case analysis.

12.1 The Case Method

The analysis and discussion of case problems has been the most popular method of teaching strategy and policy for many years. The case method provides the opportunity to move from a narrow, specialized view that emphasizes functional techniques to a broader, less precise analysis of the overall corporation. Cases present actual business situations and enable you to examine both successful and unsuccessful corporations. In case analysis, you might be asked to critically analyze a situation in which a manager had to make a decision of long-term corporate importance. This approach gives you a feel for what it is like to face making and implementing strategic decisions.

12.2 Researching the Case Situation

You should not restrict yourself only to the information written in the case unless your instructor states otherwise. You should, if possible, undertake outside research about the environmental setting. Check the decision date of each case (typically the latest date mentioned in the case) to find out when the situation occurred and then screen the business periodicals for that time period. An understanding of the economy during that period will help you avoid making a serious error in your analysis, for example, suggesting a sale of stock when the stock market is at an all-time low or taking on more debt when the prime interest rate is over 15%. Information about the industry will provide insights into its competitive activities. *Important Note: Don't go beyond the decision date of the case in your research unless directed to do so by your instructor.*

Use computerized company and industry information services such as Compustat, Compact Disclosure, and CD/International, available on CD-ROM or online at the library. On the Internet, Hoover's OnLine Corporate Directory (www.hoovers.com) and the Security Exchange Commission's Edgar database (www.sec.gov) provide access to corporate annual reports and 10-K forms. This background will give you an appreciation for the situation as it was experienced by the participants in the case. Use a search engine such as Google to find additional information about the industry and the company.

A company's **annual report** and **SEC 10-K form** from the year of the case can be very helpful. According to the Yankelovich Partners survey firm, 8 out of 10 portfolio managers and 75% of security analysts use annual reports when making decisions.[6] They contain not only the usual income statements and balance sheets, but also cash flow statements and notes to the financial statements indicating why certain actions were taken. 10-K forms include detailed information not usually available in an annual report. **SEC 10-Q forms** include quarterly financial reports. **SEC 14-A forms** include detailed information on members of a company's board of directors and proxy statements for annual meetings. Some resources available for research into the economy and a corporation's industry are suggested in **Appendix 12.A**.

A caveat: Before obtaining additional information about the company profiled in a particular case, ask your instructor if doing so is appropriate for your class assignment. Your strategy instructor may want you to stay within the confines of the case information provided in the book. In this case, it is usually acceptable to at least learn more about the societal environment at the time of the case.

12.3 Financial Analysis: A Place to Begin

Once you have read a case, a good place to begin your analysis is with the financial statements. **Ratio analysis** is the calculation of ratios from data in these statements. It is done to identify possible financial strengths or weaknesses. Thus it is a valuable part of SWOT analysis. A review of key financial ratios can help you assess a company's overall situation and pinpoint some problem areas. Ratios are useful regardless of firm size and enable you to compare a company's ratios with industry averages. **Table 12–1** lists some of the most important financial ratios, which are (1) **liquidity ratios**, (2) **profitability ratios**, (3) **activity ratios**, and (4) **leverage ratios**.

TABLE 12–1   Financial Ratio Analysis

	Formula	How Expressed	Meaning
1. Liquidity Ratios			
Current ratio	$$\frac{\text{Current assets}}{\text{Current liabilities}}$$	Decimal	A short-term indicator of the company's ability to pay its short-term liabilities from short-term assets; how much of current assets are available to cover each dollar of current liabilities.
Quick (acid test) ratio	$$\frac{\text{Current assets} - \text{Inventory}}{\text{Current liabilities}}$$	Decimal	Measures the company's ability to pay off its short-term obligations from current assets, excluding inventories.
Inventory to net working capital	$$\frac{\text{Inventory}}{\text{Current assets} - \text{Current liabilities}}$$	Decimal	A measure of inventory balance; measures the extent to which the cushion of excess current assets over current liabilities may be threatened by unfavorable changes in inventory.
Cash ratio	$$\frac{\text{Cash} + \text{Cash equivalents}}{\text{Current liabilities}}$$	Decimal	Measures the extent to which the company's capital is in cash or cash equivalents; shows how much of the current obligations can be paid from cash or near-cash assets.
2. Profitability Ratios Net profit margin	$$\frac{\text{Net profit after taxes}}{\text{Net sales}}$$	Percentage	Shows how much after-tax profits are generated by each dollar of sales.
Gross profit margin	$$\frac{\text{Sales} - \text{Cost of goods sold}}{\text{Net sales}}$$	Percentage	Indicates the total margin available to cover other expenses beyond cost of goods sold and still yield a profit.
Return on investment (ROI)	$$\frac{\text{Net profit after taxes}}{\text{Total assets}}$$	Percentage	Measures the rate of return on the total assets utilized in the company; a measure of management's efficiency, it shows the return on all the assets under its control, regardless of source of financing.
Return on equity (ROE)	$$\frac{\text{Net profit after taxes}}{\text{Shareholders' equity}}$$	Percentage	Measures the rate of return on the book value of shareholders' total investment in the company.
Earnings per share (EPS)	$$\frac{\text{Net profit after taxes} - \text{Preferred stock dividends}}{\text{Average number of common shares}}$$	Dollars per share	Shows the after-tax earnings generated for each share of common stock.
3. Activity Ratios Inventory turnover	$$\frac{\text{Net sales}}{\text{Inventory}}$$	Decimal	Measures the number of times that average inventory of finished goods was turned over or sold during a period of time, usually a year.
Days of inventory	$$\frac{\text{Inventory}}{\text{Cost of goods sold} \div 365}$$	Days	Measures the number of one day's worth of inventory that a company has on hand at any given time.

continued

TABLE 12–1   Financial Ratio Analysis, continued

	Formula	How Expressed	Meaning
Net working capital turnover	$\dfrac{\text{Net sales}}{\text{Net working capital}}$	Decimal	Measures how effectively the net working capital is used to generate sales.
Asset turnover	$\dfrac{\text{Sales}}{\text{Total assets}}$	Decimal	Measures the utilization of all the company's assets; measures how many sales are generated by each dollar of assets.
Fixed asset turnover	$\dfrac{\text{Sales}}{\text{Fixed assets}}$	Decimal	Measures the utilization of the company's fixed assets (i.e., plant and equipment); measures how many sales are generated by each dollar of fixed assets.
Average collection period	$\dfrac{\text{Accounts receivable}}{\text{Sales for year} \div 365}$	Days	Indicates the average length of time in days that a company must wait to collect a sale after making it; may be compared to the credit terms offered by the company to its customers.
Accounts receivable turnover	$\dfrac{\text{Annual credit sales}}{\text{Accounts receivable}}$	Decimal	Indicates the number of times that accounts receivable are cycled during the period (usually a year).
Accounts payable period	$\dfrac{\text{Accounts payable}}{\text{Purchases for year} \div 365}$	Days	Indicates the average length of time in days that the company takes to pay its credit purchases.
Days of cash	$\dfrac{\text{Cash}}{\text{Net sales for year} \div 365}$	Days	Indicates the number of days of cash on hand, at present sales levels.
4. Leverage Ratios Debt to asset ratio	$\dfrac{\text{Total debt}}{\text{Total assets}}$	Percentage	Measures the extent to which borrowed funds have been used to finance the company's assets.
Debt to equity ratio	$\dfrac{\text{Total debt}}{\text{Shareholders' equity}}$	Percentage	Measures the funds provided by creditors versus the funds provided by owners.
Long-term debt to capital structure	$\dfrac{\text{Long-term debt}}{\text{Shareholders' equity}}$	Percentage	Measures the long-term component of capital structure.
Times interest earned	$\dfrac{\text{Profit before taxes} + \text{Interest charges}}{\text{Interest charges}}$	Decimal	Indicates the ability of the company to meet its annual interest costs.
Coverage of fixed charges	$\dfrac{\text{Profit before taxes} + \text{Interest charges} + \text{Lease charges}}{\text{Interest charges} + \text{Lease obligations}}$	Decimal	A measure of the company's ability to meet all of its fixed-charge obligations.
Current liabilities to equity	$\dfrac{\text{Current liabilities}}{\text{Shareholders' equity}}$	Percentage	Measures the short-term financing portion versus that provided by owners.

TABLE 12–1	Financial Ratio Analysis, continued		
	Formula	**How Expressed**	**Meaning**
5. Other Ratios Price/earnings ratio	$\dfrac{\text{Market price per share}}{\text{Earnings per share}}$	Decimal	Shows the current market's evaluation of a stock, based on its earnings; shows how much the investor is willing to pay for each dollar of earnings.
Divided payout ratio	$\dfrac{\text{Annual dividends per share}}{\text{Annual earnings per share}}$	Percentage	Indicates the percentage of profit that is paid out as dividends.
Dividend yield on common stock	$\dfrac{\text{Annual dividends per share}}{\text{Current market price per share}}$	Percentage	Indicates the dividend rate of return to common shareholders at the current market price.

NOTE: In using ratios for analysis, calculate ratios for the corporation and compare them to the average and quartile ratios for the particular industry. Refer to Standard & Poor's and Robert Morris Associates for average industry data. Special thanks to Dr. Moustafa H. Abdelsamad, Dean, Business School, Texas A&M University—Corpus Christi, Corpus Christi, Texas, for his definitions of these ratios.

ANALYZING FINANCIAL STATEMENTS

In your analysis, do not simply make an exhibit that includes all the ratios (unless your instructor requires you to do so), but select and discuss only those ratios that have an impact on the company's problems. For instance, accounts receivable and inventory may provide a source of funds. If receivables and inventories are double the industry average, reducing them may provide needed cash. In this situation, the case report should include not only sources of funds but also the number of dollars freed for use. Compare these ratios with industry averages to discover whether the company is out of line with others in the industry. Annual and quarterly industry ratios can be found in the library or on the Internet. (See the resources for case research in **Appendix 12.A.**) In the years to come, expect to see financial entries for the trading of CERs (Certified Emissions Reductions). This is the amount of money a company earns from reducing carbon emissions and selling them on the open market. To learn how carbon trading is likely to affect corporations, see the **Environmental Sustainability Issue**.

A typical financial analysis of a firm would include a study of the operating statements for five or so years, including a trend analysis of sales, profits, earnings per share, debt-to-equity ratio, return on investment, and so on, plus a ratio study comparing the firm under study with industry standards. As a minimum, undertake the following five steps in basic financial analysis.

1. **Scrutinize historical income statements and balance sheets:** These two basic statements provide most of the data needed for analysis. Statements of cash flow may also be useful.

2. **Compare historical statements over time** if a series of statements is available.

3. **Calculate changes that occur in individual categories from year to year,** as well as the cumulative total change.

4. **Determine the change as a percentage** as well as an absolute amount.

5. **Adjust for inflation** if that was a significant factor.

Examination of this information may reveal developing trends. Compare trends in one category with trends in related categories. For example, an increase in sales of 15% over three years may appear to be satisfactory until you note an increase of 20% in the cost of goods sold

ENVIRONMENTAL sustainability issue

IMPACT OF CARBON TRADING

Do you know about carbon trading, emissions allowances, cap-and-trade, or CERs? These are terms you can expect to hear a lot more in the years to come. The concept of carbon trading is something that will soon be affecting the balance sheets and income statements of all corporations, especially those with international operations. It is one way to account for environmental sustainability initiatives.

The Kyoto Protocol established an emissions trading program that assigned annual limits on greenhouse gases emitted by facilities within each country's boundaries. The countries signing the pact, including Canada, Japan, and the European Union, were then able to trade emission surpluses and deficits with each other. In addition, individual countries or companies could invest in projects in developing nations that would reduce emissions and use those reductions to meet their own targets.

In 2005 the European Union initiated a trading system allowing individual facilities to sell credit allowances they had earned for reducing greenhouse gas emissions. It created a tradable commodity, the Certified Emissions Reduction (CER), which gave a facility the right to emit one metric ton of carbon dioxide annually. The CER was created by another facility that reduced its carbon dioxide emissions. (Reducing or trapping one metric ton of methane from entering the atmosphere was worth 21 CERs due to

methane's greater impact on global warming.) By 2006, a CER traded on the European market for around 25 euros with trading volume totaling one million CERs per day. Barclays, Citibank, Credit Suisse, HSBC, Lehman Brothers, and Morgan Stanley soon opened trading desks for CERs at London's Canary Wharf, the global center for carbon trading. By 2007, European and Asian traders bought and sold approximately $60 billion worth of emission CERs.

Carbon trading has created an opportunity for new and established companies. For example, Mission Point Capital Partners is one of more than 50 private equity and hedge funds specializing in carbon finance and clean energy. Mission Point created a joint venture in 2008 with GE and AES to develop large volumes of emissions credits. These would be sold to U.S. companies like Yahoo! and News Corp that wanted to become carbon neutral by offsetting their carbon emissions. Assuming that the U.S. federal government would soon establish a cap-and-trade market for emissions, the joint venture partners expected to produce 10 million tons of emission credits by 2010. According to Kevin Walsh, managing director of GE Energy Financial Services, "We think this is going to be an enormous market."

....
SOURCE: A. White, "Environment: The Greening of the Balance Sheet," *Harvard Business Review* (March 2006), pp. 27–28; M. Gunther, "Carbon Finance Comes of Age," *Fortune* (April 28, 2008), pp. 124–132.

during the same period. The outcome of this comparison might suggest that further investigation into the manufacturing process is necessary. If a company is reporting strong net income growth but negative cash flow, this would suggest that the company is relying on something other than operations for earnings growth. Is it selling off assets or cutting R&D? If accounts receivable are growing faster than sales revenues, the company is not getting paid for the products or services it is counting as sold. Is the company dumping product on its distributors at the end of the year to boost its reported annual sales? If so, expect the distributors to return the unordered product the next month, thus drastically cutting the next year's reported sales.

Other "tricks of the trade" need to be examined. Until June 2000, firms growing through acquisition were allowed to account for the cost of the purchased company, through the pooling of both companies' stock. This approach was used in 40% of the value of mergers between 1997 and 1999. The pooling method enabled the acquiring company to disregard the premium it paid for the other firm (the amount above the fair market value of the purchased company often called "good will"). Thus, when PepsiCo agreed to purchase Quaker Oats for $13.4 billion in PepsiCo stock, the $13.4 billion was not found on PepsiCo's balance sheet. As of June 2000, merging firms must use the "purchase" accounting rules in which the true purchase price is reflected in the financial statements.[7]

GLOBAL issue

FINANCIAL STATEMENTS OF MULTINATIONAL CORPORATIONS: NOT ALWAYS WHAT THEY SEEM

A multinational corporation follows the accounting rules for its home country. As a result, its financial statements may be somewhat difficult to understand or to use for comparisons with competitors from other countries. For example, British firms such as British Petroleum use the term *turnover* rather than *sales revenue*. In the case of AB Electrolux of Sweden, a footnote to an an-

nual report indicates that the consolidated accounts have been prepared in accordance with Swedish accounting standards, which differ in certain significant respects from U.S. generally accepted accounting principles (U.S. GAAP). For one year, net income of 4,830m SEK (Swedish kronor) approximated 5,655m SEK according to U.S. GAAP. Total assets for the same period were 84,183m SEK according to Swedish principle, but 86,658m according to U.S. GAAP.

The analysis of a multinational corporation's financial statements can get very complicated, especially if its headquarters is in another country that uses different accounting standards. See the **Global Issue** for why financial analysis can get tricky at times.

COMMON-SIZE STATEMENTS

Common-size statements are income statements and balance sheets in which the dollar figures have been converted into percentages. These statements are used to identify trends in each of the categories, such as cost of goods sold as a percentage of sales (sales is the denominator). For the income statement, net sales represent 100%: calculate the percentage for each category so that the categories sum to the net sales percentage (100%). For the balance sheet, give the total assets a value of 100% and calculate other asset and liability categories as percentages of the total assets with total assets as the denominator. (Individual asset and liability items, such as accounts receivable and accounts payable, can also be calculated as a percentage of net sales.)

When you convert statements to this form, it is relatively easy to note the percentage that each category represents of the total. Look for trends in specific items, such as cost of goods sold, when compared to the company's historical figures. To get a proper picture, however, you need to make comparisons with industry data, if available, to see whether fluctuations are merely reflecting industry-wide trends. If a firm's trends are generally in line with those of the rest of the industry, problems are less likely than if the firm's trends are worse than industry averages. If ratios are not available for the industry, calculate the ratios for the industry's best and worst firms and compare them to the firm you are analyzing. Common-size statements are especially helpful in developing scenarios and pro forma statements because they provide a series of historical relationships (for example, cost of goods sold to sales, interest to sales, and inventories as a percentage of assets) from which you can estimate the future with your scenario assumptions for each year.

Z-VALUE AND INDEX OF SUSTAINABLE GROWTH

If the corporation being studied appears to be in poor financial condition, use **Altman's Z-Value Bankruptcy Formula** to calculate its likelihood of going bankrupt. The *Z-value* formula combines five ratios by weighting them according to their importance to a corporation's financial strength. The formula is:

$$Z = 1.2x_1 + 1.4x_2 + 3.3x_3 + 0.6x_4 + 1.0x_5$$

where:

$$x_1 = \text{Working capital/Total assets (\%)}$$
$$x_2 = \text{Retained earnings/Total assets (\%)}$$
$$x_3 = \text{Earnings before interest and taxes/Total assets (\%)}$$
$$x_4 = \text{Market value of equity/Total liabilities (\%)}$$
$$x_5 = \text{Sales/Total assets (number of times)}$$

A score below 1.81 indicates significant credit problems, whereas a score above 3.0 indicates a healthy firm. Scores between 1.81 and 3.0 indicate question marks.[8] The Altman Z model has achieved a remarkable 94% accuracy in predicting corporate bankruptcies. Its accuracy is excellent in the two years before financial distress, but diminishes as the lead time increases.[9]

The **index of sustainable growth** is useful to learn whether a company embarking on a growth strategy will need to take on debt to fund this growth. The index indicates how much of the growth rate of sales can be sustained by internally generated funds. The formula is:

$$g^* = \frac{[P(1 - D)(1 + L)]}{[T - P(1 - D)(1 + L)]}$$

where:

$$P = \text{(Net profit before tax/Net sales)} \times 100$$
$$D = \text{Target dividends/Profit after tax}$$
$$L = \text{Total liabilities/Net worth}$$
$$T = \text{(Total assets/Net sales)} \times 100$$

If the planned growth rate calls for a growth rate higher than its g*, external capital will be needed to fund the growth unless management is able to find efficiencies, decrease dividends, increase the debt-equity ratio, or reduce assets through renting or leasing arrangements.[10]

USEFUL ECONOMIC MEASURES

If you are analyzing a company over many years, you may want to adjust sales and net income for inflation to arrive at "true" financial performance in constant dollars. **Constant dollars** are dollars adjusted for inflation to make them comparable over various years. One way to adjust for inflation in the United States is to use the Consumer Price Index (CPI), as given in **Table 12–2.** Dividing sales and net income by the CPI factor for that year will change the figures to 1982–1984 U.S. constant dollars (when the CPI was 1.0). Adjusting for inflation is especially important for companies operating in the emerging economies, like China and Russia, where inflation in 2008 rose to 6.6%, the highest in 10 years. In that same year, Zimbabwe's inflation rate was the highest in the world at 2.2 million%![11]

Another helpful analytical aid provided in **Table 12–2** is the **prime interest rate**, the rate of interest banks charge on their lowest-risk loans. For better assessments of strategic decisions, it can be useful to note the level of the prime interest rate at the time of the case. A decision to borrow money to build a new plant would have been a good one in 2003 at 4.1% but less practical in 2007 when the average rate was 8.1%.

TABLE 12–2	Year	GDP (in $ billions) Gross Domestic Product	CPI (for all items) Consumer Price Index	PIR (in %) Prime Interest Rate
U.S. Economic Indicators	1980	2,789.5	.824	15.27
	1985	4,220.3	1.076	9.93
	1990	5,803.1	1.307	10.01
	1995	7,397.7	1.524	8.83
	1996	7,816.9	1.569	8.27
	1997	8,304.3	1.605	8.44
	1998	8,747.0	1.630	8.35
	1999	9,268.4	1.666	7.99
	2000	9,817.0	1.722	9.23
	2001	10,128.0	1.771	6.92
	2002	10,469.6	1.799	4.68
	2003	10,960.8	1.840	4.12
	2004	11,685.9	1.889	4.29
	2005	12,421.9	1.953	6.10
	2006	13,178.4	2.016	7.94
	2007	13,807.5	2.073	8.08
	2008	14,280.7	2.153	5.21

NOTES: Gross Domestic Product (GDP) in Billions of Dollars; Consumer Price Index for All Items (CPI) (1982–84 = 1.0); Prime Interest Rate (PIR) in Percentages.

SOURCES: Gross Domestic Product (GDP) from U.S. Bureau of Economic Analysis, National Economic Accounts (www.bea.gov). Consumer Price Index (CPI) from U.S. Bureau of Labor Statistics (www.bls.gov). Prime Interest Rate (PIR) from www.moneycafe.com.

In preparing a scenario for your pro forma financial statements, you may want to use the **gross domestic product (GDP)** from **Table 12–2**. GDP is used worldwide and measures the total output of goods and services within a country's borders. The amount of change from one year to the next indicates how much that country's economy is growing. Remember that scenarios have to be adjusted for a country's specific conditions. For other economic information, see the resources for case research in **Appendix 12.A**.

12.4 Format for Case Analysis: The Strategic Audit

There is no one best way to analyze or present a case report. Each instructor has personal preferences for format and approach. Nevertheless, in **Appendix 12.B** we suggest an approach for both written and oral reports that provides a systematic method for successfully attacking a case. This approach is based on the strategic audit, which is presented at the end of **Chapter 1** in **Appendix 1.A**). We find that this approach provides structure and is very helpful for the typical student who may be a relative novice in case analysis. Regardless of the format chosen, be careful to include a complete analysis of key environmental variables—especially of trends in the industry and of the competition. Look at international developments as well.

If you choose to use the strategic audit as a guide to the analysis of complex strategy cases, you may want to use the **strategic audit worksheet** in **Figure 12–1**. Print a copy of the worksheet to use to take notes as you analyze a case. See **Appendix 12.C** for an example of a completed student-written analysis of a 1993 Maytag Corporation case done in an outline form

FIGURE 12–1
Strategic Audit
Worksheet

Strategic Audit Heading	Analysis		Comments
	(+) Factors	(–) Factors	
I. Current Situation			
A. Past Corporate Performance Indexes			
B. Strategic Posture: Current Mission Current Objectives Current Strategies Current Policies			
SWOT Analysis Begins:			
II. Corporate Governance			
A. Board of Directors			
B. Top Management			
III. External Environment (EFAS): Opportunities and Threats (SW_OT_)			
A. Natural Environment			
B. Societal Environment			
C. Task Environment (Industry Analysis)			
IV. Internal Environment (IFAS): Strengths and Weaknesses (_SW_OT)			
A. Corporate Structure			
B. Corporate Culture			
C. Corporate Resources			
1. Marketing			
2. Finance			
3. Research and Development			
4. Operations and Logistics			
5. Human Resources			
6. Information Technology			
V. Analysis of Strategic Factors (SFAS)			
A. Key Internal and External Strategic Factors (SWOT)			
B. Review of Mission and Objectives			
SWOT Analysis Ends. Recommendation Begins:			
VI. Alternatives and Recommendations			
A. Strategic Alternatives—pros and cons			
B. Recommended Strategy			
VII. Implementation			
VIII. Evaluation and Control			

NOTE: See the complete Strategic Audit on pages 82–89. It lists the pages in the book that discuss each of the eight headings.

using the strategic audit format. This is one example of what a case analysis in outline form may look like.

Case discussion focuses on critical analysis and logical development of thought. A solution is satisfactory if it resolves important problems and is likely to be implemented successfully. How the corporation actually dealt with the case problems has no real bearing on the analysis because management might have analyzed its problems incorrectly or implemented a series of flawed solutions.

End of Chapter SUMMARY

Using case analysis is one of the best ways to understand and remember the strategic management process. By applying to cases the concepts and techniques you have learned, you will be able to remember them long past the time when you have forgotten other memorized bits of information. The use of cases to examine actual situations brings alive the field of strategic management and helps build your analytic and decision-making skills. These are just some of the reasons why the use of cases in disciplines from agribusiness to health care is increasing throughout the world.

ECO-BITS

- A 2007 McKinsey & Company survey of 7,751 people in eight countries found that 87% of consumers worry about the environment and the social impact of the products they buy.

- The same 2007 survey found that only 33% of the consumers said that they were ready to buy green products or had already done so.

- In a 2007 *Chain Store Age* survey of U.S. consumers, only 25% of them had bought any green products other than organic food or energy-efficient lighting.[12]

DISCUSSION QUESTIONS

1. Why should you begin a case analysis with a financial analysis? When are other approaches appropriate?

2. What are common-size financial statements? What is their value to case analysis? How are they calculated?

3. When should you gather information outside a case by going to the library or using the Internet? What should you look for?

4. When is inflation an important issue in conducting case analysis? Why bother?

5. How can you learn what date a case took place?

STRATEGIC PRACTICE EXERCISE

Convert the following two years of income statements from the Maytag Corporation into common-size statements. The dollar figures are in thousands. What does converting to a common size reveal?

Consolidated Statements of Income: Maytag Corporation

	1992	%	1991	%
Net sales	$3,041,223	100	$2,970,626	100
Cost of sales	2,339,406	—	2,254,221	—
Gross profits	701,817	—	716,405	—
Selling, general, & admin. expenses	528,250	—	524,898	—
Reorganization expenses	95,000	—	0	—
Operating income	78,567	—	191,507	—
Interest expense	(75,004)	—	(75,159)	—
Other—net	3,983	—	7,069	—
Income before taxes and accounting changes	7,546	—	123,417	—
Income taxes	(15,900)	—	(44,400)	—
Income before accounting changes	(8,354)	—	79,017	—
Effects of accounting changes for postretirement benefits	(307,000)	—	0	—
Net income (loss)	$(315,354)	—	$79,017	—

KEY TERMS

activity ratio (p. 414)

Altman's Z-Value Bankruptcy Formula (p. 419)

annual report (p. 414)

common-size statement (p. 419)

constant dollars (p. 420)

gross domestic product (GDP) (p. 421)

index of sustainable growth (p. 420)

leverage ratio (p. 414)

liquidity ratio (p. 414)

prime interest rate (p. 420)

profitability ratio (p. 414)

ratio analysis (p. 414)

SEC 10-K form (p. 414)

SEC 10-Q form (p. 414)

SEC 14-A form (p. 414)

strategic audit worksheet (p. 421)

NOTES

1. M. Heimer, "Wall Street Sherlock," *Smart Money* (July 2003), pp. 103–107.
2. *Ibid.*, p. 105.
3. *Ibid.*, p. 105.
4. *Ibid.*, p. 105.
5. D. Stead, "The Secrets in SEC Filings," *Business Week* (September 1, 2008), p. 12.
6. M. Vanac, "What's a Novice Investor to Do?" *Des Moines Register* (November 30, 1997), p. 3G.
7. A. R. Sorking, "New Path on Mergers Could Contain Loopholes," *The* (Ames, IA) *Daily Tribune* (January 9, 2001), p. B7; "Firms Resist Effort to Unveil True Costs of Doing Business," *USA Today* (July 3, 2000), p. 10A.
8. M. S. Fridson, *Financial Statement Analysis* (New York: John Wiley & Sons, 1991), pp. 192–194.
9. E. I. Altman, "Predicting Financial Distress of Companies: Revisiting the Z-Score and Zeta Models," Working paper at http://pages.stern.nyu.edu/~ealtman/Zscores.pdf (July 2000).
10. D. H. Bangs, *Managing by the Numbers* (Dover, N.H.: Upstart Publications, 1992), pp. 106–107.
11. "Economic Focus: A Tale of Two Worlds," *The Economist* (May 10, 2008), p. 88; "Zimbabwe: A Worthless Currency," *The Economist* (July 19, 2008), pp. 56–57.
12. S. M. J. Bonini and J. M. Oppenheim, "Helping 'Green' Products Grow," *McKinsey Quarterly* (October 2008), pp. 1–8.

12.A
Resources
for Case Research

Company Information

1. Annual reports
2. Moody's *Manuals on Investment* (a listing of companies within certain industries that contains a brief history and a five-year financial statement of each company)
3. Securities and Exchange Commission Annual Report Form 10-K (annually) and 10-Q (quarterly)
4. Standard & Poor's *Register of Corporations, Directors, and Executives*
5. Value Line's *Investment Survey*
6. Findex's *Directory of Market Research Reports, Studies and Surveys* (a listing by Find/SVP of more than 11,000 studies conducted by leading research firms)
7. Compustat, Compact Disclosure, CD/International, and Hoover's Online Corporate Directory (computerized operating and financial information on thousands of publicly held corporations)
8. Shareholders meeting notices in SEC Form 14-A (proxy notices)

Economic Information

1. Regional statistics and local forecasts from large banks
2. *Business Cycle Development* (Department of Commerce)
3. Chase Econometric Associates' publications
4. U.S. Census Bureau publications on population, transportation, and housing
5. *Current Business Reports* (U.S. Department of Commerce)
6. *Economic Indicators* (U.S. Joint Economic Committee)
7. *Economic Report of the President to Congress*
8. *Long-Term Economic Growth* (U.S. Department of Commerce)
9. *Monthly Labor Review* (U.S. Department of Labor)
10. *Monthly Bulletin of Statistics* (United Nations)
11. *Statistical Abstract of the United States* (U.S. Department of Commerce)
12. *Statistical Yearbook* (United Nations)
13. *Survey of Current Business* (U.S. Department of Commerce)
14. *U.S. Industrial Outlook* (U.S. Department of Defense)
15. *World Trade Annual* (United Nations)
16. *Overseas Business Reports* (by country, published by the U.S. Department of Commerce)

Industry Information

1. Analyses of companies and industries by investment brokerage firms
2. *Business Week* (provides weekly economic and business information, as well as quarterly profit and sales rankings of corporations)

3. *Fortune* (each April publishes listings of financial information on corporations within certain industries)

4. *Industry Survey* (published quarterly by Standard & Poor's)

5. *Industry Week* (late March/early April issue provides information on 14 industry groups)

6. *Forbes* (mid-January issue provides performance data on firms in various industries)

7. *Inc.* (May and December issues give information on fast-growing entrepreneurial companies)

Directory and Index Information on Companies and Industries

1. *Business Periodical Index* (on computers in many libraries)

2. *Directory of National Trade Associations*

3. *Encyclopedia of Associations*

4. Funk and Scott's *Index of Corporations and Industries*

5. Thomas' *Register of American Manufacturers*

6. *Wall Street Journal Index*

Ratio Analysis Information

1. *Almanac of Business and Industrial Financial Ratios* (Prentice Hall)

2. *Annual Statement Studies* (Risk Management Associates; also Robert Morris Associates)

3. *Dun's Review* (Dun & Bradstreet; published annually in September–December issues)

4. *Industry Norms and Key Business Ratios* (Dun & Bradstreet)

Online Information

1. *Hoover's Online*—financial statements and profiles of public companies (www.hoovers.com)

2. U.S. Securities and Exchange Commission—official filings of public companies in Edgar database (www.sec.gov)

3. Fortune 500—statistics for largest U.S. corporations (www.fortune.com)

4. Dun & Bradstreet's Online—short reports on 10 million public and private U.S. companies (smallbusiness.dnb.com)

5. Ecola's 24-Hour Newsstand—links to Web sites of 2,000 newspapers, journals, and magazines (www.ecola.com)

6. Competitive Intelligence Guide—information on company resources (www.fuld.com)

7. Society of Competitive Intelligence Professionals (www.scip.org)

8. *The Economist*—provides international information and surveys (www.economist.com)

9. *CIA World Fact Book*—international information by country (http://www.cia.gov)

10. Bloomberg—information on interest rates, stock prices, currency conversion rates, and other general financial information (www.bloomberg.com)

11. The Scannery—information on international companies (www.thescannery.com)

12. CEOExpress—links to many valuable sources of business information (www.ceoexpress.com)

13. *Wall Street Journal*—business news (www.wsj.com)

14. Forbes—America's largest private companies (http://www.forbes.com/lists/)

15. CorporateInformation.com—subscription service for company profiles (www.corporateinformation.com)

16. Kompass International—industry information (www.kompass.com)

17. CorpTech—database of technology companies (www.corptech.com)

18. ADNet—information technology industry (www.companyfinder.com)

19. CNN company research—provides company information (http://money.cnn.com/news/crc/)

20. Paywatch—database of executive compensation (http://www.aflcio.org/corporatewatch/paywatch/)
21. Global Edge Global Resources—international resources (http://globaledge.msu.edu/resourceDesk/)
22. Google Finance—data on North American stocks (http://finance.google.com/finance)
23. World Federation of Exchanges—international stock exchanges (www.world-exchanges.org/)
24. SEC International Registry—data on international corporations (http://www.sec.gov/divisions/corpfin/internatl/companies.shtml)
25. Yahoo Finance—data on North American companies (http://finance.yahoo.com)

APPENDIX 12.B

Suggested Case Analysis Methodology Using the Strategic Audit

1. READ CASE

First Reading of the Case

- Develop a general overview of the company and its external environment.
- Begin a list of the possible strategic factors facing the company at this time.
- List the research information you may need on the economy, industry, and competitors.

2. READ THE CASE WITH THE STRATEGIC AUDIT

Second Reading of the Case

- Read the case a second time, using the strategic audit as a framework for in-depth analysis. (See **Appendix 1.A** on pages 82–89.) You may want to make a copy of the strategic audit worksheet (**Figure 12–1**) to use to keep track of your comments as you read the case.
- The questions in the strategic audit parallel the strategic decision-making process shown in **Figure 1–5** (pages 76–77).
- The audit provides you with a conceptual framework to examine the company's mission, objectives, strategies, and policies as well as problems, symptoms, facts, opinions, and issues.
- Perform a financial analysis of the company, using ratio analysis (see **Table 12–1**), and do the calculations necessary to convert key parts of the financial statements to a common-size basis.

3. DO OUTSIDE RESEARCH

Library and Online Computer Services

- Each case has a decision date indicating when the case actually took place. Your research should be based on the time period for the case.
- See **Appendix 12.A** for resources for case research. Your research should include information about the environment at the time of the case. Find average industry ratios. You may also want to obtain further information regarding competitors and the company itself (10-K forms and annual reports). This information should help you conduct an industry analysis. *Check with your instructor to see what kind of outside research is appropriate for your assignment.*
- Don't try to learn what actually happened to the company discussed in the case. What management actually decided may not be the best solution. It will certainly bias your analysis and will probably cause your recommendation to lack proper justification.

4. BEGIN SWOT ANALYSIS

External Environmental Analysis: EFAS

- Analyze the natural and societal environments to see what general trends are likely to affect the industry(s) in which the company is operating.

- Conduct an industry analysis using Porter's competitive forces from **Chapter 4.** Develop an Industry Matrix (**Table 4–4** on page 167).

- Generate 8 to 10 external factors. These should be the *most important* opportunities and threats facing the company at the time of the case.

- Develop an EFAS Table, as shown in **Table 4–5** (page 174), for your list of external strategic factors.

- **Suggestion:** Rank the 8 to 10 factors from most to least important. Start by grouping the 3 top factors and then the 3 bottom factors.

Internal Organizational Analysis: IFAS

- Generate 8 to 10 internal factors. These should be the *most important* strengths and weaknesses of the company at the time of the case.

- Develop an IFAS Table, as shown in **Table 5–2** (page 212), for your list of internal strategic factors.

- **Suggestion:** Rank the 8 to 10 factors from most to least important. Start by grouping the 3 top factors and then the 3 bottom factors.

5. WRITE YOUR STRATEGIC AUDIT: PARTS I TO IV

First Draft of Your Strategic Audit

- Review the student-written audit of an old Maytag case in **Appendix 12.C** for an example.

- Write Parts I to IV of the strategic audit. Remember to include the factors from your EFAS and IFAS Tables in your audit.

6. WRITE YOUR STRATEGIC AUDIT: PART V

Strategic Factor Analysis Summary: SFAS

- **Condense the list of factors from the 16 to 20 identified in your EFAS and IFAS Tables to only the 8 to 10 most important factors.**

- Select the most important EFAS and IFAS factors. Recalculate the weights of each. The weights still need to add to 1.0.

- Develop a SFAS Matrix, as shown in **Figure 6–1** (pages 226–227), for your final list of strategic factors. Although the weights (indicating the importance of each factor) will probably change from the EFAS and IFAS Tables, the numeric rating (1 to 5) of each factor should remain the same. These ratings are your assessment of management's performance on each factor.

- This is a good time to reexamine what you wrote earlier in Parts I to IV. You may want to add to or delete some of what you wrote. Ensure that each one of the strategic factors you have included in your SFAS Matrix is discussed in the appropriate place in Parts I to IV. Part V of the audit is *not* the place to mention a strategic factor for the first time.

- Write Part V of your strategic audit. This completes your SWOT analysis.

- This is the place to suggest a revised mission statement and a better set of objectives for the company. The SWOT analysis coupled with revised mission and objectives for the company set the stage for the generation of strategic alternatives.

7. WRITE YOUR STRATEGIC AUDIT: PART VI

Strategic Alternatives and Recommendation

A. Alternatives

■ Develop around three mutually exclusive strategic alternatives. If appropriate to the case you are analyzing, you might propose one alternative for growth, one for stability, and one for retrenchment. Within each corporate strategy, you should probably propose an appropriate business/competitive strategy. You may also want to include some functional strategies where appropriate.

■ Construct a corporate scenario for each alternative. Use the data from your outside research to project general societal trends (GDP, inflation, and etc.) and industry trends. Use these as the basis of your assumptions to write pro forma financial statements (particularly income statements) for each strategic alternative for the next five years.

■ List pros and cons for each alternative based on your scenarios.

B. Recommendation

■ Specify which one of your alternative strategies you recommend. Justify your choice in terms of dealing with the strategic factors you listed in Part V of the strategic audit.

■ Develop policies to help implement your strategies.

8. WRITE YOUR STRATEGIC AUDIT: PART VII

Implementation

■ Develop programs to implement your recommended strategy.

■ Specify who is to be responsible for implementing each program and how long each program will take to complete.

■ Refer to the pro forma financial statements you developed earlier for your recommended strategy. Use common-size historical income statements as the basis for the pro forma statement. Do the numbers still make sense? If not, this may be a good time to rethink the budget numbers to reflect your recommended programs.

9. WRITE YOUR STRATEGIC AUDIT: PART VIII

Evaluation and Control

■ Specify the type of evaluation and controls that you need to ensure that your recommendation is carried out successfully. Specify who is responsible for monitoring these controls.

■ Indicate whether sufficient information is available to monitor how the strategy is being implemented. If not, suggest a change to the information system.

10. PROOF AND FINE-TUNE YOUR AUDIT

Final Draft of Your Strategic Audit

■ Check to ensure that your audit is within the page limits of your professor. You may need to cut some parts and expand others.

■ Make sure that your recommendation clearly deals with the strategic factors.

■ **Attach your EFAS and IFAS Tables, and SFAS Matrix,** plus your ratio analysis and pro forma statements. Label them as numbered exhibits and refer to each of them within the body of the audit.

■ Proof your work for errors. If on a computer, use a spell checker.

SPECIAL NOTE: Depending on your assignment, it is relatively easy to use the strategic audit you have just developed to write a written case analysis in essay form or to make an oral presentation. The strategic audit is just a detailed case analysis in an outline form and can be used as the basic framework for any sort of case analysis and presentation.

Example of Student-Written Strategic Audit

(For the 1993 Maytag Corporation Case)

I. Current Situation

A. Current Performance

Poor financials, high debt load, first losses since 1920s, price/earnings ratio negative.

- First loss since 1920s.
- Laid off 4,500 employees at Magic Chef.
- Hoover Europe still showing losses.

B. Strategic Posture

1. **Mission**
   - Developed in 1989 for the Maytag Company: "To provide our customers with products of unsurpassed performance that last longer, need fewer repairs, and are produced at the lowest possible cost."
   - Updated in 1991: "Our collective mission is world class quality." Expands Maytag's belief in product quality to all aspects of operations.

2. **Objectives**
   - "To be profitability leader in industry for every product line Maytag manufactures." Selected profitability rather than market share.
   - "To be number one in total customer satisfaction." Doesn't say how to measure satisfaction.
   - "To grow the North American appliance business and become the third largest appliance manufacturer (in unit sales) in North America."
   - To increase profitable market share growth in North American appliance and floor care business, 6.5% return on sales, 10% return on assets, 20% return on equity, beat competition in satisfying customers, dealer, builder and endorser, move into third place in total units shipped per year. Nicely quantified objectives.

3. **Strategies**
   - Global growth through acquisition, and alliance with Bosch-Siemens.
   - Differentiate brand names for competitive advantage.
   - Create synergy between companies, product improvement, investment in plant and equipment.

4. **Policies**
   - Cost reduction is secondary to high quality.
   - Promotion from within.
   - Slow but sure R&D: Maytag slow to respond to changes in market.

II. Strategic Managers

A. Board of Directors

1. Fourteen members—eleven are outsiders.
2. Well-respected Americans, most on board since 1986 or earlier.
3. No international or marketing backgrounds.
4. Time for a change?

B. Top Management

1. Top management promoted from within Maytag Company. Too inbred?
2. Very experienced in the industry.
3. Responsible for current situation.
4. May be too parochial for global industry. May need new blood.

III. External Environment (EFAS Table; see Exhibit 1)

A. Natural Environment

1. Growing water scarcity
2. Energy availability a growing problem

B. Societal Environment

1. **Economic**
   a. Unstable economy but recession ending, consumer confidence growing—could increase spending for big ticket items like houses, cars, and appliances. (**O**)
   b. Individual economies becoming interconnected into a world economy. (**O**)

2. **Technological**
   a. Fuzzy logic technology being applied to sense and measure activities. (**O**)
   b. Computers and information technology increasingly important. (**O**)

3. **Political–Legal**
   a. NAFTA, European Union, other regional trade pacts opening doors to markets in Europe, Asia, and Latin America that offer enormous potential. (**O**)
   b. Breakdown of communism means less chance of world war. (**O**)
   c. Environmentalism being reflected in laws on pollution and energy usage. (**T**)

4. **Sociocultural**
   a. Developing nations desire goods seen on TV. (**O**)
   b. Middle-aged baby boomers want attractive, high-quality products, like BMWs and Maytag. (**O**)
   c. Dual-career couples increases need for labor-saving appliances, second cars, and day care. (**O**)
   d. Divorce and career mobility means need for more houses and goods to fill them. (**O**)

C. Task Environment

1. North American market mature and extremely competitive—vigilant consumers demand high quality with low price in safe, environmentally sound products. **(T)**

2. Industry going global as North American and European firms expand internationally. **(T)**

3. European design popular and consumer desire for technologically advanced appliances. **(O)**

4. **Rivalry High**. Whirlpool, Electrolux, GE have enormous resources & developing global presence. **(T)**

5. **Buyers' Power Low**. Technology and materials can be sourced worldwide. **(O)**

6. **Power of Other Stakeholders Medium**. Quality, safety, environmental regulations increasing. **(T)**

7. **Distributors' Power High**. Super retailers more important: mom and pop dealers less. **(T)**

8. **Threat of Substitutes Low**. **(O)**

9. **Entry Barriers High**. New entrants unlikely except for large international firms. **(T)**

IV. Internal Environment
(IFAS Table; see Exhibit 2)

A. Corporate Structure

1. Divisional structure: appliance manufacturing and vending machines. Floor care managed separately. **(S)**

2. Centralized major decisions by Newton corporate staff, with a time line of about three years. **(S)**

B. Corporate Culture

1. Quality key ingredient—commitment to quality shared by executives and workers. **(S)**

2. Much of corporate culture is based on founder F. L. Maytag's personal philosophy, including concern for quality, employees, local community, innovation, and performance. **(S)**

3. Acquired companies, except for European, seem to accept dominance of Maytag culture. **(S)**

C. Corporate Resources

1. **Marketing**
   a. Maytag brand lonely repairman advertising successful but dated. **(W)**
   b. Efforts focus on distribution—combining three sales forces into two, concentrating on major retailers. (Cost $95 million for this restructuring.) **(S)**
   c. Hoover's well-publicized marketing fiasco involving airline tickets. **(W)**

2. **Finance** (see **Exhibits 4 and 5**)
   a. Revenues are up slightly, operating income is down significantly. **(W)**
   b. Some key ratios are troubling, such as a 57% debt/asset ratio, 132% long-term debt/equity ratio. No room for more debt to grow company. **(W)**
   c. Net income is 400% less than 1988, based on common-size income statements. **(W)**

3. **R&D**
   a. Process-oriented with focus on manufacturing process and durability. **(S)**
   b. Maytag becoming a technology follower, taking too long to get product innovations to market (competitors put out more in last 6 months than prior 2 years combined), lagging in fuzzy logic and other technological areas. **(W)**

4. **Operations**
   a. Maytag's core competence. Continual improvement process kept it dominant in the U.S. market for many years. **(S)**
   b. Plants aging and may be losing competitiveness as rivals upgrade facilities. Quality no longer distinctive competence? **(W)**

5. **Human Resources**
   a. Traditionally very good relations with unions and employees. **(S)**
   b. Labor relations increasingly strained, with two salary raise delays, and layoffs of 4,500 employees at Magic Chef. **(W)**
   c. Unions express concern at new, more distant tone from Maytag Corporation. **(W)**

6. **Information Systems**
   a. Not mentioned in case. Hoover fiasco in Europe suggests information systems need significant upgrading. **(W)**
   b. Critical area where Maytag may be unwilling or unable to commit resources needed to stay competitive. **(W)**

V. Analysis of Strategic Factors

A. Situational Analysis (SWOT) (SFAS Matrix; see Exhibit 3)

1. **Strengths**
   a. Quality Maytag culture.
   b. Maytag well-known and respected brand.
   c. Hoover's international orientation.
   d. Core competencies in process R&D and manufacturing.

2. **Weaknesses**
   a. Lacks financial resources of competitors.
   b. Poor global positioning. Hoover weak on European continent.
   c. Product R&D and customer service innovation areas of serious weakness.
   d. Dependent on small dealers.
   e. Marketing needs improvement.

3. **Opportunities**
   a. Economic integration of European Community.
   b. Demographics favor quality.
   c. Trend to superstores.

4. **Threats**
   a. Trend to superstores.
   b. Aggressive rivals—Whirlpool and Electrolux.
   c. Japanese appliance companies—new entrants?

B. Review of Current Mission and Objectives

1. Current mission appears appropriate.
2. Some of the objectives are really goals and need to be quantified and given time horizons.

VI. Strategic Alternatives and Recommended Strategy

A. Strategic Alternatives

1. *Growth through Concentric Diversification*: Acquire a company in a related industry such as commercial appliances.
   a. *[Pros]:* Product/market synergy created by acquisition of related company.
   b. *[Cons]:* Maytag does not have the financial resources to play this game.

2. *Pause Strategy*: Consolidate various acquisitions to find economies and to encourage innovation among the business units.

    a. *[Pros]:* Maytag needs to get its financial house in order and get administrative control over its recent acquisitions.

    b. *[Cons]:* Unless it can grow through a stronger alliance with Bosch-Siemens or some other backer, Maytag is a prime candidate for takeover because of its poor financial performance in recent years, and it is suffering from the initial reduction in efficiency inherent in acquisition strategy.

3. *Retrenchment*: Sell Hoover's foreign major home appliance businesses (Australia and UK) to emphasize increasing market share in North America.

    a. *[Pros]:* Divesting Hoover improves bottom line and enables Maytag Corp. to focus on North America while Whirlpool, Electrolux, and GE are battling elsewhere.

    b. *[Cons]:* Maytag may be giving up its only opportunity to become a player in the coming global appliance industry.

B. Recommended Strategy

1. Recommend pause strategy, at least for a year, so Maytag can get a grip on its European operation and consolidate its companies in a more synergistic way.

2. Maytag quality must be maintained, and continued shortage of operating capital will take its toll, so investment must be made in R&D.

3. Maytag may be able to make the Hoover UK investment work better since the recession is ending and the EU countries are closer to integrating than ever before.

4. Because it is only an average competitor, Maytag needs the Hoover link to Europe to provide a jumping off place for negotiations with Bosch-Siemens that could strengthen their alliance.

VII. Implementation

A. The only way to increase profitability in North America is to further involve Maytag with the superstore retailers; sure to anger the independent dealers, but necessary for Maytag to compete.

B. Board members with more global business experience should be recruited, with an eye toward the future, especially with expertise in Asia and Latin America.

C. R&D needs to be improved, as does marketing, to get new products online quickly.

VIII. Evaluation and Control

A. MIS needs to be developed for speedier evaluation and control. While the question of control vs. autonomy is "under review," another Hoover fiasco may be brewing.

B. The acquired companies do not all share the Midwestern work ethic or the Maytag Corporation culture, and Maytag's managers must inculcate these values into the employees of all acquired companies.

C. Systems should be developed to decide if the size and location of Maytag manufacturing plants is still correct and to plan for the future. Industry analysis indicates that smaller automated plants may be more efficient now than in the past.

EXHIBIT 1   EFAS Table for Maytag Corporation 1993

External Factors	Weight	Rating	Weighted Score	Comments
	1	2	3	4	5
Opportunities				
■ Economic integration of European Community	.20	4.1	.82	Acquisition of Hoover
■ Demographics favor quality appliances	.10	5.0	.50	Maytag quality
■ Economic development of Asia	.05	1.0	.05	Low Maytag presence
■ Opening of Eastern Europe	.05	2.0	.10	Will take time
■ Trend to "Super Stores"	.10	1.8	.18	Maytag weak in this channel
Threats				
■ Increasing government regulations	.10	4.3	.43	Well positioned
■ Strong U.S. competition	.10	4.0	.40	Well positioned
■ Whirlpool and Electrolux strong globally	.15	3.0	.45	Hoover weak globally
■ New product advances	.05	1.2	.06	Questionable
■ Japanese appliance companies	.10	1.6	.16	Only Asian presence in Australia
Total Scores	**1.00**		**3.15**	

EXHIBIT 2   IFAS Table for Maytag Corporation 1993

Internal Factors	Weight	Rating	Weighted Score	Comments
	1	2	3	4	5
Strengths				
■ Quality Maytag culture	.15	5.0	.75	Quality key to success
■ Experienced top management	.05	4.2	.21	Know appliances
■ Vertical integration	.10	3.9	.39	Dedicated factories
■ Employer relations	.05	3.0	.15	Good, but deteriorating
■ Hoover's international orientation	.15	2.8	.42	Hoover name in cleaners
Weaknesses				
■ Process-oriented R&D	.05	2.2	.11	Slow on new products
■ Distribution channels	.05	2.0	.10	Superstores replacing small dealers
■ Financial position	.15	2.0	.30	High debt load
■ Global positioning	.20	2.1	.42	Hoover weak outside the United Kingdom and Australia
■ Manufacturing facilities	.05	4.0	.20	Investing now
Total Scores	**1.00**		**3.05**	

EXHIBIT 3 SFAS Matrix for Maytag Corporation 1993

1	2	3	4	Duration		5	6
Strategic Factors (Select the most important opportunities/threats from EFAS, Table 4–5 and the most important strengths and weaknesses from IFAS, Table 5–2)	Weight	Rating	Weighted Score	SHORT	INTERMEDIATE	LONG	Comments
▸S1 Quality Maytag culture (S)	.10	5.0	.50			X	Quality key to success
▸S5 Hoover's international orientation (S)	.10	2.8	.28	X	X		Name recognition
▸W3 Financial position (W)	.10	2.0	.20	X	X		High debt
▸W4 Global positioning (W)	.15	2.2	.33		X	X	Only in N.A., U.K., and Australia
▸O1 Economic integration of European Community (O)	.10	4.1	.41			X	Acquisition of Hoover
▸O2 Demographics favor quality (O)	.10	5.0	.50		X		Maytag quality
▸O5 Trend to super stores (O + T)	.10	1.8	.18	X			Weak in this channel
▸T3 Whirlpool and Electrolux (T)	.15	3.0	.45	X			Dominate industry
▸T5 Japanese appliance companies (T)	.10	1.6	.16			X	Asian presence
Total Scores	1.00		3.01				

EXHIBIT 4

Ratio Analysis for Maytag Corporation 1993

	1990	1991	1992	1993
1. LIQUIDITY RATIOS				
Current	2.1	1.9	1.8	1.6
Quick	1.1	1.0	1.1	1.0
2. LEVERAGE RATIOS				
Debt to Total Assets	61%	60%	76%	57%
Debt to Equity	155%	151%	317%	254%
3. ACTIVITY RATIOS				
Inventory turnover—sales	5.7	6.1	7.6	6.9
Inventory Turnover—cost of sales	4.3	4.6	5.8	6.5
Avg. Collection Period—days	57	55	56	0
Fixed Asset Turnover	3.9	3.6	3.6	3.6
Total Assets Turnover	1.2	1.2	1.2	1.1
4. PROFITABILITY RATIOS				
Gross Profit Margin	24%	24%	23%	5%
Net Operating Margin	8%	6%	3%	5%
Profit Margin on Sales	3%	3%	−0%	2%
Return on Total Assets	4%	3%	−0%	2%
Return on Equity	10%	8%	−1%	8%

EXHIBIT 5		1992	1991	1990
Common Size Income Statements for Maytag Corporation 1993	Net Sales	100.0%	100.0%	100.0%
	Cost of Sales	76.92	75.88	75.50
	Gross Profit	23.08	24.12	24.46
	Selling, general/admin. expenses	17.37	17.67	16.90
	Reorganization Expenses	.031	—	—
	Operating Income	.026	.064	.075
	Interest Expense	(.025)	(.025)	(0.26)
	Other-net	.001	.002	.009
	Income before accounting changes	.002	.042	.052
	Income taxes	.005	.015	.020
	Income before accounting changes	(.002)	.026	.032
	Effect of accounting changes for post-retirement benefits other than pensions and income taxes	(.101)	-----	-----
	Total Operating Costs and Expenses	74.9	76.0	76.3
	Net Income	**(.104)**	**.026**	**.032**

EXHIBIT 6	Implementation, Evaluation, & Control Plan for Maytag Corporation 1993					
Strategic Factor	Action Plan	Priority System (1–5)	Who Will Implement	Who Will Review	How Often Review	Criteria Used
Quality Maytag culture	Build quality in acquired units	1	Heads of acquired units	Manufacturing VP	Quarterly	Number defects & customer satisfaction
Hoover's international orientation	Identify ways to expand sales	2	Head of Hoover	Marketing VP	Quarterly	Feasible alternatives generated
Financial position	Pay down debt	1	CFO	CEO	Monthly	Leverage ratios
Global positioning	Find strategic alliance partners	2	VP of Business Development	COO	Quarterly	Feasible alternatives generated
EU economic integration	Grow sales throughout EU	3	Hoover UK Head	Marketing VP	Annually	Sales growth
Demographics favor quality	Simplify controls	3	Manufacturing VP	COO	Annually	Market research user satisfaction
Trend to super stores	Market through Sears	1	Marketing VP	CEO	Monthly	Sales growth
Whirlpool & Electrolux	Monitor competitor performance	1	Competition committee	COO	Quarterly	Competitor sales & new products
Japanese appliance companies	Monitor expansion	4	Head of Hoover Australia	Competition committee	Semi-annually	Sales growth outside Japan

Ending Case for Part Five

IN THE GARDEN

Walking with my watering can underneath the cherry tree, the apricot tree, the plum tree, and the nectarine tree, strawberry vines and raspberry canes at my feet, I gazed at my hedge and thought what would it take to avoid disease in the garden this year? I was amazed how this garden, so similar and different from previous seasons, had evolved from two saplings, purchased by chance, placed by happenstance, but planted with care. Now I wondered at the wild order.

....
This case was written by Mark Meckler, University of Portland and presented to the North American Case Research Association at its 2006 annual meeting. Copyright © 2006 by Mark Meckler. Edited for publication in *Strategic Management and Business Policy*, 12th edition and *Concepts in Strategic Management and Business Policy*, 12th edition. Reprinted by permission of Mark Meckler and the North American Case Research Association.

Was this the fruit I should be growing? How could I end up with the sweetest fruit, and what about the most fruit and the largest fruit? How would I set myself up for more success next year, and what of the years after that? And, I sadly thought, what shall I do with the wonderful apple tree I climbed as a child that now yielded so little fruit?

All these thoughts I had walking with my watering can under the cherry tree, the apricot tree, the plum tree, and the nectarine tree, strawberry vines and raspberry canes at my feet.

Cases in

Strategic Management

cases in
strategic management

CONTENTS

alphabetical listing of cases

CASE **1**

The Recalcitrant Director
at Byte Products, Inc.:

CORPORATE LEGALITY VERSUS CORPORATE RESPONSIBILITY

Dan R. Dalton, Richard A. Cosier, and Cathy A. Enz

BYTE PRODUCTS, INC., IS PRIMARILY INVOLVED IN THE PRODUCTION OF ELECTRONIC components that are used in personal computers. Although such components might be found in a few computers in home use, Byte products are found most frequently in computers used for sophisticated business and engineering applications. Annual sales of these products have been steadily increasing over the past several years; Byte Products, Inc., currently has total sales of approximately $265 million.

Over the past six years, increases in yearly revenues have consistently reached 12%. Byte Products, Inc., headquartered in the midwestern United States, is regarded as one of the largest-volume suppliers of specialized components and is easily the industry leader, with some 32% market share. Unfortunately for Byte, many new firms—domestic and foreign—have entered the industry. A dramatic surge in demand, high profitability, and the relative ease of a new firm's entry into the industry explain in part the increased number of competing firms.

Although Byte management—and presumably shareholders as well—is very pleased about the growth of its markets, it faces a major problem: Byte simply cannot meet the demand for these components. The company currently operates three manufacturing facilities in various locations throughout the United States. Each of these plants operates three production shifts (24 hours per day), 7 days a week. This activity constitutes virtually all of the company's production capacity. Without an additional manufacturing plant, Byte simply cannot increase its output of components.

This case was prepared by Professors Dan R. Dalton and Richard A. Cosier of the Graduate School of Business at Indiana University and Cathy A. Enz of Cornell University. The names of the organization, individual, location, and/or financial information have been disguised to preserve the organization's desire for anonymity. This case was edited for SMBP–9th, 10th, 11th, and 12th Editions. Reprint permission is solely granted to the publisher, Prentice Hall, for the book, *Strategic Management and Business Policy – 12th Edition* and cases in *Strategic Management and Business Policy, 12th Edition* by copyright holders Dan R. Dalton, Richard A. Cosier, and Cathy A. Enz. Any other publication of this case (translation, any form of electronic or other media), or sold (any form of partnership) to another publisher will be in violation of copyright laws, unless the copyright holders have granted an additional written reprint permission.

James M. Elliott, Chief Executive Officer and Chairman of the Board, recognizes the gravity of the problem. If Byte Products cannot continue to manufacture components in sufficient numbers to meet the demand, buyers will go elsewhere. Worse yet is the possibility that any continued lack of supply will encourage others to enter the market. As a long-term solution to this problem, the Board of Directors unanimously authorized the construction of a new, state-of-the-art manufacturing facility in the southwestern United States. When the planned capacity of this plant is added to that of the three current plants, Byte should be able to meet demand for many years to come. Unfortunately, an estimated three years will be required to complete the plant and bring it online.

Jim Elliott believes very strongly that this three-year period is far too long and has insisted that there also be a shorter-range, stopgap solution while the plant is under construction. The instability of the market and the pressure to maintain leader status are two factors contributing to Elliott's insistence on a more immediate solution. Without such a move, Byte management believes that it will lose market share and, again, attract competitors into the market.

Several Solutions

A number of suggestions for such a temporary measure were offered by various staff specialists but rejected by Elliott. For example, licensing Byte's product and process technology to other manufacturers in the short run to meet immediate demand was possible. This licensing authorization would be short term, or just until the new plant could come online. Top management, as well as the board, was uncomfortable with this solution for several reasons. They thought it unlikely that any manufacturer would shoulder the fixed costs of producing appropriate components for such a short term. Any manufacturer that would do so would charge a premium to recover its costs. This suggestion, obviously, would make Byte's own products available to its customers at an unacceptable price. Nor did passing any price increase to its customers seem sensible, for this too would almost certainly reduce Byte's market share as well as encourage further competition.

Overseas facilities and licensing also were considered but rejected. Before it became a publicly traded company, Byte's founders had decided that its manufacturing facilities would be domestic. Top management strongly felt that this strategy had served Byte well; moreover, Byte's majority stockholders (initial owners of the then privately held Byte) were not likely to endorse such a move. Beyond that, however, top management was reluctant to foreign license—or make available by any means the technologies for others to produce Byte products—as they could not then properly control patents. Top management feared that foreign licensing would essentially give away costly proprietary information regarding the company's highly efficient means of product development. There also was the potential for initial low product quality—whether produced domestically or otherwise—especially for such a short-run operation. Any reduction in quality, however brief, would threaten Byte's share of this sensitive market.

The Solution!

One recommendation that has come to the attention of the Chief Executive Officer could help solve Byte's problem in the short run. Certain members of his staff have notified him that an abandoned plant currently is available in Plainville, a small town in the northeastern United States. Before its closing eight years before, this plant was used primarily for the manufacture of electronic components. As is, it could not possibly be used to produce Byte products, but it could be inexpensively refitted to do so in as few as three months. Moreover, this plant is available at a very attractive price. In fact, discreet inquiries by Elliott's staff indicate that this plant could probably be leased immediately from its present owners because the building has been vacant for some eight years.

All the news about this temporary plant proposal, however, is not nearly so positive. Elliott's staff concedes that this plant will never be efficient and its profitability will be low. In addition, the Plainville location is a poor one in terms of high labor costs (the area is highly unionized), warehousing expenses, and inadequate transportation links to Byte's major markets and suppliers. Plainville is simply not a candidate for a long-term solution. Still, in the short run, a temporary plant could help meet the demand and might forestall additional competition.

The staff is persuasive and notes that this option has several advantages: (1) there is no need for any licensing, foreign or domestic, (2) quality control remains firmly in the company's hands, and (3) an increase in the product price will be unnecessary. The temporary plant, then, would be used for three years or so until the new plant could be built. Then the temporary plant would be immediately closed.

CEO Elliott is convinced.

Taking the Plan to the Board

The quarterly meeting of the Board of Directors is set to commence at 2:00 P.M. Jim Elliott has been reviewing his notes and agenda for the meeting most of the morning. The issue of the temporary plant is clearly the most important agenda item. Reviewing his detailed presentation of this matter, including the associated financial analyses, has occupied much of his time for several days. All the available information underscores his contention that the temporary plant in Plainville is the only responsible solution to the demand problems. No other option offers the same low level of risk and ensures Byte's status as industry leader.

At the meeting, after the board has dispensed with a number of routine matters, Jim Elliott turns his attention to the temporary plant. In short order, he advises the 11-member board (himself, 3 additional inside members, and 7 outside members) of his proposal to obtain and refit the existing plant to ameliorate demand problems in the short run, authorizes the construction of the new plant (the completion of which is estimated to take some three years), and plans to switch capacity from the temporary plant to the new one when it is operational. He also briefly reviews additional details concerning the costs involved, advantages of this proposal versus domestic or foreign licensing, and so on.

All the board members except one are in favor of the proposal. In fact, they are most enthusiastic; the overwhelming majority agree that the temporary plant is an excellent—even inspired—stopgap measure. Ten of the eleven board members seem relieved because the board was most reluctant to endorse any of the other alternatives that had been mentioned.

The single dissenter—T. Kevin Williams, an outside director—is, however, steadfast in his objections. He will not, under any circumstances, endorse the notion of the temporary plant and states rather strongly that "I will not be party to this nonsense, not now, not ever."

T. Kevin Williams, the senior executive of a major nonprofit organization, is normally a reserved and really quite agreeable person. This sudden, uncharacteristic burst of emotion clearly startles the remaining board members into silence. The following excerpt captures the ensuing, essentially one-on-one conversation between Williams and Elliott:

Williams: How many workers do your people estimate will be employed in the temporary plant?

Elliott: Roughly 1,200, possibly a few more.

Williams: I presume it would be fair, then, to say that, including spouses and children, something on the order of 4,000 people will be attracted to the community.

Elliott: I certainly would not be surprised.

Williams: If I understand the situation correctly, this plant closed just over eight years ago, and that closing had a catastrophic effect on Plainville. Isn't it true that a large portion of the community was employed by this plant?

Elliott: Yes, it was far and away the majority employer.

Williams: And most of these people have left the community, presumably to find employment elsewhere.

Elliott: Definitely, there was a drastic decrease in the area's population.

Williams: Are you concerned, then, that our company can attract the 1,200 employees to Plainville from other parts of New England?

Elliott: Not in the least. We are absolutely confident that we will attract 1,200—even more, for that matter virtually any number we need. That, in fact, is one of the chief advantages of this proposal. I would think that the community would be very pleased to have us there.

Williams: On the contrary, I would suspect that the community will rue the day we arrived. Beyond that, though, this plan is totally unworkable if we are candid. On the other hand, if we are less than candid, the proposal will work for us, but only at great cost to Plainville. In fact, quite frankly, the implications are appalling. Once again, I must enter my serious objections.

Elliott: I don't follow you.

Williams: The temporary plant would employ some 1,200 people. Again, this means the infusion of over 4,000 to the community and surrounding areas. Byte Products, however, intends to close this plant in three years or less. If Byte informs the community or the employees that the jobs are temporary, the proposal simply won't work. When the new people arrive in the community, there will be a need for more schools, instructors, utilities, housing, restaurants, and so forth. Obviously, if the banks and local government know that the plant is temporary, no funding will be made available for these projects and certainly no credit for the new employees to buy homes, appliances, automobiles, and so forth.

If, on the other hand, Byte Products does not tell the community of its "temporary" plans, the project can go on. But, in several years when the plant closes (and we here have agreed today that it will close), we will have created a ghost town. The tax base of the community will have been destroyed; property values will decrease precipitously; practically the whole town will be unemployed. This proposal will place Byte Products in an untenable position and in extreme jeopardy.

Elliott: Are you suggesting that this proposal jeopardizes us legally? If so, it should be noted that the legal department has reviewed this proposal in its entirety and has indicated no problem.

Williams: No! I don't think we are dealing with an issue of legality here. In fact, I don't doubt for a minute that this proposal is altogether legal. I do, however, resolutely believe that this proposal constitutes gross irresponsibility.

I think this decision has captured most of my major concerns. These along with a host of collateral problems associated with this project lead me to strongly suggest that you and the balance of the board reconsider and not endorse this proposal. Byte Products must find another way.

The Dilemma

After a short recess, the board meeting reconvened. Presumably because of some discussion during the recess, several other board members indicated that they were no longer inclined to support the proposal. After a short period of rather heated discussion, the following exchange took place:

Elliott: It appears to me that any vote on this matter is likely to be very close. Given the gravity of our demand capacity problem, I must insist that the stockholders' equity be protected. We cannot wait three years; that is clearly out of the question. I still feel that licensing—domestic or foreign—is not in our long-term interests for any number of reasons, some of which have been discussed here. On the other hand, I do not want to take this project forward on the strength of a mixed vote. A vote of 6–5 or 7–4, for example, does not indicate that the board is remotely close to being of one mind. Mr. Williams, is there a compromise to be reached?

Williams: Respectfully, I have to say no. If we tell the truth—namely, the temporary nature of our operations—the proposal is simply not viable. If we are less than candid in this respect, we do grave damage to the community as well as to our image. It seems to me that we can only go one way or the other. I don't see a middle ground.

CASE 2

The Wallace Group

Laurence J. Stybel

FRANCES RAMPAR, PRESIDENT OF RAMPAR ASSOCIATES, DRUMMED HER FINGERS ON THE desk. Scattered before her were her notes. She had to put the pieces together in order to make an effective sales presentation to Harold Wallace.

Hal Wallace was the President of The Wallace Group. He had asked Rampar to conduct a series of interviews with some key Wallace Group employees, in preparation for a possible consulting assignment for Rampar Associates.

During the past three days, Rampar had been talking with some of these key people and had received background material about the company. The problem was not in finding the problem. The problem was that there were too many problems!

Background on The Wallace Group

The Wallace Group, Inc., is a diversified company dealing in the manufacture and development of technical products and systems (see **Exhibit 1**). The company currently consists of three operational groups and a corporate staff. The three groups include Electronics, Plastics, and Chemicals, each operating under the direction of a Group Vice President (see **Exhibits 2, 3,** and **4**). The company generates $70 million in sales as a manufacturer of plastics, chemical products, and electronic components and systems. Principal sales are to large contractors in governmental and automotive markets. With respect to sales volume, Plastics and Chemicals are approximately equal in size, and both of them together equal the size of the Electronics Group.

Electronics offers competence in the areas of microelectronics, electromagnetic sensors, antennas, microwaves, and minicomputers. Presently, these skills are devoted primarily to the engineering and manufacture of countermeasure equipment for aircraft. This includes radar detection systems that allow an aircraft crew to know that they are being tracked by radar units on the ground, on ships, or on other aircraft. Further, the company manufactures displays that provide the crew with a visual "fix" on where they are relative to the radar units that are tracking them.

This case was prepared by Dr. Laurence J. Stybel. It was prepared for class discussion rather than to illustrate either effective or ineffective handling of an administrative situation. Unauthorized duplication of copyright materials is a violation of federal law. This case was edited for *SMBP*-9th, 10th, 11th, and 12th Editions. The copyright holders are solely responsible for case content. Reprint permission is solely granted to the publisher, Prentice Hall, for the book, *Strategic Management and Business Policy* – 12th Edition and cases in *Strategic Management and Business Policy* 12th Edition by copyright holder, Dr. Laurence J. Stybel. Any other publication of this case (translation, any form of electronic or other media), or sold (any form of partnership) to another publisher will be in violation of copyright laws, unless the copyright holder has granted an additional written reprint permission.

EXHIBIT 1
An Excerpt from the
Annual Report

To the Shareholders:

This past year was one of definite accomplishment for The Wallace Group, although with some admitted soft spots. This is a period of consolidation, of strengthening our internal capacity for future growth and development. Presently, we are in the process of creating a strong management team to meet the challenges we will set for the future.

Despite our failure to achieve some objectives, we turned a profit of $3,521,000 before taxes, which was a growth over the previous year's earnings. And we have declared a dividend for the fifth consecutive year, albeit one that is less than the year before. However, the retention of earnings is imperative if we are to lay a firm foundation for future accomplishment.

Currently, The Wallace Group has achieved a level of stability. We have a firm foothold in our current markets, and we could elect to simply enact strong internal controls and maximize our profits. However, this would not be a growth strategy. Instead, we have chosen to adopt a more aggressive posture for the future, to reach out into new markets wherever possible and to institute the controls necessary to move forward in a planned and orderly fashion.

The Electronics Group performed well this past year and is engaged in two major programs under Defense Department contracts. These are developmental programs that provide us with the opportunity for ongoing sales upon testing of the final product. Both involve the creation of tactical display systems for aircraft being built by Lombard Aircraft for the Navy and the Air Force. Future potential sales from these efforts could amount to approximately $56 million over the next five years. Additionally, we are developing technical refinements to older, already installed systems under Army Department contracts.

In the future, we will continue to offer our technological competence in such tactical display systems and anticipate additional breakthroughs and success in meeting the demands of this market. However, we also believe that we have unique contributions to make to other markets, and to that end we are making the investments necessary to expand our opportunities.

Plastics also turned in a solid performance this past year and has continued to be a major supplier to Chrysler, Martin Tool, Foster Electric, and, of course, to our Electronics Group. The market for this group continues to expand, and we believe that additional investments in this group will allow us to seize a larger share of the future.

Chemicals' performance, admittedly, has not been as satisfactory as anticipated during the past year. However, we have been able to realize a small amount of profit from this operation and to halt what was a potentially dangerous decline in profits. We believe that this situation is only temporary and that infusions of capital for developing new technology, plus the streamlining of operations, has stabilized the situation. The next step will be to begin more aggressive marketing to capitalize on the group's basic strengths.

Overall, the outlook seems to be one of modest but profitable growth. The near term will be one of creating the technology and controls necessary for developing our market offerings and growing in a planned and purposeful manner. Our improvement efforts in the various company groups can be expected to take hold over the years with positive effect on results.

We wish to express our appreciation to all those who participated in our efforts this past year.

Harold Wallace
Chairman and President

In addition to manufacturing tested and proven systems developed in the past, The Wallace Group is currently involved in two major and two minor programs, all involving display systems. The Navy-A Program calls for the development of a display system for a tactical fighter plane; Air Force-B is another such system for an observation plane. Ongoing production orders are anticipated following flight testing. The other two minor programs, Army-LG and OBT-37, involve the incorporation of new technology into existing aircraft systems.

EXHIBIT 2
Organizational Chart: The Wallace Group (Electronics)

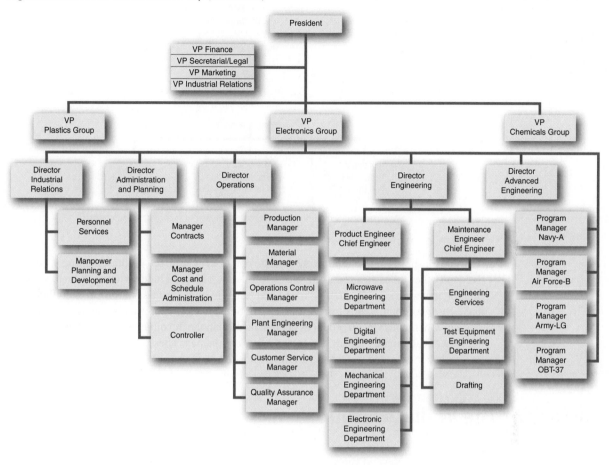

EXHIBIT 3
The Wallace Group
(Chemicals)

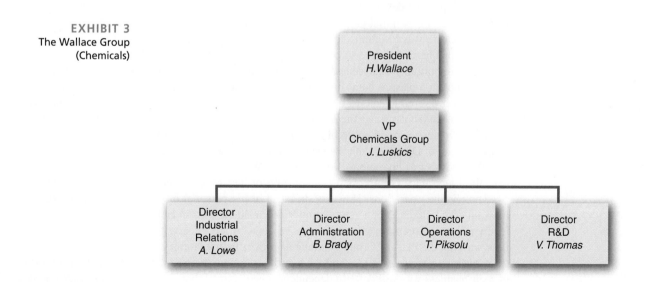

EXHIBIT 4
The Wallace Group
(Plastics)

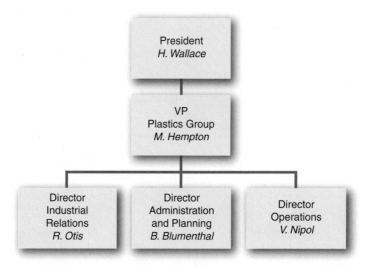

The Plastics Group manufactures plastic components utilized by the electronics, automotive, and other industries requiring plastic products. These include switches, knobs, keys, insulation materials, and so on, used in the manufacture of electronic equipment and other small made-to-order components installed in automobiles, planes, and other products.

The Chemicals Group produces chemicals used in the development of plastics. It supplies bulk chemicals to the Plastics Group and other companies. These chemicals are then injected into molds or extruded to form a variety of finished products.

History of The Wallace Group

Each of the three groups began as a sole proprietorship under the direct operating control of an owner/manager. Several years ago, Harold Wallace, owner of the original electronics company, determined to undertake a program of diversification. Initially, he attempted to expand his market through product development and line extensions entirely within the electronics industry. However, because of initial problems, he drew back and sought other opportunities. Wallace's primary concern was his almost total dependence on defense-related contracts. He had felt for some time that he should take some strong action to gain a foothold in the private markets. The first major opportunity that seemed to satisfy his various requirements was the acquisition of a former supplier, a plastics company whose primary market was not defense-related. The company's owner desired to sell his operation and retire. At the time, Wallace's debt structure was such that he could not manage the acquisition and so he had to attract equity capital. He was able to gather a relatively small group of investors and form a closed corporation. The group established a Board of Directors with Wallace as Chairman and President of the new corporate entity.

With respect to operations, little changed. Wallace continued direct operational control over the Electronics Group. As holder of 60% of the stock, he maintained effective control over policy and operations. However, because of his personal interests, the Plastics Group, now under the direction of a newly hired Vice President, Martin Hempton, was left mainly to its own devices except for yearly progress reviews by the President. All Wallace asked at the time was that the Plastics Group continue its profitable operation, which it did.

Several years ago, Wallace and the board decided to diversify further because two-thirds of their business was still defense dependent. They learned that one of the major suppliers of the Plastics Group, a chemical company, was on the verge of bankruptcy. The company's owner, Jerome Luskics, agreed to sell. However, this acquisition required a public stock offering, with most of the funds going to pay off debts incurred by the three groups, especially the Chemicals Group. The net result was that Wallace now holds 45% of The Wallace Group and Jerome Luskics 5%, with the remainder distributed among the public.

Organization and Personnel

Presently, Harold Wallace serves as Chairman and President of The Wallace Group. The Electronics Group had been run by LeRoy Tuscher, who just resigned as Vice President. Hempton continued as Vice President of Plastics, and Luskics served as Vice President of the Chemicals Group.

Reflecting the requirements of a corporate perspective and approach, a corporate staff has grown up, consisting of Vice Presidents for Finance, Secretarial/Legal, Marketing, and Industrial Relations. This staff has assumed many functions formerly associated with the group offices.

Because these positions are recent additions, many of the job accountabilities are still being defined. Problems have arisen over the responsibilities and relationships between corporate and group positions. President Wallace has settled most of the disputes himself because of the inability of the various parties to resolve differences among themselves.

Current Trends

Presently, there is a mood of lethargy and drift within The Wallace Group. Most managers feel that each of the three groups functions as an independent company. And, with respect to group performance, not much change or progress has been made in recent years. Electronics and Plastics are still stable and profitable, but both lack growth in markets and profits. The infusion of capital breathed new life and hope into the Chemicals operation but did not solve most of the old problems and failings that had caused its initial decline. For all these reasons, Wallace decided that strong action was necessary. His greatest disappointment was with the Electronics Group, in which he had placed high hopes for future development. Thus he acted by requesting and getting the Electronics Group Vice President's resignation. Hired from a computer company to replace LeRoy Tuscher, Jason Matthews joined The Wallace Group a week ago.

As of last week, Wallace's annual net sales were $70 million. By group they were:

Electronics	$35,000,000
Plastics	$20,000,000
Chemicals	$15,000,000

On a consolidated basis, the financial highlights of the past two years are as follows:

	Last Year	Two Years Ago
Net sales	$70,434,000	$69,950,000
Income (pre-tax)	3,521,000	3,497,500
Income (after-tax)	2,760,500	1,748,750
Working capital	16,200,000	16,088,500
Shareholders' equity	39,000,000	38,647,000
Total assets	59,869,000	59,457,000
Long-term debt	4,350,000	3,500,000
Per Share of Common Stock		
Net income	$.37	$.36
Cash dividends paid	.15	.25

Of the net income, approximately 70% came from Electronics, 25% from Plastics, and 5% from Chemicals.

The Problem Confronting Frances Rampar

As Rampar finished reviewing her notes (see **Exhibits 5–11**), she kept reflecting on what Hal Wallace had told her:

> Don't give me a laundry list of problems, Fran. Anyone can do that. I want a set of priorities I should focus on during the next year. I want a clear action plan from you. And I want to know how much this plan is going to cost me!

Fran Rampar again drummed her fingers on the desk.

Rampar: What is your greatest problem right now?

Wallace: That's why I called you in! Engineers are a high-strung, temperamental lot. Always complaining. It's hard to take them seriously.

Last month we had an annual stockholder's meeting. We have an Employee Stock Option Plan, and many of our long-term employees attended the meeting. One of my managers—and I won't mention any names—introduced a resolution calling for the resignation of the President—me!

The vote was defeated. But, of course, I own 45% of the stock!

Now I realize that there could be no serious attempt to get rid of me. Those who voted for the resolution were making a dramatic effort to show me how upset they are with the way things are going.

I could fire those employees who voted against me. I was surprised by how many did. Some of my key people were in that group. Perhaps I ought to stop and listen to what they are saying.

Businesswise, I think we're O.K. Not great, but O.K. Last year we turned in a profit of $3.5 million before taxes, which was a growth over previous years' earnings. We declared a dividend for the fifth consecutive year.

We're currently working on the creation of a tactical display system for aircraft being built by Lombard Aircraft for the Navy and the Air Force. If Lombard gets the contract to produce the prototype, future sales could amount to $56 million over the next five years.

Why are they complaining?

Rampar: You must have thoughts on the matter.

Wallace: I think the issue revolves around how we manage people. It's a personnel problem. You were highly recommended as someone with expertise in high-technology human resource management.

I have some ideas on what is the problem. But I'd like you to do an independent investigation and give me your findings. Give me a plan of action.

Don't give me a laundry list of problems, Fran. Anyone can do that. I want a set of priorities I should focus on during the next year. I want a clear action plan from you. And I want to know how much this plan is going to cost me!

Other than that, I'll leave you alone and let you talk to anyone in the company you want.

EXHIBIT 6
Selected Portions of
a Transcribed
Interview with
Frank Campbell,
Vice President of
Industrial Relations

Rampar: What is your greatest problem right now?

Campbell: Trying to contain my enthusiasm over the fact that Wallace brought you in!

Morale is really poor here. Hal runs this place like a one man operation, when it's grown too big for that. It took a palace revolt to finally get him to see the depths of the resentment. Whether he'll do anything about it, that's another matter.

Rampar: What would you like to see changed?

Campbell: Other than a new President?

Rampar: Uh-huh.

Campbell: We badly need a management development program for our group. Because of our growth, we have been forced to promote technical people to management positions who have had no prior managerial experience. Mr. Tuscher agreed on the need for a program, but Hal Wallace vetoed the idea because developing such a program would be too expensive. I think it is too expensive *not* to move ahead on this.

Rampar: Anything else?

Campbell: The IEWU negotiations have been extremely tough this time around, due to excessive demands they have been making. Union pay scales are already pushing up against our foreman salary levels, and foremen are being paid high in their salary ranges. This problem, coupled with union insistence on a no-layoff clause, is causing us fits. How can we keep all our workers when we have production equipment on order that will eliminate 20% of our assembly positions?

Rampar: Wow.

Campbell: We have been sued by a rejected candidate for a position on the basis of discrimination. She claimed our entrance qualifications are excessive because we require shorthand. There is some basis for this statement since most reports are given to secretaries in handwritten form or on audio cassettes. In fact, we have always required it and our executives want their secretaries to have skill in taking dictation. Not only is this case taking time, but I need to reconsider if any of our position entrance requirements, in fact, are excessive. I am sure we do not want another case like this one.

Rampar: That puts The Wallace Group in a vulnerable position, considering the amount of government work you do.

Campbell: We have a tremendous recruiting backlog, especially for engineering positions. Either our pay scales are too low, our job specs are too high, or we are using the wrong recruiting channels. Kane and Smith [Director of Engineering and Director of Advanced Systems] keep rejecting everyone we send down there as being unqualified.

Rampar: Gee.

Campbell: Being head of human resources around here is a tough job. We don't act. We react.

EXHIBIT 7
Selected Portions of
a Transcribed
Interview with
Matthew Smith,
Director of
Advanced Systems

Rampar: What is your greatest problem right now?

Smith: Corporate brass keeps making demands on me and others that don't relate to the job we are trying to get done. They say that the information they need is to satisfy corporate planning and operations review requirements, but they don't seem to recognize how much time and effort is required to provide this information. Sometimes it seems like they are generating analyses, reports, and requests for data just to keep themselves busy. Someone should be evaluating how critical these corporate staff activities really are. To me and the Electronics Group, these activities are unnecessary.

An example is the Vice President, Marketing (L. Holt), who keeps asking us for supporting data so he can prepare a corporate marketing strategy. As you know, we prepare our own group marketing strategic plans annually, but using data and formats that are oriented to our needs, rather than Corporate's. This planning activity, which occurs at the same time as Corporate's, coupled with heavy work loads on current projects, makes us appear to Holt as though we are being unresponsive.

Somehow we need to integrate our marketing planning efforts between our group and Corporate. This is especially true if our group is to successfully grow in nondefense-oriented markets and products. We do need corporate help, but not arbitrary demands for information that divert us from putting together effective marketing strategies for our group.

I am getting too old to keep fighting these battles.

Rampar: This is a long-standing problem?

Smith: You bet! Our problems are fairly classic in the high-tech field. I've been at other companies and they're not much better. We spend so much time firefighting, we never really get organized. Everything is done on an ad hoc basis.

I'm still waiting for tomorrow.

EXHIBIT 8
Selected Portions of
a Transcribed
Interview with
Ralph Kane,
Director of
Engineering

Rampar: What is your greatest problem right now?

Kane: Knowing you were coming, I wrote them down. They fall into four areas:

1. Our salary schedules are too low to attract good, experienced EEs. We have been told by our Vice President (Frank Campbell) that corporate policy is to hire new people below the salary grade midpoint. All qualified candidates are making more than that now and in some case are making more than our grade maximums. I think our Project Engineer job is rated too low.

2. Chemicals Group asked for and the former Electronics Vice President (Tuscher) agreed to "lend" six of our best EEs to help solve problems it is having developing a new battery. That is great for the Chemicals Group, but meanwhile how do we solve the engineering problems that have cropped up in our Navy-A and OBT-37 programs?

3. As you know, Matt Smith (Director of Advanced Systems) is retiring in six months. I depend heavily on his group for technical expertise, and in some areas he depends heavily on some of my key engineers. I have lost some people to the Chemicals Group, and Matt has been trying to lend me some of his people to fill in. But he and his staff have been heavily involved in marketing planning and trying to identify or recruit a qualified successor long enough before his retirement to be able to train him or her. The result is that his people are up to their eyeballs in doing their own stuff and cannot continue to help me meet my needs.

4. IR has been preoccupied with union negotiations in the plant and has not had time to help me deal with this issue of management planning. Campbell is working on some kind of system that will help deal with this kind of problem and prevent them in the future. That is great, but I need help now—not when his "system" is ready.

Rampar: What is your . . . ?

Lowell: . . . great problem? I'll tell you what it is. I still cannot get the support I need from Kane in Engineering. He commits and then doesn't deliver, and it has me quite concerned. The excuse now is that in "his judgment," Sid Wright needs the help for the Air Force program more than I do. Wright's program is one week ahead of schedule, so I disagree with "his judgment." Kane keeps complaining about not having enough people.

Rampar: Why do you think Kane says he doesn't have enough people?

Lowell: Because Hal Wallace is a tight-fisted S.O.B. who won't let us hire the people we need!

Rampar: What is your greatest problem right now?

Jones: Wheel spinning—that's our problem! We talk about expansion, but we don't do anything about it. Are we serious or not?

For example, a bid request came in from a prime contractor seeking help in developing a countermeasure system for a medium-range aircraft. They needed an immediate response and concept proposal in one week. Tuscher just sat on my urgent memo to him asking for a go/no go decision on bidding. I could not give the contractor an answer (because no decision came from Tuscher), so they gave up on us.

I am frustrated because (1) we lost an opportunity we were "naturals" to win, and (2) my personal reputation was damaged because I was unable to answer the bid request. Okay, Tuscher's gone now, but we need to develop some mechanism so an answer to such a request can be made quickly.

Another thing, our MIS is being developed by the Corporate Finance Group. More wheel spinning! They are telling us what information we need rather than asking us what we want! E. Kay (our Group Controller) is going crazy trying to sort out the input requirements they need for the system and understanding the complicated reports that came out. Maybe this new system is great as a technical achievement, but what good is it to us if we can't use it?

EXHIBIT 11
Selected Portions of
a Transcribed
Interview with
Burt Williams,
Director of
Operations

Rampar: What is your biggest problem right now?

Williams: One of the biggest problems we face right now stems from corporate policy regarding transfer pricing. I realize we are "encouraged" to purchase our plastics and chemicals from our sister Wallace groups, but we are also committed to making a profit! Because manufacturing problems in those groups have forced them to raise their prices, should *we* suffer the consequences? We can get some materials cheaper from other suppliers. How can we meet our volume and profit targets when we are saddled with noncompetitive material costs?

Rampar: And if that issue was settled to your satisfaction, then would things be O.K.?

Williams: Although out of my direct function, it occurs to me that we are not planning effectively our efforts to expand into nondefense areas. With minimal alteration to existing production methods, we can develop both end-use products (e.g., small motors, traffic control devices, and microwave transceivers for highway emergency communications) and components (e.g., LED and LCD displays, police radar tracking devices, and word processing system memory and control devices) with large potential markets.

The problems in this regard are:

1. Matt Smith (Director, Advanced Systems) is retiring and has had only defense-related experience. Therefore, he is not leading any product development efforts along these lines.

2. We have no marketing function at the group level to develop a strategy, define markets, and research and develop product opportunities.

3. Even if we had a marketing plan and products for industrial/commercial application, we have no sales force or rep network to sell the stuff.

   Maybe I am way off base, but it seems to me we need a Groups/Marketing/Sales function to lead us in this business expansion effort. It should be headed by an experienced technical marketing manager with a proven track record in developing such products and markets.

Rampar: Have you discussed your concerns with others?

Williams: I have brought these ideas up with Mr. Matthews and others at the Group Management Committee. No one else seems interested in pursuing this concept, but they won't say this outright and don't say why it should not be addressed. I guess that in raising the idea with you I am trying to relieve some of my frustrations.

CASE 3

Hershey Foods Company:

BOARD OF DIRECTORS AND STAKEHOLDERS CONFLICT OVER SALE

Cynthia Clark Williams

IN SEPTEMBER 2002, ROBERT C. VOWLER, THE CEO OF THE HERSHEY TRUST COMPANY (HTC) that owned 77% voting control of the Hershey Foods Company, was facing one of the most challenging decisions of his 25-year career as a trust officer: whether or not to recommend to his Board that the American chocolate-making icon be sold. After a summer of community opposition, including a petition to oust the Trust's Board and a lawsuit from the Pennsylvania Attorney General (AG), the HTC Board called a meeting to vote on two offers to buy Hershey Foods Company. On September 14, HTC had received two bids, one from Wm. Wrigley Jr. Co. and one from Nestle SA/Cadbury-Schweppes PLC. Although Wrigley's offer had some attractive features, including the purchase price of $12.5 billion and the promise of expanding local employment and retaining the company name and headquarters, the deal included a 60% stock purchase and 40% in cash. The second offer was a joint bid by Nestle and Cadbury-Schweppes and was an all-cash deal of $11 billion.

The Board meeting was scheduled for September 17, 2002. With the Trust having 77% voting control through its class B shares, the meeting's outcome was, in fact, the final decision regarding the fate of Hershey Foods Company, provided that the U.S. Justice Department's antitrust division approved the deal.[1]

Stepping into the conference room at the Hilton Valley Forge on September 17, Vowler considered how to phrase his recommendation to his fellow Board members seated around the rectangular table.

Events Leading Up to HTC Board Meeting Events

Richard H. Lenny, who had been the CEO of Hershey Foods since March 2001, faced a number of challenges in addition to the potential sale. Competition from Nestle and Mars had increased in recent years, causing profit margins to decline. In an effort to boost margins, Lenny announced

The author prepared this case for the sole purpose of providing material for class discussion. It was not intended to illustrate effective or ineffective handling of a managerial decision of decisions. The author wishes to thank David Wylie, Thomas L. Wheelen, three anonymous reviewers, and the journal editors for their valuable insights and guidance. Reprinted by permission from the *Case Research Journal*, Copyright © 2007 Cynthia Clark Williams and the North American case Research Association. All rights reserved. This case was published in the *Case Research Journal*, Volume 26, Issue 1, Winter 2006, pp. 13–28.

a new "value-enhancing" strategy in October 2001.[2] The plan included a $275 million business realignment that called for a voluntary workforce reduction program, the closing of three manufacturing plants and a distribution center, the elimination of non-strategic brands, a realignment of the sales force, and the outsourcing of all cocoa production.[3] However, many community members and employees were growing critical of Lenny's management style and the new strategy.[4] Shareholders, of course, were anxiously awaiting the benefits of the change in strategy. Adding to the CEO's concerns was the recent six-week strike by the local chapter of the Chocolate Worker's Union over health benefits, in the spring of 2002, following Lenny's proposed reductions to employee health coverage. The strike had been the longest in the company's history.[5]

When Lenny learned of HTC's decision to explore a sale, in March 2002, he became determined to seek alternatives. In May 2002 he met with Robert Vowler and proposed a stock buyback of the HTC's shares over a 3- to 5-year period at a 10% premium. But Vowler declined the proposal on behalf of HTC's investment committee. He reiterated that the Trust, its investment banker Morgan Stanley and the AG's office, which had oversight of all charitable trusts, wanted to explore a sale, an idea that had become increasingly popular among HTC Board members in the wake of scandals at Enron and WorldCom. Vowler thought Lenny's buyback offer left the company open to a hostile takeover, as Hershey Foods would have to accumulate debt to finance a buyback.[6] After reportedly being threatened by some of HTC's Board members that he would be fired, Lenny backed off of his buyback proposal and agreed to have his investment banker, Credit Suisse First Boston, solicit bids from potential buyers.[7] A short list was developed that included Coca-Cola, Kraft Foods, Wrigley, and Nestle. Meanwhile, Vowler made his all-cash deal preference clear to the bankers at Morgan Stanley.[8]

Vowler's pressures were also beginning to mount in the months leading up to the September board meeting. He knew after spending a lot of time on the phone with them that some of the HTC's Board members were having second thoughts. He was no doubt aware that the investment bankers and the remaining shareholders might push for the sale because they stood to earn a large sum. The fact that the relationship between the Hershey Foods' board and the HTC board had become more fractious in recent years didn't help matters either (see **Exhibit 1** for chronology). Likewise, the wishes of Pennsylvania's Attorney General (AG) were a concern. The office had just concluded an investigation into alleged mismanagement at the Milton Hershey School, for

EXHIBIT 1
Chronology of Key Events

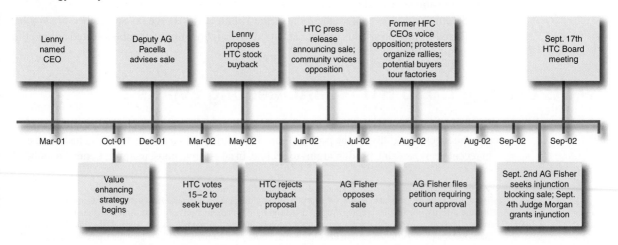

SOURCE: *Various articles quoted in case.*

which the HTC had oversight, calling for it to sell its Hershey Foods' shares in order to diversify and meet its future capital requirements. The local community of Hershey, PA—largely dependent on Hershey Foods for economic stability—was rife with sale rumors that summer.[9]

Hershey Foods Company and the Town of Hershey, PA

The Hershey Foods Company was founded in 1905 by Milton S. Hershey and went public in 1927. In 2001, its sales were $4.6 billion, which represented 43% of the domestic chocolate market. The company was headquartered in Hershey, Pennsylvania, an unincorporated village within the Derry Township, and employed some 6,200 of the township's 21,000 residents.[10]

Hershey Foods was divided into three product groups: the chocolate and confectionery group, restaurant operations, and the food products and services group. The most well-known group was the chocolate and confectionery group; it was responsible for producing such popular brands as Hershey's Kisses, Reese's Peanut Butter Cups, Twizzlers, Mounds, and Kit Kat.[11] Industry experts noted that the chocolate market was not growing. Some saw this as an explanation for the HTC's motivation to sell all of its shares.[12]

Although Hershey Foods controlled a large portion of the chocolate market, in 2002 it had increasing competition from Mars and Nestle and was determined to maintain its market share, having wrestled control from Mars in 1988.[13] Mars, a private company, held approximately 27% of the market, whereas Nestle, a public company, held 12%.[14] The more diversified companies of Mars and Nestle, both of whom sold cat and dog food products among other non-chocolate items, had sales of $64.3 billion and $16.2 billion in 2002, respectively.[15]

Exhibits 2 and 3 are the consolidated income statements and balance sheets of the Hershey Foods Corporation for 1999 through 2001.

EXHIBIT 2
Consolidated Statements of Income: Hershey Foods Company (Dollar amounts in millions)

Year Ending December 2001	2001	2000	1999
Net Sales	$4,557,241	$4,220,976	$3,970,924
Costs and Expenses:			
Cost of Sales	2,665,566	2,471,151	2,354,724
Selling, marketing, and administrative	1,269,964	1,127,175	1,057,840
Business realignment and asset impairments	228,314	—	—
Gain on the sale of business	(19,237)	—	(243,785)
Total costs and expenses	4,144,607	3,598,326	3,168,779
Income before Interest and Income Taxes	412,634	622,650	802,145
Interest expense, net	69,093	76,011	74,271
Income before Income Taxes	343,541	546,639	727,874
Provision for income taxes	136,385	212,096	267,564
Net Income	$207,156	$334,543	$460,310
Net Income Per Share—Basic	$1.52	$2.44	$3.29
Net Income Per Share—Diluted	$1.50	$2.42	$3.26
Cash Dividends Paid Per Share (in dollars):			
Common Stock	1.165	1.08	1.00
Class B Common Stock	1.05	0.975	0.905

Note: All notes were deleted.

SOURCE: *Hershey Foods Corporation, 2002 Annual Report, p. A-16.*

EXHIBIT 3
Consolidated
Balance Sheets
Hershey Foods
Company (Dollar
amounts in
thousands)

Year Ending December 31	2001	2000	1999
ASSETS			
Current Assets:			
Cash and cash equivalents	$134,147	$31,969	118,078
Accounts receivable—trade	361,726	379,680	352,750
Inventories	512,134	605,173	602,202
Deferred income taxes	96,939	76,136	80,303
Prepaid expenses and other	62,595	202,390	126,647
Total current assets	1,167,541	1,295,348	1,279,980
Property, Plant and Equipment, Net	1,534,901	1,585,388	1,510,460
Intangibles Resulting from Business Acquisitions, Net	429,128	474,448	450,165
Other Assets	115,860	92,580	106,047
Total Assets	**$3,247,430**	**$3,447,764**	**3,346,652**
LIABILITIES AND STOCKHOLDERS' EQUITY			
Current Liabilities:			
Accounts payable	$133,049	$149,232	136,567
Accrued liabilities	462,901	358,067	292,497
Accrued income taxes	2,568	1,479	72,159
Short-term debt	7,005	257,594	209,166
Current portion of long-term debt	921	529	2,440
Total current liabilities	606,444	766,901	712,829
Long-term Debt	876,972	877,654	878,213
Other Long-term Liabilities	361,041	327,674	330,938
Deferred Income Taxes	255,769	300,499	326,045
Total liabilities	2,100,226	2,272,728	2,248,025
Stockholders' Equity:			
Preferred Stock, shares issued: none in 2001 and 2000	—	—	—
Common Stock, shares issued: 149,517,064 in 2001 and 149,509,014 in 2000	149,516	149,508	149,507
Class B Common Stock, shares issued: 30,433,808 in 2001 and 30,441,858 in 2000	30,434	30,442	30,443
Additional paid-in capital	3,263	13,124	30,079
Unearned ESOP compensation	(15,967)	(19,161)	(22,354)
Retained earnings	2,755,333	2,702,927	2,513,275
Treasury—Common Stock shares, at cost: 44,311,870 in 2001 and 43,669,284 in 2000	(1,689,243)	(1,645,088)	(1,552,708)
Accumulated other comprehensive loss	(86,132)	(56,716)	(49,615)
Total stockholders' equity	1,147,204	1,175,036	1,098,627
Total Liabilities and Stockholders' Equity	**$3,247,430**	**$3,447,764**	**$3,346,652**

Note: All notes were deleted

SOURCE: *Hershey Foods Corporation, 2002 Annual Report, p. A-17, 1999 Annual Report, p A-12.*

The Sweetest Place on Earth

Milton S. Hershey had two goals when he created the Hershey Foods Company: to be a pioneer in the mass production of chocolate and to create a utopian community. His company not only was a producer of chocolate, but was the builder of houses and public buildings, manager of the town's transportation system and utilities, and creator of the town bank, the Hershey Trust Company. Milton Hershey's goal was to create the "sweetest place on earth," complete with Hershey Kiss–shaped street lights and streets named for cocoa bean producing locales such as Caracas and Java.[16] Hershey Foods is a focal point of the town with an amusement park called Hershey Park, Hotel Hershey, and the Hershey Theater, a 7,000-seat arena.[17] Tourists flocked to the town as did entertainers such as the World Wrestling Federation, Cher, and the Harlem Globetrotters. As one resident and long-time employee put it, "Hershey Foods is the life-blood of this town."[18]

Lenny's New Vision

Although the town of Hershey remained committed to the original Hershey Company's goals, as its new CEO, Lenny's primary focus had been the shareholder. Lenny was a former vice president of Kraft Foods, with oversight of its Nabisco Biscuit unit, and was the first outsider ever to head Hershey Foods. The chocolate maker had seen profits suffer in the past several years, but by 2002, Lenny had increased earnings by 10% in just three months. Part of this success was due to cost cutting from plant closures and cocoa production outsourcing, two main features of the value-enhancing strategy.

Lenny's vision for Hershey Foods Company was clearly different from that of Milton Hershey. The new CEO described his intentions by stating, "I'm here to do what the shareholders want me to do, which is increase shareholder value."[19]

Employees and community members had begun to openly express their concern with Lenny's strategy. According to Art Long, a union member at the Hershey plant for 24 years, "Lenny came here from Nabisco with an ax." Debbie Keyton, a local bar owner whose father worked at the plant, agreed: "People were angry because Hershey wasn't founded on greed."[20]

Hershey Foods' Board of Directors

As with any public company, Hershey Foods had in place a Board of Directors with overall company governance authority. In 2002 the Hershey Foods' Board of Directors consisted of nine members (see **Exhibit 4**). Each director's compensation was $55,000 annually plus $40,000 in restricted stock unit grants each year. On average the Board met six times a year with 97% of its members in attendance.[21]

Hershey Trust Company and the Milton Hershey School

In 2002, the Hershey Trust Company was headed by president and CEO, Robert Vowler, a native of Harrisburg. He and his wife Holly decided to settle there, seeing it as a good place to raise their family.[22] Vowler became an active member in the community by serving on the Harrisburg Regional Chamber of Commerce and the Susquehanna Alliance, an economic development group. He quickly rose through the ranks at various Hershey-related organizations as well. He was president of the Hershey Foundation and a member of its Board of Managers. Prior to being named CEO of the HTC, he had served as the Chief Financial Officer since

EXHIBIT 4
Board of Directors Hershey Foods Company

	Director Since	Audit	Compensation and Executive Organization Committee	Committee on Directors, Corporate Governance	Executive
Jon Boscia	2001	●			
Robert Campbell	1995	●		●	
Gary Coughlan	2001	●			
Bonnie Hill	1993	●	●		
J. Robert Hillier	2001			●	
John C. Jamison	1974	● (Chair)			●
Richard Lenny	2001			●	● (Chair)
Mackey McDonald	1996		● (Chair)		●
John M. Pietruski	1987		●	● (Chair)	●

Jon A. Boscia, age 49, Chairman and Chief Executive Officer of Lincoln Financial Group in Philadelphia, PA.

Robert H. Campbell, age 64, retired in 2000 as Chairman of the Board and CEO of Sunoco, Inc. in Philadelphia, PA.

Gary P. Coughlan, age 58, retired on March 31, 2002, as the Senior Vice President and CFO of Abbott Laboratories in Abbott Park, IL.

Bonnie G. Hill, age 60, President of B. Hill Enterprises in Los Angeles, CA.

J. Robert Hillier, age 64, Chairman of the Board and founder, The Hillier Group, Princeton, NJ. Served also on Hershey Trust Board.

John C. Jamison, age 67, Chairman of Mallardee Associates, Williamsburg, VA. Chair of Audit Committee.

Richard H. Lenny, age 50, Chairman of the Board, President and CEO of Hershey Foods Corporation, Hershey, PA. Chair of Executive Committee.

Mackey J. McDonald, age 55, Chairman, President and CEO of VF Corporation, Greensborough, NC. Chair of Compensation and Executive Organization Committee.

John M. Pietruski, age 69, Chairman of the Board of Texas Biotechnology Corporation, Houston, TX. Chair of Directors and Corporate Governance Committee.

SOURCE: *Hershey Food Corporation, SEC DEF-14A (March 15, 2002), pp. 3–5.*

1987. From 1980 to 1987 he held several financial management positions with Hershey Entertainment and Resorts, where he remained a member of the Board of Directors.[23]

The HTC not only was the community's first bank, but was trustee for the Milton Hershey School and the Hershey Foundation.[24] The HTC owned approximately 32% of Hershey Foods total equity but its class B shares, each carrying 10 votes, comprised 77% voting control as of December 31, 2002.[25] The HTC was responsible for the M.S. Hershey Foundation, the Milton S. Hershey School, and the Milton Hershey School Trust while also serving its own investment clients. The Hershey Foundation operated the Hershey Museum, Hershey Gardens, Hershey Theatre, and the Hershey Community Archives. See **Exhibit 5** for a description of the organizations owned by HTC.

The Hershey School's original purpose had been to train orphaned boys and had eventually included girls and minorities from underprivileged backgrounds in grades K–12. The school was headed by William L. Lepley, who was a voting member of the HTC and was its highest-paid member.[26]

EXHIBIT 5
Hershey Entities
Organizational
Chart, Hershey Trust
Company

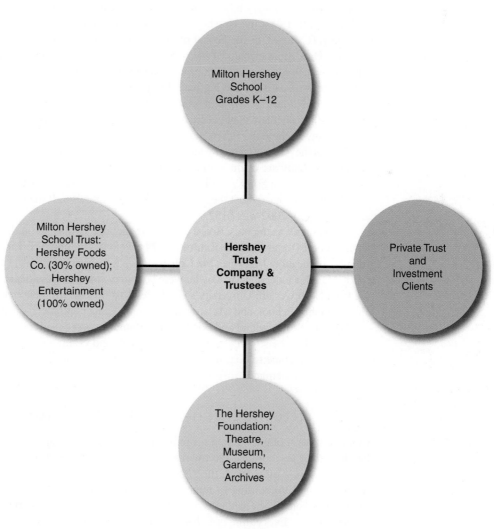

SOURCE: *Adapted from HTC organizational chart, http://www.hersheytrust.org.*

Student-related costs, including education, food, clothing, health services and housing, were $76.9 million, and in the 2000–2001 school year 1,152 students were enrolled.[27] Over 50% of the HTC's assets were common stock holdings of Hershey Foods, 27% were common stock of other companies, 12% were bond holdings, and the remainder was sprinkled among property, equipment, cash, and other investments. Stock in Hershey Foods was valued at $2.5 billion as of July 31, 2001, and unrealized gains were $770 million.[28]

The HTC Board

The Trust Board's relationship with the Hershey Foods Company Board had become more distant following Milton Hershey's death in 1945. Some described it as "frosty" at times.[29] Over the years the shared values of Hershey Trust and Hershey Foods began to appear more like conflicts of interest. Gone were the days when Milton Hershey served as the chairman of both boards. Likewise, the competitive climate began to require a sharper focus on strong numbers for shareholders. During his tenure as Hershey Foods CEO from 1994 to 2001, Ken Wolfe had laid off 400 employees to reduce fixed costs and refused to allow the school to advertise on Hershey candy bars, a long-standing goodwill gesture.

By the mid-1990s the Hershey Foods Board was mostly made up of independent directors. The HTC Board, at the behest of school president Lepley, voted on whether to remove Wolfe and Dick Zimmerman, Hershey Foods CEO from 1984 to 1993. The Trust voted against their removal, but the relationships became more fractured, with each executive stepping down from the Board on leaving his CEO post. Lepley reportedly resented the executives' higher status and lack of willingness to defer to the Trust.[30] In 2001, also to eliminate the apparent conflict of interest between running Hershey Foods and being a controlling shareholder, Lenny became the first CEO not to sit on HTC's Board, according to Vowler.[31]

The Hershey Trust Company had 17 Board members with equal voting rights in 2002 (see **Exhibit 6**).[32] Only six of these members lived in the central Pennsylvania area, and three of these members—Anthony J. Colistra, William H. Alexander, and Robert C. Vowler—were seen as likely to vote against the sale.[33] Average full-time Board member compensation at fiscal year end July 2002 was $152,950.[34]

Bob Hillier was the only Board member at the time to also sit on the board of directors at Hershey Foods (refer back to **Exhibit 4**). Ms. Pennington and Ms. Lipsitz had strong backgrounds in education. Likewise, Mr. Colistra was a former superintendent and an alumnus of the school. Mr. Alexander and Mr. Vowler were both investment professionals, and Vowler had a degree from Northwestern University's Graduate Trust School. Mr. Senser was an alumnus of the Milton Hershey School, and Ms. Rowland brought gender and racial diversity to the Board.

According to Rowland and Vowler, the community's opposition was not a factor in any of the Board's decisions.[35] Yet, with legal, political, and community pressure mounting, such pressure would come to bear on the decision-making abilities of any group facing accountability to external demands.

A Lack of Trust: The Attorney General's Investigation

Although it was not uncommon for public companies to be majority owned by a single large shareholder or to dominate the town's employee base,[36] the HTC's involvement added another challenging element to the situation: it was also a charitable trust for the Milton S. Hershey School. According to James Negley, manager of the Derry Township, "Everything here is incestuous, The Hershey Trust, Hershey Foods, Hershey Entertainment and the Milton Hershey School. Everything goes back to the school."[37] Even though selling all of its controlling shares at one time would fetch the best price and help HTC to diversify, some felt it was yet another sign of the growing separation of HTC and the township of Derry.

EXHIBIT 6
Hershey Trust Board Members in 2002

Name	Position	Comments
William H. Alexander	Managing Director, Snider Entrepreneurial Center, University of Pennsylvania	HSY (6,091 shares), PA
Robert F. Cavanaugh	Managing Director, DLJ Real Estate Partners, a Credit Suisse Company	Member, Investment Committee
Anthony J. Colistra	Superintendent, Cumberland Valley School District	PA
Don Cornwell	CEO, Granite Broadcasting, New York	Chairman, HTC Investment Committee
John Gabig, Esq.	Retired Partner, Miller Chevalier	HSY (100 shares), Chairman, HTC Board
Lucy D. Hackney	Former Senior Advisor for Child Care Policy, U.S. General Services Administration	PA
Bob Hillier	CEO, Hillier Group Architects	HSY (1,097 shares) Member, Investment Committee
Dr. William L. Lepley	President of Milton S. Hershey School	HSY (549 shares), PA
Dr. Joan S. Lipsitz	Independent consultant and author of two books on adolescence	
Dr. Michael W. Matier	Director, Institutional Research Planning, Cornell University	
Rev. John S. McDowell, Jr.	St. James the Less Episcopal Church	HSY (864 shares)
Hilary C. Pennington	Co-President, Jobs for the Future	
Wendy D. Puriefoy	President of Public Education Network	
Juliet C. Rowland	CEO, United Way of Ohio	
Joseph M. Senser	Restaurant owner in Minnesota	
Robert C. Vowler	CEO of HTC	PA, Member, Investment Committee
A. Morris Williams, Jr.	President, Williams & Company	PA

Key: PA, resident of Pennsylvania; HSY, holds stock in Hershey Foods Co.

Notes: McCollister Evarts, MD, of Hershey, PA, and Kenneth Wolfe, former CEO of Hershey Foods and resident of Hershey, PA, were board members until January 2002.

SOURCE: *Hershey School, Trust board members.* Harrisburg Patriot *(July 26, 2002), p. A15; Hershey School and School Trust IRS form 990; Marcy, B. Cutting the Ties That Bind: without Father, It's No Longer a Close-knit Hershey Family,* Sunday Patriot-News Harrisburg *(July 28, 2002), p. A1; Marcy, B., Hershey Trust Board Would See Little Profit from Sale,* Harrisburg Patriot *(August 16, 2002), p. A1.*

"It does make good business sense, but they don't have to cut the heart out of the town to do it. They're out for top dollar, and they're going to do it at the expense of the community," said Kathleen Lewis, president of the Derry Township Historical Society.[38] Bruce McKinney, a former HTC board director, said of these fissures, "I think the trust in the trust is gone."[39]

The breakdown in the relationship between the HTC and the community had begun in December 2001 with the presentation of the AG's findings. A year earlier, the Pennsylvania AG's office began receiving a number of complaints, mostly from alumni of the school, concerning Lepley, subpar education, and teacher misdeeds. In response, the office stepped in to investigate the allegations. The Public Protection Division of the AG's office oversaw all property in Pennsylvania committed to charitable purposes. The AG's jurisdiction included a mandate to ensure that the assets of the charity, in this case the Milton S. Hershey School, were being properly administered for the benefit of the public.

During the investigation, Deputy Attorney General Mark Pacella began meeting with the HTC. In these meetings he kept repeating that the Trust needed to make some changes.[40] In a meeting on December 4, 2001, he recommended that the trust diversify its holdings so that it might be better equipped to fulfill its financial obligations and manage the school's foundation. In this meeting, Pacella also proposed that the Trust explore the idea of divesting its Hershey Foods shares.[41] According to one report, Pacella implied that the trustees would be breaching their fiduciary responsibility to shareholders by passing up a financial windfall from the sale.[42] Because the HTC had controlling interest through the stock class structure, such a move would effectively force the sale of the company as a whole.

Several months later, at its quarterly meeting in March 2002, the HTC had voted 15–2 to diversify its portfolio by finding a buyer for the Hershey Foods Corporation. Juliet Rowland and Joseph Senser were the only two trustees who voted against exploring a potential sale.[43] In a statement, Mr. Vowler said, "The Trust has been extremely pleased with the Company's management. This is simply a matter of meeting our fiduciary responsibilities to diversify the assets of the Trust."[44]

Very few members of the HTC were willing to speak publicly following the investigation and had apparently made a pact against doing so, including Don Cornwell, the chair of the committee, and Bob Hillier, who also sat on the Hershey Foods Board.[45] Cornwell and Hillier were selected to meet with Richard Lenny and discuss their findings and recommendations. But as pressure on the board began to escalate in late summer, some board members decided to speak out. HTC Board Chairman John Gabig; Anthony Colistra, superintendent of Cumberland Valley School District; and Lucy Hackney, a child care policy advisor, all felt that the sale of Hershey Foods stock was a necessary, albeit painful, step. According to Gabig, "The community, in general, believes that this is their company. Well, it is a public company with shareholders, and everybody knows that a publicly held company has to be responsible to it shareholders."[46]

Public Disclosure: Company and Community Opposition

Because the buyback proposal had been rejected, Lenny preferred that the company remain under trust ownership—even though he stood to gain financially—because he relished the challenge of building the company's brands in partial fulfillment of his value-enhancing strategy.[47] Throughout the early part of the summer, the company and the Trust tried to keep the possible sale quiet as the investment bankers developed their short list.[48]

However, the HTC's intention to explore a sale was leaked to the *Wall Street Journal* on July 25, 2002.[49] Rick Kelly, a public relations specialist who had been hired by Vowler to handle the press, received a call from the newspaper telling him that it planned to run the story within hours.[50] Quickly, Kelly organized a news release to be sent from Hershey Foods. In the release issued later that morning, Lenny was quoted as follows:

> *Recognizing the School Trust's controlling position and its determination to explore a possible sale, the Hershey Foods Board of Directors has concluded that it is in the best interests of the Company and its stockholders for Hershey Foods and the School Trust to work together in a cooperative manner in this effort.[51]*

In a memo to Hershey employees, Lenny expressed his disappointment this way: "I came here to build our brands and build our people, not to manage a potential sale and subsequent integration process. Having been your CEO for only one year, I had hoped to work with you for a long time to come."[52]

The announcement caused Hershey Foods share price to soar to $80 per share—well above its 2002 trading range of $30–$40 (see **Exhibit 7**), but also caused a strong reaction from the community.[53] The week after the announcement, community leaders, school alumni, Hershey employees, and government officials mobilized. The decision to sell was seen as "a threat to an American icon and insult to Milton Hershey," according to the Derry Township paper, *Morning Call*.[54] Former trustee Bruce McKinney positioned himself as a leader in the

EXHIBIT 7
Stock Prices on
July 25, 2002 and
September 17, 2002:
Hershey Foods
Company

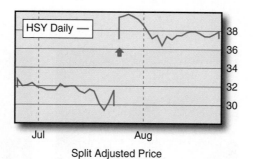

Split Adjusted Price

Hershey Foods Corporation
Wednesday, July 24, 2002

Closing Price: **62.50** Open: **60.08** High: **62.95** Low: **59.50** Volume: **965,700**

Thursday, July 25, 2002

Closing Price: **78.30** Open: **75.60** High: **78.80** Low: **74.25** Volume: **9,543,000**

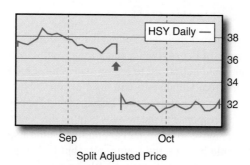

Split Adjusted Price

Hershey Foods Corporation
Monday, September 16, 2002

Closing Price: **74.81** Open: **73.67** High: **74.84** Low: **73.52** Volume: **695,600**

Tuesday, September 17, 2002

Closing Price: **73.81** Open: **74.81** High: **74.81** Low: **73.22** Volume: **1,047,600**

SOURCE: *http://www.bigcharts.com (October 2, 2005).*

opposition movement, along with two former Hershey Food's CEOs, Kenneth Wolfe and Richard Zimmerman, who claimed the sale would lead to major layoffs of local workers.[55] McKinney had particularly strong ties to the community and to the company itself. Not only had he been a student at the Milton Hershey School in the 1950s, but he had served as the Board chairman, CEO, and later a trustee of the Hershey Estates (named HERCO in 1976).[56]

On August 2, 2002, McKinney led a crowd of more than 500, including town citizens, alumni, employees and politicians, to Chocolatetown Square in the center of Hershey, PA.[57] An hour-long rally followed the march. The grassroots opposition grew to include an online petition to expel HTC board members, a "derail the sale" yard sign campaign, and union protests in the state capital of Harrisburg, about 20 miles from the town of Hershey[58] (see **Exhibit 8**).

The opposition also had tee-shirts made up with pictures of Milton Hershey and the slogan "Save the Dream" for the protesters to wear during the march. McKinney was quoted as saying, "Fortunately, the community came together in a firestorm of protest. The media across Pennsylvania, the country and even most of Western Europe was behind us."[59] A group called Friends of Hershey Foods was organized to oppose the sale and also held rallies at the middle school auditorium.

EXHIBIT 8
Signs of Opposition

  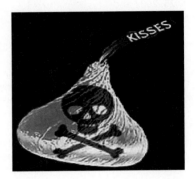

SOURCE: *The Friends of Hershey Foods.*

The Political and Legal Climate

Other voices of dissent included Pennsylvania Attorney General Mike Fisher, who was running for Governor of Pennsylvania and was currently behind in the polls. According to news articles, Fisher could not afford to let the state's most recognizable name be sold and needed mid-state voters from Hershey to win his election.[60] Members of the Trust Board, including Vowler, had previously believed that Fisher would support or ignore the sale.[61]

In reality, his response to the news was quite the contrary. Not only did Pennsylvania government officials move to enact legislation that would require companies to consider the impact the sale would have on the community, but Fisher announced his intent to legally block the company's sale and on August 12 filed a petition with Judge Morgan of the Dauphin County Orphan's Court asking that the sale be subject to its approval because of the court's jurisdiction over the HTC.

On September 3, 2002, the Dauphin County Court heard the attorney general's request for a temporary injunction to prevent the sale of Hershey Foods, which cited the potential and irreparable harm to the local community. Richard Zimmerman testified to try to stop the sale at the injunction hearing.[62] Judge Morgan granted the injunction on September 4 and stated, "The sale appears to be excessive and unnecessary."[63] The Trust then appealed the ruling by stating that the court had no jurisdiction as Hershey was incorporated in the state of Delaware.

The HTC Board Meeting

The HTC Board members met for close to 11 hours on September 17, 2002 (see **Exhibit 6**). The offer from Nestle and Cadbury-Schweppes would result in various Hershey brands being divided between the two companies. Hershey had long-standing licensing agreements with Cadbury, but reportedly shareholders from Nestle believed the $11 billion offer was too high.[64] The Wm. Wrigley Jr. Company offered a combination cash and stock bid of $12.5 billion to form a new company called Wrigley Hershey. After a series of negotiations, a deal was reached with Wrigley whereby it pledged to keep the Hershey factories intact and maintain the local workforce. The Wrigley bid reportedly represented a 42% premium over the pre-auction price of Hershey Foods stock.[65]

During the September 17 meeting, Bill Wrigley, Jr., the CEO of the Wrigley empire, spoke. The meeting began with the investment bankers from both Morgan Stanley and Credit Suisse walking the 17 Board members through each proposal. Nestle representatives were not present, but the appearance by Wrigley did not appear to persuade the HTC members.[66]

During lunch an investment banker from Morgan Stanley whispered to Vowler in the buffet line that the meeting didn't appear to be going well. Vowler mentioned again that he preferred an all-cash deal.

The meeting would last for approximately eight more hours. Sometime before 11 PM, Vowler moved to call for a vote. He began by asking each member to speak for 5 or 10 minutes to express their thoughts about the sale offers.[67] As Vowler listened to the board members' comments, he knew he'd have to address the board and present the final vote on the fate of Hershey Foods Company—his own.

NOTES

1. Class B shares typically carry more votes than common shares. In HTC's case, each class B share held 10 votes, whereas common shares held one vote. HTC held 99.6% of class B shares (see Hershey Food Corporation, "SEC DEF-14A," [March 15, 2002], pp. 9–10). Approximately 64% of the largest companies worldwide have controlling shareholders, and 30% of these are family owned (see R. La Porta, F. L. De Silanes, and A. Shleifer [1999]. "Corporate Ownership Around the World," *Journal of (Finance)*, 54:471–517).
2. Company news release, "Hershey Announces Value-Enhancing Strategy," http://www.hersheyfoods.com/news/release.asp? releaseID=219683 (May 7, 2006).
3. Ibid.
4. D. Shope, "Hershey Victory Bittersweet," *The Morning Call* (October 26, 2003), p. D1.
5. Associated Press, "Bitterness Coats Sweet Hershey," *Seattle Times* (May 30, 2002).
6. B. Marcy, "Hershey Trustees Were Blindsided, Besieged," *Knight Ridder Tribune Business News* (September 22, 2001), p. 1.
7. R. Frank and S., Ellison, "Meltdown in Chocolatetown—Controlling Trust at Hershey Bows to Opposition to Sale; Company Faces Future Alone," *Wall Street Journal* (September 19, 2002), p. B1.
8. The case author conducted an hour-long personal interview with Robert Vowler on June 3, 2005, in which he described the events leading up to the sale, the issues surrounding the sale, and the Trust's sale preferences. This interview was used throughout this case to inform or confirm the media accounts. See also D. Ackman, "Hershey Says No, Bankers Cry Foul," Forbes.com (September 18, 2002), http://www.forbes.com; R. Frank and S. Ellison, "Meltdown in Chocolatetown—Controlling Trust at Hershey" Bows to Opposition to Sale; Company Faces Future Alone, *Wall Street Journal* (September 19, 2002), p. B1.
9. Shope (2003).
10. W. Tanaka, "*Hershey Trust Again Defends Proposed Sale,*" *Philadelphia Inquirer* (August 17, 2002); Shope (2003).
11. http://www.thehersheycompany.com (May 13, 2005).
12. Tanaka (2002).
13. J. Helyar, "Sweet Surrender," *Fortune* (October 14, 2002), p. 224.
14. Deborah Ball, "Nestle Says a Takeover of Hershey Wouldn't Pass Antitrust Muster," *Wall Street Journal* (August 30, 2002), p. A1.
15. http://www.hoovers.com (April 24, 2006).
16. Shope (2003).
17. http://www.thehersheycompany.com (May 13, 2005).
18. Shope (2003).
19. Associated Press (2002).
20. Shope (2003).
21. Hershey Food Corporation, *SEC DEF-14A* (March 15, 2002), p. 7.
22. Tanaka (2002).
23. http://www.hersheytrust.org (May 26, 2005).
24. All recreation and tourism facilities in Hershey were owned by HERCO (Hershey Entertainment and Resort Company), a separate and distinct corporation wholly owned by the Milton Hershey School Trust. Hershey's Chocolate World, however, was owned by Hershey Foods Corporation. http://www.hersheyinvestorrelations.com/ireye/ir_site.zhtml?ticker5HSY&script51801.
25. HTC held 43,046,247 total shares (common and class B) in Hershey Foods Corporation as of March 1, 2002 (see Hershey Food Corporation, *SEC DEF-14A* [March 15, 2002], p. 10).
26. Helyar (2002).
27. *Milton Hershey School Annual Report, 2000–01.*
28. Ibid. and Hershey School and School Trust IRS form 990.
29. Ibid.; see also Frank and Ellison (2002).
30. Helyar (2002).
31. Marcy, B. "Cutting the Ties That Bind: Without Father, It's No Longer a Close-knit Hershey Family," *Patriot-News* (July 28, 2002), p. A1.
32. Ibid.
33. Ibid.
34. Hershey School and School Trust IRS Form 990.
35. Ibid.
36. "Passing On the Crown," *The Economist* (November 6, 2004), pp. 69–71.
37. Shope (2003).
38. Marcy (July 28, 2002).
39. B. Marcy, "Hershey Fate Rests with Out-of-Towners," *Patriot News* (September 16, 2002).
40. Frank and Ellison (2002).
41. B. Marcy, "Hershey Trustees Were Blindsided, Besieged," *Knight Ridder Tribune Business News* (September 22, 2002), p. 1.
42. Ibid.
43. B. Sulon, Harrisburg, PA—Area Trustees Prove Key in Hershey Decision. Knight Ridder Tribune Business News, (September 23, 2002), p. 1.
44. http://www.hersheytrust.org (May 13, 2005).
45. Tanaka (2002).
46. Marcy (September 22, 2002).
47. Sulon, B. "Hershey Foods Chief Spells Out Sale Discussion," *Patriot News* (July 31, 2002). See also B. March, "Hershey Trust Board Would See Little Profit," *Patriot-News* (August 16, 2002), p. A1. Lenny's change-of-control agreement entitled him to

three times his $750,000 salary if his employment was terminated because of an ownership change.

48. Marcy (September 22, 2002).

49. Ibid.

50. Ibid.

51. www.thehersheycompany.com/news/ (September 20, 2005).

52. Sulon (2002).

53. Historical financial data retrieved April 24, 2006, from www.hoovers.com. Authorized common shares as of December 31, 2002, were 450,000,000, authorized class B common shares were 75,000,000, and 132,220,137 were outstanding; see *Hershey Foods 2002 Annual Report*, p. 49.

54. Shope (2003).

55. Marcy (September 22, 2002).

56. Hershey Estates was part of the reorganization led by Milton S. Hershey during the Depression. It was charged with administering all the non-chocolate interests in the town; including the Hershey department store, the nursery and greenhouse, its water, electricity, laundry, hospital, sewer, and transit authorities, the Hershey Park, and all other public buildings. At the time of this reorganization, Hershey Estates and the Hershey Chocolate Company as well as its sugar company were held together by the Hershey Trust Company, which, as trustee for the School, owned and operated all three interests. In 1980, HERCO, Inc., became Hershey Entertainment and Resorts Company to better describe the change in focus over the years.

57. www.friendsofhershey.org (October 9, 2003).

58. Ibid.

59. Shope (2003).

60. Ibid.

61. Marcy (September 22, 2002).

62. Helyar (2002).

63. B. Marcy and P. Decoursey, "Hershey Sale Off," *Patriot-News* (September 18, 2002).

64. D. Ackman, "Hershey Says No; Bankers Cry Foul," *Forbes.com* (September 18, 2002).

65. Ibid.

66. Marcy (September 22, 2002).

67. The accounts of the board meeting were based on the June 3, 2005, interview with Robert Vowler. See also B. Marcy, "Hershey Trust's CEO Says Three Criteria, Not Protests, Drove Decision," *Knight Ridder Tribune Business News* (September 19, 2002).

CASE **4**

The Audit

Gamewell D. Gantt, George A. Johnson, and John A. Kilpatrick

SUE WAS PUZZLED AS TO WHAT COURSE OF ACTION TO TAKE. SHE HAD RECENTLY STARTED her job with a national CPA firm, and she was already confronted with a problem that could affect her future with the firm. On an audit, she encountered a client who had been treating payments to a large number, but by no means a majority, of its workers as payments to independent contractors. This practice saves the client the payroll taxes that would otherwise be due on the payments if the workers were classified as employees. In Sue's judgment this was improper as well as illegal and should have been noted in the audit. She raised the issue with John, the senior accountant to whom she reported. He thought it was a possible problem but did not seem willing to do anything about it. He encouraged her to talk to the partner in charge if she didn't feel satisfied.

She thought about the problem for a considerable time before approaching the partner in charge. The ongoing professional education classes she had received from her employer emphasized the ethical responsibilities that she had as a CPA and the fact that her firm endorsed adherence to high ethical standards. This finally swayed her to pursue the issue with the partner in charge of the audit. The visit was most unsatisfactory. Paul, the partner, virtually confirmed her initial reaction that the practice was wrong, but he said that many other companies in the industry follow such a practice. He went on to say that if an issue was made of it, Sue would lose the account, and he was not about to take such action. She came away from the meeting with the distinct feeling that had she chosen to pursue the issue, she would have created an enemy.

Sue still felt disturbed and decided to discuss the problem with some of her co-workers. She approached Bill and Mike, both of whom had been working for the firm for a couple of years. They were familiar with the problem because they had encountered the same issue when doing the audit the previous year. They expressed considerable concern that if she went over the head of the partner in charge of the audit, they could be in big trouble since they had failed to question the practice during the previous audit. They said that they realized it was probably wrong, but they went ahead because it had been ignored in previous years, and they knew their supervisor wanted them to ignore it again this year. They didn't want to cause problems. They encouraged Sue to be a "team player" and drop the issue.

This case was prepared by Professors John A. Kilpatrick, Gamewell D. Gantt, and George A. Johnson of the College of Business, Idaho State University. The names of the organization, individual, location, and/or financial information have been disguised to preserve the organization's desire for anonymity. This case was edited for *SMBP*-9th, 10th, 11th, and 12th Editions. Presented to and accepted by the refereed Society for Case Research. All rights reserved to the authors and the SCR. Copyright © 1995 by John A. Kilpatrick, Gamewell D. Gantt, and George A. Johnson. This case may not be reproduced without written permission of the copyright holders. Reprinted by permission.

CASE 5

Everyone Does It

Steven M. Cox and Shawana P. Johnson

JIM WILLIS WAS THE VICE PRESIDENT OF MARKETING AND SALES FOR INTERNATIONAL Satellite Images (ISI). ISI had been building a satellite to image the world at a resolution of one meter. At that resolution, a trained photo interpreter could identify virtually any military and civilian vehicle as well as numerous other military and non-military objects. The ISI team had been preparing a proposal for a Japanese government contractor. The contract called for a commitment of a minimum imagery purchase of $10 million per year for five years. In a recent executive staff meeting it became clear that the ISI satellite camera subcontractor was having trouble with the development of a thermal stabilizer for the instrument. It appeared that the development delay would be at least one year and possibly 18 months.

When Jim approached Fred Ballard, the President of ISI, for advice on what launch date to put into the proposal, Fred told Jim to use the published date because that was still the official launch date. When Jim protested that the use of an incorrect date was clearly unethical, Fred said, "Look Jim, no satellite has ever been launched on time. Everyone, including our competitors, publishes very aggressive launch dates. Customers understand the tentative nature of launch schedules. In fact, it is so common that customers factor into their plans the likelihood that spacecraft will not be launched on time. If we provided realistic dates, our launch dates would be so much later than those published by our competitors that we would never be able to sell any advanced contracts. So do not worry about it, just use the published date and we will revise it in a few months." Fred's words were not very comforting to Jim. It was true that satellite launch dates were seldom met, but putting a launch date into a proposal that ISI knew was no longer possible seemed underhanded. He wondered about the ethics of such a practice and the effect on his own reputation.

The Industry

Companies from four nations, the United States, France, Russia, and Israel, controlled the satellite imaging industry. The U.S. companies had a clear advantage in technology and imagery clarity. In the United States, three companies dominated: Lockart, Global Sciences, and ISI. Each of these companies had received a license from the U.S. government to build and launch a satellite able to identify objects as small as one square meter. However, none had yet been able to successfully launch a commercial satellite with such a fine resolution. Currently, all of the companies had announced a launch date within six months of the ISI published launch date. Further, each company had to revise its launch date at least once, and in the case of Global Sciences, twice. Each time a company had revised its launch date, ongoing international contract negotiations with that company had been either stalled or terminated.

Financing a Satellite Program

The construction and ongoing operations of each of the programs was financed by venture capitalists. The venture capitalists relied heavily on advance contract acquisition to ensure the success of their investment. As a result, if any company was unable to acquire sufficient advance contracts, or if one company appeared to be gaining a lead on the others, there was a real possibility that the financiers would pull the plug on the other projects and the losing companies would be forced to stop production and possibly declare bankruptcy. The typical advance contract target was 150% of the cost of building and launching a satellite. Since the cost to build and launch was $200 million, each company was striving to acquire $300 million in advance contracts.

Advance contracts were typically written like franchise licensing agreements. Each franchisee guaranteed to purchase a minimum amount of imagery per year for five years, the engineered life of the satellite. In addition, each franchisee agreed to acquire the capability to receive, process, and archive the images sent to them from the satellite. Typically, the hardware and software cost was between $10 million and $15 million per installation. Because the data from each satellite was different, much of the software could not be used for multiple programs. In exchange, the franchisee was granted an exclusive reception and selling territory. The amount of each contract was dependent on the anticipated size of the market, the number of possible competitors in the market, and the readiness of the local military and civilian agencies to use the imagery. Thus, a contract in Africa would sell for as little as $1 million per year, whereas in several European countries $5–$10 million was not unreasonable. The problem was complicated by the fact that in each market there were usually only one or two companies with the financial strength and market penetration to become a successful franchisee. Therefore, each of the U.S. companies had targeted these companies as their prime prospects.

The Current Problem

Japan was expected to be the third largest market for satellite imagery after the United States and Europe. Imagery sales in Japan were estimated to be from $20 million to $30 million per year. Although the principal user would be the Japanese government, for political reasons the government had made it clear that they would be purchasing data through a local Japanese company. One Japanese company, Higashi Trading Company (HTC), had provided most of the imagery for civilian and military use to the Japanese government.

ISI had been negotiating with HTC for the past six months. It was no secret that HTC had also been meeting with representatives from Lockart and Global Sciences. HTC had sent several engineers to ISI to evaluate the satellite and its construction progress. Jim Willis believed that ISI was currently the front-runner in the quest to sign HTC to a $10 million annual contract. Over five years, that one contract would represent one sixth of the contracts necessary to ensure sufficient venture capital to complete the satellite.

Jim was concerned that if a new launch date was announced, HTC would delay signing a contract. Jim was equally concerned that if HTC learned that Jim and his team knew of the camera design problems and knowingly withheld announcement of a new launch date until after completing negotiations, not only his personal reputation but that of ISI would be damaged. Furthermore, as with any franchise arrangement, mutual trust was critical to the success of each party. Jim was worried that even if only a 12-month delay in launch occurred, trust would be broken between ISI and the Japanese.

Jim's boss, Fred Ballard, had specifically told Jim that launch date information was company proprietary and that Jim was to use the existing published date when talking with clients. Fred feared that if HTC became aware of the delay, they would begin negotiating with one of ISI's competitors, who in Fred's opinion were not likely to meet their launch dates either. This change in negotiation focus by the Japanese would then have ramifications with the venture capitalists whom Fred had assured that a contract with the Japanese would soon be signed.

Jim knew that with the presentation date rapidly approaching, it was time to make a decision.

CASE **6**

Li & Fung—The Global Value Chain Configurator

Vivek Gupta and A. Neela Radhika

"In an age when the Internet is supposedly going to eliminate the middleman, here's a middleman, an old Asian trading company that has made itself indispensable."[1]

AN ARTICLE IN *FORBES*

"We deliver a new type of value added, truly global product that has never been seen before. We're pulling apart the value chain and optimising each step — and we're doing it globally."[2]

VICTOR FUNG, CHAIRMAN, LI & FUNG, IN JUNE 2000

Strengthening Its Fort

IN JANUARY 2004, LI & FUNG LIMITED (LI & FUNG), A HONG KONG based global consumer goods trading giant, announced that Li & Fung Trading (Shanghai), its wholly owned subsidiary, had been granted an export company license by the Ministry of Commerce of the People's Republic of China (China). After receiving the license, Li & Fung Trading (Shanghai) became the first wholly owned foreign trading company to be offered direct export rights in China. The company was authorized to export China-sourced goods directly to customers worldwide and import raw materials for manufacturing in China. Li & Fung was until then dependent on its Chinese partners for exporting from China.

According to William Fung (William), managing director, Li & Fung, the license freed the group companies (see **Exhibit 1** for Li & Fung's Major Subsidiaries & Associate Companies) from the many trading restrictions in China. It would enhance the company's competitiveness and increase its share in the global market. William said, "With the ability to directly

EXHIBIT 1
Li & Fung's Major Subsidiaries and Associated Companies

Held Directly	Place of Incorporation and Operation	Issued and Fully Paid Share Capital	Principal Activities
Li & Fung (B.V.I.) Limited	British Virgin Islands	US$400,010	Marketing services and investment holding
Basic & More Fashion Limited	Hong Kong	HK$1,000,000	Export trading
Black Cat Fireworks Limited	England	GBP£1,200,000	Wholesaling
Camberley Enterprises Limited	Hong Kong	HK$250,000	Apparel exporting
Civati Limited	Hong Kong	US$450,000	Export trading
Colby International Limited	Hong Kong	HK$1,500,000	Exporting of garments and sundry goods
Colby Tekstil ve Dis Ticaret Limited Sirketi	Turkey	TL50,000,000,000	Export trading
CS International Limited	Hong Kong	HK$1,000,000	Provision of export assistance service
Dodwell (Mauritius) Limited	Hong Kong	HK$500,000	Export trading
Golden Gate Fireworks Inc.	U.S.A.	US$600,000	Commission agent and investment holding
GSCM (HK) Limited	Hong Kong	HK$140,000	Export trading
Hillung Enterprises Limited	Hong Kong	HK$300,000	Export trading
International Sourcing Group, LLC	U.S.A.	US$300,000	Trading of apparel
Janco Overseas Limited	Hong Kong	HK$760,000	Buying agent
Kariya Industries Limited	Hong Kong	HK$1,000,000	Manufacturing and trading
LF Maclaine (Thailand) Limited	Thailand	Baht4,000,000	Export trading
Li & Fung Agencia De Compras em Portugal, Limitada	Portugal	PTE20,000,000	Export trading
Li & Fung (Exports) Limited	Hong Kong	HK$8,610,000	Export trading
Li & Fung (Fashion Accessories) Limited	Hong Kong	HK$600,000	Export trading
Li & Fung (India)	India	Rupees64,000,200	Export trading
Li & Fung (Italia) S.r.l.	Italy	Lire90,000,000	Export trading
Li & Fung (Korea) Limited	Korea	Won200,000,000	Export trading
Li & Fung (Korea) Limited	Mauritius	Rupees1,250,000	Export trading
Li & Fung Mumes sillik, Pazarlama Limited	Turkey	TL25,000,000,000	Export trading
Li & Fung (Phillippines) Inc.	The Philippines	Peso500,000	Export trading
Li & Fung (Properties) Limited	Hong Kong	HK$1,000,000	Property investment
Li & Fung Taiwan Holdings Limited	Taiwan	NT$287,996,000	Investment holding
Li & Fung Taiwan Investments Limited	British Virgin Islands	US$4,912,180	Investment holding
Li & Fung (Taiwan) Limited	Taiwan	NT$63,000,000	Export trading
Li & Fung (Thailand) Limited	Thailand	Baht6,000,000	Export trading
Li & Fung (Trading) Limited	Hong Kong	HK$10,000,200	Export trading and investment holding
Li & Fung Trading (Shanghai) Limited	The People's Republic of China	RMB50,000,000	Export trading
Li & Fung (Zhanjiang) Limited	The People's Republic of China	US$1,999,055	Packaging
Livring Limited	Mauritius	Rs250,000	Export trading

Held Directly	Place of Incorporation and Operation	Issued and Fully Paid Share Capital	Principal Activities
Lloyd Textile Trading Limited	Hong Kong	HK$1,000,000	Export trading
Maclaine Limited	Hong Kong	HK$5,570,150	Export trading
Perfect Trading Inc.	Egypt	LE2,480,000	Export trading
Shiu Fung Fireworks Company Limited	Hong Kong	HK$1,200,000	Export trading
The Millwork Trading Co., Ltd	U.S.A.	US$1,331,000	Distribution and wholesaling
Toy Island Manufacturing Company Limited	Hong Kong	HK$62,000,000	Design and marketing
Verity Enterprises Limited	Hong Kong	HK$2,000,000	Export trading
W S Trading Limited	Hong Kong	HK$1,000,000	Export trading

Notes:
1. Li & Fung (B.V.I.) Limited provides the subsidiaries with promotional and marketing services outside Hong Kong.
2. Subsidiaries not audited by PricewaterhouseCoopers, Hong Kong. The aggregate net assets of subsidiaries not audited by PricewaterhouseCoopers, Hong Kong amounted to approximately 5% of the Group's total net assets.

The above table lists out the principal subsidiaries of the Company as of 31 December 2003, which, in the opinion of the directors, principally affected the results for the year or form a substantial portion of the net assets of the Group. To give details of other subsidiaries would, in the opinion of the directors, result in particulars of excessive length.

SOURCE: *Li & Fung Annual Report, 2003.*

export products from China to our customers worldwide, Li & Fung is now able to offer an even more complete supply chain service."[3]

After China joined the World Trade Organization (WTO) in 2001, it emerged as the world's largest exporter of textiles and clothing. The country also consolidated its position as one of the world's largest and fastest growing manufacturing economies. According to the U.S. International Textiles Association, export of textiles and clothing from China to the United States doubled from US$6.5 billion in 2001 to US$11.6 billion in 2003. With export quotas among WTO members proposed to be eliminated in January 2005, China would be free of restrictions on quantity of exports to the United States, enabling further growth.

In this light, analysts felt Li & Fung stood to benefit significantly from its new license as it was one of the world's leading textile export traders, and the largest to the United States. The company was well-placed to leverage China's leadership position in textile manufacturing and exports, as that country was the company's largest manufacturing hub, from where it sourced over US$2 billion worth of products annually. Li & Fung had 16 offices in China, which it planned to take to 36 by 2007. The downside was that in early 2004, Li & Fung faced many challenges, such as a slowdown in its overall revenues and net profit growth, over dependence on the U.S. market, declining share of revenues from the European market, and negligible growth in revenues from the rapidly growing Asian markets.

Background Note

The history of Li & Fung goes back to the early 1900s, making it the oldest trading company in Hong Kong. The company was founded in 1906 by Fung Pak-Liu (Pak-Liu) and Li To-ming (To-ming) in Guangzhou (South China) and was one of the first Chinese-owned export companies.

Trade in China at that time was controlled by foreign commercial houses. Li & Fung began operations by exporting porcelain and silk, mainly to the United States. It later expanded its product portfolio to include bamboo, jade, ivory, rattan ware, fireworks, and handicrafts.

During the early 1900s, since U.S. buyers did not know Chinese, and Chinese sellers did not know English, traders who could speak both languages became essential mediators between buyers and sellers. Li & Fung, being one among this lot, prospered, earning commissions as high as 15% on each export deal. Li & Fung was formally established in Hong Kong as a limited company in 1937.

World War II disrupted trading in the early 1940s, forcing Li & Fung to cease trading for some years. In 1943, Pak-Liu passed away. Shortly after the end of the war, To-ming, who had been a silent partner, retired and sold his stake to Pak-Liu's family. With this, the Fung family became sole owners of Li & Fung.

In 1949, Pak-Liu's son, Fung Hon-chu (Hon-chu), restarted trading operations in Hong Kong, which had come under British control. Hon-chu was instrumental in leading Li & Fung into the new era. The trading business picked up momentum in Hong-Kong during the mid 1900s, driven by the influx of refugees, which transformed China into a manufacturing economy that exported labor-intensive consumer products. Li & Fung began exporting consumer products such as garments, electronics, plastic flowers and toys and was soon Hong Kong's biggest exporter.

By the early 1970s, the trading business in Hong Kong began to struggle owing to stiff competition from other manufacturing economies in Asia such as Taiwan and Singapore. Trading margins also went down significantly to 3%, as buyers and sellers became comfortable dealing directly with each other, doing away with intermediaries.

Under these circumstances, Hon-chu called his sons—William and Victor Fung (Victor)—back home from the United States. Victor was teaching at the Harvard Business School and William had just finished his MBA from the same business school. Despite their friends' warning that trading would die out in a decade, the two brothers returned to Hong Kong to join their family firm.

Victor and William worked hard to modernize and rebuild Li & Fung into a well-structured organization, professionally managed at all levels. In 1973, the company went public and was listed on the Hong Kong Stock Exchange. Li & Fung's initial public offering was oversubscribed 113 times—a record that stood for 14 years.

With the opening up of the Chinese economy in 1979, many manufacturers in Hong Kong relocated their factories to southern China, which was more cost effective thanks to low labor costs. The rapid industrialization of underdeveloped Asian countries widened the choice of supply sources. Li & Fung realized that there was a huge potential for the trading business. To benefit, the company established a regional network of sourcing offices in Asian countries such as Taiwan, Singapore, and Korea in the 1980s. It emerged as a major regional trading company in Asia.

In 1989, with trading margins decreasing further, Victor and William realized the need for drastic changes to safeguard the company's business. As a result, in that year, Li & Fung was again made a private company, in one of the first management buyouts in Hong Kong. The company was then restructured into a diversified group with export trading and retail as its core businesses. In 1992, the firm's export trading business, Li & Fung (Trading) Pvt. Limited., was re-listed on the Hong Kong Stock Exchange.

As Li & Fung expanded its business, it understood that sourcing could no longer be restricted to a few countries but required a vast network of sourcing offices to sustain the trading business. Thus, the company established sourcing offices across the world, mainly around its major markets, the United States, and Europe. Li & Fung also went in for acquisitions to strengthen its sourcing and distribution networks and expand its product lines and customer networks. It pursued an active information technology (IT) and Internet strategy to enhance the efficiency and effectiveness of its internal and external communications.

EXHIBIT 2
Revenues by
Geographic
Segments
(1999–2003)

Geographic Regions	1999	2000	2001	2002	2003
				(In percentage terms)	
North America	69%	70%	75%	76%	75%
Europe	27%	26%	21%	19%	19%
East Asia	1%	1%	1%	3%	3%
South Hemisphere	3%	3%	3%	2%	2%
Total (%)	100%	100%	100%	100%	100%
Total Revenues (in HK$ billion)	16.298	24.992	32.941	37.281	42.631

SOURCE: *Li & Fung Annual Report 2003.*

By the turn of the 20th century, Li & Fung was a premier global trading company, with more than 95% of its revenues coming from North America and Europe. East Asia and the South Hemisphere accounted for the rest. In the fiscal year 2002, North America and Europe accounted for 76% and 19% of the group's total revenues, while East Asia and the South Hemisphere were placed at 3% and 2% respectively (see **Exhibit 2** for Li & Fung's Revenues by Geographic Segments in percentage terms).

The group's major product segments were both soft and hard goods. While soft goods included garments, hard goods constituted product lines such as fashion accessories, footwear, gifts, and furnishings (see **Exhibit 3** for Li & Fung's Major Product Lines). Soft goods contributed to a majority of the group's revenues. In 2002, this segment accounted for 68% of Li & Fung's total revenues, while hard goods generated the remaining 32% (see **Exhibit 4** for Li & Fung's Revenues by Product Segments in percentage terms).

In 2002, export trading remained Li & Fung's major business, but it also actively operated in the retailing and distribution business through its privately held companies. The retailing business was confined to China and the Asian market, where it operated as a regional license holder for Toys "R" Us, the biggest United States toy products chain and was the franchisee for the Hong Kong–based Circle K convenience store chain. The distribution business too was confined to China and the Asian region. Li & Fung was also involved in other businesses such as venture capital, investment holding and property investment.

In the fiscal 2002, Li & Fung registered revenues of HK$37.3 billion, a 13% increase over HK$32.94 billion revenues in 2001. The company recorded a net profit of HK$1.08 billion in 2002, an increase of 38% over the figure of HK$782 million in 2001. The company's largest

EXHIBIT 3
Li & Fung's Major
Product Lines

Soft Goods	Hard Goods
Garments	Fashion Accessories
	Footwear
	Furnishing
	Gifts
	Handicrafts
	Home Products
	Promotional Merchandise
	Toys
	Stationery
	Sporting Goods
	Travel Goods

SOURCE: *www.lifung.com.*

EXHIBIT 4
Li & Fung's Revenues
by Product
Segments
(1999–2003)

Product Segments	1999	2000	2001	2002	2003
					(In percentage terms)
Soft Goods	75%	78%	72%	68%	67%
Hard Goods	25%	22%	28%	32%	33%
Total (%)	100%	100%	100%	100%	100%
Total Revenues (in HK$ billion)	16.298	24.992	32.941	37.281	42.631

SOURCE: *Li & Fung Annual Report 2003.*

customer in the United States was Kohl's department store chain, accounting for nearly 13% of Li & Fung's total revenues in 2002. Other major clients included Abercrombie & Fitch, Ann Taylor, Walt Disney, American Eagle Outfitters, Guess, Laura Ashley Jeans, Levi Strauss & Company (Levis), Reebok, The Limited Inc., and Warner Bros.

By this time, Li & Fung had successfully positioned itself as a cutting-edge sourcing company in the world, with a well-established sourcing network of 68 offices across 40 countries and over 4,500 employees. In 2002, Li & Fung was reportedly one of the best professionally run companies in Hong Kong. The company's commitment to excellence and high standards in corporate governance practices earned it many awards and recognitions. Li & Fung was named one of Hong Kong's best companies, by the *Euromoney* magazine, in the category "Asia's Best Company 2002." The same year, Li & Fung was named the "Best Managed Company 2002" and "Company most committed to Corporate Governance" by *Finance Asia* magazine (see **Exhibit 5** for the corporate governance structure of Li & Fung).

Analysts credited the growth and success of Li & Fung to the visionary leadership and managerial capabilities of Victor and William. Since the early 1970s, the duo had led Li & Fung through a series of transformations in line with changes in the external environment. The major factors that helped Li & Fung evolve into a major global export trading company were the focus on efficiently managing the supply chain of its clients, a unique customer-centric organizational structure, leveraging IT and the Internet, and global expansion strategies.

EXHIBIT 5
Li & Fung's
Corporate
Governance
Structure

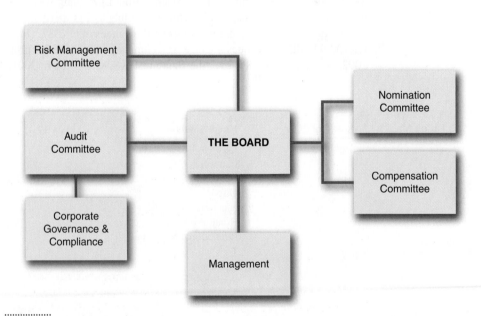

SOURCE: *Li & Fung Annual Report, 2003.*

Managing the Global Supply Chain

Li & Fung's evolution into a supply chain manager took place in three stages, driven by significant changes in the global retailing industry, customer and retailer preferences, and economic trends across Asia through the early 1970s.

In the first stage (during the 1970–78 period), Li & Fung acted as a regional sourcing agent. The company extended its geographic reach by establishing sourcing offices in Singapore, Korea, and Taiwan. Li & Fung's knowledge and reach in the Asian region held value for customers. This was because many big buyers could manage their own sourcing if they needed to deal only in Hong Kong. Dealing with the whole region was far more complex and buyers did not have the necessary resources. Commenting on the complexity of sourcing from the region, in an interview to *Harvard Business Review*, Victor said that as quotas governed world trade in the textiles industry, knowledge on which quotas had been used up in Hong Kong and which was the next best place to source textiles from, where quotas had not been exhausted, enabled Li & Fung to provide customers with a complete product package.

In the second stage (1979–82), Li & Fung evolved from a sourcing agent into a manager and deliverer of production programs. When a customer came up with an idea of a product and gave specifications such as look, color and quality, the company developed a detailed manufacturing program for that product. In other words, the firm created an entire manufacturing program for its customers for a particular fashion season. The program involved all tasks from specifying the product mix to scheduling the manufacturing process and delivery time. Li & Fung worked with factories to plan and monitor the manufacturing process, to ensure quality and on-time delivery.

This strategy worked well for Li & Fung. Yet, the 1980s brought a new challenge. This led to its third stage of evolution (1983 to the present period). Other countries in Asia such as Korea, Taiwan, and Thailand had by then emerged as labor-intensive manufacturing hubs, while Hong Kong had become an expensive and noncompetitive place to manufacture. The Chinese economy was being liberalized, and the company soon took the advantage by moving the labor-intensive portion of production to southern China.

Dispersed Manufacturing

Li & Fung broke the value chain into parts, which it called "dispersed manufacturing." Under this, the company performed all high-end value-added activities such as design and quality control in Hong Kong and outsourced low-end activities like manufacturing to the best possible locations across the world. For every order, the company aimed at customizing the supply chain to meet the client's specific requirements. For example, when Li & Fung got an order for transistor radios, it created little kits (plastic bags) filled with all the components necessary to build a radio and shipped the kits to China, where they were assembled. The assembled radios were then shipped back to Hong Kong, where they underwent final testing and inspection.

Similarly, to fulfil an order for baby dolls, Li & Fung designed them in Hong Kong, produced moulds for the dolls using sophisticated machinery, and then shipped the moulds to China; where plastic was injected into the moulds, the dolls were assembled, their fingers were painted, and their clothes were tailored. After the completion of such labor-intensive work in China, the dolls were shipped back to Hong Kong for final testing, inspection, packaging, transportation, and distribution. So, while the front and back ends of the value chain were taken care of in Hong Kong, the middle portion was performed in China.

Once Li & Fung understood the benefits of dispersed manufacturing and gained expertise in it, the company extended its network beyond southern China. It moved into the inner parts of China, where wages were even lower. Li & Fung also began searching for other labor-intensive

EXHIBIT 6
Exports and Imports of Services in Hong Kong (2000–02)

Major Service Group	Year	Exports of Services			Imports of Services			Net Exports of Services
		HK$ mn	Share (%)	Year-on-Year % Change	HK$ mn	Share (%)	Year-on-Year % Change	HK$ mn
Transportation	2000	99,513	33.0	11.5	48,628	25.4	23.9	50,885
	2001	93,675	30.4	–5.9	50,916	26.5	4.7	42,759
	2002	103,751	30.9	10.8	48,518	24.3	–4.7	55,233
Travel	2000	46,019	15.2	7.4	97,402	50.9	–4.4	–51,383
	2001	46,362	15.1	0.7	96,057	49.9	–1.4	–49,695
	2002	58,855	17.5	26.9	96,846	48.5	0.8	–37,991
Insurance services	2000	3,452	1.1	12.6	4,111	2.1	–17.4	–659
	2001	3,556	1.2	3.0	4,028	2.1	–2.0	–472
	2002	3,421	1.0	–3.8	4,618	2.3	14.6	–1,197
Financial services	2000	20,859	6.9	8.6	5,536	2.9	–3.4	15,323
	2001	21,823	7.1	4.6	5,242	2.7	–5.3	16,581
	2002	19,564	5.8	–10.4	4,876	2.4	–7.0	14,688
Merchanting and other trade-related services	2000	97,616	32.3	19.7	11,170	5.8	6.3	86,446
	2001	106,447	34.6	9.0	11,802	6.1	5.7	94,645
	2002	115,996	34.6	9.0	14,660	7.3	24.2	101,336
Other services	2000	34,355	11.4	15.8	24,695	12.9	13.7	9,660
	2001	35,794	11.6	4.2	24,408	12.7	–1.2	11,386
	2002	33,826	10.1	–5.5	30,158	15.1	23.6	101,336
All services	2000	301,813	100.0	13.7	191,543	100.0	4.1	110,270
	2001	307,657	100.0	1.9	192,453	100.0	0.5	115,204
	2002	335,412	100.0	9.0	199,676	100.0	3.8	135,736

Note:
1. Figures for exports of travel services have incorporated the new data released by the Hong Kong Tourism Board in November 2003 on destination consumption expenditure of incoming visitors and travellers. For details, please refer to the feature article "Statistics on Inbound Tourism" in the December 2003 issues of the *Hong Kong Monthly Digest of Statistics.*
2. The sum of individual items and the corresponding total shown in the table may not tally because of rounding.

SOURCE: *www.info.gov.hk.*

and potential sources of supply outside China and established a strong global network of suppliers by the late 1990s. Soon, the concept of "dispersed manufacturing" spread to other industries in Hong Kong, which led to the transformation of Hong Kong from a manufacturing economy into a service economy. By 1997, 84% of Hong Kong's gross domestic product[4] came from services (see **Exhibits 6 and 7** for Hong Kong's trade statistics).

Meanwhile, owing to maturing markets, intense competition, and changing consumer trends, many companies in the Western countries were compelled to outsource not only their

EXHIBIT 7
Hong Kong's
External Trade
Performance

	2003 (HK% Mn)	2004 Jan–May (HK$ Mn)	% Change	
			03/02	04/03 J—M
Overall				
- Domestic Exports	121,687	44,668	–7	1
- Re-exports	1,620,749	713,531	13	16
- Imports	1,805,770	816,918	12	19
- Total Trade	3,548,206	1,575,117	12	17
Balance	–63,334	–58,719	8	99
Total Exports–Major Markets				
All Markets	1,742,436	758,199	12	15
- China	742,544	334,450	21	18
- U.S.A.	324,215	122,950	–3	5
- E.U.	231,033	98,469	12	13
- Japan	94,003	41,241	12	13
- Singapore	35,704	16,866	13	27
- Taiwan	42,269	20,334	22	23
- Rep. of Korea	35,526	18,054	17	29
Total Exports–Major Products				
All Products	1,742,436	758,199	12	15
- Electronics [#]	732,653	332,023	20	23
- Clothing	180,357	65,408	3	5
- Electrical Products [#]	192,485	88,524	13	21
- Textile Yarn & Fabrics	101,923	45,067	5	9
- Toys & Games	75,008	22,538	1	–3
- Footwear	44,755	17,874	–1	–3
- Watches and Clocks	41,903	17,237	9	8
- Travel Goods & Handbags	32,070	14,333	*	12
- Plastic Articles	23,872	9,309	–8	–6
- Food	15,404	5,597	–8	–7
- Jewellery	22,231	9,794	17	21
Re-exports–with China				
Total Re-exports	1,620,749	713,531	13	16
- To China	705,787	321,126	23	19
- Of China Origin	967,104	418,816	12	16
Imports–End-use Categories				
Total Imports	1,805,770	816,918	12	19
- Foodstuffs	53,439	22,747	–3	8
- Consumer Goods	573,926	235,109	5	9
- Raw Materials	654,452	319,439	17	27
- Fuels	35,398	18,026	13	28
- Capital Goods	481,081	218,494	12	18

[#] Overlap with other products

* Insignificant

SOURCE: *http://stat.tdctrade.com*

manufacturing, but the entire supply chain management (SCM), to reap time and cost benefits. Li & Fung, with its extensive sourcing depth and network, grew from a deliverer of production programs into a potential manager of supply chains for companies looking for optimum SCM.

Li & Fung described SCM as "tackling the soft $3" in the structure—that is, if the price of a consumer product when it leaves a factory in China was $1, it would end up on retail shelves at $4. The company felt there was very little companies could do to further reduce production costs, as they had already exhausted all possible ways. It would be easier to cut on costs that were spread across distribution channels—that is, the $3 (difference between the product price on retail shelves and price when it left the factory).

Li & Fung took its dispersed manufacturing technique further, dissecting the entire value chain and optimizing every step of the chain, from product design and development, raw material sourcing, production planning, conducting quality assurance and factory inspections, managing production and logistics of exporting, timely delivery, and complying with import and export quota restrictions imposed by the buyer and seller countries, respectively. The company became a much broader intermediary by connecting and coordinating many links in the supply chain. It made its services more valuable by delivering a better product, which translated into better price and margins for customers (see **Exhibit 8** for Li & Fung's Supply Chain).

EXHIBIT 8
Li & Fung's
Supply Chain

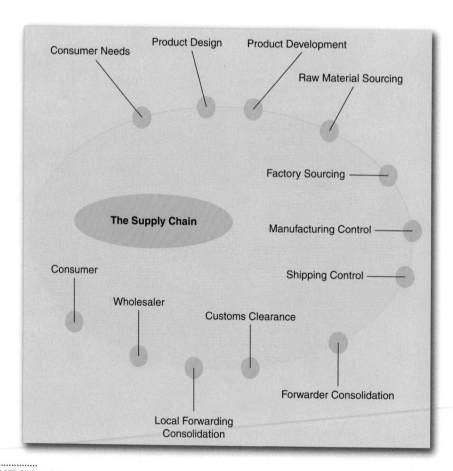

SOURCE: *Li & Fung Annual Report, 2003.*

Global Supplier Network

When Li & Fung got an order from a customer, it sifted through its global supplier network (see **Exhibit 9** for Li & Fung's Global Sourcing Network) to find the right manufacturer for the specific product and the most attractive combination of cost and quality. The company broke up its supply chain to disperse different production processes to manufacturers in various countries, based on factors such as labor costs, quality, trade barriers, transportation costs, and so on. The company coordinated all processes in the value chain, managing the logistics and arranging the shipment of the finished order to the client. Li & Fung also ensured that suppliers complied with rules and regulations pertaining to environmental standards, child labor, etc. in the importing countries (see **Exhibit 10** for Li & Fung's Code of Conduct for Suppliers).

For instance, when Li & Fung got an order from Levis, a leading retail clothes chain in the United States, with garment designs for the next fashion season, the company took the basic product concepts and researched the market to find the right kind of raw materials such as yarn, dye, and buttons. The company then assembled the raw materials to create a prototype, which was sent to Levis for inspection. Once the prototype was approved, Levis placed an order for the garments with Li & Fung, asking for delivery within six weeks.

Li & Fung immediately went to work—it distributed various tasks of the overall manufacturing process to different producers based on their capabilities and costs. It decided to purchase yarn from a Korean supplier but have it woven and dyed in Taiwan. The yarn was picked

EXHIBIT 9
Li & Fung's Global Sourcing Network

Europe & The Mediterranean	The Americas	North Asia
Amsterdam	Boston	Beijing
Bucharest	Guadalajara	Dalian
Cairo	Guatemala City	Dongguan
Denizli	Managua	Guangzhou
Florence	Mexico City	Hepu
Huddersfield	New York City	Hong Kong
Istanbul	San Francisco	Huizhu
Izmir	San Pedro Sula	Liuyang
London	Santo Domingo	Longhua
Oporto		Macau
Tunis	**Southeast Asia**	Nanjing
Turin	Bangkok	Ningbo
	Hanoi	Qingdao
South Asia	Ho Chi Minh City	Seoul
Amman	Jakarta	Shanghai
Bahrain	Makati	Shantou
Bangalore	Phnom Penh	Shenzhen
Chennai	Saipan	Taipei
Colombo	Shan Alam	Tokyo
Delhi	Singapore	Zhanjiang
Dhaka		Zhongshan
Karachi	**South Africa**	
Lahore	Durban	
Mumbai	Madagascar	
Sharjah	Mauritius	

SOURCE: *Li & Fung Annual Report, 2003.*

EXHIBIT 10

Li & Fung's Code
of Conduct
for Suppliers

Li & Fung (Trading) Limited Code of Conduct ("Code of Conduct") outlines the basic requirements on working conditions that must be satisfied by all vendors ("Vendors") to principals of Li & Fung (Trading) Limited ("Li & Fung"). Li & Fung and its principals can supplement these requirements at any time.

Child Labor: Vendors shall not use child labour. A "Child" is defined as a person who is not older than the local age for completing compulsory education, but in no event is less than 15 years old. Vendors must verify the age of their workers and maintain copies of proof of age. Vendors must follow all applicable laws and regulations regarding working hours and conditions for minors.

Involuntary Labor: Vendor shall not use involuntary labour. "Involuntary Labor" is defined as work or service extracted from any person under threat or penalty for its non-performance, and for which the worker does not offer himself or herself voluntarily. It includes prison, bonded, indentured and forced labor.

Disciplinary Practices: Vendors shall not use corporal punishment, any form of physical or psychological coercion or intimidation against workers.

Non-discrimination: Vendors shall employ workers solely on the basis of their ability to do the job. They shall not discriminate on the basis of age, gender, racial characteristics, maternity or marital status, nationality or cultural, religious or personal beliefs in relation to hiring, wages, benefits, termination or retirement.

Health and Safety: Vendors shall maintain a clean, safe and healthy workplace in compliance with applicable laws and regulations. They shall ensure that workers have access to clean drinking water, sanitary washing facilities and adequate number of toilets, fire-extinguishers and fire exits. Workplaces should provide adequate lighting and ventilation. Vendors shall ensure that these standards are also met in any canteen and/or dormitory provided for workers.

Environmental Protection: Vendors shall comply with all applicable laws and regulations to protect the environment and maintain procedures for notifying the local authorities in the event of an environmental accident resulting from the vendors' operations.

Wages and Benefits: Vendors shall provide wages and benefits that comply with all applicable laws and regulations or match prevailing local manufacturing or industry rates, whichever is higher. Overtime pay shall be calculated at the legally required rate, regardless of whether workers are compensated hourly or by piece rate.

Working Hours: Vendors shall not require workers to work, including overtime, more than 60 hours per week or more than the maximum number of hours per week set by applicable laws and regulations, whichever is less. Vendors shall guarantee that workers receive at least one day off during each seven-day period.

Freedom of Association: Vendors shall respect the right of workers to associate, organize and bargain collectively in a legal and peaceful manner.

Familiarization and Display of this Code of Conduct: Vendors shall familiarize workers with this Code of Conduct and display it, translated in the local language, at each of their facilities in a place readily visible and accessible to workers.

Legal Requirements: Vendors shall comply with all legal requirements applicable to the conduct of their businesses, including those set out above.

Contractors and Suppliers: Vendors shall ensure that their contractors and suppliers adhere to this Code of Conduct.

Monitoring of Compliance: Vendors authorize Li & Fung and its principals to conduct scheduled and unscheduled inspections of vendors' facilities for ensuring compliance with the Code of Conduct. During these inspections, Li & Fung and its principals have the right to review all employee-related books and records maintained by vendors and to interview workers.

Corrective Action: When violations are found, Li & Fung and the vendor concerned will agree on a corrective action plan that eliminates the problem in a timely manner. If it is determined that a vendor is knowingly and/or repeatedly in violation of this Code of Conduct, Li & Fung and its principals shall take appropriate corrective action. This may include cancellation of orders and/or termination of business with that vendor.

SOURCE: *www.lifung.com.*

up from Korea and shipped to Taiwan. As the Japanese offered the best quality zippers and buttons, which they were manufactured in China, Li & Fung approached the leading zipper manufacturer in Japan to order the right zippers from Chinese factories. Li & Fung decided to manufacture the final garments in Thailand, based on factors like quota availability and favorable labor conditions. It moved all the materials to Thailand. Since the order had to be fulfilled within six weeks, the order was divided across five factories in Thailand. Li & Fung ensured that within the scheduled date of delivery, the finished products, all looking as if they came from one factory, arrived at Levis retail stores.

Efficient SCM also addressed the problem of obsolete inventory, a major area of concern for fast-moving consumer goods (FMCG) companies, which were consumer-driven. FMCG companies preferred buying closer to the market as it shortened the buying cycle and gave them more time to get a better sense of the changing needs and preferences of consumers. Such quick changes led to shorter product cycles, and the problem of obsolete inventories went up significantly. This was where Li & Fung's global SCM expertise was useful, as it aimed at buying the right things at the right place, at the right cost and quality.

The SCM Strategy

To ensure shorter product delivery cycles, Li & Fung managed the whole supply chain of its customers. To shrink the delivery cycle, the company reached upstream to organize production and ensured small production runs, which resulted in improved response time for retailers, enabling them to alter production in tandem with market trends. For instance, Li & Fung got to know that Levis would order 1 million pieces of garments, but did not have specific details of style or colors. This would be disclosed only four weeks before delivery was due. Under these circumstances, Li & Fung, based on trust and its strong relationship with suppliers, reserved undyed yarn and locked up capacity at mills for weaving and dying. It told suppliers that they would receive an order for a specific size and colors, six days before delivery. Then the company intimated to factory owners that it did not know product specifications yet, but it had organized the colors, fabric and trim for them and they should deliver the order on a specific date, say two weeks from the raw materials arriving at their factories.

Having a vast network of suppliers enabled Li & Fung to configure activities as if they were modules in a process. For instance, a South Korean yarn provider might be appropriate for a product line, but an Indonesian supplier who used different raw materials and production technology might be a better choice for the needs and preferences of a specific customer. Li & Fung assembled the right modules for each job, customizing value chain solutions for its clients. Such flexible modules also meant that the company could quickly change its plans if there were unforeseen problems at the manufacturing site. The company could tap its worldwide network and send the order to another company to avoid delays in order fulfillment. For example, Li & Fung quickly shifted production from high-risk countries to lower-risk countries following the September 11, 2001, terrorist attacks in the United States.

A major supplier management strategy of Li & Fung was to utilize anywhere from 30% to 70% of factory capacity of suppliers, ensuring that at such a capacity, the company would be one of their important customers. Most times, Li & Fung would be their largest customer. Li & Fung also ensured that it did not use up the entire capacity of any manufacturer, to give itself flexibility. It did not want manufacturers to be completely dependent on the company. This strategy also enabled the company to gain exposure to new suppliers.

To improve suppliers' performance, Li & Fung managers, based on their interactions with them, provided a detailed performance feedback to each supplier, mentioning strengths and weaknesses. Faltering suppliers were dropped from a project or from the company's network if they failed to improve. According to analysts, as Li & Fung offered many economic incentives to suppliers, they willingly customized their own operations to fit Li & Fung's supply chain strategy. The major benefits to suppliers were substantial and steady business from Li & Fung and the opportunity to improve their performance, as the company set detailed benchmarks across its entire process network and gave all partners valuable insights into their specific strengths and weaknesses. It also helped them address performance gaps.

To further strengthen its supplier network, Li & Fung constantly looked out for new suppliers. The company evaluated the experience and skills of each prospect to determine whether its operational standards could be met. By the early 2000s, Li & Fung had an extensive network of over 7,500 regular suppliers, each on average having about 200 employees. Li & Fung described itself as a smokeless factory. Though it did not own any manufacturing concern, it was involved in various functions that qualified it as a manufacturer.

Customer-Centric Organizational Structure

Li & Fung had an organizational structure that masked its size. In line with the transformation of the company's business strategy during the 1980s, Li & Fung revamped its organizational structure to manage its global sourcing network better and meet customer needs. The company discarded its traditional structure of geographic division as it found inefficiencies in this. During this period, all large trading companies in the world with vast supplier networks were organized geographically with country units as profit centers. Such a structure made it tough for the companies to optimize the value chains for their customers, as the country units competed against each other for business. The lack of cooperation and coordination among country units also resulted in loss of customers, affecting a company's business.

To eliminate this, Li & Fung adopted a new customer-centric structure, where it organized itself into various small customer-centric divisions.[5] Under the new structure, an entire division focused on serving a big customer such as The Limited, Levis, Kohl's, and Abercrombie & Fitch. A single division aimed at fulfilling the needs of a group of smaller customers, with similar needs. For example, the company's theme-store division served a group of customers like Warner Bros. stores chain and Rainforest Café. According to company sources, this new model assisted them in creating a customized value chain for each customer order.

As part of its customer-centric strategy, Li & Fung created small divisions dedicated to serving one customer, and a person managing the unit as if it were his/her own company. Li & Fung hired people who were entrepreneurial in nature and whose ultimate aim was to run their own business. Thus, each division was run by a lead entrepreneur, designated as division manager, who was responsible for understanding customers' needs and fulfilling them by mobilizing resources from the group's sourcing and process network. For instance, the Gymboree division, which served Gymboree, a leading U.S.-based clothing store, was headquartered in a separate office within the Li & Fung building in Hong Kong. It had 40-plus employees focused on meeting Gymboree's needs. The division was further broken up into specialized teams in areas such as technical support, raw material purchase, quality assurance, merchandising, and shipping. Apart from the employees at its head office, the division also had dedicated sourcing teams across the branch offices of Li & Fung in China, Indonesia, and Philippines, the countries from where the division purchased in high volumes.

These divisions also promoted knowledge sharing during their interactions with customers, which benefited customers. Commenting on this, Frank Leong (Leong), CFO and head of the Operation Support Group (OSG), Li & Fung, said, "Our people sit down to share with them the latest information from the production side—what sort of material is hot, what new colors are available, where a product can be produced."[6] Such discussions not only expanded the fashion retailers' knowledge, but also gave them scope for more creativity and financial liberty in designing garments for a season. If required, the divisions also offered trade financing services to customers, through Letters of Credit (L/C).[7]

To preserve the entrepreneurial spirit, Li & Fung kept each division relatively small, with average revenues ranging between HK$30 million and HK$50 million. The company allowed each division to act as an independent unit with its own customers and profit and loss accounts. Li & Fung gave considerable freedom to division managers to run their divisions, as it believed that autonomy would encourage a free spirit. To further ensure the commitment of division managers, Li & Fung tied their compensation to their division's bottom line. To motivate them to achieve their division's targets, the company gave out substantial financial incentives. Reportedly, Li & Fung did not fix any ceilings on bonuses. The company followed the same policy of performance-based compensation and incentives for other employees too.

Li & Fung provided the divisions with all necessary financial resources and administrative support, mainly through the OSG, which provided back-end support to the entire group operations. The OSG supplied all divisions with personal computers and network connections, at a charge per PC, which covered the entire network, including order processing, production tracking, and e-mail communication. These charges were paid from the division's revenues.

The OSG also acted as an in-house HR provider, as it supplied recruitment services by internally matching staff from across various divisions, to meet some specific requirements of clients, and training them. It also acted as the divisions' chief banker as all divisional revenues finally went to the OSG. According to company sources, the divisions could take loans from the OSG at an interest rate cheaper than the market rate.

The OSG's performance was measured against its profit-and-loss account as was the case of any other division in the group. According to Leong, such a performance measurement strategy ensured that the OSG provided advanced high-quality services to its customers (other divisions) and at the same time optimized its costs.

The logic behind such an organizational structure was to allow each division to function as an independent company without worrying about back-end needs. Such a model provided the group with the flexibility of a small company, while having the strengths of a large, global company. As Leong said, "We're marrying the strength of being small and big together. Big companies tend to get bureaucratic, while small companies can do specialized products. Our small business units act extremely fast, but at the back-end, they get the level of service of a huge company."[8]

However, while Li & Fung believed in flexibility in some things, the company was highly conservative when it came to financial control and operating procedures. These were centralized and tightly managed. Li & Fung also maintained tight control over its working capital. All cash flows were centrally managed through headquarters in Hong Kong. For instance, L/Cs from all divisions came to headquarters for approval and were then reissued. The company also had a standardized and fully computerized order executing and tracking system used by all divisions.

Leveraging IT and the Internet

To leverage the potential of IT, Li & Fung took many initiatives through the mid 1990s. It tied up its global network of offices with an intranet[9] since 1995, to enable free information flow. In 1998, the company began creating dedicated extranet[10] sites for major customers. These sites enabled the company to interact with customers, track their orders, help in product development, and perform many other tasks in a cost-efficient manner. The extranet also enabled customers to track their orders and gain access to related information through Li & Fung's Electronic Trading System, known as XTS, which was linked to Li & Fung's global network of offices.

The major benefits of a dedicated extranet site can be understood from the following example. In the late 1990s, Coca-Cola, the leading soft-drink company, and many of its independent bottlers worldwide largely relied on merchandise tied to sporting events to promote the company's core brand, Coca-Cola. As Coca-Cola was mainly a beverage company, with no exposure to manufacturing, the company found managing the manufacturing activity (for its merchandise) expensive and outside its area of core expertise. The company also feared that its manufacturing process might be too slow to respond to sporting and entertainment events. As a result, in March 2001, the company turned to Li & Fung for managing its manufacturing activities. Li & Fung designed and built an extranet site, called Kodimsum.com ("KO" for Coke's stock symbol, and dimsum for a Hong Kong food delicacy), enabling Coca-Cola's executives and bottlers to place online orders. The extranet also allowed bottlers to check orders placed by other bottlers of the company, enabling them to place a similar order if they found that the product would be useful in their own markets.

With the emergence of the Internet as a major communication medium, industry observers felt it would make trading companies like Li & Fung redundant. Li & Fung opposed this view, stating that the key to its business was not hardware but information and its application to the management of client supply chains. The company believed that instead of being a threat, the Internet and e-commerce would offer more opportunities by helping it drive supply chain costs down and integrating management of supply chain via IT. Analysts too felt that this was true. They said that the real value of Li & Fung's business model lay not just in its ability to link suppliers and buyers, but in its power to influence suppliers and manufacturers, with whom the company had a strong relationship of trust.

Thus, Li & Fung used the Internet as a tool to make supply chains more transparent. When Li & Fung received an order from a customer, it used extranet sites and the Internet to fine-tune specifications. It then took instructions from customers and fed the information on to its intranet to find the right raw material suppliers and right factory or factories to assemble the product. The Web also aided customers in quickly assessing shifting consumer demands. Thus, as an order moved through different phases of production, customers could make last-minute changes through Li and Fung's Web site, which hosted real-time information on the entire production process.

This real-time tracking by customers was not possible until the mid-1990s, when Li & Fung began using phone and fax. For instance, when a customer ordered 50,000 khaki cargo pants, the company delivered the pants five months later, leaving the customer with little chance of altering their orders in line with changing market trends. By the early 2000s, once the Web-based communication system was established, customers could cancel their order until the time the material was woven, change the color until the fabric was dyed, and alter the design or size until the fabric was cut.

In March 2000, Li & Fung announced its Internet strategy to enter the e-commerce market, through its Business-to-Business (B2B) initiatives. Li & Fung aimed at creating economies of scale and scope for small- and medium-sized enterprises by bundling its orders for the same products and then customizing the mass-produced product to meet the requirements of each customer.

Commenting on this, William said, "Li & Fung has done private-label manufacturing for a long time. We can only do this if the customers are very large and they have the scale, since you need intensive interaction when you do private-label work. To capture economies of scale, we need large customers, not small ones. . . . What the Internet does is allow us to reach the small and midsize guys we could never reach before. What do they want? What the big guys have—a private label, their own differentiated line, and at the same price as the big guys. . . . The Internet allows us to reach those people—without intensive interaction—and to aggregate their orders. We can allow you different style, limited customisation using American yarn, knitted in China, assembled in Bangladesh. And we can allow you to put in your own label, embroidery, colours, packages, boxes. We can reap the economics of mass production, but with enough customisation."[11]

As part of Li & Fung's Internet strategy, StudioDirect Inc. was formed in April 2000, as an e-commerce subsidiary of the company (57% controlling stake) with an investment of US$19 million. StudioDirect's Web site, www.studiodirect.com, launched in March 2001, allowed placement of highly individualized orders from small- and medium-sized retailers, enabling them to choose from a wide variety of fabrics, colors and accessories such as cuffs, pockets, buttons, and embroidery. According to Li & Fung sources, StudioDirect had customisation options that could satisfy 90% of the smaller retailers.

StudioDirect aggregated all orders placed on its Web site and put them on to Li & Fung's manufacturers, resulting in a series of private-label lines ready for delivery. To handle the logistics needed to deliver finished goods to retailers across the world, StudioDirect tied up with Danzas AEI Intercontinental, a business division of the Danzas Group, which specialized in logistics services and had already worked with Li & Fung.

Reportedly, StudioDirect was capable of beginning production within six hours of receiving an order from a client over the Internet. For marketing its B2B initiative, the company chose the strategy of direct mailing. Through this, the company aimed at reaching about 1,000 small- and medium-sized retailers in the first year and expected to do business of $2 million with each of them, in the next five years. The initiative was launched in the United States in early 2001.

Analysts felt that Li & Fung, with its sound global sourcing network and strong financials (US$270 million in cash reserves) was poised to establish itself as a strong player in the B2B marketplace. Commenting on what Li & Fung could provide small- and medium-sized customers, with Barnett a Goldman Sachs' analyst, said, "A large company that uses Li & Fung typically pays 4% to 12% of the value of the order [because of economies of scale]. It's about 30% for a small company. Those costs come down to 4% to 12% if clients use the studiodirect.com Internet site."[12]

In the early 2000s, Li & Fung maintained Internet-based communication with all its major customers worldwide. About 75% of them were large retailers in the United States, who reaped significant benefits from the transparent SCM attained due to the use of IT and the Internet.[13] Laurence H. Alberts, managing partner, Mercer Management Consulting (Asia), said, "They [Li & Fung] are the leaders in Asia in providing this full solution of sourcing and supply-chain management. They've built up a very considerable barrier to anyone else trying to replicate it."[14]

Global Expansion

During the late 1990s, with the growing popularity of private-label brands, shortening product life cycles, and acute competition in the retailing industry, companies had to focus on their supply chain processes. As many companies did not have expertise in SCM and outsourcing was a cost-efficient alternative, the demand for companies that offered SCM services increased. Li & Fung, which already had an impressive sourcing network and SCM expertise, increased efforts to position itself as a global consumer goods trading company. The company devised an acquisition strategy to strengthen its position in the global trading market. The strategy aimed at expanding the sourcing network, product lines, and customer base.

In 1995, Li & Fung acquired Inchcape Buying Services (also known as Dodwell) from Inchcape Pacific, a leading British trading conglomerate. That company had an established network of offices in South Asia, and the Mediterranean and Caribbean regions, where Li & Fung had little or no presence. The acquisition nearly doubled the size and geographic reach of Li & Fung and brought with it a vast European customer base that complemented Li & Fung's strength in North America. The acquisition also contributed significantly to the company's success in achieving its three-year plan (1995–98) target of doubling its profits from HK$225 million in 1995 to HK$455 million in 1998.

As a part of its proximity strategy, which aimed at producing products closer to the customer market (North America and Europe), Li & Fung began establishing and expanding its sourcing networks in regions such as the Mediterranean, Eastern Europe, North Africa, South Africa, and Central America in the late 1990s.

In December 1999, Li & Fung acquired Swire & Maclaine and Camberley Enterprises, the trading businesses of the Hong Kong–based group, Swire Pacific, for HK$450 million. While Swire & Maclaine was a major provider of product sourcing and quality assurance services in Hong Kong, Camberley Enterprises made high-quality ladies sportswear, ready-to-wear garments, and home accessories. These acquisitions offered Li & Fung design process expertise and helped it further strengthen its customer base in the United States and Europe, by adding some major customers like Laura Ashley and Ann Taylor. As Swire & Maclaine had been a major competitor of Li & Fung in Hong Kong, its acquisition helped Li & Fung further consolidate its business in Hong Kong and strengthened its position as one of the world's leading sourcing and supply chain management companies.

In November 2000, Li & Fung announced the acquisition of Colby Group Holdings Limited, a Hong Kong–based leading consumer goods trading company, for HK$2.2 billion to consolidate its global competitive position further and helped it emerge as the largest consumer goods export trading group in Hong Kong. Commenting on the rationale behind the acquisition, William Fung said, "Colby has strong brand recognition, especially among U.S. department stores. Its seasoned staff and diversified sourcing capabilities will complement our existing business. With this acquisition, we will be able to expand our customer base and further penetrate what is an important new market segment."[15] Even after the acquisition, Colby continued to operate under its own company name, as a subsidiary of Li & Fung.

In the early 2000s, Li & Fung focused its acquisition strategy on hard goods companies. In mid 2002, Li & Fung acquired Janco Overseas, a Hong Kong–based buying agent, specializing in hard goods, for HK$249.6 million. According to company sources, the acquisition was expected to increase Li & Fung's turnover by HK$1.4 billion. Reportedly, Janco's strengths in the hard goods segment and focus on large food retailers, who were rapidly expanding their non-food offerings, was expected to strengthen Li & Fung's position in the hard goods segment. It was also expected to open up new customer segments and opportunities on account of expansion in its hard goods product portfolio.

In the fiscal year 2002, the hard goods segment accounted for 32% of Li & Fung's revenues compared to 28% in 2001. The segment registered a 29% increase in revenues and 70% in operating profits over 2001. Li & Fung sources said the acquisition of Janco was a major factor that contributed to such a significant growth in its hard goods business.

In August 2003, Li & Fung announced plans to purchase the remaining one-third stake in the group's New York–based garment importer unit, International Sourcing Group (ISG), for US$5.22 million, from ISG's chief executive, Alan Chartash, who owned that stake. The acquisition was expected to increase Li & Fung's profitability. Victor said, "By further leveraging the group's financial resources, management strength and entrepreneurial corporate culture, it is envisaged that a more comprehensive service will be provided to ISG's customers."[16]

During the early 2000s, Li & Fung focused on expanding its customer base in non-U.S. markets to balance the group's overall revenue portfolio, which was highly skewed toward the United States. It concentrated on the fast developing economies in Asia and the Southern Hemisphere, where more and more companies were outsourcing manufacturing and SCM on account of increasing globalization and resulting competitive pressures that were forcing companies to optimize resources.

Li & Fung identified Japan as a potential market, where the fashion retailing business was booming. In October 2003, Li & Fung entered into an alliance with Nichimen Corporation (Nichimen), a leading general trading firm in Japan, to offer higher value for Japanese retailers. This was possible due to the integration of Li & Fung's global sourcing network with Nichimen's customer servicing capabilities.

In December 2003, Li & Fung acquired the sourcing business of the Hong Kong–based Firstworld Garments Limited and the U.S.-based International Porcelain Inc. for US$27 million. These two companies would together operate under the name "International Sources." They were expected to strengthen Li & Fung's presence in the hard goods business and enable it to reach out to Mexico.

The Challenges

By the end of 2003, Li & Fung emerged as one of the few global consumer goods trading companies with geographical flexibility and depth of expertise required for success in the fiercely competitive business environment of the early 21st century. In the fiscal year ending December 31, 2003, the group's revenues amounted to HK$42.6 billion, a 14.3% rise over HK$37.3 billion in 2002. Net profits amounted to HK$1.22 billion in fiscal 2003, a 13.2% increase over the HK$1.08 billion in fiscal 2002. In December 2003, the share price of Li & Fung was quoting around HK$13 (see **Exhibit 11** for Li & Fung's Five-Year Stock Price Chart).

However, according to company sources, revenues and profits were below expectations. The Iraq War,[17] the SARS epidemic,[18] and poor business performance in the holiday season of some major customers were cited as reasons. The drop in the group's nontrading income also had an unfavorable effect on overall financial results. Reportedly, the net loss from Li & Fung's venture capital business amounted to HK$8 million in fiscal 2003.

EXHIBIT 11
Li & Fung's Five-Year Stock Price Chart (August 1999–July 2004)

SOURCE: *www.prophet.net.*

That year, the soft goods segment accounted for 67% of Li & Fung's total revenues, while hard goods accounted for the remaining 33%. Geographically, North America continued to be the company's largest export market, accounting for 75% of its total revenues. It was followed by Europe (19%), East Asia (3%), and the South Hemisphere (3%). As part of achieving its three-year plan (2001–04) goal of doubling profits by the fiscal 2004, Li & Fung announced that it would continue its aggressive acquisition drive, focused at non-U.S. companies, and new product lines that could open up more revenue opportunities.

In August 2003, Li & Fung finalized a licensing agreement with Levis, under which the former would design, manufacture, and market clothing under the latter's Levi Strauss Signature label. According to company sources, these products would be marketed in the United States by late 2004. In early 2004, Li & Fung also signed similar licensing deals with Official Pillowtex LLC, a U.S.-based company that owned the Royal Velvet linen brand. Commenting on these deals, William said, "Leveraging our strong position in the supply chain, we are building a higher-margin business model of licensing well-known brand names. This new business model will augment our core sourcing business and will be an important growth driver for the group in our next three-year plan for 2005–2007."[19]

By mid 2004, Li & Fung had an extensive network of over 65 offices in 40 countries worldwide, managed by a dedicated employee base of over 6,000. Reportedly, the company faced very little competition, which analysts attributed to its unique positioning as a supply chain manager for its clients and its focused acquisition strategy. William E. Connor & Associates (WEC&A), an American-owned, Hong Kong–based trading company, was the closest

EXHIBIT 12
A Note on Hong Kong's Export Trade Industry

THE EXPORT TRADE INDUSTRY

Hong Kong has always been one of the world's major export trade centres. Until the 1970s, Hong Kong was a manufacturing economy, supplying the world with textiles, handbags, toys, plastic flowers, watches and footwear. Most of its exports were to the U.S. and Europe. After the Chinese economy was liberalized in 1979 (initially only some coastal regions were opened up for foreign investors) many companies across all the major industrial segments and trading companies in Hong Kong moved the labour-intensive part of manufacturing to China.

The rapid industrialization of Asian countries from the 1980s resulted in expansion of production capabilities in the manufacturing sector and related supporting services especially in other low cost countries like Taiwan and Korea. This in turn led to trading companies expanding their sourcing reach beyond China to optimise sourcing costs for their clients. By the late 1990s, Hong-Kong emerged as a service economy with 84% of GDP derived from services. According to a survey by the Hong Kong Trade Development Council (TDC) in 1998, 64% of international buyers sourced China-made products through trading companies in Hong Kong. The country's strategic location, good physical infrastructure, expertise in international trade and well-established legal framework made trading reliable, simple and convenient. By the turn of the 20th century, Hong Kong became one of the world's largest export trade countries.

In 2001, Hong Kong earned HK$106 billion from exporting trade-related services, accounting for 32.7% of total services exports. In 2002, one in five employed persons in Hong Kong were engaged in the import-export trade. The sector produced a net output of HK$249 billion and accounted for 21% of Hong Kong's GDP. In 2002, there were more than 1,133 companies involved in the wholesale, retail and import and export trade businesses.

In the early 2000s, off shore export trading was increasing rapidly on account of many factors. The use of advanced technology, sophisticated production processes and on-site inspections by trading firms eliminated the need for further processing of products like final assembly, packaging and imposing quality control procedures. At the same time, the increased availability of cost-effective and reliable transport services contributed to the rise in off shore export trade. Some expected changes in the regional trade regimes including the China-ASEAN Free Trade Agreement and the Closer Economic Partnership Arrangement (CEPA) between Hong Kong and mainland China were expected to further boost the trading industry in Hong Kong.

In 2003, Hong Kong was the world's freest and 10th largest trading economy. It was a major trading centre with total merchandise trade amounting to US$457 billion, equivalent to 289% of GDP for that year. Major exports included clothing, electrical machinery, apparatus, textiles, jewellery, insurance services, financial services, transportation and travel services. In 2003, Hong Kong earned US$287.9 billion from exporting goods and services. Major export trading partners included mainland China (39.3%), US (21.3%), Japan (5.4%) and the UK (3.5%). With trading volumes of such magnitude, Hong Kong became a leading sourcing hub in the Asia-Pacific region in the early 21st century.

EXPORT TRADING FIRMS IN HONG KONG

Export trading firms in Hong Kong can be divided into three categories:

Left hand–right hand traders:

Traditional trading firms that matched sellers and buyers but did not add significant value. These firms identified goods produced in Hong Kong or neighbouring countries and shipped them to their customers.

Traders with some value-added services:

These firms, apart from sourcing raw material for their customers, offered some additional value such as providing trade finance and freight forwarding services.

Traders with sophisticated value-added services:

These exporting firms offered went beyond traditional trading services. Additional services included product designing and development, manufacturing prototypes, supply chain management services, and distribution and delivery of finished goods.

Hong Kong's export trading firms source garments, toys, electronic items and other manufactured goods. The sourcing activities are of three types:

- Sourcing goods produced in Hong Kong.
- Sourcing goods from the Asian region for re-export from Hong Kong.
- Sourcing goods from one country for direct shipping to another country, without touching Hong Kong. This is called offshore trade.

Trading firms in Hong Kong usually specialize in one product. In most cases, they offer shipping services to customers and manage their own warehousing facilities. Such facilities enable exporters of durable goods to offer better customer service, as a certain quantity of stock is always readily available for shipment. For goods like textiles, trading firms use temporary storage, with emphasis placed on prompt dispatch for shipping.

Most export trading firms in Hong Kong are closely involved in manufacturing activities, though indirectly, as actual production is usually sub-contracted. Short production cycles, a preference for smaller quantities of more product lines and keeping tight deadlines ensured that companies met customer needs. They provided supplier factories with advanced production techniques and know-how and helped solve production bottlenecks.

PROFILE OF WILLIAM E. CONNER & ASSOCIATES (LI & FUNG'S MAJOR COMPETITOR)

William E. Conner & Associates (WEC&A) was founded in 1949 in Tokyo and moved to Hong Kong in 1985. It is one of the major export trade companies in Hong-Kong in the early 21st century and the closest competitor to the market leader, Li & Fung, in the consumer goods trading market. WEC&A optimised the supply chain for its clients by managing every aspect of sourcing, right from product design & development to distribution and delivery of the finished product. The company's products included apparel, fabrics, fashion accessories, footwear, decorative accessories, textiles, house ware, furniture, lighting, office products, stationery and fashion-related products.

In the early 2000s, WEC&A had a global network of 35 offices in 20 countries. With an employee base of over 1,400, the company fulfilled the requirements of over 70 customers, which included leading department stores, specialty stores, catalogue companies, e-commerce retailers and importers, mainly in North America, Australia, Europe, Latin America and Japan.

In 2002, WEC&A's net worth amounted to US$850 million.

SOURCE: *www.tdc.trade.com & www.weconnor.com.*

competitor to Li & Fung in Hong Kong, as textiles was WEC&A's major product line. But, as WEC&A focused on large department store customers, and Li & Fung concentrated on specialty store chains, analysts felt that competition between them was not intense (see **Exhibit 12** for a Note on Hong Kong's Export Trade Industry).

While Li & Fung's business model might seem error free and its future bright, analysts were quick to point out that every business had its negative side and Li & Fung also had made miscalculations. They said the company's much-hyped B2B initiative "StudioDirect" had failed to get the expected response, forcing Li & Fung to restructure its operations. In 2002, Li & Fung converted StudioDirect from a full-service e-commerce company into a private label golf-wear specialist, offering services to customers through the Internet. The company also reduced its stake in StudioDirect from 57% to 15%. Li & Fung attributed this restructuring to changes in market conditions in the United States, which were not conducive to the growth of StudioDirect's business. It stated that it was still committed to e-commerce and its aim was to reach smaller and mid-sized retailers. However, even by early 2004, StudioDirect had failed to make major progress on this front.

The continuous fall in the annual growth of revenues and profitability through the early 2000s was also perceived as an area of concern by many analysts (see **Exhibit 13** for Li & Fung's Seven-Year Financial Summary). While Li & Fung registered a high growth in

EXHIBIT 13
Li & Fung's Consolidated Statements of Income (1997–2003)

Year Ending December 31	2003 HK$'000	2002 HK$'000	2001 HK$'000	2000 HK$'000	1999 HK$'000	1998 HK$'000	1997 HK$'000
Continuing operations	42,630,510	37,281,360	32,941,392	24,992,227	16,297,501	14,312,618	13,345,722
Discontinued operations	-	-	87,183	791	-	-	-
Total Turnover	**42,630,510**	**37,281,360**	**33,028,575**	**24,993,018**	**16,297,501**	**14,312,618**	**13,345,772**
Continuing operations	1,285,952	1,134,605	904,520	830,223	592,885	469,501	361,289
Discontinued operations	-	-	(237,955)	(39,375)	-	-	-
Gross Profit	**1,285,952**	**1,134,605**	**666,565**	**790,848**	**592,885**	**469,501**	**361,289**
Interest income	38,373	49,581	112,837	140,330	43,830	56,093	37,772
Interest expenses	(9,813)	(8,987)	(12,464)	(20,585)	(32,243)	(61,346)	(6,270)
Share of profit less losses of associated companies	2,015	393	1,443	13,677	9,389	6,850	6,666
Profit before taxation	1,316,527	1,175,592	768,381	924,270	613,861	471,098	399,457
Taxation	(105,513)	(94,896)	(55,637)	(64,178)	(36,638)	(16,425)	(25,326)
Profit after taxation	1,211,014	1,080,696	712,744	860,092	577,223	454,673	374,131
Minority interests	12,104	(228)	69,567	10,296	(2,585)	495	974
Continuing operations	1,223,118	1,080,468	782,311	860,092	574,638	455,168	375,105
Discontinued operations	-	-	(168,996)	(22,730)	-	-	-
Net Profit	**1,223,118**	**1,080,468**	**782,311**	**870,388**	**574,638**	**455,168**	**375,105**

SOURCE: *Li & Fung Annual Report, 2003.*

revenues and profit after taxation of 53.35% and 49% respectively, for the fiscal year ending December 31, 2000, the growth in revenues and profit after taxation came down to 14.35% and 12.06% respectively by the fiscal 2003. Analysts felt that the sharp decline in the share of overall revenues derived from European markets, during the early 2000s, was not a good sign for the company. They felt the company had failed to come up with effective strategies to increase revenue share from the European market, which, next to the United States, had immense potential for fashion goods, especially garments, Li & Fung's major business. They criticized Li & Fung for failing to build on the opportunities provided by its acquisition of Inchcape Buying Services, which had a strong presence in Europe.

Analysts also felt that Li & Fung's high dependence on large retailers, especially in the United States and Europe, might prove a threat for the company in the long run, given the uncertainties in the retailing industry. They pointed out that a major consolidation in the North American retailing industry, Li & Fung's largest export market, might severely affect the company's business. For instance, if a retailing giant such as Wal-Mart, which rarely outsourced its manufacturing activities, acquired other major American retailers, or put them out of business, it could lead to an 8% to 10% cut in margins for Li & Fung. Such consolidation might also result in only a few large retailing giants surviving (with other companies either having been acquired or forced to quit) in the market, which might also have severe implications on Li & Fung's revenues. This was because the company mainly derived its revenues from a large base of companies in the United States, with revenues of over US$100 million.

Analysts further added that Li & Fung's hopes of benefiting from increased manufacturing activity in China to strengthen its competitive position in the United States, after the removal of the quota system in January 2005, might fail. They were of the view that according to WTO rules, the United States and Europe were entitled to impose "anti-surge" quotas until the end of 2008, in case they felt any threat to domestic industry from exports. Anti-surge quotas restricted annual growth of imports from a country to 7.5% per product category. Analysts also said that it was very likely that the anti-surge quotas would come into existence in 2005.

Despite these challenges, industry observers felt that with Li & Fung focusing on expanding its customer base outside the United States, especially in Asia, in the years to come the company could reduce its dependence on the United States, its largest market. Meanwhile, Li & Fung had already achieved considerable success in lessening its dependence on soft goods over the years, reducing some risks in its business.

Media reports expressed optimism for Li & Fung's future. They wrote that the company, powered by its depth of sourcing knowledge and positioning as an efficient manager of global supply chains, was well poised for growth, in the light of increasing globalization. An *Economist* article had quoted in 2001, "Li & Fung appears to have as bright a future as globalization itself."[20]

NOTES

1. "Stitches in Time," www.forbes.com, June 09, 1999.
2. "Winning at a Global Game: Part Five of an Eleven Part Series," www.asiabusinesstoday.org, June 10, 2000.
3. "First Hong Kong Trading Firm to Gain China Licence," www.hktrader.net, February 2004.
4. GDP is used to measure the growth and health of an economy and is defined as the total market value of all final goods and services produced in a country in a given year, equal to total customer, investment, and government spending, plus the value of the total exports, minus the value of total imports.
5. In 2002, Li & Fung had about 120 business divisions across 40 countries.

6. "Asset Lite," www.cfoasia.com, April 2002.
7. A document, consisting of specific instructions by the buyer of goods, that is issued by a bank to the seller who is authorized to draw a specified sum of money under certain conditions (e.g., the receipt by the bank of certain documents within a given time). A confirmed L/C is one issued by a foreign bank, which is validated or guaranteed by a Hong Kong bank for a Hong Kong exporter in the case of default by the foreign buyer or bank.
8. "Asset Lite," www.cfoasia.com, April 2002.
9. An intranet is a restricted-access network that works like the Internet. Usually owned and managed by a corporation, an

intranet enables an organization to provide content and services to its employees across its various divisions, without allowing external people to view it.

10. An extranet is an Internet site that is offered to a select group of people such as customers, suppliers, and business partners, usually to provide or share non-public information.

11. "A Different Kind of B2B Play in China?" www.businessweek.com, May 08, 2000.

12. "Picking Asian Winners in the Internet Age," www.asiaweek.com, 2000.

13. However, in countries such as China, Bangladesh, Philippines, Africa, and Caribbean, where communication systems are still underdeveloped, Li & Fung relied on personal visits, phones, faxes, and couriers to communicate information and manage operations.

14. "Middleman Become Master," www.chiefexecutive.net, October 2002.

15. "Li & Fung to Acquire Colby," www.irasia.com, November 09, 2000.

16. Li & Fung to Buy Out Last Stake of US Unit, Hong Kong iMail (China), August 20, 2003.

17. The U.S. government believed that Osama Bin Laden–led terrorist organization, Al-Qaida, which was responsible for the September 11, 2001, terrorist attacks on the World Trade Center in the United States may obtain weapons of mass destruction (WMD) from Iraq. As Iraq was ruled by Saddam Hussain (Hussain), who was openly hostile to the United States, the U.S. officials considered it a severe threat to the country's security, and felt the need for pre-emptive war against Iraq to prevent further damage from occurring in the United States. In March 2003, the United States declared war against Iraq (the second war, the first being in January 1991), called "Operation Iraqi Freedom," aimed at freeing Iraq from the ruling Hussain government and gaining control over the WMD. The war ended in May 2003, following the capture of Tikrit, the birthplace of Hussain. Hussain was captured by the U.S. Army in December 2003.

18. According to www.cdc.gov, Severe Acute Respiratory Syndrome (SARS) is a viral respiratory illness caused by a corona virus called the SARS associated corona virus (SARS – CoV). The first case of SARS was reported in Asia in February 2003. Within a few months, the illness spread to more than 24 countries throughout the world. The outbreak of SARS in the Asian region severely damaged its economic performance—the hardest-hit business was the region's tourism industry.

19. "Hong Kong Li & Fung Posts 13% Net Profit Rise on Sales Growth," www.prophet.net, March 24, 2004.

20. "Li & Fung: Optimising Supply Chain for Other Companies," *The Economist*, May 31, 2001.

Starbucks Coffee Company:

THE INDIAN DILEMMA

Ruchi Mankad and Joel Sarosh Thadamalla

As the world's second most populous country, with more than 1 billion people and growing at 6% per year, we see unique and great opportunity for bringing the Starbucks experience to this market (India).[1]

HOWARD SCHULTZ, CHAIRMAN, STARBUCKS CORPORATION

India is an important long-term growth opportunity in the Asia Pacific region. We're looking at our own strategy . . . We believe there is a growing affinity for global brands.[2]

MARTIN COLES, PRESIDENT, STARBUCKS COFFEE INTERNATIONAL

IN 2006, STARBUCKS COFFEE COMPANY (STARBUCKS), the world's No.1 specialty coffee retailer had over 11,000 stores in 36 countries of the world and employed over 10,000 people (see **Exhibit 1**). Every week over 40 million customers visited Starbucks coffeehouses. The company had over 7,600 retail locations in the United States, which was its home country and its biggest market. After phenomenal success in the United States, Starbucks entered one country after another and popularized its specialty coffee worldwide.

During the 1990s, Starbucks concentrated its expansion efforts mainly in Asia. In 1995 it entered Japan and by late 1990s Japan had became the second-most-profitable market for Starbucks. In 1999, Starbucks entered China and by 2006 Starbucks had become the leader in specialty coffee in China and had moved China up to the No. 1 priority.[3]

After Japan and China, Starbucks expressed its intentions to enter India. In 2002, Starbucks announced for the first time that it was planning to enter India.[4] Later it postponed its entry as it had entered China recently and was facing problems in Japan. In 2003, there was news again that Starbucks was reviving its plans to enter India. In 2004, Starbucks

EXHIBIT 1
Starbucks Timeline

1971: The first Starbucks, under partners Gordon Bowker, Jerry Baldwin, and Zez Siegel, is opened across from Pike Place Market in Seattle, Washington.

1972: A second Starbucks store is opened in Seattle.

Early 1980s: Zev Siegel leaves the company. Jerry Baldwin takes over management of the company and functions as CEO. Gordon Bowker remains involved as a co-owner but other projects take up most of his time.

1982: Howard Schultz joins the company, taking charge of marketing and overseeing the retail stores.

1984: Starbucks acquires the five stores in San Francisco's Peet's Coffee and Tea chain.

April 1984: Starbucks opens its fifth store, the first one in downtown Seattle. Schultz convinces the owners to test an espresso bar, making this Starbucks the first to sell coffee beverages. It becomes a huge success.

Late 1984: The Starbucks founders are still resistant to installing espresso bars into other Starbucks locations and Schultz becomes increasingly frustrated. He has visited the espresso bars of Milan, Italy, and has a vision of bringing Italian-style espresso bars to America.

Late 1985: Schultz leaves Starbucks and starts the Il Giornale Coffee Company.

April 1986: The first Il Giornale store opens.

March 1987: Baldwin and Bowker decide to sell the Starbucks Coffee Company.

Aug. 1987: Schultz acquires Starbucks and rebrands all of his Il Giornale coffee houses with Starbucks name.

1992: Starbucks goes public with its initial public stock offering. At this time it has 165 outlets.

1996: The first Starbucks opens outside of North America in Tokyo, Japan.

Sept. 1997: Starbucks Chairman Howard Schultz publishes a book called *Pour Your Heart Into It: How Starbucks Built a Company One Cup at a Time*.

1999: Starbucks enters Hong Kong and China.

April 2003: Starbucks purchases Seattle's Best Coffee and Torrefazione Italia from AFC Enterprises and turns them all into Starbucks outlets. By this time, Starbucks has more than 6,400 outlets worldwide.

Oct. 4, 2004: XM Satellite Radio and Starbucks Coffee Company announce the debut of the Starbucks "Hear Music" channel on XM Radio. The station will feature 24-hour music programming featuring an "ever-changing mix of the best new music and essential recordings from all kinds of genres."

Sept. 8, 2005: Starbucks announces plans to donate funds and supplies to the Hurricane Katrina relief effort, worth monetary donations over $5 million as well as donations of coffee, water, and tea products.

Late 2005: Starbucks and Jim Beam Brands Co., a unit of Fortune Brands Inc., introduce a coffee liqueur product in the United States and announces plans to launch the product in 2006 in restaurants, bars, and retail outlets where premium distilled spirits are sold. The product will not be sold in company-operated or licensed stores.

SOURCE: *Compiled from www.starbucks.com.*

officials visited India but according to sources they returned unconvinced as they could not crystallize on an appropriate partner for its entry. In mid 2006, a Starbucks spokesperson said, "We are excited about the great opportunities that India presents to the company. We are looking forward to offering the finest coffee in the world, handcrafted beverages, the unique Starbucks experience (see **Exhibit 2**) to customers in this country within the next 18 months."[5]

EXHIBIT 2
The Starbucks
Experience

Howard Schultz believed that Starbucks did not sell just a cup of coffee but provided a Starbucks experience, which he defined as, "You get more than the finest coffee when you visit a Starbucks— you get great people, first-rate music, a comfortable and upbeat meeting place, and sound advice on brewing excellent coffee at home. We establish the value of buying a product at Starbucks by our uncompromising quality and by building a personal relationship with each of our customers. Starbucks is rekindling America's love affair with coffee, bring romance and fresh flavor back to the brew.[6]

Starbucks' outlets provided a captivating atmosphere. Its stores were distinctive, sleek, and comfortable. Though the sizes of the stores and their formats varied, most were modeled after the Italian coffee bars where regulars sat and drank espresso with their friends. Starbucks stores tend to be located in high-traffic locations such as malls, busy street corners, and even grocery stores. They were well lighted and featured plenty of light cherry wood and artwork. The people who prepared the coffee are referred to as "baristas." Jazz or opera music played softly in the background. The stores ranged from 200 to 4,000 square feet, with new units tending to range from 1,500 to 1,700 square feet.

SOURCE: *Compiled by IBS Ahmedabad Research Center.*

About Starbucks

The Initial Years

In 1971, three partners, Gordon Bowker, Jerry Baldwin, and Zev Siegel opened a store in Seattle to roast and sell quality whole coffee beans. The trio had a passion for dark-roasted coffee, which was popular in Europe but yet to catch on in the United States. They chose Starbucks Coffee, Tea and Spice as the name of their store. The name Starbucks was taken from the name of a character from the novel Moby Dick. They chose the logo of a mermaid encircled by the store's name. The store offered a selection of 30 different varieties of whole-bean coffee, bulk tea, spices and other supplies but did not sell coffee by the cup. The popularity of the store grew and within 10 years, it employed 85 people, had five retail stores which sold freshly roasted coffee beans, a small roasting facility, and a wholesale business that supplied coffee to local restaurants. Its logo had become one of the most visible and respected logos.

Howard Schultz and Starbucks

Howard Schultz, who was later to lead Starbucks, was born in 1953. He started his career as a sales trainee at Xerox.[7] After three years at Xerox, the 26-year-old Schultz joined a Swedish housewares company, Hammerplast, which sold coffee makers to various retailers and Starbucks was one of its major customers. In 1981, Schultz visited Starbucks while on a business trip to Seattle. After visiting the company and its owners, he was completely fascinated. He realized that the specialty coffee business was close to his heart and he decided to be a part of Starbucks. In 1982 Schultz joined Starbucks as director, Retail Operations & Marketing.

In 1983, while on a company trip to Milan, Italy, Schultz observed the immense popularity of coffee, which was central to the national culture. In 1983, there were around 200,000 coffee bars in Italy and 1,500 coffee bars in Milan alone. The espresso[8] bars in the cities had trained baristas[9] who used high-quality Arabica beans to prepare espresso, cappuccino, and other drinks. Schultz witnessed that though each coffee bar had its own individual character, all provided a sense of comfort and the ambience of an extended family. During his week-long stay in Milan, he made frequent visits to espresso bars. These visits were a revelation to Schultz, which he described in his book[10] thus:

> As I watched, I had a revelation: Starbucks had missed the point, completely missed it... The connection to the people who loved coffee did not have to take place only in their homes, where they ground and brewed whole-bean coffee. What we had to do was unlock the romance and mystery of coffee, firsthand, in coffee bars. The Italians understood the personal relationship that people could have to coffee, its social aspect. Starbucks sold great coffee beans, but we didn't serve coffee by the cup. We treated coffee as produce, something to be bagged and sent home with the groceries. We stayed one big step away from the heart and soul of what coffee has meant throughout the centuries.[11]

Schultz was convinced that he could recreate the Italian coffee culture in the United States through Starbucks and differentiate it from other specialty coffee suppliers. After returning, he tried to convince the owners to build Starbucks into a chain of Italian style espresso bars, but they refused. In 1985, Schultz left Starbucks and launched his own coffee bar; Il Giornale[12] coffee bar chain. The first Il Giornale store was opened in mid-1986 in a well-known office building in Seattle. The décor of the store resembled an Italian style coffee bar. The baristas wore white shirts and bow ties. All service was stand-up and no seating was provided. National and international newspapers were hung on stands. Only Italian opera was played. The store offered high-quality coffee in whole beans and in espresso drinks, such as cappuccino and caffe lattes.[13] It also offered salads and sandwiches. The menu was covered with Italian words. With the passage of time, many changes were done in the store décor based on feedback from customers. Chairs were added for those customers who wanted to stay longer in the store. Carryout business constituted a large part of the revenues, so paper cups for serving carryout customers were introduced. The store gained popularity and within six months the store was serving more than 1,000 customers a day. A second store opened in Seattle, six months after the first store. For the third store, Giornale went international and opened a store in Vancouver, British Columbia, in mid-1987. By this time, the sales in each store had reached around $500,000 a year.[14]

The New Starbucks

In early 1987 the founders of Starbucks decided to sell the assets of Starbucks, including its name. As soon as Schultz came to know about the decision, he decided to buy Starbucks. In August 1987, Schultz with the help of investors bought Starbucks, including its name, for $3.8 million.[15] All the stores were consolidated under the name Starbucks. Schultz promised the investors that Starbucks would open 125 stores in the next five years.

Starbucks first always gained a foothold in the market it entered and then moved on to the next market. Starbucks entered Chicago in 1987. Chicago proved a difficult market and presented several challenges to the company, initially. It took around three years for Starbucks to become successful in Chicago and by 1990 it was able to build a critical mass of loyal customers. Starbucks entered Los Angles in 1991 and achieved success without much struggle. As in other markets, Starbucks did not advertise its locations heavily but relied on the word-of-mouth promotions by the consumers.

Between 1990 and 1992 sales at Starbucks increased almost 300% and reached $103 million. Earnings reached to $4.4 million in 1992. Starbucks came out with an IPO[16] in 1992, which was very successful and raised $29 million for the company.

In 1993, Starbucks opened its first store in Washington, D.C. After succeeding in Washington, Starbucks opened stores in New York and Boston in 1994. Starbucks opened stores at places that were home to many opinion makers. Within a short duration, Starbucks was rated as the best coffee in New York. In Boston after opening a few company-owned stores, Starbucks acquired the leading competitor, The Coffee Connection. The Coffee Connection was founded in 1975 and had around 24 stores in Boston in 1994. It specialized in light-roasted gourmet coffee and had a loyal customer base in Boston. After the acquisition, Starbucks became the leading player in Boston overnight.

Hot drinks at Starbucks were available in four cup sizes: Venti containing 20 oz.,[17] Grande containing 16 oz., Tall containing 12 oz., and Short containing 8 oz. Cold drinks were available in three cup sizes; Iced Venti–24 oz., Iced Grande–16 oz., and Iced Tall–12 oz.[18] In 1994, Starbucks launched Frappuccino, a cold drink made from coffee, sugar, low-fat milk, and ice. It became an instant hit and drew many non–coffee drinkers also to the store. In 1995, more than three million people visited Starbucks stores each week.[19]

Over time and with experience, Starbucks developed a sophisticated store-development process based on a six-month opening schedule. The process enabled it to open a store every day. In 1996 alone, Starbucks opened 330 outlets. It also refined its expansion strategy. Schultz said, "For each region we targeted a large city to serve as a hub where we located teams of professionals to support new stores. We entered large markets quickly, with the goal of opening 20 or more stores in the first two years. Then from that core we branched out, entering nearby spoke markets, including smaller cities and suburban locations with demographics similar to our typical customer mix."[20]

Starbucks was opposed to the concept of franchising. Schultz believed that, "If we had franchised, Starbucks would have lost the common culture that made us strong. We teach baristas not only how to handle the coffee properly but also how to impart to customers our passions for our products. They understand the vision and value system of the company, which is seldom the case when someone else's employees are serving Starbucks coffee."[21]

Starbucks initially believed in selling coffee only through its own outlets. But with the passage of time, to broaden its distribution channels and product line, it started to enter into strategic alliances. Schultz said, "When we enter into any partnership, we first assess the quality of the candidate. We look for a company that has brand name recognition and a good reputation in its field, be it hotels or airlines or cruise ships. It must be committed to quality and customer service. We look for people who understand the value of Starbucks and promise to protect our brand and the quality of our coffee. All these factors are weighted before financial considerations."[22]

The first strategic alliance Starbucks entered was with the real estate company Host Marriott wherein Starbucks licensed Marriott to open Starbucks outlets at select airport locations. Starbucks licensed Aramark[23] to open Starbucks stores at a few college campuses. Other partnerships were with the department store Nordstrom, the specialty retailer Barnes & Noble, the Holland America cruise lines, Starwood hotels, Dreyer's Grand Ice Cream, and United Airlines. Under a joint venture with PepsiCo Inc.,[24] a new version of Frappuccino was bottled and sold through grocery stores.

Starbucks maintained a non-smoking policy at all its outlets worldwide. It believed that the smoke could adversely affect the aroma of its coffee. For similar reasons, its employees were required to refrain from using strong perfumes.

Focusing on Asia

In 1994, Starbucks International was formed and Howard Behar became its president. Starbucks pursued international expansion with three objectives in mind: to prevent competitors from getting a head start, to build upon the growing desire for Western brands, and to take advantage of higher coffee consumption rates in different countries.[25] Starbucks entered new markets outside the United States either through joint ventures, licenses, or by company-owned operations. In

1996, Starbucks entered Japan, Hawaii, and Singapore. In 1998, it entered Taiwan, Thailand, New Zealand, and Malaysia, and in 1999, it opened stores in Kuwait, Korea, Lebanon, and China. During the 1990s Starbucks concentrated its expansion efforts mainly in Asia. Schultz said, "The maturity of the coffee market in Europe was very strong and was not going to change much over the years. The Asian market share was in its developmental stage and we had an opportunity to position Starbucks as a leader in a new industry, and in a sense, educate a market about the quality of coffee, the experience, and the idea of Starbucks becoming the third place between home and work in those countries."[26]

Starbucks in Japan

As its first international destination, Starbucks chose Japan because it was the third-largest coffee importer in the world after the United States and Germany and the largest economy in the Pacific Rim. Japan originally was a tea-drinking country and the per capita consumption of coffee in Japan in 1965 was only 300 grams per year.[27] Owing to the decade-long promotional activities of coffee companies and coffee associations, coffee became immensely popular in Japan and by 1990s the per capita consumption of coffee had reached 3.17 kilograms.[28]

In the Japanese coffee industry, specialty blends were the fastest growing segment. Gourmet coffee accounted for 2.5% of the 1.2 billion pounds of coffee imported by Japan annually. The average per capita consumption among gourmet coffee drinkers had doubled from 1990 to 1.5 cups a day in 1997.[29] An industry analyst said, "The Japanese have taken to coffee like a baby to milk."[30]

In 1995, Starbucks entered Japan with a joint venture—Starbucks Coffee Japan, Ltd. with a leading Japanese retailer and restaurant operator, Sazaby Inc. In 1996, Starbucks opened its first shop in the upscale Ginza shopping district, Tokyo, Japan. The décor and logo of the stores were similar to its U.S. stores. The menu remained the same but with slight variations. The store also offered Starbucks coffee beans and coffee-making equipment as well as fresh pastries and sandwiches. The store gathered a huge crowd on the opening day and Japanese lined around the block to get a taste of the Starbucks coffee.

The initial sales volume in Japan was twice as that in the United States. Starbucks rapidly expanded and by 1997 it had 10 stores at prime locations. Despite the slump in economic growth in Japan in the late 1990s, Starbucks remained profitable. Japan had become the most profitable market for Starbucks outside North America. The success of Starbucks and the growing popularity of coffee propelled other players to enter Japan.

By 2002, Starbucks had opened over 360 stores in Japan. But in the same year, Starbucks incurred huge losses in its Japanese operations. According to analysts, Starbucks was opening stores too close to each other, which affected its brand image. Food menu was another reason, for Japanese consumers, food was a major part of the coffee experience. The no-smoking policy of Starbucks also displeased many. As a result many competitors took advantage and included an elaborate food menu with coffee and had separate smoking areas. Other challenges that Japan presented to Starbucks were high rent and cost of labor. The land rent rate in Tokyo was more than double that of Seattle. Moreover, Starbucks did not have a roasting facility in Japan; it had to ship coffee from its roasting facility in Kent.

After cost-cutting exercises and introduction of new products based on consumer research, Starbucks Japan returned to profitability in 2004. By 2006, Starbucks had over 600 retail locations in Japan.[31]

Starbucks in China[32]

A key component of our development in the China market was finding the right business partner who understands the marketplace, and, more importantly, share similar values, vision, and business philosophy.[33]

Howard Schultz

Starbucks had begun its groundwork for entering China since 1994 and entered China in 1999. Starbucks decided to first enter Hong Kong. In Hong Kong, Starbucks created a joint venture, Coffee Concepts (Hong Kong) Ltd., with Maxim's Caterer, a food and beverage company that had 46 years of experience in Hong Kong. Maxim had a thorough know-how of establishing and running businesses in China. Maxim was also the business partner of Hong Kong Land Company, which had cornered a lot of real estate market in Hong Kong. Maxim provided Starbucks with valuable insights about Chinese preferences.

After Hong Kong, Starbucks opened a store at Beijing through a joint venture with Beijing Mei Da Coffee Co. Ltd.[34] The first Starbucks store opened in 1999 at the China World Trade Center, Beijing. The store opening was celebrated according to Chinese traditions. The store offered a complete menu of Starbucks internationally acclaimed coffee beverages, a selection of more than 15 varieties and blends of the finest Arabica coffee beans, freshly baked local pastries and desserts, and a wide selection of coffee brewing equipment, accessories, and service-ware. The ambience and décor of the store were kept similar to its stores in the United States. After Beijing, Starbucks opened stores in Shanghai. As in other markets, Starbucks did not market, advertise, or promote its stores in China and relied mainly on word-of-mouth promotion. Starbucks selected high visibility, high traffic locations to open its stores.

By 2002 Starbucks had expanded to 50 outlets in China. Pedro Man, the then-president of Starbucks Asia Pacific said, "These are still early days of our expansion in the China market. Our approach is very focused. We plan to open one store at a time, serve one customer at a time."[35]

In 2003, Starbucks raised its stake in its joint venture operations in Shanghai to 50%. In mid-2005, Starbucks became the majority owner of its operations in Southern China. The first wholly owned and operated Starbucks store opened in Qingdao[36] in 2005 and by mid-2006, there were nine wholly owned stores in Qingdao, Dalian, and Shenyang.[37]

Starbucks had to face many challenges in China. In its initial years, many were opposed to the opening of a Western coffee chain in China, which was traditionally a tea drinking country. Another challenge it faced was the dominance of instant coffee among coffee drinkers. Specialty coffee was limited to mainly urban consumers. Competition had also grown intense and many domestic and foreign players were setting up specialty coffee shops. Despite the challenges, Starbucks achieved significant success in China and became the leader in specialty coffee. By 2005, China contributed to little less than 10% of the global sales of Starbucks and by 2008, Starbucks expected to derive 20% of its revenue from Chinese locations.[38]

The Next Destination

In 2006, Schultz said,[39] "We are equally excited about two other major markets we intend to enter during 2007—India and Russia (see **Exhibit 3**). We are in discussions with potential joint venture partners. Meanwhile, we are scouting locations, meeting with government officials—all toward gaining additional market knowledge and building critical relationships to make our market entries a success."[40]

About India

India had embarked on a series of economic reforms since 1991. The reforms included liberalization of foreign investment, significant reduction in tariffs and other trade barriers and significant adjustments in government policies.[41] The reforms over the years had resulted in higher growth rates, lower inflation, and significant increase in foreign investment (see **Exhibit 4**). In 2006, India was ranked as the fourth-largest economy in the world in terms of purchasing power parity[42] and the tenth-most-industrialized country in the world.[43] In 2006, the middle class[44] in India was estimated at around 250 million and was growing in double digits in urban and second tier[45] cities.[46] The spending power had increased considerably in the recent years (see **Exhibit 5**). According to a report[47] by KPMG,[48] disposable incomes remained concentrated in urban areas, well-off and affluent classes, and double-income households. Consumers in the age group of 20–45 years were emerging as the fastest growing consumer group.

India's population was one of the youngest in the world and was to remain the youngest in the coming years (see **Exhibit 6**). In 2000, one-third of India's population was below 15 years

EXHIBIT 3
India's Performance against Competing Nations

Parameter	India	Indonesia	China	Mexico	Philippines	Russia
Availability of workforce-quantity	◗	◗	●	◗	◗	◑
Availability of skilled workforce	◗	◔	◗	◑	◔	◗
Cost of labor	●	●	●	◑	◕	◑
English-language skills	●	◔	◑	◑	◕	◑
Cost and quality of telecom infrastructure	◕	◔	◕	◑	◑	◔
Labor productivity (PPP)[(1)]	◗	◔	◗	●	◗	◕
Perceived stability of government policies	◗	◔	◕	◑	◗	◔
Perceived operational risk • Risk of personal harm • Risk of business disruption	◕	◔	●	●	◑	◑

● Very favorable   ○ Unfavorable

(1) Labor productivity for India highest in IT services vis-à-vis competing nations
Note: Russia and China included as they will compete in specific areas despite aggregate shortages: Israel and Ireland
          not included because they are not expected to be significant competitors due to lack of manpower

SOURCE: *"India's new opportunity – 2020," Report of the High level strategic group in consultation with The Boston Consulting Group.*

EXHIBIT 4
Pricewaterhouse Coopers 2004/2005 Global Retail & Consumer Study from Beijing to Budapest–India

Key economic indicators	1999-00	2000-01	2001-02	2002-03	2003-04
GDP growth (%)	6.0	4.4	5.6	4.3	8.1
CPI (%)	3.4	3.7	4.3	4.0	4.6

SOURCE: *Reserve Bank of India.*

EXHIBIT 5
Growing Middle
Class and Increase
in Spending

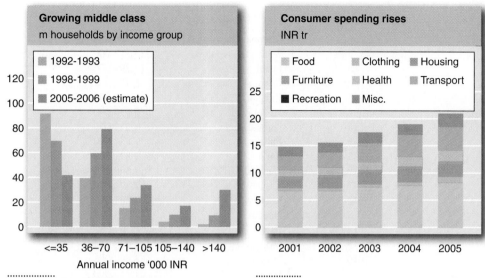

SOURCE: *NCAER, DB Research.*   SOURCE: *MSPI, DB Research.*

EXHIBIT 6
Population
Distribution

Aging population	2001	2006 (projected)	2011 (projected)	2016 (projected)
0–14 years (%)	35.6	32.5	29.7	27.1
15–59 years (%)	58.2	60.4	62.5	64.0
60 and above (%)	6.3	7	7.9	8.9

SOURCE: *Statistical Outline of India (2003–2004).*

of age and close to 20% of its people were in the age group of 15–24 years. The population of Indians in the age group of 15–24 years in 2000 was around 190 million, which increased to around 210 million by 2005. The average age of an Indian in 2020 would be 29 years, compared to 37 years in China and the United States, 45 years in Western Europe, and 48 years in Japan.[49] India had emerged as a prime destination for business process outsourcing (BPO) companies, which employed mainly the young people. The real estate market in India was also undergoing a boom.

Mumbai was considered the economic and financial center of India. It housed headquarters of numerous Indian companies and many foreign financial service providers.[50] Many IT companies, financial service providers, and business process outsourcing companies had sprung up in Mumbai. Delhi was the third biggest city in India, had the seat of the government and the most important city in the northern India. Delhi and the neighboring towns of Gurgaon and Noida were established as the call-center hubs. Another prominent city was Bangalore, which was also known as India's Silicon Valley. Many famous Indian and global IT companies were present in Bangalore. In 2005, there were a total of 35 cities with population more than 1 million in India (see **Exhibit 7**).

However, there were certain factors that constrained economic growth. The factors included inadequate infrastructure, bureaucracy, regulatory and foreign investment controls, the reservation of key products for small-scale industries, and high fiscal deficits.[51]

EXHIBIT 7
India's Largest Cities/
Urban Areas

Rank	City / Urban Area	Population
1	Mumbai (Bombay)	16,368,000
2	Kolkata (Calcutta)	13,217,000
3	Delhi	12,791,000
4	Chennai	6,425,000
5	Bangalore	5,687,000
6	Hyderabad	5,534,000
7	Ahmadabad	4,519,000
8	Pune	3,756,000
9	Surat	2,811,000
10	Kanpur	2,690,000
11	Jaipur	2,324,000
12	Lucknow	2,267,000
13	Nagpur	2,123,000
14	Patna	1,707,000
15	Indore	1,639,044
16	Vadodara	1,492,000
17	Bhopal	1,455,000
18	Coimbatore	1,446,000
19	Ludhiana	1,395,000
20	Kochi	1,355,000
21	Visakhapatnam	1,329,000
22	Agra	1,321,000
23	Varanasi	1,212,000
24	Madurai	1,195,000
25	Meerut	1,167,000
26	Nashik	1,152,000
27	Jabalpur	1,117,000
28	Jamshedpur	1,102,000
29	Asansol	1,090,000
30	Dhanbad	1,064,000
31	Faridabad	1,055,000
32	Allahabad	1,050,000
33	Amritsar	1,011,000
34	Vijayawada	1,011,000
35	Rajkot	1,002,000

SOURCE: *India's national census of 2001.*

The Retail Environment

In 2006, the Indian retail market was estimated at US$350 billion. The market was largely unorganized and dominated by small and individually owned businesses. Organized retailing accounted for only 3% of the market, but by 2010, the share was expected to reach over 10%.[52] Modern and organized retail channels such as hypermarkets, supermarkets, department stores, discount stores, etc. were sprouting in a big way. Retailing in grocery accounted for more than three-quarters of overall retailing sales.[53] In 2005, non-grocery retailing grew by 14% in sales value compared to 2004.[54] Department stores were the frontrunners in growth in non-grocery retailing and the number of department stores had grown by 24% per year since 1999–2000.[55] Department stores were largely frequented by the high-income and the upper-middle segment. Specialty retailing was also increasing (see **Exhibit 8**).

In early 2006, the Indian government permitted Foreign Direct Investment (FDI) up to 51% in retail trade of single-brand products with prior government approval. FDI was subjected

EXHIBIT 8
Key Players of the Indian Organized Retail Sector

		Food Retail Channels			
Category	**Company**	**Group Name**	**No. of Outlets**	**Net Sales (2003–04)**	**Future Plans**
Hypermarkets	Big Bazaar	Pantaloon Retail	9	2300	Over 22 stores by 2006
	Giant	RPG Group	2	900	21 stores by 2007
Supermarkets	Food World	RPG (51%) & Dairy Farm (49%)	93	3519	Not Available
	Nilgiris	Nilgiris	30	2550	20 new outlets in 3 years
	Food Bazaar	Pantaloon Retail	12	1650	Over 30 stores by 2006
Discount stores	Subhiksha	Viswapriya group	143	2350	Over 55 new stores by 2006
	Margin free markets	Independent retailer	300	540	Not Available
Cash & Carry	Metro Cash & Carry	Metro Group of Germany	2	650	Wait and watch

		Non Food Retail Channels			
Category	**Company**	**Group Name**	**No. of Outlets**	**Net Sales (2003–04)**	**Future Plans**
Department stores	Shoppers Stop	K Raheja Group	14	4040	11 new stores by 2006, venture in food retailing
	Westside	Trent Ltd.	15	1555	6 new stores by 2006, venture in food retailing
	Lifestyle	Landmark Group	7	2400	13 new stores by 2006
	Globus	R Raheja Group	7	1100	8 new stores by 2006
	Pantaloon	Pantaloon Retail	16	2500	Over 21 stores by 2006
	Ebony	DS Group	8	820	2 new stores by 2006
Specialty retailing	Music World (Music)	RPG Group	125	600	14 new stores by 2006
	Tanishq (Jewelry)	TATA	65	3900	Over 75 stores by 2006
	Health & Glow (Pharma)	RPG Group	24	282	3 new stores by 2006
	Crossword (Book)	Shoppers' Stop (51%), ICICI Ventures (49%)	18	370	Over 28 stores and turnover of 680 million by 2006

SOURCE: *Compiled by IBS, Ahmedabad Research Center from 2004/2005 Global Retail & Consumer Study from Beijing to Budapest – India, www.pwc.com.*

to three conditions; products could be sold under a single brand, the products should be sold under the same brand internationally and the products needed to be branded during manufacturing.[56] Any addition to the product or product categories under the single brand would require fresh government approval.

Many single-brand global retail giants such as Gap and Zara announced their plans to enter India and many were in the exploration stage. Many domestic conglomerates also had big plans. One of the leading Indian conglomerates, Reliance Industries, announced its plans to invest US$3.4 billion in retail in India and establish a chain of 1,575 stores by mid-2007. Another group, K Raheja Group, had plans to open 55 hypermarkets by 2015.[57] In 2006, India was ranked as the top destination for retailers according to A.T. Kearney's[58] Global Retail Development Index (GRDI) (see **Exhibit 9**).

EXHIBIT 9
A. T. Kearney's Global Retail Development Index (GRDI)

2006 Rank	Country	Region Weight	Country Risk 25%	Market Attractiveness 25%	Market Saturation 30%	Time Pressure 20%	GRDI Score
1	India	Asia	55	34	89	76	100
2	Russia	Eastern Europe	43	59	53	90	85
3	Vietnam	Asia	43	24	87	81	84
4	Ukraine	Eastern Europe	42	37	76	81	83
5	China	Asia	58	40	57	86	82
6	Chile	Americas	67	57	47	48	71
7	Latvia	Eastern Europe	58	50	31	88	69
8	Slovenia	Eastern Europe	78	52	25	70	68
9	Croatia	Eastern Europe	57	51	28	91	67
10	Turkey	Mediterranean	46	59	64	40	66
11	Tunisia	Mediterranean	58	40	79	25	65
12	Thailand	Asia	57	39	49	72	64
13	Korea, South	Asia	68	73	35	36	63
14	Malaysia	Asia	66	49	54	38	62
15	Macedonia	Eastern Europe	32	32	75	64	61
16	United Arab Emirates	Asia	78	67	33	25	60
17	Saudi Arabia	Asia	53	46	67	30	59
18	Slovakia	Eastern Europe	61	51	23	78	58
19	Mexico	Americas	54	67	47	28	57
20	Egypt	Mediterranean	45	35	81	35	60
21	Bulgaria	Eastern Europe	48	37	52	65	55
22	Romania	Eastern Europe	45	40	53	60	54
23	Hungary	Eastern Europe	65	50	17	76	53
24	Taiwan	Asia	83	69	32	6	52
25	Bosnia and Herzegovina	Eastern Europe	31	18	71	75	51
26	Lithuania	Eastern Europe	59	52	32	55	50
27	Brazil	Americas	46	56	64	16	49
28	Morocco	Mediterranean	45	31	76	30	48
29	Colombia	Americas	39	42	65	37	47
30	Kazakhstan	Asia	48	15	99	8	46
Key	□ On the radar screen ▨ Lower priority ■ To consider	**Legend**	0 = high risk 100 = low risk	0 = low attractiveness 100 = high attractiveness	0 = saturated 100 = not saturated	0 = no time pressure 100 = urgency to enter	

SOURCE: *www.atkearney.com.*

Food Habits

India had a diverse cuisine that varied from region to region. Both vegetarian and nonvegetarian cuisines were eaten. Spicy food and sweets remained popular in India (see **Exhibit 10**). In 2006, a nationwide survey[59] was conducted that threw fresh light on the eating habits of Indians (see **Exhibit 11**).

EXHIBIT 10
Indian Cuisine

In India, the food habits differed across diverse religions and regions. There was no single style of Indian cooking and no single national dish. Styles of cooking and commonly used ingredients differed from region to region and from one household to another. The Hindu and Muslim cultures played a pivotal role in the development of the Indian cuisine. The Portuguese, the Persians, and the British also made important contributions to the Indian cuisine scene.

Overall, wheat and rice were the staple foods. Gravy-based dishes were prominent throughout India. The essence of Indian cooking revolved around the use of spices, which served both as appetizers and digestives. The other main ingredients of Indian cooking were the milk products— ghee and curd. Dals or pulses were also used across the country. Vegetables differed across regions and with seasons. The style of cooking vegetables was dependent upon the main dish or cereal with which they were served. Several customs were associated with the way in which food was consumed. Traditionally, meals were eaten while sitting on the floor or on very low stools, eating with the fingers of the right hand.

The Indian cuisine included a host of beverages, desserts, and paan for a grand finale. Buttermilk, an accompaniment to Indian meals, was made by vigorously churning yogurt and water. It was called lassi in the north and mor or majige in the South. Tender coconut was available in plenty in the coastal areas and was consumed to beat the summer heat.

Coffee was more popular in South India, and tea in North India. Indian tea grown on the mountain slopes of Darjeeling, Munnar, and Coonoor was exported the world over. Coffee was primarily grown in Karnataka.

Bottled drinks included various brands of lime, orange, and cola. Other fruit-based drinks— apple, guava, mango, and tomato—were available in tetra packs and tins. Alcoholic beverages included gin and rum. Fenny, a cashew or palm extract, was popular in Goa.

SOURCE: *Compiled from http://www.geocities.com/Tokyo/Shrine/4287/cuisine.htm.*

EXHIBIT 11
Key Findings of
The Hindu-CNN-IBN
State of the Nation
Survey

Category	Persons	Families*
Vegetarians	31%	21%
Vegetarians who take eggs	9%	3%
Non-Vegetarians	60%	44%
Mixed eating habits	-	32%

*Family includes parents and spouses. Figures are for families where everyone falls in the same category. 32% of families have mixed eating habits.

Those who consume*	Rural	Urban
Tea/Coffee	83	96
Cold drinks	22	44
Eat out in restaurants	-	23

*Figures in percentage for those who consume either daily or once or twice a week or once or twice a month.

SOURCE: *Yogendra Yadav, Sanjay Sharma "The food habits of a nation," www.hinduonnet.com, August 14, 2006.*

Indian Beverage Market

The Indian beverage market is chiefly composed of milk, tea, coffee, bottled water, carbonated soft drinks, fruit beverages, distilled spirits, beer, wine, and others (see **Exhibit 12**). Consumers in different parts of the country had different tastes and preferences. The middle class was the biggest consumer of beverages. Consumption in rural areas had stagnated as a majority of the

EXHIBIT 12
Indian Beverage
Market

A. Change in volume by category—2001–2005

Segment	2000/01	2001/02	2002/03	2003/04	2004/05
Milk	3.0%	4.7%	2.1%	2.2%	2.0%
Tea	3.2%	3.1%	3.0%	3.0%	2.9%
Bottled Water	51.9%	63.7%	45.6%	32.7%	23.8%
Coffee	6.7%	6.2%	2.9%	2.0%	2.0%
Carbonated Soft Drinks	20.0%	25.0%	−5.0%	−15.0%	−5.0%
Distilled Spirits	4.3%	14.9%	11.6%	11.3%	10.4%
Beer	7.6%	8.2%	6.6%	5.3%	6.3%
Fruit Beverages	15.6%	20.6%	48.8%	23.9%	23.2%
Wine	—	—	—	18.0%	19.3%
Subtotal	**3.4%**	**4.7%**	**2.9%**	**2.8%**	**2.8%**
All Others[1]	0.8%	0.5%	0.8%	0.9%	0.9%
TOTAL	**1.2%**	**1.2%**	**1.2%**	**1.2%**	**1.2%**

Note: [1]Includes tap water, vegetable juices, powdered drinks, and miscellaneous others.

SOURCE: *Beverage Marketing Corporation.*

B. Per Capita Consumption by Category

Categories	Liters Per Person					
	1995	1996	1997	1998	1999	2000
Beer	0.5	0.5	0.6	0.6	0.7	0.7
Bottled Water	0.1	0.1	0.1	0.2	0.3	0.5
CSDs	1.0	1.2	1.2	1.5	1.6	1.8
Coffee	2.0	1.2	1.3	1.3	1.3	1.2
Distilled Spirits	0.3	0.3	0.4	0.5	0.6	0.6
Fruit Beverages	0.1	0.1	0.1	0.2	0.2	0.2
Milk	41.2	41.7	40.2	40.7	40.1	40.5
Tea	49.7	50.9	49.2	52.5	48.2	44.2
Wine	0.0	0.0	0.0	0.0	0.0	0.0
Subtotal	**94.9**	**96.0**	**93.1**	**97.5**	**93.0**	**89.7**
All Others*	631.9	630.6	633.6	629.3	633.7	637.0
TOTAL[2]	**726.7**	**726.7**	**726.7**	**726.7**	**726.7**	**726.7**

Categories	Gallons Per Capita					
	1995	1996	1997	1998	1999	2000
Beer	0.1	0.1	0.2	0.2	0.2	0.2
Bottled Water	0.0	0.0	0.0	0.1	0.1	0.1
CSDs	0.3	0.3	0.3	0.4	0.4	0.5
Coffee	0.5	0.3	0.3	0.3	0.3	0.3
Distilled Spirits	0.1	0.1	0.1	0.1	0.1	0.2
Fruit Beverages	0.0	0.0	0.0	0.0	0.0	0.1
Milk	10.9	11.0	10.6	10.8	10.6	10.7
Tea	13.1	13.4	13.0	13.9	12.7	11.7
Wine	0.0	0.0	0.0	0.0	0.0	0.0
Subtotal	**25.0**	**25.2**	**24.5**	**25.8**	**24.4**	**23.8**
All Others[1]	166.9	166.6	167.4	166.3	167.4	168.3
TOTAL[2]	**192.0**	**192.0**	**192.0**	**192.0**	**192.0**	**192.0**

Note: [1]Includes tap water, vegetable juices powders, and miscellaneous others.
[2]Rounding errors

SOURCE: *Beverage Marketing Corporation.*

rural population depended on agricultural products. Also, most of the advertisements were targeted at the urban population living in cities, and very few advertisements targeted the rural market. The Indian hot-beverage market was dominated by tea. India was the largest producer and consumer of tea in the world and accounted for 29% of the total production and over 20% of the total consumption globally.[60] Most of the Indians consumed tea at least twice a day, in the morning and in the afternoon. Tea, perceived as having health benefits, was extensively and easily available, but more than half was available in unpacked or loose form. Milk followed tea as the second-most-popular drink. Coffee was third in the hot beverage market. The total soft drink market (carbonated soft drinks and juices) was estimated at US$1 billion per year. Mineral water market in India was a US$50 million industry.[61]

Indian Coffee Market

Between 1947 and 1996, coffee consumption in India had remained stagnant at 50,000 tons per year. Since 1996, coffee consumption witnessed a steady rise reaching 85,000 tons in 2005.[62] The late 1990s saw the emergence of trendy coffee bars, specialty coffee serving chains that started replacing the conventional and old-fashioned coffee houses.

According to market research studies, coffee was mainly consumed in the urban areas (71%) and to a much lesser extent in the rural areas (29%).[63] The people in southern states of India largely consumed coffee (see **Exhibit 13**). The people in the northern states were generally not coffee drinkers, but drank coffee and experimented with various flavors as a fashion statement. The consumption of instant coffee and filter coffee[64] was almost equal on the national level. But region-wise, filter coffee was more popular in the south and the proportion of instant coffee was very high in the non-south regions.[65] The Coffee Board of India[66] undertook research studies in 2001 and 2003 regarding the consumption of coffee and attitude of coffee drinkers in India (see **Appendix 1**).

The size of the total packaged coffee market was 19,600 tones or US$87 million.[67] According to industry reports, the gourmet coffee market in India in 2004, which was still in its nascent stage, held potential for 5,000 cafes over the next five years.[68] As mentioned by Schultz, "Much like China, India has traditionally been a tea culture, yet there is a growing coffee culture emerging, especially among the country's young adults. Also like China, there is a growing interest in Western consumer brands and luxury products."[69]

Competitive Scenario

Homegrown brands dominated the retail coffee market. Coffee Café Day (CCD) pioneered the concept of specialty coffee in India followed by Qwiky's and Barista Coffee.

EXHIBIT 13
Per Capita Consumption of Coffee in India – State-wise

States	1981	1991	2001
Tamil Nadu	0.633	0.425	0.493
Karnataka	0.498	0.370	0.350
Kerala	0.179	0.070	0.143
AP	0.109	0.062	0.077
Total South	0.362	0.237	0.267
Total for Non-South	0.009	0.004	0.005
Total for all States	**0.094**	**0.076**	**0.062**

SOURCE: *http://indiacoffee.org/newsletter/2004/april/cover_story.html.*

Café Coffee Day

To be the best café chain in the country by offering a world class coffee experience at affordable prices.[70]

CCD Mission statement

CCD, India's first coffee bar was established in 1996 in Bangalore by the largest exporter of coffee in India, the Amalgamated Bean Coffee Trading Company (ABCTCL). By 2002, CCD had 50 outlets in 9 cities, which increased to 326 outlets in 65 cities by 2006.[71] CCD offered a wide variety of Indian and international flavors of hot and cold coffee, hot chocolate, cold drinks, ice creams, pastries, sundaes, quick snacks, and powder coffee.

Customer Profile at CCD

The best-selling item at CCD in summer was Frappe[72] and Cappuccino in winters. In northern states, hot coffee was the most popular. Country-wise, on an average, the sales of cold coffee exceeded the sales of hot coffee.[73]

CCD also sold merchandise such as caps, T-shirts, bags, mugs, mints, and coffee filters at its outlets. Other brands were also promoted in a CCD outlet through innovative and interactive use of posters, cards, danglers, leaflets, contest forms, etc. CCD had tied up with popular television serials and also ran promotion contests for many brands. It had also tied up with some popular Indian movies where CCD was featured in some of the scenes.

By 2006, CCD had six café formats; Music Cafés, Book Cafés, Highway Cafés, Lounge Cafés, Garden Cafés & Cyber Cafés. Music Cafés provided customers with the choice of playing their favorite music tracks on the digital audio jukeboxes installed in the café. CCD had 85 Music Cafés out of which 32 cafés also allowed the customers to watch their favorite music videos through video jukeboxes. Book Cafés offered the customers bestsellers and classic books to read while enjoying coffee. CCD had allied with a leading Indian book distributor for supplying books that would appeal to the customers. There were 15 Book Cafés in 12 cities. There were highway cafés on two important highways in the country that provided coffee and clean restrooms to relax. CCD had three Lounge Cafés at Delhi, Kolkata, and Hyderabad, which provided exquisite interiors, an exotic menu, and theme music. It had hostesses to assist who were looked upon as fashion icons. There were two Garden Cafés at Bangalore and Delhi amidst famous gardens. Cyber Cafés at Bangalore and Delhi allowed the customer to surf while enjoying coffee. CCD had plans to come out with more formats like sports Café, singles café, and fashion café.

In 2006, ABCTCL earned revenues of 3.5 billion INR.[74] It had plans to increase its outlets to 500 by June 2007 by opening 3–4 shops per week and increase its revenue to 10 billion INR.[75]

Speaking on competition with other players, Sudipta SenGupta, marketing head, CCD said: We don't have any competition because we are not competing with the others. In fact we are aiding each other in creating and growing the coffee culture. All of us have a distinct identity. We sure do![76]

Qwiky's

Two software engineers, Shashi Chimala and Shyam, opened the first Qwiky's outlet in Chennai in 1999. They were inspired by the specialty coffee bars in the United States. The menu at Qwiky's included varieties in hot Italian coffee, Indian coffee, specialty hot coffee, cold coffee, frappes, milk shakes, tea, other beverages, desserts, and snacks. It targeted youths in the age group of 18 to 30 years. By 2002, the annual revenues of Qwiky's were 43 million INR.

Qwiky's had three types of formats; Qwiky's Coffee Pubs were stand-alone coffee bars, Qwiky's Coffee Islands were outlets within big stores, multiplexes, and movie theatres, and Qwiky's Coffee Xpress were coffee kiosks. By 2006 it had over 20 outlets in nine cities in India and one franchise in Sri Lanka. Qwiky's had plans to open more outlets in metropolitan and large cities in India and abroad through franchising its business. It had joined with retailers such as Lifestyle, Music World, and Ebony to open store-in-store outlets.

Barista

The first outlet of Barista Coffee Company Limited (Barista) was established in 2000 in Delhi by an investment company,[77] promoted by Amit Judge. Barista offered a range of hot coffee, international coffee, cold coffee, ice cream, cold non-coffee, ice cream sundaes, add-ons, other beverages, and fast food in their outlets. Coffee and other products at Barista were priced high and its target audiences were youth from the upper-middle-class segment. The coffee at Barista was made with high-quality Arabica coffee beans and baristas (brew masters) were invited from Italy to make new blends. Brotin Banerjee, vice president of marketing, Barista, said, "Our inspiration was the traditional Italian Espresso bars where the idea is to create a 'home away from home.'"[78] In 2001, Barista entered into a strategic alliance with Tata Coffee Ltd. (Tata), the largest coffee producer in India. Tata later acquired a 35% stake in Barista. The alliance allowed Barista to enlarge its distribution network and set up outlets in the Taj Group of hotels owned by Tata and its other allied businesses.

The outlets also offered many merchandise such as mugs, flasks, coffee-made candles, coffee filters, coffee cup miniatures, soft toys, and chocolates.[79] The outlets also gave away gift certificates that could be redeemed at any Barista outlet. By 2003, Barista became a chain of over 100 cafés (mainly in the northern cities), had sales of 650 million INR, and served 35,000 customers daily.[80] It had surpassed CCD in sales, which had over 50 outlets by 2003. In 2004, Amit sold 65.4% stake of the company to an NRI[81] businessman, Sivasankaran (Siva), who later in 2004 bought the remaining stakes from Tata as well. After the acquisition, Siva revamped the chain, opened more Barista outlets in Southern cities, and began franchising its outlets. It started opening up a new outlet every 10 days. A new look was given to its outlets by making changes in its seating arrangements, in-store merchandise, and providing a better youthful ambience of the store.[82] The brew masters maintained friendly relations with the customers and called them by their first names.

Barista joined with specialty retailers such as the music retailer Planet M, the book retailer Crossword, and the Taj Group of hotels for setting up espresso corners in their premises. It also launched a concept called Bancafe, a coffee shop within the bank premises and joined with the bank ABN AMRO.[83] By 2006, Barista had over 130 café chains.

Others

Costa Coffee, owned by the UK-based Whitbread plc, opened its first coffee retail chain in Delhi in late 2005.[84] It entered India through a joint venture agreement with RK Jaipuria Group of India. It had plans to open 300 outlets in India by 2010. Costa coffee, which had 100 outlets in nine countries, was the first international coffee, chain to enter India. In India it priced its coffee, which was locally competitive.

After Costa Coffee, Orlando-based coffee chain Barnie's entered India through a franchising agreement with an Indian company and set up its first outlet at Delhi.[85] The company had plans to invest around 750 million INR and open 300 stores across the country in the next five years. The world's second-largest specialty coffee company, Australia-based Gloria Jean's also disclosed its plans to enter India and set up 20 outlets in seven large cities in India by 2006.[86] Illy, an Italian-based coffee chain, was also in exploration stages to enter India.[87]

The Road Ahead

In 2004, Starbucks had signed an agreement with Tata to source premium coffee beans. Tata had won a gold medal for the best Robusta[88] coffee in the world at the international cupping competition, Grands Crus de Café held at Paris.[89] The agreement was the first instance when Starbucks decided to source coffee from anyplace other than South America and Indonesia. Tata had met all the stringent standards and conditions followed by Starbucks such as quality, soil, water, pest, waste and energy management, forest and biodiversity conservation to workers' welfare, wages and benefits, living conditions, health, safety, etc. Hamid Ashraff, managing director, Tata Coffee, said, "Starbucks deal with Tata Coffee is yet another significant milestone to show how Indian coffee is gaining acceptance in the international market."[90]

In mid-2006, a Starbucks spokesperson said, "We are excited about the great opportunities that India presents to the company. We are looking forward to offering the finest coffee in the world, handcrafted beverages, the unique Starbucks experience to customers in this country within the next 18 months."[91] Starbucks was said to have been in talks with several probable partners (see **Exhibit 14**) for their much-talked-about entry in India. The marketplace was full of many such speculations that Starbucks had finalized their Indian partner but there was no confirmation from Starbucks. In an interview with a leading Indian newspaper,[92] Coles said, "When we open a new market, we take time to make sure we have the right joint venture partner or licensee to help develop the brand. As it is very important for us to find a partner with the right business and retail experience as well as cultural fit for Starbucks, the process can be a long one. We will open each market when the time is right, one store at a time."[93]

Starbucks sounded firm on its Indian ambitions and seemed prepared to meet the challenges that the Indian market could pose for Starbucks. Starbucks products were priced at a premium and the per capita income in India was lower compared to other markets where it was already present. Coles said, "We price our products competitively in each market, so product prices in India would be locally competitive."[94]

Speaking on competition with the traditional Indian beverage tea, Christine Day, president of Starbucks Asia Pacific Group said, "India is a tea-based culture. We're not saying coffee is a substitute. We're saying Starbucks is a place to hang out, to eat and drink, to see and be seen."[95]

Another significant challenge that Starbucks could face was the increasing rate of obesity and obesity related diseases such as diabetes, high blood pressure, and heart diseases in India. In 2005, 25 million Indians suffered from diabetes, which according to estimates by WHO[96] would increase to 57 million by 2025.[97] Starbucks was said to have been on the target of many consumer health groups worldwide who planned to campaign against the high-calorie and high-fat products that Starbucks sold and which could lead to increased obesity risk, heart diseases,

EXHIBIT 14
Some of the Probable Partners, Starbucks Reported to be in Discussion

Group	Assets	Financials
Anil Dhirubhai Ambani Group (ADAG)	Runs Java Green coffee chain in its Reliance Webworld stores, businesses in energy, finance, telecom. Plans to venture in pharma retail	Operating Profit ADAG Group—INR 50 billion (As on May 2005)
K Raheja Group	Owner of Shopper's Stop, 19 department stores in 10 cities in India (2006)	Shoppers' Stop Revenues—INR 6.75 billion (year ending March 2006)
Pantaloon Retail	Owner of Pantaloons, Big Bazaar, Food Bazaar. 100 stores in 25 cities in India (2005)	Group Revenues—INR 10.73 billion (year ending June 2005)
Planet Sports	Licensee of Starbucks in Indonesia, Licensee of Marks & Spencer in India, 25 stores in India	Turnover in India—INR 0.3–0.4 billion (2005)

SOURCE: *Compiled by IBS Ahmedabad, Research Center.*

and cancer.[98] For instance, Banana Mocha Frappuccino with whipped cream, offered by Starbucks, contained 720 calories and 11 grams of saturated fat.[99] According to the consumer groups, Starbucks should use healthier shortenings[100] and publicize its smallest cup size, short, which was available but did not appear on the menu card. Starbucks provided information about the nutritional value of each of its offerings on its Web site and in-store brochures. The health groups insisted that the information should also be provided on its menu card.[101] A Starbucks official said they were actively researching alternatives to high-fat products.

Starbucks had expressed its interest in entering India several times in recent history. In 2002, Starbucks announced for the first time that it was planning to enter India.[102] Later it postponed its entry as it had entered China recently and was facing problems in Japan. In 2003, there was news again that Starbucks was reviving its plans to enter India. In 2004, Starbucks officials visited India but according to sources they returned unconvinced as they could not agree on an appropriate partner for its entry. Banerjee of Barista said, "We've been hearing about them [Starbucks] coming for the last 3 to 4 years. We don't know why they are not here yet. If they do come, we still believe we have a number of factors to our advantage." Cole commented: Without sounding arrogant, we are looking at our own strategy. There is nothing that keeps us doing business in India."[103]

Appendix 1: Salient Results of the Studies Undertaken by The Coffee Board of India

Consumption of Coffee in India

- Consumption of coffee was 19% when compared to tea at 85%. Consumption was the highest in the South at 31% while it ranged between 35% in the weak coffee zones: North, East, and South.

- Per capita consumption of coffee (among all respondents—both drinkers and non-drinkers) was 0.33 cups against 1.77 cups for tea. However, coffee consumption among drinkers was at 1.76 cups compared with that of tea at 2.1 cups.

- About 41% of the respondents were non-drinkers of coffee and 40% were occasional drinkers.

- Consumption was the highest among the age groups of 15–24 and 35–44 years. The proportion of non-drinkers was the highest in the age group of 55+ years.

- Coffee consumption dipped from 11% at home to 6% outside.

- Coffee was consumed as the first cup only by 23% of coffee drinkers, including in the South.

- Penetration level was found to decrease from higher socioeconomic class (SEC) to the lower socioeconomic class. Penetration of filter coffee was highest in South India. In the rural areas of South India, instant coffee had a higher level of penetration than filter coffee.

- Visiting cafes was not a frequent habit. Of all respondents surveyed, about 12% visited cafes and there was a greater tendency among the upper SECs to visit cafes. About 10% have ever visited cafes; the highest proportion was higher among men and the younger age groups (15–34 years).

- The average number of cups of coffee consumed increased marginally from summer to winter.

- The North had an increased consumption of cold coffee in summer, showing 60% consuming cold coffee at least once a week in summer.

- Around 65% of households bought instant coffee and 18% bought filter coffee. Among filter coffee drinking households, 49% were branded coffee drinkers and 51% were unbranded coffee drinkers. In the South, filter coffee was bought mostly from R&G (Roast & Ground) outlets.

- Amongst coffee consumers in the rural areas, a majority were light drinkers, consuming 1–2 cups every day. About a fifth of rural consumers consumed coffee occasionally.

- A majority of the rural households (71%) bought packaged and branded coffee powder. Of those, 47% bought instant coffee, and 53% filter coffee.

Attitude Toward Coffee Consumption

- Coffee at home was significantly different to coffee outside. Rating for coffee outside home was better than tea outside home, specifically in the North and the East.

- Coffee from vending machines rated significantly more satisfactory in the North as compared to the East or the West. Consumers in the North believed that making filter coffee was time-consuming.

- In the weak coffee markets, the key barriers to coffee appeared to be its bitter taste (East) and its inconsistent taste outside. High price of coffee was also felt as a barrier in the South and the North.

■ The knowledge levels on coffee appeared to be relatively weak in the North and East.

■ While consumers in the North believed that instant coffee was convenient and tasted good, the seasoned coffee consumer in the South believed that all instant coffee contains chicory and that filter coffee is the gold standard in coffee.

■ Respondents in the North, followed by East, appeared to be most positively inclined to consume more coffee at home if the price was less, they were reassured on health, and they could try different recipes.

■ Respondents in the North, followed by West and East, appeared to be most positively inclined to consume more coffee outside if the price was less, consistently good coffee was more easily available outside, and they were reassured on health.

■ In South, consumers believed that they would consume more coffee at home if their family & friends consumed coffee.

■ In the East, there appeared to be a certain level of eagerness to learn about making "just right" coffee and they would make filter coffee if they knew how to make it well.

....
SOURCE: S. Radhakrishnan "Coffee consumption in India—Perspectives and Prospects," www.indiacoffee.org, April 2004.

REFERENCES

Source: www.starbucks.com

Chaitali Chakravarty, Sabarinath, Starbucks brews success recipe for Indian palate, www.indiacoffee.org, July 15, 2005.

Starbucks seeks partner for India tour, www.economictimes.com, April 8, 2005.

Starbucks sees big opportunity in China, www.msnbc.com, February 14, 2006.

Sudha Menon, Starbucks coffee firms up India plans, www.blonnet.com, May 26, 2006.

Howard Schultz, Dori Jones Yang, *Pour your heart into it: How Starbucks built a company one cup at a time.*

A V Vedpuriswar, Starbucks, www.vedpuriswar.org.

Jen-Lin Hwang, Coffee goes to China: An examination of Starbucks Market Entry Strategy, www.clas.ufl.edu, July/August 2005.

Starbucks Coffee: Expansion in Asia, www.interscience.wiley.com.

www.starbucks.com.

Ruchi Mankad, Anand Rao, Aspiration of Starbucks in China: Popularizing coffee among tea-drinkers, www.ecch.com.

Allen Liao, Starbucks brings in coffee culture to China, www.teacoffeeasia.com.

Starbucks brews a business in tea-drinking China, www.siamfuture.com, March 25, 2002.

Starbucks soars in China, www.atimes.com, June 15, 2005.

Joseph Pratt, Starbucks-China blend: A Slam Dunk Grande, www.dailyindia.com, March 12, 2006.

Investing in India, www.ibef.org, June 18, 2005.

Rules laid out for FDI in branded retail, www.economictimes.com, February 15, 2006.

Jayati Ghosh, India's potential demographic dividend, www.blonnet.com, January 17, 2006.

Parija Bhatnagar, After caffeinating China, the coffee chain has its sights set on yet another tea-drinking nation, www.cnn.com, November 1, 2004.

Starbucks Q3 2006 Earnings Conference Call Transcript, http://retail.seekingalpha.com/article/14895, August 2, 2006.

www.economictimes.com.

Starbucks seeks partner for India tour, www.economictimes.com, April 8, 2005.

India's new opportunity 2020, Report of the High level strategic group in consultation with The Boston Consulting Group.

www.ibef.org

Starbucks to source premium coffee beans from Tata coffee, www.tata.com, October 18, 2004.

www.google.com

www.pantaloon.com

www.shoppersstop.com

www.starbucks.com

www.cia.gov

www.ficci.com

www.finmin.nic.in

www.indiastat.com

www.wikipedia.org

NOTES

1. 'Starbucks Q3 2006 Earnings Conference Call Transcript,' http://retail.seekingalpha.com/article/14895, 2 August 2006.
2. Chaitali Chakravarty, Sabarinath 'Starbucks brews success recipe for Indian palate,' www.indiacoffee.org, 15 July 2005.
3. 'Starbucks sees big opportunity in China,' www.msnbc.com, February 14th 2006.
4. 'Starbucks looks for Indian entry early next year,' www.helplinelaw.com.

5. Sudha Menon 'Starbucks coffee firms up India plans,' www .blonnet.com, May 26th 2006.

6. Allen Liao, 'Starbucks brings in coffee culture to China,' www .teacoffeeasia.com.

7. A global company providing office solutions such as copiers, fax machines, etc.

8. Espresso is a strong, flavorful coffee beverage brewed by forcing hot water through finely ground roasted coffee beans. In Italian, espresso means "to press," and refers to the pressure applied to the water as it is forced through the grinds.

9. A person who made coffee drinks as a profession.

10. Howard Schultz, Dori Jones Yang 'Pour your heart into it: How Starbucks built a company one cup at a time,' Hyperion, 1997.

11. Ibid., Pg. 52.

12. Giornale was the name of the largest newspaper company in Italy and also meant 'daily' in general.

13. A shot of coffee mixed with hot steamed milk and up to a half inch of foamed milk on top.

14. Op cit 'Pour your heart into it: How Starbucks built a company one cup at a time,' Pg. 90.

15. 'Planet Starbucks (A),' www.thunderbird.edu, 2003.

16. Initial Public Offering is the first sale of stock by a private company to the public. IPOs are often done when smaller, younger companies seek capital to expand their business.

17. Oz is abbreviation for Ounce. 1 Ounce = 28.349 grams.

18. www.wikipedia.org.

19. 'Starbucks Corporation,' http://www.referenceforbusiness.com/ businesses/M-Z/Starbucks-Corporation.html.

20. Op cit 'Pour your heart into it: How Starbucks built a company one cup at a time,' Pg. 195–196.

21. Ibid., Pg. 173.

22. Ibid., Pg. 273.

23. Aramark is an international company based in US, specializing in food services for stadiums, campuses, businesses, and schools.

24. The global food and beverage company.

25. A V Vedpuriswar 'Starbucks,' www.vedpuriswar.org.

26. Jen-Lin Hwang 'Coffee goes to China: An examination of Starbucks' Market Entry Strategy,' www.clas.ufl.edu, July/August 2005.

27. 'Analysis: The Chinese Coffee Market,' www.friedlnet.com, 16 September 2003.

28. Ibid.

29. 'Starbucks Coffee: Expansion in Asia,' www3.interscience .wiley.com.

30. Ibid.

31. www.starbucks.com.

32. Information adapted from the case "Aspiration of Starbucks in China: Popularizing coffee among tea-drinkers,' authored by Ruchi Mankad under the supervision of Prof. Anand Rao, ICFAI Business School, Ahmedabad.

33. Allen Liao 'Starbucks brings in coffee culture to China,' www .teacoffeeasia.com.

34. Beijing Mei Da Coffee Co. was the distribution agent for Starbucks wholesale operations in Beijing since 1994. It was set up by the Beijing General Corp, of Agriculture, Industry, and Commerce and the Borderless Investment Group. Borderless Investment Group was headed by a former Starbucks executive.

35. 'Starbucks brews a business in tea-drinking China,' www .siamfuture.com, March 25th 2002.

36. Qingdao is situated in Eastern China's Shandong province.

37. Dalian and Shenyang are located northeastern China's Liaoning province.

38. Joseph Pratt 'Starbucks-China blend: A Slam Dunk Grande,' www.dailyindia.com, March 12th 2006.

39. Starbucks Q3 2006 Earnings Conference.

40. 'Starbucks Q3 2006 Earnings Conference Call Transcript,' http:// retail.seekingalpha.com/article/14895, August 2nd 2006.

41. 'Economy of India,' http://dictionary.laborlawtalk.com/ Economy_of_India.

42. Purchasing Power Parity (PPP) is a method of measuring the relative purchasing power of different countries' currencies over the same types of goods and services. As goods and services may cost more in one country than in another, PPP provides more accurate comparisons of standards of living across countries. PPP estimates use price comparisons of comparable items.

43. 'Investing in India,' www.ibef.org, June 18th 2005.

44. In India middle income was defined as income between 5,000 and 20,000 INR or approximately US$110 to US$450 per month.

45. Tier 1 cities included Delhi, Mumbai, & Bangalore. Tier 2 cities included Hyderabad, Pune, & Chennai. Tier 3 cities included Kolkata, Nagpur, Ahmedabad, Chandigarh, Indore, Kochi, Trivandrum, Mangalore, and 30 other cities.

46. 'The multiple beverage marketplace in India-2006 edition,' Data taken from the sample text of the report, accessible to all.

47. Consumer Markets in India: the next big thing?

48. KPMG is a global network of professional firms providing Audit, Tax and Advisory services.

49. Jayati Ghosh 'India's potential demographic dividend,' www .blonnet.com, January 17th 2006.

50. 'Building up India-Outlook for India's real estate markets,' www.dbresearch.com, May 8th 2006.

51. 'Background note: India,' http://www.state.gov/r/pa/ei/bgn/ 3454.htm, December 2005.

52. Op Cit 'Building up India-Outlook for India's real estate markets.'

53. 'Retailing in India,' www.euromonitor.com, July 2006, Data taken from the sample text of the report, accessible to all.

54. Op Cit 'Retailing in India.'

55. *2004/2005 Global Retail & Consumer Study from Beijing to Budapest – India,* www.pwc.com.

56. 'Rules laid out for FDI in branded retail,' www.economictimes .com, February 15th 2006.

57. 'Emerging market priorities for global retailers—The 2006 Global Retail Development Index,' www.atkearney.com.

58. A.T Kearney headquartered in Chicago is a management consulting firm.

59. 'State of the Nation' survey was conducted by The Hindu-CNN-IBN between August 1st and 6th 2006 whereby 14,680 respondents spread across 883 villages and urban areas in 19 states were interviewed.

60. 'Agricultural commodities: Profiles and relevant WTO negotiating issues -Sugar and beverages,' http://www.fao.org/ DOCREP/006/Y4343E/y4343e05.htm#bm05.

61. www.beveragemarketing.com.

62. 'Foreign brands to flavour Indian coffee cuppa!,' www.hindu .com, August 22nd 2006.

63. S. Radhakrishnan 'Coffee consumption in India-Perspectives and Prospects,' www.indiacoffee.org, April 2004.

64. Filter Coffee is a sweet milky coffee made from dark roasted coffee beans (70%–80%) and chicory (20%–30%), especially

popular in the southern states of India. Outside India, a coffee drink prepared using a filter is known as Filter Coffee or as Drip Coffee as the water passes through the grounds solely by gravity and not under pressure or in longer-term contact.

65. S. Radhakrishnan 'Coffee consumption in India—Perspectives and Prospects,' www.indiacoffee.org, April 2004.

66. The Coffee Board of India is an autonomous body functioning under the Ministry of Commerce and Industry, Government of India. The Board set up in the year 1942 focuses on research, development, extension, quality up-gradation, market information, and the domestic and external promotion of Indian coffee.

67. 'The great Indian bazaar,' www.ibef.org.

68. Parija Bhatnagar 'After caffeinating China, the coffee chain has its sights set on yet another tea-drinking nation,' www.cnn.com, 1 November 2004.

69. 'Starbucks Q3 2006 Earnings Conference Call Transcript,' http://retail.seekingalpha.com/article/14895, 2 August 2006.

70. www.cafecoffeeday.com.

71. Ibid.

72. Frappe is coffee and ice-cream blended together.

73. 'Interview with Café Coffee Day marketing head Sudipta Sen Gupta,' www.indiantelevision.com, May 27th 2004.

74. As on September 6th 2006, 1 US $ was equal to 46.19 INR.

75. Arthur Cundy 'Coffee Day parent brews plans to double presence,' www.cafelist.blogpost.com, May 17th 2006.

76. 'Interview with Café Coffee Day marketing head Sudipta Sen Gupta,' www.indiantelevision.com, May 27th 2004.

77. Turner Morrison.

78. Parija Bhatnagar 'Starbucks: A passage to India,' www.money.cnn.com, 1 November 2004.

79. www.barista.co.in.

80. 'A coffee-man's 'circle of influence,' www.rediff.com, 4 February 2003.

81. Non Resident Indian.

82. 'More Barista cafes,' www.chennaionline.com, 27 August 2004.

83. Ratna Bhushan 'Keeping the coffee hot,' www.thehindubusinessline.com, 22 May 2003.

84. 'Costa Coffee launch in India,' www.news.yahoo.com, 8 September, 2005.

85. 'Barnie's gourmet coffee enters India,' www.thehindubusinessline.com, 17 August 2006.

86. 'Gloria Jeans plans first outlet in Delhi by July,' http://franchise.business-opportunities.biz, 24 April 2006.

87. Sravanthi Challapalli 'There's deep interest in coffee here,' www.thehindubusinessline.com, 1 June 2006.

88. The two main types of coffee traded internationally are Arabics and Robusta. Robusta coffee is a milder variety compared to Arabica.

89. 'Starbucks to source premium coffee beans from Tata coffee,' www.tata.com, October 18th 2004.

90. Ibid.

91. Sudha Menon 'Starbucks coffee firms up India plans,' www.blonnet.com. May 26th 2006.

92. The Economic Times.

93. 'Starbucks seeks partner for India tour,' www.economictimes.com, 8 April 2005.

94. Ibid.

95. Op Cit 'After caffeinating China, the coffee chain has its sights set on yet another tea-drinking nation.'

96. World Health Association.

97. Amelia Gentleman 'India's newly rich battle with obesity,' www.indiaresource.org, 4 December 2005.

98. 'Starbucks may be next target of fatty-fighting group,' www.foxnews.com, 19 June 2006.

99. www.starbucks.com.

100. Shortening is a fat used in food preparation specially baked goods. It has 100% fat content.

101. Op Cit 'Starbucks may be next target of fatty-fighting group.'

102. 'Starbucks looks for Indian entry early next year,' www.helplinelaw.com.

103. Op Cit 'After caffeinating China, the coffee chain has its sights set on yet another tea-drinking nation.'

CASE 8

Turkcell:

THE ONLY TURK ON WALL STREET

Sue Greenfeld

WITH MORE THAN 60% OF THE TURKISH MARKET FOR MOBILE PHONES AND 16.3 MILLION subscribers as of March 31, 2003, Turkcell İletişim Hizmetleri A.Ş., or Turkcell (TKC) for short, is the only Turkish company listed on the New York Stock Exchange. As stated on TKC's Web site, "we . . . have developed the premier mobile brand in Turkey by differentiating ourselves from our competition based on quality of service . . . [We] have introduced a wide range of mobile services intended to attract and retain customers with various service needs." Simply put, there is no company in the world like Turkcell. It is a vibrant, full-of-life, and energetic firm that is all over Turkey. This is especially amazing because Turkcell only began operations in 1994.

With more than 100 different consumer services, Turkcell considers itself the leading mobile telecommunications operator in Turkey. Having launched its General Packet Radio Service (GPRS) in 2001 and a Multimedia Messaging Service (MMS) in 2002, Turkcell has believed in remaining at the forefront of technological innovation since its inception. MMS is an application that combines videotext, graphics, and voice into a single message. According to company literature, Turkcell was one of the first mobile operators in Europe to promote MMS technology to its subscribers.

By the end of 2002, Turkcell had total assets of $3.2 billion, revenues of $1.97 billion, net income of $101 million, and more than 2,000 employees. With three additional Turkish market players created since 1994, including Aycell, a state-owned company, and an onerous 66% tax burden, Turkcell wonders what steps it should take to position itself for the twenty-first century. For example, how can it reduce economic risk if the Turkish lira (TRL) takes a nosedive as it did in the year 2000? How can it increase usage per customer aside from increasing its subscriber base? Also, can it afford to take a leadership role in introducing 3G, the third generation of mobile phone systems, into Turkey? Is there anything it can do to influence the Turkish government in order to reduce its 66% tax burden? And with the Turkish government moving toward privatization of numerous industries, why would the government set up a state-owned company in the first place? These are just a few of the questions that the managers of Turkcell are asking as they think about the company and its future.

Country Background

Turkey is a fascinating country with more than 19 civilizations that date back thousands of years. Hittites, Phrygians, Urartians, Lydians, Greeks, and Romans are just a few among the many people who once roamed the rolling landscape. However, the history of modern Turkey begins October 29, 1923, with the revolution and the creation of the Republic of Turkey. This was accomplished through the inspirational leadership of Mustafa Kemal Atatürk, the "Father of the Turks," who transformed and secularized the country.

Turkey is the successor to the great Ottoman Empire, which started in the late thirteenth century but was slowly dismantled throughout the nineteenth century via wars and by the Allied powers during World War I, when the Turks sided with Germany. In fact, one of the worst battles occurred at Gallipoli, when the Australian, British, and New Zealand Armies struggled to destroy the remnants of the Ottoman Empire. More than 100,000 Allied forces and Turks lost their lives at Gallipoli, but the Allied forces were unable to vanquish the Turkish spirit. From this gruesome despair of World War I, Mustafa Kemal Atatürk emerged as a new leader for Turkey, and he quickly realized the need for a new type of government, one more democratic and more secular than had previously existed.

From 1923 to 1929, the Turkish government focused on reducing illiteracy, latinizing the language, nationalizing the economy, and decreasing the 80% dependency on agriculture as a primary source of employment. Some foreign capital was encouraged in the areas of construction and railways. This focus changed during the world depression years of 1929 to 1939, when the emphasis shifted to protectionism, nationalization of foreign firms, and the building up of financial institutions. At that time, the government created its first Five-Year Plan for industrial development, including the establishment of factories for steel, cement, paper, chemicals, sugar, and textiles. The Second Five-Year Plan of 1936 added mines, facilities in natural resources, and other heavier industry, but World War II interrupted this development. During the war years of 1939 to 1945, the government was engaged in a major land reform effort, against the wishes of Turkey's largest landholders.

During World War II, Turkey remained neutral until 1945, when it joined the Allies, and it subsequently became part of the United Nations. It was admitted into the North American Treaty Organization (NATO) in 1952. From 1947 to 1962, Turkey received funds from the Marshall Plan to mechanize agricultural output. Strong encouragement of foreign capital investment began in 1954, while 1963 to 1979 saw rapidly growing international debt. This debt was incurred in part from Turkey's low level of exports in comparison to its high dependence on imported raw material. Since 1986, Turkey has been an associate member of the European Union (EU), and it has since applied for full membership. In December 2002, Turkey received a date from the EU for accession talks to begin in December 2004.

In 2002, Turkey's economy still had a strong 40% agricultural base. Other industries were clothing, textiles, ceramics, food processing, automobiles, mining, steel, petroleum, construction, and glass. About 18.7% of Turkey's exports went to Germany, while 11.4% were directed to the United States. Turkey is highly dependent on oil imports.

Nevertheless, Turkey continues to struggle with an inflation rate that has hovered around 40% for 20 years. **Exhibit 1** indicates the exchange rate of the U.S. dollar for the TRL.

EXHIBIT 1
Exchange Rate of
the U.S. Dollar for
the Turkish Lira

Year	U. S. Dollar ($)	Turkish Lira (TRL)
1996	$1.00	81,405
1997	1.00	151,865
1998	1.00	260,724
1999	1.00	418,783
2000	1.00	677,621
2001	1.00	1,176,560
2002	1.00	1,650,000

SOURCE: *www.odci.gov/cia/publications/factbook/geos/tu.html (September 10, 2002).*

In 2001, there was a major economic crisis when overnight the Turkish lira was drastically devaluated. According to the 2001 Annual Report letter from Chairman Mehmet Emin Karamehmet to Turkcell's shareholders, "the Turkish Lira lost 114% of its value against the U.S. dollar, [Turkish] gross national product decreased by approximately 9.4%, [and] consumer inflation rose by 68% by year end." It was also the first time that Turkcell had posted a net income loss of more than $186 million. Some have blamed the crisis in part on the government printing too much money and having too many state-supported programs, inadequate collection of tax revenues, the severe drop in the Turkish stock market, insufficient privatization of industries, and inadequate reform in the banking area. In 2000, the government took over 22 different Turkish banks that had gone bankrupt and/or were considered corrupt. The International Monetary Fund (IMF) has stepped in more than one time to help assist Turkey. By the end of 2002, Turkey held $16 billion in IMF loans. To make up for lost tax revenues and the underreporting of income, the Turkish government decided to place heavy tax burdens on both the petroleum and mobile communications industries. In the case of petroleum, there is a user tax at the gas pump. In 2002, the equivalent U.S. price for a gallon of gasoline in Turkey was $4.50, and after 1999 the government added a 25% earthquake tax on mobile communications. The 2002 tax rate on Global System for Mobile Communication (GSM) communications operators/subscribers in Turkey, including Turkcell, was approximately 66% of earnings before interest charges.

To enhance foreign investment opportunities in Turkey, a foreign economic relations board (DEIK) was created in 1986. This nonprofit, private organization "attempts to improve the external economic relations with Turkish enterprises and to contribute to the integration of the Turkish economy into the world economy." According to Başak Kızıldemir from DEIK, there are 30 individuals on staff working with business councils in 59 different countries. The Turkish–U.S. Business Council is a part of DEIK. Some member organizations include Microsoft, CNN Türk, Boeing, JPMorgan, and Delta Air Lines, among many others. Literature from the DEIK reminds readers that Turkey is one of the 10 largest emerging economies, has great resiliency, is a long-term trading partner with the United States, and is one of the most trusted allies of the United States. Turkey played a major role in the 1991 Gulf War, helping the United States.

In terms of demographics, Turkey has about 70 million people in a land space approximately the size of Texas (see **Exhibit 2**). Seventy percent of the population is under the age of 35. While the country is secular, without a state-supported religion, 98.8% of Turks identify themselves as Muslim, with less than 1% Jewish or Christian. Turkey has 53 government and 19 private trust-funded universities, and students are admitted through a central placement system. Entry is extremely competitive, and students have to score very well on the multidisciplinary university entrance exam. On the university campus and elsewhere, the Turkish population dresses casually, in Western-style clothing.

EXHIBIT 2
Map of Turkey

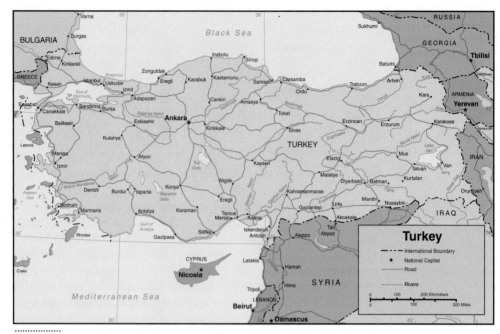

SOURCE: *Lonely Planet.*

History of Telecommunications in Turkey

Like the rest of the world, Turkey has embraced the mobile telephone communication age with a ravenous appetite, and as in many other countries, the postal service and telecommunications in Turkey have been the sole domain of the government. Except for the GSM communications, the state-owned Türk Telecom is the only authorized supplier of telecommunications. The Telecommunication Authority regulates all telecommunications activity in Turkey. Telegram and Telephone Law No. 406 was the principal law governing telecommunication, and it gave Türk Telecom complete monopoly power until December 31, 2003. Then the communications world in Turkey became a different ballgame, but the mobile telephone world of GSM had changed 16 years earlier.

In 1987, GSM was created to assist in the unification and integration of mobile communications within the EU, and it is one of four basic digital standards for mobile communications. A key component of GSM is the subscriber's identity, or SIM card. The SIM card allows the user of a handset or mobile phone to be identified. Without a valid SIM card inside, a handset does not function. Under a revenue-sharing agreement with Türk Telecom, Turkcell was formed in 1993 as Turkey's first GSM company. Turkcell started operations the following year, at the same time that a second mobile phone company, TelSim, began. In 1998, upon payment of an up-front license fee of $500 million, Turkcell was a granted a 25-year GSM license to operate in Turkey.

In the mid-1990s, the only services provided were the basic handsets for the sole mobile vocal communication market, but mobile phones in Turkey, as elsewhere, have become personal digital assistants (PDAs), among other features. The infrastructure in Turkey has been constantly updated as new technologies have emerged to provide for better mobile phone services. Turkcell introduced Dual Numbering Service, which enables the creation of two separate numbers on an individual mobile phone. Another technological advance has been the Wireless Application Protocol (WAP), which allows Internet access to anyone with a mobile phone. More specifically, WAP is an application environment and a set of communication protocols for wireless devices, designed to enable manufacturer-, vendor-, and technology-independent access to the Internet and advanced telephony services.

In 2000, the government of Turkey issued two new GSM 1800 licenses. One was to the Iştim consortium, operating under the name Aria. The other new GSM 1800 license was awarded to Türk Telecom, operating under its wholly owned subsidiary Aycell. Aria began offering services on March 21, 2001, and Aycell became operational in December 2001. By the end of 2002, there were four major players in the highly competitive Turkish market: Turkcell, TelSim, Aria, and state-owned Aycell. Each has its own marketing style, and each is working hard to become a household name in Turkey.

While TelSim also started operations in 1994 and held a respectable market share in 2002, it has become embroiled in a long-standing controversy with Motorola, the U.S. communications giant, and Nokia, the Swedish handset vendor. Both Motorola and Nokia have claimed in court papers that TelSim defaulted on $2 billion of vendor financing to help set up TelSim's infrastructure. Motorola wanted the top TelSim CEO to go to jail for up to 24 months for contempt.

Aria is a smaller player and a fast-rising star in Turkey. It is composed of a major consortium of Turkey's largest bank, Işbank, and Telecom Italia. Together, they paid $2.5 billion for the GSM 1800 license, but the real threat to the mobile communications market has been the government's entry, Aycell. Aycell has undercut prices and offers services lower than cost, especially to its own customers calling from an Aycell phone to another Aycell phone, but so far it has gotten away with it. The Turkish government covers any losses of Aycell. Through its lawyers, Turkcell has issued concerns to the regulatory body in Turkey, but wonders whether there is anything else it can do to halt what it thinks is unfair competition.

A new threat from Aycell surfaced in May 2003. The news agency Reuters announced that the Italian telecommunication giant TIM, part of the Telecom Italia group, was merging with Aycell in Turkey. Reuters reported that the two companies "agreed to merge their Turkish wireless operation in a move that would solve TIM's escalating regulatory dispute in the country." The merger of TIM with Aycell would give the Italian company entry into Turkey and would eliminate the need for roaming access to its rivals' networks, which is an important facet of the dispute in Turkey. To combat this challenge, Turkcell realizes that it must be vigilant in case there is an opportunity to merge with or acquire another company itself.

At the end of 2002, it was believed that market penetration of mobile phones ran around 34% in Turkey. This means a lot more growth can be expected if Turkey is to reach the saturation levels of other industrial countries, such as Italy (92%), Finland (82%), Portugal (91%), Spain (81%), the United Kingdom (83%), Greece (83%), Germany (69%), or France (62%). See **Exhibit 3** for mobile phone etiquette.

EXHIBIT 3
Mobile Phone
Etiquette

1. When answering or making a mobile telephone call, it is important to remember a few simple rules. Being polite is the first step.
2. Receiving or making calls should not be disruptive, intrusive, or take priority over face-to-face conversations.
3. Mobile phones should be switched off in meetings, in places of worship, in libraries, and at the cinema, the theater, or a concert.
4. Using a mobile phone should be avoided in elevators, buses, trains, and other small places where the conversation can be overheard.
5. Phones *must* be switched off on airplanes, on sea buses, and in hospitals.
6. Using a mobile phone while driving can be very dangerous. Some U.S. states have made a law against using a phone while driving. Drivers should never endanger themselves or others by using a handheld phone. Only under a dire emergency should a mobile phone be used while driving a car. It is better to pull off to the side of the road to make the call.
7. If calling for business purposes, always call during business hours.

SOURCE: *Adapted from S. Delin, "Mobile Manners Maketh Man,"* Turkcell World: The International Magazine of Turkey's Leading GSM Operator, *Issue 2 (Winter 2001).*

Company Background

Starting with only 94 employees, Turkcell commenced operations in 1994 under a revenue-sharing agreement with Türk Telecom, the state-owned fixed-line network operator. At that time, there were only 63,500 subscribers in the customer base. This number grew significantly each year to about 2.3 million in 1998, when upon a payment of an up-front license fee of $500 million, Turkcell was granted a 25-year GSM license to operate in Turkey. From 1994 to 1998, Turkcell operated with only TelSim as a primary competitor. Since 1998, the customer base has continued to grow considerably: 5.5 million at the end of 1999, 10.1 million at the end of 2000, 12.2 million at the end of 2001, and 16.3 million by the end of March 2003.

There are two basic types of Turkcell customers: prepaid and postpaid. A prepaid customer purchases a voucher card at a gas station, newsstand, kiosk, retail store, Turkcell's web site, or a bank ATM. He or she scratches the card to reveal the secret 12-digit number. When the customer calls an authorized Turkcell number and provides the 12-digit number, the service is activated or continued for a particular mobile phone. A postpaid customer receives a bill. Both types of customers have risen steadily for Turkcell, to the point where the customer base is two-thirds prepaid and one-third postpaid. By March 21, 2002, there was a nationwide network of more than 520 exclusive handset dealers selling only Turkcell services, and about 13,300 sales points (such as newspaper kiosks) for voucher cards.

In 1999, Turkcell became the first GSM operator in Turkey to be awarded the prestigious ISO 9001. The International Organization for Standardization (ISO) created worldwide guidelines to promote operating efficiency, improve productivity, and reduce costs. The ISO 9000 concept took off in the early 1990s and has helped to define world-class quality systems. There are four levels of ISO 9000: 9001, 9002, 9003, and 9004. The most rigorous of the ISO standards is ISO 9001, which has 20 components. ISO 9001 means the company has certification in design, engineering, and manufacturing.

However, one of Turkcell's most momentous events occurred on July 11, 2000, when the company completed its initial public offering (IPO) of more than 25 billion shares, in the form of ordinary shares on the Istanbul Stock Exchange and American Depository shares on the New York Stock Exchange. There was quite a bit of excitement at Turkcell as numerous company employees were on hand to make the day a big success. Turkcell took over Wall Street with a carnival-like atmosphere. A small Turkish village with street fair tents and kiosks was set up. It featured Turkish food, Turkish coffee and tea, and authentic Turkish crafts. The air had a festive feeling of celebration. There was a man on stilts whose legs were covered with long yellow pants and purple trim saying Turkcell. He wore a matching blue jacket with the Turkcell snabbit logo and a tall hat. It was a sight to behold. And who could forget the blue and white balloons tied together in a gigantic arch overreaching the tents and the wonderful Turkcell banner hanging from the sober columns of the New York Stock Exchange building? None of the Turkcell employees who attended can forget that day. By the end of 2002, they were still talking about the grand Turkcell entrance and quite proud to be the first Turkish company ever listed on the New York Stock Exchange.

In 2001, the company launched one of the world's largest mobile portals, called GPRSLand. GPRS means General Packet Radio Service; it is a data transmission service that provides faster mobile access to the Internet than WAP. GPRS is a standard for wireless communications that runs at speeds up to 115 kilobits per second, compared to GSM's speed of 9.6 kilobits per second. GPRS, which supports a wide range of bandwidths, is an efficient use of limited bandwidth and is particularly suited for sending and receiving small bundles of data, such as in e-mail and Web browsing, as well as large volumes of data. GPRS allows Turkcell postpaid customers to have permanent access to their e-mail and the Internet. GPRSLand is a collaborative effort between Turkcell and Ericsson, one of Sweden's largest companies and a supplier of mobile phones. Four software companies have worked to develop the 15 applications included in GPRS-Land. GPRSLand is a unique service that has provided Turkcell customers with access to a host of data applications. The applications were segmented into information and entertainment offerings. The launch of GPRSLand was supported by an extensive advertising campaign that made it a well-known service among Turkcell customers. In October 2002, GPRSLand won the "best new service" award at the World Communications Awards in the United Kingdom. "This is how everyone should do it," said the judges of Turkcell's GPRSLand. A panel of judges, including industry leaders, consultants, and representatives from industry groups, also commented, "Turkcell has done a great job putting a package together, not just a network. They've really thought it through and it's great to hear of this kind of sophistication." Currently there are 27 applications on GPRSLand. The business model provides financial incentives for third-party developers as well, encouraging them to create successful applications.

In 2002, Turkcell and Microsoft created another new service, called Office Mobile Service. This service allows subscribers access to Microsoft Outlook and Exchange by using a Microsoft Mobile Information Server (MMIS). Turkcell also provided 100% comprehensive coverage for all cities in Turkey that had populations of 5,000 or more. Turkcell had international roaming agreements with 319 operators in 136 countries as of June 3, 2003. Turkcell started the year 2002 with the appointment of new Chief Executive Officer Muzaffer Akpinar. He became Turkcell's second CEO, following the visionary leadership of CEO Cüneyt Türktan.

The Story of Snabbit

Snabbit is the 1994 creation of Mengül Ertel, a famous Turkish contemporary graphic designer who passed away on March 15, 2000. When Turkcell was about to be launched, the company approached Ertel to design a company logo and emblem that would be very unique and quite memorable. He turned to the animal world and created an animal like no other animal: the snabbit, partly a snail (because of its antennae) and partly a rabbit (because of its speed). According to company literature, the snabbit "reflects the energy, dynamism and total uniqueness that define Turkcell." The snabbit is featured in every Turkcell retail store. It graces numerous promotional items and can be seen at many sporting events. What Ertel produced has become a Turkish icon.

Initially, only one snabbit existed, and he was named Sinyal Bebek. For an important telecommunication fair to be held in September 2001, Sinyal Bebek was renamed Cell-O and given a whole new family. Later, in a *Turkcell World* article, Sevil Delin, a writer and translator, described all the family members. Cell-O is pictured as a technophile and joker, but he is kind-hearted and a visionary. His wife, Celly, is cautious and very economical. She is interested in astrology, and she is a great businesswoman and a great mother. Cellita, the daughter, is environmentally and fashion conscious. She needs her freedom, while Cell, Jr., the son, is an Internet addict, obsessed with soccer, voracious, and enterprising. Finally, the grandfather, Celldede, is just a teenager in his 70s who is an adventurer, a philanderer, and a generous man. By establishing an entire family, Turkcell believed that the Cell family would increase the value of the Turkcell brand and help to ensure brand loyalty to retain subscribers. Each member of the Cell family represents a different segment of Turkcell's customer base. The idea was to target products for those various market segments. Some individuals in Turkey believe the Cell family with its dad, mom, daughter, son, and grandfather may have some similarity to the popular show *The Simpsons*, which is shown on TV in English but with Turkish subtitles in Turkey.

Facilities

Turkcell's main headquarters is located at the Turkcell Plaza in Istanbul, Turkey. The highly commercial area is a mixture of upscale retail stores, various types of businesses, mosques, churches, schools, and a tramway. One side of the Turkcell offices faces the famous İstiklal Caddesi (or Independence Street) of Taksim. The headquarters building is nine stories and includes offices, underground parking, a gym, a cafeteria, and a sauna. All lunches are provided by the company through lunch tickets that are given to employees each month. The company pays for parking, and various shops in the nearby area give Turkcell employees special discounts. In the main lobby area is a display case that contains the dozens of awards that Turkcell has received. Among the awards are plaques and certificates from Ericsson, Interpro, and the Lions Club, along with Turkcell's ISO 9001 certification. The building is mostly dedicated to Turkcell's administration, finances, marketing, training, investor relations, and corporate communications.

Maltepe (on the outskirts of Istanbul) is the home of the "brains" of Turkcell—the $10 million Network Control Center, with its state-of-the-art computer technology. It houses 42 technical staff who work in shifts for the 24/7 coverage. Similar to the Houston control center that monitors space shuttle flights, the Turkcell Network Control Center has a series of curved interconnected workstations facing multifaceted sets of maps. When a red light appears, a Turkcell team of technicians is immediately sent to the location to investigate the problem. These 7,500 base stations allow Turkcell to provide 100% mobile communications coverage in Turkey for all cities in Turkey with populations of 5,000 or more. Turkcell also has numerous Turkcell customer care centers throughout Turkey, where subscribers can sign up for various services or resolve their mobile communications or billing issues.

Organizational Philosophy and Social Responsibility

The Turkcell company philosophy has been strongly influenced by the first Turkcell CEO, Cüneyt Türktan, who received bachelor's and master of business administration (MBA) degrees from Bosphorus University in Turkey. In 1980, he joined PriceWaterhouse in New York as an accountant, and then he returned to Turkey in 1985 as an audit supervisor for KPMG, and he worked for Interbank as the Head of Corporate Finance. Then in 1992, he became the Area Finance Director of PepsiCo International, in charge of Turkey and Israel. In 1994, he led the organizational team that created Turkcell.

According to Türktan, writing in a 2002 issue of *Turkcell World*, Turkcell values five structural principles: proactive approach, result orientation, minimum hierarchy, full accountability, and simplicity. The company strongly espouses both creating high employee loyalty and providing extensive employee training. Once a year in Istanbul, the company holds a major Turkcell information day that is designed strictly for the employees, and through its own educational classrooms, Turkcell provides training programs on individual development, functional, conference attending, computer and language training, and organization. The courses are given in English and Russian. Turkcell has more than 2,000 employees, divided into 49% technical, 26% customer care, 16% finance and administration, and 9% marketing. The average age of a Turkcell employee is 28. More than 80% of Turkcell's employees are university educated. Turkcell pays all its employees slightly above industry average.

Carrying on with the organizational philosophy of Turkcell is the second CEO, Muzaffer Akpinar, who was born in 1962 and has worked in the telcom sector since 1993. Akpinar speaks Turkish, French, and English, and he took part in the restructuring of Fintur. He was a founder and managing director of Penta Textile, and he worked as the CEO for KVK Mobil Telfon Hizmetleri, a major importer and distributor of handsets, as well as MV Holding Company. Like the first CEO, Akpinar is a graduate of Bosphorus University in Turkey. He started as the second CEO of Turkcell in January 2002.

Part of Turkcell's philosophy involves good customer relations and social responsibility. This means stressing the importance of customer care and being a good corporate citizen in Turkey. The company wants to increase its customer base and retain its current customers through both marketing and its visibility as a responsible company. For example, in conjunction with the Foundation for Supporting Modern Life, Turkcell has provided 5,000 young girls with scholarships and training in Eastern Turkey. Turkcell targets girls in this program because in rural Turkey, most families prefer to spend their limited funds on their sons. Daughters' educations are generally neglected. For its efforts in this area, Turkcell has received Institute of Public Relations (IPR) excellence awards in the category *Corporate Social Responsibility*. Turkcell also achieved the Cystal Obelisk award for the same project from the Foundation of Women Executives (WEPR) in New York.

As stated by A. Cüneyt Türktan, the former CEO, in an issue of *Turkcell World*, "Turkcell understands and is proud of its role as a corporate citizen and will continue to sponsor important programs." It has also sponsored the restoration of school gyms in Istanbul and the "Sharing Our Toys" campaign for children in rural areas of Turkey, and it helped set up computer laboratories in 53 schools in less developed provinces of Turkey.

Marketing

Turkcell engages in extensive marketing within Turkey. Not only does Turkcell want to increase the number of subscribers, but it wants to increase the call minutes per customer as well. Globally, the year 2001 was a difficult year for mobile telecom operators. These difficulties were compounded in Turkey by economic upheaval that led to a steep depreciation of the currency, lower purchasing power, and a contraction of economic activity. Turkcell had to manage the economic crisis with flexibility and sensitivity by taking decisive measures to control operating and capital expenditures. In order to keep up with the currency's depreciation, Turkcell had to raise the tariffs to subscribers in reasonable increments throughout the year while remaining sensitive to customer expectations and usage patterns.

In addition, Turkey's economic crisis seriously affected the monthly minutes used by subscribers. While subscribers had been using on average more than 100 minutes per month, that number drastically fell to 56.2 minutes monthly as of year end 2003. Ideally, Turkcell would like the monthly minutes per month to match the average of other industrialized or developing countries. The average U.S. subscriber spends more than 430 minutes monthly on a mobile phone, Hong Kong 350, Israel 237, China 199, Egypt 188, Norway 181, Brazil 105, and Greece 105. Turkcell wonders: Are there certain marketing campaigns that might help to achieve an improvement in the average monthly minutes? What type of marketing segmentation should we try? How can Turkish mobile phone users be encouraged to spend more time monthly on a mobile phone? Would educational campaigns be helpful?

For example, some subscribers, especially those in rural areas, appear to be quite resistant to newer technologies such as cell phones and do not know how to best use mobile communication. If an educational campaign were conducted, how much time and effort should Turkcell spend on it? One effort in the year 2000 was quite successful. Should Turkcell do it again? In that year, Turkcell sponsored the "Signal Tour 2000" project, which lasted six months. In this project, a truck was used as a symbol of wireless communication. The truck tour traveled to 82 locations throughout Turkey, met with more than 500,000 people, and covered about 18,000 miles. After the completion of this campaign, Turkcell received the Direct Marketing Association (DMA) International ECHO award, which was presented in Chicago at a gala event in 2001. But such campaigns take time and money. Would sponsorship of other events be more worthwhile? To illustrate, Turkcell also sponsors numerous athletic, cultural, theater, film, and/or music events, including the International Istanbul Jazz Festival and the International Istanbul Film Festival. Which campaigns are best geared at customer retention, getting new subscribers, or getting current consumers to use their mobile phones and services more often?

Financial Issues

The financial structure of Turkcell is highly sophisticated and involves a number of holdings inside and outside Turkey. To illustrate, on August 21, 2002, Turkcell, Sonera, and Cukurova Group, the shareholders of Fintur Holdings B.V., finalized the restructuring of two business divisions of Fintur: the international GSM businesses and the technology businesses. In line with the terms of the transaction, Turkcell bought 16.45% of Fintur International from the Cukurova Group, increasing its stake in Fintur International to 41.45%. At the same time, Sonera bought 23.24% of Fintur International from the Cukurova Group, increasing its holding to 58.8%. As part of this transaction, Turkcell and Sonera sold their entire interest in Fintur Technologies (Internet service providers, digital television, etc.) to the Cukurova Group. But because Cukurova Group is the majority shareholder of Turkcell, it will continue to create group synergies via various projects. Thus Turkcell is one of the major shareholders of Fintur Holdings B.V., which in turn holds a 51.3% interest in Azercell of Azerbaijan, an 83.2% interest in Geocell of Georgia (formerly part of the U.S.S.R.), a 51% interest in K'Cell of Kazakhstan, and a 77% interest in Moldcell of Moldova. Most of these countries have very low penetration of mobile phone usage. For example, only 3% of the Georgian market has mobile phones. Fintur International's GSM business in Azerbaijan, Kazakhstan, Georgia, and Moldova added approximately 500,000 new subscribers and reached a total of approximately 1.6 million subscribers in 2002. The combined revenue of the business was US$240 million in 2002, and the business was EBITDA positive in all countries.

Other holdings of Turkcell outside Turkey include Kuzey Kibris Turkcell (KKTCell) in the Republic of Northern Cyprus. Thus outside Turkey, there is great opportunity for Turkcell to increase its subscriber base, and this explains why Russian is one of the languages included by Turkcell in its training facilities. Should Turkcell expand into other European countries, and, if yes, which ones?

In 2001, Turkcell's loss of more than $186 million was attributed to the severe deflation of the TRL and the subsequent currency translation. Turkcell has to use U.S. funds to repay bank loans, licensing agreements, and purchasing of infrastructure, while revenues from subscribers are received in TRL. Although Turkcell raised its rates to subscribers by 101% in 2001, this was not sufficient to cover the 114% inflation and devaluation of the lira. However, Turkcell announced a $101.8 million net profit as of year end 2002. In 2002, Turkcell made debt repayments of $474.3 million in both principal and interest. At the end of 2002, Turkcell's total outstanding financial debt was reduced to approximately US$1.3 billion at the end of 2002. In addition, during the first quarter of 2003, Turkcell paid a total of $313 million of debt in principal and interest. As of March 31, 2003, Turkcell's total outstanding financial debt was reduced to approximately US$1.0 billion from US$1.3.

Also problematic for Turkcell is the fact that records have to be maintained using two vastly different accounting standards. As a company quoted on the NYSE, Turkcell has to follow U.S. Generally Accepted Accounting Principles (GAAP), while as a firm listed on the Istanbul Stock Exchange, the company also uses the Turkish SPK system. The latter does not allow for any inflation accounting, and this does not make sense to Turkcell, especially given Turkey's historical inflation rates. **Exhibits 4** and **5** are Turkcell's balance sheet and operations statement information, given in U.S. dollars.

EXHIBIT 4
Consolidated
Balance Sheets:
Turkcell (TKC)
(Dollar amounts in
thousands, except
share data)

Year Ending December 31	2001	2000
Assets		
Current Assets:		
Cash and cash equivalents	$243,114	$363,365
Trade receivables	256,143	325,636
Due from related parties	164,448	113,860
Inventories	12,154	16,402
Prepaid expenses	20,843	22,484
Other current assets	46,965	44,476
Total current assets	$743,667	$886,223
Advances to related parties		1,020
Due from related parties	10,085	
Prepaid expenses	3,300	11,765
Investments	58,329	60,068
Fixed assets	1,655,110	1,762,168
Construction in progress	119,363	233,299
Intangibles	916,920	892,995
Other long-term assets	28,996	37,382
Total Assets	$3,535,770	$3,884,920
Liabilities and Shareholders' Equity		
Current Liabilities:		
Short-term borrowings	$383,167	$438,081
Trade payables	302,039	208,890
Due to related parties	3,626	2,811
Tax payable	130	
Deferred tax liability		21,103
Other current liabilities and accrued expenses	303,425	271,194
Total Current Liabilities	992,387	942,079
Long-term lease obligations	1,218,903	1,600,676
Long-term lease obligations	37,103	34,472
Retirement pay liability	4,737	3,545
Deferred tax liabilities		3,491
Minority interest	896	12
Other long-term liabilities	6,792	5,838
Shareholders' equity:		
Common Stock	636,116	458,239
Additional paid in capital	178	
Advances for common stock	119	141
Legal reserves	5	5
Accumulated other comprehensive loss	(1,875)	(1,049)
Retained earnings	650,682	837,471
Total shareholders' equity	1,285,225	1,294,807
Total Liabilities and Shareholders' Equity	**3,546,043**	**$3,884,920**

SOURCE: *Turkcell, "2001 Annual Report," p. 46.*

EXHIBIT 5
Consolidated
Statements of
Operations: Turkcell
(TKC) (Dollar
amounts in
thousands, except
share data)

Year Ending December 31	2001	2000
Revenues	$1,786,910	$2,224,940
Direct cost of revenue	(1,173,743)	($1,197,175)
Gross profit	613,167	1,027,765
General administrative expenses	(130,681)	(187,878)
Selling and marketing expenses	(265,249)	(414,250)
Operating Income	217,237	425,637
Income from related parties	2,508	2,450
Interest income	97,268	94,654
Interest expense	(305,069)	(251,174)
Other income (expenses)	(5,135)	9,703
Equity in net loss of unsoiled investees	(51,316)	(31,645)
Gain on sale of affiliates		44,244
Minority interest	389	(316)
Translation loss	(151,454)	(21,953)
Income (loss) before taxes	(195,572)	271,600
Net Income (loss)	($186,789)	$ 227,907
Basic and dilute earnings (loss) per common share	($0.00040)	$0.00051
Weighted average number of common shares outstanding	470,348,717,330	443,740,603,721

SOURCE: *Turkcell, "2001 Annual Report," p. 4.*

Future Challenges and Issues

As Turkcell looks toward the future, it wants to maintain its leadership in the Turkish communications market, but how should it do that? Turkcell has to consider both Turkish competitors and other European competitors. Even though there are high barriers to entry, the mobile phone industry has been quite competitive. With 15.7 million mobile phone subscribers as of year end 2002, Turkcell is one of the largest operators in Europe in terms of the number of users. Besides TIM of the Telecom Italia group, other European competitors are Germany's T-Mobile, Norway's Vodafone, Spain's Telfonica, France's Orange, and Italy's Omnitel Vodafone.

In February 2003, Turkcell joined the Board of Directors of the GSM Association (GSMA), an association of the world's mobile operators, infrastructure producers, telephone manufacturers, and procurers. The GSMA, whose 700 members originate from 192 countries, with a total customer base of almost 788 million subscribers, represents 77% of the world's mobile communications market. In addition to Turkcell, the other members of the Board are well known, large, mobile operators, including Vodafone and Orange from the United Kingdom, NTT DoCoMo from Japan, Telecom Italia Mobile from Italy, and AT&T Wireless from the United States. The GSMA is established as the mobile communications sector's global trade organization, and in coming periods, the association is to focus on a series of commercial enterprises that should have significant effects on the development of the sector.

Of the major competitors on the GSMA Board, Turkcell is closely watching the mobile operators Orange, Vodafone, and Telecom Italia because these firms are expanding beyond their national borders. Orange has operations in 33 countries, Vodafone 29 countries, and Telecom Italia 20 countries. To hook the younger market, Vodafone advertises heavily on MTV Europe. Industry authorities believe that Vodafone wants to be considered the Coca-Cola of cell phone communications. A major consolidation might occur, and mergers may occur across continents, such as the partnership between Sony (Japan) and Ericsson (Sweden) or a partnership between Telia (Sweden) and Sonera (Finland). Turkcell wants to be a major player in the European market, but should it go it alone? Should it merge with another company or allow itself to become a subsidiary of a major communications giant?

One leadership approach would be to be the first to offer 3G, the third generation of mobile cell technology, in Turkey. At the end of 2002, Turkcell's infrastructure was at 2.5G. This technology allows a subscriber to use a mobile phone for data transmission, including the sending and receiving of digital pictures, as well as for the provision of wireless Internet services. The 3G technology would allow a subscriber to download and watch videos. The problem is that expected revenues would not cover the cost of adding the required infrastructure. In Europe, mobile communications companies that have moved to the 3G technology have already paid more than $150 billion for the licenses. Industry analysts believe it may take 10 years for them to get back their investments in this technology. Also, the Turkish government has not issued a license allowing Turkcell to move into the 3G technology, but given the risks, should it? Not going to 3G technology may allow another company to get an advantage in future years. The increasing demand for voice is creating capacity problems, and the quality of the service will be diminished. Going to 3G technology will help to build a better infrastructure, but will revenues be enough to cover the costs?

Thus as managers at Turkcell sip their Turkish coffee after finishing a meal at a cafe on Istiklal, they think about this vibrant and dynamic company that they have joined. They wonder: What strategies will allow us to stay a market leader, be one of the largest mobile communications operators in Europe and position ourselves for the ever-increasing communication battle that is bound to come?

BIBLIOGRAPHY

M. Bentley and W. Schomberg, "TIM: Turk Telkom Merge Turkish Mobile Units," *Reuters* (May 13, 2003).

T. Brosnahan and P. Yale, *Turkey*, 5th edition (Australia: Lonely Planet, 1997).

E. Cülcuoğlü, "Upgrading Services: A Technological Imperative," *Turkcell World: The International Magazine of Turkey's Leading GSM Operator*, Issue 1 (Autumn 2000).

DEIK, *Business Guide to Turkey* (Istanbul, Turkey: Foreign Relations Board, March 2002).

S. Delin, "And Snabbit Was Created," *Turkcell World: The International Magazine of Turkey's Leading GSM Operator*, Issue 2 (Winter 2001).

S. Delin, "Congratulations! It's a Family," *Turkcell World: The International Magazine of Turkey's Leading GSM Operator*, Issue 4 (2002).

S. Delin, "Mobile Manners Maketh Man," *Turkcell World: The International Magazine of Turkey's Leading GSM Operator*, Issue 2 (Winter 2001).

H. Dyck and S. Greenfeld, "Inland Technologies, Inc: An ISO 9001 Certified Company" (Case Study), in C. W. L. Hill and G. Jones, *Strategic Management: An Integrated Approach*, 4th ed. (Boston: Houghton Mifflin, 1998).

IGEME—Export Promotion Center of Turkey, *Turkey* (Republic of Turkey: Prime Ministry, Undersecretariat for Foreign Trade, December 2000).

O. Karagoz, Interviews and PowerPoint presentations from the office of the CEO Turkcell. (November 2002–January 2003).

A. Liel, *Turkey in the Middle East: Oil, Islam and Politics* (Boulder, CO: Lynne Riener Publishers, 2001).

N. Taits, "Uzan Fails to Appear for Questioning," *Durrants* (December 2002), p. 26.

R. B. Tekin, "Turkish Economic Conditions," unpublished paper (Marmara University, 2002).

Turkcell, *Annual Reports*, 1999 through 2001.

Turkcell, "Corporate Profile" (brochure).

"Turkey," *Encyclopedia Americana International Edition*, Vol. 27, pp. 247–254.

Turkish–U.S. Business Council (TUSBC) of DEIK, "Turkish–U.S. Economic Relations" brochure (March 2002).

www.odci.gov/cia/publications/factbook/geos/tu.html (September 10, 2002).

www.turkcell.com.tr/english/history.html (November 15, 2002).

CASE 9

Guajilote Cooperativo Forestal, Honduras

Nathan Nebbe and J. David Hunger

GUAJILOTE (PRONOUNCED WA-HEE-LOW-TAY) COOPERATIVO FORESTAL WAS A FORESTRY cooperative that operated out of Chaparral, a small village located in the buffer zone of La Muralla
National Park in Honduras' Olancho province. Olancho was one of 18 Honduran provinces
and was located inland, bordering Nicaragua. The cooperative was one result of a relatively
new movement among international donor agencies promoting sustainable economic development of developing countries' natural resources.[1] A cooperative in Honduras was
similar to a cooperative in the United States: It was an enterprise jointly owned and operated by members who used its facilities and services.

Guajilote was founded in 1991 as a component of a USAID (United States Agency for International Development) project. The project attempted to develop La Muralla National Park
as an administrative and socioeconomic model that COHDEFOR (the Honduran forestry development service) could transfer to Honduras' other national parks. The Guajilote Cooperativo Forestal was given the right to exploit naturally fallen (not chopped down) mahogany
trees in La Muralla's buffer zone. Thus far, it was the only venture in Honduras with this right.
A buffer zone was the designated area within a park's boundaries but outside its core protected
zone. People were allowed to live and engage in economically sustainable activities within this
buffer zone.

In 1998, Guajilote was facing some important issues and concerns that could affect not
only its future growth but its very survival. For one thing, the amount of mahogany wood was
limited and was increasingly being threatened by forest fires, illegal logging, and slash-and-
burn agriculture. If the total number of mahogany trees continued to decline, trade in its wood
could be restricted internationally. For another, the cooperative had no way to transport its
wood to market and was thus forced to accept low prices for its wood from the only distributor in the area. What could be done to guarantee the survival of the cooperative?

Operations

Guajilote's work activities included three operations using very simple technologies. First, members searched the area to locate appropriate fallen trees. This, in itself, could be very difficult since mahogany trees were naturally rare. These trees were found at elevations up to 1,800 meters (5,400 feet) and normally were found singly or in small clusters of no more than four to eight trees per hectare (2.2 acres).[2]

Finding fallen mahogany in La Muralla's buffer zone was hampered due to the area's steep and sometimes treacherous terrain. (*La Muralla* means "steep wall of rock" in Spanish.) The work was affected by the weather. For example, more downed trees were available during the wet season due to storms and higher soil moisture—leading to the uprooting of trees.

Second, the cooperative set up a temporary hand-sawmill as close as possible to a fallen tree. Due to the steep terrain, it was often difficult to find a suitable location nearby to operate the hand-sawmill. Once a suitable work location was found, men used a large cross-cut saw to disassemble the tree into various components. The disassembling process was a long and arduous process that could take weeks for an especially large tree. The length of time it took to process a tree depended on the tree's size—mature mahogany trees could be gigantic. Tree size thus affected how many trees Guajilote was able to process in a year.

Third, after a tree was disassembled, the wood was either carried out of the forest using a combination of mule and human power or floated down a stream or river. Even if a stream happened to be near a fallen tree, it was typically usable only during the wet season. The wood was then sold to a distributor who, in turn, transported it via trucks to the cities to sell to furniture makers for a profit.

Guajilote's permit to use fallen mahogany was originally granted in 1991 for a 10-year period by COHDEFOR. The permit was simply written, and stated that if Guajilote restricted itself to downed mahogany, its permit renewal should be granted automatically. The administrator of the area's COHDEFOR office indicated that if things remained as they were, Guajilote should not have any problem obtaining renewal in 2001. Given the nature of Honduran politics, however, nothing could be completely assured.

In 1998, Guajilote's mahogany was still sold as a commodity. The cooperative did very little to add value to its product. Nevertheless, the continuing depletion of mahogany trees around the world meant that the remaining wood should increase in value over time.

Management and Human Resources

Santos Munguia, 29 years old, had been Guajilote's leader since 1995. Although Munguia had only a primary school education, he was energetic and intelligent and had proven to be a very skillful politician. In addition to directing Guajilote, Munguia farmed a small parcel of land and raised a few head of cattle. He was also involved in local politics.

Munguia had joined the cooperative in 1994. Although he had not been one of Guajilote's original members, he quickly became its de facto leader in 1995, when he renegotiated a better price for the sale of the cooperative's wood.

Before Munguia joined the cooperative, Guajilote had been receiving between 3 and 4 lempiras ($0.37, or 11 lempiras to the dollar) per foot of cut mahogany from its sole distributor, Juan Suazo. No other distributors were available in this remote location. The distributor transported the wood to Tegucigalpa or San Pedro Sula and sold it for 16 to 18 lempiras per foot. Believing that Suazo was taking advantage of the cooperative, Munguia negotiated a price increase to 7 to 8 lempiras per foot ($0.60 to $0.62 per foot at the July 15, 1998, exchange rate) by putting political pressure on Suazo. The distributor agreed to the price increase only after a police investigation had been launched to investigate his business dealings. (Rumors circulated that Suazo was transporting and selling illegally logged mahogany by mixing it with that purchased from Guajilote.)

Munguia: El Caudillo

After renegotiating successfully with the cooperative's distributor, Munguia quickly became the group's caudillo (strong man). The caudillo was a Latin American political and social institution. A caudillo was a (typically male) purveyor of patronage. All decisions went through, and were usually made by, him. A caudillo was often revered, feared, and hated at the same time because of the power he wielded. Munguia was viewed by many in the area as an ascending caudillo because of his leadership of Guajilote.

Guajilote did not operate in a democratic fashion. Munguia made all the decisions—sometimes with input from his second in command and nephew, Miguel Flores Munguia—and handled all of Guajilote's financial matters. Guajilote's members did not seem to have a problem with this management style. The prevailing opinion seemed to be that Guajilote was a lot better off with Munguia running the show by himself than with more involvement by the members. One man put the members' view very succinctly: "Santos, he saved us (from Suazo, from COHDEFOR, from ourselves)."

Guajilote's organizational structure emphasized Munguia's importance. He was alone at the top in his role as decision maker. If, in the future, Munguia became more involved in politics and other ventures that could take him out of Chaparral (possibly for long periods of time), he would very likely be forced to spend less time with Guajilote's operations. Munguia's leadership has been of key importance to Guajilote's maturing as both a work group and as a business. In 1998, there did not seem to be another person in the cooperative that could take Munguia's place.

Guajilote's Members

When founded, the cooperative had been composed of 15 members. Members were initially selected for the cooperative by employees of USAID and COHDEFOR. The number of employees has held steady over time. Since the cooperative's founding, 3 original members have quit; 4 others were allowed to join. Although no specific reasons were given for members leaving, they appeared to be because of personality differences, family problems, or differences of opinion. No money had been paid to them when they left the cooperative. In 1998 there were 16 members in the cooperative.

None of Guajilote's members had any education beyond primary school. Many of the members had no schooling at all and were illiterate. As a whole, the group knew little of markets or business practices.

Guajilote's existence has had an important impact on its members. One member stated that before he had joined Guajilote, he was lucky to have made 2,000 lempiras in a year, whereas he made around 1,000 to 1,500 in one month as a member of the cooperative. He stated that all five of his children were in school, something that he could not have afforded previously. Before joining the cooperative, he had been involved in subsistence farming and other activities that brought in a small amount of money and food. He said that his children had been required previously to work as soon as they were able. As a simple farmer, he often had to leave his family to find work, mostly migrant farm work, to help his family survive. Because of Guajilote, his family now had enough to eat, and he was able to be home with his family.

This was a common story among Guajilote's members. The general improvement in its members' quality of life also appeared to have strengthened the cooperative members' personal bonds with each other.

Financial Situation

No formal public financial records were available. As head of the cooperative, Munguia kept informal records. Guajilote's 1997 revenues were approximately 288,000 lempiras (US$22,153). (Revenues for 1996 were not available.) Guajilote processed around 36,000 feet of wood during 1997. Very little of the money was held back for capital improvement purchases due to the operation's simple material needs. Capital expenditures for 1997 included a mule plus materials needed to maintain Guajilote's large cross-cut saws.

Each of Guajilote's 16 members was paid an average of about 1,500 lempiras (US$113) per month in 1997 and 1,300 lempiras (US$100) per month in 1996. 1998 payments per month had been similar to 1997's payments, according to Guajilote's members. Money was paid to members based on their participation in Guajilote's operations.

There was conjecture, among some workers, that Munguia and his second in charge were paying themselves more than the other members were receiving. When Munguia was asked if he received a higher wage than the others because of his administrative position in the group, he responded that everything was distributed evenly. An employee of COHDEFOR indicated, however, that Munguia had purchased a house in La Union—the largest town in the area. That person conjectured, based on this evidence, that Munguia was likely receiving more from the cooperative than were the other members.

Issues Facing the Cooperative

Guajilote's size and growth potential were limited by the amount of mahogany it could produce in a year. Mahogany was fairly rare in the forest, and Guajilote was legally restricted to downed trees. Moreover, with the difficulties of finding, processing by hand, and then moving the wood out of the forest, Guajilote was further restricted in the quantity of wood it could handle.

Lack of transportation was a major problem for Guajilote. The cooperative had been unable to secure the capital needed to buy its own truck; lending through legitimate sources was very tight in Honduras and enterprises like Guajilote did not typically have access to lines of credit. Although the prices the cooperative was receiving for its wood had improved, the men still thought that the distributor, Juan Suazo, was not paying them what the wood was worth. It was argued that when demand was high for mahogany, the cooperative gave up as much as 10 lempiras per foot in sales to Suazo. Guajilote could conceivably double its revenues if it could somehow haul its wood to Honduras' major market centers and sell it without use of a distributor. The closest market center was Tegucigalpa—three to four hours from Chaparral on dangerous, often rain soaked, mountain roads.

A Possibility

Some of the members of Guajilote wondered if the cooperative could do better financially by skipping the distributor completely. It was possible that some specialty shops (chains and independents) and catalogs throughout the world might be interested in selling high-quality mahogany furniture, i.e., chests or chairs, that were produced in an environmentally friendly manner. Guajilote, unfortunately, had no highly skilled carpenters or furniture makers in its membership. There were, however, a couple towns in Honduras with highly skilled furniture makers who worked on a contract basis.

A U.S. citizen with a furniture export business in Honduras worked with a number of independent furniture makers on contract to make miniature ornamental chairs. This exporter reviewed Guajilote's situation and concluded that the cooperative might be able to make and market furniture very profitably—even if it had to go through an exporter to find suitable markets. Upon studying Guajilote's operations, he estimated that Guajilote might be able to more than treble its revenues. In order to do this, however, the exporter felt that Guajilote would have to overcome problems with transportation and upgrade its administrative competence. Guajilote would need to utilize the talents of its members more if it were to widen its operational scope. It would have to purchase trucks and hire drivers to transport the wood over treacherous mountain roads. The role of administrator would become much more demanding, thus forcing Munguia to delegate some authority to others in the cooperative.

Concerns

In spite of Guajilote's improved outlook, there were many concerns that could affect the cooperative's future. A serious concern was the threat of deforestation through fires, illegal logging (i.e., poaching of mahogany as well as clear cutting), and slash-and-burn agriculture.

Small fires were typically set to prepare soils for planting and to help clear new areas for cultivation. Often these fires were either not well supervised or burned out of the control of the people starting them. Due to the 1998 drought, the number of out-of-control forest fires had been far greater than normal. There seemed to be a consensus among Hondurans that 1998 would be one of the worst years for forest fires. Mahogany and tropical deciduous forests are not fire resistant. Fires not only kill adult and young mahogany trees, but they also destroy their seeds.[3] Mahogany could therefore be quickly eliminated from a site. Each year, Guajilote lost more area from which it could take mahogany.

To make matters worse, many Hondurans considered the area around La Muralla National Park to be a frontier open to settlement by landless campesinos (peasant farmers). In fleeing poverty and desertification, people were migrating to the Olancho province in large numbers.[4] Not only did they clear the forests for cultivation, but they also cut wood for fuel and for use in building their homes. Most of the new settlements were being established in the area's best mahogany growing habitats.

Another concern was that of potential restrictions by CITIES (the international convention on trade in endangered species). Although trade in mahogany was still permitted, it was supposed to be monitored very closely. If the populations of the 12 mahogany species continued to decrease, it was possible that mahogany would be given even greater protection under the CITIES framework. This could include even tighter restrictions on the trade in mahogany or could even result in an outright ban similar to the worldwide ban on ivory trading.

NOTES

1. K. Norsworthy, *Inside Honduras* (Albuquerque, NM: Inter-Hemispheric Education Resource, 1993), pp. 133–138.
2. H. Lamprecht, *Silviculture in the Tropics* (Hamburg, Germany: Verlag, 1989), pp. 245–246.
3. Ibid.
4. K. Norsworthy, *Inside Honduras* (Albuquerque, NM: Inter-Hemispheric Education Resource, 1993), pp. 133–138.

CASE **10**

Apple Computer and Steve P. Jobs (2006):

PIXAR ANIMATION AND WALT DISNEY COMPANY

Moustafa H. Abdelsamad, Hitesh (John) Adhia, David B. Croll, Alan N. Hoffman, Charles E. Michaels Jr., and Thomas L. Wheelen

COMPARED TO OTHER FORTUNE 500 COMPANIES, APPLE COMPUTER HAS ALWAYS BEEN AN interesting and often exciting firm. It had been the first to make and mass-market a personal computer with its Apple IIc. The company had been the darling of the stock market in the mid-1980s when it cemented its technological advantage through the introduction of its state-of-the-art Macintosh (MAC) personal computer. Nevertheless, the Microsoft Windows operating system and Office software coupled with Intel microprocessors left Apple far behind in PC market share by the mid-1990s. Apple Computer had fallen to being just a niche player in the industry. At that time, it was rumored that the company had little future unless it merged with or sold out to another computer company. With the beginning of the 21st century, Apple's fortunes changed for the better. The introduction of the iPod catapulted Apple back into the spotlight, just at a time when Microsoft and Intel seemed to be losing momentum.

2006 was another exciting year for Apple Computer and for its management and shareholders—full of both good news and bad news.

Good News

On May 23, 2006, Apple and Nike announced a joint-technology running shoe. The new Nike shoe would have a sensor placed in a small pocket of the shoe, and a wireless receiver on the iPod Nano. The two devices were to communicate wirelessly so the runner would be able to track distances covered, calories burned, and time spent exercising. The data was to be accessible in two ways: (1) by clicking on a button and hearing it through headphones, and (2) by looking at a menu on the screen.[1]

On August 2, 2006, Coke and Apple announced that Coke would offer codes for 70 million free iTunes to German and UK Coke customers. Coke was to be allowed to link its Web site with Apple's iTunes site.[2]

On August 23, 2006, Apple partnered with General Motors, Ford Motor, and Mazda Motor to make iPods compatible with 2007 model car stereo systems. This would cover about 70% of the cars manufactured by their three companies.[3]

On October 9, 2006, Apple Computer announced that fourth-quarter (ending September 30, 2006) profits rose 27% to $546 million, and revenues rose 32% to $4.84 billion when compared with 2005 results. Mac shipments reached 1.61 million computers, which was the highest sales in the company's history. The sales were driven by the new notebooks with the faster Intel microprocessor. Apple began using the Intel chip in January, and completed the transition in August. Mac sales were up 37% to $2.21 billion. This was the eighth straight quarter that Mac sales were over a million units. Notebooks sales were up 63% and accounted for 61% of computer sales. Notebook sales outpaced the revenues for desktop systems including the Mac. Macs comprised 46% of Apple's revenues, whereas iPods and music sold through iTunes accounted for 42%.[4]

The new iPod nano and the video player with increased storage capacity were released in September 2006. These new products assisted in driving sales up 35.3% to 8.73 million units. Apple had a 75.6% market share of music portable players in the United States, SunDisk had 9.7% and Creative Technology was in third place with 4.3%.[5] Microsoft planned to release its music player for the 2006 Christmas season with a price of $250. During fiscal 2006, Apple Computer sold 41,385,000 iPods, which was more than double the 2005 sales of 20,443,000. The quarterly growth rates from year to year for the iPods ranged from a low of 32% to an extremely high growth rate of 624.2% (see **Exhibit 1**).[6]

On November 8, 2006, Apple's management announced that iTunes Latino would offer Spanish language and bilingual shows in cooperation with NBC Universal's Telemundo. It was also to offer regional Mexican baladas y boleros and pop Latino.[7]

An announcement on November 1, 2006, stated that wireless carrier Cingular was teaming with Napster and Yahoo and did not plan to work with Apple. Napster was to have a

EXHIBIT 1
Quarterly Units Shipped and Percent Change from Year to Year Apple Computer, Inc. (Units in thousands)

Year Quarter		Macintosh	Year to Year Change (%)	iPod	Year to Year Change (%)
2006	4	1,610	30	8,710	51
	3	1,327	12	8,117	32
	2	1,112	4	8,521	60.1
	1	1,254	20	14,043	207
2005	4	1,236	48	5,751	186.2
	3	1,182	35	6,155	624.2
	2	1,070	43	5,321	559.4
	1	1,046	26	4,580	525
2004	4	836	6	2,010	500
	3	876	14	850	183
	2	748	5	807	909
	1	829	12	733	235

Notes:
The 4th quarter ended on September 30th.
The 3rd quarter ended on June 30th.
The 2nd quarter ended on March 30th.
The 1st quarter ended on December 29th.

SOURCE: *Apple Computer, Inc., company quarterly press releases.*

$15 monthly fee. Cingular was jointly owned by AT&T and BellSouth. An analyst commented that this strategic alliance was not a major setback for Apple. According to analyst Jonathan Hoopers: "Apple might opt out with its upcoming iPhone to become 'a mobile virtual network operator' which could be a better deal."

On November 12, 2006, Apple announced that it had made an agreement with six airlines, Air France, Continental, Delta, Emirates, KLM, and United, to install iPod connections in their in-flight entertainment systems. This was scheduled for mid-2007.[8]

On November 16, 2006, Apple announced that its iPhone, the highly anticipated iPod cell phone, would include a 2.0-megapixel digital camera. An analyst estimated that this phone could add 22% to Apple's earnings in 2007. A Taiwanese source "has confirmed that an Apple iPod iPhone is now in production and that more than 10 million will be available in January, [so] . . . Steve Jobs can formally launch the new [iPhone] at Macworld in January." In addition to the iPhone, an iTV is expected in 2007. An industry analyst predicted "2007 to be one of the most exciting in Apple's history."[9]

Bad News

On August 3, 2006, a French law required Apple Computer to make its iPod player and iTunes online store compatible with rival offerings. This law was initially written to level the playing field to allow smaller rivals to compete with companies such as Sony and Apple. Apple argued that the opening of its formats would encourage software pirates. Other EU countries were looking at similar laws.[10]

On August 24, 2006, Apple management announced the recall of 1.8 million laptop batteries. The batteries were manufactured by Sony. Dell had a similar recall of 4.1 million of these Sony batteries.[11]

On September 1, 2006, the Chinese government told Hongfujin Precision Industry, a supplier of Apple Computer's iPod, to allow more than 200,000 workers to establish a trade union. China did not allow independent labor unions, but the Chinese government had been pressuring foreign-invested companies to allow state-sanctioned labor unions.[12]

On September 5, 2006, SpiralFrog, a new online music service, signed an agreement with EMI Music Publishing to authorize SpiralFrog to use EMI's music catalog for legal downloading in the United States. SpiralFrog had signed a similar deal with Universal Music Group, a unit of Vivendi. Artists covered in these deals included Sting, Nelly Furtado, Jay Z, and Kanye West.[13]

On October 21, 2006, Jon Loch Johansen, age 22, said that he had cracked Apple's iTunes copyright restrictions. The copyright protection stopped iPod users from playing downloaded music from music stores other than iTunes. The copyright protection also stopped music that had been used on an iPod from being played on a competitive music player. Johansen's Norwegian company, Double Twin Venture, planned to license the code to businesses that could use the code to sell downloadable music for playing on an iPod. Several analysts expected Apple to take legal action against Johansen and his company. In response, Johansen claimed "that he has developed (a legal) way around any restrictions."[14]

When only 15 years of age, Johansen worked with two other European programmers to hack the DVD protection code. The hackers created a free program, DeCSS, which was available on the Internet. DeCSS software allowed the user to unlock a DVD's copy protection. This allowed users to play and make copies of movies with their computers. Johansen earned the name "DVD Jon" for this hacking effort. There was a series of lawsuits in Norway and the United States.[15]

Real Networks, Inc., the owner of the RealPlayer Music Store, announced on October 21, 2006, that it was introducing a new product, Harmony. Harmony would let customers download music from the RealPlayer online store and allow them to use it on any portable music player. In response, an Apple spokesperson said that the company was looking into Real's actions under various laws, including the Digital Copyright Millennium Act, which prohibited the manufacture, sale, or distribution of code-breaking devices. Real Networks stood firm. A Real Networks executive said, "We remain committed to Harmony and to giving millions of consumers who own portable music devices, including the Apple iPod, choice and compatibility."[16]

Stock Option Investigation

On January 23, 2006, Apple announced "an internal probe uncovered irregularities related to the company's issuance of stock options granted between 1997 and 2001 when its shares fell 3 percent." The board of directors had hired an independent counsel to perform the investigation and to inform the U.S. Securities and Exchange Commission (SEC) of the probe.[17]

The internal probe resulted in examining more than 650,000 e-mails and documents and interviews of more than 40 current and former employees, directors, and advisors. A company representative said that "Jobs knew that some grants had given favorable dates 'in a few instances,' but he did not benefit from them and was not aware of the accounting implications." The investigative report "did not uncover any misconduct by any members of Apple's current management team, but it did raise serious concerns regarding the actions of two former executives." The investigation may have prompted the September 30, 2006, resignation of former Chief Financial Officer (CFO) Fred Anderson from the board.[18]

Steve Jobs stated: "I apologize to Apple's shareholders and employees for these problems, which happened on my watch. They are completely out of character for Apple." He further stated: "We will now work to resolve the remaining issues as quickly as possible and to put the proper remedial measures in place to ensure that this never happens again."[19]

On August 2, 2006, management announced that the company would likely need to restate earnings and delay filing its quarterly SEC report (10-Q) because of additional irregularities the company found in its accounting of stock options. Apple's stock fell 6.6% after this announcement. As of November 12, 2006, the company had not yet filed complete SEC-required financial statements or SEC 10-Q reports for the third and fourth quarters, and its yearly 10-K form.[20]

The problem of backdating stock options in order to maximize executive compensation existed in more than 120 other U.S. companies. Although backdating was not prohibited under SEC regulations, companies are now required to record non-cash charges for compensation expenses relating to these stock options and to restate past financial statements where this occurred.[21]

On October 10, 2006, McAfee announced that the board had fired President Weiss, and that George Sameriuk, CEO and Chairman, "will retire after stock option investigation into accounting problems that will require financial restatements." The restatements of $100 to $150 million "would cover a 10-year period."[22]

On October 12, 2006, the Minnesota attorney general's office was planning to investigate United Health Group Inc.'s stock options. United Health was already under investigation by federal regulators for "the stock options grant timing for 11 executives of the company."[23]

Apple Threatened with Delisting from the NASDAQ Exchange

In August 2006, Apple and more than a dozen other companies were warned by NASDAQ of their possibly delisting because they were late in filing their quarterly report (third quarter) as these companies worked to untangle their options accounting.[24]

Between 1995 and 2004, more than 7,300 companies were delisted from U.S. stock markets. About half were involuntary delisting. During the period 2000 to 2004, 3,000 companies were delisted from NASDAQ. A Georgetown study by Professor James L. Angel found that "roughly one for every five on the exchange in any given year . . . were delisted."[25]

Apple could have filed a tardy report with the SEC before its requested NASDAQ hearing. The filing was for the third quarter, which ended on July 1, 2005. As of October 10, 2006, the SEC 10-Q had not yet been filed.

History of Apple Computer[26]

The history of Apple Computer can be broken into four separate time periods, each with its own strategic issues and concerns.

1976–1984: The Founders Build a Company

Founded in a California garage on April 1, 1976, Apple created the personal computer revolution with powerful yet easy-to-use machines for the desktop. Steve Jobs sold his Volkswagen bus and Steve Wozniak hocked his HP programmable calculator to raise $1,300 in seed money to start their new company. Not long afterward, a mutual friend helped recruit A.C. "Mike" Markkula to help market the company and give it a million-dollar image. Even though all three founders had left the company's management team during the 1980s, Markkula continued serving on Apple's Board of Directors until August 1997.

The early success of Apple was attributed largely to marketing and technological innovation. In the high-growth industry of personal computers in the early 1980s, Apple grew quickly, staying ahead of competitors by contributing key products that stimulated the development of software for the computer. Landmark programs such as Visicalc (forerunner to Lotus 1-2-3 and other spreadsheet programs) were developed first for the Apple II. Apple also secured early dominance in the education and consumer markets by awarding hundreds of thousands of dollars in grants to schools and individuals for the development of education software.

Even with enormous competition, Apple revenues continued to grow at an unprecedented rate, reaching $583.3 million by fiscal 1982. The introduction of the Macintosh graphical user interface in 1984, which included icons, pull-down menus, and windows, became the catalyst for desktop publishing and instigated the second technological revolution attributable to Apple. Apple kept the architecture of the Macintosh proprietary, that is, it could not be cloned like the "open system" IBM PC. This allowed the company to charge a premium for its distinctive "user-friendly" features.

A shakeout in the personal computer industry began in 1983 when IBM entered the PC market, first affecting companies selling low-priced machines to consumers. Companies that made strategic blunders or that lacked sufficient distribution or brand awareness of their products disappeared.

1985–1997: Professional Managers Fail to Extend the Company

In 1985, amid a slumping market, Apple saw the departure of its founders, Jobs and Wozniak. As Chairman of the Board, Jobs had recruited John Sculley, an experienced executive from PepsiCo, to replace Jobs as Apple's CEO in 1983. Jobs had challenged Sculley when recruiting him by saying, "Do you want to spend the rest of your life selling sugared water, or do you want to change the world?" Jobs willingly gave up his title as CEO so that he could have Sculley as his mentor. In 1985, a power struggle took place between Sculley and Jobs. With his entrepreneurial orientation, Jobs wanted to continue taking the company in risky new directions. Sculley, in contrast, felt that Apple had grown to the point where it needed not only to be more careful in its strategic moves, but also to be better organized and rationally managed. The board of directors supported Sculley's request to strip Jobs of his duties. The board felt that the company needed an experienced executive to lead Apple into its next stage of development.

Jobs then resigned from the company he had founded and sold all but one share of his Apple stock. Under the leadership of John Sculley, CEO and Chairman, the company engineered a remarkable turnaround. He instituted a massive reorganization to streamline operations and expenses. It was during this time that Wozniak left the company. Macintosh sales gained momentum throughout 1986 and 1987. Sales increased 40% from $1.9 billion to $2.7 billion in fiscal 1987, and earnings jumped 41% to $217 million.

In the early 1990s, Apple sold more personal computers than any other computer company. Net sales grew to over $7 billion, net income to over $540 million, and earnings per share to $4.33. The period from 1993 to 1995 was, however, a time of considerable change in the management of Apple. The industry was rapidly changing. Personal computers using Microsoft's Windows operating system and Office software plus Intel microprocessors began to dominate the personal computer market place. (The alliance between Microsoft and Intel was known in the trade as Wintel.) Dell, Hewlett-Packard, Compaq, and Gateway replaced both IBM and Apple as the primary makers of PCs. The new Windows system had successfully imitated the user-friendly "look and feel" of Apple's Macintosh operating system. As a result, Apple lost its competitive edge. In June 1993, Sculley was forced to resign and Michael H. Spindler was appointed CEO of the company. At this time, Apple was receiving a number of offers to acquire the company. Many of the company's executives advocated Apple's merging with another company. When no merger took place, many executives chose to resign.

Unable to reverse the company's falling sales, Spindler was soon forced out and Gilbert Amelio was hired from outside Apple to serve as CEO. Amelio's regime presided over an accelerated loss of market share, deteriorating earnings, and stock that had lost half of its value, Apple's refusal to license the Mac operating system to other manufacturers had given Microsoft the opening it needed to take the market with its Windows operating system. Wintel PCs now dominated the market—pushing Apple into a steadily declining market niche composed primary of artisans and teachers. By 1996, Apple's management seemed be in utter disarray.

Looking for a new product with which Apple could retake the initiative in personal computers, the company bought NeXT for $402 million on December 20, 1996. Steve Jobs had formed the NeXT computer company when he left Apple. Jobs had envisioned his new company as the developer of the "next generation" in personal computers. Part of the purchase agreement was that Jobs would return to Apple as a consultant. In July of 1997, Amelio resigned and was replaced by Steve Jobs as Apple's interim CEO (iCEO). This ended Steve Jobs' 14-year exile from the company that he and Wozniak had founded. In addition to being iCEO of Apple, Jobs also served as CEO of Pixar, a company he had personally purchased from Lucasfilm for $5 million. Receiving only $1.00 a year as CEO of both Pixar and Apple, Jobs held the Guinness World Record as the "Lowest Paid Chief Executive Officer."

1998 to 2001: Jobs Leads Apple "Back to the Future"

Once in position as Apple's CEO, Steve Jobs terminated many of the company's existing projects. Dropped were the iBook and the AirPort products series, which had helped popularize the use of wireless LAN technology to connect a computer to a network.

In May 2001, the company announced the reopening of Apple Retail Stores. Like IBM and Xerox, Apple had opened its own retail stores to market its computers during the 1980s. All such stores had been closed when Wintel-type computers began being sold by mass merchandisers, such as Sears and Circuit City, and through corporate Web sites.

The iPod portable digital audio player was introduced, and the company opened its own iTunes music store to provide downloaded music to iPod users. Given the thorny copyright issues inherent in the music business, analysts doubted if the new product would be successful.

2002–2006: A Corporate Renaissance?

In 2002, Apple introduced a redesigned iMac using a 64-bit processor. The iMac had a hemispherical base and a flat-panel all-digital display. Although it received a lot of press, the iMac failed to live up to its sales expectations.

In 2004 and 2005, Apple opened its first retail stores in Europe and Canada. By November 2006, the company had 149 stores in the United States, 4 stores in Canada, 7 stores in the United Kingdom, and 7 stores in Japan.

In 2006, Jobs announced that Apple would sell an Intel-based Macintosh. Previously Microsoft had purchased all of its microprocessors from Motorola. By this time, Microsoft's operating system with Intel microprocessors was running on 97.5% of the personal computers sold, with Apple having only a 2.5% share of the market. The first Intel-based machines, the iMac and MacBook Pro, were introduced.

By this time, Apple's iPod had emerged as the market leader of a completely new industry category, which it had created. In 2006, Apple controlled 75.6% of the market, followed by SunDisk with 9.7%, and Creative Technology in third place with 4.3%. Although one analyst predicted that more than 30 million iPods would be sold in fiscal 2006, Apple actually sold 41,385,000. Taking advantage of its lead in music downloading, the company's next strategic move was to extend its iTunes music stores by offering movies for $9.99 each. An analyst reviewing this strategic move said, "Apple was able to create a $1 billion-a-year market for the legal sale of music. Apple may be able to provide the movie industry with a similar formula."

Steven P. Jobs: Entrepreneur and Corporate Executive[27]

Steve P. Jobs was born on February 24, 1955, in San Francisco and was currently married with three daughters. He was adopted by Paul and Clara Jobs in February 1955. In 1972, Jobs graduated from Homestead High School in Los Altos, California. His high school electronics teacher said, "He was somewhat of a loner and always had a different way of looking at things."[28] After graduation, Jobs was hired by Hewlett-Packard as a summer employee. This is where he met Steve Wozniak, a recent dropout from The University of California at Berkeley. Wozniak had a genius IQ and was an engineering whiz with a passion for inventing electronic gadgets. At this time, Wozniak was perfecting his "blue box," an illegal pocket-size telephone attachment that allowed the user to make free long-distance calls. Jobs helped Wozniak sell this device to customers.[29]

In 1972, Jobs enrolled at Reed College in Portland, Oregon, but dropped out after one semester. He remained around Reed for a year and became involved in the counterculture. He enrolled in various classes in philosophy and other topics. In a later speech at Stanford University, Jobs explained, "If I had never dropped in on that single course (calligraphy), that Mac would have never had multiple type faces or proportionally spaced fonts."[30]

In early 1974, Jobs took a job as a video-game designer for Atari, a pioneer in electronic arcade games. After earning enough money, Jobs went to India in search of personal spiritual enlightenment. Later that year, Jobs returned to California and began attending meetings of Steve Wozniak's "Homebrew Computer Club." Wozniak converted his TV monitor into what would become a computer. Wozniak was a very good engineer and extremely interested in creating new electronic devices. Jobs was not interested in developing new devices, but he realized the marketability of Wozniak's converted TV. Together they designed the Apple I computer in Jobs' bedroom and built the first prototype in Jobs' garage. Jobs showed the Apple I to a local electronics retailer, the Byte Shop, and received a $25,000 order for 50 computers. Jobs took this purchase order to Cramer Electronics to order the components needed to assemble the 50 computers.

The local credit manager asked Jobs how he was going to pay for the parts and he replied, "I have this purchase order from the Byte Shop chain of computer stores for 50 of my computers and the payment terms are COD. If you give me the parts on a net 30 day terms, I can build and deliver the computers in that time frame, collect my money from Turrell at the Byte Shop and pay you." With that, the credit manager called Paul Terrell who was attending an IEEE computer conference . . . and verified the validity of the purchase order. Amazed at the tenacity of Jobs, Turrell assured the credit manager if the computers showed up in his stores Jobs would be paid and would have more than enough money to pay for the parts order. The two Steves and their small crew spent day and night building and testing the computers and delivered to Turrell on time to pay his suppliers and have a tidy profit left over for their celebration and next order. Steve Jobs had found a way to finance his soon-to-be multimillion-dollar company without giving away one share of stock or ownership.[31]

Jobs and Wozniak decided to start a computer company to manufacture and sell personal computers. They contributed $1,300 of their own money to start the business. Jobs selected the name Apple for the company based on his memories of a summer job as an orchard worker. On April 1, 1976, Apple Computer Company was formed as a partnership.

During Jobs' early tenure at Apple, he was a persuasive and charismatic evangelist for Apple. Some of his employees have described him at that time as an erratic and tempestuous manager. An analyst said "many persons who look at Jobs' management style forget that he was 30 years old in 1985 and he received his management and leadership education on the job." Jobs guided the company's revenues to $1,515,616,000 and profits of $64,055,000 in 1984. Jobs was cited in several articles as having a demanding and aggressive personality. One analyst said that these two attributes described most of the successful entrepreneurs. Jobs strategically managed the company through a period of new product introduction, rapidly changing technology, and intense competition—a time when many companies have failed.

In 1985, after leaving Apple, Jobs formed a new computer company, NeXT Computer Inc. NeXT was a computer company that built machines with futuristic designs and ran the UNIX-derived NeXT step operating system. It was marketed to academic and scientific organizations. NeXT was not a commercial success, in part because of its high price. Jobs served as Chairman and CEO.[32]

In 1986, Jobs purchased Pixar Animation from Lucasfilm for $5 million. He provided another $5 million in capital, owned 50.6% of the stock, and served as Chairman and CEO. Pixar created three of the six highest domestic grossing (gross revenues) animated films of all time—*Toy Story* (1995), *A Bug's Life* (1998), and *Toy Story II* (1999). These films were released under a partnership with the Walt Disney Company. Each of these films was the highest grossing animated film for the year in which it was released. During this period, Jobs delegated more to his executives. Many analysts felt that the excellent executive staff and animators were prime reasons that Disney management subsequently wanted to acquire Pixar. Jobs served as CEO of NeXT and Pixar from 1985 to 1997. Jobs sold NeXT in 1996 to Apple for $402 million and became iCEO of Apple in July 1997.[33]

At Pixar, Jobs focused on business duties, which was different than his earlier management style at Apple. The creative staff was given a great deal of autonomy. Sources say he spent less than one day a week at the Pixar campus in Emeryville, just across the San Francisco Bay from Apple's headquarters. A Pixar employee said, "Steve did not tell us what to do." He further stated, "Steve's our benevolent benefactor."[34]

Michael D, Eisner, CEO of the Walt Disney Company, did not have a smooth relationship with Jobs during the years of the Pixar/Disney partnership. Critics explained that Eisner was unable to work with Jobs because both men were supremely confident (some said arrogant) that their own judgment was correct—regardless of what others said. In 2005, in response to Eisner's unwillingness to modify Disney's movie distribution agreement with Pixar, Jobs refused to renew the contract. At the time, Disney's own animation unit was faltering and unable to match Pixar's new computer technology and creativity. Concerned with Eisner's leadership style and his inability to support the company's distinctive competence in animation, Roy Disney led a shareholders' revolt. On October 1, 2005, Eisner was replaced by Robert A. Iger as CEO of Disney.[35]

On January 24, 2006, CEO Iger announced that Disney had agreed to pay $7.4 billion in stock to acquire Pixar Animation Studios. Since this deal made Jobs the largest stockholder (6.67%) in Disney, he was appointed to Disney's board of directors.[36]

Edward S. Woodward, Jr., former Chairman of Apple Computer, told Apple's board of directors: "He (Jobs) has a good relationship with you; there is nobody better with you; there is nobody better in the world to work with. Iger made a very wise move, and two years from now everyone will be saying that."[37]

Peter Burrows and Ronald Grover in an article said: "The alliance between Jobs and Disney is full of promise. If he can bring to Disney the same kind of industry-sharing, boundary-busting energy that has lifted Apple and Pixar sky-high, he could help the staid company become the leading laboratory for media convergences. It's not hard to imagine a day when you could fire up your Apple TV and watch net-only spin-offs of popular TV shows from Disney's ABC Inc. (DIS). Or use your Apple iPhone to watch Los Angeles Lakers superstar Kobe Bryant's video biog delivered via Disney's ESPN Inc. 'We've been talking about a lot of things, said Jobs. 'It's going to be a pretty exciting world looking ahead over the next five years.'"[38]

An expert on Jobs asked, "*So what is Jobs' secret?*" His answer: "There are many, but it starts with focus and a non-religious faith in his strategy." In his return to Apple, he took a proprietary approach as he cut dozen of projects and products. Many on Wall Street were not initially happy with Jobs' new directions for the company, but soon were impressed by the Apple's successful turnaround.[39]

Corporate Governance[40]

Exhibit 2 lists the seven members of the board of directors and the executive officers as of October 8, 2006. Steve Jobs, as CEO, was the only internal board member and the only member who had served on the original board. On September 30, 2006, Fred Anderson, who had joined the board in 2004, resigned from the board over the stock options investigation. On August 28, 2006, Dr. Eric Schmidt, CEO of Google, was appointed to the board. He did not accept the automatic 30,000 stock options available to all new board members. Shaw Nu, analyst, said, "He (Schmidt) gives Jobs and Apple more perspective on dealing with Microsoft. . . . And like Jobs, Schmidt has lost at times against (Microsoft)." As soon as Schmidt's board appointment was announced, speculation began about the potential for future partnerships between Google and Apple.

External board members received $50,000 as an annual retainer. In addition, directors were eligible to receive up to two free computer systems, and discounts on the purchase of additional products. On the fourth anniversary of joining the board, each member was entitled to receive an option to acquire 30,000 shares of stock.

Although Steve Jobs' annual salary was only $1.00 as CEO of Apple, the board gave Jobs a bonus of $84 million in 2001, consisting of $43.5 million for a private jet, a Gulfstream V, as well as $40.5 million to pay Jobs' income taxes on this bonus. Jobs owned 10,200,004 (1.25%) of Apple's stock. The closing price on November 21, 2006, was $88.60 per share. Together, the directors and executives owned 16,307,625 (1.94%) shares of stock. Barclay Bank Plc owned 67,094,321 (8.09%) shares and FMR Corporation owned 51,250,663 (6.18%) shares of Apple. These are the two financial institutions with more than 5% ownership.

EXHIBIT 2
Directors and
Executive Officers:
Apple Computer Inc.

A. Directors

Name	Position	Age	Since
Fred A. Anderson	Director	61	2004
William V. Campbell	Co-lead Director	65	1997
Millard S. Drexler	Director	61	1999
Albert A. Gore, Jr.	Director	57	2000
Steven P. Jobs	Director and CEO	50	1997
Arthur D. Levinson	Co-lead Director	55	2000
Jerome B. York	Director	67	1997

B. Executives

Steven P. Jobs
CEO, Apple
CEO, Pixar
Director, Apple
Director, Walt Disney

Timothy D. Cook
Chief Operating Officer

Nancy R. Heinen
Senior Vice President
and General Counsel

Ron Johnson
Senior Vice President Retail

Peter Oppenheimer
Senior Vice President
Chief Financial Officer

Dr. Avdias "Avie" Tevanian, Jr.
Chief Software Technology Officer

Jon Rubinstein
Senior Vice President
iPod Divison

Philip W. Schiller
Senior Vice President
Worldwide Product Marketing

Bertrand Seriet
Senior Vice President
Software Engineering

Sina Tamaddon
Senior Vice President, Applications

SOURCE: *Apple Computer, Ind., SEC 10-K Report (December 1, 2005), p. 102.*

Management's View of the Company[41]

Apple Computer's 10-K Report for the fiscal year ended September 24, 2005 contained the following analysis of the company by management:

First, the company designed, manufactured, and marketed personal computers and related software, services, peripherals, and networking solutions. The company also designed, developed, and marketed a line of portable digital music players along with related accessories and services including the online distribution of third-party music, audio books music videos, short films and television shows. The company's products and services included the Macintosh line of desktop and notebook computers, the iPod digital music player, the Xserve G5 server and the Xserve RAID storage products, a portfolio of consumer and professional software applications, the Mac OS X operating system, the iTunes Music Store, a portfolio of peripherals that support and enhance the Macintosh and iPod product lines, and a variety of other service and support offerings. The company sold its products worldwide through its online stores, its own retail stores, its direct sales force, and third-party wholesalers, resellers, and value added resellers. In addition, the company sold a variety of third-party Macintosh compatible products, including computer printers and printing supplies, storage devices, computer memory, digital camcorders and still cameras, personal digital assistants, and various other computing products and supplies through its online and retail stores. The company sells to education, consumer, creative, professional, business, and government customers.

Second, the company's business strategy leveraged its ability, through the design and development of its own operating system, hardware, and many software applications and technologies, to bring to its customers around the world compelling new products and solutions with superior ease-of-use, seamless integration, and innovative industrial design.

Third, the company participated in several highly competitive markets, including personal computers *with its* Macintosh line *of computers,* consumer electronics *with its* iPod line *of digital music players, and distribution of third-party digital content through its online* iTunes Music Store. *While the company was widely recognized as an innovator in the personal computer and consumer electronic markets as well as a leader in the emerging market for distribution of digital content, these were all highly competitive markets that are subject to aggressive pricing and increased competition. To remain competitive, the company believed that increased investment in research and development (R&D) and marketing and advertising was necessary to maintain and extend its position in the markets where it competes. The company's R&D spending was focused on delivering timely updates and enhancements to its existing line of personal computers displays, operating systems, software applications, and portable music players; developing new digital lifestyle consumer and professional software applications: and investing in new product areas such as rack-mount servers, RAID storage systems, and wireless technologies. The company also believed investment in marketing and advertising programs was critical to increasing product and brand awareness.*

Fourth, in June 2005, the company announced its plan to begin using Intel microprocessors in its Macintosh computers. The company planned to begin shipping certain models with Intel microprocessors by June 2006 (which the company did) and to complete the transition of all of its Macintosh computers to Intel microprocessors by the end of calendar year 2007.

Fifth, the company utilized a variety of direct and indirect distribution channels. The company believed that sales of its innovative and differentiated products were enhanced by knowledgeable salespersons who can convey the value of the hardware, software, and peripheral integration, demonstrate the unique digital lifestyle solutions of the Windows platform and networks. The company further believed that providing a high-quality sales and after-sales support experience was critical to attracting and retaining customers. To ensure a high-quality buying experience for its products in which service and education are emphasized, the company had expanded and improved its distribution capabilities by opening its own retail stores in the U.S. and internationally. The company had 124 stores open as of September 24, 2005.

Sixth, the company also staffs selected third-party stores with the company's own employees to improve the buying experience through reseller channels. The company had deployed Apple employees and contractors in reseller locations around the world including the U.S., Europe, Japan, and Australia. The company also sold to customers directly through its online stores around the world.

Seventh, to improve access to the iPod product line, the company had significantly expanded the number of distribution points where iPods are sold. The iPod product line can be purchased in certain department stores, member-only warehouse stores, large retail chains, and specialty retail stores, as well as through the channels listed above.

Business Strategy[42]

The company was committed to bringing the best personal computing and music experience to students, educators, creative professional, businesses, government agencies, and consumers through its innovative hardware, software, peripherals, services, and Internet offerings. The company's business strategy leverages its unique ability through the design and development of its own operating system, hardware, and many software applications and technologies, to bring to its customers new products and solutions with superior ease-of-use, seamless integration, and innovative industrial design. The company believed continual investment in research and development is critical to facilitate innovation of new and improved products and technologies. Besides updates to its existing line of personal computers and related software, services, peripherals, and networking solutions, the company continued to capitalize on the convergence of digital consumer electronics and computers by creating innovations like the iPod and iTunes Music Store. The company's strategy also included expanding its distribution network to effectively reach more of its targeted customers and provide them a high-quality sales and after-sales support experience.

Digital Hub

The company believed personal computing was in an era in which the personal computer functions for both professionals and consumers as the digital hub for advanced new digital devices such as the company's iPod digital music players, personal digital assistants, cellular phone, digital camcorders and still cameras, CD and DVD players, televisions, and other consumer electronic devices. The attributes of the personal computer included a high quality user interface, relatively inexpensive data storage, and the ability to run complex applications and easily connect to the Internet. Apple was the only company in the personal computer industry that controls the design and development of the entire personal computer—from the hardware and operating system to sophisticated application. Additionally, the company's products provided innovative industrial design, intuitive ease-of-use, and built-in networking, graphics, and multimedia capabilities. Thus, the company was uniquely positioned to offer integrated digital hub products and solutions.

The company developed products and technologies that adhere to many industry standards in order to provide an optimized user experience through interoperability with peripherals and devices from other companies. The company had played a role in the development, enhancement, promotion, and/or use of numerous of these industry standards.

Expanded Distribution

The company believed that a high quality buying experience with knowledgeable salespersons who can convey the value of the company's products and services was critical to attracting and retaining customers. The company sold many of its products and resold certain third-party products in most of its major markets directly to consumers, education customers, and businesses through its retail and online stores in the U.S. and internationally. The company had also invested in programs to enhance reseller sales, including the Apple Sales Consultant Program, which consisted of the deployment of Apple employees and contractors to selected third-party reseller locations. The company believed providing direct contact with its targeted customers is an efficient way to demonstrate the advantage of its Macintosh computer and other products over those of its competitors. The company had significantly increased the points of distribution for the iPod product family in order to make its products available at locations where its customers shop.

From inception of the retail initiative in 2001 through 2005, the company had opened 116 retail stores in the U.S. and 8 international stores in Canada, Japan, and the U.K. The company opened 2 additional stores in October of 2005. The company had typically located its stores at high traffic locations in quality shopping malls and urban shopping districts.

One of the goals of the retail initiative was to bring new customers to the company and expand its installed base through sales to computer users who currently did not own a Macintosh computer and first time personal computer buyers. By operating its own stores and building them in desirable high traffic locations, the company was able to better control the customer retail experience and attract new customers. The stores were designed to simplify and enhance the presentation and marketing of personal computing products. To that end, retail stores configurations had evolved into various sizes in order to accommodate market demands. The stores employed experienced and knowledgeable personnel who provided product advice and certain hardware support services. The stores offered a wide selection of third-party hardware, software, and various other computing products and supplies selected to complement the company's own products. Additionally, the stores provided forum in which the company was able to present computing solutions to users in areas such as digital photography, digital video, music, children's software, and home and small business computing.

Education

For more than 25 years, the company had focused on the use of technology in education and had been committed to delivering tools to help educators teach and students learn. The company believed effective integration of technology into classroom instruction can result in higher levels of student achievement, especially when used to support collaboration, information access, and the expression and representation of student thought and ideas. The company created solutions that enable new modes of curriculum delivery, better ways of conducting research, and opportunities for professional development of faculty, students, and staff. The company had designed a range of products and services to help schools maximize their investments in the needs of education customers. These products and services included the eMac™, and the iBook®, video creation and editing solutions, wireless networking, student information systems, high-quality curriculum and professional development solutions, and one-to-one (1:1) learning solutions (primarily in K–12). 1:1 learning solutions typically consisted of iBook portable computers for every student and teacher along with a wireless network connected to a central server.

Creative Professionals

Creative professionals constitutes one of the company's most important markets for both hardware and software products. This market was also important to many third-party developers who provide Macintosh-compatible hardware and software solutions. Creative customers utilized the company's products for a variety of creative activities including digital video and film production and editing; digital video and film special effects, compositing, and titling; digital still photography and workflow management; graphic design, publishing, and print production; music creation and production; audio production and sound design; and web design, development, and administration.

The company designed its high-end hardware solutions, including servers, desktops, and portable Macintosh systems, to incorporate the power, expandability, and features desired by creative professional. The company's operating system, Mac OS X, incorporated powerful graphics and audio technologies and features developer tools to optimize system and application performance when running powerful creative solutions provided by the company or third-party developers. The company also offered various software solutions to meet the needs of its creative customers.

Business Organization[43]

The company managed its business primarily on a geographic basis. The company's reportable operating segments are comprised of the Americas, Europe, Japan, and Retail. The Americas, Japan, and reportable segments did not include activities related to the Retail segments. The Americas segment included both North and South America. The Europe segment included European countries as well as the Middle East and Africa. The Retail segment currently operates Apple-owned retail stores in the U.S., Canada, Japan, and the U.K.

Other operating segments included Asia-Pacific, which included Australia and Asia except for Japan, and the company's subsidiary, FileMaker, Inc. Each reportable geographic operating segment provided similar hardware and software products and similar services.

Current Products

Apple Computer designed, manufactured and marketed PCs and related software, services, networking solutions, worldwide and peripherals. The company products and services included the (1) Macintosh line of notebooks and desktop computers (iMac, MacBook, Mac mini, Mac Pro); (2) iPod digital music players (iPod Nano, iPod, iPod Hi-Fi); (3) Mac OS X operating system; (4) Xserve, G5 server, and Xserve RAID storage products; (5) a portfolio of professional and consumer software applications; (6) Mac OS X operating system; (7) iTunes Music Store; and (8) a portfolio of peripherals that support and enhance the Macintosh and iPod product lines. The company's pro video peripherals support the Macintosh and iPod product lines. The company offered products and services for the educational industry which included the eMac, iMac, and iBook, creation and editing solutions, wireless networking and student information systems, curriculum and professional development solutions, and one-on-one learning solutions. The company makes announcements on new products and services on a continuous basis.

Competition

The company was confronted by aggressive competition in all areas of business. The market for personal computer and related software and peripheral products was highly competitive. This market continued to be characterized by rapid technological advances in both hardware and software that had substantially increased the capabilities and use of personal computers and had resulted in the frequent introduction of new products with competitive price, features, and performance characteristics. Over the past several years, price competition in the personal computer market had been particularly intense. The company's competitors that sold personal computers based on other operating systems had aggressively cut prices and lowered product quality to maintain market share. The company's results of operations and financials can be adversely affected by these and other industry-wide downward pressures on gross margins.

The principal competitive factors in the market for personal computers included price, retail price performance, product qualities and reliability, design innovation, availability of software, product features, marketing and distribution capability, service and support, availability of hardware peripherals, and corporate reputation. Further, as the personal computer industry and its customers placed more reliance on the Internet, an increasing number of Internet devices that are simpler, and less expensive, than traditional personal computers may compete for market share with the company's existing products.

The company was currently taking and will continue to take steps to respond to the competitive pressures being placed on personal computer sales. The company's future operating results and financial condition were substantially dependent on its ability to continue to develop improvements to the Macintosh platform in order to maintain perceived functional and design advantages over competing platforms.

The company's services and products relating to music, and other creative content, had already encouraged significant competition from other companies, many of whom had greater financial, marketing, and manufacturing resources than those of the company. The company faced increasing competition from other companies promoting their own digital and distribution music products services, subscription services, and free peer-to-peer music services. The company anticipated the competition will intensify as hardware, software, and content providers work more collaboratively to offer integrated products competition with the company's offering. However, the company believed it currently maintained a competitive advantage by more effectively integrating an entire solution, including the hardware (iPod), software (iTunes), and distribution of third-party digital content (iTunes Music Store).[44]

The chief iPod competitors were SunDisk and Microsoft's new MP3 player, Zune. The iPod had a 77 percent market share and SunDisk had a 10 percent market share. Peter Lewis of *Fortune* magazine reported "It [Zune] was bigger and heavier and more difficult to use." Zune will sell for around $250. Microsoft will use Universal Music Group, which was owned by Vivendi, and its artist, Microsoft will pay a fee for each song and an additional payment will be made. Apple paid the studios per song. Vivendi was the largest music company, and did not sell music to Apple[45].

The company's competitors were Dell, HP, Gateway, Toshibo, Lenovo, and Acer. U.S. market share information for the 3rd quarter of 2006 was:

Company	Market Share[46]
Dell	32.1%
HP	23.0
Gateway	6.4
Apple	6.1
Toshiba	5.1

The U.S. Mac market share had grown 31 percent in the 3rd quarter, when compared with the 3rd quarter of 2005. In 2005, 744,000 units were sold compared to 975,000 units being sold in 2006. Dell sales declined by 7.1 percent, while Hewlett-Packard's (HP) share grew from 21.2 percent to 23.0 percent.

During this period, Apple's worldwide share did not place it among the top-selling PCs. HP moved into first place with 16.1 percent market share. HP had not been in first place since first quarter of 2003. Dell was in second place with a 16.0 percent market share. Lenovo's market share was 7.5 percent, followed by Acer with a 5.1 percent, and Toshiba with 4.3 percent.

Distribution and Marketing[47]

The company believed that a high quality buying experience with a knowledgeable salesperson who can convey the values of the company's products and services was critical to attracting and retaining customers. The company sold many of its products and resold certain third-party products in most of the major markets directly to customers, education customers and business through its retail and online stores in the U.S. and internationally. The company had invested in programs to enhance reseller sales, including the Apple Sales Consumer Program, which consisted of the department of Apple employees and contractors to select third-party reseller locations. The company believed in providing direct contact with its products over those of its competitors. The company had significantly increased the points of distribution for the iPod product family, in order to make its products available at locations where its customers shopped.

One of our goals of retail initiative was to bring new customers to the company and expand its installed base through sales to computer buyers who do not own a Macintosh computer and the first time personal computer buyer. By operating in its own stores and building them in desirable high traffic locations, the company was able to better control the customer's retail experience and to attract new customers. The stores were designed to simplify and enhance the presentation and marketing of personal computing products. To that end retail store configurations had evolved into various sizes in order to accommodate market demands. The stores employ experienced and knowledgeable personnel who provided product advice and certain hardware support services. The store offered a wide selection of third-party hardware, software, and various other computing products and supplies selected to complement the company's own products. Additionally, the store provided a forum in which the company was able to present computing solutions to users in areas such as digital photography digital video, music, children's software, and home and small business computing.

Advertising[48]

Advertising costs totaled $205 million, $193 million, and $209 million for 2004, 2003, and 2002, respectively. All forms of advertising (print, internet, etc.) were used by Apple to introduce new products and sustain existing products. Advertising was focused on the target market.

Research and Development[49]

Because the personal computer and consumer electronics industries were characterized by rapid technological advances, the company's ability to compete successfully was heavily dependent upon its ability to ensure a continuing and timely flow of competitive products and technology to the market. The company continued to develop new products and technologies and to enhance existing in the areas of hardware, and peripherals, consumer electronic products, system software, application software, networking and communications software and solutions, and the Internet. The company may expand the range of its product offerings and intellectual property through licensing and/or acquisition of third-party business and technology. The company's research and development expenditures totaled $534 million, $489 million, and $471 million in 2005, 2004 and 2003, respectively.

Patents, Trademark, Copyright, and Licensing[50]

The company currently held the rights to patents and copyrights relating to certain aspects of its computer systems, iPod, peripheral, and software. In addition, the company had registered, and/or had applied to register, trademarks and service marks in the U.S. and a member of foreign countries for "Apple," the Apple logo, "Macintosh," "iPod," "iTunes," "iTunes Music Store," and numerous other trademarks and service marks. Although the company believed the ownership of such patents, copyrights, trademarks, and service marks was an important factor in its business, and that its success does depend in partly on the ownership thereof, the company relied primarily on innovative skills, technical competences, and marketing abilities of the personnel.

Many of the company's products were designed to include intellectual property obtained from third parties. While it may be necessary in the future to seek or renew licensing relating to various aspects of its products and business methods, the company believed that, based upon past experience and industry practice, such licenses generally could be obtained on commercially reasonable terms. However, there was no guarantee that such licenses can be obtained at all. Because of technologies changes in the computer industry, current extensive patent coverage, and the rapid rate of issuance of new patents it was possible certain components of the company's products and business methods may unknowingly infringe existing patents of others. From time to time, the company had been notified that it may be infringing certain patents or intellectual property rights of third-parties.

Properties[51]

The company headquarters were located in Cupertino, California. The company had manufacturing facilities in Cork, Ireland. The company owned or leased buildings in other locations.

Foreign and Domestic Operations and Geographic Data[52]

The U.S. represented the company's largest geographic marketplace. Approximately 60 percent of the company's net sales in 2005 came from sales inside the U.S. Final assembly of products sold by the company was conducted in the company's manufacturing facilities in Cork, Ireland and external vendors in Fremont and Fullerton, California, Taiwan, Korea, the People's Republic of China, and the Czech Republic. Currently, manufacture of many of the components used in the company's products and final assembly of substantially all of the company's portable products including PowerBooks, iBooks, and iPods were performed by third-party vendors in China. Margins on sales of the company's products in foreign countries, and sales of products that included components obtained from foreign suppliers, can be adversely affected by foreign currencies exchange rate fluctuations and international trade regulations, including tariffs and antidumping penalties.

Seasonality[53]

The company had historically experienced increased net sales in the first and fourth quarters compared to other quarters in the fiscal year (ending September 24, 2005) due to seasonal demand related to the holiday season and the beginning of the school year. This historical pattern should not be considered a reliable indicator of the company's future net sales or financial performance.

Raw Materials[54]

Although most components essential to the company's business were generally available from multiple sources, certain key components [including microprocessors and application-specific integrated circuits ("ASIC")] were currently obtained by the company from single or limited sources. Some other key components, while currently available to the company from multiple sources, were at times subject to industry-wide availability constraints and pricing pressures. In addition, the company used some components that were not common to the rest of the personal computers and consumer electronics industries, and new products introduced in the company often initially utilize current components.

Environmental Laws[55]

Compliance with federal, state, local, and foreign laws for the protection of the environment had to date no material effect on the company's capital expenditures, earnings, or competitive position. In the future, these laws could have a material adverse effect on the company.

Production and marketing of products in certain states and countries may subject the company to environmental and other regulations, such as the requirement that the company provide consumers with the ability to return product to the company at the end of its useful life, and place responsibility for environmentally safe disposal or recycling with the company. Such laws and regulations had recently been passed in several jurisdictions in which the company operates, including various European Union member states, Japan, and California. In the future, these laws could have a material adverse effect on the company.

Employees[56]

The company had 14,800 full-time employees and 2,200 temporary employees and contractors.

Legal Proceedings[57]

Apple Computer was subject to certain legal proceedings and claims, which have arisen in the ordinary course of business and had not been fully adjudicated in the opinion of management, the company did not have a potential liability related to any existing legal proceedings and claims that will have a material adverse effect on the financial condition and operating results. In 2005, the company settled several issues and the settlements individually or in the aggregate have a material impact on the company's financial results.

The European Commission had notified the company that it was being investigated relating to the iTune Music Store in the European Union (EU). The case focuses on EU competition law and contended that Apple was charging more for online music in the UK than in Eurozone countries.

An analyst expects legal action against Jon Loch Johansen and RealNetworld, over their breaking of the protection codes on the iPod.

Financial Performance[58]

Management's view of the company's 2005 financial performance (see **Exhibits 3–6**) follows:

> *Net sales of iPods rose $3.2 billion during 2005 compared to 2004. Unit sales of iPods totaled 22.5 million in 2005, which represented an increase of 400% from the 4.4 million iPod units sold in 2004. Strong sales of iPods during 2005 continued to be experienced in all the company's operating segments and was driven by a strong demand for the iPod Shuffle introduced in January 2005, the release of an updated version of the iPod Mini in February 2005, the release of the iPod Nano in September 2005, and expansion of the iPod distribution network. Net sales per iPod unit sold decreased 32 percent primarily due to the introduction of the lower priced iPod Shuffle in January 2005, and iPod Mini pricing reductions in February 2005. From the introduction of the iPod in 2002 through 2005, the company sold approximately 28 million iPods.*

Other music related products and services consisted of sales associated with the iTune Music Store and iPod services and accessories. Net sales of other music related products and services increased $621 million or 223 percent during 2005 compared to 2004. The company had experienced strong growth in sales of iPod services and accessories consistent with the increase in overall iPod unit sales for 2005. The increases sales from the iTune Music Store was primarily due to the substantial growth of net sales in the U.S. and expansion in Europe, Canada, and Japan.

Total Macintosh net sales increased $1.4 billion or 27 percent during 2005 compared to 2004. Unit sales of Macintosh systems increased 1.2 million units or 38 percent during 2005 compared to 2004. The increase in Macintosh net sales and unit sales related primarily to strong demand for the company's desktop products, which was experienced in all of the company's operating segments. The company believed that the success of the iPod was having a positive impact on Macintosh net sales by introducing new customers to the company's other products. Desktop demand was stimulated in 2005 due to the new iMac G5 and the introduction of the Mac Mini in January 2005. Net sales and unit sales of desktop products increased 45 percent and 55 percent, respectively, during 2005 compared to 2004. Macintosh net sales and unit sales also included sales of the company's portable products, which increased 11 percent and 21 percent, respectively, compared to 2004.

Future Possibility

On December 11, 2006, a *Fortune* article, "Happiness Is a Warm iPod," discussed the possibility that the Beatles may give Apple Computer's iTunes an exclusive to their recordings. The Beatles had refused for years to allow MP3, Microsoft's MSN, and Rhapsody to use their music.

EXHIBIT 3
Consolidated
Statements of
Operations: Apple
Computer, Inc.
(Dollar amounts in
millions, except per
share data)

Three Fiscal Years Ending September 24, 2005	2005	2004	2003
Net sales	$13,931	8,279	6,207
Cost of sales	9,888	6,020	4,499
Gross margin	4,043	2,259	1,708
Operating expenses:			
Research and development	534	489	471
Selling, general, and administrative	1,859	1,421	1,212
Restructuring costs	—	23	26
Total operating expenses	2,393	1,933	1,709
Operating income (loss)	1,650	326	(1)
Other income and expense:			
Gains on non-current investments, net	—	4	10
Interest and other income, net	165	53	83
Total other income and expense	165	57	93
Income before provision for income taxes	1,815	383	92
Provision for income taxes	480	107	24
Income before accounting changes	1,335	276	68
Cumulative effects of accounting changes, net of income taxes	—	—	1
Net income	$ 1,335	276	69
Earnings per common share before accounting changes:			
Basic	$ 1.65	$ 0.37	$ 0.09
Diluted	$ 1.56	$ 0.36	$ 0.09
Earnings per common share:			
Basic	$ 1.65	$ 0.37	$ 0.10
Diluted	$ 1.56	$ 0.36	$ 0.09
Shares used in computing earnings per share (in thousands):			
Basic	808,439	743,180	721,262
Diluted	856,780	774,622	726,932

SOURCE: *Apple Computer, SEC 10-K Report (December 1, 2005), p. 61.*

The Beatles' music was controlled by Apple Corps. Apple Corps had been in and out of courts for more than 20 years over the exclusive use of the name—"Apple." Apple Corps had opposed the use of *Apple* in *Apple* Computer. In May 2006, a London judge ruled in favor of Apple Computer in the use of the word *Apple* in the company's name. This ruling was appealed by the Beatles, and was scheduled to be heard in February 2007. Tim Arango, author of the article, said, "Clearly, if the two Apples wind up in business together, the matter is likely to be dropped."

Britain's EMi Group served as a peacemaker between Steve Jobs and Neil Aspinall, who was the Beatles' road manager and is now serving as the guardian of the Beatles' music as the business manager for Apple Corps.

The Beatles have been very protective of the use of their music. In 1987, Nike used a Beatles song as part of a TV commercial. Nike management believed it had all the legal licenses to use the song, but Nike was sued by the Beatles. Nike got caught in the crossfire between EMi and the Apple Corps. A lawyer said, "The Beatles' position is that they don't sing jingles, or anything else." Jobs would like to be able to link Paul and/or Ringo to the iPod if the deal is finalized. An analyst said that this issue could be a deal breaker. This deal could be worth hundreds of millions of dollars.

EXHIBIT 4
Consolidated
Balance Sheets:
Apple Computer,
Inc. (Dollar amounts
in millions, except
per share data)

Year Ending	September 24, 2005	September 25, 2004
Assets:		
Current assets:		
Cash and cash equivalents	$3,491	$2,969
Short-term investments	4,770	2,495
Accounts receivable, less allowances of $46 and $47, respectively	895	774
Inventories	165	101
Deferred tax assets	331	231
Other current assets	648	485
Total current assets	10,300	7,055
Property, plant, and equipment, net	817	707
Goodwill	69	80
Acquired intangible assets, net	27	17
Other assets	338	191
Total assets	$11,551	$8,050
Liabilities and Shareholders' Equity:		
Current liabilities:		
Accounts payable	$ 1,779	$1,451
Accrued expenses	1,705	1,200
Total current liabilities	3,484	2,651
Non-current liabilities	601	323
Total liabilities	4,085	2,974
Commitments and contingencies		
Shareholders' equity:		
Common stock, no par value; 1,800,000,000 shares authorized; 835,019,364 and 782,887,234 shares issued and outstanding, respectively	3,521	2,514
Deferred stock compensation	(60)	(93)
Retained earnings	4,005	2,670
Accumulated other comprehensive income (loss)	—	(15)
Total shareholders' equity	7,466	5,076
Total liabilities and shareholders' equity	$11,551	$8,050

SOURCE: *Apple Computer, SEC 10-K Report (December 1, 2005), p. 60.*

EXHIBIT 5
Geographic Data:
Apple Computer,
Inc. (Dollar amounts
in millions)

	2005	2004	2003
Americas			
Net sales	$6,590	$4,019	$3,181
Operating income	$ 798	$ 465	$ 323
Depreciation, amortization, and accretion	$ 6	$ 6	$ 5
Segment assets (a)	$ 705	$ 563	$ 494
Europe			
Net sales	$3,073	$1,799	$1,309
Operating income	$ 454	$ 280	$ 130
Depreciation, amortization, and accretion	$ 4	$ 4	$ 4
Segment assets	$ 289	$ 259	$ 252

EXHIBIT 5
(Continued)

	2005	2004	2003
Japan			
Net sales	$ 920	$ 677	$ 698
Operating income	$ 140	$ 115	$ 121
Depreciation, amortization, and accretion	$ 3	$ 2	$ 3
Segment assets	$ 199	$ 114	$ 130
Retail			
Net sales	$2,350	$1,185	$ 621
Operating income (loss)	$ 151	$ 39	$ (5)
Depreciation, amortization, and accretion (b)	$ 43	$ 35	$ 25
Segment assets (b)	$ 555	$ 351	$ 243
Other Segments (c)			
Net sales	$ 998	$ 599	$ 398
Operating income	$ 118	$ 90	$ 51
Depreciation, amortization, and accretion	$ 2	$ 2	$ 2
Segment assets	$ 133	$ 124	$ 78

Notes:
(a) The Americas asset figures do not include fixed assets held in the U.S. Such fixed assets are not allocated specifically to the Americas segment and are included in the corporate assets figures below.
(b) Retail segment depreciation and asset figures reflect the cost and related depreciation of its retail stores and related infrastructure. Retail store construction-in-progress, which is not subject to depreciation, is reflected in corporate assets.
(c) Other segments include Asia-Pacific and FileMaker.

Source: Apple Computer, SEC 10-K Report (December 1, 2005), p. 94.

EXHIBIT 6
Segment
Information:
Apple Computer,
Inc. (Dollar amounts
in millions)

Information regarding net sales by product is as follows:

Net Sales:	2005	2004	2003
Desktops (a)	$ 3,436	$2,373	$2,475
Portables (b)	2,839	2,550	2,016
Total Macintosh net sales	6,275	4,923	4,491
iPod	4,540	1,306	345
Other music related products and services (c)	899	278	36
Peripherals and other hardware (d)	1,126	951	691
Software, service, and other net sales (e)	1,091	821	644
Total Net Sales	$13,931	$8,279	$6,207

Notes:
(a) Includes iMac, eMac, Mac mini, Power Mac and Xserve product lines.
(b) Includes iBook and PowerBook product lines.
(c) Consists of iTunes Music Store sales and iPod services, and Apple-branded and third-party iPod accessories.
(d) Includes sales of Apple-branded and third-party displays, wireless connectivity and networking solutions, and other hardware accessories.
(e) Includes sales of Apple-branded operating system, application software, third-party software, AppleCare, and Internet services.

SOURCE: Apple Computer, SEC 10-K Report (December 1, 2005), p. 96.

Conclusion

Industry analysts were very impressed with Apple Computer's recent history, but were concerned about the company's future. How long would Steve Jobs continue as CEO? Can Apple be successful without Jobs' leadership? Strategically, where should Apple go from here? What does it need to do to keep its competitive advantage in iPods?

NOTES

1. Ellen Lee, "Apple, Nike Hocking Runners Up to iPods," *www.SFGate.com,* May 24, 2006.

2. Andrew Ward, "Coke and Apple in iTune Move," *www.FT.com,* August 1, 2006.

3. Mary Wong, "Apple's iPod Sweetens the Ride with Top Automakers," www.signonsandiego.com, August 3, 2006.

4. Connie Gugielmo, "Apple Shares Rise on Record Macintosh Shipments, New iPod Sales," www.Bloomberg.com, October 19, 2006.

5. Arik Hesseidahl, "Apple's Big Mac," www.business.com, October 19, 2006, p. 1.

6. Dan Nystedt, "Apple's New iPods Priced for Profits Not Market Share," www.playlistmag.com, September 16, 2006, p. 1.

7. "Apple Launchers iTunes Latino," *www.biz.yahoo.com,* November 1, 2006.

8. Staci D. Kramer, "Six Airlines Integrating iPods into In-Flight Audio, Video Systems," www.paidcontent.com, November 14, 2006.

9. Katie Dean, "Apple's iPhone in Tune," www.thestreet.com, November, 2006 and "iPhone May Bolster Apple Earnings 22%," www.macnn.com, November 25, 2006.

10. Angele Chariton, "French Law on iPod, iTune Takes Effect," www.biz.yahoo.com, August 3, 2006.

11. "Apple Get Burned, Toyota Skids," finance.yahoo.com, August 25, 2006 and Philip Goliner, "UPDATE 2-Apple to Recall 1.8 million NoteBook Batteries," www.yahoo.rueters.com, August 24, 2006.

12. Elaine Kurtenback, "Report: iPod Supplier Told to Unionize," www.biz.yahoo.com, September 1 2006.

13. "Spiral Frog in Deal with EMi Music," www.biz.yahoo.com, September 6, 2006.

14. Associated Press, "DVD Jon Says He's Cracked Apples iTunes Copy Restrictions," October 25, 2006, p. 1 of 4.

15. "Net Information About The Jon Johnsen ("DVD JON") Case," *Electronic Fotiport Norge.*

16. "Spiral Frog in Deal with EMi Music,"

17. Duncan Martell, "Apple Probe Found Option Grant 'Irregularities,'" www.Rueters.com, June 29, 2006.

18. Ibid.

19. Mu Wong, "CEO Apologizes for Apple Stock Practices," www.yahoo.finance.com.

20. Arik Heseidahl, "Apple Comes Clean on Options," www.businessweekonline.com, October 5, 2006, p. 1.

21. "What Scandal?," *www.Forbes.com,* June 7, 2006, p. 2.

22. "Stock Options Investigation," www.CBSS.com (local San Francisco CBS station) October 11, 2006, p. 1.

23. "Minnesota to Expand Investigation of United Health," www.bizjournals.com, October 12, 2006, p. 1.

24. Ibid.

25. Ibid.

26. "This section is a combination of information from previous versions of this book, *Strategic Management and Business Policy* over the past 20 years. Wikipedia, the free encyclopedia, "History of Apple Computer," pp. 1–18.

27. "Steve Jobs," Wikipedia, the free encyclopedia, pp. 1–8.

28. Ibid, pp. 1–2.

29. Ibid, p. 2.

30. Ibid.

31. "History of Apple Computer," pp. 2–3.

32. Previous Apple Computer cases.

33. Pixar, "Corporate Overview," p. 1.

34. "Steve Jobs" Magic Kingdom," *Businessweek online,* p. 3.

35. Ibid., pp. 1–5, and Vandana Sinna, "Disney, Pixar Give Marriage Second Chance," pp. 1–3.

36. "Steve Jobs' Magic Kingdom," p. 1.

37. Ibid, p. 2.

38. Ibid.

39. Ibid.

40. This section was directly quoted from *Apple Computer, Inc.,* "SEC 10-K," September 2, 2005, and (2) "SEC DEF 14A" March 13, 2006.

41. This section was directly quoted from *Apple Computer, Inc.,* "SEC 10-K," September 24, 2005, pp. 27–28.

42. This section was directly quoted from Apple computer, Inc., "SEC 10-K," September 24, 2005, pp. 2–3.

43. Ibid., p. 3.

44. The above 4 paragraphs are directly quoted from "Apple Computer Inc." "SEC 10-K," p. 13.

45. Nick Wingfield and Robert A. Gith, "Microsoft Confirms Plan for Music Video Player," *The Wall Street Journal,* July 22, 2006, p. A3.

46. Apple Insider, "Apple's Share of U.S. PC Market jumps to 6.1 percent," October 18, 2006, p. 1.

47. The 3 paragraphs directly quoted from *Apple Computer, Inc.,* "SEC 10-K," p. 22.

48. Ibid., p. 5.

49. Ibid., p. 14.

50. Ibid.

51. Ibid., p. 16.

52. Ibid., p. 15.

53. Ibid.

54. Ibid.

55. Ibid., p. 16.

56. Ibid.

57. Ibid.

58. Ibid., p. 32.

McAfee 2005:

ANTI-VIRUS AND ANTI-SPYWARE

Bethany Sweesy and Alan N. Hoffman

McAfee, Inc. proactively secures systems and networks from known and unknown threats, worldwide. Home users, businesses, service providers, the public sector, and our partners all trust McAfee's unmatched security expertise, and have confidence in our comprehensive and proven solutions to block attacks and prevent disruptions.[1]

CEO GEORGE SAMENUK STARED OUT HIS OFFICE WINDOW AND CONSIDERED THE COMPANY'S financial results from 2004. Headquartered in Santa Clara, California, McAfee, as of January 20, 2005, is the "largest dedicated security software company in the industry."[2] In the past year, McAfee had conducted several strategic transactions including the divestiture of two slow-growing product lines and investment in the high-growth security sector, in order to streamline its focus. The strategy appeared to be paying off and McAfee's product portfolio was the strongest ever in the history of the company. Furthermore, having paid down $347 million in debt, McAfee was set to enter 2005 debt-free.

Samenuk knew, however, that in the highly competitive and rapidly changing industry McAfee's success in 2004 would not be sufficient to carry the company through another year. In order to achieve the organization's goal of becoming a "worldwide leader in intrusion prevention and risk management solutions and services,"[3] McAfee must continue to offer customers innovative, quality solutions. With a corporate mission to secure "consumers and businesses from the desktop to the core of the network by delivering best-of-breed products and services that protect . . . global customer's information technology systems and infrastructure"[4] Samenuk knew his work was cut out for him.

Industry

The 1960s and 1970s was the era of the mainframe computer. During this period, "rabbits"—programs that cloned themselves—were the most common security threat. Rabbits were a local phenomenon and did not replicate from system to system and were likely to be "mistakes or pranks by system programmers servicing" the mainframes.[5] However, the first epidemic of a computer virus occurred during this time infecting the Univax 1108 system. The virus "merged itself to the end of executable files—[and] virtually did the same thing that modern viruses do."[6]

During the 1980s computers became more and more prevalent, as did viruses. In the early part of the decade, Trojan horses were especially common, as programs were frequently written by private individuals and freely distributed over general access servers. (See **Exhibit 1.**) In the latter half of the decade, several notorious and extremely debilitating viruses including *VirDem*, *Vienna*, and *Jerusalem* affected computers globally.[7] It was during the 1980s that many of the anti-virus software companies began developing software to protect users from the hazards of viruses.

In the 1990s intrusion software became more complex, forcing anti-virus software to follow suit. Additionally, with the approach of 2000 (Y2K), businesses across the globe began dumping enormous amounts of cash in technology. The anti-virus industry felt the effects of this spending and an already competitive industry became even more cutthroat. Companies began underhandedly vying for customers, causing 1997 to be littered with litigation and SEC investigations. McAfee attacked Dr. Solomon for a particular feature in the software; Dr. Solomon counterattacked McAfee for false advertising. Symantec and McAfee also had a bout in court concerning copyright infringement.[8]

Industry shakeout occurred in the early part of the 21st century with the decrease in IT spending and an overall economic slowdown. However, by 2003 conditions had improved and IDC predicted that the security software market would "grow 16.9% annually between 2003 and 2008."[9]

EXHIBIT 1
Definitions

WHAT IS A VIRUS?
A virus is a manmade program or piece of code that causes an unexpected, usually negative, event. Viruses are often disguised games or images with clever marketing titles such as "Me, nude."

WHAT IS A WORM?
Computer Worms are viruses that reside in the active memory of a computer and duplicate themselves. They may send copies of themselves to other computers, such as through email or Internet Relay Chat (IRC).

WHAT IS A TROJAN HORSE?
A Trojan horse program is a malicious program that pretends to be a benign application; a Trojan horse program purposefully does something the user does not expect. Trojans are not viruses since they do not replicate, but Trojan horse programs can be just as destructive. Many people use the term to refer only to non-replicating malicious programs, thus making a distinction between Trojans and viruses.

SOURCE: *http://us.mcafee.com/virusInfo/default.asp?cid=10371.*

History

In 1989, John McAfee formed McAfee Associates to market his anti-virus software. He advertised the company's products on computer bulletin boards, requiring users to pay for the products only if they found them useful. Individuals were so satisfied with the anti-virus software that they recommended it to their companies. Only three years after its humble beginnings, McAfee Associates was so successful that the company decided to go public.[10]

In conjunction with the decision to incorporate, McAfee Associates also "began to diversify and market other types of software compatible with the electronic channel."[11] McAfee Associates expanded product offerings primarily through acquisitions and achieved higher sales through a product bundling strategy. The growth and sales strategies proved profitable and by 1997 annual sales topped $600 million. Also in 1997, McAfee Associates merged with Network General Corporation to form Network Associates. In an effort to achieve the company's vision to become a leading network security and desktop management specialist, Network Associates continued to pursue an acquisition growth strategy acquiring companies such as Trusted Information Systems, Secure Networks, and CyberMedia.

Network Associates' fast track to success came to a sudden halt when in 1999 the company was forced to restate financial results from the previous year. Shareholder lawsuits ensued and the company suffered a loss. The following year several top executives including CEO William Larson resigned after "a surprise earnings warning."[12] This was not the end of the bad news for Network Associates as the company continued to experience repercussions from its aggressive acquisition strategy. In 2003 the company was forced to restate financial results for FYs 1998–2000 after a second SEC investigation revealed improper accounting related to the acquisitions. Despite the setbacks, Network Associates continued to pursue an acquisition growth strategy. This time, however, acquisitions and divestitures streamlined the "business to focus exclusively on security."[13] In late 2004, Network Associates changed its name to McAfee in an effort to reflect the decision to concentrate solely on security products.[14]

Corporate Governance

Exhibit 2A lists the seven members of the board of directors as of January 2005. Only George Samenuk, Chairman and CEO, was an internal member. Board members were elected to staggered three-year terms. The three board committees were audit, compensation, and governance and nominations. All directors except Mr. Samenuk were considered "independent." Mr. Dutkowsky served as lead director. Directors received an annual retainer of $40,000 plus $1,500 for each meeting attended (including committee meetings). The lead director and committee chairs received an additional $10,000 per year.

Exhibit 2B shows the key executives and their salaries. Eric Brown replaced Stephen Richards as Chief Financial Officer in January 2005 when Richards left the company. Raymond Smets, former President of Sniffer Technologies, served as a member of McAfee's top management group from October 2002 when McAfee acquired the company until July 2004 when Sniffer Technology was sold to Network General Division. In addition to salaries and bonuses, the top executives were granted a total of 775,000 shares worth of stock options in 2004.

The executive officers and directors as a group owned 209,847 shares (1.8% of outstanding shares). The financial firms of T. Rowe Price and Lord, Abbett & Company each owned 6% of the outstanding stock.

EXHIBIT 2
Board of Directors
and Key Executives:
McAfee, Inc.

A. BOARD OF DIRECTORS

George Samenuk, 49
Chief Executive Officer, McAfee, Inc. Chairman of the Board since April, 2001. Previously, he served as President and CEO of TradeOut, Inc., a private online exchange company. He had also served in various senior management positions with IBM. Board member since 2001. Term expires 2006. Owned 175,000 McAfee shares of stock.

Leslie G. Denend, 64
President of McAfee, Inc. 1997–1998. Previously, he served as CEO and President of Network General Corp. prior to its being merged into McAfee, Inc. Board member since 1995. Term expires 2006. Owned 6,297 McAfee shares of stock.

Robert Pangia, 52
General Partner and Managing Member of Ivy Capital Partners. He previously held a number of senior management positions with Paine Webber Inc. Board member since 2001. Term expires 2007. Designated "financial expert" on audit committee. Also member of compensation committee.

Robert B. Bucknam, 54
Sr. Vice President of Cross Match Technologies, Inc., a fingerprint identification provider. He previously served as Chief of Staff, Federal Bureau of Investigation and Deputy Attorney General with the U.S. Dept. of Justice. Board member since 2003. Term expires 2005. Member of governance and nominations committee.

Liane Wilson, 62
Consultant. She previously served as Vice Chairman of Washington Mutual, Inc. Board member since 2002. Term expires 2005. Member of audit and governance and nominations committees.

Robert Dutkowsky, 50
Chairman of the Board, CEO, and President of Engenera, Inc. Previously, he served as President and CEO of J. D. Edwards & Company. He also held executive positions with Teradyne, EMC Corporation, and IBM. Board member since 2001. Term expires 2007. Member of audit and compensations committees. Owned 50 McAfee shares of stock.

Denis J. O'Leary, 48
Private investor. Previously, he was Executive Vice President of J.P. Morgan Chase bank. Board member since 2003. Term expires 2007. Member of compensation and governance and nominations committees.

B. KEY EXECUTIVES

	Salary	Bonus
George Samenuk, 49 Chairman and Chief Executive Officer since January, 2001 when joined firm Previously President & CEO of TradeOut, Inc.	$773,333	$1,075,000
Gene Hodges, 53 President since October, 2001 Held various executive positions since joined firm in 1995	445,833	451,250
Kent H. Roberts, 48 Executive Vice President, Secretary and General Counsel Since January, 2001 Held various legal positions since joined firm in May, 1998	333,333	170,938

EXHIBIT 2
(Continued)

Kevin Weiss, 48 Executive Vice President of Worldwide Sales since joined firm in October, 2002 Previously Senior VP of Ariba, Inc.	441,667	463,750
Eric F. Brown, 39 Chief Financial Officer and Executive Vice President since January 2005 when joined firm Previously CFO of MicroStrategy, Inc.	998,000	

SOURCE: *2004 McAfee 10-K Form.*

Current Situation

McAfee has unleashed several initiatives to improve financial statement performance. In 2004, the company paid down $347 million in convertible debt and repurchased $220 million in common stock. In addition to altering its capitalization strategy, McAfee also implemented several cost-cutting initiatives. Revenues had declined over the past two years, while net income had increased. (See **Exhibits 3 and 4**.) The initiatives are aimed at achieving a 25% operating margin. Ongoing operations generated over $350 million in cash, ending the fiscal year with nearly $1 billion in cash, cash equivalents, and investments. Deferred revenue for the period increased by $200 million.[15]

McAfee partners with service providers (MSPs, ASPs, Telcos, and outsourcing service providers) to sell products.[16] Companies will often opt to outsource the network to a third-party provider for economic reasons. As part of the provider's responsibility it must safeguard the client's network and assets. Rather than develop its own security software, the provider relies on a company such as McAfee to provide the necessary security tools. The partnership enables McAfee to sell multiple products to multiple companies through the convenience of a single provider.

Products

The company provides two categories of products, the McAfee System Protection Solution for desktops and servers and the McAfee Network Protection Solutions for corporate networks. (See **Exhibit 5**.) Customers of both product categories include businesses, governments, and consumers. McAfee distributes products to five main geographic locations including North America, Europe, the Middle East, Africa, Japan, and Latin America.[17]

Desktop and server solutions include anti-virus, anti-hacker and anti-spyware, antispam and anti-abuse, mobile and wireless, and bundled products. Consumers purchase a license for these products and must periodically update the software to keep it current.

- **Anti-Virus**—"McAfee VirusScan detects, blocks, and removes viruses and spyware" that can damage important documents or slow PC processing.[18]
- **Anti-Hacker & Anti-Spyware**—Two products provide hacker and spyware protection. The first is "McAfee Personal Firewall Plus" which "safeguards . . . documents . . . by preventing unwanted Internet connections to or from your PC."[19] "McAfee AntiSpyware detects potentially unwanted programs (PUPs), such as spyware, adware, dialers, tracking

EXHIBIT 3
Income Statement:
McAfee, Inc.
(Dollar amounts
in thousands)

Year Ending December 31	2004	2003	2002
Net revenue			
Product	$ 294,163	$ 513,610	$ 631,550
Services and support	616,379	422,726	411,494
Total net revenue	910,542	936,336	1,043,044
Cost of net revenue:			
Product	73,058	80,895	101,019
Services and support	62,520	57,362	60,539
Amortization of purchased technology	13,331	11,369	3,153
Total cost of net revenue	148,909	149,626	164,711
Operating costs:			
Research and development	172,717	184,606	148,801
Marketing and sales	354,380	363,306	397,747
General and administrative	139,845	129,920	119,393
(Gain) loss on sale of assets and technology	(240,336)	788	(9,301)
Litigation (reimbursement) settlement	(24,991)	—	70,000
Restructuring charges	17,493	22,667	1,116
Amortization of intangibles	14,065	15,637	10,742
Severance/bonus costs related to disposition	10,070	—	—
Reimbursement from transition services agreement	(5,997)	—	—
Provision for (recovery of) doubtful accounts, net	1,716	(1,216)	(219)
Acquisition related costs not subject to capitalization	—	—	16,026
In-process research and development	—	6,600	—
Total operating costs	438,962	722,308	754,305
Income from operations	322,671	64,402	124,028
Interest and other income	15,889	15,917	27,324
Interest and other expenses	(5,315)	(7,543)	(25,085)
(Loss) gain on repurchase of convertible debt	(15,070)	(2,727)	26
(Loss) gain on investments, net	(1,704)	3,076	3,838
Impairment of strategic and other investments	—	—	(198)
Income before provision for (benefit from) income taxes, minority interest and cumulative effect of change in accounting principle	316,471	73,125	129,933
Provision for (benefit from) income taxes	91,406	13,220	(274)
Income before minority interest and cumulative effect of change in accounting principle	225,065	59,905	130,207
Minority interest in income of consolidated subsidiaries	—	—	(1,895)
Income before cumulative effect of change in accounting principle	225,065	59,905	128,312
Cumulative effect of change in accounting principle, net of taxes of $3,590	—	10,337	—
Net income	$ 225,065	$ 70,242	$ 128,312
Other comprehensive income:			
Unrealized losses on marketable securities, net of reclassification adjustment for losses recognized on marketable securities during the period and income tax	$ (2,129)	$ (709)	$ (2,667)
Foreign currency translation (loss) gain	(4,537)	10,578	10,744
Comprehensive income	$ 218,399	$ 80,111	$ 136,389

Note: All notes were deleted

SOURCE: *2004 McAfee 10-K Form, p. 35.*

EXHIBIT 4
Balance Sheet:
McAfee, Inc.
(Dollar amounts
in thousands)

Year Ending December 31	2004	2003
ASSETS		
Current assets:		
Cash and cash equivalents	$ 291,155	$ 333,651
Short-term marketable securities	232,929	174,499
Accounts receivable, net of allowance for doubtful accounts of $2,536 and $2,863, respectively	137,520	170,218
Prepaid expenses, income taxes, and other current assets	103,687	97,616
Deferred income taxes	200,459	160,550
Assets held for sale	—	24,719
Total current assets	965,750	961,253
Long-term marketable securities	400,597	258,107
Restricted cash	617	20,547
Property and equipment, net	91,715	111,672
Deferred income taxes	220,604	199,196
Intangible assets, net	107,133	105,952
Goodwill	439,180	443,593
Other assets	12,080	20,178
Total assets	$ 2,237,676	$ 2,120,498
LIABILITIES AND STOCKHOLDERS' EQUITY		
Current liabilities:		
Accounts payable	$ 32,891	$ 32,099
Accrued liabilities	197,368	147,281
Deferred revenue	475,621	342,795
Liabilities related to assets held for sale	—	23,310
Total current liabilities	705,880	545,485
Deferred revenue, less current portion	125,752	116,762
Convertible debt	—	347,397
Accrued taxes and other long-term liabilities	204,796	222,765
Total liabilities	1,036,428	1,232,409
STOCKHOLDERS' EQUITY		
Preferred stock, $0.01 par value:		
Authorized: 5,000,000 shares; Issued and outstanding: none in 2004 and 2003	—	—
common stock, $0.01 par value: authorized: 300,000,000 shares; Issued:162,266,174 shares and 162,071,798 shares for 2004 and 2003, respectively; outstanding: 162,266,174 shares and 161,721,798 for 2004 and 2003, respectively	1,623	1,621
Treasury stock, at cost: no shares in 2004 and 350,000 shares in 2003	—	(4,707)
Additional paid-in capital	1,178,855	1,087,625
Deferred stock-based compensation	(1,777)	(598)
Accumulated other comprehensive income	27,361	34,027
Accumulated deficit	(4,814)	(229,879)
Total stockholders' equity	1,201,248	888,089
Total liabilities and stockholders' equity	$ 2,237,676	$ 2,120,498

SOURCE: *2004 McAfee 10-K Form, p. 34.*

EXHIBIT 5
McAffee Solution
Focus: McAfee, Inc.

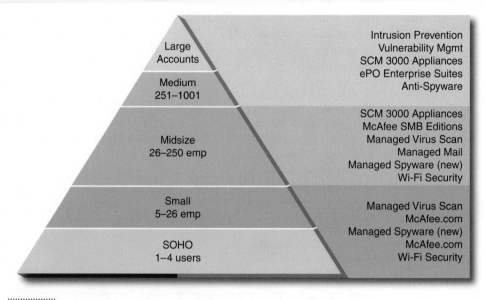

SOURCE: *McAfee, Inc.*

cookies, and other unwelcome marketing programs before they compromise . . . information, invade your privacy, or slow the performance of your PC."[20]

- **Anti-Spam & Anti-Abuse**—"McAfee SpamKiller" is designed to protect "personal and financial information against known 'phishing' scams by blocking access to known and potentially fraudulent identity theft websites."[21] While "McAfee Privacy Service helps prevent personal information . . . from being transmitted over the Internet." It also allows parents to set controls for the children's Internet activities. "In addition, McAfee Privacy Service helps block online advertisements and filter inappropriate Website, e-mail, and IM content."[22]

- **Wireless & Mobile**—McAfee Virus Scan Mobile protects mobile phones from virus, worms, and Trojan horses that may be transmitted by accessing email, instant messaging, or downloads on a wireless phone.[23] The "Wireless Home Network Security encrypts . . . data as it is sent over Wi-Fi and blocks hackers from accessing your wireless network,"[24] protecting personal wireless technologies.

Products are sold on a subscription basis. A single-user, one year license for the home computer Internet security suite is sold for $69.99 before a mail-in rebate of $20. A three-user, one year license is available for $129.99. Products for small businesses are priced depending on the size of the organization and the length of the license.

Network Protection Solutions for corporate networks incorporates two core technologies—IntruShield and Foundstone. McAfee acquired Foundstone Inc. in 2004 and immediately integrated its technology into McAfee's product offerings. Foundstone is a priority-based technology designed to identify the most important assets of the enterprise and assess their vulnerabilities. The system then responds to attacks on the network to remediate the situation. Within the Foundstone technologies, there are five protection solutions:[25]

- **Foundstone Enterprise**—is an "appliance-based solution" that "offers network infrastructure protection to ensure business continuity through asset discovery, inventory, and prioritization; threat intelligence and correlation; and enhanced remediation tracking and reporting."

- **Foundstone FS1000 Appliance**—"is a complete . . . solution that powers Foundstone Enterprise." It "is engineered to manage and mitigate the business risks associated with digital vulnerabilities."

■ **Foundstone On-Demand Service**—"performs client vulnerability assessments from the Foundstone Operations Center." It is a "subscription-based, zero deployment solution for effectively assessing vulnerabilities for Internet facing network resources."

■ **Foundstone Threat Correction Module**—an add-on module to Foundstone Enterprise that "delivers up-to-the-minute Threat Intelligence Alerts from Foundstone Labs so you can respond immediately to breaking events such as worms and wide-scale attacks."

■ **Foundstone Remediation Module**—"is a fully automated and tightly integrated [add-on] module that auto-assigns tickets based on discovered vulnerabilities and auto-closes them once the vulnerabilities have been fixed."

IntruShield is an intrusion prevention system (IPS) combining hardware and software technology that "delivers comprehensive and proactive intrusion prevention to protect business availability and critical network infrastructure by detecting and blocking attacks before they inflict damage."[26] "The . . . architecture integrates patented signature, anomaly, and Denial of Service (DoS) analysis techniques, enabling highly accurate and intelligent attack detection and prevention up to multi-gigabit speeds."

IntruShield has received several awards for technology leadership and was recently recognized as a worldwide market share leader for network based intrusion software by Infonetics Research.[27]

In the future, McAfee hopes to expand its mobile and wireless solutions. McAfee and VeriFone Holdings, Inc., collaborated to be first to market with a virus protection solution for point of sale terminals in the United States. As the trend in merchandising evolves to utilizing Internet Protocol for payment processing, VeriFone and McAfee are seizing the opportunity to provide real-time monitoring and protection for this venue. In the future the companies foresee the virus protection solution being offered on all IP-enabled systems, though for now it is only available on the Omni 3750 Ethernet-enabled payment solution.[28]

Competitors

McAfee competes against companies such as Symantec, Computer Associates, Trend Micro, Sophos, Fescure, Panda, and Dr. Ahn's in the security software market (see **Exhibit 6**). The industry is highly competitive, and Symantec is McAfee's most intimidating competitor. **Exhibit 7** shows the rapid growth predicted for security software.

EXHIBIT 6
McAfee's Competitors

Network Fault Identification and Application Performance Management	Anti-virus Software	Intrusion Detection and Protection Products
Netscout	Symantec	Symantec
WildPackets	Microsoft	Computer Associates
Agilent	Computer Associates	Cisco Systems
Cisco Systems	Trend Micro	Enterasys Security Systems
Compuware Corporation	Sophos	Netscreen
Concord Communications	Fescure	Sourcefire
Finisar	Panda	TippingPont Technologies
Fluke Networks	Dr. Ahn's	
Network Instruments		
Niksun		

SOURCE: *McAfee, Inc.*

EXHIBIT 7
Predicted Total
Available Market for
Security Software

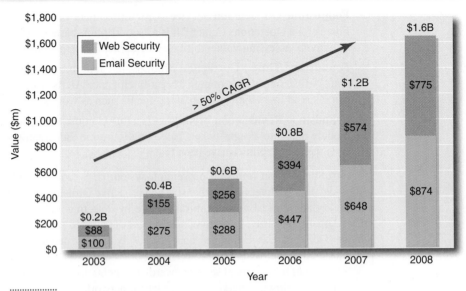

SOURCES: *IDC (August 2004); PM and Raymond James Reporting.*

Symantec Corporation

Symantec is the industry leader in security solution software and McAfee's strongest competitor. Symantec "provides a variety of content and network security software for both consumers and businesses."[29] The company's product lines include client, gateway, and server security solutions for virus protection; firewalls and VPN networks; vulnerability management; intrusion detection; and security services.

Symantec is most noted for the Norton series of personal computer security solutions. In fact, by capitalizing on the popularity of Norton, Symantec was able to expand into the corporate security market.[30] The company also provides consulting services.

Symantec's premier products include Intruder Alert, NetRecon, Norton AntiVirus, Norton SystemWords, Norton Utilities, pcANYWHERE, Symantec AntiVirus, and Symantec Ghost. These products provide everything from intrusion detection to network vulnerability management, and data transfer from remote PCs to the host. Thus Symantec is able to provide a solution to protect an entire enterprise network from the threat of viruses, worms, and Trojan horses.

Like McAfee, Symantec has also chosen an acquisition growth strategy. The company has a long history of M&A activity, but most notable was the proposed merger with VERITAS. VERITAS was an industry leader in information storage, so a merger with Symantec would enable the corporation to deliver products that incorporated both data storage and protection. Symantec's vision for the future was to enable customers to "bounce back from disruptions" and continue efficient operations.[33]

Symantec has successfully bounced back from its own business disruptions. In 1997, Symantec "filed copyright-infringement charges against Network Associates." The following year anti-virus product users filed a lawsuit against Symantec "alleging that it ignored its warranty by charging to fix a year 2000 software glitch."[34]

Despite the alleged copyright infringement and shareholder lawsuit, Symantec has had strong financial performance. Net profit margin has increased for the past three years; earnings per share has also increased over this time period. Symantec had annual sales of $1.87 billion in FY 2004 and net income of $371 million. The company's stock priced topped out at $48.09 in 2004, $13 per share more than the 2003 high.[36]

Computer Associates

Computer Associates is "one of the world's largest software" providers. Founded in 1976, the company is headquartered in Islandia, NY.[37] CA's product line is extensive and includes solutions for "business intelligence, storage, security, and network management applications."[38] With revenue of $3.5 billion in 2004, the company primarily services *Fortune* 500, Global 1000, and government organizations.[39]

Over the past 10 years the company has made significant investments in systems management and security; currently this segment of the company is greatly expanding.[40] With product offerings that support personal computers, small businesses, and large enterprises and have the ability to be customized by industry, CA delivers security solutions to diverse market segments.[41]

*e*Trust Security Management solution is designed to protect critical information in large enterprises. The software enables the company to enforce privacy policies and comply with regulations while protecting assets from viruses and worms.[42] Similarly, CA offers an *e*Trust product line designed to protect small to medium-sized businesses. Security solutions in the product line include anti-virus, anti-spyware, intrusion detection, content management, and vulnerability management.[43] CA also provides small-business security solutions bundled with their other products. For example, a small business can purchase software that includes security solutions along with backup storage solutions for quick and easy recovery of data.[44] Home and home office security solutions include *e*Trust spyware, virus, and spam protection. A bundled security solution is also available for this market segment.

The company has faced multiple setbacks over the past few years. In 2004, Computer Associates was forced to restate financial results for 2000 and 2001. The investigations began shortly after the dot-com crash in 2001. In 2003 and 2004 several executives were removed from the company. CA signed a Deferred Prosecution Agreement with the Department of Justice in September 2004 accepting full responsibility for previous activities and agreeing to pay restitution to shareholders. However, with a new CEO in place the company was making strides forward.

Panda Software

In 1990, Panda Software was established in Bilbao, Spain. By 1995, Panda had achieved a market leadership position and began international expansion. In 2005, the company employed more than 500 individuals at its headquarters in Spain, and an almost equal number of individuals are employed in subsidiaries and franchises. Products are sold in more than 200 countries around the world. Panda has enjoyed unprecedented growth as a privately owned company, achieving a revenue increase of 55% from 2003 to 2004; this is three times the industry average.[45]

Like the other antivirus vendors, Panda provides solutions for personal computers, small to medium-sized businesses, and large enterprises. The company strives to achieve rapid release of updates to customers as well as excellent customer service. One example of the company's focus on customer service is a 24-hour, 7 day a week technical center, available in every country where Panda products are sold.[46]

The software utilizes a signature-based technology to identify known threats and prevent them from damaging assets. "Unlike other companies in the industry, all of Panda Software's products include the same signature-based detection engine, and as a result they all have the same capacity to detect and eliminate threats."[47]

TruPrevent is a patented technology designed to prevent unidentified viruses from infecting the computer or system. Currently, it takes antivirus companies approximately 72 hours to update against a new threat. TruPrevent protects assets during that 72-hour window from discovery of a virus or other intrusion device and the release of an update to uniquely identify and eliminate it.[48]

In addition to its focus on quality products and excellent customer service, the company also implements several socially responsible programs. Specifically, the initiatives focus "on the protection of children, the cooperation in the fight against AIDS and other epidemics, the protection of the environment, etc." Panda also invests in improving local communities in which the company operates.[49]

Trend Micro

Trend Micro Incorporated was founded in 1988 by Steve Chang. The company is headquartered in Tokyo, Japan, and maintains 25 corporate offices throughout the world. Trend Micro has a reputation for innovation with its outbreak solution software. "Trend Micro focuses on . . . providing customers with a comprehensive approach to managing the outbreak lifecycle and the impact of network worms and virus threats to productivity and information."[50]

The company is highly focused and significantly smaller than competitors such as McAfee, Symantec, and Computer Associates. FY 2004 revenues were $587.4 million USD (62.5 billion yen at an exchange rate of JPY105.63/USD). Trend Micro experienced 29% growth in revenue between FY03 and FY04. Earnings during that time period increased by an astounding 71%, causing stockholder equity to increase by 46.5%.[51]

Although Trend Micro does not have the breadth of product offerings of McAfee, Symantec, and Computer Associates, it does have product-line depth. Security solutions include virus protection for enterprises and home users, outbreak life-cycle management, layered network virus protection, email and groupware protection, server gateway and domain protection, file storage, and mobile security.[52]

Sophos

Sophos is headquartered in Abingdon, UK, and provides products to more than 150 countries. The company's products are highly scalable and can be used in small businesses, global enterprises, or anything in between. Over the past year and a half, Sophos has focused on consolidating its product portfolio, adding anti-spam and email policy enforcement protection. The company is no longer singularly identified as an anti-virus company but rather as an entire protection solution. Notably, Sophos is recognized for its gateway and endpoint solutions.[53]

Products are designed to protect networks against virus, spam, spyware, and policy abuse. The enterprise solution is a multi-tier, cross-platform application that monitors, updates, and reports threats.[54] Small-business solutions are designed for companies with small IT budgets and less experienced IT professionals. Products are engineered for simplicity and usability. Sophos' Small Business Suite "provides anti-virus and anti-spam protection for desktops, file servers, and email servers" in a single package.[55]

Sophos also provides industry-specific solutions for educational institutions and the government. Security solutions for the education industry are developed to function on multiple platforms while remaining within a specified price point.[56] Government solutions integrate strict security policies and are also designed to function on multi-platforms.[57]

Sophos, a privately held company, has experienced substantial financial success, growing at twice the market rate in FY2004. The British company has plans to increase its workforce by 13% in the coming year to parallel financial growth.

Microsoft: A New Entrant

In an internally generated document in 2004, Microsoft stated that spyware had become a serious problem for PC users and "customers have made it clear that they want Microsoft to deliver effective solutions to protect against the threat."[59] Microsoft developed a twofold plan to assist consumers in the battle against spyware. On December 16, 2004, Microsoft acquired GIANT Company Software, Inc., an anti-spyware leader. Subsequent to the acquisition Microsoft developed a beta version of anti-spyware software that was distributed free to anyone who would like to download the program. Additionally, Microsoft has made Microsoft Windows Malicious Spyware Removal Tool available in monthly updates to assist in ridding PCs of viruses and worms.[60]

Microsoft's entry into the anti-virus, anti-spyware industry poses a serious threat for existing competitors. With nearly $4.9 billion in cash and cash equivalents as of June 30, 2005,[61] the sheer size and purchasing power of Microsoft could potentially eliminate companies such as McAfee.

Looking to the Future

The anti-virus industry is highly competitive with large, all-encompassing solution providers as well as smaller niche players that cater to specific market segments. Overseas competitors also pose a serious threat to McAfee's business. CEO George Samenuk wondered how McAfee could leverage its strengths to compete in the coming months and years. What competitive advantages does McAfee's software have that customers are willing to pay for despite the availability of free anti-spyware software from Microsoft? What strategy should McAfee pursue to remain a market leader in the anti-virus industry? With rapidly changing market conditions and the threat of Microsoft, Samenuk knew the next 12 months would be critical to the survival and success of McAfee.

NOTES

1. http://phx.corporate-ir.net/phoenix.zhtml?c=104920&p=irol-IRHome. October 26, 2005.
2. Dear shareholders.
3. Dear shareholders.
4. Company's mission statement.
5. http://www.virus-scan-software.com/virus-scan-help/answers/the-history-of-computer-viruses.shtml. November 17, 2005.
6. http://www.virus-scan-software.com/virus-scan-help/answers/the-history-of-computer-viruses.shtml. November 17, 2005.
7. http://www.virus-scan-software.com/virus-scan-help/answers/the-history-of-computer-viruses.shtml. November 17, 2005.
8. http://www.virus-scan-software.com/virus-scan-help/answers/the-history-of-computer-viruses.shtml. November 17, 2005.
9. http://www.sophos.com/pressoffice/news/articles/2005/02/pr_uk_20050207marketgrowth.html. November 16, 2005.
10. Hoovers Inc., Austin, TX 2005.
11. http://phx.corporate-ir.net/phoenix.zhtml?c=104920&p=irol-History.
12. Hoovers Inc., Austin, TX 2005.
13. http://phx.corporate-ir.net/phoenix.zhtml?c=104920&p=irol-History.
14. Hoovers Inc., Austin, TX 2005.
15. http://library.corporate-ir.net/library/10/104/104920/items/155360/AR_042205.pdf. November 18, 2005. page 2.
16. http://www.mcafee.com/us/about/partners/msp/default.asp. November 18, 2005.

17. http://www.mcafee.com/us/about/home.htm. October 21, 2005.
18. http://us.mcafee.com/root/package.asp?pkgid=100&cid=16259. November 1, 2005.
19. http://us.mcafee.com/root/package.asp?pkgid=103&cid=16260. November 1, 2005.
20. http://us.mcafee.com/root/package.asp?pkgid=206&cid=16261. November 1, 2005.
21. http://us.mcafee.com/root/package.asp?pkgid=156. November 1, 2005.
22. http://us.mcafee.com/root/package.asp?pkgid=104&cid= 16262. November 1, 2005.
23. http://us.mcafee.com/root/landingpages/afflandpage.asp?lpname=vs_mobile. November 1, 2005.
24. http://us.mcafee.com/root/package.asp?pkgid=250. November 1, 2005.
25. http://www.foundstone.com/index.hetm?subnav=products/navigation.htm&subcontent=/products/product overview.htm.
26. http://www.mcafee.com/us/local_content/datasheets/ds_instrushieldsecuirtymanagement.pdf
27. http://www.monitortoday.com/index.php?page=~~newsitems_9143
28. http://global.factiva.com/en/eSrch/ss_hl.asp. November 1, 2005.
29. Hoover's Inc. Bloomberg, L.P. October 21, 2005.
30. Hoover's Inc. Bloomberg, L.P. October 21, 2005.
31. http://library.corporate-ir.net/library/89/894/89422/items/ 163589/Final_Symantec_2005_10Kwrap.pdf. November 9, 2005.

32. Hoover's Inc. Bloomberg, L.P. October 21, 2005. page 6.

33. http://library.corporate-ir.net/library/89/894/89422/items/ 163589/ Final_Symantec_2005_10Kwrap.pdf. November 9, 2005. page 8. Symantec Corp. 2004 Annual Report.

34. Hoover's, Inc. Bloomberg, L.P. October 21, 2005.

35. http://library.corporate-ir.net/library/89/894/89422/items/163589/ Final_Symantec_2005_10Kwrap.pdf. November 9, 2005. Symantec Corp. 2004 Annual Report.

36. Hoover's Inc. Bloomberg, L.P. October 21, 2005. page 3.

37. http://www.ca.com/invest/reports/corpprofile/. November 15, 2005.

38. Hoover's Inc. Bloomberg, L.P. November 10, 2005.

39. http://investor.ca.com/phoenix.zhtml?c=83100&p=irol-home-profile. November 10, 2005.

40. http://media.corporate-ir.net/media_files/irol/83/83100/reports/ 2005arpdf.pdf. November 15, 2005. page 6.

41. http://www3.ca.com/products/. November 15, 2005.

42. http://www3.ca.com/Files/WhitePapers/etrust_security_ management_white_paper.pdf. November 15, 2005. page 2.

43. http://www3.ca.com/smb/solution.aspx?ID=5276. November 15, 2005.

44. http://www3.ca.com/smb/solution.aspx?id=5312&culture=en-us. November 15, 2005.

45. http://www.pandasoftware.com/about_panda/about_panda. December 1, 2005.

46. http://www.pandasoftware.com/about_panda/press_room/_ Best+Performer_BusinessSecure.htm. December 1, 2005.

47. http://www.pandasoftware.com/about_panda/technology. December 1, 2005.

48. http://www.pandasoftware.com/about_panda/technology. December 1, 2005.

49. http://www.pandasoftware.com/about_panda/about_panda. December 1, 2005.

50. http://www.trendmicro.com/en/about/investors/company/about/ overview.htm. November 15, 2005.

51. http://www.trendmicro.com/en/about/investors/accounts/ historical/ annual.htm. November 15, 2005.

52. http://www.trendmicro.com/en/products/global/enterprise.htm. November 15, 2005.

53. http://www.sophos.com/pressoffice/news/articles/2005/02/ pr_uk_20050207marketgrowth.html. November 16, 2005.

54. http://www.sophos.com/products/es/. November 16, 2005.

55. http://www.sophos.com/products/sb/sbs/. November 16, 2005.

56. http://www.sophos.com/products/education/. November 16, 2005.

57. http://www.sophos.com/products/government/. November 16, 2005.

58. http://www.sophos.com/pressoffice/news/articles/2005/02/ pr_uk_20050207marketgrowth.html. November 16, 2005.

59. http://www.microsoft.com/presspass/press/2004/dec04/12-16GIANTPR.mspx. December 2, 2005.

60. http://www.microsoft.com/presspass/features/2005/jan05/01-06Spyware.mspx. December 6, 2005.

61. http://www.microsoft.com/msft/ar05/flashversion/10k_fr_ bal.html. December 6, 2005.

CASE **12**

Reorganizing Yahoo!

P. Indu and Vivek Gupta

"We're putting the right people in the right places to execute our focused growth strategy. Yahoo! has an extraordinarily skilled and experienced group of senior executives and we're adding outside senior talent to this already strong team. Our new structure gives us the opportunity to draw more fully on Yahoo!'s deep bench of talent, both at the new group level and down through the organization, while also increasing accountability, reducing bottlenecks and speeding decision-making. We'll also continue to drive sustained innovation by recruiting, developing and retaining the best talent in our industry."[1]

TERRY SEMEL, CHAIRMAN & CEO, YAHOO, ON THE COMPANY'S REORGANIZATION PROGRAM ANNOUNCED IN 2006.

"This is just the beginning of what Yahoo! needs to do. It may take all of 2007. Change like this is evolutionary, not revolutionary. The new division heads will need time to grasp the enormity of the task at hand."[2]

JORDAN ROHAN, ANALYST RBC CAPITAL MARKETS[3] ON YAHOO'S REORGANIZATION, IN 2006.

Introduction

ON FEBRUARY 05, 2006, U.S.-BASED INTERNET SERVICES COMPANY YAHOO! INC. (Yahoo) moved all its advertisers to a new ranking model called 'Panama' in order to regain customers who had shifted to the Google's[4] more popular AdWords.[5] Yahoo's new algorithm and ranking model would rank the advertisements based on the highest bid on search keywords by the advertiser and the number of clicks. Industry analysts opined that with the new model, Yahoo would be in a better position to challenge Google. Panama received encouraging reviews from the customers and the advertisers. According to Marianne Wolk, analyst at Susquehanna Financial Group,[6] "The early feedback on Panama is strong. Click-through rates are better than expected."[7]

In December 2006, prior to the launch of Panama, Yahoo had announced that it was reorganizing the company. The reorganization became necessary as Yahoo found itself unable to generate enough revenues from search-related advertising despite being the most visited Web site on the Internet. Between July 2005 and July 2006, Yahoo's share in total online searches in the United States went down from 30.5% to 28.8% (see **Exhibit 1** for share of online searches by engine in July 2005 and July 2006).

	July 05	June 06	July 06	% Change
Google Sites	36.5	44.7	43.7	4.2
Yahoo! Sites	30.5	28.5	28.8	−1.7
MSN Microsoft sites	15.5	12.8	12.8	−2.7
Times Warner Network	9.9	5.6	5.9	−4.0
Ask Network	6.1	5.1	5.4	−0.7

Note:[1] Total work, home and university Internet users in the United States, Internet population is 100%.

SOURCE: *www.comscore.com.*

In spite of total revenues going up from US$5,257.67 million in 2005 to US$6,425.68 million in 2006, Yahoo's net income fell from US$1,896.2 million to US$751 million (see **Exhibit 2** for Yahoo's Income Statement between 2001 and 2006). According to analysts, the problem was that Yahoo was not focusing on any particular product, but was trying instead to cater to different customers through a single portal. Though Yahoo acquired several companies, it failed to integrate

EXHIBIT 2
Income Statement: Yahoo, Inc.
(Dollar amounts in millions)

Year Ending December 31	2006	2005	2004	2003	2002	2001
Total Revenue	**$6,425.68**	**$5,257.67**	**$ 3,574.52**	**$1,625.10**	**$953.07**	**$ 717.42**
Cost Revenue	2,669.10	2,096.20	1,342.34	370.09	162.88	157.00
Gross Profit	**3,756.58**	**3,161.47**	**2,232.18**	**1,255.01**	**790.19**	**560.42**
Selling, General, Adm Expenses	2,002.48	1,397.41	1,072.92	709.67	539.05	470.91
Research & Development	688.34	547.14	368.76	207.28	141.77	121.47
Depreciation/Amortization	124.79	109.19	101.92	42.38	21.19	64.08
Unusual Income (Expense)						63.23
Total Operating Expense	2,815.61	2,053.74	1,543.60	959.33	702.01	719.69
Operating Income	940.97	1,107.73	688.58	295.68	88.18	−159.27
Interest Income, Net Non-Operating	139.78	1,092.45	475.95	45.98	87.69	4.36
Gain (Loss) on Sales of Assets	15.16	337.96				
Other, Net	2.09	5.44	20.49	1.53	2.35	72.09
Income Before Tax	1,098.00	2,543.58	1,185.02	343.19	178.22	−82.82
Income After Tax	**458.01**	**767.82**	**437.97**	**147.04**	**71.28**	**−9.97**
Minority Interest	−0.71	−7.78	−2.50	−5.92		
Equity in Affiliates	112.11	128.24	94.99	47.65		
Net Income	**$ 751.39**	**$1,896.22**	**$ 839.54**	**$ 237.88**	**$106.94**	**$ −92.79**

Consolidated Balance Sheets Data:

	December 31,				
	2002	2003	2004	2005	2006
			(In thousands)		
Cash and cash equivalents	$ 234,073	$ 415,892	$ 823,723	$ 1,429,693	$ 1,569,871
Marketable debt securities	$1,299,965	$2,150,323	$2,918,539	$ 2,570,155	$ 1,967,414
Working capital	$ 558,190	$1,013,913	$2,909,768	$ 2,245,481	$ 2,276,148
Total assets	$2,790,181	$5,931,654	$9,178,201	$10,831,834	$11,513,608
Long-term liabilities	$ 84,540	$ 822,890	$ 851,782	$ 1,061,367	$ 870,948
Total stockholders' equity	$2,262,270	$4,363,490	$7,101,446	$ 8,566,415	$ 9,160,610

SOURCES: *finance.google.com and 2006 Annual Report, Yahoo, Inc., 1.33.*

them. Even in search-related advertising, which had emerged as a major revenue generator in the Internet business, Yahoo fell behind its competitor Google, which was generating twice as much revenue on each search ad. The challenges that Yahoo was facing externally were further compounded by the internal turmoil in the company brought about by the complex organization structure and slow decision-making process.

Yahoo delayed several product launches as it wanted to focus on Panama, which had been delayed by more than two quarters. Panama was to be launched in the second quarter of 2006 but was not launched even at the end of 2006. Yahoo's problems were reported widely in the media. At the same time, the *Wall Street Journal*[8] published an internal memo that was circulated by a senior vice president at Yahoo, about the lack of focus in the company due to which its resources were thinly spread across several business segments.

Within a month, Yahoo introduced a new organization structure, under which the company was reorganized into three operating units, namely the Audience Group, the Advertiser & Publisher Group, and the Technology Group with the focus on the customers, advertisers, and technology, respectively. The heads of the three units reported directly to Terry Semel (Semel), chairman & CEO of Yahoo.

Analysts opined that with the reorganization and Panama in place, Yahoo could well be on its way to regaining its lost glory. According to Martin Pyykkonen, analyst, Global Crown Capital,[9] "I'm not forecasting any kind of wholesale shift here, that all of a sudden Google is going to fall by the wayside … but I do think they (Yahoo) will narrow the gap."[10]

Background Note

Yahoo was founded by Jerry Yang and David Filo, who began exploring the Internet as a hobby after finishing their doctoral theses in electrical engineering at Stanford University. In April 1994, they created a directory to keep track of their personal interests on the Internet. Gradually, they began to spend more and more time on their directory. Later, Yang and Filo started categorizing Web sites as a way to keep track of all the sites they had visited. They posted this list on the Web as "Jerry and David's Guide to the Worldwide Web."

The guide became very popular and became the first choice of people browsing the Web to find sites intelligently. It helped people to discover useful, interesting, and entertaining content on the Internet. In late 1994, the duo changed the name of the guide to Yahoo,[11] positioning it as a customized database designed to serve different users. They developed customized software to help locate, identify, and edit material stored on the Internet. Yahoo rapidly became popular and attracted a lot of media attention.

Yahoo was formally incorporated in March 1995, and by mid-1995 it had implemented a business plan modeled on traditional broadcast media companies. Through its IPO in April 1996, Yahoo sold 2.6 million shares, raising US$38.8 million.

Yahoo generated its revenues mainly from online advertisements, primarily banner ads[12] and ad placement fees, promotions,[13] sponsorships, direct marketing,[14] and merchandising. It also generated revenues from monthly hosting fees and commissions on online sales from its merchant partners. These included transaction fees generated from the sale of merchandise on its site.

Within the four years from 1997 to 2000, Yahoo reported substantial growth in its revenues. More than 85% of its revenues came from the sale of banners and sponsorship advertising while the remaining came from business services and e-commerce transactions. By mid-2000, Yahoo was drawing more than 180 million unique visitors,[15] which made Yahoo a leading Internet brand.

In late 2000, Yahoo faced several problems owing to the internal rivalry between President Jeffrey Mallett and CEO Timothy A Koogle (Koogle). Its troubles were compounded by the fact that the company had grown complacent and did not adapt to the rapidly changing business environment. Yahoo was heavily dependent on the advertising revenues generated through dotcoms. Once the dotcoms began going out of business, Yahoo's ad revenues declined sharply. The online advertising market was going through major changes, and the advertisers were looking beyond the banner ads, toward ads that integrated the Internet, television, and radio. Yahoo, however, did not understand what kind of advertising would work for the customers. It failed to make any improvements in its business models, which would have allowed it to cater to a wide range of customers. Several key personnel also left the company during the time.

In the first quarter of 2001, with a sharp decline in online advertisement sales, Yahoo reduced its revenue forecast from US$230 million to US$175 million. At a board meeting convened in February 2001, it was decided that Koogle should step down, making way for Semel. Semel brought in several changes in the company and the number of business units was reduced from 44 to just five. He also announced the layoff of 400 people from Yahoo's 3,500 workforce. Several new services, including subscription-based services were introduced.

In order to consolidate its position, Yahoo entered into several partnership deals. One such deal was with Overture, a paid search services[16] provider. The acquisitions made by Yahoo included Hotjobs.com, an online careers site, in February 2002 for US$435 million, and Inktomi Corporation[17] in March 2003 for US$257 million. Yahoo also entered into a licensing agreement with Google to use its search engine technology.

At the end of 2003, Yahoo acquired Overture for around US$1.6 billion. At the time, Overture dominated search-related advertising, and its revenues were almost double that of Google. Through Overture's advertising platform, advertisers could select words and search phrases and bid for them. This enabled their advertisements to be shown along with the regular search results. As Overture was highly successful, analysts opined that Yahoo was making the right moves and could consolidate its position in the rapidly growing online advertising market by acquiring Overture. With Inktomi and Overture,[18] Yahoo was expected to become a domination force in the search advertising market (see **Exhibit 3** for online advertising market in the United States).

The Problems

Though Yahoo possessed search engine and search advertising technology, integrating both proved to be a difficult task. The engineers in the company had to be convinced that, rather than build the new technology from scratch, it was better to use the acquired technology from Inktomi and Overture. In order to convince the engineers, Semel announced the integration of Yahoo, Inktomi, and Overture to create the best search technology consumers and an effective advertising platform for the advertisers.

However, even until early 2004, Yahoo continued using Google's search engine. In February 2004, Yahoo launched a Web crawler–based[19] search engine, based on Yahoo Slurp.[20] With the prevailing optimism about Yahoo, its stock hit US$36.42 by mid-2004.

Through Overture, advertisements were placed depending on the amount the advertiser had agreed to pay per click. So the advertisements of the highest bidder were placed on the top, irrespective of their relevance. The technology used in Overture could not handle the high traffic expected out of a Yahoo search. Overture required each advertisement to be reviewed and placed with human intervention, and this required a lot of time. To display advertisements based on relevance, Yahoo needed to create new ranking software and a database to measure the clicks the advertisements were receiving. The company planned to spruce up technology and call the project Panama. However, the project ran into trouble with executives from Yahoo and Overture not being able to work together. Meanwhile, by 2004, Google had surpassed Overture in terms of revenues. There were several other areas in which Yahoo faced problems. According to analysts, Yahoo had become a victim of it own success. The company had adopted the model of being a one-stop portal, offering all the services on its website. Over the years, Yahoo's home page grew highly cluttered. The difference was quite stark when compared to Google's home page. Google's home page was simple and user-friendly while Yahoo's homepage had links to a host of products and services, such as

EXHIBIT 3
A Note on Online
Advertising Market
in the U.S.

With the increase in the number of broadband connections, especially after 2000, an Internet advertising market began growing rapidly in the United States. The faster broadband connections offered advertisers an opportunity to dabble with rich media advertising. Moreover, limitations began to surface in the til-then most popular advertising channel, the television, making advertisers look for a better alternative in their efforts to reach the right kind of audience. This led to the emergence of online advertising, especially search-based advertising, where the advertisers chose to advertise only to their target audience. One of the first Internet advertising companies was GoTo.com, later named Overture, which pioneered the concept of paid search. The next player on the horizon was Google, which came out with the idea of payment for advertising according to the clicks the advertisement received. These advertisements were also contextual and were related to the content on the page. On similar lines, companies like Microsoft launched AdCenter and eBay launched AdContext.

Online advertising techniques include banners, pop-ups, pop-unders, search and display ads, and interactive advertising, etc. In display advertising, advertisers pay the online company for space to display the ad, which could be a hyperlinked banner, logo, etc. In the case of sponsorship, the advertisers sponsor a Web site or some of the pages on the website for a particular period. Advertisers opting to advertise through e-mail place their banner ads, links, or newsletters on the e-mails. Other forms of Internet advertising are lead generation, referrals, classifieds, auctions, rich media, and slotting fees.

It is search advertising that remains highly popular. In search advertising, a fee is paid by the advertisers to the online companies to list or link their site domain name to a specific search word or a search phrase. There are different types of search advertising. In paid listings, text links appear at the top of the search results. The advertiser pays only when users click the link. In contextual search, the text links of the advertisers appear depending on the context of the content, irrespective of the search word. Even in this, the advertisers pay the online company only when users click the links. Through paid inclusion, advertisers are guaranteed that their URL is indexed on a search engine.

In the year 2003, Internet advertising was the fastest-growing advertising medium, and by 2005 Internet advertising in the United States was valued at over US$12.5 billion, showing a growth of 30% over 2004. Internet advertising accounted for around 5% of the total advertising revenues in the United States in 2005.

In 2005, keyword search accounted for 34% of the total Internet ad revenue at US$5142 million. Display advertising's share was at 20% with US$2508 million, rich media was US$1003 million, sponsorship at US$627 million, slotting fee US$125 million, classifieds US$2132 million, e-mail US$251 million, and referrals/lead generation about US$753 million.

Advertising Market in the U.S. (2005)

Media	In US$ Million
Direct mail	56.6
Newspapers	47.9
Broadcast & Syndicated TV	35.0
Radio	21.7
Cable TV	18.9
Consumer Magazines	12.9
Internet	**12.4**
Business Magazines	7.8
Outdoor	6.2

Internet Advertising – Annual Revenues

Year	Revenue (In US$ Million)
1996	267
1997	907
1998	1,920
1999	4,621
2000	8,087
2001	7,134
2002	6,010
2003	7,267
2004	9,626
2005	12,452

SOURCE: *Adapted from IAB Internet Advertising Revenue Report and PricewaterhouseCoopers.*

e-mail, music, mobile, small business services, health, finance, games, movies, personals, etc. Tucked away among all these was a search engine. Some of the Yahoo employees were of the opinion that the home page suffered "from too many cooks in the kitchen."[21] (See **Exhibit 4** for Yahoo's homepage in 1996 and see **Exhibit 5** for Yahoo's homepage in 2004.)

Yahoo seemed unclear about its identity, about whether it was a portal, search engine, or a media company. At the same time, several sites such as Google, eBay,[22] and MySpace[23] were successful in their specialized area, and consumers shifted their preferences to those sites. In the process of diversifying into several areas, Yahoo appeared to have lost its identity. According to Stewart Butterfield, director of project management, Yahoo, and cofounder of Flickr,[24] "There's always been some ambiguity about whether it's a tech company or a media company."[25]

There were other problems too. For instance, Yahoo was the most visited Web site on the Internet, with an average of 500 million monthly visitors as of mid-2006. The company's revenues for the first three quarters of 2006 stood at US$4.5 billion. On the other hand, Google, with 380 million visitors, recorded revenue of US$7.2 billion in the same period. This meant that Yahoo was failing to generate enough revenues from the users visiting its site.

Yahoo had been actively acquiring companies since 2002. Some of the companies acquired by Yahoo were Flickr, Konfabulator, Upcoming.org,[26] Del.icio.us,[27] and Webjay.[28] Konfabulator was a widget[29] engine, Upcoming.org was a social event calendar, Del.icio.us was a bookmarking site, and Webjay, a music playlist service. Yahoo launched Yahoo 360, a social networking service. However, many of these acquisitions could not be integrated with the company's operations. Though all these were part of Yahoo, a user had to log in separately for accessing each of the services (see **Exhibit 6** for some of Yahoo's acquisitions over the years).

Yahoo's problems were compounded by the company's complex matrix organization structure with overlapping responsibilities, which slowed down the decision-making process. Many

EXHIBIT 4
Home Page in 1996:
Yahoo, Inc.

EXHIBIT 5
Home Page in 2004:
Yahoo, Inc.

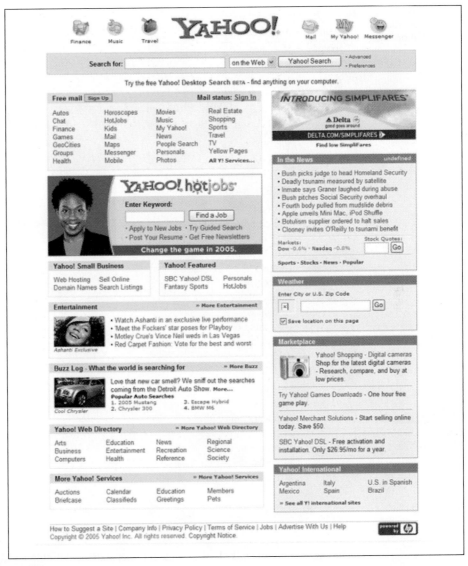

new employees in the company were of the view that the company's top-down approach did not encourage creativity. There was little cooperation between the different teams in the company. According to one of the media buyers, even the search and display teams in Yahoo did not communicate with each other. He complained, "Their organization is set up in such a way that we could spend 50 million dollars in search, and not be recognized at all by the display people."[30]

Yahoo had planned to acquire several companies with the objective of boosting its presence in the emerging social networking market. But it failed in these attempts. The company's existing sites were overrun by the competition. Yahoo's plans to acquire Facebook[31] did not meet with success as Facebook backed out of the deal, and YouTube,[32] which Yahoo was planning to acquire, was acquired by Google. Nor did the company's plan to create original content meet with success. Yahoo brought in several high-profile executives like Lloyd Brown from ABC Television Entertainment, as the head of Media group, Neil Budde from the *Wall Street Journal* Online, and David Katz from CBS Television. Yahoo planned to produce television-style programs,

EXHIBIT 6
Acquisitions:
Yahoo, Inc.

Year	Acquired Company
2002	Hotjobs
	Inktomi
2003	Overture
2004	3721 Internet Assistant
	Kelkoo
	Oddpost
	The All-Seeing Eye
	MusicMatch
	Stata Lab Inc
	WUF Networks
2005	Verdisoft
	Ludicorp Research (Flickr)
	Stadeon
	TeRespondo
	Dialpad
	blo.gs
	Konfabulator
	Alibaba
	Upcoming.org
	Whereonearth
	del.icio.us
2006	Searchfox
	Meedio
	Gmarket
	Jumpcut.com
	AdInterax
	Right Media
	Kenet Works
	bix.com
	Wretch

Compiled from various sources.

including sitcoms and talk shows for the Internet audience. Within a year, in March 2006, Yahoo announced that it was scaling back these efforts. The content development was not going as planned, and the entertainment unit suffered from the same problems. The employment listings of Yahoo, Hotjobs, could not withstand the competition from other employment sites like Monster and Careerbuilder. David A. Utter, staff writer covering technology and business for webpronews.com said, "Declining ad sales in the finance and automotive markets, a delayed launch of new contextual ad service, and splashy acquisitions by Google have left Yahoo feeling like the last grape in a wine press."[33]

According to Nick Blunden, client services director, Profero,[34] "Yahoo! has lost some of the magic that propelled it into the digital stratosphere in its heyday. While there is no single explanation for this, its quest for growth appears to have undermined the sense of purpose and identity that drove its success. Just a few years ago, Yahoo!'s services seemed to be clustered around themes of communication, content, and commerce and it was renowned for its innovation in these areas. Today, it appears to be a much looser collection of services that are united by the Yahoo! name."[35]

In July 2006, when Semel announced that the launch of Panama would be delayed by three months, the stock took a beating and fell by 22% on a single day. The price dropped from

EXHIBIT 7
Quarterly Income
Statement
(September
2005–September
2006): Yahoo, Inc.
(Dollar amounts
in millions)

Quarter Ending	Sep 30, 06	Jun 30, 06	Mar 31, 06	Sep 30, 05
Total Revenue	$1,580.32	$1,575.84	$1,567.05	$1,329.93
Cost of Revenue	681.12	645.77	657.94	520.24
Gross Profit	**899.20**	**930.07**	**909.11**	**809.69**
Selling, General, Admin. Expenses	462.00	457.75	459.46	343.44
Research & Development	202.09	208.74	217.58	141.62
Others	32.77	34.00	30.86	54.57
Total Operating Expense	**$1,377.98**	**$1,346.26**	**$1,365.84**	**$1,059.87**
Operating Income	**$202.34**	**$229.58**	**$201.21**	**$270.06**
Net Income	**$158.52**	**$164.33**	**$159.86**	**$253.77**

US$32.24 to US$25.24. When Yahoo's third quarter results were announced on October 12, 2006, profits were down by 38% as compared to third quarter of 2005 (see **Exhibit 7** for quarter-wise revenue and net income details of Yahoo). At that time, Semel realized that Yahoo needed to improve its search advertising capability in order to take advantage of growing revenues from that category. One of the founding executives of Yahoo, Ellen Siminoff, said, "A lot of people (at Yahoo) feel abused by the outside world and its perception of the company. They have missed a few quarters this year, they have lowered expectations, they were late in delivering Panama, and so they're in the penalty box with Wall Street."[36]

In October 2006, the *New York Times* published an article titled, "Yahoo's growth being eroded by new rivals" in which it was written that the company was slow in negotiating with other companies. The article particularly referred to Google's acquisition of YouTube. It was said that in spite of being the most popular website, Yahoo had suffered setbacks in advertising, both search related and display advertising. The article quoted David Cohen, senior vice president, Universal McCann,[37] saying that many clients were opting for new sites. He said, "Yahoo has lost the favor it enjoyed a year or two ago. There are more players in town, and the others are closing the gap relative to the things Yahoo is good at."[38] The article said Yahoo was late in launching new products, many of its products did not perform up to expectations, and the company was said to be demanding and inconsistent in carrying out negotiations. The new advertising upgrade was blamed for the delay in developing other products.

Yahoo was said to be competing with established players like CNN in news, ESPN in Sports, Microsoft in e-mail, AOL in instant messaging, Google in Search, and MySpace in social networking. Tim Hanlon, senior vice president, Denuo,[39] said, "It's hard to figure out what they want to be when they grow up, even though they are grown up now. Are they a content company? Are they a service company? Or are they a portal to other things? You ask three people and you may get three different answers."[40]

After the article was published, Brad Garlinghouse, senior vice president, Communications and Communities Products at Yahoo, sent an internal memo to some of the employees. The memo compared Yahoo's activities and investments to a thinly spread layer of peanut butter, as Yahoo was involved in several activities without focus on any particular activity. The memo was leaked to the press and was published in the *Wall Street Journal*. The analogy with peanut butter led to journalists and industry insiders dubbing the memo "The Peanut Butter Manifesto."

In "The Peanut Butter Manifesto," Garlinghouse wrote that Yahoo needed to reduce its workforce by 15–20% by eliminating the unit structure through which the company had spread its attention over several products and services and by decentralizing the matrix structure of the organization. Restructuring Yahoo was necessary to eliminate the existing bureaucracies. Pointing out that different units in the company lacked coordination and were competing with each other, Garlinghouse recommended a major revamp in the corporate structure. According to the *Wall Street Journal*, Garlinghouse's memo was circulated among the top brass of Yahoo.

According to Garlinghouse, Yahoo did not have a particular focus or strategy and was trying to cater to all the customer segments. He felt that the company should focus on a few key areas like video, mobile, and social networking. The memo mentioned that there were several competing silos existing in the company, such as Yahoo Music Engine (YME)[41] and Musicmatch, Yahoo Photos and Flickr, Del.icio.us and Myweb, Messenger Plug-ins and Sidebar widgets, (see **Exhibit 8** for a note on services offered by Yahoo), which were targeted at the same customers (see **Exhibit 9** for excerpts from "The Peanut Butter Manifesto"). According to Allen Weiner, an analyst from Gartner, "Yahoo is by no means out of the game, but [it's time] to execute on a more tightly focused vision. That's what's missing. Garlinghouse is right in saying there are way too many people doing way too many things."[42]

EXHIBIT 8
Services Offered
by Yahoo!

YME or Yahoo Music Jukebox is a free music player released in 2005. The features include CD burning, CD ripping, transfer of music to portable devices, playlist creation, music subscription, etc. Several plug-ins are also provided with Yahoo Music Jukebox.

Musicmatch is an audio player used to manage a digital audio library. The features include CD ripping, CD playback, Internet audio, and an online music store. Musicmatch was acquired by Yahoo in October 2004.

Yahoo Photos is the photo sharing service provided by Yahoo. Through this service, Yahoo users can store photos with a jpeg or jpg extension. The users can create their individual albums, categorize the photos, and can publish the albums for others to see. An uploader tool is provided through which photos can be dragged from the computer and dropped to Yahoo Photos. Using the other services, users can order prints, create calendars or personal stamps. Pictures stored in Yahoo Photos can be shared through Yahoo 360°, displayed on Yahoo Pages, and used through Yahoo Messenger.

Flickr is an online community platform that is popular for its photo sharing service and is widely used as a photo repository. Flickr was launched by Canada-based Ludicorp in February 2004. In March 2005, Yahoo acquired Ludicorp.

My Web was launched in June 2005 and is a social bookmarking site, which allows users to save the cached copy of their favorite Web pages. These pages are saved to the users' personal "My Web." Users can access these Web pages any time and can conduct searches through these pages. Users can save their Yahoo search results to My Web through Yahoo toolbar.

Del.icio.us is social bookmarking Web site that allows the users to store, share, and discover Web bookmarks. This Web site was launched in 2003 and Yahoo acquired it in December 2005. Del.icio.us uses non-hierarchical keyword categorization, with which users can tag bookmarks with any keyword. Most of the content on the Web site is viewable, and users can mark some bookmarks as private.

Yahoo Widgets bring the updated view of the favorite services of the users to the desktop. Widget refers to an interface element through which the computer and the user interact. Yahoo has more than 4,000 desktop widgets, with which several tasks can be performed; these include tracking information of the browsing history, weather widget, which downloads the weather forecasts from the selected place, digital clock widget, which shows the time and has an alarm facility, stock ticker widget, which shows updated stock prices, etc.

Messenger Plug-ins provide easy access to the user's favorite content. Some of the popular plug-ins include eBay plug-in, which displays the listings and bids on eBay, and Calendar plug-in, which allows users to view calendars. Other plug-ins allow users to listen to music, send invites, plan events, and view the blogs and photos of friends.

EXHIBIT 9
Excerpts from
'Peanut Butter
Manifesto'

We lack a focused, cohesive vision for our company. We want to do everything and be every-thing – to everyone. We've known this for years, talk about it incessantly, but do nothing to fun-damentally address it. We are scared to be left out. We are reactive instead of charting an unwavering course. We are separated into silos that far too frequently don't talk to each other. And when we do talk, it isn't to collaborate on a clearly focused strategy, but rather to argue and fight about ownership, strategies, and tactics.

Our inclination and proclivity to repeatedly hire leaders from outside the company results in disparate visions of what winning looks like—rather than a leadership team rallying around a sin-gle cohesive strategy.

I've heard our strategy described as spreading peanut butter across the myriad opportunities that continue to evolve in the online world. The result: a thin layer of investment spread across everything we do and thus we focus on nothing in particular.

We lack clarity of ownership and accountability. The most painful manifestation of this is the massive redundancy that exists throughout the organization. We now operate in an organiza-tional structure—admittedly created with the best of intentions—that has become overly bureau-cratic. For far too many employees, there is another person with dramatically similar and overlapping responsibilities. This slows us down and burdens the company with unnecessary costs.

Equally problematic, at what point in the organization does someone really OWN the suc-cess of their product or service or feature? Product, marketing, engineering, corporate strategy, fi-nancial operations . . . there are so many people in charge (or believe that they are in charge) that it's not clear if anyone is in charge. This forces decisions to be pushed up—rather than down. It forces decisions by committee or consensus and discourages the innovators from breaking the mold . . . thinking outside the box.

We lack decisiveness. Combine a lack of focus with unclear ownership, and the result is that decisions are either made or are made when it is already too late. Without a clear and focused vi-sion, and without complete clarity of ownership, we lack a macro perspective to guide our deci-sions and visibility into who should make those decisions. We are repeatedly stymied by challenging and hairy decisions. We are held hostage by our analysis paralysis.

We have awesome assets. Nearly every media and communications company is painfully jealous of our position. We have the largest audience, they are highly engaged and our brand is synonymous with the Internet.

Independent of specific proposals of what this reorganization should look like, two key prin-ciples must be represented:

Blow up the matrix. Empower a new generation and model of General Managers to be true general managers, Product, marketing, user experience & design, engineering, business develop-ment & operations all report into a small number of focused General Managers. Leave no doubt as to where accountability lies.

Kill the redundancies. Align a set of new BUs so that they are not competing against each other. Search focuses on search. Social media aligns with community and communications. No competing owners for Video, Photos, etc. And Front Page becomes Switzerland. This will be a delicate exercise – decentralization can create inefficiencies, but I believe we can find the right balance.

My motivation for this memo is the adamant belief that, as before, we have a tremendous op-portunity ahead. I don't pretend that I have the only available answers, but we need to get the dis-cussion going; change is needed and it is needed soon. We can be a stronger and faster company—a company with a clearer vision and clearer ownership and clearer accountability.

We may have fallen down, but the race is a marathon and not a sprint. I don't pretend that this will be easy. It will take courage, conviction, insight, and tremendous commitment. I very much—look forward to the challenge.

SOURCE: *Yahoo Memo: The 'Peanut Butter Manifesto,' The Wall Street Journal, November 18, 2006.*

The Reorganization Program

On December 5, 2006, Semel announced the reorganization of Yahoo and major changes in its executive team. Semel announced, "Yahoo! is now entering what I call its third phase—focused on customers. We're seeing the competitive and advertising landscapes evolve yet again and today we announced the realignment that we believe will let Yahoo! capture the major growth opportunities ahead."[43]

Though it was widely speculated that Yahoo's announcement of reorganization was prompted by the leaked memo, the company denied this and said that reorganization was already in the process. According to Semel, "Now, I know what you're thinking—this is all about peanut butter. Actually, we've been orchestrating this plan for a number of months as we envisioned the next phase of growth for the Internet. Following our third quarter results, I very openly discussed that we were going to become more focused and bring about change."[44] (see **Exhibit 10** for key objectives of Yahoo's reorganization).

The reorganization aimed at making Yahoo leaner, more nimble, and responsive to customers. Through the reorganization, the company planned to align its operations with the key customer segments of audiences, advertisers, and publishers and capture the emerging growth opportunities especially on the Internet, and become more customer-focused with the support of technology. Yahoo was reorganized around three groups, with two groups, the Audience Group, and the Advertising & Publishing Group, focusing on the customer. The third group, Technology Group, aimed at strengthening the technology function in the company. The heads of the three groups reported directly to Semel.

The **Audience Group's** main focus was on creating user experiences and at the same time, generating value for the advertisers. The group was a result of the merger of seven existing product groups in the company, and was created to maintain a better focus on the customer. According to Yahoo, the focus of the Audience Group was to "enhance its existing products in search, media, communities and communications; build social media environment across Yahoo!; open more opportunities for users to take advantage of Yahoo! tools and services off network and through mobile and digital devices; and pursue growth opportunities in emerging international markets."[45] The Audience Group focused on different services offered by Yahoo, which included search, e-mail, messenger, e-commerce, music, and video. Through reorganization, Yahoo aimed to bring coherence to the wide array of services it provided. The creation of the Audience Group was expected to transform the company into a social media provider and help it bring in the content that was relevant to the audience.

EXHIBIT 10
Key Objectives
of Reorganization

Expand customer-centric culture and capabilities. Yahoo! will develop rich experiences for each audience segment and deliver solutions to meet the needs of all advertisers and publishers worldwide. Yahoo! will organize its services around audience segments and advertising customers, rather than around products.

Create leading social media environments. Yahoo! will leverage its strong positions in community, communications, search, as well as media content across its global network to create leading social media environments, which will encourage every user on the Yahoo! network to participate in the consumption and publishing of information, and knowledge through tagging, reviewing, sharing of images and audio, and other social media activities.

Lead in next-generation advertising platforms. Yahoo! will extend its industry-leading breadth of offerings to give the most diverse array of advertisers, from large brand marketers to local merchants, every opportunity to connect with audiences on and off Yahoo!

Drive organizational effectiveness and scale. Yahoo! will recruit and retain the best industry talent and focus its resources on high-impact, network-wide platforms to help capture the most significant long-term growth opportunities.

The **Advertising & Publisher Group's** main task was to manage Yahoo's advertising content, build a large audience in association with Yahoo partner publishers, and create a global advertising network on and off Yahoo sites. The group's aim was to transform the way in which the advertisers connected with their target audience and provide them with more value. Susan L. Decker, who was heading Yahoo! Marketplaces business unit, took over the revamped advertising unit, while continuing to function as the CFO until a new CFO was recruited. The group, with the aim of building a global advertising network, was created combining several existing units, including a search marketing unit, publishing unit, and media sales and graphical advertising unit. The group was created to serve the customer in major customer segments such as large advertisers, large adverting agencies, businesses of small and medium size, resellers, and publishers.

The Advertising & Publisher Group was organized around three functions, which were demand channels, supply channels, and marketing products (see **Exhibit 11** for more about divisions in Advertising & Publishing Group).

The **Technology Group** was headed by Farzad Nazem, chief technology officer (CTO) of Yahoo. This group was responsible for integrated product development, and the Platform & Infrastructure sub-groups were a part of the Technology Group. The group aimed at achieving integration within product development teams. Through this group, Yahoo wanted to channel its investment toward global platforms with high impact and scalability. Leveraging on the investments in communities to create technology and advertising platforms, Yahoo aimed at expanding the advertising network and remaining focused on product development. With the

EXHIBIT 11
Divisions in
Advertising &
Publishing Group

DEMAND CHANNELS (MARKETING SOLUTIONS)
Yahoo's demand channels were organized into the Direct Sales Channel and the Online Channel, based on the advertisers. The direct sales channel catered to the advertisers who interacted directly with the company while the online channel was targeted at self-service advertisers, who used online services.

SUPPLY CHANNELS (YAHOO PUBLISHER NETWORK)
This channel catered to publishing customers, and was responsible for display and display based ad networks, by securing ad inventory from different Yahoo and non-Yahoo sites. Yahoo planned to offer its advertising customers a wide range of marketing products and also high quality customers through this channel.

MARKETING PRODUCTS DIVISION
The marketing products division connected the demand and supply channels, by connecting the marketing offers from demand channels with ad inventory generated by different Yahoo channels. This division was responsible for developing products and marketplaces that would offer effectiveness for advertising customers and monetization for publishing customers. The division comprised search and listing marketplaces, and display marketplaces. These marketplaces were supported by project management, and engineering teams.

LOCAL MARKETS & COMMERCE DIVISION
This division, formerly known as Marketplaces, was brought under the Advertising & Publishing Group. This included shopping, travel, autos, hotjobs, personals, and real estate.

STRATEGIC MARKETING & MAJOR INITIATIVES
The main task of this division was to work closely with other divisions in the Advertising & Publishing group, and bring in a unified marketing strategy and customer and market segments.

SOURCE: *Adapted from E-Mail Titled 'Update on APG Organization' Sent by Susan Decker to all Yahoo! Employees on February 14, 2007. Retrieved from www.techcrunch.com.*

centralized technology group, it was expected that users could access all the services provided by Yahoo products with a single Yahoo e-mail account. According to Justin Port, analyst with Merrill Lynch,[46] "The elevated status of the Technology Group underscores management's commitment to improving product innovation."[47]

As part of the reorganization program, which was expected to be completed by the end of March 2007, three executives—Dan Rosensweig, COO, Lloyd Braun, head Media Group, and John Marcom, senior vice president, International Operations, resigned from the organization during the first quarter 2007. The reorganization program also led to a new mission statement for Yahoo: "to connect people to their passions, their communities, and the world's knowledge." Analyst opined that the new mission statement signified the fact that Yahoo had put people at the center of their strategy. They said that by restructuring, Yahoo was changing its focus to eliminate redundancies and increase accountability and decision making and emerge as a customer-focused organization.

The Road Ahead

Yahoo's reorganization was expected to eliminate the bureaucracy that had crept into the company over a period of time. After the reorganization was announced, the company's stock price fell by 2% to US$26.86. Industry experts were of the view that it was high time Yahoo was reorganized, as the previous reorganization[48] was done about five years back (see **Exhibit 12** for Yahoo's stock price chart).

EXHIBIT 12
Stock Price Chart (April 2002–March 2007): Yahoo, Inc.

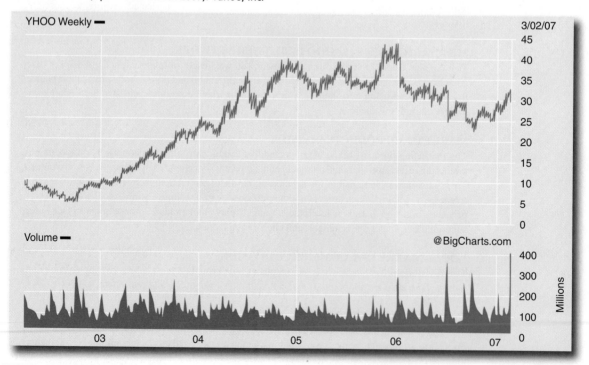

SOURCE: *www.bigchart.com*

Another strategy that Yahoo adopted was "Brand Universe" through which it planned to develop sites dedicated to high-profile entertainment brands, including television shows like *Lost*[49] and *The Office*,[50] video games like Halo[51] and The Sims,[52] and movies like *Harry Potter*.[53] Through Brand Universe, Yahoo planned to link entertainment content across different Yahoo services and Web sites. All the entertainment partners would also be informed about the traffic their content was attracting, the reach of the brands, and other such details. The fact the YouTube was planning to include short advertisements before each video clip was expected to boost Yahoo's ability to attract visitors, as visitors who wished to skip the advertisements would opt for other alternatives, such as Yahoo.

To spruce up Yahoo News, which was accessed by 34 million unique users every month as of 2006, Yahoo launched video content in association with CBS owned stations. Yahoo News served over 60 million video streams per month as of February 2007.

In November 2006, Yahoo entered into an agreement with a consortium of nine companies, representing more than 170 newspapers in the United States. The consortium included Hearst Newspapers, MediaNews Group, Cox Newspapers, Lee Enterprises, Journal Register, and EW Scripps. As per the agreement, the newspapers started using Yahoo HotJobs from December 2006 onward. Both the parties were expected to benefit from the deal, as Yahoo would get regional exposure while advertisements from local newspapers would acquire a wider reach. Over a period of time, other content such as local news and advertisements were also planned to be included.

In the first week of December 2006, Yahoo released a mobile social networking service called Mixd with which customers could coordinate outings and meetings with friends using text messages and photo messages. The activities were simultaneously posted on the Web page. The service was targeted at young users of 18–25 years of age and Yahoo started marketing the service in some university campuses in the United States.

According to industry experts, Yahoo was on the right path in proposing a restructuring plan; however, what mattered most was how the plan was executed. They said Yahoo should be careful in executing the reorganization program. Analysts also opined that the reorganization might take some time to show results. Meanwhile, Yahoo had to face competition not only from existing players but also from new ones, which were making their presence felt in the market. Yahoo needed to generate more revenues from social media and user-generated content. There were suggestions that Yahoo could consider a merger with AOL or Microsoft, as neither of these companies was strong in search engine technology. Any such deal, according to analysts, would help Yahoo compete with Google effectively.

Analysts were of the opinion that as Yahoo was one of the most popular sites attracting millions of unique visitors, through Panama, it could increase the number of clicks on the ads, and thus generate more revenues. Commenting on Panama, Paul Kedrosky, partner, Ventures West,[54] said, "It doesn't have to be as good as Google, Yahoo has this bazooka. It stomps Google in page views. And Yahoo is still the king of audience. There is a huge upside for them."[55] Yahoo also had another advantage of having specialized sites like Yahoo Finance, Yahoo Real Estate, Yahoo Tech, etc. through which it could charge a premium from advertisers who were targeting a particular set of audience.

Yahoo itself considered 2007 to be a year of transition with many challenges to face. Analysts too were of the same view, as Imran Khan, analyst at JP Morgan Chase,[56] said, "The coming year will be challenging, in terms of numbers. The management change doesn't fix the problem. There are lots of new competitors and Yahoo is not as well-positioned in search as Google."[57]

Within one month of the launch of Panama, Yahoo experienced better click-through rates for sponsored search ads. comScore[58] analyzed the click-through rates before and after the launch of Panama, by dividing the total clicks on sponsored search ads by the total search ads. It was found that after the launch of Panama, in the first week the click-through ads grew by 5% compared to a week before the launch. By the second week, the click-through rates rose to 9%.

Some analysts were of the view that Yahoo's wide array of service had attracted millions of users to the portal. These users did not need to go to different Web sites to access different services. They said that Yahoo should continue to provide all these services, and should only look at revamping its advertising services and better search engine.

Industry experts also opined that the problem lay not with Yahoo but with advertisers, who were highly optimistic about search-based advertising and its prospects. They felt that Yahoo, even if it came up with the best in terms of search engine, would not be able to compete with Google. Yahoo remained strong in financial forums and community sites like Flickr and del.icio.us. Instead of trying to attract customers from Google, Yahoo could target competitors like MSN and ask.com, opined an analyst from Standard & Poor's.

However, industry experts remained optimistic about Yahoo's future prospects after its re-organization and the launch of Panama. According to comScore Media Networks, Google's share in the Internet search market in the United States stood at 47.5% in January 2007, while Yahoo's share was at 28.1%. According to Nick Blunden, client services director, Profero, "Despite recent challenges, the Yahoo! business has a lot going for it. The brand is a fantastic asset with extraordinary levels of awareness. Yahoo! also retains one of the single biggest on-line audiences worldwide. Finally, while it may not have outright market leadership in all of its services, many of them are extremely competitive."[59]

NOTES

1. "Yahoo! Re-Aligns Organization to More Effectively Focus on Key Customer Segments and Capture Future Growth Opportunities," Yahoo press release, December 05, 2006.
2. "Yahoo Shake-up to Take on Rivals," http://news.bbc.co.uk, December 6, 2006.
3. RBC Capital Markets, a part of Royal Bank of Canada, is a corporate and investment bank providing a wide range of services and products catering to institutions, corporations, and governments across the world.
4. U.S.-based Google has specialized in Internet search and online advertising. As of December 2006, the company's revenue was at US$10.604 billion and net income stood at US$3.077 billion.
5. Adwords allows advertisers to place their advertisements on Google's search results. It provides pay-per-click advertising and site-targeted advertising for text and banner ads.
6. The Susquehanna Financial Group is a part of Susquehanna International Group of companies of SIG, which comprises several trading and investment related companies. The company's primary focus is on investment banking, trading, and institutional sales and research.
7. Paul R. La Monica, "Yahoo! Thumps Google on Wall Street," CNNMoney.com, March 05, 2007.
8. Dow Jones & Company-owned *Wall Street Journal* is a daily newspaper published from New York, with a circulation of around 2 million per day.
9. Global Crown Capital is a San Francisco–based boutique investment firm, specializing in objective and actionable research, institutional sales and trading, hedge funds, wealth management, and asset management.
10. Michele Gershberg, "Yahoo's New Ad System Could Boost Growth: Analysts," Reuters, January 24, 2007.
11. Yahoo! is the abbreviation for Yet Another Hierarchical Officious Oracle.
12. Banner advertisements appear on Web pages within various Yahoo channels. Hypertext links were embedded in each banner advertisement to give users instant access to the advertiser's Web site, to obtain additional information, or to purchase products and services.
13. Promotional sponsorships were typically focused on a particular event, such as sweepstakes. The merchant sponsorship icon advertised products. Users had to click on the icon to complete a transaction.
14. Direct marketing revenues came through e-mail campaigns targeted at Yahoo's registered users who had indicated their willingness to receive such promotions.
15. While tracking the number of visitors on a Web site, unique visitor refers to a person who visits a Web site more than once within a specified period of time. Through the use of software, a company can track and count Web site visitors and can also distinguish between visitors who visit the site only once and unique visitors who return to the site.
16. Pioneered by Overture, the "paid search" advertising model is also know as "pay-per-click" model. In this model, Overture provided an auction room for online advertisers, whose bidding determined how prominently their link will be displayed. Overture then provided a list of these advertisers to customers, including Yahoo! and shared with them the advertising revenues once the visitors on Yahoo's site clicked on those ads.
17. Based in California, Inktomi is a pioneer in Web search technology. The company was a leading provider of Web search and paid inclusion services.
18. Yahoo renamed Overture as Yahoo Search Marketing.
19. Web Crawler, also known as Spider, is a program that visits Web sites and reads their pages and other information in order to create entries for search engine index.
20. Yahoo Slurp, a Web crawler, is used to put content into the search engine. Yahoo Slurp was based on the Web search technology of Inktomi.
21. Robert Hof, "Five Steps to Get Yahoo Back on Track," Business-Week, December 7, 2006.

22. eBay.com is an online auction and shopping Web site managed by the U.S.-based Internet company eBay Inc. In 2005, eBay Inc. recorded revenues of US$4.55 billion.

23. MySpace is a social networking Web site and its content includes personal profiles, blogs, groups, photos, music, and videos. The parent company of MySpace is News Corporation.

24. Flickr is a photo sharing Web site and an online community platform. It was launched by Ludicorp in 2004. In March 2005, Yahoo acquired Ludicorp and Flickr.

25. Jeremy Caplan, Jeffrey Ressner, "How Yahoo! Aims to Reboot," Time South Pacific, February 12, 2007.

26. Upcoming.org is a social events calendar that used user-generated content and social media to capture event information. Yahoo acquired the company in October 2005.

27. Del.icio.us is a social bookmarking Web service used for storing and sharing bookmarks. Yahoo acquired the company in December 2005.

28. Webjay is a Web-based playlist service, containing links to audio files on the Web. Yahoo acquired Webjay in January 2006.

29. Widget is a small application with a graphical interface component that can be used to perform a variety of functions like search, photo, and mapping services. Widgets run on the desktops without use of browsers. Through the widgets the portals can draw visitors directly from the desktop.

30. Gavin O'Malley, "Madison Ave: Yahoo Overhaul Might Fall Short," Online Media Daily, December 8, 2006.

31. Facebook is a social networking Web site, focused on college and university students. It is the seventh most visited Web site in the United States and boasts of several photo uploads. The Web site was founded by Mark Zuckerberg, a sophomore at Harvard University, in February 2004.

32. YouTube is a video sharing Web site that allows the users to upload, share, and view video clips, and was founded in February 2005. YouTube was named Time Magazine's Invention of the Year for 2006. In October 2006, Google acquired YouTube for US$1.65 billion.

33. David A. Utter, "Yahoo Pressed from All Sides," www.webpronews.com, October 13, 2006.

34. London-based Profero, is a digital marketing agency that provides services like Web development, search and affiliate marketing, advertising, media planning and buying, and relationship marketing. The clients of Profero include CNN, Sky TV, BBC World, Black & Decker, Singapore Airlines, Johnson & Johnson, and Merrill Lynch.

35. Gemma Charles, "Yahoo!" Marketing, January 3, 2007.

36. Jeremy Caplan, Jeffrey Ressner, "How Yahoo! Aims to Reboot," Time South Pacific, February 12, 2007.

37. Universal McCann was created in 1999 through the consolidation of the media operations of McCann Erickson. The company's worldwide billings stood at US$13 billion in 2006.

38. Saul Hansell, "Yahoo's Growth Being Eroded by New Rivals," New York Times, October 11, 2006.

39. Denuo is the media futures consulting arm of the Publicis Groupe, the fourth largest communications company. The company has a presence in 104 countries across the world. Denuo is actively involved in strategic consulting, ventures and partnerships, and catalyst and activation.

40. Saul Hansell, "Yahoo's Growth Being Eroded by New Rivals," New York Times, October 11, 2006.

41. In August 2006, the Yahoo Music Engine was renamed Yahoo Music Jukebox.

42. "Peanut Butter Sticks to Yahoo," www.infoworld.com, November 27, 2006.

43. Terry Semel, "Taking Yahoo Forward," http://yodel.yahoo.com, December 5, 2006.

44. Terry Semel, "Taking Yahoo Forward," http://yodel.yahoo.com, December 5, 2006.

45. "Yahoo! Re-Aligns Organization to More Effectively Focus on Key Customer Segments and Capture Future Growth Opportunities," Yahoo press release, December 5, 2006.

46. Merrill Lynch is one of the world's leading financial management and advisory companies, with offices in 36 countries and territories and total client assets of approximately $1.8 trillion. The services provided by Merrill Lynch, its subsidiaries, and affiliates are capital market services, investment banking and advisory, wealth management, asset management, and insurance and banking. In 2005, the company recorded revenue of US$47.78 billion and net income of US$5.046 billion.

47. Robert Hof, "Five Steps to Get Yahoo Back on Track," BusinessWeek, December 7, 2006.

48. A detailed description of Yahoo's previous reorganization is covered in the ICMR case study, "reviving Yahoo!—Strategies that Turned the Leading Internet Portal Around," Reference No. BSTR064 (www.icmr.icfai.org).

49. Lost is a highly popular television drama series aired on ABC network in the United States. Lost has won several awards, including Golden Globes and Emmys. The series depicts the lives of plane crash survivors.

50. After the success of the BBC series The Office in the UK, NBC created a U.S. version of the popular show, which premiered in March 2005. This situation comedy series is set in the office of a paper supply company.

51. Halo is a video game from Bungie Studios, which featured Master Chief, a soldier with superhuman strength and technologically advanced armor.

52. Sims is a computer game published by Maxis. It is a strategic life simulation computer game, about the day-to-day activities of people in a household in fictional SimCity. The game was released in February 2000 and went on to become one of the best selling PC games.

53. Harry Potter is a series of novels written by JK Rowling, featuring Harry Potter and his fight against an evil wizard. The movies based on the Harry Potter series were distributed by Warner Brothers.

54. Ventures West is a Canada-based Venture Capital partner, which has invested in more than 150 companies.

55. Catherine Holahan, "Why Yahoo's Panama Won't be Enough," BusinessWeek, December 26, 2006.

56. Incorporated in 1800s by Janius S. Morgan, a merchant banker, JP Morgan is one of the leading banks in the United States. In 2001, JP Morgan merged with Chase Manhattan to create the second largest bank in the United States. In July 2004, JP Morgan bought Bank One Corporation, which created an entity with combined assets of US$1.1 trillion. In 2006, the revenues of the merged entity stood at US$61.437 billion and net income of US$14.44 billion.

57. Jefferson Graham, "Yahoo's Shake-up: Too Little, Too Late?" USA Today, December 7, 2006.

58. comScore provided marketing and data services to several large businesses and is one of the leading Internet market research companies. comScore provides insight into the online behavior of consumers by tracking the Internet data on the surveyed computers.

59. Gemma Charles, "Yahoo!" Marketing, January 3, 2007.

CASE 13

Google:

AN INTERNET SEARCH SERVICE COMPANY

Joseph Teye-Kofi, Robert J. Mockler, and Marc Gartenfeld

IN FEBRUARY OF 2005, ALMOST SIX MONTHS AFTER GOOGLE'S INITIAL PUBLIC OFFERING (IPO) of stock, CEO Eric Schmidt announced the need to develop an effective company-wide strategy in order to brace for the next level of services and products Google wanted to offer to stay ahead of the competition. In the last quarter of 2004, Google's operating income totaled $321 million, versus $322 million for nine-year-old eBay and $260 million for 10-year-old Yahoo. As an industry market share leader, the overall task at hand was to develop an effective differentiating enterprise-wide strategy especially for the company's Internet search segment, enabling Google to survive and prosper against aggressive competition in the intermediate and long-term future.

The company generated revenue by delivering relevant, cost-effective online advertising. Businesses used the company's AdWords program to promote their products and services with targeted advertising. In addition, the thousands of third-party Web sites that made up the Google Network used the Google AdSense program to deliver relevant ads that generated revenue and enhanced the user's experience.

As shown in **Exhibit 1,** Google had many tools and provided many services. Here, common terminologies in Internet search are defined for clarity. A web browser is a program used for displaying and viewing pages on the World Wide Web. A search engine is computer software that compiles lists of documents, most commonly those on the World Wide Web, and the contents of those documents. A blog is an easy-to-use Web site, where people can quickly post thoughts and interact with other people, and more. Browser buttons let the user search the Internet simply by highlighting a word (or phrase) on any Web page and clicking the Google Search button.

This case was prepared by Joesph Teye-Kofi, MBA student at St. John's Univeristy, under the direction of Dr. Robert J. Mockler and Professor Marc Gartenfeld of St. John's Univeristy. Dr. Mockler and Professor Marc Gartenfeld revised and edited this case. This case was reprinted from *Cases in Domestic and Multinational Strategic Management,* Publication (VIII) #44, pp. C5-1 thru C5-21, edited by Robert J. Mockler and Marc Gartenfeld. The copyright holders are solely responsible for the case content. This case was edited for *SMBP* 11th and 12th editions. Copyright © 2005 by Robert J. Mockler, Strategic Management Research Group, 114 East 90th Street (1B), New York, NY 10128. Reprinted by permission.

EXHIBIT 1
Google's Tools
and Services

Tools	Services
Blogger	Alerts
Browser Buttons	Answers
Desktop Search	Catalogs
Google In Your Language	Images
Picasa Photo Organizer	News Search
Google Tool Bar	Internet search
Translate Tool	Wireless

As for tools, Google's desktop search allowed users to find email, files, web history, and online chat on their computers offline. It allowed users to instantly view Web pages, even when not online. Adding Google Browser Buttons to a personal toolbar granted access to Google's search technology, without taking up extra screen space. "Google in Your Language" was a tool that intended to use volunteers to translate all of the world's languages into a database that could be utilized by users of the service. Picasa Photo Organizer was a free software download from Google that helped users instantly find, edit, and share all the pictures on a personal computer.

As for services, Google alerts were email updates of the latest relevant Google results (web, news, etc.) based on users' choice of query or topic. With Google Answers, more than 500 carefully screened analysts in various fields of study were ready to answer questions online for as little as $2.50, usually within 24 hours. Google Catalogs allowed patrons to search and browse mail-order catalogs from various companies online. Google Image Search allowed users to search for images online. Just type in the name of the image and a vast array of specific images were displayed as requested.

Google News allowed users access to more than 4,500 local and international news sources, updated continuously. Google's wireless adaptable search technology could be accessed from any number of devices, such as mobile phones and Palm VII handhelds. Whatever the language or platform, Google let users search the Web with ease, speed, and accuracy.

Google's main strength was the fact that it had established itself using superior Internet search technology. It had also made phenomenal strides in the international arena. Moreover, the company's successful IPO gave it the financial leverage needed to expand and easily become a large, independent web portal. A portal or portal site is a computing home site for a web browser. Portals are Internet hubs, more like Grand Central station, that serve as a connection or link to other places that might be of interest to web users. Google's raw materials were the technical proficiency and innovativeness of its employees. The question remained whether or not Google should continue primarily as an Internet search engine or morph into a large web portal.

Google's major weakness was the fact that there were virtually no switching costs in the industry, and Internet search users would try another search engine if they did not find what they were looking for using Google's search technologies. Microsoft's next version of the windows system, code-named "Longhorn" and slated for release in 2006, as "VISTA," presented a potential threat to Google's services. Microsoft's Vice President was quoted as saying, "Google is a very nice system but compared to my vision, it is pathetic."[1] Moreover, Microsoft had all the funding it needed and, if it focused on Internet search technology, was bound to vanquish many big players in the Internet search segment. The main problem to be resolved was how to further differentiate Google's Internet search segment from its competition and to achieve a winning edge over competitors within intensely competitive, rapidly changing immediate, intermediate, and long-term time frames.

Exhibit 2 provides a list of Internet terminology and concepts.

EXHIBIT 2
A Glossary of Some
Relevant Common
Internet
Technology
Concepts/
Terminology

A. GENERAL

A **Web page** is a location on the World Wide Web: a computer file, encoded in hypertext markup language [HTML] and containing text, graphics files, and sound files, that is accessible through the World Wide Web. Every Web page has a unique Uniform Resource Locator URL, or address. For example, when users type www.stjohns.edu into an Internet Explorer address bar and press **"enter,"** the page that is displayed would be Saint John's University's Web page.

A **toolbar** is a row of icons on a computer screen that are clicked on to perform certain frequently used functions. For example, when I click the printer icon on a computer screen, I convey to the computer my intentions to print that page's contents.

Web hosting is the business of supplying server space for storage of Web sites on the Internet, and sometimes the provision of ancillary services such as Web site creation and development. Most portals offer this service. Businesses that intend to grow and market their products and services over the Internet patronize this service, offered mostly by large Web portals such as Yahoo and MSN.

After a company is formed, it normally develops a Web site under its business name and engages in some form of publicity campaign to attract customers to its Web site. It needs space to store the information and communication that ensues from day-to-day transactions on its Web site. The more established large portals offer the service of handling a smaller company's storage needs using their servers for a fee.

A **Web server** is a computer that stores Web documents and makes them available to the rest of the world. A server may be dedicated, meaning its sole purpose is to be a Web server, or non-dedicated, meaning it can be used for basic computing in addition to acting as a server.

A **desktop** is a graphical computer representation of an office desk: a visible portion of a software program that forms a background on which icons representing equipment, programs, and files are displayed.

B. SEARCH SERVICES

A **search engine** is a *computer program* that searches for particular keywords and returns a list of documents in which they were found, especially a commercial service that scans documents on the Internet. For example, a Web user types "Iraq" in a Google search pane and presses **"enter."** Google's search engine (mathematical algorithms program) scans the entire Internet database for any document containing the word "Iraq" and returns links to these documents in an order based on frequency of the word "Iraq" as it appears in the documents. By definition, therefore, every Internet search company has its own unique search engine (program). The list of responses on a Google "Iraq" search would, therefore, differ from Yahoo search results, which would also differ from AOL search results or Ask Jeeves search results.

A **browser** is computer software that allows an Internet user to search for information on the World Wide Web. It is the vehicle that allows you to travel from one Web page to the other just by typing the Web address.

A **Web browser** is a program used for displaying and viewing pages on the World Wide Web. It is the actual framework that allows all Internet users to see Web pages in a particular window.

Spyware is a general term for a program that surreptitiously monitors a user's actions. Although spyware is sometimes sinister, as with a remote control program used by a hacker, software companies have been known to use spyware to gather data about customers. The practice is generally frowned on.

A **pop-up** is an ad that displays in a new browser window. Pop-up windows come in many different shapes and sizes, typically in a scaled-down browser window with only the Close, Minimize, and Maximize commands. Some Web surfers strongly resent pop-up ads. Marketers often do not realize the ill-will generated by pop-ups because it is easier to click the "close" button than send an email to complain.

A **portal** or **portal site** is a computing home site for a Web browser on the Internet. It is a Web site that provides links to information and other Web sites. By industry standards, Google is

(Continued)

EXHIBIT 2
(Continued)

not yet considered a portal. A portal is a much larger and more comprehensive Web site because of its extensive links to other equally extensive Web pages with different functions. It is the entrance to a maze of related and unrelated Web sites. Portals aggregate information from multiple sources into one Web-based entry point. Yahoo, MSN, and AOL are considered Internet portals because, aside from the Internet search services they provide, they offer a range of other services not related to search: Web hosting and storage, finance, mail, sports, publishing, personal communications, auto, shopping, and maps and driving directions are but a fraction of the services portals provide.

A **Web crawler** is a program used to search through pages on the World Wide Web in order to locate documents containing a particular set of words, a phrase, or a topic. It is tool used by Internet search companies to produce search results.[2]

SOURCE: *MSN 2005. "MSN" (online) http://finance.yahoo.com. Accessed March 27, 2005.*

Membership Services

The large Internet search companies such as AOL, MSN, and Yahoo were beginning to channel a lot of effort toward maintaining and developing their Internet search capabilities to match Google's current Internet search supremacy. These large companies already had a lot of non–search related member services in place and would enjoy a big advantage if they were able to successfully utilize the information in their large membership database—including email accounts, personals (groups and online dating services), and fantasy sports—to help them advertise to their members based on specific responses to previously asked questions. Google electronically scanned the contents of its Gmail service letters and placed relevant ads based on keywords contained in the letter beside the email once it was opened to be read by a Gmail service member. (Gmail was Google's name for its email service.) The main key to success here remained how to successfully convince members that the confidentiality of their personal information would not be compromised or shared with other marketing entities such as telemarketers.

Competition

The main competitors of Google in Internet search technology were MSN, Yahoo, and AOL. Competition was fierce in this segment for two reasons. First, a great deal of revenue was being generated by the Internet search companies, and the major Internet service providers had been awakened by Google's rise to fame and its ability to generate revenue from ads placed next to its search results. Even though MSN, AOL, and Yahoo offered many other services, they trailed Google in market share and, most importantly, user loyalty, brand identity, and easy name recognition when it came to Internet search. These four big companies all provided search services, but Google was by far the most popular. The other three companies were, however, bigger and offered more variety in non-search Internet services. This was the reason some analysts referred to these relatively bigger companies as Internet portals. The key to the future of Internet search rested with the company that was best able to register its patrons and to successfully utilize that information to advertise even more effectively.

Second, it was difficult to predict the direction in which the Internet search segment was heading with regard to innovation. Every competitor in this segment was trying to be more innovative in search solutions, because quality search results guaranteed customer loyalty and its accompanying advertising dollars.

Yahoo

Yahoo Inc. together with its consolidated subsidiaries was a global Internet brand. The company provided Internet services that were essential and relevant to users and businesses through the provision of online properties to Internet users and a range of tools and marketing solutions for businesses to market to that community of users. The company was focused on extending the marketing platform and access to Internet users beyond the Yahoo Network through the distribution network of third-party entities (affiliates) that had integrated the sponsored search offerings into their Web sites. Many of the services offered were free to users. It provided services that allowed businesses to list information on properties on the Yahoo Network. The offerings to users and businesses fell into three categories: Search and Marketplace; Information and Content; and Communications and Consumer Services.

Yahoo placed second to Google in the number of people who utilized search services and was far ahead of the competition when it came to all other Internet services such as email, shopping, online personals, and travel. The opportunity for success was for companies to offer newer and more innovative services in order to build a solid membership base that could be utilized for directory-linked target advertising. Directory-linked target advertising, the future of Internet search's continued revenue generation, first had to overcome its most demanding test of ensuring confidentiality and preventing identity theft. Yahoo had an advantage because it had a huge registered membership already in place owing to the services it offered such as email, auto information, shopping, and driving directions. On the other hand, Yahoo had weaknesses when it came to linking its search engine to an already established information source such as the online *Britannica* encyclopedia, and it also did not have a platform for online auctions.

Yahoo efficiently offered business services such as domain name registration, Web site design and development, and Web hosting for small and new businesses. This represented a great source of additional revenue. However, Yahoo was relatively weak with regard to assuring registered service members of the confidentiality and security of the personal information they shared with the company. Also, Yahoo was not considered a dominant force in Internet search technology. For the fiscal year ended December 31, 2004, Yahoo's revenues totaled $3.57 billion, up from $1.63 billion. Net income totaled $839.6 million, up from $237.9 million. Results reflected increased marketing services, fees and listings sales results from growth in Yahoo's organic sales and acquisitions and higher investment gains.[3]

AOL

Time Warner Inc. (Time Warner) was a media and entertainment company. It classified its businesses into five fundamental areas: America Online (AOL), consisting principally of interactive services; Cable, consisting principally of interests in cable systems providing video, high-speed data, and digital phone services; Filmed Entertainment, consisting principally of feature film, television, and home video production and distribution; Networks, consisting principally of cable television and broadcast networks; and Publishing, consisting principally of magazine and book publishing. AOL was a subsidiary of Time Warner Inc. It specialized in Internet services provision and more recently began to focus on Internet search services as an additional revenue source. In the Internet search segment, AOL ranked fourth behind Google, Yahoo, and MSN with regard to volume of Internet search patrons.[4]

AOL's strengths were the variety of services it provided. These included online dating services, email services, Internet service provision, news, and sports. The services it provided such as instant messaging allowed it to successfully register all its patrons. This broad membership base could be the needed catalyst for future advertising in the Internet search segment. In addition, AOL had established a very secure Web site with virus protection and spam blocking controls for its Internet service subscribers. AOL's international image and popularity remained an Achilles heel. The company, because of its inability to effectively market to non-AOL Internet service subscribers, was not popular outside of the United States and Canada. Moreover, the company's search service was not a dominant one in the Internet search segment when compared to the leading search companies. For the fiscal year ended December 31, 2004, revenues rose 6% to $42.1 billion. Net income from continuing operations and before accounting change rose 2% to $3.21 billion. Results reflected higher worldwide license fees from television series, partially offset by legal reserves expense.[5]

MSN

Microsoft Corporation developed, manufactured, licensed, and supported a wide range of software products for various computing devices. The company's software products included scalable operating systems for servers, personal computers (PCs), and intelligent devices; server applications for client/server environments; information worker productivity applications; business solutions applications; software development tools; and mobile and embedded devices. Microsoft provided consulting services and product support services and trained and certified system integrators and developers. The company sold the Xbox video game console, along with games and peripherals. Its online businesses included the MSN subscription and the MSN network of Internet products and services. The company's seven product segments were Client, Server and Tools, Information Worker, Microsoft Business Solutions, MSN, Mobile and Embedded Devices, and Home and Entertainment.

The MSN network was a subsidiary of Microsoft Corporation and offered Internet services based on membership subscription for emails, online personals, shopping, etc. Recently MSN linked its search engine to its online Encarta encyclopedia software, which was a virtual database of information updated regularly. MSN had the financial backing of Microsoft Corporation and openly expressed its intentions of improving and taking the Internet search business to a new level. MSN also offered business solutions and Web page design and development for small new businesses. On the other hand, the company's inability to mount a platform for online auctions and its ineptitude in the sale and distribution of still images and other multimedia products counted as areas that needed improvement. In addition, the company would be able to strongly capture market share only if it was able to bundle very effective search software into Microsoft's Windows computer program without raising any anti-trust concerns.

The company gained prominence when it introduced software that made both business and home computing a breeze for even the most reluctant to embrace computer technology. More recently, it seemed to be losing its technological luster and innovativeness when compared to Google. A key to success would be to successfully recruit technically proficient workers, especially in Internet search technology, and to stop the exodus of its workforce to Google. MSN could also boost its Hotmail email service membership by increasing free storage limits to at least 1 gigabyte, because Yahoo was about to offer 1 gigabyte email storage for its members and Google was already offering 2 gigabytes for its exclusive Gmail service members. For the six months ending December 31, 2004, revenues rose 9% to $20.01 billion. Net income rose 44% to $5.99 billion. Results reflected continued improvements in overall Internet technology spending and lower research and development costs.[6]

The Company

Google was founded in 1998 by Larry Page and Sergey Brin, PhD students at Stanford University who were fed up with the existing Internet search technology companies and their inability to return accurate search results. Google was basically an online company that

EXHIBIT 3
Business Model: Google, Inc.

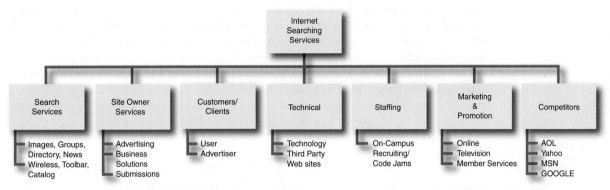

specialized in developing a reliable Internet search engine. Of all the applications on today's computers, one could argue that the search engine was second in importance only to the Web browser (such as Internet Explorer or Mozilla Firefox). This trend reflected the importance of Google as a service provider to the computer services industry.

Google Inc. offered highly targeted advertising solutions, global Internet search solutions through its own destination Internet site, and intranet solutions via an enterprise search appliance. In other words, the company maintained an online index of Web sites and other content, which it made available to anyone with an *Internet connection*. Its automated search technology helped people obtain nearly instant access to relevant information from its vast online index. In providing an avenue for search, the company also furnished ads based on keywords in a search inquiry beside the search results.[1]

The company provided an interface for more than 88 languages, and half of Google.com's traffic originated outside the United States. This clearly demonstrated a trend of international popularity and the fact that the company was satisfying an important need in the Internet jungle, where users needed a guide as to where to go looking for specific information, saving time in the process.

Most of Google's revenue came from advertising. This was done through Google AdWords, which was based on an auction system. An advertiser would bid on relevant words, and the placement of the ads was based on the bids. A big benefit for the advertiser was it paid nothing unless a user clicked on its ad. In other words, Google pursued a "performance-oriented" method of advertising. This meant that very little was wasted in terms of advertising dollars spent. Again, the ad system was based on simplicity. There were no flashy ads; instead, the ads were text-based. As a result, an advertiser did not have to spend much time creating an ad campaign. It was also easier for the advertiser to flexibly change ads based on effectiveness. Actually, it took only about 15 minutes to set up an ad campaign at an initial cost of $5.[7] The Google AdWords system had a powerful self-management system. An advertiser could easily adjust a campaign in terms of budgets: They could set a limit on how much they could pay to have their ads posted in a given time frame.

Exhibit 3 shows a detailed description of Google's business model. Each section focuses on strengths and weaknesses in key success areas.

Search Services

Google had developed a broad range of innovative search solutions. Internet search service was the core service from which additional services related to search branched off. Consumers patronized all the additional services even though Google's revenue was solely generated from Internet search services. The company generated all its revenues from selling ads that were placed beside its search results. Google charged its advertisers an undisclosed amount of money any time an ad that was related to a search inquiry was clicked by an Internet search user. The ad clicked did not have to generate a sale for Google to get paid: a phenomenon in Internet search advertising known as "cost per click" pricing. Google had built a financial powerhouse selling ads this way. More recently, the company announced a big change in how it was going to sell ads. Google was going to allow advertisers more control over where their ads appeared online and how the ads were priced. The company would allow advertisers to use flashier animated graphics. The move, which applied to thousands of other Web sites (third party) that used Google's search technology, was designed to attract more big-name advertisers and was intended to help Google better tap budgets for advertising of product brands, which represented the bulk of U.S. ad spending.[8]

Images

Google Images contained an index of 425 million still images. With Google Images, for example, a user typed "red sports car" in the Images search pane and pressed "enter." A few seconds later more than a thousand pictures of red sports cars would be made available for the user to choose from. Industry experts predicted a strong demand for multimedia search, given the spread of technology for producing, sharing, and storing digital media files. Images were a strong area for Google because the main competitors had not developed a strong buzz as far as images. With the exception of Yahoo, Google was the automatic choice for images.

Groups

With Google Groups, Google.com users could search for a discussion topic and add postings to a newsgroup. Google acquired the Usenet discussion service from Deja.com, including its archive of more than 500 million postings dating back to 1981. However, Yahoo was more advanced and had many patrons in groups and online personals. Yahoo had several million registered patrons who used its platform for online topic discussions and posting blogs.

Directory

Google used its unique search technology to arrange, by subject category, 1.5 million Uniform Resource Locators (URLs) that had been identified by thousands of volunteers using Netscape's Open Directory project. Every Web page had a unique URL, or address. Directory service was a way of classifying or listing all the millions of articles in the Google database into subject categories. AOL, Yahoo, and MSN had directory services. There were not many opportunities for revenue generation with this service on its own; it was just a way of attracting more patrons to discover other profitable services. In the future, however, directory-linked target advertising held the promise of becoming the next direction for effective Internet advertising and marketing.

News

Google News, started in early 2004, was compiled from 4,500 news sources worldwide. Google News employed computer algorithms to identify the most relevant stories within a topic area, then, by story, grouped links to different news sources, allowing users to see how different journalists covered the stories. This service summed up the most-read news articles for busy people who could not sift through volumes of news articles daily. Yahoo's news service could be described as more comprehensive and a leader in this area, which was not a strong service for Google.

Google Wireless

Google's wireless search technology translated Web pages into a language understood by handheld devices. Licensees included Sprint PCS, Cingular, Nextel, Bell Mobility (Canada), Yahoo Everywhere, Vizzavi, and Palm. This technology allowed cell-phone and handheld device subscribers to the companies just mentioned the ability to use Google search if they had wireless access to the World Wide Web. The promise of licensing patented technology and intellectual property to other companies needed to be encouraged and developed.

Google Toolbar

Google's downloadable toolbar could be embedded permanently in a user's Web browser. In addition to an Internet search box, the Google Toolbar included tools for blocking pop-up ads, automatically filling out Web page forms, and creating "blog" postings pointing to a web page (see **Exhibit 4**). Blogs, short for "web logs," were diaries in Web page form that presented personal thoughts on almost any topic. In early 2003, Google had acquired Pyra Labs and its Web site, Blogger.com, which offered tools for creating Web logs. Being able to successfully propagate Google's toolbar on Web browsers would be a step in the right direction because Internet search users would not have to go to Google.com to initiate a search query.

Google Catalog

Google's Catalog Search, a beta service started in early 2004, allowed users to search hundreds of print mail-order catalogs not previously available online. The catalogs were scanned, analyzed, and indexed by Google. The company was a pioneer in this area because none of the major competitors—AOL, MSN, and Yahoo—offered this service. This was a very useful service for prospective advertisers, because most patrons of this service had a commercial motivation. A key to success would be to reach an agreement with the companies whose catalogs were indexed to pay a fee to Google any time a sale was finalized through Google catalogs. The online catalog idea was an opportunity to begin collecting information on products and services that most companies that advertised with Google carried. This information, in the long run, could be used to enhance the quality of directory-linked target ads that were placed next to search results because it would incorporate almost everything in the inventory of advertisers and increase revenues for both Internet search companies and search engines. In addition, the transparency of advertising packages offered and a clear-cut pricing policy were keys to success for Internet search companies.

EXHIBIT 4
Google's Toolbar
Embedded
in Microsoft's
Internet Explorer
Web Browser

Google's toolbar

Site Owner Services

Site owner service referred to a platform that Internet search companies and large Internet services companies used to invite potential advertisers to the variety of advertising packages they offered. It represented a grand standpoint for a Web-based company to stake its claim to being in a unique position to help businesses advertise and help them reach a larger audience. This was the link reserved for potential advertisers looking to do business with an Internet search service company such as Google. Google's reluctance to incorporate multimedia banner ads and colorful animated graphics on its home page did not serve as an effective way of letting prospective advertisers get a visual image of Google's advertising packages, because colorful graphics tend to make a better impression.

Advertising

Businesses that intended to advertise beside Google's search results used this link to determine whether Google's offered advertising package was the right choice for their business. A business owner would access this link in order to open a business account as a potential advertiser with Google. Advertising under Site Owner Services was a link reserved only for businesses who intended to do business with Google. For example, Google's AdWords was cost-per-click advertising. Advertisers paid only when users clicked on an ad. It had features that allowed an advertiser to control its costs by setting a budget for what it was willing to spend per day. AdWords-sponsored listings were also shown on Google's partner sites. Yahoo was a segment leader as far as presenting the potential advertiser with the best possible packages and also in terms of the ease with which business was conducted.

Business Solutions

Using this link, businesses were able to assess the various ways Google could help them grow and become more profitable. In other words, with Business Solutions Google marketed the potency of its advertising methods to potential advertisers. Yahoo was the segment leader in this area with MSN and AOL closely in the hunt. All the major players in Internet search were going to great lengths to inform prospective advertisers of the various ways a search engine could help them grow and expand their clientele. The crossing point for Google was the fact that the company refused to advertise on its home page, which was supposed to be the ultimate platform. Google was the most widely visited Web site in the world. Management believed that advertising on Google's home page took away from the main reason patrons visited the site—quality Internet search.

Submissions

Case files for prospective advertisers on Google search were submitted through this link. Google had a reputation for not assigning one person or team to a case; rather, they kept switching teams assigned to a particular case. Many prospective advertisers saw Google as filled with arrogant people and found it time-consuming and difficult to do business with the company. Yahoo's effort at making submissions brisk was unmatched in the segment.

Customers and Clients

The Internet searching services' customers and clients consisted primarily of advertisers, Internet search patrons, and large Web portals, some of which had their own Internet search services: groups and licensees, among others. Customers and clients were bundled together because of the vague distinction between the two in this segment. Yahoo was a service provider to Google when it displayed Google ads on the Yahoo Web site. In this scenario, Google was the customer on Yahoo's Web site. On the other hand, if Google displayed a Yahoo service ad beside its search results as a contextual ad, Google became the service provider and Yahoo became a client of Google's search service and its related advertising. Companies in this segment normally provided email services in order to increase the number of people visiting their Web sites.

User

Most Internet search users needed guidance in finding information about goods or services in which they were interested, and Internet search engines presented an opportunity to go directly to what users needed without wasting time. Internet search users also ended up buying things or requesting services that they made queries on. This was the lure to advertisers seeking to reach consumers using Internet search companies. Google, since its launch in 1998, had grown explosively to become the most-used Web site in the world. Inducted as a verb into the Oxford English dictionary, it was each month used by 165 million people in the United Kingdom and United States alone. In the lives of tens of millions of Internet users, Google was nothing less than the front door to the Internet.[9] Yahoo was closely behind, largely because of its popular free email service, which was patronized worldwide.

Advertiser

Google had numerous loyal Web users who used its Internet search services frequently for search solutions on the Web. Quality search results made Web surfing easier. This loyal pool of patrons presented a great opportunity for advertisers to effectively reach a target audience. As Google continued to develop effective ways of linking search results to specific search-based services, advertisers would keep flocking to Google for ways in which they could help businesses reach a target audience. Contextual ads, which were a Google staple, were Internet search–based ads placed beside search results directing patrons to possible solutions to their internet search query. MSN, Yahoo, and AOL also began to incorporate colorful graphics and multimedia banner ads beside search results. These were more flashy ways of attracting an Internet search user's attention to an ad. Companies in this segment normally provided email services, online shopping, news and sports, online satellite maps, and driving directions services as a way of luring customers to their Internet search services and to also have a registered member base for future directory-linked target advertising. Directory-linked target advertising had not yet been approved because of the privacy and identity theft concerns of Internet service users, especially registered members.

Technical

This section encompasses the technology behind Google's Internet search engines and its policy in relationship to third-party Web sites.

Google's Technology

Businesses used the Google's AdWords program to promote their products and services using targeted advertising. In addition, the thousands of third-party Web sites that made up the Google network used the Google AdSense program to deliver relevant ads that generated revenue and enhanced the user experience. Google AdWords ads connected businesses with new customers at the very moment when they were looking for a product or service. The Google network reached more than 80% of Internet users. With Google AdWords, prospective advertisers could create their own ads, choose keywords to help Google match their ads to a target audience, and pay only when someone clicked on them.

Google AdSense was a fast and easy way for Web site publishers of all sizes to display relevant, unobtrusive Google ads on their Web sites' content pages and earn money. Because the ads were related to what users were looking for on a Web site, Web site publishers could finally both make money and enhance their content pages. It was also a way for Web site publishers to provide Google Internet search to their visitors, and earn money by displaying Google ads beside search results.[10] A key to success would be to remain a dominant force in Internet search technology.

Third-Party Web Sites

Google's policy on third-party Web sites read: "The sites displayed as search results or linked to by Google services are developed by people over whom Google exercises no control. The search results that appear from Google's indices are indexed by Google's automated machinery and computers, and Google cannot and does not screen the sites before including them in the indices from which such automated search results are gathered. A search using Google services may produce search results and links to sites that some people find objectionable, inappropriate, or offensive. We cannot guarantee that a Google search will not locate unintended or objectionable content and assume no responsibility for the content of any site included in any search results or otherwise linked to by the Google Services."[11] The goal here was to appeal to a large number of third-party Web sites in order to reach a larger audience and increase market share in the process.

Staffing

Eric Schmidt, Google's CEO, recently announced the company was having problems recruiting. He claimed the pool of candidates were either not of sufficient quality or not technically proficient enough. The company's headquarters in Mountain View, California, employed a little more than 2,700 people, of whom 900 were techies.

On-Campus Recruiting/Annual Code Jams

The company was notoriously picky when it came to hiring, even though it was hiring about 25 new people a week. A team of 50 recruiters combed through resumes, which had to be submitted online, then dumped them into a program that channels those chosen for an interview to the proper hiring committee and threw the rest in electronic trash. Interviewing for a job at Google could take months in a grueling process that would not guarantee a job. The company also organized annual code jams where programmers from all over the world competed for cash and ultimately a job. The school campus environment at Googleplex—the company's headquarters in Mountain View, California—encouraged employees to stay at work past work hours. There was an around-the-clock free catering service at the cafeteria. Google as well as the main players in the Internet search segment knew the future of the segment depended on the continued development and training of technical staff that came up with more effective ways of enhancing Internet search technology. The key to success, therefore, would be setting up the right administrative mechanisms to effectively handle business operations and to successfully recruit a quality and technically proficient work force while at the same time improving on the competence of existing employees.

Marketing and Promotion

Most of Google's popularity could be attributed to simple word of mouth and quality search results. The company, however, had to shift into a more proactive mode of marketing and promotion on a more serious level. Google needed to communicate to its everyday patrons that it existed, first and foremost, to offer Internet search services but also to get users to accommodate the fact that the company was evolving and was rolling out a bevy of non–search related services.

Online

Companies normally would use their own Web sites to promote their services. Google, on the other hand, did not advertise on its home page. This, Google believed, let the user know that the quality of the search result was paramount. Users would be introduced to ads only after typing their inquiries. It must be emphasized that companies encouraged their registered members to customize their Web browsers with a preferred company's search pane as the default search engine. Google encouraged its search patrons to download an inbuilt taskbar on their computers for search purposes.

Television

Television ads and radio promotions can be an effective outlet for reaching out to an older, less Internet-savvy audience. Television and radio had not been used traditionally as an outlet for marketing and promotion by Internet search companies, but could be considered as competition between Internet search companies intensified. A need may arise to pursue a marketing strategy that includes television ad campaign.

Member Services

Google needed to expand its membership-grabbing effort by offering new services, such as increasing its 1-gigabyte storage limit for its Gmail users. The company's email services were based on invitation only from an existing Gmail user. How did a person get invited to subscribe to this email service? Few potential users seemed to know. In a nutshell, Google needed to increase its membership service subscription initiatives if it was to compete in the future with companies with a large membership base such as MSN, AOL, and Yahoo.

Competition

Google's main competitors were Yahoo, AOL, and MSN. Google compared favorably with its major competitors in key areas. Google maintained an edge in the U.S. Internet search traffic market share with 31%, while Yahoo and MSN held 26% and 20% shares, respectively.[11] However, Google did not have the size, network, and existing service depth of its competitors.

Google's Internet search engine was by far the most accurate when compared with AOL, MSN, and Yahoo search results. The major concern in this area was the fact that all the major competitors had expressed keen interest in taking over the Internet search segment in a bid to reduce Google's current market share.

The main complaint leveled by Google's clients (prospective advertisers) was the company's inability to assign one team to a project. The company kept changing employees assigned to already established cases and wasted clients' time in the process because they had to start over any time a new team was assigned to an already opened case file.

EXHIBIT 5
2004 Direct
Competitor
Comparison

	Google	MSFT (MSN)	Yahoo	Industry Average
Market Cap ($):	54.05B	279.73B	46.90B	212.81M
Employees:	1,907	57,000	5,500	470
Revenue Growth (%):	117.56%	14.40%	70.50%	10.80%
Revenue ($):	3.19B	38.47B	3.57B	95.93M
Gross Margin (%):	54.29%	83.67%	63.67%	48.74%
EBITDA ($):	788.67M	13.44B	834.28M	6.71M
Operating Margins (%):	20.07%	32.73%	19.26%	8.27%
Net Income ($):	399.12M	10.00B	839.55M	3.13M
EPS ($):	1.442	0.917	0.576	0.13
PE:	137.09	28.04	59.22	27.12
PEG:	1.63	1.73	2.18	1.32
PS:	17.01	7.29	13.24	1.96

SOURCE: *http://finance.yahoo.com/q/co?s=GOOG. Accessed February 7, 2005.*

Finally, Google's main competitors in Internet search—Yahoo, MSN, and AOL—were also well-established Web portals with a wide range of products and services and millions of registered members. Google was yet to introduce a wide range of services to match its competitors. Google's revenue growth rate of 233.50% (see **Exhibit 5**) surpassed all its competitors across the computer services industry even though the major competitors were by far bigger and more independent Web portals. Google's main weakness was the fact that it had to depend on its competitors to propagate its Internet search technology. Others also suggested that Google could do without all the other services and forego the high overhead costs associated with operating a Web portal like Yahoo, AOL, and MSN.

Financial Analysis

Google ranked high among the computer services industry's well-run companies. The company's profit margin of 12.52% compared favorably with the industry average. The current management's effectiveness was positively highlighted through its ROA and ROE of 21.05% and 25.97%, respectively.

Google's revenue growth of 117.56% as of December 2004 was phenomenal and further reflected an increase in shareholder value with current revenue per share of $11.692 over the same period. With regard to Internet search technology, Google had the winning search engine. This trend was easily reflected in the company's financial position and by the fact that it was the most visited Web site in the world.

The company made all of its revenues from contextual ads that were placed beside search results. For instance, a business owner arranged with Google to pay for clicks on its ad, to be displayed beside a Google search result any time a particular keyword was searched. A corn distributor might choose "corn" as the keyword that should trigger its ad to be displayed. The business specified the number of clicks it could afford to pay for daily or weekly based on a fee that was agreed on by Google and the advertising company. Businesses were increasingly using this mode of advertising because it yielded better results as far as generating sales: Ads were relevant only to the search inquiry and were more likely to result in a sale.

EXHIBIT 6
Consolidated
Statements of
Income: Google, Inc.
(Dollar amounts in
thousands, except
per share amounts)

	2004	2003	2002
Revenues	$3,189,223	$1,465,934	$439,508
Costs and expenses:			
Cost of revenues	1,457,653	625,854	131,510
Research and development	225,632	91,228	31,748
Sales and marketing	246,300	120,328	43,849
General and administrative	139,700	56,699	24,300
Stock-based compensation	278,746	229,361	21,635
Non-recurring portion of settlement of disputes with Yahoo	201,000	—	—
Total costs and expenses	2,549,031	1,123,470	253,042
Income from operations	640,192	342,464	186,466
Interest income (expense) and other, net	10,042	4,190	(1,551)
Income before income taxes	650,234	346,654	184,915
Provision for income taxes	251,115	241,006	85,259
Net income	$399,119	$105,648	$99,656
Net income per share:			
Basic	2.07	0.77	0.86
Diluted	1.46	0.41	0.45
Number of shares used in per share calculations:			
Basic	193,176	137,697	115,242
Diluted	272,781	256,638	220,633

SOURCE: *Google, Inc. 2004 Annual Report, p. 68.*

In a nutshell, Google was one of the fastest growing companies in any industry as reflected in its revenue growth rate. The company's IPO with its Wall Street buzz and the eventual tripling of the company's stock, trading at $180, reflected the confidence that the public had vested in the future direction of the company. Financially, Google was sound. The company's expenses were minimal because it had no inventory. Google's raw materials were the innovativeness of its technical staff. **Exhibits 6 and 7** provide summarized financial information.

EXHIBIT 7
Consolidated
Balance Sheets:
Google, Inc.
(Dollar amounts
in thousands,
except par value)

	2004	2003
Assets		
Current assets:		
Cash and cash equivalents	$426,873	$148,995
Marketable securities	1,705,424	185,723
Accounts receivable, net of allowance of $4,670 and $3,962	311,836	154,690
Income taxes receivable	70,509	—
Deferred income taxes, net	19,463	22,105
Prepaid revenue share, expenses and other assets	159,360	48,721
Total current assets	2,693,465	560,234
Property and equipment, net	378,916	188,255
Goodwill	122,818	87,442
Intangible assets, net	71,069	18,114
Deferred income taxes, net, non-current	11,590	—
Prepaid revenue share, expenses and other assets, non-current	35,493	17,413
Total assets	$3,313,351	$871,458

(Continued)

EXHIBIT 7
(Continued)

	2004	2003
Liabilities, Redeemable Convertible Preferred Stock Warrant and Stockholders' Equity		
Current liabilities:		
Accounts payable	$32,672	$46,175
Accrued compensation and benefits	82,631	33,522
Accrued expenses and other current liabilities	64,111	26,411
Accrued revenue share	122,544	88,672
Deferred revenue	36,508	15,346
Income taxes payable	—	20,705
Current portion of equipment leases	1,902	4,621
Total current liabilities	340,368	235,452
Long-term portion of equipment leases	—	1,988
Deferred revenue, long-term	7,443	5,014
Liability for stock options exercised early, long-term	5,982	6,341
Deferred income taxes, net	—	18,510
Other long-term liabilities	30,502	1,512
Commitments and contingencies		
Redeemable convertible preferred stock warrant	—	13,871
Stockholders' equity:		
Convertible preferred stock, $0.001 par value, issuable in series: 164,782 and 100,000 shares authorized at December 31, 2003 and December 31, 2004, 71,662 and no shares issued and outstanding at December 31, 2003 and December 31, 2004, aggregate liquidation preference of $40,815 and none at December 31, 2003 and December 31, 2004	—	44,346
Class A and Class B common stock, $0.001 par value: 700,000 and 9,000,000 shares authorized at December 31, 2003 and December 31, 2004, 160,866, and 266,917 shares issued and outstanding, excluding 11,987, and 7,605 shares subject to repurchase (see Note 10) at December 31, 2003 and December 31, 2004	267	161
Additional paid-in capital	2,582,352	725,219
Note receivable from officer/stockholder	—	(4,300)
Deferred stock-based compensation	(249,470)	(369,668)
Accumulated other comprehensive income	5,436	1,660
Retained earnings	590,471	191,352
Total stockholders' equity	$2,929,056	$588,770
Total liabilities, redeemable convertible preferred stock warrant and stockholders' equity	3,313,351	871,458

SOURCE: *Google, Inc. 2004 Annual Report, p. 67.*

Corporate Governance

Exhibit 8 shows Google's Board of Directors and the company's executive management team.

The Google Culture

Though growing rapidly, Google still maintained a small company feel. At the Googleplex headquarters almost everyone ate in the Google café (known as "Charlie's Place"), sitting at

EXHIBIT 8
Board of Directors
and Executive
Management
Group: Google, Inc.

A. BOARD OF DIRECTORS

Dr. Eric Schmidt, Google Inc.
Sergey Brin, Google, Inc.
Larry Page, Google, Inc.
John Doerr, Kleiner Perkins Caufiled & Byers
Michael Mortiz, Sequoia Capital
Ram Sriram, Sherpalo
John Hennessy, Stanford University
Paul Otellini, Intel
Shirley M. Tilghman, Princeton University
Ann Mather

B. EXECUTIVE MANAGEMENT GROUP

Dr. Eric Schmidt, Chairman of the Executive Committee and Chief Executive Officer
Larry Page, Co-Founder & President, Products
Sergey Brin, Co-Founder & President, Technology
Shona Brown, Senior Vice President, Business Operations
W. M. Coughran, Jr., Vice President, Engineering
David C. Drummond, Senior Vice President, Corporate Development
Alan Eustace, Senior Vice President, Engineering & Research
Urs Holzle, Senior Vice President, Operations & Google Fellow
Jeff Huber, Vice President, Engineering
Omid Kordestani, Senior Vice President, Global Sales & Business Development
George Reyes, Senior Vice President & Chief Financial Officer
Jonathan Rosenberg, Senior Vice President, Product Management
Elliot Schrage, Vice President, Global Communications & Public Affairs

SOURCE: *Google, Inc., "Corporate Information," Google Web site.*

whatever table had an opening and enjoying conversations with Googlers from all different departments. Topics ranged from the trivial to the technical, and whether the discussion was about computer games or encryption or ad serving software, it was not surprising to hear someone say, "That's a product I helped develop before I came to Google."

Google's emphasis on innovation and commitment to cost containment meant each employee was a hands-on contributor. There was little in the way of corporate hierarchy, and everyone wore several hats. The international Webmaster who created Google's holiday logos spent a week translating the entire site into Korean. The chief operations engineer was also a licensed neurosurgeon. Because everyone realized they were an equally important part of Google's success, no one hesitated to skate over a corporate officer during a game of roller hockey.

Google's hiring policy was aggressively non-discriminatory and favored ability over experience. The result was a staff that reflected the global audience the search engine served. Google had offices around the globe, and Google engineering centers were recruiting local talent in locations from Zurich to Bangalore. Dozens of languages were spoken by Google staffers, from Turkish to Telugu. When not at work, Googlers pursued interests from cross-country cycling to wine tasting, from flying to Frisbee. As Google expanded its development team, it continued to look for those who shared an obsessive commitment to creating search perfection and having a great time doing it.[12]

Management Strategy

Google's President and CEO, Eric Schmidt, was committed to the continued growth of Google as a premium Internet search company while at the same time striving to further expand beyond just the Internet search–based services the company offered. The company needed to introduce new Internet-related services in order to develop a more enduring company not reliant solely on Internet search technology but diversified enough to remain an enduring entity. The company also had to further develop its international popularity.

In addition, Google needed to improve its general administrative capabilities. The primary complaint leveled by prospective advertisers trying to do business with Google was the fact that its employees were a bunch of brash arrogant people who kept switching teams assigned to cases. This led to unnecessary delays and frustrating experiences when setting up business deals with the company.

Looking to the Future

In 2005, CEO Eric Schmidt and his management team decided that Google needed to effect measures that would allow it to remain competitive as more big players focused on the Internet search segment. Despite the fact that Google was a leader in Internet search technology, the company was introducing a new line of services not related to Internet search. This new situation placed Google in a face-to-face showdown with companies that were previously considered too big to be Google's competitors. These bigger companies, namely MSN (Microsoft), AOL, and Yahoo, were feverishly working to close in on Google's Internet search supremacy and had made public their intentions to participate in the advertising dollars Internet search generates. Google, therefore, needed to differentiate itself from the other competitors in the Internet search services and to remain the household name with the largest market share. It had to achieve this using the immense human, financial, and technological expertise at its disposal.

One alternative proposed by Larry Page, co-founder, suggested the need for Google to keep focusing on doing what it does best—"Internet search solutions." He stressed the need for the company to focus on its distinctive competence by continuing to develop a superior search engine. In essence, Google should remain a company that specialized only in developing the best Internet search engine; and focusing only on Internet search applications and how they could best be utilized to effectively advertise products and services. This would keep Google on top of the pile in the Internet search segment.

The benefit of this alternative was the sustained revenues from advertising that focusing on further developing a proven Internet search engine like Google brings, through online target advertising using contextual ads. This would allow the company to remain focused on developing further what brings the company all of its revenues. It was a winning formula that had been proven because it brought the company sudden fame and fortune.

This alternative was feasible because it focused on further developing Google's main strength—Internet search services. It focused on a path successfully trod by the company—Internet search technology. Google's search engine and its associated contextual ads technology attracted advertisers and had been referred to as the future of advertising.

The alternative could be successful because Google was the segment leader in market share. Despite the hot pursuit by its competitors, Google had established brand name recognition in Internet search technology. Being the Internet search segment leader, Google could further develop its winning search service and focus on capturing market share in the international arena, where Google remained more popular than its competitors. Google could use its brand name recognition in Internet search to generate revenue using its segment-leading contextual ad technology.

The company recently announced that it was going to incorporate colorful and animated multimedia graphics beside its search results. Advertisers were also going to pay for the service whether or not users clicked on an ad. This method of Web advertising, known as "cost per impression," was based on the number of people who saw the ads and would be displayed on sites that run Google's search technology. This would allow Google's advertisers to reach more customers while expanding the list of possible advertisers who would want to consider Google as a potential source for advertising, increasing Internet search market share in the process.

A drawback to this alternative was the risk of not having a wide range of services to help absorb the shock of lost revenues in the event Internet search did not live up to its current promise as an effective advertising medium.

Another alternative, being considered by Sergey Brin, co-founder, suggested that in order to differentiate itself from the competition, Google needed to add a broad range of services and communication tools such as instant messaging, travel, news, email, paid jumbo email accounts, Web site development and hosting, sports, finance, games, and text messaging to complement its Internet search services. In other words, Google needed to expand as a business if it was to remain competitive in the future.

The benefit of this alternative would be the diverse range of new services offered by Google. It would allow the company to build a solid membership base with the introduction of fantasy sports, instant messaging, travel, and finance and other services in addition to Internet search. This would help build on Google's member services through email services that bring members to Google's Web site and also increase the likelihood of generating advertising revenues in the process.

The alternative was feasible, given Google's current profitability and financial flexibility compared to similar companies in the Internet search segment. The company's financial flexibility allowed it to branch off successfully into other areas not related to search. This alternative, therefore, placed Google in a new light as a multi-service provider in this segment. Being the market leader in Internet search technology, Google would be in a great position to introduce new services largely owing to its phenomenal success in Internet search.

The alternative could be successful simply because it made room for Google to survive any future adverse developments in the Internet search segment. By offering a variety of services to complement its Internet search segment, the company would place itself in a position to avoid total collapse should today's revenue-generating Internet search services fail to live up to their future promise. By expanding and offering new services, Google could use its current role as an Internet search powerhouse as a platform to compete and eventually beat already well-established companies such as AOL, MSN, and Yahoo, who offered an array of non–search based Internet services. Non-search Internet services would place Google in a position to have more registered members in their database. This membership database could be an advantage for more effective advertising, especially with directory-linked target advertising, which was yet to be approved but would ultimately allow Internet search companies to use previously collected information on a search user in a member database to help advertise specifically to that particular user.

Furthermore, the future of the industry may depend on directory-linked target advertising: advertising that would incorporate Internet search that analyzed the age, gender, national origin, geographical location, preferences, and previous commercial history of the search inquirer. Even though it was yet to be approved as an advertising medium in Internet search, this was touted as the future of the continued profitability of Internet search, in terms of advertising dollars. Directory-linked target advertising would tend to favor companies that had a database of registered members. This alternative could better prepare Google for competitive advantage in the future should issues of confidentiality and identity theft be tackled effectively by Internet search companies, thus paving the way for directory-linked target advertising. The industry would first have to assure members that the confidentiality of members' personal information would be guaranteed.

A drawback to this alternative was the unforeseen risks associated with rapid expansionary measures, especially in technology-centered companies. In addition, identity theft issues and confidentiality of members' personal information were affecting further development of search-based advertising.

Eric Schmidt, Google's CEO, agreed that these were worthy alternatives. Management needed further deliberation to decide the best course of action that was both efficient and effective for Google to achieve success in Internet search and related services. The best course of action should provide Google a long-term competitive edge.

NOTES

1. B. Dudley, "Putting Microsoft Brand on a New Breed: Longhorn," *Seattle Times* (February 28, 2003).

2. *MSN Encarta Encyclopedia Premium,* http://encarta.msn.com/dictionary (March 15, 2005).

3. Dudley (2003).

4. K. Delaney; "In Click Fraud, Web Outfits Have a Costly Problem," *Wall Street Journal* (April 6, 2005).

5. Profile of AOL, http://finance.yahoo.com/q/pr?s=TWX, (March 27, 2005).

6. MSN (2005).

7. Eisenmann, T. (2004). "Google, Inc. Case # 9-804-141," p. 4. http://www.hbs.edu/ (February 8, 2005).

8. Delaney, K., "Google to Target Brands in Revenue Push," Wall Street Journal (April 25, 2005).

9. Andrew Murray-Watson. "Gates v. Google: Microsoft Has Declared War on the World's Best Loved Search Engine but It May Find Its Dominance of the Software Industry Works Against It." http://premium.hoovers.com/subscribe/co/news/list.xhtml?ID=59101&Name=Google&Ticker=GOOG (February 6, 2005).

10. Google, "Google AdSense," https://www.google.com/adsense/?hl=en_US&sourceid=aso&subid=us-et-adsYahoo.com./finance (March 18, 2005).

11. Google, "Google AdWords," https://adwords.google.com/select/main?cmd=Login&sourceid=AWO&subid=US-ET-ADS&hl=en_US. (March 18, 2005).

12. Google, "Company Record."

REFERENCES

"Profile of MSN," http://finance.yahoo.com/q/pr?s=MSFT (March 27, 2005).

"Profile of Yahoo," http://finance.yahoo.com/q/pr?s=YAHOO (March 27, 2005).

T. Taulli, http://www.dealflowmanager.com/documents/Google%20Research%20Report.doc (April 26, 2005).

USA Today, http://asp.usatoday.com/search/search.aspx?q=where+most+people+click+%22search+engines+with+the+most+visitors%22&spell=1&site=USATODAY_main&client=USATODAY_main&output=xml_no_dtd&num=10&ie=UTF-8&oe=UTF-8&access=p&source=usat (April 5, 2005).

F. Vogelstein, "Google: Is This Company Worth $165 a Share?" Fortune (December 13, 2004).

F. Vogelstein, "Search and Destroy," Fortune (May 2, 2005).

Alan N. Hoffman, Rendy Halim, Rangki Son, and Suzanne Wong

CASE 14

TiVo Inc.:

TIVO VS. CABLE AND SATELLITE DVR; CAN TIVO SURVIVE?

Background

"With TiVo, TV fits into your busy life, NOT the other way around."

THE HISTORY OF TELEVISION BEGAN IN 1939 with the purpose of providing people with entertainment in their homes. It was followed in 1950 by the invention of the remote control—an extraordinarily successful invention. Forty years later, two creative Silicon Valley veterans, Mike Ramsey and Jim Barton, invented an innovative and advanced technological development, a digital video recorder (DVR) called the TiVo. They created TiVo to be "TV Your Way." According to its founders, "With TiVo, TV fits into your busy life, NOT the other way around."

By now, many people may have heard of TiVo from its being mentioned in popular TV shows and motion pictures. Even Oprah Winfrey wondered in the September 2005 issue of her "O" magazine: "Why can't life be like TiVo?" Unfortunately, even by 2007, not very many people knew what TiVo did or how it did it.

Once Upon a TiVo ...

Pioneered by Mike Ramsay and Jim Barton, TiVo redefined television entertainment by delivering the promise of technologies that up until then had only been promised. Incorporated in Delaware and originally named Teleworld, TiVo was founded as a company on August 4, 1997. As proposed, the original concept was to create a home network–based multimedia

This case was prepared by Rendy Halim, Rangki Son, and Suzanne Wong, MBA graduate, and Professor and MBA Director Alan N. Hoffman of Bentley College. This case cannot be reproduced in any form without the written permission of the copyright holder, Rendy Halim, Rangki Son, Suzanne Wong, and Alan N. Hoffman. Reprint permission is solely granted to the publisher, Prentice Hall, for the books *Strategic Management and Business Policy*—12th (and the International version of this book) and *Cases in Strategic Management and Business Policy* 12th Editions by copyright holders, Rendy Halim, Rangki Son, Suzanne Wong, and Alan N. Hoffman. This case was edited for *SMBP*-12th Edition. Copyright © 2008 by Alan N. Hoffman. The copyright holders are solely responsible for the case content. Any other publication of the case (translation, any form of electronics or other media), or sold (any form of partnership) to another publisher will be in violation of copyrights. Rendy Halim, Rangki Son, Suzanne Wong and Alan N. Hoffman have granted an additional written reprint permission.

server in which content to "thin" clients would be streamed throughout the home. In order to market such a product, a solid software foundation was first needed. The device had to operate flawlessly, be reliable, and handle power failure gracefully for the users. At the time, both founders were working at Silicon Graphics (SGI) and were very much involved in the entertainment industry. Jim Barton was then involved with an on-demand video system and was the executive sponsor of an effort to port an open source system called Linux to the SGI Indy workstation. Mike Ramsay was responsible at that time for products that created movies' special effects for such companies as ILM and Pixar. These two SGI veterans thought Linux software would serve TiVo well as its operating system foundation. The hardware was designed solely by TiVo Inc., but manufactured by other companies, including Philips, Sony, Hughes, Pioneer, Toshiba, and Humax. They created a product that was interactive, delivering a service that allowed people to assume greater control of their television viewing.

From the Server Room to the Living Room

Departing slightly from their original idea to create a home network device, the founders developed the idea of recording digitized video on a computer hard drive. Inside TiVo's Silicon Valley headquarters in Alviso, California, the founders created what they called a "fantasy living room" that they hoped would serve as a prototype for 100 million living rooms across North America. The fantasy living room was composed of an oval coffee table and a comfortable chair. The only objects on the table surface were a telephone and TiVo's distinctive peanut-shaped remote control. The sofa and chairs all faced an entertainment center containing a big-screen television that was linked to several TiVo boxes.

At the time, Ramsey and Barton both knew it would be fun to exploit and develop their concept into an actual product with a promising future—the dream of most start-ups companies. In the early days of the company, Mike Ramsay commented that they used to think: "Wow, you know, you can pause live television—isn't that a cool thing?" Jim Barton worked to store a live TV signal on a computer and play it back. That was the start of TiVo—an invention to create the world's first interactive entertainment network, in which the luxury of entertainment and control was firmly in the viewers' own hands. TiVo shipped its first unit on March 31, 1999. Since that date was considered to be a blue moon (second full moon in a month), the engineering staff code-named TiVo's first version as the "Blue Moon." Both Jim Barton and Mike Ramsay were excited by the market introduction of their innovative product. Teleworld was renamed TiVo in July 1999.

TiVo Acclamation

With the success of on-demand programs and online streaming catering to people's viewing habits, many people have found the DVR to be an essential part of their digital home entertainment center. Salespeople at big box retailers, such as Best Buy, Circuit City, Target, and Wal-Mart, often referred to any DVR as a TiVo even though TiVo was not the only DVR on the market. Both ReplayTV and TiVo launched DVRs at the 1999 Consumer Electronics Show in Las Vegas. ReplayTV won the "Best of Show" award in the video category and was later acquired by SonicBlue and D&M Holdings. Surprisingly, ReplayTV's version of the DVR failed to attract customers. TiVo, in contrast, became widely known and succeeded at becoming the only stand-alone DVR company in the industry. According to the research firm, Forrester, TiVo's brand trust among regular users scored 4.2 (out of 5 possible), while its brand potential among aspiring users scored an "A" with 11.1 million potential users.

Spending approximately 13 months to develop the first TiVo unit, the company found the wait to be worthwhile. TiVo received an Emmy award in August 19, 2006, in recognition of

TiVo's providing innovative and interactive services that greatly enhanced television viewing. Other finalists for that Emmy award included AOL Music on Demand, CNN Enhanced, and DirecTV Interactive Sports. TiVo established a well-known brand that became extremely popular among fiercely loyal customers and even non-users. Becoming a cult-like product, TiVo was transformed into a verb. Celebrities like Regis Philbin would say "TiVo it," meaning to record a program. A working wife, who had an important business dinner meeting that night and was rushing through the door, would ask her husband: "Could you TiVo Desperate Housewives for me tonight, dear?" On the other hand, TiVo felt that this verb transformation might jeopardize the TiVo brand and associate its products with the generic DVR. People might say, "I want two TiVos," when they meant DVRs. Nevertheless, thanks to TiVo's product acceptance, TiVo became publicly listed September 30, 1999, on the NASDAQ at an opening price of $16 per share with 5.5 million shares being offered. On its way to the IPO (initial product offering), TiVo established one of the most rapid adoption rates in the history of consumer electronics. According to the April 2007 issue of *PC World*, TiVo was third on its list of 50 best technology products of all time.

As of 2007, TiVo was available in four countries: the United States, United Kingdom, Canada, and Taiwan. Although TiVo was not yet being sold in Australia, New Zealand, Netherlands, or South Africa, its technology was informally being modified by end users so it could fit their systems. Nevertheless, TiVo had not generated a profit since its launching in 1997. Considered to be the best DVR system in use by a variety of top-notch publications, such as *Business Week*, *New York Times*, and *Popular Science*, TiVo achieved a 3 million subscriber milestone on February 18, 2005. TiVo's subscribers included well-known loyal subscribers, such as Oprah Winfrey, Brad Pitt, Regis Philbin, and entrepreneur Craig Newmark (the owner of *Craigslist*). TiVo's mission was simple: Connect consumers to the digital entertainment they want, where and when they want it.

The Brain Inside the Box

"It's not TiVo unless it's a TiVo"

The Surf and Turf

As people's daily life became busier and they demanded more convenience in watching TV, digital video recorders became the tool to satisfy that need. DVRs were far easier to use than VCRs (video cassette recorders) and provided more capabilities, such as replaying a program in slow motion or temporarily putting a TV program on hold while answering the door or making a phone call. The DVR platform created a massive opportunity for TiVo to continue developing creative and sophisticated applications, features, and services. As a digital video recorder, TiVo used Linux-based software to allow users to capture any TV program and record it onto internal hard disk storage for later viewing.

The TiVo device also allowed users to watch their programs without having to watch the commercials. This feature was very attractive to consumers, but not to television networks and advertising agencies. However, unlike ReplayTV, which allowed users to automatically skip advertisements (causing it to be the target of several lawsuits from ad agencies and TV networks), TiVo took a different approach. As with a VCR, viewers using TiVo could either watch the commercials or fast-forward through them.

With an inventive advertising feature, TiVo created a business opportunity. Knowing that advertising could be a source of revenue, TiVo's management tested a "pop-up" feature. While recording or watching a program, advertisements popped up at the bottom of the TV screen. If a customer was interested in any of these advertisements, he/she had the ability to click to get more information about the product being advertised. People thus had the choice to get advertisers' information or not, depending on their interests. "Product Watch" let users choose the products, services, or even brands that interested them and would automatically find and deliver the requested products straight to a viewer's list. Surprisingly, during the 2002 Super Bowl, TiVo tracked the viewing patterns of 10,000 of its subscribers and found that TiVo's instant replay feature was used more on certain commercials, notably the Pepsi ad with Britney Spears, than on the game itself. TiVo included 70 "showcase" advertising campaigns in its TiVo platforms for companies such as Acura, Best Buy, BMW, Buick, Cadillac, Charles Schwab, Coca-Cola, Dell, General Motors, GMC, New Line Cinema, Nissan, Pioneer, Porsche, and Target.

In addition to the features previously mentioned, there was much more for users to experience. A "Season Pass Manager" avoided conflicts, such as one recording canceling another. A "Wish List" platform allowed viewers to store their search accordingly to their interests, such as actor, keyword, director, etc. No other company had yet been able to match these two TiVo recording features. In addition, the easy-to-use remote control with its distinctive "Thumbs Up and Down" feature allowed users to rate the shows they had watched so that TiVo could assist and provide users with programs similar to what they had rated positively. This feature also provided TiVo with some useful market research data. The remote control had won design awards from the Consumer Electronics Association. Jakob Nielsen, a technology consultant of the Nielsen Norman Group, called the oversize yellow pause button in the middle of the remote "the most beautiful pause button I've ever seen." Steve Wozniak, the co-founder of Apple Computer, stated that "TiVo adjusts to my tastes. Its remote has been the most ergonomic and easy to use one that I have had encountered in many years."

"TiVoToGo," a feature launched in January 2005, allowed users to connect their TiVo to a computer with an Internet or a home network, transferring recorded shows from TiVo boxes to users' PCs. Through a software program developed with Sonic, customers were able to edit and save their TiVo files. In August 2005, TiVo released a software program that allowed customers to transfer MPEG2 video files from their PC to their TiVo boxes in order to play the video on the TiVo DVR.

The TiVoToGo feature included TiVo's "Central Online," which allowed users to schedule recordings on its Web site, "MultiRoom Viewing," and allowed them to transfer recordings between TiVo units in multiple rooms, download any programs in any format into the TiVo box and transfer them into other devices, such as an IPOD, laptop, or other mobile device, such as cellular phones. This provided users with the opportunity to view recordings anytime and anywhere the users desired. With various partnerships that TiVo had established regarding third-party network content, viewers could access weather, traffic condition, and even purchase a last-minute movie ticket at Fandango.com. Viewers could also use "Amazon Unbox" to buy or rent the latest movies and TV shows that would be downloaded into the TiVo box. By early 2007, Amazon had 1,500 TiVo-compatible movies listed for rent and 2,300 available for purchase.

"Behind The Box"—The Hardware Anatomy of TiVo 101

TiVo units can be installed fairly easily because they had been designed for anyone to install and operate. Parts that went into the device and its internal architecture had been made less complex. An online self-installation guide with step-by-step pictured instruction was used to complete the installation request. It was possible, however, to have professional installation service through a retailer, such as Best Buy or a customer's cable provider.

In reality, TiVo was simply a cable box with a hard drive that provided the ability to record using a fancy user interface. The main idea at the beginning was to free people from a TV network's schedule. With TiVo, the viewer could watch programs at any time using features such as pause, rewind, fast forward, and slow motion.

TiVo's model Series 2 was supported with USB ports that had been integrated into the TiVo system to support network adapters that included wired Ethernet and WiFi capabilities. It received its signal from the cable or satellite box. It also provided the ability to record a program over-the-air. The next generation, TiVo Series 3, had been built with two internal cable-ready tuners and supported a single external cable or satellite box. As a result, the Series 3 TiVo provided the ability to record two shows at once, unlike other DVRs available at that time. Moreover, the latest version of the TiVo box had a 10/1000 Ethernet connection port and a SATA port which could support external storage hardware. It also had an HDMI plug, which provided an interface between any compatible digital audio/video source, such as a DVD player, a PC, or a video game system. With the new Series 3 TiVo box, customers no longer needed their cable box. Some recent models contained DVD-R/RW drives that transferred recordings from the TiVo box to a DVD disc.

TiVo hardware could also work alone as a normal DVR. It was thus possible for TiVo users to keep the TiVo hardware but cancel their TiVo subscription. This, of course, could seriously damage TiVo's revenue stream.

What the Hack!

Where technology was involved, there were always incentives for hackers to challenge the system. Some people hacked into the TiVo boxes to improve the service and expand its recording and/or storage capacity. Others tried to make TiVo available in countries where TiVo was not currently available. In the latest version of TiVo, improved encryption of the hardware and software made it more difficult for people to hack the systems.

The Tivo Operation – Behind the Scenes ...

". . . .and I never miss an episode. TiVo takes care of the details"

Manufacturing and Supply Chain

TiVo outsourced the manufacturing of its products to third-party manufacturers. This outsourcing extended from prototyping to volume manufacturing and included activities such as material procurement, final assembly, test, quality control, and shipment to distribution centers. The majority of the company's products were assembled in Mexico. TiVo's primary distribution center was operated on an outsourced basis in Texas.

Several consumer electronics manufacturers, including Toshiba, Humax, and Pioneer, manufactured and distributed TiVo-enabled stand-alone DVRs during the last three years. The company also engaged contract manufacturers to build TiVo-enabled stand-alone DVRs.

The components that made up TiVo's products were purchased from various vendors, including key suppliers such as Broadcom, which supplied microprocessors. Some of TiVo's components, including microprocessors, chassis, remote controls, and certain discrete components were currently supplied by sole source suppliers.

Marketing

Feel the Buzzzzzz—Hail Thy TiVo

When it came to new technology, penetrating existing consumer markets was usually difficult. Customers were often slower to embrace new product than forecasters predicted and opted to choose an older and more familiar technology, like that used by VCRs. TiVo founder

Mike Ramsay would often get upset in TiVo's early days when someone said, "Oh, that's just like a VCR." He would then retort, "No, no, no, no, no. It's much more than a VCR. It does this. . . . It does that. . . . Let's personalize it and all that stuff." At that point, Ramsey found that it became difficult to describe what TiVo actually was, leading to a five- to 10-minute conversation instead of a 30-second TiVo advertisement.

In its early years, TiVo tried the standard approach of explaining the product via ads—resulting in a series of stumbles in marketing. Millions of dollars spent on advertising did not help consumers understand what TiVo actually did. A customer claimed, "I personally remember seeing TiVo ads on TV before I even knew what a TiVo was, and it took seven years for me to finally see one 'in the flesh.'"

What made TiVo DVRs different from generic DVRs could not be grasped by most people by simply seeing the differences listed in **Exhibit 1**. As a true "experience good," it could only be felt and experienced by using the product itself. TiVo's interface was vastly superior to that used by most competitive DVRs. According to Gartner analyst Van Baker, "For cable and satellite DVRs, the interface stinks. They do a really bad job of it." Once people used a TiVo, many told others about the product and how it had improved their enjoyment of television. According to a survey reported on the TiVo Web site, 98% of users said that they could not live without their TiVo.

Between 1999 and 2000, TiVo's subscriptions increased by 86%. In addition to capitalizing on its thousands of customer evangelists to move the product into the mainstream, TiVo's word-of-mouth strategy focused on celebrity endorsements and television show product placement. The firm began giving its product away to such celebrities as Oprah Winfrey, Jay Leno, Sarah Michelle Gellar, Rosie O'Donnell, and Drew Bledsoe, turning them into high-profile members of the cult of satisfied TiVo users. Total subscriptions increased from 3.3 million (1.2 million TiVo-owned plus 2.1 million DirecTV-controlled) in early 2005 to 4.4 million (1.7 million TiVo-owned plus 2.1 million DirecTV-controlled) at end-2006.

Sales and marketing expenses consisted primarily of employee salaries and related expenses, media advertising (including print, online, radio, and television), public relations activities, special promotions, trade shows, and the production of product-related items, including collateral and videos. Advertising expenses were $15.9 million, $10.4 million, and $16.1 million for the fiscal years ended January 31, 2007, 2006, and 2005, respectively.

The TiVo-owned churn rate per month was 1.0% for the fiscal year ended January 31, 2007, compared to .9% and .7% for the fiscal years ended January 31, 2006, and 2005, respectively. The churn rate measure was composed of total TiVo-owned subscription cancellations during a period divided by the average TiVo-owned subscriptions for that period divided by the number of months in the period. Management anticipated that the TiVo-owned churn rate per month would increase in future periods as a result of increased competition in the marketplace, competitive pricing issues, the growing importance of offering competitive service features such as high definition television recording capabilities, and increased churn from product lifetime subscriptions. TiVo had previously offered lifetime service subscriptions to initially attract people to purchase TiVo DVRs, but was no longer making this offer. It had been replaced by one- to three-year service contracts containing monthly fees.

Subscription acquisition costs (SAC) totaled $267 million in 2006, $196 in 2005, and $182 in 2004. Management defined SAC as the company's total acquisition costs for a given period divided by TiVo-owned subscription gross additions for the same period. Total acquisition costs were the sum of sales and marketing expenses, rebates, revenue share, and other payments to channel, minus hardware gross margin (defined as hardware revenues less cost of hardware revenues). This included all fixed costs, including headcount-related expense, such as stock-based compensation, marketing not directly associated with subscription acquisition, operating expenses for the advertising sales business, and allocations.

EXHIBIT 1
TiVo's Product Specifications+

	TiVo Series2™ Boxes	Leading Cable Service DVR*	Satellite DVR**	DIRECTV DVR with TiVo©
Record from multiple sources	**Yes** combine satellite, cable, or antenna, depending on product.	**No** Digital cable only	**No** Satellite only	**No** DIRECTV only
Easy search: Find shows by title, actor, genre, or keyword	Yes	Titles only browsing only	title, subject, and actor only	Yes
Online scheduling: Schedule recordings from the Internet	Yes	No	No	No
Dual Tuner: Record 2 shows at once[1]	Yes	Yes	Yes	Yes
Movie and TV Downloads: Purchase or rent 1000s of movies and television shows from Amazon Unbox and have them delivered directly to your television.[2]	Yes	No	No	No
Home Movie Sharing: Edit, enhance, and send movies and photo slideshows from your One True Media account to any broadband connected TiVo box.[3]	Yes	No	No	No
Online services: Yahoo! weather, traffic & digital photos, Internet Radio from Live365, Podcasts, & movie tickets from Fandango	Yes	Limited	Limited	No
Built-In Ethernet: Broadband-ready right out of the box—connecting to your home network is a snap[4]	Yes	No	No	No
TiVoToGo transfers to mobile devices: Transfer shows to your favorite portable devices, laptop, or burn them to DVD.[3]	Yes	No	No	No
Home media features: Digital photos, digital music, and more	Yes	No	No	No
Transfer shows between boxes: Record shows on one TV and watch them on another.[3, 5]	Yes	No	No	No

Notes:

*Leading cable services compared to Time Warner/Cox Communications Explorer® 8000™ DVR and Comcast DVR

**Leading satellite services compared to DISH Network 625 DVR

[1]On theTiVo® Series2™ DT DVR, you can record 2 basic cable channels, or one basic cable and one digital cable channel, at once.

[2]Requires broadband cable modem or DSL connection

[3]Requires your TiVo box to be connected to a home network wirelessly or via Ethernet

[4]Available on the new TiVo® Series2™ DT DVR and the TiVo® Series3™ DMR

[5]In order to burn TiVoToGo transfers to DVD you will need to purchase software from Roxio/Sonic Solutions.

SOURCE: http://www.TiVo.com/1.0.chart.asp.

(Continued)

EXHIBIT 1
(Continued)

Multiroom Solutions

	Diego/Maxi	Motorola	Scientific-Atlanta	EchoStar	TiVo	Microsoft
Main DVR	Cable DVR[1]	Cable DVR[2]	Cable DVR[3]	Satellite DVR[4]	Tivo box	Media Center PC
Set-top box on additional TV(s)	IP terminal	Cable box[5]	Cable box	None Analog	TiVo box	Xbox 360
How boxes share content	IP	IP	Digital broadcast	broadcast	IP[5]	IP
Physical connection	Coax	Coax	Coax	Coax	Home network	Home network
Features available on additional TVs:						
Play back recorded programs	✓	✓	✓	✓	✓	✓
Record programs	✓	✓		✓	✓	✓
Pause programs	✓	✓		✓	✓	✓
View Internet content	✓	x			✓	✓
View personal digital content	x	x			✓	✓

Notes:
[1]New product specifically designed for multiroom use
[2]Standard cable DVR plus modifications for multiroom use
[3]Requires additional IP dongle on standard digital set-top box
[4]Available, but operators have not yet deployed
[5]Requires transferring files from one TiVo box to the other

SOURCE: *Forrester Research Inc., 2006.*

The Market Research Team

The need to create an emotional connection between people and its products was significant to TiVo's success. The company's market research team was considered key to management's understanding of TiVo's target market. The market research team was supported in its work by Lieberman Research Worldwide and Nielsen Media Research. With Lieberman, the first DVR-based panel was established in August 2002. Internally, TiVo had built a mechanism in its system that sent detailed information back to TiVo on the viewing habits of its customers. TiVo also fully embraced the viewing community with community and hackers programs so that the TiVo research team better understood users' viewing needs and wants.

Financial

Fast Forward or Rewind TiVo's Stock?

Upon going public with an IPO in 1999, TiVo's stock was listed with an initial price of $16 per share. TiVo's stock soon reached $78.75, the highest price in the stock's history. After the initial enthusiasm, TiVo's stock price eventually dropped by 2002 to a low of $2.25, the lowest in its history. TiVo's stock price began to rise in 2003 when the FCC Chairman Michael Powell announced that he used TiVo—claiming TiVo was a "God's Machine"—and when the White House Press Secretary Ari Fleischer admitted to being a loyal user of TiVo. In mid-2003, when TiVo achieved one million subscribers, its stock price jumped to $14.00 per share. It then fell to a low of $3.50 per share resulting from the resignation of its founder-CEO, Mike Ramsay. With a new CEO in place, TiVo reached the 3 million subscriber milestone by mid-2005. The stock fluctuated around $6–$8 per share in 2006 and closed at $5.35 on January 31, 2007, the end of the company's 2006 fiscal year. The company followed a policy of declaring no cash dividends.

Since its founding, the company had incurred significant losses and has had substantial negative cash flow. During the 2006 fiscal year ended January 31, 2007, the firm had a net loss of $47.8 million. TiVo had a positive cash flow of $3.8 million for the year of 2006 thanks to $64.5 million raised from the sale of 8.2 million shares of its common stock in September, 2006. (See **Exhibits 2 and 3** for financial statements.)

EXHIBIT 2

Consolidated Statements of Operations: TiVo, Inc. (Dollar amounts in thousands, except per share and share amounts)

Year Ending January 31	2007	2006	2005
Revenues			
Service and technology revenues (includes $6,805 from related parties for the fiscal year ended January 31, 2005)	$ 217,985	$ 170,859	$ 115,476
Hardware revenues	88,740	72,093	111,275
Rebates, revenue share, and other payments to channel	(48,136)	(47,027)	(54,696)
Net revenues	258,589	195,925	172,055
Cost of revenues			
Cost of service and technology revenues (1)	60,177	34,961	35,935
Cost of hardware revenues	112,212	86,817	120,323
Total cost of revenues	172,389	121,778	156,258
Gross margin	86,200	74,147	15,797
Research and development (1)	50,728	41,087	37,634
Sales and marketing (1) (includes $1,100 from related parties for the fiscal year ended January 31, 2005)	42,955	35,047	37,367
General and administrative (1)	44,813	38,018	16,593
Total operating expenses	138,496	114,152	91,594
Loss from operations	(52,296)	(40,005)	(75,797)
Interest income	4,767	3,084	1,548
Interest expense and other	(173)	(14)	(5,459)
Loss before income taxes	(47,702)	(36,935)	(79,708)
Provision for income taxes	(52)	(64)	(134)
Net loss	$ (47,754)	$ (36,999)	$ (79,842)
Net loss per common share – basic and diluted	$ (0.53)	$ (0.44)	$ (0.99)
Weighted average common shares used to calculate basic and diluted net loss per share	89,864,237	83,682,575	80,263,980
(1) Includes stock-based compensation expense (benefit) as follows:			
Cost of service and technology revenues	$ 1,490	$ —	$ —
Research and development	5,596	(85)	754
Sales and marketing	1,649	55	302
General and administrative	5,977	415	—

EXHIBIT 3
Consolidated Balance Sheets: TiVo, Inc. (Dollar amounts in thousands, except share amounts)

Year Ending	January 31, 2007	January 31, 2006
ASSETS		
CURRENT ASSETS		
Cash and cash equivalents	$ 89,079	$ 85,298
Short-term investments	39,686	18,915
Accounts receivable, net of allowance for doubtful accounts of $271 and $56	20,641	20,111
Inventories	29,980	10,939
Prepaid expenses and other, current	3,071	8,744
Total current assets	182,457	144,007
LONG-TERM ASSETS		
Property and equipment, net	11,706	9,448
Purchased technology, capitalized software, and intangible assets, net	16,769	5,206
Prepaid expenses and other, long-term	1,018	347
Total long-term assets	29,493	15,001
Total assets	$ 211,950	$ 159,008
Liabilities' and Stockholders' Equity (Deficit) Liabilities		
Current Liabilities		
Accounts payable	$ 37,127	$ 24,050
Accrued liabilities	36,542	37,449
Deferred revenue, current	64,872	57,902
Total current liabilities	138,541	119,401
Long-Term Liabilities		
Deferred revenue, long-term	54,851	67,575
Deferred rent and other	1,562	1,404
Total long-term liabilities	56,413	68,979
Total liabilities	194,954	188,380
COMMITMENTS AND CONTINGENCIES		
STOCKHOLDERS' EQUITY (DEFICIT)		
Preferred stock, par value $0.001:		
Authorized shares are 10,000,000;		
Issued and outstanding shares – none	—	—
Common stock, par value $0.001:		
Authorized shares are 150,000,000;		
Issued shares are 97,311,986 and 85,376,191, respectively and	97	85
outstanding shares are 97,231,483 and 85,376,191, respectively		
Additional paid-in capital	759,314	667,055
Deferred compensation	—	(2,421)
Accumulated deficit	(741,845)	(694,091)
Less: Treasury stock, at cost – 80,503 shares	(570)	—
Total stockholders' equity (deficit)	16,996	(29,372)
Total liabilities and stockholders' equity (deficit)	$ 211,950	$ 159,008

Decontructing TiVo

Since its founding in 1997, TiVo had accumulated $741.8 million in losses. Looking at TiVo's revenue and cost structures in **Exhibit 2**, the company recorded its revenues under service and technology and hardware. In order to become profitable, the company's management needed to find ways to increase revenues faster than costs increased. In terms of service and technology revenues, for example, TiVo needed to know the actual value of TiVo-owned subscribers and not just TiVo's partnership subscribers of DirectTV and Comcast. Deconstructing the value of just this one particular matter led to larger questions, which included, how long did a TiVo subscriber remain a subscriber, how much did each of them they pay, how much were they willing to pay, and how much advertising revenue did users produce for every tag they clicked? Moreover, how long and how could TiVo maintain its subscribers as TiVo-owned subscribers?

TiVo's hardware revenue was subject to a chicken and egg problem. If management dropped the price of TiVo hardware, more people would buy TiVo DVRs and subscribe to the TiVo service. It would then, however, be selling hardware at a significant loss. Even though rebates were offered, TiVo's management in 2007 had not yet found a price point that would attract a significantly larger number of buyers. In early 2007, TiVo offered three types of boxes depending on the hours of programming storage capacity. These ranged from an 80-hour TiVo Series 2 to a 300-hour TiVo Series 3. The basic TiVo Series 2 box of 80 hours and 180 hours had a one-time price of $99.99 and $199.99, respectively, while the TiVo Series 3 box with 300-hour storage capacity was priced at $799.99. TiVo customers then needed to pay a monthly subscription fee to obtain TiVo service.

The company had been a heavy user of mail-in rebates, which were reflected on the income statement as negative revenue. According to *Business Week*, $5 million in additional positive revenue was recognized because nearly half of TiVo's 100,000 new subscribers failed to apply for a $100 rebate. This slippage, known to marketers as the "shoebox effect," was very helpful to TiVo's revenues.

Research and Development

The word "interactive" was the slogan of R&D. TiVo's R&D team made sure that they built TiVo from the user's perspective and his/her viewing habits. There was a TiVo Forum composed of communication through TiVo Community.com and TiVo hackers. In this forum, criticism was allowed and even encouraged, so long as it was constructive and helped TiVo to grow. Ideas generated through this forum helped TiVo's R&D team and developers to be innovative by continuous adjusting to people's ever-changing lifestyles. TiVo's management was also concerned with how TiVo's platform could be used inappropriately by children. As a result, TiVo had collaborated with parents to build a new feature called the TiVo Parental Zone that allowed parents to control what their kids watched. TiVo protected its users' privacy by storing personal information on a computer behind its "firewall" in a secure location and by restricting the number of employees internally who could access this data.

In its early years, TiVo's R&D staff consisted only of contract-based engineers. As the company grew, management expanded its R&D team to consist of a diverse and creative group of on-staff engineers. It had an R&D policy stating that new benefits must extend people's existing behaviors. The design team had a very detailed list of steps to follow to ensure the fit of TiVo products to user needs. As an example of TiVo's meticulous product design process, TiVo created a remote control that combined personalization and interconnectivity. TiVo's remote had a feature of thumbs up and down to be clicked by users to rate shows so that the TiVo box would know what to record. In addition, TiVo enabled Braille on its remote for vision-impaired users. Other R&D processes included product testing and development of software and platforms, integration of software to satellite systems, and product integration, such as with the DVD burner and TiVo recorder. Besides developing its main products, the TiVo R&D team also designed platforms and technology that could be used with other products to enhance the performance of TiVo's main products, such as the ability to connect with computers, other home theater technologies, and especially with cable and satellites.

Since competition was increasing in the DVR industry, TiVo's management decided to patent the company's advanced software and technology platforms. TiVo licensed its TiVo-ToGo software to chip maker AMD and digital media software, such as Sonic Solutions, to Microsoft in order to enable video playback on pocket PCs and smart phones. As of end-2006, TiVo had 85 patents granted and 117 patents pending, including both domestic and foreign patents. TiVo licensed its patents through several of its trusted partners, including Sony, Toshiba, Pioneer, and Direct TV. TiVo's management believed that licensing its technology to third parties was an excellent revenue generator.

Although total company employee headcount had increased by approximately 7% in fiscal year 2007, the company increased the number of its regular, temporary, and part-time employees engaged in research and development by 9% from a total of 264 to 288 as of January 31, 2007, compared to January 31, 2006.

Corporate Governance

Top Management

In its early years, TiVo's top management had been personally involved in operations and marketing. Founder Mike Ramsay often made overseas trips to conduct meetings and seminars with consumer electronics manufacturers. This was as an attempt to convince the manufacturers to embed TiVo's software into their products. In order to make sure everything went well and accordingly to plan, Ramsey focused on maintaining partnerships. He would rarely be in his office. He would instead be on the road talking to companies that could help TiVo build software and subscribers. During his tenure as TiVo's CEO, Ramsey did commit a number of managerial errors. For example, instead of re-doubling marketing efforts when two distribution contracts were lost during 2001, he laid-off 80 employees (approx 25% of its workforce at the time) in April, 2001, plus 40 more employees (approx 20% of its remaining workforce) in the following October. Ramsay was an engineer and knew how to be creative and build great machines, but didn't truly understand the industry or how to manage the company's growth. By 2005, the company was drowning in red ink and its future was in doubt. As a result, Mike Ramsay was forced to resign in July 2005 and a change of CEO was implemented by the board of directors. The board hired as TiVo's new CEO the former president of NBC Cable, Tom Rogers.

Mike Ramsey continued to serve on TiVo's board of directors after his resignation. The board agreed to a transition agreement with Ramsey in which Ramsay agreed to provide services to TiVo that included assistance with executive transition matters, service as chairman of the Technology Advisory Committee of TiVo's Board and TiVo's beta test program, cooperation with existing or future litigation, and the provision of other advice and assistance that fell within Mr. Ramsay's knowledge and expertise in exchange for a salary of $100,000 annually plus stock options. Ramsay's transition employment agreement had been renewed and was in effect through September 8, 2007.

In early 2007, TiVo's current top managers were:

Thomas S. Rogers, 52, was appointed by TiVo's board to serve as a director in September 2003 and was named president and chief executive officer of TiVo, effective July 1, 2005. From 2004 until July 2005, he served as the senior operating executive for media and entertainment for Cerberus Capital Management, a large private equity firm. From October 1999 until April 2003, Rogers had been chairman and CEO of Primedia Inc., a print, video, and online media company. From January 1987 until October 1999, Rogers held positions with National Broadcast Company Inc., including president of NBC Cable and executive vice president. Rogers held a B.A. degree in Government from Wesleyan University and a J.D. degree from Columbia Law School. In 2006, he earned $504,583 in salary and $294,521 in bonuses plus $4,282,000 in stock options tied to long-term performance.

Steve Sordello, 37, was named senior vice president and chief financial officer in August 2006. He replaced David H. Courtney, who had resigned from TiVo in April 2006. Prior to joining TiVo, Sordello had served as executive vice president and chief financial officer at Ask Jeeves from April 2001 until October 2005, when the company was acquired by IAC/InterActiveCorp. Prior to Ask Jeeves, Sordello held senior positions at Adobe Systems Inc. and Syntex Corporation. Sordello held a B.S. degree in Management/Accounting and an M.B.A. degree from Santa Clara University.

James Barton, 48, was a co-founder of TiVo and served as TiVo's vice president of Research and Development, chief technical officer and director since the company's inception to January 2004, and was currently chief technical officer and senior vice president. From June 1996 to August 1997, Barton had been president and chief executive officer of Network Age Software Inc., a company that he founded to develop software products targeted at managed electronic distribution. From November 1994 to May 1996, Barton had served as chief technical officer of Interactive Digital Solutions Company, a joint venture of Silicon Graphics Incorporated (SGI) and AT&T Network Systems created to develop interactive television systems. From June 1993 to November 1994, Barton had served as vice president and general manager of the Media Systems Division of SGI. From January 1990 to May 1991, Barton had served as vice president and general manager for the Systems Software Division of Silicon Graphics. Prior to joining SGI, Barton held technical and management positions with Hewlett-Packard and Bell Laboratories. Mr. Barton held a B.S. degree in Electrical Engineering and an M.S. degree in Computer Science from the University of Colorado at Boulder. In 2006, Barton earned $275,000 in salary and $133,100 in bonuses plus $151,694 in stock options tied to long-term performance.

Jeffrey Klugman, 46, was named senior vice president and general manager, Service Provider and Media and Advertising Services Division, in April 2005. Klugman had served as vice president of Technology Licensing from December 2001 until February 2004 and vice president, TiVo Platform Business, from February 2004 until April 2005. Prior to joining TiVo, Klugman had been CEO of PointsBeyond.com, an Internet-portal start-up focused on outdoor activities and adventures. In 1999, Klugman served as vice president of Marketing and Business Development for Quantum Corporation's Consumer Electronics Business Unit. Klugman held a B.S. degree in engineering from Carnegie Mellon University and an M.B.A. degree from the Stanford Business School. In 2006, he earned $225,000 in salary and $108,419 in bonuses plus $238,315 in stock options tied to long-term performance.

Mark A. Roberts, 46, was named senior vice president of Consumer Products and Operations in October 2005 responsible for Consumer Products Engineering and Product Strategy, Manufacturing, Distribution, Call Center, Service Operations, Information Technology, Facilities and Broadcast Center Operations. He had served as senior vice president of Engineering since December 2002 until October 2005 and chief information officer of TiVo from March 1999 until December 2002. Prior to joining TiVo, he had served as vice president of Information Technology at Acuson Corporation, a medical ultrasound company, from March 1996 to March 1999. From July 1990 to March 1996, Roberts was director of Information Systems at SGI. Roberts held a B.S. degree in Economics from Santa Clara University. In 2006, he earned $255,000 in salary and $148,717 in bonuses plus $222,395 in stock options based on long-term performance.

Matthew Zinn, 42, was named senior vice president, general counsel, secretary, and chief privacy officer in April 2006. Zinn had served as vice president, general counsel, and chief privacy officer since July 2000 and as corporate secretary since November 2003. From May 1998 to July 2000, Zinn was the senior attorney, Broadband Law and Policy, for the MediaOne Group, a global communications company. From August 1995 to May 1998, Zinn served as corporate counsel for Continental Cablevision, the third largest cable television operator in the United States. From November 1993 to August 1995, he was an associate with the Washington, D.C., law firm of Cole, Raywid & Braverman, where he represented cable operators in federal, state, and local matters. Zinn held a B.A. degree in Political Science from the University of Vermont and a J.D. degree from the George Washington University National Law Center.

Nancy Kato, 52, was named senior vice president of Human Resources in April 2006. Kato had served as vice president, Human Resources, since January 2005. From January 2003 to January 2005 Kato was vice president of Global Compensation at Hewlett-Packard. From December 2000 to October 2002 Kato was senior vice president of Human Resources for Ariba. She has also held senior roles at Compaq and Tandem. Kato held a B.S. in Health Sciences and M.A. in Education and Counseling from San Jose State University.

Joe Miller, 40, was named senior vice president, Consumer Sales and Distribution, in September 2006 and was responsible for all aspects of the company's TiVo-Owned sales and distribution efforts. Miller had served as TiVo's vice president, Consumer Sales and Distribution, from May 1999 to August 2006. Prior to joining TiVo. Miller was with U.S. Satellite Broadcasting from February 1994 to May 1999 as general manager of Retail Sales and prior to that Miller was a national sales manager for Cox Satellite Programming. Miller held a B.A. degree in Public Relations from Southwest Texas State.

Individual senior executives who owned shares of the company's stock in 2006 were: CEO Thomas Rogers, 960,816 shares (1.1% of total shares outstanding), Sr. VP & Chief Technical Officer James Barton, 1,135,928 shares (1.3% of total shares outstanding), Sr. VP & General Manager of Service Provider & Media Advertising Services Jeffrey Klugman, 115,887 shares (less than 1% of total shares outstanding), and Sr. VP of Consumer Products & Operations Mark Roberts, 151,173 shares (less than 1%).

Board of Directors

TiVo's board of directors consisted of three executives from the venture capital firms of Kleiner Perkins Caufield & Byers, Redpoint Ventures, and New Enterprise Associates, three senior executives from NBC, Coca-Cola, and Univision Communications, an independent consultant who had been CFO at Univision Communications, plus TiVo's current and past CEO, for a total of nine members of the board. The board selected Jeffrey Hinson as its ninth member on January 26, 2007, for his financial experience as an ex-CFO to join the board and serve as chairman of its audit committee. See **Exhibit 4** for a list of the members of the board of directors, their backgrounds, and committee assignments.

Individual non-management directors owned the following amounts of stock in 2006 (% of total in parentheses): Michael Ramsey, 3,020,102 shares (3.5%), David Zaslav, 3,777,151 shares (4.4%), Geoffrey Y. Yang, 2,663,295 shares (3.1%), Mark Perry, 849,063 shares (less than 1%), Randy Komisar, 333,963 shares (less than 1%), Joseph Uva, 75,000 shares (less than

EXHIBIT 4
Board of Directors: TiVo

1. Board of Directors: TiVo Inc.

Name of Director	Age	Principal Occupation	Term Expires	Director Since
Michael Ramsey[1]	56	Former Chairman of the Board & CEO, TiVo Inc.	2009	1997
Geoffrey Y. Yang[1]	47	Managing Director, Redpoint Ventures & General Partner, Institutional Ventures Partners	2009	1997
Randy Komisar[1]	51	Partner, Kleiner Perkins Caufield & Byers	2009	1998
David M. Zaslav	46	Executive Vice President, NBC & President, NBC Cable	2007	2000
Mark W. Perry	62	General Partner, New Enterprise Associates	2007	2003
Thomas S. Rogers	51	President & CEO, TiVo Inc.	2008	2003
Charles B. Fruit	59	Sr. Vice President, Chief Marketing Officer, Coca-Cola Company	2007	2004
Joseph Uva	50	CEO, Univision Communications, Inc.	2008	2004
Jeffrey Hinson[2]	51	Consultant. Past-CFO, Univision Communications Inc.	2007	2007

Notes:

[1]Elected at 2006 annual meeting.

[2]Added in January, 2007.

2. Board Committees
(as of 1/31/2007)
Audit: Hinson (Chair), Fruit, Perry
Compensation: Yang (Chair), Uva
Nominating & Governance: Komisar (Chair), Yang
Pricing: Zaslav (Chair), Perry
Technology: Ramsey (Chair), Komisar, Yang

1%), and Charles Fruit, 75,000 shares (less than 1%). All executive officers and directors owned as a group 16.3% of shares outstanding. Other shareholders owning more than 5% of shares outstanding were the investment firms of FMR Corporation (8.1%) and Wellington Management (7.5%).

The TiVo board used five committees to conduct its business: audit, compensation, nominating and governance, pricing, and technology committees. Non-employee (outside) directors received an annual retainer of $15,000, plus $1,000 for each committee meeting attended. (Committee chairs receive an additional $2,000 for each committee meeting attended.) In addition, each director received stock option grants to purchase 50,000 shares when elected to the board and an additional grant to purchase 25,000 shares each year thereafter.

Human Resources

TiVo employed approximately 451 employees, including 48 in service operations, 246 in research and development, 44 in sales and marketing, and 113 in general and administration. The company also employed, from time to time, a number of temporary and part-time employees as well as consultants on a contract basis. The employees were not represented by a collective bargaining organization. The company had never experienced a work stoppage or strike and management considered employee relations to be good.

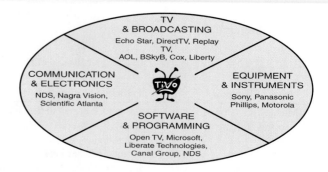

EXHIBIT 5
The Digital Video Recorder or Personal Video Recorder Market Was Located at the Convergence of Four Established Industries: TV and Broadcasting, Software and Programming, Equipment and Instruments, and Communication and Electronics.

Sleeping with Enemies

". . . So Long, TiVo! Hello DVR! . . ."

The Industry

For TiVo, the introduction of its digital video recorder was full of obstacles. The DVR was a "disruptive technology," a technology that created something new which usurped existing products and services. According to TiVo's founder Mike Ramsay, the DVR phenomenon established that "people really want to take control of television, and if you give them control, they don't want you to take it back." Although TiVo had added the software, platforms, and services that a TiVo DVR had to offer, the viewing experience was incomplete without a connection to a cable network or to satellite signals. Therefore, users who wanted a TiVo DVR needed to subscribe to the TiVo service, pay a one-time fee for a TiVo box, and subscribe to a cable or satellite provider, such as Comcast or DirecTV. Because of this requirement, the TiVo DVR had been made with a built-in cable-ready tuner for use with any external cable box or satellite receiver. TiVo had forged many alliances and sometimes even competed with cable operators and satellite networks. With cable, satellite, and electronics companies pushing to market their own DVRs, the DVR industry was expected to grow rapidly.

In terms of market share, TiVo claimed to cover the entire U.S. market (See **Exhibit 6**).

Friends or Foe?

In 2000, AOL had invested $200 million in TiVo and became the largest shareholder of the company and one of its main service partners. The AOL connection enabled TiVo to release a box that provided both TiVo's capabilities and AOL services. In addition to AOL, TiVo established other service partnerships. TiVo and Discovery Communication and NBC agreed to an $8.1 million deal in the form of advertising and promotional services. An additional $5 million was paid to NBC for promotions. TiVo also collaborated on research and development with Discover Communication, allowing TiVo to use a portion of its satellite network. AT&T supported TiVo in the marketing and selling of its service in the Boston, Denver, and Silicon Valley areas. BSkyB was the service partner for TiVo in the United Kingdom. Creative Artists Agency marketed and gave promotional support to the personal video recorder and was given in exchange 67,122 shares of TiVo's preferred stock.

Despite TiVo's many alliances, the company was faced with the difficult challenge of working with cable and satellite operators who offered their own digital video recorder-equipped

EXHIBIT 6

WE COVER the ENTIRE U.S. MARKET

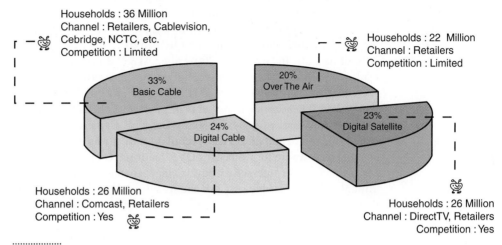

Households : 36 Million
Channel : Retailers, Cablevision,
Cebridge, NCTC, etc.
Competition : Limited

Households : 22 Million
Channel : Retailers
Competition : Limited

33% Basic Cable

20% Over The Air

24% Digital Cable

23% Digital Satellite

Households : 26 Million
Channel : Comcast, Retailers
Competition : Yes

Households : 26 Million
Channel : DirectTV, Retailers
Competition : Yes

SOURCE: *Natexis Bielchroeder, Inc., July 2005.*

set-top boxes. Cable operators like Time Warner Cable and Cox Communications offered built-in DVR capability in set-top boxes and provided the equipment free to subscribers. In August 2003, Echostar announced a free DVR promotion, an unprecedented move in the industry. TiVo's relatively expensive hardware could jeopardize the company's ability to compete with cable or satellite service providers that offered their own DVRs at a lower price. There were relatively few nationwide cable or satellite providers, leaving TiVo with little bargaining power. These cable/satellite providers could affect pricing of the TiVo technology because of their size and because of their ability to market their own version of a generic DVR unit to their subscription base. Although TiVo had to give a piece of its potential profits to partners, TiVo's management decided to form strategic relationships with competitors and cable companies for distribution.

DirecTV, the satellite service provider, had served as TiVo's backbone in its early years. This service partner had fueled most of TiVo's early growth. TiVo's current 4.4 million sub-scribers had mostly come from its partnership with DirecTV. In early 2002, subscribers to TiVo's service through DirecTV increased from 230,000 to 2.1 million, representing more than half of all DVR subscriptions. Subscription fees to Direct TV ranged from $29.99/month for 40 channels to $65.99/month for over 250 channels. Interestingly, when DirecTV first began negotiations with TiVo, the satellite provider had already been equipped with a DVR service through its partnership with Microsoft's Ultimate TV.

DirecTV decided in 2005 to develop its own DVR device in cooperation with the NDS Group. It soon informed TiVo that it would stop marketing and selling TiVo's digital recorders to its satellite TV subscribers starting in 2007. This was a serious blow to TiVo. DirecTV's DVR would cost users a $299 onetime fee, but it included unique features, such as the ability to jump to a specific scene in the program as well as allowing users to pay for downloaded pay-per-view movies only when they were being viewed. In 2006, TiVo and DirecTV reached a commercial extension agreement for three years. The agreement allowed existing DirecTV customers using the TiVo digital video recorder to continue to receive maintenance and sup-port from DirecTV. As part of the agreement, TiVo and DirecTV agreed that they wouldn't sue each other over patent rights. Since the agreement with DirecTV was facing an expiration date in 2009, TiVo has been rushing to differentiate its product and working to make other dis-tribution agreements.

In July 2000, Comcast, the nation's leading cable operator, agreed to a trial offering of TiVo boxes to its subscribers. TiVo's management hoped that the trial would lead to a bigger deal in which Comcast would integrate TiVo software into Comcast cable boxes. Unfortunately, Comcast balked and was unwilling to agree to this extension of the agreement. In April 2001, when another trial failed to lead to a larger deal, TiVo laid off approximately 25% of its staff. In November 2001, after AT&T Broadband had just agreed to offer TiVo DVRs to its customers, Comcast acquired the cable provider and its 14 million customers, and canceled the agreement. In 2002, cable operators such as Comcast ended up developing their own DVR boxes with makers such as Motorola and Scientific-Atlanta. Even though the DVR was similar to that offered by DirecTV, Comcast announced in March 2005 that it would offer its customers a video recorder service from TiVo and even would allow TiVo to develop its software for Comcast's DVR platform. Comcast and TiVo agreed to make TiVo's DVR service and interactive advertising capability (ad management system) available through Comcast's cable network and its set-top DVR boxes. This agreement also included that the first of their co-developed products would be available in mid- to late-2006 under the TiVo brand name.

Subscriptions to Comcast's basic or standard cable cost users $8.63 or $52.55, respectively. Adding a DVR feature cost an additional $13.94 with Comcast in addition to the TiVo subscription, which ranged from $12.95 to $16.95 per month depending on the length of the plan (from one to three years). Following this agreement with Comcast, TiVo's shares closed up nearly 75%, or $2.87 per share, to $6.70. Investment analysts were positive about the news, some upgrading TiVo's investment rating from a sell to a hold. Since DirecTV had started using a second company, NDS, to provide DVR service, the deal with Comcast put to rest some of these concerns by opening up a large new potential audience for TiVo's service. According to a TiVo filing with the SEC, TiVo received an upfront payment from Comcast for creating a new DVR that worked with Comcast's current service. TiVo also received a recurring monthly fee for each Comcast subscriber who used TiVo through Comcast.

Offering new technology-driven products, such as a DVR, was easier for satellite broadcasters because changes could be made in a central location. For cable operators, however, new technologies and products needed to be deployed gradually as the operators had different equipment in different areas.

TiVo and BellSouth FastAccess DSL recently agreed on a variety of co-marketing arrangements. With its strong presence and high level of customer satisfaction in the Southeastern United States, BellSouth could provide a DSL Internet pipeline for TiVo to send video content directly to the television. To expand program recording to a cellular phone, its latest TiVo Mobile feature, TiVo made an agreement with Verizon. The agreement brought the digital video recording pioneer's capabilities beyond its set-top-boxes and the television directly to cell phones for the first time. In terms of content, TiVo also had engaged in new partnerships with CBS Corp, Reuters Group PLC, Forbes magazine, New York Times Co., and the National Basketball Association, among others. This would make news and entertainment programs available for downloading onto TiVos. International Creative Management recommended films, television shows, and Internet videos that TiVo users could download onto their boxes. In addition, TiVo's management decided to offer amateur videos through an agreement with One True Media Inc., an Internet start-up that operated a Web service designed to help users easily edit their raw footage into quality home movies.

The TALKA TiVo

". . . Bring 'em on! We are talking the HD language now . . . Yeah!."

TiVo Series 2 DT

The company's basic DVR was its TiVo Series 2 DT unit. It included dual tuners (DT) so that a viewer could record two programs at the same time (but only one digital signal) or watch one program while recording another. Customers could choose between two versions: the basic 80-hour unit or the 180-hour unit. The selling price for an 80-hour unit with a one-year service commitment was $16.95 a month or $179 prepaid plus $99.99 for the box. The monthly service fee was reduced by $2 for each additional year on the service commitment. The Series 2 DT DVR could record from multiple sources, such as cable, satellite, or antenna. See **Exhibit 1** for product specifications.

High Definition Television

High definition (HD) was the most important new consumer electronic development in television. HD products radically increased the quality of the viewing and listening experience. High definition sets included HD TV, HD broadcasting, HD DVD, HD Radio, HD Photo, and even HD Audio.

High definition TV (HD TV) was first introduced in the United States during the 1990s. It was a digital television broadcasting system using a significantly higher resolution than the traditional formats, such as NTSC, PAL, and SECAM. The technology during the 1990s was very expensive. With increasing production levels, prices decreased and HD TV was being offered in an increasing number of televisions. As of 2007, HD TVs were being used in 24 million U.S. households. It was predicted that by 2009, high definition would replace standard definition television. With the price of computer hard drives becoming lower and the increasing availability of HD TV broadcasting, demand for the HD products was increasing rapidly. Compared to standard definition television, HD TV offered viewers greater screen clarity and smoother motion with richer, more natural colors, and surround sound.

TiVo Series 3

TiVo recently introduced the TiVo Series 3 to allow customers to record high definition television and digital cable. Since TiVo's management realized that great quality video needed to be supported by great quality audio, the company put a lot of effort in the audio development and received the certification of being the first digital media recorder to meet the THX performance standard in HD TV. THX was known to have developed the highest standard of audio—mainly the surround-sound systems in the entertainment as well as the media industry.

The new high definition TiVo Series 3, which was being sold for $799.000, had two tuners, giving it the ability to record two HD programs simultaneously while playing back a third previously recorded program. (This required two CableCARDS for dual-function capability through cable or antenna, but did not support satellite service.) Its larger storage capacity allowed it to record up to 300 hours of standard definition programming or 32 hours of high-definition programming. It also had two signal inputs and it accepted cable TV and over-the-air signals. Despite TiVo's ability to record and playback at high definition quality, a downside was its relatively high price—especially when some cable companies were offering non-HD DVRs free to their subscribers. The monthly service fee was, however, the same as that for the Series 2.

TiVo HD

The company was developing a new version of the TiVo box, which would be available for sale in 2007. The TiVo HD had most of the features of the Series 3, but would be sold for only $300. The new TiVo contained a 160 GB hard drive good for recording 180 hours of standard-definition programming or 20 hours of high-definition programming. Both Series 3 and HD models used the same architecture and had dual tuners, two slots for CableCARDS, and the same ports. (Like the Series 3 DVR, the TiVo HD required two CableCARDS for dual-function capability through antenna or cable, but did not support satellite service.) The TiVo HD did come with a cheaper remote control and, contrasted with the Series 3 remote, was not backlit or capable of controlling other components. The monthly service fee was the same as that for the Series 2 or 3 DVRs.

HD TiVENemies

The cable operator, Comcast, did not sell DVRs, but allowed its subscribers to rent DVR boxes for $13.94 per month (in addition to their cable subscription fee). Its HD DVR boxes were manufactured by Motorola and Scientific Atlanta. Users of these DVRs were able to navigate their own preferences as they would with TiVo, except that TiVo offered better and more features built into its boxes.

The satellite operator, DirecTV, allowed subscribers to add an additional DVR subscription service for $4.99 monthly on top of the chosen monthly subscription service package to DirecTV cable channels (ranging in cost from $29.99 to $65.99 per month). DirecTV offered its subscribers the opportunity to buy a standard definition DVR for $99.99 and an HD DVR box for $299 with a $100 rebate.

Looking to the Future

As CEO Tom Rogers looked at TiVo's financial statements for the 2006 fiscal year ending January 31, 2007, he pondered TiVo's future prospects. In some ways, the future looked very promising. Approximately 16 million households had DVRs and this number was expected to increase to 56 million by 2010 according to The Carmel Group. Given its user-friendly software interface and celebrity endorsements, TiVo should be able to obtain a large piece of that growth. Although there were many versions of the generic DVR, the TiVo DVR had perceived sex appeal. TiVo had been successful in creating a unique set of technologies, products, and services that were meeting the needs of consumers, television distributors, and the advertising community. TiVo's advantages were clear:

- Compelling, easy-to-use consumer DVR offerings
- Differentiated features
- Integrated broadband and broadcast capabilities (download movies, etc.)
- Portable technology platform
- Advanced advertising and promotion solutions

The company's current strategy included a number of key elements:

- Offer an increasingly differentiated service
- Diversify our sources of revenue to include more advertising
- Integrate TiVo technology with third-party DVR platforms to provide TiVo service
- Extend and protect TiVo's intellectual property
- Promote and leverage the TiVo brand through multiple advertising and marketing channels
- Extend the TiVo product beyond the U.S. market into countries such as China and Mexico

There were also a number of challenges to consider. During the past fiscal year, the company experienced growth in its TiVo-owned subscription base and subscription revenues.

However, this subscription growth was largely offset by the loss of a portion of TiVo's DirecTV installed subscription base. Even though management decided to invest in subscription acquisition activities in an effort to expand TiVo's subscription base and promote the TiVo brand for future partnerships, TiVo-owned subscription gross additions for the fiscal year 2007 were 429,000—down 13% from fiscal year 2006. Although it was not unusual for entrepreneurial ventures to generate losses for their first few years of operation, TiVo had not earned a profit in the 10 years since it had been founded or in the eight years since it went public. It hadn't had a profitable quarter in the past two years!

As with any publicly held U.S. company, TiVo had to list risk factors that might affect its future performance. Compared to the list of risks found in the SEC Form 10-K Report of most publicly held companies, TiVo's list of risks was extremely long—over 17 pages! Some of these risk factors were:

- We face intense competition from a number of sources, which may impair our revenues, increase our subscription acquisition cost, and hinder our ability to generate new subscriptions.

- We depend upon a limited number of third parties to manufacture, distribute, and supply critical components, assemblies, and services for the DVRs that enable the TiVo service. We may not be able to operate our business if these parties do not perform their obligations.

- DVRs could be the subject of future regulations relating to copyright law or evolving industry standards and practices that could adversely impact our business.

- A significant part of our installed subscription base results from our relationship with DirecTV which we expect to decrease in the future due to DirecTV's support of a competing DVR by NDS.

- We face a number of challenges in the sale and marketing of the TiVo service and products that enable that service. Even when consumers are aware of the benefits of our products, they may not be willing to pay for them, especially when competitors under price us.

- If we are unable to create or maintain multiple revenue streams, such as licensing, advertising, audience research measurement, revenues from programmers, and electronic commerce, we may not be able to recover our expenses and this could cause our revenues to suffer.

- The product lifetime subscriptions we offered in the past obligate the company for an indefinite period and may not be large enough to cover future increases in costs.

- If there is increased use of switched technologies to transmit television programs by cable operators (also known as switched digital) in the future, the desirability and competitiveness of our current products could be reduced.

- We need to safeguard the security and privacy of our subscribers' confidential data, and any inability to do so may harm our reputation and brand and expose us to legal action.

- Product defects, system failures or interruptions to the TiVo service may have a negative impact on our revenues, damage our reputation and decrease our ability to attract new customers.

- We have limited experience in providing service and operations internationally that are subject to different laws, regulations, and requirements than those in the U.S. and our inability to comply with such could harm our reputation, brand, and have a negative impact on revenues.

- If we are unable to raise additional capital through the issuance of equity, debt, or other financing activities on acceptable terms, our ability to effectively manage growth and build a strong brand could be harmed.

- We expect continued volatility in our stock price.

The full list of TiVo's risks was daunting, but nothing terribly unusual for a fast-growing entrepreneurial venture. The big issue facing top management was how to make the company profitable without slowing its growth. Investors have a limited amount of patience. A no-dividend policy made sense for a fast-growing entrepreneurial company, but a low, volatile stock price was not going to be acceptable for long. How long can the company continue to sell TiVo DVRs when the competition was selling DVRs at a lower price or even offering them for free? What should Rogers do?

REFERENCES

http://www.TiVo.com/

http://en.wikipedia.org/wiki/TiVo

http://en.wikipedia.org/wiki/High-definition_television

http://egotron.com/ptv/ptvintro.htm

http://news.com.com/TiVo,+Comcast+reach+DVR+deal/2100-1041_3-5616961.html

http://news.com.com/TiVo+and+DirecTV+extend+contract/2100-1038_3-6060475.html

http://www.technologyreview.com

http://www.fastcompany.com/magazine/61/TiVo.html

http://iinnovate.blogspot.com/2006/09/mike-ramsay-co-founder-of-TiVo.html

http://www.acmqueue.org/modules.php?name=Content&pa=showpage&pid=53&page=7

http://www.internetnews.com/stats/article.php/3655331

http://thomashawk.com/2006/04/TiVo-history-101-how-TiVo-built-pvr_24.html

http://www.tvpredictions.com/TiVohd030807.htm

http://www.TiVocommunity.com/TiVo-vb/showthread.php?threadid=151443

2006 Form 10-K, TiVo, Inc. (filed 4/16/2007)

2006 Form 14A, TiVo, Inc. (filed 5/31/2006)

"Jeffrey Hinson Elected to TiVo Board of Directors," press release, TiVo, Inc. (January 26, 2007).

Stafford, A., "Bargain TiVo Records HD Video Without a Cable Box," *PC World* (October, 2007), p. 62.

C A S E **15**

Marvel Entertainment Inc.:

IRON MAN TO THE RESCUE

Ellie A. Fogarty and Joyce P. Vincelette

Introduction

POW! BAM! ZAP! IN 2008, MARVEL MAN'S ENTIRE UNIVERSE SHIFTED. After 70 years of ferocious struggle, Marvel Man's domination of the printed page was strong, with occasional swipes by his long-time nemesis DC Man and some puny domestic and foreign rivals. With no longer the need to fight on every frontier to protect his formidable assets from being exploited, Marvel Man was able to share his super strengths through lucrative licensing agreements with other trusted big-name heroes who understood the ins and outs of their own competitive worlds. Marvel Man was growing up and leaving toys behind. The new skirmishes would be fought online and on the big screen. What surprises await Marvel Man in these new media worlds? Which Hollywood villains might strike first—the writers or the actors? How can Marvel Man stay fresh and relevant in these changing times? What superhuman strength will be needed to triumph over sinister intellectual property thieves? What nefarious plot would the unpredictable Wall Street Woman concoct and would it involve battling a bear or a bull? Keep alert, loyal followers, and welcome to a brand new day!

History

Today's Marvel Entertainment Inc. traces its long, complicated history back to a small comic book company, Timely Comics, which was owned by Martin Goodman in the 1930s. A New York publisher of pulp magazines, Goodman's selections featured stories about detectives, science fiction, Westerns, crime, and horror. Following closely on the heels of rival DC Comics, which had just introduced Superman and Batman, Timely Comics produced its first Marvel Comics series in 1939, featuring the Human Torch and Namor the Sub-Mariner. The issue sold well and solidified Goodman's interest in the superhero genre. By late 1940, the first Captain America issue was an instant success as he battled the emerging Nazi threat. At $.10 an issue, comic books provided the action-packed distraction that the Depression-era generation needed. Stanley Leiber, better known as Stan Lee, began working as an assistant in 1940 at his cousin Goodman's company. Lee would later become synonymous with Marvel Comics as an editor, manager, and spokesman. Goodman's company grew rapidly throughout the 1930s and 40s during the Golden Age of comic books.

In the early 1950s, Goodman created Atlas News Company, which he set up as his national distribution system. Timely Comics was renamed Atlas Publishing in 1951. During the 1950s, the entire comic book industry slowed, not only from the popularity of television, but also from a newly created censorship board, the Comics Code Authority, whose special seal of approval guaranteed inoffensive, and bland, content between the pages. Distribution operations at Atlas News Company were suspended in 1956, forcing Atlas Publishing into a distribution deal with competitor DC Comics to get a limited number of comics in the Marvel series out per month.

In the 1960s, the re-emergence of superheroes appealed to the baby boomer generation, now in high school and on college campuses. It was in 1962 that Stan Lee co-created Marvel's most recognizable character, Spider-Man. Over the next few years, with the releases of the Fantastic Four, the Incredible Hulk, the Avengers, and the X-Men, the company, now publishing under the name Marvel Comic Groups, began merchandising its products and debuted its first superhero show on the ABC television network. Although the company was still reporting strong sales, its profits had dropped due to consolidating distribution outlets. The increasing popularity of chain supermarkets, which did not carry comic books, hurt many comic book publishers that had relied on corner grocers as a primary distribution outlet. In 1968, Goodman sold Atlas, including the Marvel Comics series, to Perfect Film and Chemical Corporation, which was then re-named Cadence Industries. Marvel Comics existed within Cadence as part of a business unit called Magazine Management. By the end of the 1970s, the market for comic books was reduced to an all-time low. Readers had lost interest in comics.

In the 1980s, the growing number of comic book collectors ushered in a wave of stores dedicated to the sales of comic books. Marvel began to target different demographics in the market, and began to use new distribution outlets including shopping malls. Marvel's revenues continued to grow through character license agreements. As part of a liquidation, Marvel was sold by Cadence to New World Entertainment for $46 million in 1986. Ron Perelman, through his Andrews Group and MacAndrews & Forbes holding companies, acquired Marvel from New World Entertainment in 1988 for $82.5 million and formed Marvel Entertainment Group.

In June of 1991, Perelman announced that Marvel would sell its stock to the public for the first time. Perelman pushed Marvel to expand into other areas with the 1992 purchase of Fleer Corporation, which made trading cards, and the 1993 exchange of a 46% interest in Toy Biz, a toy company owned by Isaac Perlmutter, in return for the use of Marvel's characters. Throughout the early nineties, Marvel completed a number of acquisitions, including children's kites (Sepctra Star), stickers (Panini), toy rockets (Quest), smaller publishers (Welsh Publishing and Malibu Comics), another trading card company (SkyBox), and a distribution operation (Superhero Enterprises). Marvel Mania was opened as a theme restaurant with servers in costume and menu selections with superhero descriptions. Confusion reigned as various firms claimed specific rights to produce and distribute films with Marvel characters. For example, Columbia Tristar Home Video claimed video cassette rights and Viacom claimed television rights for a possible motion picture based on Spider-Man. By December 1996, Marvel filed for bankruptcy amid plunging sales and mounting debt.

In 1997, Perelman was accused of helping to divert over $553 million from Marvel to his other companies before the bankruptcy. The suit was finally settled when Perelman agreed to pay former shareholders $80 million in 2008.[1] Perelman was ousted by the board, and Carl Icahn, a major bondholder, won control of the company for about a year until the courts appointed a Chapter 11 trustee at the end of 1997. After Icahn's failed attempts at a plan of reorganization, the company merged and became a wholly-owned subsidiary of Toy Biz in 1998. Toy Biz became known as Marvel Enterprises Inc. and changed the trading symbol for Toy Biz stock on the New York Stock Exchange to MVL. Additional legal issues were resolved with movie studios and Marvel entered into a joint venture with Sony Pictures to develop the Spider-Man movie franchise. Also during the late nineties, the company streamlined publishing efforts, diversified with licensing agreements that would help restore Marvel's image, and expanded into foreign markets hungry for Marvel superheroes. To signal its move into the entertainment industry, Marvel Enterprises changed its name to Marvel Entertainment Inc. in September 2005. After signing a master toy licensing agreement with Hasbro in 2006, Marvel began its exit from its toy manufacturing and distributing businesses. Marvel made some of its comic book archives available online through its Digital Comics division in 2007. By the end of the decade, Marvel was well on its way to becoming a leader in the entertainment industry, with two self-produced feature films in 2008 (Iron Man and the Incredible Hulk) and the funding and creative ideas for many more.

Marvel Entertainment Inc.'s history bears a striking resemblance to one of its downtrodden superheroes that battles rivals and fights injustices. As it transitioned from a traditional publisher and toy maker into a new media and entertainment company, would Marvel emerge triumphant over the forces of intense competition and flagrant disregard for the principles of intellectual property?

Corporate Governance

Board of Directors

Exhibit 1 lists the company's board of directors and the compensation received by each in 2007. The 8 directors were:[2]

Isaac Perlmutter, 65, had been Marvel's Chief Executive Officer since January 1, 2005, and was employed by Marvel as vice chairman of the board of directors since November 2001. Mr. Perlmutter was a director since April 1993 and served as chairman of the board of directors until March 1995. Perlmutter held over 37% of the company's common stock outstanding

EXHIBIT 1
Board of Directors: Marvel Entertainment Inc.

Name	Age	Title	Compensation
Handel, Morton E.	72	Chairman of the Board	$868,160
Perlmutter, Isaac	65	Vice Chairman of the Board, Chief Executive Officer	$3,872,797
Breyer, James W.	46	Director	$273,210
Charney, Laurence N.	60	Director	$192,180
Cuneo, F. Peter	63	Vice Chairman of the Board (Non-Executive)	$387,984
Ganis, Sid	68	Director	$435,710
Halpin, James F.	57	Director	$298,210
Solar, Richard L.	68	Director	$312,984

SOURCE: *Marvel Entertainment, Inc. Proxy Statement (May 5, 2008), pp. 4–5, 7.*

as of March 2008.[3] Under the terms of a share disposition agreement in February 2008, Perlmutter agreed not to sell any of his Marvel stock until the company's share repurchase program ended in March 2010.[4]

F. Peter Cuneo, 63, was Marvel's president and chief executive officer from July 1999 through December 2002 and served as the part-time special advisor to Marvel's chief executive officer from January 2003 through December 2004. Mr. Cuneo had been a Marvel director since July 1999, and since June 2003 he served as a non-executive vice chairman of the board of directors. Mr. Cuneo was a senior advisor to Plainfield Asset Management LLC, a hedge fund based in Greenwich, CT, that specialized in special and distressed situations. Mr. Cuneo was a director of Iconix Brands Inc.

Sid Ganis, 68, had been a Marvel director since October 1999. Mr. Ganis was the president of the Academy of Motion Picture Arts and Sciences, the organization that awards the Oscars. Mr. Ganis had been president of Out of the Blue . . . Entertainment, a company that he founded, since September 1996. Out of the Blue . . . Entertainment was a provider of motion pictures, television and musical entertainment for Sony Pictures Entertainment and others. From January 1991 until September 1996, Mr. Ganis held various executive positions with Sony Pictures Entertainment, including vice chairman of Columbia Pictures and president of Worldwide Marketing for Columbia/TriStar Motion Picture Companies.

James F. Halpin, 57, had been a Marvel director since March 1995. Mr. Halpin retired in March 2000 as president and chief executive officer and a director of CompUSA Inc., a retailer of computer hardware, software, accessories and related products, with which he had been employed since May 1993. Mr. Halpin was a director of Life Time Fitness Inc.

James W. Breyer, 46, had been a Marvel director since June 2006. Mr. Breyer had served as a partner of the Silicon Valley-based venture capital firm, Accel Partners, since 1995. Mr. Breyer was a director of Wal-Mart Stores Inc. and RealNetworks Inc. Mr. Breyer also served on the boards of various privately held companies. Mr. Breyer was a member of the board of dean's advisors to Harvard Business School and was chairman of the Stanford Engineering Venture Fund.

Laurence N. Charney, 60, had been a Marvel director since July 10, 2007. Mr. Charney retired from his position as a partner of Ernst & Young LLP in 2007, having served that firm for over thirty-five years. At Ernst & Young, Mr. Charney most recently served as the Americas director of conflict management. In that role he had oversight and responsibility in ensuring compliance with global and local conflict of interest policies for client and engagement acceptance across all service lines. Mr. Charney previously served as an audit partner and was Marvel's audit partner for its 1999 through 2003 audits.

Morton E. Handel, 72, had been the chairman of the board of directors of Marvel since October 1998 and was first appointed as a director in June 1997. Mr. Handel was a director of Trump Entertainment Resorts Inc. and served from 2000 until February 2006 as a director of Linens 'N Things Inc. Mr. Handel was also a regent of the University of Hartford and was active on the boards of several not-for-profit organizations in the Hartford, CT, area.

Richard L. Solar, 68, had been a Marvel director since December 2002. Since February 2003, Mr. Solar had been a management consultant and investor. From June 2002 to February 2003, Mr. Solar acted as a consultant for Gerber Childrenswear Inc., a marketer of popular-priced licensed apparel sold under the Gerber name, as well as under licenses from Baby Looney Tunes, Wilson, Converse and Coca-Cola. From 1996 to June 2002 (when Gerber Childrenswear was acquired by the Kellwood Company), Mr. Solar was senior vice president, director and chief financial officer of Gerber Childrenswear. Mr. Solar was also vice president and treasurer of Barrington Stage Company Inc., which produced plays, developed experimental musicals and provided a program for at-risk high school students in the Berkshires.

EXHIBIT 2
Corporate Officers: Marvel Entertainment, Inc.

Name	Age	Title	Compensation
Perlmutter, Isaac	65	Vice Chairman of the Board, Chief Executive Officer	$3,872,797
West, Kenneth P.	49	Executive Vice President, Chief Financial Officer	$766,526
Fine, Alan	57	Executive Vice President, Publishing/Toy/Characters	$632,420
Maisel, David	45	Executive Vice President, Marvel Studios	$4,118,999
Turitzin, John	52	Executive Vice President, Legal/General Counsel	$1,390,212

SOURCE: *Marvel Entertainment, Inc. Proxy Statement (May 5, 2008), pp. 13, 23.*

Corporate Officers

Exhibit 2 lists Marvel's corporate officers and the compensation received by each in 2007. In addition to Mr. Isaac Perlmutter, listed earlier, there were four other key corporate officers:[5]

Alan Fine (57) had served as executive vice president and chief marketing officer of Marvel Characters Inc. (a wholly owned subsidiary of Marvel Entertainment Inc. that owned and licensed Marvel's intellectual property library) since May 2007. Mr. Fine also had served as Chief Executive Officer of Marvel's publishing division since September 2004, and as Chief Executive Officer of Marvel's toy division since August 2001 and from October 1998 to April 2001.

David Maisel (45) had served as executive vice president, Office of the Chief Executive, since September 2006 and became chairman of Marvel Studios in March 2007. From September 2005 until September 2006, Mr. Maisel served as executive vice president, Corporate Development, and from September 2005 until March 2007, Mr. Maisel served as vice chairman of Marvel Studios. From January 2004 to September 2005, Mr. Maisel served as president and chief operating officer of Marvel Studios. From October 2001 to November 2003, Mr. Maisel headed Corporate Strategy and Business Development for Endeavor Agency, a Hollywood literary and talent agency.

John Turitzin (52) had served as executive vice president, Office of the Chief Executive, since September 2006. From February 2006 until September 2006, Mr. Turitzin served as Marvel's chief administrative officer. Mr. Turitzin had also served as an executive vice president and general counsel since February 2004. From June 2000 to February 2004, Mr. Turitzin was a partner in the law firm of Paul, Hastings, Janofsky & Walker LLP.

Kenneth P. West (49) had served as executive vice president and chief financial officer since June 2002.

Corporate Structure

Primary Operating Segments

In the first quarter of 2008, Marvel Entertainment eliminated its Toy division and reorganized into three operating segments: Publishing, Licensing, and Film Production. Marvel operated in these markets both domestically and internationally, although the U.S. market made up an average of over 70% of the company's annual revenues. Because each segment depended on Marvel's extensive library of characters, the company emphasized the integrated and complementary nature of the three segments. **Exhibit 3** shows Marvel's primary business segments and **Exhibit 4** lists Marvel's subsidiaries.

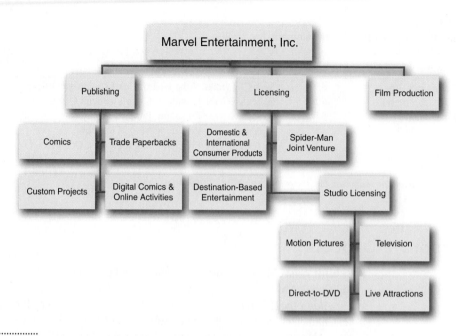

SOURCE: *Derived from Marvel Entertainment, Inc.,* Form 10-Q *(June 30, 2008), pp. 11–12 and Cuneo & Turitzin presentation at JP Morgan US Mid Cap Growth Conference, London, (Sept. 30, 2008), pp. 6–7, 13.*

For most of its history, Marvel's primary direct competitors had been other comic book publishers, such as the well-established DC Comics, a subsidiary of Warner Bros., and the publisher of Superman, Batman, and Wonder Woman comics, and the much younger Dark Horse Comics. As Marvel repositioned itself as an entertainment firm, the company faced competition from industry giants such as the Walt Disney Company and NBC Universal.

The **Publishing** segment created and published comic books, trade paperbacks, custom comics, and digital comics. Well-known characters included Spider-Man, X-Men, Fantastic Four, Iron Man, the Incredible Hulk, Captain America, and Ghost Rider. The segment also received revenues from related advertising and subscription operations. Publishing contributed between 25% to 30% of the company's annual net sales, with revenues coming overwhelmingly (85%) from the U.S. market. Segment revenues were $125,657,000, $108,464,000, and $92,455,000 in 2007, 2006, and 2005, respectively.

Over the course of 70 years, Marvel developed an extensive library of over 5,000 characters, most of which were developed and popularized through published comic books (see **Exhibit 5** for a listing of popular characters). The publishing segment had published comic books since 1939 and was able to present characters in contemporary dramatic settings that were suggestive of real people with real problems. The ability to stay relevant enabled Marvel to retain the attention of old readers, while also attracting the attention of new readers over time.

In 2008, Marvel was focused on expanding its distribution channels as well as its product lines. Comic books were distributed through three main channels: comic book specialty stores, traditional retail outlets such as bookstores and newsstands, and on a subscription basis. Approximately 70% of the Publishing segment's revenues were attributed to sales from comic book specialty stores, also known as the "direct market." Another 15% of the Publishing net sales were derived from sales to the mass market retail outlets. The final 15% of the segment's revenues came from sales of advertising and subscriptions, including its online business. Because of the growth of the Internet and the potential for online readership, online comic books were launched in 2007 through Marvel Digital Comics Unlimited, in an attempt to reach existing readers in a new medium while also further extending Marvel's reach to new readers.

EXHIBIT 4
Subsidiaries: Marvel
Entertainment, Inc.

	Name	Jurisdiction of Organization
1	Marvel Characters, Inc.	Delaware
2	Marvel Characters B.V.	The Netherlands
3	MVL International C.V.	The Netherlands
4	Marvel International Character Holdings LLC	Delaware
5	Marvel Entertainment International Limited	United Kingdom
6	Marvel Property Inc.	Delaware
7	Marvel Publishing Inc.	Delaware
8	Marvel Internet Productions LLC	Delaware
9	Marvel Toys Limited	Hong Kong
10	Spider-Man Merchandising L.P.**	Delaware
11	MRV, Inc.	Delaware
12	Marvel Studios, Inc.	Delaware
13	MVL Film Finance LLC*	Delaware
14	MVL Productions LLC*	Delaware
15	MVL Rights LLC*	Delaware
16	MVL Development LLC	Delaware
17	Marvel Film Productions LLC	Delaware
18	Iron Works Productions LLC*	Delaware
19	Incredible Productions LLC*	Delaware
20	MVL Iron Works Productions Canada Inc.*	Province of Ontario
21	MVL Incredible Productions Canada, Inc.*	Province of Ontario
22	Asgard Productions LLC	Delaware
23	Marvel Animation, Inc.	Delaware
24	Green Guy Toons LLC	Delaware
25	Squad Productions LLC	Delaware

*Wholly owned subsidiaries formed as Film Slate Subsidiaries
**Joint venture with Sony Pictures for licensing Spider-Man

SOURCE: *Marvel Entertainment, Inc., Form 10-K (Dec. 31, 2007), Exhibit 21.*

EXHIBIT 5
Popular Characters:
Marvel
Entertainment Inc.

Ant-Man	Incredible Hulk
Avengers	Iron Man
Black Panther	Mr. Fantastic
Blade	Multiple Man
Captain America	Nick Fury
Cyclops	Nightcrawler
Daredevil	Phoenix
Dr. Doom	Silver Surfer
Dr. Strange	Spider-Girl
Elektra	Spider-Man
Emma Frost	Sub-Mariner
Fantastic Four	The Punisher
Gambit	The Thing
Ghost Rider	Thor
Hawkeye	Wolverine
Human Torch	X-Men

In the publishing industry, Marvel was the number one publisher of comic books in the United States with over 40% of the market. DC Comics followed with approximately 30% in 2007. Dark Horse Comics comprised about 5% of the comic book market.[6] Throughout their histories, Marvel and other comic book publishers struggled to expand readership beyond teenage boys. Various attempts included romance comics, female superheroes, and adult-themed comics. The most recent and successful expansion in this industry was the introduction of Japanese comics called "manga" which often included stories with girl-friendly content and were distributed to both comic book shops and mainstream bookstores.[7] Some comic book publishers also entered the field of graphic novels, which was well-suited to serialized stories. In 2008, Marvel had eight product lines that targeted different age groups and interests. These included stories taken from classic literature (the Iliad), stories from best-selling authors, and an all-ages print line for Wal-Mart and Target. Rival comic book company DC Comics had five print lines including a manga-type line and one primarily for teenage girls. DC also used established novelists to draw new readers to its publications.[8]

The **Licensing** segment typically delivered over half of the company's net sales in a year. An average of 70% of these sales were generated in the U.S. market. Licensing revenues were $272,722,000, $127,261,000, and $230,063,000 in 2007, 2006, and 2005 respectively. The Licensing segment directed the licensing, promotion, and brand management for all Marvel characters worldwide. Marvel pursued a strategy of concentrating licensee relationships with fewer, larger licensees who demonstrated superior financial and merchandising capability.[9]

Revenues within this segment were broken into four categories as of 2007. This was before the restatement of Toys revenues within the segment. The Domestic Consumer Products category represented $71.8 million or about 25% of total licensing sales in 2007. International Consumer Products made up another $41.8 million. The Spider-Man Joint Venture with Sony accounted for $122 million, or 45%, of total sales in this segment. Marvel Studios licensing made up $37.1 million in 2007.[10] Marvel was ranked within the top five licensing companies by sales by *License!* magazine in 2008 (See **Exhibit 6**).

EXHIBIT 6
Top Licensing Companies, 2008

| Rank | Company | (Dollar Amounts in Billions) | | Brands |
		Sales 2007	Sales 2006	
1	Disney Consumer Brands	$26.0	$24.0	Hannah Montana, High School Musical, Disney Princesses, Disney Fairies, Pixar's Cars, Chronicles of Narnia
2	Phillips-Van Heusen	$6.7	$6.7	Van Heusen, Arrow, Izod, Bass
3	Warner Bros. Consumer Products	$6.0	$6.0	Harry Potter and the Order of the Phonenix, The Dark Knight, Speed Racer, Where the Wild Things Are
4	Iconix	$6.0	NA	Candie's, Starter, Joe Boxer, OP, Cannon, Royal Velvet, Mudd, Mossimo
5	Marvel Entertainment Inc.	$5.5	$4.8	Spider-Man, X-Men, Hulk, Iron Man, Fantastic Four, Avengers, Spider-Man & Friends
6	Nickelodeon & Viacom Cons. Prod.	$5.5	$5.3	Dora, Diego, The Backyardigans, Ni-Hao, Kai Lan, SpongeBob SquarePants, South Park, Neopets
7	Major League Baseball	$5.1	$4.7	Major League Baseball
8	Sanrio	$5.0	$5.2	Hello Kitty, Keroppi, Kuromi, Badtz-Maru
9	Cherokee Group	$4.0	NA	Cherokee, Sideout, Carole Little
10	National Football League	$3.4	$3.2	National Football League

SOURCE: License! Global's *Top 100 Licensing Companies (April 2008)*.

Marvel shifted its toy business to Hasbro during the first quarter of 2008. According to the company:

> We also completed a change in the focus of the support that we provide to Hasbro, which resulted in changes to our internal organizational structure and staff reductions. These events altered our internal reporting of segment performance, with the result that we are now including revenues earned from Hasbro (associated with toys manufactured and sold by Hasbro) and related expenses (associated with royalties that we owe on our Hasbro revenue) within our Licensing segment. Those revenues and expenses were formerly included in our Toy segment.[11]

Seeking a strategic partnership with a recognized industry giant, Marvel entered a 5-year master toy license with Hasbro for the period January 1, 2007, to December 31, 2011. The agreement gave Hasbro the exclusive right to make action figures, plush toys, and certain role-play toys, and non-exclusive rights for several other types of toys, using Marvel's characters. The Hasbro agreement was reached after the early termination of a prior 5 1/2-year agreement with Toy Biz Worldwide Limited (TBW) in December 2005, for which Marvel took a $12.5 million non-recurring expense. The agreement with TBW, a Hong Kong toy maker totally unrelated to the Toy Biz company previously owned by Perlmutter, began in 2001 and gave TBW the right to use Marvel characters, except for Spider-Man, in producing and selling action figures and accessories. During the interim year (2006), Marvel produced and sold its own toys, with TBW serving as a sourcing agent to help Marvel locate factories in China.

Marvel faced intense competition in the toy industry and relied on the expertise of Hasbro to reach two main target markets: boys, primarily ages four through 13, and collectors aged 18–44. For 2007, the last time that the company would report revenues in the Toy segment, U.S. toy sales were responsible for about 60% of Marvel's Toy segment sales. Beginning in 2008, domestic and international licensing revenues from toy sales were reflected in the licensing segment.

With such an extensive catalog of characters, Marvel partnered with numerous companies such as Activision and Sega for video games, Leapfrog for electronics, Hallmark for party supplies, General Mills and 7-11 for food and beverages, and Johnson & Johnson for health & beauty products. Footwear deals included an exclusive collection of children's sneakers for Reebok featuring Iron Man and the Incredible Hulk and sold only at Foot Locker and Kids Foot Locker, as well as another deal with Crocs Inc. Fruit of the Loom held the licensing agreement for children's underwear printed with Marvel characters. As part of the licensing agreements, Marvel received a flat fee for access to any proprietary character in addition to per unit fees for every Marvel licensed item sold.

In 2007, Marvel began to enhance the product development and merchandising of its consumer product categories. In addition to its mass market mainstays, Wal-Mart and Target, Marvel was moving into new distribution channels such as Pottery Barn Kids with Spider-Man room furnishings and accessories designed exclusively for the retailer and its more upscale consumers. Additional deals were in place with Nordstrom, Fred Segal, and H&M.[12]

Although Marvel created its own film production business unit, there were a number of outstanding licensing agreements with 20th Century Fox to produce major motion pictures featuring X-Men and the Fantastic Four. Under this agreement Marvel retained more than 50% of merchandising-based royalty revenue. Marvel also partnered with Lionsgate Entertainment Corp. for animated DVDs for the home video market and with FX, a cable network from FOX, to distribute Marvel's self-produced movies on cable.[13]

Marvel licensed its characters for use at Universal Studios theme parks in Orlando, Florida, and Osaka, Japan. In 2008, characters had been licensed for the development of a major theme park in Dubai, two theme parks in South Korea, and a Broadway musical of Spider-Man with director Julie Taymor (*The Lion King*) and music by U2's Bono and The Edge. Characters were licensed by other companies for short-term promotions of products and services, and were used in foreign-language comic books, paperbacks, and coloring books.

Spider-Man Merchandising L.P. was a joint venture between Marvel and Sony Pictures Entertainment Inc. for the purpose of pursuing licensing opportunities relating to characters based upon movies or television shows featuring Spider-Man and produced by Sony. Marvel maintained control of decision making and received the majority of the financial interest of the joint venture.[14]

The **Film Production** segment included self-produced feature films. Marvel planned to self-produce all future films based on characters that had not already been licensed to third parties. The company felt it would have more control of films and have greater flexibility with respect to the coordination of licensed products and film release timing. Marvel financed new films through a $525 million credit facility funded by Merrill Lynch that enabled Marvel to independently finance the development and production of up to 10 feature films over eight years. The theatrical film rights of 12 second-tier characters and their supporting partners or rivals were pledged as collateral to the film facility, including Ant-Man, Black Panther, Captain America, Doctor Strange, Nick Fury, and The Avengers. **Exhibit 7** shows the schedule of films and studios involved.

Marvel formed seven wholly owned subsidiaries, known as the Film Slate Subsidiaries, in connection with the film facility, that are identified in **Exhibit 4**. The first two films produced by this $525 million investment were *Iron Man* and *The Incredible Hulk*, both of which were released in mid-2008 with successful opening weekends of $98.6 million and $55.4 million, respectively.[15] Paramount Pictures distributed *Iron Man*, staring Robert Downey Jr., Gwyneth Paltrow, Terrence Howard, and Jeff Bridges, and Universal Pictures distributed *The Incredible Hulk*, staring Edward Norton, Liv Tyler, William Hurt, and Tim Roth. Marvel began reporting revenues for the Film Production segment in the second quarter of 2008. In September 2008, Marvel leased sound stages, equipment, production spaces, and corporate offices in California through its MVL Productions LLC subsidiary to make its next four self-produced films.[16]

EXHIBIT 7			
Film Schedule and Studio: Marvel Entertainment Inc.	2000	*X-Men*	Fox
	2002	*Spider-Man*	Sony
	2003	*Daredevil*	Fox
		X2: X-Men United	Fox
		Hulk	Universal
	2004	*Spider-Man 2*	Sony
	2005	*Elecktra*	Fox
		Fantastic Four	Fox
	2006	*X-Men: The Last Stand*	Fox
	2007	*Ghost Rider*	Sony
		Spider-Man 3	Sony
		Fantastic Four-ROTSS	Fox
	2008	*Iron Man*	Marvel
		Incredible Hulk	Marvel
		Punisher: War Zone	Lionsgate
	2009	*X-Men Origins: Wolverine*	Fox
	2010	*Iron Man 2*	Marvel
		Thor	Marvel
	2011	*The First Avenger: Captain America*	Marvel
		The Avengers	Marvel

SOURCE: *Cuneo & Turitzin presentation at JP Morgan US Mid Cap Growth Conference, London, (Sept. 30, 2008), pp. 14–15 and Marvel Entertainment, Inc. Form 8-K, May 9, 2008, p. 3.*

The move to self-produced films came as a result of hard learning experiences. Previous failed attempts in Hollywood and unfavorable movie deals left Marvel with nothing to show for its long history of investment in character and story development. In past arrangements, the company did not bear the production risks and in exchange it reaped a small percentage of the profits.[17] Sometimes Marvel would receive only 2 to 10 percent of profits of a feature film. For example, licensing mishandled during Ron Perelman's era brought Marvel only one million dollars from 1997's *Men in Black*, a film that generated close to $600 million worldwide. Another lesson was learned when Marvel made $25,000 from 1998's *Blade*, which brought in $133 million worldwide.[18] However, popular films produced by other companies using Marvel characters continued to generate increased licensing revenues for Marvel from toys and consumer products, and often reignited interest in the comic books themselves.

Cross-Segment Operations

Operating across segments was the company's Global Digital Media Group, established in 2008 to coordinate Marvel's expanding digital distribution strategy. This included Marvel Digital Comics Unlimited, part of the Publishing segment, as well as digital video, animated content, mobile games, and strategic partnerships.[19] In late 2007, Marvel launched its Digital Comics online subscription service, providing high-resolution Internet access and search capabilities to thousands of classic comic book titles from its archives as well as contemporary issues. Special features on the Web site included the first 100 issues of the *Amazing Spider-Man*, first-time appearances of specific super heroes, and series designed for young readers. Rival publisher DC Comics pushed technology beyond static, digitized versions of print materials by offering a hybrid of comic books and animation called "motion comics." DC's first motion comic series featured the Dark Knight and coincided with the release of the 2008 Batman movie. The series could be downloaded for game consoles, mobile phones, and video on demand.[20] Following DC's lead, Marvel partnered with thriller/horror author Stephen King to develop a 25-episode animated video of King's short-story "N," from his collection "Just After Sunset." Marvel created the episodes specifically for small screens and offered them via online and mobile channels prior to the book's release.[21]

Serious legal considerations influenced all of Marvel's operations, domestically and internationally. Marvel worked diligently to protect the most valuable assets of the company, its globally-recognized characters and stories. In addition to the company's registered trademarks and copyrights within the United States, Marvel attempted to protect its intellectual property abroad by registering trademarks in Africa, Asia, Latin America, the Middle East, and Western Europe.[22] According to the International Intellectual Property Alliance, over $18 billion in revenue was lost in 2007 by U.S. firms due to copyright piracy of software, music, and books.[23] Another $5 billion was lost by major U.S. motion picture studios.[24] Marvel's legal challenges also extend to the virtual world, including its fights to protect its intellectual property by challenging the superhero avatars designed by players of massively multiplayer online role-playing games (MMORPG). In a recent case against NCsoft, Marvel accused the videogame developers of infringement of copyright and trademarks. The case was dismissed and Marvel later settled with the NCsoft, leaving many important questions about copyright and the boundaries of fair use in game playing to be settled in the future.[25]

Marvel relied on hundreds of gifted individuals to conceive of, design, and deliver the wide-ranging and ever-changing adventures of Marvel characters. Legal issues related to talent included claims of copyright ownership made by freelance writers, disputes with former employees, and labor agreements with writers and actors. For example, Marvel faced a challenge during the 100-day strike in 2007–2008 of the Writers Guild of America (WGA), which represents writers in the motion picture, broadcast, cable, and new media industries. Progress on its ambitious film development slate stopped until Marvel negotiated an interim agreement with the WGA to put the writers back to work. Marvel revised its two-films-per-year model and amended its agreement concerning the $525 million film slate credit facility.[26] As of November 2008, the Screen Actor's Guild (SAG) had been without a contract for five months and was seeking a strike authorization from its members.[27]

Financial Performance

Licensing segment net sales accounted for 56% of total net sales in 2007. The Publishing segment accounted for 26%, and Toys made up the remaining 18%. In 2007, revenue from foreign operations accounted for 30% of Marvel's total revenues, up from just 21% in 2005. **Exhibit 8** provides revenues by segment and geographic area for Marvel in 2007. As noted earlier, the company substantially exited the Toy business in early 2008 and began reporting revenues for the Film Production segment in the second quarter of 2008. As of the third quarter of 2008, Marvel's Licensing business accounted for $237,479,000 in net sales, down from a restated 2007 amount of $267,512,000. Publishing produced $92,322,000 in net sales, also down from a restated 2007 amount of $95,356,000. Film production made up $119,105,000 of net sales in the third quarter of 2008.[28]

As of late 2008, the global economy had entered a recessionary period. On the strength of its summer 2008 film releases, Marvel's share price appeared to be weathering the storm in late 2008. Because its characters were used across business segments, Marvel was able to leverage exposure from films to create revenues from sales of licensed merchandise. However, this ripple effect was expected to slow in the absence of new films or television shows. No self-produced films were scheduled for release in 2009.

Since emerging from bankruptcy in 1998, Marvel's net sales increased 110%, averaging nearly 14% growth per year. However, a closer analysis of Marvel's financials revealed wide fluctuations over the period. For fiscal year 2007, consolidated net sales were up 38% over 2006 to $485.8 million. The increase came after a 24% drop from 2004, when net sales exceeded $513.4 million, to 2005, and a further drop of 10% from 2005 to 2006. Marvel's consolidated statement of income is provided in **Exhibit 9** and **Exhibit 10**, consolidated balance sheet.

EXHIBIT 8
Revenues by Segment and Geographic Area: Marvel Entertainment Inc.

| | (Dollar Amounts in Thousands) | | | | | |
| | 2007 | | 2006 | | 2005 | |
	U.S.	Foreign	U.S.	Foreign	U.S.	Foreign
Licensing	$ 178,534	$ 94,188	$ 83,955	$ 43,306	$ 181,959	$ 48,104
Publishing	106,858	18,799	90,924	17,540	77,312	15,143
Toys[1]	53,100	34,328	82,171	33,902	47,695	20,294
Total	$ 338,492	$ 147,315	$ 257,050	$ 94,748	$ 306,966	$ 83,541

Note 1. $38.5 million and $4.4 million of U.S. toy revenue and $32.4 million and $0.8 million of foreign toy revenue for 2007 and 2006, respectively, is attributable to royalties and service fees generated by Hasbro. $37.1 million of the U.S. toy revenue and $14.7 million of the foreign toy revenues for 2005 are attributable to royalties and service fees from toy sales generated by TBW.

SOURCE: *Marvel Entertainment, Inc.,* Form 10-K *(Dec. 31, 2007), p. F-40.*

EXHIBIT 9

Consolidated Statements of Income: Marvel Entertainment, Inc. (Dollar amounts in thousands of dollars)

Year Ending December 31	2007	2006	2005
Net Sales	485,807	351,798	390,507
Costs and expenses:	—	—	—
Cost of revenues (excluding depreciation expense)	60,933	103,584	50,517
Selling, general and administrative	147,118	123,130	166,456
Depreciation and amortization	5,970	14,322	4,534
Total costs and expenses	$214,021	$241,036	$221,507
Other income, net	2,643	1,798	2,167
Operating income	$274,429	$112,560	$171,167
Interest expense	13,756	15,225	3,982
Interest income	2,559	1,465	3,863
Income before income tax expense and minority interest	$263,232	$98,800	$171,048
Income tax expense	(98,908)	(39,071)	(62,820)
Minority interest in consolidated joint venture	(24,501)	(1,025)	(5,409)
Net Income	$139,823	$58,704	$102,819
Basic and diluted net income per share:	—	—	—
Weighted average shares outstanding:	—	—	—
Weighted average shares for basic earnings per share	79,751	82,161	99,594
Effect of dilutive stock options, warrants and restricted stock	2,716	5,069	6,464
Weighted average shares for diluted earnings per share	82,467	87,230	106,058
Net income per share:	—	—	—
Basic	1.75	0.71	1.03
Diluted	1.70	0.67	0.97

SOURCE: *Marvel Entertainment, Inc., Form 10-K (Dec. 31, 2007), p. F-5.*

EXHIBIT 10

Consolidated Balance Sheet: Marvel Entertainment, Inc. (Dollar amounts in thousands)

Year Ending December 31	2007	2006
Assets	—	—
Current assets:	—	—
Cash and cash equivalents	30,153	31,945
Restricted cash	20,836	8,527
Short-term investments	21,016	—
Accounts receivable, net	28,679	59,392
Inventories, net	10,647	10,224
Income tax receivable	10,882	45,569
Deferred income taxes, net	21,256	22,564
Advances to joint venture partner	—	8,535
Prepaid expenses and other current assets	4,245	7,231
Total current assets	**$147,714**	**$193,987**
Fixed assets, net	**2,612**	**4,444**
Product and package design costs, net	—	1,497
Film inventory	264,817	15,055
Goodwill	346,152	341,708
Accounts receivable, non–current portion	1,300	12,879
Income tax receivable, non–current portion	4,998	—
Deferred income taxes, net	37,116	36,406
Deferred financing costs	11,400	15,771
Other assets	1,249	2,118
Total assets	**$817,358**	**$623,865**

(Continued)

EXHIBIT 10
(Continued)

Year Ending December 31	2007	2006
Current liabilities:	—	—
Accounts payable	3,054	5,112
Accrued royalties	84,694	68,467
Accrued expenses and other current liabilities	37,012	38,895
Deferred revenue	88,617	140,072
Film facilities	42,264	—
Minority interest to be distributed	556	—
Total current liabilities	$256,197	$252,546
Accrued royalties, non-current portion	10,273	12,860
Deferred revenue, non-current portion	58,166	35,667
Line of credit	—	17,000
Film facilities, non-current portion	246,862	33,200
Income tax payable, non-current portion	54,066	10,999
Other liabilities	10,291	6,702
Total liabilities	$635,855	$368,974
Commitments and contingencies	—	—
Stockholders—equity:	—	—
Preferred stock, $.01 par value, 100,000,000 shares authorized, none issued	—	—
Common stock, $.01 par value, 250,000,000 shares authorized, 133,179,310 issued and 77,624,842 outstanding in 2007 and 128,420,848 issued and 81,326,627 outstanding in 2006	1,333	1,284
Additional paid-in capital	728,815	710,460
Retained earnings	349,590	228,466
Accumulated other comprehensive loss	(3,395)	(2,433)
Total stockholders—equity before treasury stock	$1,076,343	$937,777
Treasury stock, at cost, 55,554,468 shares in 2007 and 47,094,221 shares in 2006	(894,840)	(682,886)
Total stockholders equity	181,503	254,891
Total liabilities and stockholders equity	$817,358	$623,865

SOURCE: *Marvel Entertainment, Inc.,* Form 10-K *(Dec. 31, 2007), p. F-4.*

NOTES

1. "Perelman to settle Marvel suit." *New York Times*, August 8, 2008.

2. Marvel Entertainment, Inc., *Proxy Statement* (May 5, 2008), pp. 4–5. This section was directly quoted, except for minor editing.

3. Marvel Entertainment, Inc., *Proxy Statement* (May 5, 2008), p. 35.

4. Marvel Entertainment, Inc., *Form 8-K* (February 19, 2008), p. 1.

5. Marvel Entertainment, Inc., *Proxy Statement* (May 5, 2008), p. 13. This section was directly quoted, except for minor editing.

6. Market share 2007 from Diamond accessed September 6, 2008. http://comicbooks.about.com/od/diamondreports2007/a/2007publishers.htm

7. Phillips, Matt. "Pow! Romance! Comics court girls; Inspired by Japanese manga, major American publishers aim for new female fans." *Wall Street Journal*, June 8, 2007, p. B.1.

8. Lieberman, David. "Comic boom!" *USA Today*, July 25, 2008, p. 1b.

9. Marvel Entertainment, Inc., *10-Q* (September 30, 2008), p. 18.

10. Marvel Entertainment, Inc., *8-K* (February 19, 2008), p. 2.

11. Marvel Entertainment, Inc., *10-Q* (June 30, 2008), p. 16.

12. "News flash! Spidey merch spotted at Pottery Barn: Deal seeks to break Marvel out of 'commodity product' mold." *Brandweek*, February 11, 2008, p. 8.

13. "Marvel Studios enters into free TV rights deal with FX for Marvel's self-produced movies," accessed April 29, 2008. http://www.marvel.com/company/index.htm?sub=viewstory_current.php&id=1278

14. Marvel Entertainment, Inc., *10-Q* (June 30, 2008), p. 5.

15. www.boxofficemojo.com, accessed September 6, 2008.

16. Marvel Entertainment, Inc., *10-Q* (September 30, 2008), p. 16, 37.

17. Marr, Merissa. "In new film venture, Marvel hopes to be its own superhero." *Wall Street Journal*, April 28, 2005, p. B1.

18. Hamner, Susanna. "Is Marvel ready for its close-up?" *Business 2.0*, May 2006, p. 112.

19. "Marvel appoints Ira Rubenstein Executive Vice President of its newly launched Global Digital Media Group," accessed April 29, 2008. http://www.marvel.com/company/index.htm?sub=viewstory_current.php&id=1281

20. McBride, Sarah. "Web draws on comics: Online shorts boost Batman." *Wall Street Journal*, July 18, 2008, p. B.10.

21. Trachtenberg, Jeffrey A. "Author King enlists Marvel in video plot." *Wall Street Journal*, July 25, 2008, p. B.1.

22. Marvel Entertainment, Inc., *10-K* (December 31, 2007), p. 8.

23. International Intellectual Property Alliance, "2008 'Special 301' USTR decisions," accessed September 6, 2008. http://www.iipa.com/pdf/USTRdecisions2008Special301Tableof EstimatedLossesandPiracyLevels2007Final061708.pdf

24. Motion Picture Association of American, "The cost of movie piracy." Dated 2005, accessed September 6, 2008. http://www.mpaa.org/leksummaryMPA%20revised.pdf

25. Louie, Andrea W. M. "Designing avatars in virtual worlds: How free are we to play Superman?" *Journal of Internet Law*, November 2007, pp. 3–12.

26. Marvel Entertainment, Inc., *Form 8-K* (January 18, 2008), p. 1.

27. Simmons, Leslie. "Actors will vote on strike." *Adweek*, November 24, 2008, accessed November 24, 2008. http://www.adweek.com/aw/content_display/news/media/e3i550533f2636cdbd1ff5fc3bd8f91a1ad

28. Marvel Entertainment, Inc., *10-Q* (September 30, 2008), p. 13.

CASE 16

Harley Davidson Inc. 2008:

THRIVING THROUGH A RECESSION

Patricia A. Ryan and Thomas L. Wheelen

We fulfill dreams through the experience of motorcycling by providing to motorcyclists and to the general public an expanding line of motorcycles, branded products and services in selected market segments.[1]

HARLEY-DAVIDSON MISSION STATEMENT

IT WAS A PRETTY AMAZING SIGHT, DOZENS AT A TIME, THOUSANDS IN A DAY DESCENDING ON THE Sinclair gas station and Western café in Lusk, Wyoming, on their way to the 2008 Sturgis rally in the blistering heat of early August. Lusk, a town of 1,348 people that lies 147 miles southwest of Sturgis, saw bikers from all walks of life, needing fuel and small supplies, some with tattoos, some with leather to protect themselves from the winds as they cruised at 60 miles per hour along Highway 18 toward Sturgis. Some clearly were businessmen on a week-long reprieve, others were rougher in appearance. The one thing they all had in common was the love of the ride . . . the ride of the Harley-Davidson motorcycle.

There were new issues facing Harley-Davidson in their 105th year of operation. Consider the weak dollar, the probability that retail sales would continue a downward spiral, which in turn would cause excess inventory of high priced motorcycles. Then there was the customer base: the rockers who grew up in the sixties and seventies are graying and this threatens the growth of Harley-Davidson. As riders approach sixty, it is important for Harley-Davidson to recruit new riders of the younger generations. Their emphasis on recruiting women has been instrumental in recent years. They were faced with an aging baby boomer population and needed to focus on growing smaller segments of their business—women bikers and younger bikers, the latter who could not traditionally afford a Harley-Davidson motorbike.

Many things were looking good for the 105-year-old motorcycle manufacturer; however, President and CEO James Ziemer needed to continue the company's strong growth as many economists felt the economy was heading into a recession. Harley-Davidson had opened their first dealership in mainland China, and named Beijing Feng Huo Lun as the first authorized dealer. A Harley-Davidson museum was due to open in 2008 and sought to attract upwards of

350,000 tourists per year. CEO and President Ziemer worked his way up the ranks, starting 38 years ago as a freight elevator operator and most recently serving a 14-year stint at CFO, but now at the driver's seat, he faced a different set of responsibilities. As noted by one analyst,

> *There are indications that Harley-Davidson is at a turning point. "It's a well managed company with still one of the strongest brand names in consumer products, but I just question whether the company can grow its production 7 to 9 percent in an environment where demand doesn't seem to be growing at that rate"*

> Ed Aaron, *analyst with BRC Capital Markets*[2]

History[3]

In 1901, William Harley (age 21), a draftsman, and his friend, Arthur R. Davidson, began experimenting with ideas to design and build their own motorcycles. They were joined by Arthur's brothers, William, a machinist, and Walter, a skilled mechanic. The Harley-Davidson Motor Company started in a 10×15 foot shed in the Davidson family's backyard in Milwaukee, Wisconsin.

In 1903, three motorcycles were built and sold. The production increased to eight in 1904. The company then moved to Juneau Avenue, which is the site of the company's present offices. In 1907, the company was incorporated.

Ownership by AMF

In 1969, AMF Inc., a leisure and industrial product conglomerate, acquired Harley-Davidson. The management team expanded production from 15,000 in 1969 to 40,000 motorcycles in 1974. AMF favored short-term profits instead of investing in research and development and retooling. During this time, Japanese competitors continued to improve the quality of their motorcycles, while Harley-Davidson began to turn out noisy, oil-leaking, heavy vibrating, poorly finished, and hard-to-handle machines. AMF ignored the Japanese competition. In 1975, Honda Motor Company introduced its "Gold Wing," which became the standard for large touring motorcycles. Harley-Davidson had controlled this segment of the market for years. There was a $2,000 price difference between Harley's top-of-the-line motorcycles and Honda's comparable Gold Wing. This caused American buyers of motorcycles to start switching to Japanese motorcycles. The Japanese companies (Suzuki and Yamaha) from this time until the middle 1980s continued to enter the heavyweight custom market with Harley look-alikes.

During AMF's ownership of the company, sales of motorcycles were strong, but profits were weak. The company had serious problems with poor quality manufacturing and strong Japanese competition. In 1981, Vaughn Beals, then head of the Harley Division, and 13 other managers conducted a leveraged buyout of the company for $65 million.

Under New Management

New management installed a Materials As Needed (MAN) system to reduce inventories and stabilize the production schedule. Also, this system forced production to work with marketing for more accurate forecasts. This led to precise production schedules for each month, allowing only a 10% variance. The company forced its suppliers to increase their quality in order to reduce customer complaints.

Citicorp, Harley's main lender, refused to lend any more money in 1985. On New Year's Eve, four hours before a midnight that would have meant Harley's demise, the company inked a deal with Heller Financial that kept its doors open. Seven months later, amid a hot market for new stock, Harley-Davidson went public again. Ziemer, the CFO puts it more bluntly: "You throw cash at it, try to grow too fast, you'd destroy this thing."[4]

During the time Harley-Davidson was a privately held firm, management invested in research and development. Management purchased a Computer-Aided Design (CAD) system that allowed the company to make changes in the entire product line and still maintain its traditional styling. These investments by management had a quick payoff in that the break-even point went from 53,000 motorcycles in 1982 to 35,000 in 1986.

During 1993, the company acquired a 49% interest in Buell Motorcycle Company, a manufacturer of sport/performance motorcycles. This investment in Buell offered the company the possibility of gradually gaining entry into select niches within the performance motorcycle market. In 1998, Harley-Davidson owned most of the stock in Buell. Buell began distribution of a limited number of Buell motorcycles during 1994 to select Harley-Davidson dealers. Buell sales were:[5]

Year	Sales	Units (thousands)
1994	$ 6 million	576
1995	$14 million	1,407
1996	$23 million	2,762
1997	$40 million	4,415
1998	$53.5 million	6,334
1999	$63.5 million	7,767
2000	$58.1 million	10,189
2001	$61.9 million	9,925
2002	$66.9 million	10,900
2003	$76.1 million	10,000
2004	$79.0 million	9,900
2005	$93.1 million	11,200
2006	$102.2 million	12,460
2007	$100.5 million	11,513

Buell's mission "is to develop and employ innovative technology to enhance 'the ride' and give Buell owners a motorcycle experience that no other brand can provide." The European sport/performance market was four times larger than its U.S. counterpart. In 2007, there were 804 dealerships that sold Buell bikes dealerships worldwide. Most of these dealerships were combined Harley-Davidson and Buell dealerships.

In 1995, the company acquired substantially all of the common stock and common stock equivalents of Eaglemark Financial Services, Inc., a company in which it held a 49% interest since 1993. Eaglemark provided credit to leisure product manufacturers, their dealers, and customers in the United States and Canada. The transaction, valued at $45 million, was accounted for as a step acquisition under the purchase method.

Concentration on Motorcycles

In 1996, the company announced its strategic decision to discontinue the operations of the Transportation Vehicles segment in order to concentrate its financial and human resources on its core motorcycle business. The Transportation Vehicles segment was composed of the Recreation Vehicles division (Holiday Rambler trailers), the Commercial Vehicles division (small delivery vehicles), and B & B Molders, a manufacturer of custom or standard tolling and injection-molded plastic pieces. During 1996, the company completed the sale of the Transportation Vehicles segment for an aggregate sales price of approximately $105 million; approximately $100 million in cash and $5 million in notes and preferred stock.

Internal Makeover and New Products

In 1997, Harley-Davidson created an internal makeover. The unsung hero of Harley-Davidson's supply-chain makeover was an intense procurement expert named Garry Berryman, vice president of Materials Management/Product Cost from 1995 to 2003 at Honda. When Berryman joined Harley-Davidson, he found the supply-chain management neglected. There were nine different purchasing departments operating from different plant locations, fourteen separate sets of representative terms and conditions, and nearly 4,000 suppliers. Engineers with little or no expertise in supply management were doing the bulk of the buying. To top it off, "the voice of supply management was buried three layers deep in the corporate hierarchy," said Berryman.

While at Honda, Berryman studied Japanese keiretsu—huge, vertically integrated companies that foster deep, trusting relationships with suppliers. He wanted to form similar strategic alliances with Harley's top suppliers, bringing them into the design and planning process. Berryman felt that new technology and the Internet would make it easier than ever to form these bonds and collaborate. He made it clear that relationship and strategy should drive applications, not vice versa. As Dave Cotteleer, the company's manager of planning and control, explained, "We're using technology to cut back on communication times and administrative trivia, like invoice tracking, so we can focus the relationships on more strategic issues. We're not saying, 'Here's a neat piece of technology. Let's jam it into our model.'"[6]

Also, in the 1990s, Harley-Davidson saw the need to build a motorcycle to appeal to the younger and international markets who preferred sleeker, faster bikes. Harley-Davidson spent an undisclosed amount of research and development dollars over several years to develop the $17,000 V-Rod motorcycle. The V-Rod, introduced in 2001, had 110 horsepower, nearly double that of the standard Harley Bike. The V-Rod was the quickest and fastest production model the company had ever built, capable of reaching 60 miles an hour in 3.5 seconds and 100 mph in a little over 8 seconds. Its top speed is about 140 mph. All in all, the V-Rod was faster and handled better than the traditional bulky Harley bikes.

All other Harley models are powered by 45-degree V-twin air-cooled engines with camshafts in the block; the new V-Rod has a 1,130-cc 60-degree engine with double overhead cams and four values for each cylinder. The V-Rod has a very long 67.5-inch wheelbase, and it handles better than other Harleys because it is so much lighter. Furthermore, the V-Rod is only 26 inches off the ground, so it will accommodate a wide range of rides.[7] Harley-Davidson hoped to gain some of the younger markets with this new bike.

In 2000, a new Softail model was introduced and all Softail models were outfitted with the twin Cam 88B engine. Fuel injection was introduced for the Softails in 2001 and in 2000; Buell introduced the Buell Blast, which was a single-cylinder bike. Along with the Buell Blast, Harley-Davidson introduced a new beginner rider's course aimed at the first time Harley owner and rider. The course was offered in Harley-Davidson and Buell dealerships. The VRSCA V-Rod in 2002 was the first Harley bike to combine fuel injection, overhead cams, and liquid cooling along with new 115 horsepower.

In an attempt to gain further female support, Harley-Davidson announced the introduction of 17-year-old Jennifer Snyder, a champion dirt bike racer as the newest member of the Harley-Davidson racing team. Female racers were starting to enter this predominantly male sport and Harley-Davidson would not miss this opportunity to challenge market perceptions of a Harley-Davidson rider.

In 2003, Harley-Davidson introduced the Lightning XBS9. In 2004, the Sportsters were refitted with rubber engine mounting, a new frame and a wider rear tire. The FLHRSI Road King was introduced with low rear suspension and wide handlebars for a beach appearance. In 2005, the XL 883 Sportster 883 Low, featuring a lowered seating position aimed at aging baby boomers, was added to the Sportster line. The FLSTNI Softail Deluxe was added to the

Softail line with a new sleek appearance reminiscent of the 1939 Harley-Davidson bike. In the same year, the FLSTSC/I Softail Springer-Classic revived the late 1940s bike in appearance.

In 2006, the Dyna motorcycle line was developed with the first 6-speed transmission. The new FLHX/I Street Glide was introduced as a lower profile touring bike. Scheduled for opening in 2008 was the Harley-Davidson museum in Milwaukee, Wisconsin. In the area of international development, the first dealership was opened in mainland China. In 2008, the company introduced four new bikes aimed at two markets—aging baby boomers and the growing female market.

Corporate Governance

Board of Directors

The Board of Directors consisted of 11 members, of which only two were internal members— James L. Ziemer, President and Chief Executive Officer (CEO), and Thomas E. Bergman, the Chief Financial Officer. **Exhibit 1** highlights board members in 2008.

The Board of Directors serve three-year staggered terms. Each of the nine non-employee directors are compensated $100,000 per year. At least half of this amount is to be paid in common stock.

Since 2005, the board has authorized a stock repurchase. In 2007, 2006, and 2005, the Company repurchased 20.4 million, 19.3 million, and 21.4 million shares of its common stock at weighted-average prices of $56, $55, and $49, respectively. As of February 2008, all of the 20 million shares authorized in 2007 remained to be repurchased. Each of the prior two years authorizations were fully repurchased by the end of the next year.

Top Management

James C. Ziemer started with Harley-Davidson 38 years ago as a freight elevator operator and served as the CFO from 1991 to 2005. In 2005, upon the retirement of Harley veteran Jeffrey Bluestein, Ziemer assumed the top role of President and CEO. He commented, "Harley-Davidson is strong and well-positioned for the road ahead."[8] Ziemer further commented:

I believe there are three constants in our success as a company: 1. Our passion for this business, for riding, and for relating to and being one with our customers; 2. Our sense of purpose—in other words, our focus on growing demand by offering great products and unique experiences; and 3. Operational Excellence—which is the continuous, relentless drive to eliminate waste in all aspects of our operations and to run Harley-Davidson better and more efficiently with each passing day. And I believe these three things—being close to our customers, growth and Operational Excellence—hold the keys to the future.[9]

Exhibit 2 shows the corporate officers for Harley-Davidson and its business segments— motor company leadership, Buell leadership, and financial services leadership.

Through 2006, Harley-Davidson received positive attention from the popular press in terms of rankings. In 2006, Business Week/Interbrand Annual Rankings Top 100 Global Brands placed Harley-Davidson at #45, up 1 from 2005. Fortune also placed Harley-Davidson in its 2004 list of "Most Admired Companies."[10] Previously, Forbes named Harley Davidson its "Company of the Year" for 2001. Harley-Davidson did not make Fortune's list in 2008.

In 2007, Harley-Davidson experienced its first declines in 20 years. Motorcycle revenue was down 1.27% over 2006, total revenue was down 0.69% and, perhaps most importantly, operating income suffered a 10.74% decline. Harley-Davidson, which had fought back from near demise in the 1980s was to face new rivals in the competitive market, an aging customer base, and the recession. Given the recession in 2008, what did the future hold for Harley-Davidson? These were issues management wrestled with as they planned for the future. One possible solution was to gain new, younger customers as the future as their current customers aged.

EXHIBIT 1
Board of Directors: Harley-Davidson Inc.

Barry K. Allen, *President, Allen Enterprises, LLC*
Barry has been a member of the Board since 1992. His distinguished business career has taken him from the telecommunications industry to leading a medical equipment and systems business and back again. Barry's diverse experience has been particularly valuable to the Board in the areas of marketing and organization transformation.

Richard I. Beattie, *Chairman of the Executive Committee, Simpson Thacher & Bartlett*
Dick has been a valued advisor to Harley-Davidson for nearly 20 years. His contributions evolved and grew with the company over time. In the early 1980s, he provided legal and strategic counsel to the 13 leaders who purchased Harley-Davidson from AMF, taking it back to private ownership. He also advised the team when it was time to take the company public again in 1986. Dick was elected to the Board in 1996.

Jeffrey L. Bleustein, *Chairman of the Board, Harley-Davidson, Inc.*
Jeff began his association with Harley-Davidson in 1975 when he was asked to oversee the engineering group. During his tenure as Vice President-Engineering, Harley-Davidson developed the Evolution engine and established the foundations of our current line of cruiser and touring motorcycles. Jeff has demonstrated creativity and vision across a wide range of senior leadership roles. In 1996, he was elected to the Board, and in June 1997, appointed CEO until his retirement in 2005. He remains on as Chairman of the Board.

George H. Conrades, *Executive Chairman of Akamai Technologies, Inc.*
George has served as a director since 2002 and brings with him extensive experience in e-business. Akamai Technologies is a provider of secure, outsourced e-business infrastructure services and software. He is also a partner with Polaris venture Partners, an early-stage investment company.

Judson C. Green, *President and CEO, NAVTEQ Corporation*
NAVTEQ is a leading provider of comprehensive digital map information for automotive navigation systems, mobile navigation devices and Internet-based mapping applications. Judson has served as a director since 2004.

Donald A. James, *Vice Chairman and Chief Executive Officer, Fred Deeley Imports, Inc.*
Don's wisdom and knowledge of the motorcycle industry has guided the Board since 1991. As a 31-year veteran of Harley-Davidson's exclusive distributor in Canada, he has a strong sense for our core products. Don has a particularly keen understanding of the retrial issues involved with motorcycles and related products and the competitive advantage inherent in strong, long-lasting dealer relationships.

Sara L. Levinson, *ChairMom and Chief Executive Officer, ClubMom, Inc.*
Sara joined the Board in 1996. She understands the value and power of strong brands, and her current senior leadership role in marketing and licensing, together with her previous experience at MTV, give her solid insights into the entertainment industries and younger customer segments.

George L. Miles, Jr., *President and CEO, WQED Multimedia*
George has been a director since 2002 and currently serves as president and CEO of WQED Multimedia, the public broadcaster for southwestern Pennsylvania.

James A. Norling, *Executive Vice President, Motorola, Inc.; President, Personal Communications Sector, retired*
Jim has been a Board member since 1993. His career with Motorola has included extensive senior leadership assignments in Europe, the Middle East, and Africa, and he has generously shared his international experience and understanding of technological change to benefit Harley-Davidson.

James L. Zeimer, *President and CEO, Harley Davidson, Inc.*
Jim has been with Harley-Davidson for over 38 years and served as CFO until 2005 when he assumed the role of CEO upon Jeff Bluestein's retirement. He has been a director since 2004.

Jochen Zeitz, *Chief Executive Officer and Chairman of the Board, Puma AG.*
Mr. Zeitz was elected to the Board in August 2007 when the size of the Board grew from 10 to 11 members. Mr. Zeitz will serve as a Class II director with a term expiring at the Company's 2008 annual meeting of shareholders.

SOURCE: *Harley Davidson, Inc., 2007 Form 10-K, page 99.*

EXHIBIT 2

1. Corporate Officers, Harley-Davidson, Inc.

James L. Ziemer
President and Chief Executive Officer

Thomas E. Bergmann
Executive Vice President, and Chief Financial Officer

Gail A. Lione
Vice President, General Counsel and Secretary

James M. Brostowitz
Vice President, Treasure, and Chief Accounting Officer

2. Motor Company Leadership

Joanne M. Bischmann
Vice President, Marketing

David P. Bozeman
General Manager, Powertrain Operations

James M. Brostowitz
Vice President and Treasurer

Leroy Coleman
Vice President, Advanced Operations

Rodney J. Copes
Vice President and General Manager, Powertrain Operations

William B. Dannehl
Vice President, North American Sales and Dealers Services

William G. Davidson
Vice President and Chief Styling Officer

Karl M. Eberle
Vice President and General Manager, Kansas City Operations

Robert S. Farchione
General Manager, Parts and Accessories

Fred C. Gates
General Manager, York Operations

James E. Haney
Vice President and Chief Information Officer

Michael P. Heerhold
General Manager, Tomahawk

Timothy K. Hoelter
Vice President, Government Affairs

Ronald M. Hutchinson
Vice President, New Business

Michael D. Keefe
Vice President and Director, Harley Owners Group®

Kathleen A. Lawler
Vice President, Communications

Lara L. Lee
Vice President, Enthusiast Services

Matthew S. Levatich
Vice President, Materials Management

Gail A. Lione
Vice President and General Counsel

James A. McCaslin
President and Chief Operating Officer

Jeffrey A. Merten
Managing Director, Asia Pacific and Latin America

Louis N. Netz
Vice President and Director, Styling

John A. Olin
Vice President, Controller

Steven R. Phillips
Vice President, Quality, Reliability and Technical Services

Harold A. Scott
Vice President, Human Resources

Patrick Smith
General Manager, General Merchandise

W. Kenneth Sutton, Jr.
Vice President, Engineering

Michael van der Sande
Managing Director, HD Europe

Jerry G. Wilke
Vice President, Customer Relationships and Product Planning

3. Harley-Davidson Financial Services Leadership

Lawrence G. Hund
Vice President, Operations and Chief Financial Officer

Kathryn H. Marczak
Vice President, Chief Credit and Administrative Officer

Saiyid T. Naqvi
President

4. Buell Motorcycle Company Leadership

Erik F. Buell
Chairman and Chief Technical Officer

Jon R. Flickinger
President and Chief Operating Officer

SOURCE: *Harley Davidson, Inc., 2006 Annual Report, p. 32.*

Harley Owners Group (H.O.G)

A special kind of camaraderie marked the Harley Owners Group rallies and other motorcycle events. At events and rallies around the world, members of the H.O.G. came together for fun, adventure, and a love of their machines and the open road. As the largest motorcycle club in the world, H.O.G. offered customers organized opportunities to ride their famed bikes. H.O.G. rallies visibly promote the Harley-Davidson experience to potential new customers and strengthened the relationships among members, dealers, and Harley-Davidson employees.

William G. Davidson, grandson of the co-founder, biker to the core, known to all as Willie G., says, "There's a lot of beaners, but they're out on the motorcycles, which is a beautiful thing." He noted that he recently co-led a national rally of Canadian HOG groups with Harley's Chairman Jeff Bleustein.[11]

In 1995, the Buell Riders Adventure Group (BRAG) was created to bring Buell motorcycle enthusiasts together and to share their on-road experiences. Harley-Davidson plans to grow both organizations with new members and chapters in the years to come.

Exhibit 3 provides a profile of H.O.G and BRAG clubs. In 2007, H.O.G. membership grew to over 1,000,000 strong, making it the largest factory-sponsored motorcycle club in the world. The newer BRAG club for Buell riders numbered 11,000 members.

EXHIBIT 3
2007 Profile of the HOG and BRAG: Harley-Davidson Inc.

HOG Sponsored Events: In 2007, H.O.G. continued to sponsor motorcycling events on local, regional, national, and international levels. The sixteenth annual international H.O.G. Rally drew tens of thousands of members.

HOG Membership: Any Harley-Davidson motorcycle could become a member of H.O.G. In fact, their first year of membership was included with the purchase of a new Harley-Davidson motorcycle. The number of H.O.G. members had grown rapidly since the motorcycle organization began in 1983 with 33,000 members. Now, the largest factory sponsored motorcycle organization in the world, there were over 1 million H.O.G. members in 130 countries worldwide. Sponsorship of H.O.G. chapters by Harley-Davidson dealers grew from 49 chapters in 1985 to over 1,400 chapters in 2007.

A Snapshot of H.O.G.

Created in	1983
Worldwide members	>1,000,000
Worldwide dealer-sponsored chapters	1,400
Countries with members	115

A Snapshot of BRAG (Buell Riders Adventure Group)

Created in	1995
Worldwide members	11,000
Number of clubs	55

SOURCE: *Harley-Davidson, Inc, http://www.harley-davidson.com.*

The Harley-Davidson Museum

In June 2006, Harley-Davidson began construction of a 130,000 square foot museum. The museum houses a collection of motorcycles and historical mementos from the company's 105-year history. It was anticipated there will be over 350,000 visitors each year to the Milwaukee museum with an anticipated opening in summer 2008.

"With over one hundred years and millions of motorcycles behind us, Harley-Davidson has a rich history, and exciting present, and a vibrant future. In the years to come, the Harley-Davidson Museum will be a centerpiece of the Harley-Davidson experience." said CEO Ziemer.[12]

Domestic and Foreign Distribution[13]

United States

Domestically, Harley-Davidson sold its motorcycles and related products at wholesale to a network of approximately 684 independently-owned full-service Harley-Davidson dealerships. Included in this figure were 307 combined Harley-Davidson and Buell dealerships. In 2007, in partial response to a dismissed lawsuit alleging improper allocation of motorcycles, Harley-Davidson implemented a new U.S. motorcycle distribution system to better align demand with supply of bikes.

With respect to sales of new motorcycles, approximately 80% of the U.S. dealerships sold the Harley-Davidson motorcycles exclusively. Independent dealers also sold a smaller portion of parts and accessories, general merchandise, and licensed products through "non-traditional" retail outlets. The "non-traditional" outlets, which serve as extensions of the main dealerships, consist of Secondary Retail Locations (SRLs), Alternate Retail Outlets (AROs), and Seasonal Retail Outlets (SROs). Secondary retail locations are satellites of the main dealership and were developed to meet the service needs of the company's riding customers. They also provided parties and accessories, general merchandise, and licensed products and were authorized to sell and service new motorcycles. Alternate retail outlets, located primarily in high-traffic locations such as malls, airports, or popular vacation destinations, focus on selling general merchandise and licensed products. Seasonal retail outlets, located in similar high-traffic areas, operate on a seasonal basis. There were approximately 104 SRLs, 68 AROs, and 12 SROs in the United States.

Foreign Operations

Revenue from the sale of motorcycles and related products to independent dealers and distributors located outside of the United States was approximately $1.52 billion, $1.18 billion, and $1.04 billion, or approximately 27%, 20%, and 19% of net revenue of the Motorcycles segment during 2007, 2006, and 2005, respectively.

Europe/Middle East/Africa

At the end of 2007, there were 370 independent Harley-Davidson dealerships serving 32 European country markets. This included 323 combined Harley-Davidson and Buell dealerships. Buell was further represented by four dealerships that did not sell Harley-Davidson motorcycles. Harley-Davidson planned to open a new sales office in South Africa in 2008.

Asia-Pacific

In the Asia/Pacific region, Harley-Davidson sold motorcycles and related products at wholesale to independent dealers and distributors. In Japan, sales, marketing, and distribution of product are managed from its subsidiary in Tokyo, which sold motorcycles and related products through 130 independent Harley-Davidson dealers. Fifty-seven of these dealers sell both Harleys and Buells. Three dealerships sold only Buell Bikes.

In Australia and New Zealand, the distribution of Harley-Davidson products was managed by independent distributors that purchased directly from the Harley-Davidson's U.S. operation. In 2007, the Harley-Davidson's subsidiary in Sydney, Australia managed the sales, marketing, and distribution in that region. The Australia/New Zealand market was served at retail by a network of 49 independent Harley-Davidson dealerships, including 32 that sold both Harley-Davidson and Buell products.

Latin America

In Latin America, Harley-Davidson sold motorcycles and related products at wholesale to independent dealers. Harley-Davidson supplied all products sold in the Latin America region directly to independent dealers from its U.S. operations, with the exception of certain motorcycles sold in Brazil which are assembled and distributed by the Company's subsidiary in Manaus, Brazil.

In Latin America, 12 countries were served by 31 independent dealers. Brazil was the company's largest market in Latin America and was served by 10 dealers. Mexico, the region's second largest market had 11 dealers. In the remaining Latin American countries, there were 10 dealers.

Canada

In Canada, Harley-Davidson sold its motorcycles and related products at wholesale to a single independent distributor, Deeley Harley-Davidson Canada/Fred Deeley Imports Ltd. In Canada, there were 75 independent Harley-Davidson dealerships. In Canada, 45 of the 74 dealerships sell both Harley-Davidson and Buell products.

Business Segments

Harley-Davidson operates in two principal business segments: Motorcycles and Related Products (Motorcycles) and Financial Services. **Exhibit 4** provides financial information on the company's two business segments.

Motorcycles and Related Products Segment

The primary business of the Motorcycles segment is to design, manufacture, and sell premium motorcycles for the heavyweight market. They are best known for Harley-Davidson motorcycle products, but also offer a line of motorcycles and related products under the Buell brand name. Sales from the company's Motorcycle segment generated 93.2%, 93.8%, and 94.2% of the total sales during 2007, 2006, and 2005, respectively; with the remainder coming from the Financial Services segment.

The majority of the Harley-Davidson branded motorcycle products emphasizes traditional styling, design simplicity, durability, ease of service, and evolutionary change. Harley's

EXHIBIT 4
Information by Business Segments: Harley-Davidson Inc. (Dollar amounts in thousands)

A. Revenues and Income from Operations

Year ending December 31	2007	2006	2005
Net sales and Financial Services income:			
Motorcycles and Related Products net sales	$5,726,848	$5,800,686	$5,342,214
Financial Services income	416,196	384,891	331,618
	$6,143,044	$6,185,577	$5,673,832
Income from operations:			
Motorcycles and Related Products	$1,230,643	$1,408,990	$1,299,865
Financial Services	212,169	210,724	191,620
General corporate expenses	(17,251)	(22,561)	(21,474)
Operating Income	$1,425,561	$1,597,153	$1,470,011

B. Assets, Depreciation, and Capital Expenditures
(Dollar amount in thousands)

	Motorcycles and Related Products	Financial Services	Corporate	Consolidated
2007				
Identifiable Assets	$1,804,202	$3,447,075	$405,329	$5,656,606
Depreciation and Amortization	197,655	6,517	-	204,172
Net Capital Expenditures	232,139	9,974	-	242,113
2006				
Identifiable Assets	$1,683,724	$2,951,896	$896,530	$5,532,150
Depreciation & Amortization	205,954	7,815	-	213,769
Net Capital Expenditures	209,055	10,547	-	219,602
2005				
Identifiable Assets	$1,845,802	$2,363,235	$1,046,172	$5,255,209
Depreciation and Amortization	198,833	6,872	-	205,705
Net Capital Expenditures	188,078	10,311	-	198,389

SOURCE: *Harley Davidson, Inc., 2007 Form 10-K, p. 95.*

appeal straddles class boundaries, stirring the hearts of grease monkeys and corporate titans alike. Malcolm Forbes, the late owner of Forbes magazine, was pivotal in introducing Harleys to the business elite in the early 1980s.[14]

Based on data from the Motorcycle Industry Council owner survey, nearly 1 out of every 10 motorcycle owners is female[15] The average U.S. Harley-Davidson motorcycle purchaser is a married male in his late-forties, with a household income of approximately $81,300, who purchases a motorcycle for recreational purposes rather than to provide transportation and is an experienced motorcycle rider. Over two-thirds of the firm's U.S. sales of Harley-Davidson motorcycles are to buyers with at least one year of education beyond high school, and 31% of the buyers have college degrees. (See **Exhibit 5.**)

In an effort to grow and recognize the importance of female riders to Harley-Davidson, the company partnered with *Jane* magazine in 2005 in a contest called the Spirit of Freedom Contest to recognize women who overcome fears and other obstacles to become Harley riders. The grand prize winner was to receive a new Sportster 883. "The adrenaline rush of riding a motorcycle out on the open is like no other experience. Through this contest, we are saluting women

EXHIBIT 5
Purchaser
Demographic
Profile:
Harley-Davidson Inc.

	2006	2005	2004	2003	1983
Gender					
Male	88%	89%	89%	89%	98%
Female	12%	12%	11%	11%	2%
Median Age					
Years	47.1	46.5	46.1	45.2	34.1
Median Household Income ($000)	82.1	81.6	80.8	83.3	38.3

2006 Purchasers	
49%	Owned Harley-Davidson motorcycle previously
37%	Coming off of competitive motorcycle
14%	New to motorcycling or haven't owned a motorcycle for at least 5 years

SOURCE: *Harley Davidson Fact Book, posted November 5, 2007, at http://investor.harley-davidson.com/downloads/factsheet.pdf.*

who embody that spirit of adventure through small gestures, inner strength, and everyday self-less acts" commented Kathleen Lawler, Vice President of Communications, Harley-Davidson.[16]

Buell motorcycle products emphasize innovative design, responsive handling, and over-all performance. The Buell motorcycle product line has traditionally consisted of heavyweight performance models, powered by the 1200cc V-Twin engine. However, in 2000, they introduced the Buell Blast, a new vehicle designed specifically to attract new customers into the sport of motorcycling. This vehicle was considerably smaller, lighter, and less expensive than the traditional Buell heavyweight models and is powered by a 492-cc single-cylinder engine. The Buell line has continued to grow since the introduction of the lower-priced Buell Blast.

The average U.S. purchaser of the Buell heavyweight motorcycle is a male at the median age of 39 with a median household income of approximately $61,600. Internal documents indicate that half of Buell Blast purchasers have never owned a motorcycle before, and in excess of 95% of them had never owned a Buell motorcycle before. The median age of Blast purchasers is 38, with over one-half of them being female.

The heavyweight motorcycle market is comprised of four segments: standard, which emphasizes simplicity and cost; performance, which emphasizes handling and acceleration; touring, which emphasizes comfort and amenities for long-distance travel; and custom, which emphasizes styling and individual owner customization.

In 2008, Harley-Davidson manufactured and sold 30 models of Harley-Davidson touring and custom heavyweight motorcycles, with domestic manufacturer's suggested retail prices ranging from approximately $6,695 to $20,645. There were eight Buell bikes ranging from $4,695 to $11,995. (See **Exhibit 6**.) The touring segment of the heavyweight market was pioneered by Harley-Davidson and includes motorcycles equipped for long-distance touring with fairings, windshields, saddlebags, and Tour Pak luggage carriers. The custom segment of the market includes motorcycles featuring the distinctive styling associated with classic Harley-Davidson motorcycles. These motorcycles are highly customized through the use of trim and accessories.

Harley-Davidson's traditional heavyweight motorcycles are based on variations of five basic chassis designs and are powered by one of four air-cooled, twin cylinder engines with a 45-degree "V" configuration, which have displacements of 883cc, 1200cc, 1450cc, and 1550cc. The V-Rod has its own unique chassis design and is equipped with the new Revolution powertrain, a new liquid-cooled, twin-cylinder, 1130cc engine, with a 60-degree "V" configuration.

EXHIBIT 6
2008 Motorcycles
Product Line:
Harley-Davidson Inc.

Motorcycle	MSRP Base Price ($)
1. BUELL[1]	
Buell® 1125R	11,995
XB12X Ulyssest®	11,495
XB12S/XB12Scg Lightning®	10,495
XB12STT Lightning® Long	10,495
XB12STT Lightning®	10,295
XB12R Firebolt®	9,995
XB9SX Lightning® CityX	8,895
XB9SX Blast	4,695
2. HARLEY-DAVIDSON SPORTSTER	
XL1200C Sportster® Custom	9,895
XL 1200L Sportster® Low	9,695
XL1200N Sportster® Nightster™	9,695
XL1200R Sportster® Roadster	8,895
XL883C Sportster® Custom	7,945
XL883L Sportster®Low	7,145
XL883 Sportster®	6,695
3. DYNA	
FXDWG Dyna® Wide Glide 105th Anniversary Edition	17,620
FXDF Dyna® Low Rider®	14,995
FXDF Dyna® Fat Bob™	14,795
FXDB Dyna® Street Bob®	13,795
FXDC Dyna® Super Glide® Custom	12,995
FXD Dyna® Super Glide®	11,995
4. SOFTAIL	
FXCWC Softail Rocker™ C	19,840
FLSTC Heritage Softail® Classic	17,945
FLSTN Softail® Deluxe	17,445
FXCW Softail Rocker™	17,295
FLSTF Fat Boy®	17,195
FXSTC Softail® Custom	16,895
FXSTb Night Train®	15,895
5. VRSC™ Family (V-Rod)	
VRSCAW V-Rod®	16,995
VRSCDX Night Rod® Special	16,695
VRSCD Night Rod®	14,995
6. TOURING	
FLHTCU Ultra Classic® Electra Glide®	20,695
FLHTC Electra Glide® Classic	18,695
FLHX Street Glide	18,675
FLTR Road Glide®	18,145
FLHR Road King®	17,945
FLHT Electra Glide® Standard	16,545

[1]Buell Motorcycle Company partnered with Harley-Davidson in 1993 and was purchased by Harley-Davidson in 1998.

SOURCE: *http://www.harley-davidson.com/wcm/Content/Pages/2008_Motorcycles/2008_Motorcycles.jsp?locale=en_US& cwpws/dwp/cont-without-flash=true&swfdwp=&dwp_dealerid=&dwp_pg=&cwpws/dwp/dwp-dealer-id=.*

Although there are some accessory differences between the top-of-the line touring motorcycles and those of its competitors, suggested retail prices are generally comparable. The prices for the high-end of the Harley-Davidson custom product line range from being competitive to 50% more than its competitors' custom motorcycles. The custom portion of the Harley-Davidson product line represents their highest unit volumes and continues to command a premium price because of the features, styling, and high resale value associated with Harley-Davidson custom products. The smallest displacement custom motorcycle (the 883cc Sportster) is directly price competitive with comparable motorcycles available in the market. The surveys of retail purchasers indicate that, historically, over three-quarters of the purchasers of its Sportster model either have previously owned competitive-brand motorcycles or are completely new to the sport of motorcycling or have not participated in the sport for at least five years. Since 1988, research has consistently shown purchasers of Harley-Davidson motorcycles have a repurchase intent in excess of 90%, and management expects to see sales of its 883cc Sportster model partially translated into sales of its higher-priced products in the normal two-to-three-year ownership cycle.

Worldwide Parts and Accessories net sales comprised 15.2%, 14.9%, and 15.4% of net sales in the motorcycles segment in 2007, 2006, and 2005, respectively. Worldwide net sales of general merchandise, which includes MotorClothes apparel and collectibles, comprised 5.3%, 4.8%, and 4.6% of net sales in the Motorcycles segment in 2007, 2006, and 2005, respectively.

Management also provides a variety of services to its dealers and retail customers, including service training schools, customized dealer software packages, delivery of its motorcycles, an owners club membership, a motorcycle rental program, and a rider training program that is available in the United States through a limited number of authorized dealers.

President and CEO's Comments[17]

James Ziemer has served as CEO since April 2005. Thomas E. Bergman, 41, succeeded him as Chief Financial Officer. Ziemer "has the information of where we're going, but he's also rooted in where we've been" commented Kirk Topel, co-owner of Hal's Harley-Davidson dealership in New Berlin, Wisconsin.

President Ziemer said in the press release announcing 2007 financial results,

Harley-Davidson managed through a weak U.S. economy during 2007. We reduced our wholesale motorcycle shipment plan for the fourth quarter, fulfilling our commitment to our dealers to ship fewer Harley-Davidson motorcycles than we expected our dealers worldwide to sell at retail during 2007. While these are challenging times in the U.S., our international dealer network delivered double digit retail sales growth in 2007.

For 2008, the Company once again plans to ship fewer Harley-Davidson motorcycles than it expects its worldwide dealer network to sell. The Company also expects moderate revenue growth, lower operating margin, and diluted earnings per share growth rate of 4 to 7 percent compared to 2007. For the first quarter, it expects to ship between 68,000 and 72,000 Harley-Davidson motorcycles, which compares to 67,761 units in the first quarter of 2007.

Commenting on the long-term sustainability and the economy, Ziemer continued,

Looking ahead, we will continue to manage the Company to generate long-term sustainable shareholder value while protecting the brand. We expect the U.S. economy to continue to be very challenging in 2008, and we will closely monitor the retail environment and regularly assess our wholesale shipments throughout the year.

Exhibits 7 and **8** present data on divisional revenues, worldwide motorcycle shipments, income, and registrations, both worldwide and U.S, and Europe for 2007.

EXHIBIT 7
Selected
United States
and World Financial
and Sales
Information:
Harley-Davidson Inc.

A. Motor Company Revenue, 2007
(Dollar amounts in millions)

Harley-Davidson Motorcycles	$4,446.8
Parts and Accessories	868.3
General Merchandise	305.4
Buell Motorcycles	100.5
Other	6.0
Total	$5,727.0

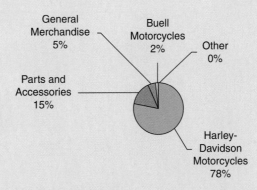

General Merchandise 5%

Buell Motorcycles 2%

Other 0%

Parts and Accessories 15%

Harley-Davidson Motorcycles 78%

B. Worldwide Motorcycle Shipments
(Units in thousands)

	2003	2004	2005	2006	2007
Exports	47.7	50.8	52.5	75.8	89.1
Total Motorcycle Shipments	291.1	317.3	329.0	349.2	330.6
Export Percentage	16.4%	16.0%	16.0%	21.7%	26.9%

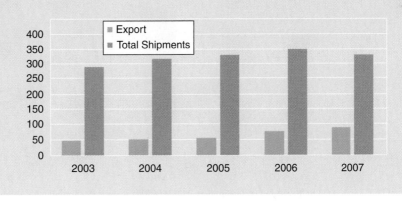

(Continued)

EXHIBIT 7
(Continued)

C. Worldwide Parts & Accessories and General Merchandise Revenue
(Dollar amounts in millions)

	2003	2004	2005	2006	2007
General Merchandise	211.4	223.7	247.9	277.5	305.4
Parts and Accessories	712.8	781.6	815.7	862.3	868.3

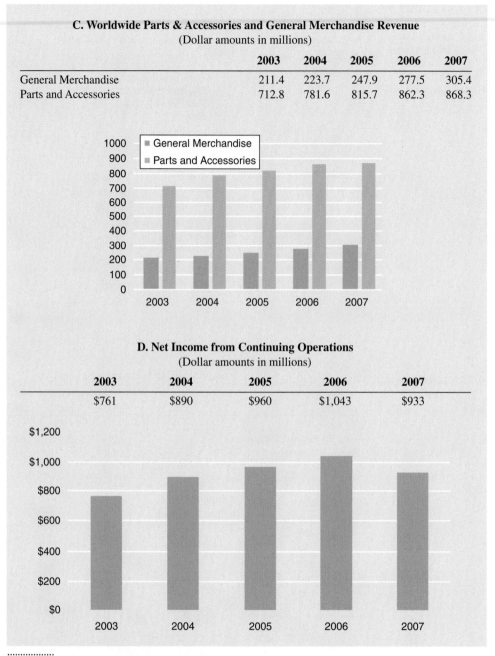

D. Net Income from Continuing Operations
(Dollar amounts in millions)

2003	2004	2005	2006	2007
$761	$890	$960	$1,043	$933

SOURCE: *Harley-Davidson, Inc., 2007 and 2005 Annual Report and 10-K.*

EXHIBIT 8
World Registrations: Harley-Davidson Inc.

A. North American 651+ cc Motorcycle Registrations
(Units in thousands)

	1997	1998	1999	2000	2001	2002	2003	2004	2005	2006	2007
Total Industry	206.1	246.2	297.9	365.4	422.8	475.0	495.4	530.8	553.5	543.0	516.1
Harley-Davidson	99.3	116.1	142.0	163.1	185.6	220.1	238.2	255.8	264.7	267.9	251.4
Harley-Davidson Market Share	48.2%	47.2%	47.7%	44.6%	43.9%	46.3%	48.1%	48.2%	47.8%	49.3%	48.2%

1997–2007 North American 651+ cc Motorcycle Registrations

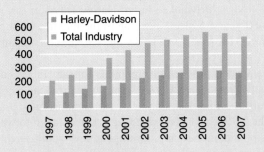

B. European 651+ cc Motorcycle Registrations

	1997	1998	1999	2000	2001	2002	2003	2004	2005	2006	2007
Total Industry	250.3	270.2	306.7	293.4	293.6	331.8	323.1	336.2	332.8	376.8	403.0
Harley-Davidson	15.1	15.7	17.8	19.9	19.6	23.5	26.3	25.9	29.7	34.3	38.7
Harley-Davidson Market Share	6.0%	5.8%	5.8%	6.8%	6.7%	7.1%	8.2%	7.7%	8.9%	9.1%	9.6%

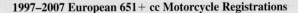

1997–2007 European 651+ cc Motorcycle Registrations

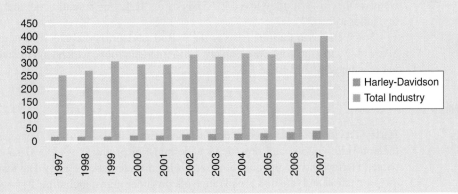

SOURCE: *Harley-Davidson, Inc., 2007 Annual Report, p. 40.*

New Millennium Bikes: The Buell and the V-Rod

Harley's new V-Rod was introduced in the Los Angeles Convention Center on July 12, 2001. More than 4,000 packed into the center for the company's long-awaited announcement. The cavernous room went black. The engines roared in the darkness. Spotlights clicked on and followed two glinting new hot-rods as they roared onto center stage.[18]

Harley-Davidson deviated from its traditional approach to styling, with the introduction of the V-Rod motorcycle. The new, liquid cooled V-Rod, inspired by Harley-Davidson's drag racing heritage, combines the characteristics of a performance motorcycle with the styling of a custom.[19] Liquid cooling allows riders to rev a little higher and hotter in each gear, boosting acceleration. It doesn't sound like a big deal, but it was a giant step for a company so stubbornly conservative that it has made only air-cooled engines for 100 years; its designers just couldn't bear the idea of placing a radiator on the front of the bike.[20]

The V-Rod is Milwaukee-based Harley-Davison Inc.'s first truly new motorcycle in more than 50 years. A sleek machine in the making for more than six years, the V-Rod is designed more for speed and handling, unlike the company's immensely popular touring bikes.[21]

As it ramped up production, premiums on many models disappeared. Chief Executive Officer James L. Ziemer says Harley wants to "narrow the gap" between supply and demand in order to curb the long-standing—but fast-diminishing—practice of selling bikes at a premium.[22] The V-Rod's $17,000 price tag has also failed to win younger buyers.[23] To that end, Harley has poured money into developing new, youth-oriented models. The V-Rod—a low-slung, high-powered number known formally as a sport performance vehicle and colloquially as a crotch rocket—was meant for hard-charging youths. Harley has also tried to go young with the Buell Firebolt ($10,000), its answer to Japanese sport bikes, and the Buell Blast ($4,400), a starter motorcycle.

At the Detroit Harley-Davidson/Buell dealership in Center Line, owner Jim Loduca commented: "This is the first time in 10 years that I've actually had product on the floor available, but our sales are also up by 14 percent this year. The company has watched this demand curve very carefully. They are simply riding the wave. They know full well that it would be catastrophic to saturate the market." He is also encouraged by Harley's biggest product departure in recent decades—the V-Rod muscle bike.[24]

Clay Wilwert, whose family has owned a dealership in Dubuque since 1959, "But guess what, as they rode it, they loved it." They said, "Hey, this is really cool that it doesn't shake my hands asleep."[25]

Some Harley traditionalists say the V-Rod, styled to compete with super-fast European bikes, strays too far from the company's all-American roots, which tend to favor heavier cruising machines.[26]

Licensing[27]

Harley-Davidson endeavored to create an awareness of the "Harley-Davidson" brand among the non-riding public and provides a wide range of product for enthusiasts by licensing the name "Harley-Davidson" and numerous related trademarks. Harley-Davidson had licensed the production and sale of a broad range of consumer items, including T-shirts, jewelry, small leather goods, toys, and numerous other products (licensed products). Although the majority of licensing activity occurs in the United States, Harley-Davidson continues to expand these activities in international markets. Royalty revenues from licensing, included in Motorcycles segment net revenue, were approximately $46 million, $45.5 million, and $43 million in 2007, 2006, and 2005, respectively.

Marketing and Distribution[28]

Marketing efforts are divided among dealer promotions, customer events, magazine and direct mail advertising, public relations, cooperative programs with Harley-Davidson/Buell dealers, and national television advertising. Harley-Davidson also sponsors racing activities and special promotional events and participates in all major motorcycle consumer shows and rallies.

E-Commerce[29]

Since 2001, Harley-Davidson utilized a highly interactive Web site at www.harley-davidson.com. Their model is unique in the industry in that, while the online catalog is viewed from the Harley-Davidson Web site, orders are actually distributed to the participating authorized Harley-Davidson dealer that the customer selects. In turn, those dealers fill the order and handle any after-sale services that the customer may require. In addition to purchasing, customers actively browse the site, create and share product wish lists, and utilize the dealer locator.

Harley-Davidson Customer Base

Harley-Davidson's customers are not what some people might expect. They see the rough and tumble riders and do not expect that a good proportion of Harley-Davidson riders are white-collar workers and executives taking the weekend relaxation on their bike. Selected quotes from customers follow:

- "It's about an image—freedom of the road, hop on your bike and go, independent living, the loosing of the chains," said Dave Sarnowski, a teacher and Harley rider from La Farge, Wisconsin.[30]
- "The Harley people I know go to church, have jobs, shop at the mall, just like everyone else," says Angie Robison, 68, of Daytona Beach, who helps her husband, Joe, run a motorcycle repair shop and Harley memorabilia/accessories store. "I can wear my silks over here and my leathers over there, and I'm still the same person."[31]
- "I worked at a computer all day for the city, and for me it's pure relaxation. I wear the leathers because they're protective."[32]
- "I love the feeling of being out on that bike on the roads—especially in the mountains. You just can't beat it, the feeling you get," says Rob Barnett, Harley-Davidson owner.
- "In general, the motorcycle industry has increased for 12 years straight, and we're expecting another increase—especially in Harley-Davidson sales—this year," says Don Brown, motorcycle analyst with DJB Associates.[33]
- "A Harley is a rolling sculpture. A piece of artwork," commented Matt Chase, sales manager of N.F. Sheldon, Harley store. "You work all week, then on the weekends you put on leathers and everyone's equal . . . all the same, brothers and sisters."[34]

Recession Resistance?

Ziemer recognized that 2008 would be a challenging year for Harley-Davidson given the pending recession. How will this affect Harley-Davidson? Harley has seen tremendous sales and stock price growth since 1986 until a slowdown in 2007. Some analysts question how Harley-Davidson will be hit in a deep recession. "For years, Harley-Davidson and the analysts that covered the company have reported that the business is recession-resistant. Given the recent changes in the economic and political landscape, this assertion is being put to the

EXHIBIT 9
Motorcycle Unit
Shipments
and Net Sales:
Harley-Davidson Inc.

	2007	2006	Increase (Decrease)	Percentage Change
Motorcycle Unit Shipments				
Touring motorcycle units	114,076	123,444	(9,368)	(11.6%)
Custom motorcycle units	144,507	161,195	(16,688)	(10.4%)
Sportster motorcycle units	72,036	64,557	7,479	11.6%
Harley-Davidson® motorcycle units	330,619	349,196	(18,577)	(5.3%)
Buell® motorcycle units	11,513	12,460	(947)	(7.6%)
Total motorcycle units	342,132	361,656	$(19,524)	(5.7%)
Net Sales ($ thousands)				
Harley-Davidson motorcycles	$4,446.6	$4,553.6	(107.0)	(2.3%)
Buell motorcycles	100.5	102.2	(1.7)	(1.7%)
Total motorcycles	$4,547.1	$4,655.8	(108.7)	(2.3%)
Parts and Accessories	$868.3	$862.3	6.0	0.7%
General Merchandise	305.4	277.5	27.9	10.1%
Other	6.0	5.1	0.9	17.7%
Total Motorcycles and Related Parts	$5,726.8	$5,800.7	$(73.9)	(1.3%)

SOURCE: *Harley-Davidson 2007 10-K, page 34.*

test, and from what we can tell, is ringing true. According the CEO Jim Ziemer, "motorcycles, the critics say, are easily deferred purchases. We always said we feel we are recession-resistant, not recession-proof."[35] (See **Exhibit 9**).

Competition [36]

The heavyweight (651+cc) motorcycle market is highly competitive. Major competitors are based outside the United States and generally have more financial and marketing resources. They also have larger worldwide sales volumes and are more diversified. In addition to these larger, established competitors, a growing segment of competition has emerged in the United States. The new U.S. competitors generally offer heavyweight motorcycles with traditional styling that compete directly with many of the Harley-Davidson's products. These competitors currently have production and sales volumes that are lower than the Harley-Davidson's and did not hold a significant market share. (See **Exhibits 10, 11, and 12**.)

Competition in the heavyweight motorcycle market is based upon a number of factors, including price, quality, reliability, styling, product features, customer preference, and warranties. Harley-Davidson emphasizes quality, reliability, and styling in its products and offers a one-year warranty for its motorcycles. Management regards its support of the motorcycling lifestyle in the form of events, rides, rallies, H.O.G., and its financing through HDFS, as a competitive advantage. In general, resale prices for used Harley-Davidson motorcycles, as a percentage of prices when new, are significantly higher than resale prices for used motorcycles of competitors.

Domestically, Harley-Davidson competes most heavily in the touring and custom segments of the heavyweight motorcycle market, which together accounted for 80%, 79%, and 80% of total heavyweight retail unit sales in the United States during 2007, 2006, and 2005, respectively. The custom and touring motorcycles are generally the most expensive vehicles in the market and the most profitable. During 2007, the heavyweight segment including standard, performance, touring, and custom motorcycles, represented approximately 54% of the total U.S. motorcycle market in terms of new units registered.

EXHIBIT 10
651+cc Motorcycle Market Regional Comparison by Segment: Harley Davidson Inc.

	2006	2005	2004	2003	2002
United States					
Custom	47.4	50.9	52.1	61.8	60.3
Touring	35.4	32.8	31.1	20.4	20.2
Performance	15.1	14.0	13.6	15.1	17.3
Standard	2.1	2.3	3.2	2.7	2.2
Total	100.1	100.0	100.0	100.0	100.0
	2006	**2005**	**2004**	**2003**	**2002**
Europe					
Custom	13.4	13.0	13.8	14.3	13.8
Touring	26.0	25.8	27.9	4.7	4.8
Performance	41.4	40.9	39.8	57.8	61.2
Standard	19.2	20.3	18.5	23.2	20.2
Total	100.1	100.0	100.0	100.0	100.0
	2006	**2005**	**2004**	**2003**	**2002**
Asia/Pacific					
Custom	30.0	30.3	29.6	32.7	26.2
Touring	9.3	9.2	9.1	9.8	8.2
Performance	47.7	47.8	54.0	53.3	60.0
Standard	13.3	12.8	7.3	4.2	5.1
Total	100.0	101.1	100.0	100.0	101.1

Notes:

Custom: Characterized by "American Styling." These bikes are often personalized with accessories.

Touring: Designed for long trips with an emphasis on comfort, cargo capacity, and reliability. These bikes often have features such as two-way radio for communication with a passenger, stereos, and cruise control.

Performance: Characterized by quick acceleration, top speed, and handling. These bikes are often referred to as sports bikes.

Standard: A basic, no frills motorcycle with an emphasis on low price. The standard percentage may also include the "adventure touring" niche.

SOURCE: *Harley Davidson Fact Book, posted November 5, 2007 at http://investor.harley-davidson.com/registrations/registrations_regional.cfm.*

EXHIBIT 11
Market Share of U.S. Heavyweight Motorcycles 1 (Engine Displacement of 651+cc)[1]

	2007	2006	2005	2004	2003	2002
New U.S. Registrations (thousands of units):						
Total market new registrations	516.2	543.0	517.6	494.0	461.2	442.3
Harley-Davidson new registrations	251.4	267.9	252.9	244.5	228.4	209.3
Buell new registrations	3.7	3.8	3.6	3.6	3.5	2.9
Total Company new registrations	255.1	271.7	256.5	248.1	231.9	212.2
Percentage Market Share						
Harley-Davidson motorcycles	48.7%	49.3%	48.9%	49.5%	49.5%	47.5%
Buell motorcycles	0.7%	0.7%	0.7%	0.7%	0.8%	0.7%
Total Company	49.4%	50.0%	49.6%	50.2%	50.3%	48.2%
Honda	14.2%	15.1%	16.6%	16.4%	18.5%	20.5%
Suzuki	12.5%	12.9%	12.4%	9.4%	9.3%	10.8%
Yamaha	9.2%	8.6%	8.9%	8.7%	8.5%	8.9%
Kawasaki	7.2%	6.8%	6.5%	6.4%	6.7%	6.9%
Other	7.5%	6.0%	6.0%	5.8%	6.3%	6.6%
Total	100.0%	99.4%	100.0%	96.9%	99.6%	101.9%

Note: [1]Motorcycle registration and market share information has been derived from data published by the Motorcycle Industry Council (MIC).

SOURCE: *Harley-Davidson, Inc., Form 10-K, 2007, page 9 and Form 10-K, 2005, page 9.*

EXHIBIT 12
Motorcycle Industry
Registration
Statistics (Units):
Harley-Davidson Inc.

	2003	2000	1997	1994	1991
U.S. and Canada					
651+cc volume	495,436	366,247	205,407	150,419	100,705
H-D volume	238,243	163,984	99,298	69,529	48,260
Buell volume	3,719	4,306	1,912	194	n/a
HOG total volume	241,962	168,290	101,210	69,723	48,260
HOG market share	**48.8%**	**45.9%**	**49.3%**	**46.4%**	**47.9%**
Europe					
651+cc volume	323,083	338,921	282,378	201,904	194,700
H-D volume	26,299	23,230	17,190	14,393	10,996
Buell volume	3,106	2,045	785	n/a	n/a
HOG total volume	29,405	25,275	17,975	14,393	10,996
HOG market share	**9.1%**	**7.5%**	**6.4%**	**7.1%**	**5.6%**
Japan and Australia					
651+cc volume	58,941	62,667	58,880	39,077	26,995
H-D volume	15,195	12,213	9,686	7,588	5,261
Buell volume	989	658	426	n/a	n/a
HOG total volume	16,184	12,871	10,112	7,588	5,261
HOG market share	**27.5%**	**20.5%**	**17.2%**	**19.4%**	**19.5%**
Total for Markets Listed					
651+cc volume	877,460	767,835	546,665	391,400	322,400
H-D volume	279,737	199,427	126,174	91,510	64,517
Buell volume	7,814	7,009	3,123	194	n/a
HOG total volume	287,551	206,436	129,297	91,704	64,517
HOG market share	**32.8%**	**26.9%**	**23.7%**	**23.4%**	**20.0%**

Notes:
1. HOG is the ticker for Harley-Davidson. These are actual registrations of motorcycles. The Harley-Davidson, Inc. registrations are typically lower than actual sales due to timing differences.
2. Data provided by R. L. Polk (1994), Giral S. A., Australian Bureau of Statistics and H-D Japan. The most recent date available is for 2003.

SOURCE: *Harley Davidson Fact Book, posted November 5, 2007, at http://investor.harley-davidson.com/downloads/factsheet.pdf.*

For the last 20 years, Harley-Davidson has led the industry in domestic (United States) unit sales of heavyweight motorcycles. Its market share in the heavyweight market was 48.7% in 2007 compared to 49.3% in 2006. The next largest competitor in the domestic market had only a 14.2% market share.

Rider Training and Safety

"Increasingly, the motorcycle riders who are getting killed are in their 40s, 50s, and 60s," says Susan Ferguson, vice president for research at the Insurance Institute for Highway Safety, which did the study.[37] Riders over 40 accounted for 40% of all fatalities in 2000, up from 14% in 1990. Part of the reason for the dramatic increase in older biker's deaths is the growing number of men and women over 40 buying motorcycles, IIHS says.

In 2000, Harley-Davidson launched an instruction program called Rider's Edge, run through dealers. Rookies pay $225 or so for a 25-hour class. This training program can be credited with bringing in more first-time riders as Harley customers. Forty-five percent are women,

86% buy something, and 25% buy a Harley-Davidson or a Buell within three months. "Going into a Harley dealership can be intimidating," says Lara Lee, who runs the program. "We give them a home base and get them riding."[38]

In March 2008, Harley-Davidson announced the company was moving the Rider's Edge program into California. There was hope the program would encourage more motorcycle sales. Julie Chichlowski, the director of Rider Services stated, "One distinct advantage of the Rider's Edge New Rider Course is that feeling of being part of something bigger. Rider's Edge teaches the skills necessary to ride a motorcycle but in an environment that is pure Harley-Davidson.[39]

Motorcycle Manufacturing[40]

Harley-Davidson designed its manufacturing process to increase capacity, improve product quality, reduce costs, and increase flexibility to respond to market changes. Harley-Davidson incorporated manufacturing techniques focused on the continuous improvement of its operations designed to control costs and maintain quality. Included in these techniques were employee involvement, just-in-time inventory principles, partnering agreements with the local unions, high performance work organizations, and statistical process control, all designed to improve product quality, productivity, and asset utilization in the production of Harley-Davidson motorcycles.

Harley-Davidson uses just-in-time inventory to minimize inventories of raw materials and work in process, as well as scrap and rework costs. This system also allows quicker reaction to engineering design changes, quality improvements, and market demands.

Raw Material and Purchase Components[41]

Harley-Davidson worked hard to establish and/or reinforce long-term, mutually beneficial relationships with its suppliers. Through these collaborative relationships, it has gained access to technical and commercial resources for application directly to product design and development. Management anticipates the focus on collaboration and strong supplier manufacturing initiatives to lead to increased commitment from suppliers. This strategy has resulted in improved product quality, technical integrity, application of new features and innovations, reduced lead times for product development, and smoother/faster manufacturing ramp-up of new vehicle introductions. Harley's initiative to improve supplier productivity and component cost has been instrumental in delivering improvements in cost and in offsetting raw material price increases.

Harley-Davidson purchased all of its raw materials, principally steel and aluminum castings, forgings, sheets and bars, and certain motorcycle components, including carburetors, batteries, tires, seats, electrical components, and instruments. Given current economic conditions in certain raw material commodity markets, and pressure on certain suppliers due to difficulties in the automotive industry, Harley-Davidson monitors supply, availability, and pricing for both its suppliers and in-house operations.

Research and Development[42]

Harley-Davidson views research and development as a significant factor in its ability to lead the custom and touring motorcycling market and to develop products for the performance segment. The company's Product Development Center (PDC) brings employees from styling, purchasing, and manufacturing together with regulatory professionals and supplier representatives to create a concurrent product and process development team. Research and development expenses were $185.5 million, $177.7 million, and $178.5 million in 2007, 2006, and 2005, respectively.

Patents and Trademarks[43]

Harley-Davidson owns patents that relate to its motorcycles and related products and processes for their production. Harley-Davidson has increased its efforts to patent its technology and certain motorcycle-related designs and to enforce those patents. Management sees such actions as important as it moves forward with new products, designs, and technologies.

Trademarks are important to the Harley-Davidson's motorcycle business and licensing activities. It has a vigorous global program of trademark registration and enforcement to strengthen the value of the trademarks associated with its products and services, prevent the unauthorized use of those trademarks, and enhance its image and customer goodwill. It believes the HARLEY-DAVIDSON trademark and its Bar and Shield trademark are each highly recognizable by the public and are very valuable assets. The BUELL trademark is well known in performance motorcycle circles, as is the associated Pegasus logo. The company is making efforts to ensure that each of these brands will become better known as the Buell business expands.

Seasonality[44]

In general, Harley-Davidson has not experienced significant seasonal fluctuations in its sales. This has been primarily the result of a strong demand for the Harley-Davidson motorcycles and related products, as well as the availability of floor plan financing arrangements for its North American and European independent dealers. Floor plan financing allows dealers to build their inventory levels in anticipation of the spring and summer selling seasons. Harley-Davidson expressed its belief that efforts to increase the availability of its motorcycles has resulted in an increase in seasonality at its independent dealers. Over the last several years they have been working to increase the availability of its motorcycles at dealers to improve the customer experience.

Regulations[45]

Federal, state, and local authorities have various environmental control requirements relating to air, water, and noise pollution that affect the business and operations. Harley-Davidson endeavors to ensure that its facilities and products comply with all applicable environmental regulations and standards.

The motorcycles are subject to certification by the U.S. Environmental Protection Agency (EPA) for compliance with applicable emissions and noise standards and by the State of California Air Resources Board (CARB) with respect to CARB's more stringent emissions standards. Motorcycles sold in California are also subject to certain tailpipe and evaporative emissions standards that are unique to California. The EPA finalized a new tailpipe emissions standard for 2006 and 2010 respectively which are harmonized with the California emission standards. Additionally, Harley-Davidson motorcycles must comply with the emissions, noise, and safety standards of the European Union, Japan, and other international markets.

Harley-Davidson, as a manufacturer of motorcycle products, is subject to the National Traffic and Motor Vehicle Safety Act, which are administered by the National Highway Traffic Safety Administration (NHTSA). They have certified to NHTSA that their motorcycle products comply fully with all applicable federal motor vehicle safety standards and related regulations. Harley-Davidson has, from time to time, initiated certain voluntary recalls. During the last three years, Harley-Davidson initiated 15 voluntary recalls at a total cost of $10.8 million.

Employees[46]

As of December 31, 2007, the Motorcycles segment had approximately 9,000 employees. Unionized employees at the motorcycle manufacturing and distribution facilities in Wauwatosa, Menomonee Falls, Franklin, and Tomahawk, Wisconsin, and Kansas City, Missouri, are represented principally by the Paper Allied-Industrial Chemical and Energy Workers International Union (PACE) of the AFL-CIO, as well as the International Association of Machinist and Aerospace Workers (IAM). Production workers at the motorcycle manufacturing facility in York, Pennsylvania, are represented principally by the IAM. The collective bargaining agreement with the Pennsylvania-IAM will expire on February 2, 2010, the collective bargaining agreement with the Kansas City-USW and IAM will expire on July 30, 2012, and the collective bargaining agreement with the Wisconsin-USW and IAM will expire on March 31, 2008.

Approximately 50% of Harley-Davidson's 9,000 employees ride a Harley-Davidson. All employees, including Ziemer and Bluestein, go through a dealer to purchase their bike. This way, the employees see the customer experience firsthand.

Properties[47]

The following is a summary of the principal operating properties of Harley-Davidson as of December 31, 2007. Seven facilities that perform manufacturing operations: Wauwatosa and Menomonee Falls, Wisconsin, suburbs of Milwaukee (motorcycle powertrain production); Tomahawk, Wisconsin (fiberglass parts production and painting); York, Pennsylvania (motorcycle parts fabrication, painting and big-twin assembly); Kansas City, Missouri (Sportster assembly); East Troy, Wisconsin (Buell motorcycles assembly); Manaus, Brazil (assembly of select models for Brazilian market). (See **Exhibit 13**.)

Financial Services Segment[48]

The Financial Services segment has office facilities in Carson City, Nevada. Wholesale, insurance, and retail operations are in Plano, Texas, and European wholesale operations in Oxford, England. Ownership and lease structures are outlined in **Exhibit 13**.

Harley-Davidson and Buell[49]

Harley-Davidson Financial Services HDFS, operating under the trade name Harley-Davidson Credit, provides wholesale financial services to Harley-Davidson and Buell dealers and retail financing to consumers. HDFS, operating under the trade name Harley-Davidson Insurance, is an agent for the sale of motorcycle insurance policies and also sells extended service warranty agreements, gap contracts, and debt protection products.

Wholesale financial services include floor plan and open account financing of motorcycles and motorcycle parts and accessories, real estate loans, computer loans, and showroom remodeling loans. HDFS offers wholesale financial services to Harley-Davidson dealers in the United States, Canada, and Europe and during 2007; approximately 96% of such dealers utilized those services. The wholesale finance operations of HDFS are located in Plano, Texas, and Oxford, England.

Retail financial services include installment lending for new and used Harley-Davidson and Buell motorcycles. HDFS' retail financial services are available through most Harley-Davidson and Buell dealers in the United States and Canada. HDFS' retail finance operations are located in Carson City, Nevada, and Plano, Texas.

EXHIBIT 13
Principal Operating Facilities: Harley Davidson Inc.

Type of Facility	Location	Square Feet	Status
Corporate Office	Milwaukee, WI	515,000	Owned
Warehouse	Milwaukee, WI	24,000	Lease expiring 2009
Airplane Hanger	Milwaukee, WI	14,600	Owned
Manufacturing	Wauwatosa, WI	430,000	Owned
Product Development Center	Wauwatosa, WI	409,000	Owned
Distribution Center	Franklin, WI	250,000	Owned
Manufacturing	Menomonee Falls, WI	868,000	Owned
Product Development and Office	East Troy, WI	58,990	Lease expiring 2011
Manufacturing	East Troy, WI	40,000	Lease expiring 2011
Manufacturing	Tomahawk, WI	211,000	Owned
Office	Ann Arbor, MI	3,400	Lease expiring 2009
Office	Cleveland, OH	23,000	Lease expiring 2013
Manufacturing and Materials Velocity Center	Kansas City, MO	450,000	Owned
Materials Velocity Center	Manchester, PA	212,000	Owned
Manufacturing	York, PA	1,321,000	Owned
Motorcycle Testing	Talladega, AL	35,000	Lease expiring 2009
Motorcycle Testing	Naples, FL	82,000	Owned
Motorcycle Testing	Mesa, AZ	29,000	Lease expiring 2009
Office and Training Facility	Monterrey, Mexico	1,100	Lease expiring 2008
Office	Morfelden-Waldorf, Germany	22,000	Lease expiring 2008
Office and Warehouse	Oxford, England	21,000	Lease expiring 2017
Office	Liederdorp, The Netherlands	9,000	Lease expiring 2010
Office	Creteil, France	8,450	Lease expiring 2016
Office and Warehouse	Arese, Italy	17,000	Lease expiring 2009
Office	Zurich, Switzerland	2,000	Lease expiring 2009
Office	Sant Cugat, Spain	3,400	Lease expiring 2017
Warehouse	Yokohama, Japan	15,000	Lease expiring 2008
Office	Tokyo, Japan	14,000	Lease expiring 2008
Manufacturing	Adelaide, Australia	485,000	Lease expiring 2011
Office	Sidney, Australia	1,100	Lease expiring 2011
Office	Shanghai, China	1,700	Lease expiring 2008
Manufacturing and Office	Manaus, Brazil	30,000	Lease expiring 2009
Office	Chicaog, IL	26,000	Lease expiring 2022
Office	Plano, TX	61,500	Lease expiring 2014
Office	Carson City, NV	100,000	Owned
Storage	Carson City, NV	1,600	Lease expiring 2008
Office	Oxford, England	6,000	Lease expiring 2017

SOURCE: *Harley-Davidson, Inc., 2007 Form 10-K, p. 20.*

Motorcycle insurance, extended service contracts, gap coverage, and debt protection products are available through most Harley-Davidson and Buell dealers in the United States and Canada. Motorcycle insurance is also marketed on a direct basis to motorcycle riders.

Funding[50]

HDFS is financed by operating cash flow, advances, and loans from Harley-Davidson, asset-backed securitizations, commercial paper, revolving credit facilities, senior subordinated debt, and redeemable preferred stock. HDFS also retains an interest in the excess cash flows from receivables and recognizes income on this retained interest. After the sale, HDFS performs billing and portfolio management services for these loans and receives a servicing fee for providing these services.

Competition[51]

The ability to offer a package of wholesale and retail financial services is a significant competitive advantage for HDFS. Competitors compete for business based largely on price and, to a lesser extent, service. HDFS competes based on convenience, service, brand association, strong dealer relations, industry experience, terms, and price.

During 2007, HDFS financed 55% of the new Harley-Davidson motorcycles retailed by independent dealers in the United States, as compared to 48% in 2006. Competitors for retail motorcycle finance business are primarily banks, credit unions, other financial institutions. In the motorcycle insurance business, competition primarily comes from national insurance companies and from insurance agencies serving local or regional markets. For insurance-related products such as extended service warranty agreements, HDFS faces competition from certain regional and national industry participants.

Seasonality[52]

In the northern United States and Canada, motorcycles are primarily used during warmer months, generally March through August. Accordingly, HDFS experiences significant seasonal variations. Retail customers typically do not buy motorcycles until they can ride them. From mid-March through August, retail financing volume increases and wholesale financing volume decreases as dealers deplete their inventories. From September through mid-March, there is a decrease in retail financing volume while dealer inventories build and turn over more slowly, substantially increasing wholesale financing volume.

Employees

At the end of 2007, the Financial Services segment had 755 employees, none of which were unionized.

Corporate Financial and Stock Price Performance

It appeared as though the weakened U.S. economy would stifle growth for Harley-Davidson. (**Exhibits 14 and 15** provide the company's income statement and balance sheet for the most recent five years. **Exhibit 16** provides a geographic breakdown of sales.) Since Harley went public, its shares have risen over 23,000% (through the end of 2006) but declined in 2007. As of February 18, 2008, there were 90,748 shareholders of record of Harley-Davidson common stock (**Exhibit 17** provides a comparison of Harley-Davidson stock and the Standard and Poor's 500 since the 1986 initial public offering.) What does the future hold for Harley-Davidson? While trading near its five-year low, analysts considered two aspects of the Harley-Davidson product.

"It's an upper-middle-class toy," says Chad Hudson of the Prudent Bear fund, one of a number of prominent short-sellers convinced that Harley will skid. "As people run out of disposable income, that's going to hurt."[53]

"The risk is that retail trends may continue to weaken at Harley-Davidson, causing inventories to build. Harley-Davidson may then lower its production numbers," says analyst Gregory Badishkanian.[54]

EXHIBIT 14
Balance Sheet 2003–2007: Harley-Davidson Inc. (Dollar amounts in thousands)

Year Ending December 31	2007	2006	2005	2004	2003
Assets					
Current Assets:					
Cash and cash equivalents	$402,854	$238,397	$140,975	$275,159	$329,329
Marketable securities	2,475	658,133	905,197	1,336,909	993,331
Account receivable, net	181,217	143,049	122,087	121,333	112,406
Current portion of finance receivables, net	2,356,563	2,101,366	0	1,207,124	1,001,990
Inventories	349,697	287,798	221,418	226,893	207,726
Deferred income taxes	103,278	73,389	61,285	60,517	51,156
Prepaid expenses and other current assets	71,230	48,501	52,509	38,337	33,189
Total Current Assets	$3,467,314	$3,550,633	$1,503,471	$3,266,272	$2,729,127
Finance Receivables, net	845,044	725,957	600,831	488,262	735,859
Property, plant and equipment, net	1,060,590	1,024,469	1,011,612	1,024,665	1,046,310
Goodwill, net	61,401	58,800	56,563	59,456	53,678
Other Assets	222,257	172,291	72,801	94,402	358,114
Total Assets	$5,656,606	$5,532,150	$4,887,044	$4,933,057	$4,923,088
Liabilities & Shareholder's Equity					
Current Liabilities:					
Accounts Payable	$300,188	$283,477	$270,614	$244,202	$223,902
Accrued expenses and other liabilities	484,936	479,709	397,525	433,053	407,566
Current portion of finance debt	1,119,955	832,491	204,973	495,441	324,305
Total Current Liabilities	$1,905,079	$1,595,677	$873,112	$1,172,696	$955,773
Finance Debt	980,000	870,000	1,000,000	800,000	670,000
Other long-term liabilities	151,954	60,694	82,281	90,864	86,337
Postretirement healthcare benefits	192,531	201,126	0	149,848	127,444
Pension Liability	51,551	47,916	-	-	-
Deferred income taxes	-	-	155,236	51,432	125,842
Total Liabilities	$3,281,115	$2,775,413	$2,110,629	$2,264,840	$1,965,396
Shareholder's Equity:					
Common Stock	3,352	3,343	$3,310	$3,300	$3,266
Additional PIC	812,224	766,382	596,239	533,068	419,455
Retained Earnings	6,117,567	5,460,629	4,630,390	3,844,571	3,074,037
Accumulated other comprehensive income	(137,258)	(206,662)	58,653	(12,096)	47,174
Less:					
Treasury Stock	(4,420,394)	(3,266,955)	(2,204,987)	(1,150,372)	(586,240)
Total Shareholder's Equity	$2,375,491	$2,756,737	$3,083,605	$3,218,471	$2,957,692
Total Liabilities and Shareholder's Equity	$5,656,606	$5,532,150	$5,255,209	$5,483,293	$4,923,088

SOURCE: *Harley-Davidson, Inc., 2007 Form 10-K, page 60 and 2005 Form 10-K, page 53.*

How does Harley-Davidson move forward and continue to grow at the pace it has seen in the past? Is this a reasonable long-term growth rate? How does it maintain interest in the 2008 model bikes? How does it grapple with the aging baby boomers, who are generally the individuals who can afford a Harley-Davidson motorcycle? These were but a few of the questions in the minds of senior management as they did strategic planning.

EXHIBIT 15
Income Statement 2003–2007: Harley-Davidson Inc. (Dollar amounts in thousands)

Year Ending December 31,	2007	2006	2005	2004	2003
Net Sales	$5,726,848	$5,800,686	$5,342,214	$5,015,190	$4,624,274
COGS	3,612,748	3,567,839	3,301,715	3,115,655	2,958,708
Gross Profit	2,114,100	2,232,847	$2,040,499	$1,899,535	$1,665,566
Financial Services Income	416,196	384,891	331,618	305,263	279,459
Financial Services Interest and Operating Expense	204,027	174,167	139,998	116,662	111,586
Operating Income from Financial Services	212,169	210,724	191,620	188,600	167,873
Selling, Admin, and Engineering Expense	900,708	846,418	(762,108)	(726,644)	(684,175)
Income from Operations	1,425,561	1,597,153	$1,470,011	$1,362,491	$1,149,264
Investment Income, net	22,258	27,087	22,797	23,101	23,088
Other, net	-	-	(5,049)	(5,106)	(6,317)
Income before Provision for Income Taxes	1,447,819	1,624,240	$1,487,759	$1,380,486	$1,166,035
Provision for Income Taxes	513,976	581,087	528,155	489,720	405,107
Net Income	$933,843	$1,043,153	$959,604	$890,766	$760,928

SOURCE: *Harley-Davidson, Inc., 2007 Form 10-K, page 31, 2005 Form 10-K, page 52.*

EXHIBIT 16
Geographic Information: Harley-Davidson Inc. (Dollar amount in thousands)

	2007	2006	2005	2004	2003
Net Revenue (1):					
United States	$4,208,016	$4,618,997	$4,304,865	$4,097,882	$3,807,707
Europe	790,150	621,069	530,124	477,962	419,052
Japan	229,759	207,884	192,268	192,720	173,547
Canada	230,230	188,993	143,204	136,721	134,319
Australia	162,689	82,792	—	—	—
Other foreign countries	106,004	80,951	171,753	109,905	89,649
Total	$5,726,848	$5,800,686	5,342,214	5,015,190	$4,624,274
Financial Services Income (1)					
United States	$381,001	$356,539	308,341	283,837	260,551
Europe	13,638	11,034	9,135	9,538	8,834
Canada	21,557	17,318	14,142	11,887	10,074
Total	$416,196	$384,891	331,618	305,262	279,459
Long-lived assets (2):					
United States	$1,173,169	$1,139,846	1,450,278	1,246,808	$1,400,772
Other foreign countries	66,988	56,214	38,002	44,300	41,804
Total	$1,240,157	$1,196,060	1,488,280	1,291,108	$1,442,576

Notes:
1. Net revenue and income is attributed to geographic regions based on location of customer.
2. Long-lived assets include all long-term assets except those specifically excluded under SFAS Number 131, such as deferred income taxes and finance receivables.

SOURCE: *Harley-Davidson 2007 Form 10-K, page 96, and 2005 Form 10-K, page 70.*

EXHIBIT 17

Year-End Market Value of $100 invested on December 31, 1986 through December 31, 2006: Harley-Davidson vs. SP 500

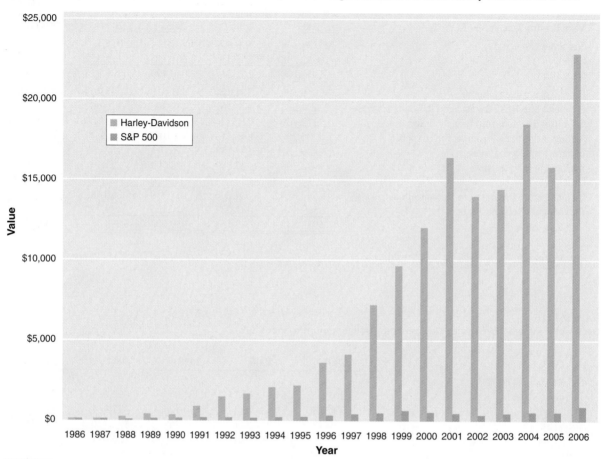

SOURCE: *http://investor.harley-davidson.com/HDvsSP500.cfm.*

NOTES

1. Harley Davidson Annual Report, 2002, back cover.

2. Nakashima, Ryan, "Potholes Ahead for Harley's New Top Hog," Associated Press Financial Wire, April 13, 2005.

3. Thomas L. Wheelen, Kathryn E. Wheelen, Thomas L. Wheelen II, and Richard D. Wheelen, "Harley-Davidson: The 95th Anniversary," Case 16, *Strategic Management and Business Policy*, 8th Ed., Prentice Hall/ Pearson Education, Inc., Upper Saddle River, NJ, 2002.

4. Jonathan Fahey, "Love into Money," *Forbes*, January 7, 2002, p. 60–65.

5. Harley-Davidson Annual Reports, 2007, 2005, 2003, 2001, 1999, 1997, 1995.

6. Missy Sullivan. "High-Octane Hog," *Forbes*, September 10, 2002, pp. 8–10. The preceding two paragraphs were directly quoted with minor editing.

7. "A Harley Takes an Engine from Porsche" *New York Times*, May 26, 2002. Accessed at http://www.nytimes.com. The preceding paragraph was directly quoted with minor editing.

8. James C. Ziemer, Letter to the Shareholders, Harley-Davidson 2005 Annual Report.

9. James C. Ziemer, Letter to the Shareholders, Harley-Davidson 2005 Annual Report.

10. Lustgarten, Abrahm, "The List of Industry Champs," *Fortune*, March 7, 2005. http://money.cnn.com/magazines/fortune/fortune_archive/2005/03/07/8253449/index.htm

11. John Helyar, "Will Harley-Davidson Hit the Wall?" *Fortune*, August 12, 2002, pp. 120–124.

12. Company press release, June 1, 2006, Harley-Davidson Kicks Off Construction of Its Museum.

13. Harley-Davidson, 2007 10-K. The following section was directly quoted with minor editing, pages 6–8.

14. Jonathan Fahey, "Love into Money," *Forbes*, January 7, 2002, pp. 60–65.

15. Discover Today's Motorcycling—Press Release "Rockefeller Center Motorcycle Show Opens with "Today Show" segment and Giant Preview Party, April 6, 2002.

16. Harley-Davidson and *Jane* magazine roll out contest to honor women with an unquenchable Spirit of Freedom, Market Wire, June 7, 2005.

17. Harley-Davidson Reports Fourth Quarter and Full Year Results for 2007. January 25, 2008. www.harley-davidson.com. Much of this section was directly quoted from President Ziemer's comments with minor editing.

18. Missy Sullivan, "High-Octane Hog," *Forbes*, September 10, 2002, pp. 8–10.

19. Harley-Davidson 10-K, 2005.

20. Jonathan Fahey, "Love into Money," *Forbes*, January 7, 2002, pp. 60–65.

21. Rich Rovito, "No Revving Needed for Sales of Harley's V-Rod Motorcycle," *The Business Journal Serving Greater Milwaukee*, January 14, 2002. Accessed at http://milwaukee.bizjournals.com/milwaukee/stories/2002/01/14/story8.html

22. Joseph Weber, "Harley Investors May Get a Wobbly Ride," *Business Week*, February 11, 2002, p. 65.

23. The Business Week 50 Ranking, *Business Week*, Spring 2002, p. 54.

24. James V. Higgins, "All Hail, Harley-Davidson" *The Detroit News*, February 22, 2002. Accessed at http://detnews.com/2002.

25. Jonathan Fahey, "Love into Money," *Forbes*, January 7, 2002, pp. 60–65.

26. Jerry Shiver, "Richer, Older Harley Riders 'Like Everyone Else,'" *USA Today*, March 8, 2002, pp. 1A–2A.

27. Harley-Davidson, 2007 10-K. The following paragraph was directly quoted with minor editing.

28. Harley-Davidson, 2007 10-K. The following two paragraphs were directly quoted with minor editing.

29. Harley-Davidson, 2007 10-K. The paragraph was directly quoted with minor editing.

30. "Harley Roars into Its Second Century," *The Tribune*, Ames Iowa, July 26, 2002, p. A2.

31. Jerry Shiver, "Richer, Older Harley Riders 'Like Everyone Else,'" *USA Today*, March 8, 2002, pp. 1A–2A.

32. Jerry Shiver, "Richer, Older Harley Riders 'Like Everyone Else,'" *USA Today*, March 8, 2002, pp. 1A–2A.

33. Ridley, Amanda, Spartanburg, S.C., "Harley-Davidson dealer moving to expanded showroom," *Herald-Journal*, July 11, 2004.

34. Pisinski, Tonya M., "Me and my Harley: Hawg riders are downright passionate about their bike riding and hitting the trail," *Worcester Telegram and Gazette*, May 25, 2005.

35. David Wells, "Lehman's Kantor Bets on Harley-Davidson: Call of Day," *Bloomberg*, November 14, 2001.

36. Harley-Davidson, Form 10-K, 2007. The following four paragraphs were directly quoted with minor editing.

37. Earle Eldrige, "More Over-40 Motorcyclists Die in Crashes" *USA Today*, January 10, 2002, p. 1B.

38. Jonathan Fahey, "Love into Money," *Forbes*, January 7, 2002, pp. 60–65.

39. "Rider's Edge, the Harley-Davidson Academy of Motorcycling, moves into California," press release, March 11, 2008, www.harley-davidson.com.

40. Harley-Davidson, Form 10-K, 2007. The following paragraph was directly quoted with minor editing.

41. Harley-Davidson, Form 10-K, 2007. The following paragraph was directly quoted with minor editing.

42. Harley-Davidson, Form 10-K, 2007. The following paragraph was directly quoted with minor editing.

43. Harley-Davidson, Form 10-K, 2007. The first three paragraphs were directly quoted with minor editing.

44. Harley-Davidson, Form 10-K, 2007. The first paragraph was directly quoted with minor editing.

45. Harley-Davidson, Form 10-K, 2007. The first paragraph was directly quoted with minor editing.

46. Harley-Davidson, Form 10-K, 2007. The first paragraph was directly quoted with minor editing.

47. Harley-Davidson, Form 10-K, 2007, the following paragraph was directly quoted with minor editing.

48. Harley-Davidson, Form 10-K, 2007, the following paragraph was directly quoted with minor editing.

49. Harley-Davidson, Form 10-K, 2007, the following three paragraphs were directly quoted with minor editing.

50. Harley-Davidson, Form 10-K, 2007, the following paragraph was directly quoted with minor editing.

51. Harley-Davidson, Form 10-K, 2007, the following two paragraphs were directly quoted with minor editing.

52. Harley-Davidson, Form 10-K, 2007, the following paragraph was directly quoted with minor editing.

53. John Helyar, "Will Harley-Davidson hit the Wall?" *Fortune*, August 12, 2002, pp. 120–124.

54. "Harley-Davidson Cut From Citi List," Associated Press, March 14, 2008.

CASE **17**

JetBlue Airways:

GROWING PAINS

S. S. George and Shirisha Regani

"We don't spend tens of millions of dollars telling people how cool we are. We put low fares out there and let them tell us."
DAVID NEELEMAN, THE FOUNDER AND THEN CEO OF JETBLUE, IN 2001[1]

"I do think they [JetBlue] had some growing pains. They were growing so fast they didn't have systems and redundancies in place."
MICHAEL MAGIERA, MANAGING DIRECTOR AT MANNING & NAPIER, A MONEY MANAGEMENT FIRM THAT OWNED JETBLUE STOCK, IN 2007[2]

A Change of Guard at JetBlue

IN MAY 2007, JETBLUE AIRWAYS INC. (JETBLUE), a low-cost carrier (LCC) based in New York, announced a new leadership structure for the company. David Barger (Barger), president and chief operating officer (COO) of the airline, replaced David Neeleman (Neeleman) as CEO. Neeleman, who founded JetBlue in 1999, had been its CEO ever since. Under the new leadership structure, Neeleman was designated as the non-executive chairman of the board. Russell Chew, a former Federal Aviation Administration (FAA)[3] executive, took over as the COO; Barger retained his position as the president of the company.

Neeleman said at that time that the board's suggestion that he step down had nothing to do with the service breakdown that JetBlue had experienced in February 2007, when the northeast region of the United States had been hit by a severe snowstorm. The airline's slow reaction to the adverse weather had left thousands of passengers stranded at airports. In addition to having serious financial repercussions, this fiasco harmed JetBlue's image as a customer-friendly airline and tarnished its reliability record.

Analysts greeted the leadership change positively. For several years after it was set up, Jet-Blue had been one of the most successful airlines in the United States, rivaling Southwest Airlines (Southwest)[4] in profitability and growth. However, it began facing various problems, both internal and external, in 2005–2006. Several analysts were of the opinion that JetBlue's growth in its early years had been too fast and unsustainable in the longer term, and that it was because of this that things started to come undone at the airline when the business environment changed.

Background

Business plans for setting up JetBlue were developed by Neeleman, along with lawyer Tom Kelly, in 1998. Neeleman raised $160 million[5] in capital from top investors such as Weston Presidio Capital, J.P. Morgan Partners, and Soros Private Equity Partners, and founded the airline in February 1999.

In September 1999, JetBlue was awarded 75 landing and takeoff slots at the John F. Kennedy International Airport (JFK) in New York, which was to serve as its base. The airline started commercial operations on February 11, 2000, with an inaugural flight from JFK to Fort Lauderdale airport in Florida.

Business Model

JetBlue's business was guided by five key values—safety, caring, integrity, fun, and passion. From its inception, it was "anti-establishment" and went against many of the accepted norms of the aviation industry. One example of this was its choice of New York, the biggest aviation market in the United States, as its base. LCCs in the United States typically avoided operating from New York because flying out of LaGuardia and Newark, the city's two domestic airports, was very expensive. Most domestic operators avoided JFK, as it mainly served international flights, and was also farther from Manhattan than the other two airports. Neeleman, however, reasoned that because JFK handled mostly international flights, JetBlue would face very little competition from domestic flights at that airport.

Positioning

From the beginning, JetBlue was positioned as a colorful and fun airline. Although it was designated as an LCC; it was in fact a "value player." The airline combined low fares with several value-added services that improved customer service without adding to operating costs.

All the planes operated at JetBlue were fitted with leather seats instead of cloth ones. Leather furnishings cost twice as much as cloth ones, but also lasted twice as long. Unlike typical LCCs, JetBlue provided assigned seating and allowed passengers to choose their seat on the plane whenever possible.

JetBlue served light snacks such as chips, cookies, and crackers, and coffee and canned drinks, which cost a fraction of a regular meal. The snacks were complimentary, unlike in LCCs that sold food to passengers. JetBlue estimated that it saved about $3 per passenger by choosing to serve sacks instead of regular food.

JetBlue provided free personal satellite television to all the passengers. The television sets reportedly cost only about $1 per passenger per flight—one-fourth the cost of a meal.

Operations

JetBlue's operations were the key to its low costs. JetBlue did not use old planes, but operated a fleet of new Airbus A-320[6] aircraft. The Airbus A-320s were chosen over the more popular Boeing-737s[7] (which Southwest used) because although they cost more initially, they would be easier to maintain and were more fuel-efficient. The planes also came with a five-year warranty. Operating a uniform fleet of planes was also economical, as it reduced costs significantly in the areas of pilot training, maintenance, and spare parts.

All the aircraft were configured in a single class, with a uniform level of service. This also allowed JetBlue to put in the maximum number of seats possible in its planes.

Initially JetBlue did not try to fly too many routes, concentrating instead on the Northeast, the West Coast, and Florida—routes for which demand was high, and it was easy to undercut the fares of rivals. In addition, JetBlue also flew to secondary cities that were neglected by major carriers.

JetBlue flew mainly to secondary airports that did not handle too much air traffic. In this way, the airline was able to avoid congestion to a great extent and to establish a good on-time record. (In 2001–2002, JetBlue had an on-time performance record of 80 percent, as against the 72 percent for the top ten airlines in the United States.) Besides, secondary airports offered better business terms than the main ones.

JetBlue tried to operate the maximum possible number of flights per day. Its average turn-around time was 35 minutes, which was comparable to Southwest and much lower than that of full service airlines (FSAs), which took an hour or more to turn around. JetBlue also operated several "red-eye" flights.[8]

JetBlue flew only point-to-point flights, avoiding the hub-and-spoke model used by major carriers. This helped it avoid the complications that resulted from connecting flights and passenger transfers, and the airline was also able to operate with far fewer airport staff.

JetBlue used electronic ticketing extensively. Typically, more than 70 percent of the tickets were booked through the airline's Web site. JetBlue also cut down on the costs of back-end operations by allowing its call-center operators and customer service executives to work from home, using voice-over-Internet protocol.

Automation and the effective harnessing of technology further helped cut costs. JetBlue was the first airline to introduce paperless cockpits, where the pilots were equipped with laptops to access flight manuals and make the requisite calculations before takeoff. This saved between 15 and 20 minutes in takeoff. JetBlue was also one of the first airlines in the United States to allow automatic check-in and electronic baggage tagging. Automation helped JetBlue maintain a lean workforce (labor costs were historically the highest component of an airline's operating costs). In 2002, JetBlue's cost per available seat mile was 7 cents, which was 25 percent less than the average of the major carriers. JetBlue was thus able to offer fares that were typically 30 to 40 percent lower than other airlines.[9]

Culture

JetBlue was also one of the few airlines in the U.S. airline industry that had a non-unionized workforce. All the employees from the CEO down to the lowest ranking ones were called "crewmembers." The top management tried to create a family-like atmosphere at the airline.

JetBlue looked for a positive attitude in its employees, as they were often called on to do things that were outside their job descriptions. For instance, JetBlue did not employ cleaning crews to clean the flights—the flight attendants and sometimes the pilots were expected to pitch in to get the flight ready for the next takeoff. Airport ground staff also loaded or unloaded baggage from the flight. However JetBlue rewarded employees frequently with bonuses and profit sharing programs. Initiative was encouraged, and all employees were free to suggest ideas to cut costs and improve operations.

Because of the positive work culture, when customers flew JetBlue, they were impressed by the energy and attitude of the employees.

JetBlue also went out of its way to avoid inconveniencing customers. The airline had a policy of never canceling flights, (all through the early 2000s, JetBlue had an average completion factor[10] of 99.5 percent). JetBlue also avoided overbooking flights. When there was a delay, passengers were informed well in advance. During extreme delays, JetBlue would hand out gift vouchers that could be redeemed for a future flight. All this was done even when the delay was because of uncontrollable factors.

JetBlue's passenger complaint numbers and baggage handling errors were among the lowest in the industry.

Growth and Expansion

JetBlue was founded during one of the most turbulent times in the history of civil aviation in the United States. September 11, 2001, terrorist attacks had hit the industry hard and any of the major airlines had either gone into bankruptcy protection, or were on the verge of doing so. In 2001, JetBlue planned to launch an IPO to fund its expansion plans.[11] The IPO had to be postponed in light of the terrorist attacks, but JetBlue continued with its expansion plans using its share of the $15 billion bailout ($5 billion in direct compensation and another $10 billion in loan guarantees)[12] the U.S. government granted the aviation industry, and a fresh infusion of funds from its original investors.

JetBlue was one of the first airlines to take a proactive approach to increase safety on aircraft. It was the first national carrier to install bulletproof, deadbolted cockpit doors on its aircraft, even before the FAA mandated their use. The airline also installed screens in the cockpit so that pilots could see what was happening in the passenger cabins.

JetBlue's message to customers after September 11 also set it apart from other airlines. It ran a newspaper advertisement that said: "We know you need time to heal. JetBlue will be here when you're ready to fly again."[13] For a few weeks after flights resumed, JetBlue aircraft flew almost empty from New York to the 17 destinations it served at that time, but the airline did not scale back operations.

Soon after the September 11 attacks, JetBlue's management identified the routes on which other airlines had cut capacity. For instance, most of the major airlines had cut down their flights from New York to Florida. JetBlue boosted its services to Florida, adding seven new flights per week on this route within a few months. JetBlue also ordered three new A-320 aircraft in 2001. JetBlue was one among only three airlines in the United States (the other two being Southwest and AirTran Airways [AirTran]) to post a profit in 2001 (The company posted a profit of $38.5 million, up from a loss of $21.3 million in 2000.)[14] (See **Exhibit 1** for Jet-Blue's annual income statements from 2002 to 2006.)

In April 2002, JetBlue launched an IPO of 5.87 million shares, raising $158 million.[15] That year, JetBlue started expanding operations on the West Coast, using Los Angeles as a second hub.

In late 2002, JetBlue acquired 100 percent ownership of LiveTV, the company that maintained its in-flight satellite TV channels, for $41 million in cash and the retirement of $39 million in debt.[16] It also started a customer loyalty program, TrueBlue, in mid-2002, collecting nearly 40,000 members by the end of the year. In 2002, JetBlue's cost per available seat mile (CASM)[17] was 6.43 cents, lower than all the other major U.S. airlines, which reported an average CASM of 9.58 cents.[18] (See **Exhibit 2** for JetBlue's key operating statistics from 2002 to 2006.)

In 2003, JetBlue placed an order for 100 Embraer-190[19] regional jets for a price of $3 billion, with options for another 100 planes[20] to serve more regional routes as a part of its expansion plans. (This was in addition to the 16 A-320 aircraft added to the fleet that year, with an order for 65 more, and options on another 50.[21]) The A-320 aircraft were configured in a 162-seat arrangement, while the Embraer aircraft, which were configured with 100 seats, were a more suitable size for regional routes. The first Embraer planes entered service in October 2005.

EXHIBIT 1
Annual Income
Statements:
JetBlue Airways

(Dollar amounts in millions except per share data)

Year Ending	2006	2005	2004	2003	2002
Operating Revenues	$ 2,363	$ 1,701	$ 1,265	$ 998	$ 635
Operating Expenses					
Salaries, wages, and benefits	553	428	337	267	162
Aircraft fuel	752	488	255	147	76
Landing fees and other rents	158	112	92	70	44
Depreciation and amortization	151	115	77	51	27
Aircraft rent	103	74	70	60	41
Sales and marketing	104	81	63	54	44
Maintenance materials and repairs	87	64	45	23	9
Other operating expenses[1]	328	291	215	159	127
Total operating expenses[2]	2,236	1,653	1,154	831	530
Operating income	127	48	111	167	105
Government compensation[3]	—	—	—	23	—
Other income (expense)	(118)	(72)	(36)	(16)	(10)
Income (loss) before income taxes	9	(24)	75	174	95
Income tax expense (benefit)	10	(4)	29	71	40
Net income (loss)	$ (1)	$ (20)	$ 46	$ 103	$ 55
Earnings (Loss) Per Common Share					
Basic	$ —	$ (0.13)	$ 0.30	$ 0.71	$ 0.49
Diluted	$ —	$ (0.13)	$ 0.28	$ 0.64	$ 0.37
Other Financial Data					
Operating margin	5.4%	2.8%	8.8%	16.8%	16.5%
Pre-tax margin	0.4%	(1.4)%	5.9%	17.4%	15.0%
Ratio of earnings to fixed charges[4]	—	—	1.6x	3.1x	2.7x
Net cash provided by operating activities	$ 274	$ 170	$ 199	$ 287	$ 217
Net cash used in investing activities	(1,307)	(1,276)	(720)	(987)	(880)
Net cash provided by financing activities	1,037	1,093	437	789	657

Notes:
[1] In 2006, we sold five Airbus A320 aircraft, which resulted in a gain of $12 million.
[2] In 2005, we recorded $7 million in non-cash stock-based compensation expense related to the acceleration of certain employee stock options and wrote-off $6 million in development costs relating to a maintenance and inventory tracking system that was not implemented.
[3] In 2003, we received $23 million in compensation under the Emergency War Time Supplemental Appropriations Act.
[4] Earnings were inadequate to cover fixed charges by $17 million and $39 million for the years ended December 31, 2006, and 2005, respectively.

SOURCE: *JetBlue Airways Annual Report 2006.*

In 2003, JetBlue received permission to build a new terminal at JFK, giving it 26 more gates. (Construction of the terminal began in late 2005.) In 2004, JetBlue announced that it planned to take delivery of one new Airbus A320 every three weeks and to hire five crew members per day during the year.[22]

During 2004, JetBlue performed well on many operating metrics, with a 99.4 percent completion factor, the highest on-time performance of 81.6 percent in the industry, and the fewest baggage mishandlings of 2.99 per 1,000 customers boarded. Its CASM also remained lower than the industry average at 6.10 cents.[23] By the end of 2004, JetBlue flew to 30 destinations, including one international destination—the Dominican Republic—launched that year. (See **Exhibit 3** for JetBlue's growth between 2000 and 2006.)

EXHIBIT 2
Operating Statistics: JetBlue Airways[1]

	2006	2005	2004	2003	2002
Revenue passengers[2] (thousands)	18,565	14,729	11,783	9,012	5,752
Revenue passenger miles[3] (millions)	23,320	20,200	15,730	11,527	6,836
Available seat miles[4] (ASMs) (millions)	28,594	23,703	18,911	13,639	8,240
Load factor[5]	81.6%	85.2%	83.2%	84.5%	83.0%
Breakeven load factor[6, 5]	81.4%	86.1%	77.9%	72.6%	71.5%
Aircraft utilization[7] (hours per day)	12.7	13.4	13.4	13.0	12.9
Average fare[8]	$ 119.73	$ 110.03	$ 103.49	$ 107.09	$ 106.95
Yield per passenger mile[9] (cents)	9.53	8.02	7.75	8.37	9.00
Passenger revenue per[10] ASM (cents)	7.77	6.84	6.45	7.08	7.47
Operating revenue per[11] ASM (cents)	8.26	7.18	6.69	7.32	7.71
Operating expense per[12] ASM (cents)	7.82	6.98	6.10	6.09	6.43
Operating expense per ASM, excluding fuel[13] (cents)	5.19	4.92	4.75	5.01	5.51
Airline operating expense per ASM (cents)[1]	7.76	6.91	6.04	6.08	6.43
Departures	159,152	112,009	90,532	66,920	44,144
Average stage length[14] (miles)	1,186	1,358	1,339	1,272	1,152
Average number of operating aircraft during period	106.5	77.5	60.6	44.0	27.0
Average fuel cost per gallon[15]	$ 1.99	$ 1.61	$ 1.06	$ 0.85	$ 0.72
Fuel gallons consumed (millions)	377	303	241	173	106
Percent of sales through jetblue.com during period	79.1%	77.5%	75.4%	73.0%	63.0%
Full-time equivalent employees at period end[5]	9,265	8,326	6,413	4,892	3,572

Notes:

[1]Excludes results of operations and employees of LiveTV, LLC, which are unrelated to our airline operations and are immaterial to our consolidated operating results.

[2]"Revenue passengers" represents the total number of paying passengers flown on all flight segments.

[3]"Revenue passenger miles" represents the number of miles flown by revenue passengers.

[4]"Available seat miles" represents the number of seats available for passengers multiplied by the number of miles the seats are flown.

[5]"Load factor" represents the percentage of aircraft seating capacity that is actually utilized (revenue passenger miles divided by available seat miles).

[6]"Breakeven load factor" is the passenger load factor that will result in operating revenues being equal to operating expenses, assuming constant revenue per passenger mile and expenses.

[7]"Aircraft utilization" represents the average number of block hours operated per day per aircraft for the total fleet of aircraft.

[8]"Average fare" represents the average one-way fare paid per flight segment by a revenue passenger.

[9]"Yield per passenger mile" represents the average amount one passenger pays to fly one mile.

[10]"Passenger revenue per available seat mile" represents passenger revenue divided by available seat miles.

[11]"Operating revenue per available seat mile" represents operating revenues divided by available seat miles.

[12]"Operating expense per available seat mile" represents operating expenses divided by available seat miles.

[13]"Operating expense per available seat mile, excluding fuel" represents operating expenses, less aircraft fuel, divided by available seat miles.

[14]"Average stage length" represents the average number of miles flown per flight.

[15]"Average fuel cost per gallon" represents total aircraft fuel costs, which excludes fuel taxes, divided by the total number of fuel gallons consumed.

SOURCE: *JetBlue Airways Annual Report 2006.*

However, in the fourth quarter of 2004, JetBlue recorded a drastic drop in profits. It announced a net income of $2.3 million compared to $19.54 million in the corresponding quarter of the previous year.[24] The drop in earnings was attributed to increased operating expenses as a result of a rise in fuel prices. The airline ended the year with a net income of $46 million, on revenues of $1.2 billion.[25] Following this, it was recognized as a "major airline" by the DOT.

EXHIBIT 3
JetBlue's Growth

| | | | Operating Aircraft | | |
Year	Destinations	Employees[1]	Owned	Leased	Total
2000	12	1174	4	6	10
2001	18	2361	9	12	21
2002	20	4011	21	16	37
2003	21	5433	29	24	53
2004	30	7211	44	25	69
2005	33	9021	61	31	92
2006	49	10,377	70	49	119

Note: [1]Employees include full time and part time employees.

SOURCE: *JetBlue Airways Annual Report 2006.*

Turbulent Times

JetBlue's performance in all the quarters of 2005 was considerably poorer than in the corresponding quarters of 2004, and in the fourth quarter of 2005, it posted a quarterly loss for the first time since its IPO. JetBlue ended the year with its first annual loss of $20 million on revenues of $1.7 billion. The airline's operating margins fell to 2.8 percent from 8.8 percent in 2004.[26]

JetBlue's performance statistics also showed a downward trend, and in 2005, the airline's on-time performance record fell to 71.4 percent, which was lower than almost all the major airlines in the United States. The turbulence continued into 2006, and JetBlue announced a loss in the first quarter of that year. JetBlue's problems were attributed to a combination of several internal and external factors.

Rising Fuel Costs

Fuel prices around the world experienced a sudden rise in 2004. Among the worst affected sectors was aviation. Fuel was the second major expense in an airline's operations after labor in the United States, and typically constituted between 10 percent and 14 percent of an airline's operating expenses. However, after the price increases, its share in operating expenses became more than 20 percent. (See **Exhibit 4** for the breakup of an airline's operating expenses in 2007.) Although the rise in fuel prices affected all airlines, its effect on LCCs such as JetBlue was greater.

In 2005, fuel prices increased by nearly 50 percent over 2004. But even as fuel prices pushed up operating expenses, JetBlue was unable to increase its fares significantly. The growing number of LCCs in the aviation industry, and the attempts of the FSAs to take away market share from the LCCs had led to a fall in the average fares. The average price for a passenger to fly a mile fell by more than 10 percent between 2000 and 2006 (see **Exhibit 5**). Added to this, JetBlue had hedged only 20 percent of its fuel requirements for 2005 at $30 per barrel, compared to the 42 percent hedged in 2004.[27] By 2005, fuel constituted nearly 30 percent of JetBlue's operating expenses, compared to 14.4 percent in 2002. It exceeded 33 percent in 2006 (see **Exhibit 6**).

Passenger Airline Cost Index First Quarter 2007	Index (2000 = 100)	% of Operating Expenses
Labor per FTE	111.1	24.5
Fuel per gallon	276.9	23.4
Aircraft ownership per operating seat	79.5	7.5
Non-aircraft ownership per enplanement	108.5	4.7
Professional services per ASM	114.9	8.6
Food & beverage per RPM	59.6	1.5
Landing fees per capacity ton landed	137.3	2.0
Maintenance material per revenue aircraft hour	53.7	1.3
Aircraft insurance as % of hull net book value	97.9	0.1
Non-aircraft insurance per rpm	221.0	0.5
Passenger commissions as % of passenger revenue	29.5	1.2
Communication per enplanement	71.0	0.9
Advertising & promotion per RPM	66.5	0.8
Utilities & office supplies per FTE	96.3	0.7
Transport-related per ASM	399.8	13.9
Other operating per RTM	111.6	8.3
Interest as % of outstanding debt	114.1	—
Composite[1]	**182.9**	**100.0**

Note: [1]Although interest is a non-operating expense, it is factored into the composite cost index to capture the role of debt in the provision of air service. It is *not* included in the composite cost per ASM or share of operating expenses.

SOURCE: *http://www.airlines.org.*

Year	Cost of Domestic Air Travel (cents per mile)[1]	U.S. Jet Fuel (cents per gallon)	U.S. CPI (1982–84) = 100
2000	14.57	90.0	172.2
2001	13.25	75.0	177.1
2002	12.00	70.8	179.9
2003	12.29	88.2	184.0
2004	12.03	120.8	188.9
2005	12.29	172.2	195.3
2006	13.00	196.8	201.6
2006 vs. 2000	−10.8%	+118.7%	+17.1%

Note: [1]Excludes government-imposed taxes and fees

SOURCE: *http://www.airlines.org/economics/energy/.*

Year Ending December 31	2006	2005	2004	2003	2002
Gallons consumed (millions)	377	303	241	173	105
Total cost ($ millions)	752	488	255	147	76
Average price per gallon	1.99	1.61	1.06	0.85	0.72
Percent of operating expenses %	33.6	29.5	22.1	17.8	14.4

SOURCE: *Compiled from JetBlue's Annual Reports.*

Industry Factors

In the period between 2001 and 2003, when JetBlue's growth was at a peak, most of the major airlines in the United States were suffering from the adverse effects of the September 11 attacks. JetBlue had taken advantage of its competitors' weakened state to boost its own growth. However, by 2004–2005, many of the airlines that were operating under Chapter 11[28] began to recapture market share. These airlines were able to undercut competition by offering very low fares, taking advantage of the protection of the bankruptcy laws. "It's too much competition from companies that are purposely allowing themselves to lose money. Companies in bankruptcy right now, such as United and US Air, have been significantly slashing their own fares," said Rick DiLisi, a spokesman for Independence Air, a low-cost airline based in Virginia.[29] JetBlue was also affected by the low fares offered by United Airlines (United) and Delta Air Lines (Delta), both of which were operating under bankruptcy protection at the time, on transcontinental routes, American Airlines (American) and Continental Airlines (Continental), which had escaped Chapter 11, also become aggressive about defending market share, and launched several new transcontinental flights at low prices.

In 2003, JetBlue launched flights from Atlanta to Los Angeles, one of the busiest routes in the United States. Atlanta was Delta's hub, and when JetBlue entered the market, Delta responded by instantly adding capacity and lowering prices on this route. It also added routes to other destinations in California, quickly establishing its dominance in the region. AirTran, another LCC that operated from Atlanta, also responded aggressively by leasing new planes to increase capacity. Eventually, JetBlue was forced to withdraw from Atlanta in December 2003, just seven months after it started its operations there.

Legacy carriers also launched low-cost subsidiaries of their own, in an effort to compete with the growing number of LCCs. Delta launched an LCC called Song in April 2003, to compete directly with JetBlue. Song was also based at JFK, and flew many of the same routes as JetBlue. Like JetBlue, Song also offered amenities such as leather seats, and a free personal entertainment system at every seat. It also served beverages, but charged for meals and liquor. The airline was promoted heavily, and for a few months was successful in capturing a large part of JetBlue's business on the New York to Florida route. However, its financial performance was not satisfactory and it was eventually integrated into Delta's mainline service in April 2006.

United also launched an LCC called "Ted" in February 2004. Although Ted was designed more along the lines of the traditional LCC model and did not serve food, it provided in-flight entertainment in the form of inflight music and videos. Ted operated mainly on central and western routes in the United States. According to analysts, the success of Ted was one of the main reasons why United was able to emerge from bankruptcy in February 2006.

Song and Ted had an advantage over the other LCCs, in that they allowed passengers to connect to the flights of their parent airlines, which had far bigger route networks than any of the LCCs. They also shared the frequent flier programs of their parents, and had access to the gates and landing/takeoff slots of their parents in large airports.

JetBlue also faced competition from LCCs such as Southwest, AirTran, America West, Spirit Airlines (Spirit), and Frontier Airlines (Frontier). Although none of these airlines offered the same kind of service as JetBlue, all of them were well established in their home markets, and had loyal customer bases. Southwest especially had the lowest cost even among the LCCs, and was very popular among passengers who were willing to give up in-flight services for cheap tickets. AirTran and Spirit operated two classes on their flights and targeted business passengers successfully with their low-fare Business Classes. With the exception of Southwest and Spirit, all the LCCs also offered some form of in-flight entertainment, although AirTran was the only other airline that offered it free.

Internal Factors

When JetBlue had first started operations, it had used new planes and fittings, which did not cost much in terms of maintenance. However, a few years later, as the fleet aged, maintenance costs began to rise. Further, JetBlue had to employ more people to meet its requirements, and also give pay increases to people who had been with the airlines for several years. In an effort to differentiate itself from its competitors, JetBlue had also kept adding new in-flight services. In 2003, the airline changed the configuration of its A-320 aircraft, removing one row of seats from the plane, in order to improve legroom for passengers (the number of seats was brought down to 156, from 162[30]). While this made the aircraft more comfortable for passengers, it also lowered JetBlue's revenue earning capacity. However, the move was expected to cut fuel costs, due to the lower weight of the aircraft.

In 2005, JetBlue upgraded its seatback televisions. All the new aircraft were fitted with larger TVs, and all the old aircraft were retrofitted. At the same time, the airline also equipped all its planes with XM Satellite radio, and increased the size of the overhead bins on the aircraft.

Most LCCs gave complimentary beverages and sold food, or served complimentary refreshments in strictly measured quantities. But JetBlue offered a range of complimentary snacks and beverages in unlimited quantities. Although the airline started out serving chips, cookies, and coffee, over the years it added several items to its line of in-flight refreshments. As of 2007, the airline offered a range of hot and cold beverages and several varieties of snacks. It also sold a variety of cocktails at $5 each.

Passengers traveling on red-eye flights were given complimentary spa amenity kits containing mint lip balm, body butter, an eyeshade, and ear plugs. JetBlue also set up a complimentary snack bar in the plane for overnight flights, and passengers were given complimentary hot towels, Dunkin Donuts coffee or tea, orange juice or bottled spring water, just before they landed the next morning.

Another issue was the problems that JetBlue experienced with its new Embraer-190 aircraft that entered service in late 2005. JetBlue faced a lot of glitches in integrating the new aircraft into its operations. To begin with, Embraer delivered the planes two weeks behind schedule, which caused several flight delays and cancellations. Second, JetBlue's employees lacked familiarity with the planes. Third, the Embraer-190 had some technical issues that caused several delayed flights and significantly lowered JetBlue's aircraft utilization rates. In the opinion of some analysts, JetBlue had been too optimistic in placing such a large order for the untried Embraer planes. After two consecutive losses in the last quarter of 2005 and the first quarter of 2006, several analysts started comparing JetBlue to People Express Airlines,[31] a low-cost airline operated in the United States between 1981 and 1987.

The Return to Profitability Plan

In April 2006, soon after announcing the first quarter loss, Neeleman and Barger announced a recovery plan for JetBlue called the "Return to Profitability" plan (RTP). The main aims of the RTP were revenue optimization, improved capacity management, cost reduction, and retaining the commitment to deliver high-quality service on every flight.

As a part of the revenue optimization goal, JetBlue announced that it would reduce the number of long-haul flights and shift its focus back to short-to-medium routes. The company said that it planned to reduce the ratio of long-haul to non–long-haul flights from 1.5:1 in 2005, to 1.2:1 during 2006. JetBlue also said that it would offer fewer tickets at very low fares and more tickets at mid-level fares on all its routes to improve the mix of fares in its revenues. The average fare was expected to rise to at least partly reflect the increased fuel prices. During 2006, JetBlue increased its lowest transcontinental fare from $349 to $399.

JetBlue also committed itself to conducting a careful scrutiny of its yield management practices to ensure it did not sacrifice revenues to increase the load factor.[32] Trying to increase the load factor put stress on an airline's operations and also led to delays as the airlines tried to get as many passengers on board as possible, even minutes before a flight's scheduled departure. In 2005, JetBlue's load factor was 85.2 percent and the yield per passenger mile was 8.02 cents. This changed to a load factor of 81.6 percent and yield per passenger mile[33] of 9.53 cents in 2006, which was nearly a 19 percent increase in yield per passenger mile over the previous year.[34]

The RTP also committed JetBlue to manage capacity better by cutting it on unprofitable routes, and adding it on high-demand routes. During 2006, JetBlue added only 21 percent capacity, instead of the previously projected 28 percent. The capacity on the New York—Florida route was cut by 15 percent, while the New York—Los Angeles route saw an 8 percent reduction in capacity.

On the other hand, JetBlue introduced short-haul routes from Boston to Washington, New York to Richmond, and Boston to Richmond; and medium-haul routes from New York to Austin, Boston to Austin, and Boston to Nassau. The airline introduced nonstop service on two high-demand long-haul routes from Burbank (California) to Orlando (Florida) and Boston to Phoenix (Arizona). On the whole, JetBlue added 16 new destinations during 2006, which mainly involved "connecting the dots" between its existing destinations using the Embraer-190 aircraft.

JetBlue sold five of its oldest A-320 aircraft during 2006, and deferred the delivery of 12 A-320 aircraft that had originally been planned for 2007–2009, to 2011–2012. The options the airline held on the A-320s were also adjusted. (See **Exhibit 7**.)

JetBlue also increased its focus on cost management. The airline managed to control its distribution cost by achieving 80 percent of its bookings through its website in 2006—the highest in the U.S. airline industry. It also implemented several initiatives to conserve fuel and improve fuel efficiency, especially by using single-engine taxi techniques, utilizing ground power units, and identifying ways to remove excess weight from the aircraft. In late 2006, JetBlue announced it would remove one more row of seats from its A-320 aircraft, bringing the total seat number down to 150.

In addition to this, JetBlue was also putting in efforts to improve the efficiency of its crew members and was trying to accomplish more with fewer full-time employees per aircraft than before. The elimination of one row of seats allowed JetBlue to operate each flight with three attendants instead of four, as federal regulations require one flight attendant for every 50 passengers. JetBlue also began to go slow on hiring people for non-operational positions. Better flight scheduling practices were also implemented to control costs. JetBlue started charging for some premium services. For instance, the company changed some of its refund policies, and increased the fees it charged for flying unaccompanied minors and the cancellation charges on confirmed flights.

EXHIBIT 7
JetBlue's A-320
Order Adjustments

	2007	2008	2009	2010	2011	2012	2013
Firm Orders Original	17	17	18	18	12	0	0
Adjusted to	12	12	16	18	18	6	0
Change	(5)	(5)	(2)	0	6	6	0
Options Original	0	2	2	2	9	20	15
Adjusted to	0	2	4	4	6	16	18
Change (%)	0	0	2	2	(3)	(4)	3

SOURCE: *http://investor.jetblue.com.*

EXHIBIT 8
A Snapshot of Jetblue's Quarterly Performance (dollar amount in millions)

Period Ending On	March 31, 2006	June 30, 2006	September 30, 2006	December 31, 2006	March 31, 2007	June 30, 2007
Operating Revenues	490	612	628	633	608	730
Operating Expenses	515	565	587	569	621	657
Operating Income (loss)	(25)	47	41	64	(13)	73
Other Income (expense)	(22)	(22)	(40)	34	(32)	(30)
Income Tax Expense (benefit)	(15)	11	1	13	(23)	22
Net Income	(32)	14	-	17	(22)	21

Compiled from JetBlue's Annual Report 2006 and 10K filings with the SEC.

The RTP started showing results by the end of 2006. In the fourth quarter of 2006, JetBlue posted a profit of $17 million on revenues on $633 million, compared to a loss of $42 million in the corresponding quarter of the previous year. Analysts had expected the company to return to profitability only in the first quarter of 2007. (See **Exhibit 8** for JetBlue's quarterly results in 2006 and 2007.) JetBlue ended 2006 with a net loss of $1 million, compared to a loss of $20 million in 2005. The operating margin also increased to 5.4 percent in 2006, compared to 2.8 percent in 2005.[35] The airline expected that the combination of higher revenues and lower costs would help it achieve savings of around $70 million by the end of 2007.[36]

The Customer Service Fiasco

Even as its financial performance started showing signs of improvement, JetBlue faced another crisis in February 2007, when a snowstorm hit the Northeast and Midwest regions of the United States, throwing the airline's operations into chaos.

Because JetBlue followed the practice of never canceling flights, even when the ice storm hit and the airline was forced to keep several flights on the ground, it desisted from calling them off. Because of this, passengers were kept waiting at airports for their flight to take off. In some cases, passengers who had already boarded their planes were kept waiting on the tarmac for several hours and not allowed to disembark. In one extreme instance, passengers were stranded on board a plane on the tarmac at JFK for 11 hours. However, after all this, the airline was eventually forced to cancel most of its flights because of bad weather.

Even after the storm cleared, JetBlue struggled to get back on its feet as the canceled flights had played havoc with its systems, which were not equipped to deal with cancellation. The airline's poor database management systems resulted in major problems in tracking and lining up pilots and flight crew who were within federal regulation limits for the number of flying hours to operate the resumed flights. In addition, the delays and cancellations had caused a baggage crisis, with several passengers losing their luggage. The airline had to give all its passengers full refunds if their flights were canceled, or rebook them on new flights, which added to the complications.

The airline had canceled nearly 1,200 flights in the days following the storm and it took several days of its operations to get back to even keel. In contrast, American, Continental, and Delta, which had canceled flights immediately after the storm broke, were able to resume operations more quickly. The fiasco reportedly cost JetBlue $30 million (which included $10 million in refunding tickets for canceled flights, $16 million for issuing travel vouchers, and $4 million for incremental costs, such as hiring overtime crews).[37]

Notwithstanding the financial loss, the loss of goodwill was expected to be much more serious for JetBlue. Traditionally, JetBlue had had one of the lowest rates of consumer complaints filed with the DOT.[38] It also usually ranked high on customer service.[39] But following the fiasco, *BusinessWeek*, a prominent business magazine, pulled JetBlue off its list of Customer Service Champs, published early in 2007. JetBlue was to have held the #4 spot on the list compiled from consumer responses from the first half of 2006.

Some analysts felt that JetBlue had taken its low-cost philosophy too far in having failed to set up the necessary systems to support its rapid growth. Following the fiasco, JetBlue published apology letters in the *New York Times* and *USA Today*, among other places. Neeleman also apologized during his appearances on the *Late Show with David Letterman* on the CBS Network, and on YouTube. "We should have acted quicker," said Neeleman. "We should have called the Port Authority quicker. These were all lessons learned from that experience."[40]

In late February 2007, Neeleman unveiled a "Customer Bill of Rights," which laid out the airline's policy on compensating passengers for delays and cancellations (see **Exhibit 9**). Additionally, JetBlue launched a new database management system to help it track crew and baggage better, and upgraded its Web site to allow online re-bookings. Employees at the airline's headquarters were being trained to help out with operations at the airport in emergency situations. JetBlue also became more proactive during bad weather conditions in the months following the storm. In March 2007, when bad weather hit the East Coast once again, JetBlue was one of the first airlines to cancel flights to and from airports on the East Coast. The airline reportedly canceled nearly 230 flights during this time.

According to analysts, JetBlue's handling of the events following the crisis was likely to go a long way in redeeming it in the eyes of the public. "The single most important thing a company needs to show in a crisis is that it cares. That's not a feeling. It's a behavior," said Bruce Blythe, the CEO of Crisis Management International[41, 42]. Several consumer polls conducted after the February 2007 crisis also showed that JetBlue's popularity with passengers continued to remain high. The crisis and its repercussions were expected to put a burden on JetBlue's already strained finances. But JetBlue managed to return to profitability in the second quarter of 2007, after a first quarter loss of $22 million.

More Turbulence Ahead?

Analysts felt that the appointment of Barger as the new CEO was likely to benefit JetBlue. According to them, the fresh leadership was likely to help JetBlue through its growing pains and provide it with a positive direction for the future. They also pointed out that Barger differed considerably from Neeleman in his leadership style. (Barger was thought to be more organized than Neeleman, and much more focused on operational issues than the latter, who enjoyed strategizing.)

However, JetBlue was likely to face many more challenges in the future than it had faced during the first few years of operations. The FSAs, most of which recovered by 2007, were ready to defend their turf against LCCs. Delta had launched a big sale of discounted tickets during the Thanksgiving weekend in 2006, triggering a price war in the industry.

In addition to this, JetBlue was likely to face competition from other LCCs such as AirTran and Frontier, which had formed an alliance in late 2006, to combine their marketing and mileage programs.[43] Competition was also expected from new airlines like Virgin America, which had been launched amidst a lot of buzz in August 2007, and was positioned as a "value" carrier. Like JetBlue, Virgin America also tried to attract passengers with amenities such as satellite TV, mood lighting, onboard self-service mini bar, and meals-on-demand. Virgin America had announced that it expected to expand to 10 cities within a year of operation and to up to 30 cities within five years.[44]

EXHIBIT 9
Jetblue's Customer
Bill of Rights

INFORMATION

JetBlue will notify customers of the following:

- Delays prior to scheduled departure
- Cancellations and their cause
- Diversions and their cause

CANCELLATIONS

All customers whose flight is canceled by JetBlue will, at the customer's option, receive a full refund or reaccommodation on a future JetBlue flight at no additional charge or fare. If JetBlue cancels a flight within 12 hours of scheduled departure and the cancellation is due to a Controllable Irregularity, JetBlue will also provide the customer with a Voucher valid for future travel on JetBlue in the amount paid by the customer for the roundtrip (or the oneway trip, doubled).

DEPARTURE DELAYS

- Customers whose flight is delayed prior to scheduled departure for 1–1:59 hours due to a Controllable Irregularity are entitled to a $25 Voucher good for future travel on JetBlue.
- Customers whose flight is delayed prior to scheduled departure for 2–3:59 hours due to a Controllable Irregularity are entitled to a $50 Voucher good for future travel on JetBlue.
- Customers whose flight is delayed prior to scheduled departure for 4–5:59 hours due to a Controllable Irregularity are entitled to a Voucher good for future travel on JetBlue in the amount paid by the customer for the oneway trip.
- Customers whose flight is delayed prior to scheduled departure for 6 or more hours due to a Controllable Irregularity are entitled to a Voucher good for future travel on JetBlue in the amount paid by the customer for the roundtrip (or the oneway trip, doubled).

OVERBOOKINGS

(As defined in JetBlue's Contract of Carriage)
Customers who are involuntarily denied boarding shall receive $1,000.

ONBOARD GROUND DELAYS

For customers who experience an onboard Ground Delay for more than 5 hours, JetBlue will take necessary action so that customers may deplane. JetBlue will also provide customers experiencing an onboard Ground Delay with food and drink, access to restrooms and, as necessary, medical treatment.

Arrivals:

- Customers who experience an onboard Ground Delay on Arrival for 30–59 minutes after scheduled arrival time are entitled to a $25 Voucher good for future travel on JetBlue.
- Customers who experience an onboard Ground Delay on Arrival for 1–1:59 hours after scheduled arrival time are entitled to a $100 Voucher good for future travel on JetBlue.
- Customers who experience an onboard Ground Delay on Arrival for 2–2:59 hours after scheduled arrival time are entitled to a Voucher good for future travel on JetBlue in the amount paid by the customer for the oneway trip, or $100, whichever is greater.
- Customers who experience an onboard Ground Delay on Arrival for 3 or more hours after scheduled arrival time are entitled to a Voucher good for future travel on JetBlue in the amount paid by the customer for the roundtrip (or the oneway trip, doubled).

Departures:

- Customers who experience an onboard Ground Delay on Departure for 3–3:59 hours are entitled to a $100 Voucher good for future travel on JetBlue.
- Customers who experience an onboard Ground Delay on Departure for 4 or more hours are entitled to a Voucher good for future travel on JetBlue in the amount paid by the customer for the roundtrip (or the oneway trip, doubled).

SOURCE: *www.jetblue.com, accessed 2007.*

Rising fuel costs were also a major concern for JetBlue in the future, as were potentially increasing operational expenses as the airline's fleet aged and operations expanded. Analysts also thought that JetBlue's growth would dilute the close-knit culture that the company enjoyed in its initial years. However, many industry experts still believed that the airline would be able to overcome most of the hurdles it faced and enjoy significant growth in the future.

NOTES

1. Eryn Brown, "A Smokeless Herb JetBlue Founder David Neeleman . . .," *Fortune*, May 28, 2001.

2. Chris Zappone, "JetBlue Struggles with 'Growing Pains,'" money.cnn.com, April 20, 2007.

3. The Federal Aviation Administration is an agency of the United States Department of Transportation with the authority to regulate and oversee all aspects of civil aviation in the United States.

4. Southwest Airlines, set up by Herb Kelleher in 1978, was the pioneer of low-cost airlines in the United States. The airline was headquartered in Dallas, Texas, and was known for its profitability record (it had posted profits for the 34th consecutive year in January 2007).

5. Eryn Brown, "A Smokeless Herb JetBlue Founder David Neeleman . . .," *Fortune*, May 28, 2001.

6. Airbus Industrie is a leading manufacturer of aircraft in the world. It was established in 1970 and is headquartered in France.

7. Boeing is a U.S.-based manufacturer of aircraft. Boeing and Airbus are the two biggest aviation companies in the world.

8. Flights operating between 9:00 p.m. and 5:00 a.m. local time are called red-eye flights. In North America, red-eye flights fly from the west to the east coast, capitalizing on the time-zone changes.

9. Amy Tsao, "Thinking of Taking Off with JetBlue?" *Business Week*, April 5, 2002.

10. The percentage of accomplished flights in relation to scheduled flight. In other words, it is the percentage of scheduled flights that were not canceled.

11. Paul C. Judge, "How Will Your Company Adapt?" *Fast Company*, November 2001.

12. "Big Airlines Benefit from Bailout Bill," www.taxpayer.net, June 7, 2002.

13. Paul C. Judge, "How Will Your Company Adapt?" *Fast Company*, November 2001.

14. Amy Tsao, "Thinking of Taking Off with JetBlue?" *Business Week*, April 5, 2002.

15. "JetBlue IPO Soars," money.cnn.com, April 12, 2002.

16. "JetBlue Closes Live TV Acquisition," *Communications Today*, September 30, 2002.

17. An airline industry metric arrived at by dividing operating expenses by available seat miles.

18. JetBlue Airways Annual Report 2002.

19. Embraer, a Brazil-based aircraft manufacturer, specialized in manufacturing regional jets.

20. Michael Bobelian, "JetBlue Lands Expansion Plans," *Forbes*, June 10, 2003.

21. JetBlue Airways Annual Report 2003.

22. JetBlue Airways Annual Report 2003.

23. JetBlue Airways Annual Report 2004.

24. "JetBlue Stays in Black," money.cnn.com, January 27, 2005.

25. JetBlue Airways Annual Report 2004.

26. JetBlue Airways Annual Report 2005.

27. JetBlue Airways Annual Report, 2005.

28. Chapter 11 is a chapter of the United States Bankruptcy Code, which permits reorganization under the bankruptcy laws of the United States. Chapter 11 bankruptcy is available to any business, whether organized as a corporation or sole proprietorship, or individual with unsecured debts of at least $336,900.00 or secured debts of at least $1,010,650.00, although it is most prominently used by corporate entities. (www.wikipedia.org)

29. Chris Isidore, "Low Fare Blues," money.cnn.com, November 24, 2004.

30. Press release on www.jetblue.com, November 13, 2003.

31. People Express had revolutionized air travel with its low fares, customer focus, and energetic staff. Within five years, the airline had reached one billion dollars in sales. However, People Express' troubles started in 1985 after it acquired several airlines in the United States, while facing aggressive competition from the FSAs. It was eventually merged with Continental in 1987. The case of People Express was often cited by airline industry analysts as an example of an airline growing too fast and not being able to sustain the growth.

32. The percentage of an aircraft seating capacity that is actually utilized.

33. The average amount one passenger pays to fly one mile.

34. JetBlue Airways Annual Report 2006.

35. JetBlue Airways Annual Report 2006.

36. www.airlinepilotforums.com

37. Grace Wong, "JetBlue Fiasco: $30M price tag," money.cnn.com, February 20 2007.

38. In 2006, the complaint rate was only 0.4 complaints per 100,000 passengers, which was the third best in the industry, behind Southwest, and a feeder airline for Continental Express called ExpressJet (Source: "JetBlue Fliers Stranded on Plane for 8 hours," *Fortune*, February 15 2007.)

39. The airline featured consistently in the University of Nebraska's national Airline Quality Rating (AQR) study every year since 2003; it ranked first in 2004, 2005, and 2006. It won the Readers' Choice Award from Condé Nast Traveler for five years until 2006, and ranked high in every measured category in the airline satisfaction ratings study conducted by J.D. Power & Associates.

40. "An Extraordinary Stumble at JetBlue," *Business Week*, March 5, 2007.

41. Crisis Management International was an Atlanta-based global consulting firm that specialized in helping organizations prepare for and manage the unexpected by offering strategic crisis management planning and related consulting services.

42. Chuck Salter, "Lessons from the Tarmac," *Fast Company*, May 2007.

43. Under the alliance, passengers could use their frequent flier miles on both the airlines.

44. Jessica Dickler, "Delays Thwart Virgin America's First Flight," money.cnn.com, August 8, 2007.

CASE **18**

Carnival Corporation & plc (2006):

TWELVE DISTINCT BRANDS SERVING SEVEN CONTINENTS

Michael J. Keeffe, John K. Ross III, Bill J. Middlebrook, and Thomas L. Wheelen

MICKEY ARISON, CHAIRMAN AND CEO, NOTED IN HIS 2005 LETTER TO THE STOCKHOLDERS that "Carnival Corporation has become the world's most profitable vacation company, with revenues surpassing $11.6 billion and net income approaching $2.3 billion. Our revenues increased by 14 percent during the past year with 8% driven by the added capacity of new ships and 6 percent from a combination of higher ticket prices, occupancies, and onboard spending." He further stated, "2005 also brought record increases in fuel prices, which cost the company an incremental $0.21 per share and drove the unit costs up 5 percent versus prior years."[1]

Arison explained, "While our targeted brands and strategic growth initiatives remain important ingredients for success, an entrepreneurial spirit is what out company thrives on. . . . Our culture empowers our brand managers to make daily decisions to the best interest of building their respective operating companies. Each brand is accountable for its individual performance."[2]

Overview

In 1972, Ted Arison founded Carnival Cruise Line with one ship, the *Mardi Gras*. Ted Arison's son, Mickey Arison, now serves as Chairman and CEO. In 2006, the company had a portfolio of 12 distinct cruise lines with 79 ships serving 7 continents.

The company's 12 cruise brands were (1) **Carnival Cruise Lines** with 21 ships; (2) **Princess Cruises** with 14 ships; (3) **Holland America Line** with 12 ships; (4) **Costa Cruises** with 10 ships; (5) **P&O Cruises** with 5 ships; (6) **AIDA Cruises** with 4 ships; (7) **Cunard Line** with 2 ocean liners; (8) **P&O Cruises Australia** with 3 ships; (9) **Ocean Village** with 1 ship; (10) **Swan Hellenic** with 1 ship; (11) **Seabourn Cruise Line** with 3 ships; and (12) **Windstar**

Cruises with 3 ships. These 79 ships had a capacity of 136,960 passengers. These ships equated to 85% of the company's total assets, and 11% of the operating cost as depreciation.

Carnival also owned a chain of 16 hotels and lodges in Alaska and the Canadian Yukon with 3,000 guest rooms. The company owned 30 domed rail cars, which were run by the Alaska Railroad as sight-seeing trains. Carnival operated two luxury day trips for tours of the glaciers in Alaska and the Yukon River.[3]

The company's occupancy rate for cruises was 105.5%, 104.5%, and 102.6% in 2005, 2004, and 2003, respectively. The company signed agreement with two shipyards to construct 16 additional ships at the cost of $8.1 billion. These 16 ships were scheduled to be delivered between 2006 and September 2009. The company has sold one of these ships. The new ships will increase passenger capacity by 41,816 lower berths or 30.5%. The company stated that it may sell a few older ships and place additional orders for new ships to be delivered in 2008 and 2009.[4]

The global cruise industry carried approximately 14 million passengers in 2005. The U.S. cruise industry grew annually by approximately by 9.1% between 1999 and 2004. In Europe, the compound growth rate was approximately 8.4% for the same time period. In 2005, Carnival had 6,848,386 passengers, which made up 48.9% of the global cruise industry's total number of passengers.

The Evolution of Cruising[5]

With the replacement of ocean liners by aircraft in the 1960s as the primary means of transoceanic travel, the opportunity for developing the modern cruise industry was created. Ships no longer required to ferry passengers from destination to destination became available to investors with visions of a new vacation alternative to complement the increasing affluence of Americans. Cruising, once the purview of the rich and leisure class, was targeted to the middle class, with service and amenities similar to the grand days of first-class ocean travel.

According to Robert Meyers, Editor and Publisher of *Cruise Travel* magazine, the increasing popularity of taking a cruise as a vacation can be traced to two serendipitously timed events. First, television's "Love Boat" series dispelled many myths associated with cruising and depicted people of all ages and backgrounds enjoying the cruise experience. This show was among the top 10 shows on television during the 1970s and provided extensive publicity for cruise operators. Second, the increasing affluence of Americans and the increased participation of women in the workforce gave couples and families more disposable income for discretionary purposes, especially vacations. As the myths were dispelled and disposable income grew, younger couples and families "turned on" to the benefits of cruising as a vacation alternative, creating a large new target market for the cruise product, which accelerated the growth in the number of Americans taking cruises as a vacation.

The Cruise Product[6]

Ted and Mickey Arison envisioned a product in which classical cruise elegance along with modern convenience could be had at a price comparable to land-based vacation packages sold by travel agents. Carnival's all-inclusive package, when compared to packages at resorts or theme parks, such as Walt Disney World, often was priced below these destinations; especially when the array of activities, entertainment, and meals were considered.

A typical vacation on a Carnival cruise ship started when the bags were tagged for the ship at the airport. On arriving at the port of embarkation, passengers were ferried by air-conditioned buses to the ship for boarding. Baggage was taken from the terminal to the cabin of the passenger by cruise/ship staff. Waiters dotted the ship offering tropical drinks to guests while the cruise staff oriented passengers to the various decks, cabins, and public rooms. In a few hours (most ships sailed in the early evening), dinner was served in the main dining rooms, where wine selection rivaled the finest restaurants and the variety of main dishes were designed to suit every palate. Diners could always order double portions if they decide not to save room for the variety of desserts and after-dinner specialties.

After dinner, cruisers could choose from among many forms of entertainment, including live music, dancing, nightclubs, and a selection of movies; or they could sleep through the midnight buffet until breakfast. (Most ships had five or more distinct nightclubs.) During the night, a daily program of activities arrived at the passengers' cabins. The biggest decisions to be made for the duration of the vacation were what to do (or not to do), what to eat and when (usually eight separate serving times, not including the 24-hour room service), and when to sleep. Service in all areas from dining to housekeeping was upscale and immediate. The service was so good that a common shipboard joke said that if you left your bed during the night to visit the head (sea talk for bathroom), your cabin steward would have made the bed and placed chocolates on the pillow by the time you returned to bed.

Carnival History

In 1972 Ted Arison, backed by the (AITS) American Travel Services, Inc., purchased an aging ocean liner from Canadian Pacific Empress Lines for $6.5 million. The new AITS subsidiary, Carnival Cruise Line, refurbished the vessel from bow to stern and renamed it the *Mardi Gras* to capture the party spirit. (Also included in the deal was another ship later renamed the *Carnivale.*) The company's start was not promising, however, as on the first voyage the *Mardi Gras,* with more than 300 invited travel agents aboard, ran aground in Miami Harbor. The ship was slow and guzzled expensive fuel, limiting the number of ports of call and lengthening the minimum stay of passengers on the ship to reach break-even. Arison then bought another older vessel from Union Castle Lines to complement the *Mardi Gras* and the *Carnivale* and named it the *Festivale.* To attract customers, Arison began adding diversions onboard such as planned activities, a casino, nightclubs, discos, and other forms of entertainment designed to enhance the shipboard experience.

Carnival lost money for the next three years, and in late 1974 Ted Arison bought out the Carnival Cruise subsidiary AITS, Inc., for $1 cash and the assumption of $5 million in debt. One month later, the *Mardi Gras* began showing a profit and through the remainder of 1975 operated at more than 100% capacity. (Normal ship capacity was determined by the number of fixed berths [referred to as lower berths] available. Ships, like hotels, could operate beyond this fixed capacity by using rollaway beds, Pullmans, and upper bunks.)

Ted Arison (then Chairman), along with Bob Dickinson (then Vice President of Sales and Marketing) and his son Mickey Arison (then President), began to alter the current approach to cruise vacations. Carnival targeted first-time cruisers and young people with a moderately priced vacation package that included airfare to the port of embarkation and home after the cruise. Per diem rates were very competitive with other vacation packages; Carnival offered passage to multiple exotic Caribbean ports, several meals served daily with premier restaurant service, and all forms of entertainment and activities included in the base fare. The only things not included in the fare were items of a personal nature, liquor purchases, gambling, and tips for the cabin steward, table waiter, and busboy. Carnival continued to add to the shipboard experience with a greater variety of activities, nightclubs, and other forms of entertainment and varied ports of call to increase its attractiveness to potential customers. It was the first modern cruise operator to use multimedia-advertising promotions and established the theme of "Fun Ship" cruises, primarily promoting the ship as the destination and ports of call as secondary. Carnival told the public that it was throwing a shipboard party and everyone was invited. Today, the "Fun Ship" theme still permeates all Carnival Cruise brand ships.

Throughout the 1980s, Carnival was able to maintain a growth rate of approximately 30%—about three times that of the industry as a whole. Between 1982 and 1988, its ships sailed with an average capacity of 104%. Targeting younger, first-time passengers by promoting the ship as a destination proved to be extremely successful. Carnival's customer profile showed that approximately 30% of the passengers at that time were between the ages of 25 and 39, with household incomes of $25,000 to $50,000.

In 1987, Ted Arison sold 20% of his shares in Carnival Cruise Lines and immediately generated over $400 million for further expansion. In 1988, Carnival acquired the Holland America Line, which had four cruise ships with 4,500 berths. Holland America was positioned to appeal to higher-income travelers with cruise prices averaging 25%–35% more than similar Carnival cruises. The deal also included two Holland America subsidiaries, Windstar Sail Cruises and Holland America Westours. This purchase allowed Carnival to begin an aggressive "superliner" building campaign for its core subsidiary. By 1989, the cruise segments of Carnival Corporation carried more than 750,000 passengers in one year, a "first" in the cruise industry.

Ted Arison relinquished the role of Chairman to his son Mickey in 1990, a time when the explosive growth of the industry began to subside. Higher fuel prices and increased airline costs began to affect the industry as a whole. The first Persian Gulf War caused many cruise operators to divert ships from European and Indian ports to the Caribbean area of operations, increasing the number of ships competing directly with Carnival. Carnival's stock price fell from $25 in June of 1990 to $13 later in that year. The company also incurred a $25.5 million loss during fiscal 1990 for the operation of the Crystal Palace Resort and Casino in the Bahamas. In 1991, Carnival reached a settlement with the Bahamian government (effective March 1, 1992) to surrender the 672-room Riviera Towers to the Hotel Corporation of the Bahamas in exchange for the cancellation of some debt incurred in constructing and developing the resort. The corporation took a $135 million write-down on the Crystal Palace for that year.

The early 1990s, even with industry-wide demand slowing, were still a very exciting time. Carnival took delivery of its first two "superliners," the *Fantasy* (1990) and the *Ecstasy* (1991), which were to further penetrate the three- and four-day cruise market and supplement the seven-day market. In early 1991, Carnival took delivery of the third superliner, *Sensation* (inaugural sailing November 1, 1993) and later in the year contracted for the fourth superliner, to be named the *Fascination* (inaugural sailing 1994).

In 1991, Carnival attempted to acquire Premier Cruise Lines, which was then the official cruise line for Walt Disney World in Orlando, Florida, for approximately $372 million. The deal was never consummated because the involved parties could not agree on price. In 1992, Carnival acquired 50% of Seabourn, gaining the cruise operations of K/S Seabourn Cruise Lines, and formed a partnership with Atle Brynestad. Seabourn served the ultra-luxury market with destinations in South America, the Mediterranean, Southeast Asia, and the Baltic.

The 1993 to 1995 period saw the addition of the superliner *Imagination* for Carnival Cruise Lines and the *Ryndam* for Holland America Lines. In 1994, the company discontinued the operations of Fiestamarina Lines, which had attempted to serve Spanish-speaking clientele. Fiestamarina had been beset with marketing and operational problems and had never reached continuous operation. Many industry analysts and observers were surprised at the failure of Carnival to successfully develop this market. In 1995 Carnival sold a 49% interest in the Epirotiki Line, a Greek cruise operation, for $25 million and purchased $101 million (face amount) of senior secured notes of Kloster Cruise Limited, the parent of competitor Norwegian Cruise Lines, for $81 million.

Carnival Corporation continued to expand through internally generated growth by adding new ships. Additionally, Carnival seemed to be willing to continue with its external expansion through acquisitions if the right opportunity arose.

In June 1997, Royal Caribbean made a bid to buy Celebrity Cruise Lines for $500 million and assumption of $800 million in debt. Within a week, Carnival had responded by submitting a counteroffer to Celebrity for $510 million and the assumption of debt. Two days later, Carnival raised the bid to $525 million. Nevertheless, Royal Caribbean announced on June 30, 1997, the final merger arrangements with Celebrity. The resulting company had 17 ships, with more than 30,000 berths.

Not to be thwarted in its expansion, Carnival announced in June 1997 the purchase of Costa, an Italian cruise company and the largest European cruise line, for $141 million. The purchase was finalized in September 2000. External expansion continued when Carnival announced the acquisition of the Cunard Line for $500 million from Kvaerner ASA on May 28, 1998. Cunard was then operationally merged with Seabourn Cruise Line. Carnival owned 100% of the resulting Cunard Line in fiscal 2000. In an attempt at further expansion, Carnival announced on December 2, 1999, a hostile bid for NCL Holding ASA, the parent company of Norwegian Cruise Lines. Carnival was unsuccessful in this acquisition attempt. The terrorist attack on New York's twin towers on 9/11/2001 caused tourists to cancel cruise plans. It caused several companies to go into bankruptcy. Some companies discounted cruise costs. Carnival soon recovered once public fears subsided.[7]

On September 30, 2006, Royal Caribbean announced the acquisition of Pullman, a privately held Spanish cruise and tour operator, for about $551 million. Pulman was the top brand in Spain—Europe's fourth-largest market. The company was very active in South America. The company's five ships ranged in age from 6 to 41 years. Pullman generated two-thirds of its revenue from cruises.[8]

Carnival's Corporate Governance

Board of Directors

Exhibit 1A shows the 14 members of Carnival's Board of Directors, of whom six were internal members. Mickey Arison had beneficial ownership of 188,054,943 shares of stock. He owned 29% of the company's stock. (He also owned the Miami Heat, a basketball team which had won the 2005 NBA Championship.) The Arison family and its trusts controlled 36% of the stock. Mickey's sister, Shari Arison, former Board member, owned 5,103,900 shares. All directors and executive officers as a group owned 190,115,930 shares (29.8% of the total shares).

According to the Board's by-laws, each outside director must own at least 5,000 shares of stock. Each year the external Board members were granted 10,000 stock options. Each director's annual retainer fee was $40,000 for serving on the Board, and extra fees were paid for attending Board and committee meetings.[9]

Exhibit 1B lists Carnival's executive officers. **Exhibit 2** shows compensation for the key executives.

EXHIBIT 1
Board of Directors and Principal Officers: Carnival Corporation & plc

A. BOARD OF DIRECTORS

Mickey Arison
Chairman of the Board and Chief Executive Officer Carnival Corporation & plc

Robert H. Dickinson
President and Chief Executive Officer Carnival Cruise Lines

Pier Luigi Foschi
Chairman and Chief Executive Officer Costa Crociere, S.p.A.

Richard J. Glasier
Former President and Chief Executive Officer Argosy Gaming Company

A. Kirk Lanterman
Chairman
Holland America Line Inc.

Sir John Parker
Chairman National Grid plc and The Peninsular and Oriental Steam Navigation Company

(Continued)

EXHIBIT 1
(Continued)

Stuart Subotnick
General Partner and Executive Vice President
Metromedia Company

B. DIRECTORS EMERITUS

Ted Arison (1924–1999)
Chairman Emeritus, Carnival Corporation

Meshulam Zonis
Director Emeritus, Carnival Corporation

Mark Birnbach
Director Emeritus, Carnival Corporation

The Lord of Plaistow GCVO, CBE
Life President pf P&O Cruises

Horst Rahe
Life President of AIDA Cruises

Richard G. Capen, Jr.
Former United States Ambassador to Spain
Corporate Director, Author and Business
Consultant

Arnold W. Donald
President and Chief Executive Officer
Juvenile Diabetes Research Foundation
International

Howard S. Frank
Vice Chairman of the Board and Chief
Operating Officer
Carnival Corporation & plc

Baroness Hogg
Chairman
3i Group plc and FrontierEconomicLtd.

Modesto A. Maidique
President
Florida International University

Peter G. Ratcliffe
Chief Executive Officer
P&O Princess Cruises International

Uzi Zucker
Private Investor

C. PRINCIPAL OFFICERS

Mickey Arison
Chairman of the Board and Chief Executive
Officer

Howard S. Frank
Vice Chairman of the Board and Chief
Operating Officer

Gerald R. Cahill
Executive Vice President and Chief Financial
and Accounting Officer

Richard D. Ames
Senior Vice President, Management Advisory
Services

Pamela C. Conover
Senior Vice President Shared Services

Ian J. Gaunt
Senior Vice President International

Arnaldo Perez
Senior Vice President, General Counsel and
Secretary

D. OPERATIONS SEGMENTS

1. AIDA CRUISES
Michael Thamm
President

2. CARNIVAL CRUISE LINES
Robert H. Dickinson
President and Chief Executive Officer

3. COSTA CROCIERE S.p.A
Pier Luigi Foschi
Chairman of the Board and Chief
Executive Officer

4. CUNARD LINE
Carol Marlow
President and Managing Director

5. HOLLAND AMERICA LINE
Stein Kruse
President and Chief Executive Officer

6. PRINCESS CRUISES
Alan Buckelew
President

7. P&O CRUISES AUSTRALIA
Gavin Smith
Managing Director

8. P&O CRUISES UK
David K. Dingle

**9. P&O PRINCESS CRUISES
  INTERNATIONAL**
Peter G. Ratcliffe
Chief Executive Officer

10. PRINCESS CRUISES
Alan B. Buckelew
President

11. SEABURN CRUISE LINE
Deborah Natansolm
President

SOURCE: *Carnival Corporation & plc, 2005 Annual Report.*

EXHIBIT 2
Key Executive Compensation: Carnival Corporation & plc

| Name and Principal Position | Year | Annual Compensation | | | Long-Term Compensation Awards | |
		Salary ($)	Bonus ($)	Other Annual Compensation ($)	Restricted Stock Awards ($)	Number of Securities Underlying Options ($)
Mickey Arison	2005	800,000	2,900,000	432,600	3,218,400	120,000
Chairman and CEO	2004	700,000	2,400,000	389,000	3,475,200	120,000
	2003	500,000	1,675,000	101,200	2,654,000	120,000
Howard S. Frank	2005	700,000	2,800,000	198,300	2,682,000	100,000
Vice Chairman	2004	600,000	2,300,000	193,400	2,896,000	100,000
and CEO	2003	400,000	1,645,000	198,100	4,913,650	100,000
Robert Dickinson	2005	741,000	1,596,400	160,100	2,070,400	80,000
President and CEO of	2004	400,000	1,393,200	137,600	1,849,200	80,000
Carnival Cruise Lines	2003	400,000	1,256,200	98,900	5,688,400	80,000
Peter G. Ratcliffe	2005	1,100,000	902,000	56,900	1,420,300	50,000
CEO of P&O Princess	2004	1,100,000	814,000	60,500	1,393,200	50,000
Cruises International	2003	966,833	419,800	57,800	864,900	51,188
Pier Luigi Foschi	2005	1,097,000	979,400	237,100	543,600	50,000
Chairman and	2004	981,000	1,033,000	150,000	—	—
CEO of Costa	2003	885,000	490,000	75,000	—	—

Note:
1. Notes were deleted

SOURCE: *Carnival Corporation & plc, SEC- DEF 14A, February 24, 2006, p. 34.*

Corporate Organization

Carnival Corporation & plc was a global cruise company and one of the largest vacation companies in the world. Its portfolio of 12 cruise brands (not including Pullman, its most recent purchase) included Carnival Cruise Lines, Princess Cruises, Holland America Line, Windstar Cruises, and Seabourn Cruise Line in North America; P&O Cruises, Cunard Line, Ocean Village and Swan Hellenic in the United Kingdom; AIDA Cruises in Germany; Costa Cruises in Europe; and P&O Cruises in Australia. These brands, which, according to management, comprised the most-recognized cruise brands in North and South America, the United Kingdom, Germany, Southern Europe, and Australia, offered a wide range of holiday and vacation products to a customer base that is broadly varied in terms of cultures, languages, and leisure-time preferences. The corporation also owned two tour companies in Alaska and the Canadian Yukon that complement its cruise operations, Holland America Tours and Princess Tours. Combined, its vacation companies attracted almost 7 million guests annually. Carnival Corporation was incorporated in Panama, and Carnival plc was incorporated in England and Wales.[10]

Mission

According to management, "Our mission is to deliver exceptional vacation experiences through the world's best-known cruise brands that cater to a variety of different lifestyles and budgets, all at an outstanding value unrivaled on land or at sea."[11]

EXHIBIT 3
Principal Operating Subsidiaries: Carnival Corporation & plc

	Country of Incorporation/ Registration	Percentage of Equity Share Capital Owned at November 30, 2005	Business Description
P&O Princess Cruises International Ltd	England	100%[1]	Shipowner
Alaska Hotel Properties LLC	U.S.A.	100%	Hotel operations
P&O Travel Ltd	England	100%	Travel agent
Royal Hyway Tours Inc.	U.S.A.	100%	Land tours
Tour Alaska LLC	U.S.A.	100%	Rail tours
CC U.S. Ventures, Inc.	U.S.A.	100%	Holding company
Costa Crociere S.p.A.	Italy	99.98%	Passenger cruising
Cozumel Cruise Terminal S.A. de C.V.	Mexico	100%	Port operations
Global Fine Arts, Inc.	U.S.A.	100%	Art sales and picture framing
Holland America Line Inc.	U.S.A.	100%	Hotel operations and land tours and rail tours

Note:
[1] Held directly by the company.

SOURCE: *Carnival Corporation & plc, 2005 Annual Report, p. 31.*

Operating Segments

The principal operating subsidiaries are shown in **Exhibit 3.**

Corporate Brands[12]

The 12 cruise ship lines competed in all of the three sectors—contemporary, premium, and luxury—of the cruise industry.

Carnival Cruise Lines (www.Carnival.com)

Carnival Cruise Lines was the most popular and most profitable cruise line in the world. The leader in the contemporary cruise sector, Carnival operated 21 ships with a total passenger capacity of 47,820. In 2005, it carried a record 3.3 million passengers—the most in the cruise industry. Its newest ship was the *Carnival Miracle.* At that time the line had two new ships, at an estimated cost of $1.0 billion, scheduled for delivery during 2006 and 2007. Carnival ships cruised to destinations in the Bahamas, Canada, the Caribbean, the Mexican Riviera, New England, the Panama Canal, Alaska, and Hawaii, with most cruises ranging from 3 to 7 days.

Princess Cruises (www.princesscruises.com)

Princess Cruises offered a "complete escape" from daily routine. It had 14 ships with a total passenger capacity of 29,152. Princess treated its passengers to world-class cuisine, exceptional service, and a myriad of resort-like amenities onboard, including the Lotus Spa, Movies Under the Stars, lavish casinos, nightclubs, and lounges. Princess was the only cruise line to offer a choice of dining experiences, so guests could dine when and where it was convenient. The Princess Fleet was growing with the addition of the *Crown Princess* in 2006 and the *Emerald Princess* in 2007. The *Crown Princess* carried more than 3,100 passengers and 1,200 crew members. The *Princess* fleet provided more than 90 unique itineraries to more than 270 destinations. Princess was classified in the industry as contemporary premium. The company offered cruises from 7 to 30 days.

Holland America Line (www.hollandamerica.com)

The Holland America Line was a leader in the premium cruise sector. Holland America operated a five-star fleet of 12 ships, with 18,930 passenger capacity. The line had two new ships scheduled for delivery during 2006 and 2007 at an estimated cost of $800 million. Holland America Line visited 280 ports in its primary destinations, which included Alaska, the Caribbean, the Panama Canal, Mexico, South America, Hawaii, Canada, New England, and Europe. The company offered cruises from 2 to 108 days. Its ships sailed to more than 300 ports of call on all seven continents. In 2005, the company had more than 300 cruises.

Seabourn Cruise Line (www.seabourn.com)

Seabourn Cruise Line epitomized luxury cruising aboard each of its three intimate all-suite ships. The Yachts of Seabourn were lavishly appointed with virtually one staff member for every guest, to ensure the highest quality service. The company owned three ships with total capacity of 624 passengers.

Ocean Village (www.oceanvillageholidays.co.uk)

Ocean Village was founded in 2004 in the United Kingdom. Its one ship sailed throughout the Mediterranean and the Caribbean. It was expecting a second ship in November 2007.

P & O Cruises (www.pocruises.com)

P & O Cruises was the largest cruise operator and the best-known contemporary cruise brand in the United Kingdom. The five-ship fleet offered cruises to the Mediterranean, the Baltic, the Norwegian Fjords, the Caribbean, and the Atlantic Islands, as well as around-the-world voyages. The passenger capacity was 8,844 people. Its principal market was the United Kingdom.

Cunard Line (www.cunard.com)

The Cunard Line offered the only regular transatlantic crossing service aboard the world-famous ocean liner *Queen Mary 2*. Her equally famous sister, *Queen Elizabeth 2*, sailed on unique itineraries worldwide serving both U.S. and U.K. guests. The passenger capacity of these two ships was 4,410. The 1,968-passenger *Queen Victoria* joined the fleet in 2005. Cunard's primary market was the United Kingdom and North America. The line proudly carried the legacy of the era of sophisticated floating palaces into the 21st century. These ships were in the luxury sector of the industry.

Swan Hellenic (www.swanhellenic.com)

Swan Hellenic operated a program of discovery cruises, targeted particularly to the United Kingdom. Itineraries included the Mediterranean, North America, South America, the Caribbean, the Indian Ocean, and the Far East.

Costa Cruises (www.costacruises.com)

Costa Cruises was Europe's leading cruise line. Headquartered in Italy, Costa offered guests on its 10 ships a multi-ethnic, multi-cultural, and multi-lingual ambiance. The line had two new ships slated to enter service during 2006 and 2007 at an estimated cost of $1.1 billion. Costa ships, including its newest, the popular *Costa Fortuna,* sailed to destinations in Europe, South America, and the Caribbean.

AIDA (www.aida.com)

AIDA was the best-known cruise brand in the fast growing German cruise industry. With its four club ships, AIDA offered cruises to the Mediterranean, the Baltic, and Norwegian Fjords, Canary Islands, and the Caribbean.

Windstar Cruises (www.windstarcruises.com)

Windstar Cruises offered luxury cruising under sail. The line's three sailing yachts offered its 148 to 308 privileged guests all ocean-view staterooms, five-star service, an eclectic selection of cuisine created by celebrity chef Joachim Splichal, and a water sports program. Windstar Cruises sailed to destinations in Europe, the Caribbean, Central America, and the South Pacific. The passenger capacity was 604. Its target market included people aged 30–50, who liked to explore new places and try new things.

Management's View of the Company[13]

Carnival's management presented its analysis of the company's operations in the 2005 SEC *10-K Report*:

> *Worldwide we continue to hear—"Carnival is the wrong end of the market for our client"— which in fact these days could hardly be further from the truth. The "New Carnival," as we have described the new ship product and delivery, is a world apart from the old Carnival. Carnival Corp. has really lifted the product to a new level where in many ways it competes against Holland America in some areas—even occasionally exceeding them in price points as well. Certainly the older ships are still the product we know from years past—the original "Fun Ships"—but gradually these are being phased out to be replaced by new ships offering every amenity found elsewhere as well as excellent food and service.*
>
> *As we all know, the European taste is in many ways more subdued than the American. Take a point in question—Costa Cruises—their ships are delightful and tastefully decorated, but done to the European expectation and as such are more "subdued" in their décor. So it should come as no surprise that Carnival has been slow in making ground in the European cruise market. That is until the "NEW Carnival" appeared on the scene.*
>
> *Carnival's Senior VP Vicki Freed acknowledged that "Carnival could not have had a full season in Europe 10 years ago—not at these price points. We didn't have the quality of the hardware and the quality of the onboard experience that we have now."*
>
> *Carnival's European ship for the 2005 season was the* Liberty. *It was not only delivered on time, but service was immediately up to the line's standards. Agents who tell clients to be wary of ships less than one year old might want to reassess that message when it comes to Carnival.*
>
> Liberty *is Carnival's sole new ship this year, but Freed says that's not the only reason it was humming from the get-go. "Remember in 2002 we had three new ships enter service, and they were all totally ready," she says. "We have a very experienced, organized team, and we're willing to spend the money to make sure the targets are made. A lot of the staff on* Liberty *have come from Carnival's* Valor; *they know how to sail on new ships, and that makes a difference."*

In a certain sense, the fact that Carnival is succeeding in Europe ties in well with today's Carnival marketing message. "If you look at our price points versus other major contemporary cruise lines, in many cases people are willing to spend a few dollars more for us," says Freed. "We're not the down and dirty pricing leader anymore."

Freed maintains that Carnival's onboard product delivers more than other brands in the contemporary market. "I just cruised on a premium cruise line, and I have to tell you, our food is equal to or better than our sister company," she says. "They won't like me saying that, but definitely our choice, our variety, even our presentation is better. Look at the Versace dishes we're using; look at the flatware, every single dish that comes out of the kitchen is a work of art, even in terms of placement of the vegetables. It's not just about throwing quantity on the plate, it's about putting quality and making it so eye-appealing that people say, 'Wow.' I think that's what today's Carnival is all about, the wow effect."

Freed says the biggest wow factor in terms of the soft goods is the bedding, a feature which has more often been promoted by premium and luxury lines. "People are sick and tired of flowered bed spreads," she notes. "They want the beautiful white clean look. We even have a pillow menu for our suite guests where they can choose from five different types of pillows, whether it's all feathers or synthetic, hard or soft."

Summer in the Tropics (Hurricanes)

Worldwide (Carnival) was fortunately a short-lived victim of hurricane Katrina—our offices lost power late on Thursday evening and happily for us power was restored in the early hours of Monday morning, so in fact we did not lose too many hours. As some of our clients might have noticed, however, more disruptive forces were at work a week or so before when somehow a virus got into our main communications server and caused havoc. After two days of hard work, our technical team was able to rebuild the system, but it was a very different period with a number of programs on the final home run.

Generally speaking, South Florida cruise lines also got fully back to business on Monday after Hurricane Katrina impacted some land-based operations on Friday. Katrina hit Thursday night as a Category 1 hurricane that downed trees and caused flooding and widespread power losses. Many who tried to reach work on Friday encountered dangerous or impassable roadways.

Fort Lauderdale companies were not affected as were those in Miami. Radisson Seven Seas never lost power, so it was business as usual for the staff that could get into the office on Friday. MSC Cruises USA also reopened on Friday, as did Silversea Cruises.

In Miami, Carnival was fully back to business today, as was Norwegian Cruise Line, where everyone was able to get to work. The Royal Caribbean/Celebrity offices reopened after staying closed on Friday. They did suffer some damage—mostly fallen trees and some damage to the roof. Oceania Cruises resumed full operations on Monday afternoon and the reservations department made up for lost time with record call volume.

New Orleans and the Gulf Coast, where Katrina packed a powerful Category 4 punch, has suffered devastating damage, but it could have been even worse as the eye of the storm jogged east at the last moment moving New Orleans out of the worst winds and rain which caused severe damage and flooding as far over as Mobile and places in western Florida. At this time there is no way of knowing how badly affected the port operations will be and when the cruise lines will be able to return to their New Orleans departures. Worldwide will be monitoring the situation and advising those of our clients with program operating from there as news comes in.

We are devastated to see the news reports coming in from the area and want to take this opportunity—on behalf of all of us and our clients—to send our condolences and best wishes for a speedy resolution to the many problems our friends and their families are having to live through in the effected area. Carnival leased three ships to the government for victims of Katrina.[14]

Advertising

The advertising expenses totaled $455 million, $464 million, and $335 million for 2005, 2004, and 2003, respectively.

Human Resource Management

Shoreside operations had approximately 9,500 full-time and 4,200 part-time/seasonal employees. Carnival also employed approximately 57,500 officers, crew, and staff onboard the 79 ships at any one time. Because of the highly seasonal nature of the Alaskan and Canadian operations, Holland America Tours and Princess Tours increased their workforce during the late spring and summer months in connection with the Alaskan cruise season, employing additional seasonal personnel, which had been included above. Carnival had entered into agreements with unions covering certain employees in the hotel, motor coach, and ship operations. Management considered its employee and union relations to be generally good.

On-board service was labor intensive, employing help from some 51 nations—mostly third-world countries—with reasonable returns to employees. For example, waiters on the *Jubilee* could earn approximately $18,000 to $27,000 per year (base salary and tips), significantly greater than could be earned in their home country for similar employment. Waiters typically worked 10 hours per day with approximately one day off per week for a specified contract period (usually 3 to 9 months). Carnival records showed that employees remained with the company for approximately eight years and that applicants exceeded demand for all cruise positions. Nonetheless, the American Maritime union had cited Carnival (and other cruise operators) several times for exploitation of its crews. The numbers of employees were 71,000, 69,000, 59,000, and 59,000 in 2005, 2004, 2003, and 2002, respectively.[15]

Government Regulations

All of Carnival's ships were registered in a country outside the United States and each ship flew the flag of its country of registration. Carnival's ships were regulated by various international, national, state, and local port authorities' laws, regulations, and treaties in force in the jurisdictions in which the ships operate. In U.S. waters and ports, the ships had to comply with U.S. Coast Guard and U.S. Public Health regulations, the Maritime Transportation Security Act, International Ship and Port Facility Security Code, U.S. Oil Pollution Act of 1990, U.S. Maritime Commission, local port authorities, local and federal law enforcement agencies, and all laws pertaining to the hiring of foreign workers. All cruise ships were inspected for health issues, and received a rating, which was published for potential cruisers to review. Terrorist threats had tightened U.S. security of ports regarding docking facilities, cargo containers and storage areas, and crews.[16]

Environmental Policy

According to Mickey Arison,

> *Our corporate culture fosters a deep commitment to preserving the marine environment and in particular the pristine condition of the waters upon which our vessels sail. We are committed to pollution prevention and continuous improvement of our environmental management. We recently announced our goal to become certified in accordance with the international recognized standard ISO 14001, which provides a framework for environmental management and measurement of environmental improvement.[17]*

The company had seven stated environmental objectives for 2006. In September 2006, Carnival Corporation & plc earned Environmental Management Certification for meeting the ISO 14001 standards established by the International Organization for Standardization. The certification was granted to Carnival's operating units. The certification was issued by four different recognized maritime regulatory agencies. The agencies were RINA of Italy, who also certified new ships as seaworthy, Germanischer Lloyd of Germany, Lloyd's Register Quality Assurance from North America, and the Maritime and Coastguard Agency of the U.K.

The California Air Resources Board adopted rules to implement legislation that barred cruise ships from burning refuse within three miles of shore. Violations result in a fine of $25,000 per violation. The law was going into effect on January 1, 2007. Similar types of legislation were being proposed for other vessels, such as cargo ships, tankers, and military carriers based in San Diego.

Suppliers

The company's largest purchases were for travel agency services, fuel, advertising, food and beverages, hotel and restaurant supplies and products, airfare, repairs and maintenance and dry-docking, port facility utilization, and communication services, and for the construction of ships. Although Carnival utilized a select number of suppliers for most of its food and beverages and hotel and restaurant supplies and products, most of these items were available from numerous sources at competitive prices. The use of a select number of suppliers enabled management to, among other things, obtain volume discounts. The company purchased fuel and port facility services at some of its ports of call from a limited number of suppliers. In addition, the company performed major dry-dock and ship improvement work at dry-dock facilities in the Bahamas, British Columbia, Canada, the Caribbean, Europe, and the United States. As of January 30, 2006, Carnival had agreements in place for the construction of 16 cruise ships by two shipyards. Management believed there were sufficient dry-dock and shipbuilding facilities to meet the company's anticipated requirements. To better manage price fluctuations, the company hedged the price of fuel oil.

Legal Issues

On July 28, 2006, four law firms filed a lawsuit on behalf of six passengers, who had been injured 10 days earlier on the *Crown Princess* after the ship had suddenly listed (tilted) between 15 and 38 degrees to the right for no apparent reason. The passengers suffered serious physical injuries after being violently thrown against the ship's deck and walls. A total of 12 passengers were seriously injured and about 70 passengers had lesser injuries. Three passengers were hospitalized. One passenger reported, "It felt like (the ship) was going to fall over," and "It was shocking."

Jim Jacobs, co-author of the musical *Grease,* had filed a $100 million class-action lawsuit against 17 cruise lines, many owned by Carnival and Royal Caribbean. Jacobs accused the 17 cruise lines of violating U.S. and international laws and exhorted them to stop producing unlicensed materials written by Jacobs and other writers. According to Jacobs, "They are doing productions not approved by the authors that they would never permit, and then don't pay." Royal Caribbean's Celebrity Cruises had presented 365 performances of *Grease* "without securing the necessary licenses or permissions." *Grease* was reportedly slated to return to Broadway in 2007.

The company was the target of several lawsuits by former employees over overtime pay issues. In addition, Carnival paid $18 million in fines in 2002 for six pollution discharges by its ships. The company pleaded guilty to six felony counts for filing false statements with the

U.S. Coast Guard. The company also agreed to cover the company's environmental-safety practices on its ships and Carnival's port facilities around the world. A written statement by the company stated, "Carnival Corp accepts responsibility for the conduct that is the subject of its guilty plea." It also stated, "The company is committed to environmental compliance, and we are adopting a compliance program that will have Carnival the industry leader in sound environmental practices."[18]

The Cruise Industry

International Council of Cruise Lines management described developments in the cruising industry as follows:

> In 2005, the cruise industry experienced a more moderate rate of capacity expansion than in recent years. Four major new cruise ships were launched, but the size of the North American fleet remained unchanged at 192 vessels as an equal number of ships were withdrawn from the market. Due to larger newly-built ships, capacity grew by 2.2 percent for a total combined capacity of 245,755 lower berths. Overall occupancy rose to 106 percent in 2005, due in part, to passenger rescheduling after a number of cruises were cancelled during the hurricane season.
>
> U.S. ports continued to handle 75 percent of all global cruise embarkations in 2005. More than 8.6 million cruise passengers began their cruises from U.S. ports, an increase of 6.3 percent over the previous year. Globally, demand for cruising remained strong in 2005, and the industry increased passenger carryings by 6 percent over 2004 to 11.5 million passengers worldwide. U.S. residents totaled 9.1 million, or 79 percent, of global passengers.
>
> The top 10 cruise embarkation ports—Miami, Port Everglades, Port Canaveral, Los Angeles, Galveston, Tampa, New York, Long Beach, Seattle, and New Orleans—accounted for 84 percent of all U.S. passenger embarkations. Higher 2005 embarkation numbers were posted by Miami (5.3 percent), Los Angeles (30.9 percent), Galveston (22.1 percent), Tampa (6 percent) and Seattle (18.2 percent).[19]

The Top 10 Most Popular Cruise Destinations in 2004 Were[20]

Caribbean	45.1%
Europe/Mediterranean	22.4%
Alaska	7.7%
Mexico (West Coast)	6.2%
Panama Canal	3.8%
Hawaii	3.4%
Canada/New England	1.9%
Transatlantic	1.8%
Bermuda	1.7%
South America	1.4%
Others	4.6%

Industry Facts

- Approximately 51 million people (17% of the U.S. population) have cruised at least once. Nearly 2.9 million have taken a cruise in the past three years.
- It was estimated that about 31,028,000 of the U.S. population will take a cruise in the next three years. Non-residents are a substantial number of total passengers.[21]

- Target U.S. market:

  - Total target market—Adults 25+ and household (HH) income
  - Affluent market—Adults 25+ and HH income of $60,000+
  - Very affluent market—Adults 25+ and HH income of $80,000+
  - Ultra affluent—Adults 25+ and HH income of $150,000[22]

- Cost of cruising per person was up $39 in 2005. There were fewer discounts or promotional offers in 2005 (52%) versus 58% in 2004.

- The average airfare was $359.

- In 2005, the cruise industry contributed $32.4 billion to the U.S. economy, a 6% increase over 2004.

- In 2005, passengers and crews were directly responsible for spending $16.2 billion in U.S. goods and services.

- **Exhibit 4** provides additional cruise industry information.

- About 80% of all cruise passengers book some of their travel through a travel agent.

EXHIBIT 4
The Cruising
Industry

A. CRUISING COSTS[24]

	Cruisers				
	Cruiser	Destinations	Luxury	Premium	Contemporary
% Receiving discount or promotional offer	52%	40%	49%	59%	54%
Mean cruise + onboard/shore	$1,690	$2,240	$2,580	$2,020	$1,640
Cruise	$1,255	$1,653	$1,948	$1,559	$1,213
Onboard and shore side expenses	$435	$587	$632	$461	$427
% Who flew to cruise	64%	72%	63%	68%	64%
Airfare	$359	$428	$614	$384	$328

Compared to 2004, cruisers report a slightly higher cruise cost per person (up $39), with fewer discounts noted—52% from 58%.

B. INCIDENCE OF CRUISING

Approximately 51 million people have cruised at least once; of these, nearly 29 million have cruised in the past three years.

	Ever Cruised	People	Cruised in Past 3 Years	People
Target Market (Age 25+, $40k+)	39%	49,608,000	22%	27,984,000
Total U.S. Population (All ages, all incomes)	17%	51,096,000	10%	28,823,000

C. CRUISER SATISFACTION AND PERCEPTIONS OF TRAVEL AGENTS

- Four out of five cruisers (79%) use travel agents to book at least some of their cruises. (Because of self-reporting, this may be understated due to confusion with 800 numbers and/or agency Web sites.)

(Continued)

EXHIBIT 4
(Continued)

- Fifty-eight percent (58%) of cruisers and 53% of non-cruisers report high satisfaction levels with their travel agents.
- The majority of cruisers believe that travel agents are:
  - More knowledgeable about travel than they are (55%)
  - Knowledgeable about hotels/resorts and destinations and their unique differences (61%)
  - Remove the hassle from travel planning (51%)
- But cruiser beliefs about travel agents present serious challenges:
  - Get the best deal on vacations—now only 28%
  - Provide good advice (42%)
  - More than half (56%) believe they get better rates when they book on their own.

D. FIRST CRUISE
The first cruise for most was in the 1990s or earlier.

Year of First Cruise	Total Cruisers
2002–2005	28%
1999–2001	28%
1990–1998	19%
1980s	13%
1970s	4%
Prior to 1970	6%
TOTAL	**100%**[1]

[1]Actually adds to 98%

E. SUMMARY OF MARKET PROJECTIONS
- Based on consumer responses, the most likely number of cruisers over the next three years (2006–2003) is 31,028,000.
- These projections understate future cruise passenger volumes.
  - Non-U.S. residents represent a substantial fraction of total passengers but are not in the survey, and . . .
  - Some of our survey respondents will take multiple trips.

Number of U.S. Travelers Likely to Cruise within Next Three Years

	Target Cruise Market[2] $40K + HHI	Affluent Cruise Market $60K + HHI	Very Affluent Cruise Market $80K + HHI	Ultra Affluent Cruise Market $150K + HHI
Best Case	50,396,000	36,766,000	24,552,000	2,254,000
Most Likely	31,028,000	23,028,000	15,444,000	1,453,000

[2]HHI, household income.

F. CRITERIA FOR MAKING VACATION DECISIONS[25]

	Cruisers	Non-Cruise Vacations
The destination	8.7	8.7
The price	7.3	7.1
Best opportunity to relax and unwind	7.1	7.1
Fit my vacation schedule/days available	6.5	7.0
Offered a unique experience	7.0	6.6
The convenience	6.8	6.6
The particular hotel/resort property or cruise ship	6.5	5.1
Good programs for children and family	3.8	4.4

Note: Data used are based on a 10-point scale where 10 is "most influence" and 1 "did not influence at all."

SOURCE: "TNS," Cruise Industry Report, www.tns-global.com.

Competitors

Carnival's primary competitors were Royal Caribbean, Disney, and Norwegian Cruise Line. **Royal Caribbean** operated two brands, Royal Caribbean International and Celebrity Lines. Royal Caribbean operated 20 cruise ships with approximately 45,470 berths. Celebrity cruises operated 16 ships with approximately 16,116 berths. Royal Caribbean was founded in 1968 and based in Miami. The company employed 38,800 employees. In 2005, the company's revenues were $4.90 billion and net income of $663.47 million. The company's gross margin was 63.17% versus Carnival's at 54.25%. In 2005, an unfortunate passenger on his honeymoon aboard a Royal Caribbean ship fell overboard and was never found. Industry-wide, this was the 25th passenger to disappear on a cruise in the past five years.

Celebrity Lines had ordered two new ships, both of which would have 2,850 berths. One ship, the *Solstice,* was to be very large in order to have larger staterooms and more balconies. Condé Nast readers listed *Celebrity* as "The Best Cruise Ship in the World." For 2005, Royal Caribbean placed an order for an energy-efficient ship that would accommodate 5,400 passengers. Royal Caribbean created a new ad campaign, "Create Your Own Adventure," that highlighted vacation experiences told by passengers.[26]

Disney Cruise Line had two cruise ships, each having 877 staterooms (3,508 berths). Disney had its own private island, Castaway Bay. Starting in May 2006, the seven-night itinerary included two stops at the islands. One analyst said, "Carnival should thank Disney for taking children off their ships." Specific areas of the ships were designated for activities preferred by adults, families, teens, and children. People could play together or in separate activities. The following summer, Disney was to have its first Mediterranean cruise.[27]

Norwegian Cruise Line was the industry's fourth largest cruise line. Its new division, "NCL America," provided Hawaii Island hopping, East Coast cruising, and California coastal cruises. No other line covered all of these areas. The ships' atmosphere was "resort casual." The company was Hawaii's cruise leader. Norwegian had two divisions—Norwegian Costal Voyages with 14 ships and 6,092 berths, and Norwegian Cruise Line with 10 ships and 17,890 berths.[28]

Carnival's management briefly described the firm's competition in the following manner:

1. Carnival competed with land-based vacation alternatives throughout the world, including, among others, resorts, hotels, theme parks, and vacation ownership properties located in Las Vegas, Nevada, Orlando, Florida, various parts of the Caribbean, and Mexico, and Bahamian and Hawaiian Island destination resorts and numerous other vacation destinations throughout Europe and the rest of the world.

2. Carnival's primary cruise competitors in the contemporary and/or premium cruise segments for North American-sourced passengers were Royal Caribbean Cruise Ltd., which owned Royal Caribbean International and Celebrity Cruises Star Cruises, plc, which owned Norwegian Cruise Line and Orient Lines and Disney Cruise Lines.

3. The three primary cruise competitors for European-sourced passengers were My Travel's Sun Cruises, Fred Olsen, Saga and Thomson in the U.K.; Festival Cruises, Hapag-Lloyd, Peter Deilmann, Phoenix Reisen, and Transocean Cruises in Germany; and Mediterranean Shipping Cruises, Louis Cruise Line, Festival Cruises, and Spanish Cruise Line in Southern Europe. We also competed for passengers throughout Europe with Norwegian Cruise Line, Orient Lines, Royal Caribbean International, and Celebrity Cruises.

4. The company's primary competitors in the luxury cruise segment for our Cunard, Seabourn, and Windstar brands included Crystal Cruises, Radisson Seven Seas Cruise Line, and Silversea Cruises.

5. Carnival brands also competed with similar or overlapping product offerings across all of our segments.[29]

Finance

Carnival's management compared the company's 2005 financial results with those of 2004. The following was included in the company's 2005 SEC *10-K Report.*

Revenues

Net cruise revenues increased $1.02 billion, or 13.9% to $8.38 billion in 2005 from $17.36 billion in 2004. (See **Exhibits 5** and **6.**) The 8.5% increase in ALBDs (net revenue yields) between 2004 and 2005 accounted for $638 million of the increase, and the remaining $528 million was from increased net revenue yields, which increased 6.5% in 2005 compared

EXHIBIT 5
Consolidated Statements of Operations: Carnival Corporation & plc (Dollar amounts in millions, except per share data)

YEARS ENDING NOVEMBER 30	2005	2004	2003
Revenues			
Cruise			
Passenger tickets	$ 8,379	$7,357	$5,039
Onboard and other	2,356	2,070	1,420
Other	352	300	259
Total Revenue	$11,087	$9,727	$6,718
Cost and Expenses			
Operating			
Cruise			
Commissions, transportation and other	1,665	1,572	1,021
Onboard and other	408	359	229
Payroll and related	1,145	1,003	744
Food	615	550	393
Fuel	709	493	340
Other ship operating	1,425	1,270	897
Other	250	210	190
Total	$ 6,217	$5,457	$3,814
Selling and administrative	1,329	1,285	936
Depreciation and amortization	902	812	585
	8,448	7,554	5,335
Operating income	2,639	2,173	1,383
Nonoperating (expense) income			
Interest income	28	17	27
Interest expense, net of capitalized interest	(330)	(260)	(195)
Other (expense) income, net	(7)	(5)	8
	(309)	(272)	(160)
Income before income taxes	2,330	1,913	1,223
Income tax expense, net	(73)	(47)	(29)
Net Income	$ 2,257	$1,866	$1,194
Earnings per Share	—	—	—
Basic	$ 2.80	$ 2.31	$ 1.66
Diluted	$ 2.70	$ 2.24	$ 1.63
Dividends per Share	$ 0.80	$0.525	$ 0.44

SOURCE: *Carnival Corporation & plc, 2005 Annual Report, p. 5.*

EXHIBIT 6
Consolidated
Balance Sheet:
Carnival
Corporation & plc
(Dollar amounts in
millions except per
share data)

Years Ending November 30	2005	2004
Assets		
Cash and cash equivalents	$ 1,178	$ 643
Short-term investments	9	17
Accounts receivable, net	408	409
Inventories	250	240
Prepaid expenses and other	370	419
Total current assets	2,215	1,728
Property and equipment, net	21,312	20,823
Goodwill	3,206	3,321
Trademarks	1,282	1,306
Other assets	417	458
Total assets	$ 28,432	$ 27,636
Liabilities and Shareholders' Equity		
Current liabilities	—	—
Short-term borrowing	$300	$381
Current portion of long-term debt	1,042	681
Convertible debt subject to current put option	283	600
Accounts payable	690	631
Accrued liabilities and other	832	868
Customer deposits	2,045	1,873
Total current liabilities	5,192	5,034
Long-term debt	5,727	6,291
Other long-term liabilities and deferred income	541	551
Commitments and contingencies (Notes 7 and 8)		
Shareholders' equity		
Common stock of Carnival Corporation; $.01 par value; 1,960 shares authorized; 639 shares at 2005 and 634 shares at 2004 issued	6	6
Ordinary shares of Carnival plc; $1.66 par value; 226 shares authorized; 212 shares at 2005 and 2004 issued	353	353
Additional paid-in capital	7,381	7,311
Retained earnings	10,233	8,623
Unearned stock compensation	(13)	(16)
Accumulated other comprehensive income	156	541
Treasury stock; 2 shares of Carnival Corporation at 2005 and 42 shares of Carnival plc at 2005 and 2004, at cost	(1,144)	(1,058)
Total shareholders' equity	16,972	15,760
Total Liabilities and Shareholder's Equity	$ 28,432	$ 27,636

SOURCE: *Carnival Corporation & plc, 2005 Annual Report, p. 6.*

to 2004 (gross revenue yields increased by 4.9%). Net revenue yields increased in 2005 primarily from higher onboard revenues and the weaker U.S. dollar relative to the euro and sterling. Net revenue yields, as measured on a constant dollar basis, increased 6.1% in 2005. Gross cruise revenues increased $1.31 billion, or 13.9%, in 2005 to $10.74 billion from $9.43 billion in 2004 for largely the same reasons as net cruise revenues.

Onboard and other revenues included concession revenues of $2,356 million in 2005 and $2,076 million in 2004. Onboard and other revenues increased in 2005 compared to 2004, primarily because of the 8.5% increase in ALBDs and increased passenger spending on our ships.

Other non-cruise revenues increased $52 million, or 17.3%, to $352 million in 2005 from $300 million in 2004 primarily due to the increase in the number of cruises/tours sold.

Costs and Expenses

Net cruise costs increased $765 million, or 14.0%, to $6.217 million in 2005 from $5.452 billion in 2004. The 8.5% increase in ALBDs between 2004 and 2005 accounted for $387 million of the increase, and the remaining $236 million was from increased net cruise costs per ALBD, which increased 4.8% in 2005 compared to 2004 (gross cruise costs per ALBD increased 3.0%). Net cruise costs per ALBD increased primarily due to a $66 increase in fuel cost per metric ton, or 34.0%, to $260 per metric ton in 2005, higher dry-dock amortization expenses, a $23 million MNOPF contribution, and a weaker U.S. dollar relative to the euro and to the pound sterling in 2005. Net cruise costs per ALDB as measured on a constant dollar basis compared to 2004 increased 4.3% in 2005 and were flat excluding fuel costs and the MNOPF contribution, compared to 2004. Gross cruise costs increased $765 million, or 11.8%, in 2004 to $7.24 billion from $6.48 billion in 2004, which was a lower percentage increase than net cruise costs primarily because of the lower proportion of passengers who purchased air transportation from us in 2005.

Other non-cruise operating expenses increased $40 million, or 19.04%, to $250 million in 2005 from $210 million in 2004 primarily due to the increase in the number of cruise/tours sold.

Depreciation and amortization expense increased by $90 million, or 11.1%, to $902 million in 2005 from $812 million in 2004 largely due to the 8.5% increase in ALBDs through the addition of new ships and ship improvement expenditures.

Other Financial Information

The company's total contracted cash obligations were $1,517,400,000 for the period of 2006 through 2010. Ship future cash costs are forecasted at $7,590,000,000 and $7,052,000,000 for long-term debt reduction. The company had repurchased 8.0 million shares for $380 million during the period December 1, 2004 through February 6, 2006. The board had authorized the repurchase of up to $1.0 billion of the common stock.

The company's dividends were 80 cents, 52.5 cents, and 41 cents for 2005, 2004, and 2003 respectively. Customers' cruise deposits, which represent unearned revenue, are included in the balance sheet (current liability account) when received and recognized as cruise revenues on completion of the voyage. Customers also were required to pay the full cruise fare (minus deposit) 60 days in advance with the fares being recognized as cruise revenue on completion of the voyage. The customer can make changes aboard ship on his/her credit cards.

In August 2006, the State of Alaska passed a ballot initiative that requires all passengers to pay a $50 head tax. There is also a gaming tax on any gambling that occurs in the state's waters. Carnival management estimated that these two taxes could lower 2007 earnings by about 3 cents per share. Chairman Arison said, "We are disappointed that the Ballot Initiative 2 has passed as we believe this will inhibit the future growth and expansion of Alaska's tourism business." Carnival currently carries about 560,000 passengers a year to Alaska on 16 ships. An analyst wondered when other states and the Caribbean will pass similar legislation.[30]

Exhibit 7 shows revenues by geographical region. The United States generated 58.1%, 59.5%, and 67.1% for 2005, 2004, and 2003, respectively.

EXHIBIT 7
Revenues by
Geographic Regions:
Carnival
Corporation & plc
(Dollar amounts
in millions)

Region	2005	2004	2003
U.S.	$6,439	$5,788	$4,513
Continental Europe	1,681	1,549	971
U.K.	1,520	1,341	724
Canada	665	562	231
Australia and New Zealand	311	215	71
Others	471	272	208
Total Revenue	$11,087	$9,727	$6,718

SOURCE: *Carnival Corporation & plc, 2005 Annual Report, p. 26.*

NOTES

1. Carnival Corporation & plc, "2005 Annual Report," p. 2.
2. Ibid.
3. Ibid.
4. Michael I. Keefe, John K. Ross III, and Bill J. Middlebrook, "Carnival Corporation: Acquiring Princess Cruise Line (2002) in *Strategic Management and Business Policy–10th Edition,* Wheelen and Hunger. This section was directly quoted.
5. Ibid.
6. Ibid.
7. Carnival Corporation & plc, "Mission," www.carnivalvcorp.com, located under Corporate Information–Mission, History.
8. "2005 Annual Report," p. 5.
9. Carnival Corporation & plc, "Mission," www.carnivalcorp.com, located under Corporate Information–Mission, History.
10. Ibid., "Carnival Corporate Brands," This section was directly quoted.
11. "The New Carnival," www.cruiseco.com, October 2005. This entire section quoted.
12. International Council of Cruise Lines, ICCL— press release. Entire section was directly quoted. www.icci.org?pressroom/pressrelease.
13. Ibid.
14. Ibid., and Florida–Caribbean Cruise Association, "Cruise Industry Overview–2005."
15. Carnival Corporation & plc, "SEC 10-K," February 9, 2006, p. 19 of 394. Internet version.
16. Royal Caribbean Cruises, Ltd., press release.
17. Royal Caribbean Cruises, Ltd., press release, 1/23/2006.
18. Disney Cruise Lines, press release.
19. Norwegian Cruise Line, company document.
20. "2005 Annual Report," p. 12.
21. Ibid., p. 34.
22. Ibid.
23. Carnival Cruise Corporation & plc, "Environmental Policy," located at www.carnivalcorp.com, Investor Relations–Corporate Responsibility.
24. "Carnival Corp. Earns Environmental Management Information," www.marinelink.com 9/12/2006.
25. Ibid.
26. "SEC 10-K," p. 36 of 394.
27. Ibid.
28. Greg Levine, "Billionaire Arison 'Cruise Line in' Grease Suit," Forbes.com, February 13, 2006.
29. "2005 Annual Report," p. 42.
30. Associated Press, "Carnival Disappointed by Alaska Taxes," 8/24/2006.

CASE 19

Wal-Mart Stores, Inc.:

UNDER ATTACK (2006)

James W. Camerius and J. David Hunger

I am asked often what my father, Sam Walton, who founded Wal-Mart in 1962, would think of our Company today. There is no doubt he'd be proud of our success and the 1.8 million associates who serve our customers every day. He also would be proud that we remain true to the fundamental principles of leadership and business that he was so instrumental in establishing.[1]

ROB WALTON, CHAIRMAN OF THE BOARD WAL-MART STORES, INC.

REFLECTING ON HIS TENURE SINCE 2000 AS CHIEF EXECUTIVE OFFICER, LEE SCOTT, President and CEO of Wal-Mart Stores, Inc., was struck not only by how successful the company had been in terms of growth and financial performance, but also by how much the firm had come under attack for its business practices. On the positive side, the company had received much acclaim for its ability to carry out Sam Walton's vision. Its policy of "everyday low prices" had enabled it to dominate U.S. retailing. In 1999, *Discount Store News* honored Wal-Mart as "Retailer of the Century." In 2000, *Fortune* magazine named it as one of the "100 Best Places to Work." By 2002, Wal-Mart officially became the world's largest company based on its $245 billion in sales—three times the size of France's Carrefour, the second largest retailer in the world. Research revealed that 82% of American households made at least one purchase at Wal-Mart annually. By 2003, not only did it lead the *Fortune* 500, Wal-Mart also sat atop *Fortune*'s list of most admired companies. Economists giddily referred to the "Wal-Mart effect" in which the company's low prices had forced competitors to keep their prices low as well, thus suppressing inflation and increasing U.S. productivity year after year. For example, one study found that a new Wal-Mart store causes competitors' prices to drop 7%–13% for goods such as toothpaste, shampoo, aspirin, and laundry detergent five years after Wal-Mart entered a city. Another study revealed that "big box" retailers, like Wal-Mart, offered households $.25 back for every dollar spent on groceries, or around $450 a year on average.[2]

By 2006, Wal-Mart's net sales had increased 9.5% over 2005 to a record $312.4 billion for the fiscal year ending January 31, 2006. At the same time, net income had risen 9.4% to a record $11.2 billion and earnings per share had grown from $2.41 in 2005 to $2.68 in 2006.

EXHIBIT 1

Eleven-Year Financial Summary: Wal-Mart Stores, Inc. (Dollar amounts in millions except per share data)

Fiscal Year Ending January 31	2006	2005	2004
1. Operating Results			
Net sales	$312,427	$285,222	$256,329
Net sales increase	9.5%	11.3%	11.6%
Comparative store sales increase in the United States[1]	3%	3%	4%
Cost of sales	$240,391	$219,793	$198,747
Operating, selling, general and administrative expenses	56,733	51,248	44,909
Interest expense, net	1,172	986	832
Effective tax rate	33.4%	34.7%	36.1%
Income from continuing operations	11,231	10,267	8,861
Net income	$ 11,231	$ 10,267	$ 9,054
Per share of common stock:			
Income from continuing operations, diluted	$ 2.68	$ 2.41	$ 2.03
Net income, diluted	2.68	2 41	2.07
Dividends	0.60	0.52	0.36
2. Financial Position			
Current assets of continuing operations	$ 43,824	$ 38,854	$ 34,421
Inventories	32,191	29,762	26,612
Property, equipment and capital lease assets, net	79,290	68,118	59,023
Total assets of continuing operations	138,187	120,154	105,405
Current liabilities of continuing operations	48,826	43,182	37,840
Long-term debt	26,429	20,087	17,102
Long-term obligations under capital leases	3,742	3,171	2,997
Shareholders' equity	53,171	49,396	43,623
3. Financial Ratios			
Current ratio	0.9	0.9	0.9
Return on assets[2]	8.91%	9.3%	9.2%
Return on shareholders' equity[3]	22.5%	22.6%	21.3%
4. Other Year-End Data			
Discount stores in the United States	1,209	1,353	1,478
Supercenters in the United States	1,980	1,713	1,471
SAM'S CLUBs in the United States	567	551	538
Neighborhood Markets in the United States	100	85	64
Units outside the United States	2,285	1,587	1,355

(1) Comparative store sales are considered to be sales at stores that were open as of February 2 of the prior fiscal year and have not been expanded or relocated since that date.
(2) Income from continuing operations before minority interest divided by average total assets.
(3) Income from continuing operations before minority interest divided by average shareholders' equity.

SOURCE: *Wal-Mart Stores, Inc., 2005 Annual Report, p. 18.*

(See **Exhibits 1–4** for Wal-Mart's financial reports.) Scott was pleased with strong international sales in Argentina, Mexico, and Brazil and with the fact that the company had more than 6,100 stores worldwide. As of January 31, 2006, Wal-Mart was operating 2,285 international stores, buying products from 70 countries, and doing 20% of its business outside the United States. (See **Exhibit 5** for the number of stores by country.) With its purchase of the retail operations of Sonae in Brazil and a majority interest of Seiyu in Japan, Wal-Mart added 537 new international stores and 50,000 new associates (employees). Its recent purchase of a majority

EXHIBIT 1
(Continued)

2003	2002	2001	2000	1999	1998	1997	1996
$229,616	$204,011	$180,787	$156,249	$130,522	$112,005	$99,627	$89,051
12.6%	12.8%	15.7%	19.7%	16.5%	12.4%	11.9%	13.7%
5%	6%	5%	8%	9%	6%	5%	4%
$178,299	$159,097	$140,720	$121,825	$102,490	$88,163	$78,897	$70,485
39,983	35,147	30,822	26,025	21,778	18,831	16,437	14,547
927	1,183	1,196	840	598	716	807	863
35.2%	36.2%	36.5%	36.8%	37.4%	37.0%	36.8%	36.8%
$ 7,818	$ 6,448	$ 6,087	$ 5,394	$ 4,240	$ 3,424	$ 2,978	$ 2,689
7,955	6,592	6,235	5,324	4,397	3,504	3,042	2,737
$ 1.76	$ 1.44	$ 1.36	$ 1.21	$ 0.95	$ 0.76	$ 0.65	$ 0.58
1.79	1.47	1.39	1.19	0.98	0.77	0.66	0.59
0.30	0.28	0.24	0.20	0.16	0.14	0.11	0.10
$ 29,543	$26,615	$25,344	$23,478	$20,064	$18,589	$17,385	$16,779
24,401	22,053	20,987	19,296	16,361	16,005	15,556	15,667
51,374	45,248	40,461	35,533	25,600	23,237	19,935	18,554
92,900	81,549	76,231	68,983	48,513	44,221	38,571	36,621
32,225	26,795	28,366	25,525	16,155	13,930	10,432	10,944
16,597	15,676	12,489	13,653	6,887	7,169	7,685	8,483
3,000	3,044	3,152	3,000	2,697	2,480	2,304	2,089
39,461	35,192	31,407	25,878	21,141	18,519	17,151	14,757
0.9	1.0	0.9	0.9	1.2	1.3	1.7	1.5
9.2%	8.4%	8.6%	9.8%	9.5%	8.5%	8.0%	7.9%
20.9%	19.4%	21.3%	22.9%	21.4%	19.2%	18.7%	19.6%
1,568	1,647	1,736	1,801	1,869	1,921	1,960	1,995
1,258	1,066	888	721	564	441	344	239
525	500	475	463	451	443	436	433
49	31	19	7	4	—	—	—
1,272	1,154	1,054	991	703	589	314	276

interest in CARHCO in Central America added stores in Costa Rica, El Salvador, Guatemala, Honduras, and Nicaragua—thus increasing the number of countries outside the United States in which Wal-Mart operated from 10 to 15. Of the almost 600 stores management planned to open during the 2007 fiscal year (February 1, 2006, to January 31, 2007), more than a third would be outside the United States.[3]

There was a negative side, however, to the Wal-Mart story. The company's stock price had fallen from $56.98 on January 31, 2002 to $46.11 on January 31, 2006. Given the company's

EXHIBIT 2

Consolidated Statements of Income: Wal-Mart Stores, Inc. (Dollar amounts in millions except per share data)

Fiscal Year Ending January 31	2006	2005	2004
Revenues:			
Net sales	$312,427	$285,222	$256,329
Other income, net	3,227	2,910	2,352
Total revenue	315,654	288,132	258,681
Costs and expenses:			
Cost of sales	240,391	210,793	198,747
Operating, selling, general and administrative expenses	56,733	51,248	44,909
Operating Income	18,530	26,091	15,025
Interest:			
Debt	1,171	934	729
Capital leases	249	253	267
Interest income	(248)	(201)	(164)
Interest, net	1,172	986	832
Income from continuing operations before income taxes and minority interest	17,358	25,105	14,193
Provision for Income taxes:			
Current	5,932	5,326	4,941
Deferred	(129)	263	177
	5,803	5,589	5,118
Income from continuing operations before minority interest	11,555	10,516	9,075
Minority interest	(324)	(249)	(214)
Income from continuing operations	11,231	10,267	8,861
Income from discontinued operation, net of tax	—	—	193
Net Income	$11,231	$10,267	$9,054
Basic net income per common share:			
Income from continuing operations	$ 2.68	$ 2.41	$ 2.03
Income from discontinued operation	—	—	0.05
Basic net income per common share	$ 2.68	$ 2.41	$ 2.08
Diluted net income per common share:			
Income from continuing operations	$ 2.68	$ 2.41	$ 2.03
Income from discontinued operations	—	—	0.04
Diluted net income per common share	$ 2.68	$ 2.41	$2.07
Weighted-average number of common shares:			
Basic	4,183	4,259	4,363
Diluted	4,188	4,266	4,373
Dividends per common share	$ 0.60	$ 0.52	$ 0.36

SOURCE: *Wal-Mart Stores, Inc., 2006 Annual Report, p. 30.*

continuous growth in sales and earnings, this was a strange development. One analyst commented that an investor who had bought Wal-Mart shares on the first day of trading in 2001 and held them through April 11, 2005, would have seen the investment decline by 9.9%! In contrast, over the same period, Costco Wholesale, Target, and J.C. Penney saw their stock prices climb 12.4%, 49.6%, and 367%, respectively. According to this analyst, the stock's lackluster performance over the previous five years was explained by competition getting tougher and growth prospects getting smaller. Once Wal-Mart had successfully expanded into every small and mid-sized city in the United States where competition was typically weak, further growth required

EXHIBIT 3
Consolidated Balance Sheets: Wal-Mart Stores, Inc. (Dollar amounts in millions except per share data)

Fiscal Year Ending January 31	2006	2005
Assets		
Current assets:		
Cash and cash equivalents	$ 6,414	$ 5.488
Receivables	2,662	1,715
Inventories	32,191	29,762
Prepaid expenses and other	2,557	1,889
Total current assets	43,824	38,854
Property and equipment, at cost:		
Land	16,643	14,472
Buildings and improvements	56,163	46,574
Fixtures and equipment	22,750	21,461
Transportation equipment	1,746	1,530
Property and equipment, at cost	97,302	84,037
Less accumulated depreciation	21,427	18,637
Property and equipment, net	75,875	65,400
Property under capital lease:		
Property under capital lease	5,578	4,556
Less accumulated amortization	2,163	1,838
Property under capital lease, net	3,415	2,718
Goodwill	12,188	10,803
Other assets and deferred charges	2,885	2,379
Total assets	$138,187	$120,154
Liabilities and shareholders' equity		
Current liabilities:	$ 3,754	$ 3,812
Commercial paper	25,373	21,987
Accounts payable	13,465	12,120
Accrued liabilities	1,340	1,281
Long-term debt due within one year	4,595	3,759
Obligations under capital leases due within one year	299	223
Total current liabilities	48,826	43,182
Long-term debt	26,429	20,087
Long-term obligations under capital leases	3,742	3,171
Deferred income taxes and other	4,552	2,978
Minority interest	1,467	1,340
Commitments and contingencies		
Shareholders' equity:		
Preferred stock ($0.10 par value: 100 shares authorized, none issued)	—	—
Common stock ($0.10 par value: 11,000 shares authorized, 4,165 and 4,234 issued and outstanding at January 31, 2006 and January 31, 2005, respectively)	417	423
Capital in excess of par value	2,596	2,425
Accumulated other comprehensive income	1,053	2,694
Retained earnings	49,105	43,854
Total shareholders' equity	53,171	49,396
Total liabilities and shareholder's equity	$138,187	$120,154

SOURCE: *Wal-Mart Stores, Inc., 2006 Annual Report, p. 31.*

EXHIBIT 4

Consolidated Statements of Cash Flows: Wal-Mart Stores, Inc. (Dollar amounts in millions except per share data)

Fiscal Year Ending January 31	2006	2005	2004
Cash flows from operating activities			
Income from continuing operations	$ 11,231	$ 10,267	$ 8,861
Adjustments to reconcile net income to net cash provided by operating activities:			
Depreciation and amortization	4,717	4,264	3,852
Deferred income taxes	(129)	263	177
Other operating activities	620	378	173
Changes in certain assets and liabilities, net of effects of acquisitions:			
Decrease (increase) in accounts receivable	(456)	(304)	373
Increase in inventories	(1,733)	(2,494)	(1,973)
Increase in accounts payable	2,390	1,694	2,587
Increase in accrued liabilities	993	976	1,896
Net cash provided by operating activities of continuing operations	17,633	15,044	15,946
Net cash provided by operating activities of discontinued operations	—	—	50
Net cash provided by operating activities	17,633	15,044	15,996
Cash flows from investing activities			
Payments for property and equipment	(14,563)	(12,893)	(10,308)
Investment in international operations, net of cash acquired	(601)	(315)	(38)
Proceeds from the disposal of fixed assets	1,049	953	481
Proceeds from the sale of McLane	—	—	1,500
Other investing activities	(68)	(96)	78
Net cash used in investing activities of continuing operations	(14,183)	(12,351)	(8,287)
Net cash used in investing activities of discontinued operations	—	—	(25)
Net cash used in investing activities	(14,183)	(12,351)	(8,312)
Cash flows from financing activities			
Increase (decrease) in commercial paper	(704)	544	688
Proceeds from issuance of long-term debt	7,691	5,832	4,099
Purchase of company stock	(3,580)	(4,549)	(5,046)
Dividends paid	(2,511)	(2,214)	(1,569)
Payment of long-term debt	(2,724)	(2,131)	(3,541)
Payment of capital lease obligations	(245)	(204)	(305)
Other financing activities	(349)	113	111
Net cash used in financing activities	(2,422)	(2,609)	(5,563)
Effect of exchange rate changes on cash	(102)	205	320
Net increase in cash and cash equivalents	926	289	2,441
Cash and cash equivalents at beginning of year	5,488	5,199	2,758
Cash and cash equivalents at end of year	$ 6,414	$ 5,488	$ 5,199
Supplemental disclosure of cash flow information			
Income tax paid	$ 5,962	$ 5,593	$ 4,538
Interest paid	1,390	1,163	1,024
Capital lease obligations incurred	286	377	252

SOURCE: *Wal-Mart Stores, Inc., 2006 Annual Report, p. 33.*

EXHIBIT 5
Fiscal 2006 End-of-
Year Store Count:
Wal-Mart Stores, Inc.
January 31, 2006

Country	Discount Stores	Supercenters	SAM's Clubs	Neighborhood Markets
Argentina	0	11	0	0
Brazil	255	23	15	2
Canada	272	0	6	0
China	0	51	3	2
Germany	0	88	0	0
Japan	2	96	0	300
South Korea	0	16	0	0
Mexico	599	105	70	0
Puerto Rico	9	5	9	31
United Kingdom	294	21	0	0
United States	1,209	1,980	567	100
TOTAL	**2,640**	**2,396**	**670**	**435**

SOURCE: *Wal-Mart Stores, Inc., 2006 Annual Report, p. 51.*

entering large cities and other countries where other discount mass merchandisers, such as Target and Carrefour, were already established. To increase sales, Wal-Mart's management added a series of new retailing concepts. The replacement of traditional discount stores with Wal-Mart Supercenters containing groceries in addition to dry goods led to higher sales, but also to the lower profit margins inherent in the grocery business. Sam's Club's sales growth was good, but far less than that of other Wal-Mart stores. International expansion required acquisition and the conversion of stores to the Wal-Mart system—often expensive, difficult, and time consuming. Investors were not as excited about a business growing at 11% to 13% annually instead of the 20% or more they had come to expect.[4]

The company has been increasingly criticized for the very management practices that had made it so successful. Its low prices, wide selection, and courteous service generated high sales and profits, but its stores tended to drive local "mom and pop" stores out of business, especially in small towns. The United Food and Commercial Workers union contended that the only reason the company could offer such low prices was that Wal-Mart underpaid its workers and offered them substandard benefits. Wal-Mart's almost legendary hard stance with suppliers was being portrayed as an abuse of power. Lawsuits alleging discrimination against women and underage workers operating dangerous machinery, among other examples, added to the firm's public relations problem. It appeared that the company had become a lightning rod for any and all criticism against big business.

Wal-Mart: A Maturing Organization

Genesis of an Idea

Sam Walton started his retail career in 1940 as a management trainee with the J.C. Penney Co. in Des Moines, Iowa. He was impressed with the Penney method of doing business and later modeled the Wal-Mart chain on "The Penney Idea" as reviewed in **Exhibit 6.** The Penney Company found strength in calling employees "associates" rather than clerks. Penney's, founded in Kemerer, Wyoming, in 1902, located stores on the main streets of small towns and cities throughout the United States.

EXHIBIT 6
The Penney Idea
(1913)

1. To serve the public, as nearly as we can, to its complete satisfaction.
2. To expect for the service we render a fair remuneration and not all the profit the traffic will bear.
3. To do all in our power to pack the customer's dollar full of value, quality, and satisfaction.
4. To continue to train ourselves and our associates so that the service we give will be more and more intelligently performed.
5. To improve constantly the human factor in our business.
6. To reward men and women in our organization through participation in what the business produces.
7. To test our every policy, method, and act in this way: "Does it square with what is right and just?"

SOURCE: *V. H. Trimble,* Sam Walton: The Inside Story of America's Richest Man *(New York: Dutton, 1990).*

Following service in the U.S. Army during World War II, Sam Walton acquired a Ben Franklin variety store franchise in Newport, Arkansas. He operated this store successfully with his brother, James L. "Bud" Walton (1921–1995), until losing the lease in 1950.

The early retail stores owned by Sam Walton in Newport and Bentonville, Arkansas, and later in other small towns in adjoining southern states, were variety store operations. They were relatively small operations of 6,000 square feet, were located on "main streets," and displayed merchandise on plain wooden tables and counters. Operated under the Ben Franklin name and supplied by Butler Brothers of Chicago and St. Louis, they were characterized by a limited price line, low gross margins, high merchandise turnover, and concentration on return on investment. The firm, operating under the Walton 5 & 10 name with 15 stores, was the largest Ben Franklin franchisee in the country in 1962. The variety stores were phased out by 1976 to allow the company to concentrate on the growth of Wal-Mart discount department stores.

Foundations of Growth

The original Wal-Mart discount concept was not a unique idea. Sam Walton became convinced in the late 1950s that discounting would transform retailing. He traveled extensively in New England, the cradle of "off-pricing." After he had visited just about every discounter in the United States, he tried to interest Butler Brothers executives in the discount store concept. The first Kmart, as a "conveniently located one-stop shopping unit where customers could buy a wide variety of quality merchandise at discount prices," had just opened in Garden City, Michigan. Walton's strategy was to operate a similar discount store in a small community. In that setting, he would offer name-brand merchandise at low prices and would add friendly service. Butler Brothers executives rejected the idea. Undeterred, Walton opened the first "Wal-Mart Discount City" in late 1962 in Rogers, Arkansas.

Wal-Mart stores sold nationally advertised, well-known-brand merchandise at low prices in austere surroundings. As corporate policy, Wal-Mart cheerfully gave refunds, credits, and rain checks. Management conceived the firm as a "discount department store chain offering a wide variety of general merchandise to the customer." Early emphasis was placed on opportunistic purchases of merchandise from whatever sources were available. Health and beauty aids (H&BA) were heavily emphasized in the product line, and "stacking it high" was the manner of merchandise presentation. By the end of 1979, there were 276 Wal-Mart stores located in 11 states.

The firm developed an aggressive expansion strategy. New stores were located primarily in communities of 5,000 to 25,000 in population. The stores' sizes ranged from 30,000 to 60,000 square feet, with 45,000 being the average. The firm also expanded by locating stores in contiguous geographic areas. When its discount operations came to dominate a market area, it moved to an adjoining area. Whereas other retailers built warehouses to serve existing outlets, Wal-Mart built the distribution center first and then spotted stores all around it, pooling advertising and distribution overhead. Most stores were less than a six-hour drive from one of the company's warehouses. The first major distribution center, a 390,000-square-foot facility, opened in Searcy, Arkansas, outside Bentonville in 1978.

Becoming National

At the beginning of 1991, the firm had 1,573 Wal-Mart stores in 35 states, with expansion planned for adjacent states. Wal-Mart had become the largest retailer and the largest discount department store in the United States. By 2006, Wal-Mart had 1,200 discount stores, 1,980 supercenters, 567 Sam's Clubs, and 100 neighborhood markets throughout all 50 states.

As a national discount department store chain, Wal-Mart Stores, Inc., offered a wide variety of general merchandise to the customer. The stores were designed to offer one-stop shopping with 40 departments that included family apparel, health and beauty aids, household needs, electronics, toys, fabric and crafts, automotive supplies, lawn and patio, jewelry, and shoes. A pharmacy, automotive supply and service center, garden center, or snack bar were also operated at certain locations. The firm operated its stores with "everyday low prices" as opposed to putting heavy emphasis on special promotions that called for multiple newspaper advertising circulars. Stores were expected to "provide the customer with a clean, pleasant, and friendly shopping experience."

Although Wal-Mart carried much the same merchandise, offered similar prices, and operated stores that looked much like the competition, there were many differences. In the typical Wal-Mart store, employees wore blue vests to identify themselves, aisles were wide, apparel departments were carpeted in warm colors, store employees followed customers to their cars to pick up their shopping carts, and the customer was welcomed at the door by a "people greeter" who gave directions and struck up conversation. In some cases, merchandise was bagged in brown paper sacks rather than plastic bags because customers seemed to prefer them. The "Wal-Mart" and the slogan "Always Low Prices" on the front of the store served to identify the firm. Yellow smiley faces were used on in-store displays along with the slogan "Watch for Falling Prices." In consumer studies it was determined that the chain was particularly adept at striking the delicate balance needed to convince customers its prices were low without making people feel that its stores were too cheap. In many ways, competitors like Kmart sought to emulate Wal-Mart by introducing people greeters, by upgrading interiors, by developing new logos and signage, and by introducing new inventory response systems.

A "satisfaction guaranteed" refund and exchange policy was introduced to allow customers to be confident of Wal-Mart's merchandise and quality. Technological advancements such as scanner cash registers, handheld computers for the ordering of merchandise, and computer linkages of stores with the general office and distribution centers improved communications and merchandise replenishment. Each store was encouraged to initiate programs that would make it an integral part of the community in which it operated. Associates were encouraged to "maintain the highest standards of honesty, morality, and business ethics" in dealing with the public.

Becoming International

Realizing that there were only so many opportunities for growth within the borders of the United States, Wal-Mart's management embarked on international expansion. It opened its first international store in 1991 when it opened a Sam's Club in Mexico City. Two years later, Wal-Mart International was created to oversee growing global opportunities.

By 2006, Wal-Mart Stores, Inc., of Bentonville, Arkansas, operated mass merchandising retail stores under a variety of names and retail formats, including 2,460 supercenters in the United States, Mexico, Brazil, Germany, the United Kingdom (ASDA), Argentina, South Korea, and Puerto Rico; 1,500 general merchandise stores in the United States, Canada, Puerto Rico, the United Kingdom, and Brazil; 930 food and drug stores in Japan, the United Kingdom, Brazil, the United States, Mexico, Puerto Rico, and China; 189 bodegas in Mexico and Brazil; 670 Sam's Clubs in the United States, Mexico, Brazil, Canada, China, and Puerto Rico; 63 George and Suburbia apparel stores in the United Kingdom and Mexico; 33 soft discount stores in Brazil and Mexico; 10 Maxxi cash and carry stores in Brazil; and 286 Vips restaurants in Mexico. Of these, 2,285 were international stores located outside the United States. Wal-Mart had either total or majority ownership of its international store operations, except for a joint venture in China.

The Sam Walton Spirit

Much of the success of Wal-Mart was attributed to the entrepreneurial spirit of its founder and past Chairman of the Board, Samuel Moore Walton (1918–1992). Many considered him one of the most influential retailers of the century. Sam Walton, or "Mr. Sam," as some referred to him, traced his down-to-earth, old-fashioned, homespun, evangelical ways to growing up in rural Oklahoma, Missouri, and Arkansas. Although he appeared to be remarkably unconcerned about his roots, some suggested that it was his simple belief in hard work and ambition that had "unlocked countless doors and showered upon him, his customers, and his employees . . . the fruits of . . . years of labor in building [this] highly successful company."

"Our goal has always been in our business to be the very best," Sam Walton said in an interview, "and, along with that, we believe that in order to do that, you've got to make a good situation and put the interests of your associates first. If we really do that consistently, they in turn will cause . . . our business to be successful, which is what we've talked about and espoused and practiced." "The reason for our success," he said, "is our people and the way that they're treated and the way they feel about their company." Many have suggested that it was this "people first" philosophy that guided the company through the challenges and setbacks of its early years and allowed it to maintain its consistent record of growth and expansion in later years.

A unique, enthusiastic, and positive individual, Sam Walton was "just your basic home-spun billionaire," a columnist once suggested. "Mr. Sam is a life-long small-town resident who didn't change much as he got richer than his neighbors," he noted. Walton had tremendous energy, enjoyed bird hunting with his dogs, and flew a corporate plane. When the company was much smaller, he could boast that he personally visited every Wal-Mart store at least once a year. A store visit usually included Walton leading Wal-Mart cheers that began, "Give me a W, give me an A. . . ." To many employees, he had the air of a fiery Baptist preacher. Paul R. Carter, a Wal-Mart Executive Vice President, was quoted as saying, "Mr. Walton has a calling." He became the richest man in America, and by 1991 had created a personal fortune for his family in excess of $21 billion. Fifteen years later, despite a division of wealth, five family members still controlled around 40% of the Wal-Mart common stock and were ranked among the top ten richest individuals in the United States.[5]

In late 1989 Sam Walton was diagnosed as having multiple myeloma, or cancer of the bone marrow. Nevertheless, he remained active in the firm as Chairman of the Board until his death in 1992.

Corporate Governance

Board of Directors

Exhibit 7 lists the 13 members of Wal-Mart's Board of Directors who were elected at the June 2, 2006, annual shareholders' meeting. Four were affiliated with the company in some manner: (1) S. Robson Walton, Chairman of the Board and son of the founder; (2) David D. Glass, Chairman, Executive Committee and CEO from 1988 to 2000; (3) Jim C. Walton, CEO of Arvest Bank Group and son of the founder; and (4) H. Lee Scott, current President and CEO. Jim Walton had been appointed to the Board September 30, 2005, to replace his older brother, John Walton, who had died in an aircraft accident. The nine other members of the Board were officially considered "independent," as defined by the New York Stock Exchange. In terms of minority membership, the Board was composed of three women, two African Americans, and two Hispanic Americans. The Board was organized into five committees: the Audit Committee; the Compensation, Nominating, and Governance Committee (CNGC); the Executive Committee (EC); the Stock Option Committee (SOC); and the Strategic Planning and Finance Committee (SPFC). The Audit and CNGC committees were composed solely of independent directors, as required by the New York Stock Exchange.

EXHIBIT 7
2006 Board of Directors: Wal-Mart Stores, Inc.

Aida M. Alvarez, 56
Former Public Finance VP, First Boston & Bear Stearns
Former member of President Clinton's Cabinet
Director since 2006

James W. Breyer, 44
Managing Partner, Accel Partners
Director since 2001

M. Michele Burns, 48
Exec VP & CFO, Marsh & McLennan Consulting Co.
Director since 2003

James J. Cash, Ph.D., 58
Retired Professor, Harvard Business School
Director since 2006

Douglas N. Daft, 63
Retired Chair & CEO, Coca-Cola Co.
Director since 2005

David D. Glass, 70
Past-President & CEO, Wal-Mart
Director since 1977

Roland A. Hernandez, 48
Retired Chair & CEO, Telemundo Group
Director since 1998

H. Lee Scott, 57
President & CEO, Wal-Mart
Director since 1999

Jack C. Shewmaker, 68
President, J-COM Consulting & Retired Wal-Mart Exec
Director since 1977

Jim C. Walton, 58
Chair & CEO, Arvest Bank Group
Director since September 28, 2005

S. Robson Walton, 61
Chairman, Wal-Mart
Director since 1978

Christopher J. Williams, 48
Chair & CEO, Williams Capital Group
Investment Bank
Director since 2004

Linda S.Wolf, 58
Former Chair & CEO, Leo Burnett Worldwide
Director since 2005

SOURCE: *Wal-Mart Stores, Inc., Notice of 2006 Annual Shareholders' Meeting, pp. 5–6.*

Non-management directors received $60,000 as an annual retainer plus $140,000 worth of Wal-Mart shares on their election to the Board. Those serving as committee chairs additionally received $15,000 to $25,000 for their service. Each non-management director was required by the Board to own within five years from election to the Board an amount of shares equal to five times the annual retainer for the year in which the director was originally elected to the Board. The Board had four regular meetings and three telephone meetings during fiscal 2006. Committee meetings were in addition to the regular Board meetings. Each director attended at least 75% of the Board and committee meetings on which he or she served. The Board typically appointed one of the non-management directors to serve as Presiding Director of any executive sessions of the non-management and independent directors.

Although the officers and directors as a group owned less than 1% of total shares, S. Robson Walton and Jim C. Walton, by virtue of their being two of the five managing members of the family's Walton Enterprises, LLC, represented the Walton family and effectively controlled close to 41% of the shares outstanding.

Top Management and Organization Structure

Exhibit 8 lists the 25 corporate officers. Lee Scott was only the third CEO in the entire history of Wal-Mart when he was elected to the position in January 2000. Its first CEO, Sam Walton, had built the company from the ground up. During the 12 years that David Glass, the previous CEO, held the position, sales grew from $16 billion to $165 billion. Lee Scott had been personally recruited by David Glass 21 years before, from a Springdale, Arkansas, trucking company, to come to Wal-Mart as the manager of the truck fleet. In his years at Wal-Mart, Glass had driven the company to a new level of growth in both domestic and international markets and continued to be active on the firm's board of directors as Chairman of the Executive Committee. Prior to his appointment as President and CEO, Lee Scott had served as Vice Chairman and Chief Operation Officer (COO), Executive Vice-President, and President and CEO of the Wal-Mart Stores unit.

On January 31, 2006, Wal-Mart Stores, Inc., was structured into three business units, Wal-Mart Stores USA, Sam's Club, and Wal-Mart International. The Wal-Mart Stores unit had 3,289 locations and included the company's supercenters, discount stores, and Neighborhood Markets in the United States, as well as walmart.com. The Sam's Club unit had 567 locations and included the warehouse membership clubs in the United States plus samsclub.com. Wal-Mart International had 2,285 locations in 10 countries. The International total was increased through the February 2006 purchase of majority control of CARHCO with 360 locations in five Central American countries. (See **Exhibit 9** for business unit data.)

In September 2005, John Menzer, President and CEO of Wal-Mart International, and Mike Duke, President and CEO of Wal-Mart Stores, USA, were promoted to Vice Chairman positions within the company and effectively traded places. Menzer was given responsibility not only for Wal-Mart Stores USA, but also for the divisions responsible for real estate, logistics, information services, benefits, global procurement, financial services, store planning, and strategic planning. Eduardo Castro-Wright, Executive Vice President and COO of Wal-Mart Stores USA, was promoted to President and CEO of that unit. He was responsible for operations, merchandising, marketing, specialty divisions, and new business development in the Wal-Mart Stores, Supercenters, and Neighborhood Markets in the United States. Duke took over leadership of Wal-Mart International, the company's fastest-growing unit. According to CEO Lee Scott, Duke's experience heading Wal-Mart's largest operating unit in the United States coupled with his previous experience as head of the company's logistics operations made him uniquely qualified to manage Wal-Mart's International unit. Doug McMillon continued as President and CEO of the Sam's Club business unit.

EXHIBIT 8
2006 Corporate
Officers: Wal-Mart
Stores, Inc.

Eduardo Castro-Wright
Exec VP, President & CEO Wal-Mart Stores
Division U.S.

M. Susan Chambers
Exec VP People Division

Patricia A. Curran
Exec VP, Store Operations Wal-Mart Stores
Division U.S.

Douglas J. Degn
Exec VP, Food, Consumables, Hardlines
Wal-Mart Stores Division U.S.

Linda M. Dillman
Exec VP
Risk Mgmt & Benefits Administration

Johnnie Dobbs
Exec V Logistics & Supply Chain

Michael T. Duke
Vice Chairman
Responsible for Wal-Mart International

Joseph J. Fitzsimmons
Sr VP Treasurer

John E. Fleming
Exec VP & Chief Marketing Officer
Wal-Mart Stores Division U.S.

Rollin L. Ford
Exec VP & Chief Information Officer

David D. Glass
Chairman of the Executive Committee
Board of Directors

Mark D. Goodman
Exec VP, Marketing, Membership &
E-commerce SAM'S CLUB

Craig R. Herkert
Exec VP, President & CEO, The Americas
Wal-Mart International

Charles M. Holley, Jr.
Sr VP Finance

Thomas D. Hyde
Exec VP & Corporate Secretary

Lawrence V. Jackson
Exec VP, President & CEO
Global Procurement

Gregory L. Johnston
Exec VP, Club Operations Sam's Club

C. Douglas McMillon
Exec VP, President & CEO Sam's Club

John B. Menzer
Vice Chairman Responsible for U.S.

Thomas M. Schoewe
Exec VP & Chief Financial Officer

H. Lee Scott
President and Chief Executive Officer

Gregory E. Spragg
Exec VP, Merchandising & Replenishment
Sam's Club

S. Robson Walton
Chairman of the Board

Claire A. Watts
Exec VP, Product Development, Apparel &
Home Merchandising, Wal-Mart Stores
Division U.S.

Eric S. Zorn
Exec VP Wal-Mart Realty

SOURCE: *Wal-Mart Stores, Inc., 2006 Annual Report, p. 52.*

EXHIBIT 9
Business Unit
Performance:
Wal-Mart Stores, Inc.
(Dollar amounts
in millions)

	2006		2005		2004	
	Sales	**Op. Income**	**Sales**	**Op. Income**	**Sales**	**Op. Income**
Wal-Mart Stores U.S.	$209,910	$15,324	$191,826	$14,163	$174,220	$12,916
Sam's Club	39,798	1,385	37,119	1,280	34,537	1,126
Wal-Mart International	62,719	3,330	56,277	2,988	47,572	2,370
Total	$312,427	$20,039	$285,222	$18,431	$256,329	$16,412

SOURCE: *Wal-Mart Stores, Inc., 2006 Annual Report, pp. 22–25.*

Competitive Environment

Wal-Mart management was aware that its business operations on a national and international level were subject to a number of factors outside of its control. Any one, or a combination, of these factors could materially affect the financial performance of the firm. These factors included the costs of goods, the cost of electricity and other energy requirements, competitive pressures, inflation, consumer debt levels, interest rate levels, and unemployment levels. They also included currency exchange fluctuations, trade restrictions, changes in tariff and freight rates, and other capital market and economic conditions.

Industry analysts labeled the decades since 1980 as an era of economic uncertainty for retailers. Although the United States had experienced one of the longest periods of economic expansion in its history during this period, increased competitive pressures, sluggish consumer spending, an energy crisis leading to higher fuel prices, lack of worldwide economic growth, and the terrorist events of September 11, 2001, converged to create a very challenging environment for all retailers at the beginning of the 21st century.

Many retail enterprises confronted heavy competitive pressure by restructuring. Sears was one example. Sears, Roebuck and Company, based in Chicago, became a more focused retailer by divesting itself of Allstate Insurance Company and its real estate subsidiaries. In 1993, the company announced it would close 118 unprofitable stores and discontinue the unprofitable Sears general merchandise catalog. It eliminated 50,000 jobs and began a $4 billion, five-year remodeling plan for its remaining multiline department stores. After unsuccessfully experimenting with an "everyday low-price" strategy, management chose to realign its merchandise strategy to meet the needs of middle-market customers, who were primarily women, by focusing on product lines in apparel, home, and automotive. The new focus on apparel was supported with the advertising campaign "The Softer Side of Sears." A later companywide campaign broadened the appeal: "The many sides of Sears fit the many sides of your life." Sears completed its return to its retailing roots by selling off its ownership in Dean Witter Financial Services, Discover Card, Coldwell Banker Real Estate, and Sears mortgage banking operations. In 1999, Sears refocused its marketing strategy with a new program that was designed to communicate a stronger whole-house and event message. A new advertising campaign introduced the slogan "The good life at a great price. Guaranteed." In 2000, a new store format was introduced that concentrated on five focal areas: appliances, home fashions, tools, kids, and electronics. Other departments, including men's and women's apparel, assumed a support role in these stores. In 2001, Sears developed another plan to reposition and restructure its core business: the full-line stores. Alan J. Lacy, Chairman and CEO, announced that this strategy would position Sears in the retail marketplace as "not a department store, not a discount store, but a broad-line retailer with outstanding credit and service capabilities." Sears' sales increased slightly from $39.4 billion in 1999 to $41.1 billion in 2003, but its net income fluctuated from $1.5 billion in 1999 to $735 million in 2001 to $3.4 billion in 2003. The lack of a consistent strategy and marketing image continued until Sears was purchased by Kmart in 2005. It was subsequently merged with Kmart to form a new firm, the Sears Holdings Corporation.

The discount department store industry by 2006 had changed in a number of ways and was thought by many analysts to have reached maturity. Several formerly successful firms such as E. J. Korvette, W. T. Grant, Atlantic Mills, Arlans, Federals, Zayre, Heck's, and Ames had declared bankruptcy and as a result either liquidated or reorganized. Venture announced liquidation in early 1998. Firms such as Target and Shopko began carrying more fashionable merchandise in more attractive facilities and shifted their emphasis to more national markets. Specialty retailers, such as Toys "R" Us, Pier 1 Imports, and Oshman's, had matured and were no longer making big inroads in toys, home furnishings, and sporting goods. The "superstores" of drug and food chains were rapidly discounting increasing amounts of general merchandise. Some firms, such as May Department Stores Company with Caldor and Venture and Woolworth Corporation with Woolco, had withdrawn from the field by either selling their discount divisions or closing them down entirely. Woolworth's remaining 122 Woolco stores in Canada were sold to Wal-Mart in 1994. All remaining Woolworth variety stores in the United States were closed in 1997.

Several new retail formats had emerged in the marketplace to challenge the traditional discount department store format. The superstore, a 100,000 to 300,000-square-foot operation, combined a large supermarket with a discount general-merchandise store. Originally a European retailing concept, these outlets where known as "malls without walls." Kmart's Super Kmart, Target's SuperTarget, and Wal-Mart's Supercenters were examples of this trend toward large operations. Warehouse retailing, which involved some combination of warehouse and showroom facilities, used warehouse principles to reduce operating expenses and thereby offer discount prices as a primary customer appeal. Home Depot combined the traditional hardware store and lumberyard with a self-service home improvement center to become the largest home center operator in the nation.

Some retailers responded to changes in the marketplace by selling goods at price levels 20%–60% below regular retail prices. These off-price operations appeared as two general types: (1) factory outlet stores, such as Burlington Coat Factory Warehouse, Bass Shoes, and Manhattan's Brand Name Fashion Outlet, and (2) independents, such as Loehmann's, T. J. Maxx, Marshall's, and Clothestime, which bought seconds, overages, closeouts, or leftover goods from manufacturers and other retailers. Other retailers chose to dominate a product classification. Some super specialists, such as Sock Appeal, Little Piggie, Ltd., and Sock Market, offered a single narrowly defined classification of merchandise with an extensive assortment of brands, colors, and sizes. Others, as niche specialists, such as Kids Foot Locker and Champs Sports, a division of Foot Locker, Inc. (formerly Woolworth Corporation), targeted an identified market with carefully selected merchandise and appropriately designed stores.

Some retailers, such as Silk Greenhouse (silk plants and flowers), Office Depot (office supplies and equipment), Home Depot (home improvement), and Toys "R" Us (toys), were called "category killers" because they had achieved merchandise dominance in their respective product categories. Stores such as The Limited, Limited Express, Victoria's Secret, and Banana Republic became mini-department specialists by showcasing new lines and accessories alongside traditional merchandise lines. The amount of specialization necessary to be a "category killer" could, however, lead to problems. Toys "R" Us, for example, made most of its sales during the Christmas season and was lucky to make break-even during the rest of the year. Wal-Mart, however, could expand its toy department during the Christmas season and then reduce it in favor of lawn and garden sales during the rest of the year. Once Wal-Mart targeted toys for merchandising emphasis during the Christmas season, Toys "R" Us could not keep up with Wal-Mart's vast selection at lower prices and was forced into bankruptcy in 2005.

Kohl's Corporation, a firm founded in 1962 in Menominee Falls, Wisconsin, operated family-focused, value-oriented department stores in 43 states as of June, 2006. The company's stores averaged 86,500 square feet in size and were typically located near but not within shopping malls. Kohl's offered moderately priced national brand-name apparel, shoes, accessories, and home products targeted to middle-income consumers in suburban areas with convenient parking. During the period 1992 and 2006, the Kohl's operation grew from 76 to 749 stores with its sales increasing from $1.1 billion in 1992 to $13.4 billion in 2006. With a quality image somewhere between J. C. Penney and Target, Kohl's earned $842 million in net income in 2006.

Kmart Corporation, headquartered in Troy, Michigan, celebrated in 1987 the 25th anniversary of its first Kmart store. At that time, it was the world's largest and most successful discount department store chain with sales of $25.6 billion. By 1990, Wal-Mart's sales of $32.6 billion surpassed Kmart's $32.1 billion and Kmart fell to second place in U.S. discount stores. By 2001, Kmart operated 2,114 stores and had sales of $36,151 million but had fallen to third place behind Wal-Mart and Target. In contrast, Wal-Mart's sales had risen to $217,799 million in 2001. Kmart was perceived by many industry analysts and consumers in several independent studies as a laggard. In the same studies, Wal-Mart was perceived as the industry leader, even though, according to the *Wall Street Journal,* "They carry much the same merchandise, offer prices that are pennies apart and operate stores that look almost exactly alike." The newspaper noted, "Even their names are similar." The original Kmart concept of a "conveniently located, one-stop shopping unit where customers could buy a wide variety of quality merchandise at discount prices," had lost its competitive edge in a changing market. As one analyst noted in an industry newsletter: "They had done so well for the past 20 years without paying attention to market changes, now they have to." Kmart changed strategic direction a number of times under different CEOs, but was unable to find a profitable niche in the increasingly competitive discount retailing industry. The firm suffered net losses in 1993, 1995, 1996, 2000, and 2001. Following its extraordinary 2001 loss of $2.4 billion, Kmart filed for bankruptcy under Chapter 11 of the federal bankruptcy laws on January 22, 2002. The firm continued to operate as an ongoing business while reorganizing. Costs were cut and marginal stores were either sold off for cash or closed. In March 2005, key investors in Kmart acquired Sears, Roebuck and Company and merged Kmart and Sears into the Sears Holdings Corporation. The management of Sears Holdings hoped to reduce costs of both Sears and Kmart by finding economies of scale in combining supply chains, IT, finance, legal, and human resources functions. During 2005, management closed 12 more Kmart stores and converted 48 Kmart stores into Sears stores. By 2006, Kmart had 1,479 stores in 49 states, Puerto Rico, and the Virgin Islands. Its stores were organized into Big Kmart stores (84,000–120,000 square feet), Kmart Super Centers (140,000–190,000 square feet), and traditional Kmart stores (80,000–110,000 square feet). For 2005, its first year of operation, Sears Holdings earned $858 million on $55 billion in sales.

Target Corporation was originally a discount unit of Dayton-Hudson, a respected department store chain headquartered in Minneapolis, Minnesota. The success of the Target unit led management to rename the company Target and to sell its department stores in 2004. By June 2006, Target had 1,418 stores in 47 states and 159 SuperTarget Stores in 21 states. Target's management viewed the company as an upscale discounter that provided high-quality, fashionable merchandise at attractive prices in clean, spacious, and guest-friendly stores. In 2003, 2004, and 2005 (years ending end-January of the following year), Target's sales were $42.0 billion, $46.8 billion, and $52.6 billion, respectively. During the same period, net earnings (not counting the sale of its department stores) were $1.6 billion, $1.9 billion, and $2.4 billion, respectively. Target's same-store sales (not including new or acquired stores) increased 5.6% in 2005 (year ending January 28, 2006) from the year earlier. As the nation's second largest retail chain, Target has become the nation's second largest retailer by successfully establishing itself in the upscale discount market niche. About 45% of Target's merchandise consisted of discretionary items, such as furniture, electonics, sporting goods, entertainment, and apparel—areas when trends and fashion were important and margins were wider, compared to only 30% for Wal-Mart, estimated Jeffrey Klinefelter, retail analyst at Piper Jaffray.[6] Wal-Mart was known as the relentless cost-cutter, but Target was the trendier place to shop and save. This upscale image coupled with management's traditional excellence in running quality department stores gave Target a competive advantage when competing against Wal-Mart in urban areas.

Some retailers, such as Kmart, had initially focused on appealing to professional, middle-class consumers who lived in suburban areas and who were likely to be price sensitive. Over time, Kmart attracted more working-class customers. Target went after an upscale consumer. Some firms, such as Fleet Farm and Pamida, served the rural consumer, whereas firms like Value City and Ames Department Stores chose to serve the urban consumer.

In rural communities Wal-Mart's success often came at the expense of established local merchants and units of regional discount store chains. Hardware stores, family department stores, building supply outlets, and stores featuring fabrics, sporting goods, and shoes were among the first to either close or relocate elsewhere. Regional discount retailers in the Sunbelt states, such as Roses, Howard's, T.G.& Y., and Duckwall-ALCO, which had once enjoyed solid sales and earnings, were forced to reposition themselves by renovating stores, opening bigger and more modern units, and re-merchandising. In many cases, stores such as Coast-to-Coast and Ben Franklin closed on a Wal-Mart announcement that it was planning to build in a specific community. "Just the word that Wal-Mart was coming made some stores close up," indicated one local newspaper editor. Ames Department Stores, Inc., which sought bankruptcy protection in 2001, announced in the summer of 2002 that it would close all 237 of its stores and liquidate inventory.

Domestic Strategies and Programs

Domestic strategies and programs at Wal-Mart were based on a set of two priorities that had guided the firm through its growth years. In the first priority, the customer was featured: "Customers would be provided with what they want, when they want it, all at a value." In the second, team spirit was emphasized: "Treating each other as we would hope to be treated, acknowledging our total dependency on our Associate-partners to sustain our success." The growth strategy included aggressive plans for new store openings; expansion to additional states; upgrading, relocating, refurbishing, and remodeling existing stores; and opening new distribution centers. For Wal-Mart management, the 1990s were considered an era in which the firm grew to become a truly nationwide retailer operating in all 50 states.

During the 1980s, Wal-Mart developed a number of new retail formats. The first Sam's Club opened in Oklahoma City, Oklahoma, in 1983. The wholesale club was an idea that had been developed by other firms earlier, but that found its greatest success and growth in acceptability at Wal-Mart. Sam's Clubs featured a vast array of product categories with limited selection of brand and model; cash-and-carry business with limited hours; large (100,000-square-foot), bare-bones facilities; rock-bottom wholesale prices; and minimal promotion. The limited membership plan permitted wholesale members who bought membership and others who usually paid a percentage above the ticket price of the merchandise. A revision in merchandising strategy resulted in fewer items in the inventory mix, with more emphasis on lower prices. A later acquisition of 100 PACE warehouse clubs, which were converted into Sam's Clubs, increased that division's units by more than one-third. A new Sam's Club format was introduced with the opening of a 154,000-square-foot store in 2001 in East Plano, Texas. The store featured an expanded product line with emphasis on fresh food, an open layout, a café, and an Internet kiosk where customers were invited to shop at the www.sams.com Web site. A new Sam's Club slogan, "It's a Big Deal!" referred to the size of the facility and the features of the prototype store.

Wal-Mart Supercenters were large combination stores. They were first opened in 1988 as Hypermarket*USA, a 222,000-square-foot superstore that combined a full general merchandise discount store with a large full-line grocery supermarket, a food court of restaurants, and other service businesses, such as banks or videotape rental stores. A scaled-down version of Hypermarket*USA was called Wal-Mart Supercenter and was similar in merchandise offerings, but with about 180,000 to 200,000 square feet of space. The company proceeded slowly with these plans and later suspended its plans for building any more hypermarkets in favor of the Supercenter concept.

Wal-Mart also tested a new concept called the Neighborhood Market in a number of locations in Arkansas. Identified by the company as "small-marts," these green-and-white stores were stocked with fresh fruits and vegetables, a drive-up pharmacy, a 24-hour photo shop, and a selection of classic Wal-Mart hard goods. Management elected to move slowly on this concept, planning to open no more than 10 a year. The goal was to ring the Superstores with these smaller stores to attract customers who were in hurry and wanted only a few items.

The McLane Company, Inc., a provider of retail and grocery distribution services for retail stores, was acquired by Wal-Mart in 1991. It was never considered a major segment of the total Wal-Mart operation and was divested in 2003.

Several programs were launched in Wal-Mart stores to highlight popular social causes. The "Buy American" program was a Wal-Mart retail program initiated in 1985. The theme was "Bring It Home to the USA," and its purpose was to communicate Wal-Mart's support for American manufacturing. In the program, the firm directed substantial influence to encourage manufacturers to produce goods in the United States rather than import them from other countries. Vendors were attracted into the program by encouraging manufacturers to initiate the process by contacting the company directly with proposals to sell goods that were made in the United States. Buyers also targeted specific import items in their assortments on a state-by-state basis to encourage domestic manufacturing. According to Haim Dabah, president of Gitano Group, Inc., a maker of fashion discount clothing that previously imported 95% of its clothing and now made about 20% of its products in the United States: "Wal-Mart let it be known loud and clear that if you're going to grow with them, you sure better have some products made in the U.S.A." Farris Fashion, Inc. (flannel shirts), Roadmaster Corporation (exercise bicycles), Flanders Industries, Inc. (lawn chairs), and Magic Chef (microwave ovens) were examples of vendors that chose to participate in the program. From the Wal-Mart standpoint, the "Buy American" program centered around value—producing and selling quality merchandise at a competitive price. The promotion included television advertisements featuring factory workers, a soaring American eagle, and the slogan "We buy American whenever we can, so you can too." Prominent in-store signage and store circulars were also included. One store poster read: "Success Stories—These items, formerly imported, are now being purchased by Wal-Mart in the U.S.A."

Wal-Mart was one of the first retailers to embrace the concept of "green" marketing. The program offered shoppers the option of purchasing products that were better for the environment in three respects: manufacturing, use, and disposal. It was introduced through full-page advertisements in the *Wall Street Journal* and *USA Today*. In-store signage identified those products that were environmentally safe. As Wal-Mart executives saw it, "Customers are concerned about the quality of land, air, and water, and would like the opportunity to do something positive." To initiate the program, 7,000 vendors were notified that Wal-Mart had a corporate concern for the environment and asked for their support in a variety of ways. Wal-Mart television advertising showed children on swings, fields of grain blowing in the wind, and roses. Green and white store signs, printed on recycled paper, marked products or packaging that had been developed or redesigned to be more environmentally sound.

The Wal-Mart private brand program began with the "Ol' Roy" brand, the private-label dog food named for Sam Walton's favorite hunting companion. Introduced to Wal-Mart stores in 1982 as a low-price alterative to national brands, Ol' Roy became the biggest seller of all dog-food brands in the United States. "We are a (national) brand-oriented company first," noted Bob Connolly, Executive Vice President of Merchandising of Wal-Mart. "But we also use private label to fill value or pricing voids that, for whatever reason, the brands left behind." Wal-Mart's private-label program included thousands of products that had brand names, such as Sam's Choice, Great Value, Equate, and Spring Valley.

Wal-Mart was the largest clothing seller in the world. Although most of the sales of its clothing business were in basics such as socks, underwear, tee-shirts, and blue jeans, the firm developed a 100-member development team to begin to focus its clothing lines on fashion and style in all sizes. Claire Watts was hired from Limited, Inc., to become the first Director of Product Development. The company also made a significant investment in technology so that all the factors of the development process, from design to production, were coordinated online among Wal-Mart, its suppliers, and factories. Rather than wait for suppliers to bring products to Wal-Mart, merchandise teams traveled to Europe four times a year to visit trendy boutiques and fashion shows and bring back racks of clothes to be evaluated at corporate headquarters on the basis of quality, fashion, and style. In 2002, Wal-Mart introduced a contemporary brand nationwide called George. George, a stylish line of clothing for women and men, had been sold exclusively for 10 years in England's ASDA supermarkets, which Wal-Mart acquired in 1999. Although the

George brand was profitable, it was never as successful as management had hoped. In 2005, management put increased emphasis on apparel and music offerings. In an attempt to upgrade its image, the company placed ads featuring women's clothing in *Vogue* magazine.

In 2000, according to DSR Marketing Systems, Wal-Mart became the largest retailer of groceries in the United States, surpassing traditional grocery retailers such as Cincinnati, Ohio–based Kroger, Boise, Idaho–based Albertson's, and Pleasanton, California–based Safeway.

Wal-Mart had become the channel commander in the distribution of many brand-name items. As the nation's largest retailer and in many geographic areas the dominant distributor, it exerted considerable influence in negotiation for the best price, delivery terms, promotion allowances, and continuity of supply. Many of these benefits could be passed on to consumers in the form of quality name-brand items available at lower-than-competitive prices. As a matter of corporate policy, management often insisted on doing business only with producers' top sales executives rather than going through a manufacturer's representative. Wal-Mart had been accused of threatening to buy from other producers if firms refused to sell directly to it. In the ensuing power struggle, Wal-Mart executives refused to talk about the controversial policy or admit that it existed. As a representative of an industry association representing a group of sales agencies representatives suggested, "In the Southwest, Wal-Mart's the only show in town." An industry analyst added, "They're extremely aggressive. Their approach has always been to give the customer the benefit of a corporate saving. That builds up customer loyalty and market share."

Another key factor in the mix was an inventory control system that was recognized as the most sophisticated in retailing. A high-speed computer system linked virtually all the stores to headquarters and the company's distribution centers. It electronically logged every item sold at the checkout counter, automatically kept the warehouses informed of merchandise to be ordered, and directed the flow of goods to the stores and even to the proper shelves. Most importantly for management, it helped detect sales trends quickly and sped up market reaction time substantially. According to Bob Connolly, Executive Vice President of Merchandising, "Wal-Mart has used the data gathered by technology to make more inventory available in the key items that customers want most, while reducing inventories overall." In April 2004, Wal-Mart began a pilot test in 150 stores and Sam's Clubs locations in the Dallas, Texas, area to test the use of radio frequency identification (RFID) to track items through the distribution channel. The new technology resulted in a 16% reduction of out-of-stocks and a threefold increase in replenishing out-of-stock items. RFID was being expanded to nearly 1,000 stores and clubs in 2006 and from 300 suppliers to more than 600 by 2007.

Hired by Wal-Mart in 1978 to help build an information technology system, Randy Mott and colleagues developed a network of computerized distribution centers in the 1980s that made it simple to open and manage new stores efficiently. Promoted to Chief Information Officer in the early 1990s, Mott persuaded management to invest in a "data warehouse" that would allow the company to collect and sift customer information to analyze buying trends. The resulting information could indicate which flavor of Pop-Tart sold best at a particular store. Since this concept was new to the industry, it gave the company another significant competitive advantage. From Wal-Mart, Mott moved to Dell and then to Hewlett-Packard to improve their information systems.[7]

At the beginning of 2000, Wal-Mart set up a separate company for its Web site, with plans to go public. Wal-Mart.com, Inc., based in Palo Alto, California, was jointly owned by Wal-Mart and Accel Partners, a Silicon Valley venture-capital firm. The site included a wide range of products and services that ranged from shampoo to clothing to lawn mowers, as well as airline, hotel, and rental car bookings. After launching and then closing a Sam's Club Web site, Wal-Mart reopened the site in mid-June 2000, with an emphasis on upscale items such as jewelry, housewares, and electronics and full product lines for small business owners. SamsClub.com was operated by Wal-Mart from the company's Bentonville, Arkansas, headquarters.

International Strategies and Programs

In 1994, Wal-Mart entered the Canadian market with the acquisition of 122 Woolco discount stores from Woolworth Corporation. When acquired, the Woolco stores were losing millions of dollars annually, but operations became profitable within three years. By the end of 2001, the company had 196 Wal-Mart discount stores in Canada. The company's operations in Canada were considered as a model for Wal-Mart's expansion into other international markets. By 2006, the number had grown to 272 discount stores and six Sam's Clubs. With a 35% share of the Canadian discount and department store market, Wal-Mart was the largest retailer in that country.

With a tender offer for shares and mergers of joint ventures in Mexico, the company in 1997 acquired a controlling interest in Cifra, Mexico's largest retailer. Cifra, later identified as Wal-Mart de Mexico, operated stores with a variety of concepts in every region of Mexico, ranging from the nation's largest chain of sit-down restaurants to a softline department store. Retail analysts noted that the initial venture involved many costly mistakes. Time after time it sold the wrong products, including tennis balls that wouldn't bounce in high-altitude Mexico City. Large parking lots at some stores made access difficult as many people arrived by bus. By 2006, Wal-Mart (known as Walmex) operated 599 stores (composed of 187 Bodegas, 16 Mi Bodegas, 1 Mi Bodega Express, 1 Mercamus, 53 Suburbias, 55 Superamas, and 286 Vips stores), 105 Supercenters, and 70 Sam's Clubs in Mexico for a total of 774 outlets, compared to just 551 outlets in 2002. The company had grown to dominate Mexico's retail market with its model of rapid expansion and low prices.

When Wal-Mart entered Argentina in 1995, it also initially faced challenges adapting its U.S.-based retail mix and store layouts to the local culture. Although globalization and U.S. cultural influences had swept through the country in the early 1990s, the Argentine market did not accept U.S. cuts of meat, bright-colored cosmetics, and jewelry that gave prominent placement to emeralds, sapphires, and diamonds, since most Argentine women preferred wearing gold and silver. The first stores even had hardware departments full of tools wired for 110-volt electric power; the standard throughout Argentina was 220. Compounding the challenges was a store layout that featured narrow aisles; stores appeared crowded and dirty. In 2006, Wal-Mart operated 11 Supercenters in Argentina, the same number as in 2002.

Wal-Mart's management concluded that Brazil offered great opportunities for Wal-Mart because it had the fifth largest population in the world and a population that had a tendency to follow U.S. cultural cues. Although financial data were not broken out on South American operations, retail analysts cited the accounts of Wal-Mart's Brazilian partner, Lojas Americanas SA, to suggest that Wal-Mart lost $100 million in start-up costs for the initial 16 stores. Customer acceptance of Wal-Mart stores was mixed. In Canada and Mexico, many customers had been familiar with the company from cross-border shopping trips. In contrast, many Brazilian customers were not familiar with the Wal-Mart name. In addition, local Brazilian markets were already dominated by savvy local and foreign competitors, such as Grupo Pao de Acucar SA of Brazil and Carrefour SA of France. Wal-Mart's insistence on doing things "the Wal-Mart way" initially alienated many local suppliers and employees. The country's continuing economic problems also presented a challenge. Realizing that it needed to take another approach to growth, management made two acquisitions. The first was Bompreco S. A. Supermercado do Nordeste, a chain of 118 hypermarkets, supermarkets, and mini-markets in Northern Brazil that was purchased in February 2004. The second was Sonae Distribuicao, a retail operation in Southern Brazil consisting of 139 hypermarkets, supermarkets, and warehouse units purchased in December 2005. By 2006, Wal-Mart operated 255 discount stores, 23 Supercenters, 15 Sam's Clubs, and 2 Neighborhood Markets in Brazil for a total of 295 outlets compared to only 12 Supercenters and 8 Sam's Clubs in 2002.

Wal-Mart entered the European market by acquiring three retail chains. Because of complex local regulations, management felt it would be easier for Wal-Mart to buy existing stores in Europe than to build new ones. The response in Europe to Wal-Mart's entry was immediate and dramatic. Competitors scrambled to match Wal-Mart's low prices, long hours, and friendly service. Some firms combined to strengthen their operations. For example, France's Carrefour SA chain of hypermarkets combined forces with competitor Promodes in a $16.5 billion deal. In 2002, Carrefour dominated the European market with three leading formats: hypermarket, supermarket, and hard discount (small food stores with low prices). It was the world's second-largest retailer, with more than 9,200 stores not only in Europe, but in Latin America and Asia as well. In 2005, Carrefour's sales rose 2.5% from the previous year to 74.5 billion euros. Although net income fell 16% to 1.44 billion euros ($1.72 billion) during the same period, the exclusion of one-time charges showed a 1.2% increase in profits to 1.81 euros ($2.15 billion). Carrefour's management planned to invest 10 billion euros ($11.9 billion) to open 100 new hypermarkets in 2006 and a total of 1,000 new stores during 2006–2008. The planned growth in hypermarkets was more than twice the average annual number of openings between 2000 and 2004. Carrefour's management expected that its growth strategy would increase sales by 10% by 2008.[8]

Wal-Mart moved into Germany at the end of 1997 by acquiring 21 stores from hypermarket operator Wertkauf. Also as part of its expansion efforts in Germany, Wal-Mart acquired 74 stores that were a part of the Interspar chain. Soon after the takeover, Wal-Mart quickly filled the top management positions with U.S. expatriates. Within weeks of the purchase, most of the top German managers left the company. Management also discovered that these stores were either cramped, unattractive, or poorly located and needed to be entirely renovated. All of these German stores were identified with the Wal-Mart name and restocked with a new and revamped selection of merchandise. In response to local laws that forced early store closings and forbade Sunday sales, the company simply opened stores earlier, to allow shopping to begin at 7 AM. In January 2000, the company launched its first big "rollback" by cutting prices on several hundred items by up to 23%. Germany was well populated with discounters such as Aldi and Lidl, which ran no-frills, cheap supermarkets. These discounters responded fiercely to price challenge by cutting their prices by up to 25%. As a result, price cuts did not have a dramatic impact on sales. Wal-Mart's store count dropped from 95 Supercenters in 2002 to 88 in 2006, less than 20% of rival Kaufland's stores. Wal-Mart's grocery market share never exceeded 2% of Germany's food sales. In a country where local discounters dominated, the leader was Aldi, which boasted a 19% market share through its 4,000 stores. According to industry analysts, Wal-Mart was in a difficult position because it needed more stores to advertise efficiently and exert purchasing power. Despite Wal-Mart's lackluster performance in Germany, management remained committed to serving this market.[9]

Wal-Mart acquired ASDA, Britain's third largest supermarket group, for $10.8 billion in July 1999. With its own price rollbacks, people greeter, "permanently low prices," and even "smiley" faces, ASDA had emulated Wal-Mart's store culture for many years. Based in Leeds, England, the firm had 232 stores in England, Scotland, and Wales. Although the culture and pricing strategies of the two companies were nearly identical, there were differences, primarily the size and product mix of the stores. The average Wal-Mart Supercenter was 180,000 square feet in size and had about 30% of its sales in groceries. In contrast, the average ASDA store had only 65,000 square feet and did 60% of sales in grocery items. By 2006, Wal-Mart operated 294 discount stores (composed of 236 ASDA stores, 10 George stores, 5 ASDA Living, and 43 ASDA small stores) and 21 Supercenters in the United Kingdom. Although ASDA was still second in the U.K. market with a 16.6% share, its sales were stagnating while its rivals J Sainsbury (16.2% share) and market leader Tesco (30.4% share) were slowly increasing their share of the market. British executives hoped to revitalize the U.K. operations sometime in 2007.[10]

Wal-Mart's initial effort to enter China fell apart in 1996, when Wal-Mart and Thailand's Charoen Pokphand Group terminated an 18-month old joint venture because of management differences. Wal-Mart decided to consolidate its operations with five stores in the Hong Kong border city of Shenzhen, one in Dalian, and another in Kunming. Analysts concluded that the company was taking a low-profile approach because of possible competitive response and government restrictions. Beijing restricted the operations of foreign retailers in China, requiring them, for instance, to have government-backed partners. In Shenzhen, it limited the number of stores Wal-Mart could open. Wal-Mart soon found another joint venture partner and continued its growth. In 2006, Wal-Mart's joint venture operated 51 Supercenters, 3 Sam's Clubs, and 2 Neighborhood Markets. This was a significant increase in China from 2002, when the company operated only 15 Supercenters, three Sam's Clubs, and one Neighborhood Market. Wal-Mart corporate management has targeted China, long a major supplier of its products, as a key market for international store growth. Management planned to open 20 additional stores in China during 2006.[11]

During December 2005, Wal-Mart purchased a majority interest in Seiyu, a retailer in Japan selling apparel, general merchandise, and food in 398 stores. 2005 was the fourth straight year Seiyu operated at a loss. Seiyu, Japan's fourth-largest retailer, had struggled unsuccessfully to adopt Wal-Mart's marketing strategy since 2002 when Wal-Mart acquired a 6% stake. Wal-Mart management was hopeful that its investment would lead to eventual success in an important market. "This market has a lot of promise and because of that we are patiently investing both management as well as capital, and we expect to get a return on that over time," reported Jeff McAllister, COO of Wal-Mart's Japanese operations.[12]

In February 2006, Wal-Mart acquired majority control of the Central American Retail Holding Company, known as CARHCO. With this purchase, Wal-Mart obtained more than 360 supermarkets and other stores in Costa Rica, El Salvador, Guatemala, Honduras, and Nicaragua. CARHCO's 2005 sales were about $2.2 billion.

On May 22, 2006, management announced that Wal-Mart was withdrawing from South Korea by selling all 16 of its outlets to Shinsegae, a local retailer for $882 million. In leaving Korea, Wal-Mart joined Carrefour, Nokia, Nestle, and Google—other firms that had also failed to adjust to South Korean tastes. According to financial analyst Na Hong Seok, "Wal-Mart is a typical example of a global giant who has failed to localize its operations in South Korea. It failed to read what South Korean housewives want when they go shopping." Analysts commented that both Wal-Mart and Carrefour had not opened stores quickly enough to build the sales needed for supply chain economies.

The international expansion accelerated management's plans for the development of Wal-Mart as a global brand along the lines of Coca-Cola, Disney, and McDonald's. "We are a global brand name," said Bobby Martin, an early President of the International Division of Wal-Mart. "To customers everywhere it means low cost, best value, greatest selection of quality merchandise and highest standards of customer service," he noted. Some changes were mandated in Wal-Mart's international operations to meet local tastes and intense competitive conditions. "We're building companies out there," said Martin. "That's like starting Wal-Mart all over again in South America or Indonesia or China." Although stores in different international markets would coordinate purchasing to gain leverage with suppliers, developing new technology and planning overall strategy was being done from Wal-Mart headquarters in Bentonville, Arkansas.

Human Resources and Corporate Culture

One principle that distinguished Wal-Mart was the unusual depth of employee involvement in company affairs. The corporation emphasized human resource management. Employees of Wal-Mart were called "associates," a name borrowed from Sam Walton's early association with the J. C. Penney Co. Input was encouraged at meetings at the store and corporate levels. The firm hired employees locally and provided training programs, and through a "Letter to the President" program, management encouraged employees to ask questions and made words such as "we," "us," and "our" a part of the corporate language. A number of special award programs recognized individual, department, and division achievement. Stock owner-ship and profit-sharing programs were introduced as part of a "partnership" concept.

The corporate culture was recognized by the editors of the trade publication *Mass Market Retailers,* when it recognized all 275,000 associates collectively as the "Mass Market Retail-ers of the Year." "The Wal-Mart associate," the editors noted, "has come to symbolize all that is right with the American worker, particularly in the retailing environment and most particu-larly at Wal-Mart." The "store within a store" concept, as a Wal-Mart corporate policy, trained individuals to be merchants by being responsible for the performance of their own departments as if they were running their own businesses. Seminars and training programs afforded them opportunities to grow within the company. "People development is not just a good 'program' for any growing company but a must to secure our future," was how Suzanne Allford, Vice President of the Wal-Mart People Division, explained the firm's decentralized approach to re-tail management development.

"The Wal-Mart Way" was a phase used by management to summarize the firm's uncon-ventional approach to business and to the development of its corporate culture. As noted in a report referring to a recent development program: "We stepped outside our retailing world to examine the best managed companies in the United States in an effort to determine the funda-mentals of their success and to 'benchmark' our own performances. The name 'Total Quality Management' (TQM) was used to identify this vehicle for proliferating the very best things we do while incorporating the new ideas our people have that will assure our future." In 1999, *Discount Store News* honored Wal-Mart Stores, Inc., as "Retailer of the Century," with a com-memorative 200-page issue of the magazine.

In many ways, Wal-Mart's corporate culture was a reflection of the values of its founder, Sam Walton, in its emphasis on everyday low prices, corporate growth, concern for people, and loyalty to the company. According to Chairman David Glass, "Sam has been gone for a num-ber of years now, but he's still alive and well in this company to a great extent. There's not a day that goes by that I don't hear conversations around here about what Sam would do or how he felt about something." An unrelenting focus on cost-cutting led to a continual search to eliminate operating inefficiencies, high pressure on suppliers to reduce costs and provide "just in time" deliveries, and frugal employee benefits. For example, even when CEO Lee Scott and CFO Tom Schoewe went on a business trip they were expected to share hotel rooms. "Sharing rooms is a very symbolic part of what we do," explained Scott.[14]

The company's cultural roots in Bentonville, Arkansas, have been considered by some to be both a key strength and a serious weakness. Management's southern, rural, conservative val-ues provided it a competitive advantage when expanding into small and mid-sized towns throughout America, but created some problems when Wal-Mart expanded into larger cities and other countries. For example, urban shoppers often preferred more fashionable merchandise than what Wal-Mart usually stocked. Brand Keys' 2006 study of top brands revealed that Wal-Mart was behind Target for the second consecutive year. According to Robert Passikoff, Presi-dent of Brand Keys, "Target means style at accessible pricing. Wal-Mart hasn't reached that point." In addition, Wal-Mart was the last major pharmacy chain to stock the "Plan B" morning-after birth control pill and only did so after it lost a lawsuit brought by three Boston women. Nevertheless, the company continued to keep its "conscientious objector" policy, which al-lowed employees who didn't feel comfortable dispensing the drugs to refer customers else-where. Wal-Mart's non-union stance was acceptable to rural southern communities, but created growing antagonism when the firm added stores in the urban Midwest and northeastern United States and in Canada. A key part of its low-cost competitive strategy, the company's non-union labor costs were 20% less than at unionized supermarkets. Management had also forced suppli-ers to hide magazine covers the company considered "racy" and refused to stock music or com-puter games with mature ratings. Nevertheless, most locations offered inexpensive firearms as part of their sporting goods offerings. The strong emphasis on Wal-Mart values offended some employees with different backgrounds. For example, many of the Canadian employees at Wal-Mart's discount store in Jonquiere, Quebec, stood silently through the mandatory Wal-Mart cheer each morning. Employee Sylvie Lavoie explained, "It's not a song. It's a military chant. I found it to be degrading."

Financial Situation

By most financial measures, Wal-Mart was in excellent financial shape and far ahead of its domestic rivals. Its net sales had steadily increased from $89.1 billion in 1996 to $204 billion in 2002 to $312.4 billion in 2006. Net income had followed a similar growth path from $2.7 billion in 1996 to $6.6 billion in 2002 to $11.2 billion in 2006. Wal-Mart's diluted earnings per share increased from $.59 in 1996 to $1.47 in 2002 to $2.68 in 2006. According to CEO Scott, "Comparative store [same store] sales in the U.S. rose a healthy 3.4%" from 2005 to 2006. By comparison, net sales and earnings of Target, its closest rival, were only $52.6 billion and $2.4 billion, respectively, in the 2005 fiscal year ending January 28, 2006. The merger of Sears and Kmart into Sears Holdings Corporation resulted in a $55 billion (in sales) company with a net income of $858 million for the 2005 fiscal year ending January 2006. (See **Exhibits 1, 2, 3,** and **4**).

During 2006, management purchased $3.6 billion of Wal-Mart common stock under a share repurchase program and paid dividends of $2.5 billion. During that year, it also issued $7.7 billion in long-term debt, repaid $2.7 billion of long-term debt, and funded a net decrease in commercial paper of $704 million. Total corporate assets of continuing operations increased from $36,621 million in 1996 to $81,549 million in 2002 to $138,187 million in 2006. Return on assets was 7.9% in 1996, 8.4% in 2002, and 8.9% in 2006. One of management's objectives was to have operating income grow faster than net sales. In fiscal year 2006, however, overall operating income increased by only 8.4% over 2005, compared to a net sales increase of 9.5%. Compared to fiscal 2005, the Wal-Mart Stores USA unit experienced an 8.4% increase in operating income and a 9.4% increase in net sales in fiscal 2006. During the same period, Sam's Club had an 8.2% increase in operating income and a 7.2% increase in net sales. At the same time, the international business unit generated 11.4% increases in both sales and operating income.

Wal-Mart's sales for the first quarter of its 2007 fiscal year ending April 30, 2006, were $79.6 billion, an increase of 12.3% over the same quarter a year earlier. The firm's net income rose to $2.62 billion from $2.46 billion the year before. This 6% increase in profits was better than expected by industry analysts, who also noted Target's 12% first-quarter profit increase.

Of special concern to management was the behavior of the company's stock. Contrary to the upward direction of the firm's sales and profits, the price of Wal-Mart's stock had fallen from $56.98 on January 31, 2002, to $46.11 on January 31, 2006. Even though the board of directors had both repurchased stock and raised dividends per share from $0.52 in 2005 to $0.60 in 2006, the stock failed to respond. When the board further raised dividends to $0.67 per share on March 2, 2006 for the 2007 fiscal year, the stock price fell 11.7% to $45.06 on the New York Stock Exchange.

Challenges to Continued Growth

Wal-Mart's management faced significant challenges in 2006—challenges that could significantly affect the achievement of its growth objectives. The company was being condemned for business practices ranging from low pay and stingy health care benefits to exporting jobs and destroying small businesses. Wal-Mart was also the subject of litigation, including a class action discrimination suit representing 1.6 million current and former female employees who accused the firm of systematic underpayment and lack of promotion. In addition, filmmaker Robert

Greenwald premiered a scathing documentary in November 2005 titled *Wal-Mart: The High Cost of Low Prices.* The movie was filled with ex-employees who trashed the company. One activist group, "Wake Up Wal-Mart," which was started in April 2005 by the United Food and Commercial Workers union, gained 115,000 members and aired TV ads to tout the new movie. "Wal-Mart Watch," another activist group, leaked an internal memo to *The New York Times* in October 2005 from Wal-Mart's Executive Vice President for Benefits to Wal-Mart's Board of Directors. The memo stated that 46% of the children of Wal-Mart workers were uninsured or on Medicaid and that Wal-Mart's health plan required such high out-of-pocket payments that the number of employees hit by a very costly illness "almost certainly would end up declaring bankruptcy." The memo proposed that Wal-Mart rewrite job descriptions to involve more physical activity, in part to "dissuade unhealthy people from coming to work at Wal-Mart."[19]

The resulting uproar over Wal-Mart's health benefits led to the Democrat-controlled legislature in Maryland passing a bill on January 12, 2006, requiring any employer with more than 10,000 employees to spend at least 8% of its payroll on health care for its workers. If it spent less, the firm must give the difference to Maryland's Medicaid program. The law was characterized as "the Wal-Mart bill" because Wal-Mart was the only company in Maryland affected. It was noted that as the nation's largest private-sector employer, Wal-Mart provided health insurance to fewer than half of its 1.3 million workers. The new law had been supported by unions who claimed that around 30 states were also considering such legislation. Nevertheless, the bill may be illegal because it could violate the federal Employment Retirement Income Security Act, which gave Congress the sole authority to regulate employee benefits.[20]

Wal-Mart's reputation took another hit when Wal-Mart's No. 2 executive and Vice Chairman of its Board of Directors, Tom Coughlin, admitted to misappropriating company funds and pleaded guilty to five counts of fraud and one count of tax evasion. Previously, he had served as President and CEO of Wal-Mart Stores and Sam's Club. Coughlin was forced to leave Wal-Mart's board in March 2005. After an internal investigation, two other Wal-Mart employees were fired for financial improprieties.[21]

In 2003, a raid on 60 Wal-Mart stores in 21 states led to the arrests of 245 illegal workers. The company paid $11 million in March 2005 without admitting guilt. In November 2005, federal agents arrested more than 120 workers on immigration violations at the construction site of a Wal-Mart distribution center. Wal-Mart's management argued that those arrested were employees of a subcontractor and that Wal-Mart has contracts with subcontractors requiring them to follow all federal, state, and local laws.[22]

Even though the company required that its suppliers certify that their factories complied with Wal-Mart's workplace standards, Jim Lynn, a Wal-Mart executive, found that these reports were routinely falsified in Honduras. When, as part of his job of checking on suppliers in Central and South America, the executive visited the Glory Garments factory near San Dedro Sula, Honduras, he found a facility "that didn't have potable drinking water, that had no toilet paper in the restrooms, and where the fire exits were padlocked. They did pregnancy testing on the women, and if it came back positive, [the women] were terminated." He also discovered that contrary to Wal-Mart's stated policy, factories received at least three-day advance notification of factory-certification visits—enough time to clean up the facilities. After notifying top management about this situation, Lynn was accused of violating company policies and fired. The case of *James Lynn v. Wal-Mart* was filed in an Arkansas state court in 2005. To its credit, Wal-Mart's management worked to rectify the problems raised by Lynn. According to Beth Keck, Wal-Mart's Director of International Affairs, the factories inspected by Lynn were either remedied or terminated as suppliers. Keck acknowledged that outside groups were still not permitted to conduct authorized inspections of their own, though she added that this was a policy that Wal-Mart was working toward.[23] She further reported in a February 13, 2006, news release: "In 2005, Wal-Mart audited on average 35 supplier factories a day or 13,600. We increased the number of unannounced audits to 20 percent."[24]

In general, Wal-Mart's management was not in favor of the unionization of its stores. Keeping labor costs down was key to "everyday low prices." Supermarket rivals paying union wages of $10 an hour and paying most health benefit costs were at a competitive disadvantage to Wal-Mart's Supercenters, where employees earned around $8 and hour and paid a higher proportion of their health costs. According to an article appearing in *The Nation,* "During the hiring process, many workers say they have had to sign forms agreeing that they would not support any effort to unionize the store, a clear violation of federal law." Although none of Wal-Mart's U.S. employees were unionized, Wal-Mart had been a defendant in 28 complaints in just one year (2002) brought by the U.S. National Labor Relations Board citing anti-union activities such as threats, interrogations, or disciplining. Critics contended that the company moved quickly to block organizing. For example, when a majority of meat cutters at a store in Jacksonville, Texas, voted to organize, the company closed its butcher departments at Jackson and other stores. When Wal-Mart's store in Jonquiere, Quebec, was certified by the Quebec government as the only unionized Wal-Mart in North America in August 2004, Wal-Mart simply closed the store and left the area. Interestingly, a union certification election two months earlier had been voted down 53% to 47%. After that union defeat, a group of Wal-Mart managers gathered just outside the front door to celebrate for the TV cameras and taunt union supporters as they left the store. Many employees who had voted against the union were so appalled by management's actions that they switched sides. Interestingly, a 2006 study reported by New England Consulting Group found that 60% of union members had visited a Wal-Mart in the past month versus 57% of all shoppers. According to Tom Hayes, a principal in the consulting group, Wal-Mart had more unionized shoppers than any other retailer—double the number for Sears and 40% more than Target. Explained Hays, "The savings are too much to resist."

Even though a recent survey found that only 8% of adults were openly hostile toward Wal-Mart, there was some indication that the company's customers were no longer pleased with the company. Based on interviews conducted in 2003 by Service Industry Research Systems, customer ratings of the staff in terms of courtesy and friendliness dropped more than 20% since 1999. The ratings had fallen to slightly below the industry average, which itself had dropped during the same period.

Opponents of "big box" retail stores were battling Wal-Mart in an increasing number of locations across the country. In 2004, the ethnically mixed Los Angeles suburb of Englewood voted to stop the building of a new Wal-Mart store, partly in the widespread belief that Wal-Mart destroyed local shopkeepers. One person attacked the company as "a modern-day plantation." A major real estate developer dropped plans to include Wal-Mart in a proposed New York City shopping mall in 2005 because of intense opposition from labor unions, neighborhood retailers, and city officials concerned about the effect the store would have on competitors. This would have been Wal-Mart's first New York City location. The company's decision to build a store in Jefferson, Wisconsin, in 2004 created a major battle among its residents. The formation of the Coalition for a Better Jefferson opposing Wal-Mart led to the launch of the pro-Wal-Mart Coalition for the Best Jefferson, headed by 69-year-old Charlotte Goers-Nevin. Goers-Nevin contended: "The number one complaint of the older people is they don't have a place to shop. Wal-Mart was going to be a good tax base for us, and it was going to be nice for the older people." Even though the town's aldermen voted against annexing the land needed for the new store, the controversy divided the city and led to a recall election against the alderman most against Wal-Mart's entry into town.[32]

In their enthusiasm to attack the company, anti-Wal-Mart interest groups sometimes used extreme measures. In December 2005, for example, the union-supported Wake Up Wal-Mart released a TV ad accusing Wal-Mart of violating religious values, supported by a letter from religious leaders attacking the company for paying low wages and offering poor benefits. The letter declared, "Jesus would not embrace Wal-Mart's values of greed and profits at any cost." The campaign was soon jokingly referred to in the media as "Where would Jesus shop?"[33]

By 2006, Wal-Mart's management was beginning to feel as if they were living in a punching bag. It appeared the company was being treated as a scapegoat for any big business wrongdoing and blamed for all of society's ills. It could be argued, for example, that low wages and benefits were typical for the retailing industry as a whole, not just Wal-Mart. Target, Kmart, and other mass merchandisers could be equally criticized for weakening downtowns, extracting public subsidies, and selling clothes made in sweatshops in developing nations. Even though Costco faced a class-action lawsuit alleging systematic discrimination against women, it never received the publicity Wal-Mart lawsuits generated.[34] In an interview with *Business Week,* Scott referred to comments made by a visiting CEO to Wal-Mart executives: "There isn't anything you are faced with, from a class action to the rest of the stuff, that we're not dealing with. The only difference is that yours is played out on the front page of the paper, and you never read about ours."[35] In response to the criticism that Wal-Mart's pay and benefits were too low, CEO Scott countered that people were continuing to apply for Wal-Mart jobs. He stated in Wal-Mart's *2006 Annual Report*: "At a store opening this year just outside Chicago, we received more than 25,000 applications for just 325 jobs."

Corporate Initiatives

To counter social criticism of the company and to regain control of its growth strategy, Wal-Mart management introduced a series of new programs.

Social Initiatives

Throughout its history, Wal-Mart has tried to be a good corporate citizen in those towns where it had facilities. When Hurricane Katrina ravaged America's Gulf Coast, Wal-Mart had its truckers haul $3 million of supplies to the area, arriving in many cases days before the Federal Emergency Management Agency (FEMA). The company also contributed $17 million in cash to relief efforts. Its long-praised efficiency was demonstrated when it reopened all but 13 of its affected stores by September 16, 2005—just three weeks after the storm. By then the company had located 97% of the employees displaced by the storm and offered them jobs at any Wal-Mart operation in the country. Thanks to the ability of Jason Jackson, Wal-Mart's Director of Business Continuity, who was able to plot the likely path of the storm, management was able to get the stores in the zone fully stocked with water, flashlights, batteries, and canned food. The result was a public relations success for the company.[36]

During October 2005, Wal-Mart offered $8.5 million worth of grants from its "Safe Neighborhood Heroes" program to recognize the efforts of hometown fire, police, rescue, and emergency medical service teams with direct financial contributions. "As a community, we must lean on each other to help those we serve," explained Betsy Reithemeyer, head of Wal-Mart & Sam's Club Foundation.[37] In addition, management announced in April 2006 that it planned to build more than 50 stores in struggling urban areas during the next two years. CEO Lee stated that the stores would generate between 15,000 and 25,000 new jobs in neighborhoods with high crime or unemployment rates, on sites that are environmentally contaminated, or in vacant buildings or malls in need of renovation.

Responding to criticism of its health care coverage, Wal-Mart's management introduced a "Value Plan." The new benefits plan offered health coverage to its employees at premiums ranging from $11 to $65 a month. The first three doctors' visits and three prescriptions were mostly paid by the company with only nominal payments needed by the employee. It did, however, contain fairly high deductibles, but the company offered tax-free health savings accounts to help employees pay out-of-pocket expenses up to the deductible amount. Wal-Mart also added health clinics to its stores to provide health care access to its associates and the local community.[38]

To deflect some of the criticism the company had been receiving regarding discrimination against women and minorities, management for the first time made public in April 2006 the data it had been providing the U.S. Equal Opportunity Employment Commission each year. The report stated that 32% of the 1.34 million Wal-Mart U.S. employees were minorities. Minorities were 21% of managers, 20% of professionals, and 33% of sales workers. Women accounted for 60% of the workforce, 39% of managers, and 75% of sales workers.[39]

Wal-Mart management realized that it had to do better in terms of dealing with its many stakeholders. Consequently, in February 2006, it established a new position of Senior Director of Stakeholder Engagement. According to the posted job description, the new position was to report to Wal-Mart's Vice President for Corporate Strategy and "will play a critical role in helping the company . . . create a new model of business engagement that uses market-based changes to create societal value." Explained spokesperson Sarah Clark, "We're trying to centralize our [social responsibility] efforts."[40] In March 2006, management announced that it planned to hire a Director of Global Ethics. The director's job was to manage the company's Global Ethics Office that had been established in 2004 and to ensure that the retailer's code of conduct was being applied across all its operations throughout the world. The person hired would lead the company's global ethics strategy and oversee ethics-related infrastructure, administration, and training.

In its quest for efficiency and low costs, Wal-Mart had inadvertently helped the environment when management decided in the early 1990s that much of the packaging being used by its suppliers was unnecessary. In one example, it told Wal-Mart suppliers to ship deodorants without their paperboard containers. Charles Fishman, in his book *The Wal-Mart Effect,* stated "It's a perfect Wal-Mart moment—the company used its insight and its muscle to help change the world. Millions of trees were not cut down, acres of cardboard were not manufactured only to be discarded, and one billion of deodorant boxes didn't end up in landfills each year. It's all unseen, all unnoticed, and all good."[41] Once they realized that business practice could be aligned with environmental needs, Wal-Mart's management expanded this program to private-label toys and other goods. In an October 24, 2005, presentation by CEO Lee Scott, he presented Wal-Mart's new environmental objectives: (1) to be supplied 100% by renewable energy, (2) to create zero waste, and (3) to sell products that sustain our resources and environment. Wanting to reduce the fuel usage of its trucking fleet, he added: "We will increase our fleet efficiency by 25% over the next three years and double it within ten years." Through improvements in technology, Scott stated that management intended to eliminate 30% of the energy used in Wal-Mart stores. Through a new process called "sandwich balers," at 99 Sam's Clubs and 548 Wal-Mart stores, the company was recycling plastic it used to throw away.

Growth Initiatives

Realizing that Target was its strongest U.S. competitor in discount mass merchandising, Wal-Mart's management felt in 2005 that it needed to overhaul its merchandise mix, stores, and image to go after higher-margin, discretionary sales. Greater emphasis was to be placed on more fashionable merchandise and more attractive advertisements. It wanted to entice its style-conscious customers who went to Wal-Mart to buy food and the basics, but avoided the fashion and home furnishings departments. Management worked to reduce clutter on the Wal-Mart sales floor. Less merchandise was to be stacked at the ends of the aisles. More room was to be allowed between apparel racks. Apparel areas were to receive imitation hardwood floors to suggest more upscale goods. More emphasis was to be placed on the George clothing line originally created in the United Kingdom by the ASDA retail chain. According to CEO Scott, the goal was not to ignore its current customers, but to offer additional goods not currently available to Wal-Mart shoppers. Said Scott: "The first thing you have to do is make sure you have the assortment that is broad enough that includes the customer's tastes and styles. That's where you end up with the new LCD TV, 400-thread-count sheets, and with more fashion."[42]

One example of the company's new upscale emphasis was management's decision in April 2006 to double its selection of organic foods in its Supercenters.

In 2003, Wal-Mart broke tradition by opening new stores in a New York City suburban shopping mall and in a Los Angeles mall where a Macy's store had once operated. For the first time, Wal-Mart built its own addition to a regional mall near San Diego. The company was actually being welcomed in cities such as Los Angeles and Portland, Oregon, where its stores' presence helped to revive fading shopping malls that served primarily minority shoppers. Although the shopping mall didn't fit the discounters' traditional model of single-story units surrounded by acres of free parking, it was the only way large retailers could find enough space in urban locations. Target Corporation, in contrast, had been locating its stores in shopping malls for 25 years. A report by Goldman, Sachs & Company estimated that Target's mall stores could grow from 30 in 2003 to 150 by 2012. Real estate analysts calculated that the higher logistical costs of a mall location would be offset by higher store traffic and more sales per square foot.[43]

Wal-Mart's management has long wanted to add financial services to its mix of offerings. Its attempt to purchase an Oklahoma bank in 1999 was thwarted, as was its 2005 attempt to buy a California industrial loan corporation (ILC). Wal-Mart Stores' application to the Federal Deposit Insurance Corporation to charter a bank drew 1,550 mostly negative comments. Most of the negative comments stressed the dangers of an unregulated commercial company owning a federally insured bank. In 2005, Wal-Mart allowed 300 local and community banks to operate branches in more than 1,000 stores on long-term leases. Opponents feared that Wal-Mart might put its own banks in stores and thus devastate community banks. "If they get their hands on an ILC and get into financial trouble, they could swamp the FDIC fund, and we could have a repeat of the savings and loan collapse," stated Camden Fine, CEO of the Independent Community Bankers of America.[44]

Recent Events

During the summer of 2006, Wal-Mart continued to be in the news. Just a few months after announcing that the company was closing its stores in South Korea, management announced that Wal-Mart was also withdrawing from Germany. The sale of its 85 hypermarkets to rival Metro AG resulted in a $863 million pretax loss for the firm. The pullout left the company with only one European operation, ASDA, Britain's second largest supermarket chain.

In a surprise decision, management decided to agree to allow officials from China's state-run union to unionize employees in Wal-Mart's 60 retail stores in China. This amazed most industry analysts because of Wal-Mart's history and because most foreign firms did not have unions in China. According to Jonathan Dong, company spokesman, it was up to the employees at each store to decide if they wished to join the union. As of August 11, 2006, six of the 60 stores had unionized.[45]

On August 8, 2006, Wal-Mart management announced that it was raising starting pay at about a third of its U.S. stores by an average of 6%. It was also introducing wage caps for the first time on each type of job in all stores. This announcement came just two weeks after Chicago's City Council passed an ordinance in July 2006 requiring all retail stores with floor space over 90,000 square feet ("big box" stores) to pay a "living wage" and provide a minimum amount for benefits.[46]

On August 15, 2006 Wal-Mart's management announced that quarterly profits had declined for the first time in 10 years. Higher gasoline prices and the closing of German operations were blamed for a 26% decline in second-quarter profit. Net income fell to $2.1 billion from $2.8 billion a year earlier. With the price of gasoline averaging $2.92 per gallon, up 33% from 2005, Wal-Mart's customers were making fewer trips to the store, but spending more each visit. Net sales for the second quarter of fiscal year 2007 (ending July 31, 2006) were $84.5 billion, an increase of 11.3% over the second quarter of fiscal 2006. Quarterly income from continuing operations was up 4.6% versus a year earlier to nearly $3 billion. The second-quarter profit decline resulted in Wal-Mart's shares falling $.55 to $44.55 at the close of business on August 15, 2006.

What Next?

H. Lee Scott would never forget his first meeting with Sam Walton. "How old are you?" Walton asked the then 30-year-old Scott, who had just taken a job managing Wal-Mart's trucking fleet. "Do you think you can do this job?" asked Walton. When Scott said yes, Walton agreed and said, "I reckon you can." More than 20 years later, as Wal-Mart's CEO, Scott faced his toughest challenge yet: keeping the world's biggest retailer on its phenomenal roll and delivering the huge sales and earnings increases that investors had come to expect from Wal-Mart over the years—all while deflecting increasing criticism of his company's business practices. Analysts had correctly projected that Wal-Mart would surpass General Motors to be ranked number one in revenue on the *Fortune* 500 list in 2000. The combination of growth and acquisition had caused revenue increases every year. Increasing profits followed higher sales. How could this be continued if Wal-Mart's management allowed costs to increase and service to lag?

Wal-Mart Stores, Inc., revolutionized American retailing with its focus on low costs, high customer service, and everyday low pricing to drive sales. Although the company had suffered through some years of lagging performance, it experienced big gains from its move into the grocery business with one-stop Supercenters and into international markets with acquisitions, joint ventures, and new ventures. To keep it all going and growing was a major challenge. As the largest retailer and firm in the world, the company and its leadership were challenged to find new areas to continue to grow sales and profits into the future. Lee Scott knew that an ambitious expansion program was called for to allow the company to meet these objectives, both at home and abroad. The company also needed a strong program to pre-empt its social critics, instead of always being on the defensive. At the same time, Scott realized that Wal-Mart could not allow itself to emphasize social over business objectives.

NOTES

1. "Letter to Shareholders," *2006 Annual Report,* Wal-Mart Stores, Inc., p. i.
2. J. Unseem, "One Nation under Wal-Mart," *Fortune* (March 3, 2003), pp. 65–78; A. Bianco and W. Zellner, "Is Wal-Mart Too Powerful?" *Business Week* (October 6, 2003), pp. 100–110; "Opening Up the Big Box," *Economist* (February 25, 2006), p. 80.
3. Letter to Shareholders, *2006 Annual Report,* pp. 12–13.
4. R. Walberg, "Can Wal-Mart's PR Campaign Save Its Stock?" *Street Patrol* (April 14, 2005).
5. "The Top Ten," *Forbes* (October 10, 2005), p. 100 and "Holdings of Major Shareholders," *Notice of 2006 Annual Shareholders' Meeting* (April 14, 2006), p. 26.
6. L. Grant, "Wal-Mart Sets Sights on Target While Keeping Core Customers," *USA Today* (August 5, 2005), pp. 1B and 2B.
7. P. Burrows, "Stopping the Sprawl at HP," *Business Week* (May 29, 2006), pp. 54–56.
8. J. Loades-Carter, "Carrefour to Open 1,000 New Stores as Profits Fall," *Financial Times* (March 9, 2006).
9. J. Ewing, "Wal-Mart: Local Pipsqueak," *Business Week* (April 11, 2005), p. 54.
10. S. Goldstein, "Wal-Mart's U.K. Market Share Eases," *MarketWatch* (March 9, 2006).
11. "Wal-Mart to Hire Up to 150,000 in China," *St. Cloud Times* (March 21, 2006), p. 6A.
12. S. Izumi, "Wal-Mart Sets $1b in Rescue for Seiyu," *Reuters* (November 2, 2005).
13. C. Sang-Hun, "Wal-Mart Selling Stores and Leaving South Korea," *International Herald Tribune* (May 23, 2006).
14. D. Faber, "With a Small-Town Culture, Wal-Mart Dominates," *CNBC* (November 10, 2004).
15. "Wal-Mart Tries to Create Hip Image," *St. Cloud Times* (February 21, 2006), p. 6A.
16. A. Bianco and W. Zellner, "Is Wal-Mart Too Powerful?" *Business Week* (October 6, 2003), pp. 100–110.
17. A. Bianco, "No Union, Please, We're Wal-Mart," *Business Week* (February 13, 2006), p. 80.
18. L. Scott, "To Our Shareholders, Associates, and Customers," *2006 Annual Report,* Wal-Mart Corporation, p. 12.
19. D. McGinn, "Wal-Mart Hits the Wall," *Newsweek* (November 14, 2005), pp. 42–44.

20. "This Year's Political Punch-Bag?" *The Economist* (January 21, 2006), p. 35.

21. C. Rousseau, "Internal Scrutiny Leads to Wal-Mart Request for Director's Resignation," *USA Today* (March 28, 2005), p. 7B.

22. S. Armour and D. Leinwand, "120 Arrested on Immigration Violations at Wal-Mart Site," *USA Today* (November 8, 2005), p. 4B.

23. H. Meyerson, "Former Wal-Mart Executive Jim Bill Lynn Blows Whistle on Factory Inspection Scam," *The American Prospect* (December 2005).

24. B. Keck, "Wal-Mart Files Motion to Dismiss Class Action Lawsuit," *Wal-Mart News Release* (February 13, 2006).

25. L. Grant, "Retail Giant Wal-Mart Faces Challenges on Many Fronts," *USA Today* (November 11, 2003), pp. 1B–2B.

26. L. Featherstone, "Will Labor Take the Wal-Mart Challenge?" *The Nation* (June 28, 2004).

27. A. Bianco (2006), pp. 78–81.

28. J. Hempel, "Labor Loves Wal-Mart's Low Prices," *Business Week* (February 13, 2006), p. 14.

29. D. McGinn (2005), p. 43.

30. "Fewer Smiles in the Aisles," *Business Week* (April 28, 2003), p. 10.

31. "The Behemoth from Bentonville," *The Economist* (February 25, 2006), pp. 85–86.

32. R. Epstein, "Wal-Mart Boosters Try to Oust Jefferson, WI Alderman Who Opposed New Store," *Milwaukee Journal-Sentinel* (July 23, 2005).

33. P. Krugman, "Big Box Balderdash," *The New York Times* (December 12, 2005).

34. J. Milchen, "Is Wal-Mart the Right Target?" *ReclaimDemocracy.org* (November 15, 2005).

35. R. Berner, "Lee Scott on Why Wal-Mart Is Playing Nicer," *Business Week* (October 3, 2005), p. 95.

36. D. Leonard, "The Only Lifeline Was the Wal-Mart," *Fortune* (October 3, 2005), pp. 74–77.

37. Press Release, "Wal-Mart Donates $8.5 Million to Benefit Police, Fire, Rescue and Emergency Medical Teams," *Wal-Mart Company* (October 12, 2005).

38. "Under Fire, a Giant Employer Offers a Useful Health Plan," *USA Today* (November 7, 2005), p. 12A.

39. "Wal-Mart Opens Books on Work Force Diversity," *St. Cloud Times* (April 12, 2006), p. 8A.

40. A. Bernstein, "A Social Strategist for Wal-Mart," *Business Week* (February 6, 2006), p. 11.

41. C. Fishman, *The Wal-Mart Effect,* Penguin Press, as reported by R. Juskalian, "A Fresh Look at Wal-Mart's Power," *USA Today* (January 30, 2006), p. 9B.

42. L. Grant (2005), pp. 1B and 2B.

43. W. Zellner, "Call It Wal-Mart," *Business Week* (July 14, 2003), pp. 40–42.

44. L. Grant, "Wal-Mart Maintains Bank Hopes Despite Greenspan Urging Change in Law," *USA Today* (January 27, 2006), p. 8B.

45. "Wal-Mart to Allow Workers to Join Unions in China," *Reuters* (August 11, 2006).

46. "Wal-Mart Raises Pay, Includes Wage Cap," *St. Cloud (MN) Times* (August 8, 2006), p. 4A.

CASE 20

The Home Depot, Inc. (2006):

EXECUTIVE LEADERSHIP

J. David Hunger and Thomas L. Wheelen

REFLECTING ON THE OVERALL PERFORMANCE OF HOME DEPOT SINCE HE BECAME CEO in December 2000, Bob Nardelli could only be pleased.

From 2000 to 2005, we opened more than 900 stores, including our 2,000th in December 2005. In 2000, we reported $45.7 billion in annual sales; five years later, our sales nearly doubled, to $81.5 billion. Over the same period, our operating margin grew 230 basis points, from 9.2 percent to 11.5 percent, and our earnings per share more than doubled from $1.10 to $2.72. Since 2000, we returned nearly $13 billion, or approximately 59 percent of our cumulative earnings, to shareholders in the form of dividends and share repurchases. And we achieved EPS growth of at least 20 percent in each of the past four years.

In short, over the past several years, we've been able to deliver sustainable, predictable, and profitable growth, creating a company that has the strongest balance sheet in the industry and tremendous potential for future growth.

Reflecting the hard work and dedication of our 345,000 associates, fiscal year 2005 was another defining year for The Home Depot. We achieved record earnings per share ($2.72, up 20.4 percent), record operating margin (11.5 percent), and record net earnings ($5.8 billion, up 16.7 percent). Our financial success has allowed us to deliver on our commitment to create shareholder value.[1]

Nardelli noted that the average ticket sale per customer had reached an all-time high of $57.98 in 2005, up 5.6% from the previous year. The Home Depot had become an important U.S. retailer of major home appliances. In just a few years, the company had gone from zero to number 3 in the core appliance market share, securing 10% of the U.S. market by the end of 2005. Nardelli had successfully pushed to improve the efficiency of Home Depot's operations through the introduction of self-checkout, Back End Automation and Re-engineering (BEAR), and centralized automated replenishment. The 21.4% growth in services revenue during 2005 was a good indication that the company had successfully extended its business from just selling home improvement products to also installing the products. To better serve the professional contractor market, the company had completed 21 acquisitions. In 2005 alone, Nardelli had announced the purchase of Hughes Supply, the largest acquisition in Home Depot's history. In addition, the company had successfully expanded across the border to become the largest home improvement retailer in both Canada and Mexico. Given this performance, it was easy to understand why Home Depot had been selected by *Fortune* magazine as the "Most Admired Specialty Retailer" for 2005!

With such positive accomplishments, why had Home Depot's common stock fallen 30% since Nardelli had taken charge of the company? The company's own Proxy Statement for the May 25, 2006 shareholders' meeting compared the performance of Home Depot's common stock with that of the S&P 500 Index and the S&P Retail Composite Index. It noted that $100 invested in January 26, 2001, in each would have resulted in $150.09 for the S&P Retail Composite, $102.99 for the S&P 500, but only $92.77 for Home Depot stock!

In addition, Nardelli was increasingly being attacked for having "excessive compensation," given the firm's poor stock performance. One shareholder proposal for the 2006 annual meeting stated the following:

> In each of the last three years, CEO Nardelli has been paid a base salary of more than $1,800,000, well in excess of the IRS cap for deductibility of non-performance-based compensation. His bonus in each of those years has been at least $4,000,000, and he was awarded restricted stock valued at over $8,000,000 in 2002, 2003, and 2004. Mr. Nardelli has also received a disturbingly large amount of compensation in the form of "loan forgiveness" and tax gross-ups related to that forgiveness, which totaled over $3,000,000 in each of the past three years.

In an interview with a *Business Week* reporter in July 2006, Nardelli was asked why he changed the metrics on which he was judged in the middle of the game: "You signed on to the idea that your performance would be gauged relative to stock price. That didn't go well, so you changed it so that your performance is tied with the performance of earnings." He responded that he and the board felt that the leadership team should be measured on things over which the team had direct control, such as earnings per share, instead of stock price compared to the retail index.[2] Even though Nardelli had been able to explain the change in his performance measurement, it didn't help that he was one of the six executives highlighted in a July 24, 2006, *Fortune* article entitled "The Real CEO Pay Problem."[3]

With sales at an all-time high and earnings per share growing 147% in the previous five years, why was the financial community downgrading Home Depot stock and why were the shareholders so upset? Although the stock price had dropped somewhat, cash dividends per share had increased from just $.05 in 1996 to $.16 in 2000 to a high of $.40 in 2005. The company had paid out a total of $857 million in cash dividends to its shareholders in 2005. Isn't Nardelli doing what he is supposed to be doing? What else do they want from a CEO?

The Home Depot, Inc.

Founded in Atlanta, Georgia, in 1978, Home Depot was the world's largest home improvement retailer and the second largest retailer (after Wal-Mart) in the United States based on net sales for the 2005 fiscal year ended January 29, 2006. The Home Depot stores sold a wide assortment of building materials and home-improvement and lawn and garden products, and they provided a number of services such as design and installation. In addition to the Home Depot stores, the company had a store format called EXPO Design Center that sold products and services primarily for home decorating and remodeling projects and two store formats focused on professional customers called Home Depot Supply and Home Depot Landscaping Supply. As of August 29, 2006, the company operated 1,832 Home Depot stores in all 50 states and the District of Columbia, Puerto Rico, and the Virgin Islands, plus 143 stores in Canada and 57 in Mexico. It also operated 34 EXPO Design Center locations in the United States, 900 Home Depot Supply locations (including 11 Contractor's Warehouse locations) in 44 states and Canada, and 11 Home Depot Landscape Supply stores in the Atlanta and Dallas–Fort Worth areas. The company also had two Home Depot Floor Stores in Texas and Florida that primarily sold flooring products.

The average Home Depot store had approximately 105,000 square feet of indoor selling space and an additional 23,000 square feet of outside garden center, including houseplant enclosures. The stores stocked approximately 35,000–45,000 different kinds of building materials, home improvement products, and lawn and garden supplies. In addition, Home Depot stores offered installation services for many products. Including its recent acquisition of Hughes Supply, the company employed approximately 355,000 associates.

Retail industry analysts had credited Home Depot with being a leading innovator in retailing, by combining the economies of warehouse-format stores with a high level of customer service. Throughout most of its history, the company augmented that concept with a corporate culture that valued decentralized management and decision making, entrepreneurial innovation and risk taking, and high levels of employee commitment and enthusiasm.

One example of the company's operational excellence was its response to Hurricane Katrina in 2005. Home Depot had started mobilizing four days before Katrina hit the U.S. Gulf Coast. Two days before landfall, maintenance teams battened down stores in the hurricane's projected path, while electrical generators and hundreds of extra workers were moved into place. A day after the storm, all but 10 of the company's 33 stores in Katrina's impact zone were open. Within a week, five of its nine New Orleans stores were open.[4]

The stores served the Do-It-Yourself (D-I-Y) person who liked to do his or her own projects and installations, the Do-It-For-Me (D-I-F-M) customer who preferred to pay someone else to do the installations, and Professional Customers, such as home improvement contractors, building maintenance professionals, interior designers, and other professionals. Although the company had been trying to increase its sales to professional customers for a number of years, it had been unable to do so through its retail stores. Home building contractors, for example, did not wish to buy carpet from Home Depot stores because they used outside contractors. The builders wanted a single company to handle both carpet and installation.

In order to better serve the professional customer, Home Depot acquired a number of businesses, such as Apex Supply Company, Contractors' Warehouse, Creative Touch Interiors, National Waterworks, White Cap Construction, Williams Brothers Lumber, and Hughes Supply, to create the Home Depot Supply business unit. Home Depot Supply distributed products and sold installation services primarily to professional business contractors, businesses, and municipalities and operated in three primary areas:

- Maintenance, Repair, and Operations (MRO) supplied maintenance, repair, and operating products primarily to multifamily housing, hospitality, and lodging facilities.
- Builder provided products and arranged installation services for production home builders.
- Professional Supply distributed specialty hardware, tools, and materials to construction contractors.

History

The Home Depot, Inc., was a great success story of three men creating a new business that redefined the industry. By 2000, the company had reached the $40 billion in revenues mark faster than had any retailer in U.S. history. The founders then left the management of the company in the hands of a new management team, who it was hoped would continue the company's success.

Founders Grow an Entrepreneurial Venture: 1978 to 2000[5]

Bernard Marcus began his career in the retail industry in a small pharmacy in Millburn, New Jersey. He later joined the Two Guys Discount Chain to manage its drug and cosmetics departments and eventually became the Vice President of Merchandising and Advertising for the parent company, Vornado, Inc. In 1972 he moved into the Do-It-Yourself home improvement sector as President and Chairman of the Board at Handy Dan/Handy City. The parent company, Daylin, Inc., was chaired by Sanford Sigoloff. He and Marcus had a strong difference of opinion over control, and one Friday at 5:00 PM in 1978, Marcus and two other Handy Dan top executives were discharged.

That weekend, Home Depot was born when the three men—Bernard Marcus, Arthur Blank, and Kenneth G. Langone—laid out plans for the Do-It-Yourself chain. Marcus and Blank were to manage the new venture with Langone providing the seed money to get started. Additional capital was provided by investment firms that included Invemed of New York as well as private investors.

When the first stores opened in Atlanta in 1979, the company leased space in three former Treasury Discount Stores with 60,000 square feet each. All three were suburban locations in the northern half of the city. Industry experts gave Home Depot 10-to-1 odds it would fail. In 1980, a fourth Atlanta stored opened, and the company had annual sales of $22.3 million. The following year, Home Depot ventured beyond Atlanta to open four stores in South Florida and also had its first public offering at $12 a share. By early 1990, its stock had soared by 7,019% and split eight times. In May 1995, an original share was worth $26,300.

The company was voted the "Retailer of the Year" in the home center industry in 1982 and had its first stock splits. By 1983, Marcus was a nationally recognized leader in the Do-It-Yourself industry. Home Depot's strong drawing power became evident as customers passively waited in long checkout lines. In 1984, Home Depot's common stock was listed on the New York Stock Exchange. It was traded under the symbol "HD" and was included in the Standard & Poor's 500 Index.

In 1989 all stores began using Universal Product Code (UPC) scanning systems to speed checkout time. The company's satellite data communications network installation improved management communication and training. On its tenth anniversary, Home Depot opened its 100th store (in Atlanta) and by the year's end had become the nation's largest home center chain.

To handle more volume per store, Home Depot developed and tested in 1990 a new store productivity improvement (SPI) program designed to make more effective use of existing and new store space and to allow for more rapid replenishment of merchandise on the sales floor. The SPI program involved the renovation of portions of certain existing stores and an improved design for new stores with the goal of enhanced customer access, reducing customer shopping time, and streamlining merchandise stocking and delivery. As part of SPI, the company also experimented with modified store layouts, materials handling techniques, and operations.

The company's SPI program proved successful and was implemented in substantially all new stores and in selected existing stores. Home Depot also continued to introduce or refine a number of merchandising programs. Included among such programs were the introduction of full-service, in-store interior decorating centers staffed by designers and an expanded assortment in its lighting department.

In 1991, management created a new division, EXPO Design Centers. EXPO Design Centers appealed to the upscale homeowner through their extensive use of computer-aided design technology by the store's creative coordination. These features were of assistance to customers remodeling their bathrooms and kitchens. From 1991 through 1995, many of the new merchandising techniques developed for the Home Depot EXPO were transferred to the entire chain.

During 1992, the company's "installed sales program," which had been tested in three selected markets in 1990, became available in 122 stores in 10 markets. This program targeted the buy-it-yourself customer, who would purchase an item but did not have either the desire or the ability to install the item.

Home Depot entered the Canadian market in 1994 through its acquisition of Aikenhead's Home Improvement Warehouse. Home Depot's first Mexican store opened in 1998. On a long-term basis, the company anticipated that success in Mexico could lead to more opportunities throughout Central and South America. In 1995, *Fortune* included Home Depot in its list of "America's Most Admired Corporations."

During 1995, the company opened CrossRoads, its first rural chain store, in Quincy, Illinois. A second store was opened in Columbus, Missouri, in 1996. The target market for this chain was farmers and ranchers who shopped in smaller, rural towns across America. At that time, there were about 100 farm and home retailers, with about 850 stores and annual sales of $6 billion. A typical CrossRoads store had 117,000 square feet of inside retail space, plus a 100,000-square-foot lumberyard. In contrast, the average Tractor Supply Company store (a competitor) was about one tenth the size of a CrossRoads store and did not have a lumberyard. In addition to carrying the typical Home Depot products, CrossRoads carried pet supplies, truck and tractor tires and parts, work clothing, farm animal medicines, feed and storage tanks, barbed wire, books (such as *Raising Sheep the Modern Way*), and other items. The company soon terminated this strategy because the stores did not generate sales and profits that Home Depot expected. The existing CrossRoads stores were renamed Home Depot stores.

In 1996, the company acquired Maintenance Warehouse/America Corporation, which was the leading direct mail marketer of maintenance, repair, and operating products to the United States building and facilities in management market. Home Depot's management felt this was "an important step towards strengthening our position with professional business customers."[6] The company's long-term goal was to capture 10% of this market.

During the 1990s, Home Depot built new stores not only within the continental United States, but also in Alaska, Puerto Rico, Canada, and Mexico. This global expansion fit the company's stated vision to be one of the most successful retailers in the next millennium.

During 2000, the company launched its online store, www.homedepot.com. The Home Depot continued to grow internationally by opening its first store in Argentina and establishing the Olympic Job Program in Puerto Rico. The company celebrated the opening of its 1,000th store and its surpassing the one-week $1 billion sales mark for the first time in May. Bernard Marcus and Arthur Blank, the two founders responsible for actively managing the growth of the company, announced that they were retiring from the company and began a search for their replacement.

Expansion Continues in the Nardelli Era: 2001–Present

In December 2000, Arthur Blank retired as President and CEO of Home Depot and joined Bernard Marcus as Co-Chairman of the Board. Blank was replaced by Robert L. Nardelli, who came to the company from a successful career at General Electric. In the last "Founders' Letter" appearing in the *2000 Home Depot Annual Report,* Blank and Marcus gave their blessing to the new management team.

We're very optimistic. Our optimism is built on our associates' dedication and commitment to our "orange-blooded" entrepreneurial spirit, which embraces change yet retains our core values of excellent customer service, respect for all people and giving back to the community. Our optimism is also built on our ability to bring new leadership into the executive ranks—to seek out new talent, experience and vision. That's why we are so excited by Bob Nardelli, one of the country's top business leaders, as President and CEO. His fresh perspective and business insight will take us to the next level. While going outside the businesses in recruiting executive talent is not rare in other industries, it is somewhat rare in retailing. But we're a unique company seeking a unique successor.

Blank left the Board of Directors after the 2001 fiscal year, followed one year later by Marcus—leaving only Kenneth Langone serving on the Board as the last member of the founding team. In addition to serving as President and CEO, Bob Nardelli assumed the position of Chairman of the Board in January 2002.

From 2001 to 2006, Home Depot continued to grow through new store locations, new store formats, and acquisitions. It opened 199 new store locations during 2001, 199 in 2002, 175 in 2003, 183 in 2004, and 152 in 2005, for a total of 908 new Home Depot stores during this period. The 100th Canadian store opened in 2003. In terms of new store formats, the company opened its first Home Depot Landscape Supply store in Atlanta and its first Home Depot Supply store in Dallas during 2002. It also launched the first home improvement online gift registry in 2004. The company spent $14 billion in renovating outdated stores, investing in new technology such as self-checkout lanes and cordless scan guns, and upgrading merchandise. At the end of fiscal 2004, the company entered into an agreement to lease commercial office space in Shanghai to support a future retail initiative in China.

Acquisitions proceeded during this time period at an increasing pace. To expand its position in Mexico, Home Depot acquired Total Home, a Mexican home-improvement chain, in 2001. It then became the market leader in Mexico in 2005 by purchasing Home Mart, the second-largest home improvement retailer in Mexico. To expand its professional service capabilities for housing contractors, the company acquired a number of firms including National Waterworks, Apex Supply Company, Creative Touch Interiors, William Brothers Lumber Company, White Cap Construction, Contractors' Warehouse, and Chem-Dry. The company completed a total of 40 acquisitions from 2001 to 2006 with 21 of these acquisitions being completed in 2005 alone. In 2006, the company acquired Hughes Supply, Inc., a leading distributor of construction and repair products at a cost of $3.5 billion—effectively doubling Home Depot Supply's size and adding $4.0 billion to Home Depot's long-term debt to finance the purchase. With the addition of Hughes Supply, Home Depot became the largest diversified wholesale distributor of construction, repair, and maintenance-related products in the United States. According to *Value Line,* by April 2006, sales at Home Depot Supply accounted for approximately 10 percent of the company's total sales.[7]

Current Strategic Posture

The company adopted a new slogan: "Improve Everything We Touch." This statement was placed on employee wristbands and break-room signs, among other locations. According to CEO Nardelli, the company did a lot of testing to find a slogan that wouldn't be time sensitive. "You can improve everything you touch whether you're a lot attendant, store manager, or chairman of the company."[8]

The company's overall strategy was composed of what Nardelli called the 3Es: *Enhancing the Core, Extending the Business, and Expanding the Market.* Enhancing the Core meant that the Home Depot stores were continually being modernized and their product lines updated to increase sales of current products to current customers. This was measured on the basis of an increasing average ticket paid by store customers and by improving store productivity. Extending the Business meant that the primary retail business of the company was being expanded into multiple channels, such as homedepot.com and catalogs, such as *10 Crescent Lane,* and by selling new products and services, such as flooring and Chem-Dry carpet-cleaning services. As another example, the company was testing gas stations outside a handful of its U.S. stores. Expanding the Market meant that the corporation was continually expanding into new markets with new products to better serve existing customers and attracts new ones. This was being accomplished by opening Home Depot stores in other countries and by offering new building supply services to professional customers, such as home building contractors. Many of the new products and services, especially those aimed at the professional market, were being obtained through acquisitions of existing companies.

In a January 2006 meeting with the financial community, Home Depot's management announced their plans for the company's growth to 2010. According to CEO Nardelli, "Over the next five years, The Home Depot expects to maintain and grow its leadership position in home improvement retail worldwide. At the same time, we expect to become the nation's largest diversified wholesale distributor, become number one in services and will dramatically increase our direct-to-consumer channels." The company's 2010 targets included:

- Compounded annual sales growth of 9%–12%
- Compounded earnings per share growth of 10%–14%
- 400–500 new store openings—adding 40–55 million new square feet
- Operating margin increases 50–100 basis points
- Cumulative operating cash flow of $50 billion
- Cumulative capital expenditures of $17–20 billion
- Grow Home Depot Supply sales to $23–27 billion

Although the planned number of new Home Depot stores was about half the number opened in the previous five years, CEO Nardelli contended that the slower growth in new retail stores would be made up by the high pace of growth in the retail business overall.[8]

Home Depot's plans for growth hinged on projected market opportunities evolving by 2010:

- $200 billion U.S. do-it-yourself market
- $110 billion services market (representing the labor component)
- More than $250 billion international do-it-yourself market
- More than $410 billion professional market

Carol Liebert, Executive Vice President of Home Depot Stores, announced that the company was leveraging technology to increase efficiency and create a fun, productive shopping environment for customers. New operational initiatives should free associates to spend more time serving customers. By 2010, according to Liebert, the company expected that 70% of operational hours would be dedicated to the selling floor, an industry-leading average. According to Frank Blake, Executive Vice President of Business Development and Corporate Operations, services should continue to grow as a percentage of total revenue. "With more than 11,000 installations per day, The Home Depot is emerging as a major force in the services area, and we expect to continue our double-digit growth through 2010, becoming number one in that market." By 2010, he expected that 5% to 6% of Home Depot sales would come from services. Although the direct-to-consumer division was a small contributor to Home Depot's 2006 revenue, CEO Nardelli felt that this division had the potential to become a billion-dollar business by 2010. He also felt that Home Depot Supply would generate 18% to 19% of overall sales by 2010. By the end of the decade, Nardelli projected that Home Depot Supply would operate more than 1,500 locations in all 50 states. "We are poised for dramatic growth over the next five years across our business," said Nardelli. "Our planned acquisition of Hughes Supply is a great example of how we are rapidly replicating in the professional market the same type of transformation that we brought to the home improvement retail market," he noted.[9]

Management's announcement of Home Depot's new five-year plan received a "lukewarm" response from the financial community. Home Depot's growth in new store openings was clearly slowing as the company reached market saturation. In contrast, rival Lowe's had announced plans to open 150 to 160 new stores in both 2006 and 2007 as it continued its expansion to large U.S. cities. In response to questions, Nardelli stated that the company planned to put fewer stores in direct competition with existing stores. "I don't want to use the word saturation, because that is a sort of self-fulfilling prophecy. . . . The new store growth has been modified to reflect the realities of the market."[10]

Corporate Culture

Entrepreneurial Culture of Founders

The culture at Home Depot had traditionally been characterized by the phrase, "Guess what happened to me at Home Depot?" This phrase showed Home Depot's bond with its customers and the communities in which it had stores and was recognition of superb service. Home Depot called this its "orange-blooded culture."

The orange-blooded culture emphasized individuality, informality, nonconformity, growth, and pride. These traits reflected those of the founders of the company. The culture was "really a reflection of Bernie and me," said Blank. "We're not formal, stuffy folks. We hang pretty loose. We've got a lot of young people. We want them to feel comfortable."[11]

Under the founders, the importance of the individual to the success of the whole venture had been consistently emphasized. Marcus's statements bear this out: "We know that one person can make a difference, and that is what is so unique about The Home Depot. It doesn't matter where our associates work in our company, they can all make a difference."[12] While emphasizing the opportunities for advancement at Home Depot, Marcus decried the kind of "cradle to grave" job that used to be the ideal in America and is the norm in Japan. To him, this was "a kind of serfdom."[13] Home Depot attempted to provide excellent wages and benefits, and superior training and advancement opportunities, while encouraging independent thinking and initiative.

Informality had always been appropriate at Home Depot during the Blank and Marcus years. Spitballs often flew at board meetings and there was always someone around to make sure that ties got properly trimmed. When executives visited stores, they went on their own without an entourage. Most managers had worked the floors and knew the business from the ground up. They were approachable and employees frequently came forward with ideas and suggestions.

Nonconformity had been evident in many different areas of the company—from the initial warehouse concept to the size and variety of merchandise to human resource practices. Both Marcus and Blank had flouted conventional corporate rules that they believed foiled innovation. Training employees at all levels was felt to be one of the most powerful means of transmitting corporate culture, and Home Depot used it extensively. One analyst noted that Home Depot (in a reverse of the "top-to-bottom" training sequence in most organizations) trained the carryout people first: "The logic is that the guy who helps you to your car is the last employee you come in contact with, and they want that contact to be positive."[14]

The Home Depot had been built on a set of values that fostered strong relationships with its key constituencies. The company's management embraced the values of taking care of its people, encouraging an entrepreneurial spirit, treating each other with respect, and being committed to the highest standards. For the customers, management believed that excellent customer service was the key to company success, and that giving back to the communities it served was part of its commitment to the customer. Importantly, management believed that if all employees lived all of these values, they would also create shareholder value.

Blank and Marcus were often asked how the company had managed to grow so fast for as long as it had and still be successful, both financially and with its customers. They responded that aggressive growth required adapting to change, but continued success required holding fast to the culture and values of the company as the company grew.[15]

Culture Change under New Management

The informal, entrepreneurial culture fostered by the founders, who relied more on instincts than on analytical tools, had successfully built Home Depot. By the end of the 1990s, however, this decentralized culture had, according to analysts, become partially responsible for the firm's stagnation in sales growth. The company "grew so fast the wheels were starting to come off," commented Edward Lawler III, a professor at the University of Southern California.[16]

The job facing Bob Nardelli when he assumed the CEO position in December 2000 was to organize the company and get Home Depot back on the fast track. Five years later, Bob Nardelli was still putting his personal stamp on what had been a decentralized entrepreneurial venture under founders Arthur Blank and Bernie Marcus. The informal (perhaps even chaotic) style of the founders was being replaced by the more military style of Nardelli. Although Nardelli had never actually served in the armed forces, he had always wanted to be in the military. He had been first alternate to the U.S. Military Academy. After graduating from Western Illinois University, his draft number was called, but he did not pass the physical. Nardelli's passion for the military is reflected in his emphasis on military efficiency and in hiring veterans. Of the 1,142 people hired into the store leadership program since it was launched in 2002, 528 of them were junior military officers known as "Bob's Army." By 2006, more than 100 of these ex-officers were managing Home Depot stores. In honor of employees serving in Iraq, Afghanistan, and elsewhere, 1,800 blue star banners hang in the main hallway of corporate headquarters.

Importing ideas, people, and management concepts from the military was one way to re-shape an increasingly unwieldy Home Depot into a more centralized and efficient organization. Under Nardelli, the emphasis was on building a disciplined manager corps, one predisposed to following orders, operating in high-pressure environments, and executing with high standards.[17] The constant flow of ideas and suggestions flowing up the organization from Home Depot's many employees was being replaced by major decisions and goals flowing down from top management. According to Joe DeAngelo, Executive Vice President of Home Depot Supply and a previous GE manager, "There's no question; Bob's the general."[18]

The cultural change in Home Depot was making it a very different type of company from Lowe's, a primary competitor. At Lowe's the culture was described as being demanding, but low-profile, collaborative, and collegial.

Interviews by *Business Week* with 11 former Home Depot executives revealed that Nardelli's culture change was facing some stiff resistance. Some described a demoralized staff and reported that a "culture of fear" was causing customer service to decline. Before Nardelli's arrival, most store managers used "tribal knowledge," based on years of experience about what sold and what didn't, to make decisions. Now they nervously clicked through Blackberries at the end of each week, hoping that they "made plan," a combination of sales and profit targets. The once-heavy ranks of full-time store employees had been replaced with part-timers to reduce labor costs. Underperforming managers were routinely asked to leave the company. Since 2001, 98% of Home Depot's 170 top executives had left the company. Fifty-six percent of headquarters personnel were hired from outside the company. Home Depot insiders sometimes referred to the firm as "Home GEpot" because of the increasing number of managers being hired from General Electric. Such poor morale was thought by some to lead to less customer satisfaction.[19]

The University of Michigan's American Customer Satisfaction Index, compiled in 2005, revealed that Home Depot, with a score of 67, had slipped to last place among major U.S. retailers. Home Depot's score had dropped from 73 in 2004 and was 11 points lower than Lowe's and three points lower than Kmart's. A former Home Depot executive stated that Nardelli's effort to measure good customer service, instead of inspiring it, was to blame. "My perception is that the mechanics are there. The soul isn't."[20]

When CEO Nardelli was asked why so many top executives left Home Depot in his first year as CEO, he responded,

You've got to understand that a lot of these people had made a ton of money. The stock split 12 or 13 times times in the early years and so, financially, they had become independent at an early age. Some said, "Bob I agree we need to transform, but I don't think I want to go through that." There are no hard feelings and I stay in touch.[21]

As of March 8, 2006, every Home Depot employee was expected to keep a copy of a 24-page booklet entitled *How to Be Orange Every Day* in their apron pockets. The booklet contained aphorisms such as "Customers cannot buy what we do not have" and "We create an atmosphere of high-energy fun." This program was introduced by Carl Liebert III, Executive Vice President of Home Depot, in an effort to better align employees with corporate goals and objectives and thus improve customer service. Commented Liebert, "I think about that line from *A Few Good Men* when Jack Nicholson says: 'Are we clear?' and Tom Cruise says: 'Crystal.' I love that." A graduate of the U.S. Naval Academy, Liebert had supervised Six Sigma programs at GE's Consumer Products unit, followed by managing a division at Circuit City. After taking over Home Depot's stores in the United States and Mexico in 2004, Liebert was working to make the company operate with a single mind rather than as a set of independent store operators. "What worked 20 years ago may not work today," explained Liebert. "It's as simple as warfare. We don't fight wars the way we used to."[22] Home Depot executives noted that internal polling showed that customer satisfaction was improving in 2006.

Although the critics of Nardelli's management style admitted to being in awe of his command of minute details, they questioned whether the manufacturing business model that worked well for him at GE—squeezing efficiencies out of the core business while acquiring new businesses—could work in a retail environment where taking care of customers is key. Steve Mahurin, Chief Merchandising Officer at True Value Company and a former Senior Vice President for merchandising at Home Depot, remarked: "Bob has brought a lot of operational efficiencies that Home Depot needed, but he failed to keep the orange-blooded, entrepreneurial spirit alive. Home Depot is now a factory."[23] For his part, Nardelli responded that this was the third time that his business model has been successful and rejected the idea that he has created a culture of fear. "The only reason you should be fearful is if you don't want to make the commitment." He made no apologies for getting rid of underperforming employees and managers in order to achieve financial objectives. "We couldn't have done this by saying, 'Run slower, jump lower, and just kind of get by,'" insists Nardelli. "So I will never apologize for setting the bar high."[24]

Community Involvement and Business Ethics

From its earliest years, Home Depot recognized its role in the community and strove to be known as a good "corporate citizen." In one community, a woman lost her uninsured home and teen-aged son to a fire. Home Depot's management responded, along with other residents, by providing thousands of dollars of free materials and supplies to assist in the rebuilding effort. In another incident, a community organization sponsored a graffiti cleanup, and the Home Depot store in the area donated paint and supplies to assist in the project. These were just a few of the stories that communities told about Home Depot, which had provided over $10 million to help fund many community projects in the United States and Canada.

Through its "Team Depot" the company helped build more than 160 homes for Habitat for Humanity and renovated more than 20,000 homes for the elderly and disabled in more than 230 communities as part of Rebuilding Together with Christmas in April.

The Home Depot's traditional concern for its stakeholders continued under the management of Bob Nardelli. As part of its philosophy of doing business, Home Depot indicated that it strove to be the employer, retailer, investment, and neighbor of choice in the home improvement industry. Management stated on the corporate Web site that the company had "a daily commitment to living values and principles that recognize our ethical obligations to our shareholders, associates (employees), customers, suppliers, and the communities in which we operate. We understand our responsibility to behave ethically, to understand the impact we have on people and communities and to fairly consider the interests of a broad base of constituencies." Home Depot's *Business Code of Conduct and Ethics* stated:

> *Acting with integrity and doing the right thing are the driving forces behind The Home Depot's extraordinary success. From the very beginning, The Home Depot, inclusive of its subsidiaries and affiliates, has been committed to conducting its business in an ethical manner—doing right by our Associates, our customers, our vendors, our suppliers, our communities and our stockholders. . . . All that we do at The Home Depot must be consistent with the values of the Company. We believe in Doing the Right Thing, having Respect for all People, building Strong Relationships, Taking Care of Our People, Giving Back, providing Excellent Customer Service, and Encouraging Entrepreneurial Spirit and providing strong Shareholder Returns.*[25]

As part of *Giving Back* to the community, Home Depot made a direct cash donation of $1.5 million in August 2005 to support Hurricane Katrina relief and rebuilding efforts in the U.S. Gulf Coast. In Pass Christian, Mississippi, The Home Depot engaged more than 500 volunteers to build the community's first permanent structure completed after Katrina—a 6,000-square-foot playground, surrounded by dozens of newly planted trees and shrubs, picnic tables, and benches in War Memorial Park. The company also offered 300,000 volunteer hours to communities across North America as part of the Corporate Month of Service in September 2005. Through the Home Depot Foundation, the company supported the building of quality, affordable housing in communities across the country. The company also sponsored a CommUnity Impacts Grant Program that funded nonprofit organizations to construct, maintain, or refurbish play spaces, community gathering spaces, affordable housing, and structures damaged in weather-related disasters. During 2005, Home Depot supported thousands of nonprofit organizations with nearly $40.6 million in material and financial contributions.

The Home Fund was one way the company was implementing *Taking Care of Our People.* The Home Fund was an emergency charitable fund supported by Home Depot associates for fellow associates. During 2005, the fund distributed over $4 million to 4,200 associates in need.

Doing the Right Thing meant that Home Depot showed its concern for the environment by following a set of principles.

- We are committed to improving the environment by selling products that are manufactured, packaged, and labeled in a responsible manner, that take the environment into consideration and that provide greater value to our customers.

- We will support efforts to provide accurate, informative product labeling of environmental marketing claims.

- We will strive to eliminate unnecessary packaging.

- We will recycle and encourage the use of materials and products with recycled content.

- We will conserve natural resources by using energy and water wisely and seek further opportunities to improve the resource efficiency of our stores.

- We will comply with environmental laws and will maintain programs and procedures to ensure compliance.

■ We are committed to minimizing the environmental health and safety risk for our associates and our customers.

■ We will train our employees to enhance understanding of environmental issues and policies and to promote excellence in job performance and all environmental matters.

■ We will encourage our customers to become environmentally conscious shoppers.[26]

Corporate Governance

Board of Directors

As of May 25, 2006, the Board of Directors of Home Depot was composed of 11 people, nine of whom were listed as independent according to the standards of the New York Stock Exchange. Robert Nardelli, as CEO of The Home Depot, was an inside director. Milledge Hart was considered a non-independent outside director because of business transactions between a company controlled by Hart and Home Depot. All members of the Nominating and Corporate Governance Committees were considered to be independent. Kenneth Langone served as Lead Director of the board.

Gregory D. Brenneman, 44, had served as director since 2000 and was Chairman and CEO of Burger King Corporation. He had previously served as CEO of Continental Airlines, PWC Consulting, and a private equity firm. He was a member of the the boards of Burger King and Automatic Data Processing. He owned 33,519 shares of Home Depot stock.

John L. Clendenin, 71, had served as director since 1996 and was retired Chairman and CEO of BellSouth Corporation. He was a member of the boards of four other companies, including Equifax and Kroger Company. He owned 38,832 shares of Home Depot stock and chaired the board's Audit Committee.

Claudio X. Gonzalez, 71, had served as director since 2001 and was Chairman and CEO of Kimberly-Clark de Mexico. He was a member of the boards of GE, Kellogg Company, Kimberly-Clark, and Investment Company of America. He owned 64,457 shares of Home Depot stock.

Milledge A. Hart, III, 72, had served as director since 1978 and was Chairman of DocuCorp International. He was Chairman of two other boards of directors. He owned 3,568,411 shares of Home Depot stock and chaired the board's Information and Technology Advisory Council.

Bonnie G. Hill, 64, had served as director since 1999 and was President of B. Hill Enterprises, a consulting firm specializing in corporate governance, and Founder and CEO of Icon Blue, Inc., a brand marketing company. She had previously served as CEO of The Times Mirror Foundation and as Vice President of the Times Mirror Company. She was a member of five other boards, including Albertson's, Hershey Foods, and Yum! Brands. She owned 22,370 shares of Home Depot stock and chaired the Leadership Development and Compensation Committee.

Laban P. Jackson, Jr., 63, had served as director since 2004 and was Chairman of Clear Creek Properties. He was also a member of the boards of J.P. Morgan Chase & Company and IPIX Corporation. He owned 7,400 shares of Home Depot stock.

Lawrence R. Johnston, 57, had served as director since 2004 and was Chairman and CEO of Albertson's. He had previously been President and CEO of GE Appliances. He owned 5,000 shares of Home Depot stock.

Kenneth G. Langone, 70, had served as a director since 1978 and was a co-founder of the company. He was Chairman and CEO of Invemed Associates, an investment banking and brokerage firm. He was a member of the boards of ChoicePoint, Yum! Brands, and Unifi, Inc. He owned 16,519,117 shares of Home Depot stock and chaired the board's Nominating and Corporate Governance Committees.

Angelo R. Mozilo, 67, had served as a director since 2006 and was Chairman and CEO of Countrywide Financial Corporation. He owned 800 shares of Home Depot stock.

Robert L. Nardelli, 57, had served as a director since 2000 when he was hired as President and CEO of The Home Depot. He previously served as President and CEO of GE Power Systems. He owned 5,332,266 shares of Home Depot stock.

Thomas J. Ridge, 60, had served as a director since 2005 and was a member of Thomas Ridge, LLC, a lecture and consulting firm. He previously served as Secretary of Homeland Security for the U.S. Federal Government and as Governor of Pennsylvania. He was also a member of the board of Exelon Corporation. He owned no shares of Home Depot stock.

Each non-management director received an annual retainer of $130,000, paid in the form of $80,000 as deferred shares of stock and $50,000 in the form of cash or stock units. In addition, each non-management director received 9,000 nonqualified stock options plus $2,000 per Board meeting attended (including the annual shareholders' meeting) and $1,500 per committee meeting attended during the year (plus travel and accommodation expenses). Chairs of Board committees were paid an additional amount of $10,000–$15,000.

The Executive Committee included Nardelli (Chair), Clendenin, Hart, and Langone. The Audit Committee included Clendenin (Chair), Brenneman, Gonzalez, Jackson, and Langone. The Nominating and Corporate Governance Committee included Langone (Chair), Brenneman, Jackson, and Ridge. The Leadership Development and Compensation Committee included Hill (Chair), Brown, Clendenin, Gonzalez, and Johnston. The Information Technology Advisory Council included Hart (Chair), Brown, Hill, Johnston, and Ridge.

The 24 directors and officers of the corporation together owned a total of 30,842,591 shares of Home Depot stock, 1.45% of shares outstanding. Stockholders owning more than 5% of the stock were FMR Corporation (5.5%) and Barclays Global Investors (5.3%).

On arriving at the annual shareholders' meeting of Home Depot on May 25, 2006, at the Hotel DuPont in Wilmington, Delaware, shareholders were surprised to note a number of changes from previous annual meetings. For one thing, except for CEO Nardelli, none of the members of the Board of Directors were present. For another, shareholders were allowed to speak about their shareholder proposals, but each had a time limit that was carefully tracked by a giant clock. Nardelli did not present a performance review, refused to acknowledge comments or answer questions, and adjourned the meeting after 30 minutes. "It's very unusual for Home Depot," commented Patrick McGurn, Executive Vice President of Institutional Shareholder Services. "It does beg the question as to whether (Home Depot) was concerned that investors were upset over pay, the performance of the stock or other issues and, as a result, decided to remove the directors from the firing line." According to Richard Metcalf, Corporate Affairs Director for Laborers International Union on North America, "This is one of the worst meetings I've seen in terms of the arrogance coming from the front table."[27]

In addition to the usual election of board members and the appointment of KPMG as the auditing firm, there were eight shareholder proposals being voted on. They dealt with issues ranging from "excessive" senior management compensation, reporting on diversity in management, separating the position of Chairman of the Board from another management position, requiring a majority (instead of plurality) vote for board member elections, shareholder approval for future "extraordinary" retirement benefits for senior executives, reporting on campaign contributions, disclosure of the monetary value of executive benefits, and affirming political non-partisanship of campaign contributions. The votes on these proposals indicated an unusually high level of shareholder dissent, with at least one-third of shareholders voting for every proposal—votes cast before the meeting. The one proposal that was passed asked to change the company's method for electing directors from a plurality to a majority of votes cast. Under the current rules, shareholders could only withhold votes for a director. All director nominees were elected at the 2006 annual meeting even though pension firms and proxy advisors had recommended votes against many Home Depot directors, some of whom had been criticized for a lack of independence. Interestingly, one third of the shareholders withheld votes for CEO Nardelli, even though they knew the vote was meaningless!

In a July 2006 interview with *Business Week,* CEO Nardelli stated that just one week after the 2006 annual meeting he decided to return to the format used at previous shareholder meetings. "I tried a new format; it didn't work. I take full responsibility for it. . . . Directors will be (at the next meeting). . . . We will do a business review."[29] Nardelli was quick to admit that he sometimes made mistakes and that he was willing to reverse himself. For example, when he first arrived at Home Depot as CEO, he made an early decision to improve inventory turnover, which he soon regretted. Said Nardelli, "I didn't understand the complexity. They complied with what I asked, but it hurt sales. We had to step back." In a separate decision, Nardelli changed the staffing mix on the sales floor from 70% full-time to 70% part-time. Unfortunately, this led to a less experienced work force and reduced customer service. Once he realized his mistake, Nardelli returned to the more traditional and heavier staffing with full-time career people.[30] Nardelli did not regret his tendency to push for action—even if it might be the wrong action. "People who do things make mistakes. The biggest mistake is doing nothing."[31]

Top Management

The Home Depot referred to its 13 Executive Officers as its Leadership Team. As of March 29, 2006, the top managers were:

Robert L. Nardelli, 57, had been President and Chief Executive Officer since 2000 and Chairman since 2002. Previously, he served as President and CEO of GE Power Systems, a division of General Electric.

Francis S. Blake, 56, had been Executive Vice President of Business Development and Corporate Operations since March 2002. He had previously served as Senior Vice President at General Electric.

Joseph DeAngelo, 44, had been Executive Vice President of Home Depot Supply since August 2005. He had previously served in other managerial positions at Home Depot and as Executive Vice President of The Stanley Works and as President and CEO of GE TIP/Modular Space, a division of General Electric.

Robert P. DeRodes, 55, had been Executive Vice President of Information Technology and Chief Information Officer since February 2002. Previously, he had been President and CEO of Delta Technology and Chief Information Officer for Delta Airlines.

Dennis M. Donovan, 57, had been Executive Vice President of Human Resources since April 2001. Previously, he had been Senior Vice President for Human Resources at Raytheon Company and Vice President of Human Resources at GE Power Systems, a unit of General Electric.

Marvin R. Ellison, 41, had been Northern Division President since January 2006. He had previously served as Senior Vice President of Logistics and as Vice President of Loss Prevention at The Home Depot since 2002. He had previously been Director of Assets Protection at Target.

Frank L. Fernandez, 55, had been Executive Vice President–Corporate Secretary and General Counsel since April 2001. Prevously, he had been Managing Partner at a law firm and Assistant Professor at The State University of New York at Albany.

Carl C. Liebert, III, 40, had been Executive Vice President of The Home Depot Stores since August 2005. He had previously been Senior Vice President of Operations at The Home Depot since August 2003 and a Division President of Circuit City.

Bruce A. Merino, 52, had been West Coast Division President since May 2000 and President, EXPO Design Center, since October 2005. Previously, he had been Merchandising Vice President at The Home Depot beginning October 1996.

Julian Paul Raines, 41, had been Southern Division President since February 2005. Previously, he had been a Regional Vice President, VP of Store Operations, and Director of Labor Management beginning in April 2000.

Thomas V. Taylor, 40, had been Executive Vice President of Merchandising and Marketing since August 2005. He had previously been Executive VP of Home Depot Stores, Eastern Division President, and various other managerial positions at Home Depot beginning in September 1996.

Carol B. Tome, 49, had been Executive Vice President and Chief Financial Officer since May 2001. Previously, she had been Senior Vice President of Finance and Accounting/Treasurer beginning 1995 and Vice President and Treasurer of Riverwood International Corporation.

Annette M. Verschuren, 49, had been President of The Home Depot Canada since March 1996. From February 2003 through October 2005, she also was President of EXPO Design Center.

Thomas Taylor, a 23-year veteran of Home Depot, resigned on July 7, 2006. Industry analysts considered Taylor to be Home Depot's only remaining retail expert and viewed his departure as a serious blow to the company. A report by Credit Suisse First Boston analyst Gary Balter on July 10 questioned if Home Depot had any retail expertise left in the top ranks.[32] This development followed a May 2006 Home Depot announcement that it would no longer report sales at stores open at least a year (same-store sales), an important performance measure in retailing.

Organization Structure

Home Depot, Inc., was legally a set of companies: Home Depot, EXPO Design Center, Home Depot Floor Store, Home Depot Landscape Supply, Home Depot Supply, Home Depot Mexico, and Home Depot Canada. For the purposes of financial reporting, operating decisions, allocation of resources, and performance evaluation, The Home Depot was composed of two business segments, Retail and Supply. The Retail segment was principally engaged in the operation of retail stores located in the United States, Canada, and Mexico. The Supply segment distributed products and sold installation services to business-to-business customers, including home builders, professional contractors, municipalities, and maintenance professionals. The Retail segment included The Home Depot stores, EXPO Design Center stores, The Home Depot Floor Stores, and The Home Depot Landscape Supply. The Retail segment also included the company's retail services business and Home Depot Direct, the company's catalog and online sales business. The Supply segment included water and sewer, industrial fasteners, MRO, professional construction supply, plumbing and HVAC, interiors, lumber, electric utilities, industrial pipes, valves and fittings, and electrical products distribution and related services.[33]

The U.S. Home Depot stores were organized and managed by geographic region, such as Southeast, Southwest, West, Northeast, and Midwest. Each geographic division was managed by a president who reported to Carl Liebert, Executive Vice President of Stores. Each store had a Manager, Assistant Managers, and Department Managers. Four to six Assistant Managers usually presided over the store's 10 departments. Each Assistant Manager was responsible for one to three departments. One Assistant Manager was responsible for receiving and the "back end" (stock storage area), in addition to his or her departments. The Assistant Managers were supported by Department Managers who were each responsible for one department. The Department Managers reported directly to the Assistant Managers and had no firing/hiring capabilities. Assistant Managers normally handled ordering, work schedules, and so on. Department Managers handled employees' questions and job assignments.

Marketing

Home Depot's marketing strategy was to offer a broad assortment of high-quality merchandise and services at low prices using knowledgeable, service-oriented personnel and strong advertising and promotion campaigns. The company used major sponsorships, such as NASCAR, the U.S. Olympics team, The Home Depot Center, ESPN College Game Day, and a number of home and garden shows. It also utilized marketing arrangements with television shows of strategic importance, such as *Trading Spaces, While You Were Out,* and *This Old House.* Home Depot's management estimated the company's share of the U.S. home improvement and professional supply market to be approximately 11%.

Advertising and Sponsorships

The company maintained an aggressive campaign, using various media for both price and institutional policy. Print advertising, usually emphasizing price, was prepared by an in-house staff to control context, layout, media placement, and cost. Broadcast media advertisements were generally institutional and promoted the company, its products, and its service, not just its pricing. These advertisements focused on the "You'll feel right at home" and "Everyday Low Pricing" ad slogans, name recognition, and the value of Home Depot's customer service. The 2005 advertising theme was: "You can do it. We can help." Although the company primarily used national advertising, the goal of its advertising was still to project a local flavor. The Western Division maintained its own creative department because of its different time zone and unique product mix. The company attempted to use information for the field in the various markets and put together an effective advertising campaign in English, Spanish, and French-Canadian. The company relied heavily on print media.

Home Depot not only sponsored the 1996 U.S. Summer Olympic Games in Atlanta, but also subsequent winter and summer Olympics, including the 2006 Winter Games in Torino, Italy. The company participated in the Olympic Job Opportunities Program, in which Home Depot provided part-time jobs for hopeful Olympic athletes while they trained for the Olympics. As the leading employer in the U.S. Olympic Committee's Olympic Job Opportunities Program (OJOP), the company had employed more than 500 Olympic and Paralympic athletes since 1992—more than any other company in the world.

Target Markets

According to management, Home Depot stores served three primary customer groups:

- **Do-It-Yourself ("D-I-Y") Customers.** These customers were typically homeowners who purchased products and completed their own projects and installations. To complement the expertise of its associates, The Home Depot stores offered "how-to" clinics taught by associates and merchandise vendors. The typical D-I-Y customer was a married male homeowner, aged 25 to 34, with a high school diploma or some college, and had an annual income of $20,000 to $40,000.

- **Do-It-For-Me ("D-I-F-M") Customers.** These customers were typically homeowners who purchased materials themselves and preferred someone else to complete the project and/or installation. The store arranged for the installation of a variety of The Home Depot products through qualified independent contractors. The typical D-I-F-M customer was an aging Baby Boomer earning an above-average income.

- **Professional Customers.** These customers were professional remodelers, general contractors, repairpeople, and tradespeople. In many stores, Home Depot offered a variety of programs to these customers, including additional delivery and will-call services, dedicated staff, extensive merchandise selections, and expanded credit programs.

Economic and Seasonal Impacts

With its combination of retail stores and professional supply, the company seemed to be recession-proof. During hard economic times and high interest rates, consumers who could not afford to buy new or bigger homes would maintain or upgrade their existing homes. This would lead to an increase in D-I-Y and D-I-F-M spending. During a period of economic growth and low interest rates, high demand for new or bigger homes would boost sales to professional builders and contractors. Home Depot's business was seasonal with the highest sales volume in the second fiscal quarter (summer) and the lowest volume during the fourth fiscal quarter (winter).

Merchandising Strategy

The merchandising strategy of Home Depot stores followed a three-pronged approach: (1) excellent customer service, (2) everyday low pricing, and (3) wide breadth of products. Merchandising included all activities involved in the buying and selling of goods for a profit. It involved long-range planning to ensure that the right merchandise was available at the right place, at the right time, in the right quantity, and at the right price. Success depended on the firm's ability to act and react with speed, spot changes, and catch trends early.

During 1994, Home Depot refined its merchandising function to be more efficient and responsive to customers. The new structure gave Division Managers responsibility for specific product categories, and specialists in each of these categories made sure the business lines were kept current. There were also field merchants who worked with the stores to ensure proper implementation of new programs as well as the maintenance of any ongoing programs. This approach strengthened product lines, got the right merchandise to the customers, reduced administration costs, and prepared Home Depot to expand into additional product lines. In 1997, Home Depot responded to the demographics of certain markets by expanding its service hours to 24 hours a day in 15 store locations.

EXPO Design Centers were a complete home decorating and remodeling resource for middle- to upper-income D-I-F-M customers. Customers were offered complete project management and installation services in each of the 34 EXPO Design Centers.

Store Location and Direct Marketing

During fiscal 2005, the company opened 140 new Home Depot stores, including four relocations, in the United States. The company also opened 21 new stores in Canada and 10 in Mexico in 2005. Most of the U.S. store openings occurred in existing markets as part of management's clustering strategy. Management intentionally cannibalized sales of existing stores by opening two other stores in a single market area. The short-run effect was to lower same-store sales, but a strategic advantage was created by raising the barrier of entry to competitors. It reduced overcrowding in the existing stores. It also allowed the company to spread its advertising and distribution costs over a larger store base, thereby lowering selling, general, and administrative costs. According to management, approximately 20% of its stores were cannibalized by new stores in 2005.

Home Depot stores were company-owned and managed. The company owned 87% of its buildings in 2005 (up from 74% in 1997 and just 40% in 1989), leasing the remainder. Although management preferred locations surrounded by shopping centers, it was not interested in having a store be attached to a shopping center or mall. Stores were placed in suburban areas populated by members of the Home Depot target market. Ownership provided Home Depot with greater operational control and flexibility, generally lower occupancy loss, and certain other economic advantages. Construction time depended on site conditions, special local requirements, and related factors.

Because of the large number of customers, older stores were being gradually remodeled or replaced with new ones to add room for new merchandise, to increase selling space for what was already there, and sometimes even to add more walking room on the inside—and more parking spaces.

Because merchandising and inventory were centrally organized, product mix varied slightly from store to store. Each, however, sported the Home Depot look: warehouse-style shelves, wide concrete-floored aisles, end displays pushing sale items, and the ever-present orange banners indicating the store's departments. Most stores had banners on each aisle to help customers locate what they were looking for. Regional purchasing departments were used to keep the stores well stocked and were preferred to a single, strong corporate department "since home improvement materials needed in the Southwest would differ somewhat from those needed in the Northeast."

Home Depot Direct offered customers expanded merchandise selection and time convenience through Web site and catalog shopping. Through www.homedepot.com, Home Depot offered an assortment of more than 30,000 items selected based on their potential for online sales. Home Depot's online sales increased 100% in 2005 from the previous year. Management estimated that its online/catalog sales had the potential to reach $1 billion.[34] In 2005, the company launched *10 Crescent Lane* and *Paces Trading,* catalogs aimed at affluent women, to compete with high-end catalogs from companies such as Williams-Sonoma.

Customer Service

Customer service differentiated Home Depot from its competitors. The availability of sales personnel to attend to customer needs had always been an objective of the Home Depot customer service strategy. The provision of highly qualified and helpful employees, professional clinics, and in-store displays had developed into a customer service approach referred to as "customer cultivation." It gave Do-It-Yourself customers the support and confidence that no home project was beyond their capabilities with Home Depot personnel close at hand. Home Depot employees went beyond simply recommending appropriate products, tools, and materials. Sales personnel cultivated the customer by demonstrating methods and techniques of performing a job safely and efficiently. This unique aspect of the company's service also served as a feedback mechanism—employees helping the next customer learn from the problems and successes of the last one.

For the Do-It-For-Me customer, the Home Depot and EXPO Design Center stores offered a variety of installation services on products such as flooring, carpeting, cabinets, countertops, and water heaters, as well as furnace and central air systems. The company's wholly owned subsidiaries, THD At-Home Services, Inc., and Home Depot Installation Services, Inc., sold and installed roofing, siding, and window programs. With the exception of Home Depot Installation Services, installation services were provided by qualified independent contractors.

All of the retail stores offered hands-on workshops on projects such as kitchen remodeling, basic plumbing, ceramic tile installation, and other activities in which customers in a particular locality had expressed interest. Offered mainly on weekends, the workshops varied in length, depending on complexity. Only the most experienced staff members, many of them former skilled craftsmen, taught at these workshops. Promotion of the workshops was done through direct mail advertising and in-store promotion.

At many Home Depot stores, customers could rent trucks by the hour through Load 'N Go, Home Depot's exclusive truck rental service. The company also expanded a tool rental service to more stores during fiscal 1998.

Home Depot offered credit programs through third-party credit providers to professional, D-I-Y, and D-I-F-M customers. In fiscal 2005, approximately 4 million new Home Depot credit accounts were opened, bringing the total number of Home Depot account holders to about 16 million. Proprietary credit card sales accounted for approximately 26% of store sales in 2005. The company also offered an unsecured Home Improvement Loan program that gave customers the opportunity to finance the purchase of large sales, such as kitchen and bath remodels.

Pricing and Suppliers

Home Depot stressed its commitment to "Everyday Low Pricing." This concept meant across-the-board lower prices and fewer deep-cutting sales. To ensure this, Home Depot employed professional shoppers to check competitors' prices regularly.

One of the major reasons that Home Depot was able to undercut the competition by as much as 25% was a dependable relationship with its suppliers. The company purchased its merchandise from suppliers located throughout the world and was not dependent on any single supplier. Most of the merchandise was purchased directly from manufacturers to eliminate "middleman" costs. The company sourced its products from more than 600 factories in approximately 35 countries. Management believed that competitive sources of supply were readily available for substantially all of the products sold in Home Depot stores.

A survey of manufacturers conducted by Shapiro and Associates found that Home Depot was "far and away the most demanding of customers." Home Depot was most vocal about holding to shipping dates. Manufacturers agreed that increased sales volume had offset concessions made to Home Depot.

Products

A typical Home Depot store stocked approximately 35,000 to 45,000 products, including variations in color and size. The products included different kinds of building materials, home improvement products, and lawn and garden supplies. In addition, Home Depot stores offered installation services for many products. Each store carried a wide selection of quality and nationally advertised brand-name merchandise. The contribution of each product group was as follows.

	Percentage of Sales		
	---	---	---
Product Group	**Year Ending 1/29/2006**	**Year Ending 1/30/2005**	**Year Ending 2/1/2004**
Building materials, lumber, and millwork	24.2%	24.4%	23.2%
Plumbing, electrical, and kitchen	29.4	29.0	28.9
Hardware and seasonal	27.1	26.9	27.6
Paint, flooring, and wall covering	19.3	19.7	20.3
Total	100.0%	100.0%	100.0%

Home Depot had formed strategic alliances and exclusive relationships with selected suppliers to market products under a variety of recognized brand names, such as Behr Premium Plus paint, Charmglow gas grills, Hampton Bay lighting, Mills Pride cabinets, Vigoro lawn care products, Husky hand tools, Pegasus faucets, Traffic Master carpets, and Ryobi power tools. Directly working with suppliers enabled the company to improve product features and quality, to import products not currently available to its customers, and to offer products at a lower price than would otherwise be available if the products had been purchased from third-party importers. According to management, this enabled the company to differentiate itself in the marketplace. Through its wholly owned subsidiary, Home TLC, Inc., Home Depot registered a variety of Internet domains, service marks, and trademarks in a number of countries. Some of these were The Home Depot: Home Depot Direct; Hampton Bay fans; Glacier Bay toilets, sinks, and faucets; Workforce tools, tool boxes, and shelving; www.10CrescentLane.com; and www.PacesTrading.com.

With the acquisition of Hughes Supply, Home Depot Supply in 2006 was composed of 36% infrastructure, 42% construction, 16% maintenance, 4% repair/remodel, and 2% international.[35]

The closest thing to research and development at Home Depot was its 88,000-square-foot Innovation Center, where the company tested everything from riding lawn mowers to displays for patio furniture sets before they arrived at its retail stores. Since it opened as an unidentified building in 2004 somewhere near corporate headquarters in Atlanta, the Center had tested not only new products, but also radically new product categories and store designs. Before the Center was built, executives had no place to test different types of displays lest they tip their hand to spies from competitors, who constantly walked Home Depot stores for new ideas. With the new facility, the company could take an Innovation Center test project to an in-store pilot project in just 30 days.[36]

Logistics

The company had established 16 import distribution centers in the United States and Canada to process its globally sourced merchandise. It also had 30 lumber distribution centers and 10 transit facilities in the United States and Canada. The transit facilities received merchandise from manufacturers and transferred it to trucks for delivery to the stores. By the end of 2005, approximately 40% of the merchandise shipped to Home Depot stores was processed through the company's network of distribution and transit facilities. The remaining merchandise was shipped directly from suppliers to the stores.

Information Systems

Each store was equipped with a computerized point-of-sale system, electronic bar code scanning system, and a UNIX server. Management believed that these systems provided efficient customer checkout, store-based inventory management, rapid order replenishment, labor planning support, and item movement information. To better serve the increasing number of customers applying for credit, the charge card approval process time had been reduced to less than 30 seconds. Store information was communicated to the Store Support Center's computers via a land-based frame relay network. These computers provided corporate, financial, merchandising, and other back-office function support.

The company was continuously assessing and upgrading its information systems to support its growth, reduce and control costs, and enable better decision making. The company opened a second technology center in 2005 in Austin, Texas, to provide redundancy and allow for growth and expansion.

In fiscal 2005, Home Depot completed an installation of back-end scanned receiving to all U.S. and Canadian stores. This system allowed the company to simplify, standardize, and automate how it received its products. By the end of fiscal 2005, self-checkout registers were in 1,272 stores and centralized automatic replenishment was increased to 20% of store sales. A Special Order Services Initiative pilot was implemented in 285 stores. In addition, the company implemented new financial systems for its Mexican retail operations, upgraded call centers, improved its Web sites, and launched several new direct-to-consumer brands.

Human Resources

Home Depot had long been noted for its progressive human resources policies, which emphasized the importance of the individual to the success of the company's operations.

Recruitment/Selection

Throughout its entire recruiting process, Home Depot looked for people who shared a commitment to excellence. Also, management recognized that having the right number of people, in the right jobs, at the right time was critical. Employee population varied greatly among stores, depending on store size, sales volume, and the season of the year. In the winter, a store could have had fewer than 75 employees and in the spring would add another 25 to 40 employees. Some of the larger northeastern stores had as many as 280 employees. Full-time employees had filled about 90% of the positions under the founders Blank and Marcus, but in 2005 filled only 68% of the positions.

When a store first opened, it attracted applications through advertisements in local newspapers and trade journals such as *Home Center News*. A new store would usually receive several thousand applications. When seasonal workers and replacements were needed, help-wanted signs were displayed at store entrances. Walk-in candidates were another source, and applications were available at the customer service desk at all times. At the management level, the company preferred to hire people at the Assistant Manager level, requiring them to work their way up to store Manager and beyond. Historically the company often hired outside talent for senior positions. This continued under Bob Nardelli as CEO.

Interviews were scheduled one per day per week; however, if someone with trade experience applied, an on-the-spot interview might be conducted. "Trade" experience included retail, construction, do-it-yourself, or hardware. The company tended to look for older people who brought a high level of knowledge and maturity to the position. In addition to related experience, Home Depot looked for people with a stable work history who had a positive attitude and were excited, outgoing, and hard workers.

The selection process included preemployment tests (honesty, math, and drugs). The stores displayed signs in the windows that said that anyone who used drugs need not apply. Interviews were conducted with three or four people—an initial qualifier, the Administrative Assistant in operations, an Assistant Manager, and the store Manager. Reference checks were completed prior to a job offer. More in-depth background checks (financial, criminal) were conducted on management-level candidates.

To help ensure that Home Depot selected the best qualified people, the company designed a proprietary automated system for identifying the best candidates for store sales associate positions. This system, which had been through extensive validation testing, screened candidates for competencies and characteristics inherent to Home Depot's best sales associates.

Retention

Employee turnover varied from store to store. In the first year of a new store's operations, turnover could run 60% to 70% but would fall below 30% in later years. The company's goal was to reduce turnover to below 20%. The major causes of turnover were students who returned to school, employees who were terminated for poor performance, and tradespeople who considered Home Depot an interim position (often returning to their trade for a position paying as much as $50,000 per year).

Career development was formally addressed during semiannual performance reviews, with goals and development plans mutually set by employees and managers. The company was committed to promotions from within and had a formal job-posting program. Vacancy lists were prepared at the regional level and distributed to the stores. Store managers were promoted from within. Affirmative action plans were used to increase female and minority representation.

Under Nardelli's tenure, people were evaluated on the basis of four performance metrics: financial, operational, customer, and people skills. Dennis Donovan, Home Depot's Executive

Vice President for Human Resources (also a GE alumnus), measured the effectiveness of Home Depot workers by using the equation $VA = Q \times A \times E$, where Value Added equals Quality of work multiplied by its Acceptance in the company, times how well the task is Executed.

Compensation

Employee Compensation

Employees were paid a straight salary. Bernard Marcus had said, "The day I'm laid out dead with an apple in my mouth is the day we'll pay commissions. If you pay commissions, you imply that the small customer isn't worth anything." Most management-level employees were eligible for bonuses that were based on such factors as a store's return on assets and sales versus budget. Assistant Managers could receive up to 25% of their base salary in bonuses, and store Managers could earn up to 50% if their stores' performance warranted.

The company maintained two employee stock purchase plans (U.S. and non-U.S. plans). These plans allowed associates to purchase up to 152 million shares of common stock, of which 117 million shares (adjusted for subsequent stock splits) had been purchased from the inception of the plans. Shares could be purchased at 85% of the stock's fair market value. During 2005, 3 million shares were purchased under these plans at an average price of $33.72 a share.

Recognition programs emphasized good customer service, increased sales, safety, cost savings, and length of service. Badges, cash awards, and other prizes were distributed in monthly group meetings.

Executive Compensation

The three components of executive compensation were base salary, annual bonus, and long-term incentives. Base salaries were established by considering total compensation, scope of responsibilities, years of experience, and the competitive marketplace. Merit increases, which occurred in April, were based on an individual's performance over the past year and potential for development. All executive officers participated in the company's Management Incentive Plan (MIP). MIP was a cash-based bonus plan that rewarded executives for the achievement of financial and non-financial objectives that had been established at the beginning of the fiscal year. Long-term incentives were offered in the form of stock options, a performance shares/cash plan, shares of restricted stock, and deferred shares or deferred stock units. These incentives were designed to reward executives for increasing long-term shareholder value and to retain them at the company.

Under the company's Executive Stock Ownership Guidelines, the executive officers were required to hold shares of common stock with a value equal to a specified multiple of base salary. This policy requires executives to hold company stock over the long term to keep their attention on long-term corporate success. The specific multiples were 6 times for CEO, 4 times for Executive Vice Presidents, and 3 times for Division Presidents/Senior Vice Presidents.

CEO Nardelli's salary for fiscal 2005 was $2,225,000. For his performance in fiscal 2005, he was awarded a cash bonus of $7,000,000 and received 380,000 shares of restricted stock, 175,000 of deferred shares, and 90,000 nonqualified stock options. The Leadership Development and Compensation Committee of the corporation's board of directors considered the strong performance of the company during 2005 when it determined compensation for Nardelli. The committee stated that it was especially impressed with the company's achievement of 20.4% growth in diluted earnings per share, net sales growth of 11.5%, comparable store sales growth of 3.8%, and total customer transaction growth of 5.6% in fiscal 2005. In addition, the committee considered progress made over the past year in the development and implementation of programs designed to transform the company to better meet the product and service needs of Home Depot's customers. The committee also used input from two compensation consulting firms to establish appropriate benchmarks for the executive officers.[37]

Training

Home Depot believed that knowledgeable salespeople were one of the keys to the company's success and spent a great deal of time training them to "bleed orange." Training costs to open a new store were about $400,000 to $500,000. Each new employee was required to go through a rigorous week-long orientation, which introduced new hires to Home Depot's culture. Training had been a crucial part of the corporate culture under the founders. When actively involved in the company, Bernard Marcus and Arthur Blank personally conducted many of the management training sessions. At that time, callers to the home office found that corporate executives spent most of their time in the stores training employees. "We teach from the top down, and those who can't teach don't become executives," said one top executive from the Blank/Marcus years. New employees were then paired with experienced associates in the stores to gain first-hand knowledge of customer service and general store operations. They trained an average of four weeks before working on their own. Even then, when there were no other customers in the department, newer employees would watch more experienced employees interact with customers to learn more about products, sales, and customer service. Employees were cross-trained to work in various departments, and even the cashiers learned how to work the sales floor.

Regular employees went through both formal and on-the-job training. Classes were held on product knowledge (giving the employee "total product knowledge . . . including all the skills a trade person might have"); merchandising concepts, and salesmanship (so that they could be sure that a customer had available, and would purchase, everything needed to complete a project); time management; personnel matters; safety and security; and how to interpret the company's various internally generated reports.

The Home Depot Television Network (called HD-TV) allowed the company to disseminate policies and philosophies, product upgrades, and so on. The fact that the programs were broadcast live, with telephone call-ins, enhanced their immediacy and made interaction possible. Every Monday night, for example, Vice Presidents Liebert and Taylor hosted a 25-minute live broadcast called *The Same Page* for senior store staff on the week's most important priorities. In recent years, however, employees had tended to mock HD-TV as "Bobaganda," referring to CEO Nardelli, for its "constant drone" of tips, warnings, and executive messages.[38]

Employees

As of the end of January 2006, the company employed approximately 345,000 people, of whom approximately 26,000 were salaried and the remainder were on an hourly or temporary basis. Approximately 68% of the company's employees were employed on a full-time basis. There were no unions. The company had never suffered a work stoppage. Management felt that its employee relations were very good.

Retail Building and Supply Industry

The retail building supply industry (also known as the home improvement industry) was moving rapidly from one characterized by small, independently run establishments to one dominated by regional and national chains of vast superstores. Home Depot developed the concept of the all-in-one discount warehouse home improvement superstore, designed to be all things to all people. The main rival to Home Depot was Lowe's, which had been expanding throughout the United States and replacing its older, smaller stores with new superstores. Other companies in the industry were facing the challenge by reconfiguring their stores and by targeting niche segments, but some were being forced to sell out to the major competitors or close their stores in the face of increased competition.

In 2006, the U.S. industry continued to be fragmented with estimated sales of approximately $700 billion, comprising of $550 billion of product demand and $150 billion for product installation. This estimate included import and export data and key end-use markets, such as residential repair and remodeling, and nonresidential construction and maintenance. It also included a wide range of product categories, including major appliances and garden supplies.[39] According to *Value Line* in mid-2006, the prospects for the industry remained generally attractive.[40]

The industry was affected by a number of factors in its general (societal) environment. Companies such as Home Depot used econometric models of the economy for planning purposes. These models included a number of variables that had been found to have some effect on home improvement sales. For example, although the U.S. economy was still strong in 2006, rising interest rates were causing a decline in home sales compared to the record-breaking sales of the preceding few years. By July 2006, the Federal Reserve had raised the federal funds rate by 25 basis points to 5.25%. This was the 17th consecutive increase since June 2004 and was in response to strong economic conditions and a low unemployment rate leading to a greater threat of inflation. Analysts were forecasting real disposable income growth of 3.4% in 2006, compared to 1.4% in 2005. Increasing gasoline prices during the spring and summer months affected retail sales as people cut back on discretionary purchases to pay for spiraling travel expenses. According to Bank of America securities analyst David Strasser, "We believe the home improvement sector is facing significant headwinds as housing turnover slows, and interest rates rise." Management at both Home Depot and Lowe's announced that they expected earnings growth for the second half of 2006 to be lower than previously expected. Nevertheless, Lowe's CEO Robert Niblock was still optimistic about the long term. He argued that most of his company's products were intended to help with the maintenance and upkeep of older homes. "That's what drives our business," he contended.[41]

A near-record level of U.S. homeownership in 2006 (after a sustained period of low interest rates) provided an established customer base for home maintenance and repair projects. In addition, the large Baby Boom generation was in its 50s—prime income-earning years, when people tended to add to their homes or purchase larger ones. Their declining interest in doing things themselves was leading to growth in the services economy. This was one reason why At-Home Services was one of Home Depot's fastest growing businesses, posting double-digit growth throughout 2005. The millennial generation, the next-largest demographic generation, were in their teens and early 20s and were just beginning to purchase their first homes and fix them up. Hispanic homeownership was growing at three times the national rate. Harvard's Joint Center for Housing estimated that between 2006 and 2016, immigration would represent at least 40% of household formation.[42]

Developments in information technology were significantly affecting multiple industries. Electronic scanning of merchandise was being used throughout the supply chain. Self-service checkouts and kiosks were being installed in most large retail stores to reduce labor costs and improve inventory procedures. In addition, the Internet was becoming increasingly important as a distribution channel. Internet research firm Nielsen/Net Ratings tracked 92.3 million online purchases in December 2005, up from 61.9 million a year earlier. Online sales by Wal-Mart were already topping $1 billion a year. According to Harvey Seegers, President of Home Depot Direct, 60% of U.S. households in 2006 had broadband Internet capability. "I envision a day when we have complete convergence between cable, satellite, and the Internet," forecasted Seegers.[43]

Home Improvement Competitors

Lowe's

Competition between Home Depot and Lowe's, the two major players in the industry, had intensified recently as Lowe's had been moving into areas previously dominated by Home Depot. As of February 3, 2006, Lowe's operated 1,234 retail stores in 49 states with 140 million square feet of retail selling space and 144,000 full-time and 41,000 part-time non-union employees. Each store averaged 113,000 square feet. Incorporated in North Carolina in 1952, Lowe's was second in market share and working hard to catch up to Home Depot, the industry leader. Lowe's opened 125 stores in 2003, 136 in 2004, and 150 in 2005. Management planned to open 155 stores in 2006—most of them in the Northeastern and Western United States, where the company had few stores. The company also planned to enter Canada with 6 to 10 stores in the Greater Toronto Area in 2007 and grow to 100 stores across Ontario and eventually to other provinces. The percentage of Lowe's stores located in the top 25 and top 100 U.S. markets was increasing (28% and 55%, respectively) at the end of 2005. More than 35% of the 400 approved future locations were in the nation's top 25 markets and more than 65% were in the nation's top 100 markets. Analysts noted that Lowe's was achieving higher increases in sales and profit than its rival Home Depot as it moved into big U.S. markets such as New York.[44]

In terms of financial performance, Lowe's management was proud of the company's growth. Net sales had been steadily rising from $30,838 million in fiscal 2004 (ending January 30, 2004) to $36,464 million in fiscal 2005, to $43,243 in fiscal 2006. During the same three-year period, net earnings increased from $1,844 million in 2004, to $2,176 million in 2005, to $2,771 million in 2006. Its same-store sales increased 6.7% in 2003, 6.6% in 2004, and 6.1% in 2005. The average ticket for comparable stores increased 6.1% in 2005 to $67.67, with comparable-store transactions increasing slightly to 639 million. Diluted earnings per share increased from $2.28 in 2003, to $2.71 in 2004, to $3.46 in 2005. Cash dividends per share had been raised from $.11 in 2003 to $.22 in 2005. Consequently, its stock price had increased from a low of $50.75 and a high of $60.42 in the fourth quarter of 2003 to a low of $59.65 and a high of $69.70 in the fourth quarter of 2005.[45] On June 30, 2006, Lowe's board of directors approved a two-for-one stock split.

Menards

After Home Depot and Lowe's, competitors in the industry were composed of regional and local chains, the most notable being Menards and 84 Lumber. Based on sales, Menards was the third largest home improvement chain in the United States, with estimated annual sales of $5.5 billion and 45,000 employees. Headquartered in Eau Claire, Wisonsin, Menards was a chain of 205 home improvement stores in the 10 Midwestern states of Ohio, Indiana, Illinois, Michigan, Wisconsin, Minnesota, Iowa, Nebraska, and both Dakotas. The privately held company planned to open a store in Saint Joseph, Missouri, in late 2006. Founded in 1962, the company in 2006 was still being operated by the Menard family, led by its founder John Menard, Jr. as CEO and his son, Charlie Menard as COO, and brother Larry Menard as Operations Manager. In 2004, Menard, Inc. ranked 20th on *Forbes'* list of "America's Largest Private Companies." Every Menards store shared a common structure divided by departments: Building Materials, Hardware, Electrical, Millwork, Wall Coverings, Plumbing, Floor Coverings, and Cabinets and Appliances. With distribution centers in Eau Claire, Wisconsin, and Plano, Illinois, the company planned to soon add two additional ones in Shelby, Iowa, and Holiday City, Ohio. In terms of its merchandise mix and its big-box stores, Menards was perceived by customers as being very similar to either Home Depot or Lowe's.

84 Lumber

The 84 Lumber Company was a low-cost (many of its stores had no heat or air conditioning) provider of lumber and building materials that operated in about 35 states—mainly in the East, Southeast, and Midwest parts of the United States. Through more than 450 stores, the company sold building materials, lumber, siding, drywall, windows, and kits to build barns, play sets, decks, and even homes. The CEO as of 2006, Joseph Hardy, Sr. had founded the company in 1956. With estimated sales of $3.5 billion and 8,000 employees, 84 Lumber was a significant regional player in the industry—even though it offered a narrower assortment of merchandise than did the industry leaders. The company's 84 Components subsidiary operated about 20 manufacturing plants that made floor and roof trusses and wall panels.[46]

Other Home Improvement Competitors

A number of other regional home improvement retailers had either gone out of business or sold out to one of the market leaders by 2006. For example, Hechinger was a 64-store chain of home improvement stores founded in 1911 and headquartered in Landover, Maryland, when it was acquired in 1987 by HQ Home Quarters Warehouse. It underwent a massive expansion in the 1990s by opening a series of "big box" stores to better compete with Home Depot and Lowe's. The chain was unable to earn a profit and was sold to private investors in 1997. The new owners merged Hechinger stores with Builders Square, formerly owned by Kmart. After filing for Chapter 11 bankruptcy protection in July 1999, it liquidated its remaining 117 stores that September. In 2004, an online retailer was created to sell to same products as the former Hechinger Company, but it did not operate any retail stores.

Eagle Hardware & Garden of Seattle, Washington, had operated 24 home improvement stores in 1995. Eagle's stores averaged 128,000 square feet, compared to Home Depot's 103,000 square feet. Eagle offered other services, namely, a custom-design section, free chain-cutting station, fences, and an idea center where customers could watch videotapes and live demonstrations of home improvement techniques. In the mid-1990s, Eagle was building the largest stores in the industry in the West Coast and Northwest markets. Eagle Hardware & Garden sold out to Lowe's in 1999 for $1 billion.

Building Supply Competitors

Since both Home Depot and Lowe's sought to expand their business by targeting the professional market, they had been coming into increasing contact with competitors that provided construction services and building products to professional homebuilders and contractors. Some of these were Building Materials Holding Corporation, Lanoga Corporation, and Stock Building Supply.

Building Materials Holding Corporation (BMHC)

Operating through two segments, BMC Construction and BMC West, BMHC was founded in 1987 in San Francisco to provide construction services and building materials to high-volume professional homebuilders and contractors in the western and southern states. BMC Construction (renamed SelectBuild Construction in 2006) provided framing, concrete, plumbing, other construction trades, managing labor, and construction schedules, as well as sourcing materials to production homebuilders. BMC West distributed building products and manufactured building components, such as lumber, millwork, floor and roof trusses, and wall panels. It also provided construction services to professional homebuilders and contractors. In 2005, BMHC had 21,000 employees and earned $137.29 million on sales of $3.44 billion.

Lanoga Corporation

Founded in the mid-1850s, Lanoga was one of the top U.S. retailers of lumber and building materials catering to professional contractors and consumers. Fidelity Capital, through its Pro-Build Holdings, owned Lanoga. Operating more than 320 stores in about 25 states, Lanoga had grown through dozens of small acquisitions. Its seven regional operating divisions included Dixieline in Southern California, Home Lumber Company in Colorado, Lumbermens Building Centers in the Northwest, Arizona, and California, Spenard Builder Supply in Alaska, Parker Lumber in Texas, Wheaton Lumber in Illinois, and United Building Centers in the Midwest and Rocky Mountain states. In February 2006, Lanoga, through its United Building Centers (UBC) subsidiary, purchased Wolohan Lumber, a privately held company in Saginaw, Michigan. UBC operated more than 300 locations with $1.2 billion in sales.

Stock Building Supply

Acquired by the United Kingdom's Wolseley plc in 1986 to be its U.S. division, Stock Building Supply provided a full line of quality building materials and installation services to professional contractors. Rated by industry trade publications as the number one building supply distributor to professional home builders and contractors in the United States, the company had 314 outlets in 33 U.S. states and employed 18,000 workers. It was headquartered in North Carolina and operated a fleet of 4,500 vehicles to move material to hubs, branches, satellites, and customers.[47]

Category Niche Competitors

Given that Home Depot, Lowe's, and Menards stocked hardware and related merchandise, they also competed against national and regional hardware stores, such as True Value Company, Ace Hardware Corporation, and Do It Best. These stores were typically small, locally owned stores with a much narrower and more locally oriented selection of merchandise than the "big box" competitors. With 2005 sales of $3,466 million, Ace Hardware was the leading hardware cooperative in the United States. Ace dealer–owners operated more than 4,600 Ace Hardware Stores, home centers, and lumber and building materials locations in all 50 states and 70 other countries. Like Ace Hardware, True Value (formerly TruServ) competed against the home improvement giants by emphasizing service and a narrower selection of merchandise. With 2005 sales of $2,043 million, the cooperative served 5,800 retail outlets throughout the United States.

As Home Depot, Lowe's, and Menards expanded their merchandise selection to boost sales, they also competed against national, regional, and local stores in individual product categories. Some of these were single category stores, such as the paint retailer Sherwin-Williams, and the flooring retailer CCA Global Partners Company, which competed under the names of Carpet One, Flooring America, Flooring One, ProSource, and International Design Guild. Given the breadth of their offerings, Home Depot, Lowe's, and Menard's also competed in some categories, such as automotive supplies and lighting, with national discounters such as Wal-Mart, Target, and Kmart and with regional discounters such as Mills Fleet Farm and Pamida.

Finance

Fiscal 2005 Performance

Home Depot's net sales for fiscal 2005 increased 11.5% to $81.5 billion from $73.1 billion in fiscal 2004. According to management, this sales growth "was driven by an increase in comparable store sales of 3.8%, sales from new stores opened during fiscal 2005 and fiscal 2004, and sales from our newly acquired businesses." The retail stores contributed 3.0% of same-store sales, with Home Depot Supply contributing the additional 0.8%. The retail store average ticket increased 5.6% to a record $57.98. Services revenue increased to $4.3 billion in fiscal 2005 compared to $3.6 billion in 2004 and $2.8 billion in 2003. Net earnings increased from $5.0 billion in fiscal 2004 to $5.8 billion in fiscal 2005. Diluted earnings per share increased from $2.26 in fiscal 2004 to $2.72 in fiscal 2005. During the four years from 2002 through 2005, the company repurchased approximately 277 million shares of common stock for a total of $9.7 billion. On February 23, 2006, the board authorized an additional $1.0 billion for share repurchases.

The company invested $3.9 billion in capital expenditures during fiscal 2005 for store modernization and technology as well as for 179 new store openings. Five of these stores were relocations of existing stores. The company also closed 22 stores during 2005. The company generated $6.5 billion in cash flow from operations in fiscal 2005. This cash was used to fund $3.9 billion in capital expenditures, $2.5 billion for acquisitions, and $3.9 billion of dividends and share repurchases. At the end of fiscal 2005, the company's return on invested capital (computed on beginning long-term debt and equity for the trailing four quarters) was 22.4% compared to 21.5% for fiscal 2004.

Second Quarter 2006 Results

At the end of the second quarter of the 2006 fiscal year (July 30, 2006), Home Depot reported six-month sales of $47,487 million compared to $41,278 for the same period a year earlier. The retail segment accounted for $41,972 million in sales during 2006 compared to $39,825 million in 2005. The supply segment accounted for $5,624 million in sales during 2006 compared to $1,478 million in 2005. (The figures do not add to total sales because of corporate adjustments.) Net earnings increased during the same period to $3,346 million in 2006 from $3,015 million in 2005. Diluted earnings per share increased to $1.60 compared to $1.40 in 2005. By the end of the second quarter of fiscal 2006, Home Depot's long-term debt to equity ratio was 24.5%, reflecting senior notes issued to purchase Hughes Supply. During the second quarter, the company repurchased 58 million shares for a total of 350 million shares repurchased since 2002—approximately 17% of outstanding shares. Retail sales per square foot were approximately $411 for the second quarter, down 2.3% from the same quarter in 2005.

Concerned about Home Depot's recent drop in customer satisfaction, management added 5.5 million more employee hours to the 2006 Fall/Winter season compared to the same period a year earlier. According to CEO Nardelli, "We are taking this step rather than adjusting payroll down in the second half, as we traditionally do coming off busy spring and summer seasons. Our investment is intended to improve the in-store experience, increase conversion, add customer transactions, and gain share." Meanwhile, Nardelli announced that the company was cutting 300 jobs at its Atlanta headquarters (5.6% of the total staff) as it shifted resources to invest in store improvements. Nardelli also stated: "In the second quarter, we launched a $30 million financial reward program for stores and associates that demonstrate a true passion for serving customers." In addition, the company was completing self-checkout at all stores and revitalizing stores with better lighting and signage. The company also planned to repair and remodel 100 bays in each of its top 500 high-volume stores. Overall, the company was spending $350 million to improve store sales in the second half of the year.[48]

Carol Tome, CFO, reported during the company's Second Quarter 2006 Earnings Conference Call on August 15, 2006, that management was returning to its historical practice of reporting comparable-store sales for the retail segment. CEO Nardelli had previously been heavily criticized for his decision in May 2006 to no longer report same-store sales. According to Tome, "Against a strong retail comp of 3.4 percent in the second quarter of 2005, comp or same store sales were a negative 0.2 percent for the second quarter of 2006. This is slightly down from our first quarter comp, which was a positive 0.2 percent. . . . In the second quarter, we cannibalized about 18 percent of our stores, which had a negative impact on comp sales of approximately 2.1 percent."

Tome also pointed out that Hughes Supply's sales grew 14% from the same quarter in 2005 and that Home Depot's growth rate (not counting acquisitions made since the previous year) was approximately 12%. "This illustrates our success in buying quality companies with strong growth potential," said Tome. She also indicated that in the second quarter Home

Depot's consolidated gross margin was 32.2% a decrease of 102 basis points from the same period in 2005. According to Tome,

> *Our consolidated gross margin rate reflects our evolving business model. As you know, Supply has a lower gross margin rate than Retail. . . . Supply's gross margin rate was approximately 26.5%. A higher penetration of lower gross margin dollars coupled with a slight decline in the Retail gross margin caused total gross margin compression in the quarter. The retail gross margin rate dropped 26 basis points to 33 percent, reflecting a changing mix of products sold due to growth in appliances. Appliances are now our largest category class.*

At the end of the management team's prepared remarks, CEO Nardelli responded to questions regarding the acquisition of Hughes Supply and the strong emphasis being placed by management on new areas for growth.

> *We have a balanced approach. We have taken the dividends from 16 cents in FY2000 to 60 cents in FY2005. At the same time, the strategic reinvestment has gone from zero to $12 billion in our Home Depot Supply which certainly broadens our customer base. . . . In 12 months we now have a billion dollar catalog business. In three years we have a billion dollar business in Mexico. . . . We have additional leverage—increasing our long-term debt to equity ratio where last year it was 9 percent. We have a tremendous amount of cash that comes off of our business; our stores are cash cows and we have access to tremendous leverage outside of the business. So we can do whatever we need to do.*

Exhibits 1 through 3 provide the company's consolidated statements of earnings, balance sheets, and 10-year selected financial and operating income highlights.

EXHIBIT 1
Consolidated Statements of Earnings: Home Depot, Inc. and Subsidiaries (Dollar amounts in millions, except per share data)

Fiscal Year Ending[1]	January 29, 2006	January 30, 2005	February 1, 2004
NET SALES	$81,511	$73,094	$64,816
Cost of Sales	54,191	48,664	44,236
GROSS PROFIT	27,320	24,430	20,580
Operating Expenses:			
Selling, General and Administrative	16,485	15,256	12,713
Depreciation and Amortization	1,472	1,248	1,021
Total Operating Expenses	17,957	16,504	13,734
OPERATING INCOME	9,363	7,926	6,846
Interest Income (Expense):			
Interest and Investment Income	62	56	59
Interest Expense	(143)	(70)	(62)
Interest, net	(81)	(14)	(3)
EARNINGS BEFORE PROVISION FOR	9,282	7,912	6,843
INCOME TAXES	9,282	7,912	6,843
Provision for Income Taxes	3,444	2,911	2,539
NET EARNINGS	$5,838	$5,001	$4,304
Weighted Average Common Shares	2,138	2,207	2,283
BASIC EARNINGS PER SHARE	$2.73	$2.27	$1.88
Diluted Weighted Average Common Shares	2,147	2,216	2,289
DILUTED EARNINGS PER SHARE	$2.72	$2.26	$1.88

[1]*Fiscal years ended January 29, 2006, January 30, 2005, and February 1, 2004, include 52 weeks.*

SOURCE: *2003 Annual Report, The Home Depot p. 36.*

EXHIBIT 2
Consolidated
Balanced Sheets:
Home Depot, Inc.
and Subsidiaries
(Dollar amounts in
millions, except per
share data)

Fiscal Year Ending	January 29, 2006	January 30, 2005
ASSETS		
Current Assets:		
Cash and Cash Equivalents	$793	$ 506
Short-Term Investments	14	1,659
Receivables, net	2,396	1,499
Merchandise Inventories	11,401	10,076
Other Current Assets	742	533
Total Current Assets	15,346	14,273
Property and Equipment, at cost:		
Land	7,924	6,932
Buildings	14,056	12,325
Furniture, Fixtures, and Equipment	7,073	6,195
Leasehold Improvements	1,207	1,191
Construction in Progress	843	1,404
Capital Leases	427	390
	31,530	28,437
Less Accumulated Depreciation and Amortization	6,629	5,711
Net Property and Equipment	24,901	22,726
Notes Receivable	348	369
Cost in Excess of the Fair Value of Net Assets Acquired	3,286	1,394
Other Assets	601	258
Total Assets	$44,482	$ 39,020
LIABILITIES AND STOCKHOLDERS' EQUITY		
Current Liabilities		
Short-Term Debt	$ 900	$ —
Accounts Payable	6,032	5,766
Accrued Salaries, and Related Expenses	1,176	1,055
Sales Taxes Payable	488	412
Deferred Revenue	1,757	1,546
Income Taxes Payable	388	161
Current Installments of Long-Term Debt	513	11
Other Accrued Expenses	1,647	1,504
Total Current Liabilities	12,901	10,455
Long-Term Debt, excluding current installments	2,672	2,148
Other Long-Term liabilities	977	871
Deferred Income Taxes	1,023	1,388

EXHIBIT 2
(Continued)

Fiscal Year Ending	January 29, 2006	January 30, 2005
STOCKHOLDERS' EQUITY		
Common Stock, par value $0.05: authorized: 10,000 shares; issued 2,401 shares at January 29, 2006 and 2,385 shares at January 30, 2005: outstanding 2,124 shares at January 29, 2006 and 2,185 shares at January 30, 2005	120	119
Paid-In Capital	7,287	6,650
Retained Earnings	28,943	23,962
Accumulated Other Comprehensive Income	409	227
Unearned Compensation	(138)	(108)
Treasury Stock, at cost, 277 shares at January 29, 2006 and 200 shares at January 30, 2005	(9,712)	(6,692)
Total Stockholders' Equity	26,909	24,158
Total Liabilities and Stockholders' Equity	$44,482	$ 39,020

SOURCE: *2005 Annual Report, The Home Depot, p. 37.*

EXHIBIT 3

10-Year Summary of Financial and Operating Results: Home Depot, Inc. and Subsidiaries (Dollar amounts in millions, except per share data)

Fiscal Year	10-Year Compound Annual Growth Rate	2005	2004	2003	2002	2001(1)	2000	1999	1998	1997	1996(1)
STATEMENT OF EARNINGS DATA											
Net sales	18.1%	$81,511	$73,094	$64,816	$58,247	$53,553	$45,738	$38,434	$30,219	$24,156	$19,535
Net sales increase (%)	—	11.5	12.8	11.3	8.8	17.1	19.0	27.2	25.1	23.7	26.3
Earnings before provision for income taxes	22.8	9,282	7,912	6,843	5,872	4,957	4,217	3,804	2,654	1,898	1,535
Net earnings	23.1	5,838	5,001	4,304	3,664	3,044	2,581	2,320	1,614	1,160	938
Net earnings increase (%)	23.1	16.7	16.2	17.5	20.4	17.9	11.3	43.7	31.9	23.7	28.2
Diluted earnings per share ($)(2)	23.1	2.72	2.26	1.88	1.56	1.29	1.10	1.00	0.71	0.52	0.43
Diluted earnings per share increase (%)	—	20.4	20.2	20.5	20.9	17.3	10.0	40.8	29.1	20.9	26.5
Diluted weighted average number of common shares	—	2,147	2,216	2,289	2,344	2,353	2,352	2,342	2,320	2,287	2,195
Gross margin—% of sales	—	33.5	33.4	31.8	31.1	30.2	29.9	29.7	28.5	28.1	27.8
Total operating expenses—% of sales	—	22.0	22.6	21.2	21.1	20.9	20.7	19.8	19.7	19.8	20.0
Net interest income (expense)—% of sales	—	—	—	—	0.1	—	—	—	—	—	0.1
Earnings before provision for income taxes—% of sales	—	11.4	10.8	10.6	10.1	9.3	9.2	9.9	8.8	7.9	7.9
Net earnings—% of sales	—	7.2	6.8	6.6	6.3	5.7	5.6	6.0	5.3	4.8	4.8
BALANCE SHEET DATA AND FINANCIAL RATIOS											
Total assets	19.7%	$44,482	$39,020	$34,437	$30,011	$26,394	$21,385	$17,081	$13,465	$11,229	$9,342
Working capital	6.9	2,445	3,818	3,774	3,882	3,860	3,392	2,734	2,076	2,004	1,867
Merchandise inventories	18.0	11,401	10,076	9,076	8,338	6,725	6,556	5,489	4,293	3,602	2,708
Net property and equipment	18.8	24,901	22,726	20,063	17,168	15,375	13,068	10,227	8,160	6,509	5,437
Long-term debt	14.0	2,672	2,148	856	1,321	1,250	1,545	750	1,566	1,303	1,247
Stockholders' equity	18.4	26,909	24,158	22,407	19,802	18,082	15,004	12,341	8,740	7,098	5,955
Book value per share ($)	18.5	12.67	11.06	9.93	8.38	7.71	6.46	5.36	3.95	3.23	2.75
Long-term debt-to-equity (%)	—	9.9	8.9	3.8	6.7	6.9	10.3	6.1	17.9	18.4	20.9
Total debt-to-equity (%)	—	15.2	8.9	6.1	6.7	6.9	10.3	6.1	17.9	18.4	20.9
Current ratio	—	1.19:1	1.37:1	1.40:1	1.48:1	1.59:1	1.77:1	1.75:1	1.73:1	1.82:1	2.01:1
Inventory turnover	—	4.8x	4.9x	5.0x	5.3x	5.4x	5.1x	5.4x	5.4x	5.4x	5.6x
Return on invested capital (%)	—	22.4	21.5	20.4	18.8	18.3	19.6	22.5	19.3	16.1	16.3
STATEMENT OF CASH FLOWS DATA											
Depreciation and amortization	24.2%	$1,579	$1,319	$1,076	$903	$764	$601	$463	$373	$283	$232
Capital expenditures(3)	11.5	3,881	3,948	3,508	2,749	3,393	3,574	2,618	2,094	1,464	1,248
Cash dividends per share ($)	25.3	0.400	0.325	0.26	0.21	0.17	0.16	0.11	0.08	0.06	0.05
STORE DATA(4)											
Number of stores	17.1%	2,042	1,890	1,707	1,532	1,333	1,134	930	761	624	512
Square footage at fiscal year-end	17.2	215	201	183	166	146	123	100	81	66	54
Increase in square footage (%)	—	7.0	9.8	10.2	14.1	18.5	22.6	23.5	22.8	23.1	21.6
Average square footage per store (in thousands)	—	105	106	107	108	109	108	108	107	106	105

STORE SALES AND OTHER DATA

Comparable store sales increase (%)[5][6][7]	—	3.8	5.4	3.8	—	—	4	10	7	7	7
Weighted average weekly sales per operating store (in thousands)	(0.3)%	$763	$766	$763	$772	$812	$864	$876	$844	$829	$803
Weighted average sales per square foot ($)[4][5]	(0.3)	377	375	371	370	388	415	423	410	406	398
Number of customer transactions[4]	13.6	1,330	1,295	1,246	1,161	1,091	937	797	665	550	464
Average ticket ($)[4]	3.3	57.98	54.89	51.15	49.43	48.64	48.65	47.87	45.05	43.63	42.09
Number of associates at fiscal year-end	15.6	344,810	323,149	298,809	280,900	256,300	227,300	201,400	156,700	124,400	98,100

[1] Fiscal years 2001 and 1996 include 53 weeks, all other fiscal years reported 52 weeks.

[2] Diluted earnings per share for fiscal 1997, excluding a $104 million non-recurring charge, were $0.55.

[3] Excludes payments for businesses acquired (net in millions) for fiscal years 2005 ($2,546), 2004 ($727), 2003 ($215), 2002 ($235), 2001 ($190), 2000 ($26), 1999 ($101), 1998 ($6), and 1997 ($61).

[4] Excludes all non-store locations since their inclusion may cause distortion of the data presented due to operational differences from our retail stores. The total number of the excluded locations and their total square footage are immaterial to our total number of locations and total square footage.

[5] Adjusted to reflect the first 52 weeks of the 53-week fiscal years in 2001 and 1996.

[6] Includes Net Sales at locations open greater than 12 months, including relocated and remodeled stores, and Net Sales of all the subsidiaries of The Home Depot, Inc. Stores and subsidiaries became comparable on the Monday following their 365th day of operation and include certain locations acquired in the current year by existing subsidiaries. Comparable store sales is intended only as supplemental information and is not a substitute for Net Earnings presented in accordance with generally accepted accounting principles.

[7] Beginning in fiscal 2003, comparable store sales increases were reported to the nearest one-tenth of a percentage. Comparable store sales increases in fiscal years prior to 2003 were not adjusted to reflect this change.

SOURCE: *2005 Annual Report, The Home Depot*, pp. F1 and F 2.

NOTES

1. B. Nardelli, "Letter to Shareholders," *2005 The Home Depot Annual Report* (March 29, 2006), p. 1.

2. M. Bartiromo, "Bob Nardelli Explains Himself," *Business Week* (July 24, 2006), pp. 98–100.

3. R. Kirkland, "The Real CEO Pay Problem," *Fortune* (July 10, 2006), pp. 78–81.

4. J. Fox, "A Meditation on Risk," *Fortune* (October 3, 2005), pp. 50–80.

5. The company's early history was summarized from Paul M. Swiercz's case "The Home Depot, Inc." in *Cases in Strategic Management,* 4th ed., Thomas L. Wheelen & J. David Hunger (Reading, MA: Addison-Wesley, 1993), pp. 367–397.

6. "Home Depot to Scale Back New-Store Openings," *Reuters* (January 19, 2006).

7. "Home Depot," *Value Line* (July 7, 2006).

8. D. Jones, "Home Depot CEO Aims for Next Level," *USA Today* (July 17, 2006), p. 3B.

9. "The Home Depot Unveils 2010 Growth Targets," *Home Depot News Release* (January 21, 2006).

10. H. R. Weber, "Investors Lukewarm About Home Depot Plan," *Associated Press* (January 19, 2006).

11. *St. Petersburg Times* (December 24, 1990), p. 11.

12. *Business Atlanta* (November 11, 1988).

13. Ibid.

14. *Chain Store Executive* (April 1983), p. 9–11.

15. The Home Depot, Inc., *1997 Annual Report,* p. 13. This was directly quoted with minor editing.

16. B. Grow, "Renovating Home Depot," *Business Week* (March 6, 2006), p. 52.

17. Ibid., pp. 50–58.

18. Ibid., p. 52.

19. Ibid., pp. 50–58.

20. Ibid., p. 56.

21. D. Jones, "Home Depot CEO Aims for Next Level," *USA Today* (July 17, 2006), p. 3B.

22. B. Grow (March 6, 2006), p. 55.

23. Ibid., pp. 57–58.

24. Ibid., p. 58.

25. "Business Code of Conduct and Ethics," The Home Depot, Inc. (January 26, 2006), http://ir.homedepot.com/governance/ethics.cfm.

26. "Environmental Principles," The Home Depot (September 14, 2006), (www.homedepot.com) corporate Web site.

27. "Lifting the Lid: Home Depot's No-Show Board Raises Ire," *Reuters* (May 26, 2006).

28. "Shareholders Still Fuming After Snub at Home Depot Meeting," *St. Petersburg Times* (June 10, 2006), p. 8D.

29. M. Bartiromo (2006), p. 98.

30. L. Grant, "CEO Bob Nardelli Sees Expansion in Home Depot's Future," *USA Today* (July 28, 2005), p. 3B.

31. D. Jones (2006), p. 3B.

32. M. Bartiromo, (2006), p. 100.

33. The first quarter of 2006 was the first time the company reported two business segments. This was due to the acquisition of Hughes Supply and the subsequent enlargement of Home Depot Supply and related activities. See The Home Depot *Report Form 10-Q* for the second quarter ending July 30, 2006.

34. K. Jacobs, "Home Depot Moves to Expand Online Sales," *Reuters* (February 20, 2006).

35. "Second Quarter 2006 Earnings Conference Call," Home Depot, Inc. (August 15, 2006).

36. B. Grow, "A Lab in a Secure, Undisclosed Spot," *Business Week* (March 6, 2006), p. 58.

37. "Proxy Statement & Notice of 2006 Annual Meeting of Shareholders," *Home Depot* (April 14, 2006), pp. 40–41.

38. B. Grow, (March 6, 2006), p. 56.

39. *Annual Report Form 10-K,* Lowe's Companies, Inc. (2005), p. 4.

40. "Retail Building Supply Industry," *Value Line* (July 7, 2006), p. 876.

41. E. Gartner, "Lowe's Expects Slowdown," *USA Today* (August 22, 2006), p. 4B.

42. *Annual Form 10-K,* Lowe's Companies, Inc. (2006), p. 3.

43. K. Jacobs, "Home Depot Moves to Expand Online Sales," *Reuters* (February 20, 2006).

44. "Lowe's First-Quarter Profit Tops Estimates," *Reuters* (May 22, 2006).

45. *Annual Form 10-K,* Lowe's Companies, Inc. (2005).

46. "84 Lumber Company Company Profile," *Yahoo! Finance* (September 11, 2006).

47. Company-owned Web site, www.wolseley.com (September 11, 2006).

48. "Quarterly Message from the CEO," Home Depot Web site (www.homedepot.com) (August 30, 2006).

CASE **21**

The Future of Gap Inc.

Mridu Verma

Gap Inc.'s heritage is based on connecting with people through great style and experiences—
and by making cultural connections along the way.
ROBERT FISHER, CHAIRMAN, GAP INC.[1]

GAP INC. WAS ONE OF THE LEADING INTERNATIONAL SPECIALTY RETAILERS OFFERING CLOTHING, accessories and personal care products for men, women, children, and babies under the Gap, Banana Republic, Old Navy, and Forth & Towne brand names. The company primarily operated in North America. The company recorded revenues of $16.023 billion during the fiscal year ended January 2006, a decrease of 1.5% over 2005. The operating profit of the company was $1.79 billion during fiscal year 2006, a decrease of 4.2% over 2005. The net profit was $1.113 billion, a decrease of 3.2% over 2005. Gap was ranked 52nd (2005 ranking—40th) by the Business Week Interbrand survey conducted in August 2006. It was valued at $6416 million ($8195 million in 2005). (See **Exhibits 1 and 2** for Gap's financial results.)

Paul Pressler (Pressler), who became Gap Inc.'s CEO in October 2002, had been heralded for his cost-cutting strategies that had restored financial discipline in the company. But there was a trade-off, analysts said. Pressler, who had little retail experience, did not steer Gap toward its customers' tastes. Realizing his mistakes, Pressler changed his strategy in mid-2004 to generate growth. Would he succeed in rejuvenating Gap Inc. and attracting customers once again? (See **Exhibit 3** for a brief SWOT analysis.)

EXHIBIT 1
Financial Results:
Gap Inc.

Year Ending	January 28, 2006	January 29, 2005	January 31, 2004
Net Sales	**$16,023**	**$16,267**	**$15,854**
Percentage change year-to-date	(2%)	3%	10%
Earnings before income taxes	$1,793	$1,872	$1,684
Percentage change year-to-date	(4%)	11%	110%
Net Earnings	**$1,113**	**$1,150**	**$1,031**
Percentage change year-to-date	(3%)	12%	116%
Cash Flows			
Net cash provided by operating activities	$1,551	$1,597	$2,160
Net cash provided by (used for) investing activites	286	183	(2,318)
Effect of exchange rate fluctations on cash	(7)	-	28
Net decrease in cash and equivalents	(210)	(16)	(261)
Net cash provided by operating activities	$1,551	$1,597	$2,160
Less: Net purchases of property and equipment	(600)	(419)	(261)
Free cash flow	$961	$1,176	$1,899

SOURCE: *Gap Inc. Annual Report 2005.*

EXHIBIT 2
Select Financial
Results: Gap Inc.

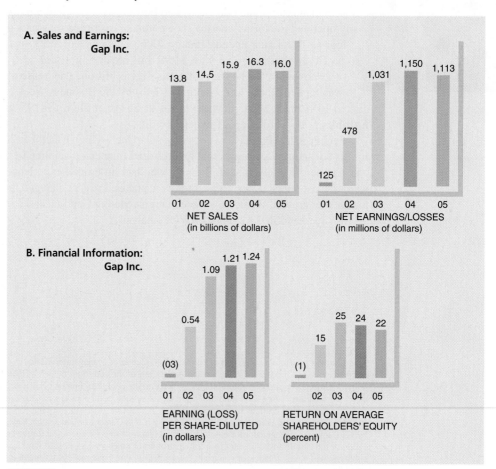

A. Sales and Earnings: Gap Inc.

NET SALES (in billions of dollars)

NET EARNINGS/LOSSES (in millions of dollars)

B. Financial Information: Gap Inc.

EARNING (LOSS) PER SHARE-DILUTED (in dollars)

RETURN ON AVERAGE SHAREHOLDERS' EQUITY (percent)

SOURCE: *Gap Inc. Annual Report 2005.*

EXHIBIT 3
SWOT Analysis:
Gap Inc.

Strengths	Weaknesses
Brand recognition	Weak performance of Gap brand
Large network of physical stores	Overdependence on North America
Low long-term debt	Declining operating cash flows
Opportunities	**Threats**
Launch of Forth & Towne	Counterfeit products
Growth in online retail spending	Slowdown in consumer spending
Markets in China and India	Emergence of private labels

SOURCE: *Gap Inc. Annual Report 2005.*

About Gap Inc.

Gap Inc. was a specialty retailer operating retail and outlet stores selling casual apparel, accessories, and personal care products for men, women, and children under the Gap, Banana Republic, Old Navy, and Forth & Towne brands. Gap division's brands also included GapKids, babyGap, and GapBody. In June 2006, the company operated 3,070 stores, including Gap, Banana Republic, and Old Navy stores throughout the U.S., as well as in Canada, the UK, France, and Japan. In addition, the company also marketed its products to its U.S. customers through three Web sites: gap.com, bananarepublic.com, and oldnavy.com.

The company primarily conducted its business through four business divisions: Old Navy, Gap, Banana Republic, and others. Old Navy targeted cost-conscious shoppers. Old Navy stores offered selections of apparel, shoes, and accessories for adults, children, and infants as well as other items, including personal care products. Old Navy also offered a line of maternity and plus sizes in its stores. The Old Navy division recorded revenues of $6.86 billion in fiscal year 2006, an increase of 1.6% over 2005. The Gap division offered extensive selections of classically styled, casual apparel at moderate price points, usually priced higher than Old Navy apparel. It also offered accessories and personal care products. The brand extensions of the Gap included GapKids, babyGap, and GapBody. During the fiscal year 2006, the Gap division recorded revenues of $6.84 billion, a decrease of 5.6% over 2005.

The Banana Republic brand offered a more sophisticated dress-casual and tailored apparel, shoes, and accessories for adults. Its products ranged from apparel, including intimate apparel, to personal care products. The Banana Republic division recorded revenues of $2.3 billion in fiscal year 2006, an increase of 1.4% over 2005. Other divisions included Forth & Towne and direct, as well as international sales programmers. Forth & Towne was the company's newest retail concept, principally targeting women over the age of 35. The "other" division recorded revenues of $29 million in fiscal year 2006, as compared to the revenues of $11 million in fiscal 2005. The bulk of Gap Inc.'s sales came from Gap and Old Navy, with Banana Republic and a new chain, Forth & Towne, representing less than 25% of its business. North America, Gap's largest geographical market, accounted for 90.9% of the total revenues in the fiscal year 2006. Revenues from North America reached $14.56 billion in 2006, a decrease of 1.4% over 2005. Europe accounted for 5.1% of the total revenues in the fiscal year 2006.

Background Note

Gap

Gap was set up by Donald Fisher in 1969. After a pair of Levi's jeans purchased by him fell short of his size requirements, Fisher sensed a gap in the market. He decided to start an only-jeans outlet that offered a wide range of sizes to the customers. With this intention, the first store was started in San Francisco. To reinforce the choices available at the stores, Gap's first advertisement carried the tag line "four tons of Levi's." The retail concept was an instant hit. Gap's "basics look" comprising signature (Levi's) blue jeans and white cotton shirts became a rage. Initially the goods were sold at Levi's controlled prices, allowing Fisher to earn hefty margins (in the region of 50%). A 1976 Federal Trade Commission (FTC) directive banned manufacturers from setting the retail price. With an increasing number of retailers discounting their retail offerings, competition in the market heated up and margins dried up. Fisher parted ways with Levi's and shifted to high-margin private labels. By 1980, 200 Gap outlets in the U.S. offered 14 different private labels, such as Foxtails, Monterey Bay, and Durango. As other retailers started taking the same private label route to bolster their margins. Gap seemed to be getting lost in the crowd. It was at this juncture that Fisher hired Millard "Mickey" Drexler (Drexler) to give a new direction to Gap.

When Drexler joined Gap in 1983, the company's turnover was just $500 million. He dumped the private-label brands and introduced Gap as a clothing brand. Soon, Gap controlled everything from manufacturing to marketing to the distribution of its offerings. Gap took advantage of America's casual-dress trend. Whenever growth appeared to slow, Drexler came up with something new: GapKids, babyGap, and then discount stores. Gap led the corporate dress-down revolution, and earnings grew at an average of 30% for the five years through 1999. In the mid-1990s, the Gap was so much a part of American pop culture that it warranted its own skit on Saturday Night Live. Unfortunately, Gap's khakis-and-blue-shirt formula proved remarkably easy to replicate. The company soon found itself competing with discount retailers such as Target and Wal-Mart.

When laid-off dot-commers stopped loading up on casual clothes, Gap took desperate measures to lift sales, stocking trendy miniskirts and low-rise jeans to chase teenage shoppers. Its purple shirts in extra large sizes did not find any buyers. Gap's core 30-and-over clientele, once Gap's mainstay, fled to rivals such as value retailers Target and Kohl's.

Banana Republic

Started by Mel and Patricia Ziegler in 1978, Banana Republic was positioned as an adventure lifestyle store. It retailed bush jackets, travel trunks, travel books, fisherman hats, and exotic maps with most of its sales coming through catalogues. Its ascent coincided with the "safari fever"[2] spreading across the U.S. in the early 1980s. When Banana Republic's sales touched the $10 million mark in 1983, its stores were bought by Gap.

Gap transformed Banana Republic from a catalog-based retailer to a physical retailer with large stores across the country. The stores offered lifestyle apparels tailored to consumers needs. By 1987, Banana Republic was a successful retail concept with sales revenue of $191 million. With safaris going out of fashion, Banana Republic's fortunes plunged. It reported a loss of $10 million in 1988. Banana underwent a makeover and shed its safari-style merchandise in favor of clothes for the dressed-down workplace, a strategy that sustained it through the dot-com era. The emphasis was on a "modern casual lifestyle" look. Banana Republic was struggling to come up with a fashion mix that its 30-and-older customers, especially men, felt more comfortable wearing.

Old Navy

Started in 1994, Old Navy targeted price-conscious customers. Old Navy apparels used different fabrics as compared to Gap and the stores were given a "fun" look.[3] Using different blends of fabric that helped keep its manufacturing costs low, Old Navy retailed basics for the whole family at two-thirds Gap's prices. It sold budget-priced jeans, T-shirts, and khaki pants to kids, teens, and young adults. Thanks to a very successful season of fleece tops and vests, Old Navy became the biggest contributor to the parent company's overall growth in 2000, even when sales declined at the core Gap chain.

Encouraged by the sales, Drexler opened 282 Old Navy stores in the next three years. Old Navy became the first-ever retail chain to reach $1 billion sales within four years. In 2004, Old Navy accounted for 41% of Gap Inc.'s total sales. Though comparatively successful, Old Navy had its own share of problems. Consumers complained that it was always bulging with merchandise, with the floor often being permanently devoted to discounted goods to boost sales. In 2000, Old Navy shifted its focus to teenagers. Initially, the brand was immensely popular among teenagers, but soon the brand became a casualty of teenagers' fickle preferences.

"Old Navy's been a bit of a problem child for them recently. In some ways it became a victim of its own success. The younger crowd went crazy for them and they met that demand, but now they're realizing that they need to appeal to a larger audience," an analyst observed.[4] Old Navy, whose merchandise mix was skewed too far toward teens in 2001, needed to win back grownups. Old Navy also needed to restore a distinct identity to avoid drawing bargain-hunting Gap shoppers.

Drexler acknowledged that each of the company's three core brands—Gap, Banana Republic, and Old Navy—had "come untethered from the tight rapport with consumers that accounted for its earlier prosperity." In the mid-1990s, Gap had embarked on an expansion spree, increasing its retail square footage by more than 20% annually. Square footage at Gap's three chains doubled between 1999 and 2002 even as sales per square foot plunged from $548 to $393 during the same period. In 2001, Gap posted a loss of $7.8 million on sales of $13.8 billion.[5] By March 2002, rating agencies had downgraded Gap Inc.'s debt from investment grade to junk. Heavy markdowns sliced Gap's gross margins by 40%. In 2002, Gap paid interest worth $145 million on the $2 billion debt it had raised to fund its expansion plans. To make things worse, Gap's per-store sales declined for 29 months straight as profits vanished. Drexler stepped down in September 2002. He was replaced by Paul Pressler (Pressler), who had been running Disney's consumer stores (which were later sold) and the Disneyland theme park (where he expanded the souvenir shops and restaurants), and oversaw all Disney parks and resorts, but had no previous fashion retail experience.

Pressler's Turnaround Strategy

Initially, Pressler focused on cost cutting, consumer research, and more targeted marketing of the three brands. Working with CFO Byron Pollitt (Pollitt), whom he had brought over from Disney, Pressler shut down hundreds of stores, consolidated production among fewer suppliers, and revamped inventory management. He reduced the inventory per square foot by 16%. He attempted to increase margins by selling clothes closer to full price. To end panicky clearance sales, Pressler ordered managers to rely increasingly on software that would tell them when and by how much to mark down merchandise. Micro-management was replaced by hands-off leadership. Pressler was not as interested in product details. He left specific color and design decisions to Gap, Old Navy, and Banana Republic division heads. Pressler devoted more attention to areas visible to the customer, including marketing and store atmosphere.

He hired what he called a "chief algorithm officer" to analyze the sales from every cash register. It turned out that Gap had been sending the same size assortments to stores with different selling patterns. He initiated customized deliveries—for instance, sending more extra-larges to places that needed them. Each chain also instituted "guardrails" that defined what portion of a store's inventory should go toward basic colors and styles regardless of how varied the floor displays were. All this served to cut the need for discounting, and profit margins improved.

When it came to the merchandise, Pressler also resorted to "numbers." Consumer-insight research showed that the three brands were losing market share. With the distinction between the products of the three brands becoming hazy, each seemed to be eating into the other's market share. He decided to reposition all the three brands, giving each a distinctive identity. While Gap stayed in the middle, Old Navy focused on lower prices and basic items, and Banana Republic raised prices and experimented with runway-influenced designs. The strategy yielded results in the early days. In 2003, the business bounced back after 29 straight months of same-store sales declines under Drexler. Cash flow from operations went up and Gap's credit rating rose.

The Decline

In July 2004 the turnaround hit a snag with each of the three chains' sales heading southward, pushing comparable sales down 5%. After initial success in distinguishing brands, Pressler's reliance on metrics prompted him to distinguish them even further, and the move backfired. Old Navy, known for its specialty style at discounted prices, disappointed its faithful by stocking commodity T-shirts and jeans similar to those sold at discount chains such as Target, in the place of the trendy-but-cheap clothes it had stocked earlier. Banana Republic went over the top, devoting too much of its space to embellished pieces unsuitable for the office. As for the Gap brand, it started marketing outfits instead of individual staples like khakis and denim. The Gap stores sported separate "going out" and "go to work" sections—making it harder for the customers to navigate. Shoppers who had once considered Banana, Gap, and Old Navy as default choices gravitated to fresher competitors like Abercrombie & Fitch, Urban Outfitters, and J. Crew (rival clothing retailers).

An exodus of sorts was underway inside the company too. Soon after Drexler's departure, a stream of talented executives who had helped make Gap great in its heyday began to head for the exits, from executive vice presidents to in-the-trenches designers (see **Exhibit 4**). Some

EXHIBIT 4
Employee Exodus:
Gap Inc.

Employee Name	Year of Departure	Name of the Company Joined
Mickey Drexler CEO	2002	J. Crew
Jeff Pfeifle EVP, product and design, Old Navy	2002	J. Crew
Henry Stafford Merchandiser, Old Navy men's	2003	American Eagle Outfitters
Jerome Jessup EVP, product development and design, Gap brands	2003	Ann Taylor
Maureen Chiquet President, Banana Republic	2003	Chanel
Neil Goldberg President, Gap Inc. outlets	2003	The Children's Place
Michael Tucci EVP, Gap Inc. online division	2003	Coach

EXHIBIT 4
(Continued)

John Goodman SVP, Gap Inc. outlets	2003	Dockers
Jennifer Foyle Divisional merchandising manager, Gap brand, women's	2003	J. Crew
Lynda Markoe Senior director, Gap Inc. HR	2003	J. Crew
Todd Snyder Senior director, Old Navy, men's product design	2003	J. Crew
John Valdivia VP, creative services, Old Navy	2003	J. Crew
Libby Wadle Div. merchandising manager, Banana Republic, women's	2003	J. Crew
Roxane Al-Fayez VP, operations, Gap Inc. online division	2003	Limited Brands
Thomas Cawley CFO, Gap brand	2003	Peet's Coffee & Tea
Patti Barkin-Camilli SVP, Old Navy, women's accessories	2003	Uniqlo
LeAnn NealzSVP, design, GapKids, babyGap SVP, design, GapKids, babyGap	2004	American Eagle Outfitters
Barbara Wambach EVP, Gap Body	2004	Bebe
Tara Poseley SVP, merchandising, GapKids, babyGap	2004	Design Within Reach
Tracy Gardner SVP, merchandising, Gap brand	2004	J. Crew
Mark Breitbard SVP, merchandising, Gap Kids, babyGap	2005	Abercrombie & Fitch
Alan Marks VP, corporate communications, Gap Inc.	2005	Nike
Pina Ferlisi EVP, design, Gap brand	2005	Generra
Jeff Jones EVP, marketing, Gap brand	2005	No announced destination
Felix Carbullido VP and general manager, Gap.com	2006	Smith & Hawken
Alan Barocas SVP, real estate, Gap Inc.	2006	No announced destination
Nick Cullen EVP, chief supply chain officer, Gap Inc.	2006	No announced destination
Jyothi Rao VP, merchandising, Forth & Towne	2006	No announced destination
Julie Rosen VP, merchandising, Gap brand	2006	No announced destination

SOURCE: *Prepared from information provided in Julia Boorstin, "Fashion Victim,"* Fortune, *4/17/2006, Vol. 153 Issue 7, p. 160–166.*

were fired, others left on their own. "From the day I got here, we've had to assess our talent," mentioned Pressler,[6] who called the turnover healthy and normal. But analysts and industry observers were not so sanguine, with some analysts downgrading the company. Morgan Stanley analyst Michelle Clark opined that with other ex-Disney players such as Gap-brand head Cynthia Harriss in key roles, the company's lack of fashion expertise at the top was being exacerbated by a drain of youthful morale and energy. Even company insiders echoed her fears. "Ten of the best 15 executives in all retail were working for the company. Now they've lost the creative people, almost all the merchandising and design leadership," observed a former head of one Gap division.[7]

By the time Pressler faced investors in Spring 2005, the momentum he had built up in his first 18 months was gone. He tried to shift Wall Street's focus to the future, announcing that the company would introduce a new store chain, Forth & Towne, for women 35 and over. More privately, he went back to the core brands, working with their respective presidents to analyze customer surveys. The identity of each chain was recalibrated: Gap would offer high-quality basics with style; Banana Republic would emphasize fashionable classics but avoid the cutting edge; Old Navy would rededicate itself to low-priced trendy items. Pressler also cut the nine-month production cycle on some Old Navy clothes to three months—so it could adapt to emerging trends more readily—by moving designers from New York to its San Francisco headquarters, positioning some merchants closer to factories in Southeast Asia, and sourcing more items in North America. Gap's 2005 fall line featured its classic navy, gray, crisp white, and denim, plus some richer materials—washed leather and cotton cashmere. Meanwhile, Banana Republic pulled back from fashion extremes and was focusing on the classics. At Old Navy—to which Pressler was looking for a big chunk of the company's growth—product quality was improved noticeably.

Gap continued to face a perception problem—a struggle to recapture customers who had abandoned it. Fiscally and operationally, Gap was a tighter, stronger business than it was in 2002. Pressler had hedged its fashion bets. Company-commissioned research was directing brand presidents on how they could expand the chains into what Pressler called "lifestyle brands," with line extensions such as accessories and baby-wear. While creating the Forth & Towne chain appeared a gamble, Pressler felt that the numbers pointed to an untapped market. Industry observers, however, opined that no matter how carefully calibrated Gap's fashion choices were, the nature of the business required a certain degree of risk taking. No one knew what consumers would actually buy until the goods were on the shelves.

Pressler also started investing more in the stores, where Gap's minimalist look too often appeared dated and shabby, replacing it with darker-wood fixtures (like Abercrombie), painted walls (like J. Crew), and more dramatic window displays. A back wall dedicated to denim and a colorful "T-shirt bar" highlighted Gap's traditional expertise. New spotlighting, hand-drawn chalk signs, and artful displays of intertwined jeans created a sense of theatricality. By year-end 2005, 60 Gap stores had been redesigned, with another 220 of the chain's 1,335 stores scheduled to get the new look in 2006. The company expected to draw customers into the stores, so that they would notice the better-designed, higher-quality products. In 2005, the company opened 198 new stores and closed 139. In 2006, the company expected to open about 175 store locations, weighted toward the Old Navy brand, and close about 135 store locations, weighted toward the Gap brand. Square footage was expected to increase between 1% and 2% for fiscal year 2006. (See **Exhibit 5.**)

All this came at a financial cost, pushing Gap's capital expenditures to among the highest in specialty retail. It also meant operating margins would drop to between 10% and 10.5% in 2006. For the year 2005, Gap group posted sales of $16 billion, a 2% drop compared with $16.3 billion for 2004. Comparative store sales for the year 2005 decreased by 5%, as against flat sales in 2004. Sales at the flagship Gap stores in the U.S. were essentially flat at $1.2 billion year-over-year in 2005, but sales on the international front lost 5.6% to $339 million from $359 million a year ago. By February 2006, customer traffic across the

EXHIBIT 5
Brand Information: Gap Inc.

A. Brand-wise Financials: Gap Inc.
(Dollars in millions)

52 Weeks Ending January 28, 2006	Gap	Old Navy	Banana Republic	Other	Total
2004 Net Sales	$7,240	$6,747	$2,269	$11	$16,267
Comparable store sales	(302)	(361)	(104)	-	(767)
Noncomparable store sales	(87)	409	130	15	467
Direct (online)	(3)	32	-	3	32
Foreign exchange	(11)	29	6	-	24
2005 Net Sales	$6,837	$6,856	$2,301	$29	$16,023

B. Brand-wise Sales: Gap Inc.
(Dollars in millions)

52 Weeks Ending January 29, 2005	Gap	Old Navy	Banana Republic	Other	Total
2003 Net Sales	$7,305	$6,456	$2,090	$3	$15,854
Comparable store sales	(76)	25	109	-	58
Noncomparable store sales	(155)	195	51	7	98
Direct (online)	16	47	14	-	77
Foreign exchange	150	24	5	1	180
2004 Net Sales	$7,240	$6,747	$2,269	$11	$16,267

C. Brand-wise Store Details: Gap Inc.

Store count and square footage as follows:

	January 28, 2006		January 29, 2005	
	Number of Store Locations	Sq. Ft. (in millions)	Number of Store Locations	Sq. Ft. (in millions)
Gap North America	1,335	12.6	1,396	13.0
Gap Europe	165	1.5	169	1.6
Gap Asia	91	1.0	78	0.8
Old Navy North America	959	18.4	889	17.3
Banana Republic North America	494	4.2	462	3.9
Banana Republic Asia	4	-	-	-
Forth & Towne	5	0.1	-	-
Total	3,053	37.8	2,994	36.6
Increase (Decrease)	2%	3%	(1%)	0%

SOURCE: *Gap Inc. Annual Report 2005.*

Gap, Banana Republic, and Old Navy brands had decreased by 13% from the same point in 2005; same-store sales were down by 11%, and a few more key executives had left.

To fill the executive vacancies, Pressler generally tapped outsiders. Karyn Hillman, senior vice president (SVP) of apparel merchandising for the Banana Republic division, had been promoted to SVP of merchandising for the Gap Adult unit of the flagship Gap brand. Pressler also hired Liz Claiborne veteran Denise Johnston to be president of Gap Adult, overseeing all aspects of Gap's women's and men's apparel and accessories. Pressler realized that fashion retail was not strictly a numbers game, and the quantitative orientation that made Pressler so appealing as an antidote to Drexler—and initially so successful—was ultimately coming back to haunt him. Running a Fortune 500 fashion retailer was a tricky balance between the art of conjuring styles and the discipline of managing an enormous and far-flung operation. Pressler seemed much more comfortable talking corporate strategy than clothing styles. He defined his task as "meeting investor expectations, building platforms, and building a vision of where we want to go."[8]

Recovery Efforts

In the summer of 2006, Gap launched a new marketing campaign called Rock Color to spotlight summer offerings. Inspired by the summer of 1969, the year the company was founded, the promotion featured a pop-up store, which was actually a converted school bus from the Sixties that would drive to summer resort spots on a mission to sell T-shirts, hoodies, flip-flops, and beach hats. The campaign also involved in-store promotions, windows, print ads, direct-mail, and outdoor ads and an online microsite offering customers the chance to win concert tickets. Color was a key component of the campaign. Gap also introduced a contest for customers in New York, Los Angeles, San Francisco, and Chicago to win tickets to concerts. Additionally, one grand-prize winner would receive a trip for two and backstage passes to Gap's private concert featuring John Legend.

Inspired by the success of Hennes & Mauritz,[9] Gap entered into a partnership with British designer Roland Mouret (Mouret) to launch a capsule collection of dresses in selected stores of Europe and a handful of units in New York. The company hoped to increase traffic to its stores through these initiatives. The move was lauded by analysts. Christine Chen, senior research analyst at Pacific Growth Equities said, "Gap needs to rejuvenate their customer, whom they have been disappointing for two years. Their problem has not been their merchandise, which I think has improved drastically, it's the stigma associated with the brand."[10] Gap had been attempting to recast its image throughout 2006 summer and back-to-school season with the return of television ads, its Audrey Hepburn campaign for the return of basic pants and, most recently, product RED.

The Mouret collection was also a part of the Gap (RED) line and featured 10 dresses, ranging in price from 45 pounds to 78 pounds, or about $85 to $148.[11] Styles included belted shirtdresses; Courreges-inspired numbers and tunics with bib fronts or ruffled V-necks in charcoal, silver-gray, navy, black, and red. The collection was seen by analysts as the next step in bringing back old customers and getting new shoppers interested in the store. Mouret said he had teamed up with Gap for a variety of reasons. "They came to me because they felt they weren't strong in the dress category. They wanted a new project that would take Gap dresses to a new level. I have always been a fan of Gap—I like their laid-back attitude, and it was the right mix of people to work with."[12]

In April 2006, Pressler decided to concentrate on Southeast Asia to generate growth. He entered into a franchise agreement with the leading retailers in Singapore, Kuala Lumpur, Malaysia, and the Middle East to open Gap and Banana Republic stores there. This was the first franchisee agreement entered into by the U.S.-based retailer that had always operated company-owned stores. The main benefit of franchise partners was that they provided the local knowledge and experience to allow the company to quickly tap new markets. The merchandise in the new stores was a franchise-specific mix of products from the North American and European collections as well as items not available in other markets. Prices were about 10 to 15% more in the new stores, mainly because of import costs and high rent.

Looking Ahead

In the third quarter of 2006, Gap Inc. reported a 10.8% decline in third-quarter earnings due in part to sagging sales at Old Navy. Foot traffic to the chains was also on the decline. At Gap, which was all but synonymous with the American mall, sales had fallen every month for the year 2006, as executives experimented with a dizzying number of fashions and store layouts. In the end, consumers appeared more confused than intrigued by the incessant changes. In the fourth quarter, overall sales fell by 8%, led by Old Navy and to some extent the flagship brand Gap. Interestingly, Banana Republic sales had rebounded. The comeback at Gap Inc. remained a work in progress. A rotating cast of designers had tried to recreate the Gap brand—with expensive handbags, bell-bottom jeans, and evening gowns—but the result was the same: sales fell.

The overall decline in sales prompted the Gap Inc. board to hire Goldman Sachs (Goldman) to explore strategies ranging from the sale of its 3,000 stores to spinning off a single division, such as Banana Republic, which had become enticing to potential buyers. Goldman was expected to conduct a full review of Gap's business lines and then present a plan to directors.

Any decision about Gap's future would be made by the company's founding family, the Fishers, who controlled more than 30% of its stock. A sale of Gap would be one of the largest buyouts ever in the retail industry. The company's prevailing market value in January 2007 was $16.4 billion, and analysts expected that a buyer would have to pay more than $18 billion.

NOTES

1. Chairman's address Gap Inc's Annual Report 2005.
2. Films such as *Raiders of Lost Ark* and *Romancing the Stone* were at their peak during this period.
3. Old Navy had a practical décor, a lively ambiance, and concrete floors unlike hardwood floors at Gap's elite stores.
4. Lee, Louise, "Gap: Missing that Ol' Micky Magic," *Business Week*, October 29, 2001 Issue 3755, p. 86.
5. Gap had posted a profit of $877 million in 2000.
6. Julia. Boorstin, "Fashion Victim," *Fortune*, April 17, 2006, Vol. 153, Issue 7, pp. 160–166.
7. Ibid.
8. Julia Boorstin, "Fashion Victim," *Fortune*, April 17, 2006, Vol. 153, Issue 7, pp. 160–166.
9. While Gap executives downplayed the comparison, the link with Mouret mirrored the strategy H&M had carried out over the last few seasons by teaming up with designers, including Karl Lagerfeld, Stella McCartney and, in 2006, with Viktor & Rolf.
10. Moin, David, "Gap Brand Taps Hillman For Merchandising," *Women's Wear Daily*, December 13, 2006, Vol. 192, Issue 124, p. 11.
11. At December 2006 exchange rate.
12. Moin, David, "Gap Brand Taps Hillman for Merchandising Post." *Women's Wear Daily*, December 13, 2006, Vol. 192, Issue 124, p. 11.

CASE 22

Rocky Mountain Chocolate Factory Inc. (2008):

RECIPE FOR SUCCESS?

Annie Phan and Joyce Vincelette

Introduction

SITTING AT HIS DESK, ADMIRING THE COLORADO MOUNTAINS IN THE DISTANCE, Frank Crail was counting his blessings at the success of Rocky Mountain Chocolate Factory Inc. (RMCF) over the past 27 years. The company had not only allowed him and his wife to raise their children in Durango, Colorado, but had also provided them a more-than-comfortable livelihood. Crail knew that for his company to continue to grow and be successful, planning for the future was necessary. How long would growth continue in the gourmet segment of the chocolate industry? Consumer tastes were changing. Competition was heating up, with smaller companies being bought by corporate giants who were eying the growth in the gourmet segment of the market. RMCF's business model had been effective, but should changes be considered? With one last glance at the beginnings of springtime in the mountains, Crail left for RMCF's annual planning meeting and his management team waiting in the board room across the hall.

History[1]

Rocky Mountain Chocolate Factory (RMCF) was built around a location and a lifestyle. RMCF began as Frank Crail's dream to move his family from crowded and bustling Southern California, where he owned CNI Data Processing Inc., a company that produced billing software for the cable TV industry, to a slower-paced and family-friendly environment. He and his wife chose the small and quaint Victorian-era town of Durango, Colorado, and began surveying the town's residents and merchants for business opportunities. "It came down to either a car wash or a chocolate shop," recalls the father of seven. "I think I made the right choice."[2]

Founded in 1981 by Crail and two partners and incorporated in Colorado in 1982, RMCF was successful from the start. In addition to the opening of the Durango store, Crail's partners opened stores in Breckenridge and Boulder, Colorado. The first franchised stores were opened in 1982 in Colorado Springs, and Park City, Utah. Crail later told *ColoradoBiz* that the "typical franchisee was a professional who wanted to set out on a second career in a small, family-oriented town,"[3] much as he himself had done. Crail's two partners left the business in 1983.

Over the years, RMCF fine-tuned its chocolates and its strategy. In February 1986, Crail took the company public, where it is now found on the NASDAQ under the symbol RMCF. *Chain Store Age* pronounced RMCF founder Frank Crail one of its Entrepreneurs of the Year for 1995. In the late 1990s most of the company-owned retail operations were closed or sold to franchisees, allowing RMCF to focus on franchising and manufacturing.

In 2008, RMCF was an international franchiser and confectionary manufacturer. The original shop "still stands on Main Street in Durango, with its sights and smells tempting tourists and locals alike to experience a cornucopia of chocolaty treats before taking part in a scenic ride on the Durango-Silverton Narrow Gauge Railroad or after a white water rafting trip through town."[4]

As of March 31, 2008, there were five company-owned and 329 franchised RMCF stores operating in 38 states (concentrated primarily on the west coast and in the Sun Belt), Canada, and the United Arab Emirates,[5] with total revenues of $31,878,183.[6]

Frank Crail believed he had created the recipe that had driven the company to success. "The number one factor is the quality of the product," said Crail. "Without that customers aren't going to stay around long."[7] "As a testament, Crail proudly points to a page from *Money* magazine mounted on his office wall, which features Rocky Mountain Chocolate winning the coveted 3-heart rating in a blind taste test. The candy maker's chocolate beat out See's Candies, Perugina, Teuscher, Godiva, and Fanny May for the richest chocolate, with intense natural flavor."[8] In addition to product quality, taste, value, and variety having been key to RMCF's business strategy, the company also believed that its store atmosphere and ambiance, its brand name recognition, its careful selection of sites for new stores and kiosks, its expertise in the manufacture, merchandising and marketing of chocolate and other candy products, and its commitment to customer service were keys to the accomplishment of its objective to build on its position as a leading international franchiser and manufacturer of high quality chocolate and other confectionary products.[9]

"A great deal has happened over the years," recounts Crail with a twinkle in his eye. "I never imagined that in my search for a place to raise a family things would turn out so sweet!"[10]

Corporate Governance[11]

The biographical sketches for the executive officers and directors as of April 30, 2008, were as follows:

Executive Officers

Franklin E. Crail (age 66) co-founded the first RMCF store in May 1981. Since the incorporation of the company in November 1982, he has served as its chief executive officer, president, and a director. He was elected chairman of the board in March 1986. Prior to founding the company, Mr. Crail was co-founder and president of CNI Data Processing Inc., a software firm that developed automated billing systems for the cable television industry.

Bryan J. Merryman (age 47) joined the company in December 1997 as vice president, Finance, and chief financial officer. Since April 1999, Mr. Merryman has also served the company as chief operating officer and as a director, and since January 2000 as its treasurer. Prior to joining the company, Mr. Merryman was a principal in Knightsbridge Holdings Inc. (a leveraged buyout firm) from January 1997 to December 1997. Mr. Merryman also served as chief financial officer of Super Shops Inc., a retailer and manufacturer of aftermarket auto parts from July 1996 to November 1997, and was employed for more than eleven years by Deloitte and Touche LLP, most recently as a senior manager.

Gregory L. Pope (age 41) became senior vice president of Franchise Development and Operations in May 2004. Since joining the company in October 1990, he has served in various positions, including store manager, new store opener, and franchise field consultant. In March 1996 he became director of Franchise Development and Support. In June 2001 he became vice president of Franchise Development, a position he held until he was promoted to his present position.

Edward L. Dudley (age 44) joined the company in January 1997 to spearhead the company's newly formed Product Sales Development function as vice president, sales and Marketing, with the goal of increasing the company's factory and retail sales. He was promoted to senior vice president in June 2001. During his 10-year career with Baxter Healthcare Corporation, Mr. Dudley served in a number of senior marketing and sales management capacities, including most recently that of director, Distribution Services from March 1996 to January 1997.

William K. Jobson (age 52) joined the company in July 1998 as director of information technology. In June 2001, he was promoted to chief information officer, a position created to enhance the company's strategic focus on information and information technology. From 1995 to 1998, Mr. Jobson worked for ADAC Laboratories in Durango, Colorado, a leading provider of diagnostic imaging and information systems solutions in the healthcare industry, as manager of technical services, and before that, regional manager.

Jay B. Haws (age 58) joined the company in August 1991 as vice president of Creative Services. Since 1981, Mr. Haws had been closely associated with the company, both as a franchisee and marketing/graphic design consultant. From 1986 to 1991 he operated two RMCF franchises located in San Francisco. From 1983 to 1989 he served as vice president of Marketing for Image Group Inc., a marketing communications firm based in Northern California. Concurrently, Mr. Haws was co-owner of two other RMCF franchises located in Sacramento and Walnut Creek, California. From 1973 to 1983 he was principal of Jay Haws and Associates, an advertising and graphic design agency.

Virginia M. Perez (age 70) joined the company in June 1996 and has served as the company's corporate secretary since February, 1997. From 1992 until joining the company, she was employed by Huettig & Schromm Inc., a property management and development firm in Palo Alto, California, as executive assistant to the president and owner. Huettig & Schromm developed, owned, and managed over 1,000,000 square feet of office space in business parks and office buildings on the San Francisco peninsula. Ms. Perez is a paralegal and has held various administrative positions during her career, including executive assistant to the chairman and owner of Sunset Magazine & Books Inc.

Directors

The company bylaws provided for no fewer than three or more than nine directors. The board had previously fixed the number of directors at six. Directors were elected for one-year terms. Crail and Merryman were the only two internal board members. Directors of Rocky Mountain Chocolate Factory who did not also serve as an executive officer were as follows:

Gerald A. Kien (age 75) became a director in August 1995. He retired in 1995 from his positions as president and chief executive officer of Remote Sensing Technologies Inc., a subsidiary of Envirotest Systems Inc., a company engaged in the development of instrumentation for vehicle emissions testing located in Tucson, Arizona. Mr. Kien has served as a director and as chairman *of the Executive Committee of Sun Electric Corporation since 1980 and as chairman, president, and chief executive officer of Sun Electric until retirement in 1993.*

Lee N. Mortenson *(age 71) has served on the board of directors of the company since 1987. Mr. Mortenson has been engaged in consulting and investments activities since July 2000, and was a managing director of Kensington Partners LLC (a private investment firm) from June 2001 to April 2006. Mr. Mortenson has been president and chief executive officer of Newell Resources LLC since 2002, providing management consulting and investment services. Mr. Mortenson served as president, chief operating officer, and a director of Telco Capital Corporation of Chicago, Illinois, from January 1984 to February 2000. Telco Capital Corporation was principally engaged in the manufacturing and real estate businesses. He was president, chief operating officer, and a director of Sunstates Corporation from December 1990 to February 2000. Sunstates Corporation was a company primarily engaged in real estate development and manufacturing. Mr. Mortenson was a director of Alba-Waldensian Inc. from 1984 to July 1999, and served as its president, chief executive officer, and director from February 1997 to July 1999. Alba was principally engaged in the manufacturing of apparel and medical products.*

Fred M. Trainor *(age 68) has served as a director of the company since August 1992. Mr. Trainor is the founder, and since 1984 has served as chief executive officer and president of AVCOR Health Care Products Inc., Fort Worth, Texas (a manufacturer and marketer of specialty dressings products). Prior to founding AVCOR Health Care Products Inc. in 1984, Mr. Trainor was a founder, chief executive officer, and president of Tecnol Inc. of Fort Worth, Texas (also a company involved with the health care industry). Before founding Tecnol Inc., Mr. Trainor was with American Hospital Supply Corporation (AHSC) for 13 years in a number of management capacities.*

Clyde W. Engle *(age 64) has served as a director of the company since January 2000. Mr. Engle is chairman of the board of directors and chief executive officer of sunstates corporation and chairman of the board of directors., president and chief executive officer of Lincolnwood Bancorp, Inc. (formerly known as GSC Enterprises, Inc.), a one-bank holding company, and chairman of the board and chief executive officer of its subsidiary, Bank of Lincolnwood.*

The Board of Directors had determined that Klein, Mortensen, Trainor, and Engle were "independent directors" under Nasdaq Rule 4200. Mortenson, Trainor, and Kien served on the Auditing Committee, Compensation Committee, and the Nominating Committee of the company's board of directors.[12]

Directors of RMCF did not receive any compensation for serving on the board. Directors received compensation for serving on board committees, chairing committees, and participating in meetings. Directors who are not also officers or employees of the company were entitled to receive stock option awards.[13]

As of June 28, 2007, there were approximately 6,080,283 shares of common stock outstanding and eligible to vote at the annual meeting. For each share of common stock held, a shareholder was entitled to one vote on all matters voted on at the annual meeting except the election of directors. Shareholders had cumulative voting rights in the election of directors.[14]

Store Concept[15]

RMCF shops were a blend of traditional and contemporary styles. The company sought to establish a fun and inviting atmosphere in all of its locations. Unlike most other confectionary stores, each RMCF shop prepared certain products, including fudge and caramel apples, in the store. Customers could observe store personnel making fudge from start to finish, including the mixing of ingredients in old-fashioned copper kettles and the cooling of the fudge on large granite or marble tables, and were often invited to sample the store's products. RMCF believed the in-store preparation and aroma of its products enhanced store ambiance, was fun and entertaining for customers, conveyed an image of freshness and homemade quality, and encouraged additional impulse purchases by customers. According to Crail, "We have a great marketing advantage with our unique in-store candy demonstrations. Customers can watch the cook spin a skewered apple in hot caramel or watch fudge being made before their eyes. Of course, everyone gets a sample!"[16]

RMCF stores opened prior to fiscal 2002 had a distinctive country Victorian décor. In fiscal 2002, the company launched its revised store concept, intended specifically for high foot traffic regional shopping malls. This new store concept featured a sleeker and more contemporary design that continued to prominently feature in-store cooking while providing a more up-to-date backdrop for newly redesigned upscale packaging and displays. The company required that all new stores incorporate the revised store design and also required that key elements of the revised concept be incorporated into existing store designs upon renewal of franchise agreements or transfers in store ownership. Through March 31, 2008, 197 stores incorporating the new design had been opened.

The average store size was approximately 1,000 square feet, approximately 650 square feet of which was selling space. Most stores were open seven days a week. Typical hours were 10 a.m. to 9 p.m., Monday through Saturday, and 12 noon to 6 p.m. on Sundays. Store hours in tourist areas may have varied depending upon the tourist season.

RMCF believed that careful selection of store sites was critical to its success, and it considered a number of factors in identifying suitable sites, including tenant mix, visibility, attractiveness, accessibility, level of foot traffic, and occupancy costs. The company believed that the experience of its management team in evaluating potential sites was one of its competitive strengths, and all final site selection had to be approved by senior management. RMCF had established business relationships with most of the major regional and factory outlet center developers in the United States and believed these relationships provided it with the opportunity to take advantage of attractive sites in new and existing real estate environments.

The company established RMCF stores in five primary environments: 1) regional centers, 2) tourist areas, 3) outlet centers, 4) street fronts, and 5) airports and other entertainment-oriented shopping centers. Each of these environments had a number of attractive features, including high levels of foot traffic. The company, over the last several years, has had a particular focus on regional center locations.

Outlet Centers

As of February 29, 2008, there were approximately 110 factory outlet centers in the United States, and there were RMCF stores in approximately 67 (up from 65 in 2007) of these centers in more than 25 states.

Tourist Areas, Street Fronts, and Other Entertainment-Oriented Shopping Centers

As of February 29, 2008, there were approximately 40 (down from 45 in 2007) RMCF stores in locations considered to be tourist areas, including Fisherman's Wharf in San Francisco, and the Riverwalk in San Antonio, Texas. RMCF believed that tourist areas offer high levels of foot traffic, favorable customer spending characteristics, and increase its visibility and name recognition. The company believed that significant opportunities existed to expand into additional tourist areas.

Regional Centers

There were approximately 1,400 regional centers in the United States, and as of February 29, 2008, there were RMCF stores in approximately 95 (down from 100 in 2007) of these centers, including locations in the Mall of America in Bloomington, Minnesota; and Fort Collins, Colorado. Although often providing favorable levels of foot traffic, regional malls typically involved more expensive rent structures and competing food and beverage concepts. The company's new store concept was designed to capitalize on the potential of the regional center environment.

Other[17]

RMCF believed there were a number of other environments that had the characteristics necessary for the successful operation of successful stores, such as airports and sports arenas. In February 2008, twelve (up from nine in 2007) franchised RMCF stores existed at airport locations: two at both Denver and Atlanta international airports, one each at Charlotte, Minneapolis, Salt Lake City, and Dallas/Fort Worth international airports, one at Phoenix Sky Harbor Airport, and three in Canadian airports, including Edmonton, Toronto Pearson, and Vancouver international airports.

On July 20, 2007, RMCF entered into an exclusive Airport Franchise Development Agreement (which expires on July 20, 2009) with The Grove Inc. The company believed this agreement would accelerate the opening of stores in high volume airport locations throughout the United States. The Grove Inc. was a privately owned retailer of natural snacks and other branded food products and, at the time of the agreement, owned and operated 65 food and beverage units, including retail stores in 13 airports throughout the United States. Under the terms of this agreement, The Grove Inc. had the exclusive right to open RMCF stores in all airports in the United States where there were no stores currently operating or under development. The Grove Inc., as of March 31, 2008, operated three stores under this agreement.

Kiosk Concept

In fiscal 2002, RMCF opened its first full-service retail kiosk to display and sell the company's products. As of March 31, 2008, there were 18 (down from 24 in 2007) kiosks in operation. Kiosks ranged from 150 to 250 square feet and incorporated the company's trademark cooking area where popular confections are prepared in front of customers. The kiosk also included the company's core product and gifting lines in order to provide the customer with a full RMCF experience.

RMCF believed kiosks were a vehicle for retail environments where real estate is unavailable or building costs and/or rent factors do not meet the company's financial criteria. The company also believed the kiosk concept enhanced its franchise opportunities by providing more flexibility in support of existing franchisees' expansion programs and allowed new franchisees that otherwise would not qualify for a store location, an opportunity to join the RMCF system.

Franchising Program

The RMCF franchising philosophy was one of service and commitment to its franchise system, and the company continuously sought to improve its franchise support services. The company's franchise concept had consistently been rated as an outstanding franchise opportunity and in January 2008, RMCF was rated the number one franchise opportunity in the candy category by *Entrepreneur* magazine. As of March 31, 2008, there were 329 franchised stores in the RMCF system.

RMCF believed the visibility of its stores and the high foot traffic at many of its locations had generated strong name recognition of and demand for its providers and franchises. RMCF stores had historically been concentrated in the western and Rocky Mountain regions of the United States, but new stores were gradually being opened in the eastern half of the country.

RMCF's continued growth and success was dependent on both its ability to obtain suitable sites at reasonable occupancy costs for both franchised stores and kiosks and its ability to attract, retain, and contract with qualified franchisees who were devoted to promoting and developing the RMCF store concept, reputation, and product quality. RMCF had established criteria to evaluate prospective franchisees, which included the applicant's net worth and liquidity, together with an assessment of work ethic and personality compatibility with the company's operating philosophy. The majority of new franchises were awarded to persons referred by existing franchisees, to interested consumers who had visited RMCF stores, and to existing franchisees. The company also advertised for new franchisees in national and regional newspapers as suitable store locations were recognized.

Prior to store opening, each domestic franchise owner/operator and each store manager for a domestic franchisee was required to complete a seven-day comprehensive training program in store operations and management at its training center in Durango, Colorado, which included a full-sized replica of a properly configured and merchandised RMCF store. Topics covered in the training course included the company's philosophy of store operation and management, customer service, merchandising, pricing, cooking, inventory and cost control, quality standards, record keeping, labor scheduling, and personnel management. Training was based on standard operating policies and procedures contained in an operations manual provided to all franchisees, which the franchisee was required to follow by terms of the franchise agreement. Additionally, trainees were provided with a complete orientation to company operations by working in key factory operational areas and by meeting with members of the senior management.

Ongoing support was provided to franchisees through communications and regular site visits by field consultants who audited performance, provided advice, and ensured that operations were running smoothly, effectively, and according to the standards set by the company.

The franchisee agreement required compliance with RMCF's procedures of operation and food quality specifications, permitted audits and inspections by the company, and required franchisees to remodel stores to conform to established standards. RMCF had the right to terminate any franchise agreement for non-compliance with operating standards. Franchisees were generally granted exclusive territory with respect to the operation of RMCF stores only in the immediate vicinity of their stores. Products sold at the stores and ingredients used in the preparation of products approved for on-site preparation were required to be purchased from the company or from approved suppliers. Franchise agreements could be terminated upon the failure of the franchisee to comply with the conditions of the agreement or upon the occurrence of certain events, which in the judgment of the company was likely to adversely affect the RMCF system. The agreements prohibited the transfer or assignment of any interest in the franchise without the prior written consent of the company and also gave RMCF the right of first refusal to purchase any interest in a franchise.

The term of each RMCF franchise agreement was 10 years, and franchisees had the right to renew for one additional 10-year term. The company did not provide prospective franchisees with financing for their stores, but had developed relationships with sources of franchisee financing to which it would refer franchisees.

In fiscal 1992, the company entered into a franchise development agreement covering Canada with Immaculate Confections Ltd. of Vancouver, BC. Under this agreement Immaculate Confections had exclusive rights to franchise and operate RMCF stores in Canada. Immaculate Confections, as of March 31, 2008, operated 38 stores under this agreement.

In fiscal 2000, RMCF entered into a franchise development agreement covering the Gulf Cooperation Council States of United Arab Emirates, Qatar, Bahrain, Saudi Arabia, Kuwait, and Oman with Al Muhairy Group of United Arab Emirates. This agreement gave the

Al Muhairy Group the exclusive right to franchise and operate RMCF stores in the Gulf Co-operation Council States. Al Muhairy Group, as of March 31, 2008, operated three stores under this agreement.

Frank Crail gives credit for the success of RMCF to the more than 200 independent franchise operators that bought into his concept. "They are the ones that really make this company a success,"[18] he remarked.

Company-Owned Stores

As of March 31, 2008, there were five company-owned RMCF stores. These stores provided a training ground for company-owned store personnel and district managers and a controllable testing ground for new products and promotions, operating, and training methods and merchandising techniques, which might then be incorporated into the franchise store operations.

The cornerstone of RMCF's growth strategy was to aggressively pursue unit growth opportunities in locations where the company had traditionally been successful, to pursue new and developing real estate environments for franchisees that appeared promising based on early sales results, and to improve and expand the retail store concept, such that previously untapped and unfeasible environments (such as most regional centers) generated sufficient revenue to support a successful RMCF location.[19]

Exhibit 1 shows the total number of RMCF stores in operation as well as those sold but not open as of February 29, 2008.

Company-owned and franchised stores were subject to licensing and regulation by the health, sanitation, safety, building, and fire agencies in the state or municipality where they were located as well as various federal agencies that regulate the manufacturing, packaging, and distribution of food products. RMCF was also subject to regulation by the Federal Trade Commission and must comply with state laws governing the fair treatment of franchisees including the offer, sale, and termination of franchises and the refusal to renew franchises.[20]

Products[21]

RMCF typically produced approximately 300 chocolate candies and other confectionery products at the company's manufacturing facility, using premium ingredients and proprietary recipes developed primarily by its Master Candy Maker. These products included many varieties of nut clusters, caramels, butter creams, mints, and truffles. During the Christmas, Easter, and Valentine's Day holiday seasons, the company may have made as many as 100 additional items, including many candies offered in packages specially designed for the holidays. RMCF continually strove to create and offer new confectionery products in order to maintain the excitement and appeal of its products and to encourage repeat business. RMCF developed a new line of sugar-free and no-sugar-added candies. According to the company, "results have been 'spectacular,' filling a need for those with special dietary requirements."[22]

EXHIBIT 1
Rocky Mountain Chocolate Factory Stores as of February 29, 2008

	Sold, Not Yet Open	Open	Total
Company-Owned Stores		5	5
Franchise Stores—Domestic Stores	14	266	280
Franchise Stores—Domestic Kiosks		18	18
Franchised Stores—International		41	41

SOURCE: *Rocky Mountain Chocolate Factory, Inc. 2008 Form 10-K, p. 34.*

In addition to RMCF's traditional chocolates and candies, special treats were prepared in each store. Besides the caramel-covered apples (some stores feature over 30 varieties), fudge (more than fifteen varieties) was made fresh every day in each store using a marble slab to literally suck the heat out of the confection while the cook shaped it with paddles into a giant 22-pound "loaf." A variety of fruits, nuts, pretzels, and cookies were also dipped by hand in pots of melted milk, dark, and even white chocolate.[23]

One of RMCF's trademarks, big, chunky chocolate concoctions, were created somewhat by accident. According to Crail, "In the early days, my partners and I did not know how to make chocolate and had to literally learn on a ping pong table." Crail recalls that "from the start we made the candy centers too big, not compensating for the added size and weight when coating the pieces in chocolate. And if they didn't look quite right we would dip them again. But the huge pieces instantly caught on and have remained the RMCF benchmark ever since."[24] One of these large-sized specialties was a king-sized peanut butter cup dubbed the Bucket™. Another signature piece, the Bear™ (turtles), was a paw-sized concoction of chewy caramel, roasted nuts and a heavy coating of chocolate. The best-selling items were caramel apples, followed by Bears.[25]

All products were produced consistent with the company's philosophy of using only the finest, highest quality ingredients with no artificial preservatives to achieve its marketing motto of "*the Peak of Perfection in Handmade Chocolates®*."[26]

RMCF believed that, on average, approximately 40 percent of the revenues of RMCF stores were generated by products manufactured at the company's factory, 50% by products made in each store using company recipes and ingredients purchased from the company or approved suppliers, and the remaining 10% by products such as ice cream, coffee, and other sundries purchased from approved suppliers. Franchisees sales of products manufactured by the company's factory generated higher revenue than sales of store-made or other products. A significant decrease in the volume of products franchisees purchase from the company would adversely affect total revenue and the results of operations. Such a decrease could result from franchisees decisions to sell more store-made products or products purchased from third-party suppliers.[27]

Chocolate candies manufactured by the company were sold at prices ranging from $14.90 to $24.00 per pound, with an average price of $18.30 per pound. Franchisees were able to set their own retail prices, though the company recommended prices for all of its products.[28]

Packaging[29]

RMCF developed special packaging for the Christmas, Valentine's Day, and Easter holidays and customers could have their purchases packaged in decorative boxes and fancy tins throughout the year.

In 2002, RMCF completed a project to completely redesign the packaging featured in its retail stores. The new packaging was designed to be more contemporary and capture and convey the freshness, fun, and excitement of the RMCF retail store experience. Sleek, new copper gift boxes were designed to reinforce the association with copper cooking kettles. And the new logo was meant to represent swirling chocolate.[30] This new line of packaging won three National Paperbox Association Gold Awards in 2002, representing the association's highest honors.[31]

Marketing[32]

RMCF sought low-cost, high-return publicity opportunities through participation in local and regional events, sponsorships, and charitable causes. The company had not historically and did not intend to engage in national advertising. RMCF focused primarily on local in-store marketing and promotional efforts by providing customizable marketing materials, including advertisements, coupons, flyers, and mail-order catalogs generated by its in-house Creative Services Department, and point-of-purchase materials. The Creative Services Department worked directly with franchisees to implement local store marketing programs. To cover its corporate marketing expenses, each franchised store paid a monthly marketing and promotions fee of 1 percent of its monthly gross sales.[33]

The trade name Rocky Mountain Chocolate Factory®, the phrases, The Peak of Perfection in Handmade Chocolates, America's Chocolatier®, The World's Chocolatier®, as well as other trademarks, service marks, symbols, slogans, emblems, logos, and designs used in the Rocky Mountain Chocolate factory system, were proprietary rights of the company. The registration for the trademark "Rocky Mountain Chocolate Factory" had been granted in the United States and Canada. Applications had been filed to register the Rocky Mountain Chocolate Factory trademark in certain foreign countries.[34] The company had not attempted to obtain patent protection for the proprietary recipes developed by the company's Master Candy Maker and was relying upon its ability to maintain confidentiality of those recipes.[35]

Operations and Distribution[36]

Manufacturing

RMCF sought to ensure the freshness of products sold in its stores with frequent shipments to distribution outlets from its 53,000-square-foot manufacturing facility in Durango, Colorado. Franchisees were encouraged to order from the company only the quantities they could reasonably expect to sell within two to four weeks because most stores did not have storage space for extra inventory.

RMCF believed that it should control the manufacturing of its own products in order to better maintain its high product quality standards, offer unique proprietary products, manage costs, control production and shipment schedules, and pursue new or underutilized distribution channels. The company believed its manufacturing expertise and reputation for quality had facilitated the sale of selected products through new distribution channels, including wholesaling, fundraising, corporate sales, mail order, and Internet sales.[37]

RMCF's manufacturing process primarily involved cooking or preparing candy centers, including nuts, caramel, peanut butter, creams and jellies, and then coating them with chocolate or other toppings. All of these processes were conducted in carefully controlled temperature ranges, employing strict quality control procedures at every stage of the manufacturing process. RMCF used a combination of manual and automated processes at its factory. Although RMCF believed that it was preferable to perform certain manufacturing processes, such as dipping some large pieces by hand, automation increased the speed and efficiency of the manufacturing process. The company had from time to time automated processes formerly performed by hand where it had become cost-effective to do so without compromising product quality or appearance. Efforts in the last several years had included the purchase of additional automated factory equipment, implementation of a comprehensive advanced planning and scheduling system, and installation of enhanced point-of-sales systems in all of its company-owned and 182 of its franchised stores through March 31, 2008. These measures had improved the company's ability to deliver its products to the stores safely, quickly, and cost effectively.

Chocolate manufacturing had been a similar process for all companies within the confectionary/chocolate industry up until 2005. In 2005, new chocolate manufacturing technology was introduced. This new manufacturing process, called NETZSCH's ChocoEasy™, enabled chocolate makers of any size to cost-effectively manufacture all varieties of chocolate from scratch. For the first time, smaller chocolate companies were no longer dependant on large chocolate manufacturers and were now free to create their own chocolate recipes and to develop their own proprietary chocolate brands.[38]

During fiscal 2008, the RMCF's manufacturing facility produced approximately 2.84 million pounds of chocolate candies, an increase of 4% from the approximately 2.73 million pounds produced in fiscal 2007. During fiscal 2008 the company conducted a study of factory capacity. As a result of this study, RMCF believed its factory had the capacity to produce approximately 5.3 million pounds per year. In January 1998, the company acquired a two-acre parcel adjacent to its factory to ensure the availability of adequate space to expand the factory as volume demands.[39]

Ingredients[40]

RMCF maintained the taste and quality of its chocolate candies by using only the finest chocolate and other ingredients. The principal ingredients used by RMCF are chocolate, nuts, sugar, corn syrup, cream, and butter. Chocolate was purchased from the Guittard Chocolate company, known for 130 years as providing the finest, most intensely flavored chocolate.[41] The factory received shipments of ingredients daily. To ensure the consistency of its products, ingredients were bought from a limited number of reliable suppliers. The company had one or more alternative sources for all essential ingredients. RMCF also purchased small amounts of finished candy from third parties on a private-label basis for sale in its stores.

Several of the principal ingredients used in RMCF's candies, including chocolate and nuts, were subject to significant price fluctuations. Although cocoa beans, the primary raw material used in the production of chocolate, were grown commercially in Africa, Brazil, and several other countries around the world, cocoa beans were traded in the commodities market, and their supply and price were therefore subject to volatility. RMCF believed its principal chocolate supplier purchased most of its beans at negotiated prices from African growers, often at a premium to commodity prices. RMCF purchased most of its nut meats from domestic suppliers who procured their products from growers around the world. Although the price of chocolate and nut meats had been relatively stable in recent years, the supply and price of nut meats and cocoa beans, and, in turn, chocolate, were affected by many factors, including monetary fluctuations and economic, political, and weather conditions in countries in which both nut meats and cocoa beans were grown.

The Ivory Coast (Cote d'Ivoire) was responsible for producing 40 percent of the world's cocoa beans that are necessary for the manufacturing of chocolate.[42] In late 2006, there was a five-day strike in which laborers refused to enter the factories because of unbearable working conditions. These strikes led to an increase of 20 percent in the price of chocolate for most companies within the industry.[43] Forty-seven percent of the total U.S. imports of cocoa beans came from the Ivory Coast.

RMCF did not engage in commodity futures trading or hedging activities. In order to assure a continuous supply of chocolate and certain nuts, the company entered into purchase contracts of between six to eighteen months for these products. These contracts permitted the company to purchase the specified commodity at a fixed price on an as-needed basis during the term of the contract.

Trucking Operations

Unable to find a suitable shipper, RMCF built its own fleet of brown and bronze semis.[44] In 2008 RMCF operated eight refrigerated trucks and shipped a substantial portion of its products from its factory on its own fleet. The company's trucking operations enabled it to deliver its products to the stores quickly and cost-effectively. In addition, the company back-hauled its own ingredients and supplies, as well as product from third parties to fill available space, on return trips as a basis for increasing trucking program economics.[45] The company's trucking operations are subject to various federal, state, and Canadian provincial regulations.[46]

Human Resources[47]

On February 29, 2008, RMCF employed approximately 190 people. Most employees, with the exception of store, factory, and corporate management, were paid on an hourly basis. RMCF also employed some people on a temporary basis during peak periods of store and factory operations. The company sought to assure that participatory management processes, mutual respect and professionalism, and high performance expectations for the employee existed throughout the organization.

RMCF believed that it provided working conditions, wages, and benefits that compared favorably with those of its competitors. The company's employees were not covered by a collective bargaining agreement. The company considered its employee relations to be good.

Chocolate and Confectionary Industry

While people enjoy chocolate across cultures, there were certain cultures that value chocolate sweets more than others. Per capita consumption of confectionary tended to be the highest in the established markets of Western Europe and North America, although these were also the most mature.[48]

The sale of chocolate and confectionary products was affected by changes in consumer tastes and eating habits, including views regarding the consumption of chocolate. In addition, numerous other factors such as economic conditions, demographic trends, traffic patterns, and weather conditions could influence the sale of confectionary products. Consumer confidence, recessionary and inflationary trends, equity market levels, consumer credit availability, interest rates, consumer disposable income and spending levels, energy prices, job growth, and unemployment rates could impact the volume of customer traffic and level of chocolate and confectionary sales.

According to the National Confectioners Association, the total U.S. candy market approximated $29.1 billion of retail sales in 2007, up from $27.9 in 2005, with chocolate generating sales of approximately $16.3 billion up from $15.7 billion in 2005. Per capita consumption of chocolate in 2006 was approximately 14 pounds per person per year nationally, an increase of 1% when compared to 2005, according to Department of Commerce figures.[49] The average U.S. consumer spent $93.92 on confectionary products in 2006, $52.16 on chocolate.[50] **Exhibit 2** shows 2007 U.S. confectionary market sales.

In 2007 the United States was the strongest market for chocolate. According to a 2004 survey, the U.S. chocolate market was far from being saturated, and considerable opportunities for growth remained, particularly in the gourmet, higher-priced premium segment.[51] Consumers in

EXHIBIT 2
The 2007 U.S. Confectionary Market

	$(in billions)	% change
Retail Sales	$29.1	+3.5%
Manufacturer Shipments	$16.9	+3.0%
Domestic Manufacturer Shipments	$17.5	+2.7%
Imports	$2.2	+4.0%
Exports	$0.9	+13.1%
Profit margin is approximately 35% for the confectionary category.		

SOURCE: *National Confectionary Association 2007 Industry Review on the United States Confectionary Market, January 2008, http://www.ecandy.com/ecandyfiles/2007_Annual_Review_Jan_08.ppt.*

the United States were shifting away from mass-produced chocolates, of the type traditionally manufactured by Hershey Foods and Mars Inc., to more expensive gourmet varieties free from chemicals and preservatives. Hershey and Mars had recognized the trend and had been increasing their interest in premium brands. Some industry observers have predicted that by 2011, premium chocolate will account for 25% of the U.S. market, generating sales of $4.5 billion.[52]

The European chocolate market had also remained lucrative for manufacturers, although there had been some degree of slowdown over the past five years. Average annual per capita chocolate consumption was cited as being about 8 kg in Europe, but this varied considerably country by country.[53] Chocolate was also used for other purposes (baking, snacks, etc.) that differed considerably across ethnic, social, regional, or religious subcultures. **Exhibit 3** shows the leading countries for per capita consumption of chocolate and confectionary.

The leading manufacturers in the European market were Mars, Nestle, Cadbury, Ferrero, and Lindt & Sprungli. These companies saw a bright future in Europe, particularly the markets of the newer members of the EU where consumers had significantly increased their chocolate consumption since 2004. Some manufacturers also believed that Russia was a key market for European growth because its rising affluence had driven a demand for premium chocolate products.[54]

Confectionary manufacturers were also looking to break into new markets such as China and India because of their growing affluence. These markets were dominated by traditional sweets, but there was a growing demand for Western goods, including chocolate, with chocolate consumption increasing at a rate of 25% a year in the Asia-Pacific region and 30% in China.[55] Many large chocolate and confectionary companies had undertaken marketing campaigns in order to lure customers in China, India, and Japan away from traditional sweets to chocolate.[56] **Exhibit 4** shows regional cocoa consumption.

EXHIBIT 3
Per Capita Consumption of Confectionary in Leading Countries in 2002 (in kilograms)

	Chocolate	Sugar	Total
Denmark	8.6	8.0	16.6
Sweden	6.4	9.6	16.0
Ireland	8.8	6.0	14.8
Switzerland	10.7	3.3	14.0
UK	9.3	4.6	13.9
Norway	8.3	4.8	13.1
Germany	7.5	4.9	12.4
Finland	4.8	7.3	12.1
Belgium	8.0	3.5	11.5
Austria	8.2	3.2	11.4

SOURCE: *Leatherheadfood International, The Global Confectionary Market—Trends and Innovations. www.leatherheadfood.com/pdf/confectionary/pdf.*

EXHIBIT 4
Regional Cocoa Consumption

Region	Percentage of global total
Europe	42.8%
Americas	25.9%
Asia and Oceania	17.0%
Africa	14.3%

SOURCE: *Kermani, Faiz, Chocolate Challenges, Report Buyer, 2007, p. 4. www.reportbuyer.com.*

Consumer Tastes and Trends

The growth in the chocolate market was heavily dependent on manufacturers satisfying consumer tastes and being aware of consumer trends in each market in which they operated. In established markets, pressure was coming from consumers for lower-fat healthier snacks and higher quality chocolate. In addition, consumers had been showing an interest in the health-related benefits of chocolate. In emerging markets, chocolate manufacturers have had to compete with traditional confectionary products. In addition, consumers were increasingly becoming concerned with the exploitation of African workers and many were choosing not to do business with "unethical" organizations that were not engaged in fair trade practices.

Gourmet Chocolate and Organic Chocolate

According to industry expert Michelle Moran, "Gourmet chocolate is expected to experience delicious growth over the next four years. Indeed, it is expected to become a nearly $1.8 billion market. According to market analysts and manufacturers, consumers are seeking better-quality chocolate at a variety of market levels. Further evidence of this trend is the recent acquisitions of small artisan chocolatiers by large manufacturing powerhouses."[57] Customers have been increasingly willing to pay higher prices for chocolates they felt were healthier; products made with quality ingredients and free from chemicals and preservatives.

In addition to growth in the gourmet segment of the chocolate industry, organic chocolate sales in the United States grew 65% to $120 million in 2006 according to Massachusetts-based Organic Trade Association, with similar growth forecasted for 2007.[58]

Health Consciousness of Consumers

Throughout history many cultures had believed in the medicinal properties of cocoa. Most historians agree that chocolate was first consumed in Central America and some evidence suggest its use by the Mayan civilization as early 500 BCE.[59] Following the Spanish conquest of Mexico, chocolate found its way to Europe in the 1500s. A number of the original European chocolate manufacturers were apothecaries (early chemists) who wanted to take advantage of the reported medicinal properties of cocoa. Dark chocolate is again being touted and researched for its health benefits. Studies have been reported in medical and scientific journals linking chocolate derived antioxidant flavonols and other compounds with the reduction in the risk of dementia, diabetes, heart-attacks, and strokes. In other studies, dark chocolate has shown health benefits such as decreased blood pressure, lower cholesterol levels, and improved sugar metabolism. Much additional research remains to be done before these health benefits can be confirmed.

According to the National Confectioners Association, dark-chocolate sales were up 50% in 2007.[60] Between 2002 and 2006, Hershey reported an 11.2% increase in the sale of dark chocolate. As a result, Hershey had been concentrating almost half of its business in this area.[61] Mars Inc. was thought to be conducting research trying to substantiate the health benefits of chocolate and had discussed partnerships with pharmaceutical companies to develop products from cocoa-derived compounds.[62] Other manufactures had been experimenting with low-fat, sugar-free products and chocolates fortified with minerals, vitamins, antioxidants, and probiotics.

Ethical and Fair Trade Chocolate

Not only were consumers more health conscious and visibly consuming darker and more premium chocolates products, they were also showing concern for the exploitation of cocoa farmers in Western Africa, particularly the use of child labor and the prices that cocoa farmers were able to charge for their crop.

Many consumers were choosing to support organizations and purchase products from companies that supported both "ethical chocolates" as well as fair trade practices. These companies had reported rising demand for their products as consumer interest in fair trade had grown.[63]

Competitors

The global market for chocolate was highly competitive. With consumer attitudes changing and new markets offering opportunities for growth, chocolate manufacturers faced a number of challenges in keeping ahead of their rivals.

RMCF and its franchisees competed with numerous businesses that offered confectionery products, from large, publically held, global conglomerates to small, private, local businesses. Many of the large competitors had greater name recognition, both domestically and globally, and greater financial, marketing, and other resources than RMCF. In addition, there was intense competition among retailers for prime locations, store personnel, and qualified franchisees.

Large confectionary companies that had traditionally concentrated on mass-produced candies, sought to make inroads into the premium market. For example, in 2005 Hershey Foods acquired two medium-sized gourmet chocolate companies, Scharffen Berger and Joseph Schmidt, for between $46.6 million and $61.1 million.[64] Mars Inc. established its catalog/retail subsidiary, Ethel M Chocolates, in 1981 when billionaire candy maker Forrest Mars developed a chain of chocolate stores in the western U.S., specializing in liquor-filled candies. In 2005 Ethel M's launched an even more premium line of chocolates called ethel's. Ethel's chocolates were available on-line and could be purchased at upscale department stores, including Nieman Marcus, Macy's, and Marshall Fields.[65] Also in 2005, Ethel's Chocolate Lounge was created as a place where sweets lovers could linger on sofas and order hot cocoa and chocolate fondue.

Principal competitors of RMCF included Alpine Confections Inc., Godiva Chocolatier Inc., See's Candies Inc., Chocoladefabriken Lindt & Sprungli AG, Fannie May (a wholly owned subsidiary of Alpine Confections), and Ethel M's/ethel's. These companies not only manufactured chocolate but also had their own retail outlets. **Exhibit 5** shows the number of stores in operation for each of these competitors in 2006.

Godiva Chocolatier, the Belgian chocolate maker, with annual sales of approximately $500 million, was one of the world's leading premium chocolate businesses. Godiva sold its products through company-owned and franchised retail stores, and wholesale distribution outlets, including specialty retailers and finer department stores and on the Internet. In January 2008, Campbell Soup company announced that it agreed to sell its Godiva Chocolatier unit to Yildiz Holdings of Turkey for $850 million. Godiva was to become part of the Ulker Group, which is owned by Yildiz. Ulker is the largest consumer goods company in the Turkish food industry.[66]

Chocoladefabriken Lindt & Sprungli AG and its subsidiaries offered products under multiple brands names, including Lindt, Ghirardelli, Caffarel, Hofbauer, and Kufferle. The company was founded in 1845 and was based in Kilchberg, Switzerland, and had six production sites in Europe, two in the United States, and distribution sites and sales companies on four continents.[67] Lindt & Sprungli was a recognized leader in the market for premium chocolate, and offered a large selection of products in more than 80 countries around the world.[68]

See's Candies, Ethel M's/ethel's, and Alpine Confections Inc. were privately held companies. Alpine Confections Inc. was based in Alpine, Utah, and had sales of approximately $125 million in 2005. Alpine owned a number of candy companies, including Maxfield Candy company, Kencraft Inc., and Harry London Candies Inc. Alpine acquired the Fanny Farmer

EXHIBIT 5
Chocolate Retailers:
Number of Stores in
Operation 2006

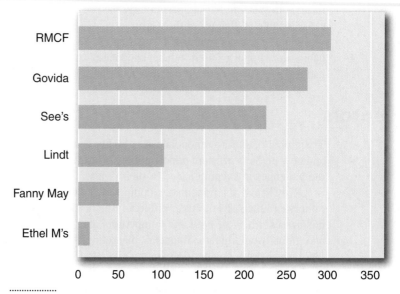

SOURCE: *Prepared by R.J. Falkner & Company Inc. on the company profile report for Rocky Mountain Chocolate Factory, November 15, 2006.*

and Fannie May brands from bankrupt Archibald Candy Corporation in 2004. The company also produced confections under license for Hallmark and Mrs. Fields. Alpine's Canadian brands included Dolce d'Or and Bottecelli, produced in British Columbia.[69]

See's Candies was founded in 1921 and headquartered in San Francisco, and had manufacturing facilities in both Los Angeles and San Francisco. See's Candies was purchased by Berkshire Hathaway Inc. (Warren Buffett) in 1972. The company manufactured over 100 varieties of candies and had over 200 retail candy shops throughout the western United States.[70]

A relatively new competitor founded in Oregon in 1993, acquired by Wayne Zink and Randy Deer in 2005, and moved to Indianapolis, Indiana, was the Endangered Species Chocolate Company. The company was the number-one seller of organic chocolate treats, with annual sales of $16 million in 2007. Its products were stocked at natural-foods stores such as Wild Oats and Whole Foods. Endangered Species Chocolate Co. was committed to making organic and healthy products that were easy on the environment, made with fair-traded ingredients, and with sustainable practices. One of Endangered Species main rivals, Oregon-based Dagoba Chocolate, sold out to Hershey in 2007.[71]

Financial Position[72]

In 2007 RMCF was ranked number 60 in Forbes annual listing of America's 200 Best Small Companies (up from number 124 in 2006). The list was compiled from publically traded companies with sales between $5 million and $750 million. Qualifying candidates were ranked according to return on equity, as well as sustained sales and earnings growth over 12-month and five-year periods.[73] **Exhibits 6 and 7** show the income statements and balance sheets for RMCF for the fiscal years ended 2004 through 2008.

RMCF's revenues were derived from three principal sources: 1) sales to franchisees and others of chocolates and other confectionery products manufactured by the company (75-72-69-68%); 2) sales at company-owned stores of chocolates and other confectionery products including product manufactured by the company (5-8-11-11%); and 3) the collection of initial franchise fees and royalties from franchisees (20-20-20-21%). The figures

EXHIBIT 6
Balance Sheets: Rocky Mountain Chocolate Factory Inc.

Year ending February 28/29	2008	2007	2006	2005	2004
Assets					
Current Assets					
Cash & cash equivalents	$675,642	$2,830,175	$3,489,750	$4,438,876	$4,552,283
Accounts receivable, less allowance for doubtful accounts of $114,271, $187,519, $46,929, $80,641, and $73,630 respectively	3,801,172	3,756,212	3,296,690	2,943,835	2,388,848
Notes receivable	22,435	50,600	116,997	451,845	313,200
Refundable income taxes	63,357			364,630	
Inventories, less reserve for slow moving inventory of $194,719, $147,700, $61,032, $127,345, and $73,269 respectively	4,015,459	3,482,139	2,938,234	2,518,212	2,471,810
Deferred income taxes	117,846	272,871	117,715	156,623	149,304
Other current assets	267,184	367,420	481,091	250,886	353,733
Total current assets	8,963,095	10,759,417	10,440,477	11,124,907	10,229,178
Property and Equipment, Net	5,665,108	5,754,122	6,698,605	6,125,898	5,456,695
Other Assets					
Notes receivable, gross	205,916	310,453	330,746	452,089	649,100
Less: Allowance		0	−52,005	−52,005	−47,005
Notes receivable, net		310,453	278,741	400,084	602,095
Goodwill, net	939,074	939,074	1,133,751	1,133,751	1,133,751
Intangible assets, net	276,247	349,358	402,469	426,827	498,885
Other assets	98,020	343,745	103,438	36,424	16,614
Total other assets	1,519,257	1,942,630	1,918,399	1,997,086	2,281,372
Total Assets	16,147,460	18,456,169	19,057,480	19,247,974	17,967,245
Liabilities and Stockholders' Equity					
Current Liabilities					
Line of Credit	300,000				
Current maturities of long-term debt	-	-		126,000	1,080,400
Accounts payable	1,710,380	898,794	1,145,410	1,088,476	952,542
Accrued salaries & wages	430,498	931,614	507,480	1,160,937	1,091,596
Other accrued expenses	467,543	585,402	750,733	324,215	474,906
Dividends payable	599,473	551,733	504,150	417,090	236,108
Deferred income	303,000	288,500	-	-	-
Total current liabilities	3,810,894	3,256,043	2,907,773	3,116,718	3,835,552
Long-term debt, less current maturities of $126,000 and $1,080,400 respectively				1,539,084	1,986,174
Deferred Income Taxes	681,529	685,613	663,889	698,602	555,567
Stockholders' Equity					
Common stock, $.03 par value; 100,000,000 shares authorized; 100,000,000, 5,980,919, 6,418,905, 4,602,135 and 4,486,461 shares issued and outstanding, respectively	179,428	192,567	188,458	138,064	134, 597
Additional paid-in capital	7,047,142	6,987,558	10,372,530	11,097,208	2,676,222
Retained earnings (accumulated deficit)	4,428,467	7,334,388	4,924,830	2,658,298	8,779,136
Total stockholders' equity	11,655,037	14,514,513	15,485,818	13,893,570	11,589,952
Total liabilities and stockholders' equity	$16,147,460	$18,456,169	$19,057,481	$19,247,891	$17,967,245

SOURCE: *Rocky Mountain Chocolate Factory Inc., 2008 form 10-K, p. 30 and 2005 Form 10-K, p. 30.*

EXHIBIT 7

Statements of Income: Rocky Mountain Chocolate Factory Inc.

Year Ending February 28/29	2008	2007	2006	2005	2004
Revenues					
Sales	$25,558,198	$253,357,39	$22,343,209	$19,380,861	$16,668,210
Franchise & royalty fees	6,319,985	6,237,594	5,730,403	5,142,758	4,464,618
Total revenues	31,878,183	31,573,333	28,073,612	24,523,619	21,132,828
Costs and Expenses					
Cost of sales, exclusive of depreciation and amortization expense of $389,273, $412,546, $381,141, and $359,633, respectively	16,678,472	15,988,620	13,956,550	11,741,205	10,535,352
Franchise costs	1,498,709	1,570,026	1,466,322	1,411,901	1,135,686
Sales & marketing expenses	1,503,224	1,538,476	1,320,979	1,294,702	1,220,585
General & administrative expenses	2,505,676	2,538,667	2,239,109	2,497,718	2,235,499
Retail operating expenses	994,789	1,502,134	1,755,738	1,453,740	1,430,124
Depreciation & amortization	782,951	873,988	875,940	785,083	796,271
Total costs & expenses	23,963,821	24,011,911	21,614,638	19,184,349	17,353,517
Operating Income (loss)	7,914,362	7,561,422	6,458,974	5,339,270	3,779,311
Other Income (Expense)					
Interest expense	(1,566)		(19,652)	(99,988)	(144,787)
Interest income	102,360	67,071	95,360	92,938	93,847
Total other income (expense), net	100,794	67,071	75,708	(7,050)	(50,940)
Income before Income Taxes	8,015,156	7,628,493	6,534,682	5,332,220	3,728,371
Income Tax Expense	3,053,780	2,883,575	2,470,110	2,015,580	1,409,325
Net Income	4,961,376	4,744,918	4,064,572	3,316,640	2,319,046
Basic Earnings per Common Share	0.78	0.74	0.62	0.53	0.38
Diluted Earnings per Common Share	0.76	0.71	0.58	0.49	0.35
Weighted average common shares outstanding	6,341,286	6,432,123	6,581,612	6,307,227	6,146,764
Dilutive effect of employee stock options	159,386	227,350	427,780	498,223	472,205
Weighted average shares outstanding-diluted	6,500,672	6,659,473	7,009,392	6,805,450	6,618,969
Year end shares outstanding	5,980,919	6,418,905	6,596,016	6,442,989	6,281,045
Total number of employees	190	200	235	185	159
Number common of stockholders	400	400	409	420	420
Number of beneficiary stockholders	800	800	800	800	800
Total number of stockholders	1,200	1,200	1,209	1,220	1,220

SOURCE: *Rocky Mountain Chocolate Factory Inc., 2008 Form 10-K, p. 31 and 2005 Form 10-K, p. 29.*

in parentheses show the percentage of total revenues attributable to each source for fiscal years ended February 28 (29), 2008, 2007, 2006, and 2005, respectively.[74]

Basic earnings per share increased 18.5% from fiscal 2006 to fiscal 2007 and from $0.74 in fiscal 2007 to $0.78 in fiscal 2008, an increase of 5.4%. Revenues increased 12.5% from fiscal 2006 to fiscal 2007, and 1% from 2007 to fiscal 2008. Operating income increased 17.1% from fiscal 2006 to fiscal 2007, and 4.7% (from $7.6 million in fiscal 2007 to $7.9 million) in fiscal 2008. Net income increased 16.7% from fiscal 2006 to fiscal 2007, and 4.6% from $4.7 million in fiscal 2007 to $5.0 million in fiscal 2008. The increase in revenue, earnings per share, operating income, and net income in fiscal 2008 compared to fiscal 2007 and 2006 was due primarily to the increased number of franchised stores in operation, the

EXHIBIT 8
Rocky Mountain
Chocolate Factory
Sources of Revenue
2005–2008
(Revenues in
thousands of
dollars)

	2008	2007	2006	2005
Factory Sales	$23,758.2	$22,709.0	$19,297.2	$16,654.4
Retail Sales	1,800.0	2,626.7	3,046.0	2,726.4
Royalty and Marketing Fees	5,696.0	5,603.8	5,047.9	4,577.5
Franchise Fees	623.1	633.8	682.5	565.3
Total	$31,877.3	$31,573.3	$28,073.6	$24,523.6

SOURCE: *Rocky Mountain Chocolate Factory, Inc. 2007 Form 10-K, p. 23 and 2006 Form 10-K, p. 20 and 23.*

increased sales to specialty markets, and the corresponding increases in revenue.[75] Details can be found in **Exhibit 8**.

Factory sales increased in fiscal 2008 compared to fiscal 2007 due to an increase of 28.8% in product shipments to specialty markets and growth in the average number of stores in operation to 324 in fiscal 2008 from 310 in fiscal 2007. Same-store pounds purchased in fiscal 2008 were down 9% from fiscal 2007, more than offsetting the increase in the average number of franchised stores in operation and mostly offsetting the increase in specialty market sales. RMCF believed the decrease in same-store pounds purchased in fiscal 2008 was due primarily to a product mix shift from factory products to products made in the stores and also the softening in the retail sector of the economy.[76]

The decrease in retail sales resulted primarily from a decrease in the average number of company-owned stores in operation from 8 in fiscal 2007 to 5 in fiscal 2008. Same-store sales at company-owned stores increased 1.1% from fiscal 2007 to fiscal 2008 and 6.9% from fiscal 2006 to fiscal 2007.[77]

Under the domestic franchise agreement, franchisees paid the company 1) an initial franchise fee; 2) a marketing and promotion fee equal to 1% of the monthly gross retail sales of the franchised store; and 3) a royalty fee based on gross retail sales. RMCF modified its royalty fee structure for any new franchised stores opening the third quarter of fiscal 2004 and later. Under the new structure no royalty was charged on franchised stores' retail sales of products purchased from the company and a 10% royalty was charged on all other sales of product sold at franchised locations. For franchise stores opened prior to the third quarter of fiscal 2004, a 5% royalty fee was charged on franchise stores gross retail sales. Franchise fee revenue was recognized upon opening of the franchise store.[78]

The increase in royalties and marketing fees resulted from growth in the average number of domestic units in operation from 266 in fiscal 2007 to 281 in fiscal 2008 partially offset by a decrease in same store sales of 0.09%. Franchise fee revenues decreased during the past two fiscal years due to a decrease in the number of franchises sold during the same period the previous year.[79]

Cost of sales increased from fiscal 2007 to 2008 due primarily to increased costs and mix of products sold. Company-store margin declined during the same period due primarily to a change in mix of products sold associated with a decrease in the average number of company stores in operation.[80]

As a percentage of total royalty and marketing fee revenue, franchised costs decreased to 23.7% in fiscal 2008, 25.2% in fiscal 2007, and 25.6% in fiscal 2006 due to lower incentive compensation costs. During this same period, sales and marketing costs and general and administrative costs also decreased due primarily to lower incentive compensation costs.[81]

In fiscal 2008 retail operating expenses decreased due primarily to a decrease in the average number of company-owned stores during fiscal 2008 versus fiscal 2007. Retail operating expenses, as a percentage of retail sales, decreased from 57.6% in fiscal 2006, to 57.2% in fiscal 2007, to 55.3% in fiscal 2008 due to a larger decrease in costs relative to the decrease in revenues associated with a decrease in the average number of company stores in operation during each fiscal year.[82]

Depreciation and amortization of $783,000 in fiscal 2008 decreased 10.4% from the $874,000 incurred in fiscal 2007 due to the sale or closure of four company-owned stores and certain assets becoming fully depreciated. Depreciation and amortization of $874,000 in fiscal 2007 was essentially unchanged from the $876,000 incurred in fiscal 2006.[83]

Other, net of $101,000 realized in fiscal 2008 represented an increase of $34,000 from the $67,000 realized in fiscal 2007, due primarily to higher average outstanding balances of invested cash during fiscal 2008. Notes receivable balances and related interest income declined in fiscal 2008 because of two notes maturing or being paid in full compared with fiscal 2007. RMCF also incurred interest expense in fiscal 2008 related to use of an operating line of credit. Other, net of $67,000 realized in fiscal 2007, represented a decrease of $9,000 from the $76,000 realized in fiscal 2006, due primarily to lower interest income on lower average outstanding balances of notes receivable and invested cash. RMCF paid its long-term debt in full during the first quarter of fiscal 2006.[84]

RMCF's effective income tax rate in fiscal 2008 was 38.1%, which was an increase of 0.3% compared to fiscal 2007. The increase in the effective tax rate was primarily due to increased income in states with higher income tax rates.[85]

In early 2008 RMCF repurchased 391,600 shares of its common stock at an average price of $11.94 because the company believed the stock was undervalued.[86] During the past eight years, the company had repurchased approximately 3,909,000 shares of its common stock (adjusted for stock splits and stock dividends), at an average price of $5.09 per share.[87] As of April 30, 2008, there were 5,980,919 shares of common stock outstanding.[88]

As of February 29, 2008, working capital was $5.2 million compared with $7.5 million as of February 28, 2007. The change in working capital was due primarily to operating results less the payment of $2.4 million in cash dividends and the repurchase and retirement of $5.9 million of the company's common stock.[89]

Cash and cash equivalent balances decreased from $2.8 million as of February 28, 2007, to $676,000 as of February 29, 2008, as a result of cash flows generated by operating and investing activities being less than cash flows used in financing activities. RMCF had a $5.0 million line of credit, of which $4.7 million was available as of February 29, 2008, that bears interest at a variable rate. For fiscal 2009, the company anticipated making capital expenditures of approximately $500,000, which would be used to maintain and improve existing factory and administrative infrastructure and update certain company-owned stores. The company believed that cash flow from operations would be sufficient to fund capital expenditures and working capital requirements for fiscal 2009. If necessary, the company had available bank lines of credit to help meet these requirements.[90]

RMCF revenues and profitability were subject to seasonal fluctuations in sales because of the location of its franchisees, which had traditionally been located in resort or tourist locations. As the company had expanded its geographical diversity to include regional centers, it had seen some moderation to its seasonal sales mix. Historically the strongest sales of the company's products had occurred during the Christmas holiday and summer vacation seasons. Additionally, quarterly results had been, and in the future are likely to be, affected by the timing of new store openings and sales of franchises.[91]

The most important factors in continued growth in the RMCF's earnings were ongoing unit growth, increased same-store sales and increased same-store pounds purchased from the factory. Historically, unit growth more than offset decreases in same-store sales and same-store pounds purchased.[92] RMCF's ability to successfully achieve expansion of its franchise system depended on many factors not within the company's control, including the availability of suitable sites for new store establishment and the availability of qualified franchises to support such expansion.[93]

EXHIBIT 9
Changes in
Systemwide
Domestic
Same-Store Sales

2003	(3.4%)
2004	(0.6%)
2005	4.8%
2006	2.4%
2007	0.3%
2008	(0.9%)

SOURCE: *Rocky Mountain Chocolate Factory, 2008 Form 10-K, p. 4, and 2007 Form 10-K, p. 4.*

For the fiscal year ended February 29, 2008, same-store pounds purchased from the factory by franchised stores decreased 9.1% from the previous fiscal year.[94] Fiscal 2007 showed a similar trend with same-store pounds purchased by franchisees decreasing 2.6% from fiscal 2006.[95] RMCF believed the decrease in same-store pounds purchased was due to a product mix shift from factory-made products to products made in the store, such as caramel apples and fudge.[96] Company efforts to reverse the decline in same-store pounds purchased from the factory by franchised stores and to increase total factory sales depended on many factors, including new store openings, competition, and the receptivity of the company's franchise system to new product introductions and promotional programs.

In addition to efforts to increase the purchases by franchisees of company manufactured products, RMCF was also sought to increase profitability of its store system through increasing overall sales at existing store locations. Changes in systemwide domestic same-store sales can be found in **Exhibit 9**. The company believed that the negative trend in fiscal 2008 was due to the overall weakening of the economy and retail environment.[97]

According to Bryan Merryman, COO and CFO, "Sales at most RMCF stores are greatly influenced by the levels of 'foot traffic' in regional shopping malls and other retail environments where the stores are located, and widely reported declines in such traffic resulted in lower revenues and earnings in the fourth quarter of our 2008 fiscal year. In light of the significant uncertainties surrounding the U.S. economy and retail trends in coming months, combined with decreasing same-store pounds purchased by franchisees, we do not feel comfortable providing specific earnings guidance for fiscal 2009 at the present time. If recent economic and consumer trends continue but do not deteriorate further, we are likely to report a modest decline in earnings for the (2009) fiscal year. Fortunately, we believe we are in excellent financial position and well able to withstand the recessionary forces currently buffeting the U.S. economy."[98]

NOTES

1. Rocky Mtn. Chocolate Profiles in Success, January 28, 2008, p. 1, www.boj.com/success/Rocky/Rocky/htm, Rocky Mountain Chocolate Factory Inc., 2008 Form 10-K, p. 3, and Rocky Mountain Chocolate Factory, Inc., www.referenceforbusiness.com//history/Qu-Ro/Rocky–Mountain-Chocolate-Factory, January 28, 2008, pp. 1–6. These sections were directly quoted with minor editing.

2. Rocky Mtn. Chocolate Profiles in Success, January 28, 2008, p. 1, www.boj.com/success/Rocky/Rocky/htm.

3. Rocky Mountain Chocolate Factory, Inc., www.referenceforbusiness.com//history/Qu-Ro/Rocky–Mountain-Chocolate-Factory, January 28, 2008, p. 2.

4. Rocky Mtn. Chocolate Profiles in Success, January 28, 2008, p. 1, www.boj.com/success/Rocky/Rocky/htm.

5. Rocky Mountain Chocolate Factory, Inc., 2008 Form 10-K, p. 3.

6. Ibid., p. 30.

7. Rocky Mtn. Chocolate Profiles in Success, January 28, 2008, p. 1, www.boj.com/success/Rocky/Rocky/htm.

8. Ibid.

9. Rocky Mountain Chocolate Factory, Inc., 2008 Form 10-K, p. 10. This section was directly quoted with minor editing.

10. Rocky Mtn. Chocolate Profiles in Success, January 28, 2008, p. 2, www.boj.com/success/Rocky/Rocky/htm. This section was directly quoted with minor editing.

11. Rocky Mountain Chocolate Factory, Inc., Proxy Statement, August 17, 2007, pp. 3–4, and Rocky Mountain Chocolate Factory, Inc., 2008 Form 10-K, pp. 11–12. These sections were directly quoted with minor editing.

12. Rocky Mountain Chocolate Factory, Inc., Proxy Statement, August 17, 2007, p. 11. This section was directly quoted with minor editing.

13. Ibid., p. 20. This section was directly quoted with minor editing.

14. Ibid., p. 1. This section was directly quoted with minor editing.

15. Rocky Mountain Chocolate Factory, Inc., 2008 Form 10-K, pp. 4–9 and 2007 Form 10-K, pp. 5–7. These sections were directly quoted with minor editing.

16. Rocky Mtn. Chocolate Profiles in Success, January 28, 2008, www.boj.com/success/Rocky/Rocky/htm, p.1. This section was directly quoted with minor editing.

17. Rocky Mountain Chocolate Factory, Inc., 2008 Form 10-K, pp. 7–8 and Rocky Mountain Chocolate Factory, Inc., Press Release, August 1, 2007, p. 1. These sections were directly quoted with minor editing.

18. Rocky Mtn. Chocolate Profiles in Success, January 28, 2008, www.boj.com/success/Rocky/Rocky/htm, p. 1.

19. Rocky Mountain Chocolate Factory, Inc., 2008 Form 10-K, p. 5. This section was directly quoted with minor editing.

20. Rocky Mountain Chocolate Factory, Inc., 2008 Form 10-K, p.13. This section was directly quoted with minor editing.

21. Rocky Mountain Chocolate Factory, Inc., 2008 Form 10-K, p. 6. This section was directly quoted with minor editing.

22. Rocky Mtn. Chocolate Profiles in Success, January 28, 2008, www.boj.com/success/Rocky/Rocky/htm, p. 2.

23. Rocky Mtn. Chocolate Profiles in Success, January 28, 2008, www.boj.com/success/Rocky/Rocky/htm, p. 2.

24. Ibid., p. 1. This section was directly quoted with minor editing.

25. Rocky Mountain Chocolate Factory, Inc., www.referenceforbusiness.com//history/Qu-Ro/Rocky–Mountain-Chocolate-Factory, January 28, 2008, p.3. This section was directly quoted with minor editing.

26. Rocky Mountain Chocolate Factory, Inc., 2008 Form 10-K, p. 9. This section was directly quoted with minor editing.

27. Ibid., p. 14. This section was directly quoted with minor editing.

28. Ibid., p. 6. This section was directly quoted with minor editing.

29. Ibid., pp. 4, 6. This section was directly quoted with minor editing.

30. Rocky Mountain Chocolate Factory, Inc., www.referenceforbusiness.com//history/Qu-Ro/Rocky–Mountain-Chocolate-Factory, January 28, 2008, p. 1. This section was directly quoted with minor editing.

31. Confectionary News.com, Rocky Mountain Chocolate Wins Packaging Award, May 31, 2002, http://www.confectionarynews.com/news/ng.asp?id=14118-rocky-mountain-chocolate.

32. Rocky Mountain Chocolate Factory, Inc., 2008 Form 10-K, p. 10. This section was directly quoted with minor editing.

33. RJFaulkner & Company, Inc.-Company Profile, Research Report, Rocky Mountain Chocolate Factory, Nov/Dec 2006, p. 5, www.rjfalkner.com/page.cfm?pageid=2140.

34. Rocky Mountain Chocolate Factory, Inc., 2008 Form 10-K, p. 10. This section was directly quoted with minor editing.

35. Ibid.

36. Ibid., pp. 9–10. This section was directly quoted with minor editing.

37. Ibid., p. 3. This section was directly quoted with minor editing.

38. NETZSCH'S ChocoEasy™, "New Chocolate Manufacturing Technology Offers Chocolatiers Independence, More Efficient Production," Press release, November 17, 2005, http://www.foodprocessingtechnology.com/contractors/processing/netzsch/press2.html.

39. Rocky Mountain Chocolate Factory, Inc., 2008 Form 10-K, p. 15. This section was directly quoted with minor editing.

40. Ibid., pp. 9, 10, 13, 27, 38. These sections were directly quoted with minor editing.

41. Rocky Mountain Chocolate Factory Corporate Site, Product Selection, p. 1, www.rmcf.com/CO/Denver50122/products.asp?.

42. Chanthavon, Samlanchith, "Chocolate and Slavery: Child Labor in Cote d'Ivoire," *TED Case Studies,* January 2001, http://www.american.edu/ted/chocolate-slave.htm.

43. Bax, Pauline. "Chocolate Industry Watching Cocoa Strike," *The Seattle Times.* October 7, 2006, http://seattletimes.nwsource.com/html/businesstechnology/2003308331_cocoa17.html.

44. Rocky Mountain Chocolate Factory, Inc., www.referenceforbusiness.com//history/Qu-Ro/Rocky–Mountain-Chocolate-Factory, January 28, 2008, p. 1. This section was directly quoted with minor editing.

45. Rocky Mountain Chocolate Factory, Inc., 2008 Form 10-K, p. 10. This section was directly quoted with minor editing.

46. Ibid., p. 12. This section was directly quoted with minor editing.

47. Ibid., p. 11. This section was directly quoted with minor editing.

48. Leatherhead Food International, The Global Confectionary Market-Trends and Innovations, www.leatherheadfood.com/pdf/confectionary/pdf.

49. Rocky Mountain Chocolate Factory, Inc., 2008 Form 10-K, p. 3. This section was directly quoted with minor editing.

50. National Confectioners Association, United States Confectionary Market, January 2008, Slide 5, http://www.ecandy.com/ecandyfiles/2007_Annual_Review_Jan_08.ppt.

51. Kermani, Faiz, "Chocolate Challenges," *Report Buyer*, 2007, p. 3, www.reportbuyer.com. This section was directly quoted with minor editing.

52. Ibid.

53. Ibid.

54. Ibid., pp. 3–4.

55. Ibid., pp. 5–6.

56. Ibid., p. 1.

57. Moran, Michelle, "Category Analysis: Chocolate: Quality Satisfies American Sweet Tooth," *Gourmet Retailer Magazine*, June 1, 2006, http://www.gourmettretiiler.com/gourmetretailer/search/article_display.jsp?vnu_content_id=1002650555.

58. Schoettle, Anthony, "Local Chocolate Firm Leads Organic Pack," *Indianapolis Business Journal*, December 17, 2007, Vol. 28, Issue 42, p. 19.

59. Kermani, Faiz, "Chocolate Challenges," *Report Buyer*, 2007, p. 2, www.reportbuyer.com.

60. National Confectioners Association, United States Confectionary Market, January 2008., Slide 26, http://www.ecandy.com/ecandyfiles/2007_Annual_Review_Jan_08.ppt.

61. Kermani, Faiz, "Chocolate Challenges, *Report Buyer*," 2007, p. 7, www.reportbuyer.com.

62. Ibid., p. 7.

63. Ibid., p. 11.

64. Ibid., p. 3.

65. Young, Lauren, "Candy's Getting Dandier," *Business Week*, February 13, 2006, Issue 3971, p. 88, and Fuller, Allisa C., "Ethel M Ready to Rule Chocolate Kingdom," *Las Vegas Business Press*, October 1986, Vol. 3, Issue 10, Section 1, p. 56.

66. Sorkin, Andrew Ross (ed.), "Campbell Soup Sells Godiva for $850 million," DealBook, *New York Times* Business, January 14, 2008, p. 1, http://dealbook.blogs.nytimes.com/2007/12/20/campbell-soup-sells-godiva-fpr-850-million/.

67. *Business Week*, Chocoladefabriken Lindt & Sprengli Ag, 2007, http://investing.businessweek.com/research/stocks/snapshot.asp?capID=876088.

68. Lindt Company Website, About Lindt, July 3, 2008, http://investors.lindt.com/cgi-bin/show.ssp?id=5101&companyName=lindt&language=Engl.

69. Alpine Confections, Inc. Company History, http://www.fundinguniverse.com/company-histories/AlpineConfections-Inc-Company-Hist

70. See's Candies Website, July 3, 2008, http://www.sees.com/history.cfm and http://www.sees.com/about.cfm.

71. Schoettle, Anthony, "Local Chocolate Firm Leads Organic Pack," *Indianapolis Business Journal*, December 17, 2007, Vol. 28, Issue 42, p. 19.

72. Rocky Mountain Chocolate Factory, Inc., 2008 Form 10-K. pp. 15–37 also 2007 and 2005 Form 10-K. This section was directly quoted with minor editing.

73. Rocky Mountain Chocolate Factory Press Release, October 24, 2007. This section was directly quoted with minor editing.

74. Rocky Mountain Chocolate Factory, Inc., 2008 Form 10-K, p. 3 and 2007 form 10-K, p. 3. These sections were directly quoted with minor editing.

75. Ibid., p. 20. These sections were directly quoted with minor editing.

76. Rocky Mountain Chocolate Factory, Inc., 2008 Form 10-K, p. 21. This section was directly quoted with minor editing.

77. Ibid. This section was directly quoted with minor editing

78. Ibid., p. 35. This section was directly quoted with minor editing.

79. Ibid., p. 21. This section was directly quoted with minor editing.

80. Ibid., p. 22.

81. Ibid., p. 22.

82. Ibid., p. 22.

83. Ibid., p. 22.

84. Ibid., p. 22.

85. Ibid., p. 22.

86. Ibid., p. 22. This section was directly quoted with minor editing.

87. Rocky Mountain Chocolate Factory. Inc. Board Authorizes New Stock Repurchase Program, PR Newswire, February 19, 2008, p. 1, www.mergentonline.com/compdetail.asp?company.

88. Rocky Mountain Chocolate Factory, Inc., 2008 Form 10-K, p. 1. This section was directly quoted with minor editing.

89. Ibid., p. 24. This section was directly quoted with minor editing.

90. Ibid., p. 24. This section was directly quoted with minor editing.

91. Rocky Mountain Chocolate Factory, Inc., 2008 Form 10-K, p. 25. This section was directly quoted with minor editing.

92. Ibid., pp. 18–19. This section was directly quoted with minor editing.

93. Ibid., p. 19. This section was directly quoted with minor editing.

94. Ibid., p. 19. This section was directly quoted with minor editing.

95. Rocky Mountain Chocolate Factory, Inc., 2007 Form 10-K, p. 19. This section was directly quoted with minor editing.

96. Rocky Mountain Chocolate Factory, Inc., 2008 Form 10-K, p. 4. This section was directly quoted with minor editing.

97. Ibid.

98. Rocky Mountain Chocolate Factory Reports Record FY2008 Revenues and Earnings, Press Release, May 8, 2008, pp. 1–2. This section was directly quoted with minor editing.

CASE 23

Inner-City Paint Corporation (Revised)

Donald F. Kuratko and Norman J. Gierlasinski

History

STANLEY WALSH BEGAN INNER-CITY PAINT CORPORATION IN A RUN-DOWN WAREHOUSE, which he rented, on the fringe of Chicago's "downtown" business area. The company is still located at its original site.

Inner-City is a small company that manufactures wall paint. It does not compete with giants such as Glidden and DuPont. There are small paint manufacturers in Chicago that supply the immediate area. The proliferation of paint manufacturers is due to the fact that the weight of the product (52½ pounds per 5-gallon container) makes the cost of shipping great distances prohibitive. Inner-City's chief product is flat white wall paint sold in 5-gallon plastic cans. It also produces colors on request in 55-gallon containers.

The primary market of Inner-City is the small- to medium-sized decorating company. Pricing must be competitive; until recently, Inner-City had shown steady growth in this market. The slowdown in the housing market combined with a slowdown in the overall economy caused financial difficulty for Inner-City Paint Corporation. Inner-City's reputation had been built on fast service: it frequently supplied paint to contractors within 24 hours. Speedy delivery to customers became difficult when Inner-City was required to pay cash on delivery (C.O.D.) for its raw materials.

Inner-City had been operating without management controls or financial controls. It had grown from a very small two-person company with sales of $60,000 annually five years ago, to sales of $1,800,000 and 38 employees this year. Stanley Walsh realized that tighter controls within his organization would be necessary if the company was to survive.

Equipment

Five mixers are used in the manufacturing process. Three large mixers can produce a maximum of 400 gallons, per batch, per mixer. The two smaller mixers can produce a maximum of 100 gallons, per batch, per mixer.

Two lift trucks are used for moving raw materials. The materials are packed in 100-pound bags. The lift trucks also move finished goods, which are stacked on pallets.

A small testing lab ensures the quality of materials received and the consistent quality of their finished product. The equipment in the lab is sufficient to handle the current volume of product manufactured.

Transportation equipment consists of two 24-foot delivery trucks and two vans. This small fleet is more than sufficient because many customers pick up their orders to save delivery costs.

Facilities

Inner-City performs all operations from one building consisting of 16,400 square feet. The majority of the space is devoted to manufacturing and storage; only 850 square feet is assigned as office space. The building is 45 years old and in disrepair. It is being leased in three-year increments. The current monthly rent on this lease is $2,700. The rent is low in consideration of the poor condition of the building and its undesirable location in a run-down neighborhood (south side of Chicago). These conditions are suitable to Inner-City because of the dusty, dirty nature of the manufacturing process and the small contribution of the rent to overhead costs.

Product

Flat white paint is made with pigment (titanium dioxide and silicates), vehicle (resin), and water. The water makes up 72% of the contents of the product. To produce a color, the necessary pigment is added to the flat white paint. The pigment used to produce the color has been previously tested in the lab to ensure consistent quality of texture. Essentially, the process is the mixing of powders with water, then tapping off of the result into 5- or 55-gallon containers. Color overruns are tapped off into 2-gallon containers.

Inventory records are not kept. The warehouse manager keeps a mental count of what is in stock. He documents (on a lined yellow pad) what has been shipped for the day and to whom. That list is given to the billing clerk at the end of each day.

The cost of the materials to produce flat white paint is $2.40 per gallon. The cost per gallon for colors is approximately 40% to 50% higher. The 5-gallon covered plastic pails cost Inner-City $1.72 each. The 55-gallon drums (with lids) are $8.35 each (see **Exhibit 1**).

	5 Gallons	55 Gallons
Sales price	$27.45	$182.75
Direct material	(12.00)	(132.00)
Pail and lid	(1.72)	(8.35)
Direct labor	(2.50)	(13.75)
Manufacturing overhead ($1/gallon)	(5.00)	(5.00)
Gross margin	$6.23	$23.65
Gross profit ratio	22.7%	12.9%

Selling price varies with the quantity purchased. To the average customer, flat white sells at $27.45 for 5 gallons and $182.75 for 55 gallons. Colors vary in selling price because of the variety in pigment cost and quantity ordered. Customers purchase on credit and usually pay their invoices in 30 to 60 days. Inner-City telephones the customer after 60 days of nonpayment and inquires when payment will be made.

Management

The President and majority stockholder is Stanley Walsh. He began his career as a house painter and advanced to become a painter for a large decorating company. Walsh painted mostly walls in large commercial buildings and hospitals. Eventually, he came to believe that he could produce a paint that was less expensive and of higher quality than what was being used. A keen desire to open his own business resulted in the creation of Inner-City Paint Corporation.

Walsh manages the corporation today in much the same way that he did when the business began. He personally must open *all* the mail, approve *all* payments, and inspect *all* customer billings before they are mailed. He has been unable to detach himself from any detail of the operation and cannot properly delegate authority. As the company has grown, the time element alone has aggravated the situation. Frequently, these tasks are performed days after transactions occur and mail is received.

The office is managed by Mary Walsh (Walsh's mother). Two part-time clerks assist her, and all records are processed manually.

The plant is managed by a man in his twenties, whom Walsh hired from one of his customers. Walsh became acquainted with him when the man picked up paint from Inner-City for his previous employer. Prior to the eight months he has been employed by Walsh as Plant Manager, his only other experience has been that of a painter.

Employees

Thirty-five employees (20 workers are part-time) work in various phases of the manufacturing process. The employees are nonunion, and most are unskilled laborers. They take turns making paint and driving the delivery trucks.

Stanley Walsh does all of the sales work and public relations work. He spends approximately one half of every day making sales calls and answering complaints about defective paint. He is the only salesman. Other salesmen had been employed in the past, but Walsh felt that they "could not be trusted."

Customer Perception

Customers view Inner-City as a company that provides fast service and negotiates on price and payment out of desperation. Walsh is seen as a disorganized man who may not be able to keep Inner-City afloat much longer. Paint contractors are reluctant to give Inner-City large orders out of fear that the paint may not be ready on a continuous, reliable basis. Larger orders usually go to larger companies that have demonstrated their reliability and solvency.

Rumors abound that Inner-City is in difficult financial straits, that it is unable to pay suppliers, and that it owes a considerable sum for payment on back taxes. All of the above contribute to the customers' serious lack of confidence in the corporation.

Financial Structure

Exhibits **2** and **3** are the most current financial statements for Inner-City Paint Corporation. They have been prepared by the company's accounting service. No audit has been performed because Walsh did not want to incur the expense it would have required.

EXHIBIT 2
Balance Sheet for
the Current Year
Ending June 30:
Inner-City Paint
Corporation

Current assets

Cash	$1,535	
Accounts receivable (net of allowance for bad debts of $63,400)	242,320	
Inventory	18,660	
Total current assets		$262,515
Machinery and transportation equipment	47,550	
Less accumulated depreciation	15,500	
Net fixed assets		32,050
Total assets		$294,565
Current liabilities		
Accounts payable	$217,820	
Salaries payable	22,480	
Notes payable	6,220	
Taxes payable	38,510	
Total current liabilities		$285,030
Long-term notes payable		15,000
Owners' equity		
Common stock, no par, 1,824 shares outstanding		12,400
Deficit		(17,865)
Total liabilities and owners' equity		$294,565

EXHIBIT 3
Income Statement
for the Current Year
Ending June 30:
Inner-City Paint
Corporation

Sales		$1,784,080
Cost of goods sold		1,428,730
Gross margin		$355,350
Selling expenses	$72,460	
Administrative expenses	67,280	
President's salary	132,000	
Office Manager's salary	66,000	
Total expenses		337,740
Net income		$17,610

Future

Stanley Walsh wishes to improve the financial situation and reputation of Inner-City Paint Corporation. He is considering the purchase of a computer to organize the business and reduce needless paperwork. He has read about consultants who are able to quickly spot problems in businesses, but he will not spend more than $300 on such a consultant.

The solution that Walsh favors most is one that requires him to borrow money from the bank, which he will then use to pay his current bills. He feels that as soon as business conditions improve, he will be able to pay back the loans. He believes that the problems Inner-City is experiencing are due to the overall poor economy and are only temporary.

CASE 24

The Haier Group:

U.S. EXPANSION

YongJun Lu, Robert J. Mockler, and Marc Gartenfeld

ON FEBRUARY 23, 2004, THE HAIER GROUP (PRONOUNCED "HIGH-ER"), A MAJOR HOME electrical appliance maker in China, was listed as the only Chinese name brand among the world's 100 most recognizable brands in a global name brand list edited by World Brand Laboratory.[1] The 20-year-old Haier had built a network composed of 18 design centers, 10 industrial parks, 30 overseas factories and manufacturing bases, 58,800 sales offices, and 96 product group categories ranging from refrigerators, washing machines, and air conditioners to cell phones and televisions. As China's domestic markets had mushroomed over the past two decades, Haier had built a reputation at home for quality, innovation, and customer service. It enjoyed leading domestic market share positions in washing machines, refrigerators, vacuum cleaners, and air conditioners.

Encouraged by the Chinese government, Haier strove to become truly international. Haier's executives believed that they could extend the company's strong domestic brand reputation into the West by introducing innovative products for niche consumer markets and then expanding into bigger markets—a strategy that would enable the company to enjoy the higher margins that came with brand sales instead of slugging it out as a low-cost supplier to Western companies.

Haier started out in 1984 as a government-owned enterprise with imported refrigerator production technology from Germany. It subsequently engaged in technical innovation, scientific management, capital operations, mergers and acquisitions, and international expansion. By 2004, it had completed its long march from a small enterprise burdened with a debit of 1.47 million RMB ($177,536) to its current position as the number one domestic electrical appliance producer in China.

Zhang Ruimin, CEO of the Haier Group, announced in November 2004 that the main goal of the company was to continuously increase the volume of products sold in the United

This case was prepared by YongJun Lu, MBA student at St. John's University, under the direction of Dr. Robert J. Mockler and Professor Marc Gartenfeld of St. John's University. Dr. Mockler and Professor Marc Gartenfeld revised and edited this case. This case was reprinted from *Cases in Domestic and Multinational Strategic Management*, Publication (VIII) #44, pp. C7-1 thru C7-26, edited by Robert J. Mockler and Marc Gartenfeld. The copyright holders are solely responsible for the case content. This case was edited for *SMBP* 11th and 12th editions. Copyright © 2005 by Robert J. Mockler, Strategic Management Research Group, 114 East 90th Street (1B), New York, NY 10128. Reprinted by permission.

States, and to modify the company's products to meet American demand.[2] Subsequently, on December 22, 2004, Haier selected A&E Factory Service, one of the leading service companies in the United States, to be its primary service provider for repairs on products under warranty and service contracts in the United States and Puerto Rico. This agreement reflected Haier's commitment to the U.S. market and to the aggressive pursuit of quality assurance. The task for Ruimin was to develop an effective strategy for Haier Group to survive and prosper against aggressive competition in the United States over the intermediate and long-term future.

In 2004, the Haier Group was organized into Haier China, Haier Europe, Haier America, Haier Middle East, Haier Spain, and Haier New Zealand divisions. Each company had its own manufacturing base and sales and marketing department. Haier America, founded in 1999, was originally a U.S. sales and marketing division. That year, it invested $40 million to purchase land in Camden, South Carolina, for its new Haier America Industrial Park. It also established a design center in Boston in 1999. Two years later, the Camden plant produced Haier's first products in America—refrigerators. Haier America also spent $15 million in 2002 to purchase the landmark Greenwich Savings Bank in Manhattan, New York City, to serve as its U.S. headquarters. In 2004, the Camden plant mainly produced large (standard-size in the United States) refrigerators to be primarily sold in the U.S. major home appliance market. Most of Haier's other products that were sold in the United States were imported from Haier China or other subsidiaries of the Haier Group that had a production cost advantage.

Although Haier had a good reputation in "white goods" (white goods referred to major home appliances such as refrigerators, washing machines, and stoves, whereas "brown goods" referred to consumer electronics such as radios and televisions), the brand was still relatively new in the United States, and the company faced a number of long-term decisions in order to build an American presence. Some of the decisions included (1) how to integrate itself with the locality and build brand recognition, (2) how to create the products that could meet American needs, (3) how to achieve the cost control needed to maintain its price advantage, and (4) how to continuously improve its services to build the trust of local customers. The main problem to be resolved for Haier was how to differentiate itself from General Electric, Whirlpool, Maytag, and Electrolux in white goods and from Sony, Panasonic, Philips, and LG in brown goods and thus achieve a winning competitive advantage in the U.S. market.

The Home Appliances and Consumer Electronics Segments of the U.S. Durable Goods Industry

Home appliances and consumer electronics were segments of the durable goods industry. Durable goods were manufactured products capable of long use (over three years), such as automobiles, jewelry, furnishings, home appliances, and consumer electronics. The durable goods industry was sensitive to business cycles. The performance of the durable goods industry was tied to the overall economy, especially to interest rates. Purchases of durable goods were typically postponed during poor economic conditions, but increased during good ones. In 2004, total durable goods shipments increased 10.3% over the previous year.[3] Home appliances included both major and small appliances. Major appliances generally included dishwashers, microwaves, washers and dryers, ranges, refrigerators, and air conditioners, whereas small appliances included less costly electric items, such as food mixers, coffee makers, and can openers. Consumer electronics included stereos, televisions, video cameras, and CD and DVD players/recorders.

For the fourth quarter of 2004, U.S. industry demand for major home appliances increased 10.7% from the prior year. For the full year, industry unit shipments grew 8.3%. Economists expected industry shipments in 2005 to increase approximately 2%. Based on sales from manufacturers to dealers, the U.S. market for consumer electronics products was expected to total

$125.7 billion in 2005, up 11% from 2004's estimated level, according to projections from the Consumer Electronics Association.[4]

Benefiting from a growing economy, U.S. consumer disposable income increased, and relatively low mortgage rates maintained a fairly high demand for new homes. These positive factors stimulated people's consumption of durable goods including home appliances and consumer electronics. The U.S. economy performed well in 2004, with consumer spending, fiscal stimulus, and low interest rates boosting a 4.1% increase of gross domestic product (GDP), up from a 3.1% increase in 2003. In addition, consumer disposable spending remained strong, ending the year at 6.1%, up from 5.2% in 2003. The number of U.S. jobs increased by 2.2 million in 2004, the best year for job growth since 1999.[5]

U.S. consumer spending on appliances and furniture outpaced overall spending, rising 7.6% for the year, compared to 2.7% for 2003. Consumer confidence was strong, with the Consumer Board's consumer confidence index at 103.4 as of January 2005, the highest level since July 2004. Housing sales were also strong, with sales of new and existing homes in 2004 up 9.4% and 8.9%, respectively, from 2003, according to the National Association of Realtors, a U.S. real estate trade association.[6] Residential housing patterns and increased remodeling activity had contributed to fairly steady growth for major home appliances since 1991. The national median existing-home price in the United States was $171,600 in late 2004, 6.6% higher than a year earlier when the median price was $161,100.[7]

Homes were also getting larger in the United States. Increased total floor space and a greater number of rooms per house translated into more appliance sales. In 2002, new homes averaged 2,320 square feet versus 1,645 square feet in 1975, according to the U.S. Census Bureau. Approximately 36% of all new houses had four or more bedrooms, up from approximately 20% in 1975.

In contrast to home appliances, the demand for consumer electronics was driven by technological innovation—especially in digital technology. The consumer electronics industry had fared better than most other industries in times of flux. Technological advances and ever-changing product lines had helped the industry avoid major saturation problems by making existing products appear outdated. The success of digital products—video players, TVs, phones, and home theater systems—had proven that consumers would often succumb to the urge to own the latest and greatest electronic gadgets, in spite of economic concerns. The consumer electronics industry surged ahead in recent years with all-time records for consumer electronics sales. DVD players, one of the fastest-selling electronics products, led this surge. In 2003, DVD rentals surpassed videocassette rentals for the first time.

As digital technology continued to fuel industry growth, products were getting quicker, smaller (except for TVs), faster, and cheaper. Rapid growth had been seen in home networking, photography, navigation, LCD, plasma, and digital radio. Sensing devices, broadband, and wireless were helping define the industry's future. Driven by demand for digital audio, video, and home information products, U.S. consumer electronics sales soared by 10.7% in 2004 to an all-time record $113.5 billion. Equally strong sales growth was anticipated for 2005, with sales expected to climb to $125.7 billion, according to the Consumer Electronics Administration.[8]

The aging of the Baby Boom generation was expected to escalate spending on appliances and electronics. With most of these people in their prime income-earning years, they were replacing old, inexpensive electronic products with new, higher-quality products and renovating their kitchens with state-of-the-art major home appliances.

Products and Markets

The common element among home appliances and consumer electronics was that they both had useful lives of more than three years. For example, the average useful life of a major home appliance in 2004 was 9 years for dishwashers, 13 years for clothes dryers, 11 years for freezers,

9 years for microwave ovens, 13 years for electric ranges, 15 years for gas ranges, 13 years for large refrigerators, 9 years for compact refrigerators, and 10 years for clothes washers and room air conditioners. In consumer electronics, the average life expectancy of color televisions was 8 years and that of VCRs was 5 years. For small home appliances, the average life expectancy ranged from 7 years for coffee percolators to 4 years for food processors.[9]

Each manufacturer tried to differentiate itself by offering products with unique features or technologically advanced products to attract either general consumers or some specific consumer bases. Further, to gain price advantage, manufacturers put more emphasis on streamlining production and implementing cost control of both production processes and supply chain and distribution management. Because competition was intense within the industry, manufacturers had been trying to gain advantages by launching aggressive mass media advertising campaigns or by doing frequent in-store promotions.

Home Appliances

Manufacturers of major home appliances generally produced washing machines, clothes dryers, dishwashers, ranges, refrigerators, freezers, and microwave ovens, and sometimes air conditioners, vacuum cleaners, and small appliances. Opportunities for home appliances were a low saturation rate (percentage of households with a particular appliance) for a particular product category and an increasing demand for new features on products. The saturation rate of major home appliances in 2004 in the United States was 100% for ranges (gas and electric), 99% for refrigerators, 98% for vacuum cleaners, 96% for microwave ovens, 95% for washing machines, 84% for clothes dryers (gas and electric), 60% for dishwashers, and 17% for compact refrigerators.[10] Some major home appliances, such as full-size refrigerators, clothes washers, and ranges, achieved significant U.S. market saturation rates decades ago. Others, such as microwave ovens, dishwashers, electric dryers, and compact refrigerators, had seen steadily rising saturation rates in recent years. For example, microwave ovens had increased from just 65.9% of U.S. homes in 1987, and compact refrigerators, which were not tracked in 1987, increased from only 7.4% saturation in 1987.[11]

The U.S. home appliance market was mature, but was still the largest market in the world. In 2004, 58,653,000 major home appliance units were sold in the United States plus 5,458,000 more in Canada.[12] Major home appliances already had high saturation levels, and no breakthrough products were looming on the horizon to create a dramatic new demand. Key factors in the appliance area were strong brand recognition, high quality of products and services, capability to provide a wide range of product categories, a strong ability to design new features on existing products, the ability to meet local consumers' needs, and price attractiveness. Brand recognition represented manufacturers' market recognition for providing consistent quality products and consistent maintenance and services in the long term.

In major home appliances, the threat of substitute products came largely from incremental improvements (such as energy-efficient washers and dryers or timed coffee makers) rather than from wholly new products that made previous products obsolete (such as the invention of the electric refrigerator, which replaced the icebox). Thus, to more effectively meet local needs, participants could devote more R&D resources to improving existing products than to developing new product categories. Manufacturers could increase their competitiveness by improving the capability of new feature designs, such as the convertible refrigerator/freezer. To continuously gain price attractiveness in a market of rising material costs in 2004, manufacturers needed to have premium product lines and raise sales in the high-end segment to offset the losses caused by increased costs. To ensure their competitive position, firms invested in technology development leading to new products, such as the robot vacuum cleaner or the home PAD refrigerator (which detected the shelf life of food and automatically displayed a list of items stored in the fridge on the door).

Because of relatively high saturation levels in the United States, the market for major home appliances was driven primarily by the demand for replacing worn-out appliances. Generally speaking, replacements accounted for 75% of sales, new housing for 20%, and new household formation for about 5% of sales of major home appliances. On average, each new home directly or indirectly represented the sales of four or five new appliances, including a refrigerator, a dishwasher, an oven and cook top (or a range), and laundry equipment.

Although housing starts had been at a relatively high level in recent years, specialists predicted that they would fall over the next several years.[13] Major home appliance manufacturers would then need to depend more on replacement demand (including purchases made during remodeling) than on housing starts. In such an environment, companies would need innovative, stylish, and attractively priced products to stimulate sales.

Consumer Electronics

Manufacturers of consumer electronics usually produced stereos, TV, CDs, DVD players/recorders, and video cameras. Opportunities for consumer electronics were the steady growth rate in such product categories as plasma TVs and DVD players/recorders and strong demand for electronic products driven by digital technology and services that offered consumers a convenient, affordable means of accessing information and communicating with other people. Benefiting from a recovering economy in 2003, sales increased 3.5%, almost hitting $100 billion. Digital TV (DTV) continued its ascent as the fastest-growing technology of all time in terms of sales. The Consumer Electronics Association projected that the sales of DTV would reach 6.97 million in 2004, 10.77 million in 2005, 16.77 million in 2006, 23.25 million in 2007, and 27.05 million in 2008.[14] Digital growth was on the rise in nearly every product category across the consumer electronics spectrum, including audio, video, imaging, information technologies, networking, and mobile electronics. The fastest growing products in 2003 as measured by sales were digital cameras, MP3 players, DVD players/recorders, and plasma TVs.

New opportunities were the flat HDTV, large LCD, plasma TV, and new display technologies with paper-thin visual displays. Despite their high prices, plasma TVs became a hot item in 2003. HDTV had become more and more popular as a subscription service in the United States, especially in public outlets such as bars and gyms. Along with the HDTV capability, plasma TVs offered a much crisper and higher-quality video and audio experience. Many specialized retail outlets, such as Best Buy, had reconfigured some of their stores to feature home theater demonstrations with plasma screen TVs. Manufacturers had responded with a continuous stream of new plasma TV products.

Key factors in consumer electronics were brand recognition, high quality of products and services, wide ranges of products, the speed of development of new technologies, and price competitiveness. Manufacturers were able to capture the high-end market by investing in new technology development and quickly translating it to technologically advanced products with unique designs. They also could satisfy some low-end market needs by offering the basic functional products with fewer features and fewer technological advances at relatively lower prices. By offering a wide range of products, manufacturers could satisfy varying needs and provide the convenience of one-stop shopping. In addition, attractive appearance design was very important for manufactures to capture consumer attention.

Manufacturing and R&D

Economic activity in the U.S. manufacturing sector grew in January 2005 for the 20th consecutive month while the overall economy grew for the 39th consecutive month, according to a report from the Institute of Supply Management.[15] The production of home appliances and consumer electronics were capital intensive; there were significant up-front and ongoing costs. Manufacturing facilities were highly mechanized, with assembly lines designed for long production runs. Consequently, the industry's fixed costs were moderately high. However, the business also had a significant variable cost element; it was somewhat sensitive to price changes in raw materials and components.

Research and development (R&D) involved ongoing expenses. New products and features must be continually introduced for a company's goods to remain competitive with otherwise undifferentiated products. In addition, consumer demand forced manufacturers to create innovative features and styles that better suited customer needs. However, in the short run, R&D spending could be reduced when cash needed to be conserved.

Home Appliances

In 2004, while many manufacturers were enjoying strong sales, major home appliance makers were significantly affected by increases in material and logistics costs. Material prices increased at an alarming rate in 2004, causing some financial loss for several companies during the third quarter of 2004. Consequently, Whirlpool, General Electric, and Maytag had passed the 5%–10% increases to their costumers. Whirlpool, an industry leader, estimated that the material cost base would increase an additional 7% to 8% during 2005.[16] Prices of electric appliances in China were in the process of rising at least 5% in 2005. For example, the price of room air conditioners was increasing 5% to 8% because of increases in costs of raw materials, such as plastics (where prices had gone up as much as 30%), steel (up 15%), and copper (up 20%).[17]

The recently volatile economy had forced most manufacturers to explore outsourcing. Many companies saw it as an opportunity to reduce costs, improve flexibility, and streamline production processes. For example, Maytag had been a vertically integrated organization for many years. However, the appliance manufacturer realized that this model was not always efficient. As a result, in 2003 Maytag developed a corporate strategy to look at each business unit and use outsourcing if it was cost effective. The company had entered into an agreement under which Daewoo Electronics of Seoul, South Korea, would manufacture top-freezer refrigerators for Maytag.

Because of the industry's high level of automation, labor was a relatively small percentage of appliance makers' costs. Labor expenses could generally be reduced when product runs were suspended temporarily, but equipment and facilities still needed to be maintained, although at a lower cost than when in full operation. As material costs increased significantly in 2004, companies worked to absorb them. Manufacturers increased productivity, restructured facilities and management, and focused on increasing product innovation. Despite attempts to curb costs, the appliance industry found itself having no choice but to pass a portion of the cost increases to consumers. Appliance manufacturers were hoping to move consumer purchases to higher-end products, where profit margins were better.

Technology was leading to improvements in products. "Smart" computerized appliances were being introduced that were expected to make life easier for users. Examples included Whirlpool's Polara combination oven/refrigerator that automatically started cooking at a programmed time and kept food either hot or cold. In Europe, Electrolux was selling the Trilobite, a robot vacuum cleaner.

The "smart kitchen" concept had captured the attention of both the appliance industry and companies that traditionally specialized in kitchen products. For instance, Samsung had introduced the "Home PAD Refrigerator," which detected the shelf life of food and automatically displayed a list of items stored in the fridge on the door. Via an Internet connection, owners of the Samsung refrigerator could retrieve that information from a remote location. LG Electronics had launched a TV refrigerator, which included a cable-ready, 13.5-inch TV screen, FM radio, two speakers, and a TV tuner.

Some new appliances used a mix of old and new technologies, such as barcode readers to recognize food items in the fridge. The engine of the smart kitchen was a broadband-equipped home network that connected all of the kitchen's products with the family's remote devices, such as a cell phone, a pager, and an office computer or a laptop. The smart kitchen featured such novelties as ovens that could download and execute recipes via the Internet, and ovens that could be temperature-controlled during the day so they could store and eventually cook food via a cell phone request while owners were still at the office.

It was becoming very important for manufacturers to continuously anticipate the trends in such new technologies as "smart appliances" and "smart kitchens" as well as to emphasize product developments and new feature designs. The manufacturer needed to maintain a highly creative and motivated technical team and achieve commitment at the corporate level to provide strong support for such development. Speed to convert innovations into mass production was another important factor that could affect the sales of the new products.

Consumer Electronics

Consumer electronics manufacturers had learned to live in a world where price, brand sensitivity, short windows for product life cycles, and the bargaining power of retailers were the norm, making time to market and time to volume the driving concerns. In order to thrive in an industry punctuated by dramatic swings in demand and short product life cycles, manufacturers had to deliver technical innovations and satisfy customer demands while containing costs. These competitive imperatives had led to the adoption of outsourced manufacturing strategies in order to reduce costs while enhancing operational flexibility.

Manufacturers either used electronics manufacturing service (EMS) providers to handle the entire product design and manufacturing process or outsourced just the manufacturing process. EMS providers offered customers a comprehensive, integrated, lower total cost of ownership approach to product design and manufacturing services. The object was to reduce total manufacturing costs and provide higher manufacturing responsiveness to changes in volume. Either way, tightly managing production and coordinating delivery to multiple distribution points had become key to supply chain profitability in these virtual supply chains.

Opportunities for consumer electronics were being generated by the U.S. transition of television broadcasting from an analog to a digital platform. Profit opportunities abounded from consumers replacing old analog televisions or adding new big-screen sets to their home theater systems. These buyers were opting to purchase displays capable of the better pixel resolution and higher-frequency scan rates of digital television (DTV) signals and took advantage of the improved video fidelity offered by popular DVD players. CEA (Consumer Electronics Administration) forecasted DTV factory revenue to climb 33% to more than $8 billion by the end of 2004, and DTV product sales to climb more than 39% to 5.8 million units. Factory sales of DTV displays exceeded CEA forecasts in 2003, with wholesale volume growing by 41% to nearly $6 billion.[18]

Portable entertainment devices were the current trend in consumer electronics. Advances in technology were changing not only the types of portable entertainment devices consumers used, but also how they were used. The outcome of this digital movement was that consumers could access their content—especially entertainment content—wherever they went. A number of consumer electronic products had emerged to meet rising consumer demand for more cutting-edge on-the-go audio and video applications. Another trend was a personal media player that integrated digital music and video from electronic files. These products allowed consumers to play back digital music much like an MP3 player, but with integrated color screens; they also enabled consumers to view digital photos and play back digitized movies, home videos, and even recorded TV shows.

Technology shifts, shorter product life cycles, and other unanticipated requirements had become part of the industry's new dynamics, but chipmakers and consumer electronics manufacturers were clearly experiencing pressure to produce new and compelling products with new features and better performance at lower production costs. It was important for manufacturers to keep up-to-date in new technologies, such as portable entertainment devices and personal media players, to continuously anticipate the trends in product development, and to improve the appearance of existing products. Time cycles to convert new technology into mass-produced products were becoming much shorter. How well manufacturers would anticipate new trends and how fast they could respond to them in a cost-efficient way were critical to their success.

Industry Supply Chain and Distribution Channels

Manufacturers had some control over retail distribution—through either outlet chain stores or independent stores. Most major manufacturers and retailers had regional distribution facilities located strategically near a cluster of stores. However, because of their high-volume purchases, major retailers such as Sears often received shipments directly from the manufacturing facility to their own warehouses. For example, Samsung put a supply-chain management program in place to reduce the number of logistics steps and deliver directly to customers' warehouses. This prompted manufacturers to provide prompt delivery of items, reduce inventory requirements at individual stores, and undertake more efficient production runs.

Manufacturers were working closely with retailers to increase the efficiency of the supply chain—from source to consumer. Manufacturers and retailers were reducing order cycle time by sharing information through collaborative planning, forecasting, and replenishment (CPFR). CPFR enabled trading partners to gain visibility into each other's demand chain, order forecasts, and promotional plans. For example, Wal-Mart created a partnership with vendors in which both sides shared information to streamline the flow of goods. Vendors tapped into the chain's computers to get a scorecard of performance and manage their own in-store inventory. A 2001 study conducted by Grocery Manufacturers of America (GMA) showed that 57% of companies using CPFR improved trading partner relationships and 38% improved service levels, stock outs, and sales. Intense pricing pressures and the drive to grow share in oversaturated markets were making the efficiency and effectiveness of the supply chain ever more important.

To enhance distribution efficiency, companies often used sophisticated cantilever racking and computer-controlled random-access inventory storage. In addition, many manufacturers employed their own drivers (rather than subcontracting the work), maintained a fleet of trucks and trailers to ensure quality control, and offered customers delivery and setup at no additional cost.

Retail distribution of home appliances and consumer electronics had historically been dominated by department stores, such as Sears Roebuck. Sears was traditionally so strong in major home appliance sales that it alone accounted for nearly two out of every five major home appliances sold in the United States. In addition to selling brand name home appliances, Sears strongly promoted its own line of Kenmore home appliances, for which it contracted with appliance manufacturers such as Whirlpool and Electrolux. These traditional retailers encountered stiff competition from mass merchandise discounters such as Wal-Mart and home improvement retailers such as Home Depot and Lowe's. Sears and other traditional retailers typically sold goods at the manufacturer's suggested retail price (Kenmore products, however, were promoted at lower prices), drawing customers with their well-stocked inventories and knowledgeable salespeople. In contrast, Wal-Mart and Home Depot sold household appliances at a discount below the suggested retail price. Although they kept limited inventory in the store and provided fewer customer services, they provided information kiosks where consumers could browse for more selections.

Sears had responded to increasing competition by lowering prices and increasing advertising, while continuing other promotional efforts such as offering low-cost financing. These recent shifts in retailing had further pressured selling prices. On the manufacturing level, appliance and electronics makers had introduced more value-added products, such as the convertible freezer/refrigerator, to differentiate their offerings and to avoid competing on price alone. Consumer demand for premium appliances and electronics with new features had helped to alleviate the industry's long-running price competition.

Because more than 80% of home appliances and consumer electronics were purchased by consumers from chain store outlets, a manufacturer's relationship with chain stores was the most important factor to affect sales performance. Good relationships translated into more shelf space, better exhibition area, and more aggressive in-store promotion. Furthermore, discount chains store such as Wal-Mart, Target, and Costco usually sold standard products with fewer features at relatively lower prices. More specialized chain stores such as Sears, Circuit City, and Bed Bath & Beyond offered more choices of a wider range of features and better services at reasonable prices.

Most major home appliances were purchased by consumers from retail outlets. The primary reason was that large products such as washers, dryers, and refrigerators usually needed professional installation, which retail outlets were able to provide by keeping trained workers on staff. In addition, consumers typically wished to inspect major appliances in person before purchasing.

Consumer electronics were generally purchased by consumers from electronics stores, such as Best Buy, Circuit City, and Radio Shack. These stores had well-trained employees who had special knowledge of the consumer electronics products and could provide appropriate recommendations to customers according to their specific needs.

Competitors in the U.S. Market

Competition in major home appliances and consumer electronics in the U.S. market came from multinational companies that manufactured both home appliances and consumer electronics as well as some large international and domestic players that focused either on home appliances or on consumer electronics. Some multinational companies, such as Matsushita, LG, and Haier, participated in both product categories. Electrolux, GE, Whirlpool, and Maytag focused mainly on major home appliances. Electrolux and Whirlpool (plus LG and Haier) had a significant presence in air conditioners, but GE and Maytag did not. Although GE had previously divested its small appliance unit to Black & Decker, Whirlpool was still active in small appliances with a 2.9% market share in 2004. Sony, Sanyo, and Philips focused mostly on consumer electronics.

Major Home Appliances

Whirlpool

Whirlpool, a worldwide manufacturer and marketer of major home appliances, was first in U.S. sales with a 33.4% market share in 2004 (see **Exhibit 1**).[19] Whirlpool manufactured in 13 countries under nine brand names and marketed products to distributors and retailers in more than 170 countries. It marketed a line of appliances and related products, primarily for home use. In addition to its presence in major home appliances, Whirlpool had a 7.1% share of the U.S. air conditioning market in 2004.

With steel, aluminum, oil, and copper costs soaring in 2004, Whirlpool took several actions to curb the rising raw material costs:

■ **Product specification.** The company worked to make improvements on and take material content out of products in order to allocate engineering and resources appropriately.

EXHIBIT 1
Shares of U.S. and Western European Market in White Goods
(Including dishwashers, dryers, ranges, ovens, refrigerators, washers)

United States Combined Market Share by Company

Company	Home Country	2001	2004	Brands
Whirlpool	USA	39.2%	33.4%	Estate, Inglis, KitchenAid, Roper, Whirlpool
GE	USA	23.2%	25.7%	GE, Hotpoint, Monogram, Profile, RCA
Maytag	USA	21.6%	15.1%	Admiral, Amana, Jenn–Air, Magic Chef, Maytag
Electrolux	Sweden	15.0%	19.0%	Frigidaire, Gibson, Kelvinator, Tappan, White-Westinghouse
Others	—	1.0%	6.8%	LG, Haier, Bosch-Siemens, Sub-Zero, Viking, etc.

Western European Combined Market Share by Company

Company	Home Country	2004
Electrolux	Sweden	16.9%
Bosch-Siemens	Germany	15.1%
Indesit/Merloni	Italy	14.2%
Whirlpool	U.S.	9.4%
Koc Group	Turkey	5.7%
Candy	Italy	3.4%
Others	—	35.3%

SOURCE: *"28th Annual Report of the U.S. Appliance Industry," Appliance (September 2005), Special Insert; "Portrait of the European Appliance Industry," Appliance (November 2005), pp. 71–74.*

- **Conversion cost consideration.** This was achieved by utilizing six-sigma and lean manufacturing practices.

- **Target setting.** Specific cost reduction targets were set for upcoming quarters.

- **Innovation rate ramp-up.** Whirlpool had introduced 25 new products in the past 3 years and it planned to double that pace in the next 2 years.

Whirlpool's strengths were its dominant U.S. market share and strong U.S. brand recognition. The company owed its leadership position to its 50-plus year relationship with Sears, to which it had been the primary supplier of Kenmore (Sears' own brand label) appliances. Even though Sears began offering appliance brands other than Kenmore in the 1990s, Whirlpool continued to be a key supplier. Whirlpool offered a wide range of product categories, high-quality products with unique designs, and a well-serviced maintenance network. Whirlpool was familiar with its major buyers' needs and responded quickly to shifts in local trends because the company designed and manufactured its major products locally. For example, Whirlpool's large refrigerators with icemaker, water filter, and water dispenser had become the most popular multi-functional refrigerator in the U.S. market. Whirlpool dominated U.S. sales of dishwashers, washers, and dryers and had a strong international and nationwide supply chain and distribution system. It maintained good relationships with chain stores, individual stores, and Internet sellers. To ensure its dominant position in the U.S. major home appliance market, the company invested heavily in R&D and spent heavily on marketing. It also had some manufacturing plants in Mexico where costs were lower.

Whirlpool's weaknesses were its relatively high prices, slightly conservative styles, fewer features, and less emphasis on compact products, such as compact refrigerators. Manufacturing primarily in the United States resulted in relatively higher production costs and a weaker ability to absorb increasing material costs compared with the other competitors from Asia such as LG and Haier.

GE Consumer & Electrical (GECI)

GE created the GECI business unit in 2004 when it combined GE consumer products and GE industrial systems. GECI's appliance division made major home appliances under the brand names of GE, Hotpoint, Monogram, RCA, and Profile. GECI was number two in U.S. sales, with a 25.7% market share in 2004, and a worldwide manufacturer and marketer of major home appliances, except in Europe, where it had only a minimal presence. GECI was the market leader in U.S. sales of gas and electric ranges and standard-size refrigerators. It was second to Haier in sales of compact refrigerators with a 17% market share in 2004.

Strong brand recognition plus good-quality product and technology capabilities led to its solid market share position in U.S. major home appliances. GECI had a strong nationwide service network. The company's strength was its standard-sized major appliances. GECI designed and manufactured its U.S. products in its appliance park near Louisville, Kentucky, and could respond quickly to shifts in the U.S. market. The company had a broad sales network and good relationships with chain stores and housing contractors. GECI kept current in technology development and manufactured some appliances in Mexico to reduce costs.

Weaknesses of GECI included relatively fewer feature designs on its existing products, relatively high U.S. production costs, a lack of compact appliances, and a weaker ability to absorb rising material costs. Consequently its products carried higher price tags. The company sold only a few products through Internet sellers.

Electrolux

With its purchase of White Consolidated Industries (WCI) in 1986, Electrolux of Sweden became a major player in the U.S. major home appliance industry. Unfortunately, WCI's many appliance brands competed against one another and were not designed for automated manufacturing. Consequently, Electrolux has been forced to invest millions into its acquired manufacturing plants to make its products competitive in the U.S. market. It sold appliances in the United States under the Frigidaire, Gibson, Kelvinator, Tappan, and White-Westinghouse brands. Electolux was ranked third in U.S. sales with a 19.0% market share in 2004. Sixty percent of Electrolux's U.S. sales were generated through major retail chains. Sears was the largest retailer of Electrolux products, followed by Lowe's, Best Buy, and Home Depot. Although Electrolux was generally second or third in most appliance categories, it dominated freezer sales with a 68% market share in 2004. In addition to its presence in major home appliances, Electrolux had 4.9% of the 2004 U.S. room air conditioning market behind LG and Fedders.

Electrolux worldwide was the world's number one producer of major home appliances under the AEG, Electrolux, Eureka, Frigidaire, and Zanussi names. It had the highest market share in Europe. Electrolux was also the world's No.1 maker of vacuum cleaners, including the Electrolux and Eureka brands. Electrolux was a presence in the commercial market as well, making products such as foodservice and laundry equipment (Electrolux, Zanussi brands), chainsaws and lawn and garden equipment (Husqvarna and Jonsered brands, which the company planned to spin off), and diamond tools (Dimas and Diamant Boart brands). Electrolux's products were sold in more than 150 countries and major home appliances accounted for more than 75% of Electrolux's sales. To increase its name recognition in the United States, Electrolux chose to name its North American division "Frigidaire" after the most well-known brand it had acquired from WCI.

The company's strength was its wide range of appliance products with trusted brand names such as AEG, Electrolux, Eureka, and Frigidaire. It had wide range of distribution networks and good relationship with retail chains, individual stores, and Internet sellers. Electrolux's U.S. products were very attractive to low- to middle-income people. As a multi-national corporation, Electrolux kept up with advances in new technology development. For example, the company sold the Trilobite 2.0, a robot vacuum cleaner, in Europe.

The company's weaknesses in the United States (Frigidaire Division) were its inefficient manufacturing facilities and the relatively poor quality reputation of its acquired brands. Because the parent corporation had grown through many acquisitions, it had a large number of brands (of varying reputations) to manage and support throughout the world. This was considered by some industry analysts to be a weakness of the parent corporation. Electrolux had implemented restructuring programs periodically in an effort to improve operating efficiencies. Citing production costs, Electrolux planned to close its Swedish factory in early 2005, moving manufacturing to Hungary. Additional plant closures included its cooker factory in France and facilities in Michigan and Texas. The company announced in 2005 that it would relocate many of its North American and European plants to Asia, Mexico, and Eastern Europe. Electrolux had also put substantial efforts into driving down costs and complexity throughout the supply chain by improving integration of the supply chain and demand flow management, but it seemed like such effort had not achieved as much costs saving as the company had expected. The company was still fighting rising material costs.

Maytag

With a 15.1% share of the U.S. market in 2004, Maytag sold appliances under the names of Admiral, Amana, Jenn-Air, Magic Chef, and Maytag. The company sold its products through national retail chains, its own retail stores, and independent dealers and distributors. In 2004, Maytag introduced several new products aimed at affluent consumers, such as the French door bottom-freezer refrigerator selling for $1,799 at Home Depot.

In June 2004, Maytag launched its most recent restructuring plan, dubbed "one company," which integrated its ailing Hoover floor care unit into its main business. Hoover's prior attempt to focus on the high end of the floor care market unfortunately coincided with shifts in consumer preference for other types of products and an influx of low-cost manufacturers. The strategy backfired, causing the company to lose market share to high-end competing brands Dyson and Bissell, and to low-cost Asian manufacturers such as LG and Haier.

In January 2005, Best Buy, which carried the low-cost competitor LG Electronics as well as other major brands, announced it would no longer carry Maytag appliances. Several domestic and foreign competitors were offering more innovative features with lower prices. LG Electronics, for example, offered a combination toaster and microwave oven and a combination clothes washer/dryer. That same month, Home Depot (which accounted for about 10% of Maytag's total sales) announced that it would begin offering LG Electronics' appliances in addition to those of Maytag. This was bad news to a company whose U.S. market share had already declined 6.5% from 2001.

Although Maytag was not in the dominant position in most appliance product categories, it had a very good reputation in terms of high product quality and moderately priced products. It was a strong second in U.S. sales of washers and dryers behind Whirlpool. Maytag had a strong nationwide service network that provided after-sale services not only for their own products but also for the other major brand products such as GE and Whirlpool. The company also invested a great amount in technology developments. It offered strong unique designs (such as the Neptune drying center) and rich features (such as the French door bottom-freezer refrigerator) in some appliance categories.

Maytag's weaknesses were its high amount of debt and relatively slow responsiveness to market shifts. Although Maytag spent a large amount on new technology development, it had difficulty in developing appropriate products to satisfy new market trends. Compared with the other major appliance manufacturers, Maytag had a relatively weak network with retail chain stores and Internet sellers. The company's products did not appeal to young people because of its conservative designs and relatively higher prices. The company's sales and promotions on the Internet and mass media were also slightly weaker than those of its major competitors, such as Whirlpool. The company's ability to absorb rising material costs was weak given that most of its products were made in the United States. Unlike its competition, Maytag was primarily a domestic company and was just beginning to establish manufacturing facilities in Mexico where costs were lower.

As a result of its acquisitions of Magic Chef, Hoover, and Amana, among others, Maytag had taken on a high amount of debt. Maytag's low profit margins had made it virtually impossible for the company to be as competitive as its peers in negotiating with retailers, leading to a significant loss of valuable store floor space.

Others

Other companies were making and selling a significant amount of major home appliances in the United States. Nevertheless, their total market share was only 6.8% in 2004—still a considerable increase from just 1% in 2001. Bosch-Siemens Hausgerate (BSH), a German joint venture between Robert Bosch and Siemens with the second largest major home appliance sales in Europe (see **Exhibit 1**), had built a dishwasher plant in North Carolina in 1997 and had expanded it in 2002 to produce cooking and laundry appliances. It also had factories in Tennessee and California. BSH made high-quality major home appliances, such as its stainless-steel dishwasher, for sale to affluent U.S. consumers. As the largest market for major home appliances in the world, the United States was considered to be a key part of Bosch-Siemens' future growth. According to CEO Kurt-Ludwig Gutberlet in a 2004 interview, "We will no doubt more than double our business in the U.S. in the next 3 to 4 years."[20]

After importing refrigerators into the U.S. since 1997, Haier built a refrigerator plant in South Carolina. By 2004 Haier's share of the standard-size refrigerator market had risen to 2% for fifth place (behind GE, Electrolux, Whirlpool, and Maytag) and 20% of the compact refrigerator market (ahead of GE's 17%) for first place in this category.

South Korea's LG Electronics (LGE) had also become a serious competitor in U.S. major home appliances. Although LGE's overall share of the U.S. major home appliance market was still low in 2004, it ranked first in U.S. microwave oven sales with a 38% market share, up from only 8% in 1999. LGE was second in the U.S. air conditioner market with a 13.8% market share. LG intended to be a global player in the industry. LGE's management wanted to achieve $14 billion in global sales by 2007, up from $8.5 billion in 2004.[21] Among the large U.S. major home appliance retailers, Best Buy was the first to carry a wide range of LG appliances, followed by Home Depot in January 2005.

In addition to Bosch-Siemens, Haier, and LGE, there were a few smaller niche competitors operating in North America, such as Sub-Zero, Viking Range, W.C. Wood, and Brown Stove Works. Most of them manufactured and sold only one category of appliance, such as specialized ranges or freezers sold at premium prices.

Competitors in Other Major Home Appliance Categories

Air conditioners and floor care appliances were not usually included with U.S. major home appliances when market shares were calculated. For example, room air conditioners were typically listed under "comfort conditioning" along with unitary (central) air conditioners and heat pumps, dehumidifiers, and furnaces. In 2004, the market share leaders in the U.S. room air conditioner market were LG Electronics (29%), Fedders (22%), Electrolux (11%), Whirlpool (11%), Haier (6%), Samsung (6%), Sharp (4%), Matsushita (2%), and Friedrich (2%), with others accounting for the remaining 7%. In the dehumidifier category, Whirlpool (35%) and LG Electronics (30%) dominated the market with the remainder going to Fedders (11%), W. C. Wood (8%), Electrolux (7%), Samsung (3%), Ebco (3%), and others (3%). The leading competitors in floor care appliances in 2004 were Panasonic and Electrolux (Eureka) in canister vacuum cleaners and Electrolux (Eureka) and Maytag (Hoover) in upright vacuum cleaners.[22] Floor care appliances were an extremely competitive category of home electric appliances.

Consumer Electronics

Sony

Sony's PlayStation home video game system was highly profitable and PlayStation 2 dominated the game console market with about 70% of global sales in 2004. Sony, one of the world's top consumer electronics firms, also made a host of other products, including PCs, digital cameras, Walkman stereos, and semiconductors. The company's TVs, stereos, and other consumer electronics accounted for more than 60% of its sales. Sony's entertainment products included recorded music and video, motion pictures, DVDs, and TV programming. In addition, Sony sold mobile phones via Sony Ericsson, its joint venture with Ericsson. Sony also owned an 8% stake in the music club Columbia House.

Internationally, Sony was the overall consumer electronics leader in market share and technology development, through a highly respected brand name, a wider variety of products than most of its competitors, greater market presence through advertising and wholly owned stores, and a higher perceived level of overall quality of its products in most sectors. Sony had a well-earned reputation for producing high-quality electronic products with unique design, attractive appearance, and good warranty service. The company had the capability to use new technology to develop and launch new products in a relatively short time. Consumers could buy Sony products either through its wide Internet networks or from its broad sales and distribution networks almost anywhere in the world. Sony had eight major manufacturing sites in North America and could respond quickly to shifts in local trends. It mainly targeted middle- and upper-income consumers.

Sony paid less attention to developing lower cost products in satisfying the low end of the market. Its weaknesses were its relatively higher prices, its cost control, and fewer in-store promotions.

Matsushita

Matsushita Electric Industrial, one of the world's top consumer electronics makers, might have had an unfamiliar name, but its brands were recognizable: Panasonic, Quasar, Technics, and JVC, to name a few. Its AVC Network sector produced TVs, VCRs, CD and DVD players, PCs, cellular phones, and fax machines. Matsushita also sold components (batteries, electric motors, displays, semiconductors), home appliances (washing machines, vacuum cleaners), and factory automation equipment (industrial robots, welding equipment). The Matsushita group included about 380 consolidated companies around the globe; its products were sold worldwide.

On February 17, 2005, Matsushita Electric Industrial Co., Ltd., at an extraordinary general meeting of shareholders, announced that it was changing the company name to Panasonic Shikoku Electronics Co., Ltd., effective April 1, 2005. The name change was part of the company's strategy to unify global brands under the Panasonic name.

Matsushita's strength was its wide range of product categories including its AVC network, home appliance, industrial equipment, and components and devices. The company offered moderate prices and relatively high-quality products with simplified functions and good warranty services. Its broad global manufacturing and distribution networks provided the company cost control advantages on production and sales. The company also cultivated good relationships with chain stores, individual stores, and Internet sellers. Technological prowess played a significant role for Matsushita to achieve its long-term goal of the ubiquitous networking society and coexistence with a global environment. With its cutting-edge technologies, the company continued to deliver "security and brand loyalty," "ease-of-use and convenience," and "inspiring" products to customers around the globe in a timely manner.

Matsushita's weakness was its diversification strategy. The company's products and brands were so broad that sometimes the company lost concentration on its core products. This was likely to improve with the name change to Panasonic.

Philips

Royal Philips Electronics made consumer electronics, including TVs, VCRs, DVD player/recorders, phones, and fax machines, as well as light bulbs (number one worldwide), electric shavers (number one) and other personal care appliances, picture tubes, semiconductors, and medical systems. Consumer electronics and small appliances accounted for about a third of the company's sales. Philips had sold its major home appliance division to Whirlpool in 1991 and was no longer involved in this industry segment. Philips had been dumping noncore businesses, such as its stake in music giant PolyGram, and acquiring and forming joint ventures in its core sectors (e.g., LG Philips Displays, a CRT display joint venture with LG Electronics).

The United States was a key market for Philips, accounting for one third ($8.9 billion) of the company's worldwide sales in 2003. All five of Philips' product divisions had a presence in the United States. Each operated independently, yet coordinated closely in sharing technologies and in developing products for the consumer and business-to-business marketplaces. Under the leadership of its corporate center in Amsterdam, this collaboration was required to unlock the full potential of the Philips brand.

Philips' strengths were its strong brand recognition, good warranty and services, and intimacy to local markets' needs. The company also implemented heavy advertising and promotion activity and built good relationships with a wide range of chain stores, individual stores, and Internet sellers. Manufacturing locally improved its response rate to the shifts of local consumption trends. Philips' strong brand image made it highly competitive in the broad product categories it provided. Another strength was its advanced technological capability. For example, Philips' high-tech campus in Eindhoven, The Netherlands, was a world-renowned technology center; the campus provided advanced facilities and an optimized working culture for thousands of top-notch engineers. It focused on crucial technological areas such as microsystems, devices, embedded systems, signal processing, and nanotechnology. Like Sony, Philips had the capability to use new technology to develop and offer new products in a relatively short time.

Philips' weaknesses were relatively high production costs and prices. Its styles and features on products that targeted the middle and low end of the market fell slightly behind its major competitors (such as Panasonic and LGE). Philip's products were so diversified that sometimes it lost concentration on its core product development, and its products did not catch much attention from young people because of their relatively high price and complicated functions.

LG Electronics (LGE)

Founded in 1958 as Gold Star, LGE was a member of South Korea's LG Group. The LG Group had 70-plus subsidiaries that designed and manufactured display and media products (TVs, VCRs, plasma display panels), home appliances (refrigerators, microwaves, air conditioners), and telecommunications devices (wireless phones, handsets, switchboards). LGE owned Zenith Electronics and launched a flat-panel display joint venture with Philips Electronics (LG Philips Displays). After Asia, LGE generated most of its sales revenue from North America; the company had established a North American headquarters in 2004. LG Electronics' new vision was to reach the top in quality and quantity by 2005 and become the best global company that had a brand synonymous with customer satisfaction and a workplace that employees were proud to call their own.

LG Electronics was best known as a leading manufacturer of televisions, VCRs, plasma display panels, and telecommunications equipment, but its share of the U.S. home appliance market was growing. Unlike its U.S. competitors, LGE had not implemented price increases to offset rising commodity costs, instead favoring aggressive efforts to increase market share.

LGE's strengths were its broad product categories, quality products with good warranty and services, and highly competitive prices compared with most of its major competitors (such as Sony, Philips, and Panasonic). LGE's products had simplified functions and were very attractive to lower-income young people. The strategic partnerships of LGE with GE, JBL, PBS, and Philips helped it secure world-leading technologies and a base from which to move forward as a leader in the multimedia business. Because LGE had established its manufacturing in Huntsville, Alabama, and Mexico, the company could quickly respond to shifts in the U.S. market. The company also had a strong capability in technology and in launching new products in a relatively short time. Its cost control ability was another one of its strengths. LGE had built good relationships with chain stores, individual stores, and Internet sellers and had implemented aggressive store promotions and mass media advertising. Internet sellers were familiar with its products and were very effective in promoting its products.

LGE's weakness was its relatively weak brand recognition in the high-end U.S. market. Its TV ads were weaker than those of its major competitors (such as Sony and Philips).

The Company

Haier had been founded in China in 1984 to produce mainly household refrigerators. Over the past 20 years, the company had witnessed significant growth and was now a transnational organization widely recognized in the world community. In 2004, Haier's global sales hit RMB 100 billion ($12 billion) and the Haier brand was valued at RMB 61.6 billion ($7.4 billion), topping all Chinese trademarks in a nationwide survey. Haier's leadership position in the Chinese home appliance industry had been solidified by obtaining a domestic market share of 21% of overall appliances, far ahead of all its competitors, with 34% of major home appliances and 14% of small electric appliances.

Haier's international promotion framework encompassed global networks for design, procurement, production, distribution, and after-sales services. According to *Euromonitor Statistics* (the world's leading provider of global business intelligence and market analysis), Haier was ranked fourth in global sales revenue of white goods in 2004. According to CEO Zhang Ruimin, Haier was on track to reaching its goal of becoming the third largest appliance maker in the world. Ruimin indicated that reaching that goal meant that the Camden facility would need to be expanded from 400,000 units in 2003 to 500,000 units in order to reach the company's objective of a 10% market share in U.S. refrigerator sales in 2005.[23]

Globally, Haier had gained first place in the United States in sales of compact refrigerators and wine coolers, in Iran for washing machines, and in Cyprus for air conditioners. The company was planning a joint venture with the Taiwan-based Sampo (an appliance manufacturer) to make compressors for air conditioners. The company had joined forces with Fujitsu Hitachi Plasma Display (a joint venture between Fujitsu and Hitachi) to develop and market plasma TVs. It had also announced plans to enter the Japanese market through partnerships with Sanyo Electric and Samsung.

On March 4, 2002, Haier opened its American headquarters in New York City, an indication that Haier had moved into a new phase in the globalization of product design, manufacturing, and sales. Haier had a strong commitment to long-term development in the United States. On August 20, 2003, Haier erected an electric billboard in the shopping district of Ginza, Tokyo, symbolizing Haier's determination to also reach the Japanese marketplace.

Haier's major markets for its consumer electronics were in China and elsewhere in Asia, where the Haier brand had broad consumer acceptance. Haier had a competitive position in the consumer electronics industry in China because of the company's strong brand recognition, rich feature designs, and well-serviced networks.

In 2004, the Haier Group acquired a controlling interest in the mobile phone company Haier-CCT Holdings Ltd., a business in which it already had a stake. Effective January 31, 2005, the name of the subsidiary was changed to Haier Electronics Group Company, Limited. The Haier Group then transferred its top-loading washing machine business to its Haier Electronics subsidiary. Haier Group management planned to eventually transfer other appliances to this unit as part of its plan to become one of the global "top three" in white goods.

In the United States, Electrolux, GE, Whirlpool, and Maytag dominated the major home appliance market with a total share of 93.2% of the major home appliance market in 2004, leaving Haier a small percentage of the total market. According to sales figures, Matsushita, Sony, Philips Electronics, Sanyo, and LG Electronics dominated the consumer electronics market in the United States. Compared with most of these major brands, Haier's consumer electronics products had no competitive advantages either in technology advances or in product quality, except for their relatively lower prices.

Products

Since the company had began exporting to the United States in the early 1990s, Haier had captured 20% of the U.S. market for compact refrigerators, the kind seen in college dorms or hotel rooms. It also pioneered electric wine cellars—inexpensive stand-alone cabinets for wine lovers. Haier started with three refrigerator products in 1998 and had advanced to more than 250 products including both home appliances and consumer electronics by 2004.

Home Appliances

Haier offered a variety of home appliance products, which included, but was not limited to, wine cellars, refrigerators, freezers, air conditioners, dishwashers, laundry products, and small appliances. Haier's core products were its major home appliances, including room air conditioners. Since 2002, Haier had grown in the major home appliance market by offering higher quality and a wider range of appliances with relatively low prices.

Haier America introduced a new line of microwave ovens at the 2005 CES Show, held during January in Las Vegas. The new line offered models ranging from compact to 1.4-cubic-foot convection grills. The units would be available in white, black, and silver colors. The company had made a long-term commitment to this category and was looking for strong and steady growth in it for years to come.

Haier's compact refrigerators were originally developed for the Chinese market, where most people liked small or medium-sized refrigerators that could save room in overcrowded living spaces. Haier applied the same concept to America and captured the niche market in college dorms, small apartments, and hotels. For example, Haier introduced a new compact refrigerator with two wooden flaps on the sides that could be folded out to make a computer table. College students could put their computer on the refrigerator. The flaps could be folded back down when extra space in the apartment was needed. Haier's new wine cellar had become one of its hottest selling products in the United States.

Other than large refrigerators made at its Camden factory, Haier America imported its products from China or the other subsidiaries of the Haier Group, where labor costs were much lower than in America. This created a price advantage for products sold in America. The company moved the production of its 14-cubic-foot refrigerator back to China in 2003 to make room for its new 21-cubic-foot models at Camden. According to Allan Guberski, VP and General Manager of Haier America Refrigerators, "It's more cost-effective to ship the 14-cubic-foot model because of how many refrigerators you can get in a container as opposed to the

21-cubic-foot."[24] Because of its lower-cost manufacturing facilities in Asia, Haier was better able to absorb rising material costs than were its U.S. competitors.

In order to increase its competitiveness and provide more consumer-friendly services, Haier had contracted with A&E Factory Service to be its primary service provider for repairs of products under the warranty and service contract in the United States and Puerto Rico.

Haier had a capability for advanced feature design on its major appliances. In terms of production, Haier tried to analyze consumer groups and understand their needs thoroughly so as to provide specific products for each distributor or customer group. For example, Haier's wine cooler had a digital thermostat operated by remote control. Its chest freezer had an innovative cooling section in addition to the freezing compartment. Unlike some portable room air conditioner models on the U.S. market, which used a water bucket that had to be emptied, all Haier's portable AC models had an "auto evaporation" function, which allowed continuous operation without water removal.

Haier did, however, have weak brand recognition in the U.S. market. Although Haier had entered the United States in 1998, the company mainly targeted niche markets, such as college dorms, hotel rooms, and the wine cellar market. Haier's aggressive expansion to the major home appliance market had captured some attention from the low end of the market, but such a strategy was not as effective in attracting the middle and high-end market segments. These segments were composed of higher-income young people and baby boomers, which together represented the largest consumer market in the U.S. major home appliance industry. Haier's unique design capability for large refrigerators fell behind its major competitors, such as GE and Whirlpool. Its development of technologically advanced products, such as smart appliances (e.g., the robot vacuum cleaner) fell slightly behind its major competitors.

Consumer Electronics

Haier offered consumer electronic products, which included plasma and flat-screen television sets, VCDs, DVDs, and TV/DVD combos. Consumer electronics was its secondary product line, a diversification designed to leverage the synergy of its existing consumer bases.

Haier's strengths were its relatively low prices and the unique designs and appearance of its electronics products. For example, at the 2005 Consumer Electronics Show in Las Vegas, Haier introduced the Haier P7 cell phone using cutting-edge technology in a unique design. The sleek P7 cell phone could be easily clipped onto a shirt pocket. It was another step forward in the evolution of the cell phone and a benchmark in the development of the Haier brand.

Haier's weaknesses were its weak brand recognition in the U.S. market and limited range of product choices. Its electronic products had no competitive advantages in either quality or warranty and services compared with the other major brands such as Sony and Philips.

Marketing

Home Appliances

For home appliances, the company primarily targeted lower-income young people and college students by offering relatively low prices on its compact appliance products. Haier was working to capture the attention of middle- and higher-income people with its large-capacity refrigerators. Middle-aged and older people preferred well-known brands such as Whirlpool, Maytag, and GE. They cared about the warranty and services of the products, but were somewhat price sensitive. If courted appropriately, they might be willing to try a new brand, especially since brand loyalty in the U.S. major home appliance industry was only 35%.[25]

Haier's primary problem was its low brand awareness in the middle and high-end markets in the United States. The company's large refrigerators, produced mainly for U.S. consumers, had not yet attracted much attention from middle- or higher-income young people, Baby Boomers, and older people. Depending so much on importing its products retarded its responsiveness to shifts in local market needs.

Consumer Electronics

For consumer electronics, Haier mainly targeted lower-income young people and college students. At the time, Haier imported most of its electronics from the Asian and Chinese manufacturing bases, where labor costs were much less than in America. Haier's price advantages on such imported electronics as the TV/DVD combo, LCD, and DVD attracted some attention from the low-end markets. Mid- to high-income and older people preferred major brand products with a reputation for quality, such as Sony and Panasonic. After-sale services were also important to these market segments.

Haier's relatively low prices on such products as the TV/DVD combo and DVD player/recorders made them attractive to younger and lower-income people. The unique designs on some of its high-tech products (e.g., the P7 cell phone) and simplified function designs attracted some attention from these consumer segments.

Haier's problem was its low brand awareness outside of its target market. Its major electronics products had no comparative advantages and had not gained recognition in the middle and high-end markets in the United States. A slow response rate to local market needs was another weakness.

Manufacturing

The Haier Group had 30 factories around the world; the one in South Carolina currently mainly manufactured large-capacity refrigerators for the American market. Although Haier had only one manufacturing base in America, the land available was large enough for continuous expansion.

Haier had a strongly motivated technician team, which was able to increase the company's product competitiveness by applying more features and style designs on its existing products. Haier could make a wide range of products in small production lots because most retailers wanted to offer products with a variety of features. To manage the costs of manufacturing many different product models, Haier designed common basic platforms. Periodically, the company changed the modules of components and subsystems to add some new features to its basic models.

Haier was relatively fast in developing new products. A large international manufacturer might spend 18 months in developing a new wine storage cabinet, but Haier took only 5 months. Because Haier could identify and meet consumer needs quickly, the company had won more than 50% of the total U.S. market share in the wine storage segment; Haier made 55,000 of the 100,000 units sold in 2002.

Haier had no advantage, however, in cost control with its large refrigerator products, making it harder to compete with such well-known brands as Whirlpool, GE, Electrolux (Frigidaire), and Maytag. Furthermore, excessive dependence on imports could cause a low response rate to local trends and relatively low speed of inventory replenishment.

Supply Chain and Distribution

In 2004, most of products that Haier sold in the United States were imported from its Asian and Chinese manufacturing facilities. The supply and distribution functions were extremely important to Haier's business development because they would determine how fast the company could respond to emerging market needs and how well the company could control its logistics costs. On October 25, 2004, COSCO, China's largest oversea shipping company, and Haier reached a strategic cooperation agreement. Under the new agreement, COSCO would provide supply-chain management based on its strong global network resources and help Haier explore business opportunities worldwide. Haier designated COSCO to be one of the leading logistics service providers for Haier's transportation and distribution of home electric appliances and supply of its raw materials and parts.

Haier's product distribution in the United States was nationwide, and its products could be found in most major chain retailers. A brief listing of outlets included Wal-Mart, Lowe's, Best Buy, Home Depot, Office Depot, Target, Sam's Club, Fortunoff, Menards, Bed Bath & Beyond, P.C. Richards, BJ's, Fry's, ABC, and BrandsMart. The list was growing every day. In 800 Wal-Mart stores, Haier had 100% of the room air-conditioner shelf space, 80% of refrigerators, and 100% of one of two SKUs in freezers. In Target stores, Haier had one of two SKUs in refrigerators. Best Buy carried Haier's digital wine cooler and advertised it as an electronic product. It was a strong, high-margin item for Best Buy.

Haier America had a strong distribution network and good relationships with both chain and individual stores. The company's recent collaboration with COSCO could further strengthen its cost savings in transportation and consolidate its price advantage.

Haier America's problems were its lack of American distribution centers and its limited exhibition space of standard appliance products compared with the other major brands such as Whirlpool, GE, Maytag, and Electrolux.

Sales and Promotion

Like most other manufacturers, Haier sold its home appliances and consumer electronics both in stores and through the Internet.

Sales

Store Sales

Since 2001, Haier products had entered the top 10 retail chain stores in the world and major chain stores in China. About 85% of Haier's orders in America and Europe came from the top 10 chain stores in those two areas. Retail sales staffs were familiar with Haier's appliances. Retailers were not as familiar, however, with Haier's electronics products, because most of them had just been introduced into the United States and the stores' shelves were already filled with products of other major brands, such as Sony, Philips, Panasonic, and LG.

Internet Sales

Haier America had broad networks with the major Internet sellers such as eBay, Amazon, and AJMadison. Haier's products could also be found on the Web sites of the top chain stores in the United States. Haier America had a broad network and good relationships with Internet sellers. Haier had price advantages over its competitors, which made it possible for Haier to offer better deals to most of the major Internet sellers. Haier did have an outdated Web site design, however, putting it behind Whirlpool, GE, Sony, and Panasonic.

Promotion

The Haier Group promoted Haier not as a Chinese or American brand, but as a global brand. The company's slogan was "What the World Comes Home To." To boost its brand image, Haier introduced its Two Brothers logo into the U.S. market.

At first, the company promoted the Haier brand mostly through outdoor advertising, airports and magazines, heavy advertising in trade publications, and on the Internet. Haier infrequently launched in-store promotions on its overstocked and outdated products. In 2004, the company sponsored an Australian basketball team, known as the Melbourne Haier Tigers.

Haier America used aggressive advertising on the Internet. The company had periodically implemented aggressive in-store promotions. Because of its labor cost advantage, Haier was able to discount its older styles or overstocked products. It did little TV advertising. Compared with heavy advertising by GE, Whirlpool, and Sony, Haier's advertising had been limited to airports, buses, billboards, and newspapers. Haier planned to launch more aggressive TV campaigns and provide sponsorships for sports teams to improve its brand recognition.

Technology

Haier had a good feature design capability in its core appliance products. The company needed relatively less time than many of its competitors to launch new products to satisfy different consumer needs. To succeed as a brand in the U.S. market, Haier had been trying to apply different features on each of its products. For example, Haier's convertible freezer/refrigerator provided the option of additional freezer or refrigerator space within one unit. Two separate temperature controls made it possible to create the type of storage needed most.

Nevertheless, Haier fell somewhat behind its major competitors in new appliance technology development. For example, Whirlpool introduced the Polara combination oven/refrigerator that could automatically start cooking at a programmed time and keep food either hot or cold. In Europe, Electrolux was selling the Trilobite, a robot vacuum cleaner. Samsung's "Home PAD Refrigerator" detected the shelf life of food and automatically displayed a list of items stored in the fridge on the door. Compared with other major brand names in consumer electronics, such as Sony, Matsushita, and LG, Haier had no competitive advantage on either product quality or technical advances. Haier's electronic products were therefore not very attractive to potential consumers in comparison with trusted and well-advertised brands such as Philips, Sony, and Panasonic.

Haier's relatively sluggish new technology development could weaken its competitiveness when facing even more serious competition in the future. Haier needed to be more effective in developing new technology for "smart appliances" and addressing more of the "smart kitchen" concept development.

International Expansion

Haier's initial stage of internationalization mainly focused on developing countries (first in Southeast Asia) to build volume and acquire international experience before it moved to the United States. In 1999, Haier established a design center in Boston, a marketing center in New York, and a manufacturing facility in South Carolina. Its strategy of localizing everything from design and manufacturing to sales and distributions indicated that Haier had a strong long-term commitment in the United States.

Haier's successful experience in the United States market supported its subsequent investment and operations in Europe and developing countries. In June 2001, Haier acquired an Italian refrigerator company. This company was to produce Haier refrigerators based on the designs provided by French and Dutch engineers. The products would be sold in the European market. Haier also implemented a strategy to localize designing and manufacturing, as well as sales and distribution. Nevertheless, Haire had no significant market share position in any major home appliance category in any European country in 2004.

In January 2002, the Haier Group signed an inclusive collaboration agreement with Japan's Sanyo Electric Co., which involved a wide-ranging business agreement to market consumer electronics products in both countries. Under the agreement, Sanyo's products would be sold in China through Haier's sales networks under the Sanyo and Haier brand names, while sales of Haier's products in Japan would be promoted by a joint venture, Sanyo-Haier Co. The Sanyo-Haier Co. started operations in April 2002 and initially sold Haier's refrigerators, freezers, and washing machines.

Warranty and Service

Haier America had recently contracted with A&E Factory Service to be its primary service provider for products under its warranty and service contract in the United States and Puerto Rico. Haier was transfering these services to A&E with the target date of February 15, 2005, for full implementation. One of the nation's leading service providers, A&E covered approximately 90% of the United States. It also serviced companies such as Whirlpool, Electrolux, Sears, GE, Fisher & Paykel, and Sharp. The commitment between Haier and A&E would provide customers with professional, courteous service from highly trained technicians and prompt service delivery using cutting-edge dispatch routing software. Only one telephone number would be needed for service inquiries and technician dispatch.

As of 2004, Haier had not yet found appropriate service providers for its consumer electronics products.

Financials

During the 17-year period from 1984 to 2001, the Haier Group had experienced a rapid growth, with an average annual growth rate of 78%, expanding from a small collectively run factory with a debt of $177,000 to the number one Chinese household appliance giant with a global sales of $7.25 billion.

In 2001, Haier group's exports from China totaled $280 million. Haier America's sales revenue at that time was $250 million. In 2002, Haier group's global sales reached $8.66 billion; its exports reached $400 million. In the United States, Haier America's sales increased to $300 million. In 2003, Haier Group's global sales reached $10 billion, its exports from China were $500 million, and it was ranked as the number one domestic electrical appliance producer in China.

In the first half of 2004, the Haier Group exported $530 million worth of products, a rise of 107% year-to-year. The Haier Group posted a 12% rise in fourth-quarter net earnings in 2004, even as fierce competition, soaring raw-materials costs, and a cut in export tax rebates reduced profits. Haier was the first Chinese brand to have more than 100 billion yuan ($12 billion) in assets. The Haier Group reported exports worth more than 1 billion U.S. dollars. Sales in the U.S. market also reached half a billion dollars. By the end of 2004, the Haier Group ranked fourth in major appliance sales worldwide behind Electrolux, Bosch-Siemens, and Whirlpool. In the United States, the company earned a 9% share of the 2,516,000-unit freezer market, a 20% share of the 2,567,000-unit compact refrigerator market, a 6% share of the 8,802,000-unit room air-conditioner market, and a 2% share of the 10,922,000-unit standard-sized refrigerator market. It was also the market share leader in home wine coolers. It had no significant U.S. market share in any other appliance category in 2004.

Exhibit 2 shows Haier's financial data from 2001 to 2004. The Haier Group's annual sales grew 1.7 times during that time, and its sales in the U.S. market doubled over the same period. Haier's total exports more than tripled, reaching $1 billion in 2004. Its brand value increased by 40% and Haier became the most valuable brand in China. Because the Haier Group was

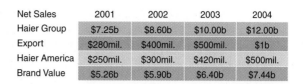

EXHIBIT 2 Haier Group Financial Data 2001–2004	Net Sales	2001	2002	2003	2004
	Haier Group	$7.25b	$8.60b	$10.00b	$12.00b
	Export	$280mil.	$400mil.	$500mil.	$1b
	Haier America	$250mil.	$300mil.	$420mil.	$500mil.
	Brand Value	$5.26b	$5.90b	$6.40b	$7.44b

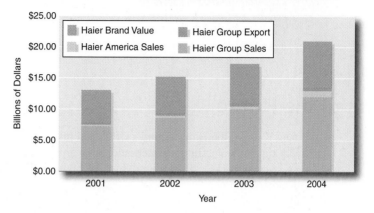

owned by the Chinese government, no other financial data were available. Haier Electronics, the Haier Group's publicly held subsidiary, which manufactured and marketed cell phones in 2004, reported sales figures of HK$3,153 million with a loss of HK$42.5 million for that year.

Strategy and Programs

To improve Haier's management efficiency, Zhang Ruimin, the CEO of the Haier Group, combined Chinese traditional culture and Western industrial experience by establishing the OEC (Overall Every Control and Clear) market-chain system. The philosophy of OEC management was to quickly identify problems, search for the causes of these problems, and find solutions one by one. On the basis of the Haier OEC management system, Haier had broken free from traditional management systems by practicing "market chain business flow renovation" and set up an order processing system comprising material, commodity, and capital subsystems, which helped realize a zero-distance contact with customers. Zhang Ruimin's management system had been widely acknowledged as superior by domestic and overseas management professionals.

Facing the challenges brought by e-commerce and China's joining the WTO, Haier began a management-restructuring program in 1998 backed by the efficient Haier market-chain system. During the first 5 years, Haier focused on organizational restructuring and management decentralizing with application of advanced information and network systems in order fulfillment, market-chain performance, logistics, capital operation, after-sales service, product inventory, and operational cost reduction. During the second 5-year period from 2003 to 2008, Haier was implementing a new management program called the "Strategic Business Units" to stimulate employee enthusiasm and to enhance Haier's competitiveness in the global marketplace. Similar to decentralized management, this program encouraged each employee to act as the manager of his or her own business unit, whether it be one job or an entire department.

Haier's growth strategy could be divided into three stages:

The first stage was the Brand Name Strategy (1984–1991). It took Haier seven years to build up a strong brand name in refrigerators through a well-planned TQC (total quality control) system. Haier products became known for quality and innovation. When Zhang Ruimin took in charge of Haier in 1984, his first act was to smash 76 poor-quality refrigerators with a hammer to drive home his intention to improve product quality.

The second stage was the Diversified Development Strategy (1992–1998). Haier spent these six years diversifying a product catalog to avoid having all of the company's eggs in one basket. When it was founded, the company had only one product and a staff of 800. By 2004, more than 30,000 Haier employees were making more than 13,000 products in 86 categories.

The third stage was the Going Multinational Strategy (1998 on). Haier's first overseas manufacturing subsidiaries were set up in developing countries, mainly in Southeast Asia. Then it entered the United States. After its successful experience in the United States, it ventured into Europe in 2001, Japan in 2002, and then into other developing countries. In early 2005, Haier had 62 distributors and more than 30,000 retail outlets around the world. The company's eventual goal was to be listed among the Fortune 500 successful companies.

Looking to the Future

Zhang Ruimin, the Haier Group's CEO, and his colleagues had turned Haier from a collectively run workshop into an international enterprise. From 2001 to 2004, Haier had won access to major U.S. distributors, but its brand still remained unfamiliar to most U.S. consumers. Many analysts were convinced that Haier had put its eggs in too many baskets, and that it ought to be focusing on appliances—its core products, which did not yet have a solid reputation in the U.S. and Europe. Haier needed to build brand recognition and enhance its brand image. There already had been some stumbling blocks, notably in personal computers, which the company exited in 2001 after four unimpressive years. Haier now faced its biggest challenge: expanding its modest U.S. footprint and becoming a genuine global brand.

Haier's management had established a goal of expanding its U.S. market share, but was not yet sure which alternative strategy to follow. Two alternatives appeared to be feasible.

The *first strategic alternative* was for Haier to introduce a wider range of products into the U.S. market. This could be achieved by building distribution centers to more effectively supply chain and individual retailers. Under this alternative, Haier would continue to import most of its products from Haier Group global manufacturing bases. Haier would improve the efficiency of its distribution networks by implementing collaborative planning, forecasting, and replenishment (CPFR).

One benefit of this alternative was that Haier could take advantage of the strength of the Haier Group as a whole and offer more choices in a wide range of product categories that could satisfy different kinds of needs. Haier could thus increase its U.S. market share by providing high-quality products at relatively low prices. This alternative was feasible because Haier America had already established fairly good relationships with most of the large chains and individual retailers and the company had the financial resources needed to build regional distribution centers. Haier products had a significant pricing advantage compared with most of its U.S. competitors because most of Haier's imported products were from its Chinese or Asian manufacturing facilities, where labor costs were much lower than in the United States. Haier's recent strategic cooperation with COSCO, China's biggest overseas logistics service provider, was expected to allow the company to save more on its supply-chain management and distribution. All of these factors could contribute more to the cost and price advantage of Haier's products and increase its competitiveness against rivals in the U.S. market.

This alternative could succeed against Asian-based multinational firms, such as Matsushita and LG, because Haier would increase its competitiveness in the low-end market segment by improving and streamlining its distribution function to solidify its cost advantage and offer relatively low prices on its newly introduced products. In addition, Haier would probably attract some consumers from the middle market segment because of the firm's ability to absorb rising material costs. It would widen Haier's range of high-quality and simplified function–designed products in both home appliances and consumer electronics. This would be attractive to one-stop shoppers, who want to stick to a quality brand with a good warranty and after-sales service. Haier had already captured 20% of the U.S. market in compact refrigerators and 2% of the U.S. standard refrigerator market, and its wine cellar was the hottest-selling product in its category in the United States. Haier's new introductions should be welcomed by its present consumer base and attract some new consumers in the low end of the U.S. market by continuously offering relatively lower prices on its even broader product categories. Because the new introductions would be produced in Haier's low-cost Chinese and other Asian manufacturing plants, Haier could achieve a price advantage on such products as microwaves and plasma TVs in the U.S. market. This could create another opportunity for Haier to attract some middle market share from its competitors.

A problem with this alternative was Haier's low response rate to shifts in local consumption trends and its relatively long lead times in transportation, which could cause temporary overstocking or a shortage of certain products. Because such a strategy mainly focused on increasing sales by offering relatively low prices of imported products, it could not help Haier build a long-term quality image in the United States. Because most of Haier America's products would continue to be sourced from Asia, import duties would reduce Haier's America's potential profits.

A *second strategic alternative* was for Haier America to develop new features for the consumer electronics and home appliances it currently sold and to expand the South Carolina facility to manufacture other home appliances, such as air conditioners, washers, and dryers. Eventually, Haier America would manufacture all its core products locally. Haier America would improve its existing refrigerator product lines by changing the modules of the components and subsystems to add new versions, such as upright freezers, chest freezers, and refrigerators with freezers on the bottom.

The benefit of this alternative was that it would enable the company to more quickly capture and respond to trends in local markets and to increase the company's competitiveness by providing more appropriate products that could satisfy specific local needs. It was also an effective way for the company to build its brand image by offering both high quality and attractive features on its products, with reasonable prices and effective after-sale services. An increase in local manufacturing would reduce import duties on goods supplied from Asia.

This alternative was feasible because Haier America had already set up a 350,000-square-foot plant on 110 acres in South Carolina, with plenty of room for both improving existing product lines and setting up new product lines. Haier had the necessary financial capability to support such an expansion. Haier also had a strong innovative design team, which could quickly and effectively add new features to its existing products in a very cost-effective way to differentiate its products from other major brands, such as Whirlpool and Maytag, and at the same time meet local market needs.

This alternative could succeed against U.S.-based major home appliance competitors because Haier should be able to implement cost controls on its manufacturing process by implementing its OEC (Overall Every Control and Clear) management to ensure its price advantages in the U.S. market. When Whirlpool, GE, and Maytag increased prices in January, 2005, this created an opportunity for Haier to steal some middle market share from its U.S.-based competitors.

Haier would continue to focus on quality control and rich feature design in its core products and launch heavy advertising campaigns. For example, Haier's new compact refrigerator having two wooden flaps on the sides that could be folded out to make a computer table was a strong feature design that satisfied college students' specific needs. Most large manufacturers were not paying attention to such minor details. Haier was able to develop new features for products to satisfy customer needs faster than its competitors. By localizing manufacturing for its core appliance products in the United States and by designing more features into them, Haier could increase its sales and market share in the short run and increase its brand recognition and reputation over the long run.

Drawbacks of this alternative were the required high initial investment in new product lines and advertising, higher local manpower rates, and higher investments in research and development, which could erode the company's profit in the short term. Nevertheless, this alternative lessened the distance between the market and the manufacturing process. Based on consumption trends fed back from the market, a design center in the manufacturing facility could quickly convert this trend information into either new feature designs or new functional products. This could increase the company's competitiveness and benefit its long-term development.

CEO Ruimin needed to decide what strategic direction to take to make Haier a major player in the U.S. market. Was there another alternative that needed to be considered?

NOTES

1. Xinhua, "Haier Listed in World's Top 100 Recognizable Brands" (February 3, 2004), http://www.china.org.cn/english/BAT/86101.htm.
2. *Business Week* (November 8, 2004), http://www.businessweek.com/magazine/content/04_45/b3907008.htm.
3. Washington, "Goods Orders Rise 0.6% in December" (January 27, 2005), http://www.mabico.com/en/news/20050127/foreign_exchange/article16574/.
4. Usernomics (January 17, 2005), http://www.usernomics.com/news/2005/01/1257-bln-of-consumer-electronics-will.html.
5. R. W. Latella, "National Retail Market Overview"(March, 2005), http://www.valuation.cushwake.com/Documents/22305.pdf.
6. A. Glynn, and M. Normand, *Home Furnishings & Appliances Analyst* (March 17, 2005).
7. NAR, "Most Metro Area Home Price Gains Strong but Cooler—NAR" (Feb. 12, 2004), http://www.realtor.org/ publicaffairsweb.nsf/Pages/MetroPrices4thQtr03?OpenDocument.
8. Twice, "CEA Says '05 Sales Will Grow 10.7%" (January 22, 2005), http://www.twice.com/article/CA498488.html?verticalid=820&industry-By+The+Numbers&industryid=23106&pubdate =01/24/2005.
9. "28th Annual Portrait of the U.S. Appliance Industry," *Appliance* (September, 2005), p. P-5.
10. Ibid., pp. P-6 and P-7.
11. A. Tewary, "Home Furnishings & Appliances Analyst" (May 6, 2004), Online.
12. "Portrait of the Canadian Appliance Industry," *Appliance* (August, 2005), pp. 57–61.
13. Russell, J., "53rd Annual Appliance Industry Forecasts—North America" (January 2005), http//www.appliancemagazine.com/zones/consumer/07_ce/editorial.php?article=699&zone=7&first=1.
14. CEA, "CEA Announces Another All-Time High for DTV as Cumulative Sales Top 13 Million Units" (November 22, 2004), http://www.ce.org/press_room/press_release_detail.asp?id=10616.
15. ISM Report, "January Manufacturing ISM Report on Business" (February 1, 2005), http://www.ism.ws/ISMReport/ROB022005.cfm.
16. Whirlpool Reports Record 2004 Sales," *Appliance* (February 3, 2005), http://www.appliancemagazine.com/news.php?article58084&zone=0&first=101.
17. China, "China's Electric Appliance Prices Expected to Rise," *Appliance* (February 17, 2005), http://www.appliancemagazine.com/news.php?article=8145&zone=0&first=51.
18. CEA, "Video Trends in 2003-2004," http://www.ce.org/publications/books_references/digital_america/video/default.asp.
19. "28th Annual Portrait of the U.S. Appliance Industry," *Appliance* (September 2005), p. P-3. All 2004 U.S. market share figures come from this article.
20. L. Bonnema, "Expanding Its Reach," *Appliance* (April 2004), p. B-8.
21. E. Biesen, "Investing in the Future," *Appliance* (September 2005), pp. 53–54.
22. "28th Annual Portrait" (2005), p. P-2.
23. L. Bonnema, "Haier: Working Its Way Up," *Appliance* (October 2003), pp. 32–37.
24. Ibid., p. 33.
25. C. Miller, VP of Marketing, North American Appliance Group, Whirlpool Corporation, quoted by R. J. Babyak and J. Jancsurak in "Product Design & Manufacturing Process for the 21st Century," *Appliance Manufacturer* (November 1994), p. 59.

CASE 25

The Carey Plant

Thomas L. Wheelen and J. David Hunger

THE GARDNER COMPANY WAS A RESPECTED NEW ENGLAND MANUFACTURER OF MACHINES and machine tools purchased by furniture makers for use in their manufacturing process. As a means of growing the firm, the Gardner Company acquired Carey Manufacturing three years ago from James Carey for $3,500,000. Carey Manufacturing was a high quality maker of specialized machine parts. Ralph Brown, Gardner's Vice President of Finance, had been the driving force behind the acquisition. Except for Andy Doyle and Rod Davis, all of Gardner's Vice Presidents (**Exhibit 1**) had been opposed to expansion through acquisition. They preferred internal growth for Gardner because they felt that the company would be more able to control both the rate and direction of its growth. Nevertheless, since both Peter Finch, President, and R. C. Smith, Executive Vice President, agreed with Brown's strong recommendation, Carey Manufacturing was acquired. Its primary asset was an aging manufacturing plant located 400 miles away from the Gardner Company's current headquarters and manufacturing facility. The Gardner Company was known for its manufacturing competency. Management hoped to add value to its new acquisition by transferring Gardner's manufacturing skills to the Carey Plant through significant process improvements.

James Carey, previous owner of Carey Manufacturing, agreed to continue serving as Plant Manager of what was now called the Carey Plant. He reported directly to the Gardner Company Executive Vice President, R. C. Smith. All functional activities of Carey Manufacturing had remained the same after the acquisition, except for sales activities being moved under Andy Doyle, Gardner's Vice President of Marketing. The five Carey Manufacturing salesmen were retained and allowed to keep their same sales territories. They exclusively sold only products made in the Carey Plant. The other Carey Plant functional departments (Human Resources, Engineering, Finance, Materials, Quality Assurance, and Operations) were supervised by Managers who directly reported to the Carey Plant Manager. The Managers of the Human Resources, Engineering, Materials, and Operations Departments also reported indirectly (shown by dotted lines in **Exhibit 1**) to the Vice Presidents in charge of their respective function at Gardner Company headquarters.

This case was prepared by Professor Thomas L. Wheelen and J. David Hunger of Iowa State University. Names and dates in the case have been disguised. An earlier version of this case was presented to the 2000 annual meeting of the North American Case Research Association. This case may not be reproduced in any form without written permission of the two copyright holders, Thomas L. Wheelen and J. David Hunger. This case was edited for *SMBP*–9th, 10th, 11th, and 12th Editions. Copyright © 2001, 2005, and 2008 by Thomas L. Wheelen and J. David Hunger. The copyright holders are solely responsible for case content. Any other publication of the case (translation any form of electronic or other media) or sale (any form of partnership) to another publisher will be in violation of copyright law, unless Thomas L. Wheelen and J. David Hunger have granted additional written reprint permission. Reprinted by permission.

EXHIBIT 1
Gardner Company Organization Chart

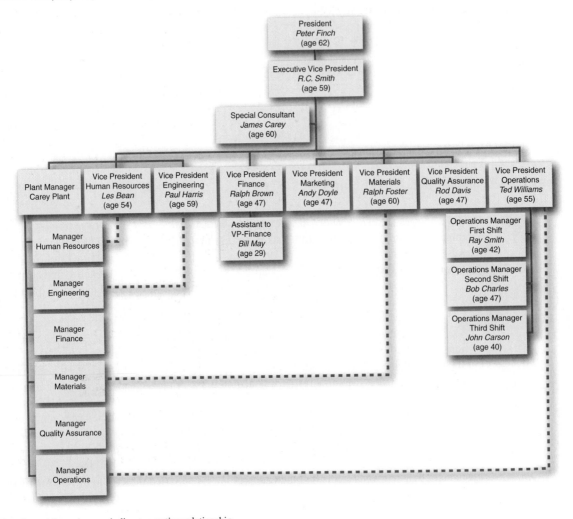

Note: Dotted lines show an indirect reporting relationship.

Until its acquisition, Carey Manufacturing (now the Carey Plant) had been a successful firm with few problems. Following its purchase, however, the plant had been plagued by labor problems, increasing costs, a leveling of sales, and a decline in profits (**Exhibit 2**). Two years ago, the Carey Plant suffered a 10-week strike called by its union in response to demands from the new management (Gardner Company) for increased production without a corresponding increase in pay. (Although Gardner Company was also unionized, its employees were represented by a different union than were the Carey Plant employees.) Concerned by both the strike and the poor performance of the Carey Plant since its purchase two years earlier, Ralph Brown initiated a study last year to identify what was wrong. He discovered that the poor performance of the Carey Plant resulted not only from its outdated and overcrowded manufacturing facility, but also from James Carey's passive role as Plant Manager. Gardner's Executive Committee (composed of the President and eight Vice Presidents) had been aware of the poor condition of the Carey Plant when it had agreed to the acquisition. It had therefore initiated

Year	Sales	Profits
5 Years Ago	$12,430,002	$697,042
4 Years Ago	13,223,804	778,050
3 Years Ago	14,700,178	836,028
2 Years Ago	10,300,000	(220,000)[1]
Last Year	13,950,000	446,812

Note:

1. Ten-week strike during October, November, and December.

plans to replace the aging plant. A new state-of-the-art manufacturing facility was being built on available property adjacent to the current plant and should be completed within a few months. The information regarding James Carey was, however, quite surprising to the Committee. Before Gardner's purchase of Carey Manufacturing, James Carey had been actively involved in every phase of his company's operations. Since selling the company, however, Carey had delegated the running of the plant to his staff, the Department Managers. One of his Managers admitted that "He was the driving force of the company, but since he sold out, he has withdrawn completely from the management of the plant."

After hearing Brown's report, the Executive Committee decided that the Carey Plant needed a new Plant Manager. Consequently, James Carey was relieved of his duties as Plant Manager in early January this year and appointed special consultant to the Executive Vice President, R. C. Smith. The current staff of the Carey Plant was asked to continue operating the plant until a new Plant Manager could be named. Vice Presidents Brown and Williams were put in charge of finding a new Manager for the Carey Plant. They recommended several internal candidates to the Executive Vice President, R. C. Smith.

The Offer

On January 31 of this year, Smith offered the Plant Manager position of the Carey Plant to Bill May, current Assistant to Ralph Brown. May had spent six years in various specialist capacities within Gardner's Finance Department after being hired with an MBA. He had been in his current position for the past two years. Brown supported the offer to May with praise for his subordinate. "He has outstanding analytical abilities, drive, general administrative skills and is cost conscious. He is the type of man we need at the Carey Plant." The other executives viewed May not only as the company's efficiency expert, but also as a person who would see any job through to completion. Nevertheless, several of the Vice Presidents expressed opposition to placing a staff person in charge of the new plant. They felt the Plant Manager should have a strong technical background and line management experience. Brown, in contrast, stressed the necessity of a control-conscious person to get the new plant underway. Smith agreed that Gardner needed a person with a strong finance background heading the new plant.

Smith offered May the opportunity to visit the Carey Plant to have a private talk with each of his future staff. Each of the six Department Managers had been with the Carey Plant for a minimum of 18 years. They were frank in their discussions of past problems in the plant and in its future prospects. They generally agreed that the plant's labor problems should decline in the new plant, even though it was going to employ the same 405 employees (half the size of Gardner) with the same union. Four of them were concerned, however, with how they were being supervised. Ever since the acquisition by the Gardner Company, the Managers of the Operations, Materials, Human Resources, and Engineering Departments reported not only to James Carey as Plant Manager, but also to their respective functional Vice Presidents and staff at Gardner headquarters. Suggestions from the various Vice Presidents and staff assistants often conflicted with orders from the Plant Manager. When they confronted James Carey about the situation, he had merely shrugged. Carey told them to expect this sort of thing after an acquisition. "It's important that you get along with your new bosses, since they are the ones who will decide your future in this firm," advised Carey.

Bill May then met in mid-February with Ralph Brown, his current supervisor, to discuss the job offer over morning coffee. Turning to Brown, he said, "I'm worried about this Plant Manager's position. I will be in a whole new environment. I'm a complete stranger to those Department Managers, except for the Finance Manager. I will be the first member of the Gardner Company to be assigned to the Carey Plant. I will be functioning in a line position without any previous experience and no technical background in machine operations. I also honestly feel that several of the Vice Presidents would like to see me fail. I'm not sure if I should accept the job. I have a lot of questions, but I don't know where to get the answers." Looking over his coffee cup as he took a drink, Brown responded, "Bill, this is a great opportunity for you. What's the problem?" Adjusting himself in his chair, May looked directly at his mentor. "The specific details of the offer are very vague in terms of salary, responsibilities, and authority. What is expected of me and when? Do I have to keep the current staff? Do I have to hire future staff members from internal sources or can I go outside the company? Finally, I'm concerned about the lack of an actual job description." Brown was surprised by his protégé's many concerns. "Bill, I'm hoping that all of these questions, except for salary, will soon be answered at a meeting Smith is scheduling for you tomorrow with the Vice Presidents. He wants it to be an open forum."

The Meeting

The next morning, May took the elevator to the third floor. As he walked down the hall to the Gardner Company Executive Committee conference room, he bumped into Ted Williams, Vice President of Manufacturing, who was just coming out of his office. Looking at Bill, Ted offered, "I want to let you know that I'm behind you 100%. I wasn't at first, but I do think you may have what it takes to turn that place around. I don't care what the others think." As the two of them entered the conference room, May looked at the eight Gardner Vice Presidents. Some were sitting at the conference table and working on their laptops while others were getting some coffee from the decanter in the corner. R. C. Smith was already seated at the head of the table. Ralph Brown, sitting on one side of the table, motioned to May to come sit in an empty chair beside him. "Want some coffee?" Brown asked. "Good idea," responded May as he walked over to the decanter. Pouring cream into his coffee, May wondered, "What am I getting myself into?"

C A S E **26**

Invacare Corporation, (2004)

Walter E. Greene and Jeff Totten

IF YOU HAD ONLY $10,000, WOULD YOU TRY TO RAISE $7.8 MILLION? MALACHI MIXON DID just that to buy Invacare from Johnson & Johnson in 1979. As the new year 2004 dawned, Mixon's concerns centered on how the changing Medicare rules on the eligibility of power wheelchairs for the elderly, intensified advertising by competitors such as The Scooter Store, and the passage of The Medicare Prescription Drug, Improvement, and Modernization Act of 2003 would affect Invacare's aggressive positioning for the near future.

History

Invacare Corporation's roots went back to the year 1885 when the Worthington Company of Elyria, Ohio, began producing "vehicles" designed for the physically handicapped. The Worthington Company merged with a manufacturer of rubber tire wheels and casters in the early 1900s and became the Colson Company. The Colson Company became a major supplier of bicycles and placed little emphasis on the wheelchair product. When the Colson Company moved its headquarters in 1952, three of its employees purchased the wheelchair operations and renamed the company Mobilaid, Inc. By 1960, Mobilaid, Inc., had annual sales of $150,000 and employed 15 individuals. It continued to grow modestly during the 1960s and was acquired in 1970 by Technicare Incorporated (Technicare), which renamed Mobilaid, Inc., as Invacare Corporation (Invacare) in 1971. Invacare focused most of its resources into the medical diagnostic imaging field and indeed became a leading manufacturer of such equipment. Invacare continued to grow at a modest rate, but with little direction and not much in the way of new products. Invacare was acquired by medical giant Johnson & Johnson in 1978.

Mal Mixon, a 39-year-old Technicare manager, became very interested in acquiring Invacare; however, the asking price was $7.8 million. Mixon, though he had only $10,000 to invest, was not dismayed by the large asking price. He believed that there was a strong growth potential for the home health care industry. Mixon was able to get real estate brokers, Cleveland-based investors,

This case was prepared by Professor Jeff Totten, Southeastern Louisana University, and Professor Walter E. Greene of University of Texas-Pan American. Copyright © 2005 by Jeff Totten and Walter E. Greene. The copyright holders are solely responsible for the case content. Reprint permission is solely granted to the publisher, Prentice-Hall, for *SMBP*–11th and 12th Editions (and the International version of this book) and Cases in *Strategic Management and Business Policy*–11th and 12th Editions, by copyright holders. Any other publication of this case (translation, any form of electronic or other media) or sale (any form of partnership) to another publisher will be in violation of copyright law, unless Jeff Totten and Walter E. Greene have granted additional written reprint permission. Reprinted by permission.

and a Chicago bank to put up approximately $7.6 million. Mixon invested his $10,000, borrowed $40,000 from two personal friends, and an additional $100,000 from the company to come up with the approximate difference from the asking price. Mixon accomplished a leveraged buyout that many would not consider feasible, but not without a high cost in debt and equity. For example, the bank loan was secured at a rate of three points over prime, which, at that time in December of 1979, equated to a rate of nearly 20%.

The buyout was structured in such a way that enabled Mixon to retain a 15% interest in Invacare. In 1979, Invacare's sales were about $19 million and net earnings after acquisition costs were approximately $100,000.[1] Invacare employed only about 350 individuals. In the first year of operations under Mixon, the profits of Invacare, which were about $1.4 million, were drained off by the high cost of debt. To further add to the obstacles of the company in its first year(s) were several well-established competitors, primarily E&J (Everest & Jennings), a California-based home health care company, which had more than 80% of the wheelchair market.

Mixon studied Invacare's product lines and eliminated those that were considered obsolete or unprofitable. In January 1981, Invacare entered the home care bed business with the acquisition of a small startup company in Sanford, Florida. Also in 1981, Invacare followed a growth strategy by expanding its product line, entering the respiratory business through the acquisition of Prime Air, Inc., a manufacturer of oxygen concentrators in Hartford, Connecticut. This operation was later moved to the Cleveland area facility in Elyria, Ohio, in 1985. Invacare entered more markets and penetrated current markets more deeply through acquisitions and partnerships throughout the 1980s and 1990s.[2] (See **Exhibit 1** for a partial list of acquisitions.)

EXHIBIT 1
Partial List of
Invacare's
Acquisitions

Date	Firm Acquired	Product
1979	Technicare (Invacare)	Wheelchairs
1981	Home Bed Care	Home beds
1981	Prime Air, Inc.	Oxygen concentrators
1984	Carters, Ltd.	Wheelchairs
1984	Gunter & Meier	Wheelchairs
1988	Invamex	Wheelchairs
1991	Canadian Posture & Seating Centre, Inc.	
1991	Canadian Wheelchair Manufacturing, Ltd.	
1992	Hovis Medical	Home medical equipment
1992	Perry Oxygen Systems	Oxygen systems
1992	Cofipar/Poirier, S.A.	Wheelchairs
1993	Top End	Athletic wheelchairs
1993	Dynamic Control, Ltd.	Wheelchairs
1993	Geomarine Systems, Inc.	Low-air-loss therapy systems
1994	Beram, AB	Wheelchairs
1994	Patient Solutions, Inc.	Ambulatory infusion pumps
1994	Rehadap, S.A.	Wheelchairs
1994	Genus Medical, Inc.	Motorized wheelchairs
1995	Special Health Systems	Wheelchair seating
1995	Medical Equipment Repair Service	Aftermarket oxygen parts and repairs
1995	Paratec, AG	Wheelchairs
1995	Group Pharmaceutical, Ltd.	Wheelchair distributor
1995	Thompson Rehab	Wheelchairs
1995	Bencraft Ltd.	Wheelchairs and seating
1995	Patient Solutions	Ambulatory infusion pumps
1995	PinDot Products	Custom seating systems
1996	Fabriorto, Lda.	Wheelchair/walking aids manufacturer

1996	Roller Chair Pty. Ltd.	Power wheelchair manufacturer
1997	Silcraft Corporation	Patient aid manufacturer
1998	Suburban Ostomy Supply Co.*	Medical supplies wholesaler
1999	Adaptive Switch Laboratories	Wheelchair devices manufacturer
1999	Dynamic Systems	Wheelchair devices manufacturer
1999	Scandinavian Mobility Int'l A/S	Bed/mobility aids manufacturer
2003	Pinnacle Medsources Inc.	Home med equipment distributor
2003	Mecc San SrL	Home med equipment manufacturer
2003	Carroll Healthcare, Inc.	Long-term-care furniture manufacturer
2003	Motion Concepts, Inc.	Seating and positioning products

*Renamed Invacare Supply Group in 2000.

SOURCE: *Invacare Reports; Datamonitor (December 8, 2003), p. 6; "Introduction to Invacare: Acquisitions," Investor Relations, www.invacare.com (January 22, 2005).*

In January 1988, Invacare began operations of it newly constructed maquiladora plant (a 78,000-square-foot manufacturing facility in Rio Bravo, Mexico, across the border from McAllen, Texas), named Invamex. This manufacturing plant enabled Invacare to manufacture low-cost manual wheelchairs that could compete with those of other foreign competitors from the Far East.

Invacare Today

The company operated in the home medical equipment (HME) industry segment. "Invacare Corporation is the world's leading manufacturer and distributor of non-acute health care products based upon its distribution channels, the breath of its product line and sales. The company designs, manufactures, and distributes an extensive line of health care products for the non-acute care environment, including the home health care, retail and extended care markets."[3]

Invacare continuously revised and expanded its product lines to meet changing market demand and offered more than two dozen product lines. The company's products were sold principally to more than 25,000 home health care and medical equipment provider locations in the United States, Australia, Canada, Europe, and New Zealand, with the remainder of its sales being primarily to government agencies and distributors. Invacare's products were sold through its worldwide distribution network by its sales force, telesales associates, and various organizations of independent manufacturers' representatives and distributors. The company also distributed medical equipment and related supplies manufactured by others.[4]

Trends in the North American Market

The home medical equipment (HME) market included home health care products, physical rehabilitation products, and other non-disposable products used for the recovery and long-term care of patients. The company believed that sales of domestic home medical equipment products would continue to grow during the next decade and beyond as a result of several factors:

- Growth in population over age 65: "The older population in 2030 is projected to be twice as large as their counterparts in 2000, growing from 35 million to 71.5 million and representing nearly 20 percent of the total U.S. population."[5]

- Treatment trends: Medical professionals and patients preferred home health care to institutional care.

- Technological trends: Medical equipment advances made home health care preferred over institutional care.

- Health care cost containment trends: The nation's health care spending was projected to increase to $3.1 trillion, growing at an annual rate of 7.3%.

- Society's mainstreaming of people with disabilities due to the 1991 Americans with Disabilities Act (ADA).

- Distribution channels: Products were now available through retail drug stores; surgical supply houses; rental, hospital, and HMO-based stores; home health agencies; direct sales; etc.

Trends in Foreign Market

The company believed that although many of the market factors influencing demand in the U.S. were also present in Europe and Australasia—aging of the population, technological trends, and society's acceptance of people with disabilities—each of the major national markets within Europe and Australasia had distinctive characteristics. The health care industry was more heavily socialized and, therefore, was more influenced by government regulations and fiscal policies. Variations in product specifications, regulatory approvals, distribution requirements, and reimbursement policies required the company to tailor its approach to each national market. Management believed that as the European markets became more homogeneous and the company continued to refine its distribution channels, the company could more effectively penetrate these markets. Likewise, the company expected to increase its sales in the highly fragmented Australian and New Zealand markets.

The home health care market in Europe was different in several aspects from that in the United States. In most European countries, socialized medicine was the norm. Consequently, governments were the largest single customers of home health care products. The rental market in countries with socialized medicine was virtually nonexistent in a market oriented more toward price than durability. In some European countries, such as Germany, the market was strongly geared toward quality and product features. Several companies, each of which possessed particular strengths in one or more countries, also dominated the European market.

A distribution network that relied on direct government outlets and on some independent medical equipment dealers characterized the European market. As the home health care equipment industry continued to develop, the roles of the medical equipment dealers were expected to strengthen.

Structure

Invacare was a highly centralized firm with headquarters in Elyria, Ohio. Invacare had a unique organizational structure that combined the benefits of both centralized and decentralized operations. During 1995 and 1996, Invacare reorganized domestic operations into a business unit to further decentralize and push decision making down to lower levels, to enable more rapid market response. Invacare realigned its management organization into three operating groups (North American, European, and Invacare Technologies), reporting to its Chief Operating Officer, Gerald Blouch. Each group consisted of several dedicated business units. Externally, Invacare had one "face to the customer" as products were sold through a single domestic sales and service organization with complete account responsibility. Executive officers are listed in **Exhibit 2.** Mixon, Blouch, and Richey are the three internal members of the 10-member Board of Directors.

A. Malachi Mixon, III	Chairman of the Board; Chief Executive Officer
Gerald B. Blouch	President; Chief Operating Officer; Director
Joseph B. Richey, II	President—Invacare Technologies; Senior VP—Electronic & Design Engineering; Director
Gregory C. Thompson	Senior VP; Chief Financial Officer
Diane J. Davie	Senior VP—Human Resources
Louis F. J. Slangen	Senior VP—Sales & Marketing
Kenneth A. Sparrow	President—Invacare Europe

SOURCES: *Summary Annual Report 2003; Datamonitor (December 8, 2005), p. 7.*

Invacare continued acquisitions over the years and in 2003 bought four businesses for cash at a total cost of $70,555,000. The four companies included the assets of Pinnacle Medsources, Inc., a Georgia corporation and distributor of home medical equipment; Mecc San SrL., an Italian corporation and manufacturer of home medical equipment; Carroll Healthcare, Inc. ("Carroll"), a Canadian corporation and a leading manufacturer of beds and furniture for the long-term care industry in North America; and Motion Concepts, Inc. ("Motion"), a Canadian corporation and a leading manufacturer of seating and positioning products in North America.

In 2003, Invacare had 34 plants in North America including four in Canada and the one in Reynosa, Mexico. Their Australasian operations comprised nine facilities, including one in Ohio and two in the United Kingdom. In Europe, Invacare operated from some 26 facilities. In total, Invacare operated more than 60 subsidiaries in approximately two dozen countries. As of December 31, 2003, the company had approximately 5,300 employees. Invacare had managed to work successfully with its employees and had no unions to contend with in the United States. That was not the case in the European market, where the labor forces were well organized up to this time. Invacare had had very little interference from the European organized labor forces, primarily because of the sluggish worldwide economy. Future labor negotiations might be an important measure of how well Invacare would perform in the European market.

Invacare made a commitment in 2004 to build a manufacturing plant in Suzhou Industrial Park in China. This followed up on the opening of an Asian procurement office in Hong Kong in 2000–2001. The company expected to achieve a low-cost delivery position in its basic product lines through overseas sourcing and manufacturing at its China plant. Additional manufacturing capacity at this plant was also planned for, while minimizing the loss of full-time jobs at its Ohio plant.[6]

Financials

Invacare issued annual audited consolidated financial statements in accordance with regulations established by the Securities and Exchange Commission. The consolidated financial statements included the accounts of Invacare Corporation and its subsidiaries. European subsidiaries were consolidated using a November 30 fiscal year-end. All significant company transactions were eliminated. Substantially all of the assets and liabilities of the company's foreign subsidiaries were translated to U.S. dollars at year-end exchange rates.[7]

See **Exhibit 3** for selected financial information over five fiscal years (1999 to 2003) and **Exhibits 4–6** for financial performance over the most recent of those fiscal years.

EXHIBIT 3
Selected Financial Information: Invacare Corporation (Dollar amounts in thousands, except per share data and ratios)

	2003	2002	2001*	2000	1999†
1. Earnings					
Net Sales	$1,247,176	$1,089,161	$1,053,639	$1,013,162	$882,774
Net Earnings‡	71,409	64,770	35,190	59,911	41,494
Net Earnings per Share—Basic	2.31	2.10	1.15	1.99	1.38
Net Earnings per Share— Assuming Dilution	2.25	2.05	1.11	1.95	1.36
Dividends per Common Share	0.05000	0.05000	0.05000	0.05000	0.05000
Dividends per Class B Common Share	0.04545	0.04545	0.04545	0.04545	0.04545
2. Balance Sheet					
Current Assets	$474,722	$398,812	$428,401	$432,408	$418,620
Total Assets	1,108,213	906,703	914,537	951,855	955,285
Current Liabilities	228,604	168,226	167,453	197,387	173,119
Working Capital	246,118	230,586	260,948	235,021	245,501
Long-Term Debt	232,038	234,134	342,724	384,316	440,795
Shareholders' Equity	613,188	480,312	381,550	349,773	318,872
3. Other Data					
Research and Development Expenditures	$19,130	$17,934	$17,394	$16,231	$15,534
Capital Expenditures, net of Disposals	30,129	19,718	19,486	26,268	32,155
Depreciation and Amortization	27,235	26,638	33,448	31,469	25,978
4. Key Ratios					
Return on Sales	5.7%	5.9%	3.3%	5.9%	4.7%
Return on Average Assets	7.1%	7.1%	3.8%	6.3%	4.9%
Return on Beginning Shareholders' Equity	14.9%	17.0%	10.1%	18.8%	14.8%
Current Ratio	2.1:1	2.4:1	2.6:1	2.2:1	2.4:1
Debt-to-Equity Ratio	0.4:1	0.5:1	0.9:1	1.1:1	1.4:1

*Reflects non-recurring and unusual charge of $31,950 ($25,250 after tax of $0.80 per share assuming dilution).
†Reflects non-recurring and unusual charge of $14,800 ($9,028 after tax or $0.29 per share assuming dilution).
‡Amortization of goodwill ceased in 2002, net earnings for prior years includes amortization expense of $8,972 in 2001, $8,899 in 2000, and $7,258 in 1999.

SOURCE: *Invacare, 2003 10-K Form.*

EXHIBIT 4
Consolidated Statement of Earnings: Invacare Corporation and Subsidiaries (Dollar amounts in thousands, except per share data)

Years Ending December 31	2003	2002	2001
Net Sales	$1,247,176	$1,089,161	$1,053,639
Cost of products sold	872,515	761,763	735,292
Gross Profit	374,661	327,398	318,347
Selling, general & admin. expenses	262,015	220,296	195,574
Amortization of goodwill	—	—	8,972
Non-recurring and unusual items	—	—	31,950
Interest expense	11,710	15,122	22,764
Interest income	(5,473)	(4,550)	(7,303)
Earnings before Income Taxes	106,409	96,530	66,390
Income taxes	35,000	31,760	31,200
Net Earnings	$ 71,409	$ 64,770	$ 35,190

EXHIBIT 4
(Continued)

Net Earnings per Share—Basic	$2.31	$2.10	$1.15
Weighted Average Shares Outstanding	30,862	30,867	30,620
Net Earnings per Share—Diluted	$2.25	$2.05	$1.11
Weighted Average Shares Outstanding— Assuming Dilution	31,729	31,664	31,683

SOURCE: *Invacare Corporation, 2003 10-K Form.*

EXHIBIT 5
Balance Sheet:
Invacare
Corporation and
Subsidiaries (Dollar
amounts in
thousands, except
per share data)

Year Ending December 31	2003	2002
Assets		
Current Assets		
Cash and cash equivalents	$16,074	$13,086
Marketable securities	214	1,350
Trade receivables, net	255,534	200,388
Installment receivables, net	7,755	20,953
Inventories, net	130,979	111,382
Deferred income taxes	24,573	26,053
Other current assets	39,593	25,600
Total Current Assets	474,722	398,812
Other Assets	53,263	51,031
Other Intangibles	14,678	4,779
Property and Equipment, net	150,051	130,963
Goodwill	415,499	321,118
Total Assets	$1,108,213	$906,703
Liabilities and Shareholders' Equity		
Current Liabilities		
Accounts payable	$110,178	$80,511
Accrued expenses	97,148	67,187
Accrued income taxes	19,107	16,049
Current maturities of long-term debt	2,171	4,479
Total Current Liabilities	228,604	168,226
Long-Term Debt	232,038	234,134
Other Long-Term Obligations	34,383	24,031
Shareholders' Equity		
Preferred Shares (Authorized 300 shares; none outstanding)	—	—
Common Shares (Authorized 100,000 shares; 30,739 and 30,294 issued in 2003 and 2002)	7,686	7,580
Class B Common Shares (Authorized 12,000 shares; 1,112, issued and outstanding)	278	278
Additional paid-in-capital	109,015	98,995
Retained earnings	477,113	407,235
Accumulated other comprehensive earnings (loss)	45,941	(18,729)
Unearned compensation on stock awards	(1,458)	(1,204)
Treasury shares (770 and 387 shares in 2003 and 2002, respectively)	(25,387)	(13,843)
Total Shareholders' Equity	613,188	480,312
Total Liabilities and Shareholders' Equity	$1,108,213	$906,703

SOURCE: *Invacare Corporation, 2003 10-K Form.*

EXHIBIT 6
Performance by Region, 2002 vs. 2003: Invacare Corporation (Dollar amounts in millions)

Region	Net Sales 2003	% Increase over 2002	% Adjusted for Foreign Currency	Net Sales 2002	% Increase over 2001	% Adjusted for Foreign Currency
North American	$897.2	13%	n/a	$793.5	3%	N/A
European	$279.8	11%	–8%	$252.07	7%	2%
Australasia	$77.44	74.8%	27%	$44.3	1%	–8%

Note:
2002 net sales for European region and 2003 net sales for Australasia region were calculated using reported percentage increases and net sales.

SOURCE: *Invacare Corporation Summary Annual Report 2003, third printed page;* Datamonitor Report *(December 8, 2003), p. 18.*

Products and Promotion

Invacare both manufactured and distributed prescription power and custom manual wheel chairs, standard wheelchairs, respiratory equipment (e.g., liquid oxygen systems), hospital-type beds for the home, motorized scooters, and other patient aids and equipment (e.g., incontinence products, canes, walkers, and shower chairs).[8]

Its products were distributed through a worldwide network of more than 25,000 home health care and medical equipment provider locations in the United States, Australia, Canada, Europe, and New Zealand, with the remainder of its sales being primarily to government agencies and distributors.[9]

The standard wheelchairs were generally purchased by older people and therefore normally reimbursed by Medicare/Medicaid. They were regarded as a commodity item and therefore a price-driven type of sale. The general price range could be from about $350 to $1,000. The power wheelchairs were Invacare's most attractive product line, with prices approaching $5,000 or higher. Power wheelchairs were purchased by people with more severe disabilities than those who purchased manual wheelchairs. Typically, users were quadriplegics who had some motor skills in at least one arm. The power wheelchair was usually controlled by a joystick, which accelerated, turned, and stopped the chair. The user needed enough control in his or her arm to operate the joystick; if not, more sophisticated "sip and puff" controls were used. Invacare was the only manufacturer who designed and manufactured its own controllers (an electronic microprocessor that controls the chair's movements). Invacare began in May of 1991 to manufacture its "Action" line of wheelchairs. These ultralight wheelchairs were the second-fastest growing segment of the market. Younger, active users with permanent disabilities generally purchased ultralight wheelchairs. These chairs allowed people with disabilities to play sports and were used in the 1996, 2000, and 2004 Paralympic games. They were light by any wheelchair standard, generally made of aluminum, and allowed the user greater mobility. However, the latest advancements in materials had enabled the production of carbon composite frames, which was lighter than the then-current frame materials.

New products introduced by the company after 2001 included the Storm Series TDX line of power wheelchairs; unbranded, low-price wheelchairs through its independent subsidiary, Professional Medical Imports; the Zoom HMV scooter; the HomeFill II oxygen system; and, for the European market, the Typhoon line of wheelchairs. Invacare also planned to enter the sleep apnea/therapy market with a new line of sleep therapy aids in 2004.[10]

New products were crucial to Invacare's success:

> *Exiting 2003, newly introduced products from the last three home care trade shows accounted for 73% of North American equipment sales in the home care channel. . . . Invacare*

has additional new products for sleep and its other product lines totaling a planned 40 new product introductions for 2004. . . . Invacare Europe has an aggressive product development plan to energize revenue growth . . . [and] Australasia benefited from a new non-healthcare customer that helped drive the top line and keep manufacturing near capacity.[11]

In 2004, through its co-op advertising program, Invacare continued to offer direct-response television commercials designed to generate demand for Invacare power chairs and scooters sold by the HME (Home Medical Equipment) provider. These commercials featured Arnold Palmer, Invacare's worldwide spokesperson. Mr. Palmer had become an integral part of Invacare's "Yes, you can" promotional and marketing efforts, encouraging consumers to achieve personal independence and participate in the activities of life, facilitated by the home health care products that Invacare manufactured, distributed, or marketed throughout the world. "Current advertising specifically highlights the HomeFill II and power mobility products."[12]

Distribution

Early on after the Mixon group acquired Invacare, marketing of its products became a priority. In a very competitive field, Mixon's strategy was to become dealer oriented. That is, in an industry that was influenced not so much by doctors but rather by therapists or dealers, Mixon began a strategy to win over the dealers because they were, for the most part, the representatives of the home health medical equipment market. In the early years, contacts and product orientation were about all they could offer dealers. In 1984 after the successful public stock offering, Invacare implemented an aggressive distribution strategy of offering dealers prepaid freight, 48-hour delivery, cheap financing, money for cooperative advertising, and volume discounts. Dealers became very familiar with Invacare's products because of the more available financing, volume discounts, etc.

During 1995, Invacare entered into retail distribution channels. Invacare kept its Invacare, Action, and PinDot brands exclusively for the HME provider channel. In early 1996, Invacare acquired Frohock-Stewart, Inc., a manufacturer of personal care products. For the first time, that acquisition permitted Invacare to offer a complete range of off-the-shelf home health care products through retail distribution channels that had no association with the company's key brands.

Evolution of the "One Stop Shopping" Proposition

Invacare's basic product strategies were simple: make its products the most attractive products for HME dealers. Invacare was known for its One Stop Shopping marketing strategy. Invacare was the only manufacturer committed to being the one source for the approximately 3,500 home health care and medical equipment dealers in the United States. Invacare distributed approximately 85% of what dealers needed. In 1992, Invacare began its One Stop Shopping Plus, a program that provided discounts to dealers as their percentage of sales exceeded 65% of Invacare products. As dealers stepped up through the percentage break point (65%), the program amounted to an exclusive distribution agreement with Invacare for the dealer in that area. The company had 100 dealers signed up for the program.

The One Stop Shopping concept was extended to Invacare's European Operations during 1995. It has since evolved into today's Total One Stop Shopping proposition, which has been credited for helping the company reach record net sales of $1.09 billion for fiscal year 2002.[13]

Competition

The home health care industry was quickly changing and becoming a global market. Former giant Everest & Jennings International (E&J) struggled and ended up becoming part

EXHIBIT 7

Major Competitors: Brands and Health Care Industry Segments

Segments Competitors	Wheel Chairs	Beds/Medical Rehab Equipment	Surgical Supplies	Sleep Therapy	Respiratory Equipment	Patient Aids
American HomePatient	X	X		X	X	X
Graham-Field	X E&J, LaBac	X (Smith & Davis)			X (John Bunn)	X (Lumex)
Hillenbrand Industries		X (Hill-Rom)			X (Vest System)	
Instrument-arium Corp.(GE)		X (Soredex, Ohmeda)			X (System 5, Ultraview)	
Mallinckrodt Inc. (Tyco)				X	X (Puritan Bennett)	
Medline Industries	X	X				
Pride Mobility	X (Jazzy Pride)	X (Quantum Rehab, Go Charis/Lifts				
Respironics				X (REMstar)	X	
Scooter Store	X					
Sunrise Medical	X (Breezy Quickie Guardian)	X		X (De Vilbiss)	X (De Vilbiss)	X

SOURCE: Plunkett's Health Care Industry Almanac 2004, *pp. 210, 389, 410, 450, 577, 612; Hoover's Online, www.hoovers.com (January 11 and January 20, 2005; subscription required); www.pridemobility.com (January 18, 2005); www.medline.com (January 20, 2005); & www.grahamfield. com (January 18, 2005).*

of Graham-Field Health Products.[14] Other major competitors included The Scooter Store (dealer), Sunrise Medical, Pride Mobility Products, American HomePatient, Medline Industries, Mallinckrodt (Tyco Healthcare), Hillenbrand, Instrumentarium (General Electric), and Respironics. See **Exhibit 7** for a competitor matrix (brands and health care segments).

Government Regulation

The company was directly affected by government regulation and reimbursement policies in virtually every country in which it operated. Government regulations and health care policy differed from country to country and within some countries. Most notably the United States, Australia, and Canada had policy differences that varied from state to state or province to province. Changes in regulations and health care policy took place frequently and often affected the size, growth potential, and profitability of products sold in each market.

Although there were a number of reimbursement-related issues in most of the countries in which Invacare competed, the issues of primary importance were in the United States. Two critical issues for Invacare were eligibility of power wheelchairs for elderly patients and the provisions of the legislation related to prescription drug coverage under Medicare.

There was a regulatory push by the Centers for Medicare and Medicaid Services (CMS) toward limiting eligibility to patients who cannot take a single step on their own. This limitation would confine many elderly patients, who are now mobile in power wheelchairs, to their beds. The impetus for the eligibility restrictions was extensive fraud that was uncovered after demand for motorized wheelchairs and scooters soared (more than 300% sales growth from 1999 through early 2003).[15] "Claims for power wheelchairs increased from 62,000 in 1999 to 168,000 in 2003. Payments in 1995 came to $22.3 million; in 2003, they rose to $666.5 million. In November 2003, The Associated Press reported the HHS inspector general identified $167 million in fraudulent power wheelchair claims and had 50 active investigations in close to 24 states."[16] CMS' "Operation Wheeler Dealer" began in Harris County, TX, home to 31,000+ power wheelchair payments in 2002 (versus 3,000+ in 2001); as a result, for example, fraudulent claims worth $84 million were found in that county alone, along with a multi-million dollar fraud uncovered in Florida, where a supplier sold $2,000 motorized scooters but billed Medicare for $6,000 power wheelchairs.[17]

In November 2003, Congress passed legislation related to providing prescription drug coverage for the elderly under the Medicare program. As part of funding the costs of this new program, a number of changes to Medicare home care reimbursement rules would take effect over the next few years. First, the home care provider (who was Invacare's customer) would not receive a cost-of-living adjustment for three years, 2004, 2005, and 2006. Also, in 2005 reimbursement for oxygen, along with several types of home care beds, wheelchairs, nebulizers, and supplies, would be lowered to the median reimbursement levels in the Federal Employee Health Benefit Plans. Third, in 2007, Congress authorized competitive bidding in the largest 10 metropolitan regions of the United States for six or fewer items and services, and the program was to be extended to 80 metropolitan regions in 2009.[18] As the law pertained specifically to power wheelchairs, section 302 stated that

> payment may not be made for such covered item unless a physician (as defined in section 1861(r)(1)), a physician assistant, nurse practitioner, or a clinical nurse specialist (as those terms are defined in section 1861(aa)(5)) has conducted a face-to-face examination of the individual and written a prescription for the item.[19]

Invacare's Mixon had this to say about the power wheelchair crackdown: "They've thrown the baby out with the bathwater. They're trying to stop the fraud, but instead, they've decided to kill the program."[20] Andrew Imparato, CEO of the American Association of People with Disabilities, stated, "They are going to force people to impoverish themselves in institutional settings. People who have not committed fraud are penalized, and the punishment doesn't fit the crime."[21]

What Next?

Invacare Corporation had grown from a minor player in the home medical equipment/health care industry to the world's largest manufacturer of home medical equipment/health care products. The company's success had come about because of the strategies it had always followed since 1979: (1) to aggressively introduce new cutting-edge products, (2) to build brand awareness and recognition in partnership with its dealers, and (3) to aggressively pursue key acquisitions that broadened its product offerings.[22] Invacare's goal for 2006 was $2 billion in sales.[23] The challenge for Mixon and his leadership team was to decide what to do about the government regulations, in particular, and the competitive environment, in general, to see that the 2006 goal was not sidetracked.

NOTES

1. Invacare Corporation, "Company Profile, History," *Datamonitor* (December 8, 2003), p. 6.
2. "History," *Datamonitor* (December 8, 2003), p. 6.
3. "Business Description," *Datamonitor* (December 8, 2003), p. 5.
4. Ibid.
5. *Older Americans 2004: Key Indicators of Well-Being,* "Indicator 1, Number of Older Americans," p. 2.
6. Invacare, *Summary Annual Report 2003*, several printed pages.

7. Invacare, *1991 Annual Report.*
8. "Invacare Corporation, Products/Operations," *Hoovers Online,* www.hoovers.com (January 11, 2005).
9. Jack W. Plunkett, *Plunkett's Health Care Industry Almanac 2004,* p. 418.
10. Invacare, *Summary Annual Report 2003,* several printed pages.
11. Ibid., third printed page.
12. Ibid., fourth printed page.
13. *Datamonitor* (December 8, 2003), p. 17.
14. For more information about Graham-Field, see its Web site: www.grahamfield.com/about.aspx (January 18, 2005).
15. Markian Hawryluk, "Medicare to Rein In Power Wheelchair Prescriptions, Sales," *American Medical News* (October 6, 2003), p. 9.
16. "Medicare: Power Wheelchair Industry Starts Lobbying," *Medical Devices & Surgical Technology Week* (March 28, 2004), p. 167.

17. Hawryluk (October 6, 2003); Markian Hawryluk, "DME: The Hard Sell," *American Medical News* (September 1, 2003), p. 5+; Michael Janofsky, "Costs and Savings in Medicare Change on Wheelchairs," *The New York Times* (January 30, 2004), http://www.aapd-dc.org/News/medicare/powerchaircov .html (January 6, 2005).
18. Invacare, *Summary Annual Report 2003,* fifth printed page.
19. *The Medicare Prescription Drug, Improvement, and Modernization Act of 2003,* section 302(a)(2)(E)(iv), p. H.R. 1–159, http://frwebgate.access.gpo.gov/cgi-bin/getdoc.cgi?dbname =108_cong_bills&docid=fih1enr.txt.pdf(January 6, 2005).
20. Janofsky (January 30, 2004).
21. Ibid.
22. Invacare, *Summary Annual Report 2003,* fourth printed page.
23. Ibid., fifth printed page.

BIBLIOGRAPHY

Brenda Hayslett, telephone interview with Human Resources, Invacare Corporation (April 12, 1993).

Invacare Corporation, *2001 Annual Report,* Elyria, OH.

Invacare Corporation, *2001 Consolidated Financial Statements,* Elyria, OH.

Invacare Corporation, *2002 Consolidated Financial Statements,* Elyria, OH.

Invacare Corporation, *2003 Consolidated Financial Statements,* Elyria, OH.

Javier Ledesma, Personal interview with Controller of Reynosa plant (April 5, 1993).

CASE 27

Wal-Mart and Vlasic Pickles

Karen A. Berger

PATRICK HUNN SAT AT HIS DESK WONDERING HOW COULD SUCH A GOOD DEAL BE VIEWED NEGA-
TIVELY? Patrick Hunn, team leader of Wal-Mart Sales, for Vlasic Foods International, had
made a record-breaking deal with Wal-Mart that resulted in selling more pickles than Vlasic
had ever sold to any one account. Wal-Mart was an important customer, accounting for 30%
of Vlasic Foods' sales. By negotiating a deal with Wal-Mart to offer a gallon jar of Vlasic pickles for $2.97 at the front of the store, Hunn had given Wal-Mart its "customer stop-
per." In addition, Hun secured an agreement that Wal-Mart would continue to buy
grocery size pickles, relishes, and peppers with each order of the gallon jar. The gallon
jar of Vlasic pickles was available in over 3,000 Wal-Mart stores in the United States. It had
been the deal of a lifetime, he had thought at the time. Why did Marketing conclude that the
deal was an enormous mistake even though Vlasic sold more product to Wal-Mart than had
ever been sold into any account? Steve Young, vice president of Grocery Marketing for Vlasic Foods International, had approved the deal. Why was Young so convinced now that Vlasic
needed to get out as soon as they could?

Background

The Vlasic brand had a long heritage of being the number one pickle brand in America. The
founders of the product line were Polish immigrants who sold their pickles through a dairy and
food distributor in Detroit. From a creamery business to a full-scale manufacturing operation,
the Vlasic brand was built on product quality and strong advertising and promotion. An advertising campaign developed in 1974 featured a stork delivering the message, "Vlasic is the best-
tasting pickle I ever heard!" This campaign helped give the brand a national identity.

In 1978 the company was sold to the Campbell Soup Company. As part of Campbell, the Vlasic brand prospered due to increased investment in both advertising expenditures and R&D. The 1994 roll-out of the Vlasic Stackers line of pickle slices intended for sandwiches continued to help build the brand into a major line of pickle products accounting for over a third of the U.S. pickle market. By 2000 the brand boasted 95% consumer awareness and was the only national pickle brand in America. However, the overall pickle market had been flat for a few years and Vlasic had only achieved small gains in the nineties. As Campbell's reconsidered its own agenda, its stock prices were sagging. Seeking to improve its profitability picture, Campbell reviewed its business units with an eye to weed out those businesses that did not meet Campbell's corporate benchmarks and objectives. Ultimately, the decision was made to spin off several non-core businesses, including Vlasic pickles as well as Open Pit Barbecue Sauce, Swanson foods, Armour meats in Argentina, and a mushroom farm business.

In March 1998 Campbell spun off a newly public company called Vlasic Foods International. This move was seen as essential to change Campbell's strategic focus and improve its long-term financial picture. The newly spun-off company, however, held debt of over $500 million along with an annual sales volume of $1.1 billion. The Vlasic line was its strongest business, accounting for sales of over $251 million in 2000.

Patrick Hunn had a long-established relationship with Wal-Mart. First, he was a major liaison between Sam's Club, a division of Wal-Mart, and Vlasic when it was part of Campbell's. His decade-long relationship with Wal-Mart made him essential to the newly formed company. He was quickly promoted from team leader of Sam's Clubs for Vlasic pickle brands to team leader of Wal-Mart for all Vlasic brands and products.

Both Hunn and Young had access to the Retail Link database that Wal-Mart had made available to its sixty-one thousand U.S. suppliers. From this database, first made accessible to vendors in 1991, Young and other selected executives from Vlasic could look at their sales data to help them understand the source and timing of their brands sold through Wal-Mart. This system helped Vlasic and other companies service Wal-Mart in the way that Wal-Mart wanted, with speed and care. In most stores, the system was connected at the individual store level allowing a given supplier to receive reports of shelf movement via real-time satellite links that update the system report each time a scan occurred at the point-of-purchase. Thus, the supplier was able to adjust its manufacturing qualities in real-time. The accuracy and timeliness of this type of system eliminated warehouse stock pile-ups, saving time and processing costs for the supplier. A supplier that did not have this type of electronic data interchange throughout the supply chain usually had higher costs and, therefore, would be likely to have difficulty meeting Wal-Mart's demands.

Like other Wal-Mart suppliers, Vlasic knew that Wal-Mart did not tolerate late orders or out-of-stocks. Wal-Mart provided the seamlessness for suppliers to maximize the efficiency of the supply chain and they expected their suppliers to respond. Vlasic had had no difficulties meeting Wal-Mart's volume requirements.

Bob Bernstock, president of the newly formed Vlasic Foods, knew that Wal-Mart was essential to his company. By 1998 it was well-established—not just at Vlasic—that a contract with Wal-Mart by definition was very important to a company's growth and success. The scale of business that Wal-Mart promised companies was unprecedented given the size of its orders and distribution capabilities. Wal-Mart was able to go national with a new item in two weeks as compared to two months in many other chains.

Hunn knew that his "charge" was to build volume for Vlasic brands and products through Wal-Mart. He had successfully worked with Wal-Mart and saw this deal as just one more opportunity to do business with this important and well-respected client. While he was not sure that the one gallon deal was a good idea at first, he had warmed up to the notion when he realized he could tie the deal to the "grocery segment," defined as pickles, relishes, and peppers 46 oz. and below.

Major deals and programs had to be approved by the president of Sales, Maurice Lane. Both Steven Young, vice president for grocery sales, and Pat Hunn, team leader for the Wal-Mart account, reported to the president of Sales.

By 1990 Wal-Mart was the number one retailer in the United States. By 1997 Wal-Mart had already had its first $100 billion sales year with combined national and international sales totaling $105 billion. Wal-Mart had become an international company with stores in Canada, Argentina, Korea, China, and Germany. As team leader of Sales for such a large, important account, Pat Hunn was an important player at Vlasic, controlling 30% of its largest line, Vlasic pickles.

The focus on the one-gallon jar of Vlasic pickles came into play when a Wal-Mart manager came up with the idea to offer the one-gallon jar usually sold in the Food Service section as a Memorial Day item at the promotion price of $2.97, instead of the everyday low price of $3.47. The Food Service section, also known as the Institutional section, was an eight-foot section near the rest of the grocery. The Food Service section contained items that small concession businesses and "Mom 'n Pop" grocery stores regularly bought. This section tended to not be as frequently shopped as the end aisles and other more prominent areas of the store. The Wal-Mart manager who wanted to do this promotion called the Bentonville headquarters, requesting promotional dollars for the one-gallon jar. Like other consumer packaged goods companies, Vlasic regularly gave its customers allowance money, part of a Marketing Investment Planning program (MIP fund for short). Once allowance money was paid, Vlasic customers could utilize the funds as they wished. Wal-Mart was a centralized organization with promotional funds controlled at the Wal-Mart headquarters. Thus, the manager of an individual store had to get promotional funding from headquarters.

According to Hunn, the allowance permitted this one Wal-Mart store to price the gallon jar at a price point of $2.97. The promotion ran over Memorial Day and "the gallon sold like crazy. . . . surprising us all."[1] News of this success spread throughout the Wal-Mart district. Soon many managers in the region wanted to duplicate this success in their stores.

In late 1998, one of the Wal-Mart grocery buyers, remembering the success of the Vlasic gallon-jar promotion, brainstormed that the gallon jar could be a "customer stopper." The overwhelming success of this limited market promotion triggered more discussions between Hunn, the Wal-Mart team leader at Vlasic, and the buying department at Wal-Mart. As team leader of the Wal-Mart account, Hunn's position required that he focus on building volume and market share. Approval of the deal needed to also come from Steve Young, vice president of grocery marketing. Both Hunn and Young were eager to build volume for their core brand.

The Deal

According to Hunn, this little promotion in a relatively low trafficked part of the store soon blossomed into a major deal, because of the newly expanded scope of the promotion. Wal-Mart executives were convinced that if consumers were enticed by a gallon of pickles at $2.97 in the Food Service section, then they would be even more enticed if the promotion was moved to an end aisle. In fact, Wal-Mart buyers saw the one-gallon jar as the "customer stopper" they wanted. The product was to be a special feature that was showcased in end stacks near or at the front of the stores. At the agreed upon price of $2.97, the jar would yield only one or two cents per jar for Vlasic. At this lower cost, Wal-Mart could price the jar at $2.97, leaving no more than a few cents profit per gallon jar for Wal-Mart as well. However, Hunn secured the deal with one proviso—all gallon-jar orders would have to be tied to a corresponding order of grocery sized items. As another control measure, the total number of cases that Vlasic would sell to Wal-Mart was established at the start of the fiscal year as part of the normal planning process.

The Results

The sales test proved right—the promotion was an enormous success for Wal-Mart. Vlasic's sales numbers skyrocketed, showing double-digit growth in the first few weeks. The gallon jar was so successful that Wal-Mart was purportedly selling on average 80 jars per store per week, or more than 240,000 gallons of pickles, just counting those sold in the gallon jars. However, the production quantities necessary to serve Wal-Mart put a strain on the procurement and production system. However, the product was selling and the Wal-Mart business grew to more than 30% of Vlasic Food International's business.[2]

Wal-Mart was very pleased with the success of the item. Wal-Mart continued to re-order gallon jars as stock became low. Since there was no cap on the order volume except for the requirement to also purchase the grocery size, the one-gallon jar was no longer a short-lived deal item, but a regular deal. From the consumer's point of view, the $2.97 deal was the Wal-Mart Every Day Low Price.

However, sources at Vlasic reported that profit was down 25%–50%. Some blamed the Wal-Mart deal for this decline. Production was pressed to provide quantities in record numbers and at times put a strain on the supply chain. Since the gallon jar used the same size and generally same product quality cucumbers as the dills and spears, this at times affected the availability of pickles for the jars of dills and spears. Since the jars of dills and spears consisted of cut pickles, they carried higher margins than the whole pickles. In addition, the pickle cost for the gallon jar could be reduced if less perfectly shaped pickles were added to the one gallon jar. However, the expansion of the distribution of the gallon jar resulted in periodic substitutions of the more perfect (and higher cost) pickles intended for the smaller but more profitable jars of dills and spears. Thus, pickles that were needed for the jars of dills and spears were sometimes in short supply and compromised the smooth flow of the supply chain. Marketing reported that over time, the few cents that Vlasic was making on the promotion was eroded, resulting in small losses per jar, given higher costs.

Supermarket sales, in non–Wal-Mart chains and independent stores, in 1999–2000 declined significantly with many customers placing smaller orders than the previous year. Marketing at Vlasic reported that predicted profits were eaten up by expenses associated with the loss of business in the non–Wal-Mart grocery sector.

On the other hand, Wal-Mart business showed real, incremental growth in its stores, based on analysis of organic growth from store expansion versus same-store growth. Not only was Wal-Mart growing due to new stores, but its existing stores were growing and showing healthy revenue and profit gains.

Through this promotion, volume of Vlasic pickles—all kinds—in Wal-Mart stores grew, so that Wal-Mart accounted for 33% of the Vlasic business. According to Hunn, sales revenue of Vlasic pickles was higher than before the gallon-jar "promotion."

The Marketing Perspective

Steve sat at his desk. His hands were full of problems due to cash flow shortages at his company. Vlasic Foods International had been spun off from Campbell's just months ago. The effect of the $500 million of debt that the spun-off company took with it was just becoming known. While this deal was only one issue in a sea of financial challenges, Steve felt that he should weigh in on the Wal-Mart part of the business given its effects on non–Wal-Mart grocery accounts. He had pleaded with Hunn to dip into his equity with Wal-Mart and end this promotion. Young was sure that this promotion had cannibalized the non–Wal-Mart business. According to Young, they "saw consumers who used to buy the spears and the chips in supermarkets buying the Wal-Mart gallons. They'd eat a quarter of a jar and throw the thing away when they got moldy. A family can't eat them fast enough."[3]

The Sales Perspective

Pat Hunn was surprised, if not disturbed, by the commentary from grocery marketing. Vlasic had financial troubles that went way beyond the sale of pickles. Wal-Mart was a great customer—sales with Wal-Mart now reached 33% of the Vlasic Foods business. On the revenue side, Vlasic's business was up with a dramatic shift upward in Wal-Mart sales. "Yes, there have been some troubles with production, but that was their job. Wal-Mart has helped build Vlasic's name as a leader in the pickle business. . . . I simply do not see why so many people are upset," thought Hunn to himself. He sat at his desk, shrugged his shoulders, and went back to work.

REFERENCES

Berman, Barry (1996), Marketing Channels. New York: John Wiley & Sons. Brynwood Partners (2005), "Pinnacle Foods," www.brynwoodpartners.com/investment/pinnacle. htm.

Dallas Business Journal (2003), "Hicks Muse Selling Pinnacle Foods for $485 million," www.bizjournals.ocm/dallas/stories/2003/08/11/daily1.html.

Fishman, Charles (2003), "The Wal-Mart You Don't Know," *Fast Company*, December 2003, p. 68, also available at pf.fastcompany.com/magazine/77/walmart.html.

Freeman, Richard (2003), "Wal-Mart 'Eats' More U.S. Manufacturers," *Executive Intelligence Review*, November 28.

Frontline (2004), "Interview with Cary Gereffi: Is Wal-Mart Good for America?" posted Nov. 23, www.pbs.org/wgbh/pages/frontline/shows/walmart/interviews/gereffi.html.

Gerard, Kim (2003), "How Levi's Got Its Jeans Into Wal-Mart," CIO Magazine, July 15.

Hannaford, Steve (2004), "Wal-Mart's oligonomy power," www.oligopolywatch.com, 10/04.

Hornblower, Sam (2004), "Wal-Mart & China: A Joint Venture: Is Wal-Mart Good for America?," *Frontline*, posted Nov. 23, www.pbs.org/wgbh/pages/frontline/shows/walmart/secrets/wmchina.html.

Hunn, Patrick (2006), Phone interviews, conducted by K. A. Berger, July 26, 2006, and August 4, 2006.

Koch, Christopher (2005), "Supply Chain and Wal-Mart," "The ABCs of Supply Chain Management," *CIO Magazine,*

http://www.cio.com/research/scm/edit/012202_scm. html, 10/4/05.

Lauster, Steffen M., and J. Neely (2004), "The Core's Competence: The Case for Recentralization in Consumer Products Companies," *strategy+Business Magazine,* Resilience Report, Booz Allen Hamilton.

Leis, Jorge (2005), transcript of radio interview, consulting expert Bain & Co., March 29, www.bain.com/bainweb.

Lewis, M. Christine, and Dogulas M. Lambert, "A Model of Channel Member Performance, Dependence, and Satisfaction," *Journal of Retailing*, Vol. 67 (Summer 1991), pp. 206–207.

Maich, Steve (2004), "Why Wal-Mart is Good," Rogers Media Inc.

Porter (1991), "Know Your Place," *Inc.* Boston, September, Vol. 13, Iss. 9, pp. 90–93.

Porter (1980), *Competitive Strategy Techniques for Analyzing Industries and Competitors*, New York: Free Press (pp. 3–5, 24–29, 180–181).

Porter (1979), "How Competitive Forces Shape Strategy," *Harvard Business Review*.

Schooley, Tim (2001), "Heinz to Acquire Vlasic Pickles," *Pittsburgh Business Times*, Jan. 29.

Wal-Mart Website (2005), visited September 28, 2005, www.walmartfacts.com/newsdesk/meet-our-partners.aspx.

Wal-Mart (2005), http://en.wikipedia.org/wiki/Wal-Mart.

NOTES

1. Fishman, 2003, p. 3 of pdf file from pf.fastcompany.com/magazine/77/walmart.html).

2. Fishman, 2003, p. 4 of pdf file.

3. Fishman, 2003, p. 4 of pdf file.

CASE **28**

Whole Foods Market (2005):

WILL THERE BE ENOUGH ORGANIC FOOD TO SATISFY A GROWING DEMAND?

Patricia Harasta and Alan N. Hoffman

REFLECTING BACK OVER HIS THREE DECADES OF EXPERIENCE IN THE GROCERY BUSINESS, John Mackey smiled to himself over his previous successes. His entrepreneurial history began with a single store, which he had now grown to the nation's leading natural food chain. Although proud of the past, John had concerns about the future direction of the Whole Foods Market chain. Whole Foods Market was an early entrant into the organic food market and had used their early mover advantage to solidify their position and continue their steady growth.

With the changing economy and a more competitive industry landscape, John Mackey was uncertain about how to meet the company's aggressive growth targets. Whole Foods Market's objective was to reach $10 billion in revenue with 300+ stores by 2010 without sacrificing quality and their current reputation. This would not be an easy task, and John was unsure of the best way to proceed.

Company Background

Whole Foods carried both natural and organic food, offering customers a wide variety of products. "Natural" refers to food that is free of growth hormones or antibiotics; "certificated organic" food conforms to the standards defined by the U.S. Department of Agriculture in October 2002.[1] Whole Foods Market was the world's leading retailer of natural and organic foods, with 172 stores in North America and the United Kingdom. John Mackey, current President and cofounder of Whole Foods, opened the Safer Way natural grocery store in 1978. The store had limited success, as it was a small location allowing only for a limited selection, focusing entirely on vegetarian foods.[2] John joined forces with Craig Weller and

Mark Skiles, founders of Clarksville Natural Grocery (founded in 1979), to create Whole Foods Market.[3] This joint venture took place in Austin, Texas, in 1980, resulting in a new company, a single natural food market with a staff of 19.

In addition to the supermarkets, Whole Foods owned and operated several subsidiaries. Allegro Coffee Company was formed in 1977 and purchased by Whole Foods Market in 1997; it then acted as their coffee roasting and distribution center. Pigeon Cove was Whole Foods' seafood processing facility, which was founded in 1985 and known as M & S Seafood until 1990. Whole Foods purchased Pigeon Cove located in Gloucester, MA, in 1996. The company is now the only supermarket to own and operate a waterfront seafood facility.[4] The last two subsidiaries are Produce Field Inspection Office and Select Fish, which was Whole Foods' West Coast seafood processing facility, acquired in 2003.[5] In addition to the foregoing, the company had eight distribution centers, seven regional bake houses, and four commissaries.[6]

"Whole Foods Market remains uniquely mission driven: The company is highly selective about what they sell, dedicated to stringent quality standards, and committed to sustainable agriculture. They believe in a virtuous circle entwining the food chain, human beings and Mother Earth: each is reliant upon the others through a beautiful and delicate symbiosis."[7] The message of preservation and sustainability is followed while providing high-quality goods to customers and high profits to investors.

Whole Foods has grown over the years through mergers, acquisitions, and several new store openings.[8] Today, Whole Foods Market is the largest natural food supermarket in the United States.[9] The Company consists of 32,000 employees operating 172 stores in the United States, Canada, and United Kingdom with an average store size of 32,000 square feet.[10] While the majority of Whole Foods locations are in the US, the company has made acquisitions expanding its presence in the UK. European expansion provides enormous potential growth due to the large population and it holds "a more sophisticated organic-foods market than US in terms of suppliers and acceptance by the public."[11] Whole Foods targets their locations specifically by an area's demographics. The Company targets locations where 40% or more of the residents have a college degree, as they are more likely to be aware of nutritional issues.[12]

Exhibit 1 lists the company's Board of Directors and key executives. John Mackey, co-founder, CEO, and Chairman of the Board, was the only internal member. A 12-year term limit was imposed on Board members in 2003.

EXHIBIT 1
Board of Directors and Key Executives: Whole Foods Market

A. Board of Directors

John P. Mackey	Chairman and CEO, Whole Foods Market
David W. Dupree	Managing Director, The Halifax Group
Dr. John B. Elstrott	Professor of Entrepreneurship, Tulane University
Gabrielle E. Greene	Chief Financial Officer, Villanueva Companies
Linda A. Mason	Co-founder & Chair, Bright Horizons Family Solutions
Morris J. Siegel	Managing Partner, Capitol Peaks investment firm
Dr. Ralph Z. Sorenson	Managing Partner, Sorenson Limited Partnership

B. Key Executive Officers

John P. Mackey	Chairman and CEO
Glenda Flanagan	Executive President and Chief Financial Officer
A.C. Galloxs	Co-president and Chief Operating Officer
Walter Robb	Co-president and Chief Operating Officer
James P. Sud	Executive Vice President of Growth and Business Development

Whole Foods Market's Philosophy

The corporate Web site defined the company philosophy as follows:

> *Whole Foods Market's vision of a sustainable future means our children and grandchildren will be living in a world that values human creativity, diversity, and individual choice. Businesses will harness human and material resources without devaluing the integrity of the individual or the planet's ecosystems. Companies, governments, and institutions will be held accountable for their actions. People will better understand that all actions have repercussions and that planning and foresight coupled with hard work and flexibility can overcome almost any problem encountered. It will be a world that values education and a free exchange of ideas by an informed citizenry; where people are encouraged to discover, nurture, and share their life's passions.*[13]

Although Whole Foods recognized that it was only a supermarket, they were working toward fulfilling their vision within the context of their industry. In addition to leading by example, they strove to conduct business in a manner consistent with their mission and vision. By offering minimally processed, high-quality food, engaging in ethical business practices, and providing a motivational, respectful work environment, management believed they were on the path to a sustainable future.[14]

Whole Foods incorporated the best practices of each location back into the chain.[15] This could be seen in the company's store product expansion from dry goods to perishable produce, including meats, fish, and prepared foods. The lessons learned at one location were absorbed by all, enabling the chain to maximize effectiveness and efficiency while offering a product line customers loved. Whole Foods carried only natural and organic products. According to management, the best tasting and most nutritious food available was found in its purest state — unadulterated by artificial additives, sweeteners, colorings, and preservatives.[16]

Whole Foods continually improved customer offerings, catering to its specific locations. Unlike business models for traditional grocery stores, Whole Foods products differed by geographic regions and local farm specialties.

Employee and Customer Relations

Whole Foods encouraged a team-based environment, allowing each store to make independent decisions regarding its operations. Teams consisted of up to 11 employees and a team leader. The team leaders typically headed up one department or another. Each store employed anywhere from 72 to 391 team members.[17] The manager was referred to as the "store team leader." The store team leader was compensated by an Economic Value Added (EVA) bonus and was also eligible to receive stock options.[18]

Whole Foods tried to instill a sense of purpose among its employees and had been named one of the "100 Best Companies to Work for in America" by *Fortune* for the preceding six years. In employee surveys, 90% of its team members stated that they always or frequently enjoyed their jobs.[19]

The company strove to take care of its customers, realizing that they were the "lifeblood of our business," and the two were "interdependent on each other."[20] Whole Foods' primary objective went beyond 100% customer satisfaction, with the goal to "delight" customers in every interaction.

Competitive Environment

American shoppers spent nearly $45.8 billion on natural and organic products in 2004, according to research published in the *"24th Annual Market Overview"* in the June issue of *Natural Foods Merchandiser*. In 2004, natural products sales increased 6.9% across all sales channels, including supermarkets, mass marketers, direct marketers, and the Internet. Sales of organic products rose 14.6% in natural products stores. As interest in low-carb diets waned, sales of organic baked goods rose 35%. Other fast-growing organic categories included meat, poultry, and seafood, up 120%; coffee and cocoa, up 64%; and cookies, up 63%.

At the time of Whole Foods' inception, there was almost no competition, with fewer than six small other natural food characteristics in the United States. Later, the organic foods industry was growing, and Whole Foods found itself competing hard to maintain its elite presence. As the population became increasingly concerned about its eating habits, natural food stores, such as Whole Foods, were flourishing. Other successful natural food grocery chains included Trader Joe's Co. and Wild Oats Market.[21] (See **Exhibit 2.**)

Trader Joe's, originally known as Pronto Markets, had been founded in 1958 in Los Angeles by Joe Coulombe. By expanding its presence and product offerings while maintaining high quality at low prices, the company had found its competitive niche.[22] The company had 215 stores, primarily on the West and East Coasts of the United States. The company "offers upscale grocery fare such as health foods, prepared meals, organic produce and nutritional supplements."[23] A low cost structure allowed Trader Joe's to offer competitive prices while still maintaining its margins. Trader Joe's stores had no service department and averaged just 10,000 square feet in store size. A privately held company, Trader Joe's enjoyed sales of $2.5 million in 2003, a 13.6% increase from 2002.[24]

Wild Oats was founded in 1987, in Boulder, Colorado. Its founders had no experience in the natural foods market, relying heavily on their employees to learn the industry. Acknowledging the increased competition within the industry, Wild Oats was committed to strengthening and streamlining its operations in an effort to continue to build the company.[25] Its product offerings ranged from organic foods to traditional grocery merchandise. Wild Oats, a publicly owned company on NASDAQ, was traded under the ticker symbol of OATS and was "the third largest natural foods supermarket chain in the United States in terms of sales." Although it fell behind Whole Foods and Trader Joe's, the company enjoyed $1,048,164 in sales in 2004, a 7.5% increase over 2003. Wild Oats operated 100 full-service stores in 24 states and Canada.[26]

Additional competition had arisen from grocery stores, such as Stop' N Shop and Shaw's, which had begun to incorporate natural foods sections in their conventional stores, placing them in direct competition with Whole Foods. Because larger grocery chains had more flexibility in their product offerings, they were more likely to promote products through sales, a strategy Whole Foods rarely practiced.

Despite being in a highly competitive industry, Whole Foods maintained its reputation as "the world's #1 natural foods chain."[27] As the demand for natural and organic food continued to grow, pressures on suppliers was rising. Only 3% of U.S. farmland was organic, so there was limited output.[28] The increased demand for these products might further elevate prices or result in goods being out of stock, with possible price wars looming.

EXHIBIT 2
Sales of Competitors in Natural and Organic Foods

Company	Sales (Dollar amounts in Millions)						
	2000	2001	% Growth	2002	% Growth	2003	% Growth
Whole Foods Market*	$1,838	$2,272	23.6%	$2,690	18.4%	$3,148	17.0%
Trader Joe's Company†	$1,670	$1,900	13.8%	$2,200	15.8%	$2,500	13.6%
Wild Oats Market‡	$ 838	$ 893	6.6%	$ 919	2.9%	$ 969	5.5%

Hoover's Online; http://www.hoovers.com/whole-foods/-ID_10952-/free-co-factsheet.xhtml (December 1, 2004).

† Hoover's Online; http://www.hoovers.com/trader-joe's-co/-ID-47619-/free-co-factsheet.xhtm (December 1, 2004).

‡ Hoover's Online; http://www.hoovers.com/wild-oats-markets/-ID_41717-/free-co-factsheet.xhtml (December 1, 2004).

The Changing Grocery Industry

Before the emergence of the supermarket, the public was largely dependent on specialty shops or street vendors for dairy products, meats, produce, and other household items. In the 1920s, chain stores began to threaten independent retailers by offering convenience and lower prices through procuring larger quantities of products. The emergence of the supermarkets in the 1930s was a result of three major changes in American society:

1. The shift in population from rural to urban areas
2. An increase in disposable income
3. Increased mobility through ownership of automobiles[29]

Perhaps the earliest example of the supermarket as we know it today was King Kullen, "America's first supermarket," which was founded by Michael Cullen in 1930. "The essential key to his plan was volume, and he attained this through heavy advertising of low prices on nationally advertised merchandise." As the success of Cullen's strategy became evident, others such as Safeway, A&P, and Kroger adopted it as well. By the time the United States entered World War II, 9,000 supermarkets accounted for 25% of industry sales.[30]

Low prices and convenience continued to be the dominant factors driving consumers to supermarkets. The industry was characterized by low margins and continuous downward pressure on prices made evident by coupons, weekly specials, and rewards cards. Over the years firms introduced subtle changes to the business model by providing additional conveniences, such as the inclusion of bakeries, banks, pharmacies, and even coffee houses co-located within the supermarket. Throughout their existence, supermarkets had also tried to cater to the changing tastes and preferences of society such as healthier diets, the Atkins diet, and low-carbohydrate foods. The moderate changes to strategy within supermarkets were imitated by competitors, which were returning the industry to a state of price competition. Supermarkets themselves faced additional competition from wholesalers such as Costco, BJ's, and Sam's Club.

A Different Shopping Experience

The setup of the organic grocery store was a key component in Whole Foods' success. The store's setup and its products were carefully researched to ensure that they were meeting the demands of the local community. Locations were primarily in cities and were chosen for their large space and heavy foot traffic. According to Whole Foods' *10-K Form*, "Approximately 88% of our existing stores are located in the top 50 statistical metropolitan areas."[31] The company used a specific formula to choose their store sites that was based on several metrics, which included but were not limited to income levels, education, and population density.

On entering a Whole Foods supermarket, it became clear that the company attempted to sell the consumer on the entire experience. Team members (employees) were well trained and the stores themselves were immaculate. There were in-store chefs to help with recipes, wine tasting, and food sampling. There were "Take Action food centers"[32] where customers could access information on the issues that affected their food such as legislation and environmental factors. Some stores offered extra services such as home delivery, cooking classes, massages, and valet parking.[33] Whole Foods went out of their way to appeal to the above-average income earner.

Whole Foods used price as a marketing tool in a few select areas, as demonstrated by the 365 Whole Foods brand-name products, priced less than similar organic products that were carried within the store. However, the company did not use price to differentiate itself from competitors.[34] Rather, Whole Foods focused on quality and service as a means of standing out from the competition.

Whole Foods spent only 0.5%[35] of their total sales from the fiscal year 2004 on advertising; they relied on other means to promote their stores. The company relied heavily on word-of-mouth advertising from their customers to help market themselves in the local community. They were also promoted in several health-conscious magazines, and each store budgeted for in-store advertising each fiscal year.

Whole Foods also gained recognition via their charitable contributions and the awareness that they brought to the treatment of animals. The company donated 5% of their after-tax profits to not-for-profit charities.[36] The company was also very active in establishing systems to make sure that the animals used in their products were treated humanely.

Aging Baby Boomers

The aging of the Baby Boomer generation was to expand the senior demographic over the next decade as their children grew up and left the nest. Urban singles were another group that had extra disposable income because of their lack of dependents. These two groups presented a growth opportunity for Whole Foods. Americans spent 7.2% of their total expenditures on food in 2001, making it the seventh highest category on which consumers spent their money.[37] Additionally, U.S. households with income of more than $100,000 per annum represented 22% of aggregate income compared with 18% a decade earlier.[38]

This shift in demographics created an expansion in the luxury store group, while slowing growth in the discount retail market.[39] To that end, there was a gap in supermarket retailing between consumers who could only afford to shop at low-cost providers such as Wal-Mart, and the population of consumers who preferred gourmet food and were willing to pay a premium for perceived higher quality.[40] "'The Baby Boomers are driving demand for organic food in general because they're health-conscious and can afford to pay higher prices,' says Professor Steven G. Sapp, a sociologist at Iowa State University who studies consumer food behavior."[41]

The perception that imported, delicatessen, exotic, and organic foods were of higher quality, therefore commanding higher prices, continued to bode well for Whole Foods Market. As John Mackey explained, "We're changing the [grocery-shopping] experience so that people enjoy it . . . It's a richer, [more fun], more enjoyable experience. People don't shop our stores because we have low prices."[42] The consumer focus on a healthy diet was not limited to food. More new diet plans had emerged in America in the last half of the 20th century than in any other country. This trend had also increased the demand for nutritional supplements and vitamins.[43]

In recent years, consumers had made a gradual move toward the use of fresher, healthier foods in their everyday diets. Consumption of fresh fruits and vegetables and of pasta and other grain-based products had increased.[44] This was evidenced by the aggressive expansion by consumer products companies into healthy food and natural and organic products.[45] "Natural and organic products have crossed the chasm to mainstream America."[46] The growing market could be attributed to the acceptance and widespread expansion of organic product offerings, beyond milk and dairy.[47] Mainstream acceptance of the Whole Foods offering could be attributed to this shift in consumer food preferences as consumers continued to list taste as the number one motivator for purchasing organic foods.[48]

With a growing percentage of women working outside the home, the traditional role of home-cooked meals, prepared from scratch, had waned. As fewer women had the time to devote to cooking, consumers were giving way to the trend of convenience through prepared foods. Sales of ready-to-eat meals had grown significantly. "The result is that grocers are starting to specialize in quasi-restaurant food."[49] Just as women entering the workforce had propelled the sale of prepared foods, it also increased consumer awareness of the need for the one-stop shopping experience. Hypermarkets such as Wal-Mart, which offered non-food items and more mainstream product lines, allowed consumers to conduct more shopping in one place rather than moving from store to store.

The growth in sales of natural foods was expected to continue at the rate of 8–10% annually, according to the National Nutritional Foods Association. The sale of organic food had largely outpaced traditional grocery products because of the consumer perception that organic food was healthier.[50] The purchase of organic food was perceived by 61% of consumers to be beneficial to consumer health, according to a Food Marketing Institute (FMI)/*Prevention* magazine study. Americans believed organic food could help improve fitness and increase longevity.[51] Much of this perception had grown out of fear of the way non-organic foods were treated with pesticides during growth and then preserved for sale. Therefore, an opportunity existed for Whole Foods to contribute to consumer awareness by funding non-profit organizations that focused on educating the public on the benefits of organic lifestyles.

Operations

Whole Foods purchased most of their products from regional and national suppliers. This allowed the company to leverage its size to receive deep discounts and favorable terms with their vendors. The company still permitted stores to purchase from local producers to keep the stores aligned with local food trends and was seen as supporting the community. The company owned two procurement centers and handled the majority of procurement and distribution themselves. Whole Foods also owned several regional bake houses, which distributed products to their stores. The largest independent vendor was United Natural Foods, which accounted for 20% of Whole Foods' total purchases for fiscal year 2004.[52] Product categories at Whole Foods included, but were not limited to:

- Produce
- Seafood
- Grocery
- Meat and poultry
- Bakery
- Prepared foods and catering
- Specialty (beer, wine, and cheese)
- Whole body (nutritional supplements, vitamins, body care, and educational products such as books)
- Floral
- Pet products
- Household products[53]

Although Whole Foods carried all the items that one would expect to find in a grocery store (and plenty that one would not), their "heavy emphasis on perishable foods is designed to appeal to both natural foods and gourmet shoppers."[54] Perishable foods accounted for 67% of their retail sales in 2004 and were the core of Whole Foods' success.[55] This was demonstrated by their own statement, "We believe it is our strength of execution in perishables that has attracted many of our most loyal shoppers."[56]

Whole Foods also provided fully cooked frozen meal options through their private label Whole Kitchen, to satisfy the demands of working families. For example, the Whole Foods Market located in Woodland Hills, CA, redesigned its prepared foods section more than three times[57] in response to a 40% growth in prepared foods sales.[58]

Whole Foods did not put just any product on its shelves. In order to make it into the Whole Foods grocery store, products had to undergo a strict test to determine whether they were "Whole Foods material." The quality standards that all potential Whole Foods products must meet included:

- Food that was free of preservatives and other additives
- Food that was fresh, wholesome, and safe to eat
- Food that was organically grown
- Food and products that promoted a healthy life[59]

Meat and poultry products had to adhere to a higher standard:

- No antibiotics or added growth hormones
- An affidavit from each producer that outlined the whole process of production and how the animals were treated
- An annual inspection of all producers by Whole Foods Market
- Successful completion of a third-party audit to attest to these findings[60]

Also, because of the lack of available nutritional brands with a national identity, Whole Foods decided to enter the private-label product business. They had three private-label product lines, with a fourth program called Authentic Food Artisan, which promoted distinctive products that were certified organic. The three private-label brands were (1) 365 Everyday Value, a well-recognized and trusted brand that met the standards of Whole Foods and was less expensive than the regular product lines; (2) Whole Kids Organic, healthy items that were directed at children; and (3) 365 Organic Everyday Value, all the benefits of organic food at reduced prices.[61]

When opening a new store, Whole Foods stocked it with almost $700,000 worth of initial inventory, which their vendors partially financed.[62] Like most conventional grocery stores, the majority of Whole Foods' inventory was turned over fairly quickly; this was especially true of produce. Fresh organic produce was central to Whole Foods' existence and turned over on a faster basis than other products.

Financial

Whole Foods Market focused on earning a profit while providing job security to its workforce to lay the foundation for future growth. The company was determined not to let profits deter the company from providing excellent service to its customers and a quality work environment for its staff. Their mission statement defined their recipe for financial success.

> Whole Foods, Whole People, Whole Planet—emphasizes that our vision reaches far beyond just being a food retailer. Our success in fulfilling our vision is measured by customer satisfaction, Team Member excellence and happiness, return on capital investment, improvement in the state of the environment, and local and larger community support.[63]

Whole Foods also capped the salary of its executives at no more than 14 times the average annual salary of a Whole Foods worker; this included wages and incentive bonuses as well.[64]

Over a five-year period from 2000 through 2004, the company experienced an 87% growth in sales, with sales reaching $3.86 billion in 2004. Annual sales increases during that period were equally dramatic: 24% in 2001, 18% in 2002, 17% in 2003, and 22% in 2004.[65] This growth was perhaps more impressive, given the relatively negative economic environment and recession in the United States.

Whole Foods' strategy of expansion and acquisition had fueled growth in net income since the company's inception. This was particularly evident when looking at the net income growth in 2002 (24.47%), 2003 (22.72%), and 2004 (27.94%).[66]

The ticker for Whole Foods, Inc. was WFMI. A review of the performance history of Whole Foods stock since its IPO revealed a mostly upward trend. The 10-year price trend showed the company increasing from under $10 per share to a high of over $100 per share, reflecting an increase of over 1,000%.[67] During 2004, the stock was somewhat volatile, but with a mostly upward trend. The August 2005 price of $136 with 65.3 million shares outstanding gave the company a market valuation of $8.8 billion.[68] See **Exhibits 3, 4,** and **5.**

EXHIBIT 3
Un-audited Quarterly Statements for the Fiscal Year ending September 26, 2004: Whole Foods Market
(Dollar amounts in thousands)

Fiscal Year 2004	First Quarter	Second Quarter	Third Quarter	Fourth Quarter
Sales	**$1,118,148**	**$902,141**	**$917,355**	**$927,306**
Cost of goods sold and occupancy costs	733,721	582,597	600,961	606,537
Gross profit	384,427	319,544	316,394	320,769
Direct store expenses	282,596	229,995	232,649	240,800
General and administrative expenses	35,869	28,783	27,551	27,597
Pre-opening and relocation costs	4,073	4,040	4,966	5,569
Operating income	**61,889**	**56,726**	**51,228**	**46,803**
Other income (expense)				
Interest expense	(2,478)	(1,859)	(1,319)	(1,593)
Investment and other income	1,464	1,503	1,782	1,707
Income before income taxes	60,875	56,370	51,691	46,917
Provision for income taxes	24,350	22,548	20,676	18,767
Net income	**$ 36,525**	**$ 33,822**	**$ 31,015**	**$ 28,150**
Basic earnings per share	$ 0.61	$ 0.55	$ 0.50	$ 0.45
Diluted earnings per share	$ 0.57	$ 0.52	$ 0.47	$ 0.43
Dividends per share	$ 0.15	$ 0.15	$ 0.15	$ 0.15

EXHIBIT 4
Balance Sheet: Whole Foods Market (Dollar amounts in thousands)

Year Ending	September 26, 2004	September 28, 2003	September 29, 2002
Assets			
Current Assets			
Cash and cash equivalents	$ 221,537	$ 165,779	$ 12,646
Short-term investments	—	—	—
Net receivables	94,421	61,554	42,356
Inventory	152,912	123,904	108,189
Other current assets	16,702	12,447	8,950
Total Current Assets	485,572	363,684	172,141
Long-Term Investments	—	2,206	4,426
Property Plant and Equipment	904,825	718,240	644,688
Goodwill	112,186	80,548	80,548
Intangible Assets	24,831	26,569	22,889
Accumulated Amortization	—	—	—
Other Assets	20,302	5,573	11,159
Deferred Long-Term Asset Charges	—	—	7,350
Total Assets	1,547,716	1,196,820	943,201

(Continued)

EXHIBIT 4
(Continued)

Year Ending	September 26, 2004	September 28, 2003	September 29, 2002
Liabilities			
Current Liabilities			
Accounts payable	328,977	233,778	170,509
Short/current long-term debt	5,973	5,806	5,789
Other current liabilities	—	—	—
Total Current Liabilities	**334,950**	**239,584**	**176,298**
Long-Term Debt	164,770	162,909	161,952
Other Liabilities	1,581	2,301	3,774
Deferred Long-Term Liability Charges	77,760	15,850	12,091
Minority Interest	—	—	—
Negative Goodwill	—	—	—
Total Liabilities	**579,061**	**420,644**	**354,115**
Stockholders' Equity			
Misc. Stocks Options Warrants	—	—	—
Redeemable Preferred Stock	—	—	—
Preferred Stock	—	—	—
Common Stock	535,107	423,297	341,940
Retained Earnings	431,495	351,255	247,568
Treasury Stock	—	—	—
Capital Surplus	—	—	—
Other Stockholders' Equity	2,053	1,624	(422)
Total Stockholders' Equity	968,655	776,176	589,086
Total Liabilities and Stockholders' Equity	**$1,547,716**	**$1,196,820**	**$943,201**

SOURCE: *http://finance.yahoo.com/q/bs?s=WFMI&annual (May 26, 2005).*

Year Ending	September 26, 2004	September 28, 2003	September 29, 2002
Total Revenue	**$3,864,950**	**$3,148,593**	**$2,690,475**
Cost of Revenue	2,523,816	2,067,939	1,757,213
Gross Profit	**1,341,134**	**1,080,654**	**933,262**
Operating Expenses			
Research & development	—	—	—
Selling general and administrative	1,107,797	893,229	771,631
Non-recurring	11,449	12,091	12,485
Others	—	—	—
Total Operating Expenses	1,119,246	905,320	784,116

EXHIBIT 5
(Continued)

Operating Income	**221,888**	**175,334**	**149,146**
Income from Continuing Operations			
Total Other Income/Expenses Net	6,456	5,593	2,056
Earnings before Interest and Taxes	228,344	180,927	151,202
Interest Expense	7,249	8,114	10,384
Income before Tax	221,095	172,813	140,818
Income Tax Expense	88,438	69,126	56,327
Minority Interest	—	—	—
Net Income from Continuing Ops	$ 132,657	$ 103,687	$ 84,491
Non-recurring Events			
Discontinued Operations	—	—	—
Extraordinary Items	—	—	—
Effect of Accounting Changes	—	—	—
Other Items	—	—	—
Net Income	**132,657**	**103,687**	**84,491**

SOURCE: *http://finance.yahoo.com/q/is?s=WFMI&annual, (July 27, 2005).*

Code of Conduct

From its inception, the company had sought to be different from conventional grocery stores, with a heavy focus on ethics. Besides an emphasis on organic foods, management also established a contract of animal rights, which stated that the company would only do business with companies that treated their animals humanely. Although they realize that animal products are vital to their business, they oppose animal cruelty.[69]

The company has a unique 14-page Code of Conduct document that addresses the expected and desired behavior for its employees. The code is broken down into the following four sections:

- Potential conflicts of interest
- Transactions or situations that should never occur
- Situations where a person may need the authorization of the Ethics committee before proceeding
- Times when certain actions must be taken by executives of the company or team leaders of individual stores[70]

This Code of Conduct covered, in detail, the most likely scenarios a manager of a store might encounter. It included several checklists that were to be filled out on a regular, or at least an annual, basis by team leaders and store managers. After completion, the checklists had to be signed and submitted to corporate headquarters and copies retained on file in the store.[71] They ensured that the ethics of Whole Foods were being followed by everyone. The ethical efforts of Whole Foods did not go unrecognized; they were ranked number 70 out of the "100 Best Corporate Citizens."[72]

Scarce Resources

Prime store locations and the supply of organic foods were potential scarce resources and could be problematic for Whole Foods Market in the future.

Whole Foods liked to establish a presence in highly affluent cities, where their target market resided. The majority of Whole Foods customers were well educated, which generally meant high salaries that enabled them to afford the company's higher prices. Whole Foods was particular when deciding on new locations, as location was extremely important for top- and bottom-line growth. However, there were a limited number of communities where 40% of the residents had college degrees.

Organic food was another possible scarce resource. Organic crops yielded a lower quantity of output and were rarer, accounting for only 3% of U.S. farmland usage.[73] Strict government requirements had to satisfied; these were incredibly time consuming, more effort intensive, and more costly to adhere to. With increased demands from mainstream super markets also carrying organics, the demand for such products could outreach the limited supply. The market for organic foods grew from $2.9 billion in 2001 to $5.3 billion in 2004, an 80.5% increase in the three-year period.[74]

Whole Foods recognized that the increasing demand for organic foods might adversely affect their earnings and informed their investors accordingly:

Changes in the Availability of Quality Natural and Organic Products Could Impact Our Business. There is no assurance that quality natural and organic products will be available to meet our future needs. If conventional supermarkets increase their natural and organic product offerings or if new laws require the reformulation of certain products to meet tougher standards, the supply of these products may be constrained. Any significant disruption in the supply of quality natural and organic products could have a material impact on our overall sales and cost of goods.[75]

NOTES

1. http://www.organicconsumers.org/organic/most071904.cfm.
2. Julia Boorstin, *Fortune* (September 15, 2003), p. 127. "No Preservatives, No Unions, Lots of Dough."
3. Whole Foods, http://www.wholefoods.com/company/timeline .html (November 4, 2004).
4. Boorstin (2003).
5. Whole Foods, http://www.wholefoods.com/company/facts .html (November 5, 2004).
6. Whole Foods, http://www.wholefoods.com/issues/org_ comments-standards0498.html (November 5, 2004).
7. Whole Foods, http://www.wholefoods.com/company/index .html (November 5, 2004).
8. Whole Foods, http://www.wholefoods.com/company/history .html (November 5, 2004).
9. "The Natural: Whole Foods Founder John Mackey Builds an Empire on Organic Eating," *Time*, Inc., 2002.
10. Whole Foods, http://www.wholefoods.com/company/facts .html (November 11, 2004).
11. "Whole Foods Buying chain of stores based in London: $38 million deal marks U.S. health-Food retailer's initial thrust into overseas market" Robert Elder Jr. (January 17, 2004.)
12. Jeanne Lang Jones, "Whole Foods is bagging locations," *Puget Sound Business Journal: Seattle* (August 13, 2004), p. 1.

13. Whole Foods, http://www.wholefoodsmarket.com/company/ sustainablefuture.html (November 5, 2004).
14. Ibid.
15. Boorstin (2003).
16. http://www.wholefoodsmarket.com/products/index.html (July 25, 2005).
17. Whole Foods, *10K-Q 2003* http://www.wholefoodsmarket .com/investor/10K-Q/2003_10K.pdf (November 11, 2004), p. 7
18. Ibid.
19. Whole Foods, *10K-Q 2004* http://www.wholefoodsmarket .com/investor/10K-Q/2004_10KA.pdf (*August 15, 2005*), p. 10.
20. http://www.wholefoodsmarket.com/company/decla-ration .html (July 29, 2005).
21. Hoovers Online: http://www.hoovers.com/whole-foods/-ID10952-/ free-co-factsheet.xhtml: (November 8, 2004).
22. Trader Joe's Company, www.traderjoes.com (November 8, 2004).
23. Hoover's Online, http://www.hoovers.com/trader-joe's-co/ -ID-47619-/free-co-factsheet.xhtm (November 8, 2004).
24. Ibid.
25. Wild Oats Market, www.wildoats.com (November 8, 2004).
26. Hoover's Online, http://www.hoovers.com/wild-oats-markets/ -ID_41717-/free-co-factsheet.xhtml (November 8, 2004).

27. Hoover's Online, http://www.hoovers.com/whole-foods/ -ID10952-/free-co-factsheet.xhtml (November 8, 2004).

28. Paul Grimaldi, "Providence, RI, Grocery Targets New Approach to Pricing,"; *Knight Ridder Tribune Business News* (September 28, 2004), p. 1.

29. David Appel, "The Supermarket: Early Development of an Institutional Innovation," *Journal of Retailing*, Vol. 48, No. 1 (Spring 1972), p. 40.

30. Ibid. p. 47.

31. Whole Foods, *10K-Q for 2003*, http://www.wholefoodsmarket .com/investor/10K-Q/2003_10K.pdf (November 11, 2004), p. 8.

32. Ibid.

33. Ibid.

34. Ibid., p. 10.

35. Whole Foods, *10K-Q 2004* http://www.wholefoodsmarket .com/investor/10K-Q/2004_10KA.pdf (August 15, 2005), p. 10.

36. Whole Foods, *10K-Q 2003*, p. 9.

37. Consumer Lifestyles in the United States (May 2003), 12.2 Expenditure on Food. *Euromonitor.* Solomon Smith Baker Library, Bentley College, Waltham, MA. (November 1, 2004).

38. John. Gapper, "Organic Food Stores Are on a Natural High," *Financial Times* (September 2004).

39. Ibid., 2004

40. Ibid.

41. Richard Murphy McGill, "Truth or Scare," *American Demographics*, Vol. 26, No. 2, (March 2004) p. 26.

42. Bob Sechler, "Whole Foods Picks Up the Pace of Its Expansion," *Wall Street Journal* (Eastern edition, September 29, 2004), p. 7.

43. Consumer Lifestyles in the United States (May 2003) 12.7 What Americans Eat. *Euromonitor.* Solomon Smith Baker Library, Bentley College, Waltham, MA. (November 1, 2004).

44. Consumer Lifestyles in the United States (May 2003) 12.4 Popular Foods. *Euromonitor.* Solomon Smith Baker Library, Bentley College, Waltham, MA. (November 1, 2004).

45. "Profile in B2B Strategy: Supermarket News Sidles into Natural, Organic Trend with New Quarterly," *Business Customer-Wire*, Regional Business News (October 25, 2004).

46. Ibid.

47. The World Market for Dairy Products (January 2004). 4.5 Organic Foods. 4.5.1 Global Market Trends in Organic Foods. *Euromonitor.* Solomon Smith Baker Library, Bentley College, Waltham, MA. (November 1, 2004).

48. The World Market for Dairy Products (January 2004). 4.5 Organic Foods. 4.5.1 Global Market Trends in Organic Foods. *Euromonitor.* Solomon Smith Baker Library, Bentley College, Waltham, MA. (November 1, 2004).

49. "Supermarkets' Prepared Meals Save Families Time," *KRTBN Knight-Ridder Tribune Business Daily News* (September 13, 2004).

50. Packaged Food in the United States (January 2004) 3.4 Organic Food. *Euromonitor.* Solomon Smith Baker Library, Bentley College, Waltham, MA. (November 1, 2004).

51. Packaged Food in the United States (January 2004) 3.4 Organic Food. *Euromonitor.* Solomon Smith Baker Library, Bentley College, Waltham, MA. (November 1, 2004).

52. Whole Foods, *10K-Q for 2004*, http://www.wholefoodsmarket .com/investor/10K-Q/2004_10KA.pdf (August 15, 2005), p. 10; http://www.wholefoodsmarket.com/investor/10K-Q/2003_10K. pdf (November 11, 2004), p. 8.

53. Whole Foods, *10K-Q for 2003*, p. 6.

54. Ibid., p. 5.

55. Whole Foods, *10K Q 2004* http://www.wholefoodsmarket.com/ investor/10K-Q/2004_10KA.pdf (August 15, 2005), p. 14.

56. Whole Foods, *10K-Q 2003*, http://www.wholefoodsmarket .com/investor/10K-Q/2003_10K.pdf (November 13, 2004), p. 6.

57. "Supermarkets' Prepared Meals," (2004).

58. Ibid.

59. Whole Foods, *10K-Q 2003*, http://www.wholefoodsmarket .com/investor/10K-Q/2003_10K.pdf (November 13, 2004), p. 5.

60. Ibid., p. 6.

61. Ibid., p. 7.

62. Ibid., p. 8.

63. Whole Foods, www.WholeFoodsmarket.com/company/ declaration.html (November 7, 2004).

64. Ibid.

65. Whole Foods, *10K-Q for 2003*, www.WholeFoodsmarket.com/ investor/10k-Q/2003_10k.pdf (November 7, 2004).

66. Ibid.

67. Nasdaq.com, "Market Symbol for Whole Foods Is WFMI," http://quotes.nasdaq.com/quote.dll?page=charting&mode=basics &intraday=off&timeframe=10y&charttype=ohlc&splits=off &earnings=off&movingaverage=None&lowerstudy=volume &comparison=off&index=&drilldown=off&symbol=WFM I&selected=WFM (November 11, 2004).

68. Ibid.

69. Whole Foods, *10K-Q for 2003*, http://www.wholefoodsmarket .com/investor/10K-Q/2003_10K.pdf (November 11, 2004), p. 6.

70. Whole Foods Code of Conduct found at company Web site, http://www.wholefoodsmarket.com/investor/codeofconduct .pdf (November 11, 2004).

71. Ibid., p. 11.

72. Business Ethics, "100 Best Companies to Work For," http://www .business-ethics.com/100best.htm (November 12, 2004).

73. Grimaldi (2004).

74. http://www.preparedfoods.com/PF/FILES/HTML/Mintel_ Reports/Mintel_PDF/Summaries/sum-OrganicFoodBeverages -Aug2004.pdf

75. Whole Foods, *10K for 2004*, http://www.wholefoodsmarket .com/investor/10K-Q/2004_10KA.pdf, p. 14.

Panera Bread Company:

RISING FORTUNES?

Ted Repetti and Joyce P. Vincelette

BREAD, ESSENTIAL AND BASIC, BUT NONETHELESS SPECIAL, TRANSCENDS MILLENNIA. A master baker combines simple ingredients to create what has been an integral part of society and culture for over 6,000 years. Sourdough bread, a uniquely American creation, is made from a "culture," or "starter." Sourdough starter contains natural yeasts, flour, and water and is the medium that makes bread rise. In order to survive, a starter must be cultured, fed, and tended to by attentive hands in the right environment. Without proper care and maintenance, the yeast, or the growth factor, would slow down and die. Without a strong starter, bread would no longer rise.

Ronald Shaich, CEO and Chairman of Panera Bread Company, created the company's "starter." Shaich, the master baker, combined the ingredients and cultivated the leavening agent that catalyzed the company's phenomenal growth. Under Shaich's guidance, Panera's total systemwide (both company and franchisee) revenues rose from $350.8 million in 2000 to $977.1 million in 2003. However, new unit expansion fueled this growth. In total, 419 Panera bakery-cafes were opened between 1999 and 2003. New unit growth masked a slowdown in the growth of average annualized unit volumes (AUVs) and year-to-year comparable sales. In 2000, systemwide comparable sales and AUVs increased 9.1% and 12.0%, respectively. Growth of these two key metrics declined in each consecutive year thereafter. In 2003, systemwide comparable sales and AUVs increased only 0.2% and 0.5%. Clearly, growth has slowed. In order to continue to rise, Panera's "starter" needs to be fed and maintained. In addition to new unit growth, new strategies and initiatives must be folded into the mix.

History

Panera Bread Company's roots began with the company that could be considered the grandfather of the fast casual restaurant concept: Au Bon Pain. In 1976, French oven manufacturer Pavailler opened the first Au Bon Pain (a French colloquialism for "where good bread is") in Boston's Faneuil Hall as a demonstration bakery.[1] Struck by its growth potential, Louis Kane, a veteran venture capitalist, purchased the business in 1978.[2] Between 1978 and 1981, Au Bon Pain struggled; it had opened 13 and subsequently closed 10 stores in the Boston area and piled up $3 million in debt.[3] Kane was ready to declare bankruptcy when he gained a new business partner in Ronald Shaich.[4]

A recent Harvard Business graduate, Shaich had opened the Cookie Jar bakery in Cambridge, Massachusetts, in 1980.[5] Shortly after opening the Cookie Jar, Shaich befriended Louis Kane. Shaich was interested in adding bread and croissants to his menu to stimulate his morning sales. Shaich recalled that "50,000 people a day were going past my store, and I had nothing to sell them in the morning."[6] In February 1981, the two merged the Au Bon Pain bakeries and the cookie store to form one business, Au Bon Pain Co., Inc. The two served as Co-CEOs until Kane's retirement in 1994. They had a synergistic relationship that made Au Bon Pain successful: Shaich was the hard-driving, analytical strategist focused on operations, and Kane was the seasoned businessman with a wealth of real estate and finance connections.[7] Between 1981 and 1984, the team expanded the business, worked to decrease the company's debt, and centralized facilities for dough production.[8]

In 1985, the partners added sandwiches to bolster daytime sales, as they noticed a pattern in customer behavior: "We had all of these customers coming and ordering a baguette cut in half. Then they'd take out these lunch bags full of cold cuts and start making sandwiches. We didn't have to be marketing whizzes to know that there was an opportunity there," recalled Shaich.[9] It was a "eureka" moment and the birth of the fast casual restaurant category.[10] According to Shaich, Au Bon Pain was the "first place that gave white collar folks a choice between fast food and fine dining."[11] Au Bon Pain became a lunchtime alternative for urban dwellers who were tired of burgers and fast food. Differentiated from other fast food competitors by its commitment to fresh, quality sandwiches, bread, and coffee, Au Bon Pain attracted customers who were happy to pay more money ($5 per sandwich) than they would have paid for fast food.[12]

In 1991, Kane and Shaich took the company public. By that time, the company had $68 million in sales and was a leader in the quick service bakery segment. By 1994, the company had 200 stores and $183 million in sales, but that growth masked a problem. The company was built on a limited growth concept, what Shaich called, "high density urban feeding."[13] The main customers of the company were office workers in locations like New York, Boston, and Washington, DC. The real estate in such areas was expensive and hard to come by. This strategic factor limited expansion possibilities.[14]

Au Bon Pain acquired the St. Louis Bread Company in 1993 for $24 million.[15] Shaich saw this as the company's "gateway into the suburban marketplace."[16] The acquired company was founded in 1987 by Ken Rosenthal and consisted of a 19-store bakery-cafe chain located in the St. Louis area. The concept of the cafe was based on San Franciscan sourdough bread bakeries.[17] The acquired company would eventually become the platform for what is now Panera.

Au Bon Pain management spent two years studying St. Louis Bread Co., looking for the ideal concept that would unite Au Bon Pain's operational abilities and quality food with the broader suburban growth appeal of St. Louis Bread.[18] Scott Davis, Panera's Chief Concept Officer, recalled the time spent trying to figure out what the new business should look like. "We didn't just look at restaurants and coffee houses," he stated. "We spent a lot of time looking at retailers. That's where our front-of-the-house bakery displays came from. We knew that people buy with their eyes, so we wanted them to walk in and crave baked goods."[19]

The restaging and development of the St. Louis Bread Co. concept was also affected by the management team's understanding of a consumer backlash against the commoditization of food service—a trend that began in the 1950s and spawned a coast-to-coast sameness (e.g., McDonald's).[20] The management team understood that a growing number of consumers wanted a unique expression of tastes and styles. Shaich and his team wrote a manifesto that spelled out what St. Louis Bread would be, from the type of food it would serve to the kind of people behind the counters and the look and feel of the physical space.[21]

Au Bon Pain began pouring capital into the chain when Shaich had another "eureka" moment in 1995. He entered a St. Louis Bread store and noticed a group of business people meeting in a corner. The customers explained that they had no other place to talk.[22] This experience opened Shaich's eyes to the fact that the potential of the neighborhood bakery-cafe concept was greater than that of Au Bon Pain's urban store concept. The bakery-cafe concept capitalized on a confluence of current trends: the welcoming atmosphere of coffee shops, the food of sandwich shops, and the quick service of fast food.[23]

While Au Bon Pain was focusing on making St. Louis Bread a viable national brand, the company's namesake unit was faltering. Rapid expansion of its urban outlets had resulted in operational problems, bad real estate deals,[24] and debt over $65 million.[25] Operating margins were on a steady decline. For example, from 1993 to 1994, margins fell from 11.5% to 8.5%.[26] Margins continued to contract because of higher food costs, stagnant sales, and decreased comparable store sales. Stiff competition from bagel shops and coffee chains such as Starbucks compounded operational difficulties. Another concern was that the fast food ambiance of the stores was not appealing to customers who wanted to sit and enjoy a meal or a cup of coffee.[27] On the other hand, the cafe-style atmosphere of St. Louis Bread, which was known as Panera (Latin for "time for bread") outside the St. Louis area, was proving to be successful. In 1996, comparable sales at Au Bon Pain locations declined 3%, while same-store sales in the Panera unit were up 10%.[28]

Lacking the capital to overhaul the ambiance of the Au Bon Pain segment, the company decided to sell the unit. This left the company the time and resources to strategically focus solely on the more successful Panera chain. Unlike Au Bon Pain, Panera was not confined to a small urban niche and had greater growth potential. Panera's per-store profit of $1.3 million over Au Bon Pain's $1 million (at the time of the sale) also proved more promising. On May 16, 1999, Shaich sold the Au Bon Pain unit to investment firm Bruckman, Sherrill, and Co. for $73 million. At the time of the divestiture, the company changed its corporate name to Panera Bread Company. The sale left Panera Bread Company debt-free, and the cash allowed for the immediate expansion of its bakery-cafe stores.[29]

General Business

From what was once a small chain acquired by Au Bon Pain, Panera Bread Company grew into the leader in the fast casual dining industry. The Panera concept combined and exploited several food service qualities: (1) the casual atmosphere of coffee shops, (2) the quality food of sandwich shops, and (3) the quick service of fast food chains. The company specialized in meeting five consumer-dining needs: breakfast, lunch, daytime "chill-out," lunch in the evening, and take-home bread. Daytime chill-out is the time between breakfast and lunch and between lunch and dinner when customers stop in to take a break from their daily activities. This niche of consumers included seniors, matineegoers, shoppers, business and sales people, and students.[30] Panera provided diners with high-quality foods, including fresh baked goods, made-to-order sandwiches on fresh baked breads, soups, salads, custom roasted coffees, and other cafe beverages. Panera targeted suburban dwellers and workers by offering a premium specialty bakery and cafe experience with a neighborhood emphasis.[31] Panera was the first in the bakery-cafe segment, and its unique concept and operational strengths led it to its leading position in the fast casual dining category.

Panera's concept was designed around meeting the needs and desires of consumers, specifically the need for efficient, time-saving service and the desire for a higher-quality dining experience—something not delivered by traditional fast food chains. The company's goal was to make Panera Bread a nationally dominant brand. Its menu, quality of operations, and design and real estate strategies were vital to the company's success.

Fast Casual

Panera's predecessor Au Bon Pain was a pioneer of the fast casual restaurant category. Fast casual, also known as quick casual, emerged to fill the gap between fast food and full-service restaurants. Technomic Information Services originally coined the term to describe restaurants that offer the speed, efficiency, and inexpensiveness of fast food with the hospitality, quality, and ambiance of a full-service restaurant. Technomic defined a fast casual restaurant by whether it met the following four criteria. *One*, the restaurant had to offer a limited-service or self-service format. *Two*, the average check had to be between $6 and $9, whereas fast food checks averaged less than $5. This pricing scheme placed fast casual between fast food and casual dining. The *third* criterion was that the food had to be made-to-order. Consumers perceived newly prepared, made-to-order foods as fresh. Fast casual menus usually also had more robust and complex flavor profiles than the standard fare at fast food restaurants. The *fourth* criterion required that the decor had to be upscale or highly developed. Decor inspired a more enjoyable experience for the customer as the environment of fast casual restaurants was more akin to that of a neighborhood bistro or casual restaurant. The decor also created a generally higher perception of quality.[32]

The fast casual market had enjoyed double-digit aggregate growth since 1999 and was expected to continue to grow by double digit figures.[33] Fast casual chain sales were expected to reach $50 billion in the next decade.[34] This large growth in fast casual was expected to come at the expense of the fast food industry.

Diverse dining offerings and higher profitability contributed to the industry's growth. Food concepts within the fast casual category ranged from Mexican, to bakeries, to Chinese. Unlike fast food restaurants that construct stand-alone stores, fast casual chains locate in strip malls, on small-town main streets, and in preexisting properties. As a result, the opening costs of a fast casual store are about a third of its average annual sales volume of $1.5 million.[35] The diversity and profitability of fast casual allowed many new players to enter the market offering new concepts and menu items.

The maturation of two large segments of the U.S. population, baby boomers and their children, was largely responsible for the growth in fast casual. Both segments had little time for cooking and grew tired of fast food, and they desired a high-quality, fresher, healthier dining experience, but did not have the time for a full dining experience. Dining trends caused fast casual to emerge as a legitimate trend in the restaurant industry as it bridged the gap between casual dining and the burgers-and-fries fast food industry.

Corporate Governance

Panera's corporate headquarters was located in St. Louis, Missouri.

Board of Directors

Shaich was the only internal board member. The biographical sketches for the board members are shown below[36]:

Ronald M. Shaich *(age 50), Director since 1981, Co-Founder, Chairman of the Board since May 1999, Co-Chairman of the Board from January 1988 to May 1999, Chief Executive Officer since May 1994, and Co-Chief Executive Officer from January 1988 to May 1994. Shaich has served as a Director of Lown Cardiovascular Research Foundation.*

Larry J. Franklin *(age 55), Director since June 2001. Franklin has been the President and Chief Executive Officer of Franklin Sports, Inc., a leading branded sporting goods manufacturer and marketer, since 1986. Franklin joined Franklin Sports, Inc., in 1970 and served as its Executive Vice President from 1981 to 1986. Franklin has served on the Board of Directors of Bradford Soap International, Inc., The Sporting Goods Manufacturers Association, The Retail Industry Leadership Association, and The New England Chapter of the Juvenile Diabetes Research Foundation.*

Fred K. Foulkes *(age 62), Director since June 2003. Professor Foulkes has been a Professor of Organizational Behavior and the Director of the Human Resources Policy Institute at Boston University School of Management since 1981 and has taught courses in human resource management and strategic management at Boston University since 1980. From 1968 to 1980, Professor Foulkes was a member of the Harvard Business School faculty. Foulkes has served on the Board of Directors of Bright Horizons Family Solutions and the Society for Human Resource Management Foundation.*

Domenic Colasacco *(age 55), Director since March 2000. Colasacco has been President and Chief Executive Officer of Boston Trust & Investment Management, a trust company formed under Massachusetts state law, since 1992. He joined Boston Trust in 1974, after beginning his career in the research division of Merrill Lynch & Co. in New York City.*

Thomas E. Lynch *(age 44), Director since June 2003. Lynch has been a Senior Managing Director of Mill Road Associates, a financial advisory firm that he founded in 2000. From 1997 through 2000, Lynch was the founder and Managing Director of Lazard Capital Partners, a private equity firm affiliated with the investment bank Lazard. From 1990 to 1997, Lynch was a Managing Director at the Blackstone Group, where he was a senior investment professional for Blackstone Capital Partners. Prior to Blackstone, Lynch was a senior consultant at the Monitor Company. Lynch has served on the Board of the City Center.*

George E. Kane *(age 99), Director since November 1988. Kane was also a company Director from December 1981 to December 1985 and a Director Emeritus from December 1985 to November 1988. Kane retired in 1970 as President of Garden City Trust Company (now University Trust Company) and served as an Honorary Director of University Trust Company from December 1985 to January 2000. Kane became a nonvoting Honorary Director Emeritus after May 2004.*

The Compensation Committee included Franklin, Foulkes, and Colasacco. The Committee on Nominations included Franklin, Lynch, and Kane. The Audit Committee included Foulkes, Colasacco, Lynch, and Kane.

Directors who were not employees received a quarterly fee ranging from $3,000 to $3,500 for serving on the Board, plus reimbursement of out-of-pocket expenses for attendance at each Board or committee meeting. Under the Directors' Plan, each Director who is not an employee or a principal stockholder received a one-time grant of an option to purchase 10,000 shares of Class A Common Stock when he or she was first elected. Each independent Director in office at the end of the fiscal year also received an option to purchase an additional 10,000 shares of Class A Common Stock.

Exhibit 1 shows the common stock ownership in the company. There were two classes of stock: (1) Class A Stock with 28,345,754 shares outstanding and one vote per share, and (2) Class B Common Stock with 1,761,521 shares outstanding and three votes per share.

EXHIBIT 1
Stock Ownership: Panera Bread Company

Name and, with Respect to Owner of More Than 5%, Address	Class A Common		Class B Common		Combined Voting Percentage
	Number	Percent	Number	Percent	
Ronald M. Shaich c/o Panera Bread Company 6710 Clayton Road Richmond Heights, MO 63117	601,660	2.1%	1,666,381	94.6%	16.5%
Domenic Colasacco	48,862	<1%	—	—	<1%
Larry J. Franklin	40,000	<1%	—	—	<1%
George E. Kane	45,912	<1%	—	—	<1%
Fred K. Foulkes	24,000	<1%	—	—	<1%
Thomas E. Lynch	20,000	<1%	—	—	<1%
Paul E. Twohig	1,000	<1%	—	—	<1%
Mark A. Borland	—	—	—	—	—
Michael E. Hood	—	—	—	—	—
Michael J. Nolan	—	—	—	—	—
All directors, director nominees, and executive officers as a group (14 persons)	818,771	2.8%	1,666,381	94.6%	17.0%
Brown Capital Management, Inc. 1201 N. Calvert Street Baltimore, MD 21202	2,014,695	7.1%	—	—	6.0%
FMR Corp 82 Devonshire Street Boston, MA 02109	4,209,696	17.9%	—	—	12.5%

SOURCE: *Panera Bread Company, Inc., 2004 Notice of Annual Meeting of Stockholders, pp. 16–17.*

Top Management

Key Executive Officers of Panera who did not also serve on the Board (as did Shaich) were as follows[37]:

Paul E. Twohig (age 50), Executive Vice President, Chief Operating Officer since January 2003. From 1993 to 2003, Twohig served as an executive at Starbucks Coffee Company, most recently as Senior Vice President responsible for retail operations development and human resources for more than 1,200 Starbucks stores in 17 states and 5 Canadian provinces. From 1986 to 1991, Twohig was a franchisee and owned and operated four Burger King units in West Palm Beach, Florida. From 1968 to 1986, Twohig was with Burger King Corporation, serving in a variety of roles, including regional manager in New England.

Neal J. Yanofsky (age 46), Executive Vice President, Chief Administrative Officer, and Corporate Staff Officer since June 2003. From June 1999 to June 2003, Yanofsky was an independent business consultant with a practice focused on strategy development for high-growth firms, including Panera. From April 1990 to June 1999, Yanofsky was Vice President of Fidelity Ventures, the private equity arm of Fidelity Investments, and served in additional capacities with Fidelity Capital, including Chief Financial Officer at Boston Coach.

Mark A. Borland (age 51), Senior Vice President, Chief Supply Chain Officer since August 2002. Borland joined the company in 1986 and held management positions within Au Bon Pain and Panera Bread divisions until 2000, including Executive Vice President, Vice President of Retail Operations, Chief Operating Officer, and President of Manufacturing Services. From

2000 to 2001, Borland served as Senior Vice President of Operations at RetailDNA and then rejoined Panera as a consultant in the summer of 2001.

Scott G. Davis *(age 40), Senior Vice President, Chief Concept Officer since May 1999. Davis joined the company in 1987 and from May 1996 to May 1999 served as Vice President, Customer Experience. From June 1994 to May 1996, Davis served as Director of Concept Services and Customer Experience.*

Mark E. Hood *(age 51), Senior Vice President, Chief Financial Officer since April 2003. Hood joined the company in August 2002, and from August 2002 to April 2003 served as Senior Vice President, Finance and Administration. From August 2000 to April 2002, Hood served as the Chief Financial and Administrative Officer of the U.S. Loyalty Corporation. From June 1995 to September 1999, Hood served as an executive at Saks Fifth Avenue, most recently as Executive Vice President and Chief Financial and Administrative Officer. Prior to joining Saks, Hood held a number of financial positions with the May Department Stores Co. from 1983 to 1995.*

Michael J. Kupstas *(age 46), Senior Vice President, Chief Franchise Officer since September 2001. Kupstas joined the company in 1996. Between August 1999 and September 2001, Kupstas served as Vice President, Franchising and Brand Communication. Between January 1996 and August 1999, Kupstas was Vice President, Company and Franchise Operations. Between April 1991 and January 1996, Kupstas was Senior Vice President/Division Vice President for Long John Silver's, Inc.*

John M. Maguire *(age 38), Senior Vice President, Chief Company and Joint Venture Operations Officer since August 2001. Maguire joined the company in April 1993. From April 2000 to July 2001, Maguire served as Vice President, Bakery Operations. From November 1998 to March 2000, Maguire served as Vice President, Commissary Operations. From April 1993 to October 1998, Maguire was a Manager and Director of Au Bon Pain/Panera Bread/St. Louis Bread.*

Michael J. Nolan *(age 44), Senior Vice President, Chief Development Officer since he joined the company in August 2001. From December 1997 to March 2001, Nolan served as Executive Vice President & Director for John Harvard's Brew House, L.L.C., and Senior Vice President, Development, for American Hospitality Concepts, Inc. From March 1996 to December 1997, Nolan was Vice President of Real Estate & Development for Apple South Incorporated, and from July 1989 to March 1996, Nolan was Vice President of Real Estate and Development for Morrison Restaurants Inc. Prior to 1989, Nolan served in various real estate and development capacities for Cardinal Industries, Inc., and Nolan Development and Investment.*

Exhibit 2 shows the executive compensation for the five highest-paid principal executives.

Concept and Strategy[38]

The company's concept focused on the Specialty Bread/Bakery-Cafe category. Its artisan breads, which were breads made with all-natural ingredients and an artisan's attention to quality and detail, and overall award-winning bakery expertise were at the heart of the concept's menu. The concept was designed to deliver against the key consumer trends, specifically the need for a responsive and more special dining experience than that offered by traditional fast food. The company's goal was to make Panera Bread a nationally dominant brand name. Its menu, prototype, operating systems, design, and real estate strategy allowed it to compete successfully in several sub-businesses: breakfast, lunch, PM chill-out, lunch in the evening, and take-home bread. On a systemwide basis, annualized AUVs increased 0.7%, to $1,852,000, for the 52 weeks ended December 27, 2003, compared to $1,840,000 for the 52 weeks ended December 28, 2002 (see **Exhibit 3**).

The distinctive nature of the company's menu offerings, the quality of its bakery-cafe operations, the company's signature cafe design, and the prime locations of its cafes were integral to the company's success. The company believed its concept had significant growth potential, which it hoped to realize through a combination of company and franchise efforts.

EXHIBIT 2

Summary Compensation Table for Executives: Panera Bread Company

| Name of Principal Position(s) | Year | Annual Compensation | | | Long-Term Compensation |
		Salary ($)	Bonus ($)	Other Annual Compensation ($)	Securities Underlying Options (#)
Ronald M. Shaich	2003	397,616	—	$49,881[2]	100,000
Chairman and Chief	2002	331,500	—[1]	$144,909[2]	40,000
Executive Officer	2001	338,000	375,000	—	—
Paul E. Twohig	2003	306,250	68,250	—	50,000
Executive Vice President,	2002	—	—	—	130,000
Chief Operating Officer	2001	—	—	—	—
Mark A. Borland	2003	238,462	47,304	—	—
Senior Vice President,	2002	120,536	30,777	—	50,000
Chief Supply Chain Officer	2001	—	—	—	—
Mark E. Hood	2003	243,365	35,551	—	5,000
Senior Vice President,	2002	83,077	18,300	—	80,000
Chief Financial Officer	2001	—	—	—	—
Michael J. Nolan	2003	238,462	51,684	—	5,000
Senior Vice President,	2002	196,153	40,000	—	—
Chief Development Officer	2001	6,539	15,821	—	80,000

Notes:
1. Shaich declined his $375,000 bonus for 2002 earned under the bonus plan approved by the Compensation Committee, in light of the chartered plane benefits he received during 2002.
2. Shaich received $144,909 in personal chartered air travel (based on the aggregate incremental cost of such travel to Panera), $5,500 in matching contributions to the 401(k) plan, and $1,947 in life insurance premiums.

SOURCE: *Panera Bread Company, Inc., 2004 Notice of Annual Meeting of Stockholders, p. 10.*

EXHIBIT 3

Selected Financial Information: Panera Bread Company (Dollar amounts in thousands)

A. Systemwide Bakery-Cafe Revenues

| | For Fiscal Year Ending | | | |
	December 27, 2003	December 28, 2002	December 29, 2001	December 30, 2000
Systemwide	$977,100	$755,400	$529,400	$350,800

B. Year-to-Year Comparable Sales

| | Fifty-Two Weeks Ending | | | | |
	December 27, 2003	December 28, 2002	December 29, 2001	December 30, 2000	December 25, 1999
Company-owned	1.7%	4.1%	5.8%	8.1%	3.3%
Franchise-operated	−0.4%	6.1%	5.8%	10.3%	2.0%
Systemwide	0.2%	5.5%	5.8%	9.1%	2.9%

EXHIBIT 3
(Continued)

C. Annualized Unit Volume (AUVs)

	For Fiscal Year Ending				
	December 27, 2003	December 28, 2002	December 29, 2001	December 30, 2000	December 25, 1999
Company-owned	$1,831,000	$1,764,000	$1,636,000	$1,471,000	$1,330,000
Franchise-operated	$1,860,000	$1,871,000	$1,800,000	$1,710,000	$1,568,000
Systemwide	$1,850,000	$1,840,000	$1,748,000	$1,617,000	$1,444,000

D. Year Percentage Change in AUVs

	For Fiscal Year Ending			
	December 27, 2003	December 28, 2002	December 29, 2001	December 30, 2000
Company-owned	3.8%	7.8%	11.2%	10.6%
Franchise-operated	−0.6%	3.9%	5.3%	9.1%
Systemwide	0.5%	5.3%	8.1%	12.0%

SOURCES: *Panera Bread Company, Inc., Media Kit and 1999 Form 10-K through 2003 Form 10-K.*

Franchising was a key component of the company's success. Utilization of franchise operating partners enabled the company to grow more rapidly because of the added resources and capabilities they provided to implement the concepts and strategy developed by Panera. As of December 27, 2003, there were 429 franchised bakery-cafes operating and signed commitments to open an additional 409 bakery-cafes. In addition, there were 173 wholly or majority-owned company bakery-cafes operating at December 27, 2003. **Exhibit 4** shows the number of bakery-cafes for the last five years.

Competition[39]

The company experienced competition from numerous sources in its trade areas. The company's bakery-cafes competed based on customers' needs for breakfast, lunch, daytime chill-out, lunch in the evening, and take-home bread sales. The competitive factors included location, environment, customer service, price, and quality of products. The company competed for leased space in desirable locations. Certain competitors had capital resources that exceeded those available to the company. Primary competitors included specialty food and casual dining restaurant retailers, including national, regional, and locally owned concepts.

Menu[40]

The menu was designed to provide the company's target customers with products that built on the strength of the company's bakery expertise and met customers' new and ever-changing tastes. The key menu groups were fresh baked goods, made-to-order sandwiches, soups, and cafe beverages. Included within these menu groups were a variety of freshly baked bagels, breads, muffins, scones, rolls, and sweet goods; made-to-order sandwiches; hearty, unique soups; and custom roasted coffees and cafe beverages such as hot or cold espresso and cappuccino

EXHIBIT 4

Company-Owned and Franchise-Operated Bakery-Cafes: Panera Bread Company

	For Fiscal Year Ending				
	December 27, 2003	December 28, 2002	December 29, 2001	December 30, 2000	December 25, 1999
Number of bakery-cafes:[1]					
Company-owned:					
Beginning of period	132	110	90	81	70
Bakery-cafes opened	29	23	21	11	12
Acquired from franchisee	15	3	—	—	—
Bakery-cafes closed	(3)	(4)	(1)	(2)	(1)
End of period	173	132	110	90	81
Franchise operated:					
Beginning of period	346	259	172	102	47
Bakery-cafes opened	102	92	88	70	56
Sold to company[2]	(15)	(3)	—	—	—
Bakery-cafes closed	(4)	(2)	(1)	—	(1)
End of period	429	346	259	172	102
System-wide:					
Beginning of period	361	252	145	66	—
Bakery-cafes opened	131	115	109	81	68
Bakery-cafes closed	(7)	(6)	(2)	(2)	(2)
End of period	485	361	252	145	66

Notes:

1. Includes majority-owned.

2. In January 2002, the company purchased the area development rights and 3 existing bakery-cafes in the Jacksonville, Florida, market from franchisees. During fiscal 2003, the company acquired 15 operating bakery-cafes' area development rights in the Louisville/Lexington, Kentucky; Dallas, Texas; Toledo, Ohio; and Ann Arbor, Michigan, markets from franchisees.

SOURCES: *Panera Bread Company, Inc., 2003 Form 10-K, p. 2, and 2001 Form 10-K, pp. 2–3.*

drinks. The company's concept emphasized the sophisticated specialty and artisan breads that supported a take-home bread business.

The company regularly reviewed and revised its menu offerings to satisfy changing customer preferences and to maintain customer interest within its target customer groups, the "bread loving trend-setters" and the "bread loving traditionalists." Both of these target customer groups sought a quality experience that reflected their discriminating tastes. The major characteristic that set these two groups apart was the more enthusiastic embrace of new and nutritional menu items by the *trend-setters*. New menu items were developed in test kitchens and then introduced in a limited number of the company's bakery-cafes to determine customer response and verify that preparation and operating procedures maintained product consistency, high quality standards, and profitability. If successful, they were then introduced in the rest of the company's bakery-cafes and franchise bakery-cafes.

Franchises[41]

Panera management believed that its specialty bakery-cafe concept had significant growth potential, which it hoped to realize through a combination of owned, franchised, and joint venture–operated stores. Franchising was a key component of the company's growth strategy. Expansion through franchise partners had enabled the company to grow more rapidly as the franchisees contributed the resources and capabilities necessary to implant the concepts and strategies developed by Panera.

The company began a broad-based franchising program in 1996. The company was actively seeking to extend its franchise relationships beyond its current franchisees and annually filed a Uniform Franchise Offering Circular to facilitate sales of additional franchise development agreements. The company offered two types of franchise opportunities: independent third-party franchisees and Area Development Agreements (ADAs). ADAs transferred all development rights within a specified geographic area to the owner of that contract and required the developer to adhere to a predetermined development time line. Franchisees were required to develop a specified number of bakery-cafes on or before specific dates. If franchisees failed to develop bakery-cafes on schedule, the company had the right to terminate the ADA and to develop company-owned locations or develop locations through new ADA developers in that market.

The franchise agreement typically required the payment of an up-front franchise fee of $35,000 (broken down into $5,000 at the signing of the ADA and $30,000 at or before the bakery-cafe opened) and continuing royalties of 4%–5% on sales from each bakery-cafe.

Franchise-operated bakery-cafes followed the same standards for product quality, menu, site selection, and bakery-cafe construction as did company-owned bakery-cafes. The franchisees were required to purchase all of their dough products from sources approved by the company. The company's fresh dough facility system supplied fresh dough products to most franchise-operated bakery-cafes. The company did not finance franchisee construction or ADA purchases. In addition, the company did not hold an equity interest in any of the franchised bakery-cafes.

The company had entered into franchise ADAs with 32 franchisee groups as of December 27, 2003. Also, as of December 27, 2003, there were 429 franchised bakery-cafes open and commitments to open 409 additional franchised bakery-cafes (see **Exhibit 5**). The company did not have any international franchise development agreements.

The high volume of franchise applicants allowed Panera to be very selective in granting franchises. Panera preferred executives with retail and restaurant franchising experience. The company chose only very strong and capable franchising partners, many of whom had experience with well-known chains, such as McDonald's and Burger King.[42] Franchisees needed to have access to financing since the company did not finance franchisee construction or ADA purchases.

Panera also saw potential in implementing a joint venture structure as an alternative to company-owned or franchised bakery-cafes to facilitate the development and operation of bakery-cafes. Unlike with franchise agreements, Panera was the major financier (where a specified interest is invested by the joint venture partner) of the bakery-cafes and earned revenues from operations. The joint venture partner managed the bakery-cafes and was entitled to a specified percentage of cash flows. The joint venture agreements forbade the partner from transferring or selling its interest to another party without the consent of Panera. After a specified term, the company had the right to purchase the joint venture partner's interest at a determined value, and the joint venture partner had the right to sell its interest back to the company at a lower value. The company saw the joint venture structure as an opportunity to attract and retain experienced and motivated operators who would want the opportunity to participate in the success of the bakery-cafes.

In 2001, Richard Postle, Panera's former Chief Operating Officer and President, left the company and through an indirect subsidiary entered into a joint venture agreement to develop 50 bakery-cafes in northern Virginia and central Pennsylvania. Under this agreement, there were 27 bakery-cafes operating in these markets at December 27, 2003. After October 2006, the company and the minority-interest owner would each have rights that could, if exercised, permit/require the company to purchase the bakery-cafes at contractually determined values based on multiples of cash flows.

EXHIBIT 5
Panera Bread/
St. Louis Bread Co.
Bakery-Cafes

State	Company Bakery-Cafes	Franchise-Operated Bakery-Cafes	Total Bakery-Cafes
Alabama	4	—	4
Arkansas	—	2	2
California	—	5	5
Colorado	—	14	14
Connecticut	1	4	5
Delaware	—	1	1
Florida	5	43	48
Georgia	8	6	14
Iowa	—	13	13
Illinois	34	32	66
Indiana	3	15	18
Kansas	—	14	14
Kentucky	4	1	5
Massachusetts	2	18	20
Maryland	—	18	18
Maine	—	2	2
Michigan	32	8	40
Minnesota	—	20	20
Missouri	36	16	52
North Carolina	1	17	18
Nebraska	—	7	7
Nevada	—	2	2
New Hampshire	—	7	7
New Jersey	—	25	25
New York	5	3	8
Ohio	6	55	61
Oklahoma	—	15	15
Pennsylvania	7	27	34
Rhode Island	—	3	3
South Carolina	—	2	2
Tennessee	1	9	10
Texas	2	9	11
Virginia	20	1	21
West Virginia	—	2	2
Wisconsin	—	15	15
Totals	**171**	**431**	**602**

SOURCE: *Panera Bread Company, Inc., 2003 Form 10-K, p. 8.*

Bakery Supply Chain[43]

According to Ronald Shaich, "Panera has a commitment to doing the best bread in America."[44] Freshly baked bread made with fresh dough was integral to honoring this commitment. Systemwide, bakery-cafes used fresh dough for sourdough and artisan breads and bagels. The company's fresh dough facility system supplied fresh dough to both company-owned and franchise-operated bakery-cafes daily. The company supplied both company-owned and franchise-operated bakery-cafes with fresh dough daily through its commissary system. The company's 16 commissaries (see **Exhibit 6**) prepared fresh, preservative-free dough daily.

Facility	Square Footage
Franklin, MA	40,300
Chicago, IL	30,900
Cincinnati, OH	14,000
Washington, DC (located in Beltsville, MD)	17,900
Warren, OH	16,300
St. Louis, MO	30,000
Orlando, FL	16,500
Atlanta, GA	18,000
Greensboro, NC	9,600
Kansas City, KS	17,000
Detroit, MI	13,500
Dallas, TX	7,800
Minneapolis, MN	8,900
Ontario, CA	13,900
Fairfield, NJ	20,200
Denver, CO	10,000

SOURCE: *Panera Bread Company, Inc., 2003 Form 10-K, p. 8.*

The commissaries assured product quality and consistency at both company-owned and franchised bakery-cafes. Panera's master artisan baker, Mile Marino, had been with the company since 1987 and oversaw all baking operations at the fresh dough facilities. A fleet of 98 temperature-controlled trucks leased by Panera and driven by Panera employees distributed the fresh dough to bakery-cafes. The optimal distribution limit was approximately 200 miles. An average distribution route delivered dough to 6 bakery-cafes. The fresh dough was then baked overnight in a $50,000 stone-bottom oven, standard in all bakery-cafes.

The company focused its expansion in areas served by commissaries in order to continue to gain efficiencies through leveraging the fixed cost of its current commissary structure. Panera selectively entered new markets that required the construction of additional facilities until a sufficient number of bakery-cafes could be opened to permit efficient distribution of the fresh dough.

The remaining baked goods that were not prepared with fresh dough (sweet goods) were prepared with frozen dough. In 1996, the company constructed a state-of-the-art frozen dough facility in Mexico, Missouri. In 1998, the company sold the facility and its frozen dough business to Bunge Food Corporation for approximately $13 million in cash. At the time of the sale, Panera entered into a five-year contract with Bunge for the supply of substantially all of its frozen dough. In November 2002, the company signed an agreement with Dawn Food Products, Inc., to prepare and deliver frozen dough from 2003 through 2007. The agreement was structured as a cost-plus agreement.

All frozen dough and related food materials were distributed to the bakery-cafes through independent distributors. Contract vendors delivered virtually all food products and supplies for retail operations (i.e. paper goods, coffee, smallwares) to the distributors, which then delivered to the individual bakery-cafes. Franchised bakery-cafes operated under individual contracts with either the company's distributor or other regional distributors. As of December 27, 2003, there were three primary distributors serving the Panera Bread system.

Marketing[45]

Panera did not rely heavily on advertising to promote its stores. In 2001, the company spent only $700,000 on media, a low 2.1% ad-to-sales ratio compared to the category average of 4%.[46] The company attempted to increase its per-location sales through menu development, product merchandising, and promotions at everyday prices and by sponsorship of local community charitable events. Advertising was intended to promote the company but not to create an identifiable image that would be synonymous with Panera, such as the McDonald's golden arches.

Franchised bakery-cafes contributed 0.4% of sales to a company-run national advertising fund and 0.4% of sales as a marketing administration fee and were required to spend 2.0% of sales in their local markets on advertising. The company contributed similar amounts from company-owned bakery-cafes toward the national advertising fund and marketing administration fee. The national advertising fund and marketing administration fee contributions received from franchised bakery-cafes were consolidated with company amounts in the company's financial statements. Liabilities for unexpended funds were included in accrued expenses in the consolidated balance sheets. The company's contributions to the national advertising fund and marketing administration fee, as well as its own media costs, were recorded as part of other operating expenses in the consolidated statements of operations. The company utilized external media when deemed appropriate and cost-effective in specific markets.

Most marketing was done through product promotion and word-of-mouth marketing. According to Shaich, "when a new store is opened in an established market, the new store benefits from the buzz and consumer familiarity created by existing locations."[47] This was akin to the "Krispy Kreme Phenomenon," which occurred when consumers greatly anticipated a new store opening in their neighborhood due to word-of-mouth praise for the quality of the food products.

Another way Panera used word-of-mouth marketing was through local charity and community work. Panera strove to add value to its surrounding neighborhoods through its products, service, employment opportunities, and citizenship and believed it had a responsibility to participate and sponsor local events. The company's most well-known program began in 1992. The "Operation Dough-Nation" program ensured that every purchase at Panera would give back in some way to the community. Cash donations could be made inside the store, with the amounts matched with fresh baked bread donated to local food drives. In addition, the company donated all unsold bread to local hunger relief agencies. The company's second community outreach program, "Dough for Funds," gave nonprofit groups a means to raise funds by profiting from the sales of Panera coupons.

The company did not compete on the basis of pricing only; its main selling point was its specialty dining experience. Yet pricing was key to promoting the company's concept. Pricing was structured so customers perceived good value with high-quality food at reasonable prices to encourage frequent visits. The company's average check per transaction at company-owned bakery-cafes for 2003 was $6.61. The average check per transaction varied by the time of day: breakfast, $4.86; lunch, $7.65; PM chill-out, $6.67; and lunch in the evening, $7.42 (see **Exhibit 7**).

The company used its store locations to market its brand image. When choosing a location to open a new store, the company carefully selected the geographic area. Better locations

EXHIBIT 7
Average Check per Transaction: Panera Bread Company

	2003	2002	2001	2000	1999
Breakfast	$4.86	$4.49	$4.30	$4.03	$3.76
Lunch	7.65	7.32	7.26	6.89	6.41
PM "Chill Out"	6.67	6.30	5.39	N/A	N/A
Evening lunch	7.42	7.02	N/A	N/A	N/A
Overall	6.61	6.26	6.19	5.80	5.44

SOURCES: *Panera Bread Company, Inc., 1999 Form 10-K through 2003 Form 10-K.*

EXHIBIT 8
Average Opening
Costs and Square
Footage: Panera
Bread Company

	2003	2002	2001	2000	1999
Opening Costs	$850,000	$737,000	$760,000	$700,000	$656,000
Square Footage	4,330	4,400	4,250	4,000	3,500

SOURCES: *Panera Bread Company, Inc., 1999 Form 10-K through 2003 Form 10-K.*

needed less marketing, and the bakery-cafe concept relied on a substantial volume of repeat business. Management used demographic and competitive information to identify areas with the best opportunity for success and that best promoted Panera's neighborhood concept. Location, real estate, and marketing teams worked in conjunction to select ideal locations. In evaluating a potential location, the company studied the surrounding trade area, obtained demographic information within that area, and examined information on breakfast and lunch competitors. Based on analysis of this information, including utilization of predictive modeling using proprietary software, the company determined projected sales and return on investment. The Panera concept had proven successful in a number of different types of real estate (i.e., in-line strip centers, regional malls, and freestanding) in 35 states.

The company also used the actual bakery-cafe as a marketing tool to promote its brand image. The company designed each bakery-cafe to provide a differentiated environment and in many cases used fixtures and materials complementary to the neighborhood location of the bakery-cafe. Many locations incorporated the warmth of a fireplace and cozy seating areas and groupings that facilitated utilization as a gathering spot. The design visually reinforced the distinctive difference between the company's bakery-cafes and other bakery-cafes serving breakfast and lunch. Many of the company's cafes also featured outdoor cafe seating.

The average construction, equipment, furniture and fixture, and signage cost for the 29 company-owned bakery-cafes opened in 2003 was $850,000 per bakery-cafe after landlord allowances (see **Exhibit 8**). The average bakery-cafe size was 4,330 square feet (see **Exhibit 8**).

All company-owned bakery-cafes were in leased premises. Lease terms were typically 10 years, with one, two, or three 5-year renewal option periods thereafter. Leases typically had charges for minimum base occupancy, a proportionate share of building and common area operating expenses and real estate taxes, and contingent-percentage rent based on sales above a stipulated sales level.

Management Information Systems[48]

Each company-operated bakery-cafe had computerized cash registers to collect point-of-sale transaction data, which was used to generate pertinent marketing information, including product mix and average check. All product prices were programmed into the system from the company's corporate office. The company allowed franchisees who elected to do so to have access to certain proprietary bakery-cafe systems and systems support.

The company's in-store information system was designed to assist in labor scheduling and food cost management, to provide corporate and retail operations management quick access to retail data, and to reduce managers' administrative time. The system supplied sales, bank deposit, and variance data to the company's accounting department on a daily basis. The company used this data to generate weekly consolidated reports regarding sales and other key elements, as well as detailed profit and loss statements for each company-owned bakery-cafe every four weeks. Additionally, the company monitored the average check, customer count, product mix, and other sales trends. The fresh dough facilities had computerized systems that allowed the fresh dough facilities to accept electronic orders from the bakery-cafes and deliver the ordered product to the bakery-cafes. The company also used network/integration systems, encompassing e-mail and all major financial systems, such as general ledger database systems, and all major operational systems, such as store operating performance database systems.

Human Resources[49]

From the beginning, Panera realized that the quality of its employees was a critical part of a successful product and a unique company. It was the company's belief that the key ingredients in the successful development of Panera ranged from the type of food served to the kind of people behind the counters. Employees included full-time associates in general or administrative positions, commissary operators, bakers, and associates at the bakery-cafes. As of December 27, 2003, the company had 3,924 full-time associates (defined as associates who averaged 25 hours or more per week), of whom 344 were employed in general or administrative functions principally at or from the company's support centers (executive offices); 676 were employed in the company's fresh dough facility operations; and 2,904 were employed in the company's bakery-cafe operations as bakers, managers, and associates. The company also had 4,078 part-time hourly associates at the bakery-cafes. There were no collective bargaining agreements. The company considered its employee relations to be good. The company placed priority on staffing its bakery-cafes, fresh dough facilities, and support center operations with skilled associates and invested in training programs to ensure the quality of its operations. Incentive programs and bonuses were available to salaried employees. Employees also received product discounts and were invited to join employee stock ownership plans. Panera believed that providing bakery-cafe operators the opportunity to participate in the success of the bakery-cafe enabled the company to attract and retain experienced and highly motivated personnel, which resulted in a better customer experience. The company developed a program and began implementation in certain markets in 2003 to allow unit general managers and multi-unit managers to own a minority interest in a bakery-cafe. Prior to full implementation of the program, the company modified the program from an ownership structure to a multi-year bonus structure, which allowed operators to participate in the success of a bakery-cafe. The company expected to continue implementation of this bonus structure where appropriate as an alternative to its traditional company-owned or franchised bakery-cafes to facilitate the development and operation of bakery-cafes.

Finance[50]

Exhibits 9 through **11** show the consolidated statement of operations, common size income statement, and consolidated balance sheets, respectively, for the company for the fiscal years ended 1999 through 2003.

The company's revenues were derived from company-owned bakery-cafe sales, fresh dough sales to franchisees, and franchise royalties and fees. Fresh dough sales to franchisees were the sales of dough products to franchisees. Franchise royalties and fees included royalty income and franchise fees. The cost of food and paper products, labor, occupancy, and other operating expenses related to company-owned bakery-cafe sales. The cost of fresh dough sales related to the sale of fresh dough products and sweet goods to franchisees. General and administrative, depreciation, and pre-opening expenses related to all areas of revenue generation.

Systemwide bakery-cafe sales for the 52 weeks ended December 27, 2003, for the company increased 29.3%, to $977.1 million from $755.4 million, for the 52 weeks ended December 28, 2002. Comparable sales increases and increases in AUVs were lower during the 52 weeks ended December 27, 2003, than during the 52 weeks ended December 28, 2002 (see **Exhibit 3**).

EXHIBIT 9

Consolidated Statement of Operations: Panera Bread Company
(Dollar amounts in thousands, except per share information)

Year Ending	December 27, 2003	December 28, 2002	December 29, 2001
Revenues:			
Bakery-cafe sales	$265,933	$212,645	$157,684
Franchise royalties and fees	36,245	27,892	19,577
Fresh dough sales to franchisees	53,708	37,215	23,856
Total revenue	355,886	277,752	201,117
Costs and expenses:			
Bakery-cafe expenses:			
Cost of food and paper products	73,727	63,255	48,253
Labor	81,152	63,172	45,768
Occupancy	17,990	14,619	11,345
Other operating expenses	36,804	27,971	20,729
Total bakery-cafe expenses	209,673	169,017	126,095
Fresh dough cost of sales to franchisees	47,151	33,959	21,965
Depreciation and amortization	19,487	13,965	10,839
General and administrative expenses	28,140	24,986	19,589
Pre-opening expenses	1,531	1,051	912
Nonrecurring charge	—	—	—
Total costs and expenses	305,982	242,978	179,400
Operating profit	49,904	34,774	21,717
Interest expense	48	32	72
Other expense (income), net	1,227	287	213
Minority interest	365	180	8
Income before income taxes	48,264	34,275	21,424
Income taxes	17,616	12,510	8,272
Income (loss) before cumulative effect of accounting change and extraordinary items	30,648	21,765	13,152
Cumulative effect of accounting change, net	(239)	—	—
Extraordinary loss from early extinguishments of debt, net	—	—	—
Net Income (loss)	**$ 30,409**	**$ 21,765**	**$ 13,152**
Per share data:			
Basic earnings per common share:			
Before cumulative effect of accounting change	$ 1.03	$ 0.75	$ 0.47
Cumulative effect of accounting change	(0.01)	—	—
Net income (loss)	$ 1.02	$ 0.75	0.47
Diluted earnings per common share:			
Before cumulative effect of accounting change	$ 1.01	$ 0.73	$ 0.46
Cumulative effect of accounting change	(0.01)	—	—
Net income (loss)	$ 1.00	$ 0.73	$ 0.46
Weighted average shares of common and common equivalent shares outstanding:			
Basic	29,733	28,923	27,783
Diluted	30,423	29,891	28,886

SOURCES: *Panera Bread Company, Inc., 2003 Form 10-K, p. 30, and 2001 Form 10-K, p. 28.*

EXHIBIT 10
Common Size Statement: Panera Bread Company (Dollar amounts in thousands, except per share information)

Year Ending	December 27, 2003	December 28, 2002	December 29, 2001	December 30 2000	December 25, 1999[1]
Revenues:					
Bakery-cafe sales	74.7%	76.6%	78.4%	82.9%	91.5%
Franchise royalties and fees	10.2%	10.0%	9.7%	8.0%	4.3%
Fresh dough sales to franchisees	15.1%	13.4%	11.9%	9.1%	4.2%
Total revenue	100.0%	100.0%	100.0%	100.0%	100.0%
Costs and expenses:					
Bakery-cafe expenses:[1]					
Cost of food and paper products	27.7%	29.7%	30.6%	32.7%	33.4%
Labor	30.5%	29.7%	29.0%	28.9%	29.0%
Occupancy	6.8%	6.9%	7.2%	7.4%	9.9%
Other operating expenses	13.8%	13.2%	13.1%	12.8%	12.9%
Total bakery-cafe expenses	78.8%	79.5%	79.9%	81.8%	85.2%
Fresh dough cost of sales to franchisees[2]	87.8%	91.3%	92.1%	88.6%	89.7%
Depreciation and amortization	5.5%	5.0%	5.4%	5.6%	3.7%
General and administrative expenses	7.9%	9.0%	9.7%	10.8%	10.0%
Pre-opening expenses	0.4%	0.4%	0.5%	0.3%	0.0%
Non-recuring charge	0.0%	0.0%	0.0%	0.3%	3.2%
Operating profit	14.0%	12.5%	10.8%	7.1%	2.2%
Interest expense	0.0%	0.0%	0.0%	0.1%	1.6%
Other expense (income), net	0.3%	0.1%	0.1%	(0.3%)	0.4%
Minority interest	0.1%	0.1%	0.0%	0.0%	0.0%
Income before income taxes	13.6%	12.3%	10.7%	7.3%	0.2%
Income taxes	4.9%	4.5%	4.1%	2.8%	0.3%
Income (loss) before cumulative effect of accounting change and extraordinary items	8.6%	7.8%	6.5%	4.5%	(0.1%)
Cumulative effect of accounting change, net	(0.1%)	0.0%	0.0%	0.0%	0.0%
Extraordinary loss from early extinguishments of debt, net	0.0%	0.0%	0.0%	0.0%	0.2%
Net Income (loss)	8.5%	7.8%	6.5%	4.5%	(0.4%)

Notes:
1. As a percentage of bakery-cafe sales.
2. As a percentage of fresh dough facility sales to franchisees.

SOURCES: *Panera Bread Company, Inc., 2003 Form 10-K, p. 14, and 2001 Form 10-K, pp. 12–13.*

Total company revenues for the 52 weeks ended December 27, 2003, increased 28.1%, to $355.9 million compared to $277.8 million, for the 52 weeks ended December 28, 2002 (see **Exhibit 9**). The growth in total revenues for the 52 weeks ended December 27, 2003, as compared to the prior year, was primarily due to the opening of 131 new bakery-cafes in 2003, as well as the increase in systemwide average weekly sales (excluding closed locations) of 0.7% for the 52 weeks ended December 27, 2003.

Bakery-cafe sales for the 52 weeks ended December 27, 2003, for the company increased 25.1%, to $265.9 million from $212.6 million, for the 52 weeks ended December 28, 2002. Bakery-cafe sales increased primarily due to the impact of a full year's operations of the 23 company-owned bakery-cafes opened in 2002, the opening of 29 company-owned bakery-cafes in 2003, and the 1.7% increase in comparable bakery-cafe sales for the 52 weeks ended December 27, 2003.

Franchise royalties and fees rose 29.7%, to $36.2 million, for the 52 weeks ended December 27, 2003, from $27.9 million for the 52 weeks ended December 28, 2002. The increase in royalty revenue was attributed to the impact of a full year's operations of the 92 franchised bakery-cafes opened in 2002 and the addition of 102 franchised bakery-cafes in 2003.

Fresh dough facility sales to franchisees increased 44.4%, to $53.7 million, for the 52 weeks ended December 27, 2003, from $37.2 million for the 52 weeks ended December 28, 2002. The increase was primarily driven by the increased number of franchise bakery-cafes opened, as well as a shift in certain products being distributed through the fresh dough facility system rather than third parties.

The cost of food and paper products included the costs associated with the fresh dough operations that sell fresh dough products to company-owned bakery-cafes, as well as the cost of food and paper products supplied by third-party vendors and distributors. The costs associated with the fresh dough operations that sell fresh dough products to the franchised bakery-cafes were excluded and are shown separately as fresh dough cost of sales to franchisees in the consolidated statements of operations. The cost of food and paper products decreased to 27.7% of bakery-cafe sales for the 52 weeks ended December 27, 2003, compared to 29.7% of bakery-cafe sales for the 52 weeks ended December 28, 2002. This decrease in the cost of food and paper products as a percentage of bakery-cafe sales was primarily due to the company's improved leveraging of its fresh dough manufacturing and distribution costs as it opened more bakery-cafes in fiscal 2003. For the 52 weeks ended December 27, 2003, there was an average of 32.7 bakery-cafes per fresh dough facility compared to an average of 27.3 for the 52 weeks ended December 28, 2002. Additionally, lower ingredient costs, including the benefits of a new sweet goods contract that commenced during the first quarter of fiscal 2003, further benefited food cost.

Labor expense was $81.2 million, or 30.5% of bakery-cafe sales, for the 52 weeks ended December 27, 2003, compared to $63.2 million, or 29.7% of bakery-cafe sales, for the 52 weeks ended December 28, 2002. The labor expense as a percentage of bakery-cafe sales increased between the 52 weeks ended December 27, 2003, and the 52 weeks ended December 28, 2002, primarily as a result of customer service initiatives in fiscal 2003 related to quality and speed of service as well as table delivery service testing and the continued commitment to training and staffing at bakery-cafes.

Occupancy costs were $18.0 million, or 6.8% of bakery-cafe sales, for the 52 weeks ended December 27, 2003, compared to $14.6 million, or 6.9% of bakery-cafe sales, for the 52 weeks ended December 28, 2002. The occupancy cost as a percentage of bakery-cafe sales declined for the 52 weeks ended December 27, 2003, due to the leveraging of these costs over higher sales volumes.

Other bakery-cafe operating expenses, which included advertising, retail field overhead, utilities, and other cafe expenses, were $36.8 million, or 13.8% of bakery-cafe sales, for the 52 weeks ended December 27, 2003, compared to $28.0 million, or 13.2% of bakery-cafe

EXHIBIT 11

Consolidated Balance Sheets: Panera Bread Company (Dollar amounts in thousands, except per share information)

Year Ending	December 27, 2003	December 28, 2002	December 29, 2001	December 30, 2000	December 25, 1999
ASSETS					
Current assets:					
Cash and cash equivalents	$ 42,402	$ 29,924	$ 18,052	$ 9,011	$ 1,936
Investments in government securities	5,019	4,102	—	—	—
Trade accounts receivable, net	9,646	7,462	4,559	3,105	2,686
Other accounts receivable	2,748	2,097	597	—	—
Inventories	8,066	5,191	3,459	2,442	1,880
Prepaid expenses	1,294	1,826	1,649	1,027	484
Refundable income taxes	—	—	—	474	98
Deferred income taxes	1,696	8,488	7,289	5,193	5,473
Other	—	172	399	—	—
Total current assets	70,871	59,262	36,004	21,252	12,557
Property and equipment, net	132,651	99,313	79,693	59,857	47,191
Other assets:					
Notes receivable	—	5,047	—	—	35
Investments in government securities	4,000	—	—	—	—
Goodwill	32,743	18,970	17,530	17,790	18,779
Deferred financing costs	—	—	—	24	88
Deposits and other	5,678	5,554	5,020	4,731	3,960
Deferred income taxes	—	294	5,687	8,035	8,419
Total other assets	42,421	29,865	28,237	30,580	31,281
Total assets	$245,943	$188,440	$143,934	$111,689	$91,029

918

LIABILITIES AND STOCKHOLDERS' EQUITY

Current liabilities:					
Accounts payable	$ 8,072	$ 5,987	$ 5,271	$ 5,396	$ 3,535
Accrued expenses	35,552	24,935	16,433	12,086	12,237
Current portion of deferred revenue	1,168	1,403	677	374	—
Current portion of computer equipment financing	—			—	
Total current liabilities	44,792	32,325	22,381	17,856	15,772
Deferred income taxes	328				
Other long-term liabilities	1,115	262	1,125	2,245	2,011
Total liabilities	46,235	32,587	23,506	20,101	17,783
Minority interest	3,771	2,197	556	—	—
Stockholders' equity:					
Common stock, $.0001 par value: Class A, shares authorized 75,000,000; issued 28,296,581 and outstanding 28,187,581 in 2003 and issued 27,446,448 and outstanding 27,337,448 in 2002	3	3	3	1	1
Class B, shares authorized 10,000,000; issued and outstanding 1,847,221 in 2003 and 1,977,363 in 2002					
Treasury stock, carried at cost	(900)	(900)	(900)	(900)	—
Additional paid-in capital	121,992	110,120	98,101	82,971	70,581
Retained earnings	74,842	44,433	22,668	9,516	2,664
Total stockholders' equity	195,937	155,853	120,428	91,588	73,246
Total liabilities and stockholders' equity	$249,714	$188,440	$143,934	$111,689	$91,029

SOURCES: *Panera Bread Company, Inc., 2003 Form 10-K, p. 29, and 2001 Form 10-K, p. 27.*

sales, for the 52 weeks ended December 28, 2002. The increase in other bakery-cafe operating expenses as a percentage of bakery-cafe sales for the 52 weeks ended December 27, 2003, was primarily due to increased organizational costs for field management, costs associated with new markets opened that did not yet have multi-unit leverage, and increased recruiting and training, repair and maintenance, and advertising costs.

For the 52 weeks ended December 27, 2003, fresh dough facility cost of sales to franchisees was $47.2 million, or 87.8% of fresh dough facility sales to franchisees, compared to $34.0 million, or 91.3% of fresh dough facility sales to franchisees, for the 52 weeks ended December 28, 2002. The decrease in the fresh dough cost of sales rate in fiscal 2003 was primarily due to favorable ingredient costs and the impact of the favorable change in the sweet goods supply agreement, which took effect during the first quarter of fiscal 2003.

Depreciation and amortization was $19.5 million, or 5.5% of total revenue, for the 52 weeks ended December 27, 2003, compared to $14.0 million, or 5.0% of total revenue, for the 52 weeks ended December 28, 2002. The increase in depreciation and amortization as a percentage of total revenue for the 52 weeks ended December 27, 2003, compared to the 52 weeks ended December 28, 2002, was primarily due to the impact of a full year's depreciation of the prior year's capital expenditures and increased capital expenditures in the current year.

General and administrative expenses were $28.1 million, or 7.9% of total revenue, and $25.0 million, or 9.0% of total revenue, for the 52 weeks ended December 27, 2003, and December 28, 2002, respectively. The decrease in the general and administrative expense rate between 2003 and 2002 resulted primarily from higher revenues, which helped leverage general and administrative expenses, and from decreased bonus costs.

Pre-opening expenses, which consisted primarily of labor and food costs incurred during in-store training and preparation for opening, exclusive of manager training costs, which were included in other operating expenses, of $1.5 million, or 0.4% of total revenue, for the 52 weeks ended December 27, 2003, were consistent with the $1.1 million, or 0.4% of total revenue, of pre-opening expenses for the 52 weeks ended December 28, 2002.

Profit for the 52 weeks ended December 27, 2003, increased to $49.9 million, or 14.0% of total revenue, from $34.8 million, or 12.5% of total revenue, for the 52 weeks ended December 28, 2002. Operating profit for the 52 weeks ended December 27, 2003, rose as a result of operating leverage that results from opening 29 company bakery-cafes in 2003 as well as the factors described above.

Other expenses for the 52 weeks ended December 27, 2003, increased to $1.2 million, or 0.3% of total revenue, from $0.3 million, or 0.1% of total revenue, for the 52 weeks ended December 28, 2002. The increase in other expense resulted primarily from increased operating fee payments to the minority interest owners. Minority interest represented the portion of the company's operating profit that was attributable to the ownership interest of the minority interest owners. The provision for income taxes increased to $17.6 million for the 52 weeks ended December 27, 2003, compared to $12.5 million for the 52 weeks ended December 28, 2002. The tax provisions for the 52 weeks ended December 27, 2003, and December 28, 2002, reflects a consistent combined federal, state, and local effective tax rate of 36.5%.

Net income for the 52 weeks ended December 27, 2003, increased $8.6 million, or 39.7%, to $30.4 million, or $1.00 per diluted share, compared to net income of $21.8 million, or $0.73 per diluted share, for the 52 weeks ended December 28, 2002. The increase in net income in 2003 is consistent with the factors described above.

NOTES

1. Hoover's Inc., "Overview: Panera Bread Company."

2. Hoover's Inc., "Overview: Panera Bread Company."

3. L. Tischler, "Vote of Confidence," *Fast Company*, No. 65 (December 2002), pp. 102–112.

4. P. O. Keegan, "Louis I. Kane & Ronald I. Shaich: Au Bon Pain's Own Dynamic Duo," *Nation's Restaurant News*, Vol. 28, No. 37 (September 19, 1994), p. 172.

5. Ibid.

6. Quoted in L. Tischler, "Vote of Confidence," *Fast Company*, No. 65 (December 2002), pp. 102–112.

7. P. O. Keegan, "Louis I. Kane & Ronald I. Shaich: Au Bon Pain's Own Dynamic Duo," *Nation's Restaurant News*, Vol. 28, No. 37 (September 19, 1994), p. 172.

8. R. L. Allen, "Au Bon Pain's Kane Dead at 69; Founded Bakery Chain," *Nation's Restaurant News*, Vol. 34, No. 26 (June 26, 2000), pp. 6–7.

9. Quoted in P. O. Keegan, "Louis I. Kane & Ronald I. Shaich: Au Bon Pain's Own Dynamic Duo," *Nation's Restaurant News*, Vol. 28, No. 37 (September 19, 1994), p. 172.

10. L. Tischler, "Vote of Confidence," *Fast Company*, No. 65 (December 2002), pp. 102–112.

11. Quoted in Ibid.

12. P. Kemp, "Second Rising," *Forbes*, Vol. 166, No. 13 (November 13, 2000), p. 290.

13. L. Tischler, "Vote of Confidence," *Fast Company*, No. 65 (December 2002), pp. 102–112.

14. Ibid.

15. Hoover's Inc., "Overview: Panera Bread Company."

16. Ibid.

17. Ibid.

18. L. Tischler, "Vote of Confidence," *Fast Company*, No. 65 (December 2002), pp. 102–112.

19. Ibid.

20. Ibid.

21. Ibid.

22. C. Y. Kwok, "Bakery-Café Idea Smacked of Success from the Very Beginning; Concept Gives Rise to Rapid Growth in Stores, Stock Price," *St. Louis Dispatch* (May 20, 2001), p. E1.

23. Ibid.

24. R. L. Allen, "Au Bon Pain Co. Pins Hopes on New President, Image," *Nation's Restaurant News*, Vol. 30, No. 47 (December 2, 1996), pp. 3–4.

25. P. Kemp, "Second Rising," *Forbes*, Vol. 166, No. 13 (November 13, 2000), p. 290.

26. R. L. Papiernik, "Au Bon Pain Mulls Remedies, Pares Back Expansion Plans," *Nation's Restaurant News*, Vol. 29, No. 34 (August 28, 1995), pp. 3–4.

27. "Au Bon Pain Stock Drops 11% on News That Loss Is Expected," *Wall Street Journal* (October 7, 1996), p. B2.

28. Ibid.

29. A. Caffrey, "Heard in New England: Au Bon Pain's Plan to Reinvent Itself Sits Well with Many Pros," *Wall Street Journal* (March 10, 1999), p. NE.2.

30. M. Sheridan, "Time Trials," *Restaurants & Institutions*, Vol. 112, No. 12 (May 15, 2002), pp. 93–102.

31. G. LaVecchia, "Fast Casual Enters the Fast Lane," *Restaurant Hospitality*, Vol. 87, No. 2 (February 2003), pp. 43–47.

32. Ibid.

33. M. Pethokoukis, "Bye-Bye Burgers," *US News & World Report*, Vol. 133, No. 21 (December 2002), p. 36.

34. Ibid.

35. S. Brooks, "Feeling Hot, Hot, Hot," *Restaurant Business*, Vol. 101, No. 15 (September 2002), p. 36.

36. Panera Bread Company, Inc., *2004 Notice of Annual Meeting of Stockholders*, pp. 4–6.

37. Ibid., pp. 7–8.

38. Panera Bread Company, Inc., *2003 Form 10-K*, p. 3. This was directly quoted, with minor editing.

39. Ibid., p. 5.

40. Ibid., p. 4.

41. Panera Bread Company, Inc., *2003 Form 10-K*, pp. 6–7. Some sentences in this section were directly quoted, with minor editing.

42. B. R. Hook and A. Stevenson, "Rising Dough," *Kiplinger's Personal Finance*, Vol. 56, No. 1 (January 2002), p. 71.

43. Panera Bread Company, Inc., *2003 Form 10-K*, pp. 5–6. Some sentences in this section were directly quoted, with minor editing.

44. L. Tischler, "Vote of Confidence," *Fast Company*, No. 65 (December 2002), pp. 102–112.

45. Panera Bread Company, Inc., *2003 Form 10-K*, pp. 4–5. Some paragraphs and sentences in this section were directly quoted, with minor editing.

46. B. Sperber, "Fast Casual Dining Ahead," *Brandweek*, Vol. 43, No. 31 (September 2, 2002), pp. 16–20.

47. J. Peters, "No Loafing Around: Panera Bread Raises Projections for Unit Growth," *Nation's Restaurant News*, Vol. 36, No. 23 (June 10, 2002), p. 12.

48. Panera Bread Company, Inc., *2003 Form 10-K*, p. 6. This section was directly quoted, with minor editing.

49. Panera Bread Company, Inc., *2003 Form 10-K*, pp. 3, 6. Sentences 4 through 8 of the first paragraph and the entire second paragraph were directly quoted, with minor editing.

50. Panera Bread Company, Inc., *2003 Form 10-K*, pp. 13–19. This section was directly quoted, with minor editing.

CASE 30

Church & Dwight Builds a Corporate Portfolio

Roy A. Cook

"**CHURCH & DWIGHT HAS UNDERGONE A SUBSTANTIAL TRANSFORMATION IN THE PAST DECADE** largely as a result of three major acquisitions which doubled the size of the total Company, created a well balanced portfolio of household and personal care businesses, and established a much larger international business."[1] As a new top management team worked to digest and integrate this series of acquisitions while scouting for new acquisition targets in consumer products, it struggled with maintaining market share in its historically core businesses. The top-line numbers looked good, but previously issued commitments to generate annual sales growth from historic core businesses of 15% had been lowered once to the 12½%–15% range and then to the 10%–12% range. Had the pieces finally been put in place for the company to compete successfully with other well-known giants in the consumer products arena, or would it remain in their shadows?

Background

For more than 160 years, Church & Dwight Co., Inc., had been working to build market share on a brand name that is rarely associated with the company. When consumers are asked, "Are you familiar with Church & Dwight products?" the answer is typically "No." Yet, a variety of Church & Dwight consumer products can be found in 95% of all U.S. households. As the world's largest producer and marketer of sodium bicarbonate–based products, Church & Dwight has achieved fairly consistent growth in both sales and earnings as new and expanded uses were found for its core sodium bicarbonate products. Although Church & Dwight may not be a household name, many of its core products bearing the Arm & Hammer name are easily recognized.

Shortly after its introduction in 1878, Arm & Hammer Baking Soda became a fundamental item on the pantry shelf as homemakers found many uses for it other than baking, such as cleaning and deodorizing. The ingredients that can be found in that ubiquitous yellow box of baking soda in almost every refrigerator can also be used as a dentrifice, a chemical agent to absorb or neutralize odors and acidity, a kidney dialysis element, a blast medium, an environmentally friendly cleaning agent, a swimming pool pH stabilizer, and a pollution control agent.

Finding expanded uses for sodium bicarbonate and achieving orderly growth had been consistent targets for the company. Over the past 30 years, average company sales had increased 10% to 15% annually. Although top-line sales growth had historically been a focal point for the company, a shift may have occurred in management's thinking as more emphasis seemed to be placed on bottom-line profitability growth. President and Chief Executive Officer James R. Craigie may have signaled this change when he stated, "Our long-term objective is to maintain the Company's track record, and continue to achieve sustained earnings growth, which we currently define as 10–12% earning per share growth on an organic basis excluding acquisitions."[2] All of this happened as Church & Dwight appeared to be shifting roles from an acquirer to an operator.

Craigie took over the helm of Church & Dwight from Robert A. Davies III in July 2004. Setting the stage to build on the successful legacy he inherited from his predecessor, Craigie proposed a new strategy of "building a portfolio of strong brands with sustainable competitive advantages."[3] The results of both Davies' and Craigie's efforts to reshape the company through acquisitions and organic growth can be seen in the financial statements shown in **Exhibits 1** and **2**.

Management

The historically slow but steady course Church & Dwight had traveled over the decades reflected stability in the chief executive office and a steady focus on long-term goals. The ability to remain focused might be attributable to the fact that about 25% of the outstanding shares of common stock were owned by descendants of the company's co-founders. Dwight C. Minton, a direct descendant of Austin Church, actively directed the company as CEO from

EXHIBIT 1
Consolidated Statements of Income: Church & Dwight Co., Inc.
(Dollar amounts in thousands, except per share data)

Year Ending December 31	2005	2004	2003
Net Sales	$1,736,506	$1,462,062	$1,056,874
Cost of sales	1,099,506	928,674	738,883
Gross Profit	637,000	533,388	317,991
Marketing expenses	183,422	161,183	88,807
Selling, general and administrative expenses	240,802	200,452	117,333
Income from Operations	212,776	171,753	111,851
Equity in earnings (loss) of affiliates	4,790	15,115	28,632
Investment earnings	3,985	3,225	1,322
Loss on early extinguishment of debt	(1,241)	(22,871)	(4,127)
Other income (expense), net	(1,329)	1,628	(313)
Interest expense	(44,098)	(41,407)	(20,400)
Income before minority interest and taxes	174,883	127,443	116,965
Minority interest	(91)	4	30
Income before taxes	174,974	127,439	116,935
Income taxes	52,068	38,631	35,974
Net Income	$ 122,906	$ 88,808	$ 80,961

EXHIBIT 2
Consolidated
Balance Sheets:
Church & Dwight
Co., Inc.
(Dollar amounts in
thousands)

Year Ending December 31	2005	2004	2003
Assets			
Current Assets			
Cash and cash equivalents	$ 126,678	$ 145,540	$ 75,634
Accounts receivable	187,863	166,203	107,553
Inventories	156,149	148,898	84,176
Deferred income taxes	11,217	7,600	14,109
Notes receivable—current	1,150	1,015	942
Net assets held for sale	—	13,300	—
Prepaid expenses	11,381	11,240	6,808
Total Current Assets	494,438	493,796	289,222
Property, plant and equipment (net)	326,903	332,204	258,010
Notes receivable	6,134	7,751	8,766
Equity investment in affiliates	10,855	13,255	152,575
Long-term supply contract	4,094	4,881	5,668
Trade names and other intangibles	541,970	474,285	119,374
Goodwill	523,676	511,643	259,444
Other assets	54,047	40,183	26,558
Total Assets	$1,962,117	$1,877,998	$1,119,617
Liabilities and Stockholders' Equity			
Current Liabilities			
Short-term borrowings	$ 105,563	$ 98,239	$ 62,337
Accounts payable and accrued expenses	255,438	242,024	148,958
Current portion of long-term debt	15,719	5,797	3,560
Income taxes payable	32,990	11,479	17,199
Total Current Liabilities	$ 409,710	$ 357,539	$ 232,054
Long-term debt	635,261	754,706	331,149
Deferred income taxes	124,882	108,216	61,000
Deferred and other long-term liabilities	40,823	39,384	33,164
Pension, postretirement and postemployment benefits	54,305	57,836	23,459
Minority interest	258	287	297
Stockholders' Equity			
Common Stock—$1 par value	69,991	69,991	69,991
Additional paid-in capital	65,110	47,444	27,882
Retained earnings	618,071	510,480	435,588
Accumulated other comprehensive income (loss)	(454)	(3,110)	(13,962)
	752,718	624,805	519,499
Less common stock in treasury, at cost	(55,840)	(64,775)	(81,094)
Stockholders' Equity Total	696,878	560,030	438,405
Total Liabilities and Stockholders' Equity	$1,962,117	$1,877,998	$1,119,528

1969 through 1995 and remained on the Board as Chairman Emeritus. He passed on the duties of CEO to the first non–family member in the company's history, Robert A. Davies III, in 1995. During his almost 10 years of leadership, Davies tripled the size of the company. Next, the future direction of the company was in the hands of James Craigie, who was serving as Chairman. **Exhibit 3** shows the 13 board members, of whom three are internal members.

Many companies with strong brand names in the consumer products field have been susceptible to leveraged buyouts and hostile takeovers. However, a series of calculated actions had spared Church & Dwight's board and management from having to make last-minute decisions to ward off unwelcome suitors. Besides maintaining majority control of the outstanding common stock, the Board amended the company's charter, giving current shareholders four votes per share but requiring future shareholders to buy and hold shares for four years before receiving the same privilege. The Board of Directors was also structured into three classes with four directors in each class serving staggered three-year terms. According to Minton, the objective of these moves was to "give the Board control so as to provide the best results for shareholders."[4]

As a further deterrent to would-be suitors or unwelcome advances, the company entered into an employee severance agreement with key officials. This agreement provides severance pay of up to two times (three times for Mr. Craigie) the individual's highest annual salary and bonus plus benefits for two years (three years for Mr. Craigie) if the individual was terminated within one year after a change in control of the company. Change of control was defined as the acquisition by a person or group of 50% or more of company common stock; a change in the majority of the board of directors not approved by the pre-change board of directors; or the approval by the stockholders of the company or a merger, consolidation, liquidation, dissolution, or sale of all the assets of the company.[5]

As Church & Dwight pushed more aggressively into consumer products outside of sodium bicarbonate–related products and into the international arena, numerous changes were made in key personnel and positions, especially in the marketing area. These changes can be seen by reviewing **Exhibits 4** and **5**. Comparing these two exhibits, which present rosters of

EXHIBIT 4
Key Officers, Management Positions, and Tenure with Company—2002

Name	Age	Position	Anniversary Date
Robert A. Davies, III	66	President & Chief Executive Officer	1995
Raymond L. Bendure, Ph.D.	58	Vice President Research and Development	1995
Mark A. Bilawsky	54	Vice President, General Counsel and Secretary	1976
Bradley A. Casper	42	Vice President, President, Domestic Personal Care	2002
Mark G. Conish	49	Vice President Operations	1993
Steven P. Cugine	39	Vice President Human Respirces	1999
Zvi Eiref	63	Vice President Finance and Chief Financial Officer	1995
Henry Kornhauser	69	Vice President Creative Services	1997
Dennis M. Moore	51	Vice President Arm & Hammer Division Sales	1980
Joseph A. Sipia, Jr.	53	Vice President, President and Chief Operating Officer/Specialty Products Division	2002
John R. Burke	50	Vice President Financial Analysis and Planning for the Arm & Hammer Division	1985
Robert J. Carroll	43	Vice President MIS	1989
Kenneth S. Colbert	46	Vice President Logistics	1979
Anthony J. Falotico	47	Vice President Research and Development, Household Products	1980
Alfred H. Falter	52	Vice President Procurement	1979
W. Patrick Fiedler	53	Vice President Basic Chemicals, Specialty Products Division	1995
Roger Fingerhut	59	Vice President Manufacturing	2001
Gary P. Halker	51	Vice President, Controller and Chief Information Officer	1977
Jaap Ketting	50	Vice President International Finance, Specialty Products Division	1987
Allison Lukacsko	51	Vice President Research and Development Personal Care	2001
Larry B. Koslow	50	Vice President Marketing, Arm & Hammer Division	1995
Ronald D. Munson	59	Vice President Animal Nutrition, Specialty Products Division	1983

SOURCE: *Church & Dwight Co., Inc., Notice of Annual Meeting of Stockholders and Proxy Statement (2001)*, pp. 5–7.

EXHIBIT 5

Key Officers,
Management
Positions, and
Tenure with
Company—2005

Name	Age	Position	Anniversary Date
James R. Craigie	52	President & Chief Executive Officer	2004
Mark G. Conish	53	Vice President, Global Operations	1975
Steven P. Cugine	43	Vice President, Global New Products Innovation	1999
Jacquelin J. Brova	52	Vice President, Human Resources	2002
Zvi Eiref	67	Vice President Finance and Chief Financial Officer	1995
Bruce F. Fleming	48	Vice President and Chief Marketing Officer	2006
Susan E. Goldy	52	Vice President, General Counsel and Secretary	2003
Joseph A. Sipia, Jr.	57	Vice President, President, and Chief Operating Officer, Specialty Products Division	2002
Gary P. Halker	55	Vice President, Finance and Treasurer	1977
Adrian J. Huns	58	Vice President, President International Consumer Products	2004
Paul A Siracusa	49	Vice President, Global Research and Development	2005
Louis H. Tursi	45	Vice President, Domestic Consumer Sales	2004

SOURCE: *Church & Dwight Co., Inc., Notice of Annual Meeting of Stockholders & Proxy Statement (2006), pp. 9–10.*

key officers along with their ages, positions, and original dates of employment for the years 2002 and 2005, shows many changes. Although Davies had retired because of age, Casper, Kornhauser, and Koslow, who had been brought in for their marketing expertise, were no longer with the company. To fill this void, several of the newer additions to a streamlined management team, including Craigie, Fleming, Huns, and Tursi, brought extensive marketing experience to the top management team from organizations such as Spalding Sports Worldwide, Johnson & Johnson, Vlasic Foods, and Carter-Wallace. In addition, Fleming and Huns along with Siracusa brought significant international experience to the team as an increasing emphasis was placed on markets outside the United States.

In addition to the many changes that had taken place in key management positions, changes had also been made in the composition of the Board of Directors. Six of the 10-member Board had served for 10 years or more; three had served for three years or less. Two women served on the board and ages of members ranged from 52 to 78. Although in a less active role as Chairman Emeritus, Dwight Church Minton, who became a board member in 1965, continued to provide leadership and a long legacy of "corporate memory."

Changing Directions

Entering the 21st century, "Management recognized a major challenge to overcome . . . was the Company's small size compared to its competitors in basic product lines of household and personal care. They also recognized the value of a major asset, the Company's pristine Balance Sheet, and made the decision to grow."[6] According to Craigie, "Church & Dwight has undergone a substantial transformation in the past decade largely as a result of three major acquisitions which doubled the size of the total company, created a well balanced portfolio of household and personal care businesses, and established a much larger international business."[7] The Mentadent, Pepsodent, Aim, and Close-Up brands of toothpaste products were purchased from Unilever in October of 2003; the purchase of the remaining 50% of Armkel, the acquisition vehicle that had been used to purchase Carter-Wallace's consumer brands such as Trojan, was completed in May of 2004; and Spinbrush was purchased from Procter & Gamble in October of 2005. The numbers spoke for themselves, as these acquisitions had pumped up total revenues. In 1995 total company sales were less than $500 million; in 2001, they had jumped to over $1 billion; and in 2005, they reached $1.7 billion.

Explosive growth through acquisitions transformed a once-small company focused on a few consumer and specialty products into a much larger competitor, across not only a broader range of products, but also geographic territory. Consumer products now encompassed a broad array of personal care, deodorizing and cleaning, and laundry products, whereas specialty products offerings were expanded to specialty chemicals, animal nutrition, and specialty cleaners. And, international consumer product sales, which had been an insignificant portion of total revenue at the turn of the century, now accounted for 17% of sales. Still, in the face of consumer products behemoths such as Procter & Gamble and Colgate-Palmolive with 2005 sales of $61.7 billion and $11.4 billion, respectively, Church & Dwight was not a major market force and struggled to retain market share.

Consumer Products

Prior to its acquisition spree, the company's growth strategy had been based on finding new uses for sodium bicarbonate. Using an overall family branding strategy to penetrate the consumer products market in the United States and Canada, Church & Dwight introduced additional products displaying the Arm & Hammer logo. This logoed footprint remains significant as the Arm & Hammer brand controls a commanding 85% of the baking soda market. By capitalizing on its easily recognizable brand name, logo, and established marketing channels, Church & Dwight moved into such related products as laundry detergent, carpet cleaners and deodorizers, air deodorizers, toothpaste, and deodorant/antiperspirants. This strategy worked well, allowing the company to promote multiple products using only one brand name, but it limited growth opportunities "in highly competitive consumer product markets, in which cost efficiency, new product offering and innovation are critical to success."[8]

From the company's founding until 1970, it produced and sold only two consumer products: Arm & Hammer Baking Soda and a laundry product marketed under the name Super Washing Soda. In 1970 under Minton, Church & Dwight began testing the consumer products market by introducing a phosphate-free, powdered laundry detergent. Several other products, including a liquid laundry detergent, fabric softener sheets, an all-fabric bleach, tooth powder and toothpaste, baking soda chewing gum, deodorant/antiperspirants, deodorizers (carpet, room, and pet), and clumping cat litter, had been added to the expanding list of Arm & Hammer brands. However, simply relying on baking soda extensions and focusing on niche markets to avoid a head-on attack from competitors with more financial resources and marketing clout limited growth opportunities.

Church & Dwight faced the same dilemma as other competitors in a mature domestic market for consumer products. New consumer products had to muscle their way into markets by taking market share from larger competitors' current offerings. With the majority of company sales concentrated in the United States and Canada, where sales are funneled through mass merchandisers such as Wal-Mart and Walgreens, Church & Dwight was well equipped to gain market share with its low-cost strategy. However, in the international arena, where growth is more product driven and less marketing sensitive, the company was less experienced. To compensate for this weakness, Church & Dwight relied on acquisitions and management changes to improve its international footprint and reach.

So, in the late 1990s, the company departed from its previous strategy of developing new product offerings in-house and bought several established consumer brands such as Brillo,

EXHIBIT 6
Selected Consumer
Product Categories

United States	**Canada**	**United Kingdom**
Laundry Products	Pure Baking Soda	Oral Care
Pure Baking Soda	Antiperspirants	Condoms
Carpet & Room Deodorizer	Oral Care	Antiperspirants
Cleaning Products	Bathroom Cleaners	Depilatories
Cat Litter	Carpet & Room Deodorizers	Pregnancy Kits
Pet Care Products	Condoms	Feminine Hygiene
Bathroom Cleaners	Depilatories	
Toilet Bowl Cleaner	Pregnancy Kits	**Spain**
Antiperspirants	Laundry Products	Depilatories
Oral Care Products		Skin Care
Condoms	**France**	
Depilatories	Skin Care	**Mexico**
Pregnancy Kits	Oral Care	Condoms
Laxatives	Depilatories	Depilatories
	Diagnostics	Oral Care
Australia		Pregnancy Kits
Baby Products	**Brazil**	
Depilatories	Skin Care	
Oral Care	Diagnostics	
Pregnancy Kits		

SOURCE: *Church & Dwight Co., Inc., 2005 Annual Report, pp. 10–11.*

Parsons Ammonia, Cameo Aluminum & Stainless Steel Cleaner, Rain Drops water softener, Sno Bowl toilet bowl cleaner, and Toss 'N Soft dryer sheets from one of its competitors, Dial Corporation. An even broader consumer product assortment including Trojan, Nair, and First Response was added to the company's mix of offering with the acquisition of the consumer products business of Carter-Wallace in partnership with the private equity group Armkel. The breadth of its expanded consumer product offerings and brand names can be seen in **Exhibits 6** and **7**.

According to Minton as the company grew, "We have made every effort to keep costs under control and manage frugally."[9] A good example of this approach to doing business could be seen in the Armkel partnership. "Armkel borrowed money on a non-recourse basis so a failure would have no impact on Church & Dwight, taking any risk away from shareholders."[10] As mentioned previously, the remaining interest in Armkel was purchased in 2005, an important move that cleared the way to increase marketing efforts behind Trojan, a brand that controlled 71% of the market.[11]

With its new stable of products and expanded laundry detergent offerings, Church & Dwight found itself competing head-on with both domestic and international consumer product giants such as Procter & Gamble, Colgate-Palmolive, Clorox, and Unilever. Even though it was smaller in size, Church & Dwight was an aggressive competitor, as its market share positions in key product categories show in **Exhibit 8**.

EXHIBIT 7
Representative
Brand Names

Arm & Hammer	Arrid	Nair
Xtra	Aim	Trojan
Brillo	Pepsodent	Natura Lamb
Scrub Free	Spinbrush	First Response

EXHIBIT 8
U. S. Market Share
Position

Product Category	Position
Laundry Detergent	3
Cat Litter	2
Bathroom Cleaner	1
Antiperspirants	5
Condoms	1
Depilatories	2
Home Pregnancy Test Kits	2

As more and more products were added to the consumer line-up, Church & Dwight brought many of its marketing tasks in-house as well as stepping out with ground-breaking marketing campaigns. The first major in-house marketing projects were in dental care. Although it entered a crowded field of specialty dental products, Church & Dwight rode the crest of increasing interest by both dentists and hygienists in baking soda for maintaining dental health, enabling it to sneak up on the industry giants. The company moved rapidly from the position of a niche player in the toothpaste market to that of a major competitor.

In a ground-breaking marketing campaign that some consider controversial, the company was to air commercials for condoms on prime-time television. "Church & Dwight executives say their new campaign is designed to shake people up, particularly those who don't think they need to use condoms. Attempts will be made to shock them out of complacency and grab their attention."[12] The company's increasing marketing strength has caught the attention of others as is evidenced by its partnership with Quidel Corporation, a provider of point-of-care diagnostic tests, to meet women's health and wellness needs. "The partnership combines Church & Dwight's strength in the marketing, distribution and sales of consumer products with Quidel's strength in the development and manufacture of rapid diagnostic tests."[13]

For the most part, Church & Dwight's acquired products and entries into the consumer products market had met with success. However, potential marketing problems might be looming on the horizon for its Arm & Hammer line of consumer products. The company could fall into the precarious line-extension snare. Placing a well-known brand name on a wide variety of products could cloud the brand's image, leading to consumer confusion and loss of marketing pull. In addition, competition in the company's core laundry detergent market continued to heat up as the market matured and sales fell, with major retailers such as Wal-Mart and Target wringing price concessions from all producers.[14] Would the addition of such well-known brand names as Xtra, Nair, Trojan, and First Response provide new avenues for consumer products growth?

Specialty Products

In addition to a large and growing stable of consumer products, Church & Dwight also had a very solid core of specialty products. The Specialty Products Division basically consisted of the manufacture and sale of sodium bicarbonate for three distinct market segments: specialty chemicals, animal nutrition products, and specialty cleaners. Manufacturers utilized sodium bicarbonate performance products as a leavening agent for commercial baked goods; an antacid in pharmaceuticals; a chemical in kidney dialysis; a carbon dioxide release agent in fire extinguishers; and an alkaline in swimming pool chemicals, detergents, and various textile and tanning applications. Animal feed producers used sodium bicarbonate nutritional products predominantly as a buffer, or antacid, for dairy cattle feeds and made a nutritional supplement that enhanced milk production of dairy cattle. Sodium bicarbonate had also been used as an additive to poultry feeds to enhance feed efficiency.

EXHIBIT 9
Percent of Net Sales

	2005	2004	2003	2002	2001
Consumer Products	87	86	82	85	82
Specialty Products	13	14	18	15	18

"Church & Dwight has long maintained its leadership position in the industry through a strategy of sodium bicarbonate product differentiation, which hinges on the development of special grades for specific end users."[15] Management's apparent increased focus on consumer products had only recently affected the significance of specialty products in the overall corporate mix of revenues, as shown in **Exhibit 9**.

Church & Dwight was in an enviable position to profit from its dominant niche in the sodium bicarbonate products market, because it controlled the primary raw material used in its production. The primary ingredient in sodium bicarbonate was produced from the mineral trona, which was extracted from the company's mines in southwestern Wyoming. The other ingredient, carbon dioxide, was a readily available chemical that could be obtained from a variety of sources. Production of the final product, sodium bicarbonate, for both consumer and specialty products was completed at one of the two company plants located in Green River, Wyoming, and Old Fort, Ohio.

The company maintained a dominant position in the production of the required raw materials for both its consumer and industrial products. It manufactured almost two-thirds of the sodium bicarbonate sold in the United States and, until recently, had been the only U.S. producer of ammonium bicarbonate and potassium carbonate. The company had the largest share (approximately 75%) of the sodium bicarbonate capacity in the United States and was the largest consumer of baking soda as it filled its own needs for company-produced consumer and industrial products.[16]

Just like the Consumer Products Division, the Specialty Products Division focused on developing new uses for the company's core product, sodium bicarbonate. Additional opportunities continued to be explored for Armex Blast Media. This is a sodium bicarbonate-based product used as a paint stripping compound. It gained widespread recognition when it was utilized successfully for the delicate task of stripping the accumulation of years of paint and tar from the interior of the Statue of Liberty without damaging the fragile copper skin. It was being considered for other specialized applications in the transportation and electronics industries and in industrial cleaning because of its apparent environmental safety. Armex also had been introduced into international markets.

Specialty cleaning products were found in blasting (similar to sand blasting applications) as well as many emerging aqueous-based cleaning technologies such as automotive parts cleaning and circuit board cleaning. Safety-Kleen and Church & Dwight teamed up through a 50–50 joint venture, Armakleen, to meet the parts cleaning needs of automotive repair shops. Safety-Kleen's 2,800-strong sales and service team marketed Church & Dwight's aqueous-based cleaners as an environmental friendly alternative to traditional solvent-based cleaners.[17]

The company's Armakleen product was also used for cleaning printed circuit boards. This non-solvent-based product may have an enormous potential market because it may be able to replace chlorofluorocarbon-based cleaning systems. Sodium bicarbonate also had been used to remove lead from drinking water and, when added to water supplies, coated the inside of pipes and prevented lead from leaching into the water. This market could grow in significance with additions to the Clean Water Bill. The search for new uses of sodium bicarbonate from pharmaceutical to environmental protection continued in both the consumer and industrial products divisions.

International Operations

Church & Dwight traditionally enjoyed a great deal of success in North American markets and was attempting to gain footholds in international markets through acquisitions. The company's first major attempt to expand its presence in the international consumer products markets was with the acquisition of DeWitt International Corporation, which manufactured and marketed personal care products including toothpaste. The DeWitt acquisition provided the company not only with increased international exposure but also with much-needed toothpaste production facilities and technology. However, until the 2001 acquisition of the Carter-Wallace line of products, only about 10% of sales were outside the United States. By 2005, international sales of consumer products had grown to 17% of total revenues.

As the company cautiously moved into the international arena of consumer products, it also continued to pursue expansion of its specialty products into international markets. Attempts to enter international markets met with limited success, probably for two reasons: (1) lack of name recognition and (2) transportation costs. Although Arm & Hammer was one of the most recognized brand names in the United States (in the top 10), it did not enjoy the same name recognition elsewhere. In addition, on a historical basis, international transportation costs were at least four times as much as domestic transportation costs. However, export opportunities continued to present themselves as 10% of all U.S. production of sodium bicarbonate was exported. Whereas Church & Dwight dominated the United States sodium bicarbonate market, Solvay Chemicals was the largest producer in Europe and Ashi Glass was the largest producer in Asia. Although demand was particularly strong in Asia, "Little of the chemical produced in North America and Europe is exported to Asia because of prohibitive transportation costs."[18]

Church & Dwight's Future

According to Craigie, developing a strong portfolio of competitive brands required a relentless commitment to the following areas:

- Improving brand positioning to ensure brands stay relevant to consumers
- Accelerating new product development to meet changing consumer needs
- Delivering significant improvement in gross margins through cost improvement programs
- Increasing global leverage through expanding product offerings into current markets and large emerging markets through global marketing campaigns and supply-chain efficiencies
- Continuing to create value through acquisitions
- Securing superior leaders for the company to ensure functional excellence[19]

The core business and foundation on which the company had been built remained the same after more than 160 years. However, as management looked to the future, could they successfully achieve a balancing act based on finding growth through expanded uses of sodium bicarbonate while assimilating a divergent group of consumer products into an expanding international footprint?

NOTES

1. Church & Dwight Co, Inc., Annual Report, 2005, p. 3.
2. Ibid., p. 5.
3. Ibid., p. 3.
4. Dwight Church Minton, personal interview (October 2, 2002).
5. *8-K, 2006.*
6. Church & Dwight, Co., Inc., *Annual Meeting, 2001*, p. 1.
7. Church & Dwight Co, Inc. *Annual Report,* 2006, p. 3.
8. *10K, 2006*, p. 20.
9. Minton (2002).
10. Ibid.
11. Jack Neff, "Trojan," *Advertising Age* (November 7, 2005).
12. Mary Ann Liebert, "Condom Maker Wants to Go Prime Time," Drug Development and STD News, *AIDS Patient Care and STDs*, Vol. 19, No. 7 (2005), p. 470.
13. Church & Dwight Co. Press Release, 2006, p. 1.
14. Doris de Guzman, "Household Products Struggle," *Chemical Market Reporter*, Vol. 269, No. 11 (2006).
15. Church & Dwight Co., *Annual Report, 2000*, p. 17.
16. Lisa Jarvis, "Church & Dwight Builds Sales Through Strength in Bicarbonate," *Chemical Market Reporter* (April 10, 2002).
17. Helena Harvilicz, "C&D's Industrial Cleaning Business Continues to Grow," *Chemical Market Reporter*, Vol. 257, No. 20 (May 15, 2000).
18. Gordon Graff, "Sodium Bicarb Supply Strong, Tags Level with Producer Costs," *Purchasing* (April 6, 2006), p. 28C1.
19. Church & Dwight Co, Inc., *Annual Report, 2005,* pp. 3–4.

CASE **31**

Dell, Inc.

J. David Hunger

DELL, INC., WAS FOUNDED IN **1984** BY MICHAEL DELL AT AGE **19** WHILE HE WAS A STUDENT living in a dormitory at the University of Texas. As a college freshman, he bought personal computers (PCs) from the excess inventory of local retailers, added features such as more memory and disk drives, and sold them out of the trunk of his car. He withdrew $1,000 in personal savings, used his car as collateral for a bank loan, hired a few friends, and placed ads in the local newspaper offering computers at 10%–15% below retail price. Soon he was selling $50,000 worth of PCs a month to local businesses. Sales during the first year reached $600,000 and doubled almost every year thereafter. After his freshman year, Dell left school to run the business full time.

Michael Dell began manufacturing his own computers in 1985 and marketed them through ads in computer trade publications. Two years later, his company witnessed tremendous change: it launched its first catalog, initiated a field sales force to reach large corporate accounts, went public, changed its name from PCs Limited to Dell Computer Corporation, and established its first international subsidiary in Britain. Michael Dell was selected "Entrepreneur of the Year" by *Inc.* in 1989, "Man of the Year" by *PC Magazine* in 1992, and "CEO of the Year" by *Financial World* in 1993. In 1992, the company was included for the first time among the *Fortune* 500 roster of the world's largest companies.

By 1995, with sales of nearly $3.5 billion, the company was the world's leading direct marketer of personal computers and one of the top five PC vendors in the world. In 1996, Dell supplemented its direct mail and telephone sales by offering its PCs via the Internet at *dell.com*. By 2001, Dell ranked first in global market share and number one in the United States for shipments of standard Intel-architecture servers. The company changed its name to Dell, Inc., in 2003 as a way of reflecting the evolution of the company into a diverse supplier of technology products and services. In 2005, Dell topped *Fortune's* list of "Most Admired Companies." In fiscal year 2006, the company earned $3,572 million in net income on $55,908 million in net revenue. Dell shipped more than 10 million systems during the fourth quarter of 2006—making it the best sales quarter in Dell's history. (Note: Dell's annual and quarterly reports and SEC filings are available via the company's Web site at *www.dell.com*.)

Problems of Early Growth

The company's early rapid growth resulted in disorganization. Sales jumped from $546 million in fiscal 1991 to $3.4 billion in 1995. Growth had been pursued to the exclusion of all else, but no one seemed to know how the numbers really added up. When Michael Dell saw that the wheels were beginning to fly off his nine-year-old entrepreneurial venture, he sought older, outside management help. He temporarily slowed the corporation's growth strategy while he worked to assemble and integrate a team of experienced executives from companies such as Motorola, Hewlett-Packard, and Apple.

The new executive team worked to get Dell's house in order so that the company could continue its phenomenal sales growth. Management decided in 1995 to abandon distribution of Dell's products through U.S. retail stores and return solely to direct distribution. This enabled the company to refocus Dell's efforts in areas that matched its philosophy of high emphasis on customer support and service. By 2004, Kevin Rollins replaced Michael Dell as Chief Executive Officer, allowing the founder to focus on being Chairman of the Board.

Business Model

Dell's business model was simple: Dell machines were made to order and delivered directly to the customer. Dell had no distributors or retail stores. Dell PCs had consistently been listed among the best PCs on the market by *PC World* and *PC Magazine*. Cash flow was never a problem because Dell was paid by customers long before Dell paid its suppliers. The company held virtually no parts inventory. As a result, Dell made computers more quickly and cheaply than any other company.

Dell Computer became the master of process engineering and supply-chain management. It spent only $463 million annually on R&D, contrasted to $534 million by Apple Computer and $4 billion by HP, but it focused all of its spending on improving its manufacturing process. Instead of spending its money on new computer technology, Dell waited until a new technology became a standard. Michael Dell explained that soon after a technology product arrived on the market, it was a high-priced, high-margin item made differently by each company. Over time, the technology standardized—the way PCs standardized around Intel microprocessors and Microsoft operating systems. At a certain point between the development of the standard and its becoming a commodity, that technology became ripe for Dell. When the leaders were earning 40% or 50% profit margins, they were vulnerable to Dell making a profit on far smaller margins. Dell drove down costs further by perfecting its manufacturing processes and using its buying power to obtain cheaper parts. Its reduction of overhead expenses to only 9.6% of revenue meant that Dell earned nearly $1 million in revenue per employee—three times the revenue per employee at IBM and almost twice HP's rate.

Although the company outsourced some operations, such as component production and express shipping, it had its own assembly lines throughout the world. The Winston-Salem, North Carolina, plant was opened in 2005 as Dell's third American plant. It was able to manufacture a complete desktop computer every five seconds.

Product Line and Structure

Over the years, Dell, Inc., broadened its product line to include not only desktop and laptop computers, but also servers, storage systems, printers, software, peripherals, and enhanced services, such as infrastructure services. By 2006, net revenue by product line was composed of desktop PCs (38%), mobility (25%), software and peripherals (15%), servers and networking (10%), enhanced services (9%), and storage (3%).

Dell's corporate headquarters was located in Round Rock, Texas, near Austin. The company was structured into three geographic business units: Dell Americas (North and South America), located in Round Rock, Texas; Dell Asia Pacific (Pacific Rim and Australia), located in Singapore; and Dell Europe, Middle East, and Africa, located in Bracknell, England. The company manufactured computer systems in seven plants in Austin, Texas; Nashville, Tennessee; Winston-Salem, North Carolina; Eldorado do Sul, Brazil; Limerick, Ireland; Penang, Malaysia; and Xiamen, China. Its 2006 revenue by region was 65% from the Americas, 23% from Europe, and 12% from the Asia-Pacific unit.

Environmental Change

By 2006, the once-torrid growth in PC sales had slowed to about 5% a year. The percentage of 2005 PC sales via the phone and Internet fell in the United States as the sales through U.S. retail stores rose. Consumers seemed to be more interested in new high-featured digital products, such as Apple's iPod, than in commodity products such as plain beige PCs. Meanwhile, Dell's rivals were becoming more competitive. Gateway, for example, had found ways to reduce its costs and had fought its way back to profitability. The same was true for Hewlett-Packard (HP) once it had digested its acquisition of Compaq. HP's market share increased from 13.8% to 14.9% in 2005, while Dell's shrank slightly. Competitors were pricing their products more aggressively and taking advantage of being in thousands of retail stores. Lenovo (previously Legend), with $13 billion in sales and 8% of the worldwide PC market, was reentering the retail notebook market with the ThinkPad it had acquired from IBM. Based in China, Lenovo specialized in consumer PCs and low-cost manufacturing. It already dominated the PC market in China with 26% market share. Contrasted with Dell, Lenovo sold its products through retailers, corporate resellers, and the IBM sales force, in addition to direct marketing.

Dell, in early 2006, was the largest PC vendor in the world, commanding 20% of the global market, 32% of the American market, and 13% of the European market. Nevertheless, the company's chief advantages—direct marketing and power over suppliers—were losing their punch. Even though the company slashed prices in 2005, it failed to gain market share. Ironically, by driving down supplier costs, Dell had also reduced its rivals' costs. In addition, the sales growth in the computer industry was in the consumer market and in emerging countries rather than in the corporate market in which Dell sold about 85% of its products. The consumer market was expected to grow 10% in 2007 versus only 7.8% for the corporate market. Consumers' desire to see and touch multiple products before a purchase made Dell's direct marketing channel less attractive to them. Sales in countries outside the United States and Canada were often based on the advice of sales staff, putting Dell's "direct only" business model at a disadvantage.

Dell's absence in retail stores had hurt the company's attempts to expand beyond PCs into consumer electronics, such as televisions. As corporate buyers increasingly purchased their computer equipment as part of a package of services to address specific problems, service oriented rivals such as IBM and HP had an advantage over Dell. Dell's close relation with Intel had been a significant advantage in past years, but this single-source agreement had created a problem recently when Intel's rival AMD offered cheaper and, in some cases, better performing microprocessors. Taken together, these facts made it clear that the environment no longer favored Dell's business model.

Internal Issues

Dell had grown in size to the point that its usual double-digit sales increases were proving to be unsustainable. Its sales growth dropped from 18.7% in fiscal year 2005 to 13.6% in 2006. Meanwhile, Dell's customer service had fallen to a new low. In 2005, Dell's customer service rating fell 6.3% to a score of 74 (average for the industry) in a survey by the University of Michigan. More than 45% of calls to Dell required at least one transfer. The Better Business Bureau reported that complaints about Dell more than doubled in 2005 to 1,533. It was not surprising to analysts when Dell's U.S. market share fell to 28% during the first quarter of 2006. Consequently, Dell's stock dropped from $40 a share in August 2005 to $25 in June 2006.

Although the company was working to improve customer satisfaction by adding more service people, more people meant increased costs. Even though more sales growth was expected in the consumer than in the corporate market, the consumer market had its disadvantages. For one thing, sales to U.S. consumers carried margins of only 6% compared with 11% for corporate buyers. Second, products had to be physically present in retail stores to compete with Gateway, HP, and Lenovo, among others.

Dell's management was working hard to regain sales growth and cut costs. It was spending more than $100 million in 2006, far more than it had spent in 2005 when its expenses were 9% of sales, compared to 13% for Apple and HP. To boost its customer service, it was expanding call centers to house 1,000 to 3,000 representatives. It was hoped that this would increase the chance that any caller's problem could be solved by someone within the building. Dell was also installing large monitors to let workers see the number of callers on hold. By early 2006, hold times had already been cut in half from those in 2005 and internal surveys of 5,000 customers revealed a 35% increase in customer satisfaction from a year earlier. To cut costs, Dell was redefining what it meant by "free shipping" for its low-end PCs. Instead of delivering them to the customer's home, Dell was planning to mail them to the nearest post office for pickup. Home delivery was an extra charge, but standard with more expensive models.

With rivals such as HP matching or undercutting its PC prices, Dell's management decided to go on the offensive. In June 2006, Dell announced a new policy of accepting old PCs, printers, and other products made by Dell for free recycling throughout the world. Management also decided to no longer single-source its purchases of microprocessor chips from Intel, but to also buy them from AMD for use in a new line of servers and desktop PCs.

In a surprise move, the company introduced its new XPS M2010, a cross between a desktop and a laptop targeted to the entertainment enthusiast. The $3,500 PC featured a detachable wireless keyboard and a monitor with adjustable height. Its black, leather-like exterior, when closed, resembled a luxury briefcase. Meanwhile, Dell's new $1,990 XPS 700 desktop was aimed at video "gamers"—a market segment that had ignored Dell's conservative offerings in the past. The company also acquired Alienware Corporation, whose sleek PCs were modeled after the beast from the movie *Alien*, to appeal to hard-core game players. Management hoped that its "gamer" PCs would generate positive responses that would spill over to Dell's other lines.

On August 17, 2006, Dell's management announced that the company's second-quarter profit fell 36% to $605 million, far short of expectations. It also admitted that the company was cooperating with an informal investigation by the Securities and Exchange Commission. This announcement came just days after Dell voluntarily recalled 4.1 million potentially flammable batteries supplied by Sony Corporation.

Future Prospects

Michael Dell refused to become negative about the future of his company. Back in the 1990s, he recalled, critics had claimed that there were limits to the firm's direct-sales model, and even suggested that Dell would never be able to make laptops or servers. Said Dell, "People say the sky has fallen, that it's the beginning of the end. I don't agree. There are lots of markets with room to grow." Management hoped to double or even triple its market share in Europe. Sales in The Netherlands, for example, were growing by 40% a year. In June 2006,

Michael Dell purchased 2.9 million shares of Dell common stock for an average price of $23.99 each, his first purchase of common stock since 2001.

Analysts, nevertheless, continued to be ambivalent about the firm's prospects in a changing industry. Should the company follow the consumer market down in price and adjusts its costs accordingly, or should it focus on business products—sacrificing market share and sales growth for profits?

CASE 32

Six Flags, Inc.:

THE 2006 BUSINESS TURNAROUND

Patricia A. Ryan

"THE BUSINESS WAS BROKEN," COMMENTED DANIEL SNYDER IN JUNE 2006, THE NEW Chairman of the Board of Six Flags.[1] Fixing the business would not occur overnight for Snyder, who owned the Washington Redskins, but clearly he thought it would be doable and profitable, as was the proxy fight to run the theme park company in late 2005. According to Mark Shapiro, CEO of Six Flags:

> We're investing more in our operations because the health of the business depends on bringing back families. Our first priority is to fix the operation and that is not going to happen overnight. We see this as a long-term investment.[2]

Over the past five years, Six Flags stock had underperformed relative to Cedar Fair, its closest competitor, as well as compared to market indices. In May 2001, Six Flags stock traded at $23.25, and it sank nearly 80% in value to the $5 range in 2005. In 2004, Snyder's company, RedZone, increased its ownership in Six Flags, as did Bill Gates' investment vehicle, Cascade Investments. Together, the two parties owned over 20% of the stock, and they demanded changes to improve financial and operating performance. Snyder and Gates used their ownership to try to influence the Board to make some drastic changes, but the parties were at odds as how to improve the performance of the company. Snyder then made a successful move to remove the old Board of Directors and senior management, replacing them with his own hand-picked executives and board members. The fight for the company was over. In 2006, Snyder had Six Flags in his hands—it was now time to implement the changes he saw necessary to increase the value of his investment.

"The company was so ground down; it won't reverse in a year or two," commented Dennis L. Speigel, President of Consultancy International Theme Park Services.[3] Clearly, it would take skill and time to turn this company around.

The Business

Six Flags operated the largest regional theme park company in the world with a sole focus on theme and water parks. Six Flags operated 29 theme parks as listed in **Exhibit 1.** Regional theme park companies such as Six Flags located parks within a day's drive for visitors and worked to place its parks near large population bases within 50 and 100 miles for a one- or

EXHIBIT 1
Theme Parks by Focus, Location, Population, and Size: Six Flags, Inc.

Theme Park	Type of Park	Location	Population within 50 and 100 Miles, Respectively (in millions)	Size (acres)
Six Flags America	Theme and water	Largo, Maryland	7.4, 12.4	523
Six Flags Darien Lake and Camping Resort	Theme and water	Darien Center, New York	2.1, 3.1	978
Six Flags Elitch Gardens	Theme and water	Denver, Colorado	2.9, 3.9	67
Six Flags Fiesta Texas	Theme and water	San Antonio, Texas	2.0, 3.6	216
Six Flags Great Adventure, Six Flags Hurricane Harbor, Six Flags Water Safari	Theme, water, safari (three separate parks)	Jackson, New Jersey	14.3, 28.1	2279
Six Flags Great America	Theme and water	Gurnee, Illinois	8.8, 13.5	324
Six Flags Kentucky Kingdom	Theme and water	Louisville, Kentucky	1.5, 4.8	59
Six Flags Magic Mountain and Six Flags Hurricane Harbor	Theme and water (two separate parks)	Valencia, California	10.6, 17.7	262
Six Flags Marine World	Theme and mammals	Vallejo, California	5.7, 10.7	135
Six Flags Mexico	Theme	Mexico City, Mexico	NA, 30	107
Six Flags New England	Theme and water	Springfield, Massachusetts	3.2, 15.8	263
Six Flags New Orleans*	Theme	New Orleans, Louisiana	NA	140
Six Flags over Georgia and Six Flags White Water Atlanta	Theme and water (two separate parks)	Atlanta, Georgia	4.8, 7.7	290
Six Flags over Texas, Six Flags Hurricane Harbor	Theme and water	Arlington, Texas	5.7, 6.8	285
Six Flags Splashdown	Water	Houston, Texas	5.1, 6.3	60
Six Flags St. Louis	Theme and water	Eureka, Missouri	2.7, 3.9	503
Six Flags Waterworld Parks	Water (two parks)	Concord and Sacramento, California	7.6, 11.3	NA
Enchanted Village and Wild Waves	Water and rides	Seattle, Washington	3.5, 4.6	66
Frontier City†	Western theme	Oklahoma City, Oklahoma	1.3, 2.6	113
La Ronde	Theme	Montreal, Canada	4.3, 5.8	146
The Great Escape and Six Flags Great Escape Lodge and Indoor Waterpark	Theme and water (two parks)	Lake George, New York	1.1, 3.2	351
White Water Bay†	Tropical theme	Oklahoma City, Oklahoma	1.3, 2.6	21
Wyandot Lake	Water and rides	Columbus, Ohio	2.2, 6.8	18

* Closed for 2006 season because of hurricane damage from Hurricane Katrina.
† Scheduled to close at the end of the 2006 season.

two-day mini-vacation. Unlike national entertainment parks such as Disneyworld and Universal Studios, they were more likely to attract visitors for a day or two as opposed to being a vacation destination. Six Flags' management estimated that their parks were within 150 miles of two thirds of the U.S. population. Specific population bases for each park are given in **Exhibit 1.**

Six Flags was founded in 1961 by Angus G. Wynne with the opening of Six Flags over Texas, a pirate-themed adventure theme park. Over the next 45 years, the company grew into a chain of theme parks with such parks as Six Flags over Georgia, and Great America in Gurnee, Illinois. Known for their fast roller coasters and adventure rides, the company successfully built a group of theme and water parks under the Six Flags name.

The theme parks changed hands several times over the 45-year history and in 1991 were sold to Time Warner. In 1998, Time Warner sold the theme parks to Premier Parks. Premier Parks continued the rapid expansion of Six Flags, using the Six Flags name for several smaller theme parks that Premier had developed including Darien Lake, Elitch Gardens, and Adventure World (CITIES). The Six Flags name was adopted for the entire firm in 2000 and by the end of 2005, the company was the largest amusement operator in the United States.

Six Flags held licenses for multiple Warner Brothers and DC Comics characters including Bugs Bunny, Tweety Bird, Daffy Duck, Yosemite Sam, Batman, and Superman. This meant they could market these characters through merchandise sold in the parks, as well as use the characters to enhance the park experience and for advertising the parks.

Multiple factors affected the business success of Six Flags. The theme parks were seasonal, with 85% of theme park attendance in the second and third quarters of the calendar year.[4] Given the outdoor nature of the theme parks, adverse weather conditions affected attendance and thus revenue. There were multiple competitors for family entertainment dollars; competition came both from direct competitors, such as Cedar Fair and Busch Entertainment, and other competitors, such as Walt Disney World, Disneyland, Sea World, and family fun centers. Cedar Fair owned 12 amusement parks and five outdoor parks including Knott's Berry Farm in California and Cedar Point in Ohio. Busch Entertainment, a subsidiary of Anheuser-Busch, owned nine theme parks in five states. It included Sea World parks in California, Florida, and Texas and two Busch Gardens parks.

The Financial Picture

Six Flags had not turned a profit since 1998. In the last six years, its net losses had been $51,959,000 in 2000, $58,102,000 in 2001, $105,698,000 in 2002, $61,713,000 in 2003, $464,809,000 in 2004, and $110,938,000 in 2005. During that time, its revenues totaled $1,041,197,000 in 2000, $1,075,989,000 in 2001, $1,059,095,000 in 2002, $1,048,643,000 in 2003, $1,037,692,000 in 2004, and $1,089,682,000 in 2005. It had been the huge loss of $5.23 per share in 2004 that had forced a management change at the company. Furthermore, long-term debt had been continually increasing during the past six years. This left Six Flags burdened with excessive debt payments. In 2000, long-term debt accounted for 52.34% of total assets, whereas at the end of 2005, long-term debt had increased to 60.94% of total assets. Six Flags was burdened with about $2,242.4 million in total indebtedness at the end of 2005. On August 2, 2006, Moody's downgraded Six Flags' $2.4 million in debt from B2 to B3. It further lowered Six Flags' senior unsecured debt to lower junk level at Caa2 from Caa3. The ratings agency expressed concern about potential higher future expense associated with management's changes on the currently weak financial position.[5] On the day the debt was downgraded, the stock price fell 22.7% to $5.76. Clearly, the stock market interpreted this as a negative signal, and one that was a surprise to the market. The annual maturities of long-term debt subsequent to December 31, 2005 were as follows:[6]

2006	$113,601,000
2007	7,148,000
2008	317,675,000
2009	314,400,000
2010	299,754,000
Thereafter	1,189,779,000
Total	$2,242,357,000

After 2000, the company had lost money each year, with losses skyrocketing in 2004 to 17.08% of sales. Total operating costs were over 80% of revenue in all but one year, with interest payments on debt swallowing the rest of the revenue. Nevertheless, the company's operating income (before debt payments and park closing costs) had been consistently positive at $195,686,000 in 2000, $205,454,000 in 2001, $230,389,000 in 2002, $188,723,000 in 2003, $149,573,000 in 2004, and $183,347,000 in 2005. The company's overall poor performance was reflected in its falling stock price. Although the stock showed strong gains during the exuberant market of the late 1990s, since the market decline in 2000 Six Flags had struggled to maintain its value in the stock market. (For financial statements, see www.sixflags.com.)

In October 2005, Six Flags AstroWorld in Houston was closed. The 104-acre site was placed on the market and Six Flags planned to use the proceeds to retire some of its debt. Six Flags New Orleans sustained extensive damage from Hurricane Katrina in August 2005 and did not open for the 2006 season. The company was in negotiation with its insurance carrier for insurance claims and planned to rebuild the park.

In January 2006, Six Flags announced it intended to sell its Oklahoma City theme and water parks after the 2006 season. The proceeds were to be used to repay some of the debt. Six Flags, according to industry analysts, had considerable potential in the theme park industry, but Snyder had his work cut out for him. Would he succeed?

Enter Bill Gates

Bill Gates, founder of Microsoft, one of the world's wealthiest men and a major shareholder of Six Flags, was not pleased with the company's recent performance. His ownership was under the name of his Canadian investment company, Cascade Investments. Gates began buying Six Flags stock in 1999 and accumulated 10,810,120 shares, which accounted for 11.5% of the firm's stock in 2004, at a market value of $54 million. It was stated in SEC filings that Gates had become increasingly dissatisfied with the financial performance of Six Flags over the past five years.[7] He expressed intent to discuss with Six Flag's board the company's strategic decision making and recent financial and operating performance.

When Gates began investing in Six Flags, the stock price had fallen about 80%.[8] Rather than recovering over time, the stock fell further. Gates and Snyder combined owned over 20% of the company's stock, and the pressure to remove old management was great.

Enter Daniel Snyder and Mark Shapiro

In 2005, there was a full management and board turnover. Unsatisfied with how things were being run, Daniel M. Snyder, owner of the Washington Redskins and Red Zone LLC, entered a proxy fight to gain control of Six Flags. Successful in his bid, he became Chairman of the

Board in late 2005. Additionally, two of his designates joined the board. This included Mark Shapiro, the new President and CEO. Shortly after this change, there were six new directors placed on the Board and five resignations, two of which were new directors.

Mark Shapiro became CEO of Six Flags on December 14, 2005. For the previous year, Shapiro had served as CEO of RedZone LLC, a private investment firm founded by Daniel Snyder. Snyder held an 11.5% interest in Six Flags.

Although the management turnaround may have been exactly what Six Flags needed, the new management team and directors did not have a proven success record with Six Flags. The management was young in age and in tenure with Six Flags. Only four members had been associated with Six Flags prior to 2005. The rest of the management team and board were new to the company in 2005 or 2006. Given the change in management and the new operational plan to turn around Six Flags, the risks of failure must be assessed.

Turnaround

At the end of 2005, Six Flags employed about 2,500 full-time employees with an additional 31,500 seasonal employees. Many of the seasonal employees were college students. According to CEO Shapiro,

> While we see 2006 as a transitional year, by reaffirming previous management's guidance we are underscoring confidence that our redefined strategy, coupled with celebration of our 45th anniversary, will broaden our customer base by attracting families as well as teenagers, boosting our per capita revenue.[9]

In June 2006, Six Flags announced that it was considering the closure of six more of its 30 theme parks. These were Six Flags Darien Lake near Buffalo, New York; Six Flags Waterworld in Concord, California; Six Flags Elitch Gardens in Denver, Colorado; Six Flags Splash-Town in Houston, Texas; Wild Waves and Enchanted Village near Seattle; and Hurricane Harbor outside Los Angeles, California.[10]

Six Flags Darien Lake, one of the six parks facing closure, announced that it would close four weeks early for the 2006 season, closing October 1 rather than November 1. The situation was becoming dire for the company. According to Robert Niles, founder of themeparkinsider.com, "In many respects, they've slid to a point where they resemble a souped-up county fair more than world-class theme parks."[11]

The Future

Six Flags changed its ticker symbol from PSK to SIX on June 5, 2006. On August 17, 2006, Shapiro rang the closing bell on the NYSE to celebrate the new ticker symbol. He commented:

> The 2006 season is winding down, and we've witnessed families returning to our parks, spending more, and driving our guest approval ratings to a five-year high. We're proud of what our employees have accomplished in this transitional year, and we're looking ahead to new horizons in 2007.[12]

There were many challenges facing Six Flags. Shapiro felt that the company's new strategy of closing the less productive theme parks and working to increase spending from guests who were in the parks was working. Management eliminated the deep discounts to maintain sales and instead focused on stronger sales techniques. Shapiro felt that the new strategy was working.

> Increased guest spending is continuing at a strong pace—a clear indication that our strategy is working. The drop-off in attendance was driven primarily by an anticipated decline in our season

pass sales, which we are no longer deeply discounting in an effort to restore price brand integrity, and to wean ourselves from those teens who don't spend money in the park.[13]

Looking to the future, Shapiro felt that management had clarified the company's mission. They were repositioning Six Flags as a set of themed parks, rather than as a collection of individual amusement parks. They were increasing the bang for the buck for visitors hoping they would stay longer, spend more, and return faster. The emphasis on customer satisfaction was stronger—as indicated by Shapiro's comments:

This means Six Flags will get back to being genuine theme parks—not merely amusement parks. It means we will restore diversified entertainment offerings such as the Chinese acrobats. It means reinvigorating the parks with "streetmosphere"—a process of enhancing the spaces between the rides with a variety of entertainment offerings. It means that daily parades, in-park celebrations, acrobatic and juggling acts will dazzle our guests. It means the casts of our Looney Tunes characters and Justice League superheroes will expand dramatically from one or two per park in 2005 to at least 30 in every Six Flags branded park, every hour of every operating day, mingling with the crowds, greeting our customers, posing with them for photographs, even riding the rides. By offering a true character program, we will have created new revenue streams that are sorely needed.[14]

Six Flags faced a number of challenges as it ended the 2006 season. Management was in the middle of implementing a new operational plan and there was uncertainly about its success. Management was young and energetic, but fairly new to the company. Given that 85% of park attendance occurred in the second and third quarters of the calendar year, Six Flags faced the challenges of managing a seasonal business.[15] This was a problem for Six Flags given that a number of its parks were in northern locations. As more recreation facilities competed for the consumer's recreation dollar, pressures would surely intensify. Finally, there was the huge mound of debt from which Six Flags needed to unbury itself. There was a risk that the company would not be able to meet its debt obligations. This would affect management's ability to obtain future funding as well as possibly force the company into bankruptcy.

What lay ahead for Six Flags? Would management's turnaround strategy save the firm, or would the heavy debt burden eventually sink the company?

ENDNOTES

1. "The Batman and Robin of Six Flags," *Business Week* (May 8, 2006).
2. "6 Flags Mulling Future of 6 Parks," Associated Press (June 22, 2006).
3. "Batman and Robin" (2006).
4. Six Flags, *2005 Annual Report*, 20.
5. "Moody's Downgrades Six Flags Debt," Associated Press (August 2, 2006).
6. *Six Flags 2005 10-K*, F-25.
7. *Six Flags 13-D* (August 27, 2004).
8. Matt Krantz, "Add Bill Gates to List of Unhappy Six Flags Investors," *USA Today* (September 1, 2004).
9. Six Flags Company Press Release (March 8, 2006).
10. Associated Press (June 22, 2006).
11. "Batman and Robin" (2006).
12. "Six Flags President and CEO Mark Shapiro Rings NYSE Closing Bell to Celebrate Company's New Stock Ticker Symbol, SIX," Six Flags Press Release (August 17, 2006).
13. Associated Press (June 22, 2006).
14. "Annual Letter to the Shareholders," *Six Flags 2005 Annual Report*.
15. *Six Flags 2005 10-K*, 22.

CASE 33

Lowe's Companies, Inc.

Maryanne M. Rouse

LOWE'S COMPANIES (LOW), THE SECOND LARGEST U.S. HOME IMPROVEMENT RETAILER, competed in the highly fragmented $400+ billion home improvement industry. Capitalizing on historically high rates of home ownership, the company had grown from 15 stores selling commodity-type products to new home builders in 1962 to a chain of almost 1,000 stores in 45 states with over 99.5 million square feet of selling space in 2004. (The total includes 46 stores opened between January 31, 2003, and August 1, 2004, the end of the second quarter of Lowe's fiscal year.) In 1989, the company redefined its business and positioned itself as a "big-box" home-improvement retailer, selling a wide array of higher-margin merchandise. Lowe's opened its first 100,000+ square-foot big-box store in 1992. Between 2003 and 2004, the company developed two prototype stores: the larger had 116,000 square feet of selling space plus an additional 31,000 square feet dedicated to lawn and garden products, while the store developed for smaller markets provided 94,000 square feet of selling space plus an additional 26,000 feet devoted to lawn and garden product lines. A typical store stocked more than 40,000 SKUs, with hundreds more available through the company's special order system. Product lines included plumbing and electrical products, tools, building materials, hardware, outdoor hardlines, appliances, lumber, mill work, paint and decorative products, cabinets, furniture, and nursery and gardening products.

Lowe's served both retail and commercial business customers. Retail customers were primarily do-it-yourself homeowners and others buying for personal and family use. Commercial business customers included repair and remodeling contractors, electricians, landscapers, painters, plumbers, and commercial and residential building maintenance professionals. Approximately 73% of the company's sales were to retail customers, with the balance to commercial customers.

Growth Strategies

With no plans for international expansion in 2004, Lowe's planned to grow domestic square footage at an annual rate of 16%–17% over the next two to three years, with 150 store openings planned for 2005 and another 150–160 store openings for 2006. The company was aggressively targeting metropolitan markets with populations of 500,000 or more, noting that currently the company's highest-volume stores were in metropolitan markets. Stores in these larger markets accounted for approximately 65% of the company's new store openings in 2003 and 2004. In line with this strategy, Lowe's announced plans to add more than 40 stores in the New York/New Jersey metro market as well as in Chicago by year-end 2005. Through September 30, 2004, Lowe's opened over 48 new stores, bringing the company's total above 1,000:

	2003	2002	2001	2000	1999
Number of stores, beginning of year	854	744	650	576	520
New stores opened	125	112	101	80	60
Relocated stores opened	5	11	14	20	31
Stores closed (including relocated stores)	(6)	(13)	(21)	(26)	(35)
Contractor yards sold	(26)	—	—	—	—
Total number of stores, end of year	952	854	744	650	576

The company believed there were significant product/market growth opportunities in three key areas: installed sales, special order sales, and commercial business customers. Additional growth strategies included increasing sales per square foot and adding high-quality product lines.

In 1998, Lowe's began a major expansion into the Western United States, with plans to build 100+ new stores in three to four years. In early 1999, the company acquired Eagle Hardware and Garden, a 41-store chain of home improvement and garden centers, accelerating Lowe's West Coast expansion and providing a stepping-stone to 10 new Western states, including a number of key metropolitan markets.

Finance

Net earnings for 2003 increased 27%, to $1.9 billion, or 6.1% of sales, compared to $1.5 billion, or 5.6% of sales, for 2002. Return on beginning assets, defined as net earnings divided by beginning total assets, was 11.7% for 2003, compared to 10.7% for 2002 and 9.0% for 2001. Return on beginning shareholders' equity, defined as net earnings divided by beginning shareholders' equity, was 22.6% for 2003, compared to 22.0% for 2002 and 18.6% for 2001. The company recorded sales of $30.8 billion in 2003, an 17% increase over 2002 sales of $26.1 billion. Sales for 2002 were 20% higher than 2001 levels. Average ticket amounts increased 4.2%, from $56.80 in 2002 to $59.21 in 2003, due in part to the success of the up-the-continuum initiative as well as the Lowe's credit programs. Comparable-store sales in 2003 increased by 6.7%, with the strongest sales increases in lumber, building materials, outdoor power equipment, paint, flooring, and home organization.

The company reported consistent sales gains across all categories, from appliances to outdoor plants. Percentage contributions to sales by product line are summarized below (dollar amounts in millions):

Category	2003	2002
Appliances	11%	11%
Lumber/Plywood	9	9
Outdoor Fashion	7	7
Millwork	7	7
Nursery	6	6
Flooring	6	6
Fashion Electrical	6	6
Fashion Plumbing	6	6
Paint	7	7
Tools	5	5
Hardware	6	6
Building Materials	5	5
Cabinets/Furniture/Shelving	4	4
Outdoor Power Equipment	3	4
Rough Plumbing	3	3
Walls/Windows	3	3
Rough Electrical	3	2
Home Organization	2	2
Other	1	1
Total sales (millions)	**$30,838**	**$26,112**

Sales in the second quarter of fiscal 2004 exceeded $10 billion for the first time in the company's history, increasing 17.3% over sales in the second quarter of fiscal 2003. For the six months ended July 30, 2004, sales increased 19.4%, and comparable-store sales increased 7.2%. Net earnings increased 17.9%, to $704 million, compared to the previous year's second quarter results. The gross margin was 33.3% of sales for the quarter ended July 30, 2004, compared to 30.3% for the previous year's comparable quarter. The gross margin for the six months ended July 30, 2004, was 33.2% versus 30.7% for the first six months of 2003. The company's aggressive new store growth gave Lowe's additional leverage with vendors, which, together with improved inventory management, resulted in a decline in cost of goods sold as a percentage of sales for fiscal 2003 and the first two quarters of 2004. (Lowe's annual and quarterly reports and SEC filings are available via the company's Web site www.lowes.com or www.wsj.com.)

Logistics

To help maintain appropriate inventory levels in stores and to improve distribution efficiency, Lowe's operated 10 highly automated regional distribution centers (RDCs). In 2004, the RDCs were strategically located in North Carolina, Georgia, Indiana, Pennsylvania, Texas, California, Ohio, Wyoming, and Florida. Each Lowe's store was served by one of these RDCs. The company also operated nine smaller support facilities to distribute merchandise that required special handling due to size or type of packaging, such as lumber, various imports, and building materials. Approximately 50% of the merchandise purchased by the company was shipped through its distribution facilities, while the remaining portion was shipped directly to stores from vendors.

Promotion

Lowe's reached target customers through a promotional mix that included television, radio, direct mail, newspaper, event sponsorships, and in-store programs. The company had developed a strategic alliance with the HGTV network, one of a half-dozen media partnerships created to build the image and equity of the Lowe's brand while complementing core media and marketing programs. Lowe's also hosted customer hospitality events through its Team 48 NASCAR sponsorship, supported the wide-ranging activities of Lowe's Home Safety Council, and used its proprietary credit programs to drive customer traffic and purchases. The easy-to-navigate Lowe's Web site was a key element in its promotional strategy. The site allowed customers to search the company's inventory on a store-by-store basis, compare products and prices, and order online or for store pickup.

Other Marketing Initiatives

In response to significant growth in the "buy-it-yourself" (BIY, or "do-it-for-me") market, Lowe's developed an installed sales program that allowed customers to arrange for installation of products in over 30 categories. A BIY customer chose and purchased the product but relied on professionals to handle installation. Lowe's had added kiosks in departments such as appliances, home decor/flooring, electrical, lighting, millwork, hardware, seasonal, plumbing, and tools to facilitate special orders. Some of these kiosks were technology based and some were literature based, but all facilitated the ability of the customer to special order to fit their home improvement needs. Special order sales allowed Lowe's to offer a variety of unique items without the investment in inventory.

The design of Lowe's stores had attracted customers, particularly women, who disliked the warehouse shopping layout of rival Home Depot. Lowe's featured wider aisles, brighter lighting, and more signs, and it stocked a larger selection of products for home decorating, including lamps, window treatments, and designer towels, than is found in a typical Home Depot.

In both 2003 and 2004, Lowe's developed a series of initiatives to better serve commercial business customers, including enhanced ordering and credit programs, increased delivery options, an increase in professional-preferred brands, and a policy of increasing in-stock quantities for bigger jobs in an effort to win the loyalty of commercial customers. Analysts estimated potential sales to this segment of the market at almost three times sales to the traditional DIY market.

Suppliers

Excluding special order vendors, Lowe's sourced its products from approximately 7,000 merchandise vendors worldwide, with no single vendor accounting for more than 4% of total purchases; however, the company had begun to develop vendor alliances with key partners under a vendor certification program. Lowe's used its Global Sourcing Division to purchase directly from foreign manufacturers and avoid higher-cost third-party importers. Growing demand for steel, plywood, and other building products, especially from China and other developing economies, had placed pressure on both suppliers and prices.

The Industry

According to the Home Improvement Research Institute (HIRI), the total retail home improvement market in the United States reached $187.6 billion in 2001 and was expected to climb to $236.7 billion in 2006. Industry sales were sensitive to a number of factors, including interest rates, housing turnover, consumer debt levels, and concern about job security. Although new housing starts were important, the sales opportunity from housing turnover was three times larger than from the sales of new homes. Even when a weakening economy forced some homeowners to delay the purchase of new homes, industry research showed that they were likely to continue to invest in improving their existing homes. Aggressive interest rate cuts during 2001, 2002, and 2003 and continued low fixed and variable first and second mortgage rates had allowed consumers to borrow more to fund home improvement projects.

Homeowners spent more to maintain and improve their living spaces than did renters. The U.S. Census Bureau estimated that home ownership increased to 69.2% in third quarter 2004, up from 65% in 1995. In addition, as baby boomers spent more time at home with their families, they were likely to spend a larger portion of disposable income on their homes than in prior years. With the bulk of the U.S. population entering the post-40 age group, demand for household products and remodeling/renovation were likely to experience strong growth.

Competition

The home improvement industry was highly fragmented, with the two largest players, Home Depot and Lowe's, controlling approximately 32% of the $192 billion do-it-yourself market and less than 5% of the $245 billion professional/commercial market. Key competitive factors in the home improvement retailing business were price, location, customer service, product and brand selection, and name recognition. As Lowe's and Home Deport pursued aggressive growth strategies, industry analysts expected consolidation, with less competitive players closing, being acquired, or merging with other retailers.

The industry leader was Home Depot, with 1,788 stores in 50 states, the District of Columbia, 5 Canadian provinces, Puerto Rico, and Mexico and an overall market share estimated at 18%, compared to 9% for Lowe's. The company's stores marketed a wide range of building materials, home improvement supplies, and lawn and garden products; EXPO Design Center stores offered interior design products and installation services.

Home Depot targeted the same three customer groups as Lowe's and, although Home Depot and Lowe's pursued many of the same competitive strategies, Home Depot's size provided the company with significant economies of scale and cost advantages. In September 2004, Home Depot opened a 105,000-square-foot superstore just off Broadway on West 23rd street, replete with such big-city touches as doormen and home delivery. After two lackluster years, Home Depot's stock had rebounded, nearly doubling to around $40 from January 2003 to mid-October 2004. Although profits at Lowe's were rising faster, Home Depot's shares were cheaper.

Other direct competitors included Building Materials Holdings, House 2 Home, Inc., Wolohan Lumber Company, Wickes, Inc., and Payless Cashways. Lowe's also competed with traditional hardware, plumbing, electrical, appliance, and home supply retailers, and with lumber yards in most of its market areas. In addition, Lowe's competed in some product categories with discount stores and membership warehouse clubs.

Movie Gallery, Inc.

J. David Hunger

MOVIE GALLERY, INC., IN AUGUST 2006 WAS THE SECOND LARGEST NORTH AMERICAN video rental company with 4,763 stores located in all 50 states plus Canada and Mexico. The company specialized in the rental and sale of DVD and VHS movies and video games under its subsidiaries, Movie Gallery, USA and Hollywood Entertainment.

The renting of videos began in the 1980s shortly after motion picture studios began selling videotapes of their movies to play on home videocassette player/recorders (VCRs). Because a typical videotape of a recent motion picture cost at that time around $15 to $25 to purchase, renting a movie for a few days for $5 made economic sense—especially if a person only wanted to view the movie once or twice. This made renting a movie much cheaper than paying about $10 for a couple to view the same film in a movie theater. Video rental stores quickly spread throughout North America as people invited friends and family to join them in eating pizza and watching rented movies in their living rooms.

Growth and Success

Movie Gallery was founded in 1985 by Joe Malugen and Harrison Parrish in Dothan, Alabama. Through its wholly owned subsidiary, M.G.A., the company's founders began operating video specialty stores in southern Alabama and the Florida panhandle, and franchising the Movie Gallery concept. By June 1987, the company owned five stores and had a franchise operation of 45 stores. Between 1988 and 1992, management consolidated the franchisees into 37 company-owned stores with annual revenues of $6 million. Using the proceeds from an initial public offering (IPO) in August 1994 to fund an aggressive expansion strategy, Movie Gallery grew to more than 850 stores by 1996 through more than 100 separate acquisitions. It also grew internally by building new retail outlets. During 1999 and 2000, for example, the company built 100 new stores each year. Additional acquisitions, including Blowout Entertainment in 1999 and Video Update in 2003, raised the total number of stores to 2,000. The purchase of Video Update launched the firm's international presence with 100 retail outlets in Canada.

This case was prepared by Professor J. David Hunger, Iowa State University and St. John's University. Copyright © 2006 by J. David Hunger. The copyright holder is solely responsible for case content. Reprint permission is solely granted to the publisher, Prentice-Hall, for the books *Strategic Management and Business Policy*–11th and 12th Editions (and the International version of this book) and *Cases in Strategic Management and Business Policy*–11th and 12th Editions, by the copyright holder, J. David Hunger. Any other publication of the case (translation, any form of electronics or other media) or sale (any form of partnership) to another publisher will be in violation of copyright law, unless J. David Hunger has granted an additional written permission. Reprinted by permission. Sources available upon request.

Movie Gallery's video stores primarily targeted small towns and suburban areas. By focusing on rural and secondary markets, the company was able to compete very effectively against the independently owned stores and small regional chains in these areas through its purchasing economies. It was able to deliver first-run movies at cheaper prices to customers in towns with fewer than 20,000 people.

The company's profits increased 57% from 2001 to 2004, resulting in its being listed Number 61 on *Business Week*'s 2005 list of the fastest-growing small companies.

Movie Gallery's top management made a strategic decision in 2005 to expand out of the company's target market by purchasing rival Hollywood Video for $1.2 billion. At the time, Hollywood Video's management had been fighting a hostile takeover bid by industry-leader Blockbuster, Inc. This acquisition raised Movie Gallery's store total to 4,700 outlets with revenues in excess of $2.5 billion annually.

Operating under the Hollywood Video and Game Crazy brands, Hollywood Entertainment primarily targeted urban centers and surrounding suburban neighborhoods and was especially strong on the West Coast where Movie Gallery was weak. It competed head-to-head with Blockbuster through excellent customer service and innovative marketing and merchandising programs. At the time of its purchase, Hollywood Entertainment operated 2,031 video rental stores and 20 free-standing video game stores throughout the United States. Its acquisition propelled Movie Gallery into second-place in the U.S. video rental market behind Blockbuster and made it a major player in large U.S. cities, such as Atlanta and Los Angeles.

In June 2005, the company added 61 retail stores to its presence in Western Canada by purchasing VHQ Entertainment. Among VHQ Entertainment's businesses was VHQ Online, a flat-fee, direct-to-home movie delivery service (http://www.VHQonline.ca). Canadian subscribers were able to choose from 52,000 movie titles, which would then be shipped by first-class mail to the customer's home for a basic monthly fee.

Consequences of Growth

The acquisition of Hollywood Entertainment left Movie Gallery heavily in debt. At the same time, the recent rise of online video rental services, such as Netflix, was cutting into retail store revenues and reducing the company's cash flow. Overall in-store sales for video rental outlets throughout the industry shrank 13% in 2005 to $7.1 billion, according to Adams Media Research, Inc. Online sales, in contrast, more than doubled to $1.4 billion in that same year.

Movie Gallery's sales slid 5% to $2 billion in 2005. By the end of the year, Movie Gallery recorded a $553 million loss. Absent one-time charges, it earned $31 million—a 38% decline from the previous year's profit. With just $135 million in cash at the end of 2005, Movie Gallery's management found itself facing possible bankruptcy. Movie Gallery's stock, worth about $3 on April 24, 2006, had lost more than 90% of its value since April 2005. Investors in mid-2006 had short positions (betting that the stock would decline further) on 18.6 million of the company's 32 million shares.

Competition

Movie Gallery was not alone in its financial difficulty. Blockbuster, the largest U.S. competitor in video rental stores, also lost money in 2005—around $450 billion.

In contrast to the situation at Movie Gallery and Blockbuster, Netflix, Inc., earned $41 million in profits on $688 in revenue during 2005. The company's shares rose 157% in the 12-month period through April 2006. With 5 million subscribers, Netflix management expected revenues to reach $990 million in 2006. CEO Reed Hastings had set the objective of Netflix reaching 20 million subscribers (around 20% of U.S. households) between 2010 and 2012.

Netflix had a different business model from that used by Movie Gallery and Blockbuster. Once Netflix subscribers selected a movie from the Web site (http://www.netflix.com), a DVD was mailed to them for $5.99 per movie. A flat rate subscription service was also available. After viewing the movie, subscribers would mail back the DVD in order to rent another movie. Pressure from Netflix, which didn't charge late fees, forced Blockbuster's management to drop most late fees, costing it approximately $400 million in 2005. Although 70% of Blockbuster's rentals were new releases, the reverse was true of Netflix. The company promoted lesser-known movies that often received little distribution in movie theaters. The average customer of Netflix was an over-35 woman with family income of $75,000 or less.

Netflix was not the only company using the movies-through-the-mail business model. Amazon had successfully copied the Netflix postal model in Britain and Germany and was thinking of launching a postal movie service in the United States. In response, Netflix management was exploring the option of delivering movies online. Apple had pioneered downloading digital music through its iTunes and was likely to expand into video. Microsoft entered the music-download business in 2006 with its Zune digital player. In August 2006, Nokia bought Loudeye, an American digital music distributor, to develop its own service for its music-enabled handsets.

Video downloads were already being offered by Movielink.com, which was owned by five large film studios. News Corp's Web sites, including MySpace.com, were planning to sell films and shows from the group's Fox network. The main problem with video downloads was the large size of video files, leading to long download times. The increasing availability of broadband cable and DSL should shorten these download times and make video downloads more popular. Broadband-equipped televisions and personal video recorders should also make the process easier.

Current Situation

In 2006, Movie Gallery's founders were still very active in the company. Joe Malugen served as Chairman of the Board, President, and Chief Executive Officer of Movie Gallery. Harrison Parrish was Vice Chairman of the Board and Senior Vice President. Both had seats on the corporation's board of directors. They were very much aware that the industry was changing and that Movie Gallery's management needed to take action to stem the losses and to position the company for future success.

For the first six months of 2006 ending July 2, total revenues were $1.3 billion compared to $1.3 billion for the same period a year earlier (assuming revenues from Hollywood Entertainment had been included in the 2005 totals). Rental revenue was 82.1% of total revenues with the remaining 17.9% coming from product sales. During this six-month period, same-store revenues decreased 5.6% from the same period in 2005. Interestingly, same-store revenues decreased only 1.3% at Movie Gallery branded stores compared to a 7.5% drop at Hollywood Entertainment branded stores. Management felt that the better performance of the Movie Gallery brand was caused by the resiliency of its Eastern-focused rural and secondary market presence as well as the success of the company's efforts to sell previously viewed titles from Hollywood stores at Movie Gallery stores.

Although the company reported a net loss of $14.9 million in the second quarter of 2006 (compared to a $12.2 million loss during the same period in 2005), the company's year-to-date net income was $25.5 million (compared to $6.2 million during the same six-month period in 2005). According to management, the company had sufficient cash to operate the business, satisfy working capital and capital expenditure requirements, and meet the company's foreseeable liquidity requirements, including financial covenants for its debt service for the remainder of 2006. Although the company's cash and cash equivalents totaled only $21,151,000 as of

July 2, 2006, compared to $51,122,000 on July 3, 2005, accounts payable had dropped from $194,000,000 on July 3, 2005, to $92,156,000 on July 2, 2006. Long-term debt (including current portion) declined slightly to $1,100,943,000 on July 2, 2006, from $1,143,359,000 on July 3, 2005.

According to Chairman, President, and CEO Malugen in Movie Gallery's *2006 Second Quarter Report*:

> *Our business continues to be affected by a weak home video release schedule and other industry-wide challenges, but we are making great progress on a number of internal initiatives intended to improve Movie Gallery's financial and operational performance. We continue to expect a slow late summer, as is typical due to the seasonality of our industry, with gradually improving business conditions beginning in October when the first of several $100 million titles will be released to home video. In the meantime, Movie Gallery is aggressively pursuing opportunities to increase revenues and further improve operating efficiencies. We have engaged Merrill Lynch to advise us on ways to improve our capital structure as well as Alvarez & Marsal, a leading turn-around management, restructuring and corporate advisory firm.*

Responding to the firm's financial problems, Movie Gallery's management twice renegotiated lending agreements with bankers to ease payment terms. Management planned to close 175 underperforming and overlapping stores and lay off 380 of its 1,800 workers by the end of 2006. Hoping to cut at least 20% from its $500 million in annual rental expenses, it was negotiating subleases in almost half of its stores. Most of the financial benefits associated with lease renegotiation were expected to begin in 2007 with the bulk of the financial benefits to be realized in 2008 and beyond. Although the company opened 30 new stores in 2006 (which were already in the pipeline), management planned to curtail new store openings over the next several years in order to maximize free cash flow. Management was also reviewing its asset portfolio to identify any non-core assets it could divest for cash. (Movie Gallery's annual and quarterly reports and SEC filings are available via the company's Web site at www.moviegallery.com.)

What Next?

Movie Gallery's stock price began to rise after the company's announcement of its first-quarter results on May 11, 2006, and by August 9, 2006 a share of its stock was selling for $6.47. Even though the financial results for the first six months of 2006 showed an improvement in the company's financial position compared to 2005, the company's stock price fell to $2.97 on August 10, 2006, with the announcement of Movie Gallery's second-quarter results.

Management's implementation of a turnaround strategy was showing some indications of success. The reduction of costs and expenses was certainly important, but what should management do to increase revenues and profits? How could Movie Gallery be positioned for future success?

GLOSSARY

10-K form An SEC form containing income statements, balance sheets, cash flow statements, and information not usually available in an annual report.

10-Q form An SEC form containing quarterly financial reports.

14-A form An SEC form containing proxy statements and information on a company's board of directors.

360-degree performance appraisal An evaluation technique in which input is gathered from multiple sources.

80/20 rule A rule of thumb stating that one should monitor those 20% of the factors that determine 80% of the results.

Absorptive capacity A firm's ability to value, assimilate, and utilize new external knowledge.

Acquisition The purchase of a company that is completely absorbed by the acquiring corporation.

Action plan A plan that states what actions are going to be taken, by whom, during what time frame, and with what expected results.

Activity ratios Financial ratios that indicate how well a corporation is managing its operations.

Activity-based costing (ABC) An accounting method for allocating indirect and fixed costs to individual products or product lines based on the value-added activities going into that product.

Adaptive mode A decision-making mode characterized by reactive solutions to existing problems, rather than a proactive search for new opportunities.

Advisory board A group of external business people who voluntarily meet periodically with the owners/managers of the firm to discuss strategic and other issues.

Affiliated directors Directors who, though not really employed by the corporation, handle the legal or insurance work for the company or are important suppliers.

Agency theory A theory stating that problems arise in corporations because the agents (top management) are not willing to bear responsibility for their decisions unless they own a substantial amount of stock in the corporation.

Altman's Bankruptcy Formula A formula used to estimate how close a company is to declaring bankruptcy.

Analytical portfolio manager A type of general manager needed to execute a diversification strategy.

Andean Community A South American free-trade alliance composed of Columbia, Ecuador, Peru, Bolivia, and Chili.

Annual report A document published each year by a company to show its financial condition and products.

Assessment center An approach to evaluating the suitability of a person for a position by simulating key parts of the job.

Assimilation A strategy that involves the domination of one corporate culture over another.

Association of South East Asian Nations (ASEAN) A regional trade association composed of Asian countries of Brunei Darussalam, Cambodia, Indonesia, Laos, Malaysia, Myanmar, Philippines, Singapore, Thailand, and Vietnam. ASEA+3 includes China, Japan, and South Korea.

Autonomous (self-managing) work teams A group of people who work together without a supervisor to plan, coordinate, and evaluate their own work.

Backward integration Assuming a function previously provided by a supplier.

Balanced scorecard Combines financial measures with operational measures on customer satisfaction, internal processes, and the corporation's innovation and improvement activities.

Bankruptcy A retrenchment strategy that forfeits management of the firm to the courts in return for some settlement of the corporation's obligations.

Basic R&D Research and development that is conducted by scientists in well-equipped laboratories where the focus is on theoretical problem areas.

BCG (Boston Consulting Group) Growth-Share Matrix A simple way to portray a corporation's portfolio of products or divisions in terms of growth and cash flow.

Behavior control A control that specifies how something is to be done through policies, rules, standard operating procedures, and orders from a superior.

Behavior substitution A phenomenon that occurs when people substitute activities that do not lead to goal accomplishment for activities that do lead to goal accomplishment because the wrong activities are being rewarded.

Benchmarking The process of measuring products, services, and practices against those of competitors or companies recognized as industry leaders.

Best practice A procedure that is followed by successful companies.

Blind spot analysis An approach to analyzing a competitor by identifying its perceptual biases.

Board of director responsibilities Commonly agreed obligations of directors, which include: setting corporate strategy, overall direction, mission or vision; hiring and firing the CEO and top management; controlling, monitoring, or supervising top management; reviewing and approving the use of resources; and caring for shareholder interest.

Board of directors' continuum A range of the possible degree of involvement by the board of directors (from low to high) in the strategic management process.

BOT (build-operate-transfer) concept A type of international entry option for a company. After building a facility, the company operates the facility for a fixed period of time during which it earns back its investment, plus a profit.

Brainstorming The process of proposing ideas in a group without first mentally screening them.

Brand A name that identifies a particular company's product in the mind of the consumer.

Budget A statement of a corporation's programs in terms of money required.

Business model The mix of activities a company performs to earn a profit.

Business plan A written strategic plan for a new entrepreneurial venture.

Business policy A previous name for strategic management. It has a general management orientation and tends to look inward with primary concern for integrating the corporation's many functional activities.

Business strategy Competitive and cooperative strategies that emphasize improvement of the competitive position of a corporation's products or services in a specific industry or market segment.

Cannibalize To replace popular products before they reach the end of their life cycle.

Cap-and-trade A government-imposed ceiling (cap) on the amount of allowed greenhouse gas emissions combined with a system allowing a firm to sell (trade) its emission reductions to another firm whose emissions exceed the allowed cap.

Capability A corporation's ability to exploit its resources.

Capital budgeting The process of analyzing and ranking possible investments in terms of the additional outlays and additional receipts that will result from each investment.

Captive company strategy Dedicating a firm's productive capacity as primary supplier to another company in exchange for a long-term contract.

Carbon footprint The amount of greenhouse gases being created by an entity and released into the air.

Cash cow A product that brings in far more money than is needed to maintain its market share.

Categorical imperatives Kant's two principles to guide actions: A person's action is ethical only if that person is willing for that same action to be taken by everyone who is in a similar situation, and a person should never treat another human being simply as a means but always as an end.

Cautious profit planner The type of leader needed for a corporation choosing to follow a stability strategy.

Cellular/modular organization structure A structure composed of cells (self-managing teams, autonomous business units, etc.) that can operate alone but can interact with other cells to produce a more potent and competent business mechanism.

Center of excellence A designated area in which a company has a core or distinctive competence.

Center of gravity The part of the industry value chain that is most important to the company and the point where the company's greatest expertise and capabilities lay.

Central American Free Trade Agreement (CAFTA) A regional trade association composed of El Salvador, Guatemala, Nicaragua, Honduras, Costa Rica, the United States, and the Dominican Republic.

Clusters Geographic concentrations of interconnected companies and industries.

Code of ethics A code that specifies how an organization expects its employees to behave while on the job.

Codetermination The inclusion of a corporation's workers on its board of directors.

Collusion The active cooperation of firms within an industry to reduce output and raise prices in order to get around the normal economic law of supply and demand. This practice is usually illegal.

Commodity A product whose characteristics are the same regardless of who sells it.

Common-size statements Income statements and balance sheets in which the dollar figures have been converted into percentages.

Competency A cross-functional integration and coordination of capabilities.

Competitive intelligence A formal program of gathering information about a company's competitors.

Competitive scope The breadth of a company's or a business unit's target market.

Competitive strategy A strategy that states how a company or a business unit will compete in an industry.

Competitors The companies that offer the same products or services as the subject company.

Complementor A company or an industry whose product(s) works well with another industry's or firm's product and without which that product would lose much of its value.

Concentration A corporate growth strategy that concentrates a corporation's resources on competing in one industry.

Concentric diversification A diversification growth strategy in which a firm uses its current strengths to diversify into related products in another industry.

Concurrent engineering A process in which specialists from various functional areas work side by side rather than sequentially in an effort to design new products.

Conglomerate diversification A diversification growth strategy that involves a move into another industry to provide products unrelated to its current products.

Conglomerate structure An assemblage of legally independent firms (subsidiaries) operating under one corporate umbrella but controlled through the subsidiaries' boards of directors.

Connected line batch flow A part of a corporation's manufacturing strategy in which components are standardized and each machine functions like a job shop but is positioned in the same order as the parts are processed.

Consensus A situation in which all parties agree to one alternative.

Consolidated industry An industry in which a few large companies dominate.

Consolidation The second phase of a turnaround strategy that implements a program to stabilize the corporation.

Constant dollars Dollars adjusted for inflation.

Continuous improvement A system developed by Japanese firms in which teams strive constantly to improve manufacturing processes.

Continuous systems Production organized in lines on which products can be continuously assembled or processed.

Continuum of sustainability A representation that indicates how durable and imitable an organization's resources and capabilities are.

Contraction The first phase of a turnaround strategy that includes a general across-the-board cutback in size and costs.

Cooperative strategies Strategies that involve working with other firms to gain competitive advantage within an industry.

Co-opetition A term used to describe simultaneous competition and cooperation among firms.

Core competency A collection of corporate capabilities that cross divisional borders and are widespread within a corporation, and is something that a corporation can do exceedingly well.

Core rigidity/deficiency A core competency of a firm that over time matures and becomes a weakness.

Corporate brand A type of brand in which the company's name serves as the brand name.

Corporate capabilities See capability.

Corporate culture A collection of beliefs, expectations, and values learned and shared by a corporation's members and transmitted from one generation of employees to another.

Corporate culture pressure A force from existing corporate culture against the implementation of a new strategy.

Corporate entrepreneurship Also called intrapreneurship, the creation of a new business within an existing organization.

Corporate governance The relationship among the board of directors, top management, and shareholders in determining the direction and performance of a corporation.

Corporate parenting A corporate strategy that evaluates the corporation's business units in terms of resources and capabilities that can be used to build business unit value as well as generate synergies across business units.

Corporate reputation A widely held perception of a company by the general public.

Corporate scenario Pro forma balance sheets and income statements that forecast the effect that each alternative strategy will likely have on return on investment.

Corporate stakeholders Groups that affect or are affected by the achievement of a firm's objectives.

Corporate strategy A strategy that states a company's overall direction in terms of its general attitude toward growth and the management of its various business and product lines.

Corporation A mechanism legally established to allow different parties to contribute capital, expertise, and labor for their mutual benefit.

Cost focus A low-cost competitive strategy that concentrates on a particular buyer group or geographic market and attempts to serve only that niche.

Cost leadership A low-cost competitive strategy that aims at the broad mass market.

Cost proximity A process that involves keeping the higher price a company charges for higher quality close enough to that of the competition so that customers will see the extra quality as being worth the extra cost.

Crisis of autonomy A time when people managing diversified product lines need more decision-making freedom than top management is willing to delegate to them.

Crisis of control A time when business units act to optimize their own sales and profits without regard to the overall corporation. See also *suboptimization*.

Crisis of leadership A time when an entrepreneur is personally unable to manage a growing company.

Cross-functional work teams A work team composed of people from multiple functions.

Cultural integration The extent to which units throughout an organization share a common culture.

Cultural intensity The degree to which members of an organizational unit accept the norms, values, or other culture content associated with the unit.

Deculturation The disintegration of one company's culture resulting from unwanted and extreme pressure from another to impose its culture and practices.

Dedicated transfer line A highly automated assembly line making one mass-produced product using little human labor.

Defensive centralization A process in which top management of a not-for-profit retains all decision-making authority so that lower-level managers cannot take any actions to which the sponsors may object.

Defensive tactic A tactic in which a company defends its current market.

Delphi technique A forecasting technique in which experts independently assess the probabilities of specified events. These assessments are combined and sent back to each expert for fine-tuning until agreement is reached.

Devil's advocate An individual or a group assigned to identify the potential pitfalls and problems of a proposal.

Dialectical inquiry A decision-making technique that requires that two proposals using different assumptions be generated for consideration.

Differentiation A competitive strategy that is aimed at the broad mass market and that involves the creation of a product or service that is perceived throughout its industry as unique.

Differentiation focus A differentiation competitive strategy that concentrates on a particular buyer group, product line segment, or geographic market.

Differentiation strategy See differentiation.

Dimensions of national culture A set of five dimensions by which each nation's unique culture can be identified.

Directional strategy A plan that is composed of three general orientations: growth, stability, and retrenchment.

Distinctive competencies A firm's competencies that are superior to those of competitors.

Diversification A corporate growth strategy that expands product lines by moving into another industry.

Divestment A retrenchment strategy in which a division of a corporation with low growth potential is sold.

Divisional structure An organizational structure in which employees tend to be functional specialists organized according to product/market distinctions.

Downsizing Planned elimination of positions or jobs.

Due care The obligation of board members to closely monitor and evaluate top management.

Durability The rate at which a firm's underlying resources and capabilities depreciate or become obsolete.

Dynamic industry expert A leader with a great deal of experience in a particular industry appropriate for executing a concentration strategy.

Dynamic capabilities Capabilities that are continually being changed and reconfigured to make them more adaptive to an uncertain environment.

Dynamic pricing A marketing practice in which different customers pay different prices for the same product or service.

Earnings per share (EPS) A calculation that is determined by dividing net earnings by the number of shares of common stock issued.

Economic value added (EVA) A shareholder value method of measuring corporate and divisional performance. Measures after-tax operating income minus the total annual cost of capital.

Economies of scale A process in which unit costs are reduced by making large numbers of the same product.

Economies of scope A process in which unit costs are reduced when the value chains of two separate products or services share activities, such as the same marketing channels or manufacturing facilities.

EFAS (External Factor Analysis Summary) table A table that organizes external factors into opportunities and threats and how well management is responding to these specific factors.

Electronic commerce The use of the Internet to conduct business transactions.

Engineering (or process) R&D R&D concentrating on quality control and the development of design specifications and improved production equipment.

Enterprise resource planning (ERP) software Software that unites all of a company's major business activities, from order processing to production, within a single family of software modules.

Enterprise risk management (ERM) A corporatewide, integrated process to manage the uncertainties that could negatively or positively influence the achievement of the corporation's objectives.

Enterprise strategy A strategy that explicitly articulates a firm's ethical relationship with its stakeholders.

Entrepreneur A person who initiates and manages a business undertaking and who assumes risk for the sake of a profit.

Entrepreneurial characteristics Traits of an entrepreneur that lead to a new venture's success.

Entrepreneurial mode A strategy made by one powerful individual in which the focus is on opportunities, and problems are secondary.

Entrepreneurial venture Any new business whose primary goals are profitability and growth and that can be characterized by innovative strategic practices.

Entry barrier An obstruction that makes it difficult for a company to enter an industry.

Environmental scanning The monitoring, evaluation, and dissemination of information from the external and internal environments to key people within the corporation.

Environmental sustainability The use of business practices to reduce a company's impact upon the natural, physical environment.

Environmental uncertainty The degree of complexity plus the degree of change existing in an organization's external environment.

Ethics The consensually accepted standards of behavior for an occupation, trade, or profession.

European Union (EU) A regional trade association composed of 27 European countries.

Evaluation and control A process in which corporate activities and performance results are monitored so that actual performance can be compared with desired performance.

Executive leadership The directing of activities toward the accomplishment of corporate objectives.

Executive succession The process of grooming and replacing a key top manager.

Executive type An individual with a particular mix of skills and experiences.

Exit barrier An obstruction that keeps a company from leaving an industry.

Expense center A business unit that uses money but contributes to revenues only indirectly.

Experience curve A conceptual framework that states that unit production costs decline by some fixed percentage each time the total accumulated volume of production in units doubles.

Expert opinion A nonquantitative forecasting technique in which authorities in a particular area attempt to forecast likely developments.

Explicit knowledge Knowledge that can be easily articulated and communicated.

Exporting Shipping goods produced in a company's home country to other countries for marketing.

External environment Forces outside an organization that are not typically within the short-run control of top management.

External strategic factor Environmental trend with both high probability of occurrence and high probability of impact on the corporation.

Externality Costs of doing business that are not included in a firm's accounting system, but felt by others.

Extranet An information network within an organization that is available to key suppliers and customers.

Extrapolation A form of forecasting that extends present trends into the future.

Family business A company that is either owned or dominated by relatives.

Family directors Board members who are descendants of the founder and own significant blocks of stock.

Financial leverage The ratio of total debt to total assets.

Financial strategy A functional strategy to make the best use of corporate monetary assets.

First mover The first company to manufacture and sell a new product or service.

Flexible manufacturing A type of manufacturing that permits the low-volume output of custom-tailored products at relatively low unit costs through economies of scope.

Follow-the-sun-management A management technique in which modern communication enables project team members living in one country to pass their work to team members in another time zone so that the project is continually being advanced.

Forward integration Assuming a function previously provided by a distributor.

Four-corner exercise An approach to analyzing a competitor in terms of its future goals, current strategy, assumptions, and capabilities, in order to develop a competitor's response profile.

Fragmented industry An industry in which no firm has large market share and each firm serves only a small piece of the total market.

Franchising An international entry strategy in which a firm grants rights to another company/individual to open a retail store using the franchiser's name and operating system.

Free cash flow The amount of money a new owner can take out of a firm without harming the business.

Full vertical integration A growth strategy under which a firm makes 100% of its key supplies internally and completely controls its distributors.

Functional strategy An approach taken by a functional area to achieve corporate and business unit objectives and strategies by maximizing resource productivity.

Functional structure An organizational structure in which employees tend to be specialists in the business functions important to that industry, such as manufacturing, sales, or finance.

GE Business Screen A portfolio analysis matrix developed by General Electric, with the assistance of the McKinsey & Company consulting firm.

Geographic-area structure A structure that allows a multinational corporation to tailor products to regional differences and to achieve regional coordination.

Global industry An industry in which a company manufactures and sells the same products, with only minor adjustments for individual countries around the world.

Globalization The internationalization of markets and corporations.

Global warming A gradual increase in the Earth's temperature leading to changes in the planet's climate.

Goal displacement Confusion of means with ends, which occurs when activities originally intended to help managers attain corporate objectives become ends in themselves or are adapted to meet ends other than those for which they were intended.

Goal An open-ended statement of what one wants to accomplish, with no quantification of what is to be achieved and no time criteria for completion.

Good will An accounting term describing the premium paid by one company in its purchase of another company that is listed on the acquiring company's balance sheet.

Grand strategy Another name for directional strategy.

Green-field development An international entry option to build a company's manufacturing plant and distribution system in another country.

Greenwash A derogatory term referring to a company's promoting its environmental sustainability efforts with very little action toward improving its measurable environmental performance.

Gross domestic product (GDP) A measure of the total output of goods and services within a country's borders.

Growth strategies A directional strategy that expands a company's current activities.

Hierarchy of strategy A nesting of strategies by level from corporate to business to functional, so that they complement and support one another.

Horizontal growth A corporate growth concentration strategy that involves expanding the firm's products into other geographic locations and/or increasing the range of products and services offered to current markets.

Horizontal integration The degree to which a firm operates in multiple geographic locations at the same point in an industry's value chain.

Horizontal strategy A corporate parenting strategy that cuts across business unit boundaries to build synergy across business units and to improve the competitive position of one or more business units.

House of quality A method of managing new product development to help project teams make important design decisions by getting them to think about what users want and how to get it to them most effectively.

Human resource management (HRM) strategy A functional strategy that makes the best use of corporate human assets.

Human diversity A mix of people from different races, cultures, and backgrounds in the workplace.

Hypercompetition An industry situation in which the frequency, boldness, and aggressiveness of dynamic movement by the players accelerates to create a condition of constant disequilibrium and change.

Idea A concept that could be the foundation of an entrepreneurial venture if the concept is feasible.

IFAS (Internal Factor Analysis Summary) table A table that organizes internal factors into strengths and weaknesses and how well management is responding to these specific factors.

Imitability The rate at which a firm's underlying resources and capabilities can be duplicated by others.

Index of R&D effectiveness An index that is calculated by dividing the percentage of total revenue spent on research and development into new product profitability.

Index of sustainable growth A calculation that shows how much of the growth rate of sales can be sustained by internally generated funds.

Individual rights approach An ethics behavior guideline that proposes that human beings have certain fundamental rights that should be respected in all decisions.

Individualism-collectivism (IC) The extent to which a society values individual freedom and independence of action compared with a tight social framework and loyalty to the group.

Industry A group of firms producing a similar product or service.

Industry analysis An in-depth examination of key factors within a corporation's task environment.

Industry matrix A chart that summarizes the key success factors within a particular industry.

Industry scenario A forecasted description of an industry's likely future.

Information technology strategy A functional strategy that uses information systems technology to provide competitive advantage.

Input control A control that specifies resources, such as knowledge, skills, abilities, values, and motives of employees.

Inside director An officer or executive employed by a corporation who serves on that company's board of directors; also called management director.

Institution theory A concept of organizational adaptation that proposes that organizations can and do adapt to changing conditions by imitating other successful organizations.

Institutional advantage A competitive benefit for a not-for-profit organization when it performs its tasks more effectively than other comparable organizations.

Integration A process that involves a relatively balanced give-and-take of cultural and managerial practices between merger partners, with no strong imposition of cultural change on either company.

Integration manager A person in charge of taking an acquired company through the process of integrating its people and processes with those of the acquiring company.

Intellectual property Special knowledge used in a new product or process developed by a company for its own use and is usually protected by a patent, copyright, trademark, or trade secret.

Interlocking directorate A condition that occurs when two firms share a director or when an executive of one firm sits on the board of a second firm.

Intermittent system A method of manufacturing in which an item is normally processed sequentially, but the work and the sequence of the processes vary.

Internal environment Variables within the organization not usually within the short-run control of top management.

Internal strategic factors Strengths (core competencies) and weaknesses that are likely to determine whether a firm will be able take advantage of opportunities while avoiding threats.

International transfer pricing A method of minimizing taxes by declaring high profits in a subsidiary located in a country with a low tax rate and small profits in a subsidiary located in a country with a high tax rate.

Intranet An information network within an organization that also has access to the Internet.

Investment center A unit in which performance is measured in terms of the difference between the unit's resources and its services or products.

ISO 9000 Standards Series An internationally accepted way of objectively documenting a company's high level of quality operations.

ISO 14000 Standards Series An internationally accepted way to document a company's impact on the environment.

Issues priority matrix A chart that ranks the probability of occurrence versus the probable impact on the corporation of developments in the external environment.

Job characteristics model An approach to job design that is based on the belief that tasks can be described in terms of certain objective characteristics and that those characteristics affect employee motivation.

Job design The design of individual tasks in an attempt to make them more relevant to the company and more motivating to the employee.

Job enlargement Combining tasks to give a worker more of the same type of duties to perform.

Job enrichment Altering jobs by giving the worker more autonomy and control over activities.

Job rotation Moving workers through several jobs to increase variety.

Job shop One-of-a-kind production using skilled labor.

Joint venture An independent business entity created by two or more companies in a strategic alliance.

Justice approach An ethical approach that proposes that decision makers be equitable, fair, and impartial in the distribution of costs and benefits.

Just-In-Time A purchasing concept in which parts arrive at the plant just when they are needed rather than being kept in inventories.

Key performance measures Essential measures for achieving a desired strategic option—used in the balanced scorecard.

Key success factors Variables that significantly affect the overall competitive position of a company within a particular industry.

Late movers Companies that enter a new market only after other companies have done so.

Law A formal code that permits or forbids certain behaviors.

Lead director An outside director who calls meetings of the outside board members and coordinates the annual evaluation of the CEO.

Lead user A customer who is ahead of market trends and has needs that go beyond those of the average user.

Leading Providing direction to employees to use their abilities and skills most effectively and efficiently to achieve organizational objectives.

Lean Six Sigma A program incorporating the statistical approach of Six Sigma with the lean manufacturing program developed by Toyota.

Learning organization An organization that is skilled at creating, acquiring, and transferring knowledge and at modifying its behavior to reflect new knowledge and insights.

Levels of moral development Kohlberg proposed three levels of moral development: pre-conventional, conventional, and principled.

Leverage ratio An evaluation of how effectively a company utilizes its resources to generate revenues.

Leveraged buy-out An acquisition in which a company is acquired in a transaction financed largely by debt—usually obtained from a third party, such as an insurance company or an investment banker.

Licensing arrangement An agreement in which the licensing firm grants rights to another firm in another country or market to produce and/or sell a branded product.

Lifestyle company A small business in which the firm is purely an extension of the owner's lifestyle.

Line extension Using a successful brand name on additional products, such as Arm & Hammer brand first on baking soda, then on laundry detergents, toothpaste, and deodorants.

Linkage The connection between the way one value activity (for example, marketing) is performed and the cost of performance of another activity (for example, quality control).

Liquidation The termination of a firm in which all its assets are sold.

Liquidity ratio The percentage showing to what degree a company can cover its current liabilities with its current assets.

Logical incrementalism A decision-making mode that is a synthesis of the planning, adaptive, and entrepreneurial modes.

Logistics strategy A functional strategy that deals with the flow of products into and out of the manufacturing process.

Long-term contract Agreements between two separate firms to provide agreed-upon goods and services to each other for a specified period of time.

Long-term evaluation method A method in which managers are compensated for achieving objectives set over a multiyear period.

Long-term orientation (LT) The extent to which society is oriented toward the long term versus the short term.

Lower cost strategy A strategy in which a company or business unit designs, produces, and markets a comparable product more efficiently than its competitors.

Management audit A technique used to evaluate corporate activities.

Management By Objectives (MBO) An organization-wide approach ensuring purposeful action toward mutually agreed-upon objectives.

Management contract Agreements through which a corporation uses some of its personnel to assist a firm in another country for a specified fee and period of time.

Market development A marketing functional strategy in which a company or business unit captures a larger share of an existing market for current products through market penetration or develops new markets for current products.

Market location tactics Tactics that determine where a company or business unit will compete.

Market position Refers to the selection of specific areas for marketing concentration and can be expressed in terms of market, product, and geographical locations.

Market research A means of obtaining new product ideas by surveying current or potential users regarding what they would like in a new product.

Market segmentation The division of a market into segments to identify available niches.

Market value added (MVA) The difference between the market value of a corporation and the capital contributed by shareholders and lenders.

Marketing mix The particular combination of key variables (product, place, promotion, and price) that can be used to affect demand and to gain competitive advantage.

Marketing strategy A functional strategy that deals with pricing, selling, and distributing a product.

Masculinity-femininity (MF) The extent to which society is oriented toward money and things.

Mass customization The low-cost production of individually customized goods and services.

Mass production A system in which employees work on narrowly defined, repetitive tasks under close supervision in a bureaucratic and hierarchical structure to produce a large amount of low-cost, standard goods and services.

Matrix of change A chart that compares target practices (new programs) with existing practices (current activities).

Matrix structure A structure in which functional and product forms are combined simultaneously at the same level of the organization.

Mercosur/Mercosul South American free-trade area including Argentina, Brazil, Uruguay, and Paraguay.

Merger A transaction in which two or more corporations exchange stock, but from which only one corporation survives.

Mission The purpose or reason for an organization's existence.

Mission statement The definition of the fundamental, unique purpose that sets an organization apart from other firms of its type and identifies the scope or domain of the organization's operations in terms of products (including services) offered and markets served.

Modular manufacturing A system in which preassembled subassemblies are delivered as they are needed to a company's assembly-line workers who quickly piece the modules together into finished products.

Moore's law An observation of Gordon Moore, co-founder of Intel, that microprocessors double in complexity every 18 months.

Moral relativism A theory that proposes that morality is relative to some personal, social, or cultural standard, and that there is no method for deciding whether one decision is better than another.

Morality Precepts of personal behavior that are based on religious or philosophical grounds.

Most favored nation A policy of the World Trade Organization stating that a member country cannot grant one trading partner lower customs duties without granting them to all WTO member nations.

Multidomestic industry An industry in which companies tailor their products to the specific needs of consumers in a particular country.

Multinational corporation (MNC) A company that has significant assets and activities in multiple countries.

Multiple sourcing A purchasing strategy in which a company orders a particular part from several vendors.

Multipoint competition A rivalry in which a large multibusiness corporation competes against other large multibusiness firms in a number of markets.

Mutual service consortium A partnership of similar companies in similar industries that pool their resources to gain a benefit that is too expensive to develop alone.

Natural environment That part of the external environment that includes physical resources, wildlife, and climate that are an inherent part of existence on Earth.

Net present value (NPV) A calculation of the value of a project that is made by predicting the project's payouts, adjusting them for risk, and subtracting the amount invested.

Network structure An organization (virtual organization) that outsources most of its business functions.

New entrants Businesses entering an industry that typically bring new capacity to an industry, a desire to gain market share, and substantial resources.

New product experimentation A method of test marketing the potential of innovative ideas by developing products, probing potential markets with early versions of the products, learning from the probes, and probing again.

No-change strategy A decision to do nothing new; to continue current operations and policies for the foreseeable future.

North American Free Trade Agreement (NAFTA) Regional free trade agreement between Canada, the United States, and Mexico.

Not-for-profit organization Private nonprofit corporations and public governmental units or agencies.

Objectives The end result of planned activity stating what is to be accomplished by when, and quantified if possible.

Offensive tactic A tactic that calls for competing in an established competitor's current market location.

Offshoring The outsourcing of an activity or function to a provider in another country.

Open innovation A new approach to R&D in which a firm uses alliances and connections with corporate, government, and academic labs to learn about new developments.

Operating budget A budget for a business unit that is approved by top management during strategy formulation and implementation.

Operating cash flow The amount of money generated by a company before the costs of financing and taxes are figured.

Operating leverage The impact of a specific change in sales volume on net operating income.

Operations strategy A functional strategy that determines how and where a product or service is to be manufactured, the level of vertical integration in the production process, and the deployment of physical resources.

Opportunity A strategic factor considered when using the SWOT analysis.

Orchestrator A top manager who articulates the need for innovation, provides funding for innovating activities, creates incentives for middle managers to sponsor new ideas, and protects idea/product champions from suspicious or jealous executives.

Organization slack Unused resources within an organization.

Organizational analysis Internal scanning concerned with identifying an organization's strengths and weaknesses.

Organizational learning theory A theory proposing that an organization adjusts to changes in the environment through the learning of its employees.

Organizational life cycle How organizations grow, develop, and eventually decline.

Organizational structure The formal setup of a business corporation's value chain components in terms of work flow, communication channels, and hierarchy.

Output control A control that specifies what is to be accomplished by focusing on the end result of the behaviors through the use of objectives and performance targets.

Outside directors Members of a board of directors who are not employees of the board's corporation; also called non–management directors.

Outsourcing A process in which resources are purchased from others through long-term contracts instead of being made within the company.

Parallel sourcing A process in which two suppliers are the sole suppliers of two different parts, but they are also backup suppliers for each other's parts.

Pattern of influence A concept stating that influence in strategic management derives from a not-for-profit organization's sources of revenue.

Pause/proceed with caution strategy A corporate strategy in which nothing new is attempted; an opportunity to rest before continuing a growth or retrenchment strategy.

Penetration pricing A marketing pricing strategy to obtain dominant market share by using low price.

Performance The end result of activities, actual outcomes of a strategic management process.

Performance appraisal system A system to systematically evaluate employee performance and promotion potential.

Performance gap A performance gap exists when performance does not meet expectations.

Periodic statistical report Reports summarizing data on key factors such as the number of new customer contracts, volume of received orders, and productivity figures.

Phases of strategic management A set of four levels of development through which a firm generally evolves into strategic management.

Piracy The making and selling counterfeit copies of well-known name-brand products, especially software.

Planning mode A decision-making mode that involves the systematic gathering of appropriate information for situation analysis, the generation of feasible alternative strategies, and the rational selection of the most appropriate strategy.

Policy A broad guideline for decision making that links the formulation of strategy with its implementation.

Political strategy A strategy to influence a corporation's stakeholders.

Population ecology A theory that proposes that once an organization is successfully established in a particular environmental niche, it is unable to adapt to changing conditions.

Portfolio analysis An approach to corporate strategy in which top management views its product lines and business units as a series of investments from which it expects a profitable return.

Power distance (PD) The extent to which a society accepts an unequal distribution of influence in organizations.

Prediction markets A forecasting technique in which people make bets on the likelihood of a particular event taking place.

Pressure-cooker crisis A situation that exists when employees in collaborative organizations eventually grow emotionally and physically exhausted from the intensity of teamwork and the heavy pressure for innovative solutions.

Primary activity A manufacturing firm's corporate value chain, including inbound logistics, operations process, outbound logistics, marketing and sales, and service.

Primary stakeholders A high priority group that affects or is affected by the achievement of a firm's objectives.

Prime interest rate The rate of interest banks charge on their lowest-risk loans.

Private nonprofit corporation A nongovernmental not-for-profit organization.

Privatization The selling of state-owned enterprises to private individuals. Also the hiring of a private business to provide services previously offered by a state agency.

Procedures A list of sequential steps that describe in detail how a particular task or job is to be done.

Process innovation Improvement to the making and selling of current products.

Product champion A person who generates a new idea and supports it through many organizational obstacles.

Product development A marketing strategy in which a company or unit develops new products for existing markets or develops new products for new markets.

Product innovation The development of a new product or the improvement of an existing product's performance.

Product life cycle A graph showing time plotted against sales of a product as it moves from introduction through growth and maturity to decline.

Product R&D Research and development concerned with product or product-packaging improvements.

Product/market evolution matrix A chart depicting products in terms of their competitive positions and their stages of product/market evolution.

Product-group structure A structure of a multinational corporation that enables the company to introduce and manage a similar line of products around the world.

Production sharing The process of combining the higher labor skills and technology available in developed countries with the lower-cost labor available in developing countries.

Professional liquidator An individual called on by a bankruptcy court to close a firm and sell its assets.

Profit center A unit's performance, measured in terms of the difference between revenues and expenditures.

Profit strategy A strategy that artificially supports profits by reducing investment and short-term discretionary expenditures.

Profitability ratios Ratios evaluating a company's ability to make money over a period of time.

Profit-making firm A firm depending on revenues obtained from the sale of its goods and services to customers, who typically pay for the costs and expenses of providing the product or service plus a profit.

Program A statement of the activities or steps needed to accomplish a single-use plan in strategy implementation.

Propitious niche A portion of a market that is so well suited to a firm's internal and external environment that other corporations are not likely to challenge or dislodge it.

Public governmental unit or agency A kind of not-for-profit organization that is established by government or governmental agencies (such as welfare departments, prisons, and state universities).

Public or collective good Goods that are freely available to all in a society.

Pull strategy A marketing strategy in which advertising pulls the products through the distribution channels.

Punctuated equilibrium A point at which a corporation makes a major change in its strategy after evolving slowly through a long period of stability.

Purchasing power parity (PPP) A measure of the cost, in dollars, of the U.S.-produced equivalent volume of goods that another nation's economy produces.

Purchasing strategy A functional strategy that deals with obtaining the raw materials, parts, and supplies needed to perform the operations functions.

Push strategy A marketing strategy in which a large amount of money is spent on trade promotion in order to gain or hold shelf space in retail outlets.

Quality of work life A concept that emphasizes improving the human dimension of work to improve employee satisfaction and union relations.

Quasi-integration A type of vertical growth/integration in which a company does not make any of its key supplies but purchases most of its requirements from outside suppliers that are under its partial control.

Question marks New products that have potential for success and need a lot of cash for development.

RFID A technology in which radio frequency identification tags containing product information is used to track goods through inventory and distribution channels.

R&D intensity A company's spending on research and development as a percentage of sales revenue.

R&D mix The balance of basic, product, and process research and development.

R&D strategy A functional strategy that deals with product and process innovation.

Ratio analysis The calculation of ratios from data in financial statements to identify possible strengths or weaknesses.

Real options approach An approach to new project investment when the future is highly uncertain.

Red flag An indication of a serious underlying problem.

Red tape crisis A crisis that occurs when a corporation has grown too large and complex to be managed through formal programs.

Reengineering The radical redesign of business processes to achieve major gains in cost, service, or time.

Regional industry An industry in which multinational corporations primarily coordinate their activities within specific geographic areas of the world.

Relationship-based governance A government system perceived to be less transparent and have a higher degree of corruption.

Repatriation of profits The transfer of profits from a foreign subsidiary to a corporation's headquarters.

Replicability The ability of competitors to duplicate resources and imitate another firm's success.

Resources A company's physical, human, and organizational assets that serve as the building blocks of a corporation.

Responsibility center A unit that is isolated so that it can be evaluated separately from the rest of the corporation.

Retired executive directors Past leaders of a company kept on the board of directors after leaving the company.

Retrenchment strategy Corporate strategies to reduce a company's level of activities and to return it to profitability.

Return on equity (ROE) A measure of performance that is calculated by dividing net income by total equity.

Return on investment (ROI) A measure of performance that is calculated by dividing net income before taxes by total assets.

Revenue center A responsibility center in which production, usually in terms of unit or dollar sales, is measured without consideration of resource costs.

Reverse engineering Taking apart a competitor's product in order to find out how it works.

Reverse stock split A stock split in which an investor's shares are reduced for the same total amount of money.

Risk A measure of the probability that one strategy will be effective, the amount of assets the corporation must allocate to that strategy, and the length of time the assets will be unavailable.

Rule-based governance A governance system based on clearly stated rules and procedures.

Rules of thumb Approximations based not on research, but on years of practical experience.

Sarbanes-Oxley Act Legislation passed by the U.S. Congress in 2002 to promote and formalize greater board independence and oversight.

Scenario box A tool for developing corporate scenarios in which historical data are used to make projections for generating pro forma financial statements.

Scenario writing A forecasting technique in which focused descriptions of different likely futures are presented in a narrative fashion.

Secondary stakeholders Lower-priority groups that affect or are affected by the achievement of a firm's objectives.

Sell-out strategy A retrenchment option used when a company has a weak competitive position resulting in poor performance.

Separation A method of managing the culture of an acquired firm in which the two companies are structurally divided, without cultural exchange.

SFAS (Strategic Factors Analysis Summary) matrix A chart that summarizes an organization's strategic factors by combining the external factors from an EFAS table with the internal factors from an IFAS table.

Shareholder value The present value of the anticipated future stream of cash flows from a business plus the value of the company if it were liquidated.

Short-term orientation The tendency of managers to consider only current tactical or operational issues and ignore strategic ones.

Simple structure A structure for new entrepreneurial firms in which the employees tend to be generalists and jacks-of-all-trades.

Six Sigma A statistically-based program developed to identify and improve a poorly performing process.

Skim pricing A marketing strategy in which a company charges a high price while a product is novel and competitors are few.

Small-business firm An independently owned and operated business that is not dominant in its field and that does not engage in innovative practices.

SO, ST, WO, WT strategies A series of possible business approaches based on combinations of opportunities, threats, strengths, and weaknesses.

Social capital The goodwill of key stakeholders, which can be used for competitive advantage.

Social entrepreneurship A business in which a not-for-profit organization starts a new venture to achieve social goals.

Social responsibility The ethical and discretionary responsibilities a corporation owes its stakeholders.

Societal environment Economic, technological, political-legal, and sociocultural environmental forces that do not directly touch on the short-run activities of an organization but influence its long-run decisions.

Sole sourcing Relying on only one supplier for a particular part.

Sources of innovation Drucker's proposed seven sources of new ideas that should be monitored by those interested in starting entrepreneurial ventures.

Sponsor A department manager who recognizes the value of a new idea, helps obtain funding to develop the innovation, and facilitates the implementation of the innovation.

Stability strategy Corporate strategies to make no change to the company's current direction or activities.

Staffing Human resource management priorities and use of personnel.

Stages of corporate development A pattern of structural development that corporations follow as they grow and expand.

Stages of international development The stages through which international corporations evolve in their relationships with widely dispersed geographic markets and the manner in which they structure their operations and programs.

Stages of new product development The stages of getting a new innovation into the marketplace.

Stage-gate process A method of managing new product development to increase the likelihood of launching new products quickly and successfully. The process is a series of steps to move products through the six stages of new product development.

Staggered board A board on which directors serve terms of more than one year so that only a portion of the board of directors stands for election each year.

Stakeholder analysis The identification and evaluation of corporate stakeholders.

Stakeholder measure A method of keeping track of stakeholder concerns.

Stakeholder priority matrix A chart that categorizes stakeholders in terms of their interest in a corporation's activities and their relative power to influence the corporation's activities.

Stall point A point at which a company's growth in sales and profits suddenly stops and becomes negative.

Standard cost center A responsibility center that is primarily used to evaluate the performance of manufacturing facilities.

Standard operating procedures Plans that detail the various activities that must be carried out to complete a corporation's programs.

Star Market leader that is able to generate enough cash to maintain its high market share.

Statistical modeling A quantitative technique that attempts to discover causal or explanatory factors that link two or more time series together.

STEEP analysis An approach to scanning the societal environment that examines sociocultural, technological, economic, ecological, and political-legal forces. Also called PESTEL analysis.

Steering control Measures of variables that influence future profitability.

Stewardship theory A theory proposing that executives tend to be more motivated to act in the best interests of the corporation than in their own self-interests.

Strategic alliance A partnership of two or more corporations or business units to achieve strategically significant objectives that are mutually beneficial.

Strategic audit A checklist of questions by area or issue that enables a systematic analysis of various corporate functions and activities. It's a type a management audit.

Strategic audit worksheet A tool used to analyze a case.

Strategic business unit (SBU) A division or group of divisions composed of independent product-market segments that are given primary authority for the management of their own functions.

Strategic choice The evaluation of strategies and selection of the best alternative.

Strategic choice perspective A theory that proposes that organizations adapt to a changing environment and have the opportunity and power to reshape their environment.

Strategic decision-making process An eight-step process that improves strategic decision making.

Strategic decisions Decisions that deal with the long-run future of an entire organization and are rare, consequential, and directive.

Strategic factors External and internal factors that determine the future of a corporation.

Strategic flexibility The ability to shift from one dominant strategy to another.

Strategic group A set of business units or firms that pursue similar strategies and have similar resources.

Strategic inflection point The period in an organization's life in which a major change takes place in its environment and creates a new basis for competitive advantage.

Strategic management A set of managerial decisions and actions that determine the long-run performance of a corporation.

Strategic management model A rational, prescriptive planning model of the strategic management process including environmental scanning, strategy formulation, strategy implementation, and evaluation and control.

Strategic myopia The willingness to reject unfamiliar as well as negative information.

Strategic piggybacking The development of a new activity for a not-for-profit organization that would generate the funds needed to make up the difference between revenues and expenses.

Strategic planning staff A group of people charged with supporting both top management and business units in the strategic planning process.

Strategic R&D alliance A coalition through which a firm coordinates its research and development with another firm(s) to offset the huge costs of developing new technology.

Strategic rollup A means of consolidating a fragmented industry in which an entrepreneur acquires hundreds of owner-operated small businesses resulting in a large firm with economies of scale.

Strategic sweet spot A market niche in which a company is able to satisfy customers' needs in a way that competitors cannot.

Strategic type A category of firms based on a common strategic orientation and a combination of structure, culture, and processes that are consistent with that strategy.

Strategic vision A description of what the company is capable of becoming.

Strategic window A unique market opportunity that is available only for a particular time.

Strategic-funds method An evaluation method that encourages executives to look at development expenses as being different from expenses required for current operations.

Strategies to avoid Strategies sometimes followed by managers who have made a poor analysis or lack creativity.

Strategy A comprehensive plan that states how a corporation will achieve its mission and objectives.

Strategy formulation Development of long-range plans for the effective management of environmental opportunities and threats in light of corporate strengths and weaknesses.

Strategy implementation A process by which strategies and policies are put into action through the development of programs, budgets, and procedures.

Strategy-culture compatibility The match between existing corporate culture and a new strategy to be implemented.

Structure follows strategy The process through which changes in corporate strategy normally lead to changes in organizational structure.

Stuck in the middle A situation in which a company or business unit has not achieved a generic competitive strategy and has no competitive advantage.

Suboptimization A phenomenon in which a unit optimizes its goal accomplishment to the detriment of the organization as a whole.

Substages of small business development A set of five levels through which new ventures often develop.

Substitute products Products that appear to be different but can satisfy the same need as other products.

Supply-chain management The formation of networks for sourcing raw materials, manufacturing products or creating services, storing and distributing goods, and delivering goods or services to customers and consumers.

Support activity An activity that ensures that primary value-chain activities operate effectively and efficiently.

SWOT analysis Identification of strengths, weaknesses, opportunities, and threats that may be strategic factors for a specific company.

Synergy A concept that states that the whole is greater than the sum of its parts; that two units will achieve more together than they could separately.

Tacit knowledge Knowledge that is not easily communicated because it is deeply rooted in employee experience or in a corporation's culture.

Tactic A short-term operating plan detailing how a strategy is to be implemented.

Takeover A hostile acquisition in which one firm purchases a majority interest in another firm's stock.

Taper integration A type of vertical integration in which a firm internally produces less than half of its own requirements and buys the rest from outside suppliers.

Task environment The part of the business environment that includes the elements or groups that directly affect the corporation and, in turn, are affected by it.

Technological competence A corporation's proficiency in managing research personnel and integrating their innovations into its day-to-day operations.

Technological discontinuity The displacement of one technology by another.

Technological follower A company that imitates the products of competitors.

Technological leader A company that pioneers an innovation.

Technology sourcing A make-or-buy decision that can be important in a firm's R&D strategy.

Technology transfer The process of taking a new technology from the laboratory to the marketplace.

Time to market The time from inception to profitability of a new product.

Timing tactics Tactics that determines when a business will enter a market with a new product.

Tipping point The point at which a slowly changing situation goes through a massive, rapid change.

Top management responsibilities Leadership tasks that involve getting things accomplished through and with others in order to meet the corporate objectives.

Total Quality Management (TQM) An operational philosophy that is committed to customer satisfaction and continuous improvement.

TOWS matrix A matrix that illustrates how external opportunities and threats facing a particular company can be matched with that company's internal strengths and weaknesses to result in four sets of strategic alternatives.

Transaction cost economics A theory that proposes that vertical integration is more efficient than contracting for goods and services in the marketplace when the transaction costs of buying goods on the open market become too great.

Transfer price A practice in which one unit can charge a transfer price for each product it sells to a different unit within a company.

Transferability The ability of competitors to gather the resources and capabilities necessary to support a competitive challenge.

Transformational leader A leader who causes change and movement in an organization by providing a strategic vision.

Transparent The speed with which other firms can understand the relationship of resources and capabilities supporting a successful firm's strategy.

Trends in governance Current developments in corporate governance.

Trigger point The point at which a country has developed economically so that demand for a particular product or service is increasing rapidly.

Triggering event Something that acts as a stimulus for a change in strategy.

Turnaround specialist A manager who is brought into a weak company to salvage that company in a relatively attractive industry.

Turnaround strategy A plan that emphasizes the improvement of operational efficiency when a corporation's problems are pervasive but not yet critical.

Turnkey operation Contracts for the construction of operating facilities in exchange for a fee.

Turnover A term used by European firms to refer to sales revenue. It also refers to the amount of time needed to sell inventory.

Uncertainty avoidance (UA) The extent to which a society feels threatened by uncertain and ambiguous situations.

Union of South American Nations An organization formed in 2008 to unite Mercosur and the Andean Community.

Utilitarian approach A theory that proposes that actions and plans should be judged by their consequences.

Value chain A linked set of value-creating activities that begins with basic raw materials coming from suppliers and ends with distributors getting the final goods into the hands of the ultimate consumer.

Value-chain partnership A strategic alliance in which one company or unit forms a long-term arrangement with a key supplier or distributor for mutual advantage.

Value disciplines An approach to evaluating a competitor in terms of product leadership, operational excellence, and customer intimacy.

Vertical growth A corporate growth strategy in which a firm takes over a function previously provided by a supplier or distributor.

Vertical integration The degree to which a firm operates in multiple locations on an industry's value chain from extracting raw materials to retailing.

Virtual organization An organizational structure that is composed of a series of project groups or collaborations linked by changing nonhierarchical, cobweb-like networks.

Virtual team A group of geographically and/or organizationally dispersed coworkers that are assembled using a combination of telecommunications and information technologies to accomplish an organizational task.

Vision A view of what management thinks an organization should become.

VRIO framework Barney's proposed analysis to evaluate a firm's key resources in terms of value, rareness, imitability, and organization.

Web 2.0 A term used to describe the evolution of the Internet into wikis, blogs, RSS, social networks, podcasts, and mash-ups.

Weighted-factor method A method that is appropriate for measuring and rewarding the performance of top SBU managers and group-level executives when performance factors and their importance vary from one SBU to another.

Whistle-blower An individual who reports to authorities incidents of questionable organizational practices.

World Trade Organization A forum for governments to negotiate trade agreements and settle trade disputes.

Z-value A formula that combines five ratios by weighting them according to their importance to a corporation's financial strength to predict the likelihood of bankruptcy.

NOTE: This glossary contains terms used in the twelve chapters of this textbook plus the three additional chapters provided on the publisher's Web site to buyers of this book.

NAME INDEX

SUBJECT INDEX

Strategic Management Model

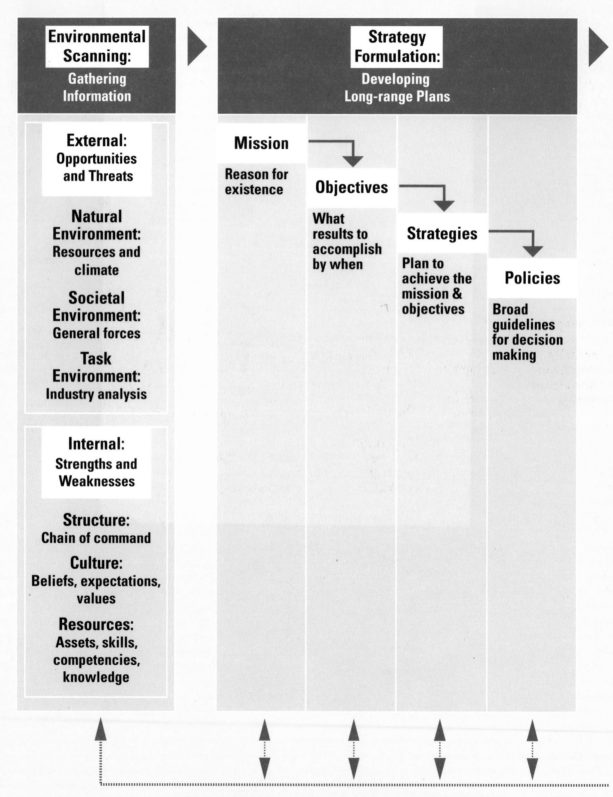

Environmental Scanning:
Gathering Information

Strategy Formulation:
Developing Long-range Plans

External: Opportunities and Threats

Natural Environment: Resources and climate

Societal Environment: General forces

Task Environment: Industry analysis

Internal: Strengths and Weaknesses

Structure: Chain of command

Culture: Beliefs, expectations, values

Resources: Assets, skills, competencies, knowledge

Mission
Reason for existence

Objectives
What results to accomplish by when

Strategies
Plan to achieve the mission & objectives

Policies
Broad guidelines for decision making

Feedback/Learning: Make corrections as needed